P9-BIJ-011

Professional ASP.NET 1.1

Professional ASP NET 1.1

Professional ASP.NET 1.1

Alex Homer

Dave Sussman

Rob Howard

Brian Francis

Karli Watson

Richard Anderson

WILEY

Wiley Publishing, Inc.

Professional ASP.NET 1.1

Published by
Wiley Publishing, Inc.
10475 Crosspoint Boulevard
Indianapolis, IN 46256
www.wiley.com

Copyright © 2004 by Wiley Publishing, Inc., Indianapolis, Indiana

Published simultaneously in Canada

Library of Congress Card Number: 2004102362

ISBN: 0-7645-5890-0

Manufactured in the United States of America

10 9 8 7 6 5 4

No part of this publication may be reproduced, stored in a retrieval system or transmitted in any form or by any means, electronic, mechanical, photocopying, recording, scanning or otherwise, except as permitted under Sections 107 or 108 of the 1976 United States Copyright Act, without either the prior written permission of the Publisher, or authorization through payment of the appropriate per-copy fee to the Copyright Clearance Center, 222 Rosewood Drive, Danvers, MA 01923, (978) 750-8400, fax (978) 646-8700. Address requests to the Publisher for permission to the Legal Department, Wiley Publishing, Inc., 10475 Crosspoint Blvd., Indianapolis, IN 46256, (317) 572-3447, fax (317) 572-4447, Email: permcoordinator@wiley.com.

LIMIT OF LIABILITY/DISCLAIMER OF WARRANTY: THE PUBLISHER AND THE AUTHOR MAKE NO REPRESENTATIONS OR WARRANTIES WITH RESPECT TO THE ACCURACY OR COMPLETENESS OF THE CONTENTS OF THIS WORK AND SPECIFICALLY DISCLAIM ALL WARRANTIES, INCLUDING WITHOUT LIMITATION WARRANTIES OF FITNESS FOR A PARTICULAR PURPOSE. NO WARRANTY MAY BE CREATED OR EXTENDED BY SALES OR PROMOTIONAL MATERIALS. THE ADVICE AND STRATEGIES CONTAINED HEREIN MAY NOT BE SUITABLE FOR EVERY SITUATION. THIS WORK IS SOLD WITH THE UNDERSTANDING THAT THE PUBLISHER IS NOT ENGAGED IN RENDERING LEGAL, ACCOUNTING, OR OTHER PROFESSIONAL SERVICES. IF PROFESSIONAL ASSISTANCE IS REQUIRED, THE SERVICES OF A COMPETENT PROFESSIONAL PERSON SHOULD BE SOUGHT. NEITHER THE PUBLISHER NOR THE AUTHOR SHALL BE LIABLE FOR DAMAGES ARISING HEREFROM. THE FACT THAT AN ORGANIZATION OR WEBSITE IS REFERRED TO IN THIS WORK AS A CITATION AND/OR A POTENTIAL SOURCE OF FURTHER INFORMATION DOES NOT MEAN THAT THE AUTHOR OR THE PUBLISHER ENDORSES THE INFORMATION THE ORGANIZATION OR WEBSITE MAY PROVIDE OR RECOMMENDATIONS IT MAY MAKE. FURTHER, READERS SHOULD BE AWARE THAT INTERNET WEBSITES LISTED IN THIS WORK MAY HAVE CHANGED OR DISAPPEARED BETWEEN WHEN THIS WORK WAS WRITTEN AND WHEN IT IS READ.

For general information on our other products and services or for technical support, contact our Customer Care Department within the U.S. at (800) 762-2974, outside the U.S. at (317) 572-3993 or fax (317) 572-4002.

Wiley also publishes its books in a variety of electronic formats. Some content that appears in print may not be available in electronic books.

Trademarks: Wiley, the Wiley Publishing logo, Wrox, the Wrox logo, Programmer to Programmer, and related trade dress are trademarks or registered trademarks of John Wiley & Sons, Inc. and/or its affiliates in the United States and other countries, and may not be used without written permission. All other trademarks are the property of their respective owners. Wiley Publishing, Inc. is not associated with any product or vendor mentioned in this book.

About the Authors

Alex Homer

Alex Homer is a software developer and a technical author living and working in the idyllic rural surroundings of Derbyshire dales, in the heart of England. Rather than doing a real job, he's discovered the raw excitement and frustration that comes with installing and playing with the latest and flakiest beta code he can find - and then he writes about it. A long-time evangelist of ASP, he has been delving deep into the world of .NET and has emerged a confirmed convert to ASP.NET. You can contact him at alex@stonebroom.com.

Alex Homer contributed Chapters 2, 5, 6, 7, 8, 9, 10, 11, 14, and 15, and all Appendices to this book.

Dave Sussman

Dave Sussman is a writer, trainer, and consultant, living in the wilds of the Oxfordshire countryside. He's been working with ASP.NET since before it was first released and still isn't bored with it. You can contact him at davids@ipona.com.

Dave Sussman contributed Chapters 1, 3, 16, 18, 22, and 23 to this book.

Rob Howard

Rob Howard is a Program Manager on Microsoft's .NET Framework Team. Within the .NET Framework Team, he specifically works on ASP.NET. He currently writes a column for *MSDN Online* entitled *Nothin' but ASP.NET*, as well as writing the .NET Framework column for *Windows 2000* magazine. You can reach Rob at rhoward@devadvice.com

Rob Howard contributed Chapters 11, 12, 19, and 20 to this book.

Brian Francis

Brian Francis is the Solution Sales Specialist for NCR's Web Kiosk Solution. Brian is responsible for supporting NCR's kiosk efforts throughout the United States. Brian has been writing books on ASP for the past 7 years, including the Beginning ASP and Professional ASP series for Wrox Press. When not working or writing, Brian spends time playing tennis and spending time with his wife Katharine and their family.

Brian Francis contributed Chapters 4, 17, and 24 to this book.

Karli Watson

Karli Watson was an in-house author for Wrox Press with a penchant for multi-colored clothing. He is now the technical director of 3form (www.3form.net). He started out with the intention of becoming a world-famous nanotechnologist, so perhaps one day you might recognize his name as he receives a Nobel Prize. For now, though, Karli's computing interests include all things mobile and upcoming technologies such as C#. He can often be found preaching about these technologies at conferences, as well as after work hours at drinking establishments. Karli is a snowboarding enthusiast, and wishes he had a cat.

Karli Watson contributed Chapter 21 to this book.

Richard Anderson

Richard Anderson is an experienced software engineer and writer who spends his time working with Microsoft technologies, day in day out. Having spent the better part of the decade doing this, he is still remarkably sane! Richard currently works for BMS software - an ADP company - where he is a technical architecture manager. Richard is currently working on the development of a large-scale Internet-based payroll and HR system.

Richard would like to say thank you to his wife Sam for giving him all the love, support, and understanding a man could ever wish for. Richard would also like to say hello and thank you to all his freinds, especially the other authors of this book, and his great workmates (Andy, Graham, Jon, Paul, Drew, Steve, Chris, and so on).

Richard Anderson was the lead author for the previous version of this book - *Professional ASP.NET 1.0 Special Edition.*

Credits

Authors
Alex Homer
Dave Sussman
Rob Howard
Brian Francis
Karli Watson
Richard Anderson

Senior Acquisitions Editor
Jim Minatel

Vice President & Executive Group Publisher
Richard Swadley

Vice President and Executive Publisher
Bob Ipsen

Vice President and Publisher
Joseph B. Wikert

Executive Editorial Director
Mary Bednarek

Project Coordinator
Mary Richards

Project Manager
Ami Frank Sullivan

Senior Production Manager
Fred Bernardi

Editorial Manager
Kathryn A. Malm

Book Producer
Peer Technical Services Pvt. Ltd.

Contents

Contents

Contents

Contents

Contents

Contents

Contents

Contents

Introduction

Right from its initial release as a preview technology, Microsoft ASP.NET has been a huge success. For those of us developing web sites using Microsoft technologies ASP.NET provides a rich programming model, allowing sites to be easily constructed. There's been a lot of talk about ASP.NET since it's release, but ignoring all the hype and press, .NET really is a product for developers, providing a great foundation for building all types of applications.

Active Server Pages (*ASP*) has been the leading web development tool from Microsoft, even though it is still a relatively young product. Its success is due to its ease of use and flexibility, providing a simple way to create dynamic web sites. This success though hasn't come without problems, many of them simply because ASP has outgrown its feature set. It was designed to work with the underlying architecture of COM, which in itself has limiting features.

ASP.NET is part of the whole .NET framework, built on top of the *Common Language Runtime* (also known as the *CLR*)–a rich and flexible architecture, designed not just to cater for the needs of developers today, but to allow for the long future we have ahead of us. What you might not realize is that, unlike previous updates of ASP, ASP.NET is very much more than just an upgrade of existing technology–it is the gateway to a whole new era of web development. This book will open the door to that gateway.

A New Kind of ASP

What does 'A New Kind of ASP' mean for the developer? After all, many products are hyped up as a major *breakthrough*, or *revolutionary*, but are in fact just point upgrades. ASP.NET isn't like that, and has been written from the ground up to provide a rich and flexible environment for developing Internet applications. Not only does it provide a host of new features, but it also changes the whole way in which you need to think about designing web-based applications.

Most of these changes come about because the architecture of ASP.NET is now much more modularized and based on the principles of components. Every page becomes a programmatically accessible, fully compiled object, and takes advantage of techniques like *object-oriented design, just-in-time compilation*, and *dynamic caching*. At the same time, the backward-compatible nature of ASP.NET means that existing pages and applications are still processed in the old way, so there is no sudden migration needed.

One of the major goals of ASP.NET is a huge improvement in the way that applications can be installed, configured, and updated. Components no longer have to be registered on the web server, and a whole application can be moved from one server to another just by using file copy commands, FTP, or specialized applications like the FrontPage Server Extensions.

What Does This Book Cover?

In this book, we attempt to explain just what ASP.NET is all about, how you can use it, and what you can use it for. We start in *Chapter 1* with a look at ASP.NET, explaining quickly the concepts and providing a layout to the rest of the book. The aim is to get you up and running with some sample pages as quickly as possible.

In *Chapter 2*, we move onto the .NET framework, examining the architecture that underpins the whole of .NET. Here, we talk about the *Common Language Runtime* (*CLR*), explaining why it is used and what benefits it brings. We also discuss the design goals of ASP.NET and show how they provide us with a great architecture for development.

Chapter 3 examines the *.NET languages* in detail, looking at the object-oriented architecture, and discusses the changes to Visual Basic and JScript, as well as the new language C#. We also discuss the benefits of the CLR with respect to these languages, and how it has freed the developer from the language wars of the past.

Chapter 4 is where we start to look at *ASP.NET in detail*, examining how ASP.NET pages are constructed. We take a look at a simple ASP page and show how this can be converted to ASP.NET, taking a look at how much cleaner and simpler the new page is. We look at how the code is managed within the new ASP.NET page, and how the new event model is much more reminiscent of Visual Basic than ASP.

Chapters 5, 6 and 7 examine the *ASP.NET server controls* in detail, starting with what these controls are and how they work. The discussion continues with the *validation controls*, which provide a declarative way of validating user input, before moving on to *web form controls* and *list controls*, which provide rich content management, and finally finishing up with *data binding*, showing how controls can automatically display data from data sources.

In *Chapter 8*, we start the discussion of *data management* in ASP.NET, looking at ADO.NET and its design goals and architecture. Moving into *Chapter 9*, we look at *relational data*, and how to manipulate data from databases, a topic continued in *Chapter 10* when we look at how to *update data* in those databases. The data discussion continues into *Chapter 11*, where we examine the use of *XML within .NET*, and how the XML objects provide a rich way of manipulating XML data.

Chapter 12 takes us to *web applications* where we look at what this term actually means, and how applications are managed. We include topics such as *state management*, the *application event architecture*, and *extending the application architecture*.

Once applications have been written, they need to be deployed, and this is explained in *Chapter 13*, along with *configuration*. We look at the *XML configuration file*, examining its *options* in detail, and look at *how ASP.NET can be extended*.

Chapter 14 covers writing *secure ASP.NET applications*, and looks at Windows 2000 and IIS security, and how ASP.NET can integrate into it. We look at both declarative and programmatic security issues, covering such topics as *forms-based and Passport authentication*.

Chapters 15 and 16 tackle the *base class libraries*, starting with a detailed look at *collections and lists*, continuing with *file system objects*, *streams*, *network classes*, and *regular expressions*. The base classes provide a huge array of functionality that can be used out of the box, and allow developers to implement sites with far less coding than was possible in ASP.

With the DNA architecture, the use of middle-tiers as a place for business components became commonplace. With .NET, the architecture has simplified and *Chapter 17* tackles *business objects* and the use of *transactional pages*. We look at the advantages of the new architecture and how applications should be designed to make the most of the new component model.

Chapter 18 deals with the topic of *extensibility*, examining server controls and how they can be easily written. It looks at the simple coding techniques used to create these controls, and how once written they can live alongside the supplied server controls.

In *Chapters 19 and 20*, we look at *Web Services* in detail. While this topic isn't specifically dedicated to ASP.NET, it is a major shift in the way applications are designed and written. Converting existing functionality to Web Services is extremely simple, and there is a huge amount of power that can be achieved using Web Services to provide and use the business-to-business model.

Chapter 21 deals with *pervasive devices*, or those that seem to be everywhere–phones, PDAs, and other such devices. The use of web sites is not just limited to computers with large screens, and the use of smaller devices is only going to increase in the future. In this chapter, we examine the *Mobile Internet Toolkit*, and how it can be used to easily produce sites accessible by small devices.

Chapter 22 deals with two important topics, *debugging* and *error handling*. Some of the new features are down to ASP.NET, while others are part of the underlying framework, and wherever they come from, these features are a great boon to developers. They provide simple and flexible ways of debugging and handling errors.

Chapter 23 discusses the topic of *migration and interoperability*. There is a large amount of existing ASP code in the world, and it is important that we examine how (if at all) existing applications can be migrated to the new framework. We also examine the topic of interoperating with existing COM components, to allow the gradual migration of middletier layers.

Finally, in *Chapter 24*, we look at a *case study* that encapsulates many of the techniques shown throughout the book. It is a sample e-commerce site, showing use of data access, server controls, class libraries, and so on.

Who Is This Book for?

This book is aimed at experienced developers who have some experience of ASP or Visual Basic. It is not aimed at beginners and does not cover general programming techniques or the basics of programming languages.

Our aim is to cover a conceptual overview of the product, including some of the background theory and explanation of why the product has developed along the lines it has. This is followed by a deeper investigation into the features that developers will use first. We show how to take advantage of the new features quickly and with the minimum of fuss.

Providing that you have used ASP before, and are reasonably comfortable with the concepts, you should be able to use this book without requiring any other reference material (other than the SDK Documentation and Help files provided with the product). You should also be comfortable with the general principles of using components, and the Visual Basic and VBScript languages. Some of the samples are written in other languages, such as JScript and C# (a new language) that are supported by the CLR, but you don't need to be fluent in these languages to be able to use this book.

What You Need To Use This Book

To run the samples in this book, you will need the following:

❑   Windows 2000, Windows Server 2003 or Windows XP.

❑   ASP.NET, which can be either the redistributable (included in the .NET SDK) or Visual Studio .NET.

The complete source code for the samples is available for download from our web site at http://www.wrox.com/. There are versions available in both Visual Basic .NET and C#. (See the Source Code section later in this introduction.)

Conventions

To help you get the most from the text and keep track of what's happening, we've used a number of conventions throughout the book.

> **Boxes like this one hold important, not-to-be forgotten information that is directly relevant to the surrounding text.**

Tips, hints, tricks, and asides to the current discussion are offset and placed in italics like this.

As for styles in the text:

❑   We *highlight* important words when we introduce them

❑   We show keyboard strokes like this: Ctrl+A

❑   We show file names, URLs, and code within the text like so: `persistence.properties`

❑   We present code in two different ways:

```
The Code Foreground style shows new, important, pertinent code. We indent
            the 2nd line to show you should enter both lines as one line.
The Code Background style shows code that's less important in the present
            context, or has been shown before.
```

Occasionally, code that needs to be placed all on one line is split over two because of the layout of the book, as shown in the preceding highlighted code. However, make sure you type it all on one line.

Source Code

As you work through the examples in this book, you may choose either to type in all the code manually or to use the source code files that accompany the book. All of the source code used in this book is available for download at http://www.wrox.com. Once at the site, simply locate the book's title (either by using the Search box or by using one of the title lists) and click the Download Code link on the book's detail page to obtain all the source code for the book.

> *Because many books have similar titles, you may find it easiest to search by ISBN; for this book the ISBN is 0-7645-5890-0.*

Once you download the code, just decompress it with your favorite compression tool. Alternately, you can go to the main Wrox code download page at http://www.wrox.com/dynamic/books/download.aspx to see the code available for this book and all other Wrox books.

Errata

We make every effort to ensure that there are no errors in the text or in the code. However, no one is perfect, and mistakes do occur. If you find an error in one of our books, like a spelling mistake or faulty piece of code, we would be very grateful for your feedback. By sending in errata you may save another reader hours of frustration and at the same time you will be helping us provide even higher quality information.

To find the errata page for this book, go to http://www.wrox.com and locate the title using the Search box or one of the title lists. Then, on the book details page, click the Book Errata link. On this page you can view all errata that has been submitted for this book and posted by Wrox editors. A complete book list including links to each book's errata is also available at www.wrox.com/misc-pages/booklist.shtml.

If you don't spot your error on the Book Errata page, go to www.wrox.com/contact/techsupport.shtml and complete the form there to send us the error you have found. We'll check the information and, if appropriate, post a message to the book's errata page and fix the problem in subsequent editions of the book.

p2p.wrox.com

For author and peer discussion, join the P2P forums at p2p.wrox.com. The forums are a Web-based system for you to post messages relating to Wrox books and related technologies and interact with other readers and technology users. The forums offer a subscription feature to email you topics of interest of your choosing when new posts are made to the forums. Wrox authors, editors, other industry experts, and your fellow readers are present on these forums.

At http://p2p.wrox.com you will find a number of different forums that will help you not only as you read this book, but also as you develop your own applications. To join the forums, just follow these steps:

1. Go to p2p.wrox.com and click the Register link.

2. Read the terms of use and click Agree.

3. Complete the required information to join as well as any optional information you wish to provide and click Submit.

4. You will receive an email with information describing how to verify your account and complete the joining process.

You can read messages in the forums without joining P2P but in order to post your own messages, you must join.

Once you join, you can post new messages and respond to messages other users post. You can read messages at any time on the Web. If you would like to have new messages from a particular forum e-mailed to you, click the Subscribe to this Forum icon by the forum name in the forum listing.

For more information about how to use the Wrox P2P, be sure to read the P2P FAQs for answers to questions about how the forum software works as well as many common questions specific to P2P and Wrox books. To read the FAQs, click the FAQ link on any P2P page.

Acknowledgments

While we depend on the software manufacturers to help us out with technical support and information for almost all the books we write, we must acknowledge the special situation within which this book was produced. Wrox have been at the forefront of ASP publishing since the first beginnings of this technology, and we are grateful for the regular support we receive from the developers and product managers at Microsoft.

The authors started working with the ASP.NET team during the writing of the *Preview to Active Server Pages+* book, and this relationship has continued through the writing of the original Professional ASP.NET book (based on Beta technology), and the rewriting of this edition. This book certainly wouldn't have been as good as it is without the generous assistance of so many of the developers. We'd like to thank everyone who answered questions, provided assistance with samples, reviewed chapters, and generally helped out, notably the ASP.NET team, the ADO.NET and XML teams, and the CLR team. There are really too many people to mention, but special thanks go to Mark Anders, Scott Guthrie, Mark Fussell, Mike Pizzo, Andres Sanabria, and Erik Olsen. We'd also like to thank Carl Grumbeck for making us more than welcome every time we visit the Microsoft labs – next time we'll remember the tea.

To all of you, thanks guys – we hope you like the result.

A Fast Track Guide to ASP.NET

Microsoft's .NET technology has attracted a great deal of press since Beta 1 was first released to the world. Since then, mailing lists, newsgroups, and web sites have sprung up containing a mixture of code samples, applications, and articles of various forms. Even if you're not a programmer using existing ASP technology, it's a good bet that you've at least heard of .NET, even if you aren't quite sure what it involves. After all, there's so much information about .NET that it's sometimes hard to filter out what you need from what's available. With new languages, new designers, and new ways of programming, you might wonder exactly what you need to write ASP.NET applications.

That's where this chapter comes in, because we are going to explain exactly what is required, and how to go about using it. The aim is to get you up and running, able to write simple ASP.NET pages as quickly as possible, and give you a solid grounding in the basics of the new framework. This will not only benefit existing ASP programmers, but also people who haven't used ASP, including Visual Basic programmers who need to write web applications. ASP.NET makes the whole job much easier, whatever your skill set.

In particular, we will look at:

- ❑ Installing and testing ASP.NET
- ❑ The benefits of the new technology
- ❑ The basic differences between ASP and ASP.NET
- ❑ The new programming model
- ❑ The rich hierarchy of server controls

We start with the simple discussion of why ASP.NET has come about.

Evolution or Revolution?

As developers, we are all used to the evolutionary cycle of software product releases, where each new release adds a few features and cures a bunch of bugs. Server–side Web technology has followed this pattern, with products such as dbWeb and the IDC rapidly settling into the Active Server Pages we know and love today. ASP 1.0 was released in 1996, and although it has gone through a further two releases, it hasn't really changed that much – until now. Be prepared to throw away many of those ingrained ASP programming habits, as you've an interesting ride ahead.

ASP.NET is where the revolution begins, because it is radically different from previous versions. Its first appearance into the world was at the Wrox Conference in Washington D.C. back in 1999, where impromptu applause showed how much the audience liked the product. Then in July 2000, ASP.NET received its first public release at PDC, where around 6,000 developers were bombarded with nothing but .NET. Consequently, they spent most of the week looking like rabbits in headlights – rather dazed and confused with all they had to take in. The concept of .NET isn't particularly difficult to understand, but ASP.NET is very different from what we are used to.

That's really the whole crux of the matter. ASP.NET is just a part of the whole .NET Framework, but to use ASP.NET effectively you have to understand the underlying architecture. In the next chapter we'll outline this new architecture and the benefits it brings, but for now we need to look at ASP.NET.

Getting Started with ASP.NET

The change to ASP.NET may seem daunting to some, but in the immortal words of Douglas Adams: *don't panic!* Even though there's been a radical change, the basics of ASP.NET are easy to grasp, especially if you've only programmed in Visual Basic before. Another important point to highlight is that ASP.NET sits alongside ASP – it doesn't touch existing ASP applications at all. Therefore, you don't have to worry about anything that you've previously done suddenly not working.

ASP.NET is supported on Windows 2000 (Professional and Server versions), Windows XP Professional, and is included in Windows Server 2003. It is not supported for Windows NT or the Windows 9x platforms. You can install Visual Studio .NET on these platforms and remotely use ASP.NET on the supported platforms. ASP.NET can be obtained from Microsoft, at http://www.Microsoft.com/net, http://www.asp.net/, or http://www.gotdotnet.com/, and is part of the MSDN Subscription service.

Installing .NET

Installation is extremely simple, consisting of one or two executables, depending on your installation requirements. The first program installs the framework, including ASP.NET – this is the least you need. During installation, you may be asked to update the Microsoft Windows Installer components, and if so, you should click the Yes button to update them. This update is required for the .NET SDK installation.

You may see a window indicating that *Microsoft Data Access Components (MDAC)* 2.7 is not installed on your system. You can press the Ignore button to continue with the setup process – MDAC 2.7 isn't required for .NET, although it is recommended. If you are installing .NET as part of the Visual Studio

.NET installation, then MDAC 2.7 is installed for you. Otherwise, you can get MDAC 2.7 or later as a free download from http://www.microsoft.com/data/.

The second program includes the samples and documentation. Once the SDK Installation Wizard starts you'll have the usual license screen followed by the options screen, as shown in Figure 1-1:

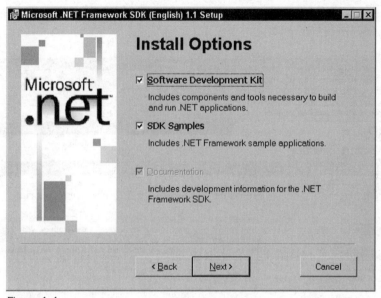

Figure 1-1

You can choose to install the required components, tools and samples, as well as the SDK samples. Leave all options ticked to ensure that everything is installed. The distributable version of the .NET Framework is around 23Mb, and doesn't contain samples or documentation.

Configuring the Samples

The installation routine creates a folder called Microsoft .NET Framework SDK containing an HTML page titled Samples and QuickStart Tutorials. From this page you should follow the steps outlined:

Step 1: Download and Install the Microsoft SQL Server 2000 Desktop Engine (MSDE): Click this link to be taken to the MSDE download page. Follow the instructions to download and install MSDE. If you already have MSDE or SQL Server installed, ensure you install Service Pack 3.

Step 2: Set up the QuickStarts: Click this link and select Run this program from its current location to configure the databases, IIS, and perform other installation routines. You may also receive another Security Warning dialog when you run this program, and you can select Yes to allow the program to run.

At this point the samples are installed, and you have the option to Launch them. You can also launch the samples by navigating to the Microsoft .NET Framework SDK menu (installed under the Programs) and selecting Samples and QuickStart Tutorials.

Running the Samples

From the main QuickStart page, select Start the ASP.NET QuickStart Tutorial, and you will be presented with the screen shown in Figure 1-2:

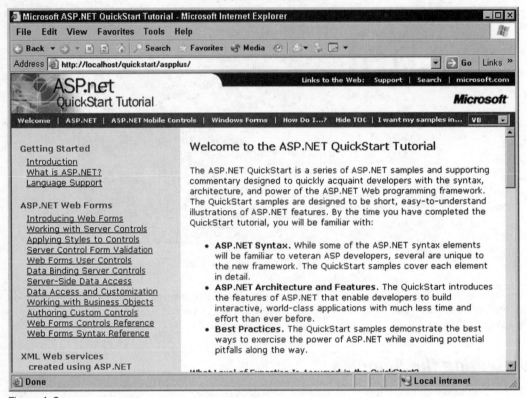

Figure 1-2

The left-hand portion of the screen shows the samples broken into their groups. You'll see examples of these topics throughout the book.

The right-hand side of the screen shows the samples, including descriptions and sourcecode. The sourcecode for all of the samples is available in Visual Basic, C#, and JScript. The use of these languages is discussed later in the chapter.

Sample Group	Consists of...
ASP.NET Web Applications	What defines an ASP.NET application, and how the global files are used.
Cache Services	The new cache features, allowing pages or data to be cached to improve performance.
Configuration	The new XML-based application configuration.
Deployment	A description of how applications are deployed.
Security	An examination of the authentication and authorization features in the .NET Framework.
Localization	Examples of how internationalization can be achieved.
Tracing	How the new tracing features of ASP.NET increase developer productivity.
Debugging	How to use the new visual debugger.
Performance	Overview, tips, and tricks on improving performance.
ASP to ASP.NET Migration	Examples showing how to migrate existing applications.
Sample Applications	Some sample applications, described below.

The Sample Applications

The sample applications give you a good idea of what can be achieved with ASP.NET, as well as showing how it can be achieved and some best practices for writing applications.

- ❑ **A Personalized Portal**: A sample portal application, allowing user login, content delivery, user preferences, configuration, and so on. It's an extremely good example of the use of *User Controls*, which are reusable ASP.NET pages.

- ❑ **An E-Commerce Storefront**: A small electronic–commerce site, based around a simple grocery store. It shows some good uses of data binding and templating, and how a shopping basket system could be implemented.

- ❑ **A Class Browser Application**: Shows how you can browse through the hierarchy of classes and objects. Not only is this useful from a learning point of view, but it also shows how the classes are queried by run–time code. This is one of the great new features of the framework, and is explained in more detail in the next chapter.

- ❑ **IBuySpy.com**: An electronic–commerce site, showing more features than the other sample store. It contains user logins, shopping baskets, and so on.

Additional Samples

The preceding list of samples describes just the ones that are installed by the SDK, but there are plenty of others available, such as a .NET version of the Duwamish site. All of the code for the samples in the book is available from the Wrox Press web site (at www.wrox.com). Microsoft has three additional sites where information and samples can be obtained:

❑ www.asp.net is the central site for downloads and links.

❑ www.ibuyspy.com is the IBuySpy application online. This code runs online as well as being available as a download (in VB.NET and C#). This site also contains links to a portal based version of IBuySpy, allowing user customization, and a news based version, aimed at content delivery.

❑ www.gotdotnet.com is a community site for all .NET developers. It's full of links and samples by both Microsoft and third parties. This site also has a list of ASP.NET hosting companies. There are also plenty of third party sites, and since this list may change, your best bet is to go to www.gotdotnet.com and follow the links page.

Visual Studio .NET 2003

Although this book is primarily aimed at ASP.NET, it is important that we mention Visual Studio .NET as well. The first thing to make clear is that Visual Studio .NET isn't required to write ASP.NET applications, but it does provide an extremely rich design environment. It provides features such as drag and drop for controls, automatic grid and list support, integrated debugging, Intellisense, and so on.

The installation of Visual Studio .NET comprises several steps, starting with Figure 1-3:

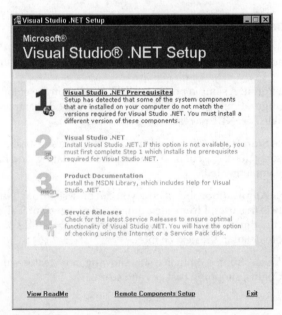

Figure 1-3

The Component Update installs the following:

- ❏ Windows 2000 Service Pack 2, if installing on Windows 2000 (this requires a reboot)
- ❏ Microsoft Windows Installer 2.0
- ❏ Microsoft FrontPage 2000 Web Extensions Client
- ❏ Setup Runtime Files
- ❏ Microsoft Internet Explorer 6.0 and Internet Tools (this requires a reboot)
- ❏ Microsoft Data Access Components 2.7
- ❏ Microsoft Visual J#.NET Redistributable Package 1.1
- ❏ Microsoft .NET Framework

The Component Update install allows you to enter a login name and password to be used during the reboots, so that the entire installation can take place without user interaction. After the Component Update has finished the Visual Studio.NET 2003 installation starts, and offers a similar setup to previous versions, as shown in Figure 1-4:

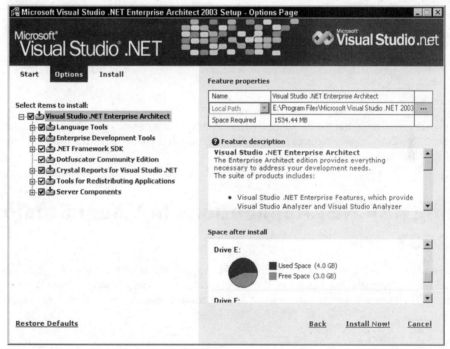

Figure 1-4

Once this step is completed, you have the option of checking for Service Releases, to allow product updates to be automatically downloaded for you.

If you've used previous version of Visual Studio, you may think that the installed menu items are rather sparse, since you only get two or three items (depending upon your installation options). What's noticeable is that the two main items are Microsoft Visual Studio .NET 2003 and Microsoft Visual Studio .NET 2003 Documentation. Because the underlying .NET architecture changes the way languages are used, Visual Studio .NET has been built to take this into account. So, no longer do you pick your language and then run the tool associated with that language. Now you just start Visual Studio .NET and then decide in which language you wish to write, and the type of application to create, as shown in Figure 1-5:

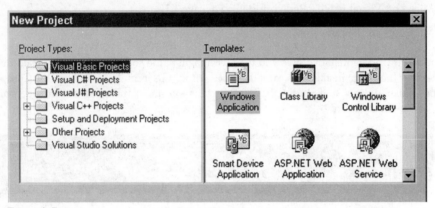

Figure 1-5

What's great about this is that the development environment is the same, whatever the language and application. This dramatically reduces training time, as you don't have to learn a different tool to do something differently.

Creating ASP.NET Applications in Visual Studio .NET 2003

When using Visual Studio .NET, select ASP.NET Web Application from the New Project dialog (shown in Figure 1-5), and this creates the named web site and creates some default pages. From that point onwards, you just use the design environment to drag controls onto the design grid, as shown in Figure 1-6:

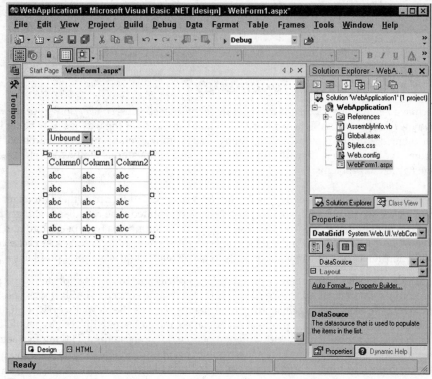

Figure 1-6

You can then use View Code (or the more familiar double-click on a control) to see the code for the web page you are creating.

We're not going to go into any more detail on using Visual Studio .NET, as it's too big a topic and really is outside the scope of this book. What we really want to concentrate on is ASP.NET itself.

How Is ASP.NET Different from ASP?

This question can be answered in one word – very! ASP.NET is not just a new version, but a whole new idea and way of programming web applications. New features weren't retrofitted into ASP to give us a new version – ASP.NET has been written from the ground up to provide the best possible application framework. This has meant that, in many areas, compatibility with ASP has been broken, but in the long run this is a good thing. It means that ASP.NET provides a much stronger platform for developing applications, and gives many more benefits.

If you're worried about the compatibility issue, then remember we mentioned earlier that ASP.NET runs alongside ASP. Even though there are many differences between the two, installing ASP.NET won't break existing applications. That's because your existing ASP pages are still processed by the same mechanism as before, and the new framework processes ASP.NET pages. This is achieved by ASP.NET pages having a new file extension (.aspx), meaning they are not processed in the same way as ASP pages.

ASP -ASP.NET compatibility and migration issues are covered in Chapter 23.

Why Do We Need a New Technology?

ASP has achieved enormous success as a way of developing web sites, so *why* do we see the need for something new? Simply put, ASP hasn't evolved to take into account the way it's now being used. Although designed with great scope and flexibility, I don't think even its authors could have seen how it would become the cornerstone of many applications. Like a tempestuous Hollywood starlet, its rapid rise to fame has led to problems:

❑   ASP is a scripted language, relying mainly on VBScript and JScript. Other languages are available if we install an interpreter, but it's still interpreted. The two disadvantages of interpreted languages are the lack of strong types (as supported by typed languages such as Visual Basic and C/C++), and the lack of a compiled environment. ASP does cache code, but it's still interpreted, and this inevitably leads to performance and scalability problems.

❑   ASP doesn't provide an inherent structure for applications. In the days of static web pages, we used to see small, focused source files. With the dynamic concept of ASP, it was possible to build code into the web page, again leading to problems. There's the eternal worry of mixing code and content, which can be a problem if you have a mixed team, with certain people designing the HTML and the interface, with different people doing the coding. Having two sets of people working on the same files is asking for trouble. Another problem was the ability to make the code complex, leading to larger source files. Include files allow a certain amount of structure and code reuse, but it was never really a great solution.

❑   You have to write code in ASP to do most things, no matter how simple. For example, consider the task of validating form fields. Just to ensure that values are entered into a field requires code. Other areas such as caching content, maintaining form state, and so on, all require code. Even adding new HTML controls requires writing the raw HTML to the page.

❑   The world of browser-compatibility has morphed into device-compatibility. While the majority of Web access still takes place from a PC and browser, how long will that remain the case? Mobile devices are becoming more prevalent, and more powerful, leading to more problems designing sites. If you want your web site to obtain maximum reach, you need to contend with these devices, and this means writing code to detect the device and render the appropriate content.

❑   Standards compatibility also plays a big part in Web development. XHTML is becoming more widely accepted, XML and XSLT are both now widely used, and talking to mobile devices might mean support for WML. Support for these standards mean that your ASP applications not only have to work with existing standards, but also be easily upgradeable to support future standards.

These are just few of the problems that are encountered when building ASP applications. The rapidly changing nature of the Internet often requires rapid changes to applications. For languages that have strong development environments, practices such as componentization, code reuse, rapid development, and so on, are a great boon to a developer, but this sort of support is lacking in ASP. The rise of Business-to-Business applications and peer-to-peer data-sharing also brings great challenges to the developer.

ASP.NET was written from the ground up to meet these needs. Not only does it answer many of the questions posed by the existing development environment, but also provides great extensibility, and brings great tool support. At its minimum, all you require is the ASP.NET redistributable, which is freely available, and you can continue to use your favorite editor of choice (come on, admit it – it's Notepad). This gives you access to everything possible with ASP.NET, including multi-language support. For a richer environment you can use Visual Studio .NET, where you get the drag and drop support, colored code (more useful than you'd think), context-sensitive help and tooltips, and all of the usual great editing features that Visual Studio has brought in the past.

Benefits of ASP.NET

From this discussion of the problems with ASP it would be easy to say that ASP.NET solves those problems, and while that is so, there's a lot more to it than that. To understand what's been done, have a look at four of the main goals of ASP.NET:

❑   Make code cleaner

❑   Improve deployment, scalability, security, and reliability

❑   Provide better support for different browsers and devices

❑   Enable a new breed of web applications

You may not see some of this support directly, as the *Common Language Runtime* (*CLR*) handles much of it. This is discussed in detail in the next chapter, but for now we shall concentrate on how ASP.NET improves our lives.

Multiple Languages

ASP has been limited to scripting engines, notably VBScript and JScript. The .NET Framework inherently supports multiple languages, so you can use whichever you feel most comfortable with. By default the CLR comes with Visual Basic .NET, C#, and JScript .NET (all compiled), and there are a number of third party languages that we can use, such as Perl, COBOL, and many others. Additionally, Visual Studio .NET adds support for Visual C++, and an implementation of Java (called J#.NET). Because this language support is part of the framework, it really doesn't matter what language you, or others in your team, use. Obviously, from your point of a view, it's probably best to maintain some degree of compatibility (for maintenance purposes if nothing else), but as far as the framework is concerned, anything goes.

This multiple language support isn't just limited to what's available, but also to how it's used. It's quite possible to write components in one language, and use (or reuse) them from another language. The server-based controls are written in C#, but they can quite conveniently be sub-classed from Visual Basic .NET, and then sub-classed again in JScript .NET (or any .NET supported language).

The framework is covered in more detail in the next chapter, while Chapter 3 delves into the languages themselves in more detail.

Server Processing

If you've done some Visual Basic programming, then you'll find the switch to the new ASP.NET Server Controls fairly painless, but they might cause some initial confusion if your programming has been limited to ASP. There's no need to worry though, as they are extremely easy to understand and use – it's just that they are very different from ASP.

One of the big problems with ASP is that pages simply define one big function, starting at the top of the page and finishing at the bottom. The page content is rendered in the page order, whether it is straight HTML or ASP-generated HTML. Therefore, our logic was dependent upon its position in the page, and there's no way to target HTML controls except by rendering them as part of the stream. Anything we do requires us to write code, and that includes the output of HTML elements.

ASP.NET solves this problem by introducing a declarative, server-based model for controls. This is where the concept may seem alien to ASP programmers, because the controls are declared on the server, can be programmed against on the server, but can be event driven from the client. This sounds pretty weird, but it's simple to use. All you have to do to turn a normal HTML control into a server control is add `runat="server"` as an attribute. For example:

```
<input id="FirstName" type="text" runat="server">
```

This is a standard HTML control, but the addition of the `runat` attribute allows the control to be programmed against with server-side code. For example, if this control is placed within a form and we submit the form back to the same page, we can do this in our server-side code:

```
Dim PersonFirstName As String
PersonFirstName = FirstName.Text
```

Making a control run on the server allows us to use the `ID` attribute to identify it directly. This allows the code to become more readable, since we don't have to refer to the form contents or copy the contents into variables. It's also more natural to refer to the control directly, which makes developing pages simpler. If you've done any Visual Basic or VBA programming, this won't seem too alien for you.

If you've only done scripting in ASP, then this may seem strange, but that's only because it's a different way of working with content to and from the browser. You've probably done database access, so you've used objects, called methods, and set properties, and the ASP.NET Server Controls aren't any different from this.

The new server processing architecture is covered in Chapter 4.

Web Form Controls

Converting existing HTML controls to server-side ones is simple, but there are still several problems with this approach:

❑ **Consistency**: We are still stuck with the rather non-intuitive nature of some HTML controls. Why for example, is there an `INPUT` tag for single line text entry, but a `TEXTAREA` tag for multi-line text entry? Surely a single control where we specify the rows and columns makes more sense?

❑ **User Experience**: How do we easily write sites that render rich content for browsers such as IE, while also preserving compatibility with down level browsers? HTML doesn't have the ability to change its content depending on the browser – we have to write the code for that.

❑ **Devices**: How do we write sites that cope with devices other than browsers? WAP-Phones, PDAs, and even fridges have browsers nowadays. Like the browser issue, we'd have to manually write code for this.

To alleviate these problems, Microsoft has created a set of server controls, identified by the `asp:` prefix. The ASP.NET server controls tackle these problems by:

❑ Providing a consistent naming standard. For example, all text entry fields are handled by the `TextBox` control. For the different modes (such as multi-line and password), we just specify attributes.

❑ Providing consistent properties. All server controls use a consistent set of properties, making it easier to remember. For example, the `Text` field of a `TextBox` is more intuitive than a `Value` field.

❑ Providing a consistent event model. Traditional ASP pages often have large amounts of code handling the posting of data, especially when one page provides multiple commands. With ASP.NET we wire-up controls to event procedures, giving our server-side code more structure.

❑ Emitting pure HTML, or HTML plus client-side JavaScript. With one minor exception (which is intentional), the server controls emit HTML 3.2 by default, giving great cross-browser compatibility. This can be changed so that by default we target up-level browsers such as IE, where the controls will emit HTML 4.0 and DHTML, providing a richer interface. All the user ever sees is the HTML content, not the server controls.

❑ Emitting device specific code. Certain controls will emit HTML when requested by a browser, but WML when requested by a WAP phone. The control handles the detection of the device and the generation of the correct markup.

The controls will be covered in detail in later chapters, but let's take a quick look at a simple example to see how these controls work:

```
<html>
<script language="VB" runat="server">
  Public Sub btn_Click(Sender As Object, E As EventArgs)
  ' some code goes here
  End Sub
</script>
<body>
<form runat="server">
 Press the button: <asp:Button runat="server"
            Text="Press Me" OnClick="btn_Click />
</form>
</body>
</html>
```

The server control in this example is a button, added to the page using the `asp:Button` element. There are several things to note about this control:

❑ It has the `runat="server"` attribute set, to tell ASP.NET that it should process this control.

❑ It uses the `Text` attribute to set the text to be shown on the button. This is consistent with other controls.

❑   It uses the `OnClick` attribute to identify the event procedure to be run when the button is clicked. Since this is a server control, this event procedure runs on the server.

The event procedure is automatically supplied with two parameters – the control that generated the event, and any additional arguments the procedure requires. Within the event procedure, we can access any other server controls, including the contents of input fields submitted during a postback.

HTML Output

In traditional ASP pages, the ASP processor runs server-side code, stripping it out so that only HTML and client-side script is sent to the client. This process is exactly the same for ASP.NET pages (the <% %> tags still work), with the server controls being converted to their HTML equivalents. For example, the preceding page code renders the following HTML to the browser:

```
<html>
<body>

<form name="ctrl2" method="post" action="test.aspx" id="ctrl2">
<input type="hidden" name="__VIEWSTATE"
    value="YTB6MTU5NDYxNjE5Ml9fX3g=2dbab7f5" />

 Press the button: <input type="submit" name="ctrl5" value="Press Me" />
</form>

</body>
</html>
```

There are several things to note here:

❑   The first is that the `form` has `method`, `action`, and `id` attributes added automatically. We can add these in ourselves (with the exception of the action attribute) if we want to, but it's not necessary.

❑   A hidden input field is added, which contains (in a compressed form) the state of the server controls. This is called the ViewState, and is how ASP.NET manages the content of the controls. View State is covered in Chapter 4.

❑   The Button is converted into a standard submit button.

So, we can see that even though we have better code on the server, it doesn't affect how the code is presented on the client. It's still standard HTML, with standard forms and elements.

Server Control Hierarchy

The server controls are logically broken down into a set of families:

❑   **HTML Server controls**: The server equivalents of the HTML elements

❑   **Web Form controls**: Map closely to individual HTML elements

❑   **List Controls**: Map to groups of HTML elements that produce grids or grid-like layout

- ❑ **Rich controls**: Produce rich content and encapsulate complex functionality, and will output pure HTML or HTML and script. A good example of this is the Calendar control, which provides the user with a calendar from only one line of code

- ❑ **Validation controls**: Non-visible controls, but allow the easy use of both server-side and client-side form validation.

- ❑ **Mobile controls**: Output HTML or WML depending upon the device accessing the page.

Chapters 5 and 6 deal extensively with most of these controls, and Chapter 21 covers the Mobile Controls.

At such an early stage in the book, you may not be able to see the implications that these controls have for you, but let's take a couple of common examples. First off, the case of displaying data from a database, perhaps in some form of grid. In ASP, we'd open the Recordset containing the data, and loop through the rows and columns building up an HTML table. We might well have this abstracted into a separate function in an include file, but we still had to write the code. With the ASP.NET DataGrid control, it's the control itself that handles this for us. The list controls (which include the DataGrid) have built in support for extracting data from a data source and creating the HTML for us. For example, consider the following ASP code:

```
<%
 Dim rs
 Dim fld

 Set rs = Server.CreateObject("ADODB.Recordset")

 rs.Open "SELECT * FROM authors", _
    "Provider=SQLOLEDB; Data Source=.; Initial Catalog=pubs; UID=sa; PWD="

 If Not rs.EOF Then
  Response.Write "<table border='1'><tr>"
  For Each fld In rs.Fields
   Response.Write "<td>" & fld.Name & "</td>"
  Next
  Response.Write "</tr>"

  While Not rs.EOF
   Response.Write "<tr>"
   For Each fld In rs.Fields
    Response.Write "<td>" & fld.Value & "</td>"
   Next
   Response.Write "</tr>"
   rs.MoveNext
  Wend

  Response.Write "</table>"
 End If
%>
```

There's nothing special about this – it just creates an HTML table. Now compare this to the equivalent ASP.NET code using a DataGrid:

```
<%@ Import Namespace="System.Data.SqlClient" %>
<script language="VB" runat="server">
 Sub Page_Load(Sender As Object, E As EventArgs)
   Dim con As New SqlConnection("Data Source=.; " & _
                 "Initial Catalog=pubs; UID=sa; PWD=")
   Dim cmd As SqlCommand
   con.Open()
   cmd = New SqlCommand("SELECT * FROM authors", con)
   DataGrid1.DataSource = cmd.ExecuteReader()
   DataGrid1.DataBind()
   con.Close()
 End Sub
</script>
<asp:DataGrid id="DataGrid1" runat="server"/>
```

Note that you should always close a database connection when you have finished with it. Either call the Close *method of the* Connection *object, or pass the value* CommandBehavior.CloseConnection *as the parameter to the* ExecuteReader *method. See Chapter 8 for more details.*

We can immediately see how much less code needs to be written. In fact, all of the code here relates to getting the data from the database and binding it to the grid. There isn't any code to create a table as the DataGrid does this.

Data binding is covered in Chapter 7.

Another great example of the power of controls is the Calendar control, which with one line of code creates a fully functional calendar on our web page:

```
<asp:Calendar runat="server"/>
```

That's it – nothing extra is needed to get it working.

This sort of simplified approach doesn't mean that the controls are simple, just simple to use. The onus on coding has moved from the web page developer to the control developer. There are also plenty of other non-Microsoft controls, either planned or released, covering everything from more advanced grids to TreeViews. Alternatively you can write your own controls. This is covered in Chapter 18.

Language Improvements

One of the greatest new features is that scripting is dead – hooray. This is a slight exaggeration, as what's really dead is the typeless, interpreted nature of these languages. VBScript is no longer supported, and is replaced with full Visual Basic support, while JScript is still supported but has the addition of types. In addition, a new language called C# (pronounced C Sharp) is introduced, with a format similar to C/C++. As ASP.NET is entirely written in C#, you can understand that this isn't a minor addition

We look at the detailed improvements in languages in Chapter 3, but for now, all we need to understand is that all languages:

❑ Support data types

❑ Use a common set of data types

❑   Are fully compiled

❑   Are object oriented, and support inheritance

What's also important is that the language support is built into the CLR, which provides this common support. This means that things such as inheritance are cross-language, so we can write components in C# and inherit and extend them in Visual Basic. The CLR manages all of this for us, as well as providing cross-language debugging, giving such features as being able to use a debugger to step through Visual Basic code in an ASP.NET page into a C# component.

Extensibility is also provided, meaning that additional languages are supported. Microsoft supply VB.NET, JScript, and C# as standard with the .NET SDK, but many other languages are being worked on by third parties.

Code and Content Separation

This is generally an unused feature of web site design, as many sites are created entirely by programmers. In itself, this isn't a bad thing, but I think programmers don't usually make great designers, and I count myself firmly in this group. ASP tended to build on this problem, as the code (ASP script) is, more often than not, intermingled with the content (HTML).

This makes it difficult for design and coding to be done at the same time, and also increases the risk of problems if updates to the page are required.

Code Inline

ASP.NET gets around this problem in one of two ways. The first is the code inline model, where code is still held within the ASP.NET page, but is not mixed with the HTML. It's easy to separate the code and content into two sections. For example:

```
<html>
<%-- This is the code section %>
<script runat="server">
Public Sub btn_Click(Sender As Object, E As EventArgs)
  YourName.Text = Name.Text
 End Sub
</script>
<body>
<%-- This is the content section %>
 <form runat="server">
  Enter your name: <asp:TextBox id="Name" runat="server"/>
  <br/>
  Press the button: <asp:Button OnClick="btn_Click"
             runat="server" Text="Press Me"/>
  <br/>
  Your name is: <asp:Label id="YourName" runat="server"/>
 </form>
</body>
</html>
```

This isn't that radical a design, but it is a marked difference from ASP where the <%...%> server blocks are often intermingled with the HTML. Don't worry about what the code does for the moment, as we'll be covering that later. What's important is that all of the script is kept separate from the content. This split is possible in ASP.NET because of the new server control architecture, which allows access to the HTML controls from server-based code. We'll be looking at this in a moment.

Code-Behind

The second way of separating code from content is the code-behind model, where the code is completely removed into a separate file. Using the previous example, our HTML file would now look like this:

```
<%@Page Language="VB" Inherits="Ch1CodeBehind"
    Src="Components\Ch1CodeBehind.vb" %>
<html>
<body>
<%-- This is the content section %>
 <form runat="server">
  Enter your name: <asp:TextBox id="Name" runat="server"/>
  <br/>
  Press the button: <asp:Button OnClick="btn_Click"
              runat="server" Text="Press Me"/>
  <br/>
  Your name is: <asp:Label id="YourName" runat="server"/>
 </form>
</body>
</html>
```

Once again don't worry too much about the code itself – it's the structure that's important. Notice how the script block has been removed, and a special Page directive has been added (these are covered in Chapter 4). This tells the CLR that the current page inherits its code from the named file, which looks like:

```
Imports System
Imports System.Web.UI
Imports System.Web.UI.WebControls

Public Class Ch1CodeBehind
        Inherits System.Web.UI.Page
 Public Sub btn_Click(Sender As Object, E As EventArgs)
  YourName.Text = Name.Text
 End Sub
End Class
```

Notice that the procedure btn_Click is the same as it was when it was inline. That's one of the great features of the code-behind model; apart from a few directives, the code remains exactly the same. And since we're now working in a compiled environment, there's no performance loss either.

Configuration

Two things govern the configuration of ASP.NET. The first is the standard IIS settings, no different from existing ASP applications. The second is the configuration file, an XML file containing the meta data for our application. There is a machine-wide file (machine.config) containing the defaults for all ASP.NET applications, and each application can have its own file (web.config) to override the defaults. The advantage of a file containing configuration information is that we don't need to touch the registry to modify settings – each application is self-contained. This has an added advantage when we look to deploy an ASP.NET application, because the configuration is just one of the files that we deploy.

> *The configuration files are covered in detail in Chapter 13.*

Deployment

Deployment is another area made significantly simpler in ASP.NET, and is generally called *XCopy Deployment*, for the simple reason that it's all we generally have to do. Each application is self-contained, including the configuration file and components. In the .NET Framework, components no longer require registration, and copying them to their target location is all that's required.

> *Deployment is covered in detail in Chapter 13.*

There are exceptions to this model of deployment. One is if we are interacting with COM/COM+ components, which still need to be registered. Another is if we are using *shared assemblies*, where .NET components are being used by more than one ASP.NET application. In this case the component isn't kept within the same directory as the rest of the ASP.NET files.

> *Interoperability with COM/COM+ is covered in Chapter 23.*

Writing ASP.NET Pages

The first part of this chapter has been a brief overview of some of the differences between ASP and ASP.NET, and Chapter 4 covers this in more detail. Now it's time to show you how to get those ASP.NET pages up and running as quickly as possible. Consider a simple form that extracts the author details from the pubs database. It will have a drop down list to show the various states where the authors live, a button to fetch the information, and a grid. This will quickly demonstrate several simple techniques you can use in your pages.

Creating a Web Site

The first thing to do is decide on where you want to create your samples. Like ASP, you can create a directory under \InetPub\wwwroot, or create a directory elsewhere and use a *Virtual Site* or *Virtual Directory* to point to it. There's no difference between the methods, it's purely a matter of preferences.

Next you can create your web pages, using whatever editor you prefer. You should give them an .aspx extension.

The Sample Page

Now let's add the code for the sample page – call this SamplePage.aspx (we'll examine it in more detail after we've seen it running). This page assumes that the Pubs database is installed on your system.

```
<%@ Import Namespace="System.Data.SqlClient" %>
<script language="VB" runat="server">
  Sub Page_Load(Sender As Object, E As EventArgs)
    If Not Page.IsPostBack Then
      state.Items.Add("CA")
```

```
                 state.Items.Add("IN")
                 state.Items.Add("KS")
                 state.Items.Add("MD")
                 state.Items.Add("MI")
                 state.Items.Add("OR")
                 state.Items.Add("TN")
                 state.Items.Add("UT")

        End If
     End Sub

     Sub ShowAuthors(Sender As Object, E As EventArgs)
        Dim con As New SqlConnection("Data Source=.; " & _
                    "Initial Catalog=pubs; UID=sa;
PWD=")
        Dim cmd As SqlCommand
        Dim qry As String
        con.Open()
        qry = "SELECT * FROM authors where state='" & _
           state.SelectedItem.Text & "'"
        cmd = New SqlCommand(qry, con)
        DataGrid1.DataSource = cmd.ExecuteReader()
        DataGrid1.DataBind()
          con.Close()
     End Sub
   </script>

<form runat="server">

   State: <asp:DropDownList id="state" runat="server" />
   <asp:Button Text="Show Authors" OnClick="ShowAuthors" runat="server"/>
   <p/>
   <asp:DataGrid id="DataGrid1" runat="server"/>

</form>
```

When initially run, you'll see the results as shown in Figure 1-7:

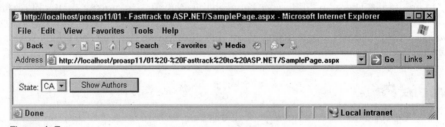

Figure 1-7

Nothing particularly challenging here, and when the button is pressed, the grid fills with authors from the selected state (Figure 1-8):

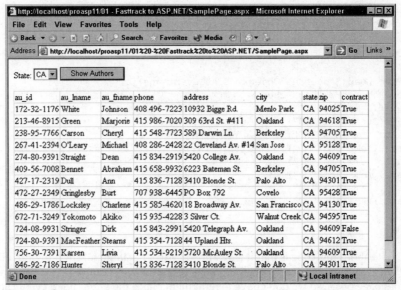

Figure 1-8

Again, nothing that couldn't be achieved with ASP, but let's look at the page code, starting with the controls:

```
<form runat="server">
  State: <asp:DropDownList id="state" runat="server" />
  <asp:Button Text="Show Authors" OnClick="ShowAuthors" runat="server"/>
  <p/>
  <asp:DataGrid id="DataGrid1" runat="server"/>
</form>
```

Here we have a form marked with the `runat="server"` attribute. This tells ASP.NET that the form will be posting back data for use in server code. Within the form, there is a `DropDownList` control(the equivalent of an HTML SELECT list) to contain the states, a `Button` (equivalent of an HTML INPUT `type="button"`) to postback the data, and a `DataGrid` control to display the authors. The button uses the `OnClick` event to identify the name of the server-side code to run when the button is pressed. Don't get confused by thinking this is the client-side, DHTML `onClick` event, because it's not. The control is a server-side control (`runat="server"`) and therefore the event will be acted upon within server-side code.

Now look at the remaining code, starting with the `Import` statement. This tells ASP.NET that we are going to use some data access code, in this case code specific to SQL Server.

```
<%@ Import Namespace="System.Data.SqlClient" %>
```

Next comes the actual code, written in Visual Basic.

```
<script language="VB" runat="server">
```

Here is the first real introduction to the event architecture. When a page is loaded, the `Page_Load` event is raised, and any code within the event procedure is run. In our case, we want to fill the `DropDownList` with a list of states, so we just manually add them to the list. In reality, this data would probably come from a database.

```
Sub Page_Load(Sender As Object, E As EventArgs)
If Not Page.IsPostBack Then
    state.Items.Add("CA")
    state.Items.Add("IN")
    state.Items.Add("KS")
    state.Items.Add("MD")
    state.Items.Add("MI")
    state.Items.Add("OR")
    state.Items.Add("TN")
    state.Items.Add("UT")
End If
End Sub
```

One thing to note about this code is that it is wrapped in an `If` statement, checking for a Boolean property called `IsPostBack`. One of the great things about the web controls is that they retain their contents across page posts, so we don't have to refill them. Since the `Page_Load` event runs every time the page is run, we'd be adding the states to the list that already exists, and the list would keep getting bigger. The `IsPostBack` property allows us to identify whether or not this is the first time the page has been loaded, or if we have done a post back to the server.

Now, when the button is clicked, the associated event procedure is run. This code just builds a SQL statement, fetches the appropriate data, and binds it to the grid.

```
Sub ShowAuthors(Sender As Object, E As EventArgs)
Dim con As New SqlConnection("Data Source=.; " & _
            "Initial Catalog=pubs; " & _
            ConfigurationSettings.AppSettings("DsnPubs"))
Dim cmd As SqlCommand
Dim qry As String
  con.Open()
qry = "SELECT * FROM authors where state='" & _
state.SelectedItem.Text & "'"
cmd = New SqlCommand(qry, con)

DataGrid1.DataSource = cmd.ExecuteReader()
DataGrid1.DataBind()
  con.Close()
End Sub
```

This code isn't complex, although it may seem confusing at first glance. The rest of the book explains many of these concepts in more detail, but we can easily see some of the benefits. The code is neatly structured, making it easy to write and maintain. Code is broken down into events, and these are only run when invoked. Chapter 4 contains a good discussion of the page events, how they can be used, and the order in which they are raised.

What's also noticeable is that there's less code to write compared to an equivalent ASP page. This means that we can create applications faster – most of the legwork is done by the controls themselves. What's also cool about the control architecture is that we can write our own to perform similar tasks. Because the entire .NET platform is object based, we can take an existing control and inherit from it, creating our own, slightly modified control. A simple example of this would be a grid within a scrollable region. The supplied grid allows for paging, but not scrolling.

Summary

This chapter has been a real whistle-stop tour! We looked at:

❑   The problems of ASP

❑   Why ASP.NET came about

❑   The differences between ASP and ASP.NET

❑   A simple example of an ASP.NET page

ASP is still a great product, and it's really important to focus on why we had to change, and the benefits it will bring in the long term. Initially there will be some pain as you learn and move towards the .NET architecture, but ultimately your applications will be smaller, faster, and easier to write and maintain. That's pretty much what most developers want from life!

Now it's time to learn about the .NET Framework itself, and how all of these great features are provided.

Understanding the .NET Framework

In the previous chapter, you saw how ASP.NET is a major evolution from ASP 3.0. ASP.NET provides a powerful new server-side control architecture, which makes the development of rich web pages easier than ever before. It has a cleaner, event-based programming model, making web development much more like traditional VB Forms programming. This results in the average ASP.NET page requiring much lesser code than an equivalent ASP page, which in turn leads to greater developer productivity and better maintainability. ASP.NET pages are also compiled, so web servers running ASP.NET applications can expect to far exceed the performance and scalability levels of previous ASP applications.

ASP.NET is part of the .NET Framework: a new computing platform that simplifies and modernizes application development and deployment on Windows. The .NET Framework is many things, but it is worthwhile listing its most important aspects. In short, the .NET Framework is:

❑ A platform designed from the start for writing Internet-aware and Internet-enabled applications that embrace and adopt open standards such as XML, HTTP, and SOAP.

❑ A platform that provides a number of very rich and powerful application development technologies, such as Windows Forms (used to build classic GUI applications) and of course ASP.NET (used to build Web applications).

❑ A platform with an extensive class library that provides wide-ranging support for data access (relational and XML), directory services, message queuing, and much more.

❑ A platform with a base class library that contains hundreds of classes for performing common tasks such as file manipulation, registry access, security, threading, and the searching of text using regular expressions.

❑ A language-neutral platform that makes all languages first class citizens. You can use the language you feel most comfortable and productive with, and not encounter any limitations.

❑ A platform that doesn't forget its origins, and has great interoperability support for existing components that you or third parties have written, using Component Object Model (COM), COM+, or standard DLLs.

❑ A platform with an independent code execution and management environment called the *Common Language Runtime (CLR)*, which ensures code is safe to run, and provides an abstract layer on top of the operating system, which allows elements of the .NET Framework to run on many operating systems and devices.

From a developer's perspective, the .NET Framework effectively supersedes the Windows development platform of old, providing an all-new, object-oriented alternative (some would say replacement) for the WIN32 API, all language runtimes, technologies like ASP, and the majority of the numerous COM object models (such as ADO) that are in use today.

This chapter looks at:

❑ The Microsoft vision for .NET, and the need for a new platform

❑ The role and power of the CLR

❑ The key elements that comprise the .NET Framework

❑ The key design goals and architecture of ASP.NET

What Is .NET?

When you first hear or read about .NET you may be a bit confused about its scope. What precisely is .NET? What technologies and products comprise .NET? Is .NET a replacement for COM? Or is it built using COM?

There is no simple answer to what .NET is. Microsoft has really blurred the boundaries of .NET, which is of course something you all know and love the Microsoft marketing division for. Ask any group of developers what Windows DNA is, and you'll get fifteen different answers. The same confusion is now happening with .NET. To make the confusion worse, Microsoft has dropped the Windows DNA name, and re-branded most of their server products (such as SQL Server 2000 and BizTalk Server 2000) as part of the all-encompassing *Windows Server System*. This has left many people thinking that .NET is just DNA renamed, which, of course, it isn't.

The Pieces of .NET

The way to cut through this confusion is to divide .NET into three main areas:

❑ **The .NET vision**: The idea that all devices will some day be connected by a global broadband network (that is, the Internet), and that software will become a service provided over this network.

❑ **The .NET Framework**: New technologies such as ASP.NET that make .NET more than just a vision, providing concrete services and technologies so that developers can build applications to support the needs of users connected to the Internet today.

❑ **The Windows Server System**: Server products, such as SQL 2000 and BizTalk 2000, which are used by .NET Framework applications but are not currently written using the .NET Framework. All future versions of these server products will support .NET, but will not necessarily be rewritten using .NET.

For developers, another important piece of the .NET platform is, of course, developer tools. Microsoft has a major new update of their premier development environment for .NET, called Visual Studio .NET. However you can still develop .NET applications using Notepad, or any other IDE, which is what a lot of the Microsoft development teams do.

The .NET Vision

For years now Microsoft has been investing heavily in the Internet, in terms of product development, technology development, and consumer marketing. I can't think of any Microsoft product or technology that isn't web-enabled these days, and I can't think of any marketing material Microsoft has released that isn't Internet-centric. The reason for this Internet focus is that Microsoft is betting its future on the success of the Internet as well as other open standards such as XML succeeding and being widely adopted. They are also betting that they can provide the best development platform and tools for the Internet in a world of open standards.

The .NET Framework provides the foundations and plumbing on which the Microsoft .NET vision is built. Assuming the .NET vision becomes reality, very soon the whole world will be predominantly Internet-enabled, with broadband access available just about anywhere, at any time. Devices of all sizes will be connected together over this network, trading and exchanging information at the speed of light. The devices will speak common languages like XML over standardized or shared protocols such as HTTP, and these devices will be running a multitude of software on different operating systems and devices. This vision is not specific to Microsoft; many other companies, such as IBM and Sun, have their own spin on it.

The .NET Framework provides the foundation services that Microsoft sees as essential for making their .NET vision a reality. It's all well and good having a global network and open standards like XML to make it easier for two parties to exchange data and work together, but history has shown that great tools and technologies to implement support for standards are an important ingredient in any vision. Marketing drivel alone doesn't make applications; great developers with great tools and a great platform do. Enter the .NET Framework.

The .NET Framework is the bricks and mortar of the Microsoft .NET vision. It provides the tools and technologies needed to write applications that can seamlessly and easily communicate over the Internet (or any other network, such as an intranet) using open standards like XML and SOAP. The .NET Framework also solves many of the problems developers face today when building and deploying Windows DNA applications. For example, have you ever cursed at having to shut down ASP applications to replace component files, wished you didn't have to register components, or spent hours trying to track down binary compatibility or versioning problems? The good news is that the .NET Framework provides a solution to problems like these; no more registering components or shutting down applications to upgrade them!

Windows DNA was the name Microsoft gave to their n-tier development methodology before .NET was launched. The name is now somewhat defunct, but the same principles (for the most part) still hold true in .NET.

Even better news is that the .NET Framework also solves many of the problems you're likely to experience in the future. For example, ever considered how you're going to adapt your applications or web sites to run on or support small hand-held devices? Have you thought about the impact of the up and coming 64-bit chips from Intel? Microsoft has, and these are all catered for as part of .NET Framework.

So, the whole push towards the Internet stems from Microsoft's belief that all devices (no matter how small or large) will one day be connected to a broadband network, the Internet. All will benefit in unimaginable ways from the advantages this global network will bring – your fridge could automatically send orders out to your local supermarket to restock itself, or your microwave could download the cooking times for the food you put in it, and automatically cook it. Wouldn't that be cool (or, in fact, hot)?

These ideas might sound a little futuristic, but manufacturers are already working on prototypes. Imagine that you were part of a team working on one of these projects. Where would you start? How many technologies and protocols would you need to use? How many languages? How many different compilers? Just thinking about some of these fairly elementary issues makes my brain hurt. However, this is just the tip of the iceberg.

If a fridge were going to restock itself automatically, wouldn't it be cool to have it connect via the Internet to the owner's local supermarket, or any other supermarket available in some global supermarket directory? The supermarket systems and fridges would need to exchange information in some standard format like XML, ordering the goods and arranging delivery. Delivery times would have to be determined, probably by the fridge, based upon the owner's electronic diary (maybe stored on a mobile device or in a central Internet location – using My .Net Services, for instance), telling the fridge when the owner will be at home to accept the delivery.

Mad as it sounds, I do believe applications like this will be available and very common in the next five to ten years. Your lives as developers really are going to change a lot in the future, especially when web services are widely adopted. I doubt if you'll all be programming fridges (although I know of people who are), but the Internet has already changed your lives and careers dramatically, and that change isn't slowing down. More and more devices are going to get connected, and if you are going to adapt quickly to these changes, you need a great toolset that enables you to meet the time-to-market requirements of the Internet, and a toolset that also provides a consistent development strategy, no matter what type of development you're doing.

Let's take a look at the former *Microsoft Windows Distributed interNet Applications (Windows DNA)* platform, and see why the existing platform and the tools need to be revamped for some of this next generation of web-enabled applications.

The Problems with Windows DNA

Microsoft Windows DNA architecture started back in late 1996 and early 1997, when Microsoft began to recognize the potential of the Internet. They released Windows DNA to help companies embrace their vision (and of course sell their platform).

Windows DNA was a programming model or blueprint that companies could use when designing n-tier distributed component-based applications for the Windows platform. At that time, development of .NET had already begun inside Microsoft, although back then it was called COM+ 2.0.

Windows DNA applications did not have to use the Internet, but the Internet was the primary focus for most companies. Over the years Windows DNA grew and came to cover the various Microsoft products and services that could be used in an n-tier application to provide functionality such as messaging and data storage.

The problem with Windows DNA was not the blueprint for design; indeed, the same n-tier designs still apply for .NET applications. The problem with Windows DNA was that the enabling toolset provided by Microsoft and others was primarily based upon old technologies like COM, whose origins date back to the early nineties, and the Win32 API utilizing proprietary languages and protocols – a bad thing these days, as you all know. This is, at least initially, rather surprising. But just think of the pains you go through as a developer today when building web applications. Do you think the Windows DNA platform is easy to use? Do you think the platform is consistent? The answer is, of course, a resounding *no*.

Let's review some of the most common problems associated with Windows DNA, and touch briefly on how .NET solves these problems. With a few of them covered, we'll really start to drill down into the driving technology behind .NET and the CLR. You'll see how these lower-level technologies really drive and enable the development of higher-level technologies such as ASP.NET.

Stopping 24 x 7 Applications

Have you ever tried replacing a COM component on a production web server? Or even on a development machine? Prior to .NET, to do this you had to stop the entire web site, copy a file across, and then restart the web site. Even worse, sometimes you had to reboot a machine because COM and IIS just seem to get confused, and do not release files correctly. This is a pain during the development of an application, and is unacceptable for production sites that must always be running. This problem is caused by the way COM manages files such as DLLs – once they are loaded, you cannot overwrite them unless they are unloaded during an idle period, which of course may never happen on a busy web server.

.NET components do not have to be locked like this. They can be overwritten at any time thanks to a feature called *Shadow Copy*, which is part of the CLR. Any applications you write, as well as Microsoft technologies like ASP.NET, can take advantage of this feature; this prevents *Portable Executable (PE)* files such as DLLs and EXEs from being locked. With ASP.NET, changes to component files that you create and place in the `bin` directory – this is where components for an application live – are automatically detected. ASP.NET will automatically load the changed components, and use them to process all *new* web requests not currently executing, while at the same time keeping the older versions of the components loaded until previously active requests are completed.

Side - by - Side

Another difficulty with Windows DNA was that it was not easy to run two different versions of the same application components side-by-side, either on the same machine, or in the same process. This problem is addressed by Windows XP, but on pre-Windows XP systems you typically have to upgrade an entire application to use the latest set of components, or go through some serious development nightmares.

.NET allows different versions of the same components to co-exist and run side-by-side on the same machine and within the same process. For example, one ASP.NET web page could be using version 1 of a component, while another, version 2 (which is not compatible with version 1, but for the most part uses the same class and method names). Based upon the dependencies for the web page (or another component) that is using this component, the correct version of a component will be resolved and loaded, even within the same process. Running multiple versions of the same code simultaneously is referred to as *side-by-side execution*.

> *Using side-by-side execution, you can run version 1.0, version 1.1, and all future versions of ASP.NET side-by-side on the same machine without conflict. The same is true for the .NET Framework itself.*

Scripting Limitations

If you're an ASP developer who is not familiar with writing components (if at all), you have probably found it annoying that you can't do everything you want to from within an ASP page. You may have had to write, find, or buy components to expose the necessary functionality to your pages, such as registry access and security, which, at the end of the day, are all a standard part of the Windows platform.

This problem is caused because ASP pages can only be written in scripting languages, which cannot directly access the Win32 API, and also have many COM-related restrictions. This can be a real pain if you haven't got the resources or time to invest in component development. Wouldn't it be nice if you could do everything within an ASP page, and just use components when you have time, and when there is a benefit such as common code reuse? Well, with ASP.NET, you can take that approach.

ASP.NET pages can use all of the functionality of the .NET Framework. You no longer have to write components to work around the problems of the scripting runtime (since there is no scripting runtime any more). You can decide what code goes into an ASP.NET page, and what goes in your components. There are no scalability issues with code in ASP.NET page (but it still is good practice to create components for reasons of code reuse and maintenance).

Versioning Hell (DLL Hell)

Undoubtedly, the biggest problem with Windows DNA is versioning. When an application is built, it typically consists of many intricately related pieces such as standard DLLs, ASP pages, and COM DLLs hosting components. ASP page X might not be able to run without COM component Y, which requires DLL Z, which in turn is dependent upon more DLLs, or specific versions of object models like ADO 2.6. All of these dependencies are implicit (not documented, visible, or enforceable by the operating system), and have to be satisfied for an application to run smoothly.

If any of these application dependencies are broken or missing, the application won't function correctly, or – worse still – might break at runtime halfway through some important operation. Many components are also dependent upon system-wide DLLs shared by many applications, and values in the system registry. It is very easy to break applications by simply installing another application, or accidentally changing the registry using a tool like Regedit. Tracking down these problems can be a very difficult task, if not impossible.

To resolve versioning problems, .NET enables developers to specify versions and dependencies between different software components. These dependencies are stored along with the component code itself in an *assembly* (think of an assembly as something like a DLL or EXE file for now), and .NET uses this information to ensure application integrity is maintained – reporting errors if components cannot be loaded, if missing dependencies are found, or even if it detects files that have been tampered with.

To further reduce registration problems, .NET no longer uses the registry for component registration. Information about the types (classes, structures, enums, etc.) is contained with the code, and this type information is retrieved directly from the files at runtime. When an application instantiates a new type, such as a business object, the CLR will scan the application directory for the component, and then look at other predefined locations for the component. Once a component is located, its information is cached (for performance reasons) and reused on subsequent requests. This decentralized registration reduces the chance that applications will interfere with each other by mistake, and also removes the need to register and unregister components. This makes deploying applications much easier, since all you have do is copy files into a directory.

> The .NET Framework supports shared components, although, unless you're a component vendor, these are not recommended. Shared components are installed in the Global Assembly Cache (GAC), which can be thought of as a system directory for holding component files.

Why Do You Need .NET?

The problems we've discussed here with Windows DNA are just a few of many that you've almost certainly encountered. These problems, combined with the inherent complexity of the Windows DNA platform, makes it a less than optimal platform for developing next generation applications, especially those that will run on non-standard devices like your fridge. Can you imagine the trouble you'd have to go to in order to actually implement the software required for an Internet-enabled e-fridge?

The good news is that .NET avoids many of the problems associated with the Windows DNA platform, by giving you a brand new Internet-centric platform.

.NET – A Clean Start

When programming applications for the Windows platform, there are a myriad of programming languages and technologies that you can use. Depending on the chosen programming language, the technologies available are typically very different – and can often be restrictive. For example, a C/C++ programmer who has to write a GUI application can use the *Microsoft Foundation Classes (MFC)*, the *Windows Template Library (WTL)*, or the lower-level WIN32 APIs. A VB programmer has to use the VB Forms package.

The problems with this approach are:

❑ Microsoft spends more time developing two or more competing technologies, rather than focusing on improving one shared technology.

❑ The availability of so many technologies that do the same thing can be confusing.

- ❑ Multi-faceted developers who know multiple languages have to learn multiple technologies to achieve the same results.

- ❑ Companies have to invest predominantly in one language, since cross-training can be time-consuming and expensive.

- ❑ Not all languages will necessarily expose the same functionality, or be as productive as each other. For example, with C/C++ and MFC you can easily write MDI applications with docking toolbars and windows. With VB, you have to buy a third-party package, or write the functionality yourselves. However, I can pretty much guarantee (from experience) that VB programmers are typically more productive because they spend less time debugging low-level pointer errors.

These issues, and many others, make the Windows DNA platform hard to understand. It often leads to confusion, and I know many companies that have chosen the wrong technology or language and then hit technical implementation limitations late in their schedules. Some people might argue that using C/C++ for everything is the best strategy, but then of course you'll probably miss your time-to-market goal because the developers are too busy debugging their code. There just aren't enough really good C/C++ programmers who actually want to develop business applications. .NET helps solve these problems.

With .NET there is now just one clean object-oriented way of accessing the functionality of the .NET Framework and building applications. All the best and most commonly used features of existing technologies have been merged together into a single framework, as shown in the schematic in Figure 2-1.

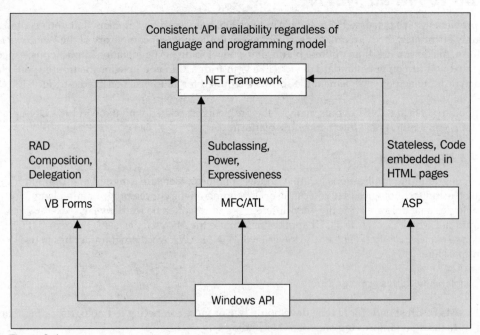

Figure 2-1

For example, Windows Forms are used when developing GUI applications. Windows Forms is a consistent GUI framework that exposes the same set of classes to any language supported by the .NET Framework. All languages typically also have the same Visual Designers. This makes the development of GUI applications simple. Use one technology, and it does not matter what language you use. The same simplicity also applies to building web applications using ASP.NET. No longer do you have to choose between writing VB Web Classes, ISAPI Extensions, or ASP; just use ASP.NET. It provides all of the features application developers need and, again, all languages are equal and can access exactly the same functionality.

> **VB Web Classes are not supported in .NET. They have been superseded by ASP.NET pages.**

Of course, there are some downsides to .NET. If you're writing applications that require absolute performance, such as real-time applications or complete packages like SQL Server, .NET might not be the platform for you. Although .NET has huge benefits for the average application developer, it simply doesn't have the raw performance of a well-written C/C++ application; certain aspects of a .NET application (such as memory allocation), however, *are* faster than C/C++. For reasons of performance and investment, many Microsoft teams will not be rewriting their applications using .NET. Instead, they will be *.NET enabling* them. For example, in SQL Server Yukon you can write stored procedures using .NET languages such as VB and C#.

No More Language Functionality Debates

If you have programmed with VB before, no doubt you are aware that C/C++ is a much more powerful language for low-level development, and suffers from far fewer limitations than VB. With .NET, all programming languages are first-class citizens. This means you can implement solutions in a programming language that your developers are productive with, without any penalties. Version 1.1 of .NET consists of four languages shipped by Microsoft:

- ❑ Visual Basic .NET
- ❑ C#
- ❑ JScript.NET
- ❑ Managed C++

There are no significant technical differences between these languages; so again, it's a matter of personal preference and company benefits. One caveat to note is that some languages may perform marginally better (about 5%) than others. My tests have shown that C# is marginally faster than VB, and Managed C++ is faster than C# since it optimizes the output it creates. At the end of the day, performance really comes down to the abilities of the compiler writers to generate good code, and this is related to how long a compiler has been under development.

If performance is crucial to your applications, you may want to do some basic performance testing before choosing a language. One would assume that eventually all these languages will be as fast as each other, so I personally wouldn't recommend spending too much time worrying about this issue. Go with the language that will give you the most productivity.

In case you're wondering, my language preference as a professional developer is C#. It's a clean, modern, and easy-to-use language that was designed specifically for the component-oriented world of the .NET Framework. It doesn't carry around any of the baggage or quirks of other languages such as VB and Managed C++.

No More ASP-Imposed Limitations

As stated earlier, there are many situations in ASP 3.0 where you end up having to create COM components. With ASP.NET, these limitations essentially disappear, since Active Scripting engines are no longer used and are replaced by proper type-safe languages such as Visual Basic .NET.

Anything that you can do from within a .NET class can be done in an ASP.NET page. This means that rather than having to always use components to develop your n-tier web application, you now have the choice of when, how, and whether you use them. This flexibility in ASP.NET stems from the fact that all ASP.NET pages are converted into classes and compiled into a DLL behind the scenes. Of course, the fact that you now have this newfound flexibility doesn't mean you should forget everything you've learned in the past. You should still use components to encapsulate data access and other common functionality used in your applications, and you certainly shouldn't go mad and do crazy things like trying to display a Windows Form in an ASP.NET page!

Multiple Platform Support

.NET has been designed with multiple platform support as a key feature. For versions 1.0 and 1.1 of .NET, this means that code written using the .NET Framework can run on all versions of Windows: Windows 95, 98, 98SE, Windows NT, Windows 2000, Windows XP, and so on. Depending upon the class libraries used, the same code will also execute on small devices on operating systems such as Windows CE, which will run a special compact edition of .NET. However, unlike Java, .NET does not promise that all classes will work on all platforms.

Rather than restricting the class libraries available in .NET to cover functionality that's only available on all platforms, Microsoft has included rich support for all platforms. As developers, it's down to you to make sure you only use the .NET classes that are supported on those platforms (although it's expected that Microsoft will provide tools to help with this process). Work in this area has already started with the definition of the CLS. Microsoft is working on the CLS with HP, Intel, IBM, and other companies, and so, who knows, you could also get non-Microsoft versions of .NET-compatible systems that run on other platforms.

An exciting prospect for companies is that the .NET code you write today will also work under 64-bit versions of Windows without change. If you ever had to port a 16-bit application to 32-bit Windows, you'll appreciate the time, effort, and pain this saves. This is possible since .NET natively supports 64-bit types such as `System.Int64`, which in VB is called the `Long` type.

Targeting multiple platforms with .NET does introduce the potential for well-known Java-like problems to hit companies. Since the code is being compiled dynamically on different platforms, the compilation process will result in different native code. Even with the best intentions in the world, this could lead to some bugs appearing in code, especially if the *Just in Time (JIT)* compiler for a given platform has bugs or just compiles things differently. You should be prepared to QA your products on the .NET platforms you are going to support. Even so, the benefits and money saved by the reduced development time make this an exciting time.

Looking forward, it is expected that .NET will run on other platforms such as UNIX, although it is unlikely that the whole of the .NET Framework will be supported, probably just the languages and the base class libraries. Microsoft is keeping these plans very quiet at the moment, but they are on the table and they are being researched. Once again though, even if Microsoft does deliver .NET on a non-Windows platform, it's unlikely they will want to invest significantly in other platforms. The amount of functionality available to .NET applications on these platforms is likely to be reduced, so you might expect to lose COM+ services such as transaction support.

Performance

Since day one, an important design goal for .NET has been great performance and scalability. For .NET to succeed, companies must be able to migrate their applications, and not suffer from poor performance due to the way code is executed by the CLR. To ensure optimal performance the CLR compiles all application code into native machine code. This conversion can either be done JIT as an application runs, on a method-by-method basis, or when an application is first installed. The compilation process will automatically make use of the processor features available on different platforms, something traditional Windows applications could never do unless you shipped different binaries for different platforms.

With the first version of ASP.NET you could expect well-written web applications to run two to four times faster than equivalent ASP applications, with similar gains in the area of scalability. Version 1.1 adds a marginal increase in performance on top of that. In other areas of .NET, such as Windows Forms, performance is likely to be similar to VB6 for most applications, with memory usage increasing slightly due to overhead introduced by the CLR. As subsequent versions of the CLR and technologies like Windows Forms are released, you'll find that each release will have a smaller memory footprint and better performance.

Hopefully, by now you're starting to understand how .NET can help solve many of the problems developers face today when writing software. It replaces a lot of older technologies like COM and COM+ (although these are certainly not dead), with better-designed equivalents. At the heart of this new platform is the CLR.

The Common Language Runtime

The CLR is one of the most radical features of .NET. Modern programming languages like VC++ and VB have always had runtimes. These are sometimes very small, like MSCRT40.DLL (used by Visual C++ applications), and other times, they can be quite big, like MSVBVM60.DLL (used by Visual Basic 6).

A language runtime's role changes depending on the language; it may actually execute the code (as in the case of Java, or VB applications compiled using p-code), or in the case of native compiled languages (like C/C++), may provide common functionality used by the application. Some of this runtime functionality may be used directly by an application (such as searching for a character sequence in a string), or indirectly by a compiler that injects additional code during the compilation process to handle error situations or exceptions (such as a user aborting an application).

The CLR is a runtime for all .NET languages. It is responsible for executing and managing *all* code written in *any* language that targets the .NET platform.

The role of the CLR in some ways is similar to Sun's *Java Virtual Machine (JVM)* and the VB runtime. It is responsible for the execution of code developed using .NET languages. However, the critical point that differentiates the CLR is that it natively compiles all code. Although .NET compilers emit *Intermediate Language (IL)* code rather than pure machine code, the IL is JIT-compiled before code is executed. IL is not interpreted, and it is not byte code like the p-code used by VB or the code used by Java. IL is a language. It is compiled, converted into machine code, and then executed. The result is that applications targeting .NET, and which execute on the CLR, have exceptionally good application performance.

To complement IL, compilers that target the CLR also emit rich *metadata* that describes the types contained with a DLL or EXE (similar to COM type libraries but much richer) and version/dependency information. This metadata allows the CLR to intelligently resolve references between different application files at runtime, and also removes the dependency on the system registry. As we discussed earlier, these are two common problem areas for Windows DNA applications.

CLR Services

The CLR provides many core services for applications, such as garbage collection, code verification, and code access security. The CLR can provide these services due to the way it manages code execution, and the fact that – thanks to the rich metadata compilers produce – it can understand all types used within code.

Garbage collection is a CLR feature that automatically manages memory on behalf of an application. You create and use objects, but do not explicitly release them. The CLR automatically releases objects when they are no longer referenced and in use. This eliminates memory leaks in applications. This memory management feature is similar in some ways to how VB works today, but, under the hood, the implementation is radically different and much more efficient. A key difference is that the time at which unused memory will be released is non-deterministic. One side effect of this feature is that you cannot assume an object is destroyed when it goes out of the scope of a function. Therefore you should not put code into a class destructor to release resources. You should always release them in the code using a method, as soon as possible.

Code verification is a process that ensures all code is safe to run prior to execution. Code verification enforces type safety, and therefore prevents code from performing illegal operations such as accessing invalid memory locations. With this feature it should *not* be possible to write code that causes an application to crash. If code does something wrong, the CLR will throw an exception before any damage is inflicted. Such exceptions can be caught and handled by an application.

Code access security allows code to be granted or denied *permissions* to do things, depending on the security configuration for a given machine, the origins of the code, and the metadata associated with types that the code is trying to use. The primary purpose of this feature is to protect users from malicious code that attempts to access other code residing on a machine. For example, with the CLR, you could protect your applications and users when writing an e-mail application by denying all rights to code contained within an e-mail so that it cannot use other classes such as the address book or file system.

The code produced for an application designed to run under the CLR is called *managed code* – self-describing code that makes use of and requires the CLR to be present. Code written with languages like VB6 that doesn't provide IL and doesn't need the CLR to run is called *unmanaged code*. For managed code, the CLR will:

❏   Always locate the metadata associated with a method at any point in time

❏   Walk the stack

❏   Handle exceptions

❏   Store and retrieve security information

These low-level requirements are necessary for the CLR to watch over code, provide the services we've discussed, and ensure its integrity for security and protection reasons.

Common Functionality

The CLR provides access to common base functionality (such as string searching) for all languages via the *Base Class Library (BCL)*. The CLR is basically a replacement for the WIN32 API and COM. It provides the foundation on which the .NET vision has been realized, since most of the Windows DNA limitations stem from features of these technologies. More importantly for VB developers, the WIN32 API provided a lot of functionality they could not easily use previously, such as process creation and free-threaded support. Since that functionality is now part of the CLR, VB (and other languages such as COBOL) can now create high-performance multi-threaded applications.

The CLR is object-oriented. All of the functionality of the CLR and the class libraries built on top of it are exposed as methods of objects. These classes are as easy to use as the ASP intrinsic objects and ADO objects you used previously, but are far richer in functionality.

Using Objects

To see how to create and use objects with the CLR, let's walk through some simple examples. In these, you will see how to create:

❏   A class in VB

❏   A class in C# that inherits from the VB class

Let's start by creating a simple VB class:

```
Namespace Wrox.Books.ProASPNet
   Public Class MyVBClass

   End Class
End Namespace
```

Don't worry about what the Namespace statement means for the moment – we'll come to that next.

Assuming this class is contained in a file called base.vb, you can compile it using the following command, which invokes the Visual Basic .NET command line compiler:

```
vbc base.vb /t:library
```

The output of the command is a DLL called `base.dll` that contains the `MyVBClass` class. The `/t:library` parameter tells the compiler that you are creating a DLL. Any other developers can now use your class in their own code written using their preferred language.

To show the in-class inheritance feature of the CLR, and to demonstrate how easy inheritance is, create a class in any other language (in this case C#) that derives from the base VB class. This C# class inherits all of the *behavior* (the methods, properties, and events) of the base class:

```
using Wrox.Books.ProASPNet;
public class MyCSharpClass : MyVBClass
{
}
```

Assuming this is contained in a file called `derived.cs`, compile it using the following command, which invokes the C# command line compiler:

```
csc /t:library /r:base.dll derived.cs
```

`csc` is the name of the C# compiler executable. `/t:library` (t is short for target) tells the compiler to create a DLL (referred to as a library). `/r:base.dll` (r is short for reference) tells the compiler that the DLL being created references types (classes etc.) in the DLL `base.dll`.

> *You'll find a more comprehensive introduction to the syntax changes in the new .NET languages, as well as the similarities and differences between them, in the next chapter. We'll also see more on the syntax of the compiler options, and discuss JScript.NET.*

This simple example doesn't have any real practical use (since there are no methods, etc.), but hopefully it goes some way in demonstrating how easy and simple building components with the CLR and Visual Basic .NET and C# is.

This code example is so clean because the CLR is effectively responsible for all of the code. At runtime, it can hook up the classes to implement the inheritance in a completely seamless way. Cross-language development and integration couldn't really be any simpler. You can create classes in any language you want, and use them in any other languages you want – either instantiating and using them, or, as in the previous example, actually deriving from them to inherit base functionality. You can use system classes (those written by Microsoft) or third-party classes in exactly the same way as you would any other class written in your language of choice. This means the entire .NET Framework is one *consistent* object-oriented class library.

Namespaces

In the next chapter, you'll create and use many different types when writing a CLR application. Within your code, you can reference types using the `Imports` keyword in Visual Basic .NET, and the `using` keyword in C#. In the VB class definition, there was the following line:

```
Namespace Wrox.Books.ProASPNet
```

The namespace declaration tells a compiler that any defined types (such as classes or enumerations) are part of the specified namespace, which in this case is called `Wrox.Books.ProASPNet`. If you want to use these classes in another application, you need to import the namespace. In C# code, you saw this namespace import definition defined as:

```
using Wrox.Books.ProASPNet;
```

This namespace import declaration makes the types within the `Wrox.Books.ProASPNet` namespace available to any of the code in your C# file.

> **In .NET, everything is referred to as a type. A type can be a class, enumeration, interface, array, or structure.**

Namespaces have two key functions:

❑ **They logically group related types**: For example, `System.Web` contains all ASP.NET classes that manage the low-level execution of a Web request. `System.Web.UI` contains all of the classes that actually render UI, and `System.Web.Hosting` contains the classes that aid in ASP.NET being hosted inside IIS or other applications.

❑ **They make name collision less likely**: In an object-oriented world, many people are likely to use the same class names. The namespace reduces the likelihood of a conflict, since the fully qualified name of a class is equal to the namespace name plus the class name. You can choose to use fully qualified names in your code, and forgo the namespace import declaration. However, you'll typically only do this if you have a namespace that contains the classes that ASP.NET uses for hosting inside IIS or the other applications.

> **Namespaces do not physically group types, since a namespace can be used in different assemblies (DLLs and EXEs).**

Namespaces are used extensively in the CLR, and since ASP.NET pages are compiled down to CLR classes, they will be used extensively in your ASP.NET pages. For this reason, ASP.NET automatically imports the most common names into an ASP.NET page. As you'll see later in the book, this list can be extended to include your own classes. It helps to think of namespaces as directories. Rather than containing files, they contain classes. However, a namespace called `Wrox.MyBook` does not mean a namespace called `Wrox` exists. It is likely that it does, but it is not mandatory.

A Common Type System

For interoperability to be smooth between languages, the CLR has a common type system. Languages like VB have built-in primitive types such as `Integer`, `String`, and `Double`. C++ has types like `long`, `ulong`, and `char*`. However, these types aren't always compatible. If you've ever written a COM component, you'll know that making sure your components have interfaces that are usable in different languages depends a great deal on types. You'll often spend a lot of time converting types, and it's a real pain.

For the CLR to make cross-language integration so smooth, all languages have to use a common type system. The following table lists the types that form part of the *CLS*, and defines the types usable in any language targeting the CLR:

Type	Description	Range/Size
System.Boolean	Represents a Boolean value.	True or False. The CLS does not allow implicit conversion between Boolean and other primitive types.
System.Byte	Represents an unsigned byte value.	Positive integer between 0 and 255.
System.Char	Represents a UNICODE character value.	Any valid UNICODE character.
System.DateTime	Represents a date and time value.	IEEE 64-bit (8-byte) long integers that represent dates ranging from 1 January 1 CE (the year 1) to 31 December 9999 and times from 0:00:00 to 23:59:59.
System.Decimal	Represents positive and negative values with 28 significant digits.	79,228,162,514,264,337,593,543,950,335 to negative 79,228,162,514,264,337,593,543,950,335.
System.Double	Represents a 64-bit, double precision, floating point number.	Negative 1.79769313486231570E+308 to positive 1.79769313486231570E+308.
System.Int16	Represents a 16-bit signed integer value.	Negative 32768 to positive 32767.
System.Int32	Represents a 32-bit signed integer value.	Negative 2,147,483,648 to positive 2,147,483,647.
System.Int64	Represents a 64-bit signed integer.	Negative 9,223,372,036,854,775,808 to positive 9,223,372,036,854,775,807.
System.Sbyte	Represents an 8-bit signed integer.	Negative 128 to positive 127.
System.Single	Represents a 4-byte, single precision, floating point number.	Negative 3.402823E38 to positive 3.402823E38.
System.TimeSpan	Represents a period of time, either positive or negative.	The MinValue field is negative 10675199.02:48:05.4775808. The MaxValue field is positive 10675199.02:48:05.4775807.

Type	Description	Range/Size
System.String	Represents a UNICODE String.	Zero or more UNICODE characters.
System.Array	Represents a single dimension array.	Range is based upon declaration and usage. Arrays can contain other arrays.
System.Object	The base type from which all other types inherit.	N.A.

Different languages use different keywords to expose these types. For example, VB will convert variables you declare as type Integer to System.Int32 during compile time, and C# will convert int into System.Int32. This makes working with different languages more natural and intuitive, while not compromising any goals of the CLR. You can of course declare the native CLR type names in any language, but you typically wouldn't do this unless the language did not have its own native mapping. This is another great feature of the CLR. If the language doesn't support a feature, you can usually find some .NET Framework classes that do.

All types derive from System.Object. This class has four methods (all of these methods are available on all types) as shown in the following table:

Method	Description
Equals	Allows two object instances to be compared for equality. Most CLR classes override this and provide a custom implementation. For example, System.ValueType has an implementation that compares all members' fields for equality. Value types are discussed shortly.
GetHashCode	Returns a hash code for the object. This function is used by classes such as Hashtable to get a unique identity for an object. Two objects of the same type that represent the same value will always return the same hash code.
GetType	Returns a Type object that can be programmatically used to explore the methods, properties, and events of a type. This feature of the CLR is called *reflection*.
ToString	Returns a string representation of the type. The default implementation returns the fully qualified type name suitable in aiding debugging. Most CLR types override this method and provide a more useful return value. For example, System.Int32 will return a string representation of a number.

Common Language Specification

Some languages can require types that other languages do not support. To allow for this, there are additional CLR types that support the functionality required for specific languages such as C#. However, one caveat with sharing CLR classes created with different languages means that there is the potential that a class will not be usable in certain languages if its types are not understood. For example, the C# language has types such as the unsigned `long` that are not available in languages such as VB, so a C# class that uses an unsigned `long` as part of its *public member definitions* cannot be used in VB. However, the same class can be used if such types are used in *non-public member definitions*. A common set of base types exists to help ensure types created by different languages are compatible. This is part of the CLS. Most CLR compilers have options to flag warnings if non-CLS types are used.

Everything in the CLR Is an Object

Every type in the CLR is an object. As seen in the previous table, all types are derived from `System.Object`. When you define your own *custom* types such as classes, structures, and enumerations, they are automatically derived from `System.Object`, even though the inheritance isn't explicitly defined. When a class is compiled, the compiler will automatically do this.

As every type has a common base type (`System.Object`), you can write some very powerful generic code. For example, the `System.Collections` namespace provides lots of collection classes that work with `System.Object` (for instance, the `Hashtable` class is a simple dictionary class populated using a name and a `System.Object` reference). By using either a name or an index, you can retrieve an object reference from the collection very efficiently. Since all types derive from `System.Object`, you can hold any type in a `Hashtable`.

Value Type and Reference Types

If you're a C/C++ developer or an experienced VB programmer, you're probably thinking that having every type in the CLR as an object is expensive, since *primitive* types such as `Integer`, `Long`, and `Structure` in VB6 and C/C++ only require space to be allocated on the stack, whereas object references require allocated space on the heap. To avoid having all types heap allocated, which would compromise code execution performance, the CLR has the following two types:

❑ **Value types**: They are allocated on the *stack*, just like *primitive* types in VBScript, VB6, and C/C++.

❑ **Reference types**: They are allocated on the *managed CLR heap*, just like object types.

It is important to understand how the CLR manages and converts these types using boxing and unboxing, to avoid writing inefficient code.

Value types are *not* instantiated using `New` (unless you have a parameterized constructor), and go out of scope when the function they are defined within returns. Value types in the CLR are defined as types that derive from `System.ValueType`. All of the CLR primitive types such as `System.Int32` derive from this class, and when structures are defined using Visual Basic .NET and C# those types automatically derive from `System.ValueType`.

Here is an example Visual Basic .NET structure that represents a CLR value type called `Person`:

```
Public Structure Person

    Dim Name As String
    Dim Age As Integer

End Structure
```

The equivalent C# structure is:

```
Public Struct Person
{
    string name;
    int age;
}
```

Both compilers will emit IL that defines a `Person` type that inherits from `System.ValueType`. The CLR will therefore know to allocate instances of this type on the stack.

Boxing

When using CLR classes such as the `Hashtable` (discussed in Chapter 15) that work with collections of `System.Object` types, you need to be aware that the CLR will automatically convert value types into reference types. This conversion happens when you assign a value type, such as a primitive type like `System.Int32`, to an `Object` reference, or vice versa.

The following code will implicitly box an `Integer` value when it is assigned to an `Object` reference:

```
//C#
int i = 32;
Object o = i;
'VB
Dim i as Integer = 32
Dim o as Object = i
```

When boxing occurs, the contents of a value type are copied from the stack into memory allocated on the managed heap. The new reference type created contains a copy of the value type, and can be used by other types that expect an `Object` reference. The value contained in the value type and the created reference types are not associated in any way (except that they contain the same values). If you change the original value type, the reference type is not affected.

The following code explicitly unboxes a reference type into a value type:

```
//C#
Object o;
int i = (int) o;
'VB
Dim o as Object
Dim i as Integer = CType(o, Integer)
```

In this example, you need to assume the object variable o has been previously initialized.

When unboxing occurs, memory is copied from the managed heap to the stack.

Understanding boxing and unboxing is important, since it has performance implications. Every time a value type is boxed, a new reference type is created and the value type is copied onto the managed heap. Depending on the size of the value type, and the number of times value types are boxed and unboxed, the CLR can spend a lot of CPU cycles just doing these conversions.

To put all this type theory into practice, take a look at the following Visual Basic .NET code, which illustrates when value types and reference types are used, and when boxing and unboxing occurs:

```
Imports System.Collections
Imports System
```

Let's start by declaring a simple structure called Person that can hold a name and an age. Since structures are always value types (remember compilers automatically derive structures from System.ValueType), instances of this type will always be held on the stack:

```
Public Structure Person
   Dim Name As String
   Dim Age As Integer
End Structure
```

Then begin your main module:

```
Public Module Main
   Public Sub Main()
   Dim dictionary As Hashtable
   Dim p As Person
```

First, create a Hashtable. This is a reference type, so use New to create an instance of the object, which will be allocated on the managed CLR heap:

```
dictionary = New Hashtable()
```

Hashtable and other collections classes are explained in more detail in Chapter 15.

Next, initialize your Person structure with some values. This is a value type, so you don't have to use New, since the type is allocated automatically on the stack when you declare your variable:

```
p.Name = "Richard Anderson"
p.Age = 29
```

Once your Person structure is initialized, add it to the dictionary using a key of Rich. This method call will implicitly cause the value type to be boxed within a reference type, as we discussed, since the second parameter of the Add method expects an Object reference:

```
dictionary.Add( "Rich", p )
```

Next, change the values of the same Person structure variable to hold some new values:

```
p.Name = "Sam Anderson"
p.Age = 28
```

Then add another person to the dictionary with a different key. Again, this will cause the value type to be boxed within a reference type and added to the dictionary:

```
dictionary.Add( "Sam", p )
```

At this point, you have a `Hashtable` object that contains two reference types. Each of these reference types contains your `Person` structure value type, with the values we initialized.

You can retrieve an item from the `Hashtable` using a key. Since the `Hashtable` returns object references, you can use the `CType` keyword to tell Visual Basic .NET that the object type returned by the `Item` function is actually a `Person` type. Since the `Person` type is a value type, the CLR knows to unbox the `Person` type from the returned reference type:

```
p = CType( dictionary.Item("Rich"), Person )
```

And now you can use the `Person` type:

```
Console.WriteLine("Name is {0} and Age is {1}", p.Name, p.Age )

    End Sub
End Module
```

Language Changes

The CLR supports a rich set of functionality. To enable languages like VB to make use of these capabilities, the language syntax has to be enhanced with new keywords. The CLR functionality may be common to all languages, but each language will expose the functionality in a way that suits that language. As the simple inheritance example showed earlier, both Visual Basic .NET and C# explicitly define the start and end of a class (VB used to do this implicitly via the file extension), but the keywords used are different.

We'll investigate the language changes in detail in Chapter 3.

Assemblies – Versioning and Securing Code

We discussed earlier how one of the biggest problems with Windows DNA applications was the number of implicit dependencies and versioning requirements. One application can potentially break another application by accidentally overwriting a common system DLL, or removing an installed component. To help resolve these problems, the CLR uses assemblies.

An assembly is a collection of one or more files, with one of those files (either a DLL or EXE) containing some special metadata known as the *assembly manifest*. The assembly manifest defines what the versioning requirements for the assembly are, who authored the assembly, what security permissions the assembly requires to run, and what files form part of the assembly.

An assembly is created by default whenever you build a DLL. You can examine the details of the manifest programmatically using classes located in the `System.Reflection` namespace. To keep our discussion focused, let's use a tool provided with the .NET SDK called *Intermediate Language Disassembler* (*ILDASM*). You can run this tool either from a command prompt, or via the Start | Run menu.

When the tool is running, you can use the File | Open menu to open up the `derived.dll` created in the simple inheritance sample earlier. Once loaded, as shown in Figure 2-2, ILDASM shows a tree control containing an entry for the assembly manifest, and an entry for each type defined in that DLL:

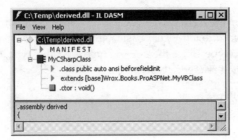

Figure 2-2

Although the type information for `MyCSharpClass` is part of your DLL, it is not part of the assembly manifest. It is, however, part of the assembly. If you double-click on the `MANIFEST` entry, you'll see the manifest definition as shown in Figure 2-3:

```
 MANIFEST                                                                    _ □ ×
.assembly extern base
{
  .ver 0:0:0:0
}
.assembly extern mscorlib
{
  .publickeytoken = (B7 7A 5C 56 19 34 E0 89 )                    // .z\U.4..
  .ver 1:0:5000:0
}
.assembly derived
{
  // --- The following custom attribute is added automatically, do not uncomment -------
  //   .custom instance void [mscorlib]System.Diagnostics.DebuggableAttribute::.ctor(bool,
  //                                                                               bool)
  .hash algorithm 0x00008004
  .ver 0:0:0:0
}
.module derived.dll
// MVID: {C5C648BF-B049-4C9C-ACF0-7C1D0E4C3BE5}
.imagebase 0x00400000
.subsystem 0x00000003
.file alignment 512
.corflags 0x00000001
// Image base: 0x07370000
```

Figure 2-3

The manifest is stored as binary data, so what you see here is a decompiled form of the manifest, presented in a readable form. The `.assembly extern` lines tell that this assembly is dependent upon two other assemblies – `base` and `mscorlib`. `mscorlib` is the main CLR system assembly, which contains the core classes for the built-in CLR types, etc. You created the assembly `base` earlier when you built your file `base.vb`. The default name of the assembly created by a compiler reflects the output filename created, minus the extension. If you'd used the following command line to build your VB DLL from earlier:

```
vbc base.vb /out:Wrox.dll
```

The assembly created would be called `Wrox`, and the output from ILDASM for `derived.dll` would show `.assembly extern` line for `Wrox` instead of `base`.

In Figure 2.3, you can see that the reference to the base assembly from within the derived assembly has two additional attributes:

❑ `.ver`: This specifies the version of the assembly compiled against. The CLR uses the `Major:Minor:Build:Revision` format for version numbers. An assembly is considered incompatible if the `Major` or `Minor` version numbers change.

❑ `.hash`: A hash value that can be used to determine if any of the files in the referenced assembly are different.

The `mscorlib` assembly reference has one additional attribute worth briefly discussing:

❑ `.publickeytoken`: This specifies part of a public key that can be used by the CLR when loading the reference assembly, to100% guarantee that only the named assembly written by a given party (in this case Microsoft) is loaded.

The `.assembly derived` section of the manifest declares the assembly information for the derived `.dll` file. This has attributes similar to the external manifests. By default the version of an assembly is `0.0.0.0`. To change this, it is necessary to specify an assembly version attribute in one of the source files. Visual Studio .NET typically creates a separate source file to contain these attributes, but you can define them anywhere you choose, providing it's not within the scope of another type definition.

In Visual Basic .NET the format for assembly attributes is:

```
<assembly: AssemblyVersion("1.0.1.0")>
```

This would make the assembly version appear as `1.0.1.0`. Within C# the format is slightly different, but has the same net effect:

```
[assembly: AssemblyVersion("1.0.1.0")]
```

> To use assembly attributes you have to import the `System.Reflection` namespace.

Attributes are a feature of CLR compilers that enables you to annotate types with additional metadata. The CLR or other tools can then use this metadata for different purposes, such as containing documentation, information about COM+ service configuration, and so on.

Are Assemblies Like DLLs?

For the most part, you can think of a DLL and an assembly as having a one-to-one relationship. Most of the time, you would probably use them this way, but for special cases you can use the more advanced features of the command line compilers to create assemblies that span multiple DLLs, a single EXE, and contain or link to either one or more resource files. Figure 2-4 shows the basic structure of a typical assembly:

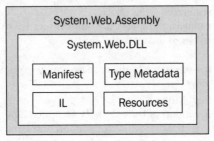

Figure 2-4

This diagram illustrates the System.Web assembly. This assembly consists of a single file, System.Web.DLL. The System.Web.DLL contains the assembly manifest, the type metadata that describes the classes located within the System.Web.DLL file, the IL for the code, and resources for embedded images. The embedded resources within this System.Web.DLL are mainly images used in Visual Studio .NET to represent Web controls. If the designers of this assembly had chosen to do so, they could have created a multi-file assembly (*complex assembly*) as the one shown in Figure 2-5:

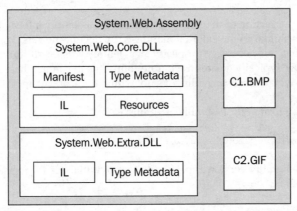

Figure 2-5

The System.Web assembly in this diagram consists of four files:

❑   System.Web.Core.DLL: Contains the assembly manifest describing all the other files and dependencies of those files, the type metadata for the classes located within the file (not the whole assembly), the IL for the code within the classes, and some embedded resources.

❑   System.Web.Extra.DLL: Contains the type metadata for the classes, etc., located within the file (not the assembly), and the IL for code within the various classes.

❑   C1.BMP: A bitmap image.

❑   C2.GIF: A Graphic Interchange Format (GIF) picture.

Although the physical file structure of these assemblies is different, to the CLR they have the same logical structure. Both expose the same types, and consumers of the types within the assemblies are not affected, since they only ever reference the types within it by name and not by physical location.

All files within an assembly are referred to as *modules*. A namespace can span one or more modules. A namespace can also span one or more assemblies. The physical structure of an assembly has no impact or relation to the namespace structure.

The reasons for creating a multi-file assembly vary. They may be appropriate if you are working in a large team and want to be able to bring individual developer's modules together within a single assembly that is version-controlled. More practically, you might want to manage memory consumption. If you know certain classes are not always needed, putting them into a separate physical file means the CLR can delay loading that file until the types within it are needed.

For most applications, using complex assemblies is probably overkill. Even if you don't use the versioning features assemblies provide, you should still be aware of how type-versioning within assemblies occurs.

It is necessary to try to make sure that your business components are kept compatible with the ASP.NET pages that call them. You create *private assemblies* when building component files like DLLs that are only used by your application. However, for the most part this is an implementation detail you can ignore. However, if you want to share component files across multiple web applications, you may need to create *shared assemblies* and put them in the GAC, and understand the more complex versioning implications they have.

No More DLL Hell

The CLR can load multiple versions of an assembly at the same time. This basically solves *DLL hell* – the problem where installing a new application might break other applications, because newer DLLs are installed that older applications are not compatible with. This is known as *side-by-side* component versioning and deployment.

Type Versioning

If you have ever written a COM component, you have probably experienced *binary-compatibility* problems. This is typified by needing to change a component's public interface (adding, changing, or deleting methods) once it has already been released. The rules of COM say that once a component is released, its interface is immutable; it should not be changed. If you do need to make changes, your component should support multiple interfaces. This approach has a number of problems:

- ❑ It's difficult to manage multiple interfaces, and almost impossible to not break compatibility by mistake.

- ❑ VB6 never really supported interfaces properly, so implementing interfaces has always been a black art.

- ❑ Most application developers don't want to version individual components.

Versioning in ASP web applications to date has shielded many developers from these problems. ASP pages always used late-binding to talk to COM components. Each time a method is called, the script engine executing the ASP page code determines whether the method exists, invoking it if it does. If a method does not exist, an error is raised.

This late-binding approach is actually pretty good in some ways. ASP developers don't have to worry too much about versioning – as long as the methods called for each object are supported, the page will work. The only drawback of this approach, which can be a significant cost, is a small performance hit per method call to find out if a method exists.

The CLR provides late-binding versioning for types in a manner similar to late-binding in COM/ASP, but without a performance hit. When the CLR loads a type such as a class, it knows what methods of other types the class is going to call. It can therefore resolve these references at runtime at a method-level, generating early-bound code to call each method. This means that the programmer only has to worry about keeping method signatures the same in order to maintain binary compatibility. It is possible to support interfaces and use the same technique as COM, but Microsoft discourages this unless it is really necessary. If an interface changes, all classes implementing the interface have to be recompiled.

If you do break compatibility in a component, it will show itself quickly. For example, if an application calls into a component that no longer supports a method it needs, the CLR will raise a `MissingMethodException`. If an application tries to use a type that has been deleted, or a type that doesn't implement all of the required methods of an interface, a `TypeLoadException` will be thrown. These can be caught by the calling application, and they usually contain detailed messages to explain what went wrong.

.NET provides a platform that enables you to start implementing next generation Internet applications, with more power and speed than ever before. It also enables you to capitalize on your existing knowledge of VB, C/++, and JScript, as well as introducing enhancements (like inheritance, polymorphism, and multi-threading) to all the languages – not to mention the brand new language C#, designed to work from the ground up with the .NET Framework.

> *The reason for not giving .NET DLL and EXE files a different extension is compatibility.*

CLR and COM

At this point you're probably beginning to ask yourself where COM fits into the CLR. The simple answer is that it doesn't. From a technology perspective, COM is *not* used as a core technology to power the CLR. The CLR is new code from the ground up, and COM is only used for interoperability and hosting. Interoperability enables you to use existing COM components within .NET languages, just as if they were CLR classes, and to use CLR classes as COM components for non-CLR applications. Hosting the CLR inside applications (such as IIS) is achieved using COM, as the CLR provides a set of COM components for loading and executing CLR code.

The fact that the CLR is not COM-based signals that COM will no longer be a mainstream technology for web applications written on the Windows platform in the future. This means that most of the concepts that you may use as a C/C++ programmer, or may have been aware of as a VB programmer, are not part of the .NET Framework. For example, in the world of COM, all objects were reference-counted, and all COM methods returned an `HRESULT`. However, the concept of interface-based programming is still prevalent within .NET, so the COM way of thinking about things in terms of interfaces is still valid. But most people will probably switch from interfaces to base classes for productivity reasons.

Internally, Microsoft is promoting the idea that teams should no longer build and release new COM components. The way forward is to create .NET components that are exposed through interop as COM components.

Intermediate Language

We're not going to cover IL in any great depth in this book, but to get a feel for it, consider this line of Visual Basic .NET code:

```
System.Console.WriteLine(".NET makes development fun and easy again")
```

It calls the `WriteLine` method of the `Console` class, which is part of the `System` namespace. A namespace, as you saw, provides a way of grouping related classes. When compiled and run as part of a console application, this line of code will basically output the simple message to a console window. You could write this same line of code in IL, as follows:

```
ldstr ".NET makes development fun and easy again"
call void [mscorlib]System.Console::WriteLine(string)
```

This code uses the same API call, except it is prefixed with `[mscorlib]`, which tells the CLR that the API we're calling is located in the file MSCORLIB.DLL. The first line shows the way in which parameters are passed to an API. The `ldstr` command loads the specified string onto the call stack, so the API being called can retrieve it.

If you took the simple VB code and used the Visual Basic .NET compiler to compile it, the output produced would be an executable file that contains IL similar to that just seen. The IL would not be identical since the VB compiler actually produces some additional initialization IL, which isn't important in this example. The important thing to note here is that the DLLs and EXEs created are *self-describing*.

Application Domains

All Windows applications run inside a process. Processes own resources such as memory and kernel objects, and threads execute code loaded into a process. Processes are protected from each other by the operating system such that one process cannot in any way unexpectedly affect the execution of another application running in another process. This level of protection is the ultimate way of having many applications run on a machine, safe in the knowledge that no matter what one application does, the others should continue as normal. Processes provide a high level of application fault tolerance, which is why IIS and COM+ use them when running in high isolation mode.

The problem with processes in Windows is that they are a very expensive resource to create and manage, and do not scale well if used in large numbers. For example, if you're using IIS and have a large number of web sites configured to run in isolation, each one has its own dedicated process that will consume a lot of resources (such as memory). If you run all these applications within the same process you'll be able to run many more web sites on one machine, since fewer resources are consumed. Less memory will be required since DLLs would only have to be loaded into one process, reducing the inter-process overhead between the various processes and the core IIS worker process. The downside to this approach is that if one site crashes, all sites will be affected. Figure 2-6 shows multiple application domains in the same .NET process:

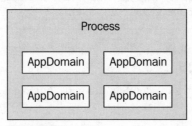

Figure 2-6

Application Domains (AppDomains) in .NET have the same benefits as a process, but multiple application domains can run within the same process, as shown in Figure 2-6. Application domains can be implemented safely within the same process, because the code verification feature of the CLR ensures that the code is safe to run before allowing it to execute. This provides huge scalability and reliability benefits. For example, with .NET, applications like IIS can achieve higher scalability by running each web site in a different application domain, rather than a different process, safe in the knowledge that inter-application isolation has not been compromised.

When running as part of IIS4/5, ASP.NET uses application domains to run each instance of an ASP.NET application, as illustrated in Figure 2-7. Each ASP.NET application runs in its own application domain, and is therefore protected from other ASP.NET applications on the same machine. ASP.NET ignores the process isolation specified in IIS.

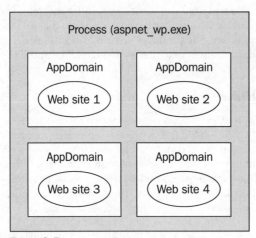

Figure 2-7

In IIS 6.0, as installed with Windows Server 2003, applications (and hence AppDomains) can be executed in separate application pools, as shown in Figure 2-8. This provides even better robustness, performance, and scalability. The allocation of each ASP.NET application or web site to a specific application pool is specified in IIS Manager. Application pools can also be used to run different versions of ASP.NET on the same box – all the applications within an application pool must run under the same version, but you can create one or more application pools for each different version.

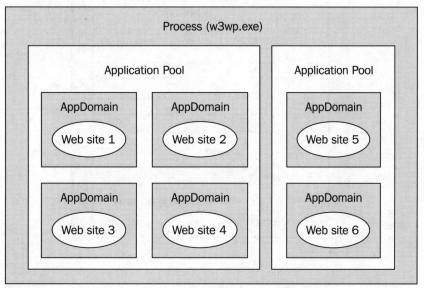

Figure 2-8

It's also possible to switch IIS 6.0 into a mode called IIS 5.0 Isolation Mode, in which case it works just like IIS 5.0 – with a consequent loss of performance and robustness. See Chapter 14 for more details.

.NET Framework Drill Down

The .NET Framework consists of four major areas:

❑   Application development technologies

❑   Class libraries

❑   Base class libraries

❑   The Common Language Runtime

These pieces sit on top of each other, with each of the higher layers making use of one or more of the lower layers, as shown in Figure 2-9:

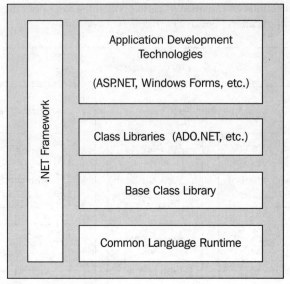

Figure 2-9

We have already discussed the CLR and base class libraries, so in the next sections we'll briefly examine the top two layers – the application development technologies and the class libraries. These layers are the primary focus for the remainder of this book.

Application Development Technologies

As you saw in Chapter 1, ASP.NET is a very exciting .NET technology for building web applications, providing many new features and a much cleaner programming mode. The features you're going to look at next are:

❑   Web services

❑   Windows Forms

Web Services

In the intelligent fridge example, we discussed the idea of a fridge talking to a supermarket over the Internet to automatically restock it. To achieve this, supermarkets would have to expose over the Internet the APIs for any fridge to call upon to place orders. It would also be necessary to locate such services, providing the fridge owner with the means to pick a supermarket to order from. This concept of locating and consuming programmatic functions over the Internet is called *web services*.

> **Web services are programmable business logic components that serve as "black boxes" to provide access to functionality via the Internet using standard protocols such as HTTP.**

Web services are based upon an application of XML called the *Simple Object Access Protocol (SOAP)*. SOAP defines a standardized format for enveloping the XML payloads exchanged between two entities over standard protocols such as HTTP. SOAP is based completely upon open standards. The consumers of a web service are therefore completely shielded from any implementation details about the platform exposing the web service – they simply send and receive XML over HTTP. This means that any web service on a Windows platform can be consumed by any other platform, such as UNIX.

> *More technical details on SOAP can be found at http://www.w3.org/TR/SOAP/.*

Web services are a core part of the .NET Framework. Using ASP.NET you can easily expose web services from a Web site, and can easily consume web services from other web sites. To make this whole model simple for .NET developers, you have to do little more than write a class to expose a web service, or consume a class to use a web service. This saves you from having to understand protocols such as SOAP in any detail, but you can be sure that anybody can access the functionality you provide.

The following Visual Basic .NET code defines a simple web service with a single function called `NameABook`:

```
<%@ WebService Language="VB" class="MyWebService" %>
Imports System
Imports System.Web.Services
Public Class MyWebService
  <WebMethod> _
  Public Function NameABook() As String
    Return "Professional ASP.NET"
  End Function

End Class
```

Here is the same web service, this time written in C#:

```
<%@ WebService Language="C#" class="MyWebService" %>
using System;
using System.Web.Services;
public class MyWebService
{
  [WebMethod]
  public string NameABook()
  {
    return "Professional ASP.NET";
  }
}
```

To host these web services within an ASP.NET page, all you have to do is copy the code into a standard text file, and save that file in the ASP.NET application directory, giving the file an `.asmx` extension. When the ASP.NET runtime sees a request for an `.asmx` file, it knows that the file being requested represents a web service. It will automatically decode the incoming SOAP request, invoke the appropriate function, and send out a SOAP/XML response.

There are more facets to web services, such as security, describing the web services available on a given site, and providing the means to locate web services via a certain discovery service. Web services are discussed in Chapters 19 and 20.

Windows Forms

For developing traditional Windows GUI applications, the .NET Framework provides you with *Windows Forms*.

> **Windows Forms is an extensive class library that exposes the functionality of Windows Common Controls using the expressive object-oriented capabilities of the .NET Framework.**

If you have ever developed a Form in VB6 using the Forms designer, or created dialogs using VC++ and MFC, you'll be right at home with Windows Forms in .NET because a lot of the classes are similar. Windows Forms uses a designer similar to previous versions of Visual Studio, but the controls expose richer functionality and are object oriented. The net result is that you produce applications that look pretty much as they do today, but with less code; the code is cleaner and easier to understand.

Another important advance with Windows Forms is that you now have a single GUI library and forms designer for all of the supported languages. Whether you program in VB, C++, or one of the newer languages such as C#, you'll be using the same classes, methods, and events, since they all use the same class library: `System.Windows.Forms`. The benefits this brings to programmers are very important. Since the same class library is being used, all of the languages have the same capabilities. This means you can use the language you're most comfortable with, and don't have to worry about whether the language you choose has the same features as are available, say, in C/C++. This is a problem you might well have encountered in the past.

Class Libraries

The .NET Framework has an extensive set of class libraries. This includes classes for:

❑ **Data access**: High-performance data access classes for connecting to SQL Server, Oracle, or any other database for which an OLEDB or ODBC provider is available. See Chapter 9.

❑ **XML support**: Next generation XML support that goes far beyond the functionality of MSXML. See Chapter 11.

❑ **Directory services**: Support for accessing Active Directory/LDAP using ADSI.

❑ **Regular expressions**: Support beyond that found in Perl 5. See Chapter 15.

❑ **Queuing support**: Provides a clean object-oriented set of classes for working with MSMQ.

These class libraries use the CLR base class libraries for common functionality.

Base Class Libraries

The base class library in the .NET Framework is huge. It covers areas such as:

❑ **Collections**: The `System.Collections` namespace provides numerous collection classes. See Chapter 15.

❑ **Thread support**: The `System.Threading` namespace provides support for creating fast, efficient, multi-threaded applications.

❑ **Code generation**: The `System.CodeDOM` namespace provides classes for generating source files in numerous languages. ASP.NET uses these classes when converting ASP.NET pages into classes, which are subsequently compiled.

❑ **IO**: The `System.IO` namespace provides extensive support for working with files and all other stream types.

❑ **Reflection**: The `System.Reflection` namespace provides support for load assemblies, examining the types within assemblies, creating instances of types, and so on.

❑ **Security**: The `System.Security` namespace provides support for services such as authentication, authorization, permission sets, policies, and cryptography. These base services are used by application development technologies like ASP.NET to build their security infrastructure.

The list of support base classes goes on forever in .NET, but if you ever find yourself lost looking for a specific class, you can use the `WinCV` tool to locate it. You can run this from the Start | Run menu. The file is usually located in the `C:\Program Files\Microsoft.NET\SDK\[version]\Bin` folder.

The WinCV tool allows you to type in a search string, and brings back a list of all the matching types it finds. For example, Figure 2-10 shows the results of typing `HttpRequest` (the ASP.NET class that is the `Request` object, also called the `Request` intrinsic). The left-hand pane shows all of the types matched. The right-hand pane shows the type definition, retrieved using the reflection classes. Using the information shown, you can determine that the `HttpRequest` class is defined as part of the `System.Web` namespace, which is contained in the `System.Web.dll` file.

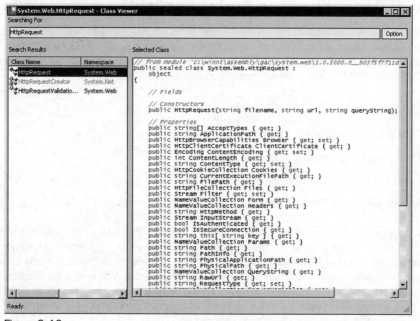

Figure 2-10

By now you should have a fairly good picture of how the .NET Framework fits together, so let's look at some of the ASP.NET design goals, and see how the .NET Framework was used to build ASP.NET.

ASP.NET Design Goals

To understand some of the reasons why ASP.NET works the way it does, we'll cover some of the key design goals of ASP.NET in this section. We'll be looking at these in more depth later in the book. Some of the key goals of ASP.NET were to:

❑   Remove the dependency on script engines, enabling pages to be type safe and compiled

❑   Reduce the amount of code required to develop web applications

❑   Make ASP.NET well factored, allowing customers to add in their own custom functionality, and extend/replace built-in ASP.NET functionality

❑   Make it easy to deploy web applications

❑   Make ASP.NET a logical evolution of ASP, where existing ASP investment and therefore code can be reused with little, if any, change

❑   Provide great tool support in terms of debugging and editing

❑   Realize that bugs are a fact of life, so ASP.NET should be as fault tolerant as possible

We'll examine each of these goals, and look at how they have been realized in ASP.NET.

Removal of Dependency on Script Engines

ASP prior to ASP.NET was built to take advantage of Active Scripting, a technology originally designed to enable developers to script and control applications in a uniform way. It isn't a technology that was really designed to write full-scale applications, which is essentially what many developers are trying to do using ASP. It is why ASP.NET was *not* written to use Active Scripting.

Active Scripting has many inherent problems:

❑   Code is interpreted, not compiled

❑   It has a weak type system – just variants

❑   It only supports late-bound calling of methods

❑   Each instance of an Active Scripting engine consumes memory

As an ASP developer you're probably aware of these problems, and will have experienced them when developing or profiling your applications. Interpreted code results in very average performance. A weak type system makes code harder to develop, read, and debug. Late-bound code is many times slower than early-bound code, and restricts what components you can use. You may have written lots of COM components to get around these problems, but even that solution has performance and maintenance implications. Creating COM objects from ASP is relatively expensive, and upgrading COM components prior to .NET typically meant stopping your web servers.

These problems are not something that the developers of ASP.NET wanted to inherit, so the decision was made early on to use compiled code. Since the .NET platform was already in development, and had the potential to deal with the problems of COM and the Windows DNA platform in general, ASP.NET was built using C# and targeted as part of the .NET Framework.

Performance

To get great performance and remove the active scripting dependency, ASP.NET pages utilize assemblies (DLLs). The basic process is shown in Figure 2-11. When a page is first requested, ASP.NET compiles the page into an assembly. The assembly created is assigned a unique name, and is placed in a sub-directory within the `%systemroot%/Microsoft.NET/Framework/[version]/Temporary ASP.NET Files` directory. The assembly contains a single generated class that derives from the `System.Web.UI.Page` class. It contains all the code needed to generate the page, and is instantiated by the framework to process a request each time the `.aspx` page is requested.

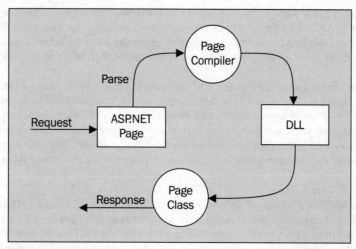

Figure 2-11

The page compilation process isn't cheap, and can take a few seconds for complex pages. However, the compilation is only ever done *once* for each `.aspx` file. All subsequent requests for the page – even after IIS has been restarted – are satisfied by instantiating the class generated, and asking it to render the page. This results in great performance. The only cost is a little disk space on the web servers.

> You can change the temporary directory location used by ASP.NET by adding a
> `tempDirectory` attribute to the compilation element in `machine.config`.

When a .NET class is generated for a `.aspx` page, the dependencies of that page – such as the `.aspx` page and any include files – form part of the compiled class. These dependencies are checked before a page is rendered, and if it's determined that any of the dependency files have changed since the page was compiled, the assembly is deleted and a new one is created. This ensures that the page rendered is always up to date.

The code generation and compilation classes and methods used by ASP.NET are a standard part of the .NET Framework, located within the `System.CodeDOM` namespace contained in the `System.DLL` assembly.

An Evolution of ASP

ASP.NET has been designed to maintain a general syntax and runtime compatibility with existing ASP pages wherever possible. The motivation behind this is to allow existing ASP pages to be initially migrated to ASP.NET by simply renaming the file to have a `.aspx` extension. Although for the most part this goal has been achieved, there are generally several basic code changes that have to be made since VBScript is no longer supported and the VB language itself has changed.

For example, you probably want to take advantage of the new architecture, viewstate, and event handling features of ASP.NET to get best performance. You may also want to use ASP.NET server controls to get better interactivity or appearance, or to generally simplify your code. In fact, in many cases, it often turns out to be easier to rewrite your pages rather than to try and update them.

However, once you have updated the pages and renamed them to have a `.aspx` extension, they become ASP.NET pages. Then you'll need to go through the process of fixing any errors so that those pages will be compiled, and can execute without problems. However, ASP.NET pages cannot share any type of state with ASP pages, so you cannot share information using any of the intrinsic objects, such as `Application` or `Session`. This means, for most applications, you'll typically have to convert all of your ASP pages at once, or convert groups of pages, so that they can work effectively together.

> You can run ASP.NET and ASP side-by-side on the same box. You can also run different versions of ASP.NET side-by-side on the same box. Version 1.1 of ASP.NET is almost completely backwards compatible with version 1.0 (see Appendix C for more details), so you can also – in most cases – run your ASP.NET 1.0 applications under ASP.NET 1.1.

Easy to Deploy

Deploying an ASP application onto a production web server could be a traumatic experience, especially if the application consisted of COM components and required configuration changes to the IIS meta-data. The scope of these problems would get a lot worse in a web farm scenario. You would have to copy the ASP files onto every server, copy and register the COM components, create COM+ applications and register the associated COM+ components, and update the IIS meta-data using ADSI according to configuration requirements. This installation wasn't an easy thing to do, and typically a skilled administrator might have been needed in addition to a lot of time and patience. Or you would have to write a fairly advanced setup program, which is the approach I've favored in the past.

The deployment of an ASP.NET application is radically simpler. Installing an application requires two steps:

1. Create a web site or virtual directory.

2. XCOPY application files into the directory.

Deleting an application is equally simple:

1. Delete or stop the web site or virtual directory.

2. Delete the files.

ASP.NET achieves this goal by making a few fundamental changes to the way web applications are developed:

❑ Configuration of applications is achieved using XML configuration files stored in the web application directories. This replaces the need to use the IIS meta-data. Also, it enables you to store your own configuration details in these files, rather than a database, which simplifies deployment. IIS 6.0 also uses an XML-based configuration persistence and backup model.

❑ ASP.NET (specifically the CLR) does not require components to be registered. As long as your component files are located within the `bin` subfolder (you can not change the name of this directory) within your virtual directory, your ASP.NET pages can create and use components within those files.

❑ ASP.NET is built using the services of the CLR rather than COM. This means you can copy updated DLLs into your application directory (the `bin` subfolder), and it will automatically start using the components within those files, unloading the previous versions from memory.

To make redeployment of an existing application simple, ASP.NET uses the CLR shadow-copy feature to ensure component files are never locked. This means that at any point in time you can upgrade components by simply copying newer component files over the old ones. The shadow-copy feature copies the component file into a cache area before it is loaded. Thus, the original file is never actually loaded from the original location.

The shadow-copy feature of the CLR works on an application domain basis. Files are shadow-copied for each application domain. To reload a component once it's changed, ASP.NET creates a new application domain, thus causing the changed file to be cached and used. However, it only works for ASP.NET component files located in the `bin` subfolder.

Great Tool Support

ASP has always been a great technology for developing web applications, but it has never had great tool support, which has made web application development less productive than it really could be.

For most people in the world of ASP, Notepad was their editor, and `Response.Write` was the preferred and – for the most part – the only reliable debugging method. To be fair, Visual Interdev wasn't a bad editor, and when it worked the debugging support was pretty good (if the sun was shining and REM was playing on the radio). However, having worked on a couple of development teams where a few people were using Visual InterDev, I can quite honestly say it always seems to cause the most grief to developers (although SourceSafe is a close second). I personally never liked Visual Interdev, since debugging from ASP pages through to COM components and back again was never supported well.

Visual Studio .NET has *first class* support for ASP.NET page development and debugging. When developing pages, you get the same type of designer mode as Visual Interdev, but the whole layout of the Visual Studio .NET designer is much more natural and flexible. Developing an ASP.NET page is pretty much the same as developing a VB form, and very productive.

There are other tools around as well, from third-party manufacturers and the excellent (and free!) Web Matrix tool that was built by the ASP.NET team to provide a lightweight and fully functional IDE that doesn't demand the use of the code-behind approach (see http://www.asp.net/ for more details).

Debugging support in ASP.NET is also excellent. You can debug from ASP.NET pages, into a .NET component, back into ASP.NET pages with great ease. Since all of the compiled code uses the CLR to execute, the orchestration between code and Visual Studio .NET is smooth and reliable, even if you debug across multiple languages. Never again will you have to use `Response.Write` or a script debugger. As if this isn't enough, ASP.NET also provides excellent tracing services, which are covered in more detail in Chapter 22.

Simpler, More Flexible Configuration

The XML-based configuration model of ASP.NET makes deployment of applications much easier. The configuration is kept in text files stored with the application, so deployment is a non-issue. Furthermore, ASP.NET provides a very powerful and flexible configuration system, which is easy to utilize within your own ASP.NET pages and components.

Configuration files in ASP.NET are hierarchical – settings defined in one directory can be overridden by settings defined in a sub-directory. A base configuration for all ASP.NET applications (machine-level) is defined in the `machine.config` file located with the ASP.NET system directory. This file defines global settings and mappings that are common to most applications, which include settings for:

❑ The time before a web request is timed out

❑ Specifying the .NET classes that should be responsible for compiling and handling files of a specific extension.

❑ The frequency with which ASP.NET should automatically recycle its worker processes.

❑ The security settings that should be used by default.

A simple XML configuration file is shown here:

```
<configuration>
 <!-- store the database connection info here -->
 <appSettings>
   <add key="DSN"
        value="server=localhost;uid=sa;pwd=;database=Northwind" />
 </appSettings>
</configuration>
```

To access and use this configuration file, you could write the following simple ASP.NET page using Visual Basic .NET:

```
<%@Page Language="VB" %>
<h3>Simple Configuration Example</h3>
<%
 Response.Write( "The DSN is " & ConfigurationSettings.AppSettings("DSN") )
%>
```

Or using C#:

```
<%@Page Language="C#" %>
<h3>Simple Configuration Example1</h3>
<%
 Response.Write( "The DSN is " + ConfigurationSettings.AppSettings["DSN"] );
%>
```

If you run either of these pages you'll see that the DSN is displayed as shown in Figure 2-12:

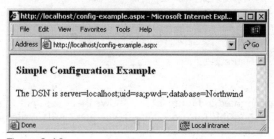

Figure 2-12

Once loaded by ASP.NET, configuration files are cached for quick access, and so performance is excellent. The files are automatically reloaded if they are changed, so configuration updates do not require the web site to be restarted. The ASP.NET configuration system is discussed in more detail in Chapter 13.

Factored Open Design

Like ASP, ASP.NET is in part implemented as an *Internet Server Application Programming Interface (ISAPI)* extension DLL. ISAPI is an arcane C API that defines a standard for having web requests processed by a DLL, rather than an EXE (as happens with CGI). The benefit of ISAPI is that DLLs are far more efficient, because executables are very expensive to create and destroy for each Web request.

IIS maps ISAPI extension DLLs to web requests by matching the extension of the URI requested to a specific DLL. These mappings are defined using the Application Configuration dialog, as shown in Figure 2-13. To display this dialog, bring up the context menu for a Web site or virtual directory, and click the Configuration button on the Home Directory or Virtual Directory tab. To view or change the path to the ISAPI extension in use for a specific file type, select it and click the Edit button:

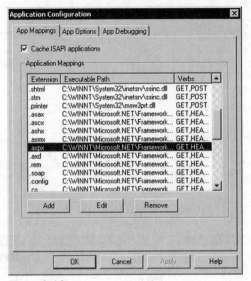

Figure 2-13

The `.aspx` extension is highlighted in Figure 2.13. It shows that the `aspnet_isapi.dll` located in the .NET system directory is responsible for processing this request. ASP implemented a lot of functionality via its ISAPI extension DLL. It:

❑ Provided state management for web clients via the `Session` object.

❑ Enabled you to share data across web applications via the `Application` object.

❑ Integrated with MTS.

❑ Provided basic security services to protect ASP files, and helped to identify users using the security support in IIS and Windows.

This is great if you're developing an ASP application. Wouldn't it be nicer if you could use some of this functionality directly from your own ISAPI extensions, or directly from COM components, without the need to have any interpreted ASP files? And wouldn't it have been nice to be able to easily replace or enhance the functionality ASP provides; for example, moving all ASP state into a database? With ASP.NET you can easily do this.

The designers of ASP.NET realized a couple of important points early on in the design phase:

❑ ASP.NET should provide an extensibility model that allows services like state management to be extended or replaced with custom alternative implementations.

❑ A lot of the services provided by ASP, such as state management, should be usable in non-ASP.NET Web applications. The services that ASP.NET requires are common requirements for all Web application types.

❑ ASP.NET should *not* require IIS to run. It should be possible to host ASP.NET on other web servers, such as Apache.

The HTTP Runtime

To achieve these goals, the HTTP runtime was created, on which ASP.NET was built. The HTTP runtime effectively provides the same base services as ISAPI extensions and ISAPI filters (filters can preprocess requests, modify them, and so on), but it's a much cleaner model. It is built using the CLR, and has a simple object-oriented approach to managing web requests:

❑   A web request is processed by an HTTP request handler class.

❑   Services (such as the state services) are exposed to the runtime using HTTP module classes.

❑   An HTTP application class manages the web execution process, effectively controlling which HTTP modules are invoked when passing a request to an HTTP request handler, and sending the output of the HTTP request handler back to the client.

The basic structure of the HTTP runtime looks something like that shown in Figure 2-14. The number of HTTP modules is not limited, and they can be defined at a directory-level by using XML configuration files. This means that different services can be made available, and consumed by different ASP.NET pages (or any type of HTTP request handler). It enables root-level configuration defined in the .NET system directory to be redefined or removed at the directory-level.

For example, the `web.config` file or `machine.config` in the .NET system directory may define that a specific HTTP module is loaded for state management by default. However, an additional `web.config` file in the same folder as a requested page (or in a parent folder of the requested page) can override this, potentially replacing the state module with another one.

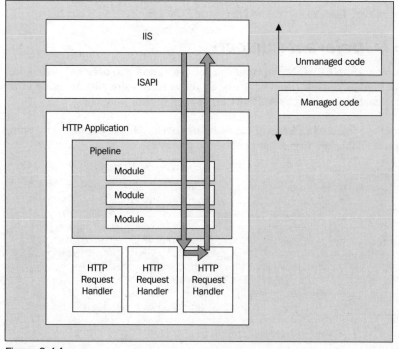

Figure 2-14

All in all, the HTTP runtime is very powerful, and a lot of the functionality and power of ASP.NET (except the server-side control architecture) comes from the HTTP runtime. You can easily extend this and use it within your applications.

Web.Config for HTTP Handlers

ASP.NET is implemented as an HTTP handler. If you look at the `machine.config` file in the .NET system `CONFIG` folder, you'll see a section called `httpHandlers`:

```
<httpHandlers>
 <add verb="*" path="*.aspx" type="System.Web.UI.PageHandlerFactory"/>
 <add verb="*" path="*.asmx"
      type="System.Web.Services.Protocols.WebServiceHandlerFactory,
            System.Web.Services, Version=1.0.5000.0, Culture=neutral,
            PublicKeyToken=b03f5f7f11d50a3a" validate="false"/>
</httpHandlers>
```

This cut-down version of the section shows that all web requests with a `.aspx` extension are handled by the `System.Web.UI.PageHandlerFactory` class, and that all requests with a `.asmx` extension are handled by `System.Web.Services.Protocols.WebServiceHandlerFactory`.

To implement your own HTTP runtime handler, you can create a class that supports the HTTP runtime interfaces, add your extension and class to the web.config file, and hence write your own web technologies.

> *When your HTTP runtime handler is hosted in IIS, you must add your extension to the IIS configuration map. Your extension should be pointed to by `aspnet_isapi.dll`.*

Language Is Irrelevant (Almost)

When developing ASP.NET pages, the language you use is down to personal preference. Whether you use VB, C#, or even JScript .NET, you have exactly the same functionality available to you. There are no limitations or penalties imposed by ASP.NET for using a specific language.

ASP.NET uses the `compilers` section of the `machine.config` file to define the mapping of a page's extension, and available languages that can be used in ASP.NET:

```
<compilers>
  <compiler language="c#;cs;csharp" extension=".cs"
          type="Microsoft.CSharp.CSharpCodeProvider,
                System, Version=1.0.3300.0, Culture=neutral,
                PublicKeyToken=b77a5c561934e089" warningLevel="1"/>
  <compiler language="vb;vbs;visualbasic;vbscript" extension=".vb"
          type="Microsoft.VisualBasic.VBCodeProvider, System,
                Version=1.0.3300.0, Culture=neutral,
                PublicKeyToken=b77a5c561934e089"/>
  <compiler language="js;jscript;javascript" extension=".js"
           type="Microsoft.JScript.JScriptCodeProvider, Microsoft.JScript,
                Version=7.0.3300.0, Culture=neutral,
                PublicKeyToken=b03f5f7f11d50a3a"/>
</compilers>
```

The compiler element has the following attributes:

❑ language: The abbreviations that can be specified by an ASP.NET page developer when using the language attribute, either as part of the <script> block, or as part of the page directive.

❑ extension: The file extension associated with the language. When a file is included as part of an ASP.NET page using one of the page directives or attributes like assembly or code behind, the extension gives ASP.NET the hint it needs to tell it how to compile the file.

❑ type: The fully qualified name of the code generator class, and the name of the assembly in which the class is located. A comma separates these two values.

For third-party languages, such as COBOL or Perl, to be usable within an ASP.NET page, the compiler vendors must provide a code generator class for their language that derives from System.CodeDOM.CodeGenerator, and it must be registered in this configuration section, so that ASP.NET knows how to make use of it.

Less Code, Cleaner Code, More Maintainability

One of the biggest problems with ASP was the amount of code that had to be written. To display data from a database, you had to write the code that connects to the database, and use Response.Write to output the HTML required for the table. To display a calendar, you had to write the code to create the calendar. With ASP.NET, you don't have to write code to do everything. ASP.NET *server controls* provide a way of declaratively building pages by using nothing but tags and attributes. These server controls encapsulate the behavior used to render the UI and respond to postback.

ASP.NET also enables you to build the following types of server controls:

❑ **Custom server controls**: You can write the server controls in a compiled form, where you develop a class that inherits from one of the ASP.NET server control classes.

❑ **User controls**: You can declare other ASP.NET pages as controls, and then use those pages to build up other pages.

Both of these approaches are shown in Chapter 18.

The ASP.NET server controls provide a great mechanism for reusing code within ASP.NET applications. Microsoft predicts that many third-party vendors will create ASP.NET server controls, and Microsoft also intends to provide more and more controls with each release of ASP.NET.

Rich Authentication Model

ASP.NET was designed to provide a rich authentication model to suit modern e-commerce application requirements. The three core modes of security supported are:

❑ **Windows authentication**: Targeted mainly at intranets, where domain accounts can be used to identify users.

❑ **Forms authentication**: Cookie-based authentication as used by sites such as Amazon.

❑ **Microsoft Passport authentication**: Cookie-based authentication performed by Passport Manager, used by sites such as Hotmail.

ASP.NET also enables different authentication models to be used within the same application. This scenario allows a single web site to be used for Intranet and Extranet purposes. The authentication models of ASP.NET are discussed in detail in Chapter 14.

Realize That Bugs Are a Fact of Life

The designers of ASP.NET appreciated from day one that nobody writes bug-free code – including Microsoft. For this reason ASP.NET deals with bugs, expecting them to happen, and has a number of cool features:

❑ It detects memory leaks and automatically restarts ASP.NET applications. You define the scope of a memory leak.

❑ It detects hung or deadlocked requests, and resolves them.

❑ It automatically restarts an ASP.NET application after a specified number of requests.

❑ It allows state to be stored externally to the main ASP.NET worker process, even in a state service or a SQL Server database. This allows ASP.NET applications to be restarted without end users losing their state.

Summary

We've taken a broad look at the scope of .NET and the various technologies involved. Initially, we explored the need for .NET, explaining some of the common deployment and versioning problems Windows DNA developers face, and how these problems are due to the underlying technologies – such as COM – on which the Windows DNA platform is built.

We showed some of the design goals for .NET, and then explored the Common Language Runtime (CLR), the core technology upon which the .NET Framework is built. This included a discussion of how the CLR architecture works, and how it solves many of the problems of the Windows DNA platform.

We discussed the four key components of the .NET Framework: Application Development Technologies, Class Libraries, Base Class Libraries, and the CLR. You saw how these are built on top of each other, and together provide a very powerful and productive development platform.

Finally, we reviewed the design goals of ASP.NET, looking at how these features work.

The next chapter will take a closer look at the syntax of some of the languages you can use to build .NET applications, investigating the advantages and disadvantages of these languages, and their similarities and differences in more detail.

The .NET Languages

In the previous two chapters, you have seen that .NET is not just a minor product release – ASP.NET is not just ASP 4.0, and Visual Studio .NET is not just another upgrade. As for the *Common Language Runtime* (*CLR*), well, that's completely new. It's a natural reaction to wonder about the changes, ask why there are new languages, why the existing ones are so different, and to question Microsoft's motives.

The Java issue has raged for a long time now; a controversy that is often mindlessly banal. Claims that 'C# is just a copy of Java' are made, often by people who apparently don't realize that each programming language builds on the ones that were developed earlier. That's what developers do – they continue to improve products, and there's no reason why languages should be treated any differently to applications. .NET 1.1 now ships with *J# .NET*, a version of Java.

Microsoft looked at the way their languages were being used and asked several questions:

- ❑ Do our languages provide developers with what they need?
- ❑ How can we improve the languages?
- ❑ How can we leverage the existing skills of developers?
- ❑ How can we enable applications to be more robust and more scalable?
- ❑ How can we provide a better development environment?
- ❑ How can the application architecture be improved?

The answers to these questions aren't necessarily compatible with each other, and with the .NET Framework Microsoft has concentrated on providing the best possible platform for future development. In some areas, this has come at the expense of compatibility with existing technologies, and risks alienating some die-hard developers. However, when weighing up the problems, the benefits easily compensate for the losses.

In the previous chapter we discussed the CLR and the benefits it brings, such as common functionality, namespaces, a common type system, versioning, and so on. In this chapter, we'll concentrate on the languages themselves, rather than any ASP.NET-specific details. In particular, this chapter will look at:

- ❑ The new features in Visual Basic .NET

- ❑ The new language of C#

- ❑ Other available languages

- ❑ How the CLR affects our use of languages

- ❑ Examples of common tasks, in VB .NET and C#, to ease conversion and migration

The Supplied Languages

The .NET Framework is supplied with four languages (Visual Basic .NET, Visual C#, Visual J#, and JScript.NET), but the whole infrastructure is designed to be language independent. We'll briefly discuss some alternative languages you can use, later in the chapter. The factored and open design of ASP.NET, which enables pluggable HTTP modules, also extends to the CLR, enabling pluggable languages.

As mentioned in the previous chapter, the compilers section of the `machine.config` file defines the languages in use:

```
<compilers>
 <compiler language="c#;cs;csharp" extension=".cs"
    type="Microsoft.CSharp.CSharpCodeProvider, System, Version=1.0.5000.0,
       Culture=neutral, PublicKeyToken=b77a5c561934e089" warningLevel="1"/>
 <compiler language="vb;vbs;visualbasic;vbscript" extension=".vb
    type="Microsoft.VisualBasic.VBCodeProvider, System, Version=1.0.5000.0,
       Culture=neutral, PublicKeyToken=b77a5c561934e089"/>
 <compiler language="js;jscript;javascript" extension=".js"
    type="Microsoft.JScript.JScriptCodeProvider, Microsoft.JScript,
       Version=7.0.5000.0, Culture=neutral, PublicKeyToken=b03f5f7f11d50a3a"/>
 <compiler language="VJ#;VJS;VJSharp" extension=".jsl"
    type="Microsoft.VJSharp.VJSharpCodeProvider, VJSharpCodeProvider,
       Version=7.0.5000.0, Culture=neutral, PublicKeyToken=b03f5f7f11d50a3a"/>
</compilers>
```

Thus, anyone can supply a language for use in the .NET Framework, as long as it has a compiler and conforms to a few basic rules. Later in the chapter, we'll look at the other languages supplied by third parties.

What Happened to VBScript?

The .NET Framework supports Visual Basic, so VBScript support has been dropped. Visual Basic provides everything that VBScript supplied, and far more. While VBScript has indeed gone, the syntax is still supported, but you now get full compilation, data types, and the added benefits of the new language. So if you've only ever used VBScript, don't worry – there will be a little adjusting to do, but for the most part you'll find using Visual Basic .NET simple.

Visual Studio or Notepad?

Most people assume that to use Visual Basic .NET or C# in your ASP.NET pages, you need Visual Studio .NET, but that isn't the case. Support for the languages is built into the CLR, and the compilers are available as part of the SDK. Thus, to write ASP.NET applications, all you need is the (freely available) SDK and your favorite editor (great news if, like me, you're a die-hard Notepad user). For compilation there's a standalone compiler for each language (described in *The .NET Language Compilers* section later in the chapter), so you can compile components from the command line.

Visual Studio .NET is far more than just an editor. It provides a rich environment for developing both ASP.NET applications (Web Forms) and Windows applications (Windows Forms), with all the usual cool features such as drag and drop, statement completion (Intellisense), debugging, and so on. As a productivity tool, it's great, but it's not forced on you if you don't want it.

Further, the open design of the .NET languages enables third parties to produce alternative editors with support for .NET.

Visual Basic .NET

The latest version of Visual Basic is a major leap forward in terms of functionality, with several features added to take advantage of the *Common Language Specification* (*CLS*) and the CLR.

Each generation of a language brings improvements. To understand why Visual Basic .NET implements the changes it does, consider for a moment some of the problems associated with previous versions of Visual Basic:

❑ **The Visual Basic runtime libraries**: These are relatively large DLLs incorporating the base functionality, and are required for all Visual Basic programs to run. Common complaints concerned the size of these DLLs, and versioning problems (different libraries for different versions of VB). You might think that these have just been replaced by the CLR, but the CLR is much more than this, and addresses far more than just VB. While size may still be considered an issue, the redistributable CLR is around 18 MB and supports multiple versions.

❑ **Poor object-oriented features**: Object-oriented programming gurus criticized Visual Basic for its lack of 'proper' functionality – not providing features such as inheritance, overloading, and so on. Although these are valid points, many of the problems really stemmed from the capabilities of COM rather than Visual Basic itself.

❑ **Inability to create multi-threaded applications**: With the introduction of *Microsoft Transaction Server* (*MTS*), n-tier architecture became a reality, and Visual Basic programmers started to get to grips with componentization. However, Visual Basic components were forced into an Apartment Threading model, a limitation that attracted much criticism from programmers who wanted to build multi-threaded components. Personally, I think much of this condemnation is misplaced, as I wonder how many people could actually write a fully threaded component (I'm not sure I could). Think about it – managing the threads, state, and so on, isn't easy.

All of these problems disappear in Visual Basic .NET. The runtime libraries are no longer needed because they're taken care of by the CLR, and the object-oriented features have been massively improved (partly because of CLR and CLS support) and the whole threading issue has gone away. With the CLR, you just don't need to think about threading (unless you want to). Let's look at some of the new features in Visual Basic .NET.

Object-Oriented Features

The OO features were probably one of the enhancements most requested by programmers. I remember being at a Microsoft event when Visual Basic 6 was in beta, and the most frequently asked question was whether inheritance will be supported. Since this is an intrinsic feature of the CLR, it is now supported, and classes are inheritable by default. In fact, since everything in .NET is class based, you have an enormous amount of flexibility, as you can not only extend and overload your own classes, but many system ones too.

Classes

As in previous versions of Visual Basic, classes are created using the `Class` statement. However, the syntax has changed a little:

```
[ Public | Private | Protected | Friend | Protected Friend ]
[Shadows]
[MustInherit | NotInheritable] Class className

End Class
```

Visual Basic still requires the underscore (_) for line continuation – to make things clearer, it's not shown in the preceding syntax outline.

Let's look at the keywords in more detail:

Keyword	Description
Public	The class is publicly accessible.
Private	The class can only be accessed within the file in which it is declared.
Protected	The class is only accessible from the containing class or types derived from the containing class.
Friend	The class is only accessible from this assembly.
Protected Friend	The class is only accessible from this program or types derived from the containing class.
Shadows	The class shadows an identically named class in a base class. `Shadows` is only available inside classes, structures, and interfaces.
MustInherit	This class is an abstract class, and the class members must be implemented by inheriting classes.
NotInheritable	This class is not inheritable.

Within a class, the member definition follows the same rules. Members that are not explicitly declared with a keyword are `Public` by default.

For example:

```
Public Class Calculator

    ' implementation goes here

End Class
```

Or:

```
Protected MustInherit Class Calculator

    ' abstract implementation goes here

End Class
```

Methods

Methods are declared as a `Sub` or a `Function`, but there are improvements to fit in with the inheritance rules. The syntax for a `Sub` is now:

```
[Overloads | Overrides | Overridable | NotOverridable | MustOverride |

 Shadows | Shared]

[Private | Public | Protected | Friend | Protected Friend]

Sub subName [(parameters)]

End Sub
```

The syntax for a `Function` is:

```
[Overloads | Overrides | Overridable | NotOverridable | MustOverride |

 Shadows | Shared]

[Private | Public | Protected | Friend | Protected Friend]

Function functionName [(parameters)] [As type]

End Function
```

The various keywords are described in the following table:

Keyword	Description
Overloads	The member is overloaded, with more than one declaration existing, each with different parameters. Overloads is not required when overloading methods in the same class, but if it is used, it must be used on all overloaded methods.
Overrides	The member overrides an identically named member from a base class. This is useful for sub-classing situations where you want to provide your own implementation of a particular member. The overridden method must have the same signature; that is, the parameters and data types must match those of the base class member.
NotOverridable	The member cannot be overridden in a derived class.
Overridable	The method can be overridden by a derived class.
MustOverride	The member *must* be overridden in a derived class. This implies Overridable.
Shadows	The method shadows a method in a parent class. This means that the method in the parent class is not available, and allows creation of methods with a different signature (parameters & data types) than that of the parent. It effectively re-declares the type.
Shared	The member is shared by all instances of the class, and it exists independently of a class instance. This is equivalent to a static method in C# or C++.
Public	The member is publicly accessible.
Private	The member is only accessible within the class.
Protected	The member is only accessible from the containing class or types derived from the containing class.
Friend	The member is only accessible from this program.
Protected Friend	The member is only accessible from this program or types derived from the containing member.

For example:

```
Public Class Calculator
   Public Function Add(Op1 As Double, Op2 As Double) As Double
      Return Op1 + Op2
   End Function
End Class
```

This is an important change from previous function syntax – the value of the function is now returned using the `Return` *keyword, rather than by setting the function name to the value.*

Properties

Properties can be implemented as `Public` member variables or by using the `Property` statement. For example:

```
Public Class Calculator
   Public Op1 As Double
   Public Op2 As Double
   Public Function Add() As Double
      Return Op1 + Op2
   End Function

End Class
```

The class could be used in the following way:

```
Dim calc As New Calculator
calc.Op1 = 123
calc.Op2 = 456
Response.Write(calc.Add())
```

The preceding example uses public variables. The alternative (and preferred) approach is to use `Property`, the syntax of which has changed as follows:

```
[Default | ReadOnly | WriteOnly] Property propertyName ([parameters])
                                                          [As type]
   Get
      ' code for getting the property
   End Get

   Set
      ' code for setting the property
   End Set

End Property
```

A property defined as `ReadOnly` can only have the `Get` block. Likewise, a property with only a `Get` block must be marked as `ReadOnly`. The same applies for `WriteOnly` and the `Set` block. There is also no longer a `Let` option, as `Set` provides the same functionality.

For example:

```
Public Class Calculator
   Private _op1 As Double
   Private _op2 As Double

   Public Property Operand1() As Double
      Get
         Operand1 = _op1
      End Get
```

```
      Set
        _op1 = value
      End Set
   End Property

   Public Property Operand2() As Double
      Get
         Operand2 = _op2
      End Get
      Set
         _op2 = value
      End Set
   End Property

End Class
```

Notice the use of the keyword `value` in the `Set` block. This is the actual code you should type, as `value` is an implicit variable that contains the value of the property being set.

Default Properties and Property Parameters

Default properties are another area of change, as they are only supported on properties with a parameter list. Therefore, you could add a property called `Result` to your `Calculator` class, to contain the last result of an operation, but you wouldn't be able to make it the `Default` property. Hence, you *can't* code it like this:

```
Default Property Result() As Double
```

This stops you doing the following:

```
Label1.Text = MyCalc
```

To declare a default property, you need to have parameters (and these cannot be declared as `ByRef`). For more details, consult the Visual Basic .NET documentation supplied with the .NET SDK.

Constructors and Object Creation

The `Class_Initialize` event has been removed from classes, but has been replaced with a member function called `New`, which enables you to inherit from constructors.

One of the cool new features of Visual Basic .NET is the use of overloading, which is perfect for providing constructors. The `New()` method is a special case for overloading, since the `Overloads` keyword is not required. For example, consider a `Person` class:

```
Public Class Person

   Private _firstName As String
   Private _lastName  As String

   Sub New()
      _firstName = """"
      _lastName = """"
```

```
    End Sub

    Sub New(firstName As String, lastName As String)
      _firstName = firstName
      _lastName = lastName
    End Sub

    Public Property FirstName() As String
      ' property code here
    End Property

    Public Property LastName() As String
      ' property code here
    End Property

End Class
```

In this example there are two occurrences of Sub New(): one *without* parameters, and another *with*. This means you can write:

```
Dim coolDude As New Person()
coolDude.FirstName = "Vince"
coolDude.LastName = "Patel"
```

Or

```
Dim coolDude As New Person("Vince", "Patel")
```

This provides a richer way of using classes and simplifies code.

Destructors and Object Destruction

Like the Class_Initialize() method, Class_Terminate() has also been replaced by a Destruct() method. For example:

```
Sub Destruct()

  ' code to clean up here

End Sub
```

There has been a big change in the way destructors are called from previous versions of Visual Basic, and it revolves around the CLR. One of the good features of the CLR is *garbage collection (GC)*, which runs in the background collecting unused object references, freeing you from having to ensure that you always destroy them. However, the downside is that since it's a background task, you don't know exactly when your destructor is called.

During the time of the beta releases, there was a wide discussion regarding this, resulting in an extensive paper from Microsoft about garbage collection and its effects (search the MSDN Web site for Deterministic Finalization for more details). Some people were concerned that there might be cases where they would need to guarantee something happening (such as resource cleanup) when the object is no longer in use. If this is the case, then the advice is to create a method to house this functionality, and call this method when you have finished with the class instance.

In reality, the time difference between releasing the object instance, and it being garbage collected, is likely to be very small, since the garbage collector is always running.

Inheritance

As mentioned in the previous chapter, everything in .NET is an object, so you can inherit from pretty much anything. Consider the `Person` class as a base class; you could create a new class from it in the following way:

```
Public Class Programmer
  Inherits Person

  Private _avgHoursSleepPerNight As Integer

  Public Sub New()
    MyBase.New()
  End Sub
  Public Sub New(firstName As String, lastName As String)
    MyBase.New(firstName, lastName)
  End Sub

  Public Sub New(firstName As String, lastName As String, _
                        hoursSleep As Integer)
    MyBase.New(firstName, lastName)
    _avgHoursSleepPerNight = hoursSleep
  End Sub

  Public Property AvgHoursSleepPerNight() As Integer
    Get
      AvgHoursSleepPerNight = _avgHoursSleepPerNight
    End Get
    Set
      _avgHoursSleepPerNight = value
    End Set
  End Property

End Class
```

This class extends the existing `Person` class and adds a new property. Let's look at the way it does this.

First, after the class declarations comes the `Inherits` statement, where the base class we are inheriting from is specified:

```
Public Class Programmer
Inherits Person
```

Next, come the definitions for the existing constructors. Our class provides an extra one, so we need to overload the base class constructors. Notice how the definitions of these match the definitions in the base class, and how we call the constructor of the base class using `MyBase`. We are not changing the existing constructors, just adding our own, so we just want to map functionality to the base class:

```
Public Sub New()
    MyBase.New()
End Sub
Public Sub New(firstName As String, lastName As String)
    MyBase.New(firstName, lastName)
End Sub
```

Now we can add our extra constructor, which calls one of the previous constructors and then sets the additional property:

```
Public Sub New(firstName As String, lastName As String, _
                                    hoursSleep As Integer)
    MyBase.New(firstName, lastName)
    _avgHoursSleepPerNight = hoursSleep
End Sub
```

Finally, we add the definition of the new property:

```
Public Property AvgHoursSleepPerNight() As Integer
  Get
    AvgHoursSleepPerNight = _avgHoursSleepPerNight
  End Get
  Set
    _avgHoursSleepPerNight = value
  End Set
End Property
```

In object-oriented terms, this is standard stuff, but it's new for Visual Basic and provides a great way to promote code reuse.

Classes and Interfaces

An interface is the description of the methods and properties a class will expose – it's an immutable contract with the outside world. The interface doesn't define any implementation – just the methods and properties. Derived classes then have to provide the actual implementation.

In Visual Basic .NET you automatically get a default interface that matches the class methods and properties, but there may be times when we want to explicitly define the interface. One good example of this is that when creating .NET-serviced components, the interface can be used to provide versioning features. See Chapter 23 for more details on this.

To create an interface, the `Interface` construct is used as follows:

```
Public Interface IPerson
   Property FirstName() As String
   Property LastName() As String
   Function FullName() As String
End Interface
```

As you can see, there is no implementation specified here. By convention, the interface name is the class name preceded by I, although this isn't enforced. To derive a class from an interface, the Implements keyword is used on the class:

```
Public Class Person
    Implements IPerson

  Private _firstName As String
  Private _lastName As String

  Public Property FirstName() As String Implements IPerson.FirstName
    ' implementation goes here
  End Property

  Public Property LastName() As String Implements IPerson.LastName
    ' implementation goes here
  End Property

  Public Function FullName() As String Implements IPerson.FullName
    Return _firstName & " " & _lastName
  End Function

End Class
```

Both the class, and the methods and properties, have to specify their implementation interface.

Multiple inheritance is allowed only in an interface. For example:

```
Public Interface Person
  Inherits IPerson
  Inherits ICleverPerson
End Interface
```

Language Changes

Along with the object-oriented features, there have been many changes to the language. We won't go into exhaustive detail here (it's well covered in the documentation), but here are some things to watch out for:

❑ **Array bounds**: The lower bound of an array is always 0, and cannot be changed. The Option Base statement is not supported.

❑ **Array declaration**: ReDim can only be used if the array has already been declared.

❑ **Array sizes**: Arrays do not have a fixed size (although the number of dimensions is fixed). For example:

```
Dim ConnectionTimes(10) As Date
```

This defines an array with an initial size of 11 elements. Arrays can also be populated on declaration:

```
Dim ConnectionTimes() As Date = {"10:30", "11:30", "12:00", "06:00"}
```

❑ **String length**: The fixed-width string is not supported unless the VBFixedString attribute is used.

❑ **Variants**: The Variant data type is no longer supported, being replaced by a more generic Object. The corresponding VarType function is also not supported, as the Object has a GetType method.

❑ **Data types**: The Currency data type is replaced by Decimal. The Integer type is now 32 bits, with Short being 16 bits and Long being 64 bits.

❑ **Short cut operators**: A new short form of addition and assignment has been added. For example:

```
counter += 1
name &= " Sussman"
```

❑ **Default properties**: As mentioned earlier, default properties are not supported, unless they take parameters.

❑ **Variable declaration**: When declaring multiple variables on the same line, a variable with no data type takes the type of the next declared type (and not Variant as was the case in VB6). For example, in the following declarations Age is an Integer:

```
Dim Age, Hours As Integer
Dim Name As String, Age, Hours As Integer
```

❑ **Variable scope**: Block scope is now supported, so variables declared within blocks (such as If blocks) are only visible within the If block. In Visual Basic 6, variables could be declared anywhere, but their scope was the entire method.

❑ **Object creation**: The As New keywords can be used freely on the variable declaration line. There is no implicit object creation, so objects that are Nothing remain set to Nothing unless an explicit instance is created.

❑ **Procedure parameters**: The rules for parameter passing and optional parameters have changed. See the section on *Parameters* later for more information on this.

❑ **Procedure calls**: Parentheses are now required on all procedure calls, not just functions.

❑ **Function return values**: The return value from a function is now supplied with the Return statement, rather than by setting the function name to the desired value.

❑ **While loops**: The Wend statement has been replaced with End While.

❑ **String and Variant functions**: The string manipulation functions that had two types of call (Trim returned a Variant and Trim$ returned a string) are replaced with overloaded method calls.

❑ **Empty and Null**: The Empty and Null keywords have their functionality replaced by Nothing.

There are many other changes, some of which don't really affect ASP.NET programmers. For a full list, consult the Visual Basic .NET documentation, or see Wrox's *Professional VB.NET, 2nd Edition, ISBN: 0-7645-4400-4.*

References

Since you're freed from using a set design tool, some of the features you are used to now require a bit more typing. One example of this is referencing other components. In Visual Basic 6, to access COM components you select **References** from the **Project** menu. There's something similar in Visual Studio .NET to reference assemblies (or even COM components), but if you're using Notepad, you have to provide the reference yourself. This is done using the `Imports` keyword. For example:

```
Imports System
Imports MyComponent
```

It's also possible to alias references using the following syntax:

```
Imports aliasName = Namespace
```

If an alias is used, the alias *must* be included in references to classes that the namespace contains. For example, if you have a namespace called `MyComponent` containing a class called `MyClass`, and import the namespace like this:

```
Imports foo = MyComponent
```

You can't then access the class like this:

```
Dim comp As MyClass
```

You have to use the following syntax:

```
Dim comp As foo.MyClass
```

Structured Exception Handling

One of the best new features of .NET is a unified structured exception-handling framework, which extends to Visual Basic .NET. Although `On Error` is still supported, a far better way of handling errors is to use the new `Try...Catch...Finally` structure. The way it works is simple, with each of the statements defining a block of code to be run.

The syntax is:

```
Try

  ' code block to run

  [
   Catch [exception [As type]] [When exception]

   ' code to run if the exception generated matches
   ' the exception and expression defined above

   [Exit Try]
  ]
Catch [exception [As.type]] [When expression]
   ' code to run if the exception generated matches
```

```
   ' the exception and expression defined above

   [Exit Try]

[Finally
   ' code that always runs, whether or not an exception
   ' was caught, unless Exit Try is called
   ]

End Try
```

This allows you to bracket a section of code and then handle generic or specific errors. For example:

```
Try
   ' connect to a database and
   ' retrieve some data
   ' ... code left out for clarity ...

   Catch exSQL As SQLException
      ErrorLabel.Text = "SQL Error: " & exSQL.ToString()

   Catch ex As Exception
      ErrorLabel.Text = "Other error: " & ex.ToString()

   Finally
      FinishedLabel.Text = "Finished"

End Try
```

You can have multiple `Catch` blocks, to make our error handling specific to a particular error. Always put the most specific `Catch` blocks first and the more generic ones last, as the `Catch` blocks are tried in the order they are declared.

The `Throw` statement can be used to throw your own errors, or even re-raise errors.

Errors and exceptions are covered in detail in Chapter 22.

Data Types and Structures

There are three new data types:

❑   `Char`: for unsigned 16-bit values.

❑   `Short`: for signed 16-bit integers. This is the equivalent to the current Visual Basic `Integer` (in Visual Basic .NET the `Integer` is now 32-bits and the `Long` 64-bits).

❑   `Decimal`: for signed integers.

Custom types are now provided by the `Structure` statement, rather than the `Type` statement. The syntax is:

```
[Public | Private | Friend] Structure structureName
End Structure
```

For example:

```
Public Structure Person
   Public  FirstName As String
   Public  LastName  As String
   Private Age       As Integer
End Structure
```

The use of structures is unified with classes, enabling structures to not only contain member variables, but also methods:

```
Public Structure Narcissist
   Public  FirstName As String
   Public  LastName  As String
   Private RealAge   As Integer

   Public Function Age() As Integer
      Return RealAge - 5
   End Function

 End Structure
```

Whether you use classes or structures is purely a coding and design decision, but the close linking of the two types provides added flexibility.

Parameters

Several things have changed regarding passing parameters to procedures. The most important is that parameters now default to `ByVal`. To achieve reference parameters, you must explicitly put `ByRef` in front of the parameter name.

Secondly, as mentioned earlier, all method calls with parameters must be surrounded by parentheses. The previous versions of Visual Basic had the inconsistency that parentheses were required for functions but not subroutines. For example, the following is no longer valid:

```
MyMethod 1, 2, "foo"
```

Instead, you must use:

```
MyMethod(1, 2, "foo")
```

For optional parameters, you now have to specify a default, and the `IsMissing()` method is removed. For example, you cannot write:

```
Sub MyMethod(Name As String, Optional Age As Integer)

   If IsMissing(Age) Then
   ...
```

You have to supply a default:

```
Sub MyMethod(Name As String, Optional Age As Integer = -1)
```

Debugging and Message Boxes

Although not relevant to ASP.NET pages, there are two things that might hit you if you are using Visual Studio .NET:

❑ The `Print` method of the `Debug` object has been replaced by four methods – `Write()`, `WriteIf()`, `WriteLine()`, and `WriteLineIf()`.

❑ The `MsgBox` statement has been replaced with the `Show` method of the `MessageBox` object.

Debugging is covered in detail in Chapter 22.

Backward Compatibility

To ease the transition from Visual Basic 6 to Visual Basic .NET, you can reference the `Microsoft.VisualBasic.Compatibility.VB6` namespace, which provides access to much of the removed or changed functionality. It's probably best not to overuse these compatibility features, though. The changes to the language have been made not only to improve it, but also to bring it in line with the CLS and the other .NET languages.

C#

Like .NET itself, C# has raised a fair amount of discussion, much of it based around raising questions such as "Another language? Why?" and "Isn't it just Java?". To understand why a new language has been introduced, think about what Microsoft is trying to achieve with .NET. Some of the key ideas are:

❑ Cross-language development

❑ A unified type system

❑ Extensibility and security

❑ Greater support for development tools

These are not the only goals, nor are they specific reasons for creating a new language, but it was clear that to build the .NET Framework the existing languages wouldn't meet these requirements. C++, for example, isn't truly component oriented, and still has many hang-ups from the C language. Java is bound by its ownership by Sun (not to mention lawsuits) and is interpreted, which leads to performance problems. Object-oriented languages such as Smalltalk and Eiffel have the stigma of being considered obscure, and would need performance increases and structural changes.

Therefore, a new language was the simplest answer, but not so new, that it wouldn't feel familiar. You can think of C# as a member of the C/C++ family – a fact that's not surprising, since the majority of development at Microsoft is done in these languages. As such, C# contains the best features of C++, but leaves out all of the bits that aren't required for a language to be part of the framework (such as typedefs, templates, and so on). Leaving out functionality hasn't been a hindrance, rather, it has made the language simpler to use and more efficient. In addition, it's not just a language being pushed on the public – ASP.NET is entirely written in C#.

If you're a Visual Basic or VBScript programmer trying out C# for the first time, there's one really important thing to note: C# is case-sensitive.

Classes

Even though C# is more like C and C++, Visual Basic or VBScript programmers won't have too much trouble with this new language. Classes are defined using the following syntax:

```
[public | protected | internal | protected internal | private |

 abstract | sealed ] class className
{
}
```

Let's look at the keywords here in more detail:

Keyword	Description
public	The class is publicly accessible.
protected	The class is only accessible from the containing class or types derived from the containing class.
internal	The class is only accessible from this program. Equivalent to Friend in Visual Basic.
protected internal	The class is only accessible from this program or types derived from the containing class. Equivalent to Protected Friend in Visual Basic.
private	The class is only accessible from within the containing class.
abstract	This class is an abstract class, and the class members must be implemented by inheriting classes. Equivalent to MustInherit in Visual Basic.
sealed	No further inheritance is allowed from this class. Equivalent to NotInheritable in Visual Basic.

For example:

```
public class Calculator
{
   // implementation goes here
}
```

Methods

In C# there is no direct distinction between a Sub and a Function, and members are just implemented as functions (that may or may not return data). The syntax is:

```
[ public | protected | internal | protected internal | private | static |
```

```
      virtual | override | abstract | extern ]
    [ type | void ] memberName([parameters])
  {
  }
```

The various keywords are described as follows:

Keyword	Description
public	The member is publicly accessible.
protected	The member is only accessible from the containing class or types derived from the containing member.
internal	The member is only accessible from this program. Equivalent to Friend in Visual Basic.
protected internal	The member is only accessible from this program, or types derived from the containing member. Equivalent to Protected Friend in Visual Basic.
private	The member is only accessible from within the containing member.
static	The member is shared by all instances of the class, and it exists independently of a class instance. Equivalent to Shared in Visual Basic.
virtual	The member can be overridden by a sub-class.
override	The member overrides an identically named member from a base class, with the same signature. The base class member must be defined as virtual, abstract or override.
abstract	This member is an abstract member, and must be implemented by a sub-class.
extern	The member is implemented in an external assembly.

For example:

```
public class calculator
{
  public double Add(double op1, double op2)
  {
    return op1 + op2;
  }
}
```

For a method that does not return a result, we declare the type as void:

```
public void updateSomething()
{
}
```

Properties

Properties in C# are very similar to Visual Basic .NET, and can be implemented as `public` member variables or by using the property accessors. For example, the following class uses public variables:

```
public class calculator
{
   public double Op1;
   public double Op2;

   public double Add()
   {
      return Op1 + Op2;
   }
}
```

The alternative (and preferred) approach is to use property accessors. For example:

```
public class calculator
{
   private double _op1;
   private double _op2;

   public double Operand1
   {
      get
      {
         return _op1;
      }
      set
      {
         _op1 = value;
      }
   }

   public double Operand2
   {
      get
      {
         return _op2;
      }
      set
      {
         _op2 = value;
      }
   }

}
```

Unlike Visual Basic, there are no specific keywords to identify `read-only` and `write-only` properties. If only the `get` accessor is provided, the property is `read-only`, and if only the `set` accessor is provided, the property is `write-only`. Both accessors imply a `read-write` property.

Constructors

Rather than using New for constructors, the C# syntax is to use a method with the same name as the class. For example:

```
public class person
{
  private string _firstName;
  private string _lastName;

  public person() {}

  public person(string firstName, string lastName)
  {
    _firstName = firstName;
    _lastName = lastName;
  }
  public string FirstName
  {
    // property accessors here
  }

  public string LastName
  {
    // property accessors here
  }
}
```

Destructors

For destructors there is no Destruct keyword. This functionality is provided by a method with the same name as the class, but with a tilde (~) preceding it. For example:

```
public class person
{
  private string _firstName;
  private string _lastName;

  public person() {}

  public person(string firstName, string lastName) { }
  ~person()
  {
    // destructor code here
  }
}
```

Like in Visual Basic .NET, destructors in C# are called by the garbage collector, and are not guaranteed to be executed at the time you destroy the class.

Inheritance

Inheritance in C# looks more like C++, where a colon (:) is used to separate the class and the base class. For example:

```
public class programmer : person
{
  private int _avgHoursSleepPerNight;

  public programmer(): base()
  {
  }

  public programmer(string firstName, string lastName):
        base(firstName, lastName)
  {
  }
  public programmer(string firstName, string lastName, int hoursSleep):
        base(firstName, lastName)
  {
    _avgHoursSleepPerNight = hoursSleep;
  }

  public int AvgHoursSleepPerNight
  {
    get { return _avgHoursSleepPerNight; }
    set { _avgHoursSleepPerNight = value; }
  }
}
```

The class definition defines that the class is called `programmer` and the base class is called `person`:

```
public class programmer : person
{
```

Next, you need to provide the constructors. Here specify the same constructors as the base class, and use the same inheritance syntax (:) to indicate that this method inherits its implementation from the base class. Any parameters should be passed to the base class constructor:

```
public programmer(): base()
{
}

public programmer(string firstName, string lastName):
        base(firstName, lastName)
{
}
```

To declare an additional constructor, follow the same rules, invoking the base constructor, but also providing additional functionality:

```
public programmer(string firstName, string lastName, int hoursSleep):
        base(firstName, lastName)
```

```
    {
       _avgHoursSleepPerNight = hoursSleep;
    }
```

Finally, you have the `new` property:

```
    public int AvgHoursSleepPerNight
    {
       get { return _avgHoursSleepPerNight; }
       set { _avgHoursSleepPerNight = value; }
    }
  }
```

The `value` keyword is implemented automatically by the CLR, providing the property with the supplied value from the calling program.

Interfaces

Interfaces work the same as in Visual Basic .NET, providing an immutable contract to the external world.

To create an interface, use the `interface` construct. For example:

```
public interface IPerson
{
   string FirstName(get; set;)
   string LastName(get; set;)

   string FullName();
}
```

To derive a class from an interface, use the same method as inheritance:

```
public class Person : IPerson
{
   private string _firstName;
   private string _lastName;

   public string FirstName()
   {
     // implementation goes here
   }

   public string LastName()
   {
     // implementation goes here
   }

   public string FullName()
   {
     return _firstName + " " + _lastName;
   }
}
```

Notice that unlike Visual Basic .NET, only the class needs to specify the interface inheritance.

References

References use the same method as Visual Basic .NET, but with the keyword `using` instead of `Imports`:

```
using System;
using MyComponent;
```

It's also possible to alias references using the following syntax:

```
using aliasName = Namespace;
```

If an alias is used, the alias *must* be included in references to classes that the namespace contains. For example, if you have a namespace called `MyComponent` containing a class called `MyClass`, and import the namespace like this:

```
using foo = MyComponent;
```

You can't then access the class like this:

```
MyClass comp = MyClass
```

You have to use the following syntax:

```
foo.MyClass comp = foo.MyClass
```

Exception Handling

The `try...catch...finally` combo is another way of performing exception handling in C#, using the following syntax:

```
try
{
  // code block to try
}
[catch[(type exception)]
{
  // code block to run if the exception matches the type above
}]
catch[(type exception)]
{
  // code block to run if the exception matches the type above
}
finally
{
  ' code that always runs, whether or not
  ' an exception was caught
}
```

For example:

```
try
{
  // connect to a database and
  // retrieve some data
  // ... code left out for clarity ...
}
catch(SQLException exSQL)
{
    ErrorLabel.Text = "SQL Error: " + exSQL.ToString();
}
catch(Exception ex)
{
    ErrorLabel.Text = "Other error: " + ex.ToString();
}
finally
{
    FinishedLabel.Text = "Finished";
}
```

The `throw` statement can be used to raise errors, even when in `try...catch` blocks. For example:

```
try
{
  // some code here
}
catch(SQLException exSQL)
{
  if (some expression)
    throw(exSQL);
}
```

XML Documentation

One great feature that C# has over Visual Basic is the ability to include inline documentation. This is done by placing a set of XML tags at various places in code, and then adding a compiler directive to pull out the comments. For example:

```
using System;

namespace peopleCS
{

  ///<remarks>
  ///The <c>programmer</c>class defines the salient
  ///attributes of every fine programmer.
  ///<seealso cref="person">Inherits from person</seealso>
  ///</remarks>

  public class programmer : person
  {
    private int _avgHoursSleepPerNight;
```

```
///<summary>Default constructor</summary>

public programmer(): base()
{ }

///<summary>Constructor using first and last names</summary>

///<param name="firstName">The first name of the programmer</param>

///<param name="lastName">The last name of the programmer</param>

///<seealso cref="string"/>

public programmer(string firstName, string lastName):
      base(firstName, lastName)
{ }

///<summary>Constructor using first and last names and

///the hours of sleep</summary>

///<param name="firstName">The first name of the programmer</param>

///<param name="lastName">The last name of the programmer</param>

///<param name="hoursSleep">The average number of hours of sleep</param>

///<seealso cref="string"/>

///<seealso cref="int"/>

public programmer(string firstName, string lastName, int hoursSleep):
      base(firstName, lastName)
{
   _avgHoursSleepPerNight = hoursSleep;
}

///<value>Defines the average number of hours of sleep.</value>

public int AvgHoursSleepPerNight

{
   get { return _avgHoursSleepPerNight; }
   set { _avgHoursSleepPerNight = value; }
}
}
}
```

The XML tags are placed after three / / / characters – not to be confused with two, as used by comments.

The tags are as follows:

Tag	Description
c	Text that indicates inline code.
code	Multiple lines of code, such as a sample.
example	Description of a code sample.
exception	Indicates an exception class. Additionally, the attribute cref can be used to reference another type (such as the exception type). This reference is checked against the imported libraries.
include	Allows XML documentation to be retrieved from another file.
list	Indicates a list of items. The type attribute can be one of: bullet, for bulleted lists number, for numbered lists table, for a table You can use a listheader element to define headings, and an item element to define the items in the list. Each of these can contain two elements: item for the item being listed, and description.
para	Allows paragraph definitions within other tags.
param	Describes the parameter of a method. The name attribute should match the name of the parameter.
paramref	Used to indicate references for parameters.
permission	Describes the permissions required to access the member. The cref can be used to reference another type (such as the security permission type). This reference is checked against the imported libraries.
remarks	Overview information about the class or type.
returns	The return value of a method.
see	The attribute cref is used to reference another type (such as a related member). This reference is checked against the imported libraries.
seealso	The attribute cref is used to reference another type (such as a related member), to be documented in the See Also section. This reference is checked against the imported libraries.
summary	Description of a member or type.
value	Description of a property.

In Visual Studio, these tags can be processed to form HTML pages that become part of the project documentation. Outside Visual Studio, you can produce an XML file for the comments by using the

/doc compiler switch (more on these in *The .NET Language Compilers* section), which produces the file as follows:

```xml
<?xml version="1.0"?>
<doc>

  <assembly>
    <name>PeopleCS</name>
  </assembly>

  <members>

    <member name="T:peopleCS.programmer">
      <remarks>
      The <c>programmer</c>class defines the salient
      attributes of every fine programmer.
      <seealso cref="T:peopleCS.person">Inherits from person</seealso>
      </remarks>
    </member>

    <member name="M:peopleCS.programmer.#ctor">
      <summary>Default constructor</summary>
    </member>

    <member name="M:peopleCS.programmer.#ctor(System.String,System.String)">
      <summary>Constructor using first and last names</summary>
      <param name="firstName">The first name of the programmer</param>
      <param name="lastName">The last name of the programmer</param>
      <seealso cref="T:System.String"/>
    </member>

    <member name="M:peopleCS.programmer.#ctor(System.String,
                                      System.String,System.Int32)">
      <summary>Constructor using first and last
              names and the hours of sleep</summary>
      <param name="firstName">The first name of the programmer</param>
      <param name="lastName">The last name of the programmer</param>
      <param name="hoursSleep">The average number of hours of sleep</param>
      <seealso cref="T:System.String"/>
      <seealso cref="T:System.Int32"/>
    </member>

    <member name="P:peopleCS.programmer.AvgHoursSleepPerNight">
      <value>Defines the average number of hours of sleep.</value>
    </member>

  </members>

</doc>
```

The compiler automatically includes the namespace and builds tags for the member names. The members are given a fully qualified name starting with one of the following prefixes:

Prefix	Description
N	Namespace
T	Type: `Class`, `Interface`, `Struct`, `Enum`, or `Delegate`
F	Field
P	Property (including indexers)
M	Method (including constructors)
E	Event
!	Error string if links cannot be resolved

You could then use an XSLT stylesheet, or XML processing code to style this into your own documentation. You could also add your own XML elements to the class descriptions, and these would be extracted along with the predefined elements.

Unsafe Code

Although C# is part of the managed code environment, Microsoft has realized that sometimes developers need total control, such as when performance is an issue, when dealing with binary structures, or for some advanced COM support. Under these circumstances, you are able to use C# code in an unsafe manner, using pointers, unsafe casts, and so on.

As an ASP.NET developer it's unlikely you'll ever need this, but knowing it's available gives you the flexibility to choose, should the need arise.

Operator Overloading

C# is the only one of the supplied languages that supports operator overloading. This works in the same way as method overloading, except for operators. The reason for this is to allow the standard operators to be used on objects such as classes.

The classic example given is a class for handling complex numbers, which have a real and imaginary part (stored as integers). Imagine a class that has two properties for these two parts, and a constructor that takes two arguments to match the properties:

```
CNumber c1 = new CNumber(12, 4);
CNumber c2 = new CNumber(5, 6);
```

When performing addition on complex numbers, you must add the real part and imaginary part independently of each other, and might consider creating this method:

```
public CNumber Add(CNumber c1, CNumber c2)
{
   return new CNumber(c1.real + c2.real, c1.imag + c2.imag);
}
```

You could then call this by:

```
CNumber c3 = CNumber.Add(c1, c2);
```

There's nothing wrong with that per se, but it would be far better to use:

```
CNumber c3 = c1 + c2;
```

To achieve this, you would have to overload the + operator:

```
public static CNumber operator +(CNumber c1, CNumber c2);
{
   return new CNumber(c1.real + c2.real, c1.imag + c2.imag);
}
```

This provides a much more intuitive way of developing, and is especially useful when building class libraries for other developers.

For more details on C#, see Professional C#, ISBN 0-7645-4398-9, from Wrox Press.

JScript.NET

Like Visual Basic, JScript has also undergone some changes, although not as radical. The first thing to realize is that JScript.NET is a full .NET language, and therefore provides the advantages that the other supported languages do. In fact, JScript.NET has been completely rewritten in C#. It now supports types and inheritance, and is fully compiled.

Although completely rewritten, JScript.NET is more evolutionary, and still supports existing JScript functionality – the new features are extra, and (apart from compilation, which is a CLR requirement) not enforced. Consult the documentation for more details on JScript.NET.

C++

Since C++ already has object-oriented features, the VC++ implementation supplied with Visual Studio .NET provides support for managed code. At the minimum, you must include the following two lines at the top of your code:

```
#using <mscorlib.dll>
using namespace System;
```

These give you access to the .NET classes. You must also add the /CLR compiler option when building the executable.

Details of working with the managed extensions for C++ are outside the scope of this book, so you should consult the documentation for more details.

Visual J#.NET

Visual J# .NET is a Microsoft implement of Java, for .NET. This is not only aimed at Java developers using Microsoft's J++ development tool, but at third party Java developers too. As part of this, the Visual J# .NET toolkit provides a tool to convert Java sourcecode into J#, migrating the language and library calls. It fully integrates with Visual Studio .NET, and supports the Microsoft extensions that J++ supported, as well as supporting (via a download) an equivalent of the JFC Swing UI library.

> *Applications developed with J# will only run within .NET. This isn't a Java virtual machine, but comprises tools and compilers for the .NET Framework. As such it doesn't produce Java byte code, and is not endorsed by Sun Microsystems.*

Other Supported Languages

We've already mentioned that the open design of .NET actively encourages the use of other languages, and Microsoft is keen for this to happen. At the time of writing, the following languages were also becoming available:

- ❑ Dyalog APL/W Version 9
- ❑ Fujitsu COBOL
- ❑ Component Pascal
- ❑ Eiffel
- ❑ Haskell
- ❑ Mercury
- ❑ Oberon
- ❑ Perl
- ❑ Python
- ❑ Scheme
- ❑ Standard ML

There are others in the pipeline, and the best resource is http://www.gotdotnet.com, which contains an up-to-date list of languages.

If you're into building your own languages, the SDK comes with some good sample compilers that show you how to do this. They are in the Tool Developers Guide. There's also plenty of documentation about assemblies, IL, and so on.

The .NET Language Compilers

When working within the Visual Studio .NET environment, you don't need to worry about the compiler, because the editor takes care of compilation. Likewise, when simply developing ASP.NET pages, you can rely on the framework to compile pages as required. However, when building components or controls, you'd want to compile code into a DLL, so you need to know how the compiler works.

There is a separate compiler for each language, but luckily, you use them all in the same way, and most of the switches and flags are identical. The compilers are:

❑   csc for C#

❑   vbc for Visual Basic .NET

❑   jsc for JScript.NET

These are automatically part of the .NET installation, and are invoked from the command line. For example:

```
vbc /t:library /out:..\bin\People.dll /r:system.dll person.vb programmer.vb
```

This compiles the `person.vb` and `programmer.vb` source files into an assembly named `People.dll`.

Compiler switches fall into two usage categories. The first includes those that enable or disable an option: in this case, the switch or the switch name followed by plus enables the option, and the switch name followed by minus disables it. For example:

/cls	Enables the option
/cls+	Enables the option
/cls-	Disables the option

The second category contains switches that specify a file or reference. Here a colon (:) separates the switch and the argument. For example:

```
/out:..\bin\People.dll
```

The full list of options including a list of which languages the option is supported in is as follows:

Option	Language	Description
@	All	Specify the file containing the compiler options.
/? /help	All	Display the options, without compiling any code.
/addmodule:module	VB / C#	Reference metadata from the specified `module`.
/autoref	JScript	Automatically reference assemblies based on imported namespaces and fully qualified names. This defaults to `on`.
/baseaddress:number	VB / C#	Specify, as a hexadecimal `number`, the base address of the DLL.
/bugreport:file	VB / C#	Create a `file` containing information that can be used when filing bug reports.
/checked	C#	Generate overflow checks
/codepage:id	JScript / C#	Specify the code page `id` used in source files.
/debug	All	Add debugging information to the created file. This is required if you need to debug into components.
/define:symbols	All	Define conditional compiler constants. You can define multiple constants by separating them with commas. For example: `/define:DBTracing=True,CustomErrors=False`
/doc:file	C#	Emit the XML documentation in the source files into the named `file`.
/delaysign	VB	Delay-sign the assembly, using only the public part of the strong name key.
/fast	JScript	Disable language features to allow better code generation.
/filealign:n	C#	Specify the alignment used for output file sections.
/fullpaths	C#	Generate fully qualified paths.

Table continued on following page

Option	Language	Description
`/imports:list`	VB	Import a namespace from the specified assembly.
`/incr` `/incremental`	C#	Enable or disable incremental compilation.
`/keycontainer`	VB	Create a unique container name for a key. Used when generating shared components as it inserts a public key into the assembly manifest, and signs the assembly with a private key. Can be used with the `sn` utility which manages keys.
`/keyfile`	VB	Specify the file containing the public and private keys to be added to a shared component. This can be used with the `sn` utility, which manages keys.
`/lcid:id`	JScript	Use the specified locale `id` for the default code page and messages.
`/lib:directories`	C# / JScript	Specify additional `directories` to search for references.
`/libpath:directories`	VB	Specify additional `directories` to search for references.

`/linkres:resinfo`
`/linkresource:resinfo`
	All	Create a link to a resource file. The first argument is the file name containing the resource, and an optional second argument specifies the identifier in the resource file. For example:
		`/linkresource:Wrox.resource,Auth`
		`orBio`

`/m:type` `/main:type`	C# / VB	Specify the class or module `type` that contains the main start-up procedure.
`/noconfig`	C#	Do not auto-include `CSC.RSP` file.
`/nologo`	C# / VB	Don't show the copyright banner during compile. This makes it a lot easier to see compilation messages.
`/nowarn`	VB	Disable warnings.
`/nostdlib`	C# / JScript	Enable or disable the import of the standard library `mscorlib.dll` compilation.

Option	Language	Description
`/nowarn:list`	C#	Disable warning messages specified in the `list`.
`/optimize`	C# / VB	Enable or disable compiler optimizations.
`/optioncompare:type`	VB	Specify the `type` of comparison used for strings. The values are `text` or `binary` (the default). For example: `optioncompare:text`
`/optionexplicit`	VB	Enable (the default) or disable explicit variable declaration.
`/optionstrict`	VB	Enables (the default) or disables strict type conversions. In strict mode the only implicit conversions are those that widen types (for example an integer to a long).
`/out:file`	All	Specify the name of the output `file`. By default a DLL will take its name from the first sourcecode file, and an EXE will take its name from the file containing the main procedure.
`/print`	JScript	Enable or disable provision of the `print()` function.
`/quiet`	VB	Quiet output mode.
`/recurse:wildcard`	C# / VB	Recurse through subdirectories compiling files. For example: `vbc /target:library /out:Foo.dll /recurse:inc\*.vb`
`/r:list` `/reference:list`	All	Reference metadata from the specified file `list`. For multiple files use a semicolon (`;`) to separate them.
`/removeintchecks`	VB	Enable or disable (the default) overflow error checking for integer variables.
`/res:resinfo` `/resource:resinfo`	All	Embed a resource into the assembly. The first argument is the file name containing the resource, and an optional second argument specifies the identifier in the resource file. For example: `/resource:Wrox.resource,AuthorBio`

Table continued on following page

Option	Language	Description
`/rootnamespace`	VB	Indicate the namespace in which all type declarations will appear.
`/target:type`	All	Indicate the `type` of file to be created. This can be one of: `exe`, for a console application `library`, for a DLL `module`, for a module `winexe`, for a Windows application The `module` option is not applicable in JScript .NET.
`/time`	C#	Display the project compile-times.
`/unsafe`	C#	Enable or disable unsafe code.
`/utf8output`	All	Output compiler messages in UTF-8 encoding.
`/verbose`	VB	Enable or disable verbose error and information messages.
`/versionsafe`	JScript	Enable or disable specification of default for members that aren't marked as `override` or `new`.
`/w:n` `/warn:n`	C# / JScript	Set the warning level to n.
`/warnaserror`	All	Enable or disable the treatment of warnings as errors.
`/win32icon:file`	C# / VB	Specify the icon `file` (`.ico`) to be added to the resource.
`/win32res:file` `/win32resource:file`	All	Insert a Win32 resource `file` into the target.

Benefits of a Common Language Runtime

❑ **Language functionality**: The choice of language is now a lifestyle choice, rather than a functionality choice, as they are all equivalent. Use whatever language you are happiest with.

❑ **Performance**: The .NET languages were designed to provide high performance. The only difference between the languages is at the compilation stage, where compilers may produce slightly different MSIL.

❑ **Platform support**: The languages sit on top of the CLR, so if the CLR is available on a platform, then so are the .NET languages. For small device support and 64-bit platforms, this makes portability far easier than with previous Windows languages.

Common API

In the previous version of Visual Studio, common functionality was always harder to implement than it should have been. For C++ programmers, the Windows API is a natural home, but Visual Basic programmers had to use custom controls and libraries, or delve into the API itself. This isn't complex, and can yield great benefits, but there is no consistency.

With .NET, you now have a common API and a great set of class libraries. For example, consider the case of TCP/IP network applications. C++ programmers generally write directly to Winsock, whereas Visual Basic programmers prefer to use custom controls on their forms. The .NET Framework provides a `System.Net.Sockets` namespace encompassing all of the networking functionality, and its usage is the same for each language.

For example, consider the case of writing to a UDP port – notice that the only differences in the code are the syntax of the language.

The code in Visual Basic .NET:

```
Dim Client       As UdpClient
Dim HostName     As String
Dim HostIP       As IPHostEntry
Dim GroupAddress As IPAddress
Dim Remote       As IPEndPoint

HostName = DNS.GetHostName()
HostIP = DNS.GetHostByName(HostName)

Client = New UdpClient(8080)
GroupAddress = IpAddress.Parse("224.0.0.1")
Client.JoinMultiCastGroup(GroupAddress, 500)
Remote = New IPEndPoint(GroupAddress, 8080)
Client.Send(".NET is great", 13, Remote)
```

The code in C#:

```
UdpClient    Client;
String       HostName;
IPHostEntry  HostIP;
IPAddress    GroupAddress;
IPEndPoint   Remote;

HostName = DNS.GetHostName();
HostIP = DNS.GetHostByName(HostName);

Client = new UdpClient(8080);
GroupAddress = IpAddress.Parse("224.0.0.1");
Client.JoinMultiCastGroup(GroupAddress, 500);
```

```
Remote = new IPEndPoint(GroupAddress, 8080);
Client.Send(".NET is great", 13, Remote);
```

Common Types

Cross-language functionality is made available by use of common types. Those Visual Basic programmers (and I was one) who delved into the Windows API always had the problem about converting types. Strings were the worst, because the API is C/C++ based, which uses Null-terminated strings, so we always had to do conversion and fixed string handling stuff. It was ugly. With the CLS, there is a common set of types, so no conversion is required. The conversion of native types into CLS types is shown in the following table:

Type	Visual Basic .NET	C#
System.Boolean	Boolean	Bool
System.Byte	Byte	Byte
System.Char	Char	Char
System.DateTime	Date	No direct equivalent. Use the CLS type.
System.Decimal	Decimal	Decimal
System.Double	Double	Double
System.Int16	Short	Short
System.Int32	Integer	Int
System.Int64	Long	Long
System.UInt16	No direct equivalent	Ushort
System.UInt32	No direct equivalent	Uint
System.UInt64	No direct equivalent.	Ulong
System.SByte	No direct equivalent	Sbyte
System.Single	Single	Float
System.String	String	String

Not all languages have equivalents of the CLS types. For example, JScript.NET implements dates using the standard JScript Date object. However, you can convert between various type formats, as well as declaring the CLS types directly.

Cross-Language Inheritance

Another area where the CLS has helped is inheritance. If you use the common types in your class interfaces, inheriting classes written in other languages is no different to that of inheriting from the same language. There was a brief example in the previous chapter, when discussing the CLR and common functionality, but a fuller example makes this clear. For example, consider the following Visual Basic class:

```
Public Class Person

    Private _firstName As String
    Private _lastName  As String

    Sub New()
    End Sub

    Sub New(firstName As String, lastName As String)
      _firstName = firstName
      _lastName = lastName
    End Sub

    Public Property FirstName() As String
      ' property code here
    End Property

    Public Property LastName() As String
      ' property code here
    End Property

End Class
```

You could write another program, perhaps in C#, that inherits from it:

```
public class programmer : Person
{
  private int _avgHoursSleepPerNight;

  public programmer(): base()
  {
  }

  public programmer(string firstName, string lastName)
                  : base(firstName, lastName)
  {
  }

  public programmer(string firstName, string lastName, int hoursSleep)
                  : base(firstName, lastName)
  {
    _avgHoursSleepPerNight = hoursSleep;
  }

  public int AvgHoursSleepPerNight
```

```
    {
      get { return _avgHoursSleepPerNight; }
      set { _avgHoursSleepPerNight = value; }
    }

    programmer()
    {
    }
  }
```

This brings great flexibility to development, especially team development.

Another great point is that many of the base classes and Web controls are inheritable. Therefore, in any language, you can extend them as you wish. A good example of this is the ASP.NET DataGrid control. Say you do not want to use paging, but want to provide a scrollable grid, so browsers that supported inline frames would allow the entire content of the grid to be rendered within a scrollable frame. You can create your own control (say, in Visual Basic), inheriting everything from the base control (perhaps written in C#), and then just output the normal content within an IFRAME. This sort of thing is extremely easy to do with the new framework.

Cross-Language Debugging and Profiling

The cross language debugging features are cool, and provide a huge leap forward over any debugging features we've ever had before. Both the framework and Visual Studio .NET come with visual debuggers, the only difference is the Visual Studio .NET debugger allows remote debugging as well as edit and continue. The debuggers work through the CLR, and allow you to step through ASP.NET pages and into components, whatever the language. Along with debugging, comes tracing and profiling, with the ability to use common techniques to track code.

Both of these topics are covered in detail in Chapter 22.

Performance Issues

Performance is always a question in people's minds, and often is raised during beta testing when there's lots of debugging code hanging around in the product. Even in the early betas, it was clear that ASP.NET was faster than ASP, with figures showing that it was 2 to 3 times as fast.

One of the reasons for this performance improvement is the full compilation of code. Many people confuse *Intermediate Language* (*IL*) and the CLR with byte-code and interpreters (notably Java), and assume that performance will drop. Their belief in this deepens when they first access an aspx page, because that first hit can sometimes be slow. It's because pages are compiled on their first hit, and then served from the cache thereafter (unless explicit caching has been disabled).

Appendix B has a list of tips and tricks to help with performance.

Languages

Although all languages compile to IL and then to native code, there may be some slight performance differences, due to the nature of the compiler and the language. In some languages, the produced IL may not be as efficient as with others (some people have said that the C# compiler is better than the VB compiler), but the effects should be imperceptible. It's only under the highest possible stress situation that you may find differences, and to be honest, I wouldn't even consider it a problem.

Late-Bound Code

One of the greatest advantages of the CLR is fully typed languages. However, you can still use JScript.NET without data types, allowing legacy code to continue working. The disadvantage is that types then have to be inferred, and this will have a performance impact.

In Visual Basic, if strict semantics are not being used (either by the `Option Strict Off` page directive or by the `/optionstrict-` compiler switch), then late-bound calls on object types are handled at runtime rather than compile time.

Common Examples

Experienced developers probably won't have much trouble using the new features of the languages, or even converting from one language to another. However, many people use ASP and VBScript daily to build great sites, but have little experience of advanced development features, such as the object-oriented features in .NET. That's actually a testament to how simple ASP is, but now that ASP.NET is moving up a gear, it's important that you make the most of these features.

To that end, this section will give a few samples in Visual Basic .NET and C#, covering a few common areas. This will help should you want to convert existing code, write new code in a language that you aren't an expert in, or perhaps just examine someone else's code. We won't cover the definition of classes and class members again in this section, as they've had a good examination earlier in the chapter.

Variable Declaration

The first point to look at is that of variable declaration. The following examples show the difference between VB.NEt and C# when declaring variables.

Visual Basic .NET

Visual Basic .NET has the same variable declaration syntax as the previous version, but now has the ability to set initial values at variable declaration time. For example:

```
Dim Name     As String = "Rob Smith"
Dim Age      As Integer = 28
Dim coolDude As New Person("Vince", "Patel")
```

C#

C# follows the C/C++ style of variable declaration:

```
string Name = "Rob Smith";
int Age = 28;
coolDude = new Person("Vince", "Patel");
```

Functions and Procedures

Declaring procedures is similar across all languages, as the following examples show.

Visual Basic .NET

Procedures and functions follow similar syntax to previous versions:

```
Private Function GetDiscounts(Company As String) As DataSet
Public Sub UpdateDiscounts(Company As String, Discount As Double)
```

The major difference is that by default all parameters are now passed by value, and not by reference. Moreover, remember that optional parameters also now require a default value:

```
' incorrect
Function GetDiscounts(Optional Comp As String) As DataSet
   ' correct
Function GetDiscounts(Optional Comp As String = "Wrox") As DataSet
```

Returning values from functions now uses the Return statement, rather than setting the function name to the desired value. For example:

```
Function IsActive() As Boolean
   ' some code here
   Return True
End Function
```

The way you call procedures has also changed. The rule is that arguments to all procedure calls must be enclosed in parentheses. For example:

```
UpdateDiscounts "Wrox", 5         ' no longer works
UpdateDiscounts("Wrox", 5)        ' new syntax
```

C#

C# doesn't have any notion of procedures – there are only functions that either return or don't return values (in which case the type is void). For example:

```
bool IsActive()
{
   // some code here

   return true;
}
void UpdateDiscounts(string Company, double Discount)
{
   return;
}
```

> To call procedures, C# requires that parentheses be used.

Syntactical Differences

A few syntactical differences confuse many people when switching languages for the firsttime. The first is that Visual Basic isn't case sensitive, but the other languages - are it still catches me out! Other things are the use of line terminators in C# and JScript, which use a semicolon. Many people switching to these languages complain about them, but the reason they are so great is that it makes the language free form – the end of the line doesn't end the current statement. This is unlike Visual Basic, where the end of the line is the end of the statement, and a line continuation character is required for long lines.

Loops

The syntax of loop constructs differs from Vb.NET to C#.

Visual Basic .NET

There are four loop constructs in Visual Basic, and the syntax of one has changed in Visual Basic .NET. The first is the For..Next loop:

```
For counter = start To end [Step step]
Next [counter]
```

For example:

```
For count = 1 To 10
   ...
Next
```

The second is the While loop, for which the syntax has changed – the new syntax is:

```
While condition
End While
```

For example:

```
While count < 10
   ...
End While
```

In previous versions of Visual Basic, the loop was terminated with a Wend *statement.*

The third is the Do...Loop, which has two forms:

```
Do [(While | Until) condition]
Loop
```

Or:

```
Do
Loop [(While | Until) condition]
```

The difference between these two is the placement of the test condition. In the first instance, the test is executed before any loop content, and therefore the content may not be executed. In the second case, the test is at the end of the loop, so the content is always executed at least once. For example:

```
Do While count < 10
Loop
```

```
Do
Loop While count < 10
```

The For Each loop construct is for iterating through collections:

```
For Each element In collection
Next [element]
```

For example:

```
Dim ctl As Control
For Each ctl In Page.Controls
   ...
Next
```

C#

C# has the same number of loop constructs as Visual Basic. The first is the for loop:

```
for ([initializers] ; [expression] ; [iterators])
```

For example:

```
for (count = 0 ; count < 10 ; count++)
```

Each of these parts is optional. For example:

```
for ( ; count < 10; count++)
for ( ; ; count++)
for (count = 0 ; ; count++)
```

```
for ( ; ; )
```

The last of these produces an infinite loop.

The second is the while loop:

```
while (expression)
```

For example:

```
while (count < 10)
```

The third is the `do...while` loop:

```
do statement while (expressions);
```

For example:

```
do
while (count < 10);
```

The `foreach` loop construct is for iterating through collections:

```
foreach (type identifier in expression)
```

For example:

```
foreach (Control ctl in Page.Controls)
```

You can also use this for looping through arrays:

```
String[] Authors = new String[]
                 {"Alex", "Brian", "Dave", "Karli", "Rich", "Rob"};

foreach (String Author in Authors)
    Console.WriteLine("{0}", Author);
```

One point to note about loops in C# is that the loop affects the code block after the loop. This can be a single line or a bracketed block; for example:

```
for (count = 0 ; count < 10 ; count++)
    Console.WriteLine("{0}", count);
```

If more than one line is required as part of the loop, this can be written as:

```
for (count = 0 ; count < 10 ; count++)
{
    Console.Write("The value is now: ");
    Console.WriteLine("{0}", count);
}
```

Type Conversion

Type conversion of one data type to another causes a great deal of confusion, especially for those programmers who are used to a typeless language such as VBScript. When dealing with strongly typed languages, you have to let the compiler or runtime convert between types (if it can) or explicitly perform the conversion yourself. The method of conversion depends upon the language.

Visual Basic .NET

In Visual Basic .NET there are two ways to do this. The first uses `CType`:

```
Dim AgeString As String
Dim Age As Integer

AgeString = "25"
Age = CType(AgeString, Integer)
```

The `CType` function takes an object and a data type, and returns the object converted to the data type.

The other way is to use the data type as a cast function:

```
Age = CInt(AgeString)
```

C#

In C# just place the type in parentheses before the expression you wish to convert. For example:

```
Age = (int)AgeString;
```

Summary

In this chapter we examined the languages supplied with .NET, and discovered that the underlying framework provides a rich development environment. The whole issue, and arguments that go along with it, of which language is better, or more suitable, has simply disappeared. The best language is the one with which you are most familiar. Apart from a few small areas, the major difference between the .NET languages is the syntax.

We also looked at the enhancements to the existing languages that bring them into line with the CLR and CLS, how these features are compatible across all languages, and the benefits they bring. Features such as cross-language development, debugging, and tracing may not seem that great if you only use one language, but the flexibility they bring is immeasurable, especially when combined with the extensive class libraries.

Now that we've examined the languages, it's time to start using them and looking in detail at the process of writing ASP.NET pages.

Writing ASP.NET Pages

You have already taken a high-level look at the .NET Framework, and seen a few quick examples of ASP.NET pages, so now let's dive in and look in more details at how to create ASP.NET pages. Whether they are called ASP.NET pages or Web forms, these files form the core of all ASP.NET applications. This chapter covers:

❑ The old way of creating ASP pages versus the new way with ASP.NET

❑ The steps a page goes through as it is processed

❑ How to use the various features of the Page object

❑ Breaking up a page into reusable objects called user controls

At the end of this chapter, you will have learned the core essentials for the rest of the ASP.NET world. The remainder of the book draws on the page framework shown in this chapter.

Coding Issues

Chapter 1 looked at some of the main disadvantages of existing ASP applications, discussed why a new version was needed, and how ASP.NET solves some of those problems. The new ASP.NET coding model will seem familiar to those who have programmed in event-driven languages such as Visual Basic. It may at first seem a little alien to programmers who have only coded in script languages such as VBScript. However, it's extremely simple, provides many advantages, and leads to much more structured code. The code is no longer intermixed with the HTML, and its event-driven nature makes it easily structured for better readability and maintainability.

The first chapter showed how this worked for an OnClick event on a server control, and how the code to be run was broken into a separate event procedure. The corresponding example showed a list of states in a DropDownList server control. Using lists like this is extremely common, and often the list of items is generated from a data store.

To understand the difference between the pre-.NET ASP architecture and the new event-driven ASP.NET architecture, let's look at a sample page and compare the old and the new.

Coding the Old Way

To produce a list of items from a data store in ASP, you have to loop through the list of items, manually creating the HTML. When the item is selected, the form is posted back to the server. It looks something like the following (`OldAsp.asp`):

```
<html>

<form action="OldAsp.asp" method="post">

    Please select your delivery method:
    <select id="ShipMethod" Name="ShipMethod" size="1">
<%
    Dim rsShip
    Dim SQL
    Dim ConnStr
    Dim ItemField

    Set rsShip = Server.CreateObject("ADODB.Recordset")

    SQL = "SELECT * FROM Shippers"
    ConnStr = "Driver={SQL Server}; Server=localhost; " & _
            "Database=Northwind; UID=sa"

    rsShip.Open SQL, ConnStr

    While Not rsShip.EOF
        Response.Write "<option value='" & _
                rsShip("ShipperID") & "'>" & _
                rsShip("CompanyName") & "</option>" & vbCrLf
        rsShip.MoveNext
    Wend

    rsShip.Close
    Set rsShip = Nothing
%>
    </select>
    <br>
    <input type="submit" value="Place Order">
</form>

<%
    If Len(Request.Form("ShipMethod")) > 0 Then
    Response.write "<br>Your order will be delivered via " & _
            Request.Form("ShipMethod")
    End If
%>
</html>
```

This code is fairly simple – it loops through a recordset building a SELECT list, allows the user to select a value, and submits that back to the server. In many situations, you'd probably build a database query or update based upon the selected value, but this example prints out the selected value.

Notice that only the value is available in the submitted page, and not the text value selected – that's the way SELECT lists work. This is fine if you are going to use the value in a data query, but not if it needs to be displayed again. Let's see how this happens by looking at the generated HTML:

```
<html>
<form action="OldAsp.asp" method="post">
    Please select your delivery method:
    <select id="ShipMethod" Name="ShipMethod" size="1">
        <option value='1'>Speedy Express</option>
        <option value='2'>United Package</option>
        <option value='3'>Federal Shipping</option>
    </select>
    <br>
    <input type="submit" value="Place Order">
</form>
<br>Your order will be delivered via 1
</html>
```

The option elements have their value attribute as the ID of the shipping method, and it's the numeric value that's accessible from server-side ASP code.

Coding in ASP.NET Pages

As ASP.NET is event-based, you need to understand the order of events, so that you can see where the equivalent code would go. Code within these events is processed sequentially, but the events are processed only when they are raised. The event order is shown in Figure 4-1:

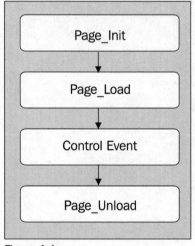

Figure 4-1

These events are:

Event	Description
Page_Init	Fired when the page is initialized
Page_Load	Fired when the page is loaded
Control Event	Fired if a control (such as a button) triggered the page to be reloaded
Page_Unload	Fired when the page is unloaded from memory

The difference between Page_Init and Page_Load is that the controls are only guaranteed to be fully loaded in the Page_Load. The controls are accessible in the Page_Init event, but the ViewState is not loaded, so controls will have their default values, rather than any values set during the postback.

For example, rewriting the original ASP page in ASP.NET yields the following (NewAspNet.aspx):

```
<%@ Import Namespace="System.Data" %>
<%@ Import Namespace="System.Data.SqlClient" %>

<html>
<head>

<script language="VB" runat="server">

   Sub Page_Load(Source As Object, E As EventArgs)

       Dim myConnection As SqlConnection
       Dim myCommand As SqlCommand
       Dim myReader  As SqlDataReader
       Dim SQL       As String
       Dim ConnStr   As String

       SQL = "SELECT * FROM Shippers"
       ConnStr = "server=localhost;uid=sa;pwd=;database=Northwind"

       myConnection = New SqlConnection(ConnStr)
       myConnection.Open()
       myCommand = New SqlCommand(SQL, myConnection)

       myReader = myCommand.ExecuteReader()

       ShipMethod.DataSource = myReader
       ShipMethod.DataBind()

   End Sub

   Sub PlaceOrder_Click(Source As Object, E As EventArgs)
       YouSelected.Text = "Your order will be delivered via " & _
```

```
                ShipMethod.SelectedItem.Text

    End Sub
</script>

<form runat="server">

    Please select your delivery method:

    <asp:DropDownList id="ShipMethod"
        DataTextField="CompanyName" DataValueField="ShipperID"
        runat="server"/>

    <br/>

    <asp:button id="PlaceOrder" Text="Place Order"
        onClick="PlaceOrder_Click"
        runat="server"/>

    <br/>

    <asp:Label id="YouSelected" runat="server"/>
</form>
</html>
```

Next, let's examine this code in detail to see what the changes are, and why they've been done, starting with the HTML form:

```
<form runat="server">

    Please select your delivery method:

    <asp:DropDownList id="ShipMethod"
        DataTextField="CompanyName" DataValueField="ShipperID"
        runat="server"/>

    <br/>

    <asp:button id="PlaceOrder" Text="Place Order"
        onClick="PlaceOrder_Click"
        runat="server"/>

    <br/>

    <asp:Label id="YouSelected" runat="server"/>
</form>
```

This example has three ASP.NET server controls – a drop-down list, a button, and a label. The next chapter discusses server controls in detail, but for the moment, let's concentrate on the event side of things. So, just remember that these are server-side controls, and can therefore be accessed from within the server-side code.

The `Import` directives are placed at the start of the page to tell ASP.NET which code libraries to use. The two shown in the following code snippet are for data access, and are covered in detail in Chapters 8 and 9:

```
<%@ Import Namespace="System.Data" %>
<%@ Import Namespace="System.Data.SqlClient" %>

<html>
<head>
```

Next, the script block is started and the `Page_Load` event is defined. Remember this runs every time the page is loaded:

```
<script language="VB" runat="server">

    Sub Page_Load(Source As Object, E As EventArgs)
```

The parameters to this event are fixed, and defined by ASP.NET. The first contains a reference to the source object that raised the event, and the second contains any additional details being passed to the event. For the `Page_Load` event, these parameters can be ignored, but later in the book you'll see where they come in useful.

Within this event, let's query the database and build the list of shipping methods. The data access code is not examined in detail, since it's covered in Chapters 8 and 9. It's roughly equivalent to the code in the previous example, simply creating a set of records from the database:

```
        Dim myConnection As SqlConnection
        Dim myCommand As SqlCommand
        Dim myReader As SqlDataReader
        Dim SQL As String
        Dim ConnStr As String

        SQL = "SELECT * FROM Shippers"
        ConnStr = "server=localhost;uid=sa;pwd=;database=Northwind"

        myConnection = New SqlConnection(ConnStr)
        myConnection.Open()

        myCommand = New SqlCommand(SQL, myConnection)

        myReader = myCommand.ExecuteReader()
```

Once the records are created, data binding is used to fill the list (`ShipMethod`). In the ASP example, you actually had to create the HTML `option` elements in the loop, but in the ASP.NET page you can use the data-binding feature that allow controls to automatically populate themselves from a set of data (data binding is covered in detail in Chapter 7). The list is declared to run server-side, so its methods and properties can be accessed server-side. This is more like the Visual Basic programming environment where you are dealing with controls.

```
        ShipMethod.DataSource = myReader
        ShipMethod.DataBind()
```

At this stage the code in the Page_Load event has finished. Since this is the first time the page has been executed, there are no control-specific events.

When you select an item in the list and click the button, the postback mechanism is invoked. The button was defined as:

```
<asp:button id="PlaceOrder" Text="Place Order"
    onClick="PlaceOrder_Click"
    runat="server"/>
```

The onClick attribute identifies the name of the server-side event procedure to be run when the button is clicked. Remember that this is server-side event processing, so there is no special client-side code. When this button is clicked, the form is submitted back to itself, and the defined event handler is run (after the Page_Load event):

```
Sub PlaceOrder_Click(Source As Object, E As EventArgs)

    YouSelected.Text = "Your order will be delivered via " & _
            ShipMethod.SelectedItem.Text

End Sub
```

This sets the text of a label to the value selected as shown in Figure 4-2:

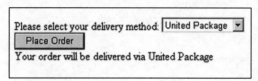

Figure 4-2

This shows an interesting point. Because the list control is a server control, you have access not only to the value, but also to the text of the selected item. Although this is possible with ASP, the code required isn't as neat as the ASP.NET solution. In ASP, the selected item from the list would have to be determined programmatically, and then its value read so that its text could be displayed. In ASP.NET, the control, and its ViewState, handles it automatically.

Let's review these points:

❑ Server-based controls can be accessed from server code. Even though these controls emit plain HTML, and are part of a standard HTML form, the architecture of ASP.NET ensures that they are accessible from server-side event procedures.

❑ The Page_Load event is run every time the page is executed. This event should be used to populate the data in controls.

❑ The control event is only run when fired by a server control. This is indicated by wiring up the event property on the control to an event procedure name.

Postback Identification

There is a big flaw in the code shown in the previous section. Because the `Page_Load` runs every time the page loads, the code in it will run even under a postback scenario – that is, even when a button is pressed. This means that you are executing the data query and filling the drop-down every time, so whatever the user selected would be overwritten (as well as being unnecessary).

The `IsPostBack` property of the `Page` is designed to counter this problem, by allowing you to identify whether or not the page is in a postback situation (as opposed to the first time the page is loaded). This property can be used in the `Page_Load` event so that the data access code is only run the first time the page is loaded:

```
Sub Page_Load(Source As Object, E As EventArgs)

    If Not Page.IsPostBack Then

        Dim myConnection As SqlConnection
        Dim myCommand As SqlCommand
        Dim myReader  As SqlDataReader
        Dim SQL       As String
        Dim ConnStr   As String

        SQL = "select * from Shippers"
        ConnStr = "server=localhost;uid=sa;pwd=;database=Northwind"

        myConnection = New SqlConnection(ConnStr)
        myConnection.Open()

        myCommand = New SqlCommand(SQL, myConnection)

        myReader = myCommand.ExecuteReader()

        ShipMethod.DataSource = myReader
        ShipMethod.DataBind()
    End If

End Sub
```

This code runs only when the page is first loaded. The contents of the list won't disappear, because the contents are held within the `ViewState` of the drop-down list. The HTML this produces is very similar to the old ASP example:

```
<html>
<head>

<form name="_ctl0" method="post" action="NewASPNet.aspx" id="_ctl0">
<input type="hidden" name="__VIEWSTATE"
value="dDw0NDY2MjMzMjt0PDtsPGk8MT47PjtsPHQ8O2w8aTwxPjtpPDU+Oz47bDx0PHQ8O3Q8aTw
    zPjtAPFNwZWVkeSBFeHByZXNzO1VuaXRlZCBQYWNrYWdlID0ZlZGVyYWwgU2hpcHBpbmc7PjtAPDE7M
    jszOz4+Oz47O2w8dDxwPHA8bDxUZXh0O00z47bDxZb3VyIG9yZGVyIHdpbGwgYmUgZGVsaXZlcmVkIHZ
    pYSBVbml0ZWQgUGFja2FnZTs+Pjs+Ozs+Oz4+Oz4+Oz4=" />

    Please select your delivery method:
```

```
<select name="ShipMethod" id="ShipMethod">
    <option value="1">Speedy Express</option>
    <option selected="selected" value="2">United Package</option>
    <option value="3">Federal Shipping</option>
</select>

<br/>

<input type="submit" name="PlaceOrder" value="Place Order" id="PlaceOrder" />

<br/>

<span id="YouSelected">Your order will be delivered via United Package</span>
</form>
</html>
```

The `asp:DropDownList` produces an HTML `select` list along with the associated `option` elements. The form posting is still handled in the same way as ASP. The major difference is the hidden `VIEWSTATE` field, containing the `ViewState` control. We'll look at this topic a little later in the chapter.

As mentioned in Chapter 1, the new model for ASP.NET is based around the separation of the visual portion of the web form (the HTML code) from the logic portion (the executable code). In this way, the operation of web forms is much closer to the way that Visual Basic forms have worked in the past than they are to traditional web pages.

Web Forms also help to solve a number of challenges in using a browser-based execution engine to provide a user experience that is similar to today's Windows applications. These challenges include:

❑ Delivering rich user interfaces on a wide variety of platforms. Web forms can free the developers from the actual client being used, allowing them to focus on providing the necessary business logic.

❑ Merging a client-server application where code is being executed in two different locations into a more traditional event-driven programming model. Web forms accomplish this by providing a single methodology for dealing with application events – no matter if the event was fired on the client, or on the server.

❑ Providing state management in an execution environment that is inherently stateless. Many different methods have been used in the past to provide for a stateful execution environment for the stateless Web world. These methods have ranged from cookies, to hidden form fields, to state information being held on the server. Yet each one of these methods presented a different programmatic interface to the developer, forcing them to choose at development time the type of state management to use. Web forms insulate developers from this by providing a standard way of maintaining state for developers, while hiding the actual implementation details.

Even though we develop the application's presentation and the logic separately, it is important to know that when they are actually executed, they come together as one unit. Even if the logic exists in one file and the presentation in another, at runtime they are compiled into a single object, which is represented by the `Page` class.

The Page Class

When a Web form is requested from the server – a client requests a URL that has an `aspx` extension on it – the components that make up that page are compiled into one unit. The components consist of:

❑ The `.aspx` file being requested

❑ The .NET class file containing the code for that page

❑ Any user controls used by the page

The unit the components are compiled into is a dynamically generated class derived from the .NET `System.Web.UI.Page` class. All the page's controls, presentation information, and logic are used to extend this class to provide an object supporting the functionality of the page that was created.

This dynamically created `Page` class can then be instantiated any time a request is made for the `.aspx` page. When it is instantiated, the resulting object is used to process the incoming requests and returns the data to the requesting client. Any web controls – intrinsic or custom – are in turn instantiated by this object and provide their results back to the `Page` object to be included in the response to the client. The executable page object is created from compiling all of the files (code-behind, user controls, and so on) associated with the page. This compilation only takes place when one of the files changes, or when the application configuration file (covered in Chapter 13) changes. This makes the process extremely efficient.

In ASP, code and presentation were either integrated into one file, or split among many files using `#include` files. When this file(s) was executed, the server would simply start at the top of the file and spit out any HTML text that it found back to the client. When it encountered some script, the script would be executed, and any additions to the HTML response stream would be added at that point. So in effect, all that existed was an HTML file with some code interspersed in it.

In ASP.NET, the page is actually an executable object that outputs HTML. But it is truly an object in that it has a series of processing stages – initialization, processing, and cleanup – just like all objects do. The difference that makes the `Page` class unique is that it performs these functions every time it is called – meaning it is a stateless object and no instances of it hang around in between client requests. Also, the `Page` class has a unique step, known as the rendering step, when HTML is actually generated for output to the client.

When we examine *code-behind* programming a little later in this chapter, you will see the file that actually contains the code is really a class definition. The class defined in that file is derived from the `Page` class. Once the class derived from the `Page` class is created, that class needs to link to the `.aspx` file in some way. This is done in the @ PAGE directive at the top of an `.aspx` file. So if the code-behind file named `mypage.cs` has a class definition such as:

```
public class MyPage: Page {..... }
```

Then the corresponding `.aspx` file includes following directive:

```
<%@ PAGE Inherits="MyPage" Code="mypage.cs" %>
```

The intrinsic `Page` class serves as a container class for all of the components that make up a page. The interface of the `Page` class can be used to manipulate certain aspects of what happens on the page. The events, properties, and methods are shown in the following table:

Attribute	Description
`Init` event	Fired when the page is initialized.
`Load` event	Fired when the page is loaded, and all controls (including their viewstate) have been loaded.
`Unload` event	Fired when the page is done processing – this happens after all the information has been sent to the client.
`PreRender` event	Fired just prior to the information being written to the client.
`AbortTransaction` event	Fired when the transaction that the page is participating in is aborted.
`CommitTransaction` event	Fired when the transaction that the page is participating in is committed.
`Error` event	The `Error` event will be fired whenever an unhandled exception occurs on the page. Handle this event to perform custom error processing (see Chapter 22 for more details).
`Application` property	Reference to the current `Application` object. For each Web application, there is exactly one instance of this object. It is shared by all of the clients accessing the Web application.
`Cache` property	The `Cache` property gets a reference to the `Cache` object that can be used to store data for subsequent server round-trips to the same page. The `Cache` object is in essence a dictionary object whose state is persisted through the use of hidden form fields or some other means, so that data can live from one page request to the next.
`ClientTarget` property	This property will override the browser detection that is built into ASP.NET and specify what the specific browser to render the page. Any controls that then rely on the browser being detected will use the specified configuration, rather than the capabilities of the actual requesting browser.
`EnableViewState` property	This `Boolean` value indicates whether or not the server controls on this page maintain their ViewState between page requests. This value affects all of the controls on the page, and supercedes any individual settings on the controls themselves.

Table continued on following page

Attribute	Description
`ErrorPage` property	If, as the page is being compiled and run, an unhandled exception is detected, then you probably want to display some kind of error message to the user. ASP.NET generates its own default error page, but to control what is being displayed, then this property can be set to the URL of the page that will be displayed instead.
`IsPostBack` property	This Boolean value is set to `true` if the page is being run as the result of a client round-trip. When it is `false`, this is the first time the page is being displayed, and that there is no ViewState stored for the server controls. When this is the case, the state of the controls need to be set manually – usually during the execution of the `Page_Load` event.
`IsValid` property	This Boolean value is set to `true` if all of the validation controls on the page report that their validation conditions have been positively met. If any one validation test fails, then this value will be set to `false`. Validation controls will be covered in Chapter 5 when Server controls are shown in detail. Checking this property can help to improve page performance by avoiding performing certain expensive functions when it is known that a validation condition has not been met.
`Request` property	Reference to the `Request` object – allowing access to information about the HTTP Request.
`Response` property	Reference to the `Response` object – allowing access to the HTTP Response.
`Server` property	Reference to the current `Server` object.
`Session` property	Reference to the current `Session` object.
`SmartNavigation` property	Boolean to indicate if smart navigation is enabled (covered later in the chapter).
`Trace` property	This property is a reference to the `Trace` object for this page. If tracing is enabled on the page, then this object can be used to write explicit information out to the trace log. This will be examined in more detail in Chapter 22.
`TraceEnabled` property	This Boolean value sets whether tracing is enabled for the page.
`User` property	Gets information about the user making the page request.

Attribute	Description
`Validators` property	This property is a reference to a collection of all of the validation controls that are on the page. Use this collection to iterate through all of the validation controls on a page to potentially check status or set validation parameters.
`ViewStateUserKey` property	This value is used to uniquely identify the user of the page. It is encoded into the viewstate, and when the page is submitted, the viewstate will be valid only this property has the proper value set. This is new in Version 1.1, and is designed to help prevent one-click attacks on the server through the page.
`DataBind` method	Performs data binding for all controls on the page.
`FindControl` method	Method to find a reference to a specific control within the page.
`LoadControl` method	Dynamically loads a User Control from a `.ascx` file.
`LoadTemplate` method	Dynamically loads a template. This is examined in Chapter 7 where data binding and templating are covered.
`MapPath` method	Retrieves the physical path for a specified virtual path.
`ResolveUrl` method	Converts a virtual URL to an absolute URL.
`Validate` method	Instructs any validation controls on the page to validate their content.

These members of the intrinsic `Page` class are accessible from within ASP.NET pages directly, without having to go through the `Page` object itself. For example, the following two lines of code are equivalent:

```
Page.Response.Write("Hello")
Response.Write("Hello")
```

There's no performance difference so you can use whichever form you prefer. Most samples only use the `Page` object when referring to `IsPostBack` purely because it's a new feature. Using the explicit convention makes it clearer that `IsPostBack` is an intrinsic property, not a user defined global variable.

HttpRequest Object

The `HttpRequest` object in ASP.NET is enhanced compared to its counterpart in legacy ASP. These changes are covered in more detail in Chapter 23, but a few of the new features are discussed here. The `HttpRequest` object is mapped to the `Request` property of the `Page` object, and is therefore available in the same way as in ASP – just by using `Request`.

One of the most evident changes is the promotion of a number of server variables to properties of the `HttpRequest` object itself. With ASP, referencing the `ServerVariables` collection was necessary to get information about the User Agent, the IP Address of the client making the request, or even the physical path to the ASP.NET source file. In ASP.NET, these values are now properties of the `HttpRequest` object, making it much easier and straightforward to access the information. For example, the following table lists some of these (the full list, including changes, is covered in detail in Chapter 23):

Property	Description
AcceptTypes	Indicates the MIME types supported by the client.
ApplicationPath	The virtual application path.
ContentLength	The length (in bytes) of the request.
ContentType	The MIME type of the request.
FilePath	The virtual path of the request.
Headers	A collection of HTTP headers.
HttpMethod	The HTTP method used for the request.
Path	The virtual path of the request.
PathInfo	Additional path information.
PhysicalApplicationPath	The physical path of the application root.
PhysicalPath	The physical path of the request.
RawUrl	The raw URL of the request.
RequestType	The HTTP method used for the request.
TotalBytes	The number of bytes in the input stream.
Url	A Uri object containing details of the request.
UrlReferrer	A Uri object detailing referrer information.
UserAgent	The browser user agent string.
UserHostAddress	The IP address of the user.
UserHostName	The DNS name of the user.
UserLanguages	An array of languages preferences.
ValidateInput	Method to validate the items in the request against an internal list of potentially dangerous string values.

Another new feature of the `HttpRequest` object is its `Browser` property. This property points to an instance of the `HttpBrowserCapabilities` object. This object contains information about the capabilities of the browser making the request. Previously, ASP developers had to use the `Browser Capabilities` component to determine the same type of information. Now, they can simply refer to the `Browser` property directly.

In the past, the information the `Browser Capabilities` component used to determine the capabilities of a browser was stored in the `BROWSCAP.INI` file. That information is now stored in the `machine.config` file in an XML format, and uses regular expression pattern matching to link a browser user agent string to the capabilities of that browser. But since the information is still contained in an updateable format, there will continue to be support for new browsers and new capabilities without requiring a completely new ASP.NET version.

The new `Params` collection is a collection of all of the `QueryString`, `Form`, `ServerVariables`, and `Cookie` items that are part of the request. In the past, this was the default collection of the `Request` object itself. To access it in ASP.NET, the `Params` collection needs to be explicitly referenced:

```
Dim strValue As String
strValue = Request.Params("param1") ' in ASP, this could have been
                        ' written as Request("param1")
```

You can still use the individual `QueryString`, `Form`, `ServerVariables`, and `Cookie` collections to access information specifically from that item if you want. You can still use the `Request("var")` syntax. The default property of the `HttpRequest` is its `Item` property.

There is now a `MapPath` method of the `HttpRequest` object. This method will take a virtual path to a file as a parameter, and return the physical path to the file on the server. This method can also be used to obtain the physical path to an object in a different application on the same server.

To help prevent malicious attacks, the `HttpRequest` object now automatically validates all input sent with the request – the contents of the `Form`, `QueryString`, and `Cookies` collections. This data is validated against an undocumented set of string values, which have been determined to be potentially dangerous. If any dangerous content is detected, then an exception is raised. This feature can be disabled in the `@Page` directive, and then explicitly called by using the `ValidateRequest` method of the `HttpRequest` object.

Finally, there is now a `SaveAs` method for the `HttpRequest` object. This method saves the contents of the current request to disk. This can be very useful during the debugging of a Web application, since the file contains the contents of the actual request. The HTTP headers can also be saved into the file along with the contents of the request:

```
If (bErrorCondition) Then
    Request.SaveAs("c:\currentRequest.txt", true)
                        ' true indicates to save the headers as well
End If
```

HttpResponse Object

The `HttpResponse` object is used to send data back to the browser as the result of a request. It also provides the page information about that response. The `HttpResponse` object is mapped to the

`Response` property of the `Page` object, and is therefore available directly within ASP.NET pages. There are several new features that are part of the `HttpResponse` object with ASP.NET.

The `Buffer` property from ASP has been deprecated and replaced by the `BufferOutput` property. This Boolean property sets the way that the response data is sent back to the client. If it is set to `true`, which is the default, the contents of the response are held on the server until the response is finished, or until the buffer is explicitly sent back to the client. When this value is `false`, the information is sent back to the browser as soon it is generated by the page.

Chapter 16 looks at some of the other classes that are part of the .NET Framework. Let's look at two classes, `TextWriter` and `Stream`. These classes allow you to work with streams of text or streams of bytes. There are methods that will take a `Stream` object or a `TextWriter` object as a parameter, and send the results from that method to that object. So what does that have to do with the `HttpResponse` object?

There are two new properties of the `HttpResponse` object – `Output` and `OutputStream` – that expose the contents of the `Response` buffer as either a `TextWriter` object or a `Stream` object. One way this object can be used is in the dynamic creation of images using ASP.NET. The `Save` method of the `Bitmap` class can accept a `Stream` object as its destination – so if you pass in the `HttpResponse.OutputStream` property to this method, the results of the save will be sent as the esponse to the client:

```
<%@ Page Language="VB" ContentType="image/jpeg" %>
<%@ Import Namespace="System.Drawing" %>
<%@ Import Namespace="System.Drawing.Imaging" %>
<%@ Import Namespace="System.Drawing.Drawing2D" %>
<%
    Response.Clear()
    Dim height As integer = 100
    Dim width As integer = 200
    Dim r As New Random
    Dim x As integer = r.Next(75)
    Dim x1 As integer = 0
    Dim a As integer = r.Next(155)
    Dim x2 As integer = r.Next(100)
    Dim bmp As new Bitmap(width, height, PixelFormat.Format24bppRgb)
    Dim g As Graphics =  Graphics.FromImage(bmp)
    g.SmoothingMode = SmoothingMode.AntiAlias
    g.Clear(Color.LightGray)
    g.DrawRectangle(Pens.White, 1, 1, width-3, height-3)
    g.DrawRectangle(Pens.Gray,  2, 2, width-3, height-3)
    g.DrawRectangle(Pens.Black, 0, 0, width, height)
    g.DrawString("Response.OutputStream Test", _
                New Font("Arial", 10, FontStyle.Bold), _
                SystemBrushes.WindowText, New PointF(10,50))
    g.FillRectangle(New SolidBrush(Color.FromArgb(a, 255, 128, 255)), _
                                    x, 20, 100, 50)
    g.FillRectangle(New LinearGradientBrush(New Point(x2, 0), _
                                    New Point(x2+75, 50+30), _
                                    Color.FromArgb(128, 0, 0, 128), _
                                    Color.FromArgb(255, 255, 255, 240)),_
                                    x2 ,50, 75, 30)
    bmp.Save(Response.OutputStream, ImageFormat.Jpeg)
    g.Dispose()
    bmp.Dispose()
```

```
    Response.End()
%>
```

There are four key lines to look at – the other drawing functions are probably worthy of an entire book to themselves! First, we tell the browser requesting this page to send back a set of bytes that represent an image – not a set of text in HTML format:

```
<%@ Page Language="VB" ContentType="image/jpeg" %>
```

Next, just to be safe, we make sure that no header information has been sent back to the browser. To do this, we need to clear the buffer. Remember that when the output to the browser is buffered, as is the default, then the buffer can be cleared out at any time before it is sent back:

```
    Response.Clear()
```

The next part of the page dynamically creates a `Bitmap` object in memory, and then draws to that object. Once the page has completed drawing the bitmap, we send it to the browser. The `Save` method of the `Bitmap` object looks like this:

```
Public Sub Save( _
    ByVal stream As Stream, _
    ByVal format As ImageFormat _
)
```

The first parameter is a `Stream` object. The `Save` method sends the bytes that make up the bitmap to this `Stream`. The second parameter defines the format that the image will be saved as. Even though the object is a `Bitmap` object, it can be used to create more than just BMP files.

```
    bmp.Save(Response.OutputStream, ImageFormat.Jpeg)
```

To save the contents of the `Bitmap` object directly to the `Response` object, we pass the `Response.OutputStream` property as the `Stream` parameter. And since earlier in the page we defined the content type as `image/jpeg`, the format of the image being saved is set to `JPEG`. Once all of the data has been sent, we explicitly end the response by calling the `End` method of the `Response` object. There are two files – `image_cs.aspx` and `image_vb.aspx` in the book's download code to try out. Figure 4-3 shows the output of this page.

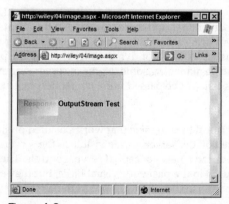

Figure 4-3

In addition to the `HttpResponse.Clear` method that you saw in the previous example, the `HttpResponse.ClearHeaders` method will just clear the headers from the response. Another new property of the `HttpResponse` object is `RedirectLocation`. This property maps to the HTTP header Location. This property can be used to either set this value directly, or can be used to read the value that will be sent as part of the header.

While the `HttpResponse.Write` method is still available in ASP.NET, the use of server controls greatly lessens the need to manually output response information using that method. However, a new method in ASP.NET, `WriteFile`, greatly simplifies the output of file-based information to the response. In previous versions of ASP, the developer was responsible for opening up a file, reading its contents into a buffer, and then outputting the contents of that buffer to the response using the `Write` method. The `WriteFile` method takes a filename as a parameter, and will do all of the necessary file handling work to open that file, read it, and then output its contents to the response buffer.

For example, this allows you to stream previously created HTML directly to the browser along with the current page:

```
<html>
Some html content here
<script language="VB" runat="server">
    Sub Page_Load(Sender As Object, E As EventArgs)
        Response.WriteFile("c:\temp\Content.html")
    End Sub
</script>
</html>
```

Page-Processing Steps

A web forms page isn't significantly different from a traditional Web page. It is still created as a result of an HTTP Request. The server creates the page, sends the data back to the client, closes the HTTP connection, and then forgets about the request. But there are many enhancements added with Web Forms. In order to best understand these enhancements, it is important to look at the steps that the page goes through when it is processed on the server.

Server Round-Trip

As with all dynamic Web generation systems, such as ASP, JSP, and Cold Fusion, there is a division of labor. There is work that the server does and there is work that the client does. The client is responsible for presenting information, capturing information from the user, and for optionally executing some client-side script. The server is responsible for dynamically creating the page and delivering the page to the client. The server may also be managing some degree of server-side state for the client – so that information about the client's task can be passed from one request by a user to the next one by that same user.

In this division of labor, it is critical to recognize that work executed on the client is usually only visible to the client and work executed on the server is only visible to the server. With the Web Forms model in ASP.NET, Microsoft has introduced a new concept of server controls. These controls act like the client-side controls that have been used in the past with Visual Basic, but they execute on the server. This means that the client has no access to these controls programmatically.

132

In order to interact with server controls, the execution must be passed from the client back to the server. The only way to do this is via an HTTP request.

> *There are other ways to pass information to the server to be executed without making an HTTP Request. You could use DCOM, Java RMI, or a simple socket communication. But within the pure Web paradigm of ASP.NET, the HTTP Request is the only method available.*

If you look at the interaction between client and server during a web forms application, you see that the execution gets passed back and forth between client and server – even within the context of the same .aspx page. This is known as a server round-trip, illustrated in Figure 4-4:

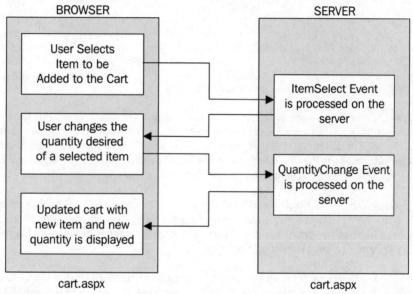

Figure 4-4

In order to trigger a round-trip, the user needs to perform some interaction with the browser. There usually isn't a case where a round-trip would be triggered without user intervention, but there is nothing that prevents that from happening. Typically, the user clicking or selecting something on a page triggers the round-trip. In either case, it takes an explicit user interaction to start a round-trip. While it is possible, you wouldn't want an event like an onmouseover to cause a round-trip. That happens too frequently and would overload the server and cause the user experience to grind to a halt.

Page ViewState

In this new round-trip model of Web Forms, there are potentially more interactions with a server than there would be in a traditional browser-server interaction. But at the core it is still stateless HTTP communication. This means that the server doesn't retain *any* information about the previous client request, such as values in form fields, or the state of objects instantiated to create the page. This would normally mean that the server is doing a lot of extra work in recreating the page each time during a round-trip. But the Web Forms architecture has a way of dealing with this.

The page will retain its `ViewState` between requests to the server. The `ViewState` contains the state of all user controls on the page. This information is stored as name-value pairs using the `System.Web.UI.StateBag` object. The `ViewState` is stored as a string variable that is passed back to the client in the page. Since the client probably doesn't know anything about ASP.NET and `ViewState`, this string is stored as a hidden form field. Take a look at the example page from earlier in this chapter, and then view its source to see the `ViewState` being stored:

```
<html>
<head>

<form name="_ctl0" method="post" action="NewASPNet.aspx" id="_ctl0">
<input type="hidden" name="__VIEWSTATE"
value="dDw0NDY2MjMzMjt0PDtsPGk8MT47PjtsPHE8O2w8TwxPjtpPDU+Oz47bDx0PHQ8O3Q8aTw
        zPjtAPFNwZWVkeSBFeHByZXNzO1VuaXRlZCBQYWNrYWdlO1ZGVyYWwgU2hpcHBpbmc7PjtAPDE7M
        jszOz4+Oz47dDxwPHA8bDxUZXh0OO0z47bDxDb3VyaW9yIG9yZGVyYXIHdpbGwgYmUgZGVsaXZlcmVkIHZ
        pYSBVbml0ZWQgUGFja2FnZTs+Pjs+Ozs+Oz4+Oz4=" />

    Please select your delivery method:
```

The contents of the `ViewState` are quite obviously not in human-readable form. But the Web Forms processor can read this and restore the values of the server controls when this page is submitted to the server. An advantage of this method is that the state of the page is held with the page, and not within the server. Another advantage is that the page can be deployed to a web farm and you do not have to worry about forcing the request from a client to come back to the same server.

But there are some minor disadvantages as well. For this rather simple page, there is a pretty sizeable set of text making up the `ViewState`. In a much more complex page, the contents of the `ViewState` could grow to a point where they begin to affect the speed at which the page is downloaded, although this isn't as much of a performance issue as it was in the past.

`ViewState` is enabled by default for all server controls. This means that you don't have to do anything explicit to take advantage of it. However, there could be performance issues in maintaining `ViewState` for a page with a large number of controls on it. There are two ways to control whether or not the `ViewState` is maintained. `ViewState` can be disabled on a page level – meaning that no state will be kept for any control on the page. To do this, use the `@Page` directive along with the `EnableViewState` attribute:

```
<%@ Page EnableViewState="false" %>
```

The second level at which to control the `ViewState` is on a control-by-control basis. To do this, simply add the same `EnableViewState` parameter to the declaration of the control:

```
<asp:DropDownList id="ShipMethod" EnableViewState="false" runat="server"/>
```

The `EnableViewState` attribute is also discussed in Chapters 6 and 7, where we look at its impact on performance.

Page-Processing Steps

The server goes through a set of distinct steps when processing a Web Forms page. At each stage, the server calls a certain set of code. This enables the developer to add code at specific points during the execution of the page. Every time a page is requested, these steps are processed. The `IsPostBack` property indicates whether this is the first time a page is being viewed, or it is being viewed as a result of a server round-trip. The four page-processing stages are:

- ❑ Configuration
- ❑ Event Handling
- ❑ Rendering
- ❑ Cleanup

There are other stages that the page goes through when it is loaded, but these are not generally used in everyday page processing. These stages are primarily used for server controls to be able to initialize themselves when the page is loading, then render themselves into the page, and finally clean themselves up. These stages will be examined in Chapter 18, when looking at creating custom server controls.

Configuration Stage

This is the first stage that is encountered in processing a page. If this is during a postback (not the initial load), then the page and control ViewStates are restored. After that is done, the `Page_Load` event is fired. This means that any code in this event handler can access the state of any control on the page. This is very important because it allows you to perform the processing necessary to get the page ready for display to the user. A typical `Page_Load` event is:

VB .NET

```
Sub Page_Load(Sender As Object, E As EventArgs)
    Dim cart As IBuyAdv.CartDB
    cart = New IBuyAdv.CartDB(getDSN())
    If Len(Request.Params("ProductCode")) > 0 Then
        cart.AddShoppingCartItem(GetCustomerID(), Request.Params("ProductCode"))
    End If
    If Not Page.IsPostBack Then
        PopulateShoppingCartList()
        UpdateSelectedItemState()
    End If
End Sub
```

C#

```
void Page_Load(Object sender, EventArgs e) {
    IBuyAdv.CartDB cart = new IBuyAdv.CartDB(getDSN());
    if (Request.Params["ProductCode"] != null) {
        cart.AddShoppingCartItem(GetCustomerID(),
                Request.Params["ProductCode"]);
    }
    if (Page.IsPostBack == false) {
    PopulateShoppingCartList();
    UpdateSelectedItemStatus();
    }
}
```

In this `Page_Load` event from the case study in Chapter 24, there are three different steps taking place. These steps are quite common. First, you create an instance of a database access object:

```
Dim cart As IBuyAdv.CartDB
cart = New IBuyAdv.CartDB(getDSN())
```

or in C#:

```
IBuyAdv.CartDB cart = new IBuyAdv.CartDB(getDSN());
```

This gives you access to a database object, which you use in the methods and events of the page. The next step is to conditionally perform some processing based on a parameter passed to this page:

```
If Len(Request.Params("ProductCode") > 0 Then
    cart.AddShoppingCartItem(GetCustomerID(), Request.Params("ProductCode"))
End If
```

or in C#:

```
if (Request.Params["ProductCode"] != null) {
    cart.AddShoppingCartItem(GetCustomerID(), Request.Params["ProductCode"]);
}
```

The `Request` object contains information about the request being made to the server. The `Params` collection is a collection of all the information contained in the `QueryString`, `Form`, `ServerVariables`, and `Cookies` collections. Based on the existence of a specific value, `ProductCode`, let's perform some processing.

```
If Not Page.IsPostBack Then
    PopulateShoppingCartList()
    UpdateSelectedItemState()
End If
```

or in C#:

```
if (Page.IsPostBack == false) {
    PopulateShoppingCartList();
    UpdateSelectedItemStatus();
}
```

The last thing we do in the `Page_Load` event is to load the data into the controls on the page. Now since these controls have their `ViewState` saved during a server round-trip, we load the data only the first time. By checking the `IsPostBack` property of the `Page` object, we can determine if this is the first time the page is being loaded.

If it is the first time that the page is loaded, we go ahead and retrieve the data from the database and add it to control. If the page is being viewed as a result of a round-trip, then we just let the `ViewState` restore the state of the control. There is no reason you couldn't populate the control from scratch each time, but why waste the server processing time if it isn't necessary.

Event Handling Stage

The server controls on an ASP.NET page can generate events that get processed on the server. This means that an action on the client can initiate a server round-trip through an HTTP POST. Now once that round-trip gets to the server, we need to identify the control that caused the event to happen and then take steps to process the event.

While there can only be one event that causes a round-trip to begin, there may be other events that have occurred for (or in) the server controls at the client which haven't been processed yet. These are also processed during the event handling stage. There is no particular order in which the prior events are processed, but they are always processed before the event that actually triggered the round-trip. The event that actually triggered the round-trip is processed last.

Let's look at some event handling routines, again from the Chapter 24 case study.

VB .NET

```
Sub Recalculate_Click(Sender As Object, E As EventArgs)
    UpdateShoppingCartDatabase()
    PopulateShoppingCartList()
    UpdateSelectedItemStatus()
End Sub

Sub Checkout_Click(Sender As Object, E As EventArgs)
    UpdateShoppingCartDatabase()
    Response.Redirect("secure/Checkout.aspx")
End Sub
```

C#

```
void Recalculate_Click(Object sender, EventArgs e) {
    UpdateShoppingCartDatabase();
    PopulateShoppingCartList();
    UpdateSelectedItemStatus();
}
void Checkout_Click(Object sender, EventArgs e) {
    UpdateShoppingCartDatabase();
    Response.Redirect("secure/Checkout.aspx");
}
```

The `Recalculate_Click` event is fired when the user clicks the **Recalculate** button on the page. Since this is a button control, the round-trip is started immediately. The next section will look at the parameters that are passed when the event is fired. The `Checkout_Click` event is fired when the user clicks the **Checkout** button on the page. In the event handler, `Response.Redirect` is called to send the browser off to another page. So an event handler even has the ability to affect whether or not a page is displayed.

Rendering Stage

The rendering stage is where the rubber meets the road. Or to be more explicit, the HTML meets the browser. In this stage all the static HTML in the page, the results of any `Response.Write` methods, and the output from all of the server controls on the page are sent to the browser. Any in-line script code is run at the same time, but no event processing occurs, since that has already happened.

Cleanup Stage

This is the final stage of the page processing. The entire HTML has been rendered and sent to the browser. The primary event that happens during this stage is the `Page_Unload` event. This event should be used to do things like closing any open database connections, closing any files you may have opened, and properly discarding any objects that may have been used in the page. Object references can simply fall out of scope, but it's not good practice to rely on this.

Since objects in .NET are garbage-collected (as seen in Chapter 2) the resources that an object uses will still be consumed, even after the object reference falls out of scope. It is the responsibility of the garbage collector to free up these resources of unused objects. Since it is not possible to predict when the garbage collector will run, you can't explicitly state when the resources will be freed. So to free up the resources as soon as possible, explicitly close the objects used in the page.

Web Form Events

Events in web forms are different to the events used in the traditional event-driven programming model. While events can still be raised on the client and handled on the client, and events raised on the server and handled on the server, the primary Web Form event model is for an event to be raised on the client and processed on the server. This transfer of control from the client to the server is accomplished through the use of an HTTP POST. A developer needs to be aware how this mechanism takes place, but the .NET Framework takes care of figuring out from the POST information what events need to be handled on the server.

There's a set of intrinsic events that server controls will support. To avoid continually passing control from the client to the server, this event set is rather limited. It's primarily user interactions, such as a button click or changing a selection, which will cause an event to be raised on the server. In this way, it takes an *explicit* user action to fire a server event – they don't usually happen without the user taking some action at the client. The event handler function declaration is the same for all events. There are two parameters that are passed to the event handler.

In C#:

```
void MyButton_OnClick(Object sender, EventArgs e)
{
    ...
}
```

or in Visual Basic .NET:

```
Sub MyButton_OnClick(Sender As Object, e As EventArgs)
    ...
End Sub
```

The first parameter, `sender`, is a reference to the server control that raised the event. When adding a server control to the page, explicitly state the events to handle, and what function will be the event handler for that particular event.

In the following example we place a `Button` server control into the page with the ID of `PlaceOrder`. When the user clicks on this button on the client, the control will be passed to the server via an HTTP POST. On the server, the `PlaceOrder_Click` function will be called:

```
<asp:Button id="PlaceOrder" Text="Place Order"
            onClick="PlaceOrder_Click" runat="server"/>
```

Remember that there is a reference to the server control passed to the event handler. In this way, one event handler can handle events for multiple controls – the specific control is identified from the value of the `sender` variable.

The second parameter is an object containing a set of information about the specific event. This parameter is usually of type `EventArgs`, which in its base implementation contains little information about the event. But it also serves as a base class for derived classes, such as the `RepeaterCommandEventArgs` class. An object of this type gets passed when using a `Repeater` control, and you have wired up the `ItemCommand` event. You can see this in the example in the Event bubbling section.

Event Bubbling

There are certain server controls that serve as containers for other controls. Controls such as the `Repeater`, the `DataList`, and the `DataGrid` can all contain server controls as children of the parent control. These child controls will not raise their events by themselves, to be handled on the page. Rather, the event is packaged by the container and passed to the page as an `ItemCommand` event. This event is raised when a button is clicked within the `Repeater`. This example looks at how to handle the events from a set of child buttons within a `Repeater` control:

```
<%@ Page Language="C#" %>

<html>
 <head>

   <script language="C#" runat="server">

      public class Authors {
         private string name;
         private string initials;
         public Authors(string name, string initials) {
            this.name = name;
            this.initials = initials;
         }

         public string Name { get { return name; } }
         public string Initials { get { return initials; } }
      }

      void Page_Load(Object Sender, EventArgs e) {
         SmartNavigation = true;
         if (!IsPostBack) {
            ArrayList values = new ArrayList();
            values.Add(new Authors("Alex Homer", "AH"));
            values.Add(new Authors("Dave Sussman", "DS"));
            values.Add(new Authors("Rich Anderson", "RA"));
            values.Add(new Authors("Rob Howard", "RH"));
            values.Add(new Authors("Brian Francis", "BF"));
            MyRepeater.DataSource = values;
```

```
                    MyRepeater.DataBind();
            }
        }
    void MyRepeater_ItemCommand(Object Sender, RepeaterCommandEventArgs e) {
        ClickInfo.Text = "You selected the  " + ((Button)e.CommandSource).Text +
                                                        " button <br>";

        }
    </script>

</head>
<body>

    <form runat="server">
    <asp:Repeater id="MyRepeater" OnItemCommand="MyRepeater_ItemCommand"
                            runat="server">

        <HeaderTemplate>
            <table border="0" cellspacing="5">
                <tr>
                    <td><b>Author</b></td>
                    <td><b>Initials</b></td>
                </tr>
        </HeaderTemplate>

        <ItemTemplate>
            <tr>
                <td> <%# DataBinder.Eval(Container.DataItem, "Name") %> </td>
                <td> <ASP:Button Text='<%# DataBinder.Eval(Container.DataItem,
                                    "Initials") %>' runat="server" /></td>
            </tr>
        </ItemTemplate>

        <FooterTemplate>
            </table>
        </FooterTemplate>

    </asp:Repeater>
    <asp:Label id="ClickInfo" font-name="Verdana" font-size="12pt"
                runat="server"/>
    </form>

</body>
</html>
```

When the page is run, there will be a list of authors and their initials. When one of the buttons is pressed, the ClickInfo label control will be populated to indicate what button was pressed (see Figure 4-5):

Figure 4-5

In this example, you have a repeater control that contains a table (simply for the sake of formatting). Each row of the table has a cell with the author name, and another cell with a button server control:

```
<td> <%# DataBinder.Eval(Container.DataItem, "Name") %> </td>
<td> <ASP:Button Text="<%# DataBinder.Eval(Container.DataItem,
                          "Initials") %>" runat="server" /></td>
```

The button control itself does not have an event handler associated with it. It does have the all-important `runat="server"` parameter, so the events generated by this control will be handled on the server. So where is the click event from this button handled? Look at the container control – the `Repeater` control:

```
<asp:Repeater id="MyRepeater" OnItemCommand="MyRepeater_ItemCommand"
        runat="server">
```

When declaring the `Repeater` control, set up an event handler function to handle the `ItemCommand` event. This event is fired whenever a control contained by the `Repeater` control raises an event. The `MyRepeater_ItemCommand` function looks like this:

```
void MyRepeater_ItemCommand(Object Sender, RepeaterCommandEventArgs e) {
    ClickInfo.Text = "You selected the  " + ((Button)e.CommandSource).Text +
                                                " button <br>";
    }
```

The second parameter of this event handler is of type `RepeaterCommandEventArgs`. This object contains enough information about the event to determine the control that raised the event. The important properties of this object are:

Property	Description
CommandSource	Reference to the child server control that actually raised the event.
Item	Reference to the specific item within the Repeater control where the event took place. This could be the header or footer template, or from an individual data row.

The child control that caused the event is a Button control, so you can cast the CommandSource object to a Button type, and then access the properties of that control. In this case, you can pull out the value of the Text property for the button, and display that in the ClickInfo label control.

Event Handling on Client and Server

In bridging the gap between client and server when it comes to handling control events, it makes sense to talk about which side handles what events. Most server controls only have one or two events that actually get processed on the server. But the HTML control that the server control is finally rendered to can generate a great number of different events for client-side use. So the question is: what gets handled where? Basically, those events that are supported by the server control will get handled on the server. So for a Button control, there is one event supported by that control – the Click event. All of the other events that can be generated by an HTML INPUT control (what a Button server control is rendered as) will need to be handled on the client. But what about the click event that can be handled at the client-side as well?

When you have an event that can be handled on either the client or the server, then the server handling of that event will take precedence. So in the case of the Button with a server-side event handler OnServerClick and a client-side event handler OnClick, the client-side code will be ignored. You could write a client-side onmouseup event handler, which would continue to run at the client – prior to the control being passed back to the server.

Page State

Since the core to the functionality in Web Forms is the server round-trip, the application is constantly going back to the server and asking it to create a new page and send it to the client. It is in this merger of the stateless Web world with the stateful world that the concept of page state needs to be discussed. How do we retain information while the client has control and the server has in essence forgotten about the client and its prior request?

The Page viewstate is the way that the information contained in the server controls is automatically persisted during a server round-trip. So how can the developer store information from request to request, when that information may not be contained in a server control? In the past, the ways to do this would be to store information in a hidden form field, or possibly in the Session object. While these ways are still available, the Web Forms framework provides another more flexible option: *State Bags*.

The state bag is a data repository that is automatically persisted from page request to page request. Let's see how to add the use of state bag to the page in the event bubbling example already discussed:

```
    void Page_Load(Object Sender, EventArgs e) {
        int viewCount;
        if (ViewState["viewCount"] != null)
            viewCount = (int)ViewState["viewCount"] + 1;
        else
            viewCount = 1;
        labelViews.Text = "Times page has been viewed: " + viewCount.ToString();
        ViewState["viewCount"] = viewCount;
        if (!IsPostBack) {
            ArrayList values = new ArrayList();
        ...
    }
    }
```

The ViewState property is a collection of the state that is maintained by the page. You can add keys to this collection, and their value is persisted along with state from all of the server controls on your page. This example stores the number of times the page is viewed, and then displays that value (Figure 4-6):

Figure 4-6

Page Directives

When creating a page, you can declaratively set a number of attributes about the page. Some of the ones you have seen already are the @ Page directive and the @ Import directive. Each of these directives has a set of associated attributes that control some aspect of the page generation.

@ Page Directive

This directive is used to assign page-specific attributes that are used by the Web Forms page parser and compiler to influence how the page is created. This directive, along will all the other ones can legally be placed anywhere on the page, but by convention they are generally at the top of the file. However, there can only be one @ Page directive in a single file. The attributes of the @ Page directive are as follows:

Attribute	Values (default in bold)	Used for
AspCompat	True or **False**	Sets the page to run in a single-thread apartment. Allows access to legacy COM components developed in VB, which could only create STA components
AutoEventWireup	**True** or False	Indicates whether or not the page events are automatically wired up. If False, events such as Page_Load must be enabled by the developer
Buffer	**True** or False	Response buffering is enabled
ClassName	Valid class name	Class name that this page is derived from
ClientTarget	Valid User Agent name	Browser (or compatible) that the page is targeting
CodePage	Valid code page value	Sets the code page of the response, if it is different from the web server
CompilerOptions	Valid compiler options	List of compiler options to be used when the page is compiled
ContentType	Valid MIME type	Sets the content type of the response
Culture	Valid culture ID	Culture ID sets the language, calendar system, and writing system.
Debug	True or **False**	Compiles page with debugging enabled
Description	n/a	Description of the page – ignored by ASP.NET
Enable SessionState	**True**, ReadOnly, or False	Page has access to the Session object. ReadOnly – the page can read but not change session variables
EnableViewState	**True** or False	Page ViewState is maintained for server controls
Enable ViewStateMac	True or **False**	Page should run a machine authentication check on the ViewState. Validates that the ViewState has not been tampered with by the client

Attribute	Values (default in bold)	Used for
ErrorPage	Valid URL	Page to be redirected to if an unhandled error occurs
Explicit	**True** or False	Uses the Visual Basic Option Explicit mode
Inherits	Valid class name	Code-behind class that this page inherits
Language	Valid .NET Language name	Language used to compile all sourcecode on the page
LCID	Valid locale ID	Locale identifier for the page, if different from the locale of the web server
ResponseEncoding	Valid character encoding name	Encoding format for the text sent by the response
SmartNavigation	True or **False**	Enables or disables the smart navigation feature (details appear later)
Src	Valid source file name	File name of the code-behind class used by this page.
Strict	True or **False**	Uses the Visual Basic Option Strict mode.
Trace	True or **False**	Tracing the page execution is enabled.
TraceMode	SortByTime or SortByCategory	Sort order for trace messages generated when the page is created.
Transaction	NotSupported, Supported, Required, RequiresNew	Indicates the transaction settings for this page.
ValidateRequest	True or False	Validate all of the information posted to the page against known dangerous string values.
WarningLevel	0, 1, 2, or 4	Compiler warning level at which compilation should be aborted.

@ Import Directive

This directive is used to explicitly import a namespace onto the page. This will make all of the classes and interfaces contained within this namespace available to code on the page. This value can either be a .NET Framework namespace name, or a valid user-created namespace:

```
<%@ Import Namespace="value" %>
```

There can only be one namespace imported per directive entry, so to import multiple namespaces into a page, add multiple @ Import directives. The .NET Framework automatically imports a set of namespaces, so these don't need to be imported explicitly. These namespaces are:

System	System.Web.Security
System.Collections.Specialized	System.Web.UI
System.Text.RegularExpressions	System.Web.UI.WebControls
System.Collections	System.Web.Caching
System.Configuration	System.Web.SessionState
System.Text	System.Web.UI.HtmlControls
System.Web	System.IO

@ Implements Directive

The @ Implements directive is used to implement a .NET interface in the page. In implementing an interface, the page will support the defined properties, methods, and events of a specific interface. This will be important when looking at implementing custom controls in Chapter 18. For a custom control to be able to respond to events like a standard server control, the control must implement the IPostBackEventHandler interface. The directive to do this is:

```
<%@ Implements Interface="System.Web.UI.IPostBackEventHandler" %>
```

Interfaces are covered in Chapter 3.

@ Register Directive

When you are adding a custom server control to a page, you need to tell the compiler something about that control. If the compiler doesn't know what namespace contains the control or what assembly that namespace is in, then it will not be able to recognize the control, and will generate an error. To give the compiler the information it needs, use the @ Register directive.

There are two forms of the @ Register directive, depending on how the location of the custom control is identified:

```
<%@ Register TagPrefix="tagprefix" TagName="tagname" Src="pathname" %>
<%@ Register TagPrefix="tagprefix" Namespace="namespace" Assembly="assembly" %>
```

The first usage of the @ Register directive is to add support for user controls to the page. The TagPrefix attribute identifies the string that will be used to decorate all instances of the custom server control on the page. For example, if this directive is at the top of the page:

```
<%@ Register TagPrefix="Ecommerce" TagName="Header"
             Src="UserControls\Header.ascx" %>
```

Then for every instance of the Header user control on the page, it will be prefixed with Ecommerce, as seen here:

```
<Ecommerce:Header id="Header" runat="server"/>
```

The TagName attribute identifies the name that will be used to refer to the control within the page. Since a user control source file, UserControls\Header.ascx, can only have one control contained within it, the tagname attribute is simply a shortcut to allow us to reference the control.

The final attribute, Src, indicates the file in which the source of the user control resides.

The second usage of the @Register directive is for adding custom server controls to the page. These custom controls are compiled and contained within assemblies. The TagPrefix attribute has the same usage seen before – it defines the namespace of the custom server control when it is used in the page. The Namespace attribute indicates the namespace in which the custom control resides. The Assembly attribute indicates the assembly where the namespace resides:

```
<%@ Register TagPrefix="Wrox" Namespace="WroxControls"
                            Assembly="RatingMeter" %>
```

When using this custom server control within the page, it looks no different than a user control in the same place:

```
<Wrox:RatingMeter runat="server" Score="3.5" Votes="1"
                  MaxRating="5" CellWidth="51" CellHeight="10" />
```

When creating a custom control, or even a user control, you can pass attributes to the control by adding them to the tag in the page. This is discussed in detail in Chapter 18.

@ Assembly Directive

The @ Assembly directive is used to reference an assembly directly, so that the classes and interfaces that it contains become available to the code in your page. Pass in the name of a compiled assembly:

```
<%@ Assembly Name="assemblyname" %>
```

or pass in the path to a source file that will be compiled when the page is compiled:

```
<%@ Assembly Src="pathname" %>
```

This tag is usually not required, as any assembly that is in the ASP.NET application's bin directory will automatically be compiled into the page. Use this directive to explicitly include an assembly that is in the global assembly cache, or to explicitly compile in an assembly source file that is residing in another directory.

@ OutputCache Directive

This directive is used to control how the page is cached on the server. ASP.NET supports a very powerful set of caching capabilities. When output caching is enabled for a page, the first time the page is requested, it is compiled and run, and the results are sent back to the browser. But instead of the server then throwing everything away, the results of that page are retained on the server. The next time a request comes in for that page, even from a different user, the server can then just spit back the results without having to rerun the page. This can tremendously increase performance, especially if there are database generated pages, but where the underlying data that creates the page doesn't change very often.

There are a series of attributes that control how the caching is performed:

```
<%@ OutputCache Duration="#ofseconds"
   Location="Any | Client | Downstream | Server | None"
   VaryByCustom="browser | customstring"
   VaryByHeader="headers"
   VaryByParam="parametername"
   VaryByControl="controlname" %>
```

The Duration attribute is used to control how long an item will stay in the cache before being invalidated. When a cache item is invalidated, the next time the page is requested, ASP.NET will run the page, deliver the results to the browser, and then store the results in the cache. This attribute is mandatory – there is no default value, and the page will not compile if you leave it out.

The Location attribute identifies where the actual data for the cache is stored. There are five possible values for this attribute:

Value	Use
Any	The cache can be located on the client, on a downstream server (like a proxy server), or on a server where the request was originally processed. This is the default.
Client	The cache is located on the client that made the request.
Downstream	The cache is located on a server downstream from the server that processed the request.
Server	The cache is located on the server where the request was processed.
None	This page does not have output caching enabled.

The VaryByCustom attribute is used to identify any custom caching requirements. If the string "browser" is passed as the value for this attribute, the cache will be varied by browser name and version. When a cache is varied, there is a different processed page stored for each condition that the cache is varied by. For example, if the cache is varied by browser, there will be one page version stored for IE 6, another one for IE 5, and yet another for Netscape 6. If someone accessed the site using Opera, then since that browser type was not cached, a new page would be generated, passed back to the browser, and then cached for the next request from an Opera browser.

The `VaryByHeader` attribute contains a list of HTTP headers (separated by semicolons) that are used to vary the output cache. The cache can vary on one header, or on a group of headers.

The `VaryByParam` attribute is used to vary the cache, based on the values of parameters passed to the server along with the request for the page. These can be `QueryString` parameters, or they can be the contents of form fields. This can contain a single parameter, multiple parameters separated by semicolons, or a `*`, which means to vary on all parameters, or `none`, which means that the cache will not be varied based on any parameters. You must supply a value for this attribute. If you don't want to vary by parameter, then pass a value of `none`. To not explicitly state which parameters to vary the cache by, then pass a `*` and the cache will be varied by all parameter values.

In a user control, the `VaryByControl` attribute can be used to vary the cache based on controls contained in the user control. The attribute contains a list of child control IDs to vary the cache by. This attribute is required in a user control that is using the `@OutputCache` directive. It is not allowed on an ASP.NET page.

@ Reference Directive

This directive is used to identify a page or control that the current page should dynamically compile and link with at runtime. This allows you to dynamically add a user control to a page at runtime. You should use this directive in conjunction with the `LoadControl` method of the `Page` object. By adding the custom control as a reference to the page, the compiler will be able to perform strong type checking against the control. Let's see how to use this in Chapter 18 when we look at custom controls.

Code-Behind

In the world of increasingly complex Web applications, it's often difficult to separate the different parts of the development process. Writing Web applications is hard enough without worrying about how to make them look good and stay maintainable over the years. Some companies have designers who create the look and feel of the site, allowing the programmers to concentrate on the coding. With the traditional ASP model, this is hard to achieve, as code and content are often intermixed.

The way to solve this problem in ASP.NET is by using Code-Behind, where the content (HTML and server controls) are in one file, and the server-side code in another. Not only does this allow different people to work on the same page at once, but it also enables either part to be redesigned (as long as the controls still stay the same) without affecting the other.

The code-behind model is no different in action to pages where the code is inline. Remember that an ASP.NET page and its associated files are compiled into an executable object. This object is essentially (as far as performance and use go) the same as any other page, allowing easier development with the same effect.

Code-Behind in Development Tools

The approach to use for code may depend on the tool used to create ASP.NET applications. For this book, most of the samples will show code inline, simply because it's easier to show, as well as being more convenient when using text editors such as Notepad.

Tools such as Visual Studio .NET take the opposite approach, using the code-behind model as default. One reason is that it allows a standard HTML designer to be used for designing the look and feel of the page, and a code editor to be used for the actual code. This gives the user the familiar feel (comparable to the Visual Basic 6 environment) of design and code windows.

Another reason is that Microsoft has taken the view that third parties may want to use write designers or code editors that integrate with .NET. The code-behind approach allows any HTML designer and any editor to be used (as long as it doesn't change ASP.NET controls).

Using Code-Behind

The principle of code-behind is to create a class for the code, and inherit this class from the ASP.NET Page object. This gives your class access to the page intrinsics, and allows it to interact with the postback architecture. You can then create the ASP.NET page and use a page directive to inherit from the newly created class.

There are some rules that you should follow to create the code-behind class, the first of which is to reference the required namespaces. At a minimum you need to reference System and System.Web.UI, although others may be required. For example, to reference controls on the page and to define the control types, you should reference System.Web.UI.WebControls. Also include any other required namespaces, such as System.Data.SqlClient for accessing SQL Server.

The second rule is create a class that inherits from the Page object (this is why the System.Web.UI namespace is needed). Within this class, you should declare public instances of ASP.NET server controls that are on the Web page, using the same name for the variables that the Web Control has. This provides a link between the code-behind class and the actual server controls (there are other ways to do this, but this method is simplest). Within this class, create event procedures, methods, and properties, just as with any class. The events can be event procedures named on server controls in the web page.

For example, consider the simple select list with Shipping Methods shown earlier in the chapter. The following code samples show the code-behind class. With the exception of the additions required for the code-behind model, the code is exactly the same as the code inline samples.

VB .NET

```
Imports System
Imports System.Web.UI
Imports System.Web.UI.WebControls
Imports System.Data
Imports System.Data.SqlClient

Public Class ShipMethodClass
    Inherits Page
```

```vb
      ' public variables to match the server controls
      Public ShipMethod   As DropDownList
      Public YouSelected   As Label
      Public PlaceOrder    As Button

      Sub Page_Load(Source As Object, E As EventArgs)

          If Not Page.IsPostBack Then
              Dim myConnection As SqlConnection
              Dim myCommand    As SqlCommand
              Dim myReader     As SqlDataReader
              Dim SQL          As String
              Dim ConnStr      As String

              SQL = "SELECT * FROM Shippers"
              ConnStr = "server=localhost;uid=sa;pwd=;database=Northwind"

              myConnection = New SqlConnection(ConnStr)
              myConnection.Open()

              myCommand = New SqlCommand(SQL, myConnection)

              myReader = myCommand.ExecuteReader()
              ShipMethod.DataTextField = "CompanyName"
              ShipMethod.DataSource = myReader
              ShipMethod.DataBind()
          End If

      End Sub

      Sub PlaceOrder_click(Source As Object, E As EventArgs)

          YouSelected.Text = "Your order will be delivered via " & _
                          ShipMethod.SelectedItem.Text

      End Sub
  End Class
```

C#

```csharp
using System;
using System.Data;
using System.Data.SqlClient;
using System.Web.UI;
using System.Web.UI.WebControls;
public class ShipMethodClass : Page
{
// public variables to match the server controls
public DropDownList   ShipMethod;
public Label          YouSelected;
public Button         PlaceOrder;

public void Page_Load(Object Source, EventArgs E)
{
```

```
if (!Page.IsPostBack)
{
    SqlConnection    myConnection;
    SqlCommand       myCommand;
    SqlDataReader    myReader;
    String       SQL;
    String       ConnStr;

    SQL = "select * from Shippers";
    ConnStr = "server=localhost;uid=sa;pwd=;database=Northwind";

    myConnection = new SqlConnection(ConnStr);
    myConnection.Open();

    myCommand = new SqlCommand(SQL, myConnection);

    myReader = myCommand.ExecuteReader();
    ShipMethod.DataTextField = "CompanyName";
    ShipMethod.DataSource = myReader;
    ShipMethod.DataBind();
    }
}

public void PlaceOrder_Click(Object Source, EventArgs E)
{
YouSelected.Text = "Your order will be delivered via " +
                    ShipMethod.SelectedItem.Text;
}
}
```

Inheriting the Code-Behind Class File in an ASP.NET Page

To connect the class file containing the code implementation to your ASP.NET page, add an `Inherits` attribute to the `<%@Page...%>` directive, and specify the location of the 'Code-Behind' file:

```
<%@Page Inherits="class_name" Src="path_to_class_file" %>
```

For example, to inherit from a Visual Basic .NET class named `ShipMethodClass` that is implemented in a file named `ShipMethodClass.vb` in the same directory as the page, you would use:

```
<%@Page Inherits="ShipMethodClass" Src="ShipMethodClass.vb" %>
```

> Use the correct file extension for your class files – **.vb** for **Visual Basic files, .js for JScript files, .cs for C# files and .cpp for C++ files. This ensures that they are passed to the correct compiler when the page is first executed.**

An alternative form of this directive allows the `Src` attribute to be omitted:

```
<%@ Page Inherits="ShipMethodClass" %>
```

In this case ASP.NET will assume that the class is pre-compiled, and in the `bin` directory of the application.

Page Caching

One of the criticisms of dynamic page creation techniques is that they are less scalable and require more server resources than when sending static HTML files to clients. A solution that many sites have adopted is batch processing the pages and saving the results to disk as static HTML files. However, this can only work if the content is not directly dependent on the client each time – in other words, the page is the same for all requests. This is the case for things like product catalogs and reports, and the update process only needs to be run when the data that the page is built from changes.

ASP.NET includes a new feature called *dynamic output caching* that provides the same effect automatically, without the need to write the pages to disk. Instead, it caches the dynamically created output (the content that the client receives), and uses this cached copy for subsequent requests. This is even better than writing the content to a disk file, as it removes the need for a disk access each time. ASP.NET will support this on Windows 2000 and Windows XP platforms.

Of course, this will only be useful where the content of the page is the same for all requests for this page. However, ASP.NET is clever – the cache can be varied based on a set of parameters, either the query string, the browser type, User Controls (see Partial Page Caching with User Controls, later in this chapter), or even a custom value, and ASP.NET will only use the cached copy if the parameters are the same as well. So, for example, pages that change depending on the contents of the query string will be served correctly – if the contents of the query string are different from those used when the cached copy was created, a new copy is created instead. This new copy is also cached, and is then available for use by clients that provide matching query string values.

An Output Caching Example

Output caching a page is quite straightforward. All that is necessary is to add the proper `@OutputCache` directive to the page, and ASP.NET will take care of the rest in caching the page. At its simplest, there are two pieces of information to provide to the `@OutputCache` directive – how long the cached item should remain in the cache, and what value should be used to vary the cache. Varying the cache means defining the value supplied by the browser that if it changes, a different page will be cached.

```
<%@ Page Language="C#" %>
<%@ OutputCache Duration="10" VaryByParam="None" %>

<Script runat="server">
   public void Page_Load(){
      // Get the Date and Time, once again this should not change after the
      // first run
      DateTime NowTime = DateTime.Now;
      DateTime Expires = NowTime.AddSeconds(10);
      CreatedStamp.InnerHtml = NowTime.ToString("r");
      ExpiresStamp.InnerHtml = Expires.ToString("r");
   }
</Script>
```

```
<Font size="3">
Output caching for 10 seconds...
<HR size="1">
Output Cache created: <Font color="red">
                     <B id="CreatedStamp" runat="server"></B></Font>
<BR>
Output Cache expires: <Font color="red">
                     <B id="ExpiresStamp" runat="server"></B></Font>
</Font>
```

In this example, let's cache the results of the page for 10 seconds. To do this, set the `Duration` attribute of the `@OutputCache` directive to 10. Also, supply a value for the `VaryByParam` attribute as well. This attribute is required, and it defines what query string parameters to vary the cache by. Since the page does not rely on a query string, it should provide the same page regardless of what parameters are passed to the page. The parameter value of `none` tells ASP.NET to always provide the same page.

When viewing the page, the time when the page was added to the cache is shown, along with when it will expire, as displayed in Figure 4-7:

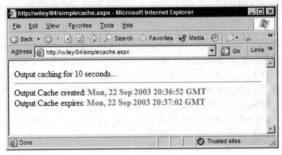

Figure 4-7

With the page displayed in the browser, press F5 to cause the page to reload. Notice that each time F5 is pressed the same page will be displayed. And after 10 seconds since the first request has elapsed, a new page will be generated and the times will change.

Caching by Browser

Just as you can vary the cache based on a query string or other parameter, you can also vary the cache based on the type of browser making the request. To do this, add the `VaryByCustom` attribute to the `@OutputCache` directive. The value for this parameter can be set to `browser`. This will tell ASP.NET to vary the cache based on the major version of the browser type. This means that IE 6 will get one version of a cached page, IE 5 will get another, and Netscape 6 will get a third. Thus a Netscape browser will not inadvertently get a page from the cache that has been customized to Internet Explorer.

```
<%@ OutputCache Duration="10" VaryByParam="*" VaryByCustom="browser" %>
```

Remember that `VaryByParam` is still a required parameter. If there is a parameter value other than browser, then the application must override the `GetVaryByCustomString` in the `global.asax` file.

> Output caching only works when using ASP.NET on the Windows 2000 and Windows XP platforms.

Smart Navigation

Smart Navigation is one of the coolest new features of ASP.NET, giving Web applications a look and feel more like those of conventional Windows applications. One of the drawbacks of Web applications is the architecture of HTTP, requiring postback to the server and a complete redrawing of the page being viewed. Not only does this cause the screen to 'flash', but for long pages it also scrolls you to the top of the page, changes control focus, and so on. With Windows applications, users are used to areas of screen content being updated without the rest of the page being affected. Smart Navigation brings this to Web applications.

The first thing to note is that this is an Internet Explorer feature only, requiring IE 5 or higher. While one of the main goals of ASP.NET is to target HTML 3.2, allowing great cross-browser compatibility, there are plenty of cases where this isn't an issue. One such case is intranets, where the browser can be controlled. However, Smart Navigation can be set to enabled or disabled at will, without affecting the application in any way. Even if you are targeting multiple browsers, Smart Navigation can remain enabled, as it detects the browser and only enables itself for supported browsers.

The four features of Smart Navigation are:

❑   No more screen flash

❑   Scroll position maintained

❑   Element focus maintained

❑   Last page in History maintained

This feature is really targeted at those applications that require a lot of postback, but where the content doesn't change a great deal.

Perhaps the most amazing thing about this feature is that you don't actually have to do any coding. Smart navigation is controlled by a `Page` directive for individual pagesand including the same in the `Web.Config` file for entire applications. For the `Page` directive, the syntax is:

```
<%@ Page SmartNavigation="true" %>
```

For `web.config` the syntax is:

```
<configuration>
    <system.web>
        <pages smartNavigation="true"/>
    </system.web>
</configuration>
```

There's no real way to show a screenshot that demonstrates how great this feature is – try it yourself to see it. It works by loading the page into a hidden IFRAME, and then only rendering those parts of the page that have changed.

User Controls

In addition to using HTML and server controls in your ASP.NET page, you can also create custom server controls. There are four primary ways for creating these custom controls – the easiest and simplest way will be covered in this chapter. A user control functions like an include file, but one with a defined interface. You can also take an existing control and derive a new control from it – retaining the desired functionality, and modifying or adding new functionality. A composite control can be created by combining the functionality of two or more server (or user) controls into a new control. Finally, a custom server control can be created from scratch – by starting with a base control class and extending it to support the functionality and the resulting HTML needed.

The idea behind user controls is that you can create reusable sections of code or content as separate ASP.NET controls, and then use them in other pages without having to change the code, or even be aware of how it works! And while code-behind techniques are primarily aimed at just inheriting code classes into a page, user controls can inherit parts of the user interface as well. In effect, they are a way of encapsulating other controls and code into a reusable package.

The programming model for writing user controls is exactly the same as that for writing ASP.NET pages – if you know how to write ASP.NET pages, then you know how to write user controls. Because they are so easy to create, user controls enable a RAD-style development model for building reusable controls.

Approaches to Building User Control

There are two approaches that you can use to build a user control. You can take an existing ASP.NET page and convert it to a user control. Or, you can set out to build a user control from scratch. The advantage to creating one from an existing (and assumed working) page is that you can test it directly as an ASP.NET page, make sure it works, and then convert it to a user control. However, to do this, let's first create a user control from scratch.

Creating a User Control

At this point in the book, you already have everything you need to create user controls from scratch. A user control is nearly identical to a Web Forms page, except for a few minor differences. A user control does not have a `<HTML>` tag, a `<BODY>` tag, or even a `<FORM>` tag. Since a user control will be inserted into another page, the other page will already have these elements. And since a page can only have one set of these elements, it is important that they are not part of the user control.

A user control can contain client script, HTML elements, ASP.NET code, and other server controls. The simplest user control would be one that simply outputs HTML when the page is rendered:

```
<hr>
<table border="0">
<tr><td colspan="2" align="center">This table is in a User Control</td></tr>
```

```
<tr><td align="right">Copyright: </td><td>2002 Wrox Press</td><tr>
<tr><td align="right">Page Created on: </td><td><%= Now() %></td></tr>
</table>
```

Create this file on the server and save it as `standardFooter.ascx`. This is now a user control. User controls must have a file suffix of `.ascx`.

To test a user control, you need to add it to a Web Forms page. There are two steps to doing this. First, use the `@ Register` directive to tell the page that there is a new user control that will be used in the page:

```
<%@ Register tagprefix="wrox" Tagname="footer" Src="standardFooter.ascx" %>
```

Next, add it to the page at the location where you want this information to be displayed:

```
<wrox:footer runat="server" />
```

The browser will display the page shown in Figure 4-8:

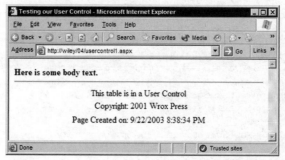

Figure 4-8

Converting a Page to a User Control

It is easy to create a user control from scratch. Now, let's look at the more common way of creating a user control. When developing ASP.NET web applications, there will be sections of code used on multiple pages. In the past, the options were to create an include file that kept the code in a single location, or maybe create a design-time control for Visual Studio. But neither of these methods was really that simple or straightforward to use. And all developers know that if something isn't simple and straightforward, then chances are it won't be used. But now with user controls, that code segment from our existing page can be taken and turned into a control that can be easily reused in multiple pages.

The example shown in the beginning of the chapter enabled you to select an item from a list of shipping methods. This page included the database code to retrieve the list as well as the controls to display the list. By packaging that logic into a reusable control, you can ensure that wherever a list of shippers is needed in your application (or applications) the data will be retrieved and displayed in the same way. A similar technique is used in Chapter 8 to build a control that returns data.

The first part of the control will be the display. The selection list is a drop-down list server control. What to do with the data in the control is up to the page that is hosting the control. Since the server control is using data binding, the code that makes up the display will be quite simple:

```
<asp:DropDownList id="ShipMethod" runat="server"/>
```

The main work of the page is done in the code that sets up the page. Since in effect the user control is a page, the code to read from the database in the Page_Load event can be the same as was used in the original page. Also, check to see if the page has a @Page directive. If it does, then change this to a @Control directive:

```
<%@ Control Language="Visual Basic" %>

<script language="VB" runat="server">
    Sub Page_Load(Source As Object, E As EventArgs)
        If Not Page.IsPostBack Then

            Dim myConnection As SqlConnection
            Dim myCommand    As SqlCommand
            Dim myReader     As SqlDataReader
            Dim SQL          As String
            Dim ConnStr      As String

            SQL = "SELECT * FROM Shippers"
            ConnStr = "server=localhost;uid=sa;pwd=;database=Northwind"

            myConnection = New SqlConnection(ConnStr)
            myConnection.Open()

            myCommand = New SqlCommand(SQL, myConnection)

            myReader = myCommand.ExecuteReader()

            ShipMethod.DataSource = myReader
            ShipMethod.DataBind()
        End If

    End Sub

</script>
```

This is exactly the same code that you had in your ASP.NET page. Since there are references to other .NET assemblies in the code, add an @Import directive to the user control. Don't rely on the page hosting this control to have imported these references. It doesn't matter to the compiler if these references are imported twice – but it will complain if they aren't there at all.

```
<%@ Import Namespace="System.Data" %>
<%@ Import Namespace="System.Data.SqlClient" %>
```

When viewing a page that contains this control, the browser will show the result (Figure 4-9):

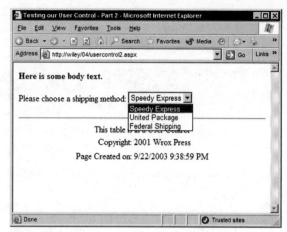

Figure 4-9

On examining the HTML that this produces, you can see that nothing special is happening on the client:

```
<html>
<head>
    <title>Testing our User Control - Part 2</title>
</head>

<body>
<form name="ctrl0" method="post" action="UserControl2.aspx" id="ctrl0">
<input type="hidden" name="__VIEWSTATE"
value="dDwzNzA5NjI5Njk7dDw7bDxpPDE+Oz47bDx0PDtsPGk8MT47PjtsPHQ8O2w8aTwwPjs+O2w8dDx0
PDtwPGw8aTwwPjtpPDE+O2k8Mj47PjtsPHA8U3BlZWR5IEV4cHJlc3M7MT47cDxVbml0ZWQgUGFja2FnZTs
yPjtwPEZlZGVyYWwgU2hpcHBpbmc7Mz47Pj47Pjs7Pjs+Pjs+QCtfh/cNp+z/JarjDm/wQX8mmt
A=" />
<strong>Here is some body text.</strong>
<P>Please choose a shipping method:
<select name="ctrl1:ShipMethod" id="ctrl1_ShipMethod">
    <option value="1">Speedy Express</option>
    <option value="2">United Package</option>
    <option value="3">Federal Shipping</option>
</select>
</P>
    <hr>
<table border=0 align=center>
<tr><td colspan=2 align=center>This table is in a User Control</td></tr>
<tr><td align=right>Copyright: </td><td>2002 Wrox Press</td><tr>
<tr><td align=right>Page Created on: </td><td>22/01/2002 15:48:09</td></tr>
</table>
</form>
</body>
</html>
```

The user control behaves just like any other control. The `Page_Load` runs and any content is transmitted to the parent page. The difference is that this user control can be dropped onto other pages.

The @ Control directive is used to assign control-specific attributes that are used by the Web Forms page parser and compiler to affect how the user control is created. There can only be one @ Control directive in a single file. The attributes are as follows:

Attribute	Values (default in bold)	Used for
AutoEventWireup	**True** or False	Indicates whether the page's events are automatically enabled
ClassName	Valid class name	Class name that this control is compiled as.
CompilerOptions	Valid compiler options	List of compiler options to be used when the page is compiled.
Debug	True or **False**	Compiles the page with debugging enabled.
Description	n/a	Description of the page – ignored by ASP.NET.
EnableViewState	**True** or False	ViewState for this user control is maintained during round-trips.
Explicit	**True** or False	Uses the Visual Basic Option Explicit mode.
Inherits	Valid class name	Code-behind class that this control inherits.
Language	Valid .NET Language name	Language used to compile all sourcecode on the page.
Src	Valid source file name	File name of the Code-Behind class used by this page.
Strict	True or **False**	Uses the Visual Basic Option Strict mode.
WarningLevel	0, 1, 2, or 4	Compiler warning level at which compilation should be aborted.

User Control Properties

You can interact with your user control by exposing a set of properties for it. This will allow you to programmatically change the behavior of the control from the page that is hosting it. It also makes it much easier to build a control that can be used on multiple pages, even if the data being displayed is somewhat different.

There are three steps to using properties with user controls. First, expose the properties from your user control. This is done using the standard property syntax that has already been covered in the book. Let's add the property syntax to the previous example to expose some properties:

```
<%@ Import Namespace="System.Data" %>
<%@ Import Namespace="System.Data.SqlClient" %>
<script language="VB" runat="server">

    Private ConnStr As String
    Property ConnectionString() As String
        Get
            return ConnStr
        End Get

        Set
            ConnStr = value
        End Set
    End Property

    Sub Page_Load(Source As Object, E As EventArgs)
        If Not Page.IsPostBack Then
            Dim myConnection As SqlConnection
            Dim myCommand    As SqlCommand
            Dim myReader     As SqlDataReader
            Dim SQL          As String
            SQL = "SELECT * FROM Shippers"
            If ConnStr = "" Then
                ConnStr = "server=localhost;uid=sa;pwd=;database=Northwind"
            End If

            myConnection = New SqlConnection(ConnStr)
            myConnection.Open()
```

One of the ways to make the user control more extensible is to not hardcode the database connection string. If the connection string is a property of the control, then the page that is using the control can pass in the proper connection string. In the code you can see that no matter what page the control is used in, a default connection string will be used if none is provided.

The first thing to do is to create a variable to hold the connection string value. Since the property assignment statement is called before Page_Load, create a place to hold the value before it is used to actually open the database:

```
Private ConnStr As String
```

The next step is to allow the user of the control to set a value for the property, as well as read the value contained by the property. This is done using the Property statement. Provide a Get method to allow for the retrieval of the value, and a Set method to allow the property value to be set.

```
Property ConnectionString() As String
    Get
        return ConnStr
    End Get
```

```
    Set
        ConnStr = value
    End Set
End Property
```

Finally, use the connection string to open the database. Since you can't guarantee that a user will have set the `Property` value, make sure there is a default value that is used if there is no value present. Alternatively, if you require that a value be set, you could throw an exception at this point if there is no value set. But in this example let's use a default value.

```
If ConnStr = "" Then
    ConnStr = "server=localhost;uid=sa;pwd=;database=Northwind"
End If
```

The last step is to use this revised user control in your ASP.NET page. To pass a property to a user control, simply add the property name and value as a parameter when adding the user control to the page. These parameters can also be set dynamically in code if desired.

```
<wrox:shipment ConnectionString="server=localhost;uid=sa; pwd=;database=Northwind"
    runat="server" />
```

User Control Events

The key thing to remember when dealing with user control events is that the event needs to be handled in the user control itself, and not in the page. In this way, the entire event handling for a user control is encapsulated within the control. You should not include event handlers for controls within a user control in the page that is hosting the user control (that is, the parent page) – the events will not be passed to the page, so the event will never be processed.

Since event handlers within a user control are handled in the same way as event handlers for server controls within pages, this is pretty similar to adding an event handler to a user control (discussed earlier in this chapter). Let's add to the current user control an event that will be fired when the user selects an item from the drop-down list. This event will cause the user's selection to be displayed in a label control just below the selection.

```
Sub ShipMethod_Change(Source As Object, E As EventArgs)
    SelectedMethod.text = "You have selected " & _
                ShipMethod.SelectedItem.Text & _
                " as your shipping method."
End Sub
</script>

<asp:DropDownList AutoPostBack="true"
                OnSelectedIndexChanged = "ShipMethod_Change"
                id="ShipMethod" runat="server"/>
<BR><asp:Label id="SelectedMethod" runat="server"/>
```

There are two changes to the `DropDownList` control that is part of the user control. First, you need to let ASP.NET know that you want to automatically trigger a postback when the selection in the drop-down list is changed. This is done by setting the `AutoPostBack` attribute to `true`. The second change is to define what method will be called whenever the user selects an item from the drop-down list. The name of the event that is fired is `OnSelectedIndexChanged` and when that event is fired, the `ShipMethod_Change` event is called.

Then you create an event handler within the user control that will be called when the selection is made. This event handler will grab the text value of the selected item from the control, and use that to populate a label control for display back to the user.

```
Sub ShipMethod_Change(Source As Object, E As EventArgs)
    SelectedMethod.text = "You have selected " & _
                    ShipMethod.SelectedItem.Text & _
                    " as your shipping method."
End Sub
```

The `SelectedItem` property of the `DropDownList` control identifies the particular item object from the list that is currently selected. The `Text` property of this object contains the actual text that was in the drop-down list. You can grab this value and use it to build a prompt to display for the user.

Code-Behind with User Controls

Earlier in this chapter, you saw how to use the `Page` class to create an object that will handle all of the code for the page. Then by placing that class definition into its own file, you can separate the code from the layout. This is the same as the code-behind technique used earlier. Since user controls are very similar to ASP.NET pages, code-behind can be used when creating user controls as well.

The first step is to import the necessary namespaces for the user control. The `System` and `System.Web.UI` namespaces are required. Since ASP.NET Server Controls are used as well, import the `System.Web.UI.WebControls` namespace. In order to retrieve the data from a database, import the `System.Data.SqlClient` namespace as well:

```
Imports System
Imports System.Web.UI
Imports System.Web.UI.WebControls
Imports System.Data
Imports System.Data.SqlClient
```

The next step is to declare a class to define the user control. To provide the necessary functionality, this class needs to inherit from the `UserControl` class. This class will contain the same initialization code, object interface code, and event handling code that is in the user control already created. One important difference is that all variables must be declared `Public` for each of the server controls that the user control needs.

```
Public Class shipMethodClass
    Inherits UserControl

    Private ConnStr As String
    Public ShipMethod As DropDownList
    Public SelectedMethod As Label
```

When saving the code-behind file, it is important to use the proper filename extension. This is the only way to inform the ASP.NET compiler what language the code-behind file is written in. If you don't use the proper extension, the compiler will fail when trying to display this page.

```
<%@ Control Inherits="shipMethodClass" Src="shipMethod.vb"
          ClassName="shipMethod" %>
```

Finally, remove the VB code from the user control and then add a @Control directive to attach the user control to the code-behind file. There are three attributes needed in the @Control directive. The Inherits attribute defines the name of the class that contains the code-behind code. The Src attribute defines the source file that actually contains the code-behind sourcecode. The ClassName attribute defines a class name for the control, needed to dynamically create the control on a page.

Partial Page Caching with User Controls

Caching can reduce the number of processing cycles required to deliver a page when it is requested by the client. By storing the output from a page on the server, and then outputting that information to a client when the same page is requested again, the need to execute the page again is eliminated. A very similar concept will allow us to cache parts of a page.

If you are wondering, "How can I tag part of the page to be cached?", think about what user controls do. They are basically separate page sections that are embedded into another page. If you could cache the output of a user control, and then insert it into a page when it is requested, you can utilize the benefits of caching. This technique is called partial page caching, or *fragment caching*.

The key to using fragment caching is through user controls. Place the portions of the page to cache into a user control, and then indicate that the user control should be cached. This is done using the @ OutputCache directive, just as when the entire page is cached:

```
<%@ OutputCache Duration="time" VaryByParam="none" %>
```

To see how fragment caching works, let's add caching to the user control created in this chapter. Since this specific user control performs database access, it will gain great performance benefits by being cached. Since the data that is being displayed does not change very frequently, it would be of great benefit if it didn't have to go to the database each time the control is used.

```
<%@ Import Namespace="System.Data" %>
<%@ Import Namespace="System.Data.SqlClient" %>
<%@ OutputCache Duration="10" VaryByParam="none" %>

<script language="VB" runat="server">
    Sub Page_Load(Source As Object, E As EventArgs)
        Dim NowTime As DateTime
        Dim Expires as DateTime
        NowTime = DateTime.Now
        Expires = NowTime.AddSeconds(10)
        CreatedStamp.InnerHtml = NowTime.ToString("r")
        ExpiresStamp.InnerHtml = Expires.ToString("r")
        If Not Page.IsPostBack Then
            Dim myConnection As SQLConnection
            ...
```

The line that enables fragment caching is the @OutputCache directive. Set the cache to hold the page for 10 seconds. Setting the VaryByParam attribute to none will return the same cached value regardless of the parameters or browser making the request.

The rest of the code added is simply to help identify that the cache is actually working. It will display the time at which the user control was run, and when the cache expires, 10 seconds afterwards. There are two Label server controls that will display that information.

```
<HR>Fragment Cache created: <Font color="red">
                            <B id="CreatedStamp" runat="server"></B></Font>
    <BR>
    Fragment Cache expires: <Font color="red">
                            <B id="ExpiresStamp" runat="server"></B></Font>
```

When viewing the page in the browser, the time that the page was created is displayed, the time that the user control was created is displayed, and when the cached version of the user control will expire is shown. The time the page was loaded was 15:48:45 – the same time shown on the fragment cache. After a refresh of the browser, the page creation time changes (it's now 15:49:24), but the user control creation time and cache expire time doesn't change – it is being drawn from the cache as shown in Figure 4-10:

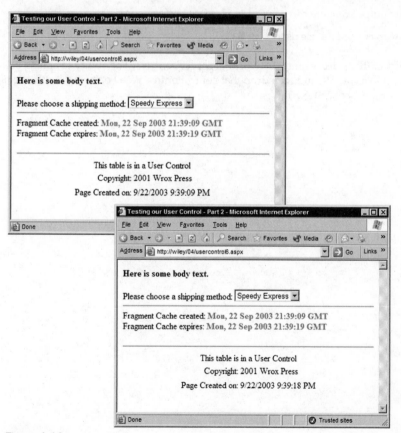

Figure 4-10

Summary

This chapter looked at the core for ASP.NET – the page. Whether referred to as a Web Form or as an ASP.NET page, the page is the central part of all that is done with ASP.NET. The page is what embodies the interface that the user has to interact with, on a web site or a Web application. The page gives us plenty of power to do things like generate non-text files such as images, or be broken up into smaller segments for reuse called user controls. But with great power comes great responsibility, and also complexity. The nice thing about the Page object and all that it represents is that you can just work with the ice of the tipberg and still function. But when you need to delve deeper, the Page object, and all that it encompasses, has the power that you need.

This chapter discussed:

❑ The old way of doing ASP pages, and contrasted that with the new ASP.NET style of pages.

❑ The Page class itself and the object model that it supports.

❑ The steps that the page goes through in its lifetime.

❑ How to use Code-Behind to separate code from layout.

❑ How output caching can be used to increase performance.

❑ How to create and use user controls.

The next chapter dives deeper into the world of server controls. The ability to embed complex functionality into a control, and then drop that control onto a Web Form page with one tag is one of the revolutionary aspects of ASP.NET.

Server Controls and Validation

We have already used server controls in many of the examples of building ASP.NET pages in previous chapters. In this chapter and the two that follow, we are going to be looking in more depth at exactly what server controls are and how we can use them. In fact, we will be examining all the different types of server controls that are supplied with the standard .NET installation.

Server controls are at the heart of the new ASP.NET techniques for building interactive web forms and web pages. They allow us to adopt a programming model based on server-side event handling that is much more like the structured event-driven approach we are used to when building traditional executable programs.

Of course, as the .NET framework is completely extensible, we can build our own server controls as well, or just inherit from existing ones and extend their behavior. We will look at how we can go about building our own server controls later in this book. In the meantime, we will stick to those that come as part of the standard .NET package.

The topics we will cover in this chapter are:

- ❑ What are server controls?
- ❑ How to build interactive forms and pages using them
- ❑ The server controls supplied with .NET
- ❑ A detailed look at the HTML and Input Validation controls

We start with the obvious question, 'What are server controls?'

What Are Server Controls?

As seen in Chapter 4, ASP.NET is designed around the concept of server controls. This stems from the fundamental change in the philosophy for creating interactive pages. In particular, with the increasing power of servers and the ease of building multi-server web farms, we can circumvent the problems of handling the increasing range of different client devices by doing much more of the work on the server.

We also end up with a client interface that looks and behaves much more like a traditional application. However, to understand how the use of server controls affects the way we build applications, it is important to grasp the way that the new ASP.NET page model changes the whole approach to web page design.

The ASP.NET Page Model Revisited

Before the advent of ASP.NET, the traditional way of creating pages dynamically has always been as shown in Figure 5-1:

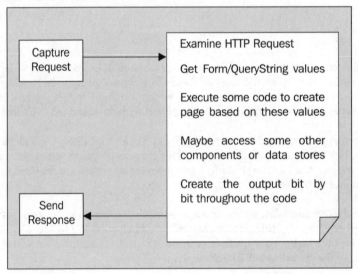

Figure 5-1

The process can be described as follows:

1. Capture the request in IIS and pipe it through a parsing engine like the ASP interpreter. This is achieved by setting the script mappings in IIS to direct all requests for .asp pages to the asp.dll ASP ISAPI DLL.

2. Within the interpreter (asp.dll), examine the page for server-side script sections. Non-script sections are simply piped back out to the client through the response. Script sections are extracted and passed to an instance of the appropriate scripting engine.

3. The scripting engine executes the code and sends any output that this code generates to the response, at that point in the page.

The problem is that the code usually ends up resembling spaghetti. It is difficult to get a well-structured design when all we are doing is interpreting the blocks of script that can be placed almost anywhere in the page.

ASP.NET Pages Are All about Events

If you think about how a traditional Windows executable application is created, it all depends on events. You create a form or window for the user to work with, and place in it the controls they will use to accomplish the required task. We create handlers for *events* that are raised as the user interacts with the controls and the page. The code in each event handler is responsible for updating the page or controls, creating output, or carrying out whatever task is required (see Figure 5-2):

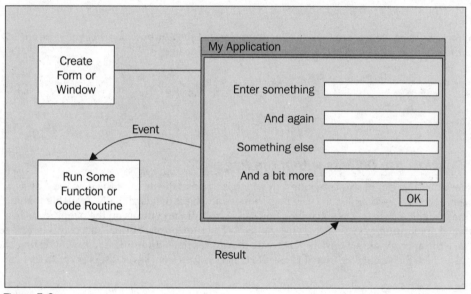

Figure 5-2

The great thing with ASP.NET is that, in conjunction with server controls and the new page model, you can build web pages and applications that work in an event-driven manner. In other words, you now have a proper event-driven architecture.

ASP.NET Is Compiled Code

Much of the theory of this new page structure was covered in previous chapters, so we will confine ourselves to the actual server controls themselves in this chapter. The important concept to grasp is that the whole page (all of the HTML, text, and other content) is compiled into a class. This class can then be executed to create the output for the client.

All the static or client-based content (text, HTML, client-side script, and so on) is sent to the client through the response when the class is executed. This content cannot be accessed using server-side code. However, all controls or elements that are marked with the `runat="server"` attribute are themselves created as objects within the page class. This means that you can write code that uses these objects. To put it more simply, if you mark an element or control as being `runat="server"`, you can access its properties, call its methods, and react to the events it raises on the server. This works because ASP.NET uses `<form>` elements to create the postback architecture described in earlier chapters. In the postback architecture, the page and its contents are posted back to the same ASP.NET file on the server when the user interacts with the controls on that page.

Server Controls Are Event-Driven

When a user clicks a button that is defined as a server control on a page, the values of the controls on that page are posted back to the server and an event is raised (on the server). We react to this event using a server-side event handler. For example, we can define a button control in the following way:

```
<input type="submit" value="Go" onserverclick="MyFunction"
       runat="server" />
```

Then, on the server, we react to the click event (notice that the attribute name is `onserverclick`, not `onclick`, which is defined in HTML 4.0 to raise a client-side event):

```
<script language="VB" runat="server">
Sub MyFunction(objSender As Object, objArgs As EventArgs)
   ... code to handle the event here ...
End Sub
</script>
```

Server Controls Are Objects within the Page

Another point that might seem obvious, but which is again at the heart of the new page design, is that each server control is compiled into the page class as an object that is globally available within the page. This means that, within an event handler, you can access all the controls on the page. So, as in a traditional application, you can access the values in other textboxes, buttons, list controls, and so on, and then take the appropriate actions and/or create the appropriate output. The following listing shows an example where the `Page_Load` event is used to collect values from several server controls.

```
<div id="divResult" runat="server" />
...
<script language="VB" runat="server">
Sub Page_Load()
  Dim strResult As String
  strResult = "MyTextBox.ID = " & MyTextBox.ID & "<p />"
  strResult += "MyTextBox.Value = " & MyTextBox.Value & "<p />"
  strResult += "MyCheckBox.Checked = " & MyCheckBox.Checked
  divResult.InnerHtml = strResult
End Sub
</script>
```

You can also set the value of the controls, as follows:

```
<script language="VB" runat="server">
Sub Page_Load()
  Dim datToday As Date = Now()
  MyTextBox.Value = datToday
End Sub
</script>
```

Experimenting with Server Controls

To show how the various server controls work, we have provided a simple example application that shows the output generated in the browser by each of the controls. You can also set the values of the common properties for each control and see the results.

The example is included in the samples that you can download for this book from http://www.daveandal.net/books/8900/, or run online at the same URL. The application is in the folder named `server-controls`, and has a `default.htm` page to start it. This opens the page `server-controls.htm`, as shown in Figure 5-3:

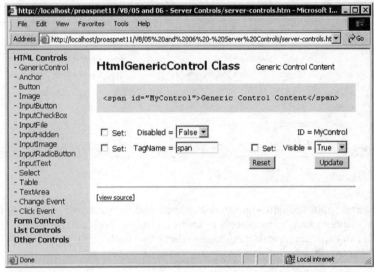

Figure 5-3

The gray background section in the main right-hand page displays the actual HTML output that the selected control generates. This is done with some client-side JScript, which creates an instance of the `XMLHTTP` object (an integral part of IE 5) and uses it to fetch the same page again as a string, after the page has finished loading into the right-hand frame of our application. The code then parses out the section containing the output of the server control and displays it (you can view the source of the page to see this code). This means that you will only be able to use IE 5 or above to view this particular example. However, this was felt to be a valid course of action in order to show the actual output of the server controls.

We could simply have queried the `OuterHtml` property of the element itself to get the HTML content, but this is actually different from the HTML that the browser receives from the server. The IE HTML DOM parses the incoming HTML and sorts and simplifies the attributes, and so you wouldn't see a true picture of the server control's output in this case.

As you can see from Figure 5-3, the left-hand frame contains a collapsible tree listing all the server controls. For each one, you can specify the values for several of the most useful properties for that control. For example, in Figure 5-4 we have selected the HTML **Anchor** control and set the `Title`, `Href`,

`Name`, and `Target` properties, and then clicked the **Update** button. You can see the effect this has on the output of the control.

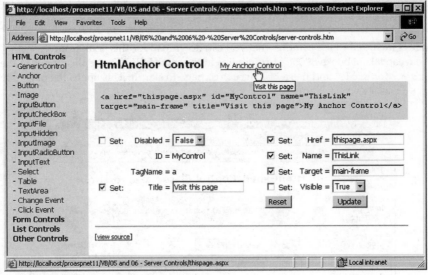

Figure 5-4

We will be using this application throughout this chapter and the next, to demonstrate the various controls. We don't have room to exhaustively examine all the methods and properties for all of the controls, but you can experiment with them to see what effect each of the properties has on the output created by the different server controls.

By comparing the generated output with the property settings you make, you can get a feel for how these controls can be used. It is a relatively simple one-to-one connection between the *properties* you set and the *attributes* created with the HTML controls. However, as you will see in the next chapter (particularly with the rich controls described there), the results from the other sets of server controls can be quite different.

About the Example Application

This chapter won't be describing how the example application works; however, the source code is available for you to look through if you want to learn more. All it does is create an instance of the selected control and then display a set of input elements for the properties specific to that control. As the page loads, it reads the values of these properties and inserts them into the input elements. When we set one or more of the properties and click the **Update** button, the server control is updated to reflect these property values.

We haven't provided inputs for all the properties, as there are a large number that are generic to many controls, and which are not commonly used. Where the property value is taken from an enumeration, such as the `ImageAlign` property for an **ASP:Image** control (Figure 5-5), we provide a drop-down list containing the enumeration values. To set the property when the page is submitted, we use the integer value of that enumeration member as stored in the value attribute of the listbox item. We will discuss this in more detail when we look at the ASP.NET Web Form controls in the next chapter. However, you can see how this works if you examine the source code for the page (`asp_image.aspx`).

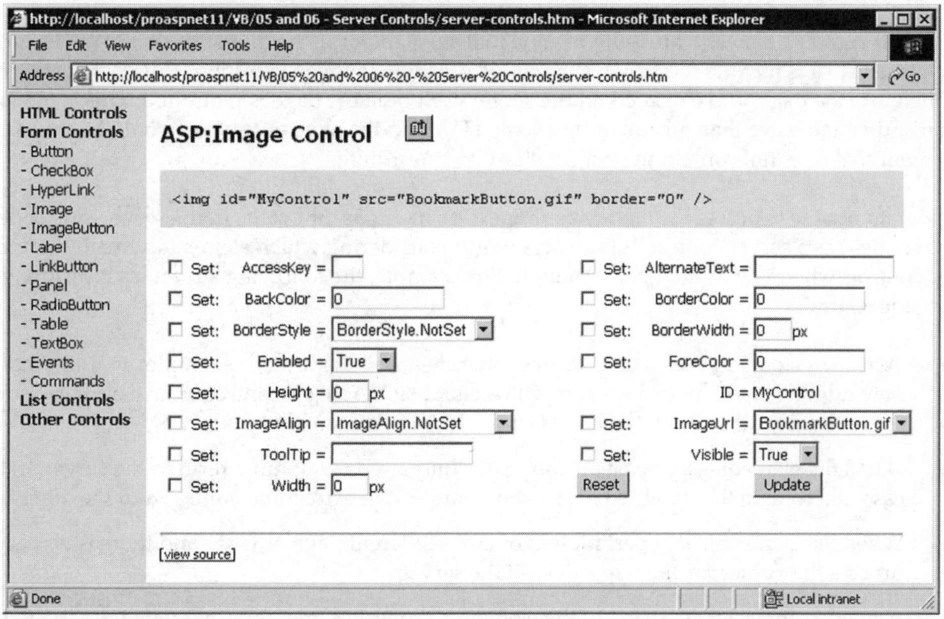

Figure 5-5

Some of the server controls demonstrated in the application (such as textboxes and lists) are interactive. However, any changes made within the control itself (the control we are demonstrating) are not reflected in the property values shown in the controls where you set these values. For example, if you change the text in the `HtmlInputText` control at the top of that particular demonstration page, it is reset to the value shown in the `Value` property input control when you click Update. At any time, you can return the control to its original state by clicking the Reset button.

When Should You Use Server Controls?

One very important topic to consider is *when* to choose server controls over normal HTML elements. For example, if you want a textbox on a form, should you use a server control or a normal `<input type="text">` element? To create a textbox, you have three options. You can use an ordinary HTML element that is displayed as a textbox in the browser, as follows:

```
<input type="text" name="mytext" />
```

You can use an `HtmlInputText` server control as well. Again, the `type` attribute is set to `"text"`, but this time the `runat="server"` attribute is included as well:

```
<input type="text" id="mytext" runat="server" />
```

You can use an `<asp:TextBox>` control (we will discuss the pros and cons of these controls in the next chapter):

```
<asp:TextBox id="mytext" runat="server" />
```

Adding the `runat="server"` attribute to an HTML element, or using one of the ASP Web Form controls (which must always include the `runat="server"` attribute in their definition) causes that control to be compiled into the page, and executed on the server each time the page is requested. This is obviously more resource-intensive than just including some HTML in the page output, as would be the case with an element that does not contain the `runat="server"` attribute.

However, to be able to access the element's properties, methods, or events in the server-side code, you *have to* create it as a server control. It is always worth considering which elements actually *need* to be server controls when you build a page, though. For example, the following situations *do not* require a server-side control:

❑ When the element is used only to run some client-side script. For example, a button that opens a new browser window, or interacts with a client-side ActiveX control or Java applet, or calculates some value for display in the page using DHTML or in an alert dialog.

❑ When the element is a Submit button that is only used to submit a form to the server. In this case, the code in the `Page_Load()` event handler can extract the values from the other controls.

❑ When the element is a hyperlink that opens a different page or URL, and there is no need to process the values for the hyperlink on the server.

❑ Any other times when access to the element's properties, methods, or events in server-side code is not required.

Remember that you can still use the `Request.Form` and `Request.QueryString` collections in the same way as in previous versions of ASP, with both ordinary HTML control elements and with server controls. HTML control elements that are on a `<form>` but are not marked with `runat="server"` (in other words, they are not server controls), will still send their values to the server in the `Request.Form` and `Request.QueryString` collections when the form is submitted.

In general, a page that uses server controls instead of HTML elements results in something like a 30 percent drop in performance each time the page is generated. However, this is only an average – you don't get a compounded 30 percent penalty hit for every control. Besides, if you use server-side code to set the values of controls using traditional ASP techniques, you generally get worse performance compared to using the ASP.NET server controls.

The Controls Available in ASP.NET

We are now in a position to appreciate the advantages we get with server controls:

❑ HTML output that creates the elements to implement the control in the browser

❑ An object within the page that we can program against on the server

❑ Automatic maintenance of the control's value (or state)

❑ Simple access to the control values without having to dig into the Request object

❑ The ability to react to events, and thus create better structured pages

❑ A common approach to building user interfaces as web pages

❑ The ability to more easily address different types of client device

The server controls provided with the .NET Framework fall quite neatly into six groups:

❑ **HTML Server Controls**: The server-based equivalents of the standard HTML controls. They create output that is the same as the definition of the control within the page, and they use the same attributes as the standard HTML elements. We will be looking at these controls in this chapter.

❑ **ASP.NET Validation Controls**: A set of special controls designed to make it easy to check and validate the values entered into other controls on a page. They perform the validation client-side, server-side, or both, depending on the type of client device that requests the page. We will also be looking at these controls in this chapter.

❑ **ASP.NET Web Form Controls**: A set of controls that are the equivalent of the normal HTML `<form>` controls, such as a textbox, a hyperlink, and various buttons. They have a standardized set of property names that make life easier at design-time, and easier for graphical page creation tools to build the page. We will see more about these controls in the next chapter.

❑ **ASP.NET List Controls**: These controls provide a range of ways to build lists. These lists can also be data bound. In other words, the content of the list can come from a data source such as an Array, a HashTable, or a range of other data sources. The range of controls provides many different display options, and some include special features for formatting the output and even editing the data in the list. We will see more about these controls in Chapter 7.

❑ **ASP.NET Rich Controls**: These controls (which include the Calendar and Ad Rotator) create complex task-specific output. We will see more about these controls in the next chapter.

❑ **ASP.NET Mobile Controls**: A separate set of controls that provide the same kind of functionality as the Web form, List, and Rich controls, but have specially extended features that completely change the output of the control, depending on the client device that is accessing the page. They are primarily designed to support mobile and small-screen devices, and they can create output that is in *Wireless Markup Language* (*WML*) as well as HTML and other formats. You will learn more about these controls in Chapter 21.

The HTML Server Controls

The HTML server controls are defined within the `System.Web.UI.HtmlControls` namespace. The controls inherit from a couple of generic base classes defined here. There are also specific classes for each of the interactive controls (those controls that are usually used on an HTML `<form>`).

The HtmlControl Base Classes

The base class for all HTML controls is `System.Web.UI.HtmlControls.HtmlControl`. This exposes methods, properties, and events that are common to all HTML controls. The ones used most often are shown in the following table.

Member	Description
`Attributes` property	Returns a collection of all the attribute name/value pairs within the `.aspx` file for this control. It can be used to read and set non-standard attributes (custom attributes that are not actually part of HTML) or to access attributes where the control does not provide a specific property for that purpose.
`ClientID` property	Returns the control identifier that is generated by ASP.NET.
`Controls` property	Returns a `ControlCollection` object containing references to all the child controls for this control within the page hierarchy.
`Disabled` property	Sets or returns a Boolean value indicating if the control is disabled.
`EnableViewState` property	Sets or returns a Boolean value indicating if the control should maintain its viewstate and the viewstate of any child controls when the current page request ends. The default is `True`.
`ID` property	Sets or returns the identifier defined for the control.
`Page` property	Returns a reference to the `Page` object containing the control.
`Parent` property	Returns a reference to the parent of this control within the page hierarchy.
`Style` property	References a collection of all the CSS style properties (selectors) that apply to the control.
`TagName` property	Returns the name of the element; for example, `a` or `div`.
`Visible` property	Sets or returns a Boolean value indicating if the control should be rendered in the page output. Default is `True`.
`DataBind` method	Causes data binding to occur for the control and all of its child controls.
`FindControl` method	Searches within the current container for a specified server control.
`HasControls` method	Returns a Boolean value indicating if the control contains any child controls.
`DataBinding` event	Occurs when the control is being bound to a data source.

A full list of all the members for this object can be found in the .NET Framework SDK Documentation under Reference, Class Library, System.Web.UI.HtmlControls, HtmlControl Class, HtmlControl Members.

The second base class is `System.Web.UI.HtmlControls.HtmlContainerControl`, which is used as the base for all HTML elements that *must* have a closing tag (elements such as `<i>`, `<b>`, and `<select>`, which, unlike `<img>` or `<input>`, make no sense as single tags). This class inherits from `HtmlControl`, and exposes the same methods, properties, and events as shown earlier. Also, because it is only used for *container* elements that themselves can have content, it adds two more very useful properties that allow us to read and set this content:

Property	Description
InnerHtml	Sets or returns the HTML and text content between the opening and closing tags of the control.
InnerText	Sets or returns just the text content between the opening and closing tags of the control.

The HtmlGenericControl Class

As you will no doubt be aware, there are around 100 elements currently defined in HTML, although some are browser-specific. Rather than provide a distinct class for each of these, the .NET Framework contains specific classes for only a few of the HTML elements. These mainly include those elements that we use on an HTML `<form>`, or which we use to build interactive parts of a page (such as hyperlinks or images).

This doesn't mean that we can't use other HTML controls as server controls. If there is no specific class for an element, the framework substitutes the `System.Web.UI.HtmlControls.HtmlGenericControl` class instead. Note that this is *not* a base class – it is a public class designed for use with elements for which there is no specific class.

For example, you may have noticed in an example earlier in the chapter that we used a `<div>` element to display the results of some code in an event handler like this:

```
<div id="divResult" runat="server" />
...
Sub Page_Load()
  ...
  divResult.InnerHtml = strResult
End Sub
```

You can see that we have defined the `<div>` as being a server control (it includes the `runat="server"` attribute, and this allows us to use the XML-style shorthand syntax of specifying a forward slash instead of a closing tag). To display the result, we simply set the `InnerHtml` property on the server. So, if the value of `strResult` is This is the result, the page output will contain:

```
<div id="divResult">This is the result</div>
```

As the `HtmlGenericControl` is based on the `HtmlContainerControl` base class (which itself inherits from `HtmlControl`), it exposes the same list of members (properties, methods, and events) that we described earlier for these classes. In our previous code, we used the `InnerHtml` property to display a value within the control. We can equally well use the other members. For example, we can force the element to be displayed or hidden (included or not included in the final page output) by setting the `Visible` property.

The Specific HTML Control Classes

The `System.Web.UI.HtmlControls` namespace includes specific classes for the HTML interactive controls, such as those used on a `<form>`. Each one inherits from either `HtmlControl` or `HtmlContainerControl` (depending on whether it has a closing tag), so it has the same members as that base class.

However, for these controls to be useful, we need to be able to access the properties and events that are specific to each type of control. For example, with a hyperlink, we might want to read and set the href, name, and target attribute values in our server-side code. We might also want to be able to detect when a user clicks on a hyperlink.

To accomplish this, each of the controls has specific properties and events that correspond to the attributes we normally use with that element. A few also have other properties that allow access to control-specific values, such as the `PostedFile` property for an `<input type="file">` element or the specific data binding properties of the `<select>` element. The button-type controls also have a `CausesValidation` property, which we will see in use when we look at the validation server controls later in this chapter. The following table lists the different HTML server controls that are available in the Framework:

HTML Element	Specific Properties	Specific Events
`<a>` Class Name: `HtmlAnchor`	`Href, Target, Title, Name`	`OnServerClick`
`<img>` Class Name: `HtmlImage`	`Align, Alt, Border, Height, Src, Width`	*- none -*
`<form>` Class Name: `HtmlForm`	`Name, Enctype, Method, Target`	*- none -*
`<button>` Class Name: `HtmlButton`	`CausesValidation`	`OnServerClick`

`<input type="button">`
`<input type="submit">`
`<input type="reset">`
Class Name: `HtmlInputButton`
	`Name, Type, Value, CausesValidation`	`OnServerClick`

HTML Element	Specific Properties	Specific Events

`<input type="text">`
`<input type="password">`
`Class Name: HtmlInputText`
	MaxLength, Name, Size, Type, Value	OnServerChange

`<input type="checkbox">`
`Class Name:`
`HtmlInputCheckBox`
	Checked, Name, Type, Value	OnServerChange

`<input type="radio">`
`Class Name:`
`HtmlInputRadioButton`
	Checked, Name, Type, Value	OnServerChange

`<input type="image">` `Class Name: HtmlInputImage`	Align, Alt, Border, Name, Src, Type, Value, CausesValidation	OnServerClick
`<input type="file">` `Class Name: HtmlInputFile`	Accept, MaxLength, Name, PostedFile, Size, Type, Value	*- none -*

`<input type="hidden">`
`Class Name:`
`HtmlInputHidden`
	Name, Type, Value	OnServerChange

`<textarea>` `Class Name: HtmlTextArea`	Cols, Name, Rows, Value	OnServerChange
`<select>` `Class Name: HtmlSelect`	Multiple, SelectedIndex, Size, Value, DataSource, DataTextField, DataValueField Items (*collection*)	OnServerChange
`<table>` `Class Name: HtmlTable`	Align, BgColor, Border, BorderColor, CellPadding, CellSpacing, Height, NoWrap, Width Rows (*collection*)	*- none -*
`<tr>` `Class Name: HtmlTableRow`	Align, BgColor, Border, BorderColor, Height, VAlign Cells (*collection*)	*- none -*
`<td>` `Class Name: HtmlTableCell`	Align, BgColor, Border, BorderColor, ColSpan, Height, NoWrap, RowSpan, VAlign, Width	*- none -*

In the next sections of this chapter, we will examine these controls in more detail using the demonstration application we have provided.

Using the HTML Server Controls

In most cases, the use of HTML controls is self-evident if you are familiar with the quirks of HTML and its inconsistent use of attribute names. The properties of the controls, as we have just seen, match the attribute names almost identically. We will look at a couple of useful techniques that apply to all the HTML controls, and to most other server controls as well.

Setting the Control Appearance Using Style Properties

All the server controls (including the ASP Web Form controls we look at in the next two chapters) provide a `Style` property that we can use to change the appearance of the control. It defines the CSS properties that will be added to the element tag when the control is created. We simply set or add the appropriate CSS style selectors to the collection for that control, using the same values as we would in a normal CSS stylesheet. For example, we can display the content of a `<div>` element in large red letters using the code shown in following listing:

```
<div id="divResult" runat="server" />
...
<script language="VB" runat="server">
Sub Page_Load()
   divResult.InnerHtml = "Some Big Red Text"
   divResult.Style("font-family") = "Tahoma"
   divResult.Style("font-weight") = "bold"
   divResult.Style("font-size") = "30px"
   divResult.Style("color") = "Red"
End Sub
</script>
```

Figure 5-6 shows the result:

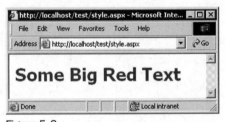

Figure 5-6

If we examine the output that is generated by the control, we see the style attribute that determines the formatting we specified in our code:

```
<div id="divResult" style="fontfamily:Tahoma;font-weight:bold;
font-size:30px;color:Red;">Some Big Red Text</div>
```

This technique is most useful with the HTML controls, as the ASP.NET Web Form controls and most of the other server controls have specific properties that can be used to change their appearance, as you will see in the next chapter.

Managing Viewstate across Postbacks

One important point you should be aware of is the effect that viewstate has on the performance of the server and the page itself. You looked at *what viewstate is* in the previous chapter, and will see more detail about its *effects on performance* in Chapter 7, when we look at the more complex list controls.

To recap, an ASP.NET page containing a server-side `<form>` control automatically generates viewstate. This is an encoded representation of all the values in all the controls on the page, and it is persisted across page loads using a `HIDDEN`-type `<input>` control. If you view the source of the page in the browser, you'll see the following:

```
<form name="ctrl0" method="post" action="mypage.aspx" id="ctrl0">
<input type="hidden" name="__VIEWSTATE" value="dDwxOTAwNDM2ODc1Ozs+" />
...
```

You can prevent a control from persisting its values within the viewstate by changing the `EnableViewState` property from its default value of `True` to `False`:

```
<ASP:TextBox id="MyTextBox" EnableViewState="False" runat="server" />
```

This is also useful if you use a control such as a `<div>` to display some kind of status or information value by setting the `InnerText` or `InnerHtml` property in your server-side code. When the page is posted back to the server, the value is persisted automatically. By changing the `EnableViewState` property to `False`, you start with a fresh new empty `<div>` (or whichever element you use it with) each time.

Examples of the HTML Server Controls

So that you can appreciate how each of the HTML server controls works, and how the properties defined affect the output that the control generates, the next few sections show each of the controls in detail, together with some pointers to be aware of when you use them.

The HtmlGeneric Control

There's not much to say about the `HtmlGeneric` control, other than this is the *only* control where the `TagName` property is read/write – it is read-only in all other controls. We can use the `HtmlGeneric` control to create any container-type HTML element that we need.

The HTML for creating the server control in the source code for the page seen in Figure 5-7 is:

```
<span id="MyControl" runat="server">
  Generic Control Content
</span>
```

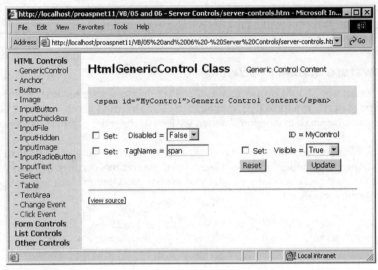

Figure 5-7

The HtmlAnchor Control

We saw the `HtmlAnchor` control in the demonstration application earlier in this chapter. The five attributes that we generally use with an HTML hyperlink or an HTML anchor are available as properties, as shown in Figure 5-8:

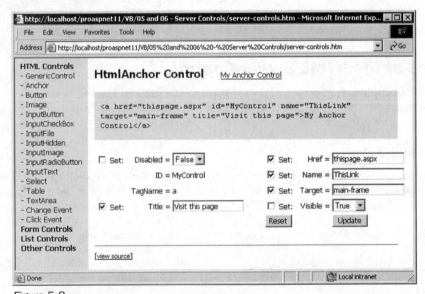

Figure 5-8

The HTML used for creating the server control in the source code for the page is:

```
<a href="html_anchor.aspx" id="MyControl" runat="server">
  My Anchor Control
</a>
```

The HtmlImage Control

To display an image, and be able to interact with this `<img>` element on the server, we can use the `HtmlImage` control. Figure 5-9 shows most of the properties set to custom values. You can see that we have changed the image, specified a five pixel wide border for it, set the height and width, and added a pop-up tool-tip.

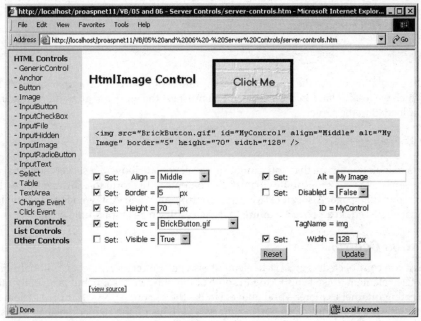

Figure 5-9

The HTML used for creating the server control in the source code for the page is:

```
<img id="MyControl" src="BookmarkButton.gif" runat="server" />
```

The HtmlForm Control

The `HtmlForm` control can't be demonstrated in our sample application. However, it can easily be used to create a form – in fact, it is how we usually do it when building ASP.NET interactive pages:

```
<form runat="server">
... form content defined here ...
</form>
```

ASP.NET automatically sets the remaining attributes so that the contents of the form are posted back to the same page. What is actually generated as output is shown next. Notice that the hidden viewstate element is automatically added:

```
<form name="ctrl0" method="post" action="test.aspx" id="ctrl0">
<input type="hidden" name="__VIEWSTATE" value="dDwxN...Oz4=" />
... form content appears here ...
</form>
```

We can also use the `HtmlForm` control to create a form with some of our own specific attributes. For example, in order to make our demonstration application work properly (due to the need to fetch the page separately with the `XMLHTTP` component to show the content), we need to use the `get` method for the form content, rather than `post`:

```
<form method="get" runat="server">
```

Also, remember that if you use the `HtmlInputFile` control or a normal `<input type="file">` element (which we look at later in the chapter), you must set the `enctype` attribute yourself to allow files to be uploaded to the server:

```
<form enctype="multipart/form-data" runat="server">
```

Other points to look out for are that you cannot set the action attribute of a server-side `<form>` element (one with a `runat="server"` attribute) to post the contents of the form to a different page. It always posts back to the same page. Also, all HTML form controls and their ASP Web Form equivalent input controls must be placed on a `<form>`. Failure to do so results in a compile-time error.

The HtmlButton Control

The `HtmlButton` control creates an HTML element of type `<button>...</button>`. This isn't a commonly used element (it isn't supported in some of the older browsers), but is actually quite useful if you are targeting Internet Explorer 4 and above. Unlike the `<input type="button">` element, `HtmlButton` is a container control, so you can place HTML inside the element instead of just text.

This means that you can display an image and text together, for example, and can even use an animated GIF image if you like. All the content is rendered on top of a standard button control background, and it *depresses* just like a normal button. Figure 5-10 shows an example:

Figure 5-10

The following code is used to create this effect:

```
<button id="cmdRemove" accesskey="R" style="font-size:9pt"
        runat="server">
  <img id="imgbtnRemove" src="remove.gif"><br />
  <u>R</u>emove
</button>
```

Note that, to change the content of an `HtmlButton` control, you have to set the `InnerHtml` property or define the content at design-time within the element. There is no specific property for the 'caption', 'text', or 'value'.

In Figure 5-11, you can see one of the few properties available for the `HtmlButton` control in use. In this case, the `Disabled` property is set to `True`, and you can see how the caption is dimmed to indicate that the button is disabled:

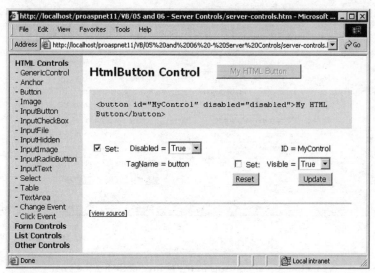

Figure 5-11

The HTML used for creating the server control in the source code for the page is:

```
<button id="MyControl" runat="server">My HTML Button</button>
```

Remember that the `Disabled` property, which adds the `disabled="disabled"` attribute to the element, only has an effect in Internet Explorer and the latest version 6 browsers from Netscape, Opera, and Mozilla. Most older browsers do not recognize this attribute.

The HtmlInputButton Control

The types of button we normally use in our interactive forms are the `<input type="submit">`, `<input type="button">`, and `<input type="reset">` elements. The `HtmlInputButton` control is used to create these three elements. The only button-specific property we can set is the `Value` (the caption). The `Disabled` and `Visible` properties are, of course, inherited from the `HtmlControl` base class.

In Figure 5-12, we have set a variety of values for the three variations of the `HtmlInputButton` control:

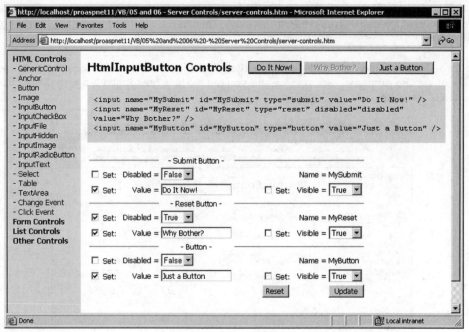

Figure 5-12

The HTML we use to create the server controls in the source code for the page is:

```
<input id="MySubmit" type="submit" runat="server" />
<input id="MyReset" type="reset" runat="server" />
<input id="MyButton" type="button" runat="server"
        Value="My Caption" />
```

The HtmlInputText Control

Probably the most common HTML form control is the textbox, and this is implemented as a server control by the HtmlInputText control. As usual with the HTML controls, the properties map one-to-one with the attributes of the <input type="text"> element that defines a textbox in the browser.

In Figure 5-13, you can see that we have set the MaxLength and Size properties. The HTML used for creating the server control in the source code for the page shown in Figure 5-13 is:

```
<input type="text" id="MyControl" value="My HTML Textbox"
        runat="server" />
```

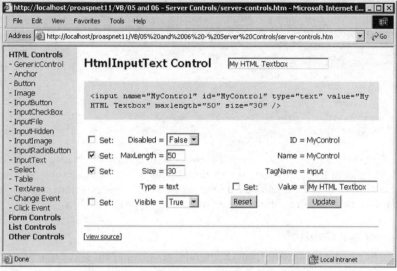

Figure 5-13

The HtmlInputCheckBox and HtmlInputRadioButton Controls

To create a checkbox or a radio button (or 'option button' as it is sometimes called) we use the `HtmlInputCheckBox` and `HtmlInputRadioButton` HTML server controls. The set of properties, and the way they work, are pretty much the same for both controls. In Figure 5-14, we show the `HtmlInputRadioButton` control:

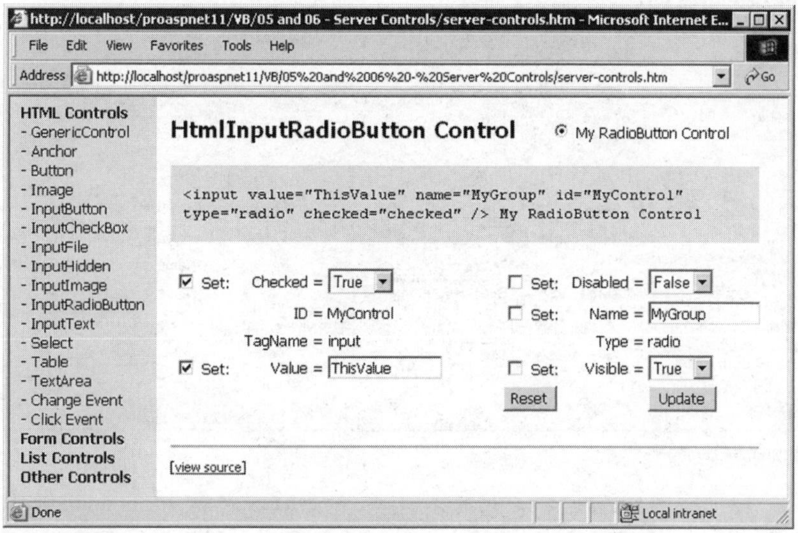

Figure 5-14

The HTML used for creating the controls in the sourcecode for these two pages is:

```
<input type="radio" id="MyControl" name="MyGroup"
       runat="server" />
My RadioButton Control
```

And:

```
<input type="checkbox" id="MyControl" runat="server" />
My Checkbox Control
```

Note that the `HtmlInputRadioButton` control allows you to specify the `Name` property (or attribute) as a value other than that of the `ID` property (or attribute). This is required to be able to create a mutually exclusive 'option' group of radio buttons on a form. The other `HtmlInputxxxx` controls do *not* allow the `Name` property to be set to a value different from that of the `ID` property.

The HtmlInputImage Control

An easy way to display an image that is *clickable* is with an `<input type="image">` element. It acts like a Submit button in that when the button is clicked, the form containing the element is submitted to the server along with the coordinates of the mouse pointer within the image. Our demonstration page, as shown in Figure 5-15, allows you to set all the commonly used properties for this type of control, including the alignment, border width, alternative text, and image source (from a selection we have provided), as well as the value:

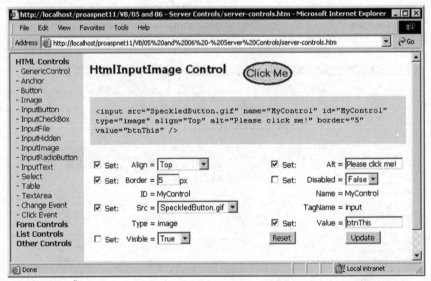

Figure 5-15

The HTML used for creating the server control in the source code for the page is:

```
<input type="image" id="MyControl" src="BookmarkButton.gif"
       runat="server" />
```

The HtmlInputFile Control

If you need to allow users to upload files to your server, you can use the `<input type="file">` element. This is implemented as a server control by `HtmlInputFile`. It has a special property just for this purpose, named `Accept` (the MIME type of the file to upload). The other properties are the same as for a textbox element. In Figure 5-16, you can see the settings we have made. And while the **Browse** button that the control creates allows you to select a file, you can't actually upload files with our demonstration application.

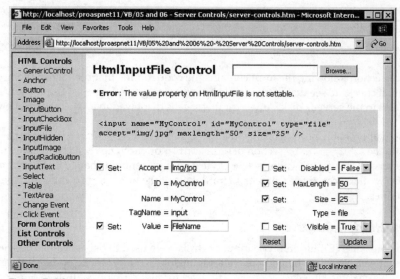

Figure 5-16

One important point to note is demonstrated by the error message you see just below the control in the page. For security reasons, you *cannot* set the `Value` property of the control (the file to download) on the server. The HTML used for creating the server control in the source code for the page is:

```
<input type="file" id="MyControl" runat="server" />
```

The Code to Upload a File

To create a working file upload page, all we need is a form with the correct value for the `enctype` attribute, an `HtmlInputFile` element, and a button to start the process, as shown in the following listing:

```
<form enctype="multipart/form-data" runat="server">
  Select File:
  <input type="file" id="MyFileInput" accept="image/*"
      runat="server" />
  <input type="button" id="SubmitButton" value="Upload"
      runat="server" onserverclick="UploadFile" />
</form>
<div id="outError" runat="server" />
```

```
...
<script language="VB" runat="server">
Sub UploadFile(objSource As Object, objArgs As EventArgs)
  If Not (MyFileInput.PostedFile Is Nothing) Then
    Try
      MyFileInput.PostedFile.SaveAs("c:\temp\uploaded.jpg")
    Catch objError As Exception
      outError.InnerHtml = "Error saving file " _
                           & objError.Message
    End Try
  End If
End Sub
</script>
```

The `<script>` section following the form contains the code routine that runs when the user clicks the Upload button. It checks to see that there is a file by referencing the `PostedFile` property of the control, and if so saves it to the server's disk. Any error message is displayed in a `<div>` control on the page.

Note that you will probably need to change the value of `maxRequestLength` in the `<httpRuntime>` element within the `<system.web>` section of `web.config` or `machine.config` to allow files to be posted to the server. The default value is 4096 (bytes), and you should change it to accommodate the largest file you wish to accept. See Chapter 13 for details of the `web.config` and `machine.config` configuration files.

The HtmlInputHidden Control

In the days before ASP.NET, hidden-type input controls were used to persist values between pages. In fact, this is what ASP.NET does behind the scenes to maintain the viewstate of the page, as seen previously in this chapter. However, there are still uses for hidden-type controls in our applications.

For example, we can use hidden-type controls to post values back to a different page on our server, or to store and manipulate values using client-side script within the page and have these values posted back to the server.

Note in Figure 5-17, that the value for the `Visible` property is `True`. Don't be confused by this – the `Visible` property simply defines whether the HTML output generated by the control will actually be included in the output for the page (the HTML that the server returns to the client). It doesn't make the control *visible* or *hidden*.

If you set the `Visible` property to `False`, the control itself will not appear in the output generated for the page (though it still remains within the control tree of the page). You can try this yourself, and you will see that the gray area showing the output from the control is then empty. This feature allows us to dynamically hide and display controls as required.

The HTML used for creating the server control in the source code for the page is:

```
<input type="hidden" id="MyControl" runat="server" />
```

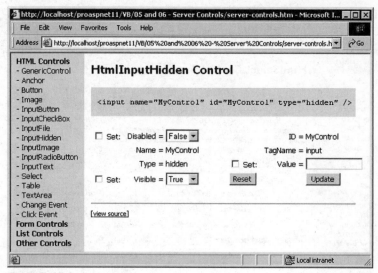

Figure 5-17

The HtmlSelect Control

HTML defines only one way to create list box controls, the HTML `<select>` element. This is implemented as the server control named `HtmlSelect`. Our demonstration page uses data binding to create the list of options for the control, using a pre-populated `HashTable` object as the `DataSource` that is created by the following code:

```
Dim tabValues As New HashTable(5)
tabValues.Add("Microsoft", 49.56)
tabValues.Add("Sun", 28.33)
tabValues.Add("IBM", 55)
tabValues.Add("Compaq", 20.74)
tabValues.Add("Oracle", 41.1)
MyControl.DataSource = tabValues
MyControl.DataBind()
```

You will see more about data binding in Chapter 7. In the meantime, you can experiment with the results here. A `HashTable` is similar to the `Dictionary` object found in ASP 3.0, with each value (in our case, the numbers) being identified by a key (in our case, the company names).

The demonstration page, as shown in Figure 5-18, allows you to set the `DataTextField` and `DataValueField` properties, which specify whether the property value should come from the `Key` or the `Value` in the `HashTable`. To see the effect that this has on the list, try swapping the values over in the page.

The HTML used for creating the server control in the source code for the page is:

```
<select id="MyControl" runat="server" />
```

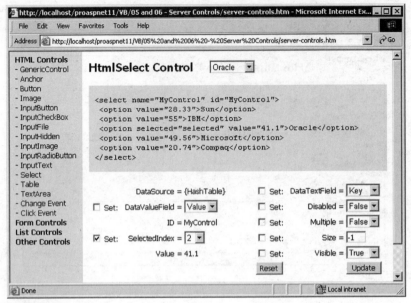

Figure 5-18

The `HashTable` is very useful in this scenario, as it allows the options in the list to use some readable text, while the actual values that are submitted to the server can be different. An example would be the use of part numbers for the values, with the text of each option showing the part name or description.

Creating List Content with ListItem Objects

Instead of populating the list using data binding, we can just use `<option>` elements in the traditional way – as shown in the following listing:

```
<select id="MyControl" runat="server">
 <option value="value1">Option 1 Text</option>
 <option value="value2">Option 2 Text</option>
 <option value="value3">Option 3 Text</option>
</select>
```

Note that we haven't marked the `<option>` elements with `runat="server"`. There is no need, as they will automatically be converted into `ListItem` objects when the page is compiled.

A `ListItem` object is not actually a server control, though it is part of the same namespace as the ASP.NET Web Form controls classes (which we will look at in more detail in the next chapter).

It is enough to know that this object exposes three useful properties, as shown in the following table:

Property	Description
Selected	Sets or returns a Boolean value indicating if this item is selected in the list. Useful for iterating through the list when the control allows multiple selections to be made by clicking while holding down the Shift and Ctrl keys.
Text	Sets or returns the text that is displayed in the list control for this item.
Value	Sets or returns the value that is returned when this item in the list is selected.

To create a multiple-selection list, just change the `Multiple` and `Size` properties in the demonstration page and click **Update**. In our example (see Figure 5-19) even after doing so, you can still only select a single item using the input control for the `SelectedIndex` property, but the demonstration control at the top of the page then works as a multiple-selection list:

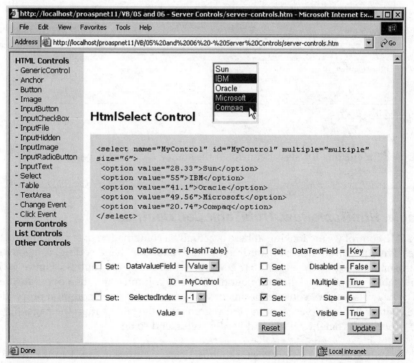

Figure 5-19

We'll see how to use the `ListItem` object in a list control to extract the list of selected items shortly, when we work with the events that the HTML controls raise.

The HtmlTextArea Control

To display a multi-line textbox in a web page, use the `<textarea>` element. This is implemented by the server control named `HtmlTextArea`. It has the specific properties required to set the number of rows and columns in the control, as well as the value. Notice in Figure 5-20 that in this case the value is actually the content rather than an attribute – the text that lies between the opening and closing `<textarea>` tags:

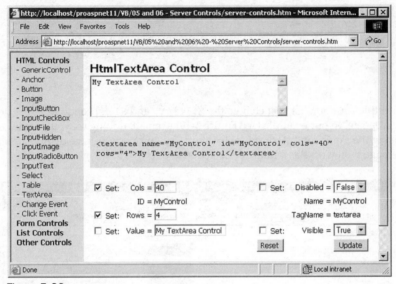

Figure 5-20

The HTML used for creating the server control in the source code for the page is:

```
<textarea id="MyControl" runat="server">My TextArea Control</textarea>
```

The HtmlTable, HtmlTableRow, HtmlTableCell Controls

The final HTML control we are looking at here is actually a combination of several controls. We can create tables dynamically on the server, and save ourselves a lot of hand coding, using an `HtmlTable` server control and the associated `HtmlTableRow` and `HtmlTableCell` controls. Figure 5-21 shows how we can build tables with the specified number of rows and columns, and then populate the cells on demand. The page also allows you to experiment with some of the other common properties of the `HtmlTable` control. For example, changing the alignment of the table within the page, the spacing and padding of the cells, the height, width, and border styles, and so on.

While we have only shown the properties for the `HtmlTable` control in our demonstration page, we can also use very similar sets of properties for the `HtmlTableRow` and `HtmlTableCell` controls. For the `HtmlTableRow` control, the commonly used properties are `Align`, `BgColor`, `Border`, `BorderColor`, `Height`, and `VAlign`. For the `HtmlTableCell` control, they are `Align`, `BgColor`, `Border`, `BorderColor`, `ColSpan`, `Height`, `NoWrap`, `RowSpan`, `VAlign`, and `Width`.

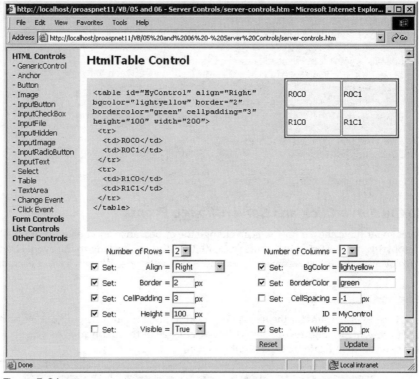

Figure 5-21

The Code to Create a Table

To create a table dynamically using the `HtmlTable`, `HtmlTableRow`, and `HtmlTableCell` server controls, we first add an `HtmlTable` control to the page like this:

```
<table id="MyControl" runat="server" />
```

Then, we have to create each cell in turn and add it to a row, and then add the row to the table. In our demonstration page, we use the code shown here:

```
    'get values for number of rows and columns from drop-down lists
Dim intRows As Integer = selRows.Value
Dim intCols As Integer = selCols.Value
    'declare the local variables we'll need
Dim intRowCount, intColCount As Integer

    'declare variables to hold an HtmlTableRow and HtmlTableCell
Dim objRow As HtmlTableRow
Dim objCell As HtmlTableCell
    'loop for the number of rows required
For intRowCount = 0 To intRows - 1
```

```
       'create a new row control
objRow = New HtmlTableRow()
       'loop for the number of columns required
For intColCount = 0 To intCols - 1
       'create a new table cell control and set the content
 objCell = New HtmlTableCell()
 objCell.InnerHtml = "R" & intRowCount & "C" & intColCount
       'add each cell to the new row
 objRow.Cells.Add(objCell)
Next
       'add the new row to the table
MyControl.Rows.Add(objRow)

Next 'go to the next row
```

Reacting to the ServerClick and ServerChange Events

Our examples so far have shown how we can change the appearance and behavior of the HTML controls by setting properties. However, we also interact with them by responding to the events that they raise. There are two events we can use, `ServerClick` and `ServerChange`. We will look at each one in turn.

Handling the ServerClick Event

The `ServerClick` event occurs for the `HtmlAnchor`, `HtmlButton`, `HtmlInputButton`, and `HtmlInputImage` controls. Figure 5-22 shows the latter three of these controls. As you click a button, a message is displayed to indicate that the event occurred:

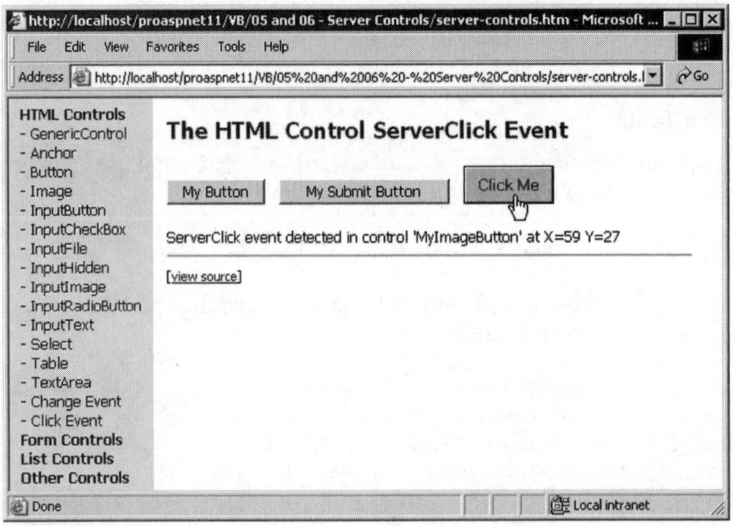

Figure 5-22

As you can see, for the image button, we can also get extra information – the x and y coordinates of the mouse pointer on the image. This could be used to create a server-side image map – code could easily examine the coordinates and take different actions, depending on which area of the image was clicked.

The following listing shows the HTML section of the code used here. It defines a form and the three button controls. Notice that the onserverclick attribute is set to one of two event handlers – MyCode or MyImageCode:

```
<form runat="server">

<input id="MyButton" type="button" value="My Button"
       onserverclick="MyCode" runat="server" />
<input id="MySubmitButton" type="submit"
       value="My Submit Button"
       onserverclick="MyCode" runat="server" />
<input id="MyImageButton" type="image" src="ClickmeButton.gif"
       onserverclick="MyImageCode" runat="server" />

</form>
```

The page also contains a <div> element where the messages about the events are displayed. Notice that we have disabled viewstate for this control so that the message will not be persisted across postbacks:

```
<div id="divResult" runat="server" enableviewstate="false" />
```

Each event handler receives two parameters when the event occurs. The first parameter is a reference to the object that raised the event (one of our button controls) from which we can get the ID of the source of the event.

The second parameter is an Args object that contains more information about the event. In the case of the HtmlInputButton, the second parameter is an EventArgs object, which contains no extra useful information. However, for the HtmlInputImage control, the object is an ImageClickEventArgs object, and this includes the two fields X and Y that contain the coordinates of the mouse pointer when the event was raised. The two event handlers are shown in the code that follows:

```
<script runat="server">
Sub MyCode(objSender As Object, objArgs As EventArgs)
  divResult.InnerHtml &= "ServerClick event detected in " _
    & "control '" & objSender.ID & "'<br />"
End Sub
Sub MyImageCode(objSender As Object, _
               objArgs As ImageClickEventArgs)
  divResult.InnerHtml &= "ServerClick event detected in " _
    & "control '" & objSender.ID & "' at X=" & objArgs.X _
    & " Y=" & objArgs.Y & "<br />"
End Sub
</script>
```

The ServerClick event is reasonably intuitive to use – when a button is clicked, the form is posted back to the server, and the event can be handled in our server-side code. Let's consider the ServerChange event.

Handling the ServerChange Event

The `ServerChange` event occurs for controls that don't automatically submit the form they are on; for example, `HtmlInputText`, `HtmlInputCheckBox`, `HtmlInputRadioButton`, `HtmlInputHidden`, `HtmlTextArea`, and `HtmlSelect`. So, how (and when) can the server-based code react to the event?

This event is raised when the page is submitted by any other control, and occurs for every control where the value has changed since the page was loaded (sent to the client). Figure 5-23 shows this. It contains three different types of controls that expose the `ServerChange` event, and a **Submit** button that simply submits the form to the server:

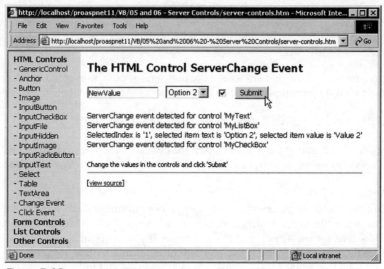

Figure 5-23

You can see that we detected three `ServerChange` events, and they occur in the order that the controls appear in the source of the page. You can also see that we are displaying the values from the option that is selected in the `HtmlSelect` control (the values for the `SelectedIndex` start at zero).

The following listing shows the declarative page syntax (the HTML source) to create the form and the server controls. The `onserverchange` attributes point to two event handlers in our page, named `MyCode` and `MyListCode`. Notice also that, in this case, the **Submit** button is *not* a server control – we haven't included the `runat="server"` attribute in the `<input type="submit">` element. We don't need to access the control on our server - we just want it to submit the form.:

```
<form runat="server">
 <input id="MyText" type="text" value="OriginalValue"
        onserverchange="MyCode" runat="server" />
 <select id="MyListBox" onserverchange="MyListCode"
          runat="server">
  <option value="Value 1">Option 1</option>
  <option value="Value 2">Option 2</option>
  <option value="Value 3">Option 3</option>
 </select>
```

```
  <input id="MyCheckBox" type="checkbox"
         onserverchange="MyCode" runat="server" />
  <input type="submit" value="Submit" />
</form>

<div id="divResult" runat="server" enableviewstate="false" />
```

The `MyCode` event handler is similar to that in the `ServerClick` event example discussed earlier, simply displaying the event name and the `ID` of the control that raised the event:

```
<script runat="server">
Sub MyCode(objSender As Object, objArgs As EventArgs)
  divResult.InnerHtml &= "ServerChange event detected for " _
    & "control '" & objSender.ID & "'<br />"
End Sub
...
```

However, the `MyListCode` event handler needs to extract the selected value from the drop-down list created by the `HtmlSelect` control. You will see how it does this, in the next section.

Getting the Selected Values from HtmlSelect List Controls

You have seen how the server control that creates listboxes or drop-down lists is made up of an `HtmlSelect` control that contains child `ListItem` elements. The `ServerClick` event handler demonstration page you just saw used code similar to the following code, for creating a list control:

```
<select id="MyListBox" runat="server"
        onserverchange="MyListCode">
<option value="Value 1">Option 1</option>
<option value="Value 2">Option 2</option>
<option value="Value 3">Option 3</option>
<option value="Value 4">Option 4</option>
<option value="Value 5">Option 5</option>
</select>
```

The simplest way to get the *value* of the currently selected item is to query the `Value` property of the list control:

```
strValue = MyListBox.Value
```

This may *not* return the expected value. As with the normal HTML `<select>` list, the `Value` of the control returns the content of the `value` attribute for the *currently* selected item, or the *first* item (the item with the lowest index) selected if there is more than one item selected. In case of *no* value attributes in the `<option>` elements, it returns the content of the first selected `<option>` element – in other words, the text displayed in the list.

We have to be more specific to extract both the content of the value attribute *and* the text content itself. To extract the values from the `ListItem` objects for each `<option>` element, we use the `Items` collection of the parent control (the `HtmlSelect` control). The `SelectedIndex` property of the `HtmlSelect` control returns the index of the first item that is selected in the list. So, we can extract the text and value of that item using:

```
strText = MyListBox.Items(MyListBox.SelectedIndex).Text
strValue = MyListBox.Items(MyListBox.SelectedIndex).Value
```

Thus, in the `MyListCode` event handler, we extract the `ID` of the `HtmlSelect` control that raised the event (so we can display it in the page), and then extract the text and value of the selected list item. The following listing shows the complete event handler for doing this:

```
...
Sub MyListCode(objSender As Object, objArgs As EventArgs)
  divResult.InnerHtml &= "ServerChange event detected " _
    & "for control '" _
    & objSender.ID & "'<br />SelectedIndex is '" _
    & objSender.SelectedIndex _
    & "', selected item text is '" _
    & objSender.Items(objSender.SelectedIndex).Text _
    & "', selected item value is '" _
    & objSender.Items(objSender.SelectedIndex).Value
  End Sub
</script>
```

Getting Multiple Selected Values from List Controls

The technique just described is fine if the list control only allows one item to be selected. In terms of the `HtmlSelect` control, when the `Multiple` property is `False`. However, if it is `True`, users can select more than one item in the list by holding the Shift or Ctrl keys while clicking. In this case, the `SelectedIndex` and `SelectedItem` properties only return the *first* item that is selected (the one with the lowest index).

To detect which items are selected in a multi-selection list (none, one, or more), we query the `Selected` property of each `ListItem` object within the list. Probably the easiest way is to use a `For Each...Next` construct. In the following listing, you can see how the event handler creates a `String` variable to hold the result, and a variable of `ListItem` type to hold each item in the list as you iterate through it.

```
Sub MyListCode(objSender As Object, objArgs As EventArgs)
  Dim strResult As String
  strResult = "The following items were selected:<br />"
  Dim objItem As ListItem
  For Each objItem in objSender.Items
    If objItem.Selected Then
      strResult &= objItem.Text & " = " & objItem.Value _
               & "<br />"
    End If
  Next
    divResult.InnerHtml = strResult
End Sub
```

In the `For Each...Next` loop, we reference each member of the `Items` collection for the list control in turn. If it is selected, we add the `Text` and `Value` properties to the results string. After examining all the items in the list, we can display the results string in a `<div>` control. Figure 5-24 shows the result:

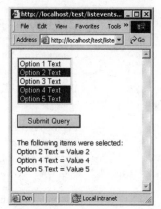

Figure 5-24

The ASP.NET Validation Controls

One of the most tiresome tasks when building interactive web forms is the requirement for validating values that the user enters into input controls. This is particularly so when you need to perform client-side validation and have to validate the values on the server when the page is submitted. For maximum browser compatibility, you should write the client-side code in JavaScript, which is often error-prone unless you are well versed with this language. It is also often a long-winded and repetitive task.Help is at hand with the range of validation controls included in ASP.NET. They cover almost all the common validation scenarios. There is even a custom validation control that you can use to integrate specific non-standard validation requirements into the overall process. The available controls are shown in the following table:

Validation Control	Description
`<asp:RequiredFieldValidator>`	Checks that the validated control contains a value. It cannot be empty. Can be used in conjunction with other validators on a control to trap empty values.
`<asp:RangeValidator>`	Checks that the value in the validated control is within a specified text or numeric range. If the validated control is empty, no validation takes place.
`<asp:CompareValidator>`	Checks that the value in the validated control matches the value in another control or a specific value. The data type and comparison operation can be specified. If the validated control is empty, no validation takes place.

Table continued on following page

201

Validation Control	Description
`<asp:RegularExpressionValidator>`	Checks that the value in the validated control matches a specified regular expression. If the validated control is empty, no validation takes place.
`<asp:CustomValidator>`	Performs user-defined validation on an input control using a specified function (client-side, server-side or both). If the validated control is empty, no validation takes place.
`<asp:ValidationSummary>`	Displays a summary of all current validation errors.

What the Input Validation Controls Do

The principle is that we associate one or more validation controls with each of the input controls we want to validate. When a user submits the page, each validation control checks the value in its associated control to see if it passes the validation test. If any fail the test, the `ValidationSummary` control will display the error messages defined for these validation controls.

The validation controls also automatically detect the browser or client device type, and generate client-side validation code in the page for Internet Explorer 5 and above (in future versions, they may support other browsers as well).

This client-side code uses Dynamic HTML to display the content of the validation control (the text or characters between the opening and closing tags of the validation control) in the page dynamically, as the user tabs from one control to the next. It also prevents the page from being submitted if any of the validation tests fail. This gives a far more responsive interface, much like traditional handcrafted client-side validation code can do. You can see an example of this in the demonstration application we provide, under the subsection Other Controls in the left-hand pane.

The validation controls also help to protect against malicious use of our pages. Client-side validation is great, but users could create their pages (or edit the page delivered to them) so that client-side validation does not take place. In this case, they could possibly 'spoof' our server by submitting invalid values. However, even if the validation controls are performing client-side validation, they always perform the same checks server-side as well when the page is submitted, so we get the best of both worlds automatically.

We can turn off client-side validation if it's not needed, and can also check the result for each validation control individually when the page is submitted. This allows us to create custom error message Strings for each control and (for example) put them into `Label` controls on the page, rather than using the `ValidationSummary` control.

We can also specify that particular submit buttons or controls will not cause validation to occur (as we will see later in this chapter). This allows us to include a Cancel button in a page that allows the user to abandon the page without having to fill in valid values for the controls.

The BaseValidator Class

All of the validation controls inherit from the `BaseValidator` base class, which is part of the `System.Web.UI.WebControls` class library namespace. The `BaseValidator` class exposes a series of properties and methods that are common to all the validation controls.

The most commonly used ones are shown in following table:

Member	Description
`ControlToValidate` property	Sets or returns the name of the input control containing the value to be validated
`EnableClientScript` property	Sets or returns a `Boolean` value indicating whether client-side validation is enabled where the client supports this
`Enabled` property	Sets or returns a `Boolean` value indicating if validation will be carried out
`ErrorMessage` property	Sets or returns the text of the error message that is displayed by the `ValidationSummary` control when validation fails
`IsValid` property	Returns a `Boolean` value indicating if the value in the associated input control passed the validation test
`Validate` method	Performs validation on the associated input control and updates the `IsValid` property

The Specific Validation Control Members

Each validation control also has properties and methods (and in the case of `CustomValidator`, an event) that are specific to that control type.

As shown in the following table, most are self-explanatory. However, we will look at all the validation controls in the next section and see how these properties and the single event are used.

Control	Properties	Events
RequiredFieldValidator	InitialValue	*- none -*
RangeValidator	MaximumValue, MinimumValue, Type	*- none -*
CompareValidator	ControlToCompare, Operator, Type, ValueToCompare	*- none -*
RegularExpression Validator	ValidationExpression	*- none -*
CustomValidator	ClientValidationFunction	OnServerValidate
ValidationSummary	DisplayMode, ShowHeaderText, ShowMessageBox, ShowSummary	*- none -*

Using the Validation Controls

The demonstration application provided includes a page that you can use to experiment with the validation controls (open the Other Controls section of the left-hand menu). The page contains several textboxes where you have to enter specific values in order for validation to be successful.

If you enter invalid values and then click the Submit button, a summary of all the errors is displayed, as shown in Figure 5-25. Notice also that there is an asterisk next to each control where validation failed.

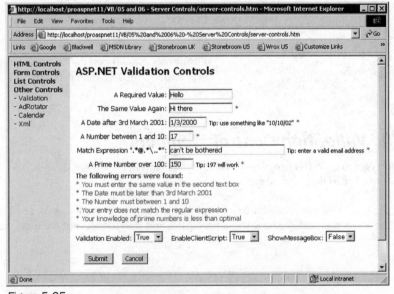

Figure 5-25

Once you enter valid values for all the controls and click Submit, a message is displayed showing that validation at page-level succeeded, as shown in Figure 5-26:

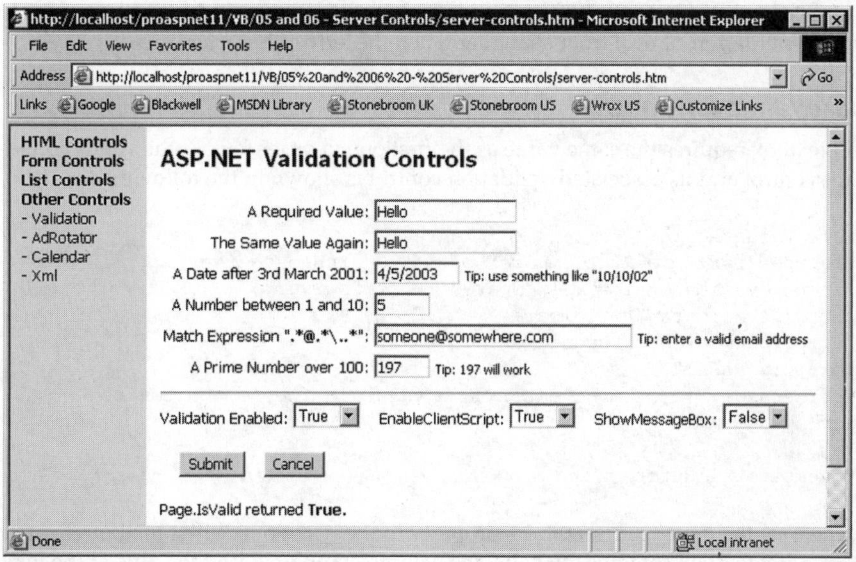

Figure 5-26

We will now examine each of the validation controls used in this demonstration page, and then move on to look at other issues, such as checking if the complete page is valid during postback, *and* enabling and disabling client-side and server-side validation.

The RequiredFieldValidator Control

The first textbox requires a value to be entered before validation can succeed. The source code used for this is as follows:

```
A Required Value:
<input type="text" id="txtRequired" size="20" runat="server" />
<asp:RequiredFieldValidator id="valRequired" runat="server"
   ControlToValidate="txtRequired"
   ErrorMessage="* You must enter a value in the first textbox"
   Display="dynamic">
   *
</asp:RequiredFieldValidator>
```

We have specified the `<input>` control named `txtRequired` as the control to be validated, and an error message that will be displayed by the `ValidationSummary` control if validation fails when the user attempts to submit the page. An asterisk is used as the content of the control in our example, though any content placed within the element will be displayed in the output (at the point where the validation control is actually located in the page) to indicate to the user that the associated control contains an invalid value. We can change the color of this text from the default of red using the `ForeColor` attribute if required.

The `Display` property determines if the text content of the validation control will take up space in the page even when *not* displayed (that is, whether it will be set to hidden but still inserted into the page, or just omitted from the page when not required). This means that we can control the layout of, for example, a table by setting the attribute `Display="static"` to prevent the width of the column containing the validation control from changing when the 'error' characters are displayed.

The CompareValidator Control

The second textbox requires the same value as the first one in order to pass the validation test. The code used for this control and its associated validation control is shown in the following listing:

```
The Same Value Again:
<input type="text" id="txtCompare" size="20" runat="server" />
<asp:CompareValidator id="valCompare" runat="server"
    ControlToValidate="txtCompare"
    ControlToCompare="txtRequired"
    Operator="Equal"
    ErrorMessage="* You must enter same value in the second textbox"
    Display="dynamic">
    *
</asp:CompareValidator>
```

In this case, we set the `ControlToCompare` property to the name of the first textbox (`txtRequired`). The `txtRequired` textbox contains the value we want to compare with the value of the textbox we're validating now (`txtCompare`). We also get to specify the type of comparison (`Equal`, `GreaterThan`, `LessThanOrEqual`, and so forth).

Remember that only the `RequiredFieldValidator` returns an invalid result when a text control on the page is left empty. This is intentional, and you have to associate a `RequiredFieldValidator` *and* any other specific validation controls you require if you don't want the user to be able to submit empty values.

The third textbox in the demonstration page also uses a `CompareValidator` control, but this time we compare the value in this textbox to a fixed value, and using a comparison based on a date instead of the default `String` type (as returned by a textbox control):

```
A Date after 3rd March 2001:
<input type="text" id="txtCompareDate" size="10" runat="server" />
<asp:CompareValidator id="valCompareDate" runat="server"
    ControlToValidate="txtCompareDate"
    ValueToCompare="3/3/2001"
    Operator="GreaterThan"
    Type="Date"
    ErrorMessage="* The Date must be later than 3rd March 2001"
    Display="dynamic">
    *
</asp:CompareValidator>
```

We specify the fixed value in the `ValueToCompare` property, an `Operator` for the comparison, and the `Type` of comparison. This is simply the data type of the fixed value we are comparing to, and can be one of `Currency`, `Double`, `Date`, `Integer`, or `String`.

The RangeValidator Control

The fourth textbox requires a value that is between two specified values. We use the RangeValidator here, and indicate the MaximumValue and MinumumValue in the respective properties. We also specify the Type of comparison to use when validating the content of the associated control:

```
A Number between 1 and 10:
<input type="text" id="txtRange" size="5" runat="server" />
<asp:RangeValidator id="valRange" runat="server"
   ControlToValidate="txtRange"
   MaximumValue="10"
   MinimumValue="1"
   Type="Integer"
   ErrorMessage="* The Number must between 1 and 10"
   Display="dynamic">
   *
</asp:RangeValidator>
```

The RegularExpressionValidator Control

To validate complex text values, we can use a RegularExpressionValidator control. The fifth textbox on our demonstration page uses this control to force the entry of a valid e-mail address. An appropriate regular expression is provided for the ValidationExpression property:

```
Match Expression "<b>.*@.*\..*</b>":
<input type="text" id="txtRegExpr" size="40" runat="server" />
<asp:RegularExpressionValidator id="valRegExpr" runat="server"
   ControlToValidate="txtRegExpr"
   ValidationExpression=".*@.*\..*"
   ErrorMessage="* Your entry does not match the regular expression"
   Display="dynamic">
   *
</asp:RegularExpressionValidator>
```

The CustomValidator Control

When the validation to be performed is too complex for any of the standard validation controls, we can use a CustomValidator control. The final textbox in the page, which in fact has two validation controls associated with it, demonstrates this. We use a CompareValidator *to ensure* that a value greater than 100 has been entered, and a CustomValidator *to validate* the value itself:

```
A Prime Number over 100:
<input type="text" id="txtCustom" size="5" runat="server" />
<asp:CompareValidator id="valComparePrime" runat="server"
   ControlToValidate="txtCustom"
   ValueToCompare="100"
   Operator="GreaterThan"
   Type="Integer"
   ErrorMessage="* The Prime Number must be greater than 100"
   Display="dynamic">
   *
</asp:CompareValidator>
<asp:CustomValidator id="valCustom" runat="server"
```

```
      ControlToValidate="txtCustom"
      ClientValidationFunction="ClientValidate"
      OnServerValidate="ServerValidate"
      ErrorMessage="* Your knowledge of prime numbers is not optimal"
      Display="dynamic">
      *
   </asp:CustomValidator>
```

The CustomValidator control provides two properties named ClientValidationFunction and OnServerValidate, where we specify the names of custom functions created (and included within the page) to validate the value.

Client-Side Validation

The ClientValidationFunction is usually written in JavaScript for maximum compatibility, as it must be included in the page we send to the browser so that the validation can be carried out on the client-side. In the example page, we used the code shown in the following listing:

```
<script language="JavaScript">
<!--
// client-side validation function for CustomValidator
function ClientValidate(objSource, objArgs) {
  var blnValid = true;
  var intNumber = objArgs.Value;
  if (intNumber % 2 == 1) {
    var intDivisor = Math.floor(intNumber / 3);
    if (intDivisor > 2) {
      for (var i = 3; i <= intDivisor; i = i + 2) {
        if (intNumber % intDivisor == 0) {
          blnValid = false;
          break;
        }
      }
    }
    else
      blnValid = false;
  }
  else
    blnValid = false;
  objArgs.IsValid = blnValid;
  return;
}
//-->
</script>
```

Notice how the validation control supplies a reference to itself (objSource) and an object containing the arguments for the function call (objArgs). We get the value of the associated control from the Value field of objArgs, and set the IsValid field of objArgs to indicate whether the custom validation succeeded or not.

Server-Side Validation

For server-side validation, we use the same logic. However, as our page is written in VB.NET, we have to use VB.NET to create the server-side validation function as well (in the current version of ASP.NET there can only be one language server-side per page). In this case, our function receives as parameters a reference to the validation control and a `ServerValidateEventArgs` object that contains the value of the associated control as its `Value` property. The function is shown in the following listing:

```vb
Sub ServerValidate(objSource As Object, objArgs As ServerValidateEventArgs)
  Dim blnValid As Boolean = True
  Try
    Dim intNumber As Integer = objArgs.Value
    'check that it's an odd number
    If intNumber Mod 2 = 1 Then
      'get the largest possible divisor
      Dim intDivisor As Integer = intNumber \ 3
      If intDivisor > 2 Then
        Dim intLoop As Integer
        'check using each divisor in turn
        For intLoop = 3 To intDivisor Step 2
          If intNumber Mod intDivisor = 0 Then
            blnValid = False
            Exit For
          End If
        Next
      Else
        blnValid = False
      End If
    Else
      blnValid = False
    End If
  Catch objError As Exception
    blnValid =False
  Finally
    objArgs.IsValid = blnValid
  End Try
End Sub
```

The ValidationSummary Control

The list of errors that is shown when the page is submitted with any invalid value is created automatically by a `ValidationSummary` control within our demonstration page. In our example, the heading we want is specified in the `HeaderText` property and the `ShowSummary` property is set to `True` so that the value of the `ErrorMessage` property of each of the other validation controls that fail to validate their associated textbox is displayed:

```
<asp:ValidationSummary id="valSummary" runat="server"
  HeaderText="<b>The following errors were found:</b>"
  ShowSummary="True" DisplayMode="List" />
```

The `DisplayMode` allows us to choose the type of output for the error messages. The options are `List`, `BulletList`, and `SingleParagraph`, and we can also use the `ForeColor` property to set the color for the messages. Another useful property is `ShowMessageBox`. Setting it to `True` causes the validation error messages to be displayed in an `Alert` dialog on the client instead of the page, as shown in Figure 5-27. You can try this in the demonstration page by setting the `ShowMessageBox` drop-down list to `True`.

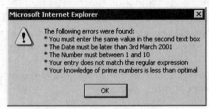

Figure 5-27

Checking If a Page Is Valid

The demonstration page contains two buttons marked **Submit** and **Cancel**. Both are HTML `<input type="submit">` buttons that submit the page to the server for processing. The **Submit** button calls the `ConfirmEntry` server-side routine, which would be used in an application to carry out the process for which you collected the values from the user:

```
<input type="submit" id="cmdConfirm" value="Submit"
       onserverclick="ConfirmEntry" runat="server" />
```

Each validation control, and the `Page` object itself, exposes an `IsValid` property. Our demonstration page displays the value of the `Page.IsValid` property when you click the **Submit** button. Bear in mind that, unless you first disable client-side validation by making use of the `EnableClientScript` drop-down list, you won't be able to submit an invalid page using this button:

```
Sub ConfirmEntry(objSender As Object, objArgs As EventArgs)
   outMessage.InnerHtml = "Page.IsValid returned <b>" _
                          & Page.IsValid & ".</b>"
End Sub
```

If you want to only determine the state of an individual validation control (perhaps to check which ones contain invalid values), you can query the control's `IsValid` property. For example, to get the value for the validation control with the id of `valRegExpr`, you could use:

```
blnValidated = valRegExpr.IsValid
```

Canceling Validation of a Page

The **Cancel** button (for abandoning data entry and closing the page) calls the `CancelEntry` server-side routine. This button also has to submit the page to the server, but if client-side validation is in use (the default on most script-enabled browsers), the user can't submit the page while it contains invalid values. In other words, a traditional `<input type="submit">` button that you might use as a **Cancel** button to abandon the page will still cause validation to occur, and will prevent the page from being submitted.

The solution is to set the `CausesValidation` property for this button to `False`. All button-type controls (`HtmlButton`, `HtmlInputButton`, `HtmlInputImage`, and the equivalents in the ASP Web Form controls that we'll look at in the next chapter) have this property. The default value is `True`, which means that they will cause validation unless we *turn it off*.

So, our Cancel button looks like this:

```
<input type="submit" id="cmdCancel" value="Cancel" runat="server"
       CausesValidation="False" onserverclick="CancelEntry" />
```

The `CancelEntry` event handler that is executed when the button is clicked simply displays a message indicating that validation was not carried out.

The Enabled and EnableClientScript Properties

You can also disable client-side, server-side, or both types of validation in your server-side code by changing the value of the `Enabled` and `EnableClientScript` properties of the appropriate validation control(s). This allows you, for example, to force the browser to use only server-side validation even if it supports dynamic client-side validation. The following code -listing, taken from the demonstration page, shows how you can iterate through the collection of validation controls and set these properties:

```
Sub Page_Load()
  Dim objValidator As BaseValidator
  For Each objValidator In Page.Validators
    objValidator.Enabled = lstEnabled.SelectedItem.Text
    objValidator.EnableClientScript = lstClientScript.SelectedItem.Text
  Next
End Sub
```

In our example, this code is executed each time the page loads, and the property settings are controlled by two drop-down lists near the bottom of the page, labeled Validation Enabled and Enable Client Script.

Summary

In this chapter, we have explored the concept of server controls in general, and concentrated on the set of HTML server controls and the validation controls that are provided with ASP.NET. Server controls are at the heart of ASP.NET development techniques, providing us with a programming model that is event-driven, and which is much closer to the way that we build traditional executable applications using environments like Visual Basic, C++, and other languages.

In conjunction with other features in ASP.NET and the .NET Framework as a whole (such as the postback architecture and the comprehensive class library), building powerful, intuitive, and attractive Web-based applications just got a lot easier.

In fact, we can summarize the advantages of using server controls. They automatically provide:

❑   HTML output that creates the elements to implement the control in the browser

❑   An object within the page that we can program against on the server

❑   Automatic maintenance of the control's value (or state)

❑   Simple access to the control values without having to dig into the Request object

❑   The ability to react to events, and so create better structured pages

- ❑ A common approach to building user interfaces as web pages
- ❑ The ability to more easily address different types of client device

In the next chapter, we look at another set of server controls that are provided with ASP.NET. These are the useful and powerful Web Form controls.

ASP.NET Web Form Controls

The previous chapter discussed the range of HTML server controls and validation controls that are part of ASP.NET. You saw how they are part of the fundamental foundations on which ASP.NET is built. These controls cause ASP.NET pages to output HTML that implements the control elements in the browser (for example, an `<input>` or `<select>` element). However, the server controls are also objects compiled within the page on the server, and so you can interact with them while dynamically building the page.

Moreover, the basic concept of using server controls allows the change to a more structured *event-driven-programming model*. This provides a cleaner programming environment that is easier to work in and debug when things go wrong.

However, the server controls you saw in the previous chapter (with the exception of the validation controls) are really nothing more than server-side equivalents of the normal HTML elements that implement controls for use on a `<form>`. They still provide a valid model for building interactive forms, but this can be bettered.

This chapter looks at:

❑ The ASP.NET Web Form controls in general

❑ The basic Web Form input and navigation server controls

❑ The Web Form server controls used for building lists

❑ The 'rich' Web Form controls that provide complex compound interface elements

We start with the basic Web Form input and navigation controls.

The Basic ASP.NET Web Form Controls

Apart from creating HTML elements using the HTML server controls, you can also use a set of controls that are part of ASP.NET, called the *Web Form controls* (or just *Web Controls*, after the namespace where they reside). These are all defined within the `System.Web.UI.WebControls` namespace. The basic controls that you can use and the equivalent HTML output that they generate are shown in the following table (the various types of list control will be covered in *The ASP.NET List Controls* section in this chapter):

ASP.NET Web Form control	Creates HTML element(s)
`<ASP:HyperLink>`	`<a>...</a>`
`<ASP:LinkButton>`	`<a><img/></a>`
`<ASP:Image>`	`<img/>`
`<ASP:Panel>`	`<div>...</div>`
`<ASP:Label>`	`<span>...</span>`
`<ASP:Button>`	`<input type="submit"/>` or `<input type="button"/>`
`<ASP:TextBox>`	`<input type="text"/>` or `<input type="password"/>` or `<textarea>...</textarea>`
`<ASP:CheckBox>`	`<input type="checkbox"/>`
`<ASP:RadioButton>`	`<input type="radio"/>`
`<ASP:ImageButton>`	`<input type="image"/>`
`<ASP:Table>`	`<table>...</table>`
`<ASP:TableRow>`	`<tr>...</tr>`
`<ASP:TableCell>`	`<td>...</td>`

Why Have Another Set of Controls?

It may seem odd to have a second set of server controls that apparently duplicate the existing HTML controls. In fact, there are a couple of good reasons for this. The ASP.NET Web Form controls are designed primarily to:

❑ Make it easier for manufacturers and developers to build tools or applications those automatically generate the UI.

❑ Simplify the process of creating interactive Web Forms, requiring less knowledge of the way that HTML controls work and making the task of using them less error-prone.

Both these requirements are met by providing a consistent and structured interface for the controls. Unlike HTML controls, all Web Form controls use the same property name for a specific *value* for the control. Contrast this with the HTML controls, where the `size` property (attribute) of a control might be the number of rows visible in a list box or the number of characters wide for a textbox. Meanwhile the number of characters wide for a `<textarea>` element is actually the `cols` property.

In the Web Form controls, the same property name is used across the controls. The property names are also more intuitive, for example the `ASP:TextBox` control has properties named `TextMode`, `Rows`, and `Columns`. By setting these in different combinations, the control will generate the appropriately sized `<input>` element or `<textarea>` element. You don't have to know the actual HTML output required; just set the control's properties of the control. It can even create a password-type `<input>` element if you set the appropriate value for the `TextMode`.

On top of this, the controls add extra features that are not usually available in the basic HTML controls. You can specify *automatic postback* of a form when a value in a control is changed. Several controls also create more than one HTML element; for example, they automatically add a text label to a checkbox or radio button.

The WebControl Base Class

Like the HTML controls, most Web Form controls inherit their members (properties, method, and events) from a base class. In this case, it is `WebControl`, defined within the `System.Web.UI.WebControls` namespace. This class provides a wide range of members, many of which are only really useful if you are building your own controls that inherit from `WebControl`. The public members used most often are shown in the following table:

Member	Description
`Attributes` property	Returns a collection of all the attribute name/value pairs within the `.aspx` file for this control. Can be used to read and set non-standard attributes (custom attributes that are not actually part of HTML) or to access attributes where the control does not provide a specific property for that purpose.
`AccessKey` property	Sets or returns the keyboard shortcut key that moves the input focus to the control.
`BackColor` property	Sets or returns the background color of the control.
`BorderColor` property	Sets or returns the border color of the control.
`BorderStyle` property	Sets or returns the style of border for the control, in other words, solid, dotted, double, and so on.
`BorderWidth` property	Sets or returns the width of the control border.
`ClientID` property	Returns the control identifier that is generated by ASP.NET.

Table continued on the following page

Member	Description
Controls property	Returns a ControlCollection object containing references to all the child controls for this control within the page hierarchy.
Enabled property	Sets or returns a Boolean value indicating whether the control is enabled.
EnableViewState property	Sets or returns a Boolean value indicating if the control should maintain its viewstate and the viewstate of any child controls when the current page request ends.
Font property	Returns information about the font used in the control.
ForeColor property	Sets or returns the foreground color used in the control, usually the color of the text.
Height property	Sets or returns the overall height of the control.
ID property	Sets or returns the identifier specified for the control.
Page property	Returns a reference to the Page object containing the control.
Parent property	Returns a reference to the parent of this control within the page hierarchy.
Style property	References a collection of all the CSS style properties (selectors) that apply to the control.
TabIndex property	Sets or returns the position of the control within the tab order of the page.
ToolTip property	Sets or returns the pop-up text displayed when the mouse pointer is over the control.
Visible property	Sets or returns a Boolean value indicating whether the control should be rendered in the page output.
Width property	Sets or returns the overall width of the control.
DataBind() method	Causes data binding to occur for the control and all its child controls.
FindControl() method	Searches within the current container for a specified server control.
HasControls() method	Returns a Boolean value indicating whether the control contains any child controls.
DataBinding() event	Occurs when the control is being bound to a data source.

The Specific Web Form Control Classes

Each of the Web Form controls inherits from WebControl (or from another control that itself inherits from WebControl), and adds its own task-specific properties, methods, and events. Those commonly used (for each control) are listed in the following table:

Control	Properties	Events
HyperLink	ImageUrl, NavigateUrl, Target, Text	- *none* -
LinkButton	CommandArgument, CommandName, Text, CausesValidation	OnClick(), OnCommand()
Image	AlternateText, ImageAlign, ImageUrl	- *none* -
Panel	BackImageUrl, HorizontalAlign, Wrap	- *none* -
Label	Text	- *none* -
Button	CommandArgument, CommandName, Text, CausesValidation	OnClick(), OnCommand()
TextBox	AutoPostBack, Columns, MaxLength, ReadOnly, Rows, Text, TextMode, Wrap	OnTextChanged()
CheckBox	AutoPostBack, Checked, Text, TextAlign	OnCheckedChanged()
RadioButton	AutoPostBack, Checked, GroupName, Text, TextAlign	OnCheckedChanged()
ImageButton	CommandArgument, CommandName, CausesValidation	OnClick(), OnCommand()
Table	BackImageUrl, CellPadding, CellSpacing, GridLines, HorizontalAlign, Rows	- *none* -
TableRow	Cells, HorizontalAlign, VerticalAlign	- *none* -
TableCell	ColumnSpan, HorizontalAlign, RowSpan, Text, VerticalAlign, Wrap	- *none* -
Literal	Text	- *none* -
PlaceHolder	- *none* -	- *none* -

It should be obvious from the names what most of the properties are for, but we will examine each control in the following sections, and indicate some of the things to look out for when you use them. The sample application (already seen in Chapter 5) shown in Figure 6-1 contains pages for most of the ASP.NET Web Form controls, and we will use these pages to demonstrate the properties of each control:

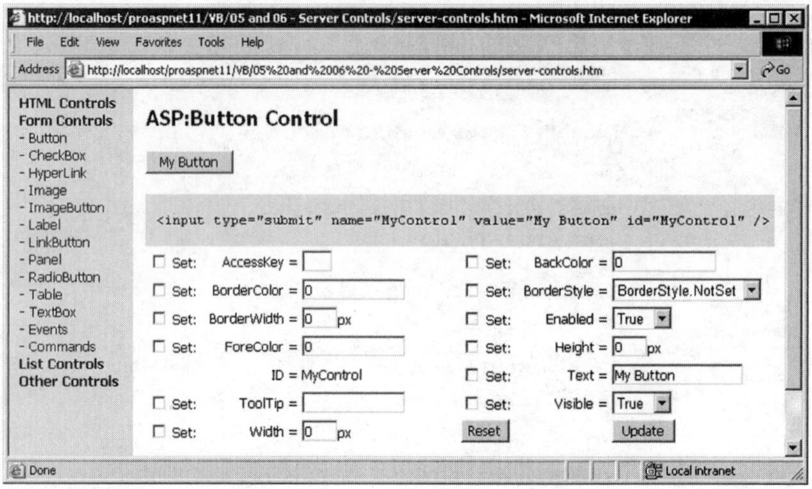

Figure 6-1

You can get the sample files for this chapter from http://www.daveandal.net/books//. The application is in the `server-controls` *folder. You can also run many of the examples online at the same URL.*

Using the Web Form Controls

To add an ASP.NET Web Form server control to your page, define it just like an ordinary HTML element; by adding the appropriate 'attributes' for the properties you want to set. For example, you can add an `ASP:TextBox` control to the page to output an HTML textbox element using:

```
<ASP:TextBox id="MyTextBox" BackColor="Red" Text="Enter a value..."
             runat="server" />
```

Notice that the Web Form controls all have the `ASP` namespace prefix (uppercase or lowercase, it doesn't matter which) to denote that they are from the `System.Web.UI.WebControls` namespace.

Setting Property Values from Enumerations

One thing that makes working with the HTML server controls used in the previous chapter easy is that all the properties are simple `String` values. For example, specify the string value `right` for the `Align` property of an `HtmlImage` control to align the image to the right of any following page content.

It is not always so straightforward with the ASP.NET Web Form controls. Many of the properties for the ASP.NET Web Form controls use values from an enumeration, or a reference to an object. For example, to align an image to the right of any following content when using an ASP.NET `Image` server control, set the `ImageAlign` property to the integer value that is defined for the enumeration member `ImageAlign.Right`.

In this example, the enumeration is named `ImageAlign`, and the member is named `Right`. Of course, this isn't a problem when you explicitly define the properties declaratively (in other words, by setting the *attributes* of a server control in the source of the page). The control knows from the property name which enumeration to use:

```
<ASP:Image Src="mypic.gif" ImageAlign="Right" runat="server" />
```

This produces the following HTML output (notice that in the `Image` control, `border="0"` is the default):

```
<img src="mypic.gif" align="Right" border="0" />
```

However, to assign a value to the property within the executable code of the page, you have to use the following:

```
objMyImage.ImageAlign = ImageAlign.Right
```

Even this is no good if you want to assign property values dynamically at runtime.

Creating Enumeration Values Dynamically

To assign property values dynamically at runtime (such as when they are selected from a list, as in our demonstration pages), you have to use the *numeric value* of the appropriate enumeration member. In the case of `ImageAlign.Right`, this value is 2.

If you use a `<select>` list control for the values, you can set the `Text` of each `<option>` to the name in the enumeration, and set the `Value` to the integer that this equates to. The following code shows a `<select>` list containing the complete `ImageAlign` enumeration:

```
<select id="selAlign" runat="server">
  <option value="0">ImageAlign.NotSet</option>
  <option value="1">ImageAlign.Left</option>
  <option value="2">ImageAlign.Right</option>
  <option value="3">ImageAlign.Baseline</option>
  <option value="4">ImageAlign.Top</option>
  <option value="5">ImageAlign.Middle</option>
  <option value="6">ImageAlign.Bottom</option>
  <option value="7">ImageAlign.AbsBottom</option>
  <option value="8">ImageAlign.AbsMiddle</option>
  <option value="9">ImageAlign.TextTop</option>
</select>
```

Then, to set the `ImageAlign` property, just assign the value from the list directly to it:

```
objMyImage.ImageAlign = selAlign.Value
```

Or you can be more specific and use the `SelectedIndex` property of the list:

```
objMyImage.ImageAlign = selAlign.Items(selAlign.SelectedIndex).Value
```

Finding Enumeration Values

Of course, the next obvious question would be, "how do I go about finding out the values to use for an enumeration?" In fact there are a few options here. Most enumerations provide a type converter that can be used to get the value given the enumeration member as a string. In Visual Basic, you can use:

```
TypeDescriptor.GetConverter(GetType(enumeration)).ConvertFromString("member")
```

To be able to create a `TypeDescriptor` object and use its methods in your code, import the `System.ComponentModel` namespace that contains the definition of the `TypeDescriptor` class:

```
<%@Import Namespace="System.ComponentModel" %>
```

For example, to get the value of `HorizontalAlign.Left`, you can use:

```
TypeDescriptor.GetConverter(GetType(HorizontalAlign)).ConvertFromString("Left"
)
```

Alternatively, for enumerations that don't provide a type converter, you can usually cast the enumeration member directly to an `Integer` variable:

```
Dim intValue = CType(HorizontalAlign.Left, Integer)
```

Another technique is to use the excellent *WinCV utility* that is included with the frameworks. Simply type in all or part of the name of the enumeration, select it in the left-hand pane and the values are displayed in the right-hand pane (see Figure 6-2). You can even click on the **Option** button in the top right-hand side of the window to copy them to the clipboard to paste into your code (but note that the values are *hexadecimal*):

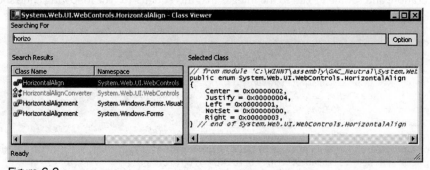

Figure 6-2

WinCV is installed in the `Program Files\Microsoft Visual Studio.NET\FrameworkSDK\Bin` folder if you have VS.NET, or the `Program Files\Microsoft.NET\SDK\[version]\FrameworkSDK\Bin` folder if you just installed the .NET Framework.

Setting Properties That Are Objects

The second area where working with the ASP Web Form controls can be a little tricky is when you want to set (or retrieve) property values that are actually references to other objects. A typical example of something that should be simple but actually isn't when you first try it is setting the value of a 'color' property. It's not that Microsoft's developers were trying to make life awkward—it's done on purpose to provide extra features within the controls and the framework as a whole. It also allows strong typechecking to be achieved by the compiler and better support in a designer tool such as Visual Studio, which would not be possible if they were string values.

As an example, the ASP Web Form controls have several properties (BackColor, ForeColor, BorderColor) that reference a Color object rather than a simple string value. When you explicitly define the colors for the controls in your source code, use the color names directly:

```
<asp:textbox id="MyText" Text="This is a textbox" runat="server"
            BackColor="Red" ForeColor="White" />
```

However, to assign colors at runtime, you have to first create a Color object and then assign this object to the appropriate property. For this, use the shared properties and methods that the Color class exposes.

The System.Drawing.Color Class

The Color class defines shared properties for all of the standard HTML color names, such as AliceBlue, AntiqueWhite, and so on. It also exposes three shared methods that create a Color object, as shown in the following table:

Method	Description
FromArgb	Creates a Color object from its 32-bit component values that define the alpha, red, green, and blue elements.
FromKnownColor	Creates a Color object from a specified HTML standard 'known color' name; for example, AliceBlue or Gainsboro.
FromName	Creates a Color object using the specified name, which can be a 'known color' name, a 32-bit value or a hexadecimal HTML-style color value such as #ff0000 (red).

Each Color object also has properties that return the individual components of the current color. For example, the properties A, B, G, and R return the alpha, blue, green, and red components respectively. To get the name of the color if it is one of the 'known colors', query the Name property of the Color object.

To be able to create a Color object and use its shared properties and methods in your code, import the System.Drawing namespace, which contains the definition of the Color class:

```
<%@Import Namespace="System.Drawing" %>
```

In our demonstration pages, there are textboxes where you can enter the colors you want for various properties of the control. For example, to set the BackColor property of a control, call the FromName()

method (passing it the value that was entered), and then assign the object that this method creates to the `BackColor` property of the control:

```
MyControl.BackColor = Color.FromName(txtBackColor.Value)
```

To retrieve the color from the `BackColor` property, extract the `Name` of the `Color` object that the property references:

```
txtForeColor.Value = MyControl.ForeColor.Name
```

The System.Web.UI.WebControls.Unit Class

Several properties of the ASP Web Form controls are references to a `Unit` object; for example, the `Width` and `Height` of an `Image` control and the `BorderWidth` of a `Table` control. As with the `Color` properties, you don't have to concern yourself with this when explicitly defining the values in your sourcecode:

```
<asp:image id="MyImage" Src="mypic.gif" runat="server"
           Height="100px" Width="50%" />
```

However, to assign values at runtime, you have to use the properties and methods exposed by the `Unit` object. The class that defines the `Unit` object is part of the same namespace as the ASP.NET Web Form controls, and so it is imported by default into your ASP pages. It exposes the two properties shown in the following table:

Property	Description
Type	The type of unit that the value is measured in. Member of the `UnitType` enumeration (`Cm`, `Mm`, `Em`, `Ex`, `Inch`, `Percentage`, `Pica`, `Pixel`, or `Point`).
Value	The number of units (as defined in the `Type` property) that make up the value.

The `Unit` class also provides three shared methods that you can use to create a `Unit` object with a specific `Type` property value. These are shown in the following table:

Method	Description
Percentage()	Creates a `Percentage` type `Unit` object using specified 32-bit signed integer.
Pixel()	Creates a `Pixel` type `Unit` object using specified 32-bit signed integer.
Point()	Creates a `Point` type `Unit` object using specified 32-bit signed integer.

So, if you have an `Integer` variable named `intTheHeight` that contains the value in pixels to be set for the `Height` property of a control named `MyControl`, use:

```
MyControl.Height = Unit.Pixel(intTheHeight)
```

If the value comes from a textbox with the `id` of `txtHeight`, use:

```
MyControl.Height = Unit.Pixel(txtHeight.Value)
```

To set the value as a percentage (say you wanted the control to be 50 percent of the width of the page or its container), use:

```
MyControl.Height = Unit.Percentage(50)
```

To retrieve the value of the `Height` property from the control, query the `Unit` object's `Value` property. The following code returns `100` for the `Image` control used earlier in this section:

```
txtHeight.Value = MyControl.Height.Value
```

If you want to know the type of unit, query the `Type` property of the `Unit` object, but this returns the integer equivalent of the `UnitType` enumeration. For a unit in pixels, for example, this property returns `1`. However (in a way similar to the example with the `HorizontalAlign` enumeration), you can use a type converter to get the text name. This time, use the `ConvertToString()` method rather than the `ConvertFromString()` method:

```
TypeDescriptor.GetConverter(GetType(UnitType)).ConvertToString _
                                        (MyControl.Height.Type)
```

Finally, the easiest way to get the complete value in human-readable form (including the unit type) is to use the `ToString()` method. For the same control, the following code returns `100px`:

```
txtHeight.Value = MyControl.Height.Value.ToString()
```

Using the AutoPostBack Feature

Certain Web Form server controls in ASP.NET (`TextBox`, `CheckBox`, and `RadioButton`), and all the list controls provide a property named `AutoPostBack`. By default, this property is `False`. If you set it to `True` for a control, that control will automatically post its value, and the values of the rest of the controls on the same form, back to the server when the user selects a value.

This also raises an event on the server that you can handle and use to update the contents of the page. You can experiment with `AutoPostBack` in the samples provided; handling the events on the server is discussed later in the chapter.

The mechanism to implement automatic postback is simple. It uses exactly the same techniques as when you program it in a `<form>` page. When the `AutoPostBack` property is `True`, the server control adds a client-side event to the control–for a button-type control, it is the `onclick` event, and for textboxes and list controls, it is the `onchange` event:

```
<input id="MyControl" type="checkbox" name="MyControl"
       onclick="javascript:__doPostBack('MyControl','')" />
```

This causes a client-side function named __doPostBack to run when the control is clicked, when the selection is changed in a list, or when the user edits the content of a textbox and moves to another control. The ID of the control is passed to this function as well.

At the same time, the <form> on which the control resides has two extra hidden-type <input> controls added to it. These are used to pass back to the server the ID of the control that was clicked or changed, and any value for the second parameter that the __doPostBack() function receives:

```
<input type="hidden" name="__EVENTTARGET" value="" />
<input type="hidden" name="__EVENTARGUMENT" value="" />
```

And, of course, the client-side __doPostBack() function is added to the page as well. It just collects the control name and any arguments, puts them into the hidden controls, and submits the form to the server:

```
<script language="javascript">

<!--
    function __doPostBack(eventTarget, eventArgument) {
    var theform;

    if (window.navigator.appName.toLowerCase().indexOf("netscape") > -1) {
      theform = document.forms["_ctl0"];
    }

    else {
      theform = document._ctl0;
    }
    theform.__EVENTTARGET.value = eventTarget.split("$").join(":");
    theform.__EVENTARGUMENT.value = eventArgument;
    theform.submit();
}

// -->
</script>
```

Microsoft issues a hot fix to solve some issues with the doPostBack code in v1.1. If you find that Netscape browsers do not work correctly with your pages, you may need to install this hotfix. More details are available from http://support.microsoft.com/default.aspx?scid=kb;en-us;818803

Examples of the ASP Web Form Controls

This section briefly looks at each of the basic ASP.NET Web Form controls to give you a flavor for what they do and how they can be used. We will bring out any particularly important points about each control as we go.

The ASP:CheckBox and ASP:RadioButton Controls

These controls create individual checkboxes and radio buttons (later you'll see two controls that can create lists of checkboxes or radio buttons automatically). One extremely useful feature of the `CheckBox` and `RadioButton` controls is that they automatically create a label for the control using the value of the `Text` property. You can place this label to the left or right of the control using the `TextAlign` property, as shown in Figure 6-3:

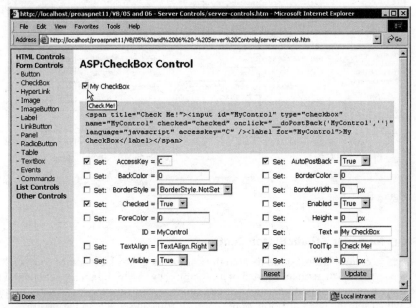

Figure 6-3

The sourcecode used for creating the server control in this page is:

```
<ASP:CheckBox id="MyControl" Text="My CheckBox" runat="server" />
```

You can also use this page to experiment with the effects of the `AutoPostBack` property discussed earlier. Also notice the `AccessKey` and `ToolTip` that make it seem like a real Visual Basic style control. These are, of course, client-side features (`ToolTip` sets the `title` attribute of the element), but they are part of the HTML 4.0 standards.

Adding Styles to Web Form Controls

The formatting features that apply to all the ASP Web Form controls are demonstrated in the screenshot of the `CheckBox` control in Figure 6-4. You can see how they add a set of CSS-style properties (or selectors) to the element:

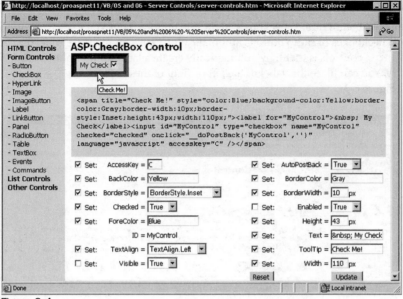

Figure 6-4

Setting the Group Name for a RadioButton Control

The RadioButton control is almost identical to the CheckBox control, except (of course) that it creates an <input type="radio"> element instead of an <input type="checkbox"> element. However, there is one more fundamental difference. The RadioButton control exposes an extra property called GroupName, which sets the name attribute of the control. You can see this in Figure 6-5:

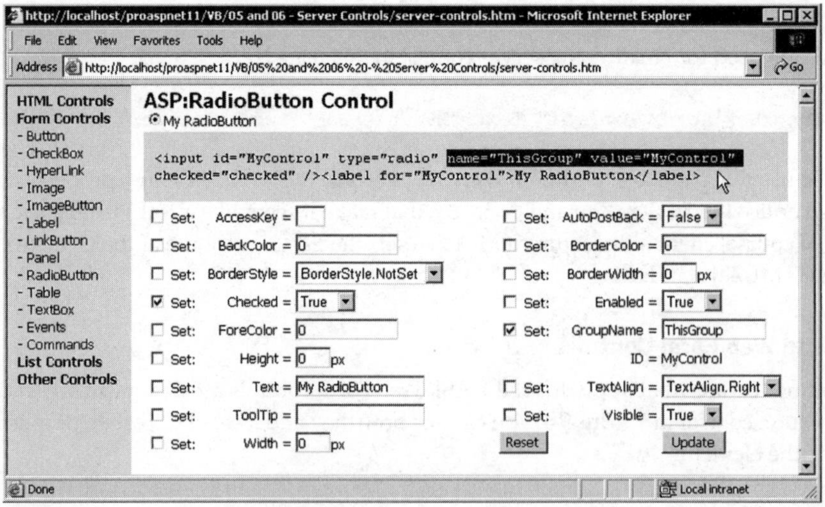

Figure 6-5

The sourcecode used for creating the server control in this page is:

```
<ASP:RadioButton id="MyControl" Text="My RadioButton" runat="server" />
```

This feature is required for two reasons. One is the obvious reason that you must use the same `name` attribute for all radio buttons that you want to be part of the same mutually exclusive group. The second reason is that all the controls on a page must have a unique `ID` property, and this is automatically used as the `name` attribute as well (as you can see if you refer back to the screenshot of the `CheckBox` control). Unlike the HTML radio button control there is no `Name` property for the ASP.NET Web Form `RadioButton` control, so the `GroupName` is the only way to set the `name` attribute.

The ASP:HyperLink Control

This control provides an easy way to create hyperlink `<a>` elements. In addition to the usual formatting, `AccessKey`, and `ToolTip` properties, it provides specific properties for the `NavigateUrl` (which sets the `href` attribute) and the `Target` property (which sets the `target` attribute). One other great feature is that you can set the text that appears as the hyperlink (the content of the resulting `<a>` element) using the `Text` property, as shown in Figure 6-6:

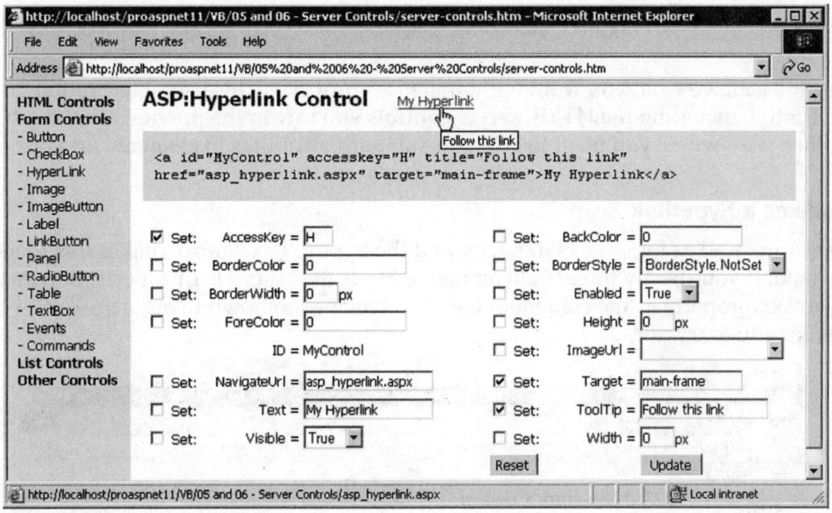

Figure 6-6

The sourcecode used for creating the server control in this page is:

```
<ASP:Hyperlink id="MyControl" Text="My Hyperlink"
               NavigateUrl="asp_hyperlink.aspx" runat="server" />
```

Notice that once again there is no `Name` property. This seems to indicate that the control can't be used to create an *anchor* in a page that another hyperlink can target. An HTML anchor element requires the `name` attribute to be set:

```
<a name="para1">Paragraph One</a>
```

The location is targeted in the page using an HTML element such as:

```
<a href="thepage.aspx#para1">Go To Paragraph One</a>
```

However, you can add a `name` attribute to a `Hyperlink` control either declaratively or programmatically. It can be declaratively done by specifying it within the element in the source of the page:

```
<ASP:Hyperlink Name="para1" id="MyAnchor" Text="text-for-link"
               NavigateUrl="url-to-go-to" runat="server" />
```

Using the Attributes Property with Server Controls

One other solution at runtime is to use the `Attributes` property to add the attribute programmatically. This property gives you access to a collection of all the HTML attributes on a server control. So, you can access the `name` attribute using:

```
strNameAttr = MyAnchor.Attributes("name")
```

And can set or change the `name` attribute using:

```
MyAnchor.Attributes("name") = strNewName
```

So, you can still achieve what you want without a `Name` property. This useful technique can be applied to any server control, including the HTML server controls you saw in the previous chapter. It may be useful in other cases where you want to add non-standard attributes to elements for your own purposes.

Using an Image as a Hyperlink

Often, images are used as hyperlinks in pages, and the `Hyperlink` control makes this much easier than coding by hand. If you specify the path to an image file as the `ImageUrl` property, that image is used in place of the `Text` property as the content of the `<a>` element, as shown in Figure 6-7. We've provided a few images for you to try out.

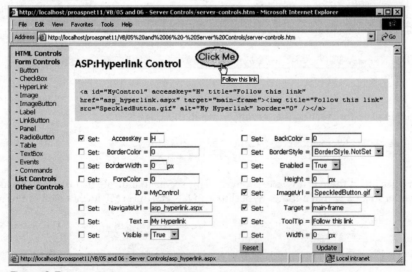

Figure 6-7

The ASP:LinkButton Control

The LinkButton control demonstrates an interesting extension to the use of an HTML <a> element. By default it uses the AutoPostBack feature described earlier, specifying the client-side __doPostBack JavaScript function as the href attribute of an <a> element. This means that whenever the link is clicked, the form will be posted back to the server, where a Click event will be raised. You can see the JavaScript function in the status bar in Figure 6-8:

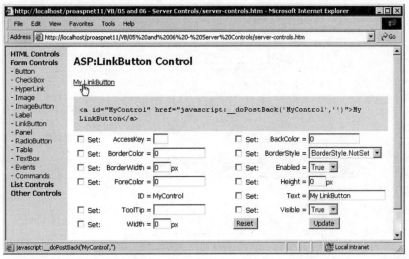

Figure 6-8

The sourcecode used for creating the server control in this page is:

```
<ASP:LinkButton id="MyControl" Text="My LinkButton" runat="server" />
```

The clickable text is specified using the Text property in the same way as with a Hyperlink control, but in this control there is no option to use an image instead of text. For that, use an ImageButton control (described shortly) instead.

The ASP:Image Control

To display an image in your page and be able to access the control in your server-side code, you can use the ASP.NET Image server control. There are properties available that specify all the usual attributes for an <img> element, including the size, an AccessKey, the ToolTip, the alignment in relation to surrounding content, the border style, and the border and background colors, as shown in Figure 6-9:

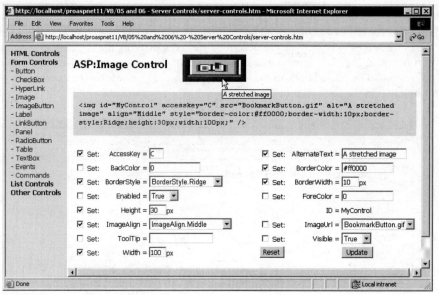

Figure 6-9

The sourcecode for creating the server control in this page is:

```
<ASP:Image id="MyControl" ImageUrl="BookmarkButton.gif" runat="server" />
```

We have provided a few images for you to experiment with. Notice how you can specify the values for the `Color` properties (`BorderColor` in the screenshot) using a standard HTML-style hexadecimal color value.

The ASP:Panel Control

While it might sound like an exotic new feature to use in your pages, the `Panel` control is actually just a way of creating a formatted HTML `<div>` element. You can specify the size and style of the element, and add a background image (though you should realize that as with all the server controls, some browsers may not support all the style properties you apply). Figure 6-10 shows the results:

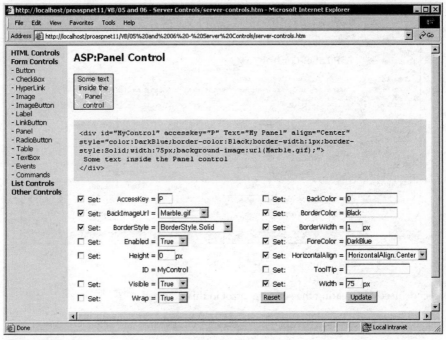

Figure 6-10

The sourcecode used for creating the server control in this page is:

```
<ASP:Panel id="MyControl" Text="My Panel" runat="server">
Some text inside the Panel control</ASP:Panel>
```

A useful feature is the ability to set the width of the control, and then turn text wrapping on and off using the `Wrap` property. Remember that you can also add extra style properties to any server control using the `Style` collection:

```
MyControl.Style("selector-name") = "value"
```

You could specify that the `<div>` should be absolutely positioned on the page, add scroll bars to it, change the font, and so on, just by adding the appropriate CSS selector values.

The ASP:Label Control

The `Panel` control you just saw creates an HTML `<div>` element, and this is not always ideal. For example, it automatically wraps to the next line and causes other content to be wrapped below it. To place content inline with other elements and text, you need an HTML `<span>` element instead. This is just what the ASP.NET `Label` control provides. This control has the usual set of properties that define the appearance: `ToolTip`, `AccessKey`, and so on. It also has the `Text` property that can be used to specify the content of the `<span>` element, as shown in Figure 6-11:

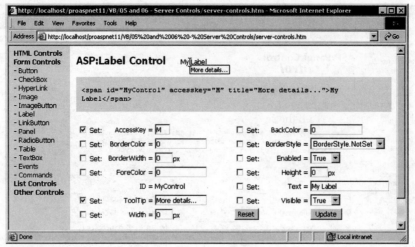

Figure 6-11

The sourcecode used for creating the server control in this page is:

```
<ASP:Label id="MyControl" Text="My Label" runat="server" />
```

The ASP:Button Control

The ASP.NET `Button` control is used to create a standard HTML button that you can access in server-side code. Again, its properties are the usual set seen in all the other controls. Notice that the type of `<input>` element it creates is a `submit` button. Clicking the button will automatically submit the form on which it resides to your server, where you can handle the `Click` event it raises in your server-side code. Figure 6-12 shows the `Button` control:

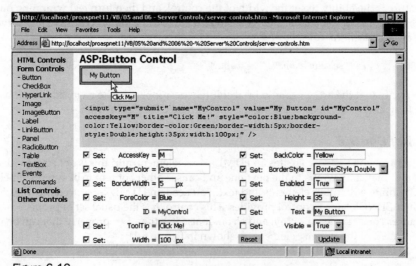

Figure 6-12

The sourcecode used for creating the server control in this page is:

```
<ASP:Button id="MyControl" Text="My Button" runat="server" />
```

The ASP:ImageButton Control

Instead of using a normal text-captioned button to raise a `Click` event on the server, you can use a clickable image instead. The `ImageButton` control creates an `<input type="image">` element that submits the form it resides on to the server when clicked. Also, as shown in Figure 6-13, you can control the size and appearance of the image to get the desired effect:

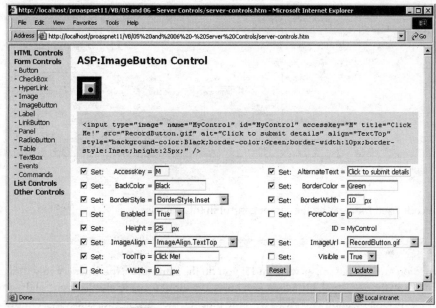

Figure 6-13

The sourcecode used for creating the server control in this page is:

```
<ASP:ImageButton id="MyControl" ImageUrl="BookmarkButton.gif"
                 runat="server" />
```

The ASP:TextBox Control

One of the most complex of the basic Web Form input controls is the `TextBox` control. You can use this to create several different types of HTML elements, including a normal single-line textbox, a multi-line textbox (where it actually creates an HTML `<textarea>` element), and a password input box that displays asterisks instead of text.

In its simplest form, to create a normal `<input type="text">` element, the default property values suffice. However, the `MaxLength`, `ReadOnly`, and `ToolTip` properties are set as seen in Figure 6-14. The `Columns` property, which equates to the `size` attribute for an `<input type="text">` element is also set:

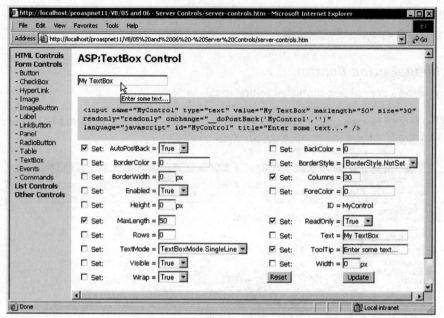

Figure 6-14

The sourcecode used for creating the server control in this page is:

```
<ASP:TextBox id="MyControl" Text="My TextBox" runat="server" />
```

We've turned on AutoPostBack as well, and if you do the same and experiment, you will find that you can type in the textbox as usual, but when you move the input focus to another control (by pressing the Tab key or by clicking on another control with the mouse), the page is automatically submitted to the server where it will raise a Change event that you could create an event handler for. You'll see more about this later in this chapter.

Creating a Multi-Line Textbox

Figure 6-15 shows how to create an HTML <textarea> element that acts as a multi-line textbox using the ASP.NET TextBox control. Just change the value of the TextMode property to TextBoxMode.MultiLine, and specify the appropriate number of Rows and Columns:

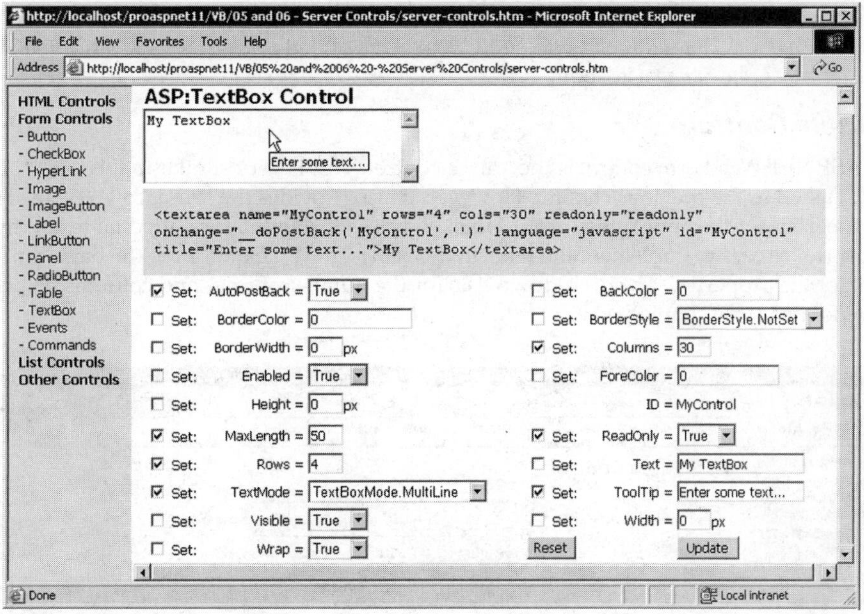
http://localhost/proaspnet11/VB/05 and 06 - Server Controls/server-controls.htm - Microsoft Internet Explorer
File Edit View Favorites Tools Help
Address http://localhost/proaspnet11/VB/05%20and%2006%20-%20Server%20Controls/server-controls.htm
HTML Controls
Form Controls
- Button
- CheckBox
- HyperLink
- Image
- ImageButton
- Label
- LinkButton
- Panel
- RadioButton
- Table
- TextBox
- Events
- Commands
List Controls
Other Controls
ASP:TextBox Control
My TextBox
Enter some text...
<textarea name="MyControl" rows="4" cols="30" readonly="readonly" onchange="__doPostBack('MyControl','')" language="javascript" id="MyControl" title="Enter some text...">My TextBox</textarea>
Set: AutoPostBack = True
Set: BorderColor = 0
Set: BorderWidth = 0 px
Set: Enabled = True
Set: Height = 0 px
Set: MaxLength = 50
Set: Rows = 4
Set: TextMode = TextBoxMode.MultiLine
Set: Visible = True
Set: Wrap = True
Set: BackColor = 0
Set: BorderStyle = BorderStyle.NotSet
Set: Columns = 30
Set: ForeColor = 0
ID = MyControl
Set: ReadOnly = True
Set: Text = My TextBox
Set: ToolTip = Enter some text...
Set: Width = 0 px
Reset
Update
Done
Local intranet

Figure 6-15

Creating a Password Input Element

The third option for the `TextMode` property is `TextBoxMode.Password`. When this is selected, as shown in Figure 6-16, the control creates an `<input type="password">` HTML element:

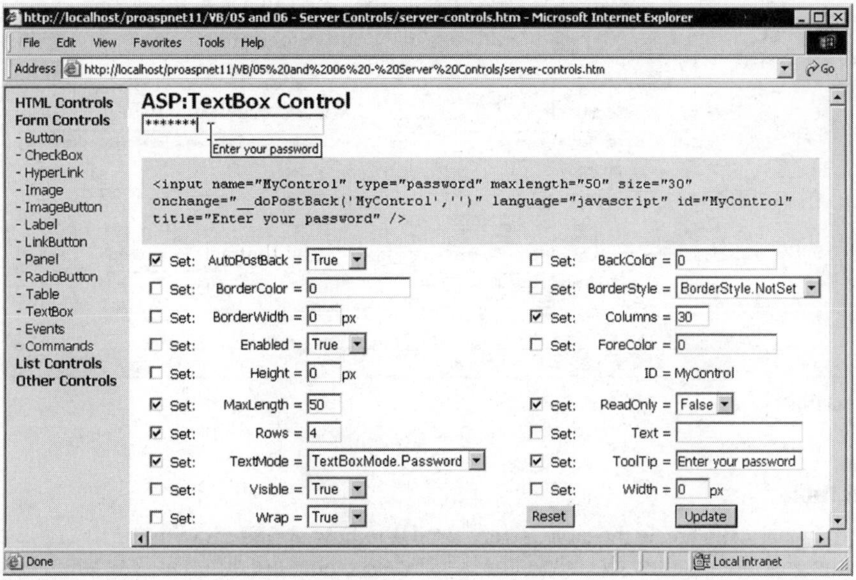
http://localhost/proaspnet11/VB/05 and 06 - Server Controls/server-controls.htm - Microsoft Internet Explorer
File Edit View Favorites Tools Help
Address http://localhost/proaspnet11/VB/05%20and%2006%20-%20Server%20Controls/server-controls.htm
HTML Controls
Form Controls
- Button
- CheckBox
- HyperLink
- Image
- ImageButton
- Label
- LinkButton
- Panel
- RadioButton
- Table
- TextBox
- Events
- Commands
List Controls
Other Controls
ASP:TextBox Control
****
Enter your password
<input name="MyControl" type="password" maxlength="50" size="30" onchange="__doPostBack('MyControl','')" language="javascript" id="MyControl" title="Enter your password" />
Set: AutoPostBack = True
Set: BorderColor = 0
Set: BorderWidth = 0 px
Set: Enabled = True
Set: Height = 0 px
Set: MaxLength = 50
Set: Rows = 4
Set: TextMode = TextBoxMode.Password
Set: Visible = True
Set: Wrap = True
Set: BackColor = 0
Set: BorderStyle = BorderStyle.NotSet
Set: Columns = 30
Set: ForeColor = 0
ID = MyControl
Set: ReadOnly = False
Set: Text =
Set: ToolTip = Enter your password
Set: Width = 0 px
Reset
Update
Done
Local intranet

Figure 6-16

Textboxes always persist their state (text) when placed on an HTML form, even if you turn off viewstate by setting `EnableViewState=False`. *This is because they always post their value back to the server from a form and cause an update event.*

The ASP:Table Control

A useful ASP.NET Web Form control is the `Table` control. This is very similar to the `HtmlTable` server control discussed in the previous chapter. However, it also provides the standard Web Form range of control properties for the appearance of the table. Figure 6-17 shows a formatted table and the output that the control creates to implement the table in the browser. At the bottom of the page, you can see the values set for the properties. The drop-down lists for the number of rows and columns help specify what size the generated table should be:

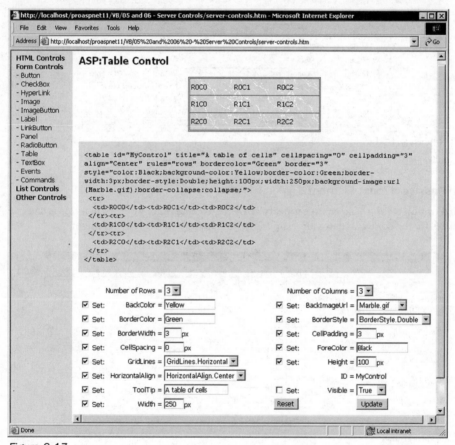

Figure 6-17

Creating the Table

The way to dynamically create the table is very similar to how you did it with the `HtmlTable` server control in the previous chapter. Of course, the object class names are different (`TableRow` and

`TableCell` instead of `HtmlTableRow` and `HtmlTableCell`). The differences between the example in the previous chapter and this one are highlighted in the following code:

```
Dim intRows As Integer = selRows.Value
Dim intCols As Integer = selCols.Value
Dim intRowCount, intColCount As Integer
Dim objRow As TableRow
Dim objCell As TableCell
For intRowCount = 0 To intRows - 1
  objRow = New TableRow()
    For intColCount = 0 To intCols - 1
      objCell = New TableCell()
      objCell.Controls.Add(New LiteralControl ("R" & intRowCount _
                                        & "C" & intColCount))
      objRow.Cells.Add(objCell)
    Next
  MyControl.Rows.Add(objRow)
Next
```

Also, you have to use a different technique to insert the values into the cells of the table. In the `HtmlTable` example, you simply set the `InnerHtml` property of the cells. You can't do that here because the `TableCell` object doesn't have an `InnerHtml` property. Instead, use `LiteralControl` objects to generate the cell content.

Using a LiteralControl Object to Generate Content

The `LiteralControl` object provides no inherent formatting or content–in other words, it doesn't create any HTML elements. It simply inserts an instruction into the code when the page is compiled (actually a `Write` statement) that outputs the value of the control.

So, to output the content for each cell, just instantiate a new `LiteralControl` object and pass as the single `String`-type parameter the text, HTML or other content that you want to be generated. You can, of course, use a `LiteralControl` where you want to generate some content without placing it inside another HTML element.

The ASP:Literal and ASP:PlaceHolder Controls

Two controls not included in the demonstration application, but which you may find uses for in your own pages, are the `ASP:Literal` and the `ASP:PlaceHolder` controls. We will describe these two controls here for completeness.

The ASP:Literal Control

The `ASP:Literal` control was used in the previous example where you dynamically created a table using the `ASP:Table` control. Other than the common members inherited from the base class `Control`, it has only a single property named `Text`. This defines the text that is output by the control. It generates no other output (no HTML elements, for example), and so it is useful where all you want to do is place some text in the page:

```
<ASP:Literal Text="Some Text Here" runat="server" />
```

The value used for the Text property can, however, contain HTML. For example, you can use it to create custom elements in the output for which there is no server control available:

```
<ASP:Literal Text="<gloop>A custom element</gloop>" runat="server" />
```

As you'd expect, this produces the following (probably not very useful) output:

```
<gloop>A custom element</gloop>
```

The ASP:PlaceHolder Control

The final control you will look briefly at is the ASP:PlaceHolder control. This is used when creating controls dynamically in a page, rather than by declaring them explicitly within the source of the page. For example, you can insert an ASP:PlaceHolder into the page like this:

```
<ASP:PlaceHolder id="MyPlaceHolder" runat="server" />
```

Then, you can insert three ASP:TextBox controls into the page using the following code:

```
<script runat="server">
Sub Page_Load()
  Dim intLoop As Integer
  Dim objTextBox As TextBox
  For intLoop = 1 To 3
    objTextBox = New TextBox()
    MyPlaceHolder.Controls.Add(objTextBox)
  Next
End Sub
</script>
```

The result when viewed in the browser is just the three new textboxes – the PlaceHolder control doesn't create any output of its own:

```
<input name="ctrl0" type="text" /><input name="ctrl1" type="text" />
<input
name="ctrl2" type="text" />
```

Reacting to Click and Change Events

As with the HTML controls, the ASP.NET Web Form controls raise events that you can react to on the server. The *Events* demonstration page (see Figure 6-18) shows the Click and Change events that are exposed by most of the Web Forms. It neatly demonstrates the way that the Change event is raised when you edit the content of a textbox and then press the Tab key or move to another control by clicking with the mouse. A message indicating that a Change event was detected, and showing the source control's id, is displayed at the bottom of the page:

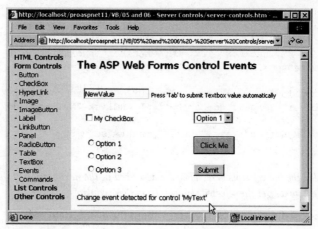

Figure 6-18

The code in the page also detects events for any of the other controls. For example, you can click the `ImageButton` control, and in this case you get the coordinates of the mouse pointer within the control displayed (see Figure 6-19):

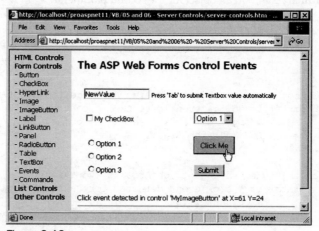

Figure 6-19

The Code in the Events Demonstration Page

The code used in this page is very similar to that used for the HTML controls in the previous chapter. Each of the non-button controls on the page has the `AutoPostBack` property set to `True`, so that clicking or changing the control's contents will automatically submit the page to the server (the button-type controls do this automatically). Also, each control has an event handler specified for the appropriate `Click` or `Change` property. Notice that they have specific event names depending on the control type:

```
<asp:TextBox id="MyText" Text="OriginalValue" runat="server"
    OnTextChanged="MyChangeCode" AutoPostBack="True" />

<asp:CheckBox id="MyCheckbox" Text="My CheckBox" runat="server"
    OnCheckedChanged="MyChangeCode" AutoPostBack="True" />

<asp:ImageButton id="MyImageButton" ImageUrl="ClickmeButton.gif"
    runat="server" ImageAlign="absbottom" OnClick="MyImageCode" />

<asp:Button id="MyButton" Text="Submit" runat="server"
    OnClick="MyClickCode" />
```

We haven't included the list controls here. They are described in the next section of the chapter, where we will investigate how we get the selected value(s) from these controls.

There is also a `<div>`, for displaying the messages about the events detected:

```
<div id="divResult" runat="server" EnableViewState="False" />
```

The event handlers for the textbox, checkbox, and button controls are shown in the code that follows. You can see that the `ImageButton` event code accepts an `ImageClickEventArgs` object as the second argument (from where it extracts the coordinates of the mouse pointer), while the handlers for the other controls accept an ordinary `EventArgs` object for the second parameter:

```
Sub MyChangeCode(objSender As Object, objArgs As EventArgs)
    divResult.InnerHtml &= "Change event detected for control '" _
                    & objSender.ID & "'"
End Sub

Sub MyImageCode(objSender As Object, objArgs As ImageClickEventArgs)
    divResult.InnerHtml &= "Click event detected in control '" _
                    & objSender.ID & "' at X=" & objArgs.X _
                    & " Y=" & objArgs.Y
End Sub

Sub MyClickCode(objSender As Object, objArgs As EventArgs)
    divResult.InnerHtml &= "Click event detected for control '" _
                    & objSender.ID & "'"
End Sub
```

Working with Command Controls

Three of the button-type controls—`Button`, `ImageButton`, and `LinkButton`—provide a *command* feature as well as supporting the standard events. You can set the two properties `CommandName` and `CommandArgument` to any string values you want. When that button is clicked, it raises a `Command` event on the server to which you can respond. You can see this in the *Commands* demonstration page shown in Figure 6-20:

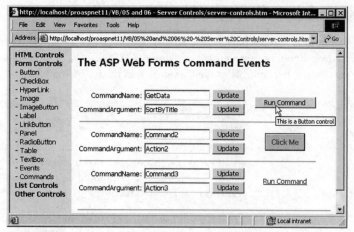

Figure 6-20

The Code in the Commands Demonstration Page

Each time the page is loaded, it assigns the values from the textboxes on the page to the `CommandName` and `CommandArgument` properties of the three button controls. The page also contains the event handler shown in the following code, which is executed when a `Command` event occurs. It extracts the `ID`, `CommandName`, and `CommandArgument` properties of the button control that raised the event, and displays them:

```
Sub MyCommandCode(objSender As Object, objArgs As CommandEventArgs)
    divResult.InnerHtml &= "Command event detected for control '" _
                        & objSender.ID & "'<br />" _
                        & "CommandName is '" _
                        & objSender.CommandName _
                        & "', CommandArgument is '" _
                        & objSender.CommandArgument & "'"
End Sub
```

This feature is useful in some couple of scenarios. Suppose you have more than one button control on a form, you can use this feature to detect which button was clicked to submit the form. In previous versions of ASP, this was normally achieved by examining the `Request.Form` collection (or `Request.QueryString` if the form has its `method` set to `GET`) to see which button was clicked. You just looked for the specific name or value of the button.

With a `Command` event, you can use a `Select Case` construct to figure out which button raised the event instead of searching the `Request.Form` and `Request.QueryString` collections. You only have to check the `CommandName` value. This provides a far better structure to your code, and means that it is easier to add more buttons or change the caption or name of existing ones without breaking the code. You can also use different values for the `CommandArgument` property to pass your own custom control-specific or task-specific values to the event handler. The second useful scenario is when you work with the complex list controls, in particular the `DataGrid` control. By setting pre-defined values for the `CommandName` property, you can use the buttons for control-specific tasks when editing data in the `DataGrid` control. This is described in Chapter 7.

The ASP.NET List Controls

The fourth group of controls that are part of ASP.NET is the range of *list controls*. This includes the familiar listbox and drop-down list, implemented using the HTML `<select>` element. However, there are several other very useful list controls as well, as shown in the following table:

Control	Description
`<ASP:DropDownList>`	Creates a `<select>` list element that includes the `size="1"` attribute to create a drop-down listbox with only a single row visible. The list can be populated using `<ASP:ListItem>` controls or through data binding.
`<ASP:ListBox>`	Creates a `<select>` list element that includes the `size="x"` attribute to create a normal single-select or multi-select list box with more than one row visible. The list can be populated using `<ASP:ListItem>` controls or through data-binding.
`<ASP:CheckBoxList>`	Creates an HTML `<table>` or a simple list containing HTML checkboxes. The list can be populated using `<ASP:ListItem>` controls or through data-binding.
`<ASP:RadioButtonList>`	Creates an HTML `<table>` or a simple list containing a mutually exclusive group of HTML radio buttons. The list can be populated using `<ASP:ListItem>` controls or through data-binding.
`<ASP:ListItem>`	Not actually a control, but an object that is used to create an item within a list control. The type of item that is created in the list depends on the type of the list control. For example, an `<ASP:ListItem>` creates an `<option>` element in a listbox, and a new checkbox control in a `CheckBoxList` control.
`<ASP:Repeater>`	Repeats content defined once, for each source item within the data source specified for the control. No integral formatting is applied except the layout and content information you define. This control is described in Chapter 7.
`<ASP:DataList>`	Creates an HTML `<table>` with a row for each source item you specify. You create templates that define the content and appearance of each row. This control is described in Chapter 7.
`<ASP:DataGrid>`	Creates an HTML `<table>` that is designed for use with server-side data-binding, and includes built-in features to support selection, sorting, and editing of the content rows. This control is described in Chapter 7.

These controls further reinforce the fact that the Web Form controls can save huge amounts of effort when creating interactive web pages, in particular when the values for the lists come from some dynamic data source such as a database. We will look in detail at the concepts of data binding in Chapter 7, and we will postpone the discussion of the three more complex types of list control until then. In this chapter, let's concentrate on the first five of the controls just listed.

The ListControl Base Class

The four list controls described in this chapter are derived from the base class `ListControl`, which is part of the namespace `System.Web.UI.WebControls`. This class itself inherits from `WebControl`, and so provides the same properties, methods, and events as described in the previous section on the Web Form controls. It adds to these some other members, as the next table suggests, which are therefore available for all the list controls:

Member	Description
`AutoPostBack` property	Sets or returns a Boolean value indicating whether the page will be posted back to the server automatically when the user changes the selection in the list.
`DataMember` property	Sets or returns the name of the table within the `DataSource` that will supply the values for the list when data binding is used to populate it. Used when the `DataSource` object contains more than one table (for example, when using a `DataSet`).
`DataSource` property	Sets or returns a reference to the object that provides the values to populate the list.
`DataTextField` property	Sets or returns the name of the field within the current `DataSource` that provides the text to be used for the list items.
`DataTextFormatString` property	Sets or returns the formatting string that controls how the data bound to the list is displayed; for example, `{0:C}` for currency.
`DataValueField` property	Sets or returns the name of the field or column within the current `DataSource` that provides the values for the list items.
`Items` property	Returns a collection of the items (rows or `<option>` elements) within the list control.
`SelectedIndex` property	Sets or returns the integer index of the first selected item in the list. To set or retrieve multiple selected items use the `Selected` property of each individual `ListItem` object.

Table continued on the following page

Member	Description
SelectedItem property	Returns a reference to the first selected item within the list control. To set or retrieve multiple selected items use the Selected property of each individual ListItem object.
SelectedValue property	Sets or returns the value of the currently selected item in the list, or the first selected item if more than one is selected. The Value property is returned if the list item has a value set for this property. If not, the value of the Text property (the visible text) is returned. Setting this property to a value that exists in the list selects that item. This property was added in version 1.1.
OnSelectedIndexChanged() event	Occurs on the server when the selection in the list is changed and the page is posted back to the server.

The Specific List Control Classes

All the list controls described in this chapter add properties and a method to the base class from which they inherit, as shown in the following table:

Control/Object	Properties	Methods
DropDownList	- *none* -	- *none* -
ListBox	Rows	- *none* -
CheckBoxList	CellPadding, CellSpacing, RepeatColumns, RepeatDirection, RepeatLayout, TextAlign	- *none* -
RadioButtonList	CellPadding, CellSpacing, RepeatColumns, RepeatDirection, RepeatLayout, TextAlign	- *none* -
ListItem	Attributes, Selected, Text, Value	FromString()

Using the ASP List Controls

In general, use the list controls in the same way as the basic ASP.NET Web Form controls examined in the previous section of this chapter. Properties like AutoPostBack, AccessKey, ToolTip, and the various formatting properties work in just the same way. We have also used a HashTable as the data source for the examples in our demonstration application, in the same way as the HtmlSelect control in the previous chapter.

Here, we will concentrate on the properties specific to list controls, as shown in the previous tables. We will follow this up towards the end of this section with a look at the way details about the selected items in a list control are retrieved.

The ASP:DropDownList Control

The ASP.NET `DropDownList` control creates basically the same output in the browser as the default `HtmlSelect` list in the previous chapter. It generates an HTML `<select>` element with no `size` attribute. Thus, only one item in the list is visible and it behaves as a 'drop-down' selection list.

Since the control is bound to the same `HashTable` as the one used with the `HtmlSelect` control, you can see that it creates the same five `<option>` elements within the `<select>` element. Setting the `BackColor`, `BorderColor`, and `ForeColor` properties performs the formatting of the control, and we have also turned on `AutoPostBack`. This adds the `onchange` attribute to the `<select>` element, as shown in Figure 6-21:

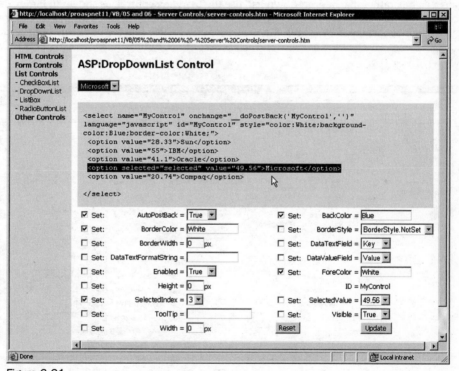

Figure 6-21

Notice the `SelectedValue` property. We set the `SelectedIndex` property to 3, and this selected the item **Microsoft**. The code in the example page then reads the properties of the control, including the `SelectedValue`, and sets the drop-down list in the lower half of the page to the matching values (in this case 49.56). As an alternative, uncheck the **Set** box next to the `SelectedIndex` property, choose a value in the `SelectedValue` drop-down list, and then click **Update**. This selects the item you choose in the list.

> You get a runtime error if you set the `SelectedValue` to a value that does not exist in the list.

The sourcecode used for creating the server control in this page is:

```
<ASP:DropDownList id="MyControl" runat="server" />
```

To see the effects of data binding to the `HashTable` data source, swap over the `DataTextField` and `DataValueField` properties. The list will show the contents of the 'field' selected as the `DataTextField` property, and use the contents of the 'field' specified as the `DataValueField` to fill the `value` attributes of each `<option>` element.

The ASP:ListBox Control

To create a listbox rather than a drop-down list, use the `ListBox` control, as shown in Figure 6-22. This has a couple of extra properties that specify the size and behavior of the list. Firstly, you can specify how many items will be displayed by setting the `Rows` property (which sets the `size` attribute–notice how the property names are common across the Web Form controls, hiding the inconsistent HTML attribute names).

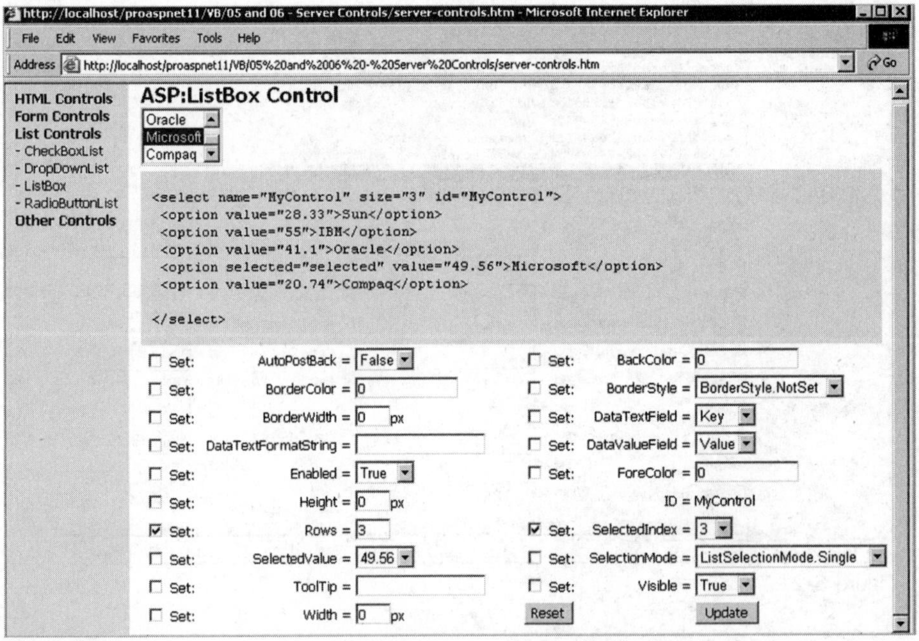

Figure 6-22

The sourcecode used for creating the server control in this page is:

```
<ASP:ListBox id="MyControl" runat="server" />
```

You can also permit multiple selections to be made in the list by setting the `SelectionMode` property to a value from the `ListSelectionMode` enumeration. The `Multiple` value simply adds the `multiple="multiple"` attribute to the output so that the Shift and Ctrl key can be used to select more than one item in the list.

The ASP:CheckBoxList and ASP:RadioButtonList Controls

Two exciting and useful controls are part of the Web Form list control range: the `CheckBoxList` and `RadioButtonList`. These create a list containing one or more checkboxes or radio buttons, and they automatically set the value and the text (for the caption) of each one. When used in conjunction with data binding, as in the demonstration pages, these controls can really reduce development time.

Figure 6-23 shows the standard results for a `RadioButtonList` control when data-bound to the same `HashTable` as that used in the previous examples. The `CheckBoxList` control is identical except that it creates a list of checkboxes (as you'd expect). You can see that the output generated is an HTML table containing `<input type="radio">` and `<label>` elements:

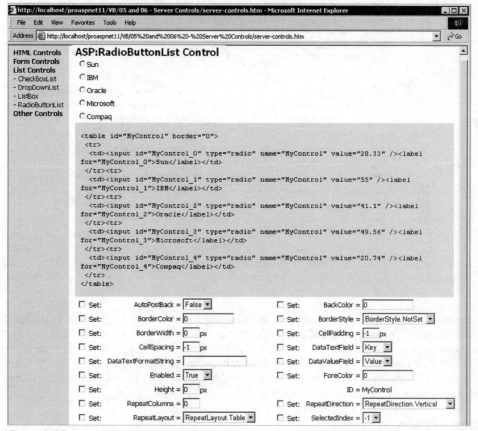

Figure 6-23

The sourcecode for creating the server control in this page is:

```
<ASP:CheckBoxList id="MyControl" runat="server" />
```

However, this is not the only output *format* you can create. In Figure 6-24, you can see that the controls are laid out inline, rather than in a table. This is because the RepeatLayout property is set to Flow, and the RepeatDirection to Horizontal (using members of the appropriate enumerations). Also, the RepeatColumns property is set to 3 so that the controls appear in threes across the page:

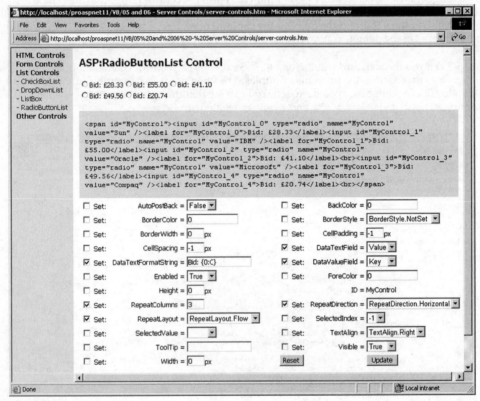

Figure 6-24

The captions are now the values rather than the company names, which are now the value attributes of the radio buttons. This was achieved by simply swapping the DataTextField and DataValueField settings. As the numeric values are now visible for each option, they are formatted as currency by setting the DataTextFormatString to a suitable format expression. This example used Bid:{0:C} to output the literal characters Bid: and convert the numerical value to currency format, but you can substitute others to experiment.

Reacting to Change Events

The Events demonstration page used in the previous section to show the events for button controls also shows how you can react to the Change event exposed by all the Web Form list controls. When you make a selection in the RadioButtonList or the DropDownList control, the page displays information about that event (see Figure 6-25):

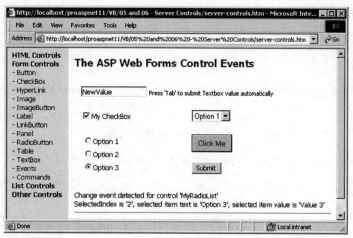

Figure 6-25

The RadioButtonList and DropDownList controls are defined in the page using explicit values for their contents, rather than data-binding as in the previous examples. However, you *must* define the contents using ListItem elements rather than <option> elements. Notice that the Text property is set to the string you want appearing in the visible portion of the list in this example, and not provided as the content of the element as is done when <option> elements are used. However, either approach is valid.

```
<asp:DropDownList id="MyDropDownList" runat="server"
       OnSelectedIndexChanged="MyListChangeCode" AutoPostBack="true">
  <asp:ListItem Text="Option 1" Value="Value 1" />
  <asp:ListItem Text="Option 2" Value="Value 2" />
  <asp:ListItem Text="Option 3" Value="Value 3" />
</asp:DropDownList>

<asp:RadioButtonList id="MyRadioList" runat="server"
       OnSelectedIndexChanged="MyListChangeCode" AutoPostBack="true">
  <asp:ListItem Text="Option 1" Value="Value 1" />
  <asp:ListItem Text="Option 2" Value="Value 2" />
  <asp:ListItem Text="Option 3" Value="Value 3" />
</asp:RadioButtonList>
```

You can also see how easy it is to define the individual radio buttons that make up the RadioButtonList control (the same technique is used with a CheckBoxList control). You have to specify only the ListItem element and its properties. The list control knows what type of items to create for the list, and automatically generates the correct HTML.

Extracting Values from List Controls

The two list controls have their AutoPostBack property set to True, so the page will be submitted to the server when the current selection is changed. They have their OnSelectedIndexChanged property set to point to an event handler named MyListChangeCode, which (as usual) is executed on the server when the page is submitted.

The Code for Handling Selection Changes

The code for the `MyListChangeCode` event handler is shown in the following code. It displays the `ID` of the control that raised the event, and then extracts the selected item `Text` and `Value` and displays these as well:

```
Sub MyListChangeCode(objSender As Object, objArgs As EventArgs)
    divResult.InnerHtml &= "Change event detected for control '" _
                    & objSender.ID & "'<br />SelectedIndex is '" _
                    & objSender.SelectedIndex _
                    & "', selected item text is '" _
                    & objSender.SelectedItem.Text _
                    & "', selected item value is '" _
                    & objSender.SelectedItem.Value & "'<br />"
End Sub
```

Notice how, in this case, you simply access the `SelectedItem` property of the list control, which returns a reference to the first item in the list that is selected. In version 1.1, the alternative is simply to query the `SelectedValue` property instead:

```
    ...
    & "', selected item value is '" _
    & objSender.SelectedValue & "'<br />"
    ...
```

Bear in mind that this returns the value of the `Value` property (or the `value` atttribute) of the first selected item. If there is no `Value` property or `value` attribute, it returns the value of the `Text` property (or the literal content of the `ASP:ListItem` element).

Extracting Multiple Selected Values from List Controls

Both the lists in the previous example allow only a single selection to be made. This is always the case with a `RadioButtonList`. However, you can specify that a `ListBox` control will accept multiple selections by setting the `SelectionMode` property to the value `ListSelectionMode.Multiple`. In a `CheckBoxList`, you will usually allow multiple item selection, as this is generally the sole reason for using this type of control.

Multiple selected values from a list control are extracted using exactly the same technique as with the `HtmlSelect` control in the previous section. Iterate through all the `ListItem` elements in the `Items` collection exposed by the list control, checking the `Selected` property of each one, and extracting the `Text` and `Value` properties for those that are selected:

```
Sub MyCode(objSender As Object, objArgs As EventArgs)
    Dim strResult As String
    strResult = "The following items were selected:<br />"
    Dim objItem As ListItem
    For Each objItem in objSender.Items
        If objItem.Selected Then
            strResult &= objItem.Text & " = " & objItem.Value & "<br />"
        End If
    Next
    outMessage.InnerHtml = strResult
End Sub
```

Other ASP.NET Rich Controls

To finish off this chapter, we will look briefly at three other controls that are provided with ASP.NET. *Rich controls* create the entire HTML required for implementing a complex task in one simple operation. A typical example of this is the `Calendar` control, which can create a complete working calendar within a web page. All you do is add the control to your page and set a few properties. The three controls covered here are:

Control	Description
`<ASP:AdRotator>`	Displays an advertisement banner that changes on a predefined schedule.
`<ASP:Calendar>`	Displays a calendar showing single months and allows selection of a date.
`<ASP:Xml>`	Displays the content of an XML document or the result of an XSL or XSLT transformation.

Using the Rich Controls

The rich controls mentioned in this section are very useful when you need to perform the specific tasks for which they are designed. We don't have room to provide exhaustive coverage here, but by now you should be familiar with the way that server controls work, and you should have no problem getting to grips with these. You can use the demonstration application provided (open the OtherControls section of the left-hand menu) to see the output they generate, and experiment with the various property settings.

The ASP:AdRotator Control

The `AdRotator` control has been part of ASP almost since the beginning, and is a popular way to display advertisement banners on a quasi-random pre-defined schedule. A new version is included as part of the default ASP.NET installation and it has a couple of extra features.

Probably the most useful feature is the ability to dynamically *filter* the list of banners that will be displayed, so that you can, for example, display banners for products or organizations that are relevant to a specific page or user. The filtering is carried out through the `KeywordFilter` property. This property is set in our demonstration application, as shown in Figure 6-26:

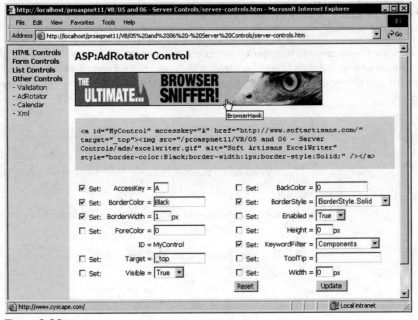

Figure 6-26

The code used for inserting the control into the page for this example is:

```
<ASP:AdRotator id="MyControl" AdvertisementFile="adverts.xml"
                runat="server" />
```

Previous versions of the `AdRotator` control relied on a text file to specify the advertisements and the schedule for displaying each one. The new control uses an XML file to define the schedules. The file path is specified in the `AdvertisementFile` property, as shown in the source code for the page above (you can't change this property in the demonstration page).

The AdRotator Schedule File

An example of the format of the XML schedule file is shown in the following code:

```
<Advertisements>
  <Ad>
    <ImageUrl>ads/asptoday.gif</ImageUrl>
    <NavigateUrl>http://www.asptoday.com/</NavigateUrl>
    <AlternateText>ASPToday</AlternateText>
    <Impressions>20</Impressions>
    <Keyword>Articles</Keyword>
  </Ad>
  <Ad>
    <ImageUrl>ads/wrox.gif</ImageUrl>
    <NavigateUrl>http://www.wrox.com/</NavigateUrl>
    <AlternateText>Wrox Press</AlternateText>
    <Impressions>20</Impressions>
```

```
        <Keyword>Books</Keyword>
      </Ad>
      ... more <Ad> elements here ...
    <Advertisements>
```

The `ImageUrl` and `NavigateUrl` are self-explanatory. The `AlternateText` is used as the HTML `alt` attribute of the `<img>` element that the `AdRotator` control creates, and the `Impressions` value is used to control how often this banner will appear. The total for this element in all the `<Ad>` elements in the schedule file is calculated, and the ratio of impressions can then be calculated by the control and used to select the advertisement to display.

The `Keyword` element is used to allocate each advertisement to a *category* with that name. When you set the `KeywordFilter` property, only advertisements with the specified value for their `Keyword` element are included in the selection and display process.

The ASP:Calendar Control

By far the most complex server control in ASP.NET is the `Calendar` control. This creates a fully interactive *one-month-at-a-time* calendar as an HTML table. Figure 6-27 shows the default output from the `Calendar` control, and you can see that it really is a *rich* control in that it saves an incredible amount of effort on behalf of the developer:

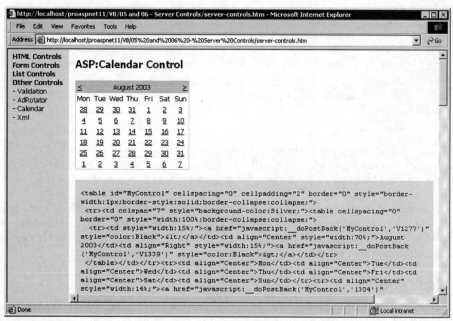

Figure 6-27

The code used for inserting the control into the source of the page is:

```
<ASP:Calendar id="MyControl" runat="server" />
```

Notice that it automatically defaults to the current date (shown in the `TodaysDate` property in the next screesnhot) if you don't specify a date. If you scroll to the bottom of this page, you can see some of the properties that can be set to change the appearance. These don't include the various calendar-specific style properties that are available, such as `DayHeaderStyle`, `DayStyle`, `MonthStyle`, and so on (see Figure 6-28):

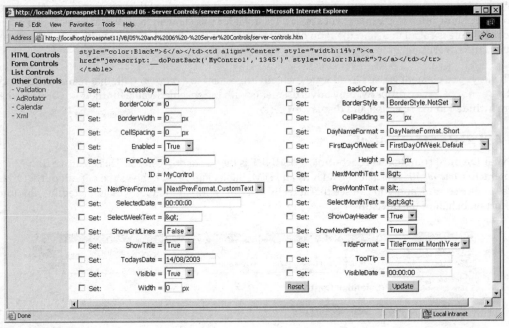

Figure 6-28

The `Calendar` control also exposes a couple of events that you can use to detect when the user interacts with the control. You can write an event handler for the `SelectionChanged` event, and obtain the date that the user selected by querying the `SelectedDate` property of the control within that event handler.

You can also create an event handler for the `VisibleMonthChanged` event. In this case, the second parameter of the event handler is a `MonthChangedEventHandler` object, which exposes two properties named `NewDate` and `PreviousDate` that contain the original (before the month was changed) and current dates (the date after the month was changed).

The ASP:Xml Control

The final control we're covering is the `ASP:Xml` server control. This can be used to display the content of an XML document, or to perform a server-side transformation on the document using a suitable XSL or XSLT stylesheet. Note that this control does not inherit from `WebControl`. It inherits directly from `Control`, and so doesn't have all the display-oriented properties that the other Web Form controls do.

Don't be confused into thinking that this control creates an IE 5-style <xml> element–it doesn't. It is a server-side object that outputs XML or the result of an XSL or XSLT transformation to the client.

There are six properties available for the `Xml` control. You can specify the source document using one of the first three properties in the following table, and the stylesheet (if you're using one) in one of the next two properties shown in:

Property	Description
Document	A reference to an `XmlDocument` object that contains the XML document we want to display or transform. The `XmlDocument` object is covered in Chapter 11.
DocumentContent	A string containing the text of the XML document you want to display or transform.
DocumentSource	A string that contains the physical or virtual path to the XML document you want to display or transform.
Transform	A reference to an `XslTransform` object that contains the XSL or XSLT stylesheet to use for transforming the XML document before displaying it. The `XslTransform` object is covered in Chapter 11.
TransformSource	A string that contains the physical or virtual path to the XSL or XSLT stylesheet you want to use for the transformation.
TransformArgumentList	A reference to an XsltArgumentList object that contains the arguments to be passed to the stylesheet.

In Figure 6-29, the `DocumentSource` property in the demonstration page is set to `books.xml`. The control loads this document from disk and displays it in the page. Of course, the XML elements aren't visible, because the browser attempts to render the XML as though it were HTML and so only the text content of the elements is shown in the page. If you view the source in your browser, however, you'll see the XML that the control sends to the client. We have also included a hyperlink in the page so that you can open the XML document in a separate browser window and see it.

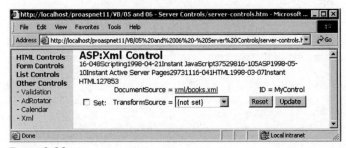

Figure 6-29

The code used for inserting the control into the source of the page is:

```
<ASP:Xml id="MyControl" DocumentSource="xml/books.xml" runat="server" />
```

If you compare the original disk file with the output of the control, you will also see that the control has removed *insignificant whitespace* from the result. In other words, it strips out all the carriage returns, spaces, and tab characters.

Using an XSL Stylesheet

We have provided three simple XSL stylesheets that you can use to transform the XML document. They transform the XML into HTML (because we are displaying it in the browser in our application). For example, Figure 6-30 shows how the `reportview.xsl` stylesheet generates a sales report from the data in the XML document:

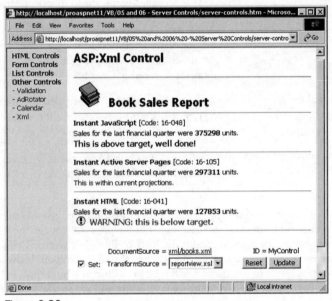

Figure 6-30

The code used to apply the XSL stylesheet detects whether this is a postback and, if it is, sets the `TransformSource` property of the `Xml` control to the relative path to the XSL file:

```
If IsPostBack() Then

    If chkTransformSource.Checked _
    And Left(selTransformSource.Value, 1) <> "{" Then
        MyControl.TransformSource = "xml/" & selTransformSource.Value
    End If

End If
```

Summary

This chapter looked at the second major set of server controls that are provided as part of the default ASP.NET installation–the Web Form controls. These are a mixture of simple controls that emulate the HTML controls you looked at in the previous chapter, and more complex controls that provide 'rich' output containing more than one HTML element.

The Web Form controls also have other advantages over the HTML controls. They provide a consistent object model, using the same property name in all the controls for the same 'value'. An example is the `Text` property that sets the visible text within the control irrespective of which HTML element is output, and which HTML attribute carries the text content. This makes working with them easier, and also simplifies the task of building tools or applications that will create a user interface automatically.

The Web Form controls examined in this chapter fall into three groups:

❑   The basic controls, such as `Image`, `Hyperlink`, `TextBox`, and `RadioButton`

❑   The list controls, such as `ListBox`, `DropDownList`, and `RadioButtonList`

❑   The rich controls, such as `AdRotator`, `Calendar`, and `Xml`

We showed you the common properties for each one, and demonstrated them through a sample application. You also saw how to react to events that these controls expose, and some of the other issues involved when you use them.

However, we didn't examine all the list controls in this chapter, as there are some very complex ones, such as `Repeater`, `DataList`, and `DataGrid`. These are covered in the next chapter.

7
List Controls and Data Binding

Most dynamic web sites, and just about every web application, will need to access a data source at some point. ASP has long been capable of accessing various kinds of data store, such as relational databases, email servers, XML documents, or text files and it's relatively simple to manipulate, format, and display data in a range of ways. However, although it's simple to do, it always requires writing code – and that code can become quite extensive, making it difficult to manage and debug.

ASP.NET introduces some new ways to manage and present data of all kinds. In later chapters, you'll look at the whole concept of data management for both relational and XML data. However, in this chapter you will look at new ways to display data in your web pages and applications.

Data presentation in ASP.NET is managed mainly through a series of new *server controls* that are specially designed to work with a whole range of types of data – not just relational or XML data. Thus, the techniques for working with these controls are akin to the techniques for creating ASP.NET pages that we've examined in previous chapters.

What's more, you don't need a deep understanding of where the data comes from, or how it is extracted from a data store, to be able to use the new data presentation controls. The fundamentally disconnected design of the data management features within the .NET Framework enables you to easily separate the business rules that create and expose the data from the code that creates the display.

In this chapter, you'll deal with the way the controls work, and how you use them. In later chapters, we'll be free to examine relational and XML data management techniques, without getting bogged down with presentation issues. The topics covered here are:

- ❑ What data binding actually is, and how it works
- ❑ How to bind controls to single data values

❑   How to bind list controls to sets of data values

❑   How to change the appearance of data-bound controls

❑   How to use data-bound controls to edit and update the source data

Obtaining the Sample Files

The examples used in this chapter are included with the sample files available for this book from http://www.daveandal.net/books/8900/. You can also run many of them online at the same URL. You'll find a `default.htm` menu page, as shown in Figure 7-1, in the folder named `data-binding`:

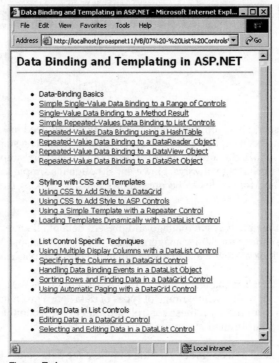

Figure 7-1

Some of the examples require a connection to a database. We've provided a Microsoft Access .mdb *database file and two SQL scripts to create the database in SQL Server. These files, and instructions on creating the database, are included in the* `data-binding/database` *folder.*

Data Binding – The Concepts

The exact meaning of *data binding* can be quite difficult to pin down. In programming languages such as Visual Basic and applications such as Microsoft Access, the term data binding describes the way that values from a collection of data, such as a recordset, are connected to controls on a form. As the form is used to navigate through the records, the values of each of the columns are automatically displayed in the controls. The controls are *bound* to the columns in the recordset, and you don't have to write any code to display the values or update the original data source.

However, the disconnected nature of the HTTP protocol means that the traditional client/server data binding used in Visual Basic and Access cannot be used over an HTTP-based network connection. When Internet Explorer 4 appeared, it included some clever client-side and server-side COM components that allowed a similar technique to be used over HTTP. This was referred to as *client-side data binding*, and worked well. However, the browser-specific requirements of this technology, combined with suspicions about security that it raised, meant that it didn't really catch on in a big way.

Doing It All on the Server

The continuing diversification of client devices means that any browser-specific technology is unlikely to have long-term appeal. Accordingly, the .NET Framework vision is to provide support for *all* types of client. Ultimately, this means either you have to build applications that detect the client device type and change their behavior accordingly, or implement all the functionality on the server.

In many cases doing it all on the server is a good plan, as it allows you to exert control over output and security within your applications. Developments in server and web farm technologies make it much easier to provide scalable and reliable sites, and ASP.NET is designed to create fast responses to client requests through pre-compilation and caching.

So how does this relate to the topics of this chapter? The answer is that in .NET you move towards the concept of *server-side data binding*. You can take advantage of the time saving and code saving features of data binding – just as you would with Visual Basic and Access – but use it across HTTP in a disconnected environment like the Web.

With data binding in ASP.NET, you simply tell the controls or the page where to find the data. It extracts the values and builds the page with this data in it as seen in the next section.

Displaying Data – ASP versus ASP.NET

With ASP 3.0 and earlier, you could use components or a technology such as ADO to create a `Recordset` object that contains rows of data for display. To get them into the page, you would usually iterate through the rows – extracting values, formatting them, and inserting them into the output as follows:

```
...' assuming we've got a Recordset object containing the data ...
Response.Write "<table>"
Response.Write "<tr><th>Date</th>"
Response.Write "<th>Subject</th>"
Response.Write "<th>User Name</th>"
Response.Write "<th>Content</th></tr>"
Do While Not objRecs.EOF
```

```
        strDate = FormatDateTime(objRecs("dtDate").value, vbLongDate)
        Response.Write "<tr><td>" & strDate & "</td>"
        Response.Write "<td>" & objRecs("tSubject").value & "</td>"
        Response.Write "<td>" & objRecs("tUserName").value & "</td>"
        Response.Write "<td>" & objRecs("tContent").value & "</td></tr>"
        objRecs.MoveNext
    Loop
    Response.Write "</table>"
    objRecs.Close
```

You had to do all this just to get a simple unformatted table containing values from the rows in the recordset. In ASP.NET you can do the same in only two lines of code by using a server control:

```
<!-- the server control located in the HTML section of the page -->
<ASP:DataGrid id="MyDataGrid" runat="server" />
...' assuming we've got a DataView object containing the data ...
MyDataGrid.DataSource = objDataView
MyDataGrid.DataBind()
```

Data access objects such as `DataView` are covered in detail in the Chapters 8 to 10.

The server control does much the same as the ASP 3.0 code you saw. It automatically creates an HTML table with the column names in the first row, followed by a series of rows that contain the values from each of the source data rows. What's more, you can now change the appearance of the table by just setting a few properties of the `ASP:DataGrid` control. You can add:

❑   Automatic sorting with only a two-line subroutine.

❑   Automatic paging, with each page showing the number of rows required and with links to the other pages, by just setting one property and creating two lines of code.

And this only scratches the surface. This control can be used in ways that will cater for almost any dataset presentation requirement. What's more, there are several other controls that are designed to display repeated data such as this, and even more that work with a single item of data at a time through server-side data binding.

Data Binding Syntax

Data binding was used in a couple of the examples in Chapters 5 and 6, but was not discussed in depth. Let's concentrate on the theory here, and then look at how to use the new ASP.NET server controls to really get the benefits of server-side data binding.

The principle behind server-side data binding is to get ASP.NET to insert one or more values from a data source into the page, or into a control on the page. The basic syntax uses a construct that looks like a server-side script block, with a # character as an indicator that this is actually a data-binding statement:

```
<%# name-of-data-source %>
```

Code to be executed cannot be placed within this block, as although it looks like a server-side script block, it isn't. Only specific data-binding syntax expressions can be used within the block.

There are two basic scenarios in which you would want to bind a control:

❑ **Single-value data binding**: When you have a single value to bind to a control. For example, you might want to set one of the properties (or attributes) of that control. In this case, the bound value is often used to set the displayed content of the control (the `Text` or `Value` property), and is suited to controls that only display a single value, such as the `<input>`, `ASP:TextBox`, and `ASP:Hyperlink` controls.

❑ **Repeated-value data binding**: When the data source contains more than one value. For example, you might want to bind a list, a collection, or a rowset to a control that can display more than one value. Examples include the various types of list controls such as `<select>`, `ASP:ListBox`, and `ASP:CheckBoxList`.

Although the techniques for both these types of binding are fundamentally similar let's examine the concepts of each separately.

Single-Value Data Binding

When you bind controls to single values such as properties, methods, or expressions, you use one of the following simple types of syntax:

```
<%# property-name %>
```

Or:

```
<%# method-name(parameter, parameter, ...) %>
```

Or:

```
<%# expression %>
```

This shows there are several possible sources for the value that will be bound to the control, and let's look at these next.

Sources of Data for Single-Value Binding

The source of the value that can be used with single-value data binding includes:

❑ The value of a property declared in either the page, or in another control or object

❑ The result returned from a method declared in either the page or in another control or object

❑ The result of evaluating an expression

All of these must return a single value that can be bound to a control or placed directly within a page. For example, you can declare a property named `ImageURL` within the code of the page as follows:

```
ReadOnly Property ImageURL() As String
   Get
       'read-only property for the Page
       Dim strURL As String
```

```
            'some code would be here to calculate the value
            'we just set it to a fixed value for illustration
            strURL = "myimage.gif"
         Return strURL
      End Get
End Property
```

Then insert the value directly into the page itself, or as the value of an attribute for a control, using:

```
<%# ImageURL %>
```

The only remaining task is to activate the binding when the page is loaded. This is done using the `DataBind` method (we'll look at this in detail shortly):

```
Sub Page_Load()
   DataBind()
End Sub
```

Using Controls with Bound Values

The real advantage in using bound values is that the data binding statement block can be used within other controls, and the value of one control can come from another control. For example, you can link a label to a textbox by specifying the `Text` property of the `TextBox` control as the `Text` property of the `Label` control.

Now, each time the page is submitted, the value in the `Label` control named `MyLabel` will be the value that was present in the `TextBox` control named `MyTextBox` – and to accomplish this you don't need to write any code other than to call the `DataBind` method:

```
<form runat="server">
  <ASP:TextBox id="MyTextBox" runat="server" />
  <ASP:Label id="MyLabel" Text="<%# MyTextBox.Text %>" runat="server" />
  <input type="submit" />
</form>
<script language="VB" runat="server">
Sub Page_Load()
   DataBind()
End Sub
</script>
```

This technique isn't limited to just setting the `Text` property of a control. You can use it to insert a value into almost any control.

For example, to specify the `Src` property of an `ASP:Image` control you could use:

```
<ASP:Image Src="<%# ImageURL %>" ImageAlign="middle" runat="server" />
```

To specify the text caption of an `ASP:CheckBox` control you could use:

```
<ASP:CheckBox Text="<%# ImageURL %>" runat="server" />
```

To specify the text and target URL for an `ASP:Hyperlink` control you could use:

```
<ASP:Hyperlink Text="<%# ImageURL %>" NavigateUrl="<%# ImageURL %>"
               runat="server" />
```

This technique works in the same way for HTML controls and elements that aren't actually server controls.

To specify the text that appears in an HTML text control element, you would use:

```
<input type="text" value="<%# ImageURL %>" />
```

To specify the caption of an HTML `submit` button, you would use:

```
<input type="submit" value="<%# ImageURL %>" />
```

Or to specify the target URL and hotlink text in an HTML `<a>` element, you would use:

```
<a href="<%# ImageURL %>"><%# ImageURL %></a>
```

If required, you can concatenate explicit values with the bound value. For example, it can be used to specify just the file name part of a complete URL:

```
<a href="http://mysite.com/images/<%# ImageURL %>">
   View the file named '<%# ImageURL %>'</a>
```

Activating the Binding

As noted earlier, once you've specified the data binding statement blocks in a page, you must activate the binding when some other event occurs (usually when the page is loaded) to get the appropriate values inserted. If you don't, the ASP engine ignores the data binding blocks when the page is compiled, and they won't be replaced by the intended value. The binding process is activated using the `DataBind` method, which is available at several places within the hierarchy of the page:

- ❑ To bind all the controls on the page, call the `DataBind` method of the `Page` object (as `Page` is the default object, `Page.DataBind` or just `DataBind` can be used as done in the examples so far). This is the only way to activate the binding for controls that are not specifically designed for use with data binding. It also binds any values that are inserted directly into a page, rather than into a control of some kind.

- ❑ To bind just a single control, call the `DataBind` method of that control. This only applies to those list controls that are designed specifically for use with data binding.

- ❑ To bind just one row or item object from the data source within a control, call the `DataBind` method of that object. Again, this only applies to list controls that are designed specifically for use with data binding.

A Single-Value Data Binding Example

Figure 7-2 shows a Simple Single-Value Data Binding (provided in the code download as `simple-single-binding.aspx`) sample page. It shows how single-value data binding can be used with a whole range of controls.

You can click on the [view source] link at the bottom of the page to see the complete sourcecode for the page. It uses the code you saw earlier to expose a simple ImageURL property.

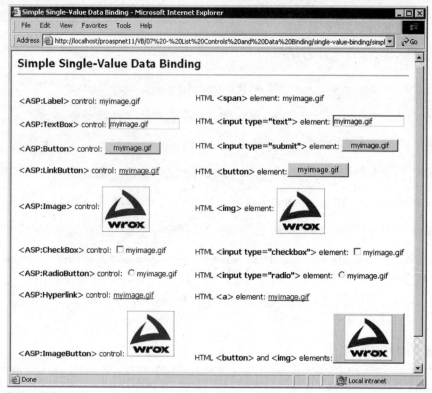

Figure 7-2

Each of the controls in the page then uses the `ImageURL` property value to set one or more of their properties. Finally, the code in the `Page_Load` event handler calls the `DataBind` method of the `Page` object to bind all the controls on the page to the property value:

```
Sub Page_Load()
  Page.DataBind()  'bind all the controls on the page
End Sub
```

We've also provided a similar example page that binds to the result of a method rather than a property value. This page, Single-Value Data Binding to a Method Result (`method-single-binding.aspx`) looks identical to the previous example when it's displayed in a browser. However, it differs in its definition of a method named `ImageURL`, which returns the value `"myimage.gif"`:

```
Function ImageURL() As String
   Return "myimage.gif"
End Function
```

The only other difference is that now the expressions in the data binding blocks include parentheses, because the data source is a method (although in Visual Basic it works just as well without them):

```
<ASP:Label Text="<%# ImageURL() %>" runat="server" />
```

Repeated-Value Data Binding

Single-value data binding is a useful technique, but data binding becomes a lot more valuable when there are repeating sets of values to display – for example, a rowset from a relational database, or an array of values.

ASP.NET provides eight *list controls* that are designed to work with repeated-value data binding. They have a set of properties and methods that allow them to be connected to a data source. Then, they automatically create a display row or display item for each row or item in the data source. For example, a <select> list control will automatically create an appropriate set of <option> elements to display all the rows or items in the data source.

One obvious advantage with these controls is that you don't have to provide any of the HTML elements or other content. The control does it all automatically (although you can add HTML elements to the output to customize it if required).

The List Controls Designed for Repeated Binding

The eight controls specifically designed for use with server-side data binding are:

- ❑ The HTML <select> element, implemented by the System.Web.UI.HtmlControls.HtmlSelect .NET class. When presented with a suitable source of repeating data values it creates a standard HTML <select> list with repeating <option> elements.

- ❑ The ASP:ListBox control, implemented by the System.Web.UI.WebControls.ListBox .NET class. This control also creates a standard HTML <select> list with repeating <option> elements. By default, it creates a list-box rather than a drop-down list like the <select> element, though the appearance of both can be changed by setting the number of items to display.

- ❑ The ASP:DropDownList control, implemented by the System.Web.UI.WebControls.DropDownList .NET class. Again, this control creates a standard HTML <select> list with repeating <option> elements. However, by default, it creates a drop-down list rather than a listbox.

- ❑ The ASP:CheckBoxList control, implemented by the System.Web.UI.WebControls.CheckBoxList .NET class. This control creates a list of standard HTML <input type="checkbox"> elements – one for each row or item in the data source.

- ❑ The ASP:RadioButtonList control, implemented by the System.Web.UI.WebControls.RadioButtonList .NET class. This control creates a list of standard HTML <input type="radio"> elements – one for each row or item in the data source. It also sets the HTML name attribute (represented by the GroupName property of the control) to the same value so that the radio buttons in the list are associated.

❑   The ASP:Repeater control, implemented by the System.Web.UI.WebControls.Repeater
    .NET class. By default, this control generates no visible interface or formatting and no HTML
    content. It simply repeats the content defined within the control once for each row or item in the
    data source.

❑   The ASP:DataList control, implemented by the System.Web.UI.WebControls.DataList
    .NET class. This control repeats the content defined within the control once for each row or item
    in the data source, either enclosing each item in an HTML table row, or delimiting the items
    using an HTML <br /> element to create a list. It can also lay the content out in more than one
    column, and process items vertically or horizontally within the columns.

❑   The ASP:DataGrid control, implemented by the System.Web.UI.WebControls.DataGrid
    .NET class. This is a fully featured grid control designed for use with data contained in a
    DataView, DataSet, or DataReader object, or a collection. It generates a visible interface by
    way of an HTML table, automatically adding the column or item names to the header row.
    There are also many other useful features built in to make it easy to customize the display
    (which will be discussed later on).

Figure 7-3 (taken from the example page you'll see shortly) shows the physical appearance of these
controls:

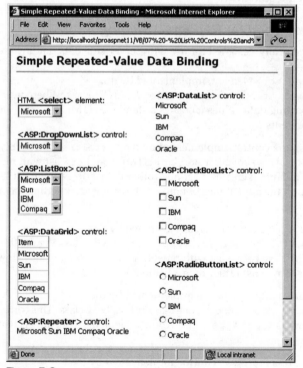

Figure 7-3

The Properties of a Repeated Binding Control

All the controls designed for use with server-side data binding expose properties and methods that are used to manage the binding. The properties are shown as follows:

Property	Description
DataTextField	Specifies which field or column in the data source contains the values to be used for display. For example, the values used as the text for `<option>` elements in a listbox, or the captions of the checkboxes in a `CheckBoxList` control.
DataValueField	Specifies which field or column in the data source contains the values to be used as the `Value` property of the control elements. For example, the values used as the `value` attribute for `<option>` elements in a listbox.
DataTextFormatString	The format string to be used for the values from the column or field specified in the `DataTextField` property when displaying these values in the control. For example, `"{0:C}"` for formatting currency values, or `"{0:dddd MMMM dd yyyy}"` for formatting dates.
DataMember	Specifies the set of rows to bind to when the data source contains more than one rowset. For example, the name of the table when binding to a `DataSet` object.

Many other properties are specific to individual controls, and govern how the content is displayed. You'll look at most of these in some example pages that use the controls later in this chapter.

The Methods of a Repeated-Value Binding Control

All of the controls designed for use with repeated-value data binding expose the two methods shown in the following table for working with bound data:

Method	Description
DataBind	Causes the control to populate itself with the data from the data source – in effect activating the bindings that are specified within the declaration of the control.
FindControl	Used to get a reference to a child control within the container (that is, within the bound control). This is useful when you want to check the value in another child control (such as a table cell) within the same row as the current control. It is normally used within event handlers that are executed once for each row or item – for example, the `DataBinding` event.

The Events of a Repeated-Value Binding Control

There is a wide range of events raised by the list controls, of which many are specific to the control type. However, there are two that are common across all list controls designed for use with data binding, as shown in the following table:

Event	Description
DataBinding	Occurs for each row or item in the data source as that row or item is created within the control during the execution of the DataBind method. The row or item is passed to the event within the event parameters, and code can examine and modify the content of that row or item as the container control is populated.
SelectedIndexChanged	Occurs when the currently selected item changes and the page is posted back to the server. It allows code to change the display to reflect the user's selection.

Sources of Data for Repeated-Value Binding

So, having looked at the controls, the next question is what kind of data source can you bind to them? In technical terms, the list controls can be bound to any data source that implements the IEnumerable, ICollection, or IListSource interface. In practical terms, the list controls can be bound to:

❑ A Collection, such as the collection of values in Request.Form, the collection of tables in a DataSet object's Tables collection, or a collection you create and populate.

❑ An ArrayList, which contains a simple list of values. This is a good way to create a list of items for display in such as a listbox.

❑ A HashTable, which contains items that are identified by a key, rather like a Dictionary object. Each item has a Key and a Value property, which makes this type of data source ideal for things like listboxes, in which the text to be displayed and the value to be returned when that item is selected are different.

❑ An ADO.NET DataView object, which contains rows from a DataTable that is populated from a database, or is manually created and populated using code (the whole topic of creating and manipulating relational data is discussed in Chapters 8 to 10).

❑ An ADO.NET DataSet object, which contains one or more DataTable objects that are populated from a database, or which are manually created and populated using code. This is a disconnected object that is easy to pass between the tiers of an application. The actual table to which the control is bound is specified in the DataMember property of the control.

❑ An ADO.NET DataReader object, which provides connected forward-only and read-only access to a database for extracting data. It can expose one or more rows of data, and essentially behaves in the same way as a DataView object for binding. For performance reasons, use a DataReader rather than a DataView or DataSet when possible. We'll explore the scenarios that do require the use of a DataView or DataSet, later in the chapter.

Chapter 15 provides a full examination of the various types of collection in the .NET Framework. Chapters 8, 9, and 10 contain a full examination of how to work with relational data and the `DataView`, `DataSet`, *and* `DataReader` *objects.*

The Syntax for Repeated-Value Data Binding

To bind controls to single values (properties, methods, or expressions as seen earlier), use the following:

```
<%# name-of-data-source %>
```

However, data sources used for repeated-value binding often have more than one *field* (that is, more than one value in each row or *list item*). Examples include the `HashTable`, which contains a `Key` and a `Value`, and the `DataView` or `DataReader` object, where each item is a `DataRow` object. Here, specify *which* field or column (that is, which value from each row or list item) you want to bind to the control.

Many of the list controls are also capable of displaying or using more than one value for each item in the list. For example, a `<select>` element can use one value for the content of an `<option>` element, and one value for that `<option>` element's `value` attribute:

```
<select>
  <option value="value1">Text1</option>
  <option value="value2">Text2</option>
  ...
</select>
```

Mapping Fields in the Data Source to Control Properties

There are two ways to map (or connect) specific fields in each row of the data source to the properties or attributes of a control; which method to use depends on the type of control you are binding to:

❑ If the control supports *templates,* declaratively create a template that defines the content of each 'row' or item that the control will display.

❑ If the control does not support templates, dynamically assign the fields in the data source to the attributes of the control by setting the properties of the control at runtime.

The controls in ASP.NET that do support templates are `Repeater`, `DataList`, and `DataGrid`. So, for one of these controls, you can declare a template within the control element and place the data binding instructions within it. Reference the row or list item as a `DataItem` object within the control's `Container`, and specify the field or column that you want to connect to. For example, when binding to a `HashTable`, specify either the `Key` property:

```
Key: <%# Container.DataItem.Key %>
```

Or the `Value` property:

```
Value: <%# Container.DataItem.Value %>
```

When binding to a `Collection`, `DataView`, or `DataReader` object, specify the property, field, or column name itself:

```
Value from DataView/DataReader: <%# Container.DataItem("BookTitle") %>
```

Or:

```
Value from Collection: <%# Container.DataItem("ForeColor") %>
```

You could, for example, use a `Repeater` control to display the `Key` and `Value` in each row of a `HashTable` as follows:

```
<ASP:Repeater id="MyRepeater" runat="server">
  <ItemTemplate>
    <%# Container.DataItem.Key %> =
    <%# Container.DataItem.Value %><br />
  </ItemTemplate>
</ASP:Repeater>
```

Then, in your `Page_Load` event handler, simply assign the data source to the control and call its `DataBind` method:

```
MyRepeater.DataSource = tabValues
MyRepeater.DataBind()
```

Mapping Fields Dynamically at Runtime

For controls that don't support templates, you must set the properties (listed earlier) at runtime. These properties specify the field from the data source that will provide the visible output for the control (the `DataTextField` property) and the field that will provide the non-displayed values for the control (the `DataValueField` property).

So, using the previous example of a `<select>` list populated from a `HashTable`, you could use one 'column' (probably the `Key`) as the `value` attribute of each `<option>` element, and the other 'column' (the `Value`) as the text of the `<option>` element. Declare the control as follows:

```
<select id="MySelectList" runat="server" />
```

Then set the properties of the control in the `Page_Load` event to display the appropriate fields from the data source:

```
MySelectList.DataSource = tabValues
MySelectList.DataValueField = "Key"
MySelectList.DataTextField = "Value"
MySelectList.DataBind()
```

The `DataGrid` control is clever enough to be able to figure out fields in the data source automatically, and display all the values. This works when the data source is an `Array`, a `DataView`, a `DataSet`, or a `DataReader`, but *not* when the data source is a `HashTable`.

We'll look at the `DataGrid` control in detail towards the end of this chapter.

Evaluating Expressions with the Eval Method

The data binding statement block in a control that uses templates (such as the `Repeater`, `DataList`, and `DataGrid`) can contain instances of only the following expression and derivatives of it.

In its simplest form, this expression is:

```
<%# Container.DataItem("field-name") %>
```

A common derivative is the use of the `Eval` method of the `DataBinder` object to specify a value within a data source (where it contains more than one value per row), and optionally format the value for display. In fact, there are three ways to use the `Eval` method:

❑   When each row or list item in the data source contains more than one value (more than one column or field) – for example, a row from a `DataView` based on a database table, or a `HashTable` object

❑   When you want to use a different object than the one the control is bound to as the source of the value

❑   When you want to format the value for display – for example, by taking a numeric value and formatting it as currency

The first of these is just an extension of the syntax used in the previous section, and adds nothing to the process other than a performance hit. In general it should be avoided. Here is an example, however, in which the required value is in the column named `BookTitle` within a row in a `DataView` object:

```
<%# DataBinder.Eval(Container.DataItem, "BookTitle") %>
```

The `DataBinder.Eval` method uses a technique called late-bound reflection to evaluate the expression. Therefore, it carries a noticeable performance overhead compared to the standard data binding syntax in which just the value name is specified.

Another important point is that you have to include a line continuation character in Visual Basic when using the `Eval` statement if you need to break the statement over more than one line. It's not really necessary, but should be kept in mind when you are reading published code listings in which the code could wrap to the next line.

The second way to use the `Eval` method is when you want to bind to an object that is not defined in the `DataSource` for the control. This allows you to reference specific values in that object, which are then used in every row that is displayed.

For example, if you have a `DataView` named `objCityData` that contains information about cities, you can specify the value of the `CityName` column in the fourth row (rows are indexed from zero) of the `DataView` with:

```
<%# DataBinder.Eval(objCityData, "[3].CityName") %>
```

However, the most common and useful application of the `Eval` method is to format values for display.

The `Eval` method takes three parameters, the last of which is optional. This third parameter, which we didn't use in the previous examples, is a *format string* that defines the format of the output.

For example, you can specify that the content of the `PublicationDate` field in your data source should be displayed in standard date format using:

```
<%# DataBinder.Eval(Container.DataItem, "PublicationDate", "{0:D}") %>
```

The result from this example is something like "*10 March 2001*" (it depends on the regional settings of the server). When you use the `Eval` method, you can only have one value in each expression, so the first number in the curly braces (a placeholder for the variable containing the value to be formatted) must always be zero.

The character(s) after the colon (in this case D) denote the format itself. The common format strings used with numeric values are shown as follows:

Format character	Description	Example (US English culture)
C or c	Currency format	$1,234.60, ($28.15), $28.75
D or d	Decimal format	205, 17534, -65
E or e	Scientific (exponential) format	3.46E+21, -1.2e+3, 3.003E-15
F or f	Fixed-point format	34.300, -0.230
G or g	General format	Depends on actual value
N or n	Number format	3,456.23, 12.65, -1.534
P or p	Percent format	45.6%, -10%
X or x	Hexadecimal format	&H5f76, 0x4528 (depends on actual value)

The following table shows the specific format strings used with dates:

Format character	Description	Example (US English culture)
d	Short date	M/d/yyyy
D	Long date	dddd, MMMM dd, yyyy
f	Full (long date and short time)	dddd, MMMM dd, yyyy HH:mm aa
F	Full (long date and long time)	dddd, MMMM dd, yyyy HH:mm:ss aa
g	General (short date and short time)	M/d/yyyy HH:mm aa
G	General (short date and long time)	M/d/yyyy HH:mm:ss aa
M or m	Month and day	MMMM dd
R or r	RFC1123 format	ddd, dd MMM yyyy HH':'mm':'ss'GMT'
s	ISO 8601 sortable using local time	yyyy-MM-dd HH:mm:ss
t	Short time	HH:mm aa
T	Long time	HH:mm:ss aa
u	ISO 8601 sortable using universal time	yyyy-MM-dd HH:mm:ss
U	Universal sortable date/time	dddd, MMMM dd, yyyy HH:mm:ss aa
Y or y	Year and month	MMMM, yyyy

It's also possible to use pre-defined characters to create a *picture* for numeric values. For example, the format string 00#.##, when applied to the number 1.2345 would produce 001.23. If you want to specify positive, negative, and zero formats, separate each with semi-colons. So given the format string 00#.##;(00#.##);[0], you would get (001.23) for -1.2345 and [0] for zero. All other characters are copied directly to the output, so the format string My value is: #.00 would, with the number 42, produce My value is: 42.00. The picture format characters for numbers are shown as follows:

Format character	Description
0	Displays a zero if there is no significant value – that is, it adds a zero in front of a number, or at the end of the number after the decimal point.
#	Digit placeholder, replaced only with significant digits. Other occurrences of this symbol are ignored if there is no significant digit.
.	Displays the decimal point character used by the current culture.
,	Separates number groups with the character used by the current culture, such as 1,000 in the US English culture. Can also be used to divide the value of a number – for example, the format string 0,, will display the number 100,000,000 as just 100 in the US English culture.
%	Displays the percent character used by the current culture.
E+0, E-0, e+0, or e-0	Formats the output as scientific or exponential notation.
\	Displays the following character as a literal – it is not interpreted as a format character.
" or '	Any characters enclosed in single or double quotes are interpreted as a literal string.
{ and }	Double curly brackets are used to display a single literal curly brace – for example, {{ displays { and }} displays }.
;	Separates the two or three sections for positive, negative, and zero values in the format string.

Remember that the DataBinder.Eval method carries a noticeable performance overhead compared to the standard data binding syntax of specifying just the value name, and you should use it only when necessary. In particular, avoid it when formatting of the value is not actually required. You can often format values as you extract them from a database, or within the definition of the property or method that provides the bound values.

Simple Repeated-Value Data Binding Examples

We've provided five example pages that are fundamentally similar, but demonstrate the different types of data source you can use with repeated-value data binding. There are examples of binding to an ArrayList, a HashTable, a DataView, a DataSet, and a DataReader. Let's start with the ArrayList example, and then see the differences between this and each of the other examples in turn.

Repeated-Value Binding to an ArrayList Object

The simplest example of repeated-value data binding uses a one-dimensional `ArrayList` that is created and populated with values in the `Page_Load` event handler. This example page, Simple Repeated-Value Data Binding (`simple-repeated-binding.aspx`) shown in Figure 7-4 includes one of each of the eight list controls bound to your `ArrayList`:

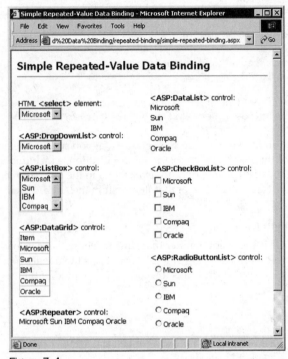

Figure 7-4

The HTML section of the page contains the definition of the eight list controls as shown in the following code. You can see that, with the exception of the `Repeater` and `DataList` controls, all you do is declare the control itself:

```
HTML <b>&lt;select&gt;</b> element:<br />
<select id="MySelectList" runat="server" /><p />


<b>&lt;ASP:DropDownList&gt;</b> control:<br />
<ASP:DropDownList id="MyDropDown" runat="server" /><p />


<b>&lt;ASP:ListBox&gt;</b> control:<br />
<ASP:ListBox id="MyASPList" runat="server" /><p />
<b>&lt;ASP:DataGrid&gt;</b> control:<br />
<ASP:DataGrid id="MyDataGrid" runat="server" /><p />


<b>&lt;ASP:Repeater&gt;</b> control:<br />
<ASP:Repeater id="MyRepeater" runat="server">
```

```
   <ItemTemplate>
     <%# Container.DataItem %>
   </ItemTemplate>
</ASP:Repeater><p />
<b>&lt;ASP:DataList&gt;</b> control:<br />
<ASP:DataList id="MyDataList" runat="server">
   <ItemTemplate>
     <%# Container.DataItem %>
   </ItemTemplate>
</ASP:DataList><p />

<b>&lt;ASP:CheckBoxList&gt;</b> control:<br />
<ASP:CheckBoxList id="MyCheckList" runat="server" /><p />

<b>&lt;ASP:RadioButtonList&gt;</b> control:<br />
<ASP:RadioButtonList id="MyRadioList" runat="server" /><p />
```

However, the `Repeater` and `DataList` controls require that you specify the output required for each repeated item, and so for these an `<ItemTemplate>` specification is included as well. The content placed inside the `<ItemTemplate>` is repeated once for every item in the data source. In your code, you're just specifying the `DataItem` itself – the value of that item within the `ArrayList`.

The Page_Load Event Handler

The remainder of the page is the event handler that runs when the page is loaded. It simply creates a new `ArrayList` and fills it with five string values. Then it sets the `DataSource` property of each of the eight list controls to this `ArrayList` and calls the `DataBind` method of the `Page` object to bind all the controls:

```
Sub Page_Load()

   'create an ArrayList of values to bind to
   Dim arrValues As New ArrayList(4)
   arrValues.Add("Microsoft")
   arrValues.Add("Sun")
   arrValues.Add("IBM")
   arrValues.Add("Compaq")
   arrValues.Add("Oracle")

   'set the DataSource property of the controls to the array
   MySelectList.DataSource = arrValues
   MyDropDown.DataSource = arrValues
   MyASPList.DataSource = arrValues
   MyDataGrid.DataSource = arrValues
   MyRepeater.DataSource = arrValues
   MyDataList.DataSource = arrValues
   MyCheckList.DataSource = arrValues
   MyRadioList.DataSource = arrValues

   'bind all the controls on the page
   Page.DataBind()
End Sub
```

How the Controls Are Bound

To understand what the controls are doing when data binding takes place, it's worth taking a look at the actual HTML that is created. You can do this by viewing the source of the page in your browser (if you're using Internet Explorer, right-click the page and select View Source). The following code shows how the simple list controls (the HTML <select>, ASP:DropDownList, and ASP:ListBox controls) are all persisted to the client as <select> elements. Each <option> element within the list has the value from the ArrayList items as both the value attribute and the text of the <option> element:

```
<select name="MySelectList" id="MySelectList">
  <option value="Microsoft">Microsoft</option>
  <option value="Sun">Sun</option>
  <option value="IBM">IBM</option>
  <option value="Compaq">Compaq</option>
  <option value="Oracle">Oracle</option>
</select>
```

The DataList control creates an HTML <table> and populates it with rows and cells containing the values from the ArrayList. The DataGrid control does the same, but adds a row containing the column name (in this case Item) as well:

```
<table cellspacing="0" rules="all" border="1">
  <tr><td>Item</td></tr>
  <tr><td>Microsoft</td></tr>
  <tr><td>Sun</td></tr>
  <tr><td>IBM</td></tr>
  <tr><td>Compaq</td></tr>
  <tr><td>Oracle</td></tr>
</table>
```

Both the CheckBoxList and RadioButtonList produce a table, but this time each cell contains either a checkbox control or a radio button control. The CheckBoxList control, which uses the values from the ArrayList as the captions for each checkbox – it doesn't set the value attribute of each one – is shown as follows:

```
<td>
  <span>
    <input id="MyCheckList_0" type="checkbox" name="MyCheckList:0" />
    <label for="MyCheckList_0">Microsoft</label>
  </span>
</td>
```

However, the RadioButtonList control does set the value as well as the caption for each radio button, and all the radio buttons have the same name attribute (the name given to the control), so they operate as a radio button group as shown:

```
<td>
  <span value="Microsoft">
    <input id="MyRadioList_0" type="radio" name="MyRadioList"
           value="Microsoft" />
    <label for="MyRadioList_0">Microsoft</label>
  </span>
</td>
```

Finally, the output from the `Repeater` control is just a list of the values with no formatting, as shown:

```
Microsoft
Sun
IBM
Compaq
Oracle
```

Repeated-Value Binding to a HashTable Object

To demonstrate the differences in the way you handle other types of data source, the next example page binds the eight types of list control to a `HashTable` object rather than an `ArrayList`. Run the **Repeated-Value Data Binding to a HashTable** (`hashtable-binding.aspx`) example page to see the difference. One thing you'll immediately notice in Figure 7-5 is that two of each of the first three controls are included, and they contain different sets of values:

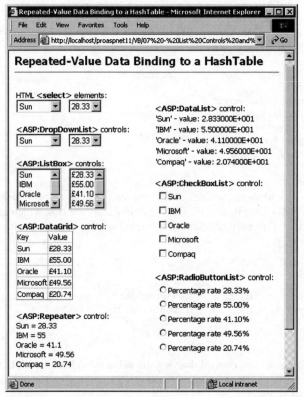

Figure 7-5

In this case, the data source is not a simple array of values, but a `Dictionary`-style object known as a `HashTable`. Each of the repeated items in the `HashTable` contains a `Key` and a `Value`. So, in this case, you can specify which of these you want to bind each control to. In the case of the first three list controls (the HTML `<select>`, `ASP:DropDownList`, and `ASP:ListBox` controls), we've bound one control to the Key of the `HashTable` and the other to the `Value`. The HTML section of the page is shown as follows:

```
HTML <b>&lt;select&gt;</b> elements:<br />
<select id="MySelectList1" runat="server" />  
<select id="MySelectList2" runat="server" /><p />

<b>&lt;ASP:DropDownList&gt;</b> controls:<br />
<ASP:DropDownList id="MyDropDown1" runat="server" />  
<ASP:DropDownList id="MyDropDown2" runat="server" /><p />

<b>&lt;ASP:ListBox&gt;</b> controls:<br />
<ASP:ListBox id="MyASPList1" runat="server" />  
<ASP:ListBox id="MyASPList2" runat="server" /><p />

<b>&lt;ASP:DataGrid&gt;</b> control:<br />
<ASP:DataGrid id="MyDataGrid" runat="server" AutoGenerateColumns="false">
  <Columns>
    <ASP:BoundColumn HeaderText="Key" DataField="Key" />
    <ASP:BoundColumn HeaderText="Value" DataField="Value"
                     DataFormatString="{0:C}" />
  </Columns>
</ASP:DataGrid><p />

<b>&lt;ASP:Repeater&gt;</b> control:<br />
<ASP:Repeater id="MyRepeater" runat="server">
  <ItemTemplate>
    <%# Container.DataItem.Key %> =
    <%# Container.DataItem.Value %><br />
  </ItemTemplate>
</ASP:Repeater><p />

<b>&lt;ASP:DataList&gt;</b> control:<br />
<ASP:DataList id="MyDataList" runat="server">
  <ItemTemplate>
    '<%# Container.DataItem.Key %>' - value:
    <%# DataBinder.Eval(Container.DataItem, "Value", "{0:E}") %>
  </ItemTemplate>
</ASP:DataList><p />

<b>&lt;ASP:CheckBoxList&gt;</b> control:<br />
<ASP:CheckBoxList id="MyCheckList" runat="server" /><p />

<b>&lt;ASP:RadioButtonList&gt;</b> control:<br />
<ASP:RadioButtonList id="MyRadioList" runat="server" /><p />
```

The declaration of the HTML `<select>`, `ASP:DropDownList`, and `ASP:ListBox` controls at the top of the page, and the `ASP:CheckBoxList` and `ASP:RadioButtonList` controls at the bottom of the page, is the same as the previous example – you just define the control itself. However, the definition of the other three list controls has to take into account the new structure of the data source.

Binding a DataGrid Control to a HashTable

The `DataGrid` control cannot figure out by itself how to handle a `HashTable`, and needs some help. This is done by setting the `AutoGenerateColumns` property of the control to `False`, and then using a `<Columns>` element and `ASP:BoundColumn` controls to specify where the values should come from. The two columns are bound to the `Key` and `Value` fields in each item. A `DataFormatString` is also specified for the `Value` column so that it is displayed in currency format:

```
<ASP:DataGrid id="MyDataGrid" runat="server" AutoGenerateColumns="false">
  <Columns>
    <ASP:BoundColumn HeaderText="Key" DataField="Key" />
    <ASP:BoundColumn HeaderText="Value" DataField="Value"
                     DataFormatString="{0:C}" />
  </Columns>
</ASP:DataGrid>
```

Binding a Repeater and a DataList Control to a HashTable

The `Repeater` and the `DataList` controls contain an `<ItemTemplate>` entry as in the previous example, where you used an `ArrayList`. However, now you can include two values in each template – the `Key` property and the `Value` property. We refer to these as properties of the `DataItem` object.

Let's add some extra layout information in these two controls. In the `Repeater` control, add the equals sign between the `Key` and the `Value`, and a line break after each `Key`/`Value` pair. In the `DataList` control, wrap the output for each `Key` in single quotes, adding the word `value:` and formatting the `Value` property in scientific notation using the format string `"{0:E}"`. The code is repeated as follows:

```
<b>&lt;ASP:Repeater&gt;</b> control:<br />
<ASP:Repeater id="MyRepeater" runat="server">
  <ItemTemplate>
    <%# Container.DataItem.Key %> =
    <%# Container.DataItem.Value %><br />
  </ItemTemplate>
</ASP:Repeater><p />

<b>&lt;ASP:DataList&gt;</b> control:<br />
<ASP:DataList id="MyDataList" runat="server">
  <ItemTemplate>
    '<%# Container.DataItem.Key %>' - value:
    <%# DataBinder.Eval(Container.DataItem, "Value", "(0:E}") %>
  </ItemTemplate>
```

The Page_Load Event Handler

When the page loads, first create the `HashTable` and fill in some values, as shown:

```
Sub Page_Load()

    'create a HashTable of values to bind to
    Dim tabValues As New HashTable(5)
    tabValues.Add("Microsoft", 49.56)
    tabValues.Add("Sun", 28.33)
    tabValues.Add("IBM", 55)
```

```
tabValues.Add("Compaq", 20.74)
tabValues.Add("Oracle", 41.1)
```

Then set the DataSource property of each of the controls on the page. In this case, you have to set at least the DataSource and DataTextField properties of the HTML <select>, ASP:DropDownList, and ASP:ListBox controls so that they know which field in the data source contains the values to display. In fact, this *is* exploited by having the first control in each pair display the Key values from the HashTable, and the second display the actual values of each item in the HashTable. You can also provide different values for the value attribute of the control if required as done for the second one of each control in the following code:

```
'first <select> displays the Keys in the HashTable
MySelectList1.DataSource = tabValues
MySelectList1.DataTextField = "Key"

'second one displays the Values in the HashTable
'and uses the Keys as the <option> values
MySelectList2.DataSource = tabValues
MySelectList2.DataValueField = "Key"
MySelectList2.DataTextField = "Value"

'same applies to ASP: controls, except here
'we can also specify the format of the Key
MyDropDown1.DataSource = tabValues
MyDropDown1.DataTextField = "Key"
MyDropDown2.DataSource = tabValues
MyDropDown2.DataValueField = "Key"
MyDropDown2.DataTextField = "Value"
MyDropDown2.DataTextFormatString = "{0:F}"

MyASPList1.DataSource = tabValues
MyASPList1.DataTextField = "Key"
MyASPList2.DataSource = tabValues
MyASPList2.DataValueField = "Key"
MyASPList2.DataTextField = "Value"
MyASPList2.DataTextFormatString = "{0:C}"
```

If you look back at Figure 7-5, you can also see the results of setting the DataTextFormatString property of the ASP:DropDownList and ASP:ListBox controls. For example, in the last four lines of the preceding code, the second ASP:ListBox control was bound to the HashTable so that the text of each <option> element is automatically formatted as a currency value.

Binding the DataGrid, Repeater, and DataList controls is easy because you specified how the columns should be mapped to the data source in the control definitions. You just need to set the DataSource property of each one:

```
MyDataGrid.DataSource = tabValues
MyRepeater.DataSource = tabValues
MyDataList.DataSource = tabValues
```

For the final two list controls, the CheckBoxList and RadioButtonList, you can specify both the DataValueField and the DataTextField properties. This is like the simple list controls such as the

`<select>` list, and allows you to use different fields from the `HashTable` for the `value` attribute and the text for the control's caption:

```
        'in the CheckboxList we'll display the Title and
        'use the Value as the control value
    MyCheckList.DataSource = tabValues
    MyCheckList.DataValueField = "Value"
    MyCheckList.DataTextField = "Key"
        'in the RadioList we'll display and format the
        'Value and use the Key as the control value
    MyRadioList.DataSource = tabValues
    MyRadioList.DataValueField = "Key"
    MyRadioList.DataTextField = "Value"
    MyRadioList.DataTextFormatString = "Percentage rate {0:F}%"
```

The final part of the code in the `Page_Load` event simply calls the `DataBind` method of the page to perform the data binding:

```
    Page.DataBind() 'bind all the controls on the page
End Sub
```

How the Controls Are Bound

If you view the output that this page creates in the browser, you'll see that (unlike in the previous `ArrayList` example, where the value and text were the same) the second list in each group has the `Key` from each item in the `HashTable` as the `value` attribute of the `<option>` elements, and the `Value` from each item in the `HashTable` as the text of each `<option>` element. A section of this output is shown here:

```
<select name="MySelectList2" id="MySelectList2">
   <option value="Sun">28.33</option>
   <option value="IBM">55</option>
   <option value="Oracle">41.1</option>
   <option value="Microsoft">49.56</option>
   <option value="Compaq">20.74</option>
</select>
```

With the `RadioButtonList`, this technique also gives an output that specifies the `Key` from each item in the `HashTable` as the `value` attribute. The `Value` of each item in the `HashTable` is formatted and used as the text caption of the checkbox or radio button:

```
<span value="Microsoft">
   <input id="MyRadioList_3" type="radio" name="MyRadioList" value="Microsoft" />
   <label for="MyRadioList_3">Percentage rate 49.56%</label>
</span>
```

Repeated-Value Binding to a DataView Object

Our third example of data binding is to a `DataView` object. For this example, we're using a custom user control that returns a `DataView` object from a database. We've provided the scripts and instructions for creating this database with the sample files, as well as a Microsoft Access database that you can use instead. All these are in the `database` folder of the examples for Chapters 8 to 11 (the data management examples).

> *We'll discuss data access techniques later in the book — it's not a vital topic here as long as you appreciate that basically each of the objects provides you with a set of data rows (a rowset) to which you can bind your controls. The next chapter discusses how to use these objects to extract data from a relational database.*

The example page shown in Figure 7-6, Repeated-Value Data Binding to a DataView Object (`dataview-binding.aspx`), contains the same eight list controls used in the previous two examples. However, now we are displaying information drawn from our database of Wrox books:

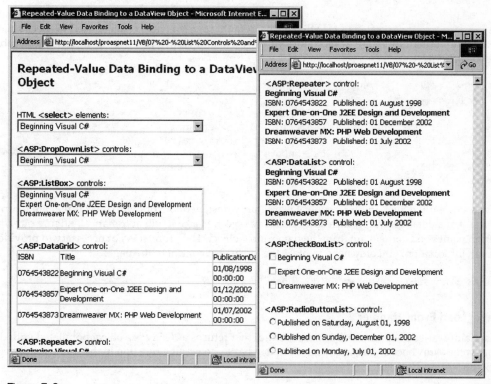

Figure 7-6

The HTML section of this page is basically the same as the first `ArrayList` example. The difference is the definition of the `Repeater` and the `DataList` controls. In each case, you need to specify the way to generate the content of the control from the values that are available in each list item (that is, each data row) within the source `DataView`.

The `Repeater` control generates no layout information by default, so you have to create a template using an `<ItemTemplate>` element. Specify a `<div>` element to get each item on a separate line, because the `Repeater` does not provide any intrinsic formatting. Inside the `<div>` element place the text, HTML, and definitions of the fields in the data source that you want to display. The following code displays the contents of three columns from the DataView – the Title, ISBN, and PublicationDate – *and* the way to format the PublicationDate column using the DataBinder.Eval method:

```
<ASP:Repeater id="MyRepeater" runat="server">
  <ItemTemplate>
    <div>
      <b><%# Container.DataItem("Title") %></b><br />
      ISBN: <%# Container.DataItem("ISBN") %>  
      Published: <%# DataBinder.Eval(Container.DataItem, _
                      "PublicationDate", "{0:D}") %>
    </div>
  </ItemTemplate>
</ASP:Repeater>
```

The DataList control creates an HTML table by default, so in this case you just need to specify the column and formatting information, along with any text and HTML you want to include in the table cells in each row:

```
<ASP:DataList id="MyDataList" runat="server">
  <ItemTemplate>
    <b><%# Container.DataItem("Title") %></b><br />
    ISBN: <%# Container.DataItem("ISBN") %>  
    Published: <%# DataBinder.Eval(Container.DataItem, _
                    "PublicationDate", "{0:D}") %>
  </ItemTemplate>
</ASP:DataList>
```

As you saw earlier, the DataGrid control is primarily designed to work with objects that are returned as the result of a database query, such as a DataView object. Hence it will automatically figure out what the column names and content are from the data source object. Therefore, it is not necessary to provide column information; you only need to place the DataGrid control in the page:

```
<ASP:DataGrid id="MyDataGrid" runat="server" />
```

The Page_Load Event Handler

This example uses a separate custom user control that returns a DataView object populated with details about some Wrox books. All the code in this page has to do is call a function in the user control to get back the DataView object:

```
'get connection string from web.config
Dim strConnect As String
strConnect = ConfigurationSettings.AppSettings("DsnWroxBooksOleDb")

'create a SQL statement to select some rows from the database
Dim strSelect As String
strSelect = "SELECT * FROM BookList WHERE ISBN LIKE '18610053%'"

'create a variable to hold an instance of a DataView object
Dim objDataView As DataView

'get dataset from get-dataset-control.ascx user control
```

```
objDataView = ctlDataView.GetDataView(strConnect, strSelect)
If IsNothing(objDataView) Then Exit Sub
```

The details of how the control is inserted into the page, and how it gets the data from the database and creates the `DataView` object are covered in Chapter 8.

The next step is to set the `DataSource` and other properties of the controls in the page. The HTML `<select>` list and `ASP:DropDownList` and `ASP:ListBox` controls are mapped to the `ISBN` and `Title` columns in the `DataView` using the `DataValueField` and `DataTextField` properties of the controls:

```
'<select> list displays values from the Title column
'and uses the ISBN as the <option> values

MySelectList.DataSource = objDataView
MySelectList.DataValueField = "ISBN"
MySelectList.DataTextField = "Title"

'do same with ASP: list controls
MyDropDown.DataSource = objDataView
MyDropDown.DataValueField = "ISBN"
MyDropDown.DataTextField = "Title"

MyASPList.DataSource = objDataView
MyASPList.DataValueField = "ISBN"
MyASPList.DataTextField = "Title"
```

As mentioned earlier, the `DataGrid` control can figure out what the `DataView` contains, so just set the `DataSource` property:

```
MyDataGrid.DataSource = objDataView
```

The column information is specified in the definition of the `Repeater` and `DataList` controls; you only need to set their `DataSource` properties:

```
MyRepeater.DataSource = objDataView
MyDataList.DataSource = objDataView
```

For the `CheckBoxList` control, use the `ISBN` as the `value` attribute, and the `Title` as the text to be displayed for each checkbox caption:

```
MyCheckList.DataSource = objDataView
MyCheckList.DataValueField = "ISBN"
MyCheckList.DataTextField = "Title"
```

Specify the `value` property of each radio button in the `RadioButtonList` control to be `ISBN`, but this time display the content of the `PublicationDate` as the caption. It is formatted using a custom format string to display a *long* date:

```
MyRadioList.DataSource = objDataView
MyRadioList.DataValueField = "ISBN"
MyRadioList.DataTextField = "PublicationDate"
MyRadioList.DataTextFormatString = "Published on {0:dddd, MMMM dd, yyyy}"
```

All that's left is to activate the binding for all the controls on the page by calling the `DataBind` method of the `Page` object:

```
Page.DataBind()
```

Repeated-Value Binding to a DataSet Object

Our next example of data sources is the `DataSet`, and this is used in the Repeated-Value Data Binding to a DataSet Object (`dataset-binding.aspx`) page. This page creates exactly the same result as the previous example. The only difference is the creation of the data source, and how you actually perform the binding. The page includes some code that creates a `DataSet` object, and we'll discuss how this works until the next chapter. We'll focus here on the use of an object that has (or can have) multiple members as a data source.

As you'll see in the next chapter, a `DataSet` object can contain several tables of data (in `DataTable` objects). Therefore, when you bind to a `DataSet`, specify which table you want the values for the control to come from. This is done with the `DataMember` property of each control. For example, to set the binding for the `<select>` list with the `id` of `MySelectList`, use:

```
MySelectList.DataSource = objDataSet 'specify the DataSet as the source
MySelectList.DataMember = "Books"    'use values from the table named "Books"
MySelectList.DataValueField = "ISBN" 'specify column to use for control values
MySelectList.DataTextField = "Title" 'specify column with text to display
```

And, of course, the same technique is used for the rest of the controls on the page.

Repeated-Value Binding to a DataReader Object

The Repeated-Value Data Binding to a DataReader Object (`datareader-binding.aspx`) example page uses a `DataReader` as the data source for the bound controls. In general, using a `DataReader` is the preferred source of data for server-side data binding.

However, there is one important difference between this and the other data sources used. A `DataReader` is really just a *pipe* to the result of executing a query in a database. Once the database has processed the query and built up the result set, the `DataReader` gives a forward-only connection to that result set. You can only read the rows once.

So, you can't create a `DataReader` and bind it to multiple controls as in the previous examples. They worked because all of the other data sources (an `ArrayList`, `HashTable`, `DataView`, and `DataSet`) are *disconnected* from the database.

Unlike the `DataReader`, these objects actually hold the data, which allows you to read the contents as many times as you like. Figure 7-7 shows the `DataReader` example page only, which contains just one data-bound control – a `DataGrid`:

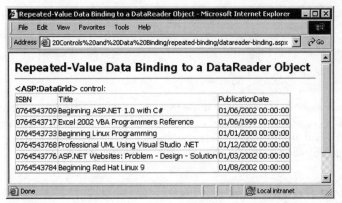

Figure 7-7

All you do is create your `DataReader` object in a variable named `objDataReader`, and bind it to the `DataGrid` control. The control can figure out what columns are in the rowset, and it displays the columnnames and the data automatically when you call the `DataBind` method:

```
    'create a DataReader object
Dim objDataReader As OleDbDataReader
...
    'code to connect to the database and build the rowset
...
    'set the DataSource property of the control
MyDataGrid.DataSource = objDataReader
MyDataGrid.DataBind() 'and bind the control
```

You are calling the `DataBind` method of the control, rather than the `DataBind` method of the `Page` object as done in previous examples (as you've only got this one control).

Adding Styles and Templates

You've seen how easy data binding is to use, and how much code and effort it saves. Next, we'll look at how to change the appearance of the data-bound controls. This can be done in three ways:

❑   Adding CSS styles to the control – either directly using a `<style>` element in the page, or by setting the specific style properties of the controls

❑   Creating templates that specify the appearance of individual sections of the control's output

❑   Using a combination of the two techniques

All of the example pages include a standard HTML `<style>` element in the `<head>` element, which specifies the font name and font size for the page. The controls are generating ordinary HTML, so their output is automatically formatted inline with these styles by the browser. The style section is as follows:

```
<style type="text/css">

    body, td {font-family:Tahoma,Arial,sans-serif; font-size:10pt}
    input {font-family:Tahoma,Arial,sans-serif; font-size:9pt}

</style>
```

So, all of the `<input>` elements (including those that are created by the `ASP:ListBox` control and `ASP:DropDownList` control) are formatted with the style specified within your `<style>` element. Also, specific CSS style definitions for the `<td>` elements are included in the `<style>` section, so that the HTML tables created by some of the list controls will be formatted as well.

Using the Style Properties

The list controls designed for use with data binding have a set of style properties that override the CSS styles defined in the page. These can be used to change the appearance of the control. The one exception is the `Repeater` control, which provides no visible interface elements (it simply repeats the content of the templates defined within it). Some of the properties that can be set are shown as follows (a full list for each control is included in the .NET SDK Documentation):

Properties	Description
`BackColor, BackImageUrl`	Sets the appearance of the control's background
`BorderStyle, BorderColor, BorderWidth`	Sets the appearance of the control's border
`GridLines, CellPadding, CellSpacing`	Specifies the appearance of each cell
`Font-Name, Font-Size, Font-Bold`	Specifies the text style within the control
`HeaderStyle, ItemStyle, FooterStyle AlternatingItemStyle`	Specifies the style for various parts of the control's output, such as the header or the content items

Adding Style to a DataGrid Control

If you run the Using CSS to Add Style to a DataGrid (`css-style-datagrid.aspx`) example page, you will see how these style properties can be used, and the effect they have on the appearance of a `DataGrid` control. The styles selected are shown in Figure 7-8, and thankfully, the alternating green and red text is not visible in these monochrome screenshots. You can edit the code yourself to experiment with the different styles.

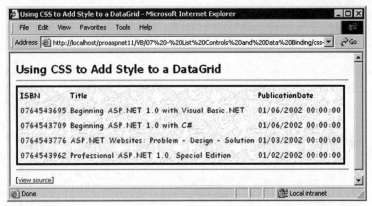

Figure 7-8

All of the work of formatting the output of this example is done using the style properties of the `DataGrid` object. The definition of the `DataGrid` within the HTML section of the page is as follows:

```
<ASP:DataGrid id="MyDataGrid" runat="server"

  ShowHeader="True"
  ShowFooter="False"
  BackColor="darkgray"
  BackImageUrl="background.gif"
  ToolTip="A List of Wrox Books"
  GridLines="None"
  BorderStyle="Solid"
  BorderColor="black"
  BorderWidth="3"
  CellPadding="2"
  CellSpacing="2"
  Font-Name="Comic Sans MS"
  Font-Size="10pt"
  Font-Bold="True" >

    <HeaderStyle ForeColor="blue" />
    <ItemStyle ForeColor="red" />
    <AlternatingItemStyle ForeColor="green" />

</ASP:DataGrid>
```

This specifies that the grid should display a header but not a footer row (although, in fact, these are the defaults). Also specified are the background color and an image to be used to fill the grid, a tool-tip that is displayed when the mouse hovers over the grid, as well as turning off the grid lines display.

Next come the properties that define a 3-pixel wide black border for the control, and the padding within and spacing between the cells. You also specify the font name and size, and make it bold. Finally come the style definitions for the header, each item (row) in the grid, and each alternating item.

All that's being done here is specifying a color for the ForeColor property (via the ForeColor attribute), though in fact you can include values for the other properties such as BackColor, BorderWidth, Font, and so on.

In the Page_Load event, all you have to do now is create a DataReader object, set it as the DataSource property of the grid, and then call the DataBind method. In this case, as there's only the one control to deal with, the DataBind method is called for your DataGrid control rather than at Page-level:

```
...
'create a suitable DataReader object here
...

'set the DataSource property of the DataGrid
MyDataGrid.DataSource = objDataReader

'and bind the control to the data
MyDataGrid.DataBind()
```

Using Templates with Data-Bound Controls

The second way to manage the appearance of the ASP list controls designed for use with data binding is through the addition of *templates* to the control definition. In fact (as seen in earlier examples), templates can do a lot more than just change the appearance of a control – you can use them to specify which columns are displayed in a control, and how the values appear.

Three of the ASP list controls – the Repeater, DataList, and DataGrid – accept a series of templates that define the appearance and content of specific parts of the output. All the templates are optional (depending on the control and the data source, as you'll see shortly). Figure 7-9 demonstrates the complete list:

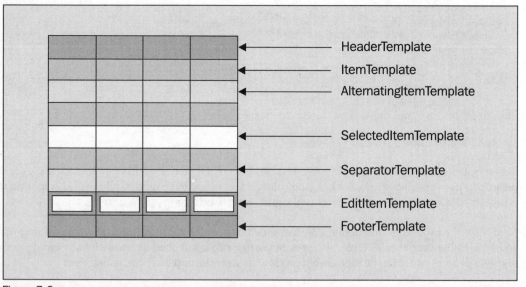

Figure 7-9

The names of each template are self-explanatory; you can optionally specify a different appearance for the header row (usually where the names of each field or column appear), the item rows, the alternating item rows, the separator used between each item row, and the footer row (often used to display navigation controls if there is more than one 'page' of rows available).

The remaining two templates require a little more explanation:

❑   The DataList and DataGrid controls allow you to specify one item or row that is "selected" (by setting the SelectedIndex property). The SelectedItemTemplate is then used to specify the appearance of this item or row.

❑   The DataList and DataGrid controls also allow you to switch them into edit mode (by setting the EditItemIndex property). The EditItemTemplate is used to specify the appearance of this item or row; for example, by changing the controls used to display the values in the row from labels to input controls.

Specifying Style and Content in a Repeater Control

You'll recall that a Repeater control is the simplest of all list controls, and is designed simply to repeat the content of the item or row without adding any formatting or layout information. To specify the content of each item when using a Repeater control (as in earlier examples), you have to add at least an <ItemTemplate> element to the control declaration. For example, to bind to an ArrayList, the code used is as follows:

```
<ASP:Repeater id="MyRepeater" runat="server">

  <ItemTemplate>
    <%# Container.DataItem %>
  </ItemTemplate>

</ASP:Repeater>
```

This specifies that the value in each row of the one-dimensional ArrayList should be displayed within the control. The <ItemTemplate> is used to define the content of the output.

The Using a Simple Template with a Repeater Control (simple-repeater-template.aspx) example page demonstrates how to use templates to specify both the content and the appearance of a Repeater control.

In this case you're displaying an image, a subheading, and some text for each item, and are also displaying a header, a footer with a hyperlink to the Wrox web site, and separating each row with a dark red *horizontal rule* image, as shown in Figure 7-10:

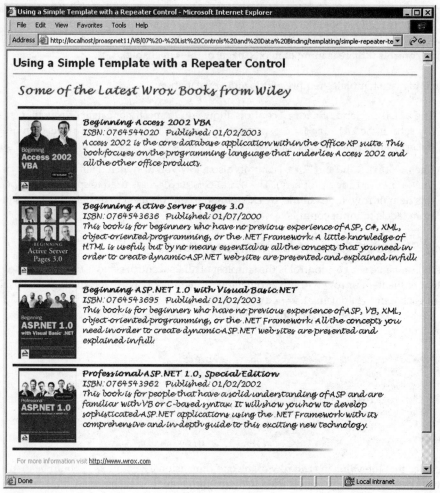

Figure 7-10

This example applies style to a `Repeater` control through the use of four templates – one each for the header, item, separator, and footer of the control – and through a set of CSS styles defined within a `<style>` element in the `<head>` section of the page. Each template specifies the formatting, layout, and content of that section of the control's output – it has to do so as the `Repeater` control produces no layout information of its own.

The following code shows how the control definition starts with the opening `<ASP:Repeater>` tag, and then contains the first template definition. This is the `<HeaderTemplate>` (although template definitions don't have to be placed in any particular order within the control definition). It uses a `<div>` element to place the heading text and a ruler-style image on the page. This `<div>` element uses the `rHead` CSS style class to format the appearance of the text in the header:

```
<ASP:Repeater id="MyRepeater" runat="server">
  <HeaderTemplate>
    <div class="rHead">
      Some of the Latest Wrox Books from Wiley<br />
      <img src="images/redrule.gif">
    </div>
  </HeaderTemplate>
```

This is followed by the `<ItemTemplate>` definition, which again is a `<div>` element. However, this time it takes its style from the `rItem` CSS style class. Inside the `<div>` element is an `<img>` element that contains the cover image – it uses the value of the column `ImageURL` as the `src` attribute of the image. This is followed by definitions of the text and bound values – similar to those used in earlier examples – that display the book title, the ISBN, the publication date, and a short description obtained from a column named `Precis`. Then comes a `<br />` element that prevents the next item from wrapping to the cover image in this row.

```
<ItemTemplate>
  <div class="rItem">
    <img src="images/<%# Container.DataItem("ImageURL") %>"
         align="left" hspace="10" />
    <b><%# Container.DataItem("Title") %></b><br />
    ISBN: <%# Container.DataItem("ISBN") %>  
    Published: <%# DataBinder.Eval(Container.DataItem, _
          "PublicationDate", "{0:d}") %><br />
    <%# Container.DataItem("Precis") %>
  </div><br clear="all" />
</ItemTemplate>
```

A line-continuation character has been included in the Eval statement for the Published value. As this code is executed within the control at runtime to obtain the values, you can't have line breaks within it when using Visual Basic unless you include the line-continuation character.

Next comes the `<SeparatorTemplate>` definition. This is simply the red *horizontal rule* image:

```
<SeparatorTemplate>
  <img src="images/redrule.gif">
</SeparatorTemplate>
```

Finally, you have the `<FooterTemplate>` definition. This also contains the red *horizontal rule* image. The `SeparatorItem` template is only rendered *between* items in the control, and not before the first one or after the last one. After the image comes the *more information* link, and then the closing `</ASP:Repeater>` tag:

```
<FooterTemplate>
  <img src="images/redrule.gif">
  <div class="rFoot">
    For more information visit
    <a href="http://www.wrox.com">http://www.wrox.com</a>
  </div>
</FooterTemplate>
</ASP:Repeater>
```

The Page_Load Event Handler

In this example, we provide the `Repeater` control with a `DataView` object created in code within the `Page_Load` event handler, rather than using a separate user control as seen in some of the earlier examples. The first part of the `Page_Load` event handler is responsible for creating a `DataTable` object from which you can obtain a `DataView`. The code follows in abridged form – we'll discuss the concepts of relational data access in depth in Chapters 8 to 10:

```
Sub Page_Load()

    'create a new empty DataTable object
    Dim objTable As New DataTable("NewTable")

    'define four columns (fields) within the table
    objTable.Columns.Add("ISBN", System.Type.GetType("System.String"))
    objTable.Columns.Add("Title", System.Type.GetType("System.String"))
    objTable.Columns.Add("PublicationDate", _
                         System.Type.GetType("System.DateTime"))
    objTable.Columns.Add("ImageURL", System.Type.GetType("System.String"))
    objTable.Columns.Add("Precis", System.Type.GetType("System.String"))

    'declare a variable to hold a DataRow object
    Dim objDataRow As DataRow

    'create a new DataRow object instance in this table
    objDataRow = objTable.NewRow()

    'and fill in the values
    objDataRow("ISBN") = "1861004478"
    objDataRow("Title") = "Professional Application Center 2000"
    objDataRow("PublicationDate") = "2001-03-01"
    objDataRow("ImageURL") = "appcenter.gif"
    objDataRow("Precis") = "This book takes you through ... etc."
    objTable.Rows.Add(objDataRow)

    ...
    'repeat process for other rows
    ...

    'assign the DataTable's DefaultView object to the Repeater control
    MyRepeater.DataSource = objTable.DefaultView
    MyRepeater.DataBind() 'and bind (display) the data

End Sub
```

The penultimate line of code simply assigns the `DataView` object that is returned from the `DefaultView` property of the table to the `DataSource` property of the `Repeater` control. The `DataBind` method of the control is then executed to display the contents of the `DataView`.

Loading Templates Dynamically at Runtime

The templates used in the previous example were hardcoded into the source of the page. But what happens if you want to change the template you use at runtime? The Loading Templates Dynamically with a DataList Control (`datalist-load-template.aspx`) example page shown in Figure 7-11 demonstrates how to do this by dynamically loading templates using code. The page includes a drop-down list from which you can select a color scheme for the output, and it loads the appropriate set of header, footer, item, and alternating item templates from disk each time:

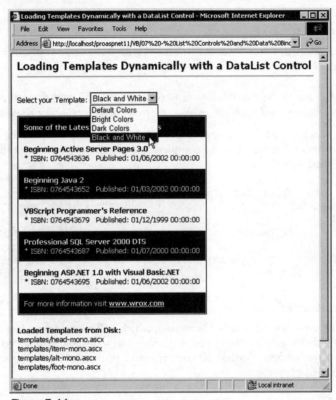

Figure 7-11

The HTML section of the page defines a `<form>` element containing the drop-down list that is used to select the color scheme. By setting the `AutoPostback` property to `True` (as described in Chapter 6), the need for a separate button is avoided, as the form will be posted to the server automatically whenever the selection in the list is changed. The remainder of the HTML defines the `DataList` control with minimal formatting, and a `Label` control where the names of the template files currently in use are displayed:

```
<form runat="server">
  Select your Template:
  <ASP:DropDownList runat="server" id="TemplateList" AutoPostback="True">
    <ASP:ListItem Value="default" Text="Default Colors" />
    <ASP:ListItem Value="bright" Text="Bright Colors" />
    <ASP:ListItem Value="dark" Text="Dark Colors" />
    <ASP:ListItem Value="mono" Text="Black and White" />
  </ASP:DropDownList>
</form>
<ASP:DataList id="MyDataList" runat="server"
```

```
            BorderStyle="None"
            Font-Name="Tahoma"
            Font-Size="10pt" />
<p><ASP:Label id="lblFileNames" runat="server" /></p>
```

The Dynamic Template Files

Dynamically loaded templates must be disk files stored within the same application's root folder or a subfolder of the page that uses them.

We've provided four templates for each color scheme (one each for the header, item, alternating item, and footer), placed in a folder named templates *below the folder that contains our example page.*

These template files contain just the contents of each of the templates, and omit the enclosing `<xxxxTemplate>` element. For example, the complete `ItemTemplate` section for items when the bright color scheme is selected is as follows:

```
<div style="color:white; background-color:blue; padding=10px">
<b><%# DataBinder.Eval(CType(Container,DataListItem).DataItem, "Title") %></b>
<br />* ISBN:
<%# DataBinder.Eval(CType(Container,DataListItem).DataItem, "ISBN") %>  
Published:
<%# DataBinder.Eval(CType(Container,DataListItem).DataItem, "PublicationDate") %>
</div>
```

The Page_Load Event Handler

When the page loads, a `DataReader` object is created, which will return some data rows from the sample database. We then create the filenames of the four templates for the selected color scheme. If this is the first time the page has been loaded (meaning it's not a postback, so no color scheme has been selected yet), the default templates are used:

```
Sub Page_Load()
      'create a suitable DataReader object here
   Dim strFileName As String
   If Page.IsPostBack Then
     strFileName = TemplateList.SelectedItem.Value & ".ascx"
   Else
     strFileName = "default.ascx"
   End If
   Dim strHeadFile As String = "templates/head-" & strFileName
   Dim strItemFile As String = "templates/item-" & strFileName
   Dim strAltIFile As String = "templates/alt-" & strFileName
   Dim strFootFile As String = "templates/foot-" & strFileName
```

Now that you have the filenames, you can load the templates by calling the `LoadTemplate` method of the `Page` object. The reference returned by this method is assigned to the appropriate property of the `DataList` control:

```
MyDataList.HeaderTemplate = Page.LoadTemplate(strHeadFile)
MyDataList.ItemTemplate = Page.LoadTemplate(strItemFile)
MyDataList.AlternatingItemTemplate = Page.LoadTemplate(strAltIFile)
MyDataList.FooterTemplate = Page.LoadTemplate(strFootFile)
```

The final tasks are to display the names of the templates in the `Label` control, and then to bind the `DataReader` object containing your data rows to the `DataList` control:

```
lblFileNames.Text = "<b>Loaded Templates from Disk:</b><br />" _
   & strHeadFile & "<br />" & strItemFile & "<br />" _
   & strAltIFile & "<br />" & strFootFile & "<br />"
MyDataList.DataSource = objDataReader
MyDataList.DataBind()
End Sub
```

Multiple Column Layouts with a DataList Control

The `DataList` control used in the previous example creates output that is, by default, an HTML table that contains the items you bind it to. One very useful aspect of this control is the ability to change the layout of the table content by specifying the number of columns to use, and the order in which the columns are filled from the data source (that is, from top to bottom or from left to right).

The Using Multiple Display Columns with a DataList Control (`columns-datalist-template.aspx`) example page shows this technique in use. It displays six book cover images in two columns of three when the page is opened. However, you can use the controls in the page to change the number of columns and the layout direction, as shown in Figure 7-12:

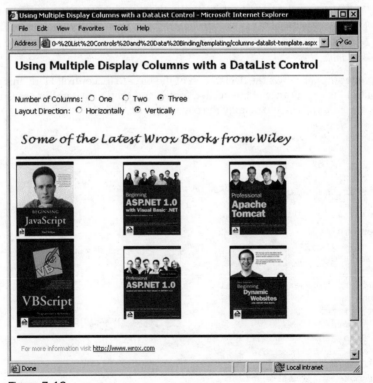

Figure 7-12

The HTML section of this page contains a `<form>` element with the five radio buttons that control how the `DataList` should lay out the content. Use the `AutoPostback` feature so that any change to the current settings automatically posts the values to the server, which regenerates the page with the new layout:

```
<form runat="server">
  Number of Columns:
  <ASP:RadioButton id="Cols1" GroupName="Cols" AutoPostback="True"
                   runat="server" /> One  
  <ASP:RadioButton id="Cols2" GroupName="Cols" AutoPostback="True"
                   runat="server" /> Two  
  <ASP:RadioButton id="Cols3" GroupName="Cols" AutoPostback="True"
                   runat="server" /> Three<br />
  Layout Direction:
  <ASP:RadioButton id="Horiz" GroupName="Dir" AutoPostback="True"
                   runat="server" /> Horizontally  
  <ASP:RadioButton id="Vert" GroupName="Dir" AutoPostback="True"
                   runat="server" /> Vertically<p />
</form>
```

The `DataList` control lays out its content using an HTML `<table>`. If you include a definition of a `<table>` and the corresponding `<tr>` and `<td>` elements within a `DataList` control's template, the contents of this table are ignored by default. To display the content for each data item in a nested table, you must set the `ExtractTemplateRows` attribute to `True` for the `DataList` control, and use the `<ASP:Table>`, `<ASP:TableRow>`, and `<ASP:TableCell>` server controls within the templates to create the nested table.

The following code snippet shows the declaration of the `DataList` control. Here, three templates are specified to control the appearance of the header, footer, and each item – in this case, using an `<img>` element in the `<ItemTemplate>` to display the cover images:

```
<ASP:DataList id="MyDataList" runat="server" RepeatLayout="Table">

  <HeaderTemplate>
    <div class="rHead">
      Some of the Latest Wrox Books from Wiley
    </div>
    <img src="images/redrule.gif">
  </HeaderTemplate>

  <ItemTemplate>
    <span>
      <img src="images/<%# Container.DataItem %>" />
    </span>
  </ItemTemplate>

  <FooterTemplate>
    <img src="images/redrule.gif">
    <div class="rFoot">
      For more information visit
      <a href="http://www.wrox.com">http://www.wrox.com</a>
    </div>
```

```
    </FooterTemplate>
  </ASP:DataList>
```

The Page_Load Event Handler

The layout styles for the `DataList` are set in the `Page_Load` event handler code. Let's start by checking if this is a postback, or if it's the first time the page has been loaded. If it's a postback, you will already have the data source (an `ArrayList` in this case) available, so you only need to check what values were selected in the radio buttons and set the appropriate values for the `RepeatColumns` and `RepeatDirection` properties of the `DataGrid`. This automatically lays out the contents in the required way, without the need to rebind the data source:

```
Sub Page_Load()

  If Page.IsPostBack Then

    'set the number of columns to display
    If Cols1.Checked = True Then MyDataList.RepeatColumns = 1
    If Cols2.Checked = True Then MyDataList.RepeatColumns = 2
    If Cols3.Checked = True Then MyDataList.RepeatColumns = 3

    'set the repeat direction of the items in the columns
    If Horiz.Checked = True Then
      MyDataList.RepeatDirection = RepeatDirection.Horizontal
    End If
    If Vert.Checked = True Then
      MyDataList.RepeatDirection = RepeatDirection.Vertical
    End If
```

However, if this is the first time that the page has been loaded (that is, it's not a postback), you must create and populate the `ArrayList` and bind it to the `DataList` control. You also have to set the default values for the radio buttons, and set appropriate initial values for the properties of your `DataList` control:

```
  Else

    'create an ArrayList of values to bind to
    Dim arrValues As New ArrayList(5)
    arrValues.Add("4055.gif")
    arrValues.Add("3679.gif")
    arrValues.Add("3695.gif")
    arrValues.Add("3962.gif")
    arrValues.Add("3725.gif")
    arrValues.Add("3741.gif")

    'bind the ArrayList to the DataList control
    MyDataList.DataSource = arrValues
    MyDataList.DataBind()

    'set default columns and direction when page first loads
    Cols2.Checked = True
    MyDataList.RepeatColumns = 2
    Horiz.Checked = True
```

```
        MyDataList.RepeatDirection = RepeatDirection.Horizontal

    End If

End Sub
```

You only have to create the data source once – when the page is first loaded – and not every time the user changes the layout. The values from the `ArrayList` are persisted through the viewstate of the page. However, you should be aware of issues that can arise from this. We'll look at the whole concept of managing the viewstate in the section on sorting and filtering the rows displayed in a list control.

Custom and Hidden Columns in a DataGrid

Templates are immensely powerful when used with the `Repeater`, `DataList`, and `DataGrid` controls. In fact, when you use a `DataGrid` control, they become almost indispensable.

The `DataGrid` control is very clever. It automatically figures out how many columns are needed to display the contents of a data source such as a `DataView` or `DataReader` object, and adds the column names to the header row. Unlike the `Repeater` and `DataList` controls, you don't *have to* include templates that define the content. In other words, just use a simple definition of the control and bind it to the data source:

```
<ASP:DataGrid id="MyDataGrid" runat="server" />
...
MyDataGrid.DataSource = objDataView
MyDataGrid.DataBind()
```

But what if you don't want to display all of the columns in the data source or if want to add custom columns to the output? It would be a shame to have to abandon the `DataGrid`, with all the extra features it provides, and go back to using a `DataList` or `Repeater` control.

Specifying a Custom Column Layout

You can use templates to specify the column layout of the `DataGrid` control, rather than relying on it to automatically generate the columns. You can set the `AutoGenerateColumns` property to `False` and then use a `<Columns>` element to specify the columns to be displayed. Within the `<Columns>` element, you can place a series of `ASP:BoundColumn` controls that define the column properties:

```
<ASP:DataGrid id="MyDataGrid" runat="server" AutoGenerateColumns="False">
  <Columns>
    <ASP:BoundColumn HeaderText="Book Code" DataField="ISBN" />
    <ASP:BoundColumn HeaderText="Book Title" DataField="Title" />
  </Columns>
</ASP:DataGrid>
```

The preceding code specifies that the control should display only the `ISBN` and `Title` columns from your data source, and that the columns should have the names `Book Code` and `Book Title` in the header row of the final output rather than the column name.

Adding Unbound Columns

You can also add extra columns that are not part of the original dataset by using an ASP:TemplateColumn control and an ItemTemplate element. For example, the declaration of a DataGrid control as shown in the following code includes a column with the heading Information. In each row of this column is an (unbound) ASP:Button control with the caption More Info:

```
<ASP:DataGrid id="MyDataGrid" runat="server" AutoGenerateColumns="False">
  <Columns>
    ...
    <ASP:TemplateColumn HeaderText="Information">
      <ItemTemplate>
        <ASP:Button id="cmdInfo" Text="More Info" runat="server" />
      </ItemTemplate>
    </ASP:TemplateColumn>
  </Columns>
</ASP:DataGrid>
```

Formatting the Column Contents

You can change the appearance of each of the custom columns, and format the values they contain. The following code declares a DataGrid like that described earlier, but now it has a column with the heading Released that displays the value of the PublicationDate column in the source dataset. The value is formatted as a date using the format string "{0:D}", and right-aligned in the column on a yellow background:

```
<ASP:DataGrid id="MyDataGrid" runat="server" AutoGenerateColumns="False">
  <Columns>
    <ASP:BoundColumn HeaderText="Book Code" DataField="ISBN" />
    <ASP:BoundColumn HeaderText="Book Title" DataField="Title" />
    <ASP:BoundColumn HeaderText="Released" DataField="PublicationDate"
            DataFormatString="{0:D}"
            ItemStyle-BackColor="yellow"
            ItemStyle-HorizontalAlign="right" />
    <ASP:TemplateColumn HeaderText="<b>Buy Now</b>"
            ItemStyle-BackColor="silver"
            ItemStyle-HorizontalAlign="center">
      <ItemTemplate>
        <ASP:CheckBox id="chkBuy" runat="server" />
      </ItemTemplate>
    </ASP:TemplateColumn>
  </Columns>
</ASP:DataGrid>
```

There is also a column with the heading Buy Now in bold text. It has a silver background with the content aligned centrally in the column, and each row contains an unbound checkbox control. You can see all of the effects we've just been describing by running the Specifying the Columns in a DataGrid Control (columns-datagrid.aspx) example page. The result is shown in Figure 7-13:

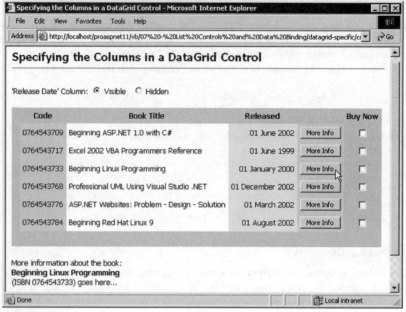

Figure 7-13

Clicking any of the **More Info** buttons produces some text at the foot of the page (it's displayed in a `Label` control). This text would probably be extracted from the same database table (or another table). However, it's not implemented in the example, as we're more interested in the way that the `DataGrid` control is used.

The first part of the HTML is the definition of the two radio buttons that control the display of the **Released** column. As in previous examples, you can use automatic postback to make it more intuitive to use:

```
<form runat="server">

  'Release Date' Column:
  <ASP:RadioButton id="chkVisible" GroupName="Col2Visible" runat="server"
                   AutoPostback="True" /> Visible  
  <ASP:RadioButton id="chkNotVisible" GroupName="Col2Visible" runat="server"
                   AutoPostback="True" /> Hidden<p />
```

Next comes the `DataGrid` control definition. It's on the `<form>` because it contains controls that you want to use for posting the page back to your server (that is, the **More Info** buttons). It uses the techniques we've just been discussing to create a custom column layout (including columns that contain only a non-breaking space and are simply there to give the required appearance for the control).

The penultimate `ASP:TemplateColumn` control contains an `<ItemTemplate>` element that specifies that each row will contain an `ASP:Button` control with the caption **More Info**. It also specifies that the `CommandName` property of the button is `Info`. You'll see how to use this when you look at the code in the page shortly.

```
<ASP:DataGrid id="MyDataGrid" runat="server"
    AutoGenerateColumns="False"
    CellPadding="5"
    GridLines="None"
    HeaderStyle-BackColor="silver"
    HeaderStyle-HorizontalAlign="center"
    FooterStyle-BackColor="silver"
    ShowFooter="True"
    OnItemCommand="ShowInfo">
  <Columns>
    <ASP:TemplateColumn HeaderText="" ItemStyle-BackColor="silver">
      <ItemTemplate> </ItemTemplate>
    </ASP:TemplateColumn>
    <ASP:BoundColumn HeaderText="<b>Code</b>" DataField="ISBN"
          ItemStyle-BackColor="lightblue" />
    <ASP:BoundColumn HeaderText="<b>Book Title</b>" DataField="Title"/>
    <ASP:BoundColumn HeaderText="<b>Released</b>"
            DataField="PublicationDate"
            DataFormatString="{0:D}" ItemStyle-BackColor="yellow"
            ItemStyle-HorizontalAlign="right" />
    <ASP:TemplateColumn HeaderText="" ItemStyle-BackColor="lightblue">
      <ItemTemplate>
        <ASP:Button id="cmdInfo" Text="More Info"
            CommandName="Info" runat="server" />
      </ItemTemplate>
    </ASP:TemplateColumn>
    <ASP:TemplateColumn HeaderText="Buy Now" ItemStyle-BackColor="silver"
            ItemStyle-HorizontalAlign="center">
      <ItemTemplate>
        <ASP:CheckBox id="chkBuy" runat="server" />
      </ItemTemplate>
    </ASP:TemplateColumn>
  </Columns>
</ASP:DataGrid>
```

The only other control is the `Label` named `lblInfo` used for displaying information about each book in the table:

```
<ASP:Label id="lblInfo" runat="server" />

</form>
```

Binding the DataGrid

The code in this page is divided into three subroutines:

❏ `Page_Load` is executed each time the page is loaded. It sets the visibility of the `Released` column and then calls the `BindDataGrid` routine.

❏ `BindDataGrid` fetches the data from the database and returns it as a `DataReader` object. Then it binds this to the `DataGrid` control to display the values.

❏ `ShowInfo` runs when any of the command buttons in the grid is clicked. It retrieves the ISBN and title of the book from the row, and displays it in the `Label` control at the foot of the page.

Showing and Hiding Columns

When you click the relevant radio button at the top of the page, the Released column is hidden or shown in the grid as shown in Figure 7-14. Compare this with Figure 7-13 to see the difference.

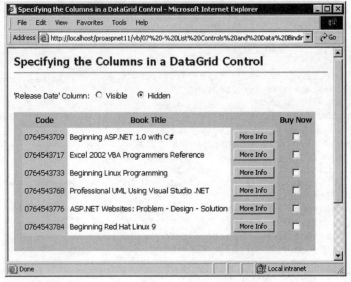

Figure 7-14

The radio buttons have their AutoPostback property set to True so that the page is reloaded each time the selection is changed. In the Page_Load event, check to see if this is the first time the page has been loaded. If not (that is, if it's a postback), you have to set the Visible property of the appropriate column using its index within the Columns collection of the DataGrid control. If it's not a postback, you have to set the default value for the radio buttons and bind the grid to the data source. In this case, the Released column will be displayed, because the default is to show all columns:

```
Sub Page_Load()

   If Page.IsPostBack Then
      'display or hide the "Released" column
      'have to use the index of the column not the column name
      MyDataGrid.Columns(3).Visible = (chkVisible.Checked = True)
   Else
      chkVisible.Checked = True 'set default value
      BindDataGrid()          'create dataset and bind grid
   End If

End Sub
```

Reacting to the ItemCommand Event

The other interesting feature of the example page is how it displays information about each book in response to a click on the More Info button. In the definition of the DataGrid control, we specified the name of an event handler for the `ItemCommand` event by setting the `OnItemCommand` property of the `DataGrid`:

```
OnItemCommand="ShowInfo"
```

When any control within the grid is activated – in this case, the `ASP:Button` control with the caption **More Info** – this event handler is executed. The parameters sent to the event handler contain a reference to the control that initiated the event, and a `DataGridCommandEventArgs` object that contains details of the event as well as references to the current row in the control (the row containing the control that was activated).

Within the event handler, you can access the `CommandName` of the `CommandSource` object (the **More Info** button) to see which control activated the event (there could be more than one in each row). The button has a `CommandName` property value of `Info`, so you can choose the action to take based on this:

```
Sub ShowInfo(objSender As Object, objArgs As DataGridCommandEventArgs)

    'runs when any command button in the grid is clicked
    'see if the CommandName of the clicked button was "Info"
    If objArgs.CommandSource.CommandName = "Info" Then
        ...
```

Now that you've identified that it was the **More Info** button that was clicked, you can access the values in that particular row of your control. The `DataGridCommandEventArgs` object (named `objArgs`) exposes the items in the current row of a `DataGrid` control as a `Cells` collection. As shown in the following code, you can access the cell by specifying its index within the row (starting at zero), and get the value from the `Text` property. These values can then be used to create the output and place it in the `Label` control located below the grid on the page.

```
    ...
    'get values of ISBN and Title from Text property of the table cells
    'for the current row returned in the objArgs parameter values
    Dim strISBN As String = objArgs.Item.Cells(1).Text
    Dim strTitle As String = objArgs.Item.Cells(2).Text

    'display the information in the page - possibly extract from database?
    lblInfo.Text = "More information about the book:<br /><b>" & strTitle _
        & "</b><br />(ISBN " &strISBN & ") goes here..."
    End If

End Sub
```

Using this technique, you could extract the ISBN and use it to look up information about the book in another table. You could even use it to access another web site or a web service to get information to display to the user.

Handling Data Binding Events

The content of each cell or item in a list control is created with a control's execution, as part of the overall page creation process. This means the content of each cell is controlled only by the value in the data source and the formatting applied by the template or style properties in the control definition. However, it's often useful to be able to access and modify the content at runtime, based on the actual value that occurs in the source dataset. You can do this by reacting to events that the control raises. The most useful event in this scenario is `DataBinding`, which occurs *after* the values for the column have been determined but *before* they are output to the client. This event is supported in all the list controls designed for data binding, including the `ASP:DataGrid`, `ASP:DataList`, `ASP:Repeater`, and `HtmlSelect` controls.

In essence, you just have to create a handler for the event, and tell the control where to find this event handler. It is then called for each row in the data source as the binding takes place. Within the event handler, you can access the entire row of data, and modify the content of any of the controls within that row.

The Handling Data Binding Events in a DataList Object (`datalist-bind-events.aspx`) example page, shown in Figure 7-15, demonstrates this technique by adding the slogan Great for ASP Programmers! to any book title that contains the text ASP or ADO:

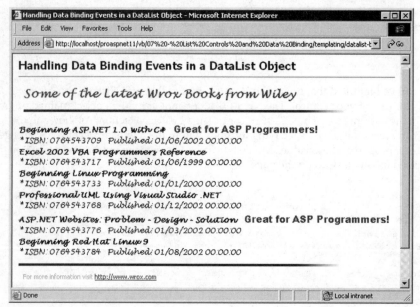

Figure 7-15

The definition of the `DataList` control used in this example is much the same as in previous examples. You have `<HeaderTemplate>`, `<ItemTemplate>`, and `<FooterTemplate>` elements along with some CSS styles to specify how to format the output from the control. It's also important to set the `OnItemDataBound` property of the `DataList` object to the name of an event handler that you want executed as each row in the list is bound to the data source:

```
<ASP:DataList id="MyDataList" runat="server" RepeatLayout="Table"
   OnItemDataBound="CheckTitle">
   ...
</ASP:DataList>
```

We use the same `Page_Load` event handler as in previous examples to get a `DataView` object that contains the source data from the separate custom user control, and bind it to the grid for display. What makes this example different is the event handler specified for the `ItemDataBound` event.

Reacting to the ItemDataBound Event

When the `CheckTitle` event handler is called by the control, as each row is bound to the source data, it is passed two parameters. The first is the usual reference to the object that caused the event, and the second is a `DataListItemEventArgs` object that contains information about the event, and the row that was being bound.

First, in your event handler, check what type of row was being bound – whether it's a header row, footer row, item row, alternating item row, and so forth (this is determined by the type of template used to create the row). You can obtain the row type from the `ItemType` property of the current row in the `DataListItemEventArgs` as follows:

```
Sub CheckTitle(objSender As Object, objArgs As DataListItemEventArgs)

    'see what type of row (header, footer, item, etc.) caused the event
    Dim objItemType As ListItemType = CType(objArgs.Item.ItemType, ListItemType)

    'only format the results if it's an Item or AlternatingItem event
    If objItemType = ListItemType.Item _
    Or objItemType = ListItemType.AlternatingItem Then
    ...
```

Once you know that this is a row you want to process, you can get the values from the `DataItem` property of this row. This returns a `DataRowView` object – basically a collection of the columns within this row. You can access the value of the column you want (in this case, the `Title` column) by specifying the column name as follows:

```
    ...
    'objArgs.Item.DataItem returns the data for this row of items
    Dim objRowVals As DataRowView = CType(objArgs.Item.DataItem, DataRowView)

    'get the value of the Title column
    Dim strTitle As String = objRowVals("Title")
```

You need to test the value to see if it's one that you want to modify. Look for book titles that contain the text strings "ASP" or "ADO". If you find one that matches, use the `FindControl` method of the row to get a reference to the control with an `ID` value of `TitleLabel`. This is the control that was bound to the `Title` column within the definition of the `DataList` control earlier in the page. Once you get a reference to this control, you can append the extra text (Great for ASP Programmers!), putting it in a `<span>` element that specifies the large red font style:

```
    If strTitle.IndexOf("ASP") >= 0 _
    Or strTitle.IndexOf("ADO") >= 0 Then

        'get a reference to the "Title" ASP:Label control in this row
        Dim objLabel As Label = _
            CType(objArgs.Item.FindControl("TitleLabel"), Label)
```

```
         'add a message to this Label control
         objLabel.Text += "    <span class='bigRed'>" _
                 & "Great for ASP Programmers!</span>"

      End If
   End If

 End Sub
```

If you look back at Figure 7-15, you'll see that the slogan text appears only for the two books that contain your search text within their title. This gives a useful technique for dynamically modifying the contents of a list control based on the current values of the data – something you can't always do by hardcoding logic into the page.

This technique isn't limited to just adding text to a `Label` control. You could place other controls that are not visible (such as `<img>` elements), in the output of a `DataList`, and then change their properties in the `ItemDataBound` event handler based on the values in the bound data. Or you could just change the formatting of existing bound content based on the current value. The possibilities are almost endless.

Sorting and Filtering Rows in a DataGrid

When you need to display more than a few rows of data, it's helpful for users to be able to sort the rows based on values in a specific column, and filter the rows based on the values in any column. Both techniques make it much easier for users to find what they are looking for. It means extra trips to the server using the current generation of controls, but it's a useful feature to add to applications nonetheless.

You can provide both these facilities easily when using a `DataGrid` control. The `DataGrid` can do most of the work required to provide a "sort by column" facility. And if the data source for the control is a `DataView` object, you can take advantage of the sorting and filtering features that it includes:

❑ To *sort* the rows within a `DataView`, just set the `Sort` property to a string containing the name of the column, and optionally the keyword `DESC` to sort in descending order. You can sort by more than one column by separating the column names with a comma.

❑ To *filter* the rows that appear in the `DataView`, set the `RowFilter` property to an expression that specifies the rows to be displayed. A simple example is `Title LIKE 'ASP'`. More details on the `Sort` and `RowFilter` properties are provided in the upcoming data access chapters.

The big advantage in using a `DataGrid` control is that it has a property named `AllowSorting`, and it exposes an event named `SortCommand`. When the `AllowSorting` property is set to `True` (usually done within the definition of the control), each column heading automatically becomes a hyperlink. When these are clicked, a postback occurs and the event handler specified for the `SortCommand` property is executed. You can see the way that we implement both sorting and filtering in the **Sorting Rows and Finding Data in a DataGrid Control** (`sort-find-datagrid.aspx`) example page, as shown in Figure 7-16:

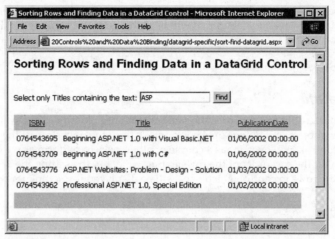

Figure 7-16

The `<form>` section of the HTML for this page contains the textbox and button used to filter the rows based on the title of the book. These controls are followed by the definition of the `DataGrid` used to display the matching titles:

```
<form runat="server">

   Select only Titles containing the text:
   <ASP:TextBox id="txtFindText" runat="server" />
   <ASP:Button id="cmdFind" Text="Find" runat="server" /><p />

   <ASP:DataGrid id="MyDataGrid" runat="server"
     Enableviewstate="False"
     CellPadding="5"
     GridLines="None"
     HeaderStyle-BackColor="silver"
     HeaderStyle-HorizontalAlign="center"
     FooterStyle-BackColor="silver"
     ShowFooter="True"
     AllowSorting="True"
     OnSortCommand="SortRows" />

</form>
```

Other than some minimal styling information, the two properties set for the `DataGrid` that are of interest here are the `AllowSorting` and `OnSortCommand` properties. These properties specify the appearance of the `LinkButton` controls that make up the column names in the header row, as well as the name of the event handler that is executed when one of the column names is clicked.

The code section of the page contains three subroutines. Apart from the `Page_Load` event handler, you have a `BindDataGrid` routine that is responsible for fetching the data sorted and filtered as required. The third routine, named `SortRows`, is executed when the column headings are clicked. You can see that it is attached to the DataGrid in the preceding code as the OnSortCommand property. The page also defines two global (Page-level) variables that will hold the current sort order and filter expression:

```
Dim gstrSortOrder As String    'to hold the sort order
Dim gstrFindText As String     'to hold the filter expression
```

Binding the DataGrid

The first subroutine, BindDataGrid, uses the same custom user control as some of the earlier examples to fetch a DataView object containing some book details from the data store. It then binds this DataView to the DataGrid control. However, it has a couple of other tasks to perform as well. It uses the two global variables to set the sort order of the rows in the DataView (by setting the Sort property), and applies a filter to the rows to control which ones will be displayed (by setting the RowFilter property):

```
Sub BindDataGrid()

  ...
  'get dataset from get-dataset-control.ascx user control
  ...

  'sort the rows in the DataView into the specified order
  objDataView.Sort = gstrSortOrder

  'select the rows in the DataView that match the filter
  objDataView.RowFilter = gstrFindText

  'set the DataSource property of the DataList and bind it
  MyDataGrid.DataSource = objDataView
  MyDataGrid.DataBind()

End Sub
```

The Page_Load Event Handler

The second subroutine is the Page_Load event handler. This is executed when the page first loads and when the user clicks a column heading to change the sort order, or clicks the Find button to filter the rows that are displayed. In the event handler, if this is a postback, the global filter expression variable is changed to reflect the value in the textbox. If it's the first time that the page has been loaded, set default values for the textbox and the global string that specifies the sort order of the rows.

The result is that you start out with the value **ASP** in the textbox when you first load the page, and from then on the global string variable will always hold the expression used to filter the rows. You also call the BindDataGrid subroutine (the one we just examined) each time the page is loaded, so that the DataView object and the grid are recreated with the current sort order and row filter:

```
Sub Page_Load()

  If Page.IsPostBack Then
    'set the value to be used for the RowFilter on the DataView
    gstrFindText = "Title LIKE '*" & txtFindText.Text & "*'"
  Else
    'set the default values for the sort string and filter textbox
```

```
        gstrSortOrder = "ISBN"
        txtFindText.Text = "ASP"
    End If

    'create the data set and bind to the DataGrid control
    BindDataGrid()

End Sub
```

When the page is first loaded, the `Page_Load` event handler sets the `Page`-level variable holding the sort order to the value `"ISBN"`, so the rows will be sorted in the order of the `ISBN` column values. But how do you change the sort order?

Sorting the Rows in the DataGrid

The `DataGrid` control raises the `SortCommand` event whenever the user clicks on a column heading `LinkButton`. The `SortRows` subroutine that is specified as the handler for this event is shown next:

```
Sub SortRows(objSender As Object, objArgs As DataGridSortCommandEventArgs)
    'runs when the column headings in the DataGrid are clicked

    'get the sort expression (name of the column heading that was clicked)
    gstrSortOrder = objArgs.SortExpression.ToString()

    'recreate the data set and bind to the DataGrid control
    BindDataGrid()

End Sub
```

As you can see, the code required is minimal. The `DataGridSortCommandEventArgs` object that's automatically passed to your event handler when a column heading is clicked exposes a `SortExpression` property, which contains the name of the column. All you do is ensure that it's converted to a string and assign it to the `Page`-level *sort order* variable, and then call the routine that recreates the `DataView` and binds it to your grid.

Controlling the Size of the Viewstate

One issue that you really must be aware of when using the ASP.NET list controls is the effect that they have on the amount of data being transmitted across the wire – with each postback and with each newly generated page. As discussed in the previous chapter, an ASP.NET page containing a server-side `<form>` control automatically generates *viewstate*. This is an encoded representation of all the values in all the controls on the page, and it is persisted across page loads using a `HIDDEN`-type `<input>` control. If you view the source of the page in your browser, you'll see something like this:

```
...
<form name="ctrl0" method="post" action="mypage.aspx" id="ctrl0">
<input type="hidden" name="__VIEWSTATE" value="dDwxOTAwNDM2ODc1Ozs+" />
...
```

If you place a list control on a page and fill it with data, all that data is encoded into the viewstate and passed across the wire with each page load and postback. In fact, it's even worse than that; when the user loads the page, you actually send all the values twice – once as the visible output of the list control, and once as the content of the viewstate.

Of course, you might want this to occur as a feature of the way that the page works. If you create the output for the list control and bind it only during the first page load (and not during each postback), you depend on the viewstate to maintain the values in the list control. If getting the values from the data source is an expensive process in terms of resources or time, then persisting them in the viewstate is a good idea.

However, if you are limited in bandwidth or are serving devices such as mobile phones that can't cope with large volumes of form content, you might instead decide to recreate the values on each postback, and not include them in the viewstate. Bear in mind that this option requires a deliberate decision – if you take no action, the values will be included in the viewstate.

Persisting List Control Values Automatically Across Postbacks

If you are persisting values across postbacks, use the `IsPostback` property of the `Page` object so that the values are only created when the page is executed for the first time. For example, the values that are automatically included in the viewstate will be used to populate the `DataGrid` control when the page is reloaded:

```
Sub Page_Load()
   If Not Page.IsPostback Then
      objDataView = GetDataView(.....)      'get or build a DataView object
      MyDataGrid.DataSource = objDataView   'specify the data source
      MyDataGrid.DataBind()                 'bind data to grid control
   End If
End Sub
```

Preventing List Control Values from Being Persisted Across Postbacks

There may be occasions when you wouldn't want to persist the values in a list control across postbacks. As well as the concern over bandwidth, you might have other reasons for recreating the data set or rebinding the list control each time you load the page. The simplest scenario is when the page does not actually include a `<form>` element. Many of our previous examples were like this. With non-interactive pages, there is no requirement to post values back to the server – just load the page and view it. In this case, there is no viewstate, but no user interaction either.

However, if the page does contain a `<form>` section, the values from the list control are automatically included in the viewstate. If the list control contains any interactive elements (such as buttons or edit controls where the value must be posted back to the server) the control has to be on an HTML `<form>`. This is the case with the sorting and filtering example you've just seen, where the column headings are automatically rendered as `LinkButton` controls.

However, to sort and filter the rows, you have to rebind the data grid to the `DataView` object each time. The whole `DataSet` and `DataView` is recreated with each postback, so there is no need to maintain the values in the viewstate. For this reason, you need to set the `Enableviewstate` property of the `DataGrid` object to `False` in the control definition so that the contents of this control are not included in the viewstate:

```
<ASP:DataGrid id="MyDataGrid" runat="server"
    Enableviewstate="False"
```

You can always check how much data is included in the viewstate of a page by using *page tracing*. In the `Page` directive, add `Trace="True"`:

```
<%@Page Language="VB" Trace="True"%>
```

Then run the page locally (that is, in a browser running on the web server itself). In the **Control Tree** section of the output, shown in Figure 7-17, you can see that the viewstate of the `DataGrid` control named **MyDataGrid** is 528 bytes. However, this does not include child controls. In fact, the `DataGrid` including all its child controls has a viewstate size of over 5 kB in this example!

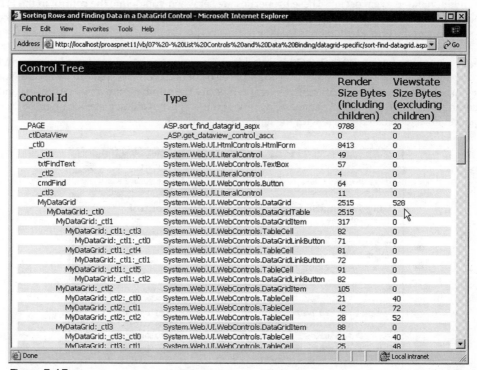

Figure 7-17

To save you adding all the values together, there is another simple way to get an indication of the total viewstate in a page – just view the source in the browser so that you can see the `HIDDEN`-type `<input>` control. From that you can get a good idea of the amount of data being sent to the client and back to the server each time.

Automatic Paging in a DataGrid

Our final example of using the `DataGrid` control just to display data demonstrates the use of *paging*. When there are a large number of rows to display, sending them all to the client in one go doesn't make sense. Users will get impatient waiting for them to arrive, and may find that they actually wanted to see something else instead. To prevent this aggravation and waste of bandwidth, you can divide the output into pages containing, for example, 10 or 20 rows (depending on the content), and then provide navigation controls so that users can view other pages of rows as required.

The `DataGrid` control makes it easy to provide a paging feature. It contains logic that can automatically create pages containing the number of rows you require, and it can render the navigation controls in a range of ways. You can also take over paging entirely and implement all the features yourselves in order to provide a custom interface.

To turn on the automatic paging feature, you simply need to set the `AllowPaging` property of the `DataGrid` control to `True`, and specify the name of an event handler that will run when the `PageIndexChanged` event occurs. These properties are set when you define the control in the HTML of the page. You can also specify the position of the *Pager* navigation controls. By default they are located in the footer row of the grid, aligned on the left.

The Using Automatic Paging with a DataGrid Control (`paging-datagrid.aspx`) example shown in Figure 7-18 uses the automatic paging feature This example also contains controls that can be used to specify other properties of the paging feature. For example, specify the number of rows in each page, and the style of the navigation controls. After changing any of the property values, just click on one of the navigation links to reload the page with the new options set.

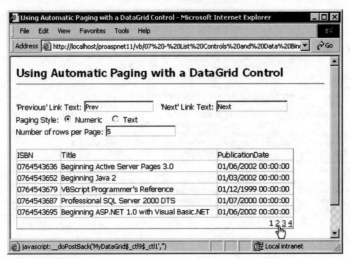

Figure 7-18

As usual, the HTML section of the page starts with the controls where you can specify how the `DataGrid` behaves:

```
<form runat="server">

  'Previous' Link Text:
  <ASP:TextBox id="PrevText" runat="server" />  
  'Next' Link Text:
```

```
<ASP:TextBox id="NextText" runat="server" /><br />

Paging Style:
<ASP:RadioButton id="PageNumeric" GroupName="Style"
        runat="server" /> Numeric  
<ASP:RadioButton id="PageText" GroupName="Style"
        runat="server" /> Text<br />

Number of rows per Page:
<ASP:TextBox id="PageRows" runat="server" /><p />
```

This is followed by the definition of the DataGrid control. Set the three properties that control the paging behavior: set AllowPaging to True, specify that the paging controls should be right-aligned within the footer row, and specify that the ChangeGridPage event handler (which we'll look at shortly) will be executed when the user selects a page using the paging controls:

```
<ASP:DataGrid id="MyDataGrid" runat="server"
    Width="90%"
    AllowPaging="True"
    PagerStyle-HorizontalAlign="Right"
    OnPageIndexChanged="ChangeGridPage" />

</form>
```

The Page_Load Event Handler

Whenever the page loads, either when the user opens the page for the first time or in response to a click by the user on the paging controls, the Page_Load event handler is executed. However, we only want to execute code when the page is first opened so check the value of the IsPostback property first. If it's False, you can set the default values for the controls in the page and call the BindDataGrid subroutine to bind and display the source data values in the DataGrid control:

```
Sub Page_Load()
  If Not Page.IsPostback Then

    'set the default values in the controls on the page
    PrevText.Text = "Prev"
    NextText.Text = "Next"
    PageNumeric.Checked = True
    PageRows.Text = "10"

    'set the initial page in the DataGrid to zero
    '(not actually required as this is the default)
    MyDataGrid.CurrentPageIndex = 0

    'create the dataset and bind it to the DataGrid control
    BindDataGrid()

  End If
End Sub
```

The BindDataGrid Routine

Before you bind the source data to the `DataGrid`, you first have to set the values of the properties that control the paging feature. You can get the number of rows that are to be shown in each page from the `PageRows` textbox on the page, and assign this value to the `PageSize` property of the `DataGrid` control.

See which type of paging controls the user specified (either page numbers, or Previous and Next text captions), and set the `PagerStyle.Mode` property of the `DataGrid`.

You can also retrieve and set the values that the user wants for the text captions (in reality, we actually only need to set this if the pager mode is text captions but it makes no difference to the operation of the page). The code is as follows:

```
Sub BindDataGrid()

  'set the value of the number of rows per page
  MyDataGrid.PageSize = CInt(PageRows.Text)

  'set the type of pager to include in the DataGrid
  If PageNumeric.Checked = True Then
    MyDataGrid.PagerStyle.Mode = PagerMode.NumericPages
  Else
    MyDataGrid.PagerStyle.Mode = PagerMode.NextPrev
  End If

  'set the text for the pager to use when in NextPrev mode
  MyDataGrid.PagerStyle.NextPageText = NextText.Text
  MyDataGrid.PagerStyle.PrevPageText = PrevText.Text
```

Now get the `DataView` object and bind it to the grid. We're using the same custom user control as in previous examples here:

```
  ...
  'get dataset from get-dataset-control.ascx user control
  ...

  MyDataGrid.DataSource = objDataView
  MyDataGrid.DataBind()

End Sub
```

In Figure 7-19, the text-style paging option has been selected, and different text for the pager links has been chosen. The number of rows that should appear in each page has also been changed:

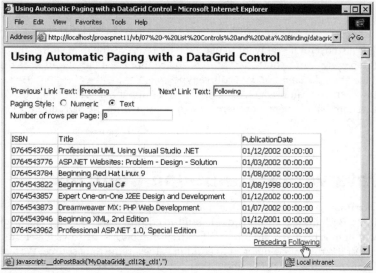

Figure 7-19

Changing the Displayed Page

We've set all the properties of the `DataGrid` control that affect the appearance, and bound and displayed the data content starting from the first *page* of rows. All that remains is to handle the `PageIndexChanged` event that occurs when the user clicks one of the page navigation links. We specified an event handler named `ChangeGridPage` in the original definition of the `DataGrid` control, the code for which is shown as follows:

```
Sub ChangeGridPage(objSender As Object, _
        objArgs As DataGridPageChangedEventArgs)
  'runs when one of the pager controls is clicked

  'update the current page number from the parameter values
  MyDataGrid.CurrentPageIndex = objArgs.NewPageIndex

  'recreate the dataset and bind it to the DataGrid control
  BindDataGrid()

End Sub
```

All you have to do is collect the index number of the page that the user selected from the `NewPageIndex` property of the `DataGridPageChangedEventArgs` object that is passed to the event handler when the event occurs. You can assign this value to the `CurrentPageIndex` property of the `DataGrid`, and then call the `BindDataGrid` routine to fetch, bind, and display the appropriate page of data rows.

Building paging into applications that display rows of data was always a notoriously error-prone task, but is easy with the `DataGrid`. You can also specify custom paging controls – building your own with buttons, hyperlinks, images, and so on. This involves setting the `AllowCustomPaging` and `AllowPaging` properties to `True`. This means that the paging controls will not appear, but you can still

319

react to the `PageIndexChanged` event to display the appropriate set of rows, and display your own paging controls.

Custom paging is also useful if you want to use a `DataReader` as the data source for your control. When using the built-in paging feature of the `DataGrid`, you cannot use a `DataReader` as the data source – it must be one of the other *disconnected* data source types, such as a `DataView`, `DataSet`, `ArrayList`, or `HashTable`. However, you can use a `DataReader` if you implement custom paging. We aren't demonstrating custom paging here, but there are examples in both the SDK and the QuickStart samples included with ASP.NET.

Editing Data with Data-Bound Controls

The final topic for this chapter shows a rather more specialized technique for use with the `DataList` and `DataGrid` controls. Both these controls provide built-in editing features. They allow you to change the way that a row or item is displayed to indicate to a user that one of the rows is 'selected' (is the 'current row'), or that one of the rows is being used to edit the values in the data source. We'll show an example of editing data with both the `DataGrid` and `DataList` controls next.

Editing Data with a DataGrid Control

The `DataGrid` provides the most automated developer support for inline editing. You can define an `EditCommandColumn` within the grid, which will automatically handle most of your plumbing and navigation. The Editing Data in a DataGrid Control (`edit-datagrid.aspx`) example page, shown in Figure 7-20, demonstrates what this control can do. When you first open the page, it displays a list of books. However, there is an extra column on the right that contains an Edit hyperlink for each row. When you click on the link, that row goes into edit mode, and the Title and Published columns show textboxes rather than just the values for that row:

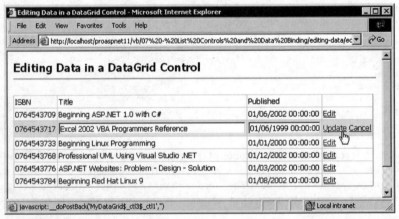

Figure 7-20

After editing the details, click the Update link to save the changes, or the Cancel link to abandon them. As we haven't looked at data management techniques so far, the example page simply creates a suitable

SQL statement that would perform the update and displays it. It doesn't actually update the original data (see Figure 7-21):

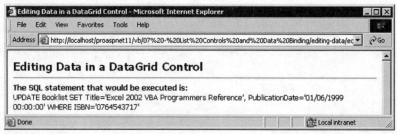

Figure 7-21

Let's see how this works. The HTML section of this page contains a `<form>` element, which contains the `DataGrid` control. The definition of the `DataGrid` specifies that the background color of the item being edited is yellow. It also specifies that the `DataKeyField` in the source dataset is the `ISBN` column. This useful feature of the list controls means that even if you need to access it to perform data updates, you don't have to include the primary key of the source dataset in your columns (as long as it's in the source rowset you are binding the control to). For any row, you can access the primary key from this collection, as seen later in this example.

The next three attributes in the opening `DataGrid` tag are used to specify the names of the event handlers that will be executed in response to the user clicking the **Edit**, **Update**, and **Cancel** links that the `EditCommandColumn` will generate for you. Finally, you set the `AutoGenerateColumns` property to `False` as you want to create your own column structure for the grid:

```
<form runat="server">

  <ASP:DataGrid id="MyDataGrid" runat="server"
    CellPadding = "2"
    EditItemStyle-BackColor="yellow"
    EditItemStyle-ForeColor="black"
    DataKeyField="ISBN"
    OnEditCommand="DoItemEdit"
    OnUpdateCommand="DoItemUpdate"
    OnCancelCommand="DoItemCancel"
    AutoGenerateColumns="False">
```

As the automatic generation of the columns is turned off, you must specify the columns that you want to appear within the `<ASP:DataGrid>` definition. Include a `BoundColumn` that displays values from the `ISBN` column in your data source, a custom `TemplateColumn` that displays the `Title`, followed by another `BoundColumn` that displays the `PublicationDate`. Include the attribute `ReadOnly="True"` for the `ISBN` column; you wouldn't want the user to be able to edit values in this column (as it is the primary key of the source table).

A custom `TemplateColumn` is used instead of a `BoundColumn` for the `Title` column for a couple of reasons. Firstly, the automatic editing feature displays a textbox instead of a simple text value in all the columns that are not read-only. However, this textbox isn't large enough to comfortably accommodate a long string, so you need to specify the editing control yourselves and make it 60 characters long.

Secondly, this gives you the chance to see how you can provide non-standard edit controls for a column if required. Just specify an `<ItemTemplate>` element to be used to display the column values in normal mode, and an `<EditItemTemplate>` element that defines the control to be used in edit mode. All the template declarations are as follows:

```
    <Columns>
      <ASP:BoundColumn DataField="ISBN" HeaderText="ISBN" ReadOnly="True" />
      <ASP:TemplateColumn HeaderText="Title">
        <ItemTemplate>
          <ASP:Label Text='<%# Container.DataItem("Title") %>' runat="server" />
        </ItemTemplate>
        <EditItemTemplate>
          <ASP:TextBox id="txtTitle" Size="60"
            Text='<%# Container.DataItem("Title") %>' runat="server" />
        </EditItemTemplate>
      </ASP:TemplateColumn>
      <ASP:BoundColumn DataField="PublicationDate" HeaderText="Published" />
      <ASP:EditCommandColumn EditText="Edit"
          CancelText="Cancel" UpdateText="Update" />
    </Columns>
    </ASP:DataGrid>

  </form>
```

As you can see, the last column is the `EditCommandColumn` mentioned earlier. While there are many attributes that can be applied to this column to control the formatting (basically the same as for the list controls themselves such as the font style, column heading, wrapping behavior, and so on), you've just specified the text you want to use for the three commands that can appear in this column. That completes the definition of your `DataGrid` control.

The Page_Load Event Handler

When the page first loads, you must create the data set being used as the source of the `DataGrid` control. As shown in the following code, this is done in the `Page_Load` event handler – but only if this is not a postback (as you've seen in plenty of earlier examples):

```
Sub Page_Load()
  If Not Page.IsPostback Then
    BindDataGrid() 'create dataset and bind to grid control
  End If
End Sub
```

The `BindDataGrid` routine is responsible for fetching the data from the database through a `DataReader` object, binding it to the control, and then calling the `DataBind` method of the `DataGrid` to display the data. Again, this is the same routine as used in previous examples:

```
Sub BindDataGrid()
  ...
    'create a DataReader object to retrieve the data
  ...

  MyDataGrid.DataSource = objDataReader
```

```
        MyDataGrid.DataBind()

    End Sub
```

Displaying the UPDATE SQL Statement

Another subroutine that's used in this page is responsible for displaying the SQL statement that you generate, and display it in a `Label` control in the HTML section at the top of the page:

```
<ASP:Label id="lblSQL" runat="server" />
```

This routine, named `ExecuteSQLStatement`, would normally be responsible for executing the SQL statement against the back-end database or other data source in order to update the values in line with the edits made in the `DataGrid`. However, in this example page, we just display the SQL statement as shown:

```
Sub ExecuteSQLStatement(strSQL)
    lblSQL.Text = "The SQL statement is: <br />" & strSQL
End Sub
```

Handling Item Edit Events

All that remains is to handle the three events you specified in the definition of the `DataGrid` control. You have to react to the `EditCommand`, `UpdateCommand`, and `CancelCommand` events.

The `EditCommand` event is raised when the user clicks the **Edit** link in any row within the grid. For this event, you specified the `DoItemEdit` event handler routine. Within this routine, first clear any existing SQL statement from the `Label` at the top of the page (to avoid any confusion). Then set the `EditItemIndex` property of the `DataGrid` control to the index of the row that contained the **Edit** link the user clicked.

You get this index from the parameters of the event handler – the code is passed a `DataGridCommandEventArgs` object that exposes the `ItemIndex` property of the item that was selected. Finally, the grid is rebound to display the new layout:

```
Sub DoItemEdit(objSource As Object, objArgs As DataGridCommandEventArgs)

    lblSQL.Text = ""  'clear text from label that shows SQL statement
        'set the EditItemIndex property of the grid to this item's index
    MyDataGrid.EditItemIndex = objArgs.Item.ItemIndex
    BindDataGrid() 'bind the data and display it

End Sub
```

The default value of the `EditItemIndex` property is -1, which indicates that none of the rows is in edit mode. When the `DataGrid` control comes to render the grid, it will detect that the `EditItemIndex` has been set to a different value, and will automatically render the specified row with the contents of your `<EditItemTemplate>` element, or with textboxes instead of plain text for ordinary bound columns where you haven't specified a custom `<EditItemTemplate>` element.

Handling the Update and Cancel Events

Now that the grid is in edit mode, you just need to handle the Update and Cancel events. A click on the Cancel link should execute the `DoItemCancel` event handler. In this event handler, all you need to do is switch the grid back out of edit mode by setting the `EditItemIndex` property back to –1:

```
Sub DoItemCancel(objSource As Object, objArgs As DataGridCommandEventArgs)
    'set EditItemIndex property of grid to -1 to switch out of Edit mode
  MyDataGrid.EditItemIndex = -1
  BindDataGrid() 'bind the data and display it
End Sub
```

However, if the user clicks the Update link, the `DoItemUpdate` event handler will be called. Here, you have to create a suitable SQL statement, or execute some stored procedure or other code to update the original source data. We're just generating a simple SQL UPDATE statement in the example, and for this it's necessary to get the edited values from the `DataGrid` row that the user is working on.

Two different techniques are used in this example (in order to illustrate the options and demonstrate how it can be done). After declaring two variables to hold references to the textboxes that contain the edited values, first access the Title textbox (named `txtTitle`) using the `FindControl` method of the item that is contained in the `DataGridCommandEventArgs` object (which was passed to the event handler as a parameter). You have to convert (cast) the return value to the correct type – in this case a `TextBox` object.

For the second textbox, access the `Cells` collection for the item contained in the `DataGridCommandEventArgs` object. From the third cell in the row (the `PublicationDate` column), you can use the `Controls` collection of that cell to get a reference to the textbox it contains. This technique is best used when the column is a normal `BoundColumn` or auto-generated column – it doesn't work with a custom column created with templates (which is why you used the `FindControl` technique with your `Title` column).

```
Sub DoItemUpdate(objSource As Object, objArgs As DataGridCommandEventArgs)
    'get a reference to the title and publication date textboxes
  Dim objTitleCtrl, objPubDateCtrl As TextBox
  objTitleCtrl = CType(objArgs.Item.FindControl("txtTitle"), TextBox)
  objPubDateCtrl = objArgs.Item.Cells(2).Controls(0)
```

Once you've got references to the two controls, you can create the SQL UPDATE statement and call the `ExecuteSQLStatement` routine to execute it against the data source (or just display it in the example page). You get the value of the primary key for the current row (the ISBN) from the `DataKeys` collection. Recall that you included the `DataKeyField="ISBN"` attribute in the definition of your `DataGrid` control, so you can get the value of the ISBN column for this row using the row index against the `DataKeys` collection. Finish off by switching the grid out of edit mode by setting the `EditItemIndex` property of the `DataGrid` control back to –1, and rebind the control to display the result:

```
    'create a suitable SQL statement and execute it
  Dim strSQL As String
  strSQL = "UPDATE Booklist SET Title='" & objTitleCtrl.Text & "', " _
      & "PublicationDate='" & objPubDateCtrl.Text & "' " _
      & "WHERE ISBN='" & MyDataGrid.DataKeys(objArgs.Item.ItemIndex) & "'"
  ExecuteSQLStatement(strSQL)
```

```
          'set EditItemIndex property of grid to -1 to switch out of Edit mode
     MyDataGrid.EditItemIndex = -1
     BindDataGrid() 'bind the data and display it
   End Sub
```

It's taken a while to explain this example, but there really isn't a lot of code in it. The code that is required is relatively simple and well structured. We are just reacting to events that the DataGrid control raises, so debugging and modifying the page is far less error-prone than with any technique used for the same thing in previous versions of ASP.

Selecting and Editing Data with a DataList Control

The second control that provides inline editing capabilities automatically is the DataList. In fact, you can do more with this control as far as selecting or editing data goes, but it requires more code and greater effort to use. One additional feature is its ability to easily switch the control into *selected* mode, where one row becomes the current row and is highlighted by applying different styles or formatting to that row.

The example page shown in Figure 7-22, Selecting and Editing Data in a DataList Control (select-edit-datalist.aspx), demonstrates both selecting and editing rows in a DataList control. When first opened, it displays a list of book titles. Each one has an Info button at the left-hand end of the row. If you click one of these buttons, that row becomes selected – and both the format and content change to reflect the following:

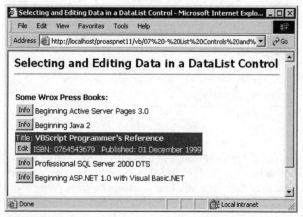

Figure 7-22

An Edit button also appears in the selected row. When you click this button, that row goes into edit mode, as shown in Figure 7-23. The book title and publication date appear in textboxes in which they can be edited. At the same time, three other buttons appear in the row – allowing you to update the row with your changes, delete the current row, or cancel your updates:

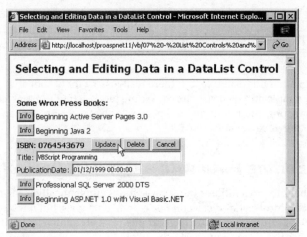

Figure 7-23

When you select the Update or Delete option, a suitable SQL UPDATE or DELETE statement is generated and displayed in the page as shown in Figure 7-24. As in the previous example, it doesn't actually execute the statement against the data store:

Figure 7-24

While this example looks quite different from the previous DataGrid example, they have a lot of similarities and they share a lot of code. The HTML section of the page contains a <form>, and within this is the definition of the DataList control. In this case, you have some extra style properties, because you now have a selected mode as well as an edit mode. As before, set the DataKeyField attribute to "ISBN" (the name of the primary key column in your data source). You also have to specify the event handlers for your edit commands. In this case, you have to react to the ItemCommand event as well, so that you can detect a click on the Info button and put that row into selected mode:

```
<ASP:DataList id="MyDataList" runat="server"
    CellSpacing = "2"
    SelectedItemStyle-BackColor="red"
    SelectedItemStyle-ForeColor="white"
    EditItemStyle-BackColor="yellow"
    EditItemStyle-ForeColor="black"
    DataKeyField="ISBN"
    OnItemCommand="DoItemSelect"
```

```
      OnEditCommand="DoItemEdit"
      OnUpdateCommand="DoItemUpdate"
      OnDeleteCommand="DoItemDelete"
      OnCancelCommand="DoItemCancel">
```

The remainder of the control definition contains the four templates needed. The `<HeaderTemplate>` element defines what appears at the top of the control, followed by the `<ItemTemplate>` element that defines the normal content for rows that are not selected or being edited. An ordinary `ASP:Button` control is used for the Info button in each row, with the `CommandName` property set to `Select`, and this button and the book title are displayed:

```
<HeaderTemplate>
  <b>Some Wrox Press Books:</b><br />
</HeaderTemplate>
<ItemTemplate>
  <ASP:Button CommandName="Select" Text="Info" runat="server" />
  <%# Container.DataItem("Title") %>
</ItemTemplate>
```

Next is the `<SelectedItemTemplate>` element, which is used for the row that is currently in selected mode. This is the row specified by the `SelectedIndex` property of the `DataList` (as with the `EditItemIndex` property of the `DataGrid` control, the value of this property is –1 if no row is selected). As shown in the following code, we display the book title, a button with the caption and `CommandName` value of `Edit`, the ISBN for this book, and the publication date, for the selected row:

```
<SelectedItemTemplate>
  Title: <b><%# Container.DataItem("Title") %></b><br />
  <ASP:Button CommandName="Edit" Text="Edit" runat="server" />
  ISBN: <%# Container.DataItem("ISBN") %>  
  Published:
  <%# DataBinder.Eval(Container.DataItem, "PublicationDate", "{0:D}") %>
</SelectedItemTemplate>
```

This provides the *selected row* appearance you saw earlier, repeated here in Figure 7-25:

Figure 7-25

The Edit button will be used to put the `DataList` row into edit mode. When this happens, the control will use the contents of the `<EditItemTemplate>` element to render the content for this row. As shown in the following code, display the ISBN followed the Update, Delete, and Cancel, buttons. Then, on the next line, display two textboxes that are bound to the `Title` and `PublicationDate` columns in the data source.

```
<EditItemTemplate>
  <b>ISBN: <%# Container.DataItem("ISBN") %></b>  
  <ASP:Button CommandName="Update" Text="Update" runat="server" />
  <ASP:Button CommandName="Delete" Text="Delete" runat="server" />
  <ASP:Button CommandName="Cancel" Text="Cancel" runat="server" /><br />
```

```
      Title:
      <ASP:TextBox id="txtTitle" Text='<%# Container.DataItem("Title") %>'
            size="46" runat="server" /><br />
      PublicationDate:
      <ASP:TextBox id="txtPubDate" size="20" runat="server"
            Text='<%# Container.DataItem("PublicationDate") %>' />
   </EditItemTemplate>
  </ASP:DataList>
```

This is a deliberate design feature of our example page, and is not a requirement. In your applications, you are free to put a row into edit mode without having to put it into selected mode first.

Figure 7-26 shows how the row we're editing looks like when edit mode, in this example:

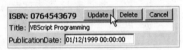

Figure 7-26

The `Page_Load` event handler is the same as used for the previous `DataGrid` example, as is the `BindDataGrid` routine. The page also contains the same `ExecuteSQLStatement` routine that displays the SQL statement you'll build when the **Update** or **Delete** buttons are clicked. What are slightly different are the routines that perform the switch to select mode and edit mode, and those that generate the SQL statements.

Selecting a Row

The `ItemCommand` event handler, for which you specified the `DoItemSelect` routine, is executed when any command button or link within the rows of the control is clicked. All you need to do to select a row in your `DataList` is set the `SelectedIndex` property of the control. Before you do this, clear any existing text from the `Label` control at the top of the page that displays your SQL UPDATE or DELETE statements.

However, there is an important issue to be aware of here. We specified other command buttons in the templates for the `DataList` – those that activate the `Update`, `Delete`, and `Cancel` commands when the grid is in edit mode. These three events will automatically call the event handlers that you specified when you defined the control. But they also call the `ItemCommand` event handler – they raise the `ItemCommand` event as well as their *own* event.

This means that you must check which control was used to raise the event in the `ItemCommand` event handler (the `DoItemEvent` routine). Select the row only if it is the Info button, which has the `CommandName` value of `Select`. Now, the grid will automatically render your `<SelectedItemtemplate>` contents for the row indicated by the `SelectedIndex` property.

```
   Sub DoItemSelect(objSource As Object, objArgs As DataListCommandEventArgs)

     lblSQL.Text = "" 'clear any content from SQL statement Label
     'see if it was the Select button that was clicked
     If objArgs.CommandName = "Select" Then
       'set the SelectedIndex property of the list to this item's index
```

```
        MyDataList.SelectedIndex = objArgs.Item.ItemIndex
        BindDataGrid() 'bind the data and display it
    End If

End Sub
```

Editing a Row

Once you put a row into selected mode in your example, it displays a button that can be used to put that row into edit mode. The Edit button has the `CommandName` value `Edit`, which means that it will raise the `EditCommand` event (as well as the `ItemCommand` event) when clicked. Specify your `DoItemEdit` routine (shown in the following code) as the event handler for the `EditCommand` event, and in it first unselect this row by setting the `SelectedIndex` property of the control to -1, and then set the `EditIndex` property to this row index and rebind the grid. The contents of the `<EditItemTemplate>` will be used when this row is rendered.

```
Sub DoItemEdit(objSource As Object, objArgs As DataListCommandEventArgs)

    'set the SelectedIndex propery of the list to -1 to "unselect" it
    MyDataList.SelectedIndex = -1

    'set the EditItemIndex property of the list to this item's index
    MyDataList.EditItemIndex = objArgs.Item.ItemIndex
    BindDataGrid() 'bind the data and display it

End Sub
```

Updating a Row

Once in edit mode, the row displays the Update, Delete, and Cancel buttons. The Update button has the `CommandName` value `Update`, and so it will raise the `UpdateCommand` event when clicked. This will execute the `DoItemUpdate` routine, which was specified as the handler for this event in the definition of the `DataList` control.

In this routine, as in the previous `DataGrid` example, get a reference to the `txtTitle` and `txtPubDate` textboxes in this row, and use their values to build a SQL statement to update the row in the original data source. Again, you get the ISBN (the primary key for the row) from the `DataKeys` collection.

Then, after executing the SQL statement (or, in this example, just displaying it), switch the row out of edit mode by setting the `EditItemIndex` of the `DataList` control to -1, and rebind the control to display the updated results:

```
Sub DoItemUpdate(objSource As Object, objArgs As DataListCommandEventArgs)

    'get a reference to the title and publication date textboxes
    Dim objTitleCtrl, objPubDateCtrl As TextBox
    objTitleCtrl = CType(objArgs.Item.FindControl("txtTitle"), TextBox)
    objPubDateCtrl = CType(objArgs.Item.FindControl("txtPubDate"), TextBox)

    'create a suitable SQL statement and execute it
    Dim strSQL As String
    strSQL = "UPDATE Booklist SET Title='" & objTitleCtrl.Text & "', " _
```

```
        & "PublicationDate='" & objPubDateCtrl.Text & "' " _
        & "WHERE ISBN='" & MyDataList.DataKeys(objArgs.Item.ItemIndex) & "'"
    ExecuteSQLStatement(strSQL)

    'set EditItemIndex property of grid to -1 to switch out of Edit mode
    MyDataList.EditItemIndex = -1
    BindDataGrid() 'bind the data and display it

End Sub
```

Deleting a Row

The `DeleteCommand` event handler specified in the definition of the `DataList` control is the routine named `DoItemDelete`. This is a relatively simple routine when compared to the *update* event handler. As shown in the following code, you can build a SQL `DELETE` statement, using the ISBN value obtained from the `DataKeys` collection, execute it, switch the row back out of edit mode, and rebind the grid to display the results:

```
Sub DoItemDelete(objSource As Object, objArgs As DataListCommandEventArgs)

    'create a suitable SQL statement and execute it
    Dim strSQL As String
    strSQL = "DELETE FROM Booklist WHERE ISBN='" _
        & MyDataList.DataKeys(objArgs.Item.ItemIndex) & "'"
    ExecuteSQLStatement(strSQL)

    'set EditItemIndex property of grid to -1 to switch out of Edit mode
    MyDataList.EditItemIndex = -1
    BindDataGrid() 'bind the data and display it

End Sub
```

Canceling Edit Mode

Canceling edit mode is the same as that on the `DataGrid` example previously. In the definition of the `DataList` control we'd specified the `DoItemCancel` routine as the event handler for the `CancelCommand` event. In this routine, just set the `EditItemIndex` property of the `DataList` control to -1 and rebind the grid:

```
Sub DoItemCancel(objSource As Object, objArgs As DataListCommandEventArgs)

    'set EditItemIndex property of grid to -1 to switch out of Edit mode
    MyDataList.EditItemIndex = -1
    BindDataGrid() 'bind the data and display it

End Sub
```

That's it. You've built a responsive, intuitive, and attractive data update page with only a handful of controls and relatively few lines of code. To do the same using ASP 3.0 would take a great deal longer, and require a great deal more effort and a lot more code.

We haven't looked very deeply at how the relational data management processes are carried out. We've used fairly simple data access code to get sets of data from a database, and displayed the explicit SQL statements you could use to perform updates. However, the next four chapters of this book are devoted to data management, using both relational data and XML.

Summary

In this chapter, we've looked in some detail at a specific new feature that is available when using ASP.NET, namely *server-side data binding*. This allows you to insert values from a range of different types of data source into a page, or into controls on a page. Together with the eight special list controls that are part of the .NET Framework, this allows you to build data-driven pages with a minimum of code and effort.

There are two basic types of data binding supported in ASP.NET – single-value binding to any control, and repeated-value binding to the special list controls. Single-value binding can be used with a property, method result, or an expression to create a value that is then used to set a property or the content of any other control – effectively just inserting this value. A simple example would be setting the `Text` property of a `Label` control to the same value as currently selected in a listbox.

Repeated-value data binding takes a data source such as an `ArrayList`, a `HashTable`, a `Collection`, a `DataView`, a `DataReader`, or a `DataSet` object. Using any of the eight special list controls, it will then display the contents of the data source as a series of repeated rows or items. Depending on the type of control, you can add formatting and specify the actual content in a range of ways. For example, you can specify the number of columns and the layout direction for a `Repeater` control, or could hide columns, add custom columns, sort and filter rows, and use automatic paging in a `DataGrid` control.

As well as looking at how to use these list controls to display data, we also (briefly) introduced the features they provide for updating data. This gives you an easy way to build an intuitive interface for managing all kinds of data – in particular, data extracted from and updated to a relational database.

We've talked quite a lot about working with relational data through objects like the `DataReader` and `DataView` in this chapter, without really explaining much about them. However, this is because we wanted to cover the wide range of server controls that are part of ASP.NET first so that you would be comfortable with creating dynamic pages. We make up for this omission by now starting a detailed exploration of the various ways of working with data in ASP.NET over the next four chapters.

Introducing .NET Data Management

We've looked at the basics of Microsoft's new .NET Framework and ASP.NET in particular. It changes the way you program with ASP, adding a whole range of new techniques that make it easier to create dynamic pages, web services, and web applications. However, there is one fundamental aspect of almost all applications that we've not yet explored. This is how we access and work with data that is stored in other applications or files. In general terms, these sources of information are called *data stores*. This chapter looks at how the .NET Framework provides access to the many different kinds of data store that you may have to interface with.

The .NET Framework includes a series of classes that implement a new data access technology that is specifically designed for use in the .NET world. We'll look at why this has come about, and how it relates to the techniques used in ASP. In fact, the new framework classes provide a whole lot more than just a .NET version of ADO. Like the move from ASP to ASP.NET, they involve fundamental changes in the approach to managing data in external data stores.

While *data management* is often assumed to relate to relational data sources such as databases, we will also explore the other types of data that are increasingly encountered today. There is extended support within .NET for working with *Extensible Markup Language* (*XML*) and its associated technologies. Apart from comprehensive support for the existing XML standards, .NET provides new ways to handle XML. These include integration between XML and traditional relational data access methods.

So, the topics for this chapter are:

- ❑   The various types of data storage used today and into the future
- ❑   The need for another data access technology
- ❑   An overview of the new relational data access techniques in .NET

❑   An overview of the new techniques for working with XML in .NET

❑   Choosing an appropriate data access technology and a data format

Let's start with a look at the way data is stored and accessed today.

Data Stores and Data Access

The term *data store* usually meant a database of some kind. Databases were usually file-based, often using fixed-width records written to disk – rather like text files. A database program or data access technology read the files into buffers as tables, and applied rules defined in other files to connect the records from different tables together. As technologies matured, relational databases evolved to provide better storage methods, such as variable-length records and more efficient access techniques.

However, the basic storage medium was still the *database* – a specialist program that managed the data and exposed it to clients. Obvious examples are Oracle, Informix, Sybase, DB2, and Microsoft's own SQL Server. All are enterprise-oriented applications for storing and managing data in a relational way.

At the same time, *desktop* database applications matured and became more powerful. In general, this type of program provides its own interface for working with the data. For example, Microsoft Access can be used to build forms and queries that can access and display data in very powerful ways. They often allow the data to be separated from the interface over the network, so that it can reside on a central server. But, again, we're still talking about relational databases.

Moving to a Distributed Environment

In recent years, the requirements and mode of operation of most businesses have changed. Without consciously realizing it, we've moved away from relying on a central relational database to store all the data that a company produces and needs to access. Now, data is stored in email servers, directory services, Office documents, and other places – as well as the traditional relational database.

The move to a more distributed computing paradigm means that the central data store, running on a huge computer in an air-conditioned IT department, is often only a part of the whole corporate data environment. Modern data access technologies need to be able to work with a whole range of different types of data store, as shown in Figure 8-1.

You can see that the range of storage techniques has become quite quite wide. It's easy to see why the term *database* is no longer appropriate for describing the many different ways that data is often stored today. Distributed computing means that we have to be able to extract data in a suitable format, move it around across a range of different types of network, and change the format of the data to suit many different types of client device.

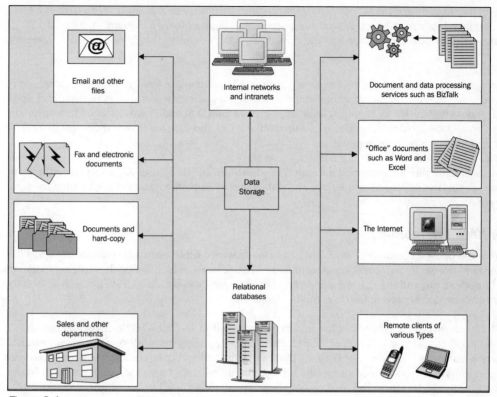

Figure 8-1

The next section explores one of the areas where data storage and management is changing completely – the growth in the use of *XML*.

XML – A Data Format for the Future?

One of the most far-reaching of the new ideas in computing is the evolution of XML. The *World Wide Web Consortium* (*W3C*) issued proposals for XML some three years ago (at the time of writing), and these have matured into standards that are being adopted by almost every sector of the industry.

XML scores when it comes to storing and transferring data – it is an accepted industry standard, and it is just plain text. The former means that we have a way of transferring and exposing information in a format that is independent of platform, operating system, and application. Compare this to, for example, the MIME-encoded recordsets that Internet Explorer's *Remote Data Service* (*RDS*) uses. Instead, XML means that you don't need a specific object to handle the data. Any manufacturer can build one that will work with XML data, and developers can use one that suits their platform, operating system, programming language, or application.

XML is just plain text, and so you no longer have to worry about how to store and transport it. It can be sent as a text file over the Internet using HTTP (which is effectively a 7-bit only transport protocol). You don't have to encode it into a MIME or UU-encoded form. You can also write it to a disk as a text file, or store it in a database as text. OK, so it often produces a bigger file than the equivalent binary representation, but compression and the availability of large cheap disk drives generally compensate for this.

Applications have already started exposing data as XML in many ways. For example, Microsoft SQL Server 2000 includes features that allow you to extract data directly as XML documents, and update the source data using XML documents. Databases such as Oracle 8i and 9i are designed to manipulate XML directly, and the most recent office applications like Word and Excel will save their data in XML format either automatically or on demand.

XML is already directly ingrained into many applications. ASP.NET uses XML format configuration files, and web services expose their interface and data using an implementation of XML called the *Simple Object Access Protocol* (*SOAP*).

Other XML Technologies

As well as being a standard in itself, XML has also spawned other standards that are designed to interoperate with it. Two common examples are *XML Schemas*, which define the structure and content of XML documents, and the *Extensible Stylesheet Language for Transformation* (*XSLT*), which is used to perform transformations of the data into new formats.

XML schemas also provide a way for data to be expressed in specific XML formats that can be understood globally, or within specific industries such as pharmaceuticals or accountancy applications. There are also several server applications that can transform and communicate XML data between applications that expect different specific formats (or, in fact, other non-XML data formats). In the Microsoft world, this is BizTalk Server, and there are others such as Oasis and Rosetta for other platforms.

Just Another Data Access Technology?

To quote a colleague of mine, "Another year, another Microsoft data access technology". We've just got used to *ActiveX Data Objects* (*ADO*), and it's all-change time again. Is this some fiendish plan on Microsoft's behalf to keep us on our toes, or is there a reason why the technology that seemed to work fine in previous versions of ASP is no longer suitable?

In fact, there are several reasons why we really need to move on from ADO to a new technology. We'll examine these next, then later on take a high-level view of the changes that are involved in moving from ADO to the new .NET Framework data access techniques.

.NET Means Disconnected Data

You've seen a bit about how relational databases have evolved over recent years. However, it's not just the data store that has evolved – it's the whole computing environment. Most of the relational databases still in use today were designed to provide a solid foundation for the client-server world. Here, each client connects to the database server over some kind of permanent network connection, and remains connected for the duration of their session.

For example, with Microsoft Access, the client opens a *Form* window (often defined within their client-side interface program). This form fetches and caches some or all of the data that is required to populate the controls on the form from the server-side database program, and displays it on the client. The user can manipulate the data, and save changes back to the central database over their dedicated connection.

For this to work, the server-side database has to create explicit connections for each client, and maintain these while the client is connected. As long as the database software and the hardware it is running on are powerful enough for the anticipated number of clients, and the network has the bandwidth and stability to cope with the anticipated number of client connections, it all works very well.

But when this is moved to the disconnected world of the Internet, it falls apart very quickly. The concept of a stable and wide-band connection is hard enough to imagine, and the need to keep this connection permanently open can quickly cause problems to appear. It's not so bad if you are operating in a limited-user scenario, but for a public web site, it's obviously not going to work out.

In fact, there are several aspects to being disconnected. The nature of the HTTP protocol that is used on the Web means that connections between client and server are only made during the transfer of data or content. They aren't kept open after a page has been loaded or a recordset has been fetched.

On top of this, there is often a need to use the data extracted from a data store while not even connected to the Internet at all. Maybe while the user is traveling with a laptop computer, or the client is on a dial-up connection and needs to disconnect while working with the data then reconnect again later.

This means that we need to use data access technologies where the client can access, download, and cache the data required, then disconnect from the database server or data store. Once the clients are ready, they then need to be able to reconnect and update the original data store with the changes.

Disconnected Data in N-Tier Applications

Another aspect of working with disconnected data arises when you move from a client-server model into the world of *n*-tier applications. A distributed environment implies that the client and the server are separate, connected by a network. To build applications that work well in this environment, you can use a design strategy that introduces more granular differentiation between the layers, or *tiers*, of an application.

As Figure 8-2 shows, it's usual to create components that perform the data access in an application (the *data tier*), rather than having the ASP code hit the data store directly. There is often a series of rules (usually called *business rules*) that have to be followed, and these can be implemented within components.

They might be part of the components that perform the data access, or they might be separate – forming the *business tier* (or application logic tier). There may also be a separate set of components within the client application (the *presentation tier*) that perform specific tasks for managing, formatting, or presenting the data.

The benefits of designing applications along these lines are many, such as reusability of components, easier testing, and faster development.

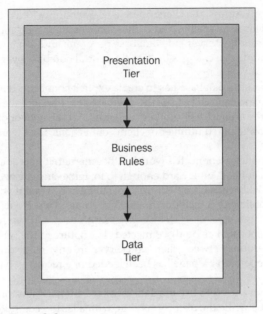

Figure 8-2

Let's take a look at how this influences the process of handling data. Within an *n*-tier application, the data must be passed between the tiers as each client request is processed. So, the data tier connects to the data store to extract the data, perhaps performs some processing upon it, and then passes it to the next tier. At this point, the data tier will usually disconnect from the data store, allowing another instance (another client or a different application) to use the connection.

By disconnecting the retrieved data from the data store at the earliest possible moment, we improve the efficiency of the application and allow it to handle more concurrent users. However, it again demonstrates the need for data access technologies that can handle disconnected data in a useful and easily manageable way – particularly when we need to update the original data in the data store.

The Evolution of ADO

Pre-ADO data access technologies, such as *Data Access Objects* (*DAO*) and *Remote Data Objects* (*RDO*) were designed to provide open data access methods for the client-server world – and are very successful in that environment. For example, if you build Visual Basic applications to access SQL Server over your local network, they work well.

However, with the advent of ASP 1.0, it was obvious that something new was needed. It used only active scripting (such as VBScript and JScript) within the pages, and for these a simplified ActiveX or COM-based technology was required. The answer was ADO 1.0, included with the original ASP installation. ADO allows you to connect to a database to extract recordsets, and perform updates using the database tables, SQL statements, or stored procedures within the database.

However, ADO 1.0 was really only an evolution of the existing technologies, and offered no solution for the disconnected problem. You opened a recordset while you had a connection to the data store, worked with the recordset (maybe updating it or just displaying the contents), then closed it and destroyed the connection. Once the connection was gone, there was no easy way to reconnect the recordset to the original data.

To some extent, the disconnected issue was addressed in ADO 2.0. A new recordset object allowed you to disconnect it from the data store, work with the contents, then reconnect and flush the changes back to the data store. This worked well with relational databases such as SQL Server, but was not always an ideal solution. It didn't provide the capabilities to store relationships and other details about the data – basically all you stored was the rowset containing the values.

Another technique that came along with ADO 2.0 was the provision of a *Data Source Object* (*DSO*) and *Remote Data Services* (*RDS*) that could be used in a client program such as Internet Explorer to cache data on a client. A recordset can be encoded as a special MIME type and passed over HTTP to the client where it is cached. The client can disconnect and then reconnect later and flush changes back to the data store. However, despite offering several useful features such as client-side data binding, this non-standard technique never really caught on – mainly due to the reliance on specific clients and concerns over security.

To get around all these limitations, the .NET Framework data access classes have been designed from the ground up to provide a reliable and efficient disconnected environment for working with data from a whole range of data stores.

.NET Means XML Data

As you saw earlier in this chapter, the computing world is moving ever more towards the adoption of XML as the fundamental data storage and transfer format. ADO 1.0 and 2.0 had no support for XML – it wasn't around as anything other than vague proposals at that time. In fact, at Microsoft, it was left to the Internet Explorer team to come up with the first tools for working with XML – the MSXML parser that shipped with IE 5 and other applications.

Later, MSXML became part of the ADO team's responsibilities and surfaced in ADO 2.1 and later as an integral part of *Microsoft Data Access Components* (*MDAC*). Along with it, the DSO used for remote data management and caching had XML support added. Methods were also added to the integral ADO objects.

The `Recordset` object gained methods that allowed it to load and save the content as XML. However, it was never anything more than an add-on, and the MSXML parser remained distinct from the core ADO objects.

Now, to bring data access up to date in the growing world of XML data, .NET includes a whole series of objects that are specifically designed to manage and manipulate XML data. This includes native support for XML formatted data within objects like the `Dataset`, as well as a whole range of objects that integrate a new XML parsing engine within the framework as a whole.

.NET Means Managed Code

As mentioned before, the .NET Framework is not a new operating system. It's a series of classes and a managed runtime environment within which code can be executed. The framework looks after all the complexities of garbage collection, caching, memory management and so on – but only as long as you use managed code. Once you step outside this cozy environment, the efficiency of your applications reduces (the execution has to move across the process boundaries into unmanaged code and back).

The existing ADO libraries are all unmanaged code, and so we need a new technology that runs within the .NET Framework. While Microsoft could just have added managed code wrappers to the existing ADO libraries, this would not have provided an ideal or efficient solution.

Instead, the data access classes within .NET have been designed from the ground up as managed code. They are integral to the framework and so provide maximum efficiency. They also include a series of objects that are specifically designed to work with MS SQL Server, using the native *Tabular Data Stream* (*TDS*) interface for maximum performance. Alternatively, managed code OLEDB, ODBC and Oracle providers are included with the framework to allow connections to all kinds of other data stores.

.NET Means a New Programming Model

One of the main benefits of moving to .NET is the ability to get away from the mish-mash of HTML content and script code that traditional ASP always seems to involve. Instead, there is a whole new structured programming model and approach to follow. You should use server controls (and user controls) to create output that is automatically tailored to each client, and react to events that these controls raise on the server.

Write in *proper* languages, and not script. Instead of VBScript, you can use Visual Basic, C#, as well as a compiled version of the JScript language. And, if you prefer, you can use C++, COBOL, Active Perl, or any one of the myriad other languages that are available or under development for the .NET platform.

This move to a structured programming model with server controls and event handlers provides improvements over existing data handling techniques using traditional ADO. For example, in ADO you need to iterate through a recordset to display the contents. However, the .NET Framework provides extremely useful server controls such as the DataGrid, which look after displaying the data themselves – all they need is a data source such as a set of records (a *rowset*).

So, instead of using Recordset-specific methods like MoveNext to iterate through a rowset, and access each field in turn, you just bind the rowset to the server control. It carries out all the tasks required to present that data, and even makes it available for editing. Yet, if required, you can still access data as a read-only and forward-only rowset using the new DataReader object instead. Overall, the .NET data access classes provide a series of objects that are better suited to working with data using server controls, as well as manipulating it directly with code.

Introducing Data Management in .NET

Having seen why we need a new data access technology, let's look at what .NET actually provides. In this section, you'll get a high-level overview of all of the .NET data management classes, and see how each of the objects fits with the disconnected and structured programming environment that .NET provides. The remainder of this chapter is divided into two sections; relational data management (techniques such as those you used traditional ADO for) and XML data management (for which, traditionally, you would use an XML parser such as MSXML).

System Namespaces for Data Management

The new relational data management classes are in a series of namespaces based on `System.Data` within the class library. The combination of the classes from the namespaces in the following table is generally referred to as *ADO.NET*:

Namespace	Description
System.Data	Contains the basic objects and public classes used for accessing and storing relational data, such as `DataSet`, `DataTable`, and `DataRelation`. Each of these is independent of the type of data source, and independent of the connection type.
System.Data. Common	Contains the base classes used by other public classes in the provider-specific namespaces, in particular those used by the classes in the `OleDb`, `Odbc`, `OracleClient`, and `SqlClient` namespaces. In general, this namespace is not specifically imported into applications.
System.Data. Odbc	Contains the public classes used to connect to and work with a data source via an ODBC driver, such as `OdbcConnection` and `OdbcCommand`. These objects inherit properties, methods, and events from the base classes in the `Common` namespace.
System.Data. OleDb	Contains the public classes used to connect to and work with a data source via an OLE-DB provider, such as `OleDbConnection` and `OleDbCommand`. These objects inherit properties, methods, and events from the base classes in the `Common` namespace.
System.Data. OracleClient	Contains the public classes used to connect to and work with an Oracle database, such as `OracleConnection` and `OracleCommand`. These objects inherit properties, methods, and events from the base classes in the `Common` namespace, and add Oracle-specific features as well.
System.Data. SqlClient	Contains the public classes used to connect to and work with a data source via the TDS interface of Microsoft SQL Server (only), using classes such as `SqlConnection` and `SqlCommand`. These classes provide better performance by removing some of the intermediate layers required by an OLEDB or ODBC provider. These objects inherit properties, methods, and events from the base classes in the `Common` namespace.
System.Data. SqlServerCe	Contains the public classes used to connect to and work with a data source running under Windows CE. These classes are not used or discussed in this book.
System.Data. SqlTypes	Contains public classes to implement the data types normally found in relational databases such as SQL Server, and which are different to the standard .NET data types. Examples are `SqlMoney`, `SqlDateTime`, and `SqlBinary`. Using these can improve performance and avoid type conversion errors.

There is also a separate series of namespaces containing the classes used to work with XML rather than relational data. These namespaces are based on `System.Xml`:

Namespace	Description
`System.Xml`	Contains the public classes required to create, read, store, write, and manipulate XML documents in line with W3C recommendations. Includes `XmlDocument` and a series of classes that represent the various types of node in an XML document.
`System.Xml.Schema`	Contains the public classes required to create, store, and manipulate XML schemas, and the nodes that they contain.
`System.Xml.Serialization`	Contains public classes that can be used to convert XML documents to other persistence formats, such as SOAP, for streaming to disk or across the wire.
`System.Xml.XPath`	Contains the public classes required to implement reading, storing, writing, and querying XML documents using a fast custom XPath-based document. Includes `XPathDocument`, `XPathNavigator`, and classes that represent XPath expressions.
`System.Xml.Xsl`	Contains the public classes required to transform XML into other formats using XSL or XSLT stylesheets. The main object is `XslTransform`.

Importing the Required Namespaces

Pages that use objects from the framework's class libraries must import the namespaces containing all the classes that they explicitly create instances of. Many of the common namespaces are imported by default, but this does not include the data management namespaces.

> To use any type of data access code, you must import the appropriate namespace.

Importing the System.Data Namespaces

To access relational data, you need at least `System.Data` *and* either `System.Data.OleDb`, `System.Data.SqlClient`, or `System.Data.Odbc` (depending on the way you're connecting to the data source). In ASP.NET, the `Import` page directive is used:

```
<%@Import Namespace="System.Data" %>
<%@Import Namespace="System.Data.OleDb" %>
```

Or:

```
<%@Import Namespace="System.Data" %>
<%@Import Namespace="System.Data.SqlClient" %>
```

In Visual Basic .NET code inside a class or module, use the `Imports` statement:

```
Imports System.Data
Imports System.Data.OleDb
```

In C#, use the `using` statement:

```
using System.Data;
using System.Data.OleDb;
```

At times when you need to specifically import other `System.Data` namespaces. For example, to create a new instance of a `DataTableMapping` class, you need to import the `System.Data.Common` namespace, and to use an SQL-specific data type, you need to import the `System.Data.SqlTypes` namespace.

Importing the System.Xml Namespaces

To access XML data using the objects in the framework class library, you can often get away with importing just the basic `System.Xml` namespace. However, to create an `XPathDocument` instance, you have to import the `System.Xml.XPath` namespace as well. To use the `XslTransform` class to perform server-side transformations of XML documents, you need to import the `System.Xml.Xsl` namespace.

The `System.Xml.Schema` namespace is usually only required when working with collections of schemas. Most XML validation objects are in `System.Xml`, so you can create an `XmlValidatingReader` (for example) without referencing the `System.Xml.Schema` namespace. But to create a new `SchemaCollection` instance, you must import the `System.Xml.Schema` namespace.

Type-Not-Found Compilation Errors

If you forget to import any required namespace, you'll get an error as that shown in Figure 8-3. In this case, it indicates that you have forgotten to import the namespace that contains the class for `OleDbConnection`. To solve this particular error, you just need to import the namespace `System.Data.OleDb`.

To find out which namespace contains a particular class, you can simply look in the .NET SDK Class Library section within the Reference section, or search for the object/class name using the *Index* or *Search* feature of the SDK. Alternatively, use the excellent *WinCV* (Windows Class Viewer) tool that comes with the .NET installation.

> *For help on using the tools that come with .NET, check out the SDK section .NET Framework Tools from within the Tools and Debugger section. The WinCV utility is described in detail in the subsection Windows Forms Class Viewer (`Wincv.exe`).*

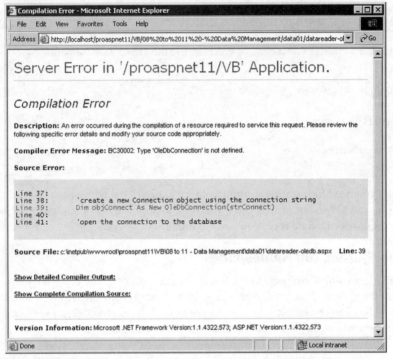

Figure 8-3

The Fundamental ADO.NET Classes

Traditional data access with ADO revolves around one fundamental data storage object – the Recordset. The technique used here is to create a connection to a data store using either an OLEDB provider or an ODBC through OLEDB driver (depending on the data store and the availability of the provider) and then execute commands against that connection to return a Recordset object containing the appropriate data. This can be done using a Command object or directly against the Connection object. Alternatively, to insert or update the data, just execute a SQL statement or a stored procedure within the data store using the Connection object or Command object directly, without returning a Recordset object.

Data access in .NET follows a broadly similar principle, but uses a different set of objects. So, switching to .NET does not involve learning a completely different technique. However, the objects used are quite different underneath, providing much better performance with more flexibility and usability.

The .NET data access object model is based around two fundamental objects – the DataReader and the DataSet. Together, they replace the Recordset from traditional ADO, providing many new features that make complex data access techniques much more efficient, while remaining as easy to use as the Recordset object. The main differences are that a DataReader provides forward-only and read-only access to data (like a *firehose* cursor in ADO), while the DataSet object can hold more than one table (in other words, more than one rowset) from the same data source as well as the relationships between them.

You can create a `DataSet` from existing data in a data store, or fill it directly with data one row at a time using code. It also allows you to manipulate the data held in the `DataSet`'s tables, and build as well as modify the relationships between the tables within it.

Each table within a `DataSet` maintains details of the original values of the data as you work with it, and any changes to the data can be pushed back into the data store at a later date.

The `DataSet` also contains metadata describing the table contents, such as the columns types, rules, and keys. Remember that the whole ethos with a `DataSet` is to be able to work accurately and efficiently in a disconnected environment.

The `DataSet` object can also persist its contents, including more than one data table or rowset, directly as XML, and load data from an XML document that contains structured data in the correct format. In fact, XML is the *only* persistence format for data in .NET – bringing it more into line with the needs of disconnected and remote clients.

Comparison of Techniques in ADO and ADO.NET

As we expect most of our readers to be at least partly familiar with traditional ADO programming techniques, we will start with a quick overview of how the new ADO.NET classes and techniques relate to the traditional approach:

Traditional ADO approach	ADO.NET equivalent
Connected access to data using a `Connection` (and possibly a `Command` as well) to fill a `Recordset` then iterate through the `Recordset`.	Use a `Connection` and a `Command` to connect a `DataReader` object to the data store and read the results iteratively from the data store.
Updating a data store using a `Connection` and `Command` object to execute a SQL statement or stored procedure.	Use a `Connection` and a `Command` to connect to the data store and execute the SQL statement or stored procedure.
Disconnected access to data using a `Connection` (and possibly a `Command` as well) to fill a `Recordset` then remove the connection to the data source.	Use a `Connection` and a `Command` to connect a `DataAdapter` to the data source and then fill a `DataSet` with the results.
Updating a data store from a disconnected `Recordset` by reconnecting and using the `Update` or `UpdateBatch` method.	Use a `Connection` and a `Command` to connect a `DataAdapter` and `DataSet` to the data source and then call the `Update` method of the `DataAdapter`.

The major differences are:

❑ There is no direct equivalent of a `Recordset` class. Depending on the task you want to achieve, you use a `DataReader` or a `DataSet` instead.

❑ Client-side and server-side (database) cursors are not used in ADO.NET. The disconnected model means that they are not applicable.

❑ Database locking is not supported or required. Again, due to the disconnected model, it is not applicable.

❑ All data persistence is as XML. There are no MIME-encoded or binary representations of rowsets or other data structures.

Let's look at the new ADO.NET classes in more detail.

The Connection Classes

These classes are similar to the ADO `Connection` class, with similar properties. They are used to connect a data store to a `Command` instance.

❑ The `OleDbConnection` class is used with an OLE-DB provider

❑ The `SqlConnection` class uses Tabular Data Services (TDS) with MS SQL Server

❑ The `OdbcConnection` class is used with an ODBC driver

❑ The `OracleConnection` class is used to connect to an Oracle database

In traditional ADO, it was common to use the `Connection` to directly execute a SQL statement against the data source or to open a `Recordset`. This *cannot* be done with the .NET `Connection` classes. However, they do provide access to transactions that are in progress against a data store.

The Commonly Used Methods of the Connection Classes

The most commonly used methods for the `OleDbConnection`, `OdbcConnection`, `OracleConnection`, and `SqlConnection` classes are shown in the following table:

Method	Description
Open	Opens a connection to the data source using the current settings for the properties, such as `ConnectionString` that specifies the connection information to use
Close	Closes the connection to the data source
BeginTransaction	Starts a data source transaction and returns a `Transaction` instance that can be used to commit or abort the transaction.

*An excellent reference to all the properties, methods, and events of the classes discussed here is included within the .NET SDK that is provided with the framework. Simply open the **Class Library** topic within the **Reference** section, or search for the class by name using the **Index** or **Search** feature of the SDK. Many of the common ones have been demonstrated, including those shown in the preceding table.*

Remember that there are at least two implementations of some of the .NET data access classes, each one being specific to the data store you are connecting to.

Classes prefixed with `OleDb` or `Odbc` are used with a managed code OLEDB provider or ODBC driver against any database that has a suitable provider or driver. The classes prefixed with `Sql` are used only with Microsoft SQL Server (we'll concentrate on just these three types of data store connection).

Other than that, the classes are identical as far as programming with them is concerned. However, you must use the appropriate one depending on which data store you connect to, so your code must be rewritten to use the correct ones if you change from one set of classes to the other.

This is generally only a matter of changing the prefixes in the class declarations. For this reason, you may prefer to avoid including the prefix in your variable and method names, and in comments within your code.

As an aside, it is possible to use the .NET Activator class's `CreateInstance` method to create an instance of a class using a variable to specify the class name. This would allow generic code routines to be created that instantiate the correct class type (`OleDb` or `Sql`) depending on some external condition you specify. The details of this topic can be found in the SDK.

The Command Classes

These classes are similar to the equivalent ADO `Command`, and have similar properties. They are used to connect the `Connection` class to a `DataReader` or a `DataAdapter` instance:

- ❑   The `OleDbCommand` class is used with an OLE-DB provider.
- ❑   The `SqlCommand` class uses Tabular Data Services with MS SQL Server.
- ❑   The `OdbcCommand` class is used with an ODBC driver.
- ❑   The `OracleCommand` class is used to access an Oracle database.

The `Command` class allows you to execute a SQL statement or stored procedure against a data source. This includes returning a rowset (in which case you use another class such as a `DataReader` or a `DataAdapter` to access the data), returning a single value (a *singleton*), or returning a count of the number of records affected for queries that do not return a rowset.

The Commonly Used Methods of the Command Classes

The most commonly used methods for the `OleDbCommand`, `OdbcCommand`, `OracleCommand`, and `SqlCommand` classes are shown in the following table:

Method	Description
ExecuteNonQuery	Executes the command defined in the CommandText property against the connection defined in the Connection property for a query that does not return any rows (an UPDATE, DELETE, or INSERT). Returns an Integer indicating the number of rows affected by the query.
ExecuteReader	Executes the command defined in the CommandText property against the connection defined in the Connection property. Returns a "reader" instance that is connected to the resulting rowset within the database, allowing the rows to be retrieved. The derivative ExecuteXmlReader method can be used with the SQL Server 7.0 SQLXML technology to return an XML document fragment in an XmlReader instance. We look at the various "reader" classes later.
ExecuteScalar	Executes the command defined in the CommandText property against the connection defined in the Connection property. Returns only a single value (effectively the first column of the first row of the resulting rowset). Any other returned columns and rows are discarded. Fast and efficient when only a "singleton" value is required.

The DataAdapter Classes

Some classes in the framework connect one or more Command instances to a Dataset. They provide the pipeline and logic that fetches the data from the data store and populates the tables in the DataSet, or pushes the changes in the DataSet back into the data store.

❑ The OleDbDataAdapter class is used with an OLE-DB provider.

❑ The SqlDataAdapter class uses Tabular Data Services with MS SQL Server.

❑ The OdbcDataAdapter class is used with an ODBC driver.

❑ The OracleDataAdapter class is used to access an Oracle database.

These classes provide four properties that define the commands used to manipulate the data in a data store: SelectCommand, InsertCommand, UpdateCommand, and DeleteCommand.

Each one of these properties is a reference to a Command instance (these Command instances can all share the same Connection instance). Figure 8-4 shows how these classes are related:

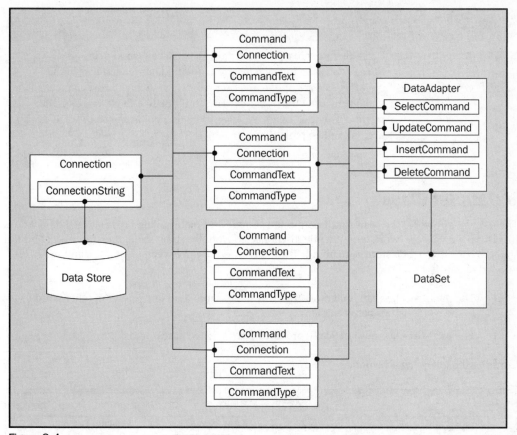

Figure 8-4

The Commonly Used Methods of the DataAdapter Classes

The `OleDbDataAdapter`, `OdbcDataAdapter`, `OracleDataAdapter`, and `SqlDataAdapter` classes provide a series of methods for working with the `DataSet` that they apply to. The three most commonly used methods are shown in the following table:

Method	Description
Fill	Executes the `SelectCommand` to fill the `DataSet` with data from the data source. Can also be used to update (refresh) an existing table in a `DataSet` with changes made to the data in the original data source if there is a primary key in the table in the `DataSet`.
FillSchema	Uses the `SelectCommand` to extract just the schema for a table from the data source, and creates an empty table in the `DataSet` with all the corresponding constraints.

Table continued on following page

Method	Description
Update	Calls the respective `InsertCommand`, `UpdateCommand`, or `DeleteCommand` for each inserted, updated, or deleted row in the `DataSet` so as to update the original data source with the changes made to the content of the `DataSet`. This is a little like the `UpdateBatch` method provided by the ADO `Recordset`, but in the `DataSet` it can be used to update more than one table.

The DataSet Class

The `DataSet` provides the basis for disconnected storage and manipulation of relational data. You can fill it from a data store, work with it while disconnected from that data store, then reconnect and flush changes back to the data store as required. The main differences between a `DataSet` and the ADO `Recordset` are:

❑   The `DataSet` class can hold more than one table (more than one rowset in other words), as well as the relationships between them.

❑   The `DataSet` class automatically provides disconnected access to data.

Consider the following schematic:

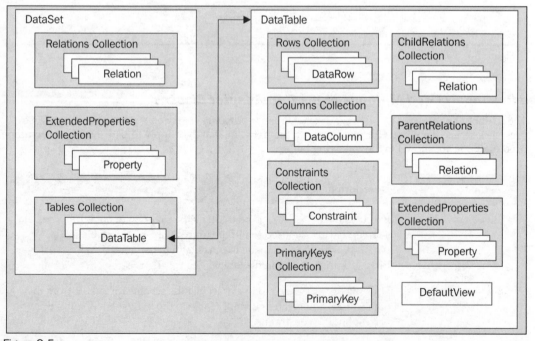

Figure 8-5

Figure 8-5 shows a schematic view of the relationship between all the classes discuss now. Each table in a `DataSet` is a `DataTable` instance within the `Tables` collection. Each `DataTable` contains a collection of `DataRow` instances and a collection of `DataColumn` instances. There are also collections for the primary keys, constraints, and default values used in this table (the `Constraints` collection), and the parent and child relationships between the tables.

There is also a `DefaultView` instance for each table. This is used to create a `DataView` based on the table, so that the data can be searched, filtered or otherwise manipulated – or bound to a control for display (we look at the `DataTable` and `DataView` classes later).

The Commonly Used Methods of the DataSet Class

The `DataSet` class exposes a series of methods that can be used to work with the contents of the tables, or the relationships between them. For example, you can clear the `DataSet`, or merge data from a separate `DataSet` into this one. The following table summarizes the methods available:

Method	Description
Clear	Removes all data stored in the `DataSet` by emptying all of the tables it contains. However, it is often more efficient to destroy the instance and create a new one unless you need to hold a reference to the existing one.
Merge	Takes the contents of a `DataSet` and merges it with another `DataSet` so that it contains all the data from both of the source `DataSet` instances.

We mentioned earlier that the default persistence format in .NET is XML. The following table shows the methods provided by the `DataSet` class for reading and writing this XML data.

Methods	Description
ReadXml *and* ReadXmlSchema	Takes an XML document or an XML schema and reads it into the `DataSet`.
GetXml *and* GetXmlSchema	Returns a `String` containing an XML document or an XML schema that represents the data in the `DataSet`.
WriteXml *and* WriteXmlSchema	Writes the XML document or XML schema that represents the data in the `DataSet` to a disk file, to a "reader/writer" instance, or to a `Stream`. We look at the "reader/writer" classes later.

The `DataSet` class, together with all the `DataTable` instances it contains, keeps a record of the values for the content when it was originally created and loaded (filled with data). This is a fundamental requirement to allow the changes to be pushed back into the original data store in a multi-user scenario.

There are four methods provided that allow you to control when and how the original values are stored, as shown in the following table:

Method	Description
AcceptChanges	Commits all the changes made to the tables or relations within the DataSet since it was loaded, or since the last time AcceptChanges was executed.
GetChanges	Returns a DataSet containing some or all of the changes made since it was loaded, or since the last time AcceptChanges was executed.
HasChanges	Indicates if any changes have been made to the contents of the DataSet since it was loaded, or since the last time AcceptChanges was executed.
RejectChanges	Abandons all the changes made to values in the tables within the DataSet since it was loaded, or since the last time AcceptChanges was executed. Returns it to the original state and removes all stored changes information.

The DataTable Class

Each of the tables or rowsets stored within a DataSet class is exposed through a DataTable class instance, as was shown in Figure 8-5. Each DataTable has a Rows property that references a DataRowCollection class instance. This is a collection of DataRow class instances.

The Commonly Used Methods of the DataTable Class

The DataTable class exposes a series of properties and methods that allow you to interact with each table individually while it is stored in the DataSet. The most commonly used methods are Clear, AcceptChanges, and RejectChanges. These are fundamentally the same as the methods just described for the DataSet class, but operate only on the specific table to which the DataTable class refers.

The following methods allow you to manipulate the contents of the table:

Method	Description
NewRow	Creates a new row for the table. The values can then be inserted into it using code, and the new row added to the table.
Select	Returns the set of rows that match a filter, in the order specified. Used to create subsets of rows.

The Commonly Used Methods of the DataRowCollection Class

This is a collection of all the rows in a `DataTable`, as referenced by the `Rows` property of the table. It provides methods to add and remove rows, and to find a row based on a value for the primary key (or more than one value for a multiple-column primary key). These methods are summarized in the following table:

Method	Description
Add	Adds a new row created with the `NewRow` method of the `DataTable` to the table
Remove	Permanently removes the specified `DataRow` class from the table
RemoveAt	Permanently removes a row specified by its index position from the table
Find	Takes an array of primary key values and returns the matching row as a `DataRow` instance

The Commonly Used Methods of the DataRow Class

This class represents the row itself within the table, and within the `DataRowCollection`. It has the `AcceptChanges` and `RejectChanges` methods, which work the same way as for the `DataTable` class.

The `DataRow` class also has methods that are used to manipulate individual rows in a table, as shown in the following table:

Methods	Description
BeginEdit, EndEdit, *and* CancelEdit	Used to switch the row into "edit mode" and save or abandon the changes made in this mode.
Delete	Marks the row as being deleted, though it is not removed from the table until the `Update` or `AcceptChanges` method is executed.
GetChildRows	Returns a collection of rows from another table that is related to this row as child rows.
SetColumnError *and* GetColumnsInError	Used to set and return the error status for this row. In conjunction with the `HasErrors` and `RowError` properties, this allows bulk edit errors to be reported separately afterwards.

The DataView Class

As shown in the earlier schematic, you can retrieve a `DataView` containing the data from a table within a `DataSet`. The `DataView` class exposes a complete table or a subset of the rows from a table. It can be created using the `DefaultView` of the table, or from a `DataTable` instance that selects a subset of rows from a table.

The Commonly Used Methods of the DataView Class

In general, to manipulate the contents of a table within a `DataSet`, it's best to create a `DataView` from the table and use the methods it provides. The most commonly used methods are shown in the following table:

Method	Description
AddNew	Adds a new row to the `DataView`. The values can then be inserted into it using code.
Delete	Removes the current or specified row from the `DataView`.
Find	Takes a single value or an array of values, and returns the index of the row that matches these value(s).
FindRows	Takes a single value or an array of values, and returns a collection of `DataRow` instances that match these value(s).

The DataReader Classes

While the `DataSet` provides a comprehensive platform for disconnected data access, there are many occasions when you just want a fast and efficient way to access a data store without actually extracting data that will be *remoted* (disconnected). This might be to extract one or a few records or specific field values, or to execute a simple INSERT, UPDATE, or DELETE SQL statement. Or, it might be where there is too much data to fit into a `DataSet` and to remote sensibly. It's also the ideal solution for server-side data binding in most cases, as mentioned in the previous chapter. For all these tasks you can use a `DataReader` class.

❑ The `OleDbDataReader` class is used with an OLEDB provider.

❑ The `SqlDataReader` class uses Tabular Data Services with MS SQL Server.

❑ The `OdbcDataReader` class is used with an ODBC driver.

❑ The `OracleDataReader` class is used to access an Oracle database.

As Figure 8-6 suggests, the `DataReader` provides the equivalent of a *firehose* cursor for direct connected access and retrieval of data from a data store. It's somewhat like the way an ADO `Recordset` is used to extract data and then iterate through it.

We execute a SQL statement or stored procedure to get a set of data rows that are referenced by a `DataReader`, and then iterate through them – while all the time remaining connected to the data store.

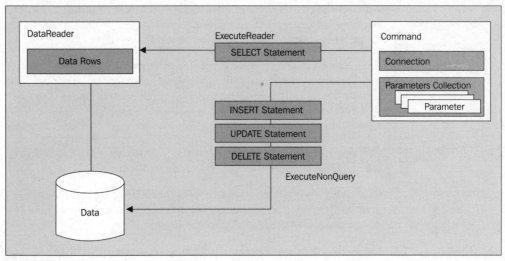

Figure 8-6

The important points to bear in mind with the `DataReader` are:

❑ It provides a partial equivalent of a cursor against a data store, using a SQL statement or stored procedure to extract a rowset.

❑ It provides the ability to execute a SQL statement or stored procedure to update the data store content.

❑ It does not provide disconnected access to data.

❑ Access to the rowset referenced by a `DataReader` is read-only and forward-only.

You can extract XML formatted data fragments directly from MS SQL Server 2000 using a reader instance (in this case an `XmlReader`) together with the in-built SQL-XML technology.

The Commonly Used Methods and Properties of the DataReader Classes

To use a `DataReader` class, create a `Command` class and then use this to execute your SQL statement or stored procedure and return a `DataReader`. You can then iterate through the rows and columns, using the `DataReader` to extract the results from the data store.

The following table shows the most commonly used methods exposed by the `DataReader` classes:

Method	Description
Read	Advances the current row pointer to the next row so that the values of the columns can be accessed using the column name or ordinal position. Returns `False` when there are no more rows to read.
GetValue	Returns one value from the current row in its native format (as the native data type in the data source) by specifying the integer column index. The simpler but less efficient alternative to using the column index is to specify the column name directly as: *value* = `DataReader("`*column-name*`")`.
GetValues	Gets one or more values from the current row in their native format (as the native data type in the data source) into an array.
Getxxxxxx	Returns a value from the current row as the data type specific to each method, by specifying the integer column index. Examples are `GetBoolean`, `GetInt16`, and `GetChars`.
NextResult	Moves the current row pointer to the next set of results when the statement is a SQL stored procedure or a batch SQL statement that returns more than one result set. Note that this is not a `MoveNext` operation like that of an ADO `Recordset` – it moves the current row pointer from one *rowset* to the first row in the *next rowset*.
Close	Closes the `DataReader` and releases the reference to the rowset.

The `DataReader` classes also expose some useful properties that allow you to discover details about the rowset that it is referencing, as shown in the following table:

Method	Description
FieldCount	Returns the number of columns (fields) in the rowset returned by the query or stored procedure.
HasRows	Returns a `Boolean` value of `True` if the execution of the query or stored procedure returned any rows, and `False` if there are no rows in the resulting rowset. This method was added in version 1.1.
IsClosed	Returns a `Boolean` value that is `True` if the `DataReader` has been closed, or `False` if it is still open following execution of the query or stored procedure.

Method	Description
RecordsAffected	Returns an Integer value that is the number of rows in the result set referenced by the DataReader. Only valid after all the rows have been read from the DataReader by a server control such as a DataGrid, or after iterating through until the Read method returns False.

Should I Use a DataReader or a DataSet?

When you start building applications that access a data store, think about what kind of access you actually need, and how the data will be used. It should be obvious from the descriptions of the classes that the DataSet carries a noticeable overhead in terms of complexity when compared to a DataReader, with the corresponding negative effect on performance and memory usage.

So, wherever it's possible, aim to use a DataReader rather than a DataSet. The kinds of occasions that require a DataSet are:

❑   When you need to remote the data (disconnect from the data store and pass the data to another tier in the application) to a client application, store it ready for use in a process, edit the data, or in some similar scenario.

❑   When you need to store, transport, or access more than one table (more than one DataTable instance), and optionally the relationships between these tables.

❑   When you need to update data in the source database using the in-built methods of the DataSet and DataAdapter rather than executing individual SQL UPDATE statements or stored procedures. The DataSet also stores the original (as well as the current) values of each column in each row, so it better manages a situation where multiple users are concurrently updating the data.

❑   When you need to take advantage of the synchronization between an XML document and the equivalent "relational" rowset. This topic is discussed in Chapter 11.

❑   In certain data binding scenarios, such as binding the same data to several controls or using automatic record paging in a DataGrid control, you cannot use a DataReader as the data source. In such cases, it's usual to use a DataView created from a table in a DataSet.

❑   If you are iterating through the data rows, and need the freedom to be able to move backwards and forwards in the rowset. You can't use a DataReader for this, as it is a forward-only data source.

Relational Data Providers for .NET

.NET uses managed code data providers to connect to a data store. The following table shows the .NET Data Providers that ship with version 1.1 of the .NET Framework:

Provider Name	Description
SQLOLEDB	OLEDB provider SQL Server
MSDAORA	OLEDB provider for Oracle
Microsoft.Jet.OLEDB.4.0	OLEDB provider for Access and other Jet data sources
SQL Server	ODBC driver for SQL Server
Microsoft ODBC for Oracle	ODBC driver for Oracle
Microsoft Access Driver (*.mdb)	ODBC driver for Microsoft Access
Oracle	Microsoft provider for Oracle (requires the Oracle client software version 8.1.7 or later to be installed)

Only the first three of the providers listed were included with.NET Framework version 1.0. A managed provider for ODBC was developed as a beta product during the version 1.0 timeframe, and can still be obtained from the *Microsoft Data* web site at http://www.microsoft.com/data/. More managed providers are planned, such as those for Microsoft Exchange, Active Directory, and other data stores. The existing unmanaged OLEDB providers for these data stores cannot be used in .NET.

> *The beta version of the ODBC driver installs in a different namespace from the driver included in version 1.1 of the .NET Framework. The current namespace is* `System.Data.Odbc`, *whereas the beta version was installed as* `Microsoft.Data.Odbc`.

Common Data Access Tasks with .NET

To demonstrate the basics of working with relational data in .NET, we've put together a series of sample pages that show the various objects in action. Figure 8-7 shows the `default.htm` main menu page for the samples:

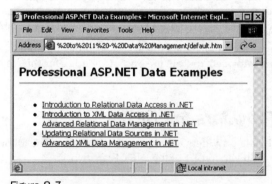

Figure 8-7

You can download the samples to run on your own server at http://www.daveandal.net/books/8900/. You can also run many of them online at the same URL. The samples are available in both VB and C#, and you can choose which to install – or install both sets.

The examples for this chapter are in the Introduction to Relational Data Access in .NET section, and this link displays the `default.htm` page for these sample pages, as shown in Figure 8-8.

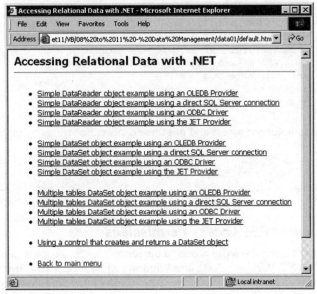

Figure 8-8

The first three groups of links show the three basic techniques for accessing relational data. Each group demonstrates four different connection types: an OLEDB provider for SQL Server, a direct SQL Server TDS connection, a connection through the .NET ODBC driver, and a connection to an Access database file through the Jet provider for Microsoft Access. There is also an example of using a user control that returns a `DataSet`. We'll be examining all these sample pages.

Setting Up the Samples on Your System

The downloadable sample files contain a `WroxBooks.mdb` Access database, which you can use with the Jet examples, and a set of SQL scripts that you can use to create the sample `WroxBooks` database on your own local SQL Server. Instructions for using the scripts are in the `readme.txt` file located within the `database` folder of the samples.

You'll also need to edit the connection strings in the `web.config` file that is installed in the root folder of the examples to suit your setup. The `<appSettings>` section of the `web.config` file contains declarations of the connection strings for all of the examples for this book, but the ones that are relevant to this chapter are highlighted in the following code. Notice that there are four, one for each of the providers/drivers used in the example pages:

```
<configuration>
    ... other settings here ...
  <appSettings>
    <add key="DsnWroxBooksSql"
         value="server=delmonte; database=WroxBooks; user id=sa; password=" />
    <add key="DsnWroxBooksOleDb"
         value="provider=SQLOLEDB.1; data source=delmonte;
                initial catalog=WroxBooks; uid=sa; pw=" />
    <add key="DsnWroxBooksJet"
         value="Provider=Microsoft.Jet.OLEDB.4.0;Data Source=" />
    <add key="DsnWroxBooksOdbc"
         value="DRIVER={SQL Server}; SERVER=delmonte;
                DATABASE=WroxBooks; uid=sa; pw=;" />
    ... other settings here ...
  </appSettings>
</configuration>
```

Any page within the samples can access and use these connection strings by using:

```
strSQLConnect = ConfigurationSettings.AppSettings("DsnWroxBooksSql")
strOLEDBConnect = ConfigurationSettings.AppSettings("DsnWroxBooksOleDb")
strJetConnect = ConfigurationSettings.AppSettings("DsnWroxBooksJet")
strOdbcConnect = ConfigurationSettings.AppSettings("DsnWroxBooksOdbc")
```

Setting Up the Required File Access Permissions

Some of the examples files require write access to the server's wwwroot folder and subfolders below this. By default in Windows NT, Windows 2000, and Windows XP, ASP.NET runs under the context of the ASPNET account that is created by the installation and setup of the .NET Framework. This is a relatively unprivileged account that has similar permissions by default as the IUSR_machinename account that is used by Internet Information Services.

To give folders on your test server write access for ASP.NET, right-click on the wwwroot folder in Windows Explorer and open the Properties dialog. In the Security tab, select the ASPNET account and give it Write permission or Full Control. Then click Advanced and tick the checkbox at the bottom of this page (Reset permissions on all child objects...).

Alternatively, configure ASP.NET to run under the context of the local System account by editing the machine.config file located in the config directory of the installation root. By default, this is the C:\WINNT\Microsoft.NET\Framework\[version]\CONFIG\ directory. Change just the userName attribute in the <processModel> element within the <system.web> section of this file to:

```
<processModel userName="system" password="autogenerate" ... />
```

> **Do this only while experimenting and only on a development server. For production servers, set up only the minimal permissions required for your applications to run.**

ASP.NET with IIS 6.0 and Windows Server 2003

While all the this is true for IIS 4.0 and IIS 5.0, as installed with Windows NT, Windows 2000, and Windows XP, the new version of IIS supplied with Windows Server 2003 (IIS 6.0) works in a slightly different way. Security and account permissions are discussed in Chapter 14. However, to enable the example pages to run on Windows Server 2003 you only need to know the basics here.

By default, in Windows Server 2003, web sites run within Application Pools and the worker processes used for accessing resources run under the context of an account named NETWORK SERVICE. Windows Server 2003 creates an account group called IIS_WPG, of which the IWAM_machinename, LOCAL SERVICE, NETWORK SERVICE and SYSTEM accounts are automatically members.

It means that you can use this group to configure access to resources for ASP.NET running under the default IIS 6.0 configuration. Alternatively, you can just assign the necessary Write permission directly to the NETWORK SERVICE account if you prefer more fine-grained control.

You can also configure IIS 6.0 to run in a special *compatibility* mode called *IIS 5.0 Isolation Mode* (in the Service tab of the Properties dialog for the Web Sites entry in the IIS Manager). In this case, IIS 6.0 runs ASP.NET just like it does under IIS 5.0, and the accounts used and permission settings you make are the same as in IIS 5.0.

So, the ASPNET account is used for ASP.NET resources, and the IWAM_machinename account is used for other resources. And an account named IWAM_machinename is used for out-of-process execution of components in this mode, just as in IIS 5.0.

> *For more information of the IIS and ASP.NET security model in Windows Server 2003, open the Help file from IIS Manager and navigate to the Server Administration Guide | Security | Access Control | Web Site Permissions section.*

Using a DataReader Object

The first group of links in the relational data access menu shows the `DataReader` in action. This is the nearest equivalent to the `Connection/Recordset` data access technique used in traditional ADO. Figure 8-9 shows the result of running the OLEDB example. The others from the same group (the SQL TDS, ODBC and Jet provider examples) provide identical output, but with different connection strings.

The code in the page (`datareader-oledb.aspx`) is placed within the `Page_Load` event handler. So, it runs when the page loads. The code inserts the connection string, SQL `SELECT` statement, and the results into `<div>` elements within page. All the code is fully commented, and we've included elementary error handling to display any errors. However, only the relevant data access code has been shown here. You can examine the entire source code for any of the pages by clicking the [view source] link at the bottom.

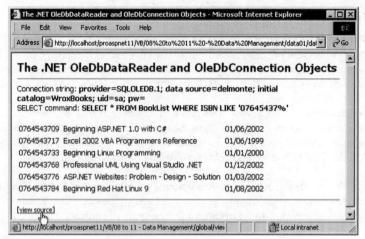

Figure 8-9

The DataReader Example Code

The following code has been used in this example:

```
'get connection string from web.config file and display it
strConnect = ConfigurationSettings.AppSettings("DsnWroxBooksOleDb")
outConnect.InnerText = strConnect

'specify the SELECT statement to extract the data and display it
strSelect = "SELECT * FROM BookList WHERE ISBN LIKE '07645437%'"
outSelect.InnerText = strSelect

'create a new Connection object using the connection string
Dim objConnect As New OleDbConnection(strConnect)

'open the connection to the database
objConnect.Open()

'create a new Command using the connection object and select statement
Dim objCommand As New OleDbCommand(strSelect, objConnect)

'declare a variable to hold a DataReader object
Dim objDataReader As OleDbDataReader

'execute the SQL statement against the command to fill the DataReader
objDataReader = objCommand.ExecuteReader()
```

The first step is to get the connection string from the web.config file, and then specify the SQL statement. These are displayed as the code runs in <div> elements named outConnect and outSelect (located within the HTML of the page). Then, we create a new instance of an OleDbConnection object, specifying the connection string as the single parameter of its constructor.

After opening the connection by calling the Open method, you need an OleDbCommand object. This will be used to execute the statement and return a new OleDbDataReader object through which you can access the results of the query. The SQL statement and the active Connection object are specified as the parameters to the OleDbCommand object constructor: You can then call the ExecuteReader method of the OleDbCommand object. This returns an OleDbDataReader object that is connected to the result rowset.

Displaying the Results

A DataReader allows you to iterate through the results of a SQL query, much like you do with a traditional ADO Recordset object. However, unlike in the ADO Recordset, in a DataReader you must call the Read method first to be able to access the first row of the results. Afterwards, just call the Read method repeatedly to get the next row of the results until it returns False (which indicates that the end of the results set has been reached).

> *We no longer have a MoveNext method. Forgetting to include this statement was found by testers to be the most common reason for problems when working with the Recordset object in ADO.*

As was common practice in ASP 3.0 and earlier, you can build up an HTML <table> to display the data. However, as you're working with ASP.NET now, this example actually creates the definition of the table as a string and then inserts it into a <div> element elsewhere in the page (rather than the ASP-style technique of using Response.Write directly). The following code was used to create the output shown in Figure 8-9:

```
Dim strResult As String = "<table>"

'iterate through the records in the DataReader getting field values
'the Read method returns False when there are no more records
Do While objDataReader.Read()
    strResult += "<tr><td>" & objDataReader("ISBN") & "</td><td>  " _
            & objDataReader("Title") & "</td><td>  " _
            & objDataReader("PublicationDate") & "</td><td></tr>"
Loop

'close the DataReader and Connection
objDataReader.Close()
objConnect.Close()

'add closing table tag and display the results
strResult += "</table>"
outResult.InnerHtml = strResult
```

> *You could, of course, simply declare an ASP.NET list control such as a DataGrid in the page, and then bind the DataReader to the control to display the results. However, the technique used here to display the data demonstrates how we can iterate through the rowset.*

Closing the DataReader and the Connection

You have to explicitly close the DataReader. You also have to explicitly close the connection by calling the Connection object's Close method. Although the garbage collection process will close the DataReader when it destroys the object in memory after the page ends, it's good practice to always close *reader* objects connections as soon as you are finished with them.

It's even more important to close the connection after you finish with it. Database connections are a precious resource, and the number available is usually limited. For this reason, as you'll see in the next section, ADO.NET provides a useful method that will close a connection automatically.

The CommandBehavior Enumeration

One useful technique to bear in mind when using a `DataReader` is to take advantage of the optional parameter for the `Command` object's `ExecuteReader` method. It can be used to force the connection to be closed automatically as soon as we call the `Close` method of the `DataReader` object:

```
objDataReader = objCommand.ExecuteReader(CommandBehavior.CloseConnection)
```

This is particularly useful if you pass a reference to the `DataReader` to another routine, say if you return it from a method. By using the `CommandBehavior.CloseConnection` option, you can be sure that the connection will be closed automatically when the routine using the `DataReader` destroys the object reference.

Other values in the `CommandBehavior` enumeration that you can use with the `ExecuteReader` method (multiple values can be used with `And` or +) are:

❑   `SchemaOnly`: The execution of the query will only return the schema (column information) for the results set, and not any data. It can be used, for example, to find the number of columns in the results set.

❑   `SequentialAccess`: Can be used to allow the `DataReader` to access large volumes of binary data from a column. The data is accessed as a stream rather than as individual rows and columns, and is retrieved using the `GetBytes` or `GetChars` methods of the `DataReader`.

❑   `SingleResult`: Useful if the query is only expected to return a single value, and can help the database to fine-tune the query execution for maximum efficiency. Alternatively, use the `ExecuteScalar` method of the `Command` object.

❑   `SingleRow`: Useful if the query is only expected to return one row, and can help the database to fine-tune the query execution for maximum efficiency.

Overall, the techniques used in this example are not that far removed from working with traditional ADO in ASP. However, there are far more opportunities available in .NET for accessing and using relational data. These revolve around the `DataSet` rather than the `DataReader`.

A Simple DataSet Example

A `DataSet` is a disconnected read/write container for holding one or more tables of data, and the relationships between these tables. In this example, we just extract a single table from the database and display the contents.

Figure 8-10 shows what the Simple DataSet object example using an OLEDB Provider (`simple-dataset-oledb.aspx`) sample looks like when it's run:

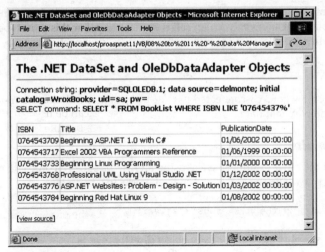

Figure 8-10

The Simple DataSet Example Code

We've used the same connection string and SQL statement as in the `DataReader` example. We also create a new `OleDbConnection` object using this connection string as before:

```
Dim objConnect As New OleDbConnection(strConnect)
```

To execute the SQL statement for the `OleDbDataReader` object in the previous example, we used the `ExecuteReader` method of the `OleDbCommand` object. In this example, to fill a `DataSet` object with data, we use an alternative object to specify the SQL statement – an `OleDbDataAdapter` object. Again, we provide the SQL statement and the active `Connection` object as the parameters to the object constructor:

```
Dim objDataAdapter As New OleDbDataAdapter(strSelect, objConnect)
```

> *This technique still creates and uses a Command object. When you create a DataAdapter, a suitable Command instance is created automatically behind the scenes, and assigned to the SelectCommand property of your DataAdapter. You could do this yourself, but it would mean writing the extra code, and there is no advantage in doing so.*

Now create an instance of a `DataSet` object and then fill it with data from the data source by calling the `Fill` method of the `DataAdapter` object. Specify as parameters the `DataSet` object and the name of the source table in the database:

```
Dim objDataSet As New DataSet()
objDataAdapter.Fill(objDataSet, "Books")
```

Filling the Schema in a DataSet

The `Fill` method of the `DataAdapter` object that was used here creates the table in the `DataSet`, and then creates the appropriate columns and sets the data type and certain constraints such as the column *width* (the number of characters). It doesn't automatically set the primary keys, unique constraints, read-only values, and defaults. However, you can call the `FillSchema` method first (before you call `Fill`) to copy these settings from the data source into the table:

```
objDataAdapter.FillSchema(objDataSet, SchemaType.Mapped)
```

After all this, you've now got a disconnected `DataSet` object that contains the results of the SQL query. The next step is to display that data.

Displaying the Results

In this and many of the other examples, we're using an ASP `DataGrid` control to display the data in the `DataSet` object. You saw how the `DataGrid` control works in Chapter 7:

```
<asp:datagrid id="dgrResult" runat="server" />
```

However, you can't simply bind the `DataSet` object directly to a `DataGrid` and have the correct rows displayed, as a `DataSet` can contain multiple tables. One solution is to create a `DataView` based on the table you want to display, and bind the `DataView` object to the `DataGrid`. You get the default `DataView` object for a table by accessing the `Tables` collection of the `DataSet` and specifying the table name:

```
Dim objDataView As New DataView(objDataSet.Tables("Books"))
```

Then, assign the `DataView` to the `DataSource` property of the `DataGrid`, and call the `DataBind` method to display the data:

```
dgrResult.DataSource = objDataView
dgrResult.DataBind()
```

However, it's actually better performance-wise, though not as clear when you read the code, to perform the complete property assignment in one statement:

```
dgrResult.DataSource = objDataSet.Tables("Books").DefaultView
```

There is also a third option, as the ASP.NET Server Controls provide a `DataMember` property that defines which table or other item in the data source will supply the data. So you could use:

```
dgrResult.DataSource = objDataSet
dgrResult.DataMember = "Books"
```

We use a mixture of techniques in our examples.

A Multiple Tables DataSet Example

Having seen how to use a `DataSet` to hold one *results* table, you'll now see how to add multiple tables to a `DataSet` object. The Multiple tables DataSet object example using an OLEDB Provider (`multiple-dataset-oledb.aspx`) example creates a `DataSet` object and fills it with three tables. It also creates relationships between these tables.

As you can see in Figure 8-11, the page displays the connection string and the three SQL statements that extract the data from three tables in the database. Following this are two `DataGrid` controls showing the contents of the `DataSet` object's `Tables` collection and `Relations` collection. Further down the page (not visible here) are two more `DataGrid` controls, which show the related data that is contained in the `Authors` and `Prices` tables within the `DataSet`.

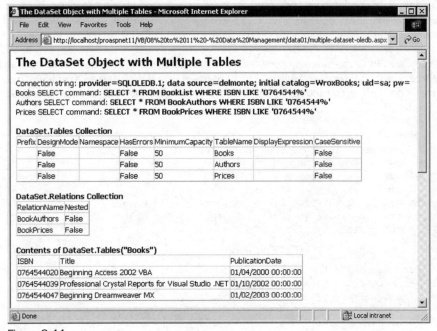

Figure 8-11

The Multiple Tables DataSet Example Code

While the principle for this example is similar to the previous Simple DataSet example, the way we've coded it is subtly different. We've demonstrated another way of using the `Command` and `DataAdapter` objects.

As before, first create a `Connection` object using your connection string, shown in the following code. However, this time create a `Command` object next using the default constructor with no parameters, and then set the properties of the `Command` object in a way similar to that used in *traditional* ADO.

Specify the connection string, the command type (in this case `Text`, as a SQL statement is being used), and the SQL statement itself for the `CommandText` property. By doing it this way, you can change the SQL statement later to get a different set of rows from the database without having to create a new `Command` object.

```
'create a new Connection object using the connection string
Dim objConnect As New OleDbConnection(strConnect)
'create a new Command object
Dim objCommand As New OleDbCommand()
```

```
'set the properties
objCommand.Connection = objConnect
objCommand.CommandType = CommandType.Text
objCommand.CommandText = strSelectBooks
```

Once you have a `Command` object, you can use it within a `DataAdapter`. You need a `DataAdapter` to extract the data from the database and squirt it into your `DataSet` object. After creating the `DataAdapter`, assign the `Command` object to its `SelectCommand` property. This `Command` will then be used when you call the `Fill` method to get the data:

So, you've got a valid `DataAdapter` object, and you can set about filling your `DataSet`. Call the `Fill` method three times, once for each table you want to insert into it. In between, you have to change the `CommandText` property of the active `Command` object to the appropriate SQL statement, as shown in the following code:

```
'create a new DataAdapter object
Dim objDataAdapter As New OleDbDataAdapter()
'and assign the Command object to it
objDataAdapter.SelectCommand = objCommand

'get the data from the "BookList" table in the database and
'put it into a table named "Books" in the DataSet object
objDataAdapter.Fill(objDataSet, "Books")

'change the SELECT statement in the Command object
objCommand.CommandText = strSelectAuthors
'then get data from "BookAuthors" table into the DataSet
objDataAdapter.Fill(objDataSet, "Authors")

'and do the same again to get the "BookPrices" data
objCommand.CommandText = strSelectPrices
objDataAdapter.Fill(objDataSet, "Prices")
```

Opening and Closing Connections with the DataAdapter

In the examples that use a `DataAdapter`, we haven't explicitly opened or closed the connection. This is because the `DataAdapter` looks after this automatically. If the connection is *closed* when the `Fill` method is called, it is opened, the rows are extracted from the data source and pushed into the `DataSet`, and the connection is automatically closed again.

However, if the connection is *open* when the `Fill` method is called, the `DataAdapter` will leave it open after the method has completed. This provides you with a useful opportunity to maximize performance by preventing the connection being opened and closed each time you call `Fill` (if you are loading more than one table in the `DataSet`). Just open the connection explicitly before the first call, and close it again after the last one, as shown by the highlighted lines in the following code:

```
Dim objDataSet As New DataSet()
objCommand.CommandText = strSelectBooks
objConnect.Open()
objDataAdapter.Fill(objDataSet, "Books")
objCommand.CommandText = strSelectAuthors
objDataAdapter.Fill(objDataSet, "Authors")
```

```
objCommand.CommandText = strSelectPrices
objDataAdapter.Fill(objDataSet, "Prices")
objConnect.Close()
```

Adding Relationships to the DataSet

You've got three tables in your `DataSet`, and can now create the relationships between them. Define a variable to hold a `DataRelation` object and create a new `DataRelation` by specifying the name you want for the relation (`BookAuthors`), the name of the primary key field (`ISBN`) in the parent table named `Books`, and the name of the foreign key field (`ISBN`) in the `Authors` child table.

Then add the new relation to the `DataSet` object's `Relations` collection, and do the same to create the relation between the `Books` and `Prices` tables in the `DataSet`. As the relations are added to the `DataSet`, an integrity check is carried out automatically. If, for example, there is a child record that has no matching parent record, an error is raised and the relation is not added to the `DataSet`.

```
'declare a variable to hold a DataRelation object
Dim objRelation As DataRelation

'create a Relation object to link Books and Authors
objRelation = New DataRelation("BookAuthors", _
                objDataSet.Tables("Books").Columns("ISBN"), _
                objDataSet.Tables("Authors").Columns("ISBN"))
'and add it to the DataSet object's Relations collection
objDataSet.Relations.Add(objRelation)

'now do the same to link Books and Prices
objRelation = New DataRelation("BookPrices", _
                objDataSet.Tables("Books").Columns("ISBN"), _
                objDataSet.Tables("Prices").Columns("ISBN"))
objDataSet.Relations.Add(objRelation)
```

Displaying the Results

Having filled the `DataSet` with three tables and two relations, you can now display the results. You use five `DataGrid` controls to do this, as shown in the following code listing. The `DataSet` object's `Tables` and `Relations` collections are bound directly to the first two `DataGrid` controls, and for the tables within the `DataSet`, we assign the `DataView` returned by the `DefaultView` property of the tables to the remaining three `DataGrid` controls.

```
'bind the collection of Tables to the first DataGrid on the page
dgrTables.DataSource = objDataSet.Tables
dgrTables.DataBind()

'bind the collection of Relations to the second DataGrid on the page
dgrRelations.DataSource = objDataSet.Relations
dgrRelations.DataBind()

'create a DataView object to use with the tables in the DataSet
Dim objDataView As New DataView()

'get the default view of the Books table into the DataView object
objDataView = objDataSet.Tables("Books").DefaultView
```

```
        'and bind it to the third DataGrid on the page
dgrBooksData.DataSource = objDataView
dgrBooksData.DataBind()
        'then do the same for the Authors table
objDataView = objDataSet.Tables("Authors").DefaultView
dgrAuthorsData.DataSource = objDataView
dgrAuthorsData.DataBind()
        'and finally do the same for the Prices table
objDataView = objDataSet.Tables("Prices").DefaultView
dgrPricesData.DataSource = objDataView
dgrPricesData.DataBind()
```

A User Control That Returns a DataSet Object

The preceding code is used in several examples in this and subsequent chapters, and to make it easier we've encapsulated it as a user control that returns a fully populated DataSet. Change the page's file extension to .ascx and change the Page directive to a Control directive:

```
<%@Control Language="VB"%>
```

Then, instead of placing the code in the Page_Load event handler, place it in a Public Function to which you provide the connection string and the WHERE clause for the SQL statement as parameters. The function returns a DataSet object, as shown in the following code. Note that the parameters passed to this function allow you to select a different set of books by varying the strWhere parameter value when you use the control.

```
Public Function BooksDataSet(strConnect As String, _
                             strWhere As String) _
                             As DataSet
    ...
    strSelectBooks = "SELECT * FROM BookList WHERE " & strWhere
    strSelectAuthors = "SELECT * FROM BookAuthors WHERE " & strWhere
    strSelectPrices = "SELECT * FROM BookPrices WHERE " & strWhere
    Dim objDataSet As New DataSet()
    ...
    ... code to fill DataSet as before ...
    ...
    Return objDataSet
End Function
```

The Using a control that creates and returns a DataSet object (use-dataset-control.aspx) example page contains the Register directive and matching element to insert the user control containing the function just described into the page. Then, to get a DataSet from the control, just create a variable of the correct type and set it to the result of the BooksDataSet method – specifying the values for the connection string and WHERE clause parameters when you make the call.

```
<%@ Register TagPrefix="wrox" TagName="getdataset"
             Src="..\global\get-dataset-control.ascx" %>
...
<wrox:getdataset id="ctlDataSet" runat="server"/>
Dim objDataSet As DataSet
objDataSet = ctlDataSet.BooksDataSet(strConnect, "ISBN LIKE '0764544%'")
```

The investigation of the `DataSet` object will be continued in Chapters 9 and 10. You'll see how to use more complex data sets, and update and edit data using the ADO.NET relational data access classes. We'll also explore the ways that .NET combines the traditional relational database access techniques with the more recent developments in XML-based data storage and management.

An Introduction to XML in .NET

The previous section described the features of .NET that are aimed at accessing relational data, and how they relate to the way you work with data compared to the traditional techniques used in previous versions of ADO. However, there is another technique for working with data within the .NET Framework.

XML is fast becoming the lingua franca of the Web, and is being adopted within many other application areas as well. We discussed the reasons for this earlier, and now look at how XML is supported within .NET. This relates to the .NET support for relational data, as XML is the standard persistence format for data within the .NET data access classes. However, there are also several other techniques for reading, writing, and manipulating XML data and the associated XML-based data formats.

In this book, we're assuming that the reader is familiar with XML as a data storage mechanism, and how it is used through an XML parser and with the associated technologies such as XSLT. Our aim is to show the way that the .NET Framework and ASP.NET can be used with XML data.

> *For a primer and other reference materials covering XML and the associated standards and technologies, check out the Wrox Press list of XML books at http://www.wrox.com/.*

The Fundamental XML Objects

The W3C (at http://www.w3.org/) provides standards that define the structure and interfaces that should be provided by applications used for accessing XML documents. This is referred to as the XML *Document Object Model (DOM)*, and is supported under .NET by the `XmlDocument` and `XmlDataDocument` objects, as shown in Figure 8-12. They provide full support for the XML DOM Level 2 Core. Within their implementation are the node types and objects that are required for the DOM interfaces, such as the `XmlElement` and `XmlAttribute` objects:

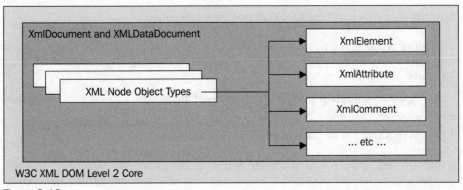

Figure 8-12

However, .NET extends the support for XML to provide much more in the way of techniques for manipulating XML documents, XML Schemas, and stylesheets. Figure 8-13 shows the main classes that are used when working with XML documents within .NET applications, and how they are related by showing the kinds of paths that you can follow when working with XML data:

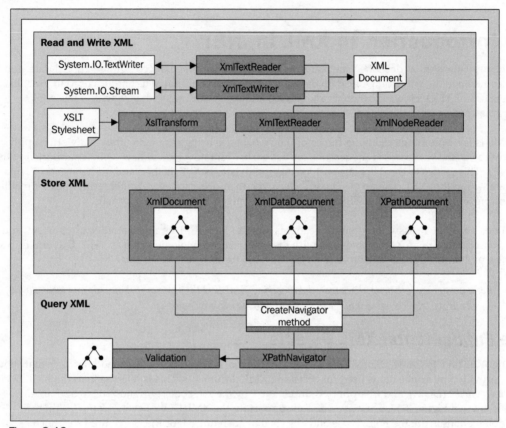

Figure 8-13

Basically, the classes shown in Figure 8-13 fall into three categories:

❑ **Reading, writing, and transforming XML**: The `XmlTextReader`, `XmlNodeReader`, and `XmlTextWriter` – plus the `XslTransform` object for creating files in a different format to the original XML document.

❑ **Storing and manipulating XML**: The function of the `XmlDocument`, `XmlDataDocument`, and `XPathDocument` objects.

❑ **Querying XML**: The function of `XPathNavigator` object.

There is some overlap between these functions, of course. To validate an XML document while reading it, you can use an `XmlValidatingReader`, and there are other objects for creating and editing XML

Schemas that aren't covered in this book. You can also use the `XslTransform` object to perform querying of a document as well as transforming it into different formats.

In this section, we'll briefly overview the objects and their commonly used methods, and then to show some simple examples. We'll come back to XML again in Chapter 11 and see some more advanced techniques.

The Document Objects

There are three implementations of the document object for storing and working with XML:

❑ The `XmlDocument` object is the .NET implementation of the standard DOM Level 2 `XMLDocument` interface. The properties and methods it exposes include those defined by W3C for manipulating XML documents, plus some extensions to make common operations easier.

❑ The `XmlDataDocument` object is an extension of the `XmlDocument` object, providing the same set of properties and methods. However, it also acts as a "bridge" between XML and relational data access methods. Once loaded with an XML document, it can expose it as a `DataSet` object. This allows you to use relational data programming techniques to work with the data, as well as the same XML DOM techniques that are used with an `XmlDocument` object.

❑ The `XPathDocument` object is a fast and compact implementation of an XML storage object that is designed for access via an `XPathNavigator` object, using only XPath queries or navigation element-by-element using the "pull" technique.

The Commonly Used XML Document Methods

The `XPathDocument` object has no really useful public methods other than `CreateNavigator`, as it is designed solely to work with an `XPathNavigator` object. However, the other two document objects expose the full set of properties and methods specified in the W3C XML DOM Level 2 Core. The extensions to these properties and methods include several very useful methods regularly used to work with XML documents.

The following table shows the extensions for creating specific types of node, and accessing existing nodes in the `XmlDocument` and `XmlDataDocument` objects:

Method	Description
`Createxxxxxx`	Creates a node in the XML document depending on the actual method name. Examples are `CreateElement`, `CreateComment`, and `CreateTextNode`.
`CloneNode`	Creates a duplicate of an XML node (for example, a copy of an element).
`GetElementById`	Returns the single node with the specified value for its `ID` attribute.
`GetElementsByTagname`	Returns a collection of nodes that contains all the elements with the specified element name.

The following table shows the series of useful methods that are available for loading and saving XML to and from the XmlDocument and XmlDataDocument objects:

Method	Description
Load	Loads an XML document from a disk file, a Stream, or an XmlTextReader
LoadXml	Loads an XML document from a String
Save	Saves the entire XML document to a disk file, a Stream, or an XmlTextWriter
ReadNode	Loads a node from an XML document that is referenced by an XmlTextReader or XmlNodeReader
WriteTo	Writes a node to another XML document that is referenced by an XmlTextWriter
WriteContentTo	Writes a node and all its descendents to another XML document that is referenced by an XmlTextWriter

To use an XPathNavigator with any of the three types of XML document object, create it using the CreateNavigator method as shown in the following table:

Method	Description
CreateNavigator	Creates and returns an XPathNavigator based on the currently loaded document. Applies to all three document objects. Optionally, for the XmlDocument and XmlDataDocument only, accepts a parameter that is a reference to a node within the document that will act as the start location for the navigator.

The XmlDataDocument adds a single property to those exposed by the XmlDocument class, as shown in the following table:

Property	Description
DataSet	Returns the contents of the XML document as an ADO.NET DataSet.

The XmlDataDocument also adds methods that provide extra access to the contents of the document, treating it more like a rowset or data table, as shown in the following table:

Method	Description
GetRowFromElement	Returns a `DataRow` representing the element in the document.
GetElementFromRow	Returns an `XmlElement` representing a `DataRow` in a table within a `DataSet`.

The XPathNavigator Class

In order to make working with XML documents easier, the `System.Xml` namespace classes include the `XPathNavigator`, which can be used to navigate within an XML document or to query the content of the document using an XPath expression. Note that an `XPathNavigator` can be used with *any* of the XML document objects – not just an `XPathDocument`. You can create an `XPathNavigator` based on an `XmlDocument` or an `XmlDataDocument` as well.

❑ The `XPathNavigator` provides methods and properties that allow cursor-style navigation through the XML document; for example, by stepping through the nodes (elements and attributes) in order, or by skipping to the next node of a specific type.

❑ The `XPathNavigator` provides methods that accept an XPath expression, the name of a node or a node type, and return one or more matching nodes. You can then iterate through these nodes.

An `XPathNavigator` can *only* be created from an existing document object. This is done using the `CreateNavigator` method:

```
Dim objNav1 As XPathNavigator = objXMLDoc.CreateNavigator()
Dim objNav2 As XPathNavigator = objXMLDataDoc.CreateNavigator()
Dim objNav3 As XPathNavigator = objXPathDoc.CreateNavigator()
```

The Commonly Used XPathNavigator Methods

The `XPathNavigator` is designed to act as a *pull* model interface for an XML document. It allows you to navigate across a document, and select and access nodes within that document. You can also create two (or more) navigator objects against the same document, and compare their positions.

To edit the XML document(s), you can use the reference to the current node exposed by the navigator, or an `XPathNodeIterator` that contains a collection of nodes, and call the methods of that node or collection. At the same time, the `XPathNavigator` exposes details about the current node directly, so there are two ways to get information about each node.

The table that follows shows methods used to move around within the document, making different nodes current in the navigator, and to create a new navigator:

Method	Description
MoveToxxxxxx	Moves the current navigator position. Examples are MoveToFirst, MoveToFirstChild, MoveToParent, MoveToAttribute, and MoveToRoot.
Clone	Creates a new XPathNavigator that is automatically located at the same position in the document as the current navigator.
IsSamePosition	Indicates if two navigators are at the same position within the document.

The following table shows the methods used to access and select parts of the content of the document:

Method	Description
GetAttribute	Returns the value of a specified attribute from the current node in the navigator
Select	Returns an XPathNodeIterator (a NodeList) containing a collection of nodes that match the specified XPath expression
SelectAncestors	Returns an XPathNodeIterator (a NodeList) containing a collection of all the ancestor nodes in the document of a specific type or which have a specific name
SelectDescendants	Returns an XPathNodeIterator (a NodeList) containing a collection of all the descendant nodes in the document of a specific type or which have a specific name
SelectChildren	Returns an XPathNodeIterator (a NodeList) containing a collection of all the child nodes in the document of a specific type or which have a specific name

The XmlTextWriter Class

When using an XmlDocument to create a new XML document, you must create document fragments and insert them into the document in a specific way – a technique that can be error-prone and complex. The XmlTextWriter can be used to create an XML document node by node in serial fashion by simply writing the tags and content to the output stream using the comprehensive range of methods that it provides.

❑ The XmlTextWriter takes as its source either a TextWriter that refers to a disk file, the path and name of a disk file, or a Stream that will contain the new XML document. It exposes a series of properties and methods that can be used to create XML nodes and other content, and output them to the disk file or stream directly.

❑ The `XmlTextWriter` can also be specified as the output device for methods in several other objects, where it automatically streams the content to a disk file, a `TextWriter`, or a `Stream`.

The `TextReader`, `TextWriter`, and `Stream` classes are discussed in Chapter 16.

The Commonly Used XmlTextWriter Methods

The most commonly used methods of the `XmlTextWriter` are listed in the following table:

Method	Description
`WriteStartDocument`	Starts a new document by writing the XML declaration to the output.
`WriteEndDocument`	Ends the document by closing all un-closed elements, and flushing the content to disk.
`WriteStartElement`	Writes an opening tag for the specified element. The equivalent method for creating attributes is `WriteStartAttribute`.
`WriteEndElement`	Writes a closing tag for the current element. The equivalent method for completing an attribute is `WriteEndAttribute`.
`WriteElementString`	Writes a complete element (including opening and closing tags) with the specified string as the value. The equivalent method for writing a complete attribute is `WriteAttributeString`.
`Close`	Closes the stream or disk file and releases any references held.

The XmlReader Classes

You need to be able to read documents from other sources, rather than creating them from scratch. The `XmlReader` class is a base class from which two public classes, `XmlTextReader` and `XmlNodeReader`, inherit.

❑ The `XmlTextReader` takes as its source either a `TextReader` that refers to an XML disk file, the path and name of an XML disk file, or a `Stream` containing an XML document. The contents of the document can be read one node at a time, and the object provides information about each node and its value as it is read.

❑ The `XmlNodeReader` takes a reference to an `XmlNode` instance (usually from within an `XmlDocument`) as its source, allowing you to read specific portions of an XML document rather than having to read all of it, if you only want to access a specific node and its children.

❑ The XmlTextReader and XmlNodeReader can be used standalone to provide simple and efficient access to XML documents or as the source for another object whereby they automatically read the document and pass it to the parent object.

Like the XPathNavigator, the XmlTextReader provides a *pull* model for accessing XML documents node-by-node, rather than parsing them into a tree in memory as is done in an XML parser. This allows larger documents to be accessed without impacting on memory usage, and can also make coding easier, depending on the task you need to accomplish.

Furthermore, if you are just searching for a specific value, you won't always have to read the whole document. Taking a broad average, you will reach the specific node you want after reading only half the document. This is considerably faster and more efficient than reading and parsing the whole document every time.

The Commonly Used XmlReader Methods

The XmlTextReader and the XmlNodeReader objects have almost identical sets of properties and methods. The most commonly used methods are shown in the following table:

Method	Description
Read	Reads the next node into the reader object where it can be accessed. Returns False if there are no more nodes to read.
ReadInnerXml	Reads and returns the complete content of the current node as a string, containing all the markup and text of the child nodes.
ReadOuterXml	Reads and returns the markup of the current node and the complete content as a string, containing all the markup and text of the child nodes as well.
ReadString	Returns the string value of the current node.
GetAttribute	Returns the value of a specified attribute from the current node in the reader.
GetRemainder	Reads and returns the remaining XML in the source document as a string. Useful if you are copying XML from one document to another.
MoveToxxxxxx	Moves the current reader position. Examples are MoveToAttribute, MoveToContent, and MoveToElement.
Skip	Skips the current node in the reader and moves to the next one.
Close	Closes the stream or disk file.

The XmlValidatingReader Class

There is another object based on the `XmlReader` base class – the `XmlValidatingReader`. You can think of this as an `XmlTextReader` that does document validation against a schema or DTD. You can create an `XmlValidatingReader` from an existing `XmlReader` (an `XmlTextReader` or `XmlNodeReader`), from a `Stream`, or from a `String` that contains the XML to be validated.

Once the `XmlValidatingReader` is created, it can be used just like any other `XmlReader`. However, it raises an event when a schema validation error occurs, allowing you to ensure that the XML document is valid against one or more specific schemas.

The XslTransform Class

One common requirement when working with XML is the need to transform a document using XML Stylesheet Language (XSL or XSLT). The .NET Framework classes provide the `XslTransform` object, which is specially designed to perform either XSL or XSLT transformations.

The Commonly Used XslTransform Methods

The `XslTransform` class has two methods that are used for working with XML documents and XSL/XSLT stylesheets, as shown in the following table:

Method	Description
Load	Loads the specified XSL stylesheet and any stylesheets referenced within it by `xsl:include` elements
Transform	Transforms the specified XML data using the currently loaded XSL or XSLT stylesheet, and outputs the results

Let's look at some of the common tasks that need to be carried out using XML documents.

Common XML Tasks in .NET

The default page for the samples contains a link Introduction to XML Data Access in .NET. The menu page that this opens, shown in Figure 8-14, contains links to several examples of the basic .NET Framework XML data access techniques.

The first two pairs of links show how to access XML data stored in a document object in two distinct ways – using the methods and properties provided by the XML DOM, and through the new .NET `XPathNavigator` class. The next pair of links demonstrates use of the `XmlTextWriter` and `XmlTextReader` classes, and the final one shows a simple example of using the `XslTransform` class. We look at all of these classes in Chapter 11.

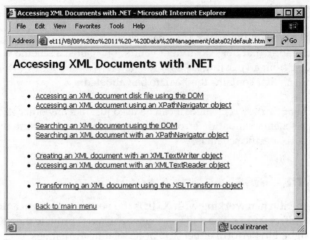

Figure 8-14

XML Document Access via the DOM

The .NET XML classes provide an XML parser object named XmlDocument that is W3C DOM-compliant. This is the core object for most XML-based activities carried out in .NET. You can use it to access an XML document using the same kind of code as you would with (say) the MSXML parser object. The first example page, Accessing XML documents using the DOM (xml-via-dom.aspx), is shown in Figure 8-15:

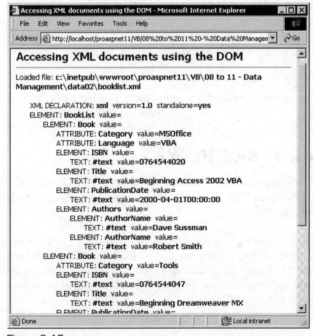

Figure 8-15

This screenshot displays the results of recursively parsing a simple XML document using DOM methods. As with all the examples in this chapter, you can use the [view source] link at the bottom of any of the sample pages to see the entire code

The XML DOM Example Code

This example, like the earlier relational data access examples, uses code in the Page_Load event handler to access the data and present the results within <div> elements located in the page. It first creates a string containing the path to the XML document, which is located in the same folder as the ASP.NET page, and then creates a new XmlDocument object and loads the XML file. The example contains some elementary error-handling code that we've removed here for clarity.

Now you can display the contents of the XML document by calling a custom function that recursively extracts details of each element. A function named GetChildNodes used here accepts a parameter an XmlNodeList object containing the collection of the child nodes of the current node – in this case, all the children of the document node.

> An XML document has a single document node that has as its children the XML declaration node (such as <?xml version="1.0"?>), the root node of the XML (in this case <BookList>) and any comment nodes or processing instructions.

The function also accepts an integer that indicates the nesting level. This is used to create the indentation of the output to show the structure more clearly. So, by calling this function initially with objXMLDoc.ChildNodes and 0 as the parameters, we'll start the process with the XML declaration and the root element of the document:

```
'create physical path to booklist.xml sample file (in same folder as ASPX page)
Dim strCurrentPath As String = Request.PhysicalPath
Dim strXMLPath As String = Left(strCurrentPath, InStrRev(strCurrentPath, "\")) _
                      & "booklist.xml"

'create a new XmlDocument object
Dim objXMLDoc As New XMLDocument()

'load the XML file into the XmlDocument object
objXMLDoc.Load(strXMLPath)
outDocURL.innerHTML = "Loaded file: <b>" & strXMLPath & "</b>"
```

The Custom GetChildNodes Function

The complete listing of the GetChildNodes function is shown in the following code. The techniques are standard W3C DOM coding practice. The principle is to iterate through all the nodes in the current NodeList, displaying information about each one. There are different properties available for different types of node – check the NodeType first, and then access the appropriate properties.

Next, if it is an Element-type node, iterate through all the attributes adding information about these. Finally, check if this node has any child nodes, and if so, iterate through these recursively calling the same GetChildNodes function.

```
Function GetChildNodes(objNodeList As XMLNodeList, intLevel As Integer) _
                                                     As String

  Dim strNodes As String = ""
  Dim objNode As XmlNode
  Dim objAttr As XmlAttribute

  'iterate through all the child nodes for the current node
  For Each objNode In objNodeList

    'display information about this node
    strNodes = strNodes & GetIndent(intLevel) _
           & GetNodeType(objNode.NodeType) & ": <b>" & objNode.Name

    'if it is an XML Declaration node, display the 'special' properties
    If objNode.NodeType = XMLNodeType.XmlDeclaration Then

      'cast the XMLNode object to an XmlDeclaration object
      Dim objXMLDec = CType(objNode, XmlDeclaration)
      strNodes = strNodes & "</b>  version=<b>" _
             & objXMLDec.Version & "</b>  standalone=<b>" _
             & objXMLDec.Standalone & "</b><br />"
    Else

      'just display the generic 'value' property
      strNodes = strNodes & "</b>  value=<b>" _
             & objNode.Value & "</b><br />"

    End If

    'if it is an Element node, iterate through the Attributes
    'collection displaying information about each attribute
    If objNode.NodeType = XMLNodeType.Element Then

      'display the attribute information for each attribute
      For Each objAttr In objNode.Attributes
        strNodes = strNodes & GetIndent(intLevel + 1) _
               & GetNodeType(objAttr.NodeType) & ": <b>" _
               & objAttr.Name & "</b>  value=<b>" _
               & objAttr.Value & "</b><br />"
      Next

    End If

    'if this node has child nodes, call the same function recursively
    'to display the information for it and each of its child node

    If objNode.HasChildNodes Then
      strNodes = strNodes & GetChildNodes(objNode.childNodes, intLevel + 1)
    End If

  Next  'go to next node

  Return strNodes   'pass the result back to the caller
End Function
```

There are a couple of other minor functions that the preceding code uses. The GetIndent function simply takes an integer representing the current indent level and returns a string containing a suitable number of   non-breaking space characters. The GetNodeType function looks up the numeric node type value returned from the NodeType property of each node, and returns a text description of the node type. Remember that you can view the code for these functions in the sample page using the [view source] link at the bottom of the page.

XML Document Access with an XPathNavigator

The second example, shown in Figure 8-16, demonstrates how you can achieve the same results as the previous example, by using the XPathNavigator object. The Accessing XML documents using an XPathNavigator (xml-via-navigator.aspx) sample page produces output that is fundamentally similar to the previous example. Notice, however, that now you get the complete content of all the child elements for the value of an element (all the #text child nodes of all the children concatenated together):

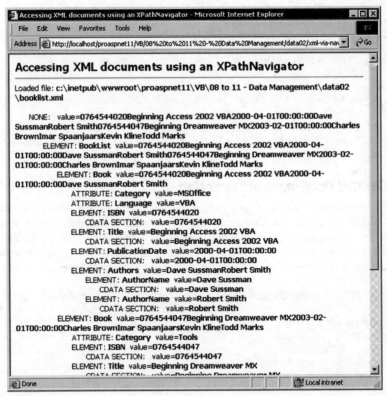

Figure 8-16

The XPathNavigator Example Code

As in the previous example, start out by locating and loading the XML document into an XmlDocument object (see the code that follows). If there is no error, you know that the document is well formed and loaded successfully. However, here the code differs considerably – you create an XPathNavigator object based on the XmlDocument object (shown highlighted in the code).

To display the output, first move the current position (pointer) of the XPathNavigator to the document itself. Then you can call a custom recursive function named GetXMLDocFragment that iterates through all the nodes in the document and inserts the result into your <div> element elsewhere in the page. Note that this time you are calling your custom function with the new XPathNavigator object as the first parameter (the second is the same *indent level* parameter as used in the previous example):

```
'create physical path to booklist.xml sample file (in same folder as ASPX page)
Dim strCurrentPath As String = Request.PhysicalPath
Dim strXMLPath As String = Left(strCurrentPath, _
                           InStrRev(strCurrentPath, "\")) & "booklist.xml"

'create a new XmlDocument object and load the XML file
Dim objXMLDoc As New XmlDocument
objXMLDoc.Load(strXMLPath)
outDocURL.innerHTML = "Loaded file: <b>" & strXMLPath & "</b>"
'now ready to parse the XML document
'it must be well-formed to have loaded without error
'create a new XPathNavigator object using the XMLDocument object
Dim objXPNav As XPathNavigator = objXMLDoc.CreateNavigator()

'move the current position to the root #document node
objXPNav.MoveToRoot()

'call a recursive function to iterate through all the nodes in the
'XPathNavigator, creating a string that is placed in the <div> above
outResults.innerHTML = GetXMLDocFragment(objXPNav, 0)
```

The Custom GetXMLDocFragment Function

The XPathNavigator object exposes a series of properties, methods, and collections that make it easy to navigate an XML document. We use a range of these in our custom function, shown in the following code. The first step, after declaring a couple of necessary local variables, is to get the information about the current node. Notice that you use the same GetNodeType function as in the previous example to convert the numeric NodeType value into a text description of the node type.

```
Function GetXMLDocFragment(objXPNav As XPathNavigator, intLevel As Integer) _
                                                          As String

   Dim strNodes As String = ""
   Dim intLoop As Integer

   'display information about this node
   strNodes = strNodes & GetIndent(intLevel) _
            & GetNodeType(objXPNav.NodeType) & ": " & objXPNav.Name _
            & "  value=" & objXPNav.Value & "<br />"
```

In the previous XML DOM example, you extracted the value of the node through the XmlNode object's Value property, which returned just the value of this node. In this example, the content of the XML document is being accessed through an XPathNavigator, and not by using the XML DOM methods. For example, to get the value of the node, we are using the Value property of our objXPNav object – an

$XPathNavigator$ that is currently pointing to the node being queried. The $Value$ property of a node returned by an $XPathNavigator$ is a concatenation of all the child node values.

Reading the Attributes of a Node

Now you can check if this node has any attributes. If it does, iterate through them collecting information about each one. You can see in the following code how this is different from using the DOM methods, where you could iterate through the $Attributes$ collection. Using an $XPathNavigator$ is predominantly a forward-only *pull* technique. You need to extract the nodes from the document in the order that they appear. So, for a node that does have attributes, we move to the first attribute, process it, move to the next attribute until there are no more to process, and then move back to the previous position using the $MoveToParent$ method:

```
'see if this node has any Attributes
If objXPNav.HasAttributes Then
   'move to the first attribute
   objXPNav.MoveToFirstAttribute()
   Do
     'display the information about it
     strNodes = strNodes & GetIndent(intLevel + 1) _
             & GetNodeType(objXPNav.NodeType) & ": " & objXPNav.Name _
             & "  value=" & objXPNav.Value & "<br />"

   Loop While objXPNav.MoveToNextAttribute()

   'then move back to the parent node (that is the element itself)
   objXPNav.MoveToParent()

End If
```

Reading the Child Nodes for a Node

You can see if the current node has any child nodes by checking the $HasChildren$ property. If it does, you need to move to the first child node and recursively call the function for that node – incrementing the *level* parameter to get the correct indenting of the results. Then you can move back to the previous position (the parent) and continue, as shown:

```
'see if this node has any child nodes
If objXPNav.HasChildren Then

   'move to the first child node of the current node
   objXPNav.MoveToFirstChild()
   Do
     'recursively call this function to display the child node fragment
     strNodes = strNodes & GetXMLDocFragment(objXPNav, intLevel + 1)

   Loop While objXPNav.MoveToNext()

   'move back to the parent node - the node we started from when we
   'moved to the first child node - could have used Push and Pop instead
   objXPNav.MoveToParent()

End If
```

Reading the Sibling Nodes for a Node

So far you've only processed the current node, its attributes, and its child nodes (if any). You need to repeat the process for all the following sibling (element) nodes as well. This is achieved using the `MoveToNext` method, and by calling the recursive function again for each one, as shown:

```
Do While objXPNav.MoveToNext()

    'recursively call this function to display this sibling node
    'and its attributes and child nodes
    strNodes = strNodes & GetXMLDocFragment(objXPNav, intLevel)

Loop

Return strNodes  'pass the result back to the caller

End Function
```

Searching an XML Document

The second pair of links in the menu page opens two examples that search for specific element values within an XML document, rather than displaying the entire document. The two examples are Searching an XML document using the DOM (`search-dom.aspx`) and Searching an XML document with an XPathNavigator (`search-navigator.aspx`). The task is to retrieve the values of all the `<AuthorName>` elements within the document. You can run these samples to see the results. Figure 8-17 shows the XML DOM version:

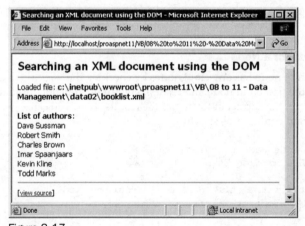

Figure 8-17

Using the DOM Methods

Using the DOM methods, you can take advantage of the very useful `GetElementsByTagname` method that the `XmlDocument` object exposes. This method can be used to create a collection of matching elements as an `XmlNodeList`, as shown in the following code, and then iterate through the collection displaying the values of the `#text` child node for each one.

```
Dim strResults As String = "<b>List of authors</b>:<br />"

'create a NodeList collection of all matching child nodes
Dim colElements As XmlNodeList
colElements = objXMLDoc.GetElementsByTagname("AuthorName")

'iterate through collection getting values of child #text nodes for each one
For Each objNode In colElements
  strResults += objNode.FirstChild().Value & "<br />"
Next
'then display the result
outResults.innerHTML = strResults
```

Remember that an element's value is stored in a #text-type child node of the element node – it's not the value of the element node itself. You can clearly see this in the previous examples that displayed all the nodes in the document.

Using an XPathNavigator

You've already seen how to create an XPathNavigator for an XmlDocument and use it to traverse the document. The XPathNavigator also provides the Select method, which takes an XPath expression and selects all matching nodes or fragments within the document. You can then traverse the set of selected nodes and extract the values you want.

You can also improve performance by using the lighter and faster XPathDocument object to hold your XML document rather than the W3C-compliant XmlDocument object.

Creating an XPathDocument and XPathNavigator Object

The following code in the Page_Load event handler first creates an XPathDocument instance and loads the XML document into it. However, in this case, you must use the constructor for the XPathDocument to load the XML, because there is no Load method for this class. While you can create an XPathDocument from a Stream, a TextReader or an XmlReader, the easiest way when you have an XML disk file is to specify the path and name of that file. The code then creates an XPathNavigator object for this document.

```
'declare a variable to hold an XPathDocument instance
Dim objXPathDoc As XPathDocument

'create XPathDocument object and load the XML file
objXPathDoc = New XPathDocument(strXMLPath)

'create an XPathNavigator based on this document
Dim objXPNav As XPathNavigator = objXPathDoc.CreateNavigator()
```

Selecting the Nodes and Displaying the Results

Now you can execute the Select method of the XPathNavigator with an appropriate XPath expression. The result will be an XPathNodeIterator object that contains the matching node(s). Then, as shown in the following code, it's simply a matter of iterating through the selected nodes collecting their values. Each *node* in the XPathNodeIterator is itself an XPathNavigator based on this node within the document. This new `XPathNavigator` has `Name` and `Value` properties that reflect the values for the current node.

```
Dim strResults As String = "<b>List of authors</b>:<br />"
     'select all AuthorName nodes into XPathNodeIterator object
     'using an appropriate XPath expression
Dim objXPIter As XPathNodeIterator
objXPIter = objXPNav.Select("descendant::AuthorName")

Do While objXPIter.MoveNext()
  'get the value and add to the 'results' string
  strResults += objXPIter.Current.Value & "<br />"
Loop

outResults.innerHTML = strResults    'display the result
```

You need to consider the task you want to achieve quite carefully when deciding whether to use an `XPathNavigator` object or the XML DOM methods. Of course, as you can create an `XPathNavigator` based on an existing `XmlDocument` object (as well as on an `XPathDocument`), you can use both where this is appropriate. Also remember to choose the lighter and faster `XPathDocument` if you don't need to access the XML DOM (in other words when you can perform all the tasks you require using an `XPathNavigator`).

An XML TextWriter Object Example

The Creating an XML document with an XMLTextWriter object (`xml-via-textwriter.aspx`) example demonstrates how to use the `XmlTextWriter` object to quickly create a new XML document as a disk file. It writes to the file a series of elements and attributes that make up the document, and then reads the document back from disk and displays it, as shown in Figure 8-18:

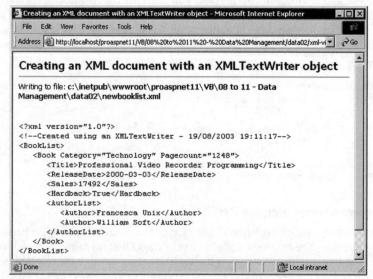

Figure 8-18

The XMLTextWriter Example Code

To create the new XML document, first create a suitable path and filename so that the new file will be placed in the same folder as the ASP page, as shown in the following code. Then create the `XmlTextWriter` object instance. Specify the path to the new file as the first parameter to the constructor, and `Nothing` (`null` in C#) for the second. The second parameter is the encoding required for the file, defined as an `Encoding` object. If you set this parameter to `Nothing`, the default encoding UTF-8 is used.

Next, set the properties of the `XmlTextWriter`. In the example, we want the document to be indented (to show the structure more clearly), with each level of indent being three space characters. Then we're ready to start writing the new document. The `WriteStartDocument` method creates the opening XML declaration, and this is followed with a comment indicating the date and time that the document was created:

```
'create physical path for the new file (in same folder as ASPX page)
Dim strCurrentPath As String = Request.PhysicalPath
Dim strXMLPath As String = Left(strCurrentPath, InStrRev(strCurrentPath, "\")) _
                   & "newbooklist.xml"

'declare a variable to hold an XmlTextWriter object
Dim objXMLWriter As XmlTextWriter

'create a new objXMLWriter object for the XML file
objXMLWriter = New XmlTextWriter(strXMLPath, Nothing)
outDocURL.innerHTML = "Writing to file: <b>" & strXMLPath & "</b>"

'now ready to write (or "push") the nodes for the new XML document
'turn on indented formatting and set indent to 3 chararcters
objXMLWriter.Formatting = Formatting.Indented
objXMLWriter.Indentation = 3

'start the document with the XML declaration tag
objXMLWriter.WriteStartDocument()

'write a comment element including the current date/time
objXMLWriter.WriteComment("Created using an XMLTextWriter - " & Now())
```

Writing Elements and Attributes

The next step is to write the opening tag of the `<BookList>` root element. The `WriteStartElement` does this for you; follow it with the opening `<Book>` element tag, as shown in the following code. We also want to add two attributes to the `<Book>` element. For these, use the `WriteAttributeString` method to create an attribute from a text string. Where the value for the attribute is a numeric (or other non-`String`) data type, you must convert it to a string first:

```
objXMLWriter.WriteStartElement("BookList")
objXMLWriter.WriteStartElement("Book")

'add two attributes to this element's opening tag
objXMLWriter.WriteAttributeString("Category", "Technology")
Dim intPageCount As Integer = 1248    'numeric value to convert
objXMLWriter.WriteAttributeString("Pagecount", intPageCount.ToString("G"))
```

The next step is to write the four elements that form the content of the `<Book>` element that's already opened. Use the `WriteElementString` method, which writes a complete element (not just the opening tag like the `WriteStartElement` method we used earlier does). Note that the actual *content* of the element in the final document is always text (XML documents are plain text). Therefore, you have to convert non-`String` type values to a string first, as shown:

```
'write four elements, using different source data types

objXMLWriter.WriteElementString("Title", _
                        "Professional Video Recorder Programming")
Dim datReleaseDate As DateTime = #02/02/2002#
objXMLWriter.WriteElementString("ReleaseDate", _
                        datReleaseDate.ToString("yyyy-MM-dd"))
Dim intSales As Integer = 17492
objXMLWriter.WriteElementString("Sales", intSales.ToString("G"))
Dim blnHardback As Boolean = True
objXMLWriter.WriteElementString("Hardback", blnHardback.ToString())
```

Next, as shown in the following code, we want to write the `<AuthorList>` element and its child `<Author>` elements. You need to open the `<AuthorList>` element and then write the child elements. Afterwards, you can create the closing `</AuthorList>` tag simply by calling the `WriteEndElement` method. This automatically closes the most recently opened element.

```
'write the opening tag for the <AuthorList> child element
objXMLWriter.WriteStartElement("AuthorList")

'add two <Author> elements
objXMLWriter.WriteElementString("Author", "Francesca Unix")
objXMLWriter.WriteElementString("Author", "William Soft")

'close the <AuthorList> element
objXMLWriter.WriteEndElement()
```

To finish the document, just close the `<Book>` element and the root `<BookList>` element. Then flush the output to the disk file and close the `XmlTextWriter`, as shown in the following code. Always remember to call the `Close` method; otherwise the disk file will remain locked. You don't actually *have* to call the `Flush` method here, as closing the `XmlTextWriter` has the same effect, but you can call `Flush` to force the part-formed document to be written to disk whenever you wish:

```
'close the <Book> element
objXMLWriter.WriteEndElement()

'close the root <BookList> element
objXMLWriter.WriteEndElement()
objXMLWriter.Flush()
objXMLWriter.Close()
```

Displaying the New XML Document

Now that you've got your new XML document written to a disk file, you can read it back and display it. To do this, use a `StreamReader` object, as shown in the following code. Open the file, read the entire content into a string variable, and close the file. Then you can insert the string into a `<div>` element elsewhere on the page to display it. Add `<pre>` elements (you could use `<xmp>` instead) to maintain the indentation and line breaks in the document when displayed in the browser.

```
Dim strXMLResult As String
Dim objSR As StreamReader = File.OpenText(strXMLPath)
strXMLResult = objSR.ReadToEnd()
objSR.Close
objSR = Nothing
outResults.innerHTML = "<pre>" & Server.HtmlEncode(strXMLResult) & "</pre>"
```

An XML TextReader Object Example

OK, so you can create an XML document as a disk file with an `XmlTextWriter`. The obvious next step is to read a disk file back using an `XmlTextReader` object. The **Accessing an XML document with an XMLTextReader object** (`xml-via-textreader.aspx`) example does just that (though with a different XML document).

Figure 8-19 shows a list of the nodes found in the sample `booklist.xml` document. For each node, the page shows the type of node, and the node name and value (if applicable – some types of node have no name and some types have no value):

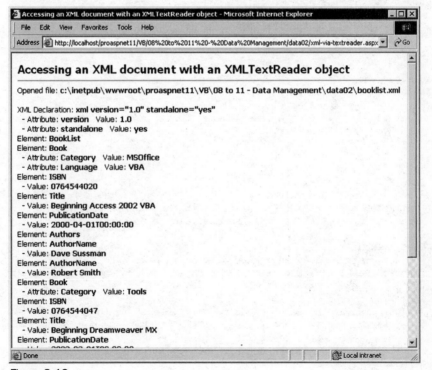

Figure 8-19

The XMLTextReader Example Code

As in the previous example, the first step is to build the path to the file that'll be opened – in this case, `booklist.xml` in the same folder as the ASP page. Next, as shown in the following code, you can declare an `XmlTextReader` object, passing the path to the file that you want to open as the parameter to the constructor.

Reading the XML document is just a matter of calling the `Read` method to return each node. This returns `False` if there are no more nodes to read. For each node you find, examine the `NodeType` property to see what kind of node it is. Depending on the node type, there are different properties available that you can access to build your `results` string.

```
'create physical path to booklist.xml sample file (in same folder as ASPX page)
Dim strCurrentPath As String = Request.PhysicalPath
Dim strXMLPath As String = Left(strCurrentPath, InStrRev(strCurrentPath, "\")) _
                & "booklist.xml"

'declare a variable to hold an XmlTextReader object
Dim objXMLReader As XmlTextReader

'create a new XmlTextReader object for the XML file
objXMLReader = New XmlTextReader(strXMLPath)
outDocURL.innerHTML = "Opened file: <b>" & strXMLPath & "</b>"

'now ready to read (or "pull") the nodes of the XML document
Dim strNodeResult As String = ""
Dim objNodeType As XmlNodeType

'read each node in turn - returns False if no more nodes to read
Do While objXMLReader.Read()

  'select on the type of the node (these are only some of the types)
  objNodeType = objXMLReader.NodeType

  Select Case objNodeType

    Case XmlNodeType.XmlDeclaration:
      'get the name and value
      strNodeResult += "XML Declaration: <b>" & objXMLReader.Name _
                & " " & objXMLReader.Value & "</b><br />"

    Case XmlNodeType.Element:
      'just get the name, any value will be in next (#text) node
      strNodeResult += "Element: <b>" & objXMLReader.Name & "</b><br />"

    Case XmlNodeType.Text:
      'just display the value, node name is "#text" in this case
      strNodeResult += "  - Value: <b>" & objXMLReader.Value _
                & "</b><br />"

  End Select
```

The `XmlTextReader` returns the document node-by-node when you call the `Read` method. However, an element-type node that has attributes is returned as a complete entity during a single `Read` method call, and so you have to examine each node as you read it to see if it is an element that has attributes. If it does, as shown in the following code, iterate through these by using the `MoveToFirstAttribute` or the `MoveToNextAttribute` methods. After processing the current node, you go back and handle the next one. And after the `Do` loop is complete (in other words, after you've processed all the nodes returned by successive `Read` method calls), close the `XmlTextReader` object and display the results in a `<div>` element elsewhere in the page:

```
  'see if this node has any attributes
If objXMLReader.AttributeCount > 0 Then
   'iterate through the attributes by moving to the next one
   'could use MoveToFirstAttribute but MoveToNextAttribute does
   'the same when the current node is an element-type node
   Do While objXMLReader.MoveToNextAttribute()
      'get the attribute name and value
      strNodeResult += "- Attribute: " & objXMLReader.Name _
                    & " Value: " & objXMLReader.Value & "<br />"
   Loop
 End If

Loop    'and read the next node
objXMLReader.Close()    'finished with the reader so close it
outResults.innerHTML = strNodeResult    'display the results in the page
```

An XSL Transform Object Example

The final example in this chapter shows one other task that is regularly required when working with XML data, and which .NET makes easy. You can use XML stylesheets written in XSL or XSLT to transform an XML document into another format, or to change its structure or content.

The Transforming an XML document using the XSLTransform object (`xsl-transform.aspx`) example page demonstrates a simple transformation using the `booklist.xml` file from the previous example and an XSLT stylesheet named `booklist.xsl`. The result of the transformation is written to disk as `booklist.html`. As shown in Figure 8-20, you can use the links in the page to open the XML document, the stylesheet, and the final HTML page:

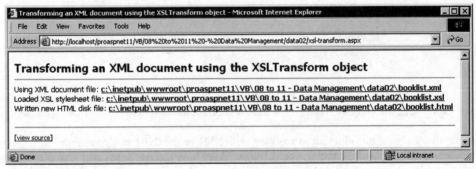

Figure 8-20

You must run this page in a browser running on the same machine as the web server to be able to open the linked files using the absolute physical paths.

The XSLTransform Example Code

There is surprisingly little code required to perform the transformation (you can view the code in the example using the [view source] link at the bottom of the page). First, create an `XslTransform` object and load the XSL stylesheet into it from disk. Then you can perform the transformation directly using the XSL file in the `XslTransform` object and the XML file path held in a variable named `strXMLPath`, as shown in the following code:

```
'create a new XslTransform object
Dim objTransform As New XslTransform()

'load the XSL stylesheet into the XslTransform object
objTransform.Load(strXSLPath)

'perform the transformation
objTransform.Transform(strXMLPath, strHTMLPath)
```

The result is sent to the disk file specified by the variable named `strHTMLPath`. Figure 8-21 shows the resulting HTML page:

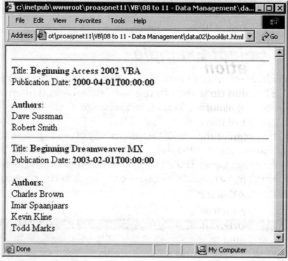

Figure 8-21

This is just one way to use the `XslTransform` object (in fact, the simplest way) and you'll see a more complex example at the end of Chapter 11, where XML data management techniques are discussed.

This section was a basic introduction to working with XML in the .NET environment. The next two chapters look at relational data management, but we'll see how the relational and XML data models are quite thoroughly integrated under .NET. Then, in Chapter 11, we'll come back to XML and look in more depth at some of the other techniques that .NET provides to make even the most complex tasks much easier that ever before. Let's try to make some sense of the whole relational versus XML issue.

Choosing a Data Storage Methodology

Having seen both relational and XML data access in action within the .NET Framework (albeit in a fairly basic way), how do you decide on a data storage methodology? The simple answer is that, with the advent of .NET, you really don't need to worry about this anymore.

Years ago, one of the main directions in data storage and access was the construction of huge data depositaries or data warehouses where all the data your organization required was stored in a massive central database. While this might still suit some situations (such as a government tax office) it has become clear that it is not a generally practical approach in today's distributed and disconnected computing world.

In fact, there has been even less centralization of data over recent years, and the drive now is far more towards the provision of access through common methods to all kinds of remote and non-centralized data. As an example, the Internet contains vast quantities of data in myriad different formats, but we increasingly need to be able to get at this data in a structured and standard way.

Likewise, in an office environment, the promised takeover of thin client computing has not really taken place yet. People like to store information locally as they work, and use it when disconnected from the corporate network. In some cases, such as the traveling salesperson with a laptop computer, this is the prime requirement when working with corporate data.

Access and Manipulation Is the Key

In fact, it's obvious that *where* and (to some extent) *how* we store data is not important. The crux of the matter is how we can *access* and *manipulate* that data – in whatever format it's stored and wherever it resides. As you saw at the start of this chapter, this is what has been the driving force behind the adoption of XML, and the design of the .NET data access libraries.

So, what issues should one consider when implementing a data store, and which data access technique is most appropriate for that data? The answer lies more in the nature of the data, and the way we need to use it. For example, highly structured data, such as stock lists or customer details, is well suited to storage in a relational database such as SQL Server or Oracle, or MS Access on the desktop. However, unstructured data, such as reports, data sheets, email messages, family trees, and other common everyday scenarios, is more suited to storage using the tree-like metaphor of XML.

Likewise, if we regularly need to access parts of the data in specific ways, or all the data on a very regular basis, the relational database is probably the most efficient. It is optimized to provide indexing and other features to give the best performance. But if we usually access the entire data entity in one go, or access it only rarely, an XML-based approach is probably the best choice. And, being basically just text files, XML documents are easy to archive and retrieve.

Of course, in some cases, you don't actually get to choose the data storage format. For example, your email server and your fax server probably have dedicated storage mechanisms that can't be changed. In such cases, you have to make do with what's there, or change to another product.

A New Approach to Querying

Another point to be aware of is that you should not base your data format decision on *current* querying technologies. One of the major issues at the moment is that each data storage format has its own specific techniques for querying and extracting data; for example, SQL for relational data and XSLT for XML data. If you want to perform a query across different types of data, you generally have to convert the all to the same *type* first.

However, this is set to change with the growing realization that a new querying technology, called XML Query Language or XQuery, will be able to integrate different types of data under a universal query mechanism. XQuery has been called *SQL querying for XML data* because it uses a syntax that is similar to the widely accepted SQL standards, and yet can be applied to XML documents.

And as relational data stores such as SQL Server become increasingly XML-capable, and the tools to access and manage XML data inside a relational database improve, XQuery can also be used with suitable relational databases. In future releases of .NET, this scenario will become a core part of the way you query data in mixed environments.

There is a preview of the way Microsoft are approaching XQuery, at least as far as working with XML is concerned, on the special Web site they have set up at http://xqueryservices.com. You can experiment with XQuery online, or download the Microsoft XQuery demo to run on your server.

Transport Protocols Are the Future

Once you've decided on the storage mechanism for your data, the next important decision comes when you consider how you will transport this data from one place to another. Here, there is probably only one good solution that matches the requirements of the future. There's no doubt that we'll face increasing needs to interface with other systems and other organizations as time goes by, and for this, a standard data interchange format will be an absolute necessity.

The only obvious choice today is XML (and the associated standards such as SOAP and other industry-specific implementations of XML). XML is independent of the platform, application, and operating system, and so it provides the best chance for interoperability.

In fact, Microsoft BizTalk Server and similar systems can handle the transmission and guaranteed delivery of data in XML format over almost any kind of network, as well as the conversion to and from other formats. Using the tools available today and in the near future, you can transform an XML document into almost any other document type on demand – and often transform any non-XML document or data into XML as well.

And .NET Is a Great Solution

So, if the transport protocol and transmission format for data are going to be XML-based, and the data storage and manipulation could be through any existing or new technology, what you really need is a solid, reliable, and wide-ranging technique to connect to any kind of data store, and work with any kind of data.

This is where the combination of the relational and XML data access techniques provided by the .NET Framework comes in. As you've seen (and will see), you can use the .NET data access classes to connect to almost any kind of data store – be it a mail server, a relational database, an office application document, an XML document, or whatever. Then, once you have extracted data, you can convert it between XML and traditional relational rowsets at will – and update the data store or save it to disk in almost any format you need.

Summary

In this chapter, we've started to explore the possibilities for working with data within the .NET Framework, based on ASP.NET, the .NET data access classes, and the extended XML technologies that they provide. We overviewed the two main topic areas, relational and XML data access, then examined in more depth the core objects that are provided within these topic areas.

One of the problems with learning to use the new techniques is the complexity that can arise from the huge number of properties, methods, and events that these new objects expose. Many are rarely used, and so we've tried to make it easier by just concentrating on the commonly used techniques rather than trying to document each one in minute detail.

*An excellent reference to all the properties, methods, and events of all the .NET Framework objects is included within the SDK that is provided with the framework. Simply open the **Class Library** within the **Reference** section, or search for the object or class name using the Index or Search feature of the SDK.*

What you should have gained by now is an understanding of the core objects and the basic techniques we use when working with them. We'll continue this in the next three chapters as well.

The next chapter looks specifically at relational data access within .NET, and how to use more advanced techniques – in particular working with relational data sets and tables, editing them, and displaying the data they contain.

Working with Relational Data

In the last chapter, you saw how easy it is to access both relational and XML data using the .NET data access libraries. In this and the next chapter, we will concentrate on what has traditionally been the major use of data access in ASP – working with relational data – and will see some of the more advanced features that .NET provides. This chapter is mainly concerned with the ways the `DataReader`, `DataSet`, and `DataTable` objects are used. In the next chapter, you'll look at how to update data sources using .NET.

While simple data access through a `DataReader` object will fulfill many of the tasks previously accomplished with ADO `Connection` and `Recordset` objects in earlier versions of ASP, you will regularly want to build more complex data structures. Plus, the fundamentally disconnected nature of the .NET data access techniques means that you will often decide to use a `DataSet` to implement a selection of information as a *package* that can be easily stored and transported between application tiers – including across the network.

The `DataSet` object is at the heart of the .NET disconnected data access strategy, so let's look at all the important aspects of using one in this chapter.

The topics covered in this chapter are:

- ❑ Accessing complex data with `DataReader` and `DataSet` objects
- ❑ Using stored procedures with `DataReader` and `DataSet` objects
- ❑ Building and editing data in a `DataTable` object
- ❑ Sorting and filtering data with `DataTable` and `DataView` objects

Obtaining the Sample Files

All the examples used in this chapter are available for you to run on your own server, in both VB.NET and C# versions. The download files can be obtained from http://www.daveandal.net/books/8900/, and include SQL scripts and instructions for creating the database that the examples use. You can also run these examples online at the same URL.

The main menu page for the data management chapter examples shown in Chapter 8 contains links to all the sample files. The third link in that page, Advanced Relational Data Management with .NET leads to another menu page (shown in Figure 9-1) that contains links to all the examples for this chapter:

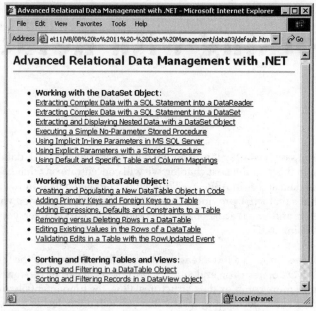

Figure 9-1

Accessing Complex Data

The relational data access examples in the previous chapter were fairly simple, concentrating on extracting data from a single table and multiple tables into the `DataSet` and `DataReader` objects. However, often the results you want are not just rows from a single table. They may require a more complex SQL query that joins several tables, or they might be the result of running a stored procedure within the database.

This section shows some examples that use both complex SQL statements and stored procedures to return sets of rows or just individual values from a data source. The first shows how you can use a `DataReader` object to efficiently extract the data for display, and the second uses the `DataSet` object.

Accessing Complex Data with a DataReader

You can use the `DataReader` object to quickly and efficiently extract a rowset from a data store. Simply create a `Connection` object, use it to create a `Command` object for this connection, and then call the `ExecuteReader` method of the `Command` object. It returns the new `DataReader` object.

The example code, like many of the relational data access examples in the previous and in this chapter, uses one of the connection strings that are defined in the `web.config` file in the root folder of the samples. Remember to edit this file to suit your own setup (as demonstrated in Chapter 8) before running the samples on your own server.

Also, the example pages in this chapter use server-side `<div>` elements to display the connection string, the SQL statements being used, and any error message. Many pages also use the ASP `DataGrid` control to display the results. For example, the following code shows the relevant controls within the HTML section of the example page:

```
<div>Connection string: <b><span id="outConnect"
                runat="server"></span></b></div>
<div>SELECT command: <b><span id="outSelect" runat="server"></span></b></div>
<div id="outError" runat="server"> </div>
<asp:datagrid id="dgrResult" runat="server" />
```

Figure 9-2 shows what the example page that opens from the link in the main menu **Extracting Complex Data with a DataReader** (`complex-datareader.aspx`) looks like when it runs:

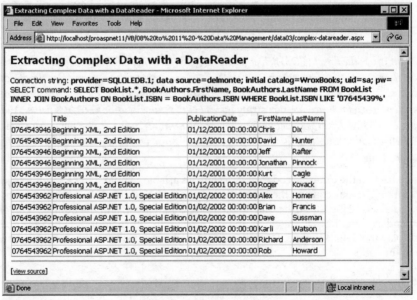

Figure 9-2

All the examples contain a [view source] link at the bottom of the page that you can use to view the source code for the page.

The Code for the DataReader Example

The code for this page is compact and quite simple. An OLEDB provider is used to access SQL Server in this example, so you need to use the OleDb-prefixed objects from the System.Data.OleDb namespace of the .NET class libraries. Add the appropriate Import declarations to the head of your page so that they are available, as shown at the start of the following code.

The most complex part is the SQL statement itself, which selects data from two joined tables. In the Page_Load event collect the connection string from the user control we discussed earlier, and use it in the constructor for a Connection object. Also create the SQL statement in a string variable named strSelect:

```
<%@Import Namespace="System.Data" %>
<%@Import Namespace="System.Data.OleDb" %>
...
Sub Page_Load()

  'get connection string from web.config file
  Dim strConnect As String
  strConnect = ConfigurationSettings.AppSettings("DsnWroxBooksOleDb")
  outConnect.innerText = strConnect 'and display it

  'specify the SELECT statement to extract the data
  Dim strSelect As String
  strSelect = "SELECT BookList.*, BookAuthors.FirstName, " _
            & "BookAuthors.LastName FROM BookList INNER JOIN " _
            & "BookAuthors ON BookList.ISBN = BookAuthors.ISBN " _
            & "WHERE BookList.ISBN LIKE '07645439%'"
  outSelect.innerText = strSelect    'and display it
```

If you want to use the direct (TDS) driver for MS SQL Server, you will need to import the System.Data.SqlClient namespace instead of System.Data.OleDb, and use the objects prefixed with Sql, as demonstrated in the previous chapter. Also remember to use the DsnWroxBooksSql value from web.config for the connection string instead of the DsnWroxBooksOleDb value. And if you are using the ODBC driver you will need to import the System.Data.Odbc namespace and use the objects prefixed with Odbc, and use the DsnWroxBooksOdbc value from web.config for the connection string.

Now, let's go back to the example code. First declare a variable to hold a DataReader object. Next, create the new Connection object using the connection string and, within a Try..Catch construct create a new Command object using the string that holds the SQL statement, and the Connection object. Open the connection and execute the SQL statement in the Command to return your DataReader object. If there is an error, display the details in the <div> element created in the HTML part of the page, and stop execution of the code:

```
'declare a variable to hold a DataReader object
Dim objDataReader As OleDbDataReader

'create a new Connection object using the connection string
Dim objConnect As New OleDbConnection(strConnect)

Try
```

```
        'create new Command using connection object and SQL statement
        Dim objCommand As New OleDbCommand(strSelect, objConnect)

        'open connection and execute command to return the DataReader
        objConnect.Open()
        objDataReader = objCommand.ExecuteReader()

    Catch objError As Exception

        'display error details
        outError.innerHTML = "* Error while accessing data.<br />" _
                        & objError.Message & "<br />" & objError.Source
        Exit Sub  ' and stop execution

    End Try
```

If all goes well and you've got your rowset, you can go ahead and display it. This example uses a `DataGrid`, but you could just iterate through the rows and create the output that way, as demonstrated in the Using a DataReader Object example in the previous chapter. Finally you must remember to close the connection, and also destroy the `DataReader` object, although this will be destroyed when the page ends anyway:

```
        'assign the DataReader object to the DataGrid control
        dgrResult.DataSource = objDataReader
        dgrResult.DataBind     'and bind (display) the data
        objConnect.Close()     'then close the connection

        'finished with the DataReader
        objDataReader = Nothing

    End Sub
```

So, using a complex SQL statement to access multiple tables is easy enough. In fact, often the hardest part is creating the statement itself. An easy way to do this is to take advantage of the Query Designers in programs like Visual Studio or Microsoft Access, both of which can easily link to a set of database tables in SQL Server and other OLEDB- or ODBC-enabled data sources.

Accessing Complex Data with a DataSet

Having seen how to use a complex SQL statement with a `DataReader`, let's see how the same SQL statement works with a `DataSet` object. The Extracting Complex Data with a SQL Statement into a DataSet (`complex-dataset.aspx`) example is very similar to the previous `DataReader` example. The only differences, as shown in the following code, are the declaration of the `DataSet` object (notice that a `DataSet` object instance is created with the `New` keyword here, whereas a variable of type `DataReader` was created in the previous example), and the use of a `DataAdapter` object instead of a `Command` object.

Then, once the `DataSet` is filled, you can display the contents of the single table within it. Again, you're using a `DataGrid` to show the results, but this time you have to use a `DataView` object (as returned by the `DefaultView` property of the table in the `DataSet`) as the `DataSource`:

```
'declare a variable to hold a DataSet object
Dim objDataSet As New DataSet()

Try

   'create a new Connection object using the connection string
   Dim objConnect As New OleDbConnection(strConnect)

   'create new DataAdapter using connection and SQL statement
   Dim objDataAdapter As New OleDbDataAdapter(strSelect, objConnect)

   'fill the dataset with data via the DataAdapter object
   objDataAdapter.Fill(objDataSet, "Books")

Catch objError As Exception

   'display error details
   outError.innerHTML = "* Error while accessing data. " _
                      & objError.Message & " " & objError.Source
   Exit Sub  ' and stop execution

End Try

'assign the table DefaultView to the DataGrid control
dgrResult.DataSource = objDataSet.Tables("Books").DefaultView
dgrResult.DataBind()  'and bind (display) the data
```

Accessing and Displaying Nested Data

The previous two examples demonstrated how to use complex SQL statements that join data from several tables and return it as a single table or rowset. There is also another situation, where you extract data from the tables in the data source using simple SQL statements and store the resulting rowsets as individual tables (plus the relationships between them) in a DataSet.

In the previous chapter, we showed you a custom user control that creates and returns a DataSet object containing three tables and the relationships between these tables. In that example (use-dataset-control.aspx), the contents of the DataSet were displayed using several ASP DataGrid controls so that you could see the contents of all the tables.

In an application, however, you generally should be able to access the data in a nested and structured fashion so that it can be displayed in a format that is meaningful to the user. In other words, you want to be able to display it in a hierarchical format, perhaps using some clever type of UI control widget. What we'll demonstrate here is how you can access the data in that way (though you're just going to display it as text in the page in your example).

Figure 9-3 shows the Displaying Nested Relational Data example (nested-data-access.aspx). It lists several of the books stored in the sample database, and for each one shows the authors (where available) and the prices in three currencies:

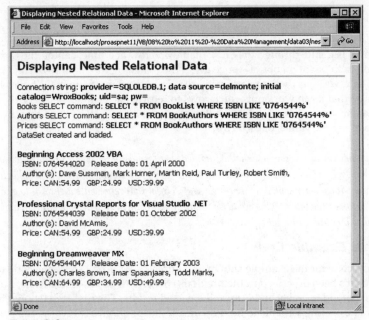

Figure 9-3

The Database Tables Structure and Relationships

In the previous chapter, you saw how the WroxBooks database holds three tables that contain all the information shown in this page. As shown in Figure 9-4, the BookList table contains the ISBN (the primary key), the title, and the publication date. The BookAuthors table contains the ISBN as a foreign key and the first and last name of each author. There is a row for each author for each book. The BookPrices table holds the ISBN as a foreign key, the currency name (CAN, GBP, or USD), and the price in that currency. Again, there is one row for each currency for each book.

Figure 9-4

The DataSet returned by the custom user control contains three tables named Books, Authors, and Prices, each containing matching subsets of rows from the three tables in the database. It also has the relationships between the tables defined (you can review the code in the previous chapter for creating a multiple-table DataSet to see how it works).

The GetChildRows Method

To be able to create the output shown in Figure 9-3, you need a way of navigating from one table to another so that you can pull out the child rows in the Authors and Prices tables in the DataSet object that match each row in the `Books` table in the `DataSet`. The technique is to use the `GetChildRows` method that is exposed by the `DataRow` object.

All you have to do is iterate through the `Books` table one row at a time, calling the `GetChildRows` method twice on each `DataRow` object – once to get the matching `Authors` rows, and once to get the matching `Prices` rows. Specify the relationship that links the parent and child tables in the call to `GetChildRows` so that it can work out which rows to return. Each call to `GetChildRows` returns a collection of matching `DataRow` objects from the specified child table. You can then iterate through these collections displaying the values of each row.

> *Interestingly, there is also a converse method named* `GetParentRows` *that, in conjunction with the members of the* `ParentRelations` *collection of the* `DataTable` *object, returns a collection of the matching parent rows when called using a* `DataRow` *object that represents a child row and a relationship between the tables. This could be useful if you wanted to list the results in a different order – perhaps by author instead of by book.*

The Nested Data Example Code

Let's examine the code for the example shown in Figure 9-3. We won't show the code to build the `DataSet` here, as it's been described in the previous chapter. We're interested in how to use the `GetChildRows` method to create and output the nested results. The first step (shown in the code that follows) is to create a string variable to hold the result (insert it into a `<div>` on the page in customary fashion afterwards). Then you can get references to all the objects you'll need.

As shown in the next section of code, you need a reference to the `Books` table to be able to iterate through the rows. Notice also that you just need references to the relationship objects and not to any of the columns – the `GetChildRows` method uses the previously defined relationships (which already contain the column information) to figure out which rows you want:

```
'create a string to hold the results
Dim strResult As String = ""

'create a reference to our main Books table in the DataSet
Dim objTable As DataTable = objDataSet.Tables("Books")

'create references to each of the relationship objects in the DataSet
Dim objAuthorRelation As DataRelation = objTable.ChildRelations("BookAuthors")
Dim objPriceRelation As DataRelation = objTable.ChildRelations("BookPrices")
```

As shown in the following code, you can iterate through the rows in the parent `Books` table. For each row, extract the values of the `Title`, `ISBN`, and `PublicationDate` columns and add them to the *results* string. Next, get a collection of the rows that are related to the current row by specifying the reference to the relationship between the `Books` and `Authors` tables in the `DataSet` in your call to `GetChildRows`. Also add a subheading `Author(s)` to the *results* string, and then iterate through the collection of `DataRow` objects returned by the `GetChildRows` method. For each one, extract the first and last name of the author, and add it to the *results* string – followed by an HTML line break:

```
Dim objRow, objChildRow As DataRow
For Each objRow In objTable.Rows
  'get the book details and append them to the "results" string
  strResult &= "<b>" & objRow("Title") & "</b><br />  ISBN: " _
```

```
                & objRow("ISBN") & "   Release Date: " _
                & FormatDateTime(objRow("PublicationDate"), 1) & "<br />"

    'get a collection of all the matching Authors table rows for this row
    Dim colChildRows() As DataRow = objRow.GetChildRows(objAuthorRelation)
    strResult &= "  Author(s): "

    'iterate through all matching Authors records adding to result string
    For Each objChildRow In colChildRows
      strResult &= objChildRow("FirstName") & " " _
              & objChildRow("LastName") & ", "
    Next
    strResult &= "<br />"
```

Repeat the process, but this time using the relationship between the Books and Prices tables. As shown in the following code, extract the currency name and the price for each matching child row and add them to the *results* string. Then, having completed one book, you can go back and repeat the process for the next book in the parent Books table. After processing all the book rows, present the results in the <div> element named divResults:

```
    'repeat using Prices table relationship for data from Price records
    colChildRows = objRow.GetChildRows(objPriceRelation)
    strResult &= "  Price: "

    For Each objChildRow In colChildRows
      strResult &= objChildRow("Currency") & ":" _
              & objChildRow("Price") & "   "
    Next
    strResult &= "<p />"

  Next  'and repeat for next row in Books table

  divResults.innerHTML = strResult  'display the results
```

So, while you *can* take advantage of clever client-side display controls such as the ASP DataGrid when working with tables in a DataSet, there is an alternative if you want to create nested output from more than one table. Of course, third-party suppliers are already offering other data grid controls, including those that can bind directly to a DataSet and display the nested data automatically.

Using Database Stored Procedures

So far, you've used SQL statements to extract the data from your data source directly. In real-world applications, it is often preferable to use a stored procedure within the data store to return the required row set. This can provide better performance, allow finer control over access permissions, and help hide the structure of the data store tables from inquisitive users.

As in traditional ADO, the .NET data access classes can work with stored procedures just as easily as they can with SQL statements. The simplest stored procedures require that you specify only the name of the procedure, and they return a set of results that can't be controlled by the ASP code used. However, stored procedures can also be written so that they accept parameters. This allows the actual content of the returned rowset to be controlled by ASP code that sets the parameter values and calls the procedure.

We've provided three examples that demonstrate the techniques for calling a stored procedure. The first example uses a simple stored procedure that does not accept parameters. The second uses a simplified *inline* or *implicit* syntax, by just adding the parameters for the stored procedure to the name of the stored procedure. The third example uses an *explicit* syntax by creating the parameter objects directly within the ASP code and then adding them to the Command object that executes the procedure.

This last technique often turned out to be difficult in traditional ADO. It was hard to arrive at the correct data types, and often programmers resorted to using the Refresh *method to create the collection of parameters with the appropriate types. The .NET Framework does not provide a direct equivalent to* Refresh, *but it is no longer really required anyway, as parameters of all types are now extremely easy to create (as you'll see shortly). However, there is the* DeriveParameters *method of the* CommandBuilder *object, which you look at in more detail in the next chapter.*

Using a Simple 'No Parameters' Stored Procedure

The Executing a Simple Stored Procedure example page (simple-stored-proc.aspx) shown in Figure 9-5 demonstrates how you can use a Command object to execute a stored procedure that does not require any parameters. This is often the case with stored procedures that perform some fixed operation (such as removing redundant rows, or selecting specific values like a count of products sold or the largest value in a column) on the data:

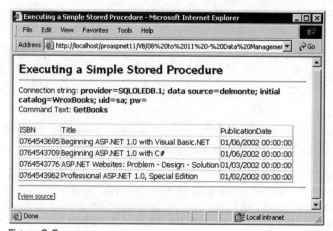

Figure 9-5

The Code for the Simple Stored Procedure Example

Our example uses a stored procedure named GetBooks that returns a fixed subset of rows from the BookList table – books with the word ASP in their title. This is what the stored procedure looks like:

```
CREATE PROCEDURE GetBooks AS
SELECT * FROM BookList WHERE Title LIKE '%ASP%'
```

The SQL scripts we provide to create the database will also create all the stored procedures used in this chapter.

As usual, in the example page, you're getting the connection string for the database from the `web.config` file, and displaying the output in an ASP `DataGrid` control. What's of interest here is the way that you specify the stored procedure in the `Command` object. As shown in the following code, the first step is to create a string that will be used as the command to be executed. In this example, it's simply the name of the stored procedure, and you display it in the page as well.

You can carry on as before when using a `DataReader` by creating a `Connection` object and a `Command` object. However, for maximum efficiency, indicate to the `Command` object that the string supplied for the first parameter of the object constructor is the name of a stored procedure. This saves SQL Server from having to check what objects with the name `GetBooks` are contained in the database when it executes the command.

> *The `CommandType` enumeration is defined within the `System.Data` class library, and the possible values are `StoredProcedure`, `TableDirect` (the name of a table), and `Text` (the default – a SQL statement).*

Finally, you can declare your `DataReader` object variable, open the connection, and execute the command. Afterwards the `DataReader` object you get back is bound to a `DataGrid` for display as usual. Also, remember to close the connection afterwards (this code is not shown here):

```
    'create the SQL statement that will call the stored procedure
Dim strCommandText As String = "GetBooks"
outCommandText.InnerText = strCommandText 'and display it
Dim objCommand As New OleDbCommand(strCommandText, objConnect)
    'set the CommandType to 'Stored Procedure'
objCommand.CommandType = CommandType.StoredProcedure
    'declare a variable to hold a DataReader object
Dim objDataReader As OleDbDataReader
    'open the connection and execute the command
objConnect.Open()
objDataReader = objCommand.ExecuteReader()
```

Using Implicit Inline Parameters with a Stored Procedure

Using a non-parameter stored procedure is as easy as using a SQL statement. However, it gets more complicated when the stored procedure expects you to provide parameters as well. One option is the simple in-line or implicit technique, which works fine with Microsoft SQL Server. You can use the `Sql`-prefixed objects (via TDS) or the `OleDb`-prefixed or `Odbc`-prefixed objects to perform the data access.

> *This syntax might not work in all database applications (other than Microsoft SQL Server), because the in-line syntax for stored procedure parameters is not always supported by other database systems.*

The Using Implicit In-line Parameters in MS SQL Server example (`sql-stored-proc.aspx`) uses a stored procedure named `FindFromTitleAndDate`. This stored procedure expects two parameters to be provided, the title (or part of it) and the publication date. It returns a rowset containing all matching books. The following code shows the stored procedure code:

```
CREATE PROCEDURE FindFromTitleAndDate
@Title varchar(50), @Date datetime
AS
SELECT *  FROM BookList
WHERE (Title LIKE @Title) AND (PublicationDate = @Date)
```

Figure 9-6 shows the result of running the example page:

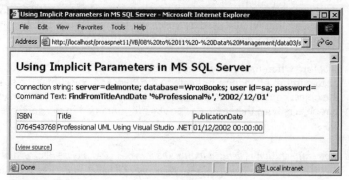

Figure 9-6

The Code for the Inline Parameters Stored Procedure Example

The only real differences between the ASP code for this example and the previous one are in the command text and the use of the `Sql`-prefixed data access objects. The command text contains the values used for the parameters. They're hardcoded in this case, but would usually be created dynamically from a user's input:

```
Dim strCommandText As String = _
    "FindFromTitleAndDate '%Professional%', '2002/12/01'"
```

However, there is one other important issue. SQL Server treats this command text as a SQL query (it automatically locates the stored procedure name within the string and parses out the parameter values). Therefore, you *cannot* set the `CommandText` property of the command object to `CommandType.StoredProcedure` as in the previous example – if you do, you'll get an error saying that the stored procedure can't be found. Instead, you can either specify `CommandType.Text` (a SQL statement) or just omit setting the property (as was done in the example). The default is `CommandType.Text`.

The rest of the code, a section of which follows, functions the same as previous examples – it creates a `Connection` object, a `Command` object, and declares a variable to hold a `DataReader` object. Then it opens the connection and executes the command to get the `DataReader`:

```
Dim objConnect As New SqlConnection(strConnect)
Dim objCommand As New SqlCommand(strCommandText, objConnect)
Dim objDataReader As SqlDataReader
objConnect.Open()
objDataReader = objCommand.ExecuteReader()
```

The rest of the code just assigns the `DataReader` to an ASP `DataGrid` as before to display the contents of the returned rows and then closes the connection to the database.

Using Explicit Parameters with a Stored Procedure

As seen in the previous example, using inline or implicit parameters when executing a stored procedure is quick and easy to program. It also provides more compact (and therefore faster) code. However, once you start using more than a couple of parameters, or need to use a return parameter to pass a result from the database to the code, the implicit technique is not really suitable. There is also the limitation that some data stores might not support it. For a more general approach, you can create each parameter for a stored procedure explicitly, and assign values to them before executing the query.

The `Command` objects (such as `SqlCommand` and `OleDbCommand`) expose a `Parameters` collection that can contain multiple `Parameter` objects. Each `Parameter` object has a range of properties that you can access and set. When you call the `ExecuteReader`, `ExecuteNonQuery`, or `ExecuteScalar` method of the `Command` object, the parameters are sent to the data store as part of the command.

The Using Explicit Parameters with a Stored Procedure (`parameter-stored-proc.aspx`) example page demonstrates how you can use these `Parameter` objects. It uses a stored procedure named `FindFromISBN` that (given the ISBN code of a book) returns two values – the title and the publication date. The stored procedure is as follows:

```
CREATE PROCEDURE FindFromISBN
@ISBN varchar(12), @Title varchar(50) OUTPUT, @Date datetime OUTPUT
AS
SELECT @Title = Title, @Date = PublicationDate
FROM BookList WHERE ISBN = @ISBN
```

Note that this differs in several ways from the `FindFromTitleAndDate` stored procedure used in the previous examples. That procedure returns a rowset containing all books that match the criteria in the two parameters. However, the `FindFromISBN` procedure used in this example returns the values in two `OUTPUT` parameters, and accepts only a single `INPUT` parameter. So, to get the results, you have to explicitly create the three parameters you need and feed them to the stored procedure when you execute it.

Figure 9-7 shows the example page in action. You can see that we're displaying not only the command text (the name of the stored procedure) but also the parameters that are explicitly created and added to the `Command` object's `Parameters` collection:

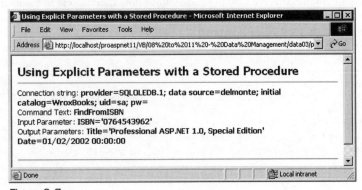

Figure 9-7

The Code for the Explicit Parameters Stored Procedure Example

Much of the code is the same as that used in previous examples. The page contains `<div>` elements into which you insert the values seen in the screenshot. However, as there is no rowset returned from the execution of the stored procedure, you don't need a `DataSet` or `DataReader` object. Remember, all the *result* values are returned as parameters.

As you're specifying the parameters explicitly this time, you only need to use the stored procedure name as the `CommandText` property of your `Command` object. Then, as shown in the following code, you can create your `Connection` and `Command` objects as before, remembering this time to set the `CommandType` property to `CommandType.StoredProcedure`:

```
'create a string to hold the name of the stored procedure
Dim strCommandText As String = "FindFromISBN"
outCommandText.InnerText = strCommandText 'and display it

Dim objConnect As New OleDbConnection(strConnect)
Dim objCommand As New OleDbCommand(strCommandText, objConnect)
objCommand.CommandType = CommandType.StoredProcedure
```

Creating the Parameter Objects

The syntax for creating and adding parameters to the `Command` object's `Parameters` collection is not immediately obvious. You can create a new `Parameter` object using the `New` operator, set the properties, and then pass it to the `Add` method of the `Parameters` collection. This technique is useful if you need to specify all the properties of a parameter – there are several properties such as `Direction`, `IsNullable`, `Precision`, `Scale`, and `SourceVersion` that you can't set through a call to the `Add` method of the `Parameters` collection.

> See the *Reference | Class Library* section of the .NET SDK for more details of the constructors and properties for the various `Parameter` object types such as `OleDbParameter` and `SqlParameter`.

Alternatively, you can use a version of the `Add` method that creates a new parameter, adds it to the `Parameters` collection, and then returns a reference to it. While this technique doesn't allow you to set some of the properties of the parameter directly, you can always set these extra properties after creating and adding the parameter to the `Parameters` collection, using the reference to the parameter that is returned from the `Add` method. The following code shows how this is done in the example:

```
'create a variable to hold a Parameter object
Dim objParam As OleDbParameter

'create a new Parameter object named 'ISBN' with the correct data
'type to match a SQL database 'varchar' field of 12 characters
objParam = objCommand.Parameters.Add("ISBN", OleDbType.VarChar, 12)

'specify that it's an Input parameter and set the value
objParam.Direction = ParameterDirection.Input
objParam.Value = "0764543962"
```

Notice the three arguments to the version of the `Add` method used here: the name of the parameter, the data type (using the `OleDbType` enumeration), and the size – in this case, 12 characters. For numeric types, you can omit the size and the default size for that data type is automatically applied. Other common data types used are `Boolean`, `Char`, `DBDate`, `Single`, `Double`, and `Integer`.

There are around 40 different data types specified for the `OleDbType` enumeration, and around 25 for the matching `SqlDbType` enumeration (as used with the `SqlCommand` object). Search the .NET Frameworks SDK for OleDbType enumeration or SqlDbType enumeration to see the complete list.

Once you've got a reference to the parameter, you can set the other properties. In the preceding code, specify the direction of the parameter (the options specified by the `ParameterDirection` enumeration are `Input`, `Output`, `InputOutput`, and `ReturnValue`). Also specify the `Value` property.

The Add Method of the ParameterCollection

Our example doesn't demonstrate all the properties that can be set for a parameter, or all the ways of creating a `Parameter` object.

There are several variations (or overloads) of the `Add` method available, ranging from the simplest one, which adds an existing `Parameter` object to the collection:

```
Parameter = Command.Parameters.Add(parameter-object)
```

To the most complex version that creates the `Parameter` object using the specified values for the properties:

```
Parameter = Command.Parameters.Add(parameter-name, db-type, _
                          size, source-column-name)
```

The meanings of the arguments to the `Add` method are as follows:

Argument	Description
parameter-name	The name for the parameter.
db-type	A data type from the `OleDbType`, `OdbcType`, `OracleType`, or `SqlDbType` enumerations.
size	The size as an integer value.
source-column-name	Sets the `SourceColumn` property of the parameter – the name of the column in a table from which the parameter value will be taken when updating the source data from a `DataSet`. Works in hand with the `SourceVersion` property. You'll see these in more detail in the next chapter.

Many of the data access examples you'll see here and in later chapters use parameter names that are not prefixed by the @ symbol when adding parameters to the `ParametersCollection`. This works fine when using the `OleDb` data access classes, because parameters are passed by position and not by name (as was the default with ADO prior to ADO.NET). In fact, any name can be used for the parameters –

the names don't have to match the parameter names in the stored procedure. However, if you use the
SqlClient classes, the parameters are passed by name, and so all parameter names must be prefixed by
@ in this case.

A Short-Cut Approach to Parameter Creation

There is also a shorter way of adding a parameter to a Command object, when all you want to specify is
the parameter name and value. You can use the following syntax:

```
Parameter = Command.Parameters.Add("param-name", param-value)
```

For example:

```
objParam = objCommand.Parameters.Add("ISBN", "1861007035")
```

And if you don't need to access the new parameter in your code, you can disregard the reference
returned by the Add method:

```
objCommand.Parameters.Add("ISBN", "1861007035")
```

As mentioned earlier, it is possible to create parameters using the DeriveParameters method of the
CommandBuilder object. However, this can only be done if you are using a DataAdapter to access
the data source and not directly with a Command object. There is no direct method equivalent to the
Refresh method that was available in previous versions of ADO. The CommandBuilder object is
discussed in the next chapter.

Getting Back to the Example Code

Getting back to the example code, you now need to create the two output parameters that will hold the
values returned by the stored procedure. The only real difference is that you specify the direction as
ParameterDirection.Output rather than ParameterDirection.Input as you did for the ISBN
parameter. The following code shows how to create the parameters for the Title and Date values that
will be returned from the stored procedure:

```
'create a new Parameter object named 'Title' with the correct data
'type to match a SQL database 'varchar' field of 50 characters
'and specify that it's an output parameter (so no value required)
objParam = objCommand.Parameters.Add("Title", OleDbType.VarChar, 50)
objParam.Direction = ParameterDirection.Output

'create another output Parameter object named 'Date' with the correct
'data type to match a SQL database 'datetime' field
objParam = objCommand.Parameters.Add("Date", OleDbType.DBDate)
objParam.Direction = ParameterDirection.Output
```

Now, you can display the value of the input parameter in the page, and execute the stored procedure. As
shown in the following code, open the connection, call the ExecuteNonQuery method of the Command
object (because you are executing a query that will not return a rowset), and close the connection again.

```
'display the value of the input parameter
outInParams.InnerText = "ISBN='" & objCommand.Parameters("ISBN").Value & "'"

'execute the stored procedure
objConnect.Open()
objCommand.ExecuteNonQuery()
objConnect.Close()

'collect the values of the output parameters - note the use of
'the ToString() method as they will contain DBNull if there was no
'match for the ISBN and this will cause an error if displayed
strTitle = objCommand.Parameters("Title").Value.ToString()
strDate = objCommand.Parameters("Date").Value.ToString()
outOutParams.InnerHtml = "Title='" & strTitle & "'   Date=" & strDate
```

Afterwards, provided there was no error (although not shown here, you should include some basic error handling code in your pages), you can extract the returned values from the two output parameters and display them.

Working with the DataTable Object

This section explores some of the ways that you can work with DataSet objects and their contents. This is by no means an exhaustive exploration of the capabilities of the DataSet – you'll be seeing more as you proceed through this chapter and the next.

Here we're interested in looking at the ways that DataSet objects can be created and filled with data, extending the techniques introduced in the previous chapter. Along the way, you'll see:

❑ How to fill a DataSet and the DataTable objects using code

❑ How to specify the columns in a table

❑ How to work with constraints, calculated columns, and default values

❑ How to add and remove rows in the tables in a DataSet

❑ How to use table and column mappings in a DataSet

❑ How to sort and filter the data in a table

There are often occasions when you'd want to create a data table directly in code, rather than filling it from a data store. Under .NET, this is a useful technique when you want to insert values into a data store. You can create a DataTable object containing the new data within a DataSet, and then push the data into a database or other type of data store. Creating a DataSet dynamically is also a useful approach when you just want to package data up into a format that you can pass from one tier of an application to another, or use as the DataSource property of a data-bound control like a DataGrid, a listbox or some other type of ASP.NET list control.

The Creating and Populating a New DataTable example page (create-new-datatable.aspx) shown in Figure 9-8 demonstrates the basic techniques for creating a DataTable object. In this case, you aren't specifically creating a `DataSet` object – you're just creating the `DataTable` as a standalone object and binding it to an ASP.NET `DataGrid` control to display the contents.

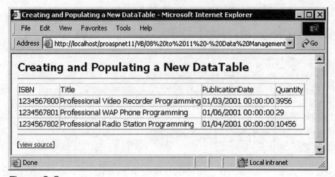

Figure 9-8

The Code to Create and Fill a New DataTable

Creating a new `DataTable` object is simply a matter of calling the constructor. You can give the table a name at the same time by providing this as the parameter to the constructor. Then you need to define the columns in the new table, as shown in the following code. Call the `Add` method of the `Columns` collection for the table, and specify the column name and the data type. The data types that you can use are listed in the `System` namespace of the class library, and are basically the same as the data types (such as `Int16`, `Int32`, `Single`, `Double`, `Char`, `String`, and `Boolean`) available for use with all the .NET languages.

```
Dim objTable As New DataTable("NewTable")

'define four columns (fields) within the table
objTable.Columns.Add("ISBN", System.Type.GetType("System.String"))
objTable.Columns.Add("Title", System.Type.GetType("System.String"))
objTable.Columns.Add("PublicationDate", _
     System.Type.GetType("System.DateTime"))
objTable.Columns.Add("Quantity", System.Type.GetType("System.Int32"))
```

Adding Data Rows to the Table

Having defined the four columns in your new table, you can now add some data rows. The following code shows how to define a variable to hold a `DataRow` object, and then call the `NewRow` method of the `DataTable` object. This creates the new row based on the schema for this table, and returns a reference to it.

You can then fill in the values for that row. Once complete, call the `Add` method of the table's `Rows` collection to add the row to the table, and repeat the process to add two more rows. Finish by assigning the `DefaultView` property of the new table to the `DataSource` property of the `DataGrid` that was placed in the HTML section of the page. A call to the `DataBind` method then causes the contents of your table to be displayed.

```
'create a new row that matches the schema of the table
Dim objDataRow As DataRow
objDataRow = objTable.NewRow()

'and fill in the values
objDataRow("ISBN") = "1234567800"
objDataRow("Title") = "Professional Video Recorder Programming"
objDataRow("PublicationDate") = "2001-03-01"
objDataRow("Quantity") = 3956
objTable.Rows.Add(objDataRow)

'repeat for two more rows
objDataRow = objTable.NewRow()
objDataRow("ISBN") = "1234567801"
objDataRow("Title") = "Professional WAP Phone Programming"
objDataRow("PublicationDate") = "2001-06-01"
objDataRow("Quantity") = 29
objTable.Rows.Add(objDataRow)

objDataRow = objTable.NewRow()
objDataRow("ISBN") = "1234567802"
objDataRow("Title") = "Professional Radio Station Programming"
objDataRow("PublicationDate") = "2001-04-01"
objDataRow("Quantity") = 10456
objTable.Rows.Add(objDataRow)

dgrResult.DataSource = objTable.DefaultView
dgrResult.DataBind()   'and bind (display) the data
```

Adding a Table to a DataSet

In the previous example, you created a standalone `DataTable` object purely to be able to use it to populate an ASP.NET `DataGrid` (and, of course, to demonstrate the technique). However, a physical `DataTable` object cannot exist alone, and must be part of a `DataSet`. What happened in the previous example was that a `DataSet` was created automatically behind the scenes and your new table is part of that `DataSet`.

However, sometimes you may want the table to be part of an existing, or an explicitly created new `DataSet` object. You can create a new instance of a `DataSet` object from scratch as follows:

```
Dim objDataSet As New DataSet("BooksDataSet")
```

The parameter is the name of the new `DataSet`, and is optional.

Alternatively, you can use an existing `DataSet` that is empty, or that already has some tables in existence. Once you've got a reference to the `DataSet` object, just declare a variable to hold a `DataTable` object and set it to the result of a call to the `Tables` collection's `Add` method:

```
Dim objTable As DataTable
objTable = objDataSet.Tables.Add("NewTable")
'populate the DataTable with the required values here
....
```

417

Managing Constraints and Default Values

If the `DataSet` object is going to be any use as a package that can be used to store and transport disconnected data, you need the ability to exert fine control over the structure and content of that `DataSet`. You saw in the previous chapter how to add relationships between the tables in a `DataSet` to check and enforce referential integrity.

You've also seen how you can add tables to a `DataSet` and fill them with data. In earlier examples, you did this simply by filling them from an existing data source, for example with a SQL `SELECT` statement that returns a rowset from a relational database.

And in the previous example, you saw how to do the same directly, using code. The data in that example was hardcoded into the page, but could just as easily have come from user input, or from processing data collected from some other kind of data store – perhaps one that doesn't support the SQL-based data access methods you've been using so far.

When you fill a table in a `DataSet` from an existing data source using the `Fill` method of a `DataAdapter` object, information about each column's data type is automatically collected from the data source and added to the table. If you use the `DataAdapter` object's `FillSchema` method first, the column constraints (that is, primary keys, default values, unique values, nullability, and so on) are also added to the table. So, if a column in the original source table in the database is an integer data type that does not accept `Null` values, the table in the `DataSet` will exhibit the same properties.

Of course, when you create tables in a `DataSet` using code (or if the `FillSchema` method was not used), you have to specify all these extra properties *yourselves*. The example page shown in Figure 9-9, and the following example, demonstrates how this can be done. The Adding Expressions, Defaults and Constraints to a Table example (`column-constraints.aspx`) shows how you can create a table that has non-nullable columns, default column values, and calculated columns (that is, columns that use an expression based on other column values as their value source).

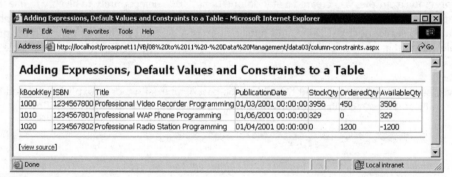

Figure 9-9

The example demonstrates several ways that you can add properties to the columns. The `kBookKey` column is an `AutoNumber` or `Auto-Increment` (`IDENTITY`) column that has `1000` as the seed value and `10` as the increment value, so the values in this column are created automatically as you add new rows to the table. The `ISBN` column cannot contain `Null` values, and each value must be unique.

The StockQty and OrderedQty columns are Integer types and have a default value specified so that they will contain zero (rather than Null) when a new record is created, if there is no value specified for one or both of these fields. Finally, the AvailableQty field is based on an expression. The value in this column is automatically adjusted when rows are added or edited to reflect the actual quantity available (StockQty minus OrderedQty).

The Code for This Example

The following code is similar to that of the previous example in that you first create a new DataTable object. However, in this case you should be able to access each of the new DataColumn objects as you add the columns to the table, so that you can set the extra properties. So, you also declare a variable that will be used to hold DataColumn objects as you create them:

```
'create a new empty DataTable object
Dim objTable As New DataTable("NewBooks")

'declare a variable to hold a DataColumn object
Dim objColumn As DataColumn
```

Creating the Columns

The first column created is the kBookKey auto-increment column with a data type of Int32. In the code that follows, you can see the property settings made for specifying that it's an auto-increment column. Next, the ISBN column is added to the table. This is a String, which cannot contain Null, can be a maximum of ten characters, and must be unique. Then come two columns to hold the Title and the PublicationDate. As you don't need to set any extra properties on these, don't collect the column reference returned from the Add method of the Columns collection.

```
'add an IDENTITY column named kBookKey
objColumn = objTable.Columns.Add("kBookKey", _
                                 System.Type.GetType("System.Int32"))
objColumn.AutoIncrement = True
objColumn.AutoIncrementSeed = 1000
objColumn.AutoIncrementStep = 10

'add a unique String column with max length 10 chars for the ISBN
objColumn = objTable.Columns.Add("ISBN", System.Type.GetType("System.String"))
objColumn.AllowDBNull = False
objColumn.Unique = True
objColumn.MaxLength = 10

'add two String columns for the Title and PublicationDate
objTable.Columns.Add("Title", System.Type.GetType("System.String"))
objTable.Columns.Add("PublicationDate",System.Type.GetType("System.DateTime"))
```

Specifying Column Default Values and Expressions

The next two columns, StockQty and OrderedQty, are of data type Int32, which you want to automatically have a default value of zero if no value is specified for new rows. As shown in the following code, this is easy – just set the DefaultValue property for each column.

The final column is a calculated column that shows the available stock quantity. Again, it's of type `Int32`. To make it a calculated column, just set the `Expression` property to a string that contains the expression to evaluate for each row:

```
'add columns for stock and order quantities with default values of zero
objColumn = objTable.Columns.Add("StockQty", _
                                 System.Type.GetType("System.Int32"))
objColumn.DefaultValue = 0
objColumn = objTable.Columns.Add("OrderedQty", _
                                 System.Type.GetType("System.Int32"))
objColumn.DefaultValue = 0

'add a column containing an expression showing the quantity availability
objColumn = objTable.Columns.Add("AvailableQty", _
                                 System.Type.GetType("System.Int32"))
objColumn.Expression = "[StockQty] - [OrderedQty]"
```

Note that column names containing special characters (. ~ () #\/=><+-*%&|^'" []) or spaces must be enclosed in square brackets. Doing this even when not actually *required* probably makes more complex expressions easier to read.

> *If any of your column names contains a closing square bracket, you must escape it with a backslash character; for example, a column named* `Tax[Basic]Value` *would be expressed as* `[Tax[Basic\]Value]`.

Adding Data Rows to the New Table

The table schema is now complete, and you can add some rows. Although the technique is the same as the previous example, we've shown the code used in this example so that you can see how the end result compares to the values placed in the columns:

```
Dim objDataRow As DataRow
objDataRow = objTable.NewRow()
objDataRow("ISBN") = "1234567800"
objDataRow("Title") = "Professional Video Recorder Programming"
objDataRow("PublicationDate") = "2001-03-01"
objDataRow("StockQty") = 3956
objDataRow("OrderedQty") = 450
objTable.Rows.Add(objDataRow)
objDataRow = objTable.NewRow()
objDataRow("ISBN") = "1234567801"
objDataRow("Title") = "Professional WAP Phone Programming"
objDataRow("PublicationDate") = "2001-06-01"
objDataRow("StockQty") = 329
'note - no "OrderedQty" provided so default value used
objTable.Rows.Add(objDataRow)
objDataRow = objTable.NewRow()
objDataRow("ISBN") = "1234567802"
objDataRow("Title") = "Professional Radio Station Programming"
objDataRow("PublicationDate") = "2001-04-01"
'note - no "StockQty" provided so default value used
objDataRow("OrderedQty") = 1200
objTable.Rows.Add(objDataRow)
```

The final step (not shown here) is to assign the `DefaultView` of the new table to a `DataGrid` object declared elsewhere in the page, so that the contents of the table are visible.

Specifying Primary and Foreign Keys

You've seen how to create a `DataSet`, add tables and relationships, fill the tables with data, and set several properties on each column. The one remaining aspect to consider is how to create columns that act as primary keys and foreign keys.

The Adding Primary Keys and Foreign Keys to a Table example (`key-constraints.aspx`) shown in Figure 9-10 illustrates the techniques:

Figure 9-10

When you open the page, you can see that data is being selected from two tables in your data store and used to fill a `DataSet` object. This automatically sets the appropriate data types for the columns. What it doesn't do is specify within the `DataSet` *which* columns are the primary key and foreign key in the tables.

Obviously, you can create a relationship between the tables within the `DataSet`. You can then use this relationship to navigate from parent row to child row and back when accessing the data in the tables, as demonstrated earlier in this chapter. But again, this does not change the table structure or specify which columns are the primary and foreign keys for each table.

So, you need to be able to create these keys yourself. Unlike the previous example, where you set the values of properties for each *column* object to define nullability and expressions, you have to create the primary and foreign key constraints as objects and add them to the `Constraints` collection of the *table* object.

This is because a primary or foreign key can encompass more than one column – for example, the only possible primary key for the `BookPrices` table in the database is the combination of the ISBN code and the currency name. None of the individual columns has values that are unique within the table, and only a combination of columns can provide a unique key value. However, the ISBN column alone provides the link to the parent `BookList` table, and so it is specified as a foreign key in the `BookPrices` table.

You can see from the `DataSet.Tables` collection that there are two tables in the `DataSet`: `Books` and `Authors`. These are filled with a subset of values from the `BookList` and `BookAuthors` tables in the database. Also shown is the content of the `Constraints` collection for both the tables in the `DataSet`, followed by the data in the two tables.

The Code for the Primary and Foreign Keys Example

The example page uses exactly the same techniques as earlier examples to fill the two tables with data from the database, so you won't be looking at that part of the code again here. What we're interested in is how to specify the primary and foreign keys for the two tables within the `DataSet`, after they have been filled with data.

As shown in the code that follows, start by getting a reference to each of the tables and to the columns that will become the primary and foreign keys. For one or more columns to become the primary key, you first need to create a `UniqueConstraint` object for that table which refers to the column(s) in question, and make sure that they cannot contain `Null` values. The new constraint in our example is named `Unique_ISBN`.

Then you can specify that it is the primary key. As we discussed, the primary key could include more than one column, and so the way you specify it is through an array of columns (even though in this case there is only one). Create an array that will contain `DataColumn` objects, and set the first and only item (at index zero) to the column that will be the primary key in the `Books` table. Afterwards, you can simply specify this array as the `PrimaryKey` property of the table itself.

```
'declare variables to refer to the DataTable and DataColumn objects
Dim objParentTable As DataTable = objDataSet.Tables("Books")
Dim objChildTable As DataTable = objDataSet.Tables("Authors")
Dim objParentColumn As DataColumn = objParentTable.Columns("ISBN")
Dim objChildColumn As DataColumn = objChildTable.Columns("ISBN")
```

```
'create a new UniqueConstraint object and add to Constraints collection
Dim objUnique As New UniqueConstraint("Unique_ISBN", objParentColumn)
objParentTable.Constraints.Add(objUnique)

'prevent the column from accepting Null values
objParentColumn.AllowDBNull = False

'create an array of columns containing this column only
Dim objColumnArray(0) As DataColumn
objColumnArray(0) = objParentColumn

'and set this array as the columns for the Primary Key of the table
objParentTable.PrimaryKey = objColumnArray
```

The next step is to specify the primary key for the Authors table. In this case, the ISBN cannot be used on its own, as the values in it are not unique – there could be more than one author row for each book row. While not strictly the correct approach (the ideal would be a unique author reference number), we've chosen, as an illustration, to use the combination of the ISBN and the last name in each row as the primary key for the table. However, it will suffice for this example where there are no authors with the same last name for any one book.

As shown in the following code, the process is the same as for the Books table, except that – as there is more than one column in the primary key – you have to add the other (Lastname) column to the array as well before assigning it to the table's PrimaryKey property:

```
'now we can process the child table named "Authors"
'create an array of columns containing the ISBN and Lastname columns
ReDim objColumnArray(1)
objColumnArray(0) = objChildColumn      'the ISBN column
objColumnArray(1) = objChildTable.Columns("Lastname")

'prevent either of these columns containing Null
objColumnArray(0).AllowDBNull = False
objColumnArray(1).AllowDBNull = False

'set this column array as the primary key
objChildTable.PrimaryKey = objColumnArray
```

Creating the Foreign Key Constraint

The foreign key constraint can now be added to the child table named Authors. This is just the ISBN column, which forms the link between the two tables in the DataSet. The code that follows shows how to create a ForeignKeyConstraint object (named here FK_BookAuthors), and specify the parent and child columns to which it applies.

You can then specify the other properties that apply to a foreign key. In this case, you're specifying that any deletes should cascade; in other words, deleting a row in the parent table will automatically delete all matching child rows. Also specify that any updates to the primary key value in the parent table should be cascaded to all matching child rows; the value of the foreign key in each matching row will be changed to the new value of the parent row's primary key (the Rule enumeration will be discussed later in this section). Finally, this constraint is added to the table's Constraints collection:

```
'create a new ForeignKeyConstraint object
Dim objFKey As New ForeignKeyConstraint("FK_BookAuthors", _
                                    objParentColumn, objChildColumn)

'set the "update" properties
objFKey.DeleteRule = Rule.Cascade
objFKey.UpdateRule = Rule.Cascade

'and add it to the Constraints collection
objChildTable.Constraints.Add(objFKey)
```

Displaying the DataSet Contents

Most of the code that displays the contents of the DataSet object is the same as used in previous examples, so it is not repeated here. You can examine the sourcecode for this (and any other) page using the [view source] link at the bottom of the page. However, notice how the contents of the Constraints collections for the two tables are displayed. As these are collections, you can bind them directly to the DataSource of a couple of ASP.NET DataGrid controls declared within the HTML section of the page:

```
'bind the collections of Constraints to DataGrids on the page
dgrBookCons.DataSource = objDataSet.Tables("Books").Constraints
dgrBookCons.DataBind()
dgrAuthorCons.DataSource = objDataSet.Tables("Authors").Constraints
dgrAuthorCons.DataBind()
```

And you can see the new foreign key constraint, and the primary key constraints created earlier for this table and the Books table, in the Constraints collections that are displayed in the page (repeated in Figure 9-11):

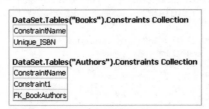

Figure 9-11

Notice that we haven't explicitly specified a named UniqueConstraint *object for this table, so it has the default name* Constraint1.

The DeleteRule and UpdateRule Property Values

You used a couple of values from the Rule enumeration in the code shown for creating the ForeignKeyConstraint, to specify how deletes and updates should be handled for related child rows in the Authors table, by setting the DeleteRule and UpdateRule properties of a ForeignKeyConstraint instance.

In most cases like this, to provide the highest level of integrity maintenance for your data, you'll use Cascade. Other choices will leave unlinked (orphan) rows in the child table. However, depending on how you want to edit and manage your data (particularly when doing bulk updates), you may prefer to specify a different setting and perform manual integrity checks afterwards. The values of the `Rule` enumeration are summarized in the following table:

Value	Description
Cascade	Updates to the primary key value in the parent table are copied to the foreign key in all linked child rows. Deleting a parent row deletes all linked child rows.
SetDefault	Updates to the primary key value in the parent table or deletion of a parent row both cause the foreign key in all linked child rows to be set to its default value.
SetNull	Updates to the primary key value in the parent table or deletion of a parent row both cause the foreign key in all linked child rows to be set to `Null`.
None	Updates to the primary key value in the parent table or deletion of a parent row have no effect on child rows.

Adding, Modifying, Removing, and Deleting Rows

You've now seen all the important techniques available for building `DataTable` objects within a `DataSet`, and filling them with data.

Next we'll confirm just how easy it is to add and edit the data in your `DataSet` tables, and then show how you can delete and/or permanently remove existing rows.

Adding Rows to a DataTable

Adding rows to a `DataTable` was demonstrated in several of the previous examples. The `NewRow` method of the `DataTable` object returns a new empty `DataRow` object for the table. After filling in the values, use the `Add` method of a table's `Rows` collection to add the new row.

At a minimum, you must provide appropriate (legal) values for any primary and foreign keys in the table, and for any columns that cannot accept `Null`. Any other columns you don't set a value for will be `Null` when the row is added to the table (unless, of course, they have a default value constraint assigned to them):

```
objDataRow = objTable.NewRow()
objDataRow("ISBN") = "1234567801"
objDataRow("Title") = "Professional WAP Phone Programming"
objDataRow("PublicationDate") = "2001-06-01"
objDataRow("Quantity") = 329
objTable.Rows.Add(objDataRow)
```

Adding Rows with an Object Array

You can also add a row to a table using an array of the basic `Object` types. As shown in the following code, you can simply create a one-dimensional array to hold the correct number of column values, fill in the values, and call the `Add` method of the `Rows` collection with the array as the single parameter:

```
'add a new row using an array of values
Dim objValsArray(3) As Object
objValsArray(0) = "1234567900"
objValsArray(1) = "Impressionist Guide to Painting Computers"
objValsArray(2) = "05-02-2002"
objValsArray(3) = 150
objTable.Rows.Add(objValsArray)
```

Editing Values in a DataTable

To change the contents of a row in a table, you can simply access the row through the table's `Rows` collection, and access the column through the collection of items in the `DataRow` object that represents that row, as shown in the following code:

```
objTable.Rows(0)("Title") = "Amateur Theatricals for Windows 2000"
objTable.Rows(2)("PublicationDate") = "01-01-2002"
objTable.Rows(5)("ISBN") = "200000000"
```

Remember that the first row in the table is at row index zero. And if you specify a row index that is greater than the number of rows in the tables minus one (a row that is past the end of the table), you'll obviously get an error.

Using the BeginEdit, CancelEdit, and EndEdit Methods

An alternative technique is to use the `BeginEdit`, `EndEdit`, and `CancelEdit` methods of the `DataRow` object. Unlike the previous technique of just referencing the column and poking a new value into it, you can perform a controlled update to several values in a row without the values being immediately persisted to the row.

The `BeginUpdate` method effectively creates a copy of the row so that all the changes are made to this copy rather than to the original row. This means that all the updates made to any of the columns can be cancelled with a call to the `CancelEdit` method of that row, whereupon the original row is unchanged. To accept all the changes, effectively replacing the original row with the updated row, you can simply call the `EndEdit` method.

The Editing Existing Values in the Rows of a DataTable example page (`edit-rows.aspx`) demonstrates this technique in action. After filling the `Books` table in a `DataSet` object with some rows from your database, as shown in Figure 9-12, it changes the `ISBN` value of the first row but then calls the `CancelEdit` method. Next it changes the value again, but this time calls the `EndEdit` method. You can see only in this case is the value persisted into the table.

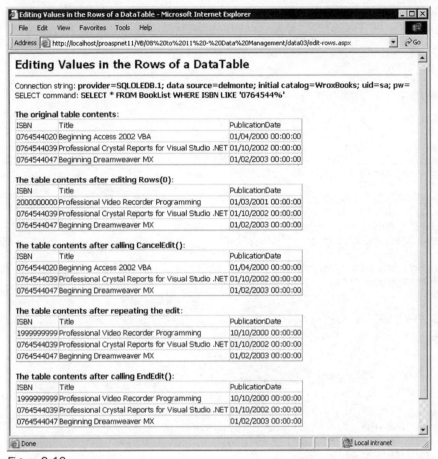

Figure 9-12

The Code for the Example Page

After filling the table from the WroxBooks database as demonstrated several times previously, the code in this page creates a reference to the table and displays the original values of the rows in the first DataGrid control on the page (as shown in the code that appears next).

Then call BeginEdit and update the first row in the table, after which the current values in the next DataGrid control are displayed. Next, perform some arbitrary test (is the value greater than 1999999999) and based on this make a decision whether to keep the changes made to the row. Notice that the *copy* of the row that is being edited is referenced using the Proposed value of that row. We'll discuss this in more detail later on. In the first case, this test fails and so the CancelEdit method is executed. After this, the contents of the table are displayed again.

To demonstrate the effect of the EndEdit method, the next section of code repeats the whole process. This time it sets the value of the ISBN field to "1999999999" so that the subsequent test succeeds, and the `EndEdit` method is called. Again, the contents of the table are displayed during and after the edit process (see the following code):

```
'get a reference to a DataTable in an existing DataSet
Dim objTable As DataTable = objDataSet.Tables("Books")

'assign the DataTable's DefaultView object to the DataGrid control
dgrResult1.DataSource = objTable.DefaultView
dgrResult1.DataBind()  'and bind (display) the data

'now edit the first row
Dim objRow As DataRow = objTable.Rows(0)
objRow.BeginEdit()

'change some of the values in the row
objRow("ISBN") = "2000000000"
objRow("Title") = "Professional Video Recorder Programming"
objRow("PublicationDate") = "2001-03-01"

'display the edited values
dgrResult2.DataSource = objTable.DefaultView
dgrResult2.DataBind()

'now check if the values are valid
If objRow("ISBN", DataRowVersion.Proposed) > "1999999999" Then
  objRow.CancelEdit()
Else
  objRow.EndEdit()
End If

'display the values after canceling the update
dgrResult3.DataSource = objTable.DefaultView
dgrResult3.DataBind()

'now repeat edit, but this time using value that will pass the test
objRow.BeginEdit
objRow("ISBN") = "1999999999"
objRow("Title") = "Professional Video Recorder Programming"
objRow("PublicationDate") = "2000-10-10"

'display the edited values
dgrResult4.DataSource = objTable.DefaultView
dgrResult4.DataBind()

'now we can check if the values are valid
If objRow("ISBN", DataRowversion.Proposed) > "1999999999" Then
  objRow.CancelEdit
Else
  objRow.EndEdit
End If

'display the values after accepting the update
dgrResult5.DataSource = objTable.DefaultView
dgrResult5.DataBind()
```

The Original, Current, and Proposed Column Values

In the previous code, notice a special syntax used when accessing the value of a column:

```
If objRow("ISBN", DataRowVersion.Proposed) > "1999999999" Then ...
```

As you'll see in more detail in the next chapter, every column in every row of a table maintains three values for that item. These values are defined in the `DataRowVersion` enumeration, shown in the following table, and are used to help maintain concurrency when updating data:

Value	Description
Original	The value that was in the column when the `DataTable` was created and filled with data. It is compared to the value in the original database table when an update is performed, to see if another user or process has changed the value since the `DataTable` data was created.
Proposed	The proposed value for this column after changes have been made following `BeginEdit`, but before `EndEdit`, `CancelEdit`, `AcceptChanges` or `RejectChanges` has been executed.
Current	The actual column value after changes have been made to it, and after these changes have been accepted (after `EndEdit` or `AcceptChanges` has been executed).

The `AcceptChanges` and `RejectChanges` methods mentioned in the table are described next.

Accepting and Rejecting Changes in a Row, Table, or DataSet

As you saw earlier, you can access any of the three values that are stored for every column in every row of a table at any time to get the appropriate value for a comparison test, or to check whether values in a row have been changed or are in the process of being changed.

Apart from using the `BeginEdit`, `EndEdit`, and `CancelEdit` methods to manage updates to a table row, you can also use the `AcceptChanges` and `RejectChanges` methods. Their actions are self-explanatory, with `AcceptChanges` effectively calling `EndEdit` on any rows currently being edited, and `RejectChanges` effectively calling `CancelEdit` on any rows currently being edited.

As far as the `DataRow` is concerned:

❑ After execution of the `BeginEdit` method, if you change the value in any column, the `Current` and `Proposed` values of all the columns become accessible. The `Proposed` value is the same as the `Current` value until you edit that particular column.

❑ After execution of the `EndEdit` method, the `Current` value for each column is replaced by the `Proposed` value.

❑ After execution of the `CancelEdit` method, the `Proposed` value is discarded and the `Current` value is unchanged.

❑ After execution of the `AcceptChanges` method, the `Original` value for each column is replaced by the `Current` value.

❑ After execution of the `RejectChanges`, the `Current` value is discarded and the `Original` value is unchanged.

Notice that the effects of the `AcceptChanges` and `RejectChanges` methods are subtly different from `BeginEdit`, `EndEdit`, and `CancelEdit`. The `AcceptChanges` and `RejectChanges` methods affect the `Current` and the `Original` values (rather than the `Current` and `Proposed` values).

The `AcceptChanges` and `RejectChanges` methods can also be used at `DataTable`- and `DataSet`-level. After execution of the `DataTable` (rather than the `DataRow`) object's `AcceptChanges` method, the `Original` value for every column in *all rows* in the table is set to the same as the `Current` value. After execution of the `DataSet` object's `AcceptChanges` method, the `Original` value for every column in every row in *all tables* in the `Dataset` is set to the same as the `Current` value.

It's important to *not* call these methods on a `DataSet` or a `DataTable` if you intend to update the original source data from the `DataSet` object, as it depends on the difference between the `Original` and `Current` values to be able to correctly detect any concurrency errors. The next chapter looks at this topic in detail.

The RowState Property of the DataRow Object

Each row in a table exposes another useful property named `RowState`. This is related to inserting, editing, and deleting rows in a table, and provides a useful indication of the current state of each row. The `DataRowState` enumeration values are summarized in the following table:

Value	Description
Unchanged	No changes have been made to the row since it was created or since the last call to the `AcceptChanges` method of the row, table, or `DataSet`.
Added	The row has been added to the table and `AcceptChanges` has not yet been executed.
Modified	At least one value or property of the row has been changed since the last call to the `AcceptChanges` method of the row, table, or `DataSet`.
Deleted	The row has been deleted from the table using the `Delete` method and `AcceptChanges` has not yet been executed.
Detached	The row has been created with the `NewRow` method but has not yet been added to the table with the `Add` method. Hence, it is not actually classed as being a row within that table.

You can access the `RowState` property at any time to see the state of any row. However, it is most useful when you come to update the original source data. You'll see this in the next chapter.

Deleting and Removing Rows from a DataTable

Deleting a row from a table is easy – all you do is call the `Delete` method of the `DataRow` object you want to delete. You can specify the index of the row to delete within the `Rows` collection:

```
'delete first and third rows in table referenced by objTable
objTable.Rows(0).Delete()
objTable.Rows(2).Delete()
```

Or you can use a reference to the actual `DataRow` object you want to delete:

```
objThisRow.Delete()
objOtherRow.Delete()
```

The deleted rows remain in the table. The `Delete` method just sets the `RowState` property to `DataRowState.Deleted` (as you saw in the previous section). However, the next time you call `AcceptChanges` for the table, or for the `DataSet` object that *contains* the table, the row is removed from the table. This means that you can *undelete* rows simply by calling `RejectChanges` instead of `AcceptChanges`.

Thus, you can write code to delete some rows (or update and insert rows for that matter) in a table, and then carry out some comparison tests to decide whether to accept or reject all the changes in one go. Of course, (as you saw a little earlier) you can access the appropriate `DataRowVersion` for each column, as you do so to get the `Original`, `Current`, or `Proposed` value.

Removing Versus Deleting Rows

Removing a row from a table is an alternative and entirely different process from deleting a row. When you execute the `Remove` method, you immediately and irretrievably remove the row from the table in the `DataSet`. It isn't marked as deleted – it just disappears from the table. As a result, the row indices change to reflect the new *row positions* as they all shuffle up to fill the gap left by the removed row.

Notice the difference in syntax, as shown in the following code. The `Delete` method is a member of the `DataRow` object. The `Remove` method is a member of the `Rows` collection:

```
'remove the third row from the table
objTable.Rows.Remove(2)

'using the Remove method on row 2 (rather than marking it as deleted
'with the Delete method) means that the next row then becomes row 2
'so, to remove the next row from the table as well we repeat the use of
objTable.Rows.Remove(2)
```

If you intend to use the `DataSet` to update the original data store, avoid using `Remove` to delete rows. Always use the `Delete` method so that the rows remain in the table but are marked as being deleted. These deletes will then be made in the original data source when you call the `Update` method.

To see how the `Delete` and `Remove` methods work, you can try the example Removing versus Deleting Rows in a DataTable (`remove-delete-rows.aspx`). Figure 9-13 shows this example page in action:

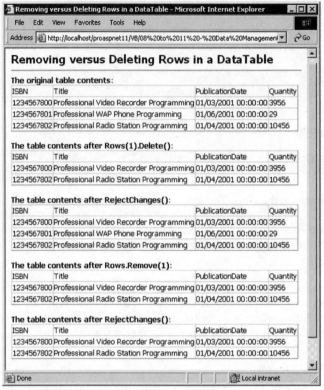

Figure 9-13

The Code for the Deleting versus Removing Rows Example

The code in this example is relatively straightforward. Start by creating a new `DataSet` and inserting three rows into it using the same kind of code as in earlier examples. All these rows will now have a `RowState` property of `DataRowState.Added`, so call the `AcceptChanges` method to *fix* (accept) these changes – which updates the `RowState` property of all the rows to `DataRowState.Unchanged`.

Then, after displaying the contents of the table in the first `DataGrid` control, call the `Delete` method on the second row, and then display the contents again in the second `DataGrid` control. The `RowState` property of the deleted row is set to `DataRowState.Deleted` and it disappears from view. However, the next line of code calls the `RejectChanges` method of the table, and then displays the contents again in the third `DataGrid` control. The `RowState` property of the deleted row is set back to `DataRowState.Unchanged` and it reappears in the table.

```
'create a new empty Table object
Dim objTable As New DataTable("NewTable")
```

```
... fill table with three new rows using code here ...

'call AcceptChanges to accept the changes to the table so far
objTable.AcceptChanges()

'assign the DataTable's DefaultView object to the DataGrid control
dgrResult1.DataSource = objTable.DefaultView
dgrResult1.DataBind()  'and bind (display) the data

'now Delete the second row and display the contents again
objTable.Rows(1).Delete()
dgrResult2.DataSource = objTable.DefaultView
dgrResult2.DataBind()

'call RejectChanges to restore deleted row and display contents again
objTable.RejectChanges()
dgrResult3.DataSource = objTable.DefaultView
dgrResult3.DataBind()
```

Next, call the `Remove` method of the `Rows` collection of the table, specifying the second row as the one to be removed. Then display the contents of the table again in the fourth `DataGrid` control to show that it has been removed. Finally, call the `RejectChanges` method of the table and display the rows again in the final `DataGrid` control. However, this time, the row does not reappear. It has been permanently removed from the table and cannot be restored:

```
'now Remove the second row from the table
'note that this is a method of the Rows collection not the Row object
objTable.Rows.Remove(1)
dgrResult4.DataSource = objTable.DefaultView
dgrResult4.DataBind()

'call RejectChanges - the deleted row is not restored
objTable.RejectChanges()
dgrResult5.DataSource = objTable.DefaultView
dgrResult5.DataBind()
```

Working with DataTable Events

The `DataTable` object exposes a series of events that you can use to monitor changes to the content of a table in a `DataSet`. The `ColumnChanging` event is raised for a column in a row that is being edited, *before* the change is applied to that column (allowing the change to be cancelled). The `ColumnChanged` event is raised *after* the column has been changed and the change has been persisted to the column.

Some events occur for the row as a whole, rather than for each column in a row. The `RowChanging` and `RowChanged` events are raised when the content of any row in the table is changed – the first event occurring before the change is applied to the row (allowing the change to be cancelled) and the second event occurring after the change has been persisted in the table.

Finally, there are two events that occur when a row is deleted from a table. The `RowDeleting` event occurs before the row is deleted, allowing the deletion to be cancelled, and the `RowDeleted` event occurs

after the row has been deleted from the table. We don't have room to demonstrate all these events –
however, we will show you an example of how they can be used.

Using the RowUpdated Event

The Validating Edits in a Table with the RowUpdated Event example page (`update-check-errors.aspx`)
demonstrates how you can use the `RowUpdated` event of a `DataTable` object to validate the values that
are entered into each row. Code in this page fills a `DataSet` object with data from the sample database
and then changes the values in two rows. Then, as shown in Figure 9-14, it displays the changed rows in
a `DataGrid`.

At the bottom of the page, you can see that two errors have been reported. You placed an event handler
in the page that detects when a row is updated, and it applies a couple of simple validation rules to the
data in the row. Code in the page then checks the data for errors, and summarizes any it finds.

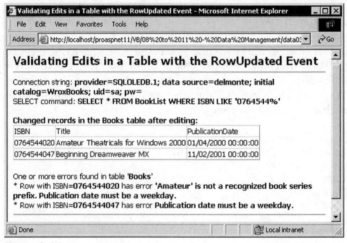

Figure 9-14

The Code for the Validating Edits Example

We've used the same techniques as most of the earlier examples to fill the `DataSet` with a `Books` table
that contains details of several books from the `WroxBooks` database. We won't repeat this code here.

After filling the `DataSet`, call the `AcceptChanges` method to *fix* the current contents. Then set up the
event handler you need to react to the `RowChanged` event. You can use the `AddHandler` method in
Visual Basic, specifying the event you want to react to and the name of the event handler
(`OnRowChanged`) that is defined elsewhere in the page. This event handler will be called when any row
is updated, after the changes have been applied to it.

In the event handler code, you can apply your validation rules. If the update is not valid, you need to be
able to flag this up, though not at this point. You want to be able to detect errors at some point in the
future, perhaps before you submit the `DataSet` back to the database to update the original data. Of
course, if you only wanted to flag up errors at the point when the users entered them, you could validate
the values in the page where they were entering the data:

```
'accept changes to "fix" current state of the DataSet contents
objDataSet.AcceptChanges()
'set up event handler to react to changes to rows in the table
Dim objTable As DataTable = objDataSet.Tables("Books")
AddHandler objTable.RowChanged, _
            New DataRowChangeEventHandler(AddressOf OnRowChanged)
```

This VB.NET code adds an event handler to the `DataTable`, using the `AddHandler` statement. However, in C#, you just append the event handler to the event property, as follows:

```
objTable.RowChanged += new DataRowChangeEventHandler(OnRowChanged);
```

Row Errors and DataRow Actions

Each `DataRow` object has a `RowError` property, which is basically just a `String` value. You can write an error message to this string property, and then later detect if there is an error in the row (and retrieve this error message). Thus, all your event handler has to do if it detects an invalid value is write this error message to the `RowError` property of the row that has just been updated.

The event handler receives a `DataRowChangeEventArgs` object that contains details of the row that is being updated. This includes a reference to the `DataRow` object that has changed, and the `Action` that is being taken on the row. The `Action` can be one of the `DataRowAction` enumeration values shown in the following table:

Value	Description
Add	The row has been added to the table
Change	One or more column values in the row have been changed
Delete	The row has been deleted from the table
Nothing	The row has not changed
Commit	The changes to the row have been committed as part of a database transaction
Rollback	The changes to the row have been abandoned following the rolling back of a database transaction

The OnRowChanged Event Handler

As you can see from the preceding table, the `RowChanged` event is actually raised in several circumstances, not just when values in a row are modified. Therefore, in the example page event handler, you need to ensure that you react only to the event when the `Action` is `DataRowAction.Change`. The following is the complete code for the event handler you use. You can see that the code applies two simple validation tests and sets the appropriate value(s) in the `RowError` property if either or both of the tests fail:

```
Sub OnRowChanged(objSender As Object, objArgs As DataRowChangeEventArgs)
   'only react if the action is "Change"
   If objArgs.Action = DataRowAction.Change Then
      'validate a new title
      If InStr(objArgs.Row("Title"), "Amateur") > 0 Then
         objArgs.Row.RowError &= "'Amateur' is not a recognized " _
                              & "book series prefix"
      End If
      'validate a new publication date
      If objArgs.Row("PublicationDate").DayOfWeek = 0 _
      Or objArgs.Row("PublicationDate").DayOfWeek = 6 Then
         objArgs.Row.RowError &= "Publication date must be a weekday"
      End If
   End If
End Sub
```

Back to the Page_Load Event Code

Having seen what happens if an edit produces an invalid value in the row, let's go back to where you were in the `Page_Load` event code that runs when the page is opened from the server. So far, you've created the `DataSet` and filled a table within it, and set up the event handler that will validate the values in the rows as they are edited.

So, as shown in the code that follows, the next step is to perform some edits. As these edits are applied to the rows, the `RowChanged` event is fired and the validation tests are carried out in your `OnRowChanged` event handler. The values being used will cause a validation error in both rows, and so the `RowError` property will be set to a text description of the error for these rows (notice that the error message is appended to any value that might already be there).

Next you can display the contents of the changed rows in the page using a `DataGrid` as before. To display just the changed rows, create a `DataView` based on the table and then set the `RowStateFilter` property of the `DataView` to `DataRowState.Modified` (data row states will be looked in detail later in this chapter and in the next chapter):

```
'change some records in the Books table
objTable.Rows(0)("Title") = "Amateur Theatricals for Windows 2000"
objTable.Rows(2)("PublicationDate") = "11-02-2001"

'declare a variable to hold a DataView object
Dim objDataView As DataView

'get DataView and set to show only modified rows
objDataView = objDataSet.Tables(0).DefaultView
objDataView.RowStateFilter = DataRowState.Modified

'display the contents of the modified rows
dgrResult.DataSource = objDataView
dgrResult.DataBind()
```

Checking for Invalid DataRows

Finally, you can check the data to see if any of the rows contain an error. Thankfully, you don't have to query the `RowError` property of every row in all the tables in a `DataSet` to find out if there actually are any errors. Both the `DataSet`, *and* each of the `DataTable` instances it contains, provide the `HasErrors` property, which is `True` if any row in that `DataSet` or `DataTable` has a non-empty value for its `RowError` property.

In the example page, as shown in the following code, first query the `HasErrors` property of the `DataSet` to see if there are any errors at all. If so, iterate through the `Tables` collection looking at the `HasErrors` property of each `DataTable` because you then know that one (or possibly more if there are several tables) contains a row that has an error.

Once the search is narrowed down to the appropriate table, iterate through each row checking if it contains an error. You can use the `HasErrors` property of each row here, which is much faster than comparing the string value of the `RowError` with an empty string. When you find a row with an error, add the value of the `RowError` property to the output message string. And having completed this table, go round and look for the next table that contains errors:

```
Dim strResult As String = ""  'to hold the result
    'see if there are any update errors anywhere in the DataSet
If objDataSet.HasErrors Then
    'check for errors in each table
  Dim objThisTable As DataTable
  For Each objThisTable In objDataSet.Tables
    If objThisTable.HasErrors Then
      strResult &= "One or more errors found in table '" _
              & objThisTable.TableName & "'<br />"
      'check each row in this table for errors
      Dim objThisRow As DataRow
      For Each objThisRow In objThisTable.Rows
        If objThisRow.HasErrors Then
          strResult &= "* Row with ISBN=" & objThisRow("ISBN") _
                & " has error " & objThisRow.RowError & "<br />"
        End If
      Next 'row
    End If
  Next 'table
End If
outResult.InnerHtml = strResult   'display the result
```

After extracting all the error messages, display them in a `<div>` at the bottom of the page. Figure 9-15 shows just this section of the page again so that you can see the results:

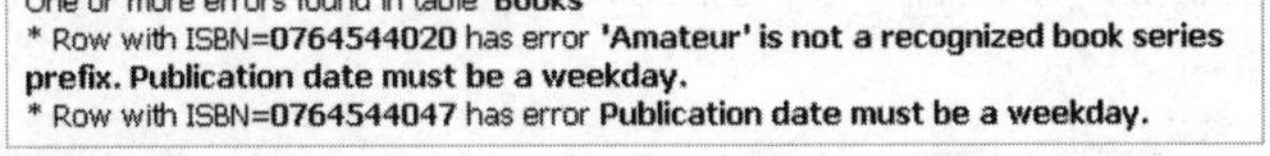

> One or more errors found in table **'Books'**
> * Row with ISBN=**0764544020** has error **'Amateur' is not a recognized book series prefix. Publication date must be a weekday.**
> * Row with ISBN=**0764544047** has error **Publication date must be a weekday.**

Figure 9-15

An alternative approach is to use the GetErrors method of each DataTable object to get an array of all the rows in that table that contain an error. This is also somewhat more efficient if there is only a small percentage of the total number of rows where an error has occurred.

The DataTable events you've seen here are very useful for validating data when you have a remoted DataSet object. There are also similar events that are raised by the DataAdapter object when you update the original data source from your DataSet. We'll look at these in the next chapter.

Using Table and Column Mappings

The next topic to consider when working with DataSet and DataTable objects is how to specify custom mappings for columns and tables. When you fill a table in a DataSet from a data source such as a relational database, you specify the name of the table within the database as the (optional) second parameter of the DataAdapter object's Fill method. For example, in this code the table is named Books:

```
objDataAdapter.Fill(objDataSet, "Books")
```

However, in this case you have no direct control over the names of the *columns* in the newly filled table. They automatically adopt the names of the columns returned by the stored procedure, table name, or SQL statement that fills the table. One way round this is to specify the column names within the SQL statement or stored procedure. For example, in a SQL statement, you can change the column names as follows:

```
SELECT ISBN AS BookCode, Title AS BookTitle, PublicationDate AS Published
FROM BookList WHERE ISBN LIKE '18610053%'
```

Now the data set returned by the SQL statement will have the new name (or alias) for each of the columns, and these will be used for the table's column names within your DataSet. Figure 9-16 shows the results viewed in SQL Server's *Query Analyser* tool:

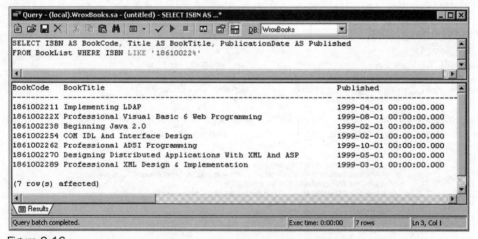

Figure 9-16

However, it's convenient to be able to specify the names of both the tables and the columns within the DataSet independently. That way, you can create reusable code that automatically maps data to the correct column and table names. It also allows you to push the changes to the data *back* into the database by simply calling the Update method – something you wouldn't be able to do if you renamed the columns in the SQL statement or stored procedure.

The Using Default and Specific Table and Column Mappings example page (table-mappings.aspx) demonstrates how you can use table and column mappings to manage the *connection* between the original table and its column names in the database with the table and column names in the DataSet. The result of running this page is shown in Figure 9-17:

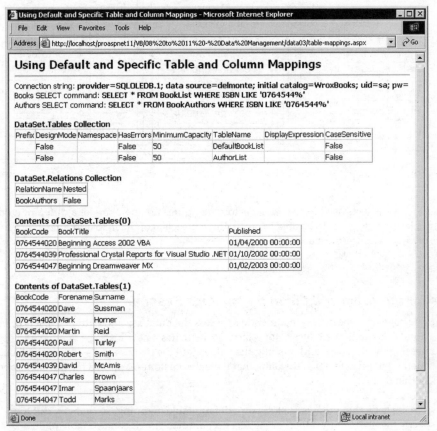

Figure 9-17

The code and data used to build the DataSet shown in Figure 9-17 is the same as in many of the examples earlier in this chapter. However, the names of the tables and the columns in each table are different from the ones you got in the earlier examples. All these are defined as custom mappings, and the conversion from the default to the custom name is automatically applied when you load the data.

All the mappings for both table names and column names are stored in the `DataAdapter` object that is used to fill the `DataSet`. This means that you can create multiple `DataAdapter` objects for a `DataSet` object with different mappings, and use the one that meets the requirements of the current task.

Figure 9-18 shows the way that the `DataAdapter` uses a `TableMappings` collection to store individual mappings between tables (`TableMapping` instances). Also, each `TableMapping` contains a collection of `ColumnMapping` instances that define the aliases relevant to that table:

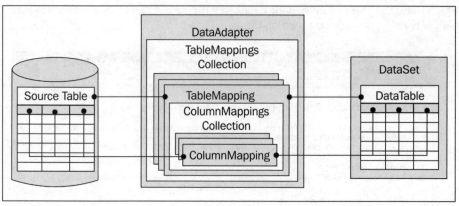

Figure 9-18

Note that the two objects used for creating custom mappings are members of a different namespace than the other objects used so far. To be able to create these objects, you have to add a reference to the `System.Data.Common` namespace to your page:

```
<%@Import Namespace="System.Data.Common" %>
```

The Code for the Table and Column Mappings Example

The example page uses the now familiar code to access the database and extract subsets of rows from the `BookList` and `BookAuthors` tables. Along the way, it creates a new instance of a `DataAdapter` object to use for accessing the database and pushing the values into the `DataSet`. It's at this point, before calling the `Fill` method to actually fetch the data, that it creates custom mappings for the tables and the columns within them.

As shown in the code that follows, you create a default table mapping, so that any call to `Fill` that doesn't specify the name of the table (in the second parameter) will create a table named `DefaultBookList`. First declare a variable to hold a `DataTableMapping` object, and then call the `Add` method of the `DataAdapter` object's `TableMappings` collection.

The `Add` method takes two parameters: the name of the source table that will be specified in the `Fill` method, and the name to use for the new table in the `DataSet` instead of the source tablename. For a default mapping, use the value `"Table"` for the first parameter.

> *The names used in the mappings are case-sensitive for the `OleDb`-prefixed and `Odbc`-prefixed objects, but not for the `Sql`-prefixed objects.*

```
'create a new DataAdapter object
Dim objDataAdapter As New OleDbDataAdapter()

'declare a variable to hold a DataTableMapping object
Dim objTableMapping As DataTableMapping

'add the default table mapping "Table" - this table name will be used
'if you don't provide a table name when filling the DataSet
objTableMapping = objDataAdapter.TableMappings.Add("Table", "DefaultBookList")
```

Specifying the Column Mappings

Once you've created the `TableMapping` object, its `ColumnMappings` collection can be accessed to create the column mappings. The simplest syntax is to use the `With` construct, as shown in the following code. You can call the `Add` method of the `ColumnMappings` collection to create each column mapping, specifying the name of the column in the data source and the name you want that column to have in the table within the `DataSet`.

You can then do the same to create the custom mappings for the `AuthorList` table. There's already a default table mapping (using the value `Table`), so you can only create specific table mappings now. First specify that a table in the data source named `BookAuthors` will create a table in the `DataSet` named `AuthorList`, and then finish up by specifying the column mappings from the source `Authors` database table to the new `AuthorList` table in the `DataSet`:

```
     'now add the column mappings for this table
With objTableMapping.ColumnMappings
   .Add("ISBN", "BookCode")
   .Add("Title", "BookTitle")
   .Add("PublicationDate", "Published")
End With
     'add a table mapping so that data from the table named "BookAuthors" in
     'the database will be placed in a table named "AuthorList"
objTableMapping = objDataAdapter.TableMappings.Add("BookAuthors", _
     "AuthorList")
     'add the column mappings for this table
With objTableMapping.ColumnMappings
   .Add("ISBN", "BookCode")
   .Add("FirstName", "Forename")
   .Add("LastName", "Surname")
End With
```

Using the Column Mappings

One point to be aware of is that the mapped table and column names are now the ones that must be used for all operations with the `DataSet` and its contents. When you create a relationship between the tables, for example, use the mapped tablenames as shown in the following code:

```
'create a Relation object to link the two tables
'note that it uses the new mapped table and column names
objRelation = New DataRelation("BookAuthors", _
             objDataSet.Tables("DefaultBookList").Columns("BookCode"), _
             objDataSet.Tables("AuthorList").Columns("BookCode"))
```

The same applies, of course, when you access tables and columns in the `DataSet` in code. The only other issue is that you must be sure to specify the same table and column mappings in the `DataAdapter` that you use when you come to update the original data source. If not, the `DataAdapter` will not be able to associate the tables and columns in the `DataSet` with the ones in the source data store or database. You'll see how all this works in the next chapter.

Sorting and Filtering Data

Let's look at one more topic concerned with `DataTable` and `DataView` objects. Once you've loaded a `DataTable` or a `DataView` object with data, you wouldn't really want to go back to the data store and reload it every time you want to sort the rows into a different order, or filter the rows so that only a subset is displayed. Thankfully, both the `DataTable` and `DataView` provide sorting and filtering features, even if the way they work is fundamentally different for each object. We'll look at both next.

Sorting and Filtering in a DataTable

The Sorting and Filtering in a DataTable Object example page (`select-in-table.aspx`) demonstrates how you can sort and filter data that is stored in a `DataTable` object. For example, in Figure 9-19, we've loaded the page and then clicked the By Date button to sort the rows into order by the values in the `PublicationDate` column and then by the values in the `Title` column. You can see from the message in the page that your code executed the `Select` method of the `DataTable` object with two parameters: an empty string, and a string containing the two column names for the sort operation:

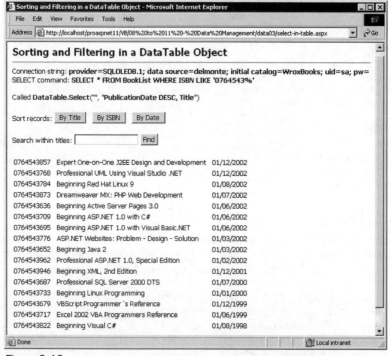

Figure 9-19

Figure 9-20 demonstrates how the page also provides a *Search* feature. We've entered ASP into the textbox and clicked the Find button to give the result shown. The `DataTable.Select` method was executed again, and this time the first parameter is the expression `Title LIKE '*ASP*'`, while the second is an empty string. Only the rows containing `ASP` anywhere within the `Title` column appear in the page.

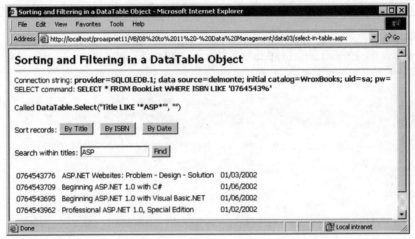

Figure 9-20

In the example page, you'll notice that code is recreating the `DataSet` and its content each time you change the sort order or perform a search. This is only because you don't persist the data elsewhere between requests.

If you remote the `DataSet` to another tier of your application, or receive it from something like a web service, you do not need to recreate it each time. Instead, simply execute the `Select` method on the table within your cached `DataSet` object.

The DataTable.Select Method

It's clear from the example that the `DataTable` object's `Select` method takes two parameters – an expression that filters the rows and a list of column names by which the rows are sorted:

```
DataTable.Select(filter-expression, sort-order)
```

The example page only uses *one* of these parameters at a time, but you can use both together:

```
objDataTable.Select("Title LIKE '*ASP*'", "PublicationDate DESC, Title")
```

Notice that the syntax for the sorting parameter is the same as for most other data access techniques – you add `DESC` to force reverse sort order. There is a second overload of this method that only accepts a parameter for the fiter expression, so you can use the following code if you want to filter the rows but don't want to sort them:

```
DataTable.Select("Title LIKE '*ASP*'")
```

Specifying the DataRowState

There is also an overload of the `Select` method that accepts a third parameter. This is used to specify the `DataViewRowState` of the rows that will be included. By using the value of each row's `RowState` property, this allows you to include *all* rows, or select only rows that are unchanged, new, modified, or deleted. For example, the following code will only include rows that have not been changed or deleted:

```
DataTable.Select("Title LIKE '*ASP*'", "Title", DataViewRowState.Unchanged)
```

The default for this parameter, if you don't specify a different value, is `DataViewRowState.None`, and the result reflects the current state of all the rows in the table. The full set of values for the `DataViewRowState` enumeration is shown in the following table:

Value	Description
CurrentRows	Includes unchanged, new, and modified rows
OriginalRows	Includes only unchanged and deleted rows
ModifiedCurrent	Includes the current values of any modified rows
ModifiedOriginal	Includes the original values of any modified rows
Unchanged	Includes only unchanged rows
Added	Includes only new rows added to the table
Deleted	Includes only deleted rows
None	No filtering on the `RowState` of the rows is applied

The Filter Expression Syntax

In general, the expression syntax used in the first parameter of the `Select` method is much as you'd expect – following the expression syntax of the .NET languages. For example:

Simple *comparison expressions* are:

```
"Lastname = 'Jones'"            'string literals in single quotes
"StockQty > 1000"               'numbers are not in quotes
"PublicationDate > #10/10/99#"  'special syntax for date/time
```

The supported comparison operators are: <, >, <=, >=, <>, =, IN, and LIKE.

For numeric column values, the operators that can be used are: +, -, *, /, % (modulus).

String concatenation is always with the '+' character. Case-sensitivity during string comparisons depends on the current setting of the parent `DataSet` object's `CaseSensitive` property. This property value can be changed in code as required.

The LIKE operator supports *wildcards for string comparisons*. The '*' or '%' character (these characters are equivalent) can be used to represent any series of characters, and can be used at the start, at the end, or at both the start and end of other literal text. They cannot be used within the text of a search string:

```
"Lastname LIKE 'Peter%'"    is the same as    "Lastname LIKE 'Peter*'"
"Lastname LIKE '%Peter'"    is the same as    "Lastname LIKE '*Peter'"
"Lastname LIKE '%Peter%'"   is the same as    "Lastname LIKE '*Peter*'"
```

To include the wildcards where they are part of the literal text in the search string, they must be escaped with a preceding backslash:

```
"WebWord LIKE '\*BOLD\*'"     'filters on the string "*BOLD*"
```

The AND, OR, and NOT operators are supported, with AND having precedence unless you use parentheses to force a different evaluation order:

```
"Title LIKE '*ASP*' AND StockQty > 1000"
"(LastName = 'Smith' OR LastName = 'Jones') AND FirstName = 'John'"
```

The following characters cannot be used directly in a column name within a filter expression:

```
~ ( ) # \ / = > < + - * % & | ^ ' " [ ]
```

If a column name contains one of these characters or a space, it must be enclosed in square brackets:

```
"[Stock#] > 1000"        'column named "Stock#"
```

If a column name contains a closing square bracket, this must be escaped with a preceding backslash:

```
"[Number[\]Cols] > 1000"       'column named "Number[]Cols"
```

There is also a range of *functions* supported in filter expressions, including:

```
Sum, Avg, Min, Max, Count, StDev, Var, Convert, Len, IsNull, IIF, SubString
```

The Code for the DataTable Sorting and Filtering Example

Look at the code for the example page you saw a little earlier. The HTML section of the page, shown in the following code, contains a `<form>` that holds the command buttons and textbox for the filter expression and this is followed by a `<div>` where the results are displayed:

```
<form runat="server">
Sort records:
  <input type="submit" id="cmdTitle" value="By Title" runat="server" />  
  <input type="submit" id="cmdISBN" value="By ISBN" runat="server" />  
  <input type="submit" id="cmdDate" value="By Date" runat="server" /><p />
Search within titles:
  <input type="text" id="txtFind" size="20" runat="server" />
  <input type="submit" id="cmdFind" value="Find" runat="server" />
</form>
<div id="outResult" runat="server"></div>
```

The code that makes it work is in the Page_Load event handler of the page. It first collects a subset of rows from the original data store – the example WroxBooks database – and places them in a table named Books within a DataSet. This table contains all the books you saw in Figure 9-19.

Then, as shown in the code that follows, you can create the filter *and* sort expressions based on the details provided by the user. In the case of a filter expression, you can add a preceding and trailing asterisk wildcard character so that it will match column values containing this text.

If this is the first time that the page has been loaded, there will be no values from the <form> in the request, and so no filter or sort expression will be created. Otherwise, after the previous code is executed, you'll have a non-empty value in either the strSortString or strFilterExpr string.

The values of these two strings are displayed in another <div> element placed before the <form> section of the page:

```
'create the Sorting expression

Dim strSortString As String = ""
If Len(Request.Form("cmdTitle")) > 0 Then strSortString = "Title"
If Len(Request.Form("cmdISBN")) > 0  Then strSortString = "ISBN"
If Len(Request.Form("cmdDate")) > 0  Then strSortString = _
                                     "PublicationDate DESC, Title"


'or create the Filter expression

Dim strFilterExpr As String = ""
If Len(Request.Form("cmdFind")) > 0 Then
    strFilterExpr = "Title LIKE '*" & txtFind.Value & "*'"
End If


'display the parameters we're using

outMessage.innerHTML = "Called DataTable.Select(""" & strFilterExpr _
                & """, """ & strSortString & """)"
```

Executing the Select Method

Finally, you can apply the filter or sort to the table. As shown in the following code, you first get a reference to the DataTable object. The Select method returns an array of DataRow objects that match the applied filter and sort, so the next step is to create a suitable array variable. Then you can execute the Select method and assign the result to this variable ready for display:

```
Dim objTable As DataTable = objDataSet.Tables("Books")

'create an array to hold the results then call the Select method

Dim objResults() As DataRow
objResults = objTable.Select(strFilterExpr, strSortString)
```

Displaying the Results

To display the results, you have to iterate through the array of `DataRow` objects that is returned by the `Select` method – you can't just bind it to a `DataGrid` as in earlier examples. The following code shows how you build an HTML table containing the column values for each `DataRow` in the array and then display this table in the `<div>` element named `outResult`:

```
'the result is an array of DataRow objects not a DataTable object

'so we have to iterate through to get the row contents

Dim objRow As DataRow
Dim strResult As String = "<table>"
For Each objRow In objResults
    strResult &= "<tr><td>" & objRow(0) & "</td><td>  " & objRow(1) _
            & "</td><td>  " & objRow(2) & "</td></tr>"

Next
strResult &= "</table>"
outResult.InnerHtml = strResult    'and display the results
```

Sorting and Filtering in a DataView Object

Another opportunity for sorting and filtering rows for display is within a `DataView` object. It's common to create a `DataView` based on a `DataTable` when using server-side data binding; you've been doing this throughout these chapters with a `DataGrid` server control.

The example page **Sorting and Filtering Records in a DataView object** (`sort-find-in-dataview.aspx`) demonstrates how easy it is to sort and filter the rows in a `DataView`.

This example page looks similar to the previous one (sorting and filtering a `DataTable`). However, rather than using a `Select` method (like was done with the `DataTable`), specify the filter and sort order for a `DataView` by setting its properties. Set the `Sort` property to change the sorting order of the rows, and the `RowFilter` property to apply a filter.

Figure 9-21 shows the rows being sorted. Notice the code that has been executed after clicking the **By Date** button this time. You can simply assign the column names (and optionally the `DESC` keyword) to the `Sort` property of the `DataView`.

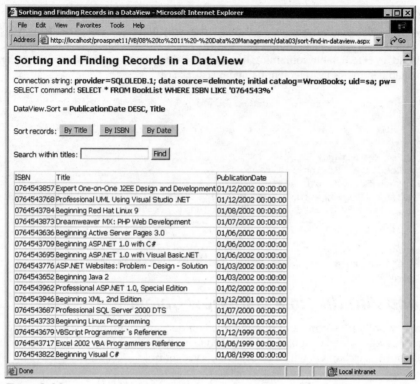

Figure 9-21

Meanwhile, as shown in Figure 9-22, the result of entering the search text **ASP** and clicking the Find button is to set the `RowFilter` property of the `DataView`:

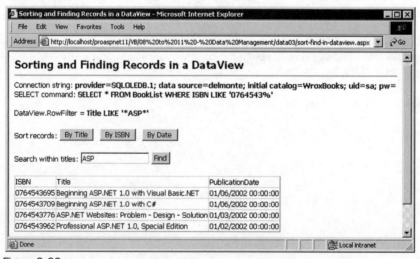

Figure 9-22

As you saw earlier in the example of using the RowUpdated *event, the* DataView *object also has a* RowStateFilter *property. This works just the same as with the* DataTable *object, and you can also use this to filter the rows.*

The Code for the DataView Sorting and Filtering Example

As you'll expect, most of the code for this example is the same as that used in the previous example. It uses the same HTML form and the same code to create and fill a DataSet with some book details. However, the next step is to get a reference to the DataView object that you'll be working with. Create a new DataView based on the Books table in the DataSet:

```
'create a DataView object for the Books table in the DataSet
Dim objDataView As New DataView(objDataSet.Tables("Books"))
```

Of course, if you already have a DataTable object available, perhaps as the result of some other code you've used to create it specifically, you can simply access the DefaultView property of the table to get back a DataView object.

Collecting the User's Values and Applying the Sort and Filter

Now you can check for user input and build the appropriate string for the Sort and RowFilter properties of the DataView, as shown in the following code. If the user clicked a 'sort' button, you can simply build the sort expression as one or more column names (including DESC for a descending sort order) and set the Sort property of the DataView object.

Following a postback where the user clicked the Find button, the code in the page builds a filter expression (using the same syntax as the previous example), and assigns it to the RowFilter property of the DataView object. As in the previous example, a preceding and trailing asterisk wildcard character is added so that it will match column values containing this text. The expression used is also displayed in the page. Finally, the sorted or filtered DataView object is assigned to the DataSource property of an ASP.NET DataGrid control declared elsewhere in the page to display the contents:

```
'sort the records into the correct order
If Len(Request.Form("cmdTitle")) > 0 Then
    objDataView.Sort = "Title"
    outMessage.innerHTML = "DataView.Sort = " & objDataView.Sort
End If
If Len(Request.Form("cmdISBN")) > 0 Then
    objDataView.Sort = "ISBN"
    outMessage.innerHTML = "DataView.Sort = " & objDataView.Sort
End If
If Len(Request.Form("cmdDate")) > 0 Then
    objDataView.Sort = "PublicationDate DESC, Title"
    outMessage.innerHTML = "DataView.Sort = " & objDataView.Sort
End If
'or find matching records
If Len(Request.Form("cmdFind")) > 0 Then
    objDataView.RowFilter = "Title LIKE '*" & txtFind.value & "*'"
    outMessage.innerHTML = "DataView.RowFilter = " & objDataView.RowFilter
End If
'assign the DataView object to the DataGrid control
dgrResult.DataSource = objDataView
dgrResult.DataBind()  'and bind (display) the data
```

Summary

This chapter addressed all the important topics regarding working with data within the three fundamental .NET data access objects – the `DataReader`, the `DataTable`, and the `DataSet` objects. You've seen how you can extract data from a data store using complex SQL statements and different types of stored procedures. You've also seen how to build `DataSet` and `DataTable` objects from scratch using code, and then set a range of properties on each data column to accurately specify their behavior.

Then you saw how you can add, delete, edit, and completely remove rows in a table. We examined the various properties that indicate the state of each row and each column in that row, and saw how to cancel changes to a row, a table, and a complete `DataSet` object.

Finally, you looked at a couple of ways to filter and sort data – in a `DataTable` object and in a `DataView` object.

Now that you are comfortable with the way that .NET data access works, as well as the fundamental objects, their common properties and methods, it's time to look at the final major relational data topic. How do you go about updating the original data in your database or other data store? This is the core topic of the next chapter.

10

Updating Relational Data Sources

In the previous two chapters, we explored how to use the major objects within the .NET Framework for relational data access. This includes the `DataReader`, `Connection`, `Command`, `DataAdapter`, `DataTable`, and `DataSet` objects. We also explored the use of subsidiary objects such as the `DataRelation`, `DataRow`, `Parameter`, and others. You've seen how to use these objects in a range of combinations to extract data from a relational data store and work with that data.

The techniques demonstrated included examination of the ways you can update the data that is held within the confines of the disconnected `DataSet` objects that you created. What you haven't looked at is how you can perform that final step required in any application used fundamentally for updating a data store—how to push your changes back into the data store.

Even in a connected environment, such as a traditional client-server application, the process of managing updates to the source data is not without its own problems, in particular the managing of concurrent updates to the source data. While .NET does not introduce any new problems, the concept of working with data in a fundamentally disconnected way (such as .NET provides) means that you need to be fully aware of the issues and know how to handle them. This is the core topic of this chapter. You will look at:

❑ Updating data sources with a `Command` object

❑ Using transactions when updating data sources

❑ Updating data sources from a `DataSet` object

❑ A detailed look inside the `DataAdapter Update` method

❑ Managing concurrent updates to a data source

Obtaining the Sample Files

All the examples used in this chapter are available for you to run on your own server, in both VB.NET and C# versions. The download files can be obtained from http://www.daveandal.net/books/8900/, and include SQL scripts and instructions for creating the database that the examples use. You can also run these examples online at the same URL.

The main menu page for the data management chapter examples, shown in Chapter 8, contains links to all the sample files. The fourth link in that page, Updating Relational Data Sources in .NET leads to another menu page (shown in Figure 10-1) that contains links to all the examples for this chapter.

Figure 10-1

Updating Data with a Command Object

Traditionally, for simple single or multiple row updates to a data store, an ADO `Connection` or `Command` object with a SQL statement or a stored procedure is used. This technique is particularly useful for tasks like inserting a new row into a database, perhaps in response to a user submitting feedback to your web site or registering for a monthly email bulletin. It's also useful for the equivalent 'delete' operation to remove one or more rows, or for updating row values.

Under the .NET Framework, you can do the same thing using one of the new `Command` objects. The `SqlCommand` object is used only with Microsoft SQL Server (via TDS), while the `OleDbCommand` object can be used for any type of data store for which an OLEDB provider is available. Other `Command` objects specially designed for use with ODBC and Oracle databases are also provided with the framework, as discussed in Chapter 8.

We have provided two pages that demonstrate data updates using a `Command` object—one that uses a SQL `UPDATE` statement to modify a row in the database, and one that uses a stored procedure within the database to add a new row or delete an existing row. Like all the examples, they develop on the techniques covered in the previous data access chapters, and so we'll be concentrating on the new features that the examples introduce, and the code that implements these features.

Using a Command Object with a SQL Statement

The simplest way to perform a quick update to a data source is to create a suitable SQL statement and then execute it against that data source using a `Command` object. The example page Updating Data with a Command Object (`update-with-command.aspx`) shown in Figure 10-2 does just that. When you open the page, code in the `Page_Load` event handler creates a SQL `UPDATE` statement that changes the title of a book with a specified ISBN code in your `BookList` table.

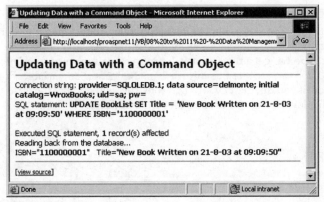

Figure 10-2

Remember that all the example pages have a [view source] link you can use to view the sourcecode of the page.

The SQL statement used is visible in the screenshot, and you can see that one row was affected by the execution of that statement. The code in the page then uses a `DataReader` object with the same connection to read back the newly updated row from the source table and display the values.

The Code for the SQL Statement Update Example

As with most of the examples in previous chapters, the pages in this chapter use a database named `WroxBooks`, and one of the connection strings defined in the `web.config` file in the root folder of the samples.

Remember to edit the `web.config` file to suit your own setup (as demonstrated in Chapter 8) before running the samples on your own server.

The first section of code shows how to create the SQL statement that will update the book title. As shown in the following code, the current date and time in the title is included so that it changes every time you run the page. After displaying the SQL statement in a `<div>` element named `outSQL` (elsewhere in the page), you can create a new `Connection` object using your previously obtained connection string. Then specify this `Connection` and your SQL statement in the constructor for a new `Command` object. Also declare an `Integer` variable to hold the number of rows that are updated.

```
        'specify the SQL statement to update the data
Dim datNow As DateTime = Now()
Dim strNow As String = datNow.ToString("dd-M-yy \a\t hh:mm:ss")
Dim strSQL As String
strSQL = "UPDATE BookList SET Title = 'New Book Written on " _
        & strNow & "' WHERE ISBN='1100000001'"
outSQL.InnerText = strSQL    'and display it
        'create Connection and Command
Dim objConnect As New OleDbConnection(strConnect)
Dim objCommand As New OleDbCommand(strSQL, objConnect)
Dim intRowsAffected As Integer  'to hold number of rows affected by update
```

Executing the SQL Statement

Now you can execute the `Command`, as shown in the following code. Open the connection to the database, and then call the `ExecuteNonQuery` method of the `Command` object. This method is used whenever you don't expect to get a rowset back. It returns the number of rows affected by the execution of the statement, and you can capture this in your `intRowsAffected` variable. Provided that you didn't get an execution error (if you do, the `Try..Catch` construct will display the error and stop execution of the code), you can display the number of rows that were updated.

```
Try
    'execute the command
  objConnect.Open()
  intRowsAffected = objCommand.ExecuteNonQuery()
Catch objError As Exception
    'display error details
  outError.InnerHtml = "* Error while updating original data.<br />" _
                    & objError.Message & "<br />" & objError.Source
  Exit Sub  ' and stop execution
End Try
    'declare string to display results and show number of rows affected
Dim strResult As String
strResult = "Executed SQL statement, " & intRowsAffected.ToString() _
        & " record(s) affected<br />Reading back from the database..."
```

Displaying the Updated Row

Now you can read the updated row back from the database to prove that the process worked. The following code shows how to create a suitable SQL `SELECT` statement and assign it to the `CommandText` property of your existing `Command` object. Then declare a variable to hold a `DataReader` object, and execute the `SELECT` statement. The result is obtained by reading the rows returned by the `DataReader` (this technique was demonstrated several times in previous chapters). Finally, display the contents of the updated row that you captured in the 'result' string in another `<div>` element named `outResult`.

```
objCommand.CommandText = "SELECT * FROM BookList WHERE ISBN='1100000001'"
Try
    Dim objDataReader As OleDbDataReader
    objDataReader = objCommand.ExecuteReader()
    Do While objDataReader.Read()
        strResult &= "ISBN=""" & objDataReader("ISBN") _
                & """   Title=""" & objDataReader("Title") & """"
    Loop
```

```
      objDataReader.Close()
      objConnect.Close()
   Catch objError As Exception
      'display error details
      outError.InnerHtml = "* Error while accessing updated data.<br />" _
                       & objError.Message & "<br />" & objError.Source
      Exit Sub  ' and stop execution
   End Try
   outResult.InnerHtml = strResult  'display the result
```

So, using a SQL statement and Command object to modify the contents of a data store is very similar to the way you would have carried out the operation in previous versions of ADO. And you can use INSERT and DELETE statements in exactly the same way as the UPDATE statement in this example.

However, it's often preferable to use a stored procedure defined within the data store to perform data updates. Stored procedures can provide a useful increase in performance, hide the structure of a database table from inquisitive users, and allow finer control over security permissions. The next example demonstrates how you can use a technique similar to the preceding technique that we saw (that is with a stored procedure instead of a SQL statement).

Using a Stored Procedure with a Command Object

Using a stored procedure with a Command object is a fundamentally similar process to using a SQL statement, as mentioned in the previous chapter when data was extracted from a data store. The example Updating Data with a Stored Procedure (update-with-storedproc.aspx) shown in Figure 10-3 demonstrates how you can use a Command object to execute a stored procedure that updates the source data.

The stored procedure named AddNewBook is created within the WroxBooks database by the SQL script we provide in the samples. It inserts a new row into the BookList table using values provided in parameters to the stored procedure, and returns zero (0) if it succeeds in inserting the new row.

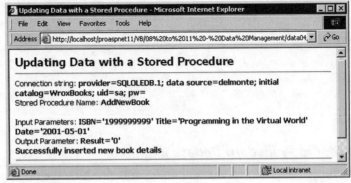

Figure 10-3

However, to make the process repeatable when you are experimenting with the samples, we've added a rather unusual twist to the procedure (one which is unlikely to be found in a real-world application). If this were not done, you would only be able to run the procedure once unless you manually deleted the row in the database, or edited the procedure to insert a different row.

As you can see from Figure 10-4, the procedure first checks to see if a book with the specified ISBN (the primary key of the table) already exists. If it does exist, it deletes this row from the table instead–and returns minus one (-1) as the result. This way, you can run the page as many times as you wish.

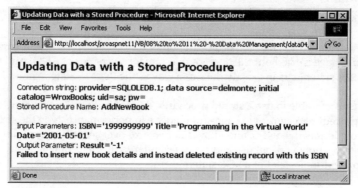

Figure 10-4

The AddNewBook Stored Procedure

The stored procedure for this example takes as input parameters the ISBN code, title, and publication date of the book to be inserted, and it has a fourth `Integer`-type output parameter to hold the result:

```
CREATE PROCEDURE AddNewBook
    @ISBN varchar(12), @Title varchar(100), @Date datetime,
    @Result integer output AS
SELECT ISBN FROM BookList WHERE ISBN=@ISBN
IF @@ROWCOUNT = 0
  BEGIN
    INSERT INTO BookList(ISBN, Title, PublicationDate)
          VALUES (@ISBN, @Title, @Date)
    SELECT @Result = 0
  END
ELSE
  BEGIN
    DELETE FROM BookList WHERE ISBN=@ISBN
    SELECT @Result = -1
  END
```

The Code for the Stored Procedure Update Example

In this example you're executing a stored procedure, so your command text is just the name of the stored procedure–`AddNewBook`–as shown in the following code. You can start by specifying this and displaying it in the page. Then create your connection and command objects as before. However, for maximum execution efficiency, you need to specify this time that the command text is the name of a stored procedure.

```
'specify the stored procedure name
Dim strSQL As String = "AddNewBook"
outSQL.InnerText = strSQL    'and display it

Dim objConnect As New OleDbConnection(strConnect)
Dim objCommand As New OleDbCommand(strSQL, objConnect)
objCommand.CommandType = CommandType.StoredProcedure
```

Creating the Parameters

Next create the parameters you'll need within the `Parameters` collection of the `Command` object. The first is for the ISBN code and is of type `OleDbType.VarChar` and length `12` characters. Also specify that it's an input parameter, and set the value.

The process is repeated for the next two input parameters, the book title and publication date. Note that the publication date parameter (named `Date`) is of type `OleDbType.DBDate`, and you have to specify the value in a format that corresponds to the column in the database. In the case of a SQL `datetime` column, the format `"yyyy-mm-dd"` will work.

The final parameter is named `Result`, and is an output parameter that will return the result of executing the stored procedure. It returns an integer value, and so you can specify `OleDbType.Integer` in this case. Finally, before executing the stored procedure, display the input parameter values in the page within a `<div>` element named `outInParams`. You can read their current values directly from the `Parameters` collection by specifying the name of each one.

```
'create a variable to hold a Parameter object
Dim objParam As OleDbParameter

'create a new Parameter object named 'ISBN' with the correct data
'type to match a SQL database 'varchar' field of 12 characters
objParam = objCommand.Parameters.Add("ISBN", OleDbType.VarChar, 12)

'specify that it's an Input parameter and set the value
objParam.Direction = ParameterDirection.Input
objParam.Value = "1999999999"

'create a new Parameter object named 'Title' with the correct data
'type to match a SQL database 'varchar' field of 50 characters
'specify that it's an Input parameter and set the value
objParam = objCommand.Parameters.Add("Title", OleDbType.VarChar, 50)
objParam.Direction = ParameterDirection.Input
objParam.Value = "Programming in the Virtual World"

'create another input Parameter object named 'Date' with the correct
'data type to match a SQL database 'datetime' field
'specify that it's an Input parameter and set the value
objParam = objCommand.Parameters.Add("Date", OleDbType.DBDate)
objParam.Direction = ParameterDirection.Input
objParam.Value = "2001-05-01"

'create an output Parameter object named 'Result' with the correct
'data type to match a SQL database 'integer' field
'specify that it's an Output parameter so no value required
```

```
objParam = objCommand.Parameters.Add("Result", OleDbType.Integer)
objParam.Direction = ParameterDirection.Output

'display the value of the input parameters
outInParams.InnerText = "ISBN='" & objCommand.Parameters("ISBN").Value _
            & "' Title='" & objCommand.Parameters("Title").Value _
            & "' Date='" & objCommand.Parameters("Date").Value & "'"
```

Many of the data access examples you'll see here and in later chapters use parameter names that are not prefixed by the @ symbol when adding parameters to the `ParametersCollection`. This works fine when using the OleDb data access classes, because parameters are passed by position and not by name (as was the default with ADO prior to ADO.NET). In fact, any name can be used for the parameters – the names don't have to match the parameter names in the stored procedure. However, if you use the `SqlClient` classes, the parameters are passed by name, and so all parameter names must be prefixed by @ in this case.

Executing the Stored Procedure

The next step is to execute the stored procedure. In this case, you don't have any returned value for the number of rows affected, so you don't need to capture the result of the `ExecuteNonQuery` method. Once the stored procedure has been executed, the parameter named `Result` will contain the result of the process and you can collect its value from the `Parameters` collection of the `Command` object. The value is displayed – plus an accompanying explanation message – in a `<div>` element named `outOutParams` within the page.

```
Try
  'execute the stored procedure
  objConnect.Open()
  objCommand.ExecuteNonQuery()
  objConnect.Close()
Catch objError As Exception
  outError.InnerHtml = "* Error while updating original data.<br />" _
                  & objError.Message & "<br />" & objError.Source
  Exit Sub
End Try
'collect and display the value of the output parameter
Dim intResult As Integer = objCommand.Parameters("Result").Value
Dim strResult As String = "Result='" & CStr(intResult) & "'<br />"
If intResult = 0 Then
  strResult &= "Successfully inserted new book details"
Else
  strResult &= "Failed to insert new book details and instead " _
          & "deleted existing record with this ISBN"
End If
outOutParams.InnerHtml = strResult
```

Updating Data Sources with Transactions

One of the features of most database systems, and some other types of data store, is the ability to use *transactions*. Simply put, a transaction is a series of events that are all completed, or of which none are completed–there is never an intermediate result where some but not all of the events within the transaction occur.

The name transaction comes from real-world scenarios such as purchasing an item in a store where you give the seller money in exchange for goods. Unless one of you gets cheated, the transaction will either succeed with both parties happy at the outcome (you pay your money and get your goods), or fail where neither action occurs. There should never be an outcome where you pay money and don't get the goods, or where you get goods but don't pay the money.

In this section, you'll look at two types of transactions:

❑ **Database transactions**, where database-specific statements control the transaction and it is carried out within the database itself. Usually the stored procedure within the database contains the transaction statements.

❑ **Connection-based transactions**, where the statements that control the transaction, and the execution and management of that transaction are outside the database. Usually these are a feature of the `Connection` object that executes a SQL statement or stored procedure.

While it is possible to write stored procedures that perform transactions across different databases on the same server, this is outside the scope of this chapter. It is also possible to use the services of another application, such as Windows 2000 Component Services (or MTS in Windows NT4) to perform a distributed transaction, where a series of events spread across different databases and applications on different servers are managed as a single transaction. Chapter 17 looks briefly at this topic.

Database Transactions

In a database system such as SQL Server, you can specify transaction operations within a stored procedure using vendor-specific statements like BEGIN TRANSACTION to start a new transaction, COMMIT TRANSACTION to accept all the updates and permanently commit the changes to the data, and ROLLBACK TRANSACTION to cancel all the changes made within the current transaction.

We've provided an example page that uses a transacted stored procedure. The stored procedure, named `DoBookArchive`, is created within the `WroxBooks` database by the SQL script provided with the samples.

The DoBookArchive Stored Procedure

The `DoBookArchive` stored procedure moves a row from the `BookList` table into another table named `ArchiveBooks`, within the same database. If the process succeeds, the transaction is committed and the updates are permanently applied to the database tables. If there is an error when writing to the `ArchiveBooks` table, or when deleting the book from the `BookList` table, both actions are rolled back and the tables are left in exactly the same state as before–neither is affected by the procedure.

However, to make it repeatable while you are experimenting with the example, the stored procedure always starts by deleting any existing book with the same ISBN (the primary key) in the `ArchiveBooks` table. This action will also be rolled back if the complete transaction fails, so if a book has been archived (and hence deleted from the `BookList` table) it will not be deleted from the `ArchiveBooks` table if you run the stored procedure again with the same ISBN. In this case, the INSERT statement will fail because the book is not in the `BookList` table, and so the entire transaction is rolled back undoing the DELETE operation on the `ArchiveBooks` table. The code for the stored procedure follows:

```
CREATE PROCEDURE DoBookArchive
    @ISBN varchar(12), @Result integer output AS
DECLARE @verror int
BEGIN TRANSACTION
DELETE FROM ArchiveBooks WHERE ISBN=@ISBN
INSERT INTO ArchiveBooks (ISBN, Title, PublicationDate)
    SELECT * FROM BookList WHERE ISBN LIKE @ISBN
SELECT @verror = @@ERROR, @Result = @@ROWCOUNT
IF @verror <> 0 GOTO on_error
IF @Result > 0
  BEGIN
    DELETE FROM BookList WHERE ISBN=@ISBN
    IF @@ERROR <> 0 GOTO on_error
    COMMIT TRANSACTION
  END
ELSE
  ROLLBACK TRANSACTION
RETURN
on_error:
SELECT @Result = -1
ROLLBACK TRANSACTION
RETURN
```

The Transacted Stored Procedure Example

The example page Updating Data with a Transacted Stored Procedure (`transacted-storedproc.aspx`) uses the stored procedure just described. We've arranged for it to use the same ISBN code as the previous example that inserts and deletes a book in the `BookList` table, so that you can see the results of this example by running it after inserting the new book and after deleting it. As shown in Figure 10-5, the stored procedure in this example will succeed providing that you have run the previous example to insert the new book row:

Figure 10-5

If you then run the page again, as in Figure 10-6, it will show that the stored procedure failed to find the book in the `BookList` table (because, of course, it's just been moved to the `ArchiveBooks` table):

Figure 10-6

The Code for the Transacted Stored Procedure Example

As in the earlier examples, let's start by specifying the name of the stored procedure and displaying it in the page, and then create the `Connection` and `Command` objects you'll need to execute it. Also set the `CommandType` of the `Command` object to indicate that you'll be executing a stored procedure. Then you can create the parameters for the command. This time there are only two–an input parameter to hold the ISBN of the book you want to archive and an output parameter to hold the result.

```
        'specify the stored procedure name
Dim strSQL As String = "DoBookArchive"
outSQL.InnerText = strSQL    'and display it


        'create connection and command
Dim objConnect As New OleDbConnection(strConnect)
Dim objCommand As New OleDbCommand(strSQL, objConnect)
objCommand.CommandType = CommandType.StoredProcedure


        'create an input Parameter object named 'ISBN' with the correct data
        'type to match a SQL database 'varchar' field of 12 characters
Dim objParam As OleDbParameter
objParam = objCommand.Parameters.Add("ISBN", OleDbType.VarChar, 12)
objParam.Direction = ParameterDirection.Input
objParam.Value = "199999999"


        'create an output Parameter object named 'Result' with the correct
        'data type to match a SQL database 'integer' field
        'specify that it's an Output parameter so no value required
objParam = objCommand.Parameters.Add("Result", OleDbType.Integer)
objParam.Direction = ParameterDirection.Output


        'display the value of the input parameter
outInParams.InnerText = "ISBN='" & objCommand.Parameters("ISBN").Value & "'"
```

Executing the Stored Procedure and Displaying the Results

The next step is to open your connection and execute the stored procedure. Then you can collect the result from the output parameter and display it, along with some accompanying explanatory text.

461

```
Try
   'execute the stored procedure
   objConnect.Open()
   objCommand.ExecuteNonQuery()
   objConnect.Close()
Catch objError As Exception
   outError.InnerHtml = "* Error while updating original data.<br />" _
      & objError.Message & "<br />" & objError.Source
   Exit Sub   'stop execution
End Try
'collect and display the value of the output parameter
Dim intResult As Integer = objCommand.Parameters("Result").Value
Dim strResult As String = "Result='" & CStr(intResult) & "'<br />"
Select Case intResult
   Case -1:   strResult &= "Error occurred while attempting archive"
   Case 0:    strResult &= "Failed to archive book - no matching book found"
   Case > 0:  strResult &= "Successfully archived the specified book"
End Select
outOutParams.InnerHtml = strResult
```

Notice that you didn't have to do anything extra to benefit from the transaction within the stored procedure–you just executed it and checked the result to see what actually happened. This is not the case, however, when you use the other type of transaction, a connection-based transaction. You'll see how different working with this type of transaction is next.

Connection-Based Transactions

The previous example shows how you can use a transaction within a stored procedure (a database transaction) to ensure that operations on your data either all succeed or are all rolled back. A second way of using a transaction is through the capabilities of the `Connection` object. All `Connection` objects (`SqlConnection`, `OelDbConnection`, `OdbcConnection`, and `OracleConnection`) can be used to perform transacted data updates.

While the way you actually apply a transaction is different from the stored-procedure transaction used in the previous example, the terminology is broadly the same. The three methods of the `Connection` class concerned with managing transactions are shown in the following table.

`Connection.BeginTransaction`	Starts a new transaction on this connection and all subsequent changes to the data become part of the transaction until it is committed or rolled back.
`Transaction.Commit`	Commits all changes made to the data within this transaction since it was started. The changes are made permanent in the target data store.
`Transaction.Rollback`	Abandons all changes made to the data within this transaction since it was started. The changes are removed from the target data store.

The Transaction Class

In ADO.NET, there are separate classes that implement transactions, one for each of the different types of `Connection`. To start a transaction, call the `BeginTransaction` method of the current `Connection` object. This returns a `Transaction` object that you must then assign to any `Command` objects that you want to enroll into that transaction.

To end a transaction and commit all the changes to the database, call the `Commit` method of the `Transaction` object (note that it's *not* a method of the `Connection` object as you might at first have expected). To abandon all changes to the data, you can call the `Transaction` object's `Rollback` method instead.

Notice also that you have to manually enroll any `Command` objects into the transaction. While this might seem odd, it does allow you to have multiple transactions in progress, and use whichever is appropriate for each command you carry out on the database. You can also create a nested transaction (that is a transaction that executes within another transaction) by creating a new `Transaction` object and calling the `Begin` method.

A Connection-Based Transaction Example

To see the transaction methods in action, open the example Transactional Data Updates with a Command Object (`update-with-transaction.aspx`) shown in Figure 10-7. This page creates three SQL statements that are used to update the titles of three books in the `BookList` table to reflect the current date and time, and then it executes these statements. Afterwards, it reads the rows back from the database and displays the details to confirm that the updates were successful.

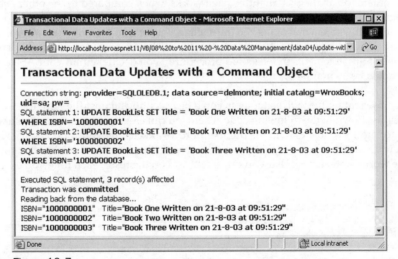

Figure 10-7

You can see in Figure 10-7 that the transaction was committed, and the three rows were updated. However, this is only because the page contains logic that uses the current time in seconds to decide whether to commit or roll back the transaction. While not a real-world scenario, it is done so that you can see the result of rolling back a transaction as well as committing it. After running the page again where the time has an even number of seconds, as shown in Figure 10-8, the transaction is rolled back and so the titles are not updated.

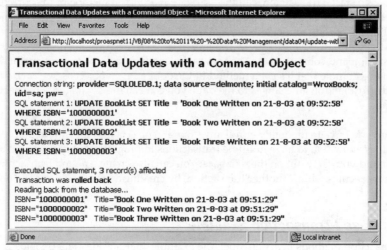

Figure 10-8

The Code for the Connection-Based Transaction Example

The only real differences in the way that this page works, when compared to the other examples that use SQL statements to update the data source, is that you have to call the transaction methods at the appropriate times–effectively managing the transaction yourself. Instead of a stored procedure within the database itself deciding whether to commit or rollback the changes (usually dependent on the outcome of one of the statements in the stored procedure), you decide within your ASP code if the transaction should be committed or rolled back.

As usual, start by creating the SQL statements you'll be executing against the `BookList` table to update the book titles, as shown in the following code. Then you can create your `Connection` and `Command` objects, and declare a variable to hold the number of rows affected by your updates. The initial value is set to zero here, though this is not actually required (zero is the default value), but it helps to illustrate how the code works, and ensures that you can safely add on the result each time you execute a SQL statement.

```
'specify the SQL statements to update the data
Dim strNow, strSQL1, strSQL2, strSQL3 As String
Dim datNow As DateTime = Now()
strNow = datNow.ToString("dd-M-yy \a\t hh:mm:ss")
strSQL1 = "UPDATE BookList SET Title = 'Book One Written on " _
         & strNow & "' WHERE ISBN='1100000001'"
outSQL1.InnerText = strSQL1    'and display it
strSQL2 = "UPDATE BookList SET Title = 'Book Two Written on " _
         & strNow & "' WHERE ISBN='1100000002'"
outSQL2.InnerText = strSQL2    'and display it
strSQL3 = "UPDATE BookList SET Title = 'Book Three Written on " _
         & strNow & "' WHERE ISBN='1100000003'"
```

```
outSQL3.InnerText = strSQL3    'and display it

'create connection and command and variable to hold result
Dim objConnect As New OleDbConnection(strConnect)
Dim objCommand As New OleDbCommand()
Dim intRowsAffected As Integer = 0
```

Starting a Transaction

You need a variable to hold the `Transaction` object that will be returned when we start a transaction, and so declare this next, as shown in the following code. Then open your connection, and execute the `BeginTransaction` method to start a new connection-based transaction. You can assign the `Transaction` object that is returned to your `objTransaction` variable.

Now you are ready to execute your three SQL UPDATE statements using the `Command` object you created earlier on. You created it without providing any values for the constructor parameters, so you have to assign your `Connection` object to its `Connection` property. Also set the `CommandType` to indicate that you're using a SQL statement (though this is the default if not specified). Once your `Command` object is set up, you also have to enroll it into the current transaction.

Notice that you can only do so after you've set the `Connection` property, and if you want to change the `Connection` property afterwards you first have to un-enrol it by setting the `Transaction` property of the `Command` object to `Nothing`.

```
'declare a variable to hold a Transaction object
Dim objTransaction As OleDbTransaction

Try

    'open connection before starting transaction
    objConnect.Open()

    'start a transaction for this connection
    objTransaction = objConnect.BeginTransaction()

    'specify the Connection object and command type for the Command
    objCommand.Connection = objConnect
    objCommand.CommandType = CommandType.Text

    'attach the current transaction to the Command object
    'must be done after setting Connection property
    objCommand.Transaction = objTransaction
```

Executing the Commands and Committing or Rolling Back

The next step is to assign each SQL statement to the `CommandText` property in turn and execute it. Then the next place where you need to consider how to handle the transaction that you've started is if an error occurs while executing the SQL statements. In an error situation, you would usually call the `Rollback` method of the `Transaction` object to cancel any changes that have been applied to the source data as shown.

If there is no error, and all three SQL statements have successfully executed, you would normally call the Commit method of the Transaction object to permanently apply the changes to the data store. However, in this example, check the number of seconds in the current time and only call Commit if this is an odd number. If it's an even number, you can call the Rollback method to abandon all updates.

```
'specify the select statement to use for the first update
objCommand.CommandText = strSQL1

'execute the SQL statement against the command to fill the DataReader
'keep track of number of records originally updated
intRowsAffected += objCommand.ExecuteNonQuery()

'repeat using the select statement for the second update
objCommand.CommandText = strSQL2
intRowsAffected += objCommand.ExecuteNonQuery()

'repeat using the select statement for the third update
objCommand.CommandText = strSQL3
intRowsAffected += objCommand.ExecuteNonQuery()

Catch objError As Exception

    'error encountered so roll back all the updates
    objTransaction.Rollback()
    'display error details
    outError.InnerHtml = "* Error while updating original data.<br />" _
                      & objError.Message & "<br />" & objError.Source
    Exit Sub  ' and stop execution

End Try

'all seems OK so can now commit all the updates. However as an
'illustration of the technique only do so if the current time
'has an odd number of seconds. If not, rollback all changes
Dim strCommit As String
If Second(datNow) Mod 2 = 0
    objTransaction.Rollback()
    strCommit = "rolled back"
Else
    objTransaction.Commit()
    strCommit = "committed"
End If
```

Afterwards you can read the values of the rows using a DataReader object and display them in the page. This is identical to the way you did it in the first example in this chapter, so the code is not repeated here.

Having looked briefly at how you can use transactions to ensure multiple data updates all succeed, or all fail, we'll move on to a different topic. The DataSet object introduced in previous chapters has the facility to automatically update the source data from which it was created–or in fact any data store for which the structure and contents of the tables within the DataSet are of the appropriate format. This is the focus of the next section.

Updating Data from a DataSet Object

In previous chapters you've regularly used a `DataSet` object to store data extracted from a database, or to hold data that you've created dynamically using code. You also looked at the ways to edit and modify the data that the `DataSet` contains. This section looks in detail at how to get those changes back into a data source such as a relational database.

ADO.NET includes the `DataAdapter` object, which is used to provide the connection between a data store and a disconnected `DataSet`. This object was seen in action in Chapter 8, but only so far as collecting rows from a database and pushing them into a `DataSet`. To understand how the update process works for a `DataSet`, we need to examine the `DataAdapter` object in more depth.

Inside the DataAdapter Object

In order to understand and take advantage of many of the features of the .NET disconnected data model, especially when we discuss at concurrent data update issues later in this chapter, you must be comfortable with what's going on behind the scenes when you use the `DataSet` and `DataAdapter` objects to push changes made to the data back into a data source.

The full chain of objects that are required to pull data from a data store into a `DataSet`, and push the changes back into the data store after updating is shown in Figure 10-9. You can see the four main objects involved in the process–the `Connection`, `Command`, `DataAdapter`, and `DataSet`:

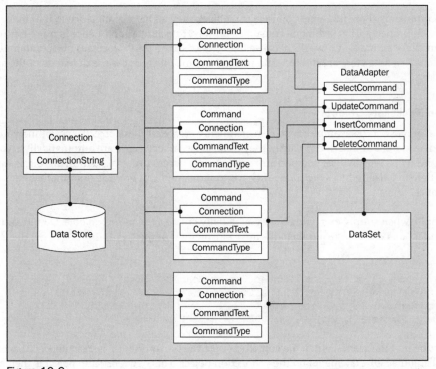

Figure 10-9

The DataSet Object Chain

The four objects in the schematic were briefly discussed in Chapter 8. Here is a detailed look at how the whole process works:

❑　The `Connection` object defines the way that the data store will communicate with `Command` objects, using a connection string and the appropriate data store provider such as SQL TDS, OLE-DB, or the ODBC driver.

❑　The `Command` object performs the task of executing the SQL statement, query, or stored procedure, etc. against the data store via the `Connection` object. It contains details about that SQL statement, query or stored procedure, and the way that it should be processed.

❑　The `DataAdapter` object is the bridge between the `DataSet` and the `Command` objects. It specifies the organization of the tables within the `DataSet` through table and column mappings, and is responsible for managing the whole process of fetching data from the data source and pushing it back to the data source.

❑　The `DataSet` is the disconnected data storage and processing unit that actually holds the data. It does so using one or more tables, and (optionally) relationships between these tables.

Notice in the schematic that there are four `Command` objects involved in the process. Why? You only need one to fill a `DataSet` from a data store–a suitable `SelectCommand` such as a SQL `SELECT` statement or the equivalent stored procedure (or table name). However, to be able to update the original data, you need the other three–`UpdateCommand`, `InsertCommand`, and `DeleteCommand`.

All four commands share the same `Connection` object; they all have a reference to it in their `Connection` property. This technique consumes far fewer resources (and hence is more efficient) than using four different ones, and works because the `DataAdapter` only processes one command at a time. Connections to a data store are limited, and using the same one reduces the demands of the application considerably.

Creating the Necessary Objects

Of course, in most of the examples, you don't explicitly create all these objects every time you want to access a data store. But that doesn't mean they don't exist. In fact many are automatically created in the background when required, as you perform various data access processes. Allowing the system to create them on demand also reduces the code you have to write, and can provide marginally better performance.

For example, when simply extracting data you usually create a `Connection` object, a `DataAdapter` object, and a `DataSet` object–and then use the `Fill` method of the `DataAdapter` to get the data into the `DataSet`:

```
Dim objConnect As New OleDbConnection(strConnectString)
Dim objDataAdapter As New OleDbDataAdapter(strSQLStatement, objConnect)
Dim objDataSet As New DataSet()
objDataAdapter.Fill(objDataSet, "table-name")
```

However, behind the scenes, when the constructor for the `DataAdapter` is executed, a `Command` object is created using the SQL statement and the connection object. This new `Command` object is then assigned to the `SelectCommand` property of the `DataAdapter` object.

You can even dispense with creating a `Connection` object yourself. Just pass the connection string itself into the constructor for the `DataAdapter` object:

```
Dim objDataAdapter As New OleDbDataAdapter(strSQLStatement, strConnectString)
```

Again, behind the scenes, the `DataAdapter` constructor is creating a new `Command` object by calling its constructor with the SQL statement and (this time) the connection string. Then the `Command` object constructor creates a new `Connection` object using the connection string. The whole process still takes place to create the chain of four objects, even if you don't specifically code this.

Specifying the SelectCommand

At minimum, when creating a `DataAdapter` object to `Fill` a `Dataset`, only the `SelectCommand` is required and this must *always* be provided. As you've seen, this is usually specified as a string (the SQL statement, query string, table name, or stored procedure name) in the constructor for the object. Of course, there's nothing to stop you creating a `Command` object directly and assigning this to the `SelectCommand` property of the `DataAdapter`:

```
Dim objConnect As New OleDbConnection(strConnectString)
Dim objCommand As New OleDbCommand(strSQLStatement, objConnect)
Dim objDataAdapter As New OleDbDataAdapter(objCommand)
```

Or, in an even more verbose way:

```
Dim objConnect As New OleDbConnection(strConnectString)
Dim objCommand As New OleDbCommand(strSQLStatement, objConnect)
Dim objDataAdapter As New OleDbDataAdapter()
objDataAdapter.SelectCommand = objCommand
```

While it's hard to see when you could use the last of these, it could be a useful technique when you already have a `DataAdapter` that you want to reuse by just changing the `SelectCommand` to reference a different `Command` object.

Specifying the Other Commands

To be able to fill a `DataSet`, you only need a `SelectCommand`–but to push the changes back to the data store, you must provide the appropriate `Command` objects for the `UpdateCommand`, `DeleteCommand`, and `InsertCommand` properties of the `DataAdapter`.

You don't always need all three, for example if you are only changing existing rows within the data source (if the `DataSet` object only contains modified rows, and no added or deleted rows), you only need to specify a suitable `Command` object for the `UpdateCommand` property of the `DataAdapter`. The same logic applies if you are only deleting rows or inserting new rows. However, if the `DataSet` contains modified, deleted, and added rows, you have to specify suitable `Command` objects for all the matching `DataAdapter` properties.

What is a suitable `Command` object? It's pretty obvious that this is a `Command` with a connection specified to the appropriate data store (via its associated `Connection` object), and which specifies a suitable SQL statement or stored procedure that will add, delete, or update the rows. We'll show some examples later in this section in more detail. However, ADO.NET can also help out by generating suitable SQL statements automatically for us.

Command Builder Objects and Auto-generated Commands

ADO.NET tries to make your life easier when you use a `DataSet` to update a data store by providing `CommandBuilder` objects, such as the `SqlCommandBuilder` for use with SQL TDS and the `OleDbCommandBuilder` for use with an OLE-DB provider. These objects can create suitable *auto-generated commands* for use when pushing changes back to a data store via a `DataAdapter` object.

All you have to do is create a `CommandBuilder` object, specifying as the parameter to its constructor the `DataAdapter` you want to use it with:

```
Dim objCommandBuilder As New OleDbCommandBuilder(objDataAdapter)
```

Then, when you call the `Update` method of this `DataAdapter`, it will automatically use the `CommandBuilder` to create the INSERT, DELETE, and UPDATE commands for the process, and assign them to the `InsertCommand`, `DeleteCommand`, and `UpdateCommand` properties of the `DataAdapter`. Once the `Update` methods ends, the `InsertCommand`, `DeleteCommand`, and `UpdateCommand` properties are set back to `Nothing` (null in C#).

However, if the `InsertCommand`, `DeleteCommand`, or `UpdateCommand` properties are not `Nothing` (null) when the `Update` method is called, the `CommandBuilder` does not replace any existing statement. This means you can assign your own custom SQL statements or stored procedure details to one or more of these properties before calling the `Update` method. In this case, the specified SQL statement or stored procedure is used for that part of the `Update` process, and will remain assigned to the `InsertCommand`, `DeleteCommand`, or `UpdateCommand` property afterwards.

Notice that you can provide a SQL statement or stored procedure for one or two of the `InsertCommand`, `DeleteCommand`, and `UpdateCommand` properties and allow the `CommandBuilder` to automatically set the remaining ones.

The `CommandBuilder` also exposes three methods that you can use if you want to retrieve the auto-generated commands for the current operation. While you probably don't need to use these methods in your applications, they are useful for displaying the auto-generated commands in your example pages. Remember that the `CommandBuilder` sets the `InsertCommand`, `DeleteCommand`, and `UpdateCommand` properties back to `Nothing` once the `Update` process completes, so you can't access these properties to see the auto-generated commands it used.

In your example pages, you can take advantage of the `GetDeleteCommand`, `GetInsertCommand`, `GetUpdateCommand` methods of the `CommandBuilder` to assign the auto-generated commands to the `InsertCommand`, `DeleteCommand`, and `UpdateCommand` properties of the `DataAdapter` before you call the `Update` method. You can then access them afterwards as shown in the following code:

```
    'create a CommandBuilder instance for the current DataAdapter
Dim objCommandBuilder As New OleDbCommandBuilder(objDataAdapter)
    'set the update, insert and delete commands for the DataAdapter
objDataAdapter.DeleteCommand = objCommandBuilder.GetDeleteCommand()
objDataAdapter.InsertCommand = objCommandBuilder.GetInsertCommand()
objDataAdapter.UpdateCommand = objCommandBuilder.GetUpdateCommand()
```

```
        'call the Update method
objDataAdapter.Update(objDataSet)
        'read back the auto-generated commands
strDeleteCommand = objDataAdapter.DeleteCommand
strInsertCommand = objDataAdapter.InsertCommand
strUpdateCommand = objDataAdapter.UpdateCommand
```

The `CommandBuilder` creates and returns `Command` objects that specify the appropriate SQL statements for an `Update` process through the `DataAdapter` it is attached to. It can figure these out by looking at the `SelectCommand` property of the `DataAdapter`, the table structure, and table and column mappings. You'll see what the SQL statements that these methods create look like in the next example in this chapter. In the meantime, however, you should be aware of a few limitations of the auto-generated command feature:

❑ The rows in a table in the `DataSet` must have originally come from a single table, and can be used only to update a table of the same format (generally the same source table).

❑ The source table must have a primary key defined (it can be a multiple-column primary key), or it must have at least one column that contains unique values. This column (or columns) must be included in the rows that are returned by the SELECT statement or query that is used for the `SelectCommand`.

❑ Table names that include special characters such as spaces, periods, quotation marks, or other non-alphanumeric characters cannot be used (even if delimited by square brackets). However, fully qualified table names that do include the period character (such as `dbo.BookList`) can be used.

Of course, you can create your own command strings if required, rather than using the auto-generated commands provided by the `CommandBuilder`, and have the `DataAdapter` use these instead of the auto-generated ones. In later examples, you'll see how this is useful when working with stored procedures that perform the updates to the data store, and with custom SQL statements.

The DeriveParameters Method

One other useful feature that the `CommandBuilder` provides is the ability to automatically create appropriate `Parameter` objects. This includes both the situation when we are using stored procedures to update the data source, as well as when you are using them to extract data from a data store.

The `DeriveParameters` method of the `CommandBuilder` object takes as its single parameter a reference to a `Command` object, and returns this `Command` object with its `Parameters` collection populated with the appropriate `Parameter` objects. All that's required then is to fill in the values:

```
        'create the Connection, Command and DataAdapter
Dim objConnect As New OleDbConnection(ConnectionString)
Dim objCommand As New OleDbCommand(SQLStatement, objConnect)
Dim objDataAdapter As New OleDbDataAdapter(objCommand)
        'create a CommandBuilder for this DataAdapter
Dim objCommandBuilder As New OleDbCommandBuilder(objDataAdapter)
        'derive the parameters and set their values
objCommandBuilder.DeriveParameters(objCommand)
objCommand.Parameters("param1-name").Value = thevalue1
objCommand.Parameters("param2-name").Value = thevalue2
...etc...
```

However, be aware that the `DeriveParameters` method requires an extra call to the data store to get information about the parameters, and so is generally inefficient. You might use it during development to find out what parameters are required (you can iterate through the `Parameters` collection examining them after calling `DeriveParameters`), but you should avoid using it in release code unless absolutely necessary.

Using the DataAdapter.Update Method

The example page Updating Data with a DataAdapter and DataSet Object (`update-with-dataset.aspx`) demonstrates the simplest way to use a `DataAdapter` object to update the source data with changes made to the rows stored in a `DataSet` object. This example simply reads in a rowset from the `BookList` table in your `WroxBooks` sample database, changes some of the rows, then pushes the changes back into the data store. As shown in Figure 10-10, the code in the page deletes or removes four rows from the original table, modifies values in three other rows, and adds a new row. You can see this by comparing the contents of the table in the two `DataGrid` controls on the page:

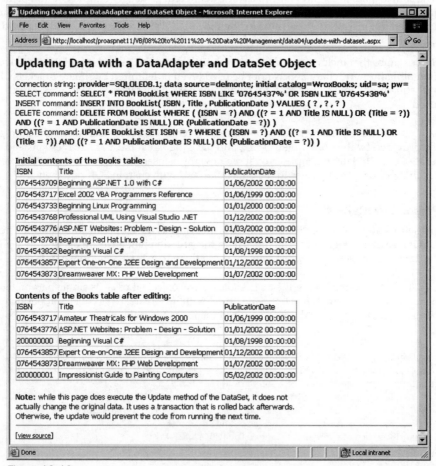

Figure 10-10

As you can see from the note at the bottom of the page, the code uses a connection-based transaction to prevent the changes being permanently applied to the source data. If they were, the example page would fail to work the next time, as some of the rows would have been deleted and primary key violations would occur due to the new row already being present in the source table. However, you can change the code to commit the transaction to verify that it actually works and does update the original data.

You can also see the auto-generated commands that are used by the DataAdapter to update the source data. It's obvious that these are SQL statements, with question-mark characters as placeholders for the values used to update the table in our target data source. We'll look at them in more detail shortly.

The Code for the 'Updating with a DataAdapter' Example

As shown in the following code, the SELECT statement used is simple enough–it just selects a subset of the rows in your BookList table. Then you can use the now familiar technique to create and fill the DataSet with your source data. This is covered in detail in previous chapters, so we're simply listing the code here:

```
strSelect = "SELECT * FROM BookList WHERE ISBN LIKE '07645437%' " _
        & "OR ISBN LIKE '07645438%'"
Dim objDataSet As New DataSet()
Dim objConnect As New OleDbConnection(strConnect)
Dim objDataAdapter As New OleDbDataAdapter(strSelect, objConnect)
Try
    objDataAdapter.Fill(objDataSet, "Books")
Catch objError As Exception
    outError.innerHTML = "* Error while accessing data.<br />" _
        & objError.Message & "<br />" & objError.Source
    Exit Sub
End Try
```

In your example, you want to be able to see which rows have been changed, and the Update method also depends on this information to be able to correctly update the original data in your database. One way to *fix* the current state of all the rows in all the tables in a DataSet (as seen in the previous chapter) is to call the AcceptChanges method to accept all the changes that have been made to the DataSet.

In fact, in your example it's not strictly necessary because the Fill method automatically sets the status of all the rows to Unchanged. However (as shown in the following code) it illustrates the process, and would be necessary if you had made any changes since you originally filled the DataSet that you don't want to flush back into the database. In later examples, we'll take advantage of this.

You'll also need to refer to the Books table in your DataSet in several places within your code, so create this reference next. Then you can display the contents of the Books table that is currently held in your DataSet. Simply bind the default view of the table to a DataGrid control named dgrResult1 that is declared elsewhere in the HTML section of the page.

```
'accept the changes to "fix" the current state of the DataSet contents
objDataSet.AcceptChanges()

'declare a variable to reference the Books table
Dim objTable As DataTable = objDataSet.Tables("Books")
```

473

```
'display the contents of the Books table before changing data
dgrResult1.DataSource = objTable.DefaultView
dgrResult1.DataBind() 'and bind (display) the data
```

Changing the Rows in the DataSet

Now you're ready to make some changes to the data. The following code shows that you can use exactly the same technique as in the previous chapter examples. After making these changes to the Books table in your DataSet display the contents again. Notice that you have to use a date string that is in the correct format for the column in your table. In the example where the value of a parameter object is set, use the format "yyyy-mm-dd" as this is a suitable format for the SQL DateTime field. Here you're using the format "mm-dd-yyyy" as this is the format of the ADO.NET table column.

```
'now change some records in the Books table
objTable.Rows(0).Delete()
objTable.Rows(1)("Title") = "Amateur Theatricals for Windows 2000"
objTable.Rows(2).Delete()
objTable.Rows(3).Delete()
objTable.Rows(4)("PublicationDate") = "01-01-2002"  'see note below
objTable.Rows.Remove(5)

    'notice that using the Remove method on row 5 (rather than marking
    'it as deleted) means that the next row then becomes row 5
objTable.Rows(5)("ISBN") = "200000000"
    'add a new row using an array of values
Dim objValsArray(2) As Object
objValsArray(0) = "200000001"
objValsArray(1) = "Impressionist Guide to Painting Computers"
objValsArray(2) = "05-02-2002"   'see note below
objTable.Rows.Add(objValsArray)

    'display the contents of the Books table after changing the data
dgrResult2.DataSource = objTable.DefaultView
dgrResult2.DataBind() 'and bind (display) the data
```

Creating the Auto-Generated Commands

OK, so now you can update your data source. The first step in this part of the process is to create the commands that the DataAdapter will use to push the changes into the database. You can use a CommandBuilder to create the three Command objects it requires, and assign these to the appropriate properties of the DataAdapter so that you can retrieve and display them afterwards.

```
'create command builder commands to update insert and delete rows
Dim objCommandBuilder As New OleDbCommandBuilder(objDataAdapter)

    'set the update, insert and delete commands for the DataAdapter
    'this is only required because we want to access them afterwards
    'if omitted, commands are set to null when update completes
objDataAdapter.DeleteCommand = objCommandBuilder.GetDeleteCommand()
objDataAdapter.InsertCommand = objCommandBuilder.GetInsertCommand()
objDataAdapter.UpdateCommand = objCommandBuilder.GetUpdateCommand()
```

Pushing the Changes Back into the Data Source

As your example uses a transaction (so that you can re-run the page) you have to explicitly open the connection to the database. If you weren't using a transaction, you could remove the Open method call as well (the DataAdapter automatically opens the connection when you call the Update method, then closes it afterwards). Then, as shown in the following code, make a call to the BeginTransaction method of the connection.

Next (only because you're using a transaction in your example) you have to explicitly enroll all the Command objects into the transaction. Then you can call the Update method of the DataAdapter to push all the changes you've made to the rows in the DataSet back into the data source automatically. Notice that the name of the table that contains the changes we want to push back into the data source is specified.

Normally that's all you would need to do. However, you are performing the update within a transaction so that you can roll it back again afterwards – allowing you to run the same page again without getting the errors that would occur from inserting and deleting the same rows again. So finish off by rolling back this transaction.

```
'start a transaction so we can roll back changes if required
objConnect.Open()
objConnect.BeginTransaction()

'attach the current transaction to all the Command objects
'must be done after setting Connection property
objDataAdapter.DeleteCommand.Transaction = objTransaction
objDataAdapter.InsertCommand.Transaction = objTransaction
objDataAdapter.UpdateCommand.Transaction = objTransaction

'perform the update on the original data
objDataAdapter.Update(objDataSet, "Books")
objTransaction.Rollback()
```

Viewing the Auto-Generated Commands

The example page displays the auto-generated commands that were created by the CommandBuilder object so that you can see what they look like. The code is placed at the end of the page, extracting the command strings and placing them in <div> elments located within the HTML section of the page.

```
'display the SQL statements that the DataSet used
'these are created by the CommandBuilder object
outInsert.InnerText = objDataAdapter.InsertCommand.CommandText
outDelete.InnerText = objDataAdapter.DeleteCommand.CommandText
outUpdate.InnerText = objDataAdapter.UpdateCommand.CommandText
```

If you examine these command strings (shown again in Figure 10-11), you can see that they are *outline* or *pseudo* SQL statements, containing question-mark placeholders where the values from each row are inserted when the statements are executed. Notice how they only perform the action on the source table if the row has not been changed by another process in the meantime (that is, while the DataSet was holding the rows). The DataSet is a disconnected data repository, and so the original rows could have been updated, existing rows deleted, or new rows added with the same primary key by another user or process.

```
SELECT command: SELECT * FROM BookList WHERE ISBN LIKE '07645437%' OR ISBN LIKE '07645438%'
INSERT command: INSERT INTO BookList( ISBN , Title , PublicationDate ) VALUES ( ? , ? , ? )
DELETE command: DELETE FROM BookList WHERE ( (ISBN = ?) AND ((? = 1 AND Title IS NULL) OR (Title = ?))
AND ((? = 1 AND PublicationDate IS NULL) OR (PublicationDate = ?)) )
UPDATE command: UPDATE BookList SET ISBN = ? WHERE ( (ISBN = ?) AND ((? = 1 AND Title IS NULL) OR
(Title = ?)) AND ((? = 1 AND PublicationDate IS NULL) OR (PublicationDate = ?)) )
```

Figure 10-11

Later in this chapter you'll be looking in detail at how ADO.NET manages concurrent updates to a data store, and how you can manage them yourself. In the meantime, there are a few other issues that you need to look at when using the `Update` method of the `DataAdapter` object.

Checking How Many Rows Were Updated

The `Update` method returns the number of rows that were updated in the source table. While you didn't take advantage of this in your examples, it's pretty easy to do. Simply declare an `Integer` variable and assign the result of the `Update` method to it:

```
Dim intRowsUpdated As Integer
intRowsUpdated = objDataAdapter.Update(objDataSet, "table-name")
```

Specifying the Tables When Updating Data

As you've seen, the `DataAdapter` object's `Update` method provides a really easy and efficient way to update the source data. If you have more than one table in the `DataSet`, simply call the method once for each table to automatically update the source data with all the changes to rows in that table. The changes are applied in the order that the rows exist within the table in the `DataSet`.

There is one point to watch out for, however. If the source data tables contain foreign keys, in other words there are enforceable relationships between the tables then the order that the tables are processed can cause errors to occur. It all depends on the type of updates you're carrying out, and the rules or triggers you have inside the source database.

For example, if your `DataSet` contained rows that originally came from the `BookList`, `AuthorList`, and `BookPrices` tables, you could add a new book to the `Books` table in the `DataSet` and add matching rows (based in the ISBN that acts as the primary and foreign keys) to the `Authors` and `Prices` tables in the `DataSet`.

When you execute the `Update` method, however, it will only work if the `Books` table is the first one to be processed. If you try to process the `Authors` or `Prices` table first, the database will report an error because there will be no parent row with an ISBN value to match the newly inserted child rows. You are trying to insert orphan rows into the database table, and thus breaking referential integrity rules.

In other words, to insert a new book in our example, you would have to use:

```
objDataAdapter.Update(objDataSet, "Books")
objDataAdapter.Update(objDataSet, "Authors")
objDataAdapter.Update(objDataSet, "Prices")
```

However, if you have deleted a book and all its child rows from the `Authors` and `Prices` tables in the `DataSet`, the opposite applies. You can't delete the parent row while there are child rows in the database table, unless the database contains rules or triggers that cascade the deletes to remove the child rows.

And if it does, the delete operations carried out for the child tables would fail, because the rows would have already been deleted. This means that you probably want to process the Books table in your DataSet last rather than first:

```
objDataAdapter.Update(objDataSet, "Authors")
objDataAdapter.Update(objDataSet, "Prices")
objDataAdapter.Update(objDataSet, "Books")
```

But if you have carried out both insert and delete operations on the tables, neither method will work correctly. In this case, you need to process the updates in a more strictly controlled order. Let's look at what this involves when we examine concurrency issues later on in this chapter (in the section *Marshalling the Changed Rows in a DataSet*). First, we'll briefly examine some of the other ways that you can use the Update method.

Automatically Updating the Default Table in a DataSet

If you have created a table mapping in the DataSet for the default table, you can execute the Update method without specifying the table name. We discussed how to create table mappings in the previous chapter. Basically, create a variable to hold a TableMapping object and then call the Add method of the DataAdapter object's TableMappings collection to create the new table mapping. Specify the string "Table" to indicate that you are creating a default table mapping, and the name of the table:

```
Dim objTableMapping As DataTableMapping
objTableMapping = objDataAdapter.TableMappings.Add("Table", "DefaultBookList")
```

Now you can call the Update method without specifying the name of the table:

```
objDataAdapter.Update(objDataSet)
```

An error occurs if this mapping does not exist when the Update method is called without specifying the name of a table.

Updating Subsets of Rows from a Table

The DataAdapter object's Update method can also be used to push changes from a collection or array of DataRow objects into the data source. All the rows must come from the same source table, and there must be a default table mapping set up as described in the previous section. The updates are then processed in the order that they exist in the array.

To create an array of DataRow objects you can use the All property of a table's Rows collection:

```
Dim arrRows() As DataRow
arrRows = objDataSet.Tables(0).Rows.All
```

Then you can push the changes in this array of rows into the data source using the Update method and specifying this array:

```
objDataAdapter.Update(arrRows)
```

This technique is useful if you have an array of rows that contain our changed records, rather than one that contains all the rows in the original table.

Updating from a DataSet Using Stored Procedures

Near the start of the chapter, we showed you how to use stored procedures within a database to update the source data. In that example, you used a `Command` object to execute the stored procedures. Meanwhile, the previous example showed how to use the auto-generated commands with a `DataSet` to update data automatically.

Of course, you don't have to use auto-generated commands with a `DataSet`. Instead you can use your own custom SQL statements or stored procedures to do the same thing. Just create the appropriate `Command` objects for the `InsertCommand`, `DeleteCommand`, and `UpdateCommand` properties of the `DataAdapter`, and call the `Update` method as before. Then your custom SQL statements or stored procedures are used to push the changes back into the data store.

The previous example also updated only a single table (a pre-requisite when using the auto-generated commands). However, often you have a more complex task to accomplish when updating the source data. For example, the rows in the table in your `DataSet` might have originally been created from several source tables, perhaps by using a `JOIN` statement in the SQL query or some complex stored procedure. This was demonstrated at the beginning of the previous chapter, where you had a table containing data drawn from both the `BookList` and the `BookAuthors` tables in your sample database. When you come to push changes to data like this back into your database, you need to use some process that can disentangle the values in each row and perform a series of staged updates to the original tables, thereby maintaining integrity within the database.

The example page Updating Complex Data with a DataSet and Stored Procedures (`complex-dataset-update.aspx`) shown in Figure 10-12 demonstrates all of these techniques and features.

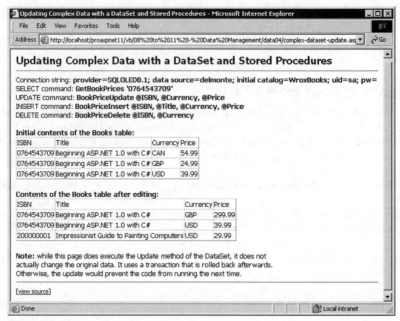

Figure 10-12

It extracts some data from the sample database using a stored procedure that joins two tables, and displays it in a `DataGrid`. Then it changes some of the rows in the original table and displays the data again. Finally, it pushes the changes back into the data source using stored procedures that we've provided within the database.

At the top of the page you can see the values of the four `Command` objects' `CommandText` properties. The `SelectCommand` is a stored procedure named `GetBookprices` that takes a single parameter (the ISBN) – which we provide inline. This stored procedure joins the `BookList` and `BookPrices` tables, and returns a rowset containing values from both tables.

```
CREATE PROCEDURE GetBookPrices
@ISBN varchar(10) AS
SELECT BookList.ISBN, BookList.Title, BookPrices.Currency, BookPrices.Price
FROM BookList JOIN BookPrices ON BookList.ISBN = BookPrices.ISBN
WHERE BookList.ISBN LIKE @ISBN
```

The other three commands shown in Figure 10-12 are obviously not auto-generated SQL statements, and they don't contain the question-mark placeholders. They are of course the names of three stored procedures within the sample database, and the names of the parameters are added to the display as well–these are not actually part of the command strings.

At the bottom of the page is a note about the transaction that is used to prevent the updates being permanently committed to the data store so that you can re-run the page (without this the updates to the source data would prevent the page from working next time).

The Update Stored Procedures for the Example Page

Your `DataSet` table holds rows that are created from two different tables in the database, and so the auto-generated commands from a `CommandBuilder` cannot be used to persist inserts, deletes, or updates that are made to rows in the table in the `DataSet`. Instead you can use three stored procedures.

The `BookPriceUpdate` stored procedure takes as parameters the ISBN of the book (which is the primary key in the `BookList` table and part of the primary key in the `BookPrices` table), the name of the currency in the `BookPrices` table (which is the other half of the primary key in this table), and the actual value for the `Price` column in the `BookPrices` table. It uses these values to update the matching row in the `BookPrices` table:

```
CREATE PROCEDURE BookPriceUpdate
@ISBN varchar(10),
@Currency varchar(3),
@Price money
AS
UPDATE BookPrices SET Price=@Price WHERE Currency=@Currency AND ISBN = @ISBN
```

The `BookPriceInsert` stored procedure takes as parameters the ISBN, title, currency, and price values that it will use to insert a new row into the `BookList` table and a new row into the `BookPrices` table. Note that, as shown in the following code, it first checks to see if a book with the specified ISBN already exists in the `BookList` table (as it might if we are only inserting a price in a different currency). In this case, it just inserts the new `BookPrices` row.

```
CREATE PROCEDURE BookPriceInsert
@ISBN varchar(10),
@Title varchar(100),
@Currency varchar(3),
@Price money
AS
SELECT ISBN FROM BookList WHERE ISBN = @ISBN
IF @@ROWCOUNT = 0
    INSERT INTO BookList(ISBN, Title) VALUES (@ISBN, @Title)
INSERT INTO BookPrices(ISBN, Currency, Price) VALUES (@ISBN, @Currency,@Price)
```

Finally, the `BookPriceDelete` stored procedure takes only two parameters–the ISBN of the book and the name of the currency for the row it will delete in the `BookPrices` table (see the following code). However, if there are no price rows left for this book after deleting the specified one, it also deletes the matching row from `BookList` table. OK, so it's a pretty contrived example, but it demonstrates the way that you can use stored procedures to manipulate multiple tables from the `Update` method of the `DataAdapter`.

```
CREATE PROCEDURE BookPriceDelete
@ISBN varchar(10),
@Currency varchar(3)
AS
DELETE FROM BookPrices
  WHERE ISBN = @ISBN AND Currency = @Currency
SELECT ISBN FROM BookPrices WHERE ISBN=@ISBN
IF @@ROWCOUNT = 0
    DELETE FROM BookList WHERE ISBN=@ISBN
```

The Code for the 'Updating with Stored Procedures' Example

So, all you need to do now is use these three stored procedures as the command text for the `Command` objects in the `DataAdapter` object's `UpdateCommand`, `InsertCommand`, and `DeleteCommand` properties. The first part of the code in the page simply fills the `DataSet` from the database using the same techniques as discussed in earlier examples and earlier chapters, so we aren't repeating that here.

Next, the code changes some of the values in the rows in the `DataSet`, deleting the first row, updating the price in the second row, and adding a new row:

```
    'declare a variable to reference the Books table
Dim objTable As DataTable = objDataSet.Tables("Books")
    'change some rows in the DataSet table
    'delete the first row
objTable.Rows(0).Delete()
    'update price in the second row
objTable.Rows(1)("Price") = 299.99
    'add a new row using an array of values
Dim objValsArray(3) As Object
objValsArray(0) = "200000001"
objValsArray(1) = "Impressionist Guide to Painting Computers"
objValsArray(2) = "USD"
objValsArray(3) = "29.99"
objTable.Rows.Add(objValsArray)
```

Using Dynamic Parameters with a Stored Procedure

The important point to note in this example is that you're specifying which columns will provide the values for the parameters when the Command is executed, rather than specifying actual values for the parameters. You are creating a *dynamic parameters* that are the equivalent to the question-mark placeholders you saw in the SQL statements for the update, delete, and insert command in the previous example. The appropriate one of these commands will be executed for each row in the DataSet table that has been modified (has a RowState property value of DataRowState.Modified), deleted (has a RowState property value of DataRowState.Deleted), or inserted (has a RowState property value of DataRowState.Added).

To specify a dynamic parameter, set the SourceColumn property of the Parameter object to the name of the column from which the value for the parameter will come. However, you'll recall that each column can expose four different values (the DataRowVersion): Original, Current, Default, and Proposed. You can specify which of these values you want the parameter to use by setting the SourceVersion property of the Parameter object as well.

This means you can specify the Original value of the column as the parameter value (useful if it is being used to look up or match a value with the original value of that column in the source table), or the Current value of the column if you are updating that column in the table. In other words, you would specify that the parameter should use the Original value of this column from each row when it's part of the SQL WHERE clause (and so should match the existing value in the database tables) or the Current value when it's part of the SET clause.

The UpdateCommand and the Dynamic Parameters

So let's get on and build the necessary Command objects. Let's start with the one for the UpdateCommand. Create a new Command object and specify that the CommandType is a stored procedure. Then you can create the parameters that to be used with this Command object.

The first parameter is used to match the ISBN code, and so it uses the Original value of that column. The code is similar for the remaining two parameters (Currency and Price). However, while the Currency parameter also uses the Original value of the column, the Price must use the Current version of the data for this column in the rows, because this value will be used to update the original rows in the database table. It will become part of the SET clause in the SQL statement that is executed by the stored procedure.

Then, once all the parameters are ready, you can specify that this Command object be used as the update command by assigning it to the DataAdapter object's UpdateCommand property.

```
    ' create the UpdateCommand and parameters
Dim objUpdateCommand As New OleDbCommand("BookPriceUpdate", objConnect)
objUpdateCommand.CommandType = CommandType.StoredProcedure
    'now create the Parameter objects and add to the Command object
Dim objParam As OleDbParameter
objParam = objUpdateCommand.Parameters.Add("ISBN", OleDbType.VarChar, 10)
objParam.Direction = ParameterDirection.Input
objParam.SourceColumn = "ISBN"
objParam.SourceVersion = DataRowVersion.Original    'used in SQL WHERE clause

objParam = objUpdateCommand.Parameters.Add("Currency", OleDbType.VarChar, 3)
```

```
objParam.Direction = ParameterDirection.Input
objParam.SourceColumn = "Currency"
objParam.SourceVersion = DataRowVersion.Original    'used in SQL WHERE clause

objParam = objUpdateCommand.Parameters.Add("Price", OleDbType.Double)
objParam.Direction = ParameterDirection.Input
objParam.SourceColumn = "Price"
objParam.SourceVersion = DataRowVersion.Current    'used in SQL SET clause
    'now specify this Command object as the UpdateCommand
objDataAdapter.UpdateCommand = objUpdateCommand
```

The InsertCommand and the Dynamic Parameters

The InsertCommand requires four parameters, as shown in the following code. Note that in this case the stored procedure uses the ISBN value in the SET clause of the SQL statement rather than the WHERE clause, to set the value of the newly inserted rows, so it must use the Current value of the column and not the Original value.

The remaining three parameters are the Title that is placed, along with the ISBN, into the new row in the BookList table; and the currency and price to be instered, along with the ISBN, into the BookPrices table. Finally you can specify that this Command object is the insert command by assigning it to the DataAdapter object's InsertCommand property.

```
Dim objInsertCommand As New OleDbCommand("BookPriceInsert", objConnect)
objInsertCommand.CommandType = CommandType.StoredProcedure

objParam = objInsertCommand.Parameters.Add("ISBN", OleDbType.VarChar, 10)
objParam.Direction = ParameterDirection.Input
objParam.SourceColumn = "ISBN"
objParam.SourceVersion = DataRowVersion.Current    'used in SQL SET clause

objParam = objInsertCommand.Parameters.Add("Title", OleDbType.VarChar, 100)
objParam.Direction = ParameterDirection.Input
objParam.SourceColumn = "Title"
objParam.SourceVersion = DataRowVersion.Current    'used in SQL SET clause

objParam = objInsertCommand.Parameters.Add("Currency", OleDbType.VarChar, 3)
objParam.Direction = ParameterDirection.Input
objParam.SourceColumn = "Currency"
objParam.SourceVersion = DataRowVersion.Current    'used in SQL SET clause

objParam = objInsertCommand.Parameters.Add("Price", OleDbType.Double)
objParam.Direction = ParameterDirection.Input
objParam.SourceColumn = "Price"
objParam.SourceVersion = DataRowVersion.Current    'used in SQL SET clause

objDataAdapter.InsertCommand = objInsertCommand
```

The DeleteCommand and the Dynamic Parameters

The third and final stored procedure is used to delete rows from the source table(s). It requires just two parameters (the ISBN and the currency) and these take their values from the Original row values.

Otherwise, the code to create them is very similar to that you've just been using with the other Command objects.

```
Dim objDeleteCommand As New OleDbCommand("BookPriceDelete", objConnect)
objDeleteCommand.CommandType = CommandType.StoredProcedure

objParam = objDeleteCommand.Parameters.Add("ISBN", OleDbType.VarChar, 10)
objParam.Direction = ParameterDirection.Input
objParam.SourceColumn = "ISBN"
objParam.SourceVersion = DataRowVersion.Original   'used in SQL WHERE clause

objParam = objDeleteCommand.Parameters.Add("Currency", OleDbType.VarChar,3)
objParam.Direction = ParameterDirection.Input
objParam.SourceColumn = "Currency"
objParam.SourceVersion = DataRowVersion.Original   'used in SQL WHERE clause

objDataAdapter.DeleteCommand = objDeleteCommand
```

Displaying the Command Properties

Now that the three new Command objects are ready, you can display the CommandText and the parameters for each one in the page. Notice that you can iterate through the Parameters collection with a For Each construct to get the values.

```
    'get stored procedure name and source column names for each parameter
Dim strSQL As String = objDataAdapter.UpdateCommand.CommandText
For Each objParam In objDataAdapter.UpdateCommand.Parameters
    strSQL &= " @" & objParam.SourceColumn & ","
Next
strSQL = Left(strSQL, Len(strSQL) -1)   'remove trailing comma
outUpdate.InnerText = strSQL   'and display it
...
'repeat the process for the Insert command
...
'repeat the process for the Delete command
...
```

Executing the Update

Simply call the Update method of the DataAdapter to push your changes into the database via the stored procedures in exactly the same way as you did in previous examples. As in earlier examples, this page uses a transaction to make it repeatable, so the code is a little more complex than is actually required simply to push those changes into the database. Basically, all you need is:

```
objDataAdapter.Update(objDataSet, "Books")
```

The code to create the transaction is the same as used in the previous example, and you can use the [view source] link at the bottom of the page to see it. To prove that the updates do actually get carried out, you can also change the code so that the transaction is committed, or remove the transaction code altogether.

Using the NOCOUNT Statement in Stored Procedures

One point to be aware of when using stored procedures with the Update method is that the DataAdapter decides whether the update succeeded or failed based on the number of rows that are actually changed by the SQL statement(s) within the stored procedure.

When a SQL INSERT, UPDATE, or DELETE statement is executed (directly or inside a stored procedure) the database returns the number of rows that were affected. If there are several SQL statements within a stored procedure, it adds up the number of affected rows for all the statements and returns this value. If the returned value for the number of rows affected is zero, the DataAdapter will assume that the process (INSERT, UPDATE, or DELETE) failed. However, if any other value (positive or negative) is returned, the DataAdapter assumes that the process was successful.

In most cases this is fine and it works well, especially when you use CommandBuilder-created SQL statements rather than stored procedure to perform the updates. But if a stored procedure executes more than one statement, it may not always produce the result you expect. For example, if the stored procedure deletes child rows from one table and then deletes the parent row in a different table, the 'rows affected' value will be the sum of all the deletes in both tables. However, if the delete succeeds in the child table but fails in the parent table, the 'rows affected' value will still be greater than zero. So, in this case, the DataAdapter will still report success, when in actual fact it should report a failure.

To get around this problem, you can use the NOCOUNT statement within a stored procedure. When NOCOUNT is ON, the number of rows affected is not added to the return value. You could use it to prevent the deletes to the child rows from being included in your 'rows affected' return value.

```
SET NOCOUNT ON
DELETE FROM ChildTable WHERE KeyValue = @param-value
SET NOCOUNT OFF
DELETE FROM ParentTable WHERE KeyValue = @param-value
```

Update Events in the DataAdapter

In the previous chapter you saw how to write event handlers for several events that occur for a row in a table when that row is updated. In the examples, the row was held in a DataTable object within a DataSet, and the events occurred when the row was updated. There is another useful series of events that can be handled, but this time they occur when you come to push the changes back into the original data store using a DataAdapter object.

The DataAdapter exposes two events: the RowUpdating event occurs before an attempt is made to update the row in the data source, and the RowUpdated event occurs after the row has been updated (or after an error has been detected—a topic we'll look at later). This means that you can monitor the updates as they take place for each row when you use the Update method of the DataAdapter.

Handling the RowUpdating and RowUpdated Events

The example page Handling the DataAdapter's RowUpdating and RowUpdated Events (rowupda ted-event.aspx) demonstrates how you can use these events to monitor the update process in a DataAdapter object. When you open the page, shown in Figure 10-13, you see the now familiar DataGrid objects containing the data before and after it has been updated by code within the page. You can also see the SQL SELECT statement that is used to extract the data, and the three auto-generated statements that are used to perform the update. This page uses exactly the same code as the earlier DataAdapter.Update example to extract and edit the data, and to push the changes back into the database. The extra features can be seen once you scroll down, as shown in Figure 10-14.

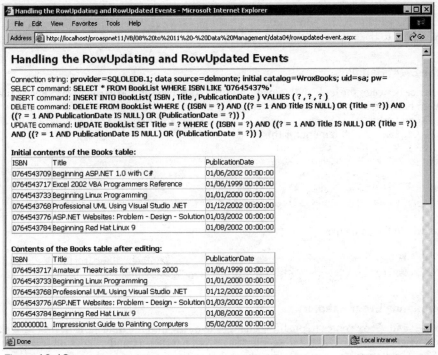

Figure 10-13

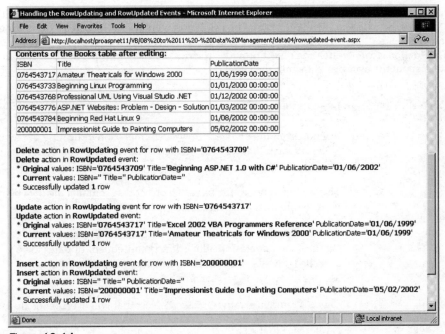

Figure 10-14

The remainder of the page contains three sets of output that is generated by the handlers you've provided for the `RowUpdating` and `RowUpdated` events—one each for a deleted row, an updated row, and a row added to the `DataSet` table.

Attaching the Event Handlers

One difference between the code in this page, and the code used in the earlier examples, is the addition of two event handlers. Attach these event handlers, which are named `OnRowUpdating` and `OnRowUpdated` to the `DataAdapter` object's `RowUpdating` and `RowUpdated` properties. In VB.NET, you can use the `AddHandler` statement for this:

```
AddHandler objDataAdapter.RowUpdating, _
          New OleDbRowUpdatingEventHandler(AddressOf OnRowUpdating)
AddHandler objDataAdapter.RowUpdated, _
          New OleDbRowUpdatedEventHandler(AddressOf OnRowUpdated)
```

In C# you can do the same using:

```
objDataAdapter.RowUpdating += new OleDbRowUpdatingEventHandler(OnRowUpdating);
objDataAdapter.RowUpdated  += new OleDbRowUpdatedEventHandler(OnRowUpdated);
```

The OnRowUpdating Event Handler

When the `DataAdapter` comes to push the changes to a row into the data store, it first raises the `RowUpdating` event, which will now execute your event handler named `OnRowUpdating`. The code receives two parameters, a reference to the object that raised the event, and a reference to a `RowUpdatingEventArgs` object.

Of course, as you're using the objects from the `System.Data.OleDb` namespace in this example, you actually get an `OleDbRowUpdatingEventArgs` object. If you were using the objects from, for example, the `System.Data.SqlClient` namespace you would get a reference to a `SqlDbRowUpdatingEventArgs` object. The `RowUpdatingEventArgs` object provides a series of *fields* or properties that contain useful information about the event, as shown in the table:

Property	Description
`StatementType`	A value from the `StatementType` enumeration indicating the type of SQL statement that will be executed to update the data. Can be `Insert`, `Update`, or `Delete`.
`Row`	This is a reference to the `DataRow` object that contains the data being used to update the data source.
`Status`	A value from the `UpdateStatus` enumeration that reports the current status of the update and allows it and subsequent updates to be cancelled. Possible values are: `Continue`, `SkipCurrentRow`, `SkipAllRemainingRows`, and `ErrorsOccurred`.
`Command`	This is a reference to the `Command` object that will execute the update.
`TableMapping`	A reference to the `DataTableMapping` that will be used for the update.

The example page's event handler collects the statement type by querying the `StatementType` enumeration (one of the values `Delete`, `Insert`, `Select`, or `Update`) and uses this value to decide where to get the row values for display. If it's an `Insert` statement, the `Current` value of the `ISBN` column in the row will contain the new primary key for that row, and the `Original` value will be empty. However, if it's an `Update` or `Delete` statement, the `Original` value will be the primary key of the original row in the database that corresponds to the row in your `DataSet`.

So, you can extract the primary key of the row that is about to be pushed into the database and display it, along with the statement type, in your page:

```
Sub OnRowUpdating(objSender As Object, _
                  objArgs As OleDbRowUpdatingEventArgs)

    'get the text description of the StatementType
    Dim strType = System.Enum.GetName(objArgs.StatementType.GetType(), _
                                      objArgs.StatementType)

    'get the value of the primary key column "ISBN"
    Dim strISBNValue As String

    Select Case strType
        Case "Insert"
            strISBNValue = objArgs.Row("ISBN", DataRowVersion.Current)
        Case Else
            strISBNValue = objArgs.Row("ISBN", DataRowVersion.Original)
    End Select

    'add result to display string
    gstrResult &= strType & " action in RowUpdating event " _
            & "for row with ISBN='" & strISBNValue & "'<br />"

End Sub
```

The OnRowUpdated Event Handler

After the row has been updated in the database, or when an error occurs, your `OnRowUpdated` event handler will be executed. In this case, you get a reference to a `RowUpdatedEventArgs` object instead of a `RowUpdatingEventArgs` object. It exposes the same five properties as the `RowUpdatingEventArgs` class, plus two more useful fields, as shown in the following table:

Property	Description
Errors	An `Error` object containing details of any error that was generated by the data provider when executing the update.
RecordsAffected	The number of rows that were changed, inserted, or deleted by execution of the SQL statement. Expect one (1) on success and zero or −1 if there is an error.

So, in your `OnRowUpdated` event handler, you can provide information about what happened after the update. Collect the statement type again; also collect all the `Original` and `Current` values from the columns in the row. Of course, if it is an `Insert` statement there won't be any `Original` values, as the row has been added to the table in the `DataSet` since the `DataSet` was originally filled. Likewise, there won't be any `Current` values if this row has been deleted in the `DataSet`.

And this time you can also include details about the result of the update. You can query the `RecordsAffected` value to see if a row was updated (as we expect), and if not include the error message from the `Errors` field.

```
'event handler for the RowUpdated event
Sub OnRowUpdated(objSender As Object, objArgs As OleDbRowUpdatedEventArgs)

    'get the text description of the StatementType
    Dim strType = System.Enum.GetName(objArgs.StatementType.GetType(), _
                                       objArgs.StatementType)
    'get the value of the columns
    Dim strISBNCurrent, strISBNOriginal, strTitleCurrent As String
    Dim strTitleOriginal, strPubDateCurrent, strPubDateOriginal As String

    Select Case strType
       Case "Insert"
          strISBNCurrent = objArgs.Row("ISBN", DataRowVersion.Current)
          strTitleCurrent = objArgs.Row("Title", DataRowVersion.Current)
          strPubDateCurrent = objArgs.Row("PublicationDate", _
                                          DataRowVersion.Current)
       Case "Delete"
          strISBNOriginal = objArgs.Row("ISBN", DataRowVersion.Original)
          strTitleOriginal = objArgs.Row("Title", DataRowVersion.Original)
          strPubDateOriginal = objArgs.Row("PublicationDate", _
                                           DataRowVersion.Original)
       Case "Update"
          strISBNCurrent = objArgs.Row("ISBN", DataRowVersion.Current)
          strTitleCurrent = objArgs.Row("Title", DataRowVersion.Current)
          strPubDateCurrent = objArgs.Row("PublicationDate", _
                                          DataRowVersion.Current)
          strISBNOriginal = objArgs.Row("ISBN", DataRowVersion.Original)
          strTitleOriginal = objArgs.Row("Title", DataRowVersion.Original)
          strPubDateOriginal = objArgs.Row("PublicationDate", _
                                           DataRowVersion.Original)

    End Select

    'add result to display string
    gstrResult &= strType & " action in RowUpdated event:<br />" _
            & "* Original values: ISBN='" & strISBNOriginal & "' " _
            & "Title='" & strTitleOriginal & "' " _
            & "PublicationDate='" & strPubDateOriginal & "'<br />" _
            & "* Current values: ISBN='" & strISBNCurrent & "' " _
            & "Title='" & strTitleCurrent & "' " _
            & "PublicationDate='" & strPubDateCurrent & "'<br />"

    'see if the update was successful
```

```
        Dim intRows = objArgs.RecordsAffected
        If intRows > 0 Then
            gstrResult &= "* Successfully updated " & intRows.ToString() _
                        & " row<p />"
        Else
            gstrResult &= "* Failed to update row <br />" _
                        & objArgs.Errors.Message & "<p />"
        End If

    End Sub
```

AcceptChanges and the Update Process

One important point to bear in mind is how the update process affects the `Original` and `Current` values of the rows in the tables in a `DataSet`. Once the `DataAdapter.Update` process is complete (in other words all the updates for all the rows have been applied), the `AcceptChanges` method is called for those rows automatically. So, after an update, the `Current` values in all the rows are moved to the `Original` values.

However, during the update process (as you can see from the example), the `Current` and `Original` values are available in both the `RowUpdating` and the `RowUpdated` events. Therefore you can use these events to monitor changes and report errors (more in a later example).

The techniques used in this section of the chapter (and in earlier examples) work fine in circumstances where there are no concurrent updates taking place on the source data. In other words, there is only ever one user reading from and writing to any particular row in the tables at any one time. However, concurrency rears its ugly head in many applications and can cause all kinds of problems if you aren't prepared for it.

Managing Concurrent Data Updates

To finish off looking at relational data handling in .NET, we'll examine some of the issues that arise when you have multiple users updating your data—a problem area normally referred to as *concurrency*. It's easy enough to see how such a problem could arise:

❑   Alice in accounts receives a fax from a customer indicating that their address has changed. She opens the customer record in her browser and starts to change the address column values.

❑   Just at this moment, Dave in dispatch (who received a copy of the fax) decides to update the customer's delivery route code. He also opens the customer record in his browser and changes the routing code column value.

❑   While Dave is doing this, Alice finishes editing the address and saves the record back to the database.

❑   Shortly afterwards, Dave saves his updated record back to the database.

What's happened is that Dave's record, which was opened before Alice saved her changes, contains the old address details. So when he saves it back to the database, the changes made by Alice are lost. And while concurrency issues aren't solely confined to databases (they can be a problem in all kinds of multi-user environments) it is obviously something that you can't just ignore when building data access applications.

Avoiding Concurrency Errors

Various database systems and applications use different approaches to control the concurrent updates problem. One solution is the use of *pessimistic record locking*. When a user wants to update a record, they open it with pessimistic locking; preventing any other user opening the same record in update mode. Other users can only open the record in 'read' mode until the first user saves their copy and releases their lock on the record.

> *For maximum runtime efficiency, many database systems actually lock a 'page' containing several contiguous records rather than just a single one–but the principle is the same.*

However, in a disconnected environment (particularly one with occasionally unreliable network links such as the Internet) pessimistic locking is not really feasible. If a user opens a record and then goes away, or the network connection fails, it will not be released. It requires some other process to monitor record locks and take decisions about when and if the user will come back to update the record so that the lock can be released.

Instead, within .NET, all data access is through *optimistic record locking*, which allows multiple users to open the same record for updating–possibly leading to the scenario we described at the start of this section. It means that you have to use some kind of code that can prevent errors occurring when you need to support concurrent updates. There are a few options you can take, such as:

❑ Write stored procedures that do lock records and manage the updates to prevent concurrency errors. For example, you could add a column called "Locked" and set this when a user fetches a row for updating. While it's set, no other user could open the row for updating, only for reading. This is not a favored approach in .NET as it takes away the advantages of the disconnected model.

❑ Arrange for your code to only update the actual columns that it changes the value of, minimizing the risk of (but not guaranteeing to prevent) concurrency errors. For example, in the previous scenario, if Dave in dispatch had only updated the route code column that he changed the value of, Alice's changes to the address columns would not have been lost.

❑ Compare the existing values in the records with the values that were there when you created your disconnected copy of the record. This way you can see if another user has changed any values in the database while you were working on your disconnected copy. This is the preferred solution in .NET, and there are built-in features that help you to implement it.

A Concurrency Error Example

To illustrate how concurrency error can be detected, try the example page Catching Concurrency Errors When Updating the Source Data (`concurrency-error.aspx`) shown in Figure 10-15. This page extracts a row from the source data table and displays the values in it. Then it executes a SQL statement directly against the *original* table in the database to change the `Title` column of the row while the disconnected `DataSet` is holding the original version of the row. You can see this in the screenshot after the first `DataGrid` control.

Next the code changes a couple of columns in the disconnected `DataSet` table row, then calls the `Update` method of the `DataAdapter` to push this change back into the original source table. A `CommandBuilder` object is used to create the SQL statement that performs the update, and you can see this statement displayed in the preceding page the `SELECT` statement that originally fetched the row. Notice that it uses a `WHERE` clause that tests all the values of the row in the database against the values held in the `DataSet`. This means, of course, that (because the concurrent process has changed the row) the update fails and an error is returned. What's happened is that the `Update` process expects a single row to be updated, and when this didn't happen it reports an error. The error message is displayed at the bottom of the page.

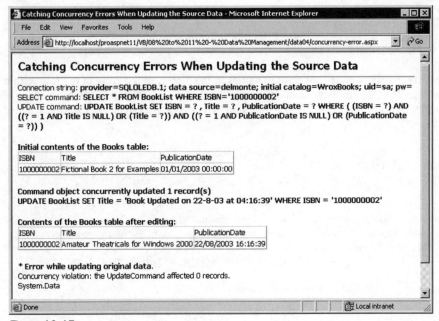

Figure 10-15

At this point, the developer would usually indicate to the user that this error had occurred, and give them the chance to reconcile the changes. Exactly how this is done and what options the user has depends on the application requirements. The usual process is to provide the user with the values that currently exist in the row as well as the values they entered, and allow them to specify which should be persisted into the data store.

The Code for the 'Catching Concurrency Errors' Example

The only section of the code for this example that you haven't seen before is that which performs a concurrent update to the source table in the database while the `DataSet` is holding a disconnected copy of the rows. It's simply a matter of creating a suitable SQL statement, a new `Connection` and `Command` object, and executing the SQL statement. Collect the number of rows affected by the update and display this in the page, along with the SQL statement you executed against the original data in the database.

```
'change one of the rows concurrently - i.e. while the
'DataSet is holding a disconnected copy of the data
Dim strUpdate As String
Dim datNow As DateTime = Now()
Dim strNow As String = datNow.ToString("dd-M-yy \a\t hh:mm:ss")
strUpdate = "UPDATE BookList SET Title = 'Book Updated on " _
          & strNow & "' WHERE ISBN = '1000000002'"
Dim intRowsAffected As Integer
Dim objNewConnect As New OleDbConnection(strConnect)
Dim objNewCommand As New OleDbCommand(strUpdate, objNewConnect)
objNewConnect.Open()
intRowsAffected = objNewCommand.ExecuteNonQuery()
objNewConnect.Close()
outUpdate.InnerHtml = "Command object concurrently updated " _
       & CStr(intRowsAffected) & " record(s)<br />" & strUpdate
```

Next, the code changes a couple of column values in the disconnected copy of the row within the
DataSet table. Then all you have to do is execute the Update method of the DataAdapter object. The
error is trapped by the Try..Catch construct (like that we've used in all the examples) and details are
displayed in the page.

```
'change the same row in the table in the DataSet
objTable.Rows(0)("Title") = "Amateur Theatricals for Windows 2000"
objTable.Rows(0)("PublicationDate") = Now()
Try
  'create an auto-generated command builder and set UPDATE command
  Dim objCommandBuilder As New OleDbCommandBuilder(objDataAdapter)
  objDataAdapter.UpdateCommand = objCommandBuilder.GetUpdateCommand()
  'display the auto-generated UPDATE command statement
  outUpdate.InnerText = objDataAdapter.UpdateCommand.CommandText
```

Now do the update (in this case we know it will fail):

```
  intRowsAffected = objDataAdapter.Update(objDataSet, "Books")
  outResult.InnerHtml = "<b>* DataSet.Update</b> affected <b>" _
                    & CStr(intRowsAffected) & "</b> row."
Catch objError As Exception
  'display error details
  outError.innerHTML = "* Error updating original data.<br />" _
        & objError.Message & "<br />" & objError.Source
End Try
```

Updating Just the Changed Columns

In general, it is the process of modifying existing rows in a data store that is most likely to create a
concurrency error. The process of deleting rows is usually less error-prone, and less likely to cause data
inconsistencies in your database. Likewise, providing data entry programs are reasonably clever about
how they create the values for unique columns; the process of inserting new rows is generally less of a
problem.

One of the ways that you can reduce the likelihood of a concurrency error during row modification, as
we suggested right at the start of this section of the chapter, is to push only the modified column values

(the ones that have been changed by this user or process) into the original data store, rather than blindly updating all of the columns. Of course, this means that you can't use the `Update` method–you have to build and execute each SQL statement yourselves.

An Example of Updating Individual Columns

The example page Managing Concurrent Updates to Individual Columns (`concurrency-columns.aspx`) demonstrates the process we've just been discussing. Rather than updating all the columns in every row that has been modified, it only attempts to update the column values that have actually changed. The code extracts a series of rows from the `BookList` table and displays them, then changes some of the column values and displays the rows again.

In Figure 10-16, you can see the original values of the rows in the database, and the values of the rows in our disconnected `DataSet` table after the code has changed some of the values. This code changed the title of the first book, the title and publication date of the third book, and (highlighted in the screenshot) just the publication date for the fourth book.

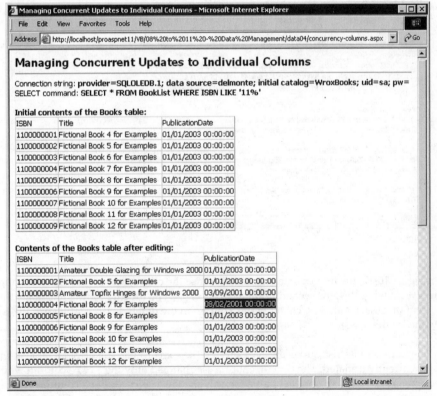

Figure 10-16

Lower down the the page, as shown in Figure 10-17, you can see that the code then concurrently updates two of the rows in the source database table while the `DataSet` is holding a disconnected copy of the data. It changes the titles of the third and fourth books. Below this is another `DataGrid` that shows just the modified rows in the `DataSet`.

Finally, at the bottom of the page you can see that–after the concurrent updates have taken place–we attempt to push our changes in the `DataSet` back into the data store. However, in this case, the `Update` method of the `DataAdapter` is not used. Instead, each of the modified rows is processed individually by executing a custom SQL statement for each one. As you can see from comparing these, the statements used only update the columns that have been changed within the table in the `DataSet`, and only check the existing values of these columns (as part of the `WHERE` clause) in the database.

Figure 10-17

As seen in Figure 10-17, the first update succeeds because the concurrent process hasn't changed the original row. Following this, the second update fails because you are attempting to change the title while the concurrent process has already changed this column in the database (look at Figure 10-16 to see the original values of the rows).

However, the third update also succeeds–even though the same row in the original table in the database has been concurrently updated. The concurrent process changed only the `Title` column while our disconnected copy contains an updated value for only the `PublicationDate` column. Hence, because the update code is clever enough to only update the changed columns, both updates can occur concurrently without the risk of inconsistencies arising.

The Code for the 'Updating Individual Columns' Example

There are several things going on in this example page that we need to look at in more depth. For example, you need to be able to get at just the modified rows in the table within your DataSet so that you can iterate through these rows processing the update for each one. Secondly, you need to look in more detail at how to create the values that you use in the WHERE clause of your SQL statements to compare to a DateTime column in SQL server.

Marshalling the Changed Rows in a DataSet

As mentioned in the previous chapter, every row in a table within a DataSet has a RowState property that indicates whether that row has changed since the table was filled, or since the last time the AcceptChanges or RejectChanges method was called. So, to get a list of the changed rows you could iterate through the table looking at this property in each row, and extract just the ones we want into an array–or into another table.

The general process of collecting together data and transferring it to another location is often referred to as *marshalling*. In your case, you want to marshal the changed rows from one table into another table, and the .NET data access classes make it easy through the GetChanges method of the DataSet object. It returns a DataSet object containing just the changed rows. You can use the GetChanges method in two ways:

❑   With no parameters, whereupon it returns a DataSet object with the default table (at index zero) filled with all the changed rows–e.g. all the rows that have been modified, deleted, or inserted.

❑   With a DataRowState value as the single parameter, whereupon it returns a DataSet object with the default table (at index zero) filled with just the changed rows having that value for their RowState property–e.g. just the rows that have been modified, or just the rows that have been deleted, or just the rows that have been inserted.

This process would also allow you to take a table that contained updated, deleted, and inserted rows and extract these into separate arrays of rows–one each for changed rows, deleted rows, and updated rows. You could then use the Update method of the DataAdapter with each table or array of rows in turn (as discussed earlier in this section of the chapter)–in the correct order to avoid any errors due to parent/child relationships within the source data tables.

Getting the Modified Rows into a New DataSet

The code in your page creates a variable to hold a DataSet object, and then executes the GetChanges method with the value DataRowState.Modified as the single parameter. The new DataSet object is returned and assigned to your variable objChangeDS, and you can display the contents in the usual way using a DataGrid control defined within the HTML section of the page.

```
'declare a variable to hold another DataSet object
Dim objChangeDS As DataSet

'get *changed* records into the new DataSet
'copy only rows with a RowState property of "Modified"
objChangeDS = objDataSet.GetChanges(DataRowState.Modified)

'display the modified records from the table in the new DataSet
```

```
dgrResult3.DataSource = objChangeDS.Tables(0).DefaultView
dgrResult3.DataBind()   'and bind (display) the data
```

As an aside (we don't actually do it in our example here) you can use the same technique to get the inserted, deleted, or unchanged rows as well. To get the inserted rows into a `DataSet` just specify the value `DataRowState.Added` in the parameter to the `GetChanges` method:

```
objChangeDS = objDataSet.GetChanges(DataRowState.Added)
```

The same applies to the deleted rows; specify `DataRowState.Deleted` in the parameter to the `GetChanges` method:

```
objChangeDS = objDataSet.GetChanges(DataRowState.Deleted)
```

However, if you then bind this data to a `DataGrid` object, nothing will be displayed because all of the rows have been deleted! To get round this you can create a `DataView` object explicitly for the table and then set the `RowStateFilter` property to `DataViewRowState.Deleted` as well (this topic was covered in previous chapters). Then it shows the deleted rows:

```
Dim objDataView As DataView = objChangeDS.Tables(0).DefaultView
objDataView.RowStateFilter = DataViewRowState.Deleted
dgrResult.DataSource = objDataView
dgrResult.DataBind()
```

Finally, to get the unchanged rows specify `DataRowState.Unchanged` in the parameter to the `GetChanges` method:

```
objChangeDS = objDataSet.GetChanges(DataRowState.Unchanged)
```

Getting Back to Our Example

After that short aside, let's get back to the code for your example page. While there is quite a lot of code in this page, most of it is stuff that you've seen several times before. Basically, you extract the rowset from the database into a `DataSet` and display it, execute a couple of SQL UPDATE statements to change the original data store contents, then change some values in the same rows in the disconnected copy held within the `DataSet` object. All these steps can be seen in the page.

What we want to concentrate on here is how to create and execute the SQL statements that you'll use to perform the updates to the original data from the rows in the disconnected `DataSet`.

Building the SQL Statements

The plan is to create the two 'root' parts of the SQL statement (the SET clause and the WHERE clause) separately as you iterate through each column in the row, then assemble the complete statement afterwards. You've already marshaled the modified rows into a new `DataSet` named `objChangeDS`, so you can iterate through the single table in that `DataSet` processing each modified row using a For Each construct.

As you process each row, create your two sections of SQL statement. For the WHERE clause include the test for the `Original` value of the ISBN (the primary key). Then you can start the nested For Each construct that will iterate through each column in this row, and collect the column name in a string variable.

The next step is to see if the value of the column has been changed since you loaded your DataSet, by comparing the Original and the Current values. Note that this is nothing to do with checking the original values in the source table in the database. You're disconnected from the database, and so you can't see any concurrent updates going on. What you're checking for here is if the contents of the disconnected row have been changed within the DataSet since it was originally extracted from the source database.

```
'iterate through all the modified rows in the table
For Each objRow in objChangeDS.Tables(0).Rows

    'create the two root parts of the SQL statement
    strSQL = "UPDATE BookList SET "
    strWhere = " WHERE ISBN='" & objRow("ISBN", DataRowVersion.Original) & "'"

    'iterate through all the columns in this row
    For Each objColumn In objChangeDS.Tables(0).Columns

        'see if this column has been changed since the DataSet was
        'originally created by comparing Original and Current values
        strColName = objColumn.ColumnName
        If objRow(strColName, DataRowVersion.Current) <> _
           objRow(strColName, DataRowVersion.Original) Then
            ...
```

Matching a SQL Server DateTime Column

If the column has been changed, you need to add it to both sections of the SQL statement you're constructing. However, if the value is a DateTime, you have to format the Original value (which will be used in the WHERE clause) to match the column in the source table in the database. To perform a match against a SQL DateTime column, you have to specify the value in your disconnected row in a suitable format so that it can be compared properly.

The next part of the code extracts the original value of the PublicationDate column from the row and formats it if it is a date/time–if not it just extracts the value. Then add the column name and values to the two sections of the SQL statement. You can use the Current value in the SET clause and the Original value in the WHERE clause.

After this, you can go round and process the next column. And once all the changed columns have been processed, tidy up the SQL statement by stripping off the extra comma and space you added and assemble it into one string. Then you can display it in the page.

```
        ...
        'have to get format of DateTime exactly right for a comparison
        If objColumn.DataType.ToString() = "System.DateTime" Then
            datRowDateValue = objRow(strColName, DataRowVersion.Original)
            strRowValue = datRowDateValue.Format("yyyy-MM-dd\ HH:mm:ss", _
                          Nothing)
        Else
            strRowValue = objRow(strColName, DataRowVersion.Original)
```

```
        End If

        strSQL &= strColName & "='" _
                & objRow(strColName, DataRowVersion.Current) & "', "
        strWhere &= " AND " & strColName & "='" & strRowValue & "'"

      End If

  Next   'go to next column

  'strip off extra comma and space from end of string
  strSQL = Left(strSQL, Len(strSQL) -2) & strWhere

  'display the SQL statement
  strResults &= "* " & strSQL & " ... "
  objCommand.CommandText = strSQL
  ...
```

Executing the SQL Statement

Now you can execute this SQL statement, check the number of rows affected, and display a suitable message for this row. If the number of rows affected is less than 1 you know there was a concurrency error–the original row in the source table has changed while you were holding the disconnected copy. Then, after processing this row, go back and do the next one in your modified rows table. When all the rows have been processed, display the result in a `<div>` element located in the HTML of the page.

```
  ...
  Try

    intRowsAffected = objCommand.ExecuteNonQuery()
    If intRowsAffected > 0 Then
      strResults &= "... updated <b>" & intRowsAffected & "</b> row(s)"
    Else
      strResults &= "<b>Error</b>: Row was changed by another user"
    End If

  Catch objError As Exception

    'display error details
    strResults &= "Error: " & objError.Message & " -" _
                & objError.Source & "<br />"
  End Try

  Next       'repeat for next row if any

outUpdates.InnerHtml = strResults    'then display the results
```

Handling Concurrency Errors

Your example simply displays the errors that were encountered due to concurrent updates in the page. It doesn't provide any way to reconcile these errors. In fact, the .NET data access objects don't provide any features for this, as there is no fixed way to do it. It all depends on what your application is doing, how the updates are being carried out, and what business rules you want to apply. The next example demonstrates another approach for managing concurrency errors.

Capturing Errors with the RowUpdated Event

The previous example attempted to reduce the likelihood of concurrency errors occurring by taking over the *update* process and replacing it with a custom system of SQL statements. This allows updates to be monitored individually. However, this kind of process is going to produce a performance hit when compared to the `Update` method exposed by the `DataAdapter`.

You saw in an earlier section of this chapter that the `DataAdapter` raises two events for each row as the `Update` method is being executed. These events allow you to examine each row before it is pushed into the original table (the `RowUpdating` event) and after the update has been processed for that row (the `RowUpdated` event). By writing handlers for these events, you can deal with many concurrency issues.

Of course, you don't usually detect a concurrency error until you actually perform the update to a row against the original data source. You could use the `RowUpdating` event to fetch the data again from the database before you attempted to perform your update, and see if it had changed, but this is an inefficient approach unless you really need to actually prevent update *attempts* that might result in a concurrency error.

Generally, a better solution is to trap any errors that occur during the update process and report these back so that the user (or some other process) can reconcile them. The next example demonstrates how you can do this, and also introduces a couple more features of ADO.NET.

Concurrent Updates and the RowUpdated Event

The example page Managing Concurrent Updates with the RowUpdated Event (`concurrency-rowupdated.aspx`) demonstrates how we can capture information about concurrency errors while updating a data source. It handles the `RowUpdated` event, and creates a `DataSet` object containing a single table that details all the errors that occurred. This `DataSet` could be returned to the user, or passed to another process that will decide what to do next. In your example, you simply display the contents in the page.

So, as shown in Figure 10-18, when you open the example page you see the rowset with its original values when you fetched it from the database, and then the contents after you've made some changes to this disconnected data. We've deleted the first row (ISBN 1100000001), changed the title and publication date in the second row (ISBN 1100000002), and just the publication date in the third row (ISBN 1100000003).

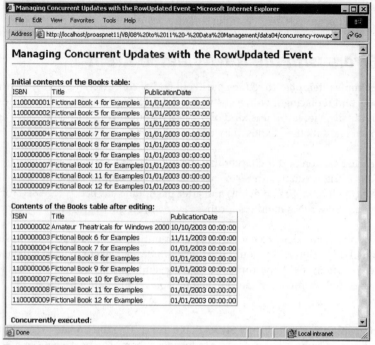

Figure 10-18

Next, as shown in Figure 10-19, the code in the page executes three SQL UPDATE statements directly against the database (as in the previous example) to change the values in the three rows that you have just edited in the disconnected DataSet.

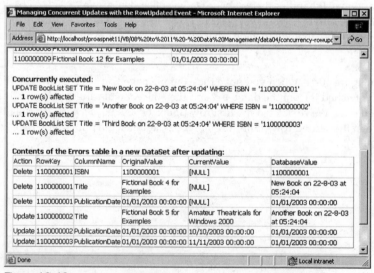

Figure 10-19

At the bottom of the page you can see a third DataGrid control. This displays the contents of the new *errors* table that you've dynamically created in response to errors that occurred during the update process.

In the *errors* table, you can see that you've got several errors, and for each one the table provides information about the type of operation that was being executed (the *Action*, equivalent to the statement type), the primary key of the row, the name of the column that was modified in the DataSet, and three values for this column. These are:

❑ OriginalValue: The value when the DataSet was first filled (the value that was in the database at that time)

❑ CurrentValue: The current value in the DataSet after the updates we made

❑ DatabaseValue: The value of this column at the present moment within the database (the value set by the concurrently executed SQL UPDATE statement)

If you look at the result, the first three error rows indicate that you deleted a row in the DataSet that was concurrently changed within the database. You can see that the Title column was changed while you had the DataSet open. These rows show the Original values, but of course they cannot show the Current values in the DataSet because the row was deleted.

The fourth and fifth rows in the *errors* table are for the second row that you modified in your DataSet. You changed the Title and PublicationDate columns in your DataSet, while the concurrent process changed the Title column–so the value for this column in the database is different from the Original value.

In the last of the error rows, the update failed because the concurrent process had changed a different column than was changed in the DataSet within that row. The database value and the Original value are the same for this column, so it must have been a different column that caused the concurrency error.

If you intend to use a page like this to extract data that will be presented to a user so that they can manually reconcile the data, you may prefer to include all the columns from rows where a concurrency error occurred in the *errors* table. We'll discuss this at the appropriate point as we work through the code.

The Code for the 'RowUpdated Event' Example

The majority of the code in this example is the same as in our earlier *concurrency* examples. One difference is that you declare some of the variables you use as being global to the page, rather than within the Page_Load event handler as you've done before. This is because you want to be able to access these variables within your RowUpdated event handler.

```vb
<script language="vb" runat="server">
Dim gstrResult As String          'to hold the result messages
Dim gstrConnect As String         'to hold connection string
Dim gobjDataSet As DataSet        'to hold rows from database
Dim gobjErrorTable As DataTable   'to hold a list of errors
Dim gobjErrorDS As DataSet        'to hold the Errors table
Sub Page_Load()
      page load event handler is here
```

In the `Page_Load` event, fill a table in the `DataSet` with some rows from the `BookList` table in your example database and display these rows in the first `DataGrid` control. Then change three of the rows in the `DataSet` in exactly the same way as you did in the previous examples, and display the rowset in the second `DataGrid` control.

Next create a new connection to the source database, and through it execute three SQL UPDATE statements that change three of the rows in the database. These statements are displayed in the preceding page the second `DataGrid` control. At this point, you are ready to push the updates back to the database. But before you do so, add your `OnRowUpdated` event handler to the `DataAdapter` so that it will be executed each time a row is updated in the original data source:

```
AddHandler objDataAdapter.RowUpdated, _
            New OleDbRowUpdatedEventHandler(AddressOf OnRowUpdated)
```

Creating and Displaying the 'Errors' DataSet

Before you start the update process, you need to create the new `DataSet` that will contain details of errors that occur during the process. Create a `DataTable` object named `Errors`, and define the columns for this table (you saw how this works in the previous chapter). Then you can create a new `DataSet` object and add the table you've just defined to it (notice that all these objects are referenced by global variables that you declared outside the `Page_Load` event handler so that you can access them from other event handlers).

Now you can carry on as in other examples by creating the auto-generated commands for the update and executing them by calling the `DataAdapter` object's `Update` method (not shown in this code). Once the update is complete, display the contents of your *errors* `DataSet` in the third `DataGrid` control at the bottom of the page.

```
'create a new empty Table object to hold error rows
gobjErrorTable = New DataTable("Errors")

'define the columns for the Errors table
gobjErrorTable.Columns.Add("Action", System.Type.GetType("System.String"))
gobjErrorTable.Columns.Add("RowKey", System.Type.GetType("System.String"))
gobjErrorTable.Columns.Add("ColumnName", System.Type.GetType("System.String"))
gobjErrorTable.Columns.Add("OriginalValue", _
                          System.Type.GetType("System.String"))
gobjErrorTable.Columns.Add("CurrentValue", _
                          System.Type.GetType("System.String"))
gobjErrorTable.Columns.Add("DatabaseValue", _
                          System.Type.GetType("System.String"))

'create a new empty DataSet object to hold Errors table
gobjErrorDS = New DataSet()
gobjErrorDS.Tables.Add(gobjErrorTable)

... execute Update method here to push changes into database ...

'display the contents of the Errors table
dgrResult3.DataSource = gobjErrorDS
dgrResult3.DataMember = "Errors"
dgrResult3.DataBind()    'and bind (display) the data
```

In this case, you've bound the `DataGrid` to the `DataSet` object itself (using the `DataSource` property) and then specified that it should display the contents of the `Errors` table within that `DataSet` by setting the `DataMember` property.

Getting the Current Value from the Database Table

Of course, the code shown so far won't actually put any rows into the *errors* `DataSet`. These rows are created within the `RowUpdated` event handler whenever a concurrency error is detected. We know that we want to include in each row the current value of the column in the original database table at the point that the update process was executed–it will be different from the `Original` value of that column in the `DataSet` if that column in the row was changed by a concurrent process.

So, we have written a short function within the page that – given a connection string, primary key (ISBN) value, and a column name–will return the value of that column for that row from the source database. The function is named `GetCurrentColumnValue`:

```
Function GetCurrentColumnValue(strConnect As String, strISBN As String, _
                              strColumnName As String) As String
  'select existing column value from underlying table in the database
  Dim strSQL = "SELECT " & strColumnName _
            & " FROM BookList WHERE ISBN='" & strISBN & "'"
  Dim objConnect As New OleDbConnection(strConnect)
  Dim objCommand As New OleDbCommand(strSQL, objConnect)
  Try
    objConnect.Open()
    'use ExecuteScalar for efficiency, it returns only one item
    'get the value direct from it and convert to a String
    GetCurrentColumnValue = objCommand.ExecuteScalar().ToString()
    objConnect.Close()
  Catch objError As Exception
    GetCurrentColumnValue = "*Error*"
  End Try
End Function
```

One interesting point is that we use the `ExecuteScalar` method of the `Command` object to get the value. The `ExecuteScalar` method returns just a single value from a query (rather than a rowset, for which we'd have to use a `DataReader` object).

So, it is extremely efficient when compared to a `DataReader`, where we have to call the `Read` method to load the first row of results, and then access the column by name or ordinal index.

The `ExecuteScalar` method is especially appropriate for queries that calculate a value, such as summing values or working out the average value in a column for some or all of the rows. In our case, it's useful because our SQL statement also only returns a single value (sometimes referred to as a singleton).

So, this simple function will return the value of a specified column in a specified row, or the string value "`*Error*`" if it can't access it (for example if it has been deleted).

The OnRowUpdated Event Handler

Finally, the page contains the `OnRowUpdated` event handler itself. Remember that this is called after each row has been updated in the source database, whether or not there was an error. So, the first thing we do is check the `RecordsAffected` field of the `RowUpdatedEventArgs` object to see if the update for this row failed. If it did, we need to add details of the error to our *errors* `DataSet`.

We want to know what type of update this is, so we extract the `StatementType` as a `String` using the enumeration's `GetName` method, and store this in a local variable for use later. We also need to extract the value of the ISBN column from the row, as this is the primary key we'll need for locating the row later. Being the primary key means that it should not be possible for the user to change the value in that row of the `DataSet`, which would mean that we could just access the Original value.

However, if they were allowed to change the value, we would have to use the Current value of that column to extract the updated value. But if this row has been deleted in the `DataSet`, there will be no Current value. In our example, to demonstrate the technique, we first check to see if it is a deleted row by examining the `RowState` property, and then extract the value from the appropriate version of the column.

```
'event handler for the RowUpdated event
Sub OnRowUpdated(objSender As Object, objArgs As OleDbRowUpdatedEventArgs)
  'see if the update failed
  If objArgs.RecordsAffected < 1 Then
    'get the text description of the StatementType
    Dim strType = System.Enum.GetName(objArgs.StatementType.GetType(), _
                              objArgs.StatementType)
    'get the primary key of the row (the ISBN). Must look at Original
    'version in deleted rows because they have no Current version
    Dim strRowKey As String
    If objArgs.Row.RowState = DataRowState.Deleted Then
      strRowKey = objArgs.Row("ISBN", DataRowVersion.Original)
    Else
      strRowKey = objArgs.Row("ISBN", DataRowVersion.Current)
    End If
    ...
```

Handling the Columns for Deleted Rows

Now we can check which column(s) caused the concurrency error to occur, or simply collect all the column values if the concurrency error occurred for a row that was deleted in the `DataSet`. We start by getting a reference to the table in our original `DataSet`, the one we filled with rows from the database, and we declare a couple of other variables that we'll need as well.

Then we iterate through the `Columns` collection of this table, extracting the column name and again checking whether this is a deleted row. If it is, we want to add the values from this column to our *error* database. We create a new `DataRow` based on the `Errors` table, and then we can start filling in the values:

We saved the values for the first three columns of our `Errors` table (the statement type, row key and column name) as strings earlier on in our event handler. The next value comes from the row referenced by the `RowUpdatedEventArgs` object that is passed to our event handler. Because it is a deleted row, we

can only access the `Original` value, and we set the `CurrentValue` column of our `Errors` table to
"`[NULL]`".

The final value comes from the custom `GetCurrentColumnValue` function we described earlier, and
contains the current value of this column in this row within the source database. And after we've filled
in all the values for the new row we add it to the `Errors` table.

```
...
'get a reference to the original table in the DataSet
Dim objTable As DataTable = gobjDataSet.Tables(0)

Dim objColumn As DataColumn      'to hold a DataColumn object
Dim strColumnName As String      'to hold the column name

'iterate through the columns in the current row
For Each objColumn In objTable.Columns

  'get the column name as a string
  strColumnName = objColumn.ColumnName

  'if this is a deleted row, insert all the original columns values
  If objArgs.Row.RowState = DataRowState.Deleted Then

      'create a new DataRow object instance in this table
      Dim objDataRow As DataRow = gobjErrorTable.NewRow()

      'and fill in the values
      objDataRow("Action") = strType
      objDataRow("RowKey") = strRowKey
      objDataRow("ColumnName") = strColumnName
      objDataRow("OriginalValue") _
          = objArgs.Row(strColumnName, DataRowVersion.Original)
      objDataRow("CurrentValue") = "[NULL]"
      objDataRow("DatabaseValue") _
          = GetCurrentColumnValue(gstrConnect, strRowKey, strColumnName)

      'add new row to the Errors table
      gobjErrorTable.Rows.Add(objDataRow)

  Else
    ...
```

Handling the Columns for Modified Rows

The preceding code handles the case of a deleted row, but for a modified row the `Else` section of the
`If..Then` construct we started will be executed. This section of the event handler code is shown in the
following code. The first step here is to compare the `Current` and `Original` values of the row. If they
are different, we know that this column in the current row has been modified within the `DataSet` since
it was filled from the database table.

Notice that this is why we only get the *modified* columns in our *errors* table. If the concurrent process
changes a different column to the one(s) that are modified in the `DataSet`, a row will not appear in the
`Errors` table. We could simply remove this `If..Then` construct, which will cause all the values from all
the columns in a row that caused a concurrency error to be included in the table. However, in that case

we would probably also want to change the way we extract the current values from the database, as using a separate function call for each column would certainly not be the most efficient technique.

Returning to the code in our example, since we know that this row caused a concurrency error and that this column has been changed since the DataSet was filled, we add details about the values in this column to our table named Errors within the new *errors* DataSet we created earlier as we did for a deleted row, though this time using the Current value of the column for the CurrentValue column in the Errors table. And, as before, after filling in the row values we add it to the Errors table.

The Next statement at the end means we can go back, look at the next column and repeat the process.

```
      ...
   Else
      'see if this column has been modified
      If objArgs.Row(strColumnName, DataRowVersion.Current) _
         <> objArgs.Row(strColumnName, DataRowVersion.Original) Then
         'create a new DataRow object instance in this table
         Dim objDataRow As DataRow = gobjErrorTable.NewRow()
         'and fill in the values
         objDataRow("Action") = strType
         objDataRow("RowKey") = strRowKey
         objDataRow("ColumnName") = strColumnName
         objDataRow("OriginalValue") _
            = objArgs.Row(strColumnName, DataRowVersion.Original)
         objDataRow("CurrentValue") _
            = objArgs.Row(strColumnName, DataRowVersion.Current)
         objDataRow("DatabaseValue") _
            = GetCurrentColumnValue(gstrConnect, strRowKey, strColumnName)
         'add new row to the Errors table
         gobjErrorTable.Rows.Add(objDataRow)
      End If
   End If
Next  'go to next column
```

So that you can see the result and better understand what the code does, we've repeated the relevant section of the screenshot of this example page again in Figure 10-20:

Contents of the Errors table in a new DataSet after updating:					
Action	RowKey	ColumnName	OriginalValue	CurrentValue	DatabaseValue
Delete	1100000001	ISBN	1100000001	[NULL]	1100000001
Delete	1100000001	Title	Fictional Book 4 for Examples	[NULL]	New Book on 22-8-03 at 05:24:04
Delete	1100000001	PublicationDate	01/01/2003 00:00:00	[NULL]	01/01/2003 00:00:00
Update	1100000002	Title	Fictional Book 5 for Examples	Amateur Theatricals for Windows 2000	Another Book on 22-8-03 at 05:24:04
Update	1100000002	PublicationDate	01/01/2003 00:00:00	10/10/2003 00:00:00	01/01/2003 00:00:00
Update	1100000003	PublicationDate	01/01/2003 00:00:00	11/11/2003 00:00:00	01/01/2003 00:00:00

Figure 10-20

Handling the Columns for Inserted Rows

Notice that we aren't specifically handling errors for new (inserted) rows in our example. In general, a concurrency error can only occur in this situation if the page allocates an existing primary key to the new row, or perhaps because a parent row was deleted when we are trying to add a related row to a child table. However, it's not hard to add the code to handle insert errors as well. The `StatementType` property of the `RowUpdatedEventArgs` that is passed to the event handler will be `StatementType.Insert` in this case, and the rows will have `DataRowState.Added` as their `RowState` property.

The one point to be aware of is that there will be no `Original` value in the row in the `DataSet`, in the same way as there is no `Current` value for a deleted row (hence our example code would fail when trying to access the `Current` value). And, of course, in this case the `GetCurrentColumnValue` function will return the value of the column inserted by another user, or an *error* value if the insert fails for some other reason.

Returning an UpdateStatus Value

The other important point when using the `RowUpdating` and `RowUpdated` event handlers that we haven't mentioned so far is how we manage the status value that is exposed by the `Status` field of the `RowUpdatingEventArgs` and `RowUpdatedEventArgs` objects. In our earlier example of using the `RowUpdating` and `RowUpdated` events (`rowupdated-event.aspx`) we just ignored these values, but that was really only acceptable because we didn't get any concurrency errors during the update process.

When the `DataAdapter` object's `Update` method is executing, each call to the `RowUpdating` and `RowUpdated` event handler includes a status *flag* value. We can set this to a specific value from the `UpdateStatus` enumeration to tell the `Update` method what to do next, as shown in the following table:

`Continue`	Default. The `DataAdapter` will continue to process rows (including the current one if this is a `RowUpdating` event) as part of the `Update` method call.
`ErrorsOccurred`	The `DataAdapter` will stop processing rows and treat the `RowUpdating` or `RowUpdated` event as raising an error.
`SkipAllRemainingRows`	The `DataAdapter` will stop processing rows and end the `Update` method, but it will not treat the `RowUpdating` or `RowUpdated` event as an error.
`SkipCurrentRow`	The `DataAdapter` will not process this row (if this is a `RowUpdating` event), but will continue to process all remaining rows as part of the `Update` method call.

Because the default is `Continue`, the `Update` process will actually stop executing and report a runtime error when the first concurrency error occurs if we just ignore this status flag. So, as we're handling the concurrency errors ourselves, we must set the value to `UpdateStatus.SkipCurrentRow` so that the concurrency error doesn't cause the `Update` process to be terminated. This is the last step in our event handler, as shown in the code:

```
...
'set the Status property of the row to skip current row update
'if there is an error. Default is Continue, which means an error
```

```
      'will halt execution for this failed update and not process the
      'remaining updated or deleted rows
      objArgs.Status = UpdateStatus.SkipCurrentRow
   End If
End Sub
```

In this example, you've seen how we can capture information on concurrency errors, allowing the user or another process to take a reasoned decision on how to reconcile the values. Because we've placed the information in a disconnected `DataSet` object, it could easily be remoted to a client via HTTP or a Web Service, or passed directly to another tier of the application.

Locating Errors After an Update Is Complete

There is one final approach to managing concurrent updates that we can take advantage of in ADO.NET when using the `Update` method of the `DataAdapter` object. Instead of reacting to each `RowUpdated` event, we can force the `DataAdapter` to continue processing the updates for each row even if it encounters an error (rather than terminating the `Update` process when the first concurrency or other error occurs).

All we need to do is set the `ContinueUpdateOnError` property of the `DataAdapter` object that is performing the `Update` to `True`. Then, whenever an error is encountered, the `DataAdapter` will simply insert the error message that it receives into the `RowError` property of the relevant row within the `DataSet`, and continue with the next updated row.

The `RowError` property is a `String` value. You saw how to use this in the example from the previous chapter where we used the `RowUpdated` event of the `DataTable` object (rather than the event of the same name exposed by the `DataAdapter` object that we've been using in this chapter).

So, if we can wait until after the `Update` process has finished to review and fix errors, we have an easier option for managing concurrency errors. The process is:

❑   Once the appropriate `DataAdapter` is created and ready to perform the `Update`, set the `ContinueUpdateOnError` property of the `DataAdapter` object to `True`

❑   Call the `Update` method of the `DataAdapter` object to push the changes into the data source

❑   After the `Update` process completes, check the `HasErrors` property of the `DataSet` object to see if any of the rows contain an error (e.g. have a non-empty value for their `RowError` property)

❑   If there are (one or more) errors, check the `HasErrors` property of each `DataTable` object in the `DataSet` to see which ones contain errors

❑   Iterate through the rows of each `DataTable` that does contain errors, checking the `RowError` property of each row—or use the `GetErrors` method of the `DataTable` to get an array of the rows with errors in them

❑   Display or feed back to the user the error details and column values so that they can retry the updates as required

Using the ContinueUpdateOnError Property

We've provided an example that carries out this series of steps while attempting to update a data source. The page Locating Concurrency Errors After Updating the Source Data (`concurrency-continue.aspx`) shown in Figure 10-21 displays the rows that it extracts from our sample database, edits two of the rows (the first and second ones), then displays the rowset again to show the changes.

After that, the same process as we used in earlier examples changes the same two rows in the source database using a separate connection, while we are holding a disconnected copy of the data in our `DataSet`. Then, as you can see at the bottom of the page, it displays the errors found in the `DataSet` after the update process has completed. It shows the error message (the value of the `RowError` property for that row), and the original, current, and underlying (database) values for the row.

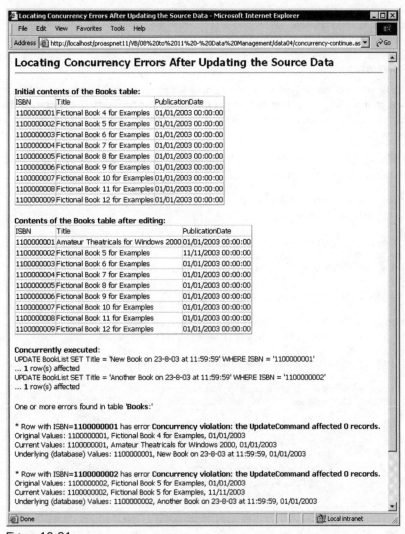

Figure 10-21

The Code for the ContinueUpdateOnError Example

Most of the code we use in this example is identical to the previous example. The only real differences are in the preparation for the Update process, and in the way that we extract and display the row values afterwards. We don't set up any event handlers of course, because we're not going to be reacting to the RowUpdated event in this case. However, as shown in the code, at the point where we're ready to call the Update method of the DataAdapter, we set the DataAdapter object's ContinueUpdateOnError property to True.

```
...
'prevent exceptions being thrown due to concurrency errors
objDataAdapter.ContinueUpdateOnError = True

'perform the update on the original data
objDataAdapter.Update(objDataSet, "Books")
...
```

Checking for Row Errors

After the Update process has finished, we must check for row errors. The process is the same as we used in the previous chapter when we were looking at the RowError property in general, and as we described in the introduction to the current example. The complete code for this part of the process is shown in the following code:

```
'see if there are any update errors anywhere in the DataSet
If objDataSet.HasErrors Then

   Dim objThisRow As DataRow
   Dim intIndex As Integer

   'check each table for errors in that table
   Dim objThisTable As DataTable
   For Each objThisTable In objDataSet.Tables

     If objThisTable.HasErrors Then

       strResult &= "One or more errors found in table '<b>" _
               & objThisTable.TableName & "</b>':<p />"

       'get collection containing only rows with errors
       'using the GetErrors method of the DataTable object
       'check each row in this table for errors
       For Each objThisRow In objThisTable.GetErrors()

         'display the error details and column values
         strResult &= "* Row with ISBN=<b>" _
                 & objThisRow("ISBN") _
                 & "</b> has error <b>" _
                 & objThisRow.RowError & "</b><br />" _
                 & "Original Values: "

         'iterate through row collecting original and current values
         For intIndex = 0 To objThisTable.Columns.Count - 1
```

```
              strResult &= objThisRow(intIndex, DataRowVersion.Original) & ", "
          Next
          strResult = Left(strResult, Len(strResult) - 2)
          strResult &= "<br />Current Values: "
          For intIndex = 0 To objThisTable.Columns.Count - 1
              strResult &= objThisRow(intIndex, DataRowVersion.Current) & ", "
          Next
          strResult = Left(strResult, Len(strResult) - 2)
          'use function declared later in page to get underlying values
          strResult &= "<br />Underlying (database) Values: " _
                     & GetUnderlyingValues(strConnect, objThisRow("ISBN")) _
                     & "<p />"

      Next

    End If

  Next 'table

End If

'display the results of the Update in <div> elsewhere on page
outResult.InnerHtml = strResult
```

Extracting the Underlying Row Values

The only other *new* code in this page is the GetUnderlyingValues function that extracts the underlying database values, so that they can be displayed along with the Original and Current values from the row in the DataSet. As shown in the following code, It works in much the same way as the GetCurrentColumnValue function we used in the previous example, but this time we want all the row values. So we use a DataReader to read the row and then return a String that we build up containing all the column values.

```
Function GetUnderlyingValues(strConnect As String, strRowKey As String) _
                                                As String
   'select existing column values from underlying table in database
   Dim strSQL = "SELECT * FROM BookList WHERE ISBN='" & strRowKey & "'"

   'create connection and command to access database
   Dim objConnect As New OleDbConnection(strConnect)
   Dim objCommand As New OleDbCommand(strSQL, objConnect)

   'declare the variables we'll need
   Dim objReader As OleDbDataReader
   Dim strValues As String = ""
   Dim intIndex As Integer

   Try

      'get a DataReader containing the specified row data
      objConnect.Open()
      objReader = objCommand.ExecuteReader()

      'put values from row into a string to return
```

```
        If objReader.Read() Then
          For intIndex = 0 To objReader.FieldCount - 1
              strValues &= objReader.GetValue(intIndex) & ", "
          Next
        End If


        'close connection and return result
        objConnect.Close()
        GetUnderlyingValues = Left(strValues, Len(strValues) - 2)

    Catch objError As Exception

        GetUnderlyingValues = "*Error*"

    End Try

End Function
```

Summary

This chapter has been devoted entirely to the often-thorny problems we encounter when updating a relational data source such as a SQL database from within our applications. While the techniques have focused on using the .NET data access classes with a relational database, bear in mind that the connection between our code and the data store is via standard methods such as OLE-DB and ODBC. This means that, as new managed providers become available, we can use the same techniques to work with other data stores such as mail servers, active directory, indexing services, etc.

The chapter began with a look at the techniques we often use to perform single operations against a data store – such as inserting a user's name and e-mail address into a database, or deleting rows in response to a user's input. We demonstrated how to do this with both SQL statements and with stored procedures. We also looked at how we can use transactions to provide better data integrity. We used both database transactions and .NET connection-based transactions.

However, the main focus of the chapter was on how we use the new DataSet object to store and then update data in a disconnected environment. We saw how we can use the Update method of the DataAdapter to push updates into a data store automatically, and how we can carry out the task ourselves in a staged and more controllable manner.

We finished up with a look at a major issue in all multi-user environments–concurrent data updates. We saw how we can work round the problem using our own custom methods, and how the .NET data access classes provide other techniques that make it much easier than the data access technologies we used in previous versions of ASP.

This chapter completes our look at how to work with relational data within .NET using the new data-access classes that the framework provides. However, the ceaseless advance of XML into our daily data-handling lives requires us to be competent in handling this new type of data format, as well as being proficient in handling relational data. And, to help us out, the .NET classes provide useful integration between relational and XML data. In the next chapter we'll explore this topic, and see other ways that we can access and manipulate XML.

XML Data Management in .NET

The previous three chapters have largely been concerned with working with relational data in ASP.NET. Even though XML is gradually spreading into most areas of computing, databases such as Microsoft SQL Server, Oracle, DB2, and Sybase still form the backbone of most commercial environments. However, to conclude our study of data management techniques within ASP.NET, this chapter looks in more detail at how to work with XML documents.

Unlike ASP versions 3.0 and earlier, you don't need to use add-ons such as an XML parser or other specialist components to be able to work with XML-formatted data. All the necessary tools are built into the .NET Framework as a set of useful and extensible classes. You can use these to read, write, and edit XML in its native format, and convert from relational data to XML and back again.

This chapter will look at:

❑   Accessing relational data as XML and vice versa

❑   Synchronization between an XML document and the `DataSet` object

❑   Validating XML documents using a schema

❑   Creating and editing XML documents in a range of different ways

❑   Some alternatives available when transforming XML using stylesheets

Part of Chapter 8 explored the whole object model for XML under .NET, and the way this changes working with XML. We also demonstrated many of the more simple techniques. Here, we'll take a detailed look at the interchangeability of XML and relational data.

Obtaining the Sample Files

The examples used in this chapter are available in both VB.NET and C# versions. The files can be downloaded from http://www.daveandal.net/books/8900/, and include SQL scripts and instructions for creating the database that the examples use. You can also run these examples online at the same URL.

The main menu page for the data management chapter examples, shown in Chapter 8, contains links to all the sample files. The final link in that page, Advanced XML Data Management in .NET, leads to another menu page (shown in Figure 11-1) that contains links to all the examples for this chapter.

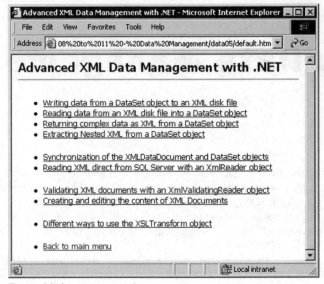

Figure 11-1

XML and the DataSet Object

Despite the ubiquitous presence of relational databases as the powerhouses of most commercial environments today, the use of XML as a data format is growing steadily. The ease of transmission and storage of XML as a text document (or within a database table as text), and its inherent cross-platform nature make it ideal for many situations. In fact, within the .NET Framework, XML is actually the foundation for all data storage and serialization. Now, there are no MIME-encoded Recordset or COM objects that hold data in their own specific formats.

A good example is the DataSet object used throughout the previous chapters. We've viewed it as a container for one or more data tables (rather like some wrapper around multiple Recordset objects). This is a reasonable approach when you need to access the data using relational techniques. However, the DataSet can persist its contents as a disk file, or into another object such as a Stream. The format of the data at this point is XML.

The XML-Based Methods of the DataSet

The `DataSet` object exposes several methods for working with an XML representation of the data it contains or will contain. These are summarized in the following table:

Method	Description
GetXml	Returns a string containing the XML representation of the data stored in the `DataSet`. No schema information is output.
GetXmlSchema	Returns just the schema for an XML representation of the data stored in the `DataSet`.
InferXmlSchema	Takes an XML document provided in a `TextReader`, `XmlReader`, `Stream` object, or a specified disk file, to infer the structure for the data in a `DataSet`.
ReadXml	Reads XML data (including a schema if present) into the `DataSet` from a `TextReader`, `XmlReader`, `Stream` object, or a specified disk file.
ReadXmlSchema	Reads an XML schema (only) into the `DataSet` from a `TextReader`, `XmlReader`, `Stream` object, or a specified disk file.
WriteXml	Writes the contents of the `DataSet` object to an XML document via a `TextWriter`, `XmlWriter`, or `Stream` object, or directly to a specified disk file. May include a schema - see the notes following the next example.
WriteXmlSchema	Writes a schema describing the contents of the `DataSet` object to a `TextWriter`, `XmlWriter`, or `Stream` object, or directly to a specified disk file.

In general, when extracting XML from a `DataSet` (unless you actually need a string representation of the data) the `GetXml` and `GetXmlSchema` methods should be avoided. It's much more efficient to create a `Stream` or disk file directly, or take advantage of a `TextWriter` or `XmlWriter` when using the `WriteXml` and `WriteXmlSchema` methods. The next two examples demonstrated these two methods, and the `ReadXml` and `ReadXmlSchema` methods.

Some of the example files in this chapter require write access to the server's wwwroot folder and subfolders. You will get an "Access Denied" message for these examples when running under the default configuration of ASP.NET. See the Setting Up the Samples section in Chapter 8 to configure the relevant permissions.

Writing Data from a DataSet to an XML File

This example (`write-data-as-xml.aspx`) demonstrates how to write data from a `DataSet` directly to a disk file as an XML document. As the `DataSet` is being filled from a relational database, you need to include the relevant .NET namespaces in the page, and collect the database connection string from the `web.config` file as in the examples in earlier chapters. The page also contains three `<div>` elements where the information and results are output.

```
<%@Import Namespace="System.Data" %>
<%@Import Namespace="System.Data.OleDb" %>

<div>Connection string: <span id="outConnect" runat="server" /></div>
<div>SELECT command: <span id="outSelect" runat="server" /></div>
<div id="outMessage" runat="server" />
```

Filling the DataSet

In the `Page_Load` event, we fill the `DataSet` using a SQL statement that joins two tables. The way the `DataSet` is being filled is identical to the techniques and code used in the previous chapters, and you can use the [view source] link at the bottom of the page to see the complete code. We won't be describing it in detail again here.

```
Sub Page_Load()

    Dim strConnect As String
    strConnect = ConfigurationSettings.AppSettings("DsnWroxBooksOleDb")
    outConnect.innerText = strConnect

    Dim strSelect As String
    strSelect = "SELECT BookList.*, BookAuthors.FirstName, " _
            & "BookAuthors.LastName FROM BookList INNER JOIN " _
            & "BookAuthors ON BookList.ISBN = BookAuthors.ISBN " _
            & "WHERE BookList.ISBN LIKE '18610033%'"
    outSelect.innerText = strSelect

    Dim objDataSet As New DataSet
    Try
        Dim objConnect As New OleDbConnection(strConnect)
        Dim objDataAdapter As New OleDbDataAdapter(strSelect, objConnect)
        objDataAdapter.Fill(objDataSet, "Books")

    Catch objError As Exception
        outError.innerHTML = "Error while accessing data.<br />" _
            & objError.Message & "<br />" & objError.Source
        Exit Sub

    End Try
```

Creating the XML Data and Schema Files

Now that there is a `DataSet` containing the data, you can write it out to a disk file as XML. All you have to do is create the appropriate path and name for the two files, and then call the `WriteXml` and `WriteXmlSchema` methods. This is done within a `Try..Catch` construct to trap any errors that might arise while writing the files – for example, if ASP.NET does not have the relevant permission or if the path does not exist. Note that you have to provide a physical path to the XML document files, not the virtual path. And if all goes well, the confirmation messages and hyperlinks to the new files are displayed.

```
Try
    'use the path to the current virtual application
    Dim strVirtualPath As String = Request.ApplicationPath _
                                & "/XML-from-DataSet.xml"
    Dim strVSchemaPath As String = Request.ApplicationPath _
                                & "/Schema-from-DataSet.xsd"

    'write data and schema from DataSet to documents on disk
    'use the Physical path to the file not the Virtual path
    objDataSet.WriteXml(Request.MapPath(strVirtualPath))

    outMessage.innerHTML = "Written file: <a href=" & Chr(34) _
                        & strVirtualPath & Chr(34) & ">" _
                        & strVirtualPath & "</a><br />"

    objDataSet.WriteXmlSchema(Request.MapPath(strVSchemaPath))
    outMessage.innerHTML &= "Written file: <a href=" & Chr(34) _
                        & strVSchemaPath & Chr(34) & ">" _
                        & strVSchemaPath & "</a></b>"

Catch objError As Exception
    'display error details
    outMessage.innerHTML = "Error while writing disk file.<br />" _
        & objError.Message & "<br />" & objError.Source
    Exit Sub  ' and stop execution
End Try
```

The result can be seen in Figure 11-2. The page includes two hyperlinks to the files created – the XML data itself and the XSD schema that defines the structure of the XML document:

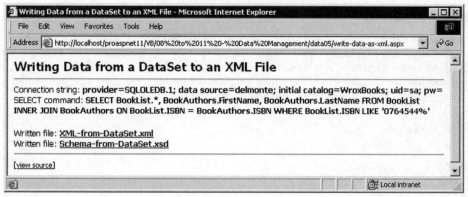

Figure 11-2

The Resulting XML Document

If you click the hyperlinks in the page, you can view the created XML document and schema. The XML document is shown in Figure 11-3. IE 5's ability to collapse elements enables you to see the overall structure of the document. Each <Books> element describes one row from the original rowset that was loaded into the DataSet object.

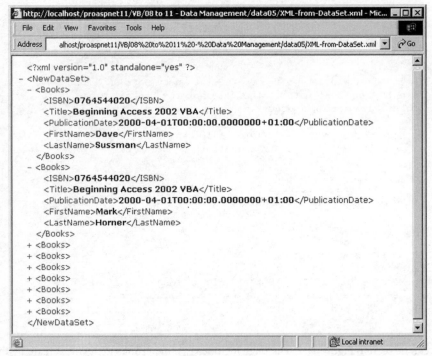

```
<?xml version="1.0" standalone="yes" ?>
- <NewDataSet>
  - <Books>
      <ISBN>0764544020</ISBN>
      <Title>Beginning Access 2002 VBA</Title>
      <PublicationDate>2000-04-01T00:00:00.0000000+01:00</PublicationDate>
      <FirstName>Dave</FirstName>
      <LastName>Sussman</LastName>
    </Books>
  - <Books>
      <ISBN>0764544020</ISBN>
      <Title>Beginning Access 2002 VBA</Title>
      <PublicationDate>2000-04-01T00:00:00.0000000+01:00</PublicationDate>
      <FirstName>Mark</FirstName>
      <LastName>Horner</LastName>
    </Books>
  + <Books>
  + <Books>
  + <Books>
  + <Books>
  + <Books>
  + <Books>
  + <Books>
  </NewDataSet>
```

Figure 11-3

The Resulting XML Schema

The second link in the example page shown in Figure 11-2 displays the schema that was created as a separate disk file. Figure 11-4 shows that the structure is specified quite loosely – for example, the schema allows elements to be optional (minOccurs="0"). It means that you may want to modify the schema if you use the XML for situations where a tighter definition is required – perhaps when communicating with BizTalk Server or some other application.

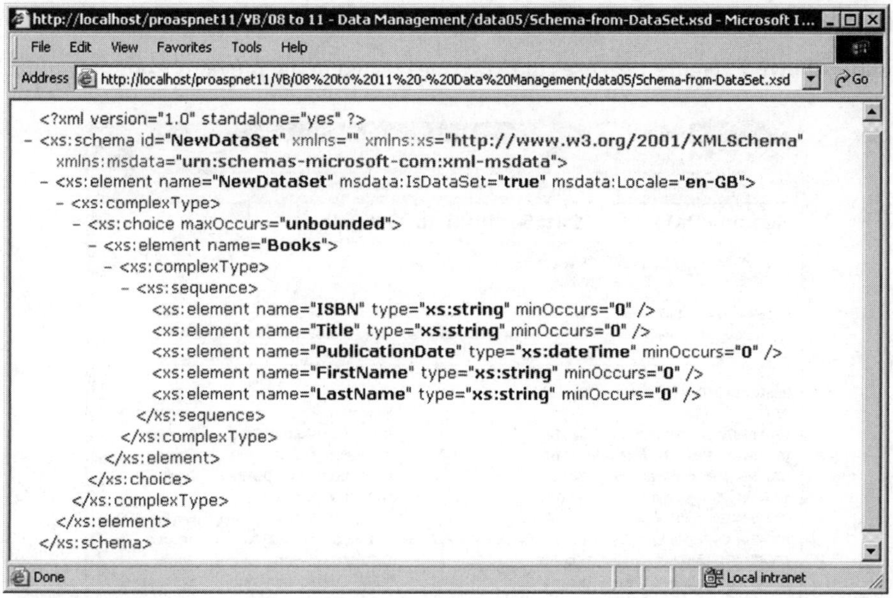

Figure 11-4

The XmlWriteMode Enumeration

The `WriteXml` method can be used with an optional second parameter that specifies in more detail how the data will be output as XML. The following code writes the data from a `DataSet` object into a disk file in `DiffGram` format:

```
DataSet.WriteXml(file-path, XmlWriteMode.DiffGram)
```

This method accepts a value from the `XmlWriteMode` enumeration:

Value	Description
WriteSchema	The default. Specifies that any loaded schema should be written out along with the XML data stored in the `DataSet`. If no schema was loaded (as in our example) then no schema is included.
IgnoreSchema	Even if there is a schema loaded it will not be written out with the XML data.
DiffGram	The data is written out in a form that includes all the original values, and any current values for columns in each row that have been changed since the `DataSet` was loaded. This allows any changes made to the data within the `DataSet` to be persisted within the XML. So, if the XML data is used to fill a `DataSet` again, the changes are persisted into the `Original` and `Current` versions of each column.

Reading Data into a DataSet from an XML File

This example, shown in Figure 11-5, uses the XML file created in the previous example.

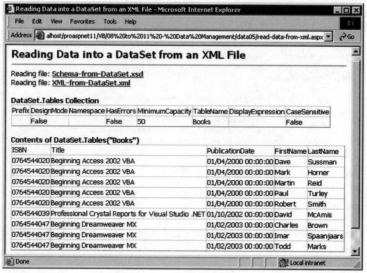

Figure 11-5

The XML data and schema are loaded into a new `DataSet` object. You can then display the content using `DataGrid` server controls. In other words, the data is accessed as a data table using relational methods. Figure 11-5 shows what the example page, Reading Data Into a DataSet from an XML File (`read-data-from-xml.aspx`) looks like when you run it

The Code for This Example

Because we're creating a `DataSet` object, an `Import` directive for the `System.Data` namespace has to be included. Next comes a `<div>` for output messages, followed by two ASP.NET `DataGrid` controls. The following code shows the relevant HTML sections:

```
<%@Import Namespace="System.Data" %>

<div id="outMessage" runat="server" /><br />

<b>DataSet.Tables Collection</b>
<asp:datagrid id="dgrTables" runat="server" /><br />

<b>Contents of DataSet.Tables("Books")</b>
<asp:datagrid id="dgrValues" runat="server" />
```

Loading the XML Documents

The code in the `Page_Load` event handler first creates a new empty `DataSet` instance, and then builds up the path and name for each of the two XML documents that we'll be loading; the schema and the data. Next, it's simply a matter of calling the `ReadXmlSchema` and `ReadXml` methods to first load the schema and then the data. As with the previous example, you have to provide a physical path to the XML document files, rather than a virtual path.

```
'create a new DataSet object
Dim objDataSet As New DataSet()

Try
    'use the path to the current virtual application
    Dim strVirtualPath As String = Request.ApplicationPath _
                                  & "/XML-from-DataSet.xml"
    Dim strVSchemaPath As String = Request.ApplicationPath _
                                  & "/Schema-from-DataSet.xsd"

    'read schema and data into DataSet from documents on disk
    'use the Physical path to the file not the Virtual path
    objDataSet.ReadXMLSchema(Request.MapPath(strVSchemaPath))
    outMessage.InnerHTML = "Reading file: <a href=" & Chr(34) _
                & strVSchemaPath & Chr(34) & ">" _
                & strVSchemaPath & "</a><br />"

    objDataSet.ReadXML(Request.MapPath(strVirtualPath))
    outMessage.InnerHTML &= "Reading file: <a href=" & Chr(34) _
                & strVirtualPath & Chr(34) & ">" _
                & strVirtualPath & "</a>"

Catch objError As Exception
    'display error details
    outMessage.InnerHTML = "Error while reading disk file.<br />" _
        & objError.Message & "<br />" & objError.Source
    Exit Sub  ' and stop execution

End Try
```

Displaying the Data

The data is now loaded into the `DataSet` and ready to use. We simply bind the `Tables` collection and the contents of the `Books` table (the tablename is automatically inferred from the repeated element name in the XML file) to a pair of `DataGrid` server controls to display the contents.

```
'assign the DataView.Tables collection first to the DataGrid control
dgrTables.DataSource = objDataSet.Tables
dgrTables.DataBind()  'and bind (display) the data

'create a DataView object for the Books table in the DataSet
Dim objDataView As New DataView(objDataSet.Tables("Books"))

'assign the DataView object to the second DataGrid control

dgrValues.DataSource = objDataView
dgrValues.DataBind()  'and bind (display) the data
```

With or Without a Schema – That Is the Question

Our example page explicitly tells the DataSet what to expect. The schema loaded first contains a definition of the structure of the XML data that's loaded afterwards. However, you may not want to use a schema, or you may not have one available.

This is often the case if the XML structure is not constant over time. To avoid creating new schemas for dynamically generated XML data, you can omit the schema altogether and just use the ReadXml method to load the XML data. The DataSet will infer the structure of the data automatically from the structure of the XML document. However, if for some reason it can't do so (usually because the document structure is not consistent), you may not get any data in the DataSet.

Bear in mind that without a schema, the DataSet may get a different idea about the structure, so it's wise to include a schema whenever possible. As long as the XML document is well-formed, it will be loaded – but the results might not be what you expect. You can create the schema as in the previous example, by loading the appropriate data into the DataSet and then calling the WriteXmlSchema method.

> *The DataSet does not validate the XML data against the schema – it just uses it to infer the structure required for the tables in the DataSet. We'll look at the issues of validating an XML document against a schema later in this chapter.*

You can also include a schema within the XML data file or document, rather than as a separate file. In this case, the structure of the data is specified automatically when you load the document and there is (of course) no need to execute ReadXmlSchema.

Getting XML as a String from a DataSet

You can use the GetXml and GetXmlSchema methods to extract XML from a DataSet. Bear in mind that it is not the recommended technique, unless you specifically want it as a string for use in your code. The WriteXml method is more efficient. However, we've provided a simple example page that uses the GetXml and GetXmlSchema methods to extract data from a DataSet and display it in the page.

Figure 11-6 shows what the Returning XML from a DataSet (get-data-as-xml.aspx) example looks like when you run it and click the Display XML Data checkbox:

Figure 11-6

The two checkboxes simply execute an appropriate combination of the GetXml and GetXmlSchema methods of the DataSet (which is filled with data using exactly the same code as the previous example). The two methods return a String, which is assigned to the InnerHtml property of an HTML <xmp> element.

The HTML <xmp> element automatically displays content as text, without attempting to render it, so the XML elements are visible. An alternative approach would be to use the Server.HtmlEncode method on the string. It could then be displayed directly in the page with the elements visible.

```
'display the data and/or schema in the DataSet as an XML document
xmpResults.InnerHtml = ""
If chkSchema.checked Then
    xmpResults.InnerHtml = objDataSet.GetXmlSchema() & vbCrlf & vbCrlf
End If
If chkXML.checked Then
    xmpResults.InnerHtml &= objDataSet.GetXml()
End If
```

Clicking the other checkbox in the page displays just the schema (as shown in Figure 11-7). You can check them both to display the schema and the XML data together. If you do this and copy the result to a new document, you'll get the appropriate combined document and schema as one file that represents the contents of this DataSet.

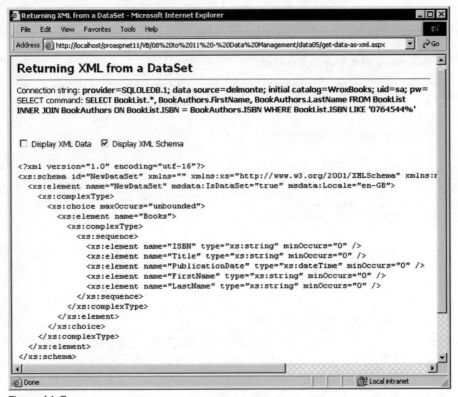

Figure 11-7

Nested XML and Related Data in a DataSet

When you export data from a `DataSet` as XML, you don't have much control over the actual format of the XML itself. There are several interesting arguments for and against the two basic approaches to the structure of an XML document that contains repeating data (a representation of a rowset or data table):

❑ Place the data within the elements as the text content.

❑ Use a single element for each data row, and place the data itself in attributes of that element.

The first option tends to give a more human-readable result, but produces a bigger document as there is more markup (element tags). Using attributes produces smaller documents, but accessing the content using other XML techniques such as the DOM methods can be more difficult.

Later in this chapter, you'll see how to use SQL Server's built-in XML data-handling function to create different formats of XML. In the meantime, you also need to consider how the format of the XML is affected when you export data from more than one data table into an XML document.

The DataRelation.Nested Property

You've seen in the previous few chapters that a `DataSet` can contain more than one table *plus* the relationships between these tables. These relationships can be used to extract the child rows from one table that were related to the current row in the parent table.

Each relationship (`DataRelation` object) in a `DataSet` also has a `Nested` property. This is `False` by default, and has no effect when accessing the data using relational techniques – for example, when you bind the data to a `DataGrid` or iterate through the `Rows` collection of a table. However, it does influence the way that the data is exported as XML when you use the `GetXML` or `WriteXml` methods. Our next example demonstrates this.

The Nested XML Data Example Page

The Extracting Nested XML from a DataSet (`nested-xml-from-dataset.aspx`) example page demonstrates how useful the `Nested` property of a `DataRelation` object is when it comes to exporting data as XML. We use the same custom user control (`get-dataset-control.ascx`) that was introduced in Chapter 8 to create a `DataSet` object, and fill it with three tables named `Books`, `Authors`, and `Prices` that contain data from the WroxBooks database. The control also creates two relationships between these tables.

The HTML section of the page, shown in the following code, includes three ASP.NET `DataGrid` controls. The first is used to display the `DataSet` object's `Tables` collection, and the other two are used to show the contents of the `Relations` collection before and after the `Nested` property is set. Also, two `<div>` elements are used to display the links to the non-nested and nested format XML files that are created.

```
<%@ Register TagPrefix="wrox" TagName="getdataset"
             Src="..\global\get-dataset-control.ascx" %>
...
<b>DataSet.Tables Collection</b>
<asp:datagrid id="dgrTables" runat="server" /><br />
<b>DataSet.Relations Collection</b>
<asp:datagrid id="dgrRelsNormal" runat="server" />
<div id="outResultNormal" runat="server" /><p />
<b>DataSet.Relations Collection</b>
<asp:datagrid id="dgrRelsNested" runat="server" />
<div id="outResultNested" runat="server" /><p />
```

Displaying the DataSet Contents

In the page code, we first create the `DataSet` using the custom control. Then we can display information about it. The first `DataGrid` control on our page is bound to the `Tables` collection, and the second to the `Relations` collection, as shown in the following code:

```
Dim strConnect As String = _
                ConfigurationSettings.AppSettings("DsnWroxBooksOleDb")
Dim objDataSet As DataSet
objDataSet = ctlDataSet.BooksDataSet(strConnect, "ISBN LIKE '0764544%'")
If IsNothing(objDataSet) Then Exit Sub
    'bind the collection of Tables to the first DataGrid on the page
dgrTables.DataSource = objDataSet.Tables
dgrTables.DataBind()
```

```
          'bind the collection of Relations to the second DataGrid on the page
dgrRelsNormal.DataSource = objDataSet.Relations
dgrRelsNormal.DataBind()
```

Exporting the Data to an XML Disk File

Next, we write the data in the `DataSet` to an XML document on disk. We build up a virtual path and name for the file, write it with the `WriteXml` method, and display a hyperlink so that it can be viewed:

```
'save as a disk file and create hyperlink to load it
Dim strVirtualPath As String = Request.ApplicationPath _
                    & "/Normal-XML-from-DataSet.xml"
objDataSet.WriteXml(Request.MapPath(strVirtualPath))
outResultNormal.innerHTML = "Written file: <a href=" & Chr(34) _
                    & strVirtualPath & Chr(34) & ">" _
                    & strVirtualPath & "</a>"
```

Figure 11-8 shows the results of running the page:

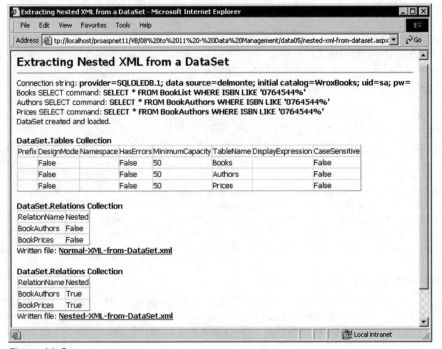

Figure 11-8

You can see the two `DataGrid` controls populated so far, and following them is the hyperlink to the `Normal-XML-from-DataSet.xml` file just created. In the second `DataGrid` in the page, you can see the contents of the `DataSet.Relations` collection at this point in the code. The two relations, named `BookAuthors` and `BookPrices`, have the default value `False` for their `Nested` property.

The Resulting XML Document

If you click the first hyperlink in the page, you will see the XML file format that is created by default from a `DataSet` containing more than one table. This is shown in Figure 11-9, with some elements *collapsed* (using this feature of IE 5) so that you can see the structure.

It's pretty clear that the document contains separate `<Books>`, `<Authors>`, and `<Prices>` elements. There is no concept of hierarchy between the parent and child elements. They are all at the same level (they are siblings, in XML terminology).

However, they also all contain the primary key (the ISBN code), so an application could read and work with the data in a related manner if required.

Figure 11-9

Nesting the XML Result

The format you've just seen is not really what you might expect after making creating the relationships between the tables. This is where the `Nested` property comes to the rescue. The code in the example page continues by setting the `Nested` property to `True` for both the `DataRelation` objects. Then it redisplays the contents of the `Relations` collection in the third `DataGrid` control. If you look back at Figure 11-8, you can see that the third `DataGrid` shows the `Nested` property of both `Relations` as being `True` now. So you can now create another XML document by exporting the contents of the `DataSet` again.

```
        'set the Nested property of the two relation objects
objDataSet.Relations("BookAuthors").Nested = True
objDataSet.Relations("BookPrices").Nested = True
        'bind the collection of Relations to the third DataGrid on the page
dgrRelsNested.DataSource = objDataSet.Relations
dgrRelsNested.DataBind()
        'save as a disk file and create hyperlink to load it
Dim strVirtualPath As String = Request.ApplicationPath _
                              & "/Nested-XML-from-DataSet.xml"
objDataSet.WriteXML(Request.MapPath(strVirtualPath))
outResultNested.innerHTML = "Written file: <a href=" & Chr(34) _
                          & strVirtualPath & Chr(34) & ">" _
                          & strVirtualPath & "</a>"
```

The Resulting XML Document

If you open and view the second XML document, you can see the difference:

Figure 11-10

As shown in Figure 11-10, each `<Books>` element is a child of the document root, and the `<Authors>` and `<Prices>` elements are nested within their respective books. This is pretty much an ideal format both for readability and usability, and is probably similar to what you would have come up with had you crafted the XML by hand. Perhaps the only downside is the repeated occurrence of the primary key within the child elements. Later in this chapter, we'll discuss a way to extract the XML from a SQL Server database so that the values are in attributes rather than as the content of elements.

Working with the XmlDataDocument Object

The `DataSet` provides an excellent vehicle for transferring data from one or more relational-style rowsets to XML documents and XML schemas, and vice versa. But you can do even better if you are predominantly concerned with accessing data as XML, rather than starting out with relational data.

Figure 11-11 repeats the diagram you saw in the data management introduction chapter:

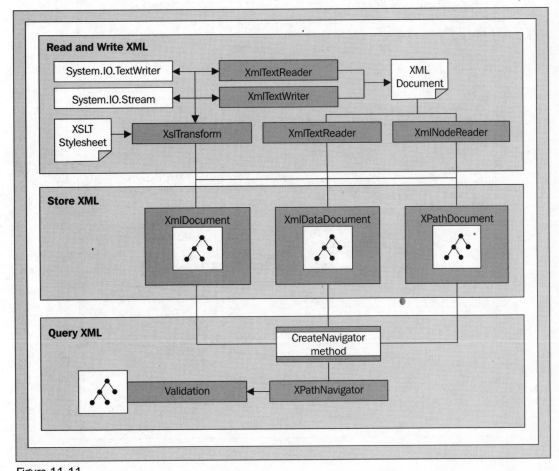

Figure 11-11

Figure 11-11 describes how there are three types of object that can be used to access XML and hold it in memory as a document: XmlDocument, XmlDataDocument, and XPathDocument. We discussed the reason for having these three different *document* objects in Chapter 8; the XmlDataDocument is designed to act as a bridge between relational and XML data.

XmlDataDocument and DataSet Synchronization

The only real external difference between an XmlDocument object and an XmlDataDocument object is that the latter has a few extra properties and methods. The most useful is the DataSet property. This returns a reference to an object that contains the data in the XML document, but which is exposed as a DataSet object. This is a useful read-only property.

Figure 11-12 conceptualizes the way it works:

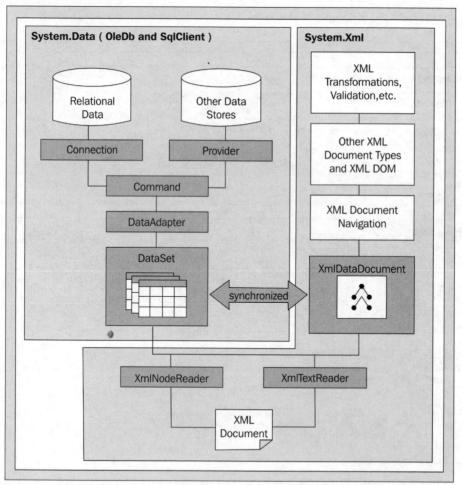

Figure 11-12

The XML document can be accessed through various `Reader` objects, loaded into an `XmlDataDocument` object (as mentioned in Chapter 8), and can also be loaded into a `DataSet`.

However, after you load the XML into an `XmlDataDocument` object, you can reference a `DataSet` object that contains the same data; this is equivalent to reading the data into that `DataSet`. More to the point, as you change the data in either the `DataSet` or the `XmlDataDocument`, the changes are reflected in both. They are completely and automatically synchronized.

This means there is no longer a distinction between the *relational* or *XML* types of data – they are just two views of the same data. This works in part because behind the scenes, the .NET Framework data management objects all use XML as their standard persistence format.

Once you've got the data in an `XmlDataDocument`, you can access it using any of the techniques available in the relational and XML armories. The next example page demonstrates a few.

The DataSet-XML Synchronization Example

The Synchronization of the XmlDataDocument and DataSet objects (`xml-to-dataset.aspx`) example page shown in Figure 11-13 demonstrates some of the features of the integration we've just discussed. It takes an XML document and the matching XSD schema and loads them into a new `XmlDataDocument` object. As shown, there are hyperlinks in the page so that you can examine the XML and schema files – they are basically the same ones used in the first couple of examples in this chapter.

You must run the page in a browser on the web server itself to be able to open the XML document and schema using the physical paths in the hyperlinks in the page.

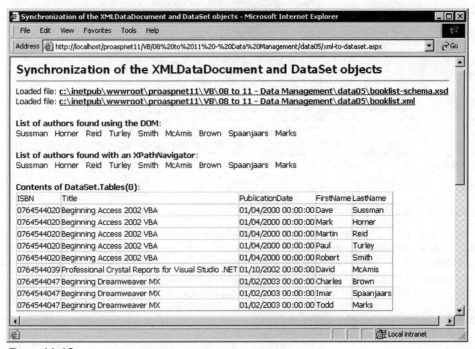

Figure 11-13

After loading the data into the `XmlDataDocument`, the code carries out four different tasks with it. It first displays a list of last names of all the authors in our data. We do this first using the standard methods exposed by the XML DOM (as per the W3C recommendations), and then using an `XPathNavigator` object with a recursive search function.

Then a `DataGrid` control displays all the rows in the table within the `DataSet`. Of course, you can get this `DataSet` from the `XmlDataDocument` object's `DataSet` property, but notice how we are already freely mixing our relational and XML terminology.

Finally, if you scroll to the bottom of this page (as shown in Figure 11-14), you'll see a heap of XML. This has been extracted from the `DataSet` object, using the `GetElementFromRow` method. Using this method, you can pull out specific rows of data and return just those rows as XML. We've got a simple and efficient automated relational-based technique for manipulating data and creating the equivalent XML.

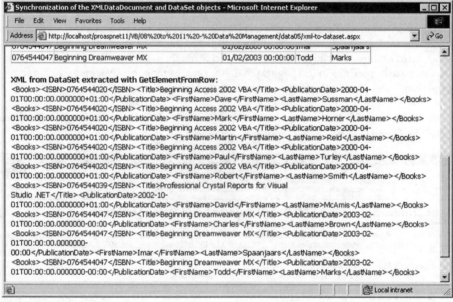

Figure 11-14

The Code for This Example Page

There is a lot of code in this page, as you can confirm if you view the source. However, it is commented and divided into the four tasks being performed, and so is easy enough to follow. In the code listings here, we'll confine ourselves to the features that are relevant to the four tasks, and omit much of the surrounding code (code that creates links in the page, error messages, and so on). The first step is to create the `XmlDataDocument` and load the schema and XML from disk:

```
'create a new XmlDataDocument object
Dim objXMLDataDoc As New XmlDataDocument()
```

```
'load the XML schema into the XmlDataDocument object
objXMLDataDoc.DataSet.ReadXmlSchema(strSchemaPath)

'load the XML file into the XmlDataDocument object
objXMLDataDoc.Load(strXMLPath)
```

Using the XML DOM Methods of the Document

Now you can use the `XmlDataDocument` object. First, the code demonstrates that the object behaves like a normal W3C-standard `XMLDocument` object by using the `GetElementsByTagname` method to create an `XmlNodeList` containing all the `<LastName>` elements in the document: Then you can iterate through this `NodeList` (collection) displaying all the element values:

```
Dim objNode As XmlNode
Dim strResults As String = ""

'create a NodeList collection of all matching child nodes
Dim colElements As XmlNodeList
colElements = objXMLDataDoc.GetElementsByTagName("LastName")

'iterate through the collection getting the values of the
'child #text nodes for each one
For Each objNode In colElements
  strResults &= objNode.FirstChild().Value & "   "
Next

'then display the result
outDOMResult.innerHTML = strResults
```

Using an XPathNavigator Object

As discussed in Chapter 8, the .NET Framework introduces a new object that can be used to navigate within an XML document. An `XPathNavigator` can be created from an XML document object of any type, by calling the `CreateNavigator` method of that document object. In the following code, we use an `XPathNavigator` to fetch the values of all the `<LastName>` elements in the `XmlDataDocument` by moving to the root element of the document and then calling a recursive function, which searches each child of the current element in turn looking for matches and extracting the values:

```
'create a new XPathNavigator object using the XmlDataDocument object
Dim objXPNav As XPathNavigator
objXPNav = objXMLDataDoc.CreateNavigator()

'move to the root element of the document
objXPNav.MoveToRoot()

'and display the result of the recursive 'search' function
outXPNavResult.innerHTML = SearchForElement(objXPNav, "LastName")
```

We haven't listed our recursive `SearchForElement` function again here, as it's identical to the technique used in Chapter 8.

Displaying the Content of the DataSet

The next part of the page output is easy to create. The following code shows how to reference the `DataSet` property of the `XmlDataDocument` object, and from that access the first member of the `Tables` collection. This gives us a reference to the default `DataTable` within the `DataSet`.

We can use this reference to create a `DataView` object, and then assign the `DataView` to an ASP.NET `DataGrid` control that was previously defined within the page. This gives us a picture of the data as a standard relational rowset – just as though we'd filled our `DataSet` table using a `Connection`, `Command`, and `DataAdapter`.

```
'create a DataView object for the Books table in the DataSet
Dim objDataView As New DataView(objXMLDataDoc.DataSet.Tables(0))

'assign the DataView object to the DataGrid control
dgrResult.DataSource = objDataView
dgrResult.DataBind()   'and bind (display) the data
```

Extracting XML Elements from the DataSet

The final task in this page is to demonstrate how to query the `DataSet` to extract individual rows as XML. The `GetElementFromRow` method takes as its parameter an object that represents a row in a `DataTable` – a `DataRow` object. It returns an XML representation of that row.

You can create a reference to the `DataTable` in the `DataSet`, and then iterate through the rows. For each one, the `GetElementFromRow` method of the `XmlDataDocument` object is called, which returns an `XmlElement` object. You get a string representation of the element from its `OuterXml` property and HTML-encode it before displaying it in the page:

```
'create a DataTable object for the Books table in the DataSet
Dim objDataTable As DataTable = objXMLDataDoc.DataSet.Tables(0)
Dim objRow As DataRow
Dim objXMLElement As XmlElement

'iterate through all the rows in this table
For Each objRow In objDataTable.Rows
   'get an XML element that represents this row
   objXMLElement = objXMLDataDoc.GetElementFromRow(objRow)
   'HTMLEncode it because it contains XML element tags
   strResults &= Server.HtmlEncode(objXMLElement.OuterXML) & "<br />"
Next

outFromRowResult.innerHTML = strResults      'and display the result
```

Getting a DataRow Object from an XML Element

Interestingly, there is a mirror of this method, named `GetRowFromElement`. You can iterate through the elements in an XML document using the DOM methods or an `XPathNavigator` to get an `XmlNodeList` of element objects, or individual `XmlElement` references.

For each one, the `GetRowFromElement` method of the `XmlDataDocument` object that holds the document will return a `DataRow` object. This can then be accessed to extract field information, or even used to update the original XML document. So now there is even a way to edit an XML document using relational techniques.

```
objThisRow = objXmlDataDoc.GetRowFromElement(objElement)
objThisRow("MyFieldName") = "This is the new value"
```

Reading XML Data Direct from SQL Server

Our earlier discussion of the format of the XML returned from a `DataSet` mentioned an alternative format of using the attributes of a row element to hold the individual column or field data items. This was, in fact, the default format introduced with ADO 2.0/2.1 when XML support was added to ADO. It's also the default format for the XML created by the new features of Microsoft SQL Server 2000 (and the *SQLXML Technology Preview* that is still available for SQL Server 7.0).

The Reading XML Direct From SQL Server With An XmlReader (`xmldatareader-sql.aspx`) example page demonstrates this feature. To use it you must have SQL Server 2000 installed – the SQLXML Technology Preview does not work with .NET.

When you run the page, as shown in Figure 11-15, you see the connection string and the SQL SELECT statement used. Notice that it includes the FOR XML AUTO instruction. Below this is a series of XML elements that are created automatically by SQL Server in response to the instruction in the SQL statement:

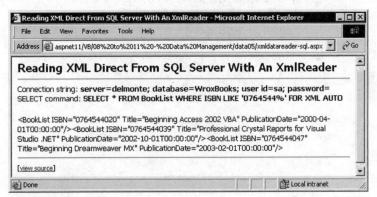

Figure 11-15

It's hard to see what the structure of the XML is from the screenshot, but if you break out one of the elements, you will see the structure quite clearly:

```
<BookList ISBN="1861003110" Title="Professional XML"
          PublicationDate="2000-01-01T00:00:00"/>
```

There are a couple of things to note. This is *not* an XML document, as there is no document type declaration or root element. All you get back is a series of elements that contain the row values as attributes. This is the default format for the AUTO part of the instruction used in the SQL statement. You would probably use the elements to build up your own specific XML documents, depending on the task your application has to achieve.

> *The XML technology built into SQL Server 2000 is very powerful, allowing updates to be made to the source data as well as extracting it. The Help topic "Retrieving and Writing XML Data" within the "XML and Internet Support" section of SQL Server Books Online contains complete details of the various formats and options that are available when using this technology.*

The Code for the SQLXML Example Page

The ability to extract data as XML from SQL Server using the SQLXML feature has proved very useful to developers already, and it's extremely fast and efficient. To support it in .NET simply entailed including an option to return an object that could hold XML document fragments.

The answer is a special version of the *execute* methods available in the `Command` object used for relational data access, but which returns an `XmlReader` object instead of a `DataReader` object. This method is called, not surprisingly, `ExecuteXmlReader`.

The code used in the example page demonstrates this. First we collect the connection string from the `web.config` file, and then create the SQL statement that will extract the XML. Then we create a `StringBuilder` object to hold the large strings that we expect to get back from the database. We also create the customary `Connection` and `Command` objects.

Notice that the objects from the `System.Data.SqlClient` namespace are being used here (prefixed `Sql`). This page is only going to work with SQL Server 2000 anyway, and so we might as well take advantage of the performance boost that comes with the SQL TDS provider:

```
Dim strConnect As String
strConnect = ConfigurationSettings.AppSettings("DsnWroxBooksSql")
Dim strSelect As String
strSelect = "SELECT * FROM BookList WHERE " _
        & "ISBN LIKE '1861003%' FOR XML AUTO"

'create a new StringBuilder to hold the results
Dim objStrBuilder As New StringBuilder()

'create a new Connection object using the connection string
Dim objConnect As New SqlConnection(strConnect)

'create new Command using the connection object and select statement
Dim objCommand As New SqlCommand(strSelect, objConnect)
```

Executing the Command

We need an object to *receive* the results of executing the SQL statement. The following code shows how to declare a variable to hold an `XmlTextReader` object (a public class based on `XmlReader`) for this. You can then open the connection and call the `ExecuteXmlReader` method. It returns the `XmlTextReader` all ready to go:

```
'declare a variable to hold an XmlTextReader object
Dim objXTReader As XmlTextReader
```

```
'open the connection to the database
objConnect.Open()

'execute the SQL statement against the command to create the XmlReader
objXTReader = objCommand.ExecuteXmlReader()
```

Retrieving the XML Result

To retrieve the data once the SQL statement is executed, we call the ReadString method of the XmlTextReader to initialize it. Then we call the GetRemainder method to read to the end of the results, and append it all to the StringBuilder created earlier. To finish off, the reader and the connection are closed, and the results are displayed:

```
'read the first result to initialize the reader
objXTReader.ReadString()

'and then read remainder into the StringBuilder as well
objStrBuilder.Append(objXTReader.GetRemainder().ReadToEnd())

'close the XmlReader and Connection
objXTReader.Close()
objConnect.Close()

'display the results as Text to show XML elements
outError.InnerText = objStrBuilder.ToString()
```

Validating XML Documents

An XML document must follow the specific standards laid down by W3C in order to be acceptable – in particular, it must be *well-formed*. It must:

❑   Have a single root element that encloses all other content except the document declaration, processing instructions, and comments.

❑   Have matching closing tags for all the opening tags (or use the shorthand syntax of ending the element with a forward slash character).

❑   Be properly nested so that elements are fully enclosed. You can't open an element as a child of another element and then close the parent element before closing the child element.

❑   Contain only valid characters. All non-valid content must be escaped or replaced by the correct entity equivalents, such as & for an ampersand character.

An XML document can be well-formed and still not be *valid*. The validity of a document is defined using a schema or *Document Type Definition* (*DTD*). This lays out the structure of the elements, attributes and other content, the ordering of the elements, and the permissible value ranges for the elements and attributes. The XML storage objects parse the XML to ensure that it's well-formed when they load it (it can't be loaded otherwise), but don't automatically validate the XML. You have to look after that yourself.

The XmlValidatingReader Object

Documents are validated against a given XML schema or DTD using the `XmlValidatingReader` object. This isn't actually a reader, but a *helper* object that is attached to a reader. Figure 11-16 shows the way it works. The document is read using an `XmlTextReader` (or an `XmlNodeReader`, if you only want to validate part of a document). This object automatically raises an error if the document is not well-formed.

When you attach an `XmlValidatingReader` to the `XmlTextReader`, it automatically checks for the presence of a schema or DTD within the document, and validates the content of the document against that schema or DTD. Errors found during validation are raised through the `Validation` event, and the handler for this event receives a `ValidationEventHandler` object that contains a description of the error. You can access this object's properties when the event occurs to determine the validation errors that are present (you'll see how this is done shortly in the example page), or you can leave it to the default event handler to raise an error.

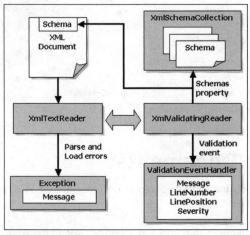

Figure 11-16

Creating an XmlValidatingReader Instance

Creating an `XmlValidatingReader` for use with a document that contains an inline schema or DTD (or which specifies an external schema or DTD) is easy. You just need to create the `XmlTextReader`, specifying the XML document to load, and then use this as the basis for creating the `XmlValidatingReader`. Afterwards, you can set the `ValidationType` property to specify the type of schema you're using:

```
'create the new XmlTextReader object and load the XML document
objXTReader = New XmlTextReader(strXMLPath)

'create an XmlValidatingReader for this XmlTextReader
Dim objValidator As New XmlValidatingReader(objXTReader)

'set the validation type to use an XML Schema
objValidator.ValidationType = ValidationType.Schema
```

The acceptable values for the `ValidationType` property are shown in the following table:

Value	Description
Auto	The default. Validation is automatically performed against whichever type of schema or DTD is encountered.
DTD	Validate against a DTD. This actually creates an XML1.0-compliant parser. Default attributes are reported and general entities can be resolved by calling the `ResolveEntity` method. The `DOCTYPE` is not used for validation purposes.
Schema	Validate against a W3C-compliant XML Schema (XSD), including an inline schema. Schemas are specified using the `schemaLocation` attribute.
XDR	Validate against a schema that uses Microsoft's XML Data Reduced (XDR) syntax, including an inline schema. XDR schemas use the "`x-schema`" namespace prefix or the `Schemas` property.
None	No validation is performed. Can be used to "switch off" validation when not required.

Figure 11-16 also shows how to use a separate (not inline or linked) schema or DTD to validate the document. And, as schemas can inherit from each other, there could be several schemas that you'd want to apply to the XML document (thought there can only be one DTD). To cope with this, the `XmlValidatingReader` exposes a reference to an `XmlSchemaCollection` through the `Schemas` property. This collection contains all the desired schemas.

Validating XML When Loading a Document Object

If you are familiar with using the MSXML parser in ASP 3.0 or other environments, you may expect to be able to validate a document when you load it simply by setting some property. For example, with MSXML, the `ValidateOnParse` property can be set to `True` to validate a document that contains an inline schema or DTD, or a reference to an external schema or DTD.

However, things are different when using the .NET `System.Xml` classes. Loading a combined schema or DTD and the XML data content (that is, an inline schema) or an XML document that references an external schema or DTD into any of the XML *storage* objects such as `XmlDocument`, `XmlDataDocument`, and `XPathDocument` does not automatically validate that document. And there is no property that you can set to make it do this.

Instead, you can load the document via an `XmlTextReader` object to which you have attached an `XmlValidatingReader`. The `Load` method of the `XmlDocument` and `XmlDataDocument` objects can accept an `XmlValidatingReader` as the single parameter instead of a file path and name. Meanwhile, the constructor for the `XPathDocument` object can accept an `XmlValdiatingReader` as the single parameter.

So all you have to do is set up the XmlValidatingReader and XmlTextReader combination, and pass this to the Load method or the constructor function (depending on which document object you're creating). The document will then be validated as it is loaded:

```
'create XmlTextReader, load XML document and create Validator
objXTReader = New XmlTextReader(strXMLPath)
Dim objValidator As New XmlValidatingReader(objXTReader)
objValidator.ValidationType = ValidationType.Schema

'use the validator/reader combination to create XPathDocument object
Dim objXPathDoc As New XPathDocument(objValidator)

'use the validator/reader combination to create XmlDocument object
Dim objXmlDoc As New XmlDocument()
objXmlDoc.Load(objValidator)
```

The XmlValidatingReader can also be used to validate XML held in a String. So, you can validate XML that's already loaded into an object or application by simply extracting it as a String object (using the GetXml method with a DataSet object, or the OuterXml property to get a document fragment, for example) and applying the XmlValidatingReader to this.

Validating XML When Loading a DataSet

Like the XML document objects, a DataSet does not automatically validate XML that's provided for the ReadXml method against any schema that is already in place within the DataSet or which is inline with the XML (that is, in the same document as the XML data content). In a DataSet, the schema is used solely to provide information about the intended structure of the data. It's not used for actual validation at all.

When you load the schema, the DataSet uses it as a specification for the table names, column names, data types, and so on. Then, when you load the XML data content, it arranges the data in the appropriate tables and columns as new data rows. An encountered value or element that doesn't match the schema is ignored, and that particular column in the current data row is left empty.

This makes sense, because the DataSet is designed to work with structured relational data, and so any superfluous content in the source file cannot be part of the correct data model. So, you should think of schemas in a DataSet as being a way to specify the data structure (rather than inferring the structure from the data, as happens if no schema is present). Don't think of this as a way of validating the data.

A Document Validation Example

The Validating XML documents with an XmlValidatingReader object (validating-xml.aspx) example page shown in Figure 11-17 demonstrates how you can validate an XML document. When first opened, it displays a list of source documents that you can use in a drop-down list, and it performs validation against the selected document. As you can see from the screenshot, it reports no validation errors in a valid document.

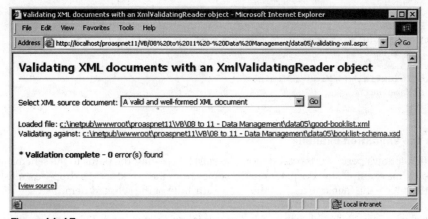

Figure 11-17

You must run the page in a browser on the web server itself to be able to open the XML document and schema using the physical paths in the hyperlinks in the page.

However, if you select the well-formed but invalid document, it reports a series of validation errors, as shown in Figure 11-18:

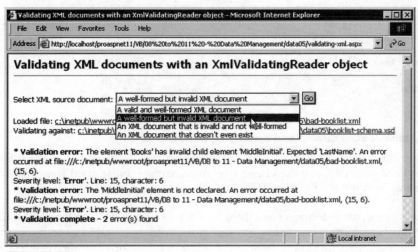

Figure 11-18

In this case the XML document contains an extra `<MiddleInitial>` child element within one of the `<Books>` elements, which is not permitted in the schema that's being used to validate it.

The following code shows the offending element. You can view the document and the schema using the hyperlinks provided in the page:

```
<Books>
  <ISBN>0764544020</ISBN>
  <Title>Beginning Access 2002 VBA</Title>
  <PublicationDate>2000-04-01T00:00:00.0000000+01:00</PublicationDate>
  <FirstName>Mark</FirstName>
  <MiddleInitial>J</MiddleInitial>
  <LastName>Horner</LastName>
</Books>
```

The Code for the Validation Example

The code that follows performs the validation. We start by creating the paths to the schema and XML document. In this example, the document name comes from the `selXMLFile` drop-down list defined earlier in the page – the filename itself is the `value` attribute of the selected item.

We then declare a variable to hold the number of validation errors found. This is followed by code to create an `XmlTextReader` object, specifying the XML document as the source. Also provided is a hyperlink to this document:

```
'create physical path to sample files (in same folder as ASPX page)
Dim strCurrentPath As String = Request.PhysicalPath
Dim strXMLPath As String = Left(strCurrentPath, _
    InStrRev(strCurrentPath, "\")) & selXMLFile.SelectedItem.Value
Dim strSchemaPath As String = Left(strCurrentPath, _
    InStrRev(strCurrentPath, "\")) & "booklist-schema.xsd"

'variable to count number of validation errors found
Dim intValidErrors As Integer = 0
'create the new XmlTextReader object and load the XML document
objXTReader = New XmlTextReader(strXMLPath)
outXMLDoc.innerHTML = "Loaded file: <a href=""" & strXMLPath _
                 & """>" & strXMLPath & "</a><br />"
```

Creating the XmlValidatingReader and Specifying the Schema

The next step is to create the `XmlValidatingReader` object with the `XmlTextReader` as the source, and specify the validation type to suit the schema (you could have, of course, used `Auto` to automatically validate against any type of schema or DTD).

The schema is in a separate document and there is no link or reference to it in the XML document. So it's necessary to specify which schema to use. You can create a new `XmlSchemaCollection`, and add the schema to it using the `Add` method of the `XmlSchemaCollection`. You then specify this collection as the `Schemas` property, and display a link to the schema:

```
'create an XmlValidatingReader for this XmlTextReader
Dim objValidator As New XmlValidatingReader(objXTReader)

'set the validation type to use an XSD schema
objValidator.ValidationType = ValidationType.Schema

'create a new XmlSchemaCollection
Dim objSchemaCol As New XmlSchemaCollection()
```

```
'add the booklist-schema.xsd schema to it
objSchemaCol.Add("", strSchemaPath)

'assign the schema collection to the XmlValidatingReader
objValidator.Schemas.Add(objSchemaCol)
outXMLDoc.innerHTML &= "Validating against: <a href=""" _
                    & strSchemaPath & """>" & strSchemaPath & "</a>"
```

In version 1.1, Microsoft has suggested an updated approach to loading stylesheets that are not fully trusted. See the Loading Stylesheets and Schemas with an XmlResolver section at the end of this chapter for details.

Specifying the Validation Event Handler

The `XmlValidatingReader` will raise an event whenever it encounters a validation error in the document, as the `XmlTextReader` reads it from the disk file. If you don't handle this event specifically, it will be raised to the default error handler. In our case, this is the `Try...Catch` construct included in the example page.

However, it's often better to handle the validation events separately from other (usually fatal) errors such as the XML file not actually existing on disk. To specify your own event handler for the `ValidationEventHandler` event in Visual Basic, use the `AddHandler` method, and pass to it the event you want to handle and a pointer to the handler routine (named `ValidationError` in this example):

```
'add the event handler for any validation errors found
AddHandler objValidator.ValidationEventHandler, AddressOf ValidationError
```

In C#, you can add the validation event handler using the following syntax:

```
objValidator.ValidationEventHandler += new
                ValidationEventHandler(ValidationError);
```

Reading the Document and Catching Parser Errors

You are now ready to read the XML document from the disk file. In this case, you're only reading through to check for validation errors. In an application, you would have code here to perform whatever tasks you need against the XML, or alternatively use the `XmlValidatingReader` as the source for the `Load` method of an `XmlDocument` or `XmlDataDocument` object, or in the constructor for an `XPathDocument` object.

Once validation is complete, you can display a count of the number of errors found and close the reader object to release the disk file. If the document is not well-formed or cannot be loaded for any other reason (such as it doesn't exist), a parser error occurs. In this case, you can include a statement in the `Catch` section that displays the error. That's all you need to do to validate the document:

```
Try
  'iterate through the document reading and validating each element
  While objValidator.Read()
    'use or display the XML content here as required
  End While
```

```
      'display count of errors found
      outXMLDoc.innerHTML &= "Validation complete " & intValidErrors _
                           & " error(s) found"

   Catch objError As Exception
      'will occur if there is a read error or the document cannot be parsed
      outXMLDoc.InnerHTML &= "Read/Parser error: " & objError.Message

   Finally
      'must remember to always close the XmlTextReader after use
      objXTReader.Close()

   End Try
```

The ValidationEvent Handler

The `XmlValidatingReader` raises the `Validation` event whenever a validation error is discovered in the XML document, and it's been specified that the `ValidationError` event handler will be called when this event is raised. This event handler receives the usual reference to the object that raised the event, plus a `ValidationEventArgs` object containing information about the event.

In the event handler, we first increment the error counter, and then check what kind of error it is by using the `Severity` property of the `ValidationEventArgs` object. A displayed message describes the error, the line number, and character position if available (although these are generally included in the error message anyway):

```
   Public Sub ValidationError(objSender As Object, _
                              objArgs As ValidationEventArgs)

      'event handler called when a validation error is found
      intValidErrors += 1    'increment count of errors

      'check the severity of the error
      Dim strSeverity As String
      If objArgs.Severity = 0 Then strSeverity = "Error"
      If objArgs.Severity = 1 Then strSeverity = "Warning"

      'display a message
      outXMLDoc.InnerHTML &= "Validation error: " & objArgs.Message _
                           & "<br /> Severity level: '" & strSeverity
      If objXTReader.LineNumber > 0 Then
         outXMLDoc.InnerHTML &= "Line: " & objXTReader.LineNumber _
                              & ", character: " & objXTReader.LinePosition
      End If

   End Sub
```

The previous screenshot displayed validation error messages caused by a well-formed but invalid document. We've also provided an XML document that is not well-formed, so that you can see the parser error that is raised and trapped by the `Try...Catch` construct. This also prevents the remainder of the document from being read, as shown in Figure 11-19:

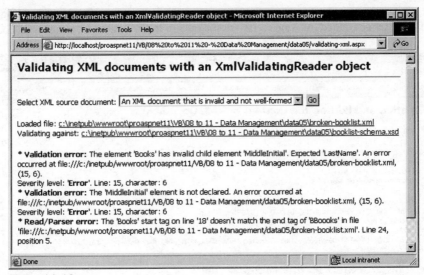

Figure 11-19

In this case, there is an illegal closing tag for one of the <Books> elements. One of the options provided even tries to load a non-existent XML document, so you can see that the page traps this error successfully as well.

```
<Books>
   <ISBN>1861003382</ISBN>
   <Title>Beginning Active Server Pages 3.0</Title>
   <PublicationDate>1999-12-01T00:00:00</PublicationDate>
   <FirstName>David</FirstName>
   <LastName>Sussman</LastName>
</BBoooks>
```

Creating and Editing XML Documents

We've discussed how to read and write XML documents, access them in a range of ways, and validate the content against a schema or DTD. Let's now look at Creating and Editing the Content of XML Documents (edit-xml.aspx).

The example page loads an XML document named bookdetails.xml and demonstrates four different techniques you can use for editing and creating documents:

❑   Selecting a node, extracting the content, and deleting that node from the document

❑   Creating a new empty document and adding a declaration and comment to it

❑   Importing (that is, copying) a node from the original document into the new document

❑   Selecting, editing, and inserting new nodes and content into the original document

Figure 11-20 shows the page when you run it. You can see the four stages of the process, though the second and third are combined into one section of the output in the page:

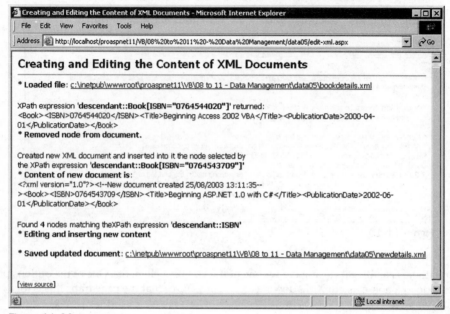

Figure 11-20

You must run the page in a browser on the web server itself to be able to open the XML documents using the physical paths in the hyperlinks in the page.

The Code for This Example Page

The page contains the customary `<div>` elements to display the results and messages, and details of any errors encountered. It also creates the paths to the existing and new documents, and displays a hyperlink to the existing document. This is identical to the previous example, and so we aren't repeating the code here. Instead, here's the part that loads the existing document into a new `XmlDocument` object:

```
Dim objXMLDoc As New XmlDocument()
Try
    objXMLDoc.Load(strXMLPath)
Catch objError As Exception
    outError.innerHTML = "Error while accessing document.<br />" _
                       & objError.Message & "<br />" & objError.Source
    Exit Sub  ' and stop execution
End Try
```

Selecting, Displaying, and Deleting a Node

To select a specific node in the document, you can use an *XPath expression*. In our example, the expression is `descendant::Book[ISBN="0764544020"]`, which – when the current node is the root element of the document – selects the `<Book>` node with the specified value for its `<ISBN>` child node. This expression is used in the `SelectSingleNode` method, and it returns a reference to the node you want. To display this node and its content, you just have to reference its `OuterXml` property.

If you only want the content of the node, use the `InnerXml` property, and if you only want the text values of all the nodes concatenated together, use the `InnerText` property.

To delete the node from the document, you can call the `RemoveChild` method of the parent node (the root of the document, which is returned by the `DocumentElement` property of the document object), and pass it a reference to the node to be deleted.

```
'specify XPath expression to select a book element
Dim strXPath As String = "descendant::Book[ISBN=" & Chr(34) _
                    & "0764544020" & Chr(34) & "]"

'get a reference to the matching <Book> node
Dim objNode As XmlNode
objNode = objXMLDoc.SelectSingleNode(strXPath)

'display node and content using the OuterXml property
outResult1.InnerHtml = "XPath expression '<b>" & strXPath _
                    & "</b>' returned:<br />" _
                    & Server.HtmlEncode(objNode.OuterXml) & "<br />"

'delete this node using RemoveChild method from document element
objXMLDoc.DocumentElement.RemoveChild(objNode)
outResult1.InnerHtml &= "Removed node from document.<br />"
```

Creating a New Document and Adding Nodes

We create a new empty XML document, simply by instantiating an `XmlDocument` (or `XmlDataDocument`) object. Nodes can then be created and inserted into this document. In the code that follows, we're creating a new XML declaration (the `<?xml version="1.0"?>` element) and inserting it into the new document with the `InsertBefore` method:

```
'create new empty XmlDocument object
Dim objNewDoc As New XmlDocument()

'create a new XmlDeclaration object
Dim objDeclare As XmlDeclaration
objDeclare = objNewDoc.CreateXmlDeclaration("1.0", Nothing, Nothing)

'and add it as the first node in the new document
objDeclare = objNewDoc.InsertBefore(objDeclare, objNewDoc.DocumentElement)
```

The second and third parameters of the `CreateXmlDeclaration` method are used to specify the encoding type used in the document, and the standalone value (in other words, if there is a schema available to validate the document). We set both to `Nothing`, so we'll get neither of these optional attributes in the XML declaration element. An XML parser will then assume the default values "UTF-8" and "yes" when it loads the document.

When the new node is created, a reference to this new node is returned from the `CreateXmlDeclaration` method. This reference is used as the first parameter to the `InsertBefore` method. The second parameter is a reference to the node that we want to insert before, and in this case we specify the root of the document.

Notice that `DocumentElement` is not the root element of the document, as it doesn't yet have one. This sounds confusing, but you can think of it as a reference to the placeholder where the root element will reside.

Next we create a new `Comment` element, and insert this into the new document after the XML declaration element:

```
'create a new XmlComment object
Dim objComment As XmlComment
objComment = objNewDoc.CreateComment("New document created " & Now())

'and add it as the second node in the new document
objComment = objNewDoc.InsertAfter(objComment, objDeclare)
```

Importing Nodes into the New Document

To get some content into the newly created document, our example page imports a node from the existing document loaded from disk at the start of the page. We again use an XPath expression with the `SelectSingleNode` method to get a reference to the `<Book>` element that is to be imported.

We then create a new `XmlNode` object in the target document to hold the imported node, and call the `Import` method of this new node to copy the node from the original document. The second parameter to the `Import` method specifies whether we want a *deep* copy – in other words, if we want to import all the content of the node as well as the value.

Once you've got the new node into the document, you have to insert it into the tree – it is only an unattached fragment at the moment. As before, you can use the `InsertAfter` method, using the reference you've already got to the new node, and the reference created earlier to the `Comment` node so that the imported node becomes the root element of the new document.

We finish this section by displaying the contents of the new document. We've got a reference to the `XmlDocument` object that contains it, so we just query the `OuterXml` property to get the complete content. You can see the new document displayed in the example page.

```
strXPath = "descendant::Book[ISBN=" & Chr(34) & "0764543709" & Chr(34) & "]"
objNode = objXMLDoc.SelectSingleNode(strXPath)

'create a variable to hold the imported node object
Dim objImportedNode As XmlNode

'import node and all children into new document as unattached fragment
objImportedNode = objNewDoc.ImportNode(objNode, True)

'insert new unattached node into document after the comment node
objNewDoc.InsertAfter(objImportedNode, objComment)
```

```
'display the contents of the new document
outResult2.InnerHtml = "Created new XML document and inserted " _
                     & "into it the node selected by<br />" _
                     & "the XPath expression '" & strXPath & "'" _
                     & "Content of new document is:<br />" _
                     & Server.HtmlEncode(objNewDoc.OuterXml)
```

Inserting and Updating Nodes in a Document

The final part of the example page edits some values in the original document. This time, an XPath expression that will match more than one node is necessary, and so we use the `SelectNodes` method of the document to return an `XmlNodeList` object containing references to all the matching nodes (in our example, all the `<ISBN>` nodes). We can then display the number of matches found.

The plan is to add an attribute to all of the `<ISBN>` elements, and replace the text content (value) of these elements with two new elements that contain the information in a different form. After declaring some variables that are needed, we can iterate through the collection of `<ISBN>` nodes using a `For Each` construct.

```
strXPath = "descendant::ISBN"

'get a reference to the matching nodes as a collection
Dim colNodeList As XmlNodeList
colNodeList = objXMLDoc.SelectNodes(strXPath)

'display the number of matches found
outResult3.InnerHtml = "Found " & colNodeList.Count _
                     & " nodes matching the" _
                     & "XPath expression '" & strXPath & "'<br />" _
                     & "Editing and inserting new content<br />"

'create variables to hold an XmlAttribute and other values
Dim objAttr As XmlAttribute
Dim strNodeValue, strNewValue, strShortCode As String

'iterate through all the nodes found
For Each objNode In colNodeList
  ...
```

Within the loop, we first create a new attribute named `formatting` and set the value to `hyphens` (all the `<ISBN>` nodes will have the same value for this attribute). You can add this attribute to the `<ISBN>` element node by calling the `SetAttribute` method. However, there is a minor hitch – the members of an `XmlNodeList` are `XmlNode` objects, which don't have a `SetAttribute` method. In Visual Basic, you can get around this by casting the object to an `XmlElement` object using the `CType` (convert type) function.

To change the content of the `<ISBN>` elements, you only have to set the `InnerXml` property. This is much easier than using the `InsertBefore` and `InsertAfter` methods demonstrated earlier, and provides a valid alternative when the content you want to insert is available as a string (recall that you had references to the element node and its new content node when you used `InsertBefore`).

Our code extracts the existing ISBN value, creates the new *short code* from it, formats the existing ISBN with hyphens, and then creates a string containing the new content for the element. The final step is to insert these values into the `<ISBN>` node by setting its `InnerXml` property, before going round to do the next one. You can then end the page by writing the complete edited XML document to a disk file and displaying a hyperlink to it so that it can be viewed.

```
...
'create an XmlAttribute named 'formatting'
objAttr = objXMLDoc.CreateAttribute("formatting")

'set the value of the XmlAttribute to 'hyphens'
objAttr.Value = "hyphens"

'and add it to this ISBN element – have to cast the object
'to an XmlElement as XmlNode doesn't have this method
CType(objNode, XmlElement).SetAttributeNode(objAttr)

'get text value of this ISBN element
strNodeValue = objNode.InnerText

'create short and long strings to replace content
strShortCode = Right(strNodeValue, 4)
strNewValue = Left(strNodeValue, 1) & "-" _
            & Mid(strNodeValue, 2, 6) & "-" _
            & Mid(strNodeValue, 8, 2) & "-" _
            & Right(strNodeValue, 1)

'insert into element by setting the InnerXml property
objNode.InnerXml = "<LongCode>" & strNewValue _
                 & "</LongCode><ShortCode>" _
                 & strShortCode & "</ShortCode>"
Next
'write the updated document to a disk file
objXMLDoc.Save(strNewPath)
'display a link to view the updated document
outResult3.InnerHTML &= "Saved updated document: <a href=""" _
                 & strNewPath & """>" & strNewPath & "</a>"
```

Viewing the Results

If you open both documents – the original and the edited version (Figures 11-21, 11-22) – you can see the effects of our editing process. The first contains the `<Book>` node with the `<ISBN>` value `0764544020`, which is not present in the second. You can also see the updated `<ISBN>` elements in the second document:

Figure 11-21

Figure 11-22

In this example, we've demonstrated several techniques for working with an XML document using the `System.Xml` classes provided in .NET. Some of the techniques use the XML DOM methods as defined by W3C, and some are specific *extensions* available with the `XmlDocument` (and other) objects. In general, these extensions make common tasks a lot easier – for example, the ability to access the `InnerText`, `InnerXml`, and `OuterXml` of a node makes it remarkably easy to edit or insert content and markup.

We haven't covered all the possibilities for accessing XML documents, as you'll see if you examine the list of properties, methods, and events for each of the relevant objects in the SDK. However, by now, you should have a flavor for what is possible, and how easy it is to achieve.

Using XSL and XSLT Transformations

Let's come back to a topic first discussed in Chapter 8. There, you saw how easy it is to perform an XSL or XSLT transformation against an XML document using the new `XslTransform` object. However, we only applied it to two disk files (an XML document and a style sheet) by specifying the paths to these files.

You can use the `XslTransform` object to perform transformations when the document is not actually a disk file. This could well be the case in an application that processes XML. For example, it could be referenced by an `XmlTextReader`, or stored in the `XmlDocument` object returned by a web service or business component, or even pointed to by an existing `XPathNavigator`. And you might not want the results to be written to disk as a file – you might need them as a `String` or a `StringBuilder` object. The next example attempts to demonstrate several of these scenarios.

In version 1.1, Microsoft suggests an updated approach to loading stylesheets that are not fully trusted. See the Loading Stylesheets and Schemas with an XmlResolver section of this chapter for details.

An XSL Transformation Example

The Different ways to use the XslTransform object (`multi-xsl-transform.aspx`) example page is shown in Figure 11-23.

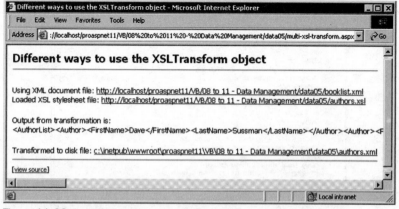

Figure 11-23

It loads the XML document and the stylesheet from disk at the start of the page, but then references the XML document in a range of ways to demonstrate the possibilities. It also performs a transformation to a `String`, and displays this in the page before writing it to disk separately – rather than directly through the `XslTransform` object:

Notice that the XML string is not wrapped, and appears a single line in the page. However, if you open the hyperlink at the bottom of the example page (shown in Figure 11-24), you'll see the transformed result. Some of the nodes have been collapsed to reduce the overall size of the page in the screenshot:

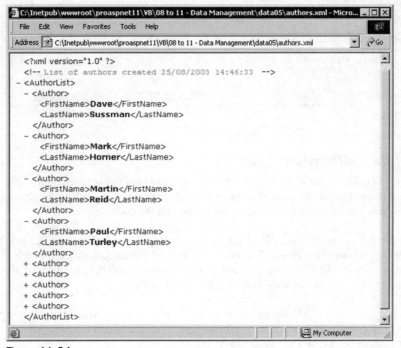

Figure 11-24

As with earlier examples, you must run this page in a browser on the web server itself to be able to open the transformed file using the physical path in the hyperlink at the bottom of the page.

Figure 11-25 shows the simple stylesheet being used. It extracts the `<AuthorName>` elements from the XML source document and generates a new XML document containing these – within a root element named `<AuthorList>`:

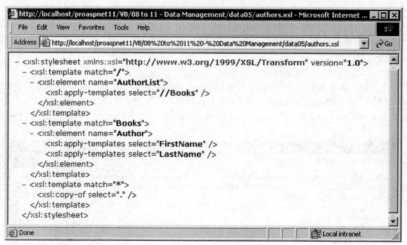

Figure 11-25

The Code for the XslTransform Example

After creating the paths to the XML document and XSL stylesheet being used, the code in the page displays hyperlinks to these documents. Here, we're only interested in loading the documents and executing the transformation itself, and so haven't repeated the code.

We start by creating a new XslTransform object and loading the stylesheet into it, using the Load method with the path and filename of the stylesheet. To load the XML document in this example, an XmlTextReader is used. This isn't the quickest or shortest way to do it, but it aims to give you some ideas about how you can use the various objects in your projects.

For example, by loading the XML document with an XmlTextReader, you'd have the opportunity to validate it at the same time if this is a requirement. You would just need to assign an XmlValidatingReader to the XmlTextReader.

So, the code creates the XmlTextReader for the XML document and then creates a new XPathDocument from this XmlTextReader. The constructor for the XPathDocument automatically loads the XML from disk into the new XPathDocument. You can then create a new XPathNavigator based on the XPathDocument by calling the CreateNavigator method:

```vb
'create a new XslTransform object to do the transformation
Dim objTransform As New XslTransform()

'load the XSL stylesheet into the XslTransform object
objTransform.Load(strXSLPath)

'create a new XmlTextReader object to fetch XML document
Dim objXTReader As New XmlTextReader(strXMLPath)

'create a new XPathDocument object from the XmlTextReader
Dim objXPDoc As New XPathDocument(objXTReader)
```

```
'create a new XPathNavigator object from the XPathDocument
Dim objXPNav As XPathNavigator
objXPNav = objXPDoc.CreateNavigator()
```

Displaying the Transformed Result with an XmlReader

The `Transform` method of the `XslTransform` object can output the result of a transformation to an `XmlReader` object, a `TextReader` object, or an `XmlWriter` object. If you want the result to be available as a string, for use elsewhere in your applications, you can use an `XmlReader` or a `TextReader` object (depending on whether the result is XML that you want to parse as you use it, or some other format that can't be used with an `XmlReader`).

Our example transforms the XML into an `XmlReader` object. We declare a variable to hold the object, and call the `Transform` method of the `XslTransform` object, passing it the `XPathNavigator` created for the XML document. The second argument allows us to pass in an `XsltArgumentList` object that can contain the parameters or arguments used by the stylesheet. As there are no parameters in our stylesheet, we use the value `Nothing` for this argument.

Once we get back the `XmlReader` object, we can display the contents – the result of the transformation. The easiest way is to use the `ReadOuterXml` method of the reader:

```
'create a variable to hold the XmlReader object that is
'returned from the Transform method
Dim objReader As XmlReader

'perform the transformation using the XSL file in the
'XslTransform and the XML document referenced by the
'XPathNavigator. The result is in the XmlReader object
objReader = objTransform.Transform(objXPNav, Nothing)

'display the contents of the XmlReader object
objReader.MoveToContent()
outResults.InnerText = objReader.ReadOuterXml()
```

Writing the Transformed Result to Disk

The alternative *output device* for the `Transform` method of the `XslTransform` object is an `XmlWriter` object. This is ideal for piping the output back to a disk file.

In our example, we create an `XmlTextWriter` object (a public class that inherits from `XmlWriter`), using a path and filename created earlier in the page. The second parameter to the constructor is the encoding to be used – if we specify `Nothing`, it sets the encoding to the default UTF-8.

Now we can use the `XmlTextWriter` to create the disk file. We start with an XML declaration (by simply calling the `WriteStartDocument` method) and add a comment element. We can then perform the transformation, sending the results directly to the `XmlTextWriter` – which writes them straight to the disk file.

We finish by calling the `WriteEndDocument` method, to close any open elements and finalize the document, and then close it and display a hyperlink so that the results can be examined.

```
'create an XmlTextWriter object to write result to disk
Dim objWriter As New XmlTextWriter(strOutPath, Nothing)

'write the opening <?xml .. ?> declaration and a comment
objWriter.WriteStartDocument()
objWriter.WriteComment("List of authors created " & Now())

'transform the XML into the XmlTextWriter
objTransform.Transform(objXPNav, Nothing, objWriter)

'ensure that all open elements are closed and end the document
objWriter.WriteEndDocument()

'flush the buffer to disk and close the file
objWriter.Close()
outFile.InnerHtml = "<a href=""" & strOutPath & """>" & strOutPath & "</a>"
```

Loading Stylesheets and Schemas with an XmlResolver

One of the major changes to the `System.Xml` namespace in version 1.1 is a revision of the best practice and the various approaches available for loading an XSLT stylesheet into instances of the `XslTransform` class. These changes are associated with the percieved increasing risks from loading stylesheets that can contain script code, and references to other external resources. In version 1.0, once the stylesheet is loaded into the `XslTransform` object, it runs as fully trusted, irrespective of the source. To some extent, the same issue applies when loading a schema, though this is less likely to be a security risk than a stylesheet.

When you call the `Load` or `Transform` method of the `XslTransform` class, the `Add` method of the `XmlSchemaCollection` class, or the `Compile` method of the `XmlSchema` class, they automatically create an `XmlUrlResolver` instance for the schemas or stylesheets you reference, and use these to resolve any references to external entities, DTDs, other schemas, and resources pointed to by `xsl:include` and `xsl:import` statements.

However, where you are not able to verify whether a stylesheet or schema is safe – for example, when loading it over the Web from an untrusted source – you should instead create instances of the `XmlUrlResolver` or `XmlSecureResolver` classes that apply the security constraints you want to apply.

The `XmlUrlResolver` is the same as in verison 1.0 of the .NET Framework, but the `XmlSecureResolver` class is new in version 1.1. It is used for the same purposes as the `XmlUrlResolver`, but allows you to restrict the permissions available to the resources you use it to access.

Creating and Populating a CredentialCache

The `XmlUrlResolver` and `XmlSecureResolver` classes expose a `Credentials` property, which is a reference to a `CredentialCache` instance that can hold one or more credentials. Each credential is itself an instance of the `NetworkCredential` class. To create a `NetworkCredential`, you provide the user name or ID, the matching password, and (optionally) the domain in which that password should be validated in a call to the constructor:

```
Dim objCred As New System.Net.NetworkCredential("userid", "password","domain")
```

The `CredentialCache` can be used to associate `NetworkCredential` instances with specific URLs so that the appropriate one is used when the stylesheet or schema is loaded.

To create a `CredentialCache` that contains more than one `NetworkCredential`, you create each one and add it to the cache, specifying the URL to which it applies in the `Add` method:

```
' create two NetworkCredential objects
Dim objCred1 As New System.Net.NetworkCredential("bob", "fH8$o3")
Dim objCred2 As New System.Net.NetworkCredential("alice", "TR3$3aq")

' create and populate CredentialCache object
Dim objCC As New CredentialCache()
objCC.Add(New Uri("http://www.site1.com/"), "Basic", objCred1);
objCC.Add(New Uri("http://www.site2.com/"), "Basic", objCred1);
objCC.Add(New Uri("http://www.site3.com/"), "Digest", objCred2);
```

Loading a Stylesheet with an XmlUrlResolver

Once you've created your `NetworkCredential` or `CredentialCache`, you can assign it to the `Credentials` property of a new `XmlUrlResolver`. You can then specify the `XmlUrlResolver` when calling the `Load` or `Transform` method of the `XslTransform` class, the `Add` method of the `XmlSchemaCollection` class, or the `Compile` method of the `XmlSchema` class – for example, when you have a single `NetworkCredential`:

```
Dim objResolver As New XmlUrlResolver()
objResolver.Credentials = objMyNetworkCredential
Dim objTransform As New XslTransform()
objTransform.Load(stylesheet-url, objResolver)
```

Or when you have a `CredentialsCache` instance:

```
Dim objResolver As New XmlUrlResolver()
objResolver.Credentials = objMyCredentialsCache
Dim objTransform As New XslTransform()
objTransform.Load(stylesheet-url, objResolver)
```

As a result of this new approach, the recommended overloads of the `Load` method of the `XslTransform` class are now limited to these five (all others are obsolete). The first overload should only be used where you can verify the stylesheet is safe, or from a fully trusted source:

- ❑   Load (*stylesheet-url*)

- ❑   Load (*stylesheet-url*, *XmlResolver*)

- ❑   Load (*XPathNavigator*, *XmlResolver*, *Evidence*)

- ❑   Load (*XmlReader*, *XmlResolver*, *Evidence*)

- ❑   Load (*XPathNavigator*, *XmlResolver*, *Evidence*)

The *Evidence* parameter required for the last three overloads is a reference to an instance of the `Evidence` class. Microsoft's documentation covers four different scenarios, with different levels of security risk, when deciding how to manage the permissions that a stylesheet will have:

❏ Where the stylesheet is self-contained, is located on a local disk, or comes from a source that you trust, and you want to allow it to execute with the same permissions as the code performing the transformation (the current assembly):

```
objTransform.Load("stylesheet-url", objResolver, _
                  Me.GetType().Assembly.Evidence)
```

❏ Where the XSLT stylesheet comes from an outside source that is known, and is a verifiable URL, Evidence can be created from that URL using the CreateEvidenceForUrl method of the XmlSecureResolver object:

```
Dim objEvidence As Evidence _
    = XmlSecureResolver.CreateEvidenceForUrl("stylesheet-url")
objTransform.Load("stylesheet-url", objResolver, objEvidence)
```

❏ Where the XSLT stylesheet comes from an outside source that is not known or not trusted, and you want to ensure that script blocks are not processed, the XSLT document function is not supported, and privileged extension objects are disallowed, you can set the Evidence parameter to Nothing (null in C#):

```
objTransform.Load("stylesheet-url", objResolver, Nothing)
```

❏ Where the XSLT stylesheet comes from an outside source that is not known or not trusted, and in addition to these limitaions, you want to ensure that xsl:import and xsl:include elements are not processed, you can set the XmlResolver parameter to Nothing (null in C#):

```
objTransform.Load("stylesheet-url", Nothing)
```

For the recommended overloads of the XslTransform.Transform method, see the .NET SDK topic Reference | Class Library | System.Xml.Xsl | XslTransform Class | Methods | Transform Method.

For the recommended overloads of the XmlSchemaCollection.Add method, see the .NET SDK topic Reference | Class Library | System.Xml.Schema | XslTransform Class | Methods | Transform Method.

For the recommended overloads of the XmlSchemaCollection.Compile method, see the .NET SDK topic eference | Class Library | System.Xml.Schema | XmlSchemaCollection Class | Methods | Add Method.

Summary

This chapter ends our exploration through the exciting techniques now available for accessing data under the .NET Framework. Over the previous four chapters, we've examined the main objects used for both relational data and XML document access, seen how to program with them, and how these two traditionally opposing data-handling technologies are now integrated together.

This chapter concentrated on the ways you can work with objects drawn mainly from the System.Xml namespaces – in particular, we saw how to read, write, validate, and edit XML documents using a variety of methods. We also explored the way that integration between XML and relational data is achieved through the XmlDataDocument and DataSet objects.

Then, after looking at some of the options available for creating and editing XML documents, we finished up with a more detailed look at the capabilities of the `XslTransform` object. This object makes it easy to perform server-side XSL and XSLT transformations using stylesheets.

Although we couldn't cover all the topics of XML handling in .NET, you should now be familiar with the basics, the objects that are available, and how they can be used within your applications. To summarize, in this chapter we introduced:

❏ Accessing relational data as XML and vice versa

❏ Synchronization between an XML document and the `DataSet` object

❏ Validating XML documents using a schema

❏ Creating and editing XML documents in a range of different ways

❏ Some alternatives available when transforming XML using stylesheets

We now leave data management, and in the next two chapters we'll discuss how to configure ASP.NET applications.

12

Web Applications and global.asax

Classic ASP supported the concept of a *Web application*. This was primarily a collection of .asp files, plus the `global.asa` file. ASP.NET expands upon this concept, but includes additional resources such as ASP.NET pages, web services, user controls, configuration data, `global.asax`, and several other files (both user-defined and defined by ASP.NET).

This chapter has two key themes. First, you will look at how to create an ASP.NET web application, and then move on to look at how to use `global.asax`. Here is a breakdown of what this chapter covers:

❑ **IIS web roots and applications:** In the first section, we will look at what a web application is, and how to create new web applications using the Internet Information Services (IIS) Manager. The steps covered in this section do not discuss ASP.NET features in their own right, but are relevant for using IIS as a host for ASP.NET.

❑ **ASP.NET web applications:** In this section, we will focus on two aspects of ASP.NET web applications: the `\bin` directory for compiled code deployment and the `global.asax` file format.

❑ **Application state management:** Here, we will look at the three options in ASP.NET for maintaining application state: `Application`, `Session`, and `Cache`.

❑ **Application events:** After discussing our choices for managing state in ASP.NET, we will look at the supported application-level events, such as `Application_OnStart` and `Application_Error`. Then, we will discuss the ordering of the events as well as some code examples showing their use.

❑ **Advanced topics:** In this last section of the chapter, we will cover some advanced topics, such as asynchronous application events and using static variables.

In the following chapter, you will look at specific details of how to configure your applications – for example, how to set the Session state timeout using ASP.NET's new configuration system.

IIS Web Roots and Applications

An ASP.NET application consists of a collection of resources such as configuration information, global application files, compiled components, and other ASP.NET resources (pages, web services, and so on). These applications are defined using IIS application roots in the same manner as classic ASP. By default, the *root directory* of a web site in IIS is an *application root*. This is the root level of a particular web site. For example, on a default Windows 2000 IIS 5.0 installation, the root directory of the default web site is http://localhost/ or http://*<servername>*, while the physical path of the root directory is `C:\Inetpub\wwwroot`.

An application root is the starting point of an ASP.NET application and contains resources like the `global.asax` file and the `\bin` directory. We will discuss these in detail later in this chapter.

We can create applications in IIS by using the IIS *Microsoft Management Console* (*MMC*) snap-in. Alternatively, both Visual Studio .NET and the command line scripts included with IIS can be used to create web applications.

Let's look at two of the most common ways of creating an application:

❑ **Create a new web site:** By default, the root directory of the web site will be an application root.

❑ **Mark a folder (virtual or physical) as an application:** The root of the folder will be defined as an application root.

The IIS MMC displays both physical and virtual directories:

❑ A *physical directory* lives within the web site, for example, `C:\Inetpub\wwwroot\Wrox\`, where `C:\Inetpub\wwwroot\` is the physical directory and `Wrox` is a directory beneath it. This appears on the web server as `http://localhost/Wrox/`.

❑ A *virtual directory* is an alias that points to a physical directory on the server. It appears as a directory in the web site, but it exists in a separate physical path. For example, `C:\Wrox\` appears to be a directory available through the server as `http://localhost/Wrox/`. This is in fact a virtual directory, since `C:\Wrox\`'s physical path is obviously not part of the root directory of our web site. For this reason, virtual directories are very useful, since multiple virtual directories can point to a common set of files or live on the same file share. Virtual directories also hide the actual path of the files on the server from a user, and hence increase security.

Although we will go through the steps of creating both virtual directories and IIS applications, this is only necessary if you want to create ASP.NET applications in directories other than the web root directory, (usually `C:\Inetpub\wwwroot\`), as the web root is, by default, an application root. Most likely, you will be creating applications that are part of an existing site. For example, to host the HR site for your company, you'd have separate applications defined for Benefits, Claims, Hiring, and so on.

Let's walk through creating a virtual directory and an IIS application.

Creating IIS Virtual Directories

Let's say you have a physical directory, `C:\Wrox\`, and want to expose that directory as a virtual directory in the web root of your web site, for example http://localhost/Wrox.

To create a virtual directory you need to use the IIS MMC, available from Start | Programs | Administrative Tools | Internet Services Manager, or by selecting Start | Run and then typing inetmgr. You will get a screen similar to Figure 12-1:

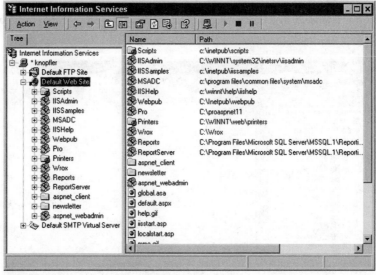

Figure 12-1

To create the Wrox virtual directory in the Default Web Site (highlighted), rightclick on Default Web Site and select New | Virtual Directory. This opens the Virtual Directory Creation Wizard, where you need to go through the following steps:

1. When the wizard opens, select Next to get past the opening screen. You will then be asked for the alias to use with the virtual directory. For this example, enter Wrox, but this can be anything you like – you are not restricted to using the same name as the physical directory.

2. You are then asked for the path to an existing directory to use as a virtual directory. Enter C:\Wrox (assuming you have already created it).

3. Next, you're asked for the access permissions for the directory. The only required selections are Read and Run scripts (such as ASP). These defaults already selected by default.

4. Finally, you are told that the virtual directory has been created. Press the Finish button to exit the wizard.

Now, if you view the available folders in Default Web Site, you will find a folder named Wrox. There are three types of icons next to folders in the root of this web site:

❑ **Normal explorer-style folders:** For example, if FrontPage server extensions are installed, you will see folders named _vti_cnf, _vti_log, and so on. These folders exist as physical directories on the web server.

❑ **Normal explorer-style folders with small globes in the bottom right corner**: These are virtual directories. Some common virtual directories include Scripts and _vti_bin.

❑   **Web application folders:** These folders are represented by a package icon. Any virtual or physical directory on our server can be converted to a web application. By default, the virtual directories we create are web application folders.

So, the `Wrox` virtual directory that you just created is a web application as well. The fact that it is a web application takes precedence over it being a virtual directory, so it is represented by a package icon, as shown in Figure 12-2:

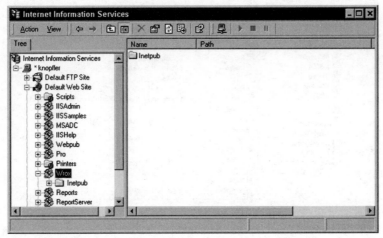

Figure 12-2

Marking a Folder as an Application

Instead of creating the `Wrox` directory as `C:\Wrox` and marking it as a virtual directory, you could have created a directory `C:\Inetpub\wwwroot\Wrox`. `Wrox` is then a physical directory for the Default Web Site.

> The default directory of the Default Web Site is `C:\Inetpub\wwwroot\`.

`C:\Inetpub\wwwroot\Wrox` is a physical directory. Therefore, to use it as an ASP.NET application root, you will have to manually mark it as an application. You can do this by right-clicking on any virtual or physical folder in any IIS web site and selecting Properties.

This brings up a properties dialog for that folder and is shown in Figure 12-3:

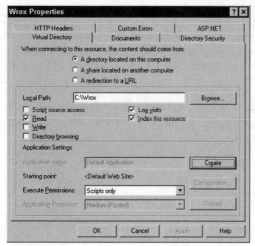

Figure 12-3

This displays the settings for the Wrox folder, the Local Path value, and the permissions that the folder allows. In this case, the default permissions of Read, Log visits, and Index this resource are set.

The lower half of the dialog box is the Application Settings section . This is of interest, because these settings enable the physical directory as a web application. To do this, press the Create button. This changes some of the settings in the Application Settings section, as shown in Figure 12-4:

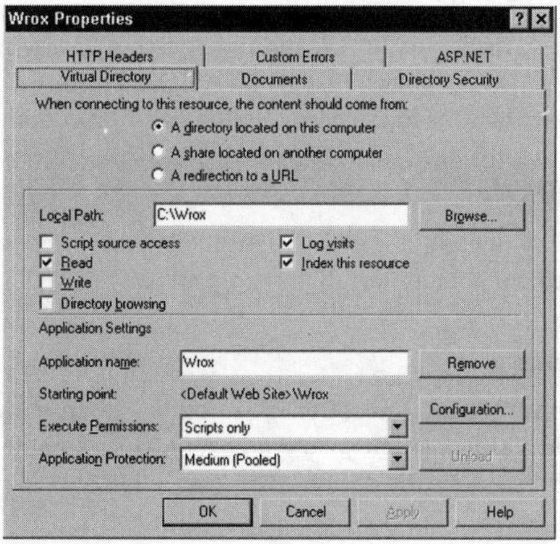

Figure 12-4

The Application name value has changed from Default Application (the name of the parent web application for this folder) to Wrox. The Starting point value has changed from <Default Web Site> to <Default Web Site>\Wrox, again noting that the application has changed. For simplicity, we will skip over the smaller, unimportant changes, except to note that the Create button has now become a Remove button.

> For more detailed information on what the remaining options within the **Properties** dialog do, please see the Internet Information Server documentation, as they do not relate to further discussions of ASP.NET in this chapter. The only exception is mapping custom extensions to ASP.NET, covered later in the Advanced Topics section.
>
> Users familiar with the **Application Protection** settings should note that these do not affect ASP.NET, since that runs in its own process, which is separate from IIS. Please see the IIS documentation for more information on this option.

Finally, click Apply and then OK. The `Wrox` folder is now an application root, just as it was when you created it as a virtual directory.

Removing the Application

Removing a web application is just as simple, if not easier than creating it. Right-click on a folder marked as an application and select Properties. Within the Application Settings section of the dialog, click the Remove button, then select Apply and OK. In the Tree view of the Default Web Site, you will now see the standard virtual or physical folder icon for Wrox.

When we remove the application, we are simply changing a configuration option in IIS. Removing the application does not delete any associated files.

Windows Server 2003

ASP.NET 1.1 ships with Windows Server 2003. Windows Server 2003 also includes the latest version of Internet Information Server (IIS) version 6.0. IIS 6.0 and ASP.NET 1.1 are designed to integrate seamlessly and ASP.NET now defaults to the new IIS 6.0 worker process model.

Installing IIS 6.0 and ASP.NET 1.1

ASP.NET 1.1 is *not* installed by default, nor is IIS. To install ASP.NET you will need to either run the Configure Your Server Wizard or manually install IIS and ASP.NET.

The Configure Your Server Wizard

To use the Configure Your Server Wizard select Configure Your Server from the Administrative Tools group. The first two screens include a welcome screen and an overview of what the Wizard does. On the third screen shown in Figure 12-5, you have the option of picking a Server Role:

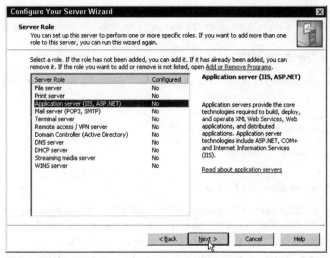

Figure 12-5

Selecting a Server Role will instruct Windows Server 2003 to configure and optimize your server for a specific task, such as an Application server for running IIS and ASP.NET. In this case, select Application server (IIS, ASP.NET) and then click Next. The next screen gives you the option to install FrontPage Server Extensions and ASP.NET. Make sure the Enable ASP.NET checkbox is checked before clicking Next.

The wizard will take you through some more screens. After the wizard has completed, both IIS 6.0 and ASP.NET 1.1 will be installed on your server.

Installing IIS and ASP.NET Manually

To install IIS and ASP.NET without using the Configure Your Server Wizard, open the Control Panel and select Add/Remove Windows Components. The Windows Components Wizard opens; see Figure 12-6:

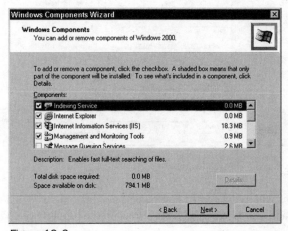

Figure 12-6

Select the Application Server option and then click the Details button. When the Details dialog is displayed, check ASP.NET. Press OK to close the dialog. The selected components are now installed.

Configuring IIS 6.0 for ASP.NET

There are several recommended changes you should make to IIS 6.0 before running ASP.NET applications:

❑   Configuring worker process memory limits

❑   Configuring worker process recycling

Configuring Worker Process Memory Limits

The ASP.NET 1.0 worker process model placed a limit upon how much memory the worker process was allowed to use – 60%. ASP.NET 1.1 uses the new IIS 6.0 process model, which defaults to no fixed limit. This can cause problems for ASP.NET applications. For example, if your application uses the Cache extensively, the Cache's scavenging algorithm will never kick in, because the process will never report that it is memory constrained. We recommend that you configure the IIS 6.0 worker processes to work within a memory limit based on the available memory in your server.

To configure the memory limits, open Internet Information Server Manager (from the Administrative Tools menu) and expand the new Application Pools node, shown in Figure 12-7:

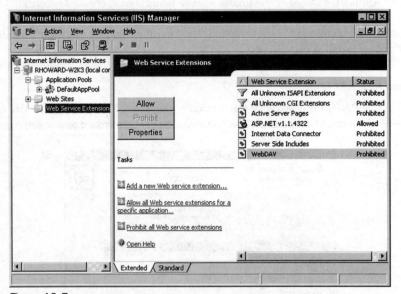

Figure 12-7

Next, right-click on items within the application pool (if you are only using one application pool, this will be DefaultAppPool) and select Properties. This brings up the property dialog, shown in Figure 12-8:

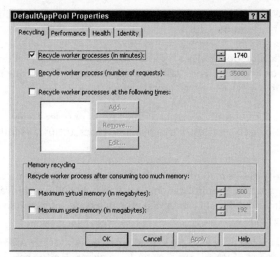

Figure 12-8

Check **Maximum used memory (in megabytes)** and set the value to 60 percent of the physical memory (or less, depending upon how you want your server configured). We recommend that the value never be larger than 800MB when using a 2 GB address space. However, if you have 3GB of addressable memory, you can set the limit to as high as 1,800MB.

Configuring Worker Process Recycling

Worker process recycling is different for the IIS 6.0 worker process model. The IIS 6.0 worker process is automatically configured to recycle the process every 29 hours. This is much too aggressive for an ASP.NET application and the ASP.NET team recommends that the automatic worker process recycling feature of IIS 6.0 be disabled.

To disable worker process recycling, follow the same steps for configuring worker process memory limits to view the properties of an Application Pool. By default, the **Recycle worker process (in minutes)**: is checked. Simply uncheck this option and click **OK**.

For more information on running ASP.NET 1.1 and IIS 6.0 together, please review the **Running ASP.NET 1.1 and IIS 6.0** article at http://www.asp.net/faq/AspNetAndIIS6.aspx.

Now that you have had a quick overview of creating a web application in IIS as well as using IIS 6.0 on Windows Server 2003, let's look at how this is related to ASP.NET.

ASP.NET Web Applications

ASP.NET makes use of IIS web applications to identify distinct *application domains*. Application domains are a feature of the CLR. Each application domain is separate, secure, and does not share memory with other domains. For example, each of the three web applications **Wrox1**, **Wrox2**, and **Wrox3** will be treated separately, so **Wrox1** will not share data such as `Session` or `Application` state with the others, and likewise for Wrox2 and Wrox3. Many application domains may be hosted within a single process – this is completely transparent thanks to the CLR.

You can think of an application domain as a logical process. When it fails, it doesn't take down the host process, so one failure won't crash all your ASP.NET applications. This is one of many new features provided by the CLR that ASP.NET takes advantage of.

An ASP.NET web application typically consists of three types of (user-created) resources, in addition to standard ASP.NET pages or web services. These resource types are always found in the root of the application, and include:

❑ `bin`: This directory lies immediately below the root of the application, and is used to hold .NET assemblies to be used by the application. (An assembly is the technical term used to describe a component built with .NET. It is compiled reusable code, an example of which is `System.Data.dll`.)

❑ `global.asax`: This file is ASP.NET's logical replacement for the ASP file `global.asa`. It allows us to execute code for ASP.NET application-level events, and to set application-level variables.

❑ `web.config`: Each web application can have its own ASP.NET configuration settings. These settings, depending upon the security configuration of the system, can override settings found in ASP.NET's `machine.config`.

The `machine.config` file applies global default settings for all ASP.NET applications. We will cover ASP.NET configuration in more detail in Chapter 13.

Let's start by briefly looking at the ASP.NET `bin` directory, as it relates to ASP.NET web applications.

Registering Components

Rather than relying upon the system registry, ASP.NET uses a special directory (`bin`) to register components as part of an application.

The next section illustrates the differences between classic ASP/COM component registration and the new ASP.NET/Assembly registration.

Prior to .NET

To use COM (reusable compiled code) in ASP, you always had to register the components on the server. For example, if you developed a simple data access component using Visual Basic 6 and wished to use it in an ASP application, you would need to explicitly register the component before you could use it.

Registering components was done either through a command line tool, `regsvr32.exe`, or with COM+ Services (Start | Programs | Administrative Tools | Component Services). In either case, an entry was made in the Windows registry describing the component, its threading model, and the location of the `.dll` file. You could then write code in your ASP application using the `erver.CreateObject` method:

```
<%
Dim myObject
Set myObject = Server.CreateObject("Example.DataAccess")
%>
```

Behind the scenes, the `ProgID` (in this case `Example.DataAccess`) would find the entry for the required component in the registry. Once found, an instance of the component would be created and a reference set to the local variable `myObject`.

This is all well and good, and many successful applications were (and still are!) built using this model. However, there are some caveats associated with using COM in ASP:

❑ **Deployment and update**: Deploying the component to multiple servers and replacing running components requires local server access to perform the registration/un-registration.

❑ **Global registration and versioning**: In addition to requiring local server access to manage the components, registered components are available to *all* applications on the server where the component is registered. Versioning the component can be rather difficult since the components are global to the server. So, they are most often versioned by `ProgID`, which in turn means changes must be made to the software using those newly versioned instances.

> *One of the most common problems that ASP developers ran into when using COM was the 'locking' of components by IIS when they attempted to replace an existing DLL with a new version.*

You will be pleased to know that these kinds of ASP/COM issues – deployment, updates, global registration, and versioning – are no longer a problem in ASP.NET.

.NET Components

As mentioned earlier, in .NET the term 'assemblies' is used to describe components – packaged units of reusable, compiled code – built with .NET. Unlike ASP, ASP.NET does not require local server access to register a component. Instead, you can simply copy your assemblies to an ASP.NET `bin` directory using FTP, DAV, XCOPY, and so on, collectively referred to as XCOPY deployment. Assemblies found in the `bin` directory are then automatically loaded by ASP.NET, and the components made available to your application.

> There can only be one `bin` directory per ASP.NET application.

Local Server Access Not Required

Deploying components in ASP.NET is simple. Local server access is not required and all you need is the ability to copy the compiled assembly to the `bin` directory. Once it is there, ASP.NET and the CLR takes care of everything else, and you can start using the component in your code right away.

So how does this type of registration work? Well, unlike a COM component, whose location and internal architecture need to be explicitly logged in the registry, a .NET assembly is *self-describing*. That is to say, the assembly's contents include meta data that describes exactly what the compiled component can and cannot do. All information required to successfully use that component is held in one place, and no extra configuration is required.

Components Are Application-Specific

Again, unlike ASP, the .NET components you register in a specific application's `bin` directory are only available to that application – by contrast, classic ASP COM components were registered for the entire server.

It is possible to register an assembly to be global for all applications using the Global Assembly Cache (GAC), which is covered in more detail in Chapter 23, but this is not the default behavior.

Component Updates

In ASP, if you wanted to replace a component, you needed to restart IIS since the component was loaded in the IIS process. ASP.NET never locks the file, and thus, you can simply delete or copy over the assembly when removing or changing the application – a procedure that does not require local server access.

This dynamic loading and unloading of the components in the `bin` directory works because ASP.NET specifically listens for file change notification events within the `bin` directory. When a change is detected (such as the addition or deletion of a component), ASP.NET will create a new application domain to begin servicing the new requests. As soon as the original application domain has completed servicing any outstanding requests, it is removed.

As far as the client is concerned, this process is completely transparent, and for the developer, it means that updates can be implemented very simply without incurring any application downtime.

An Example Use

Let's look at a simple example using the Wrox web application. You will first need to create a `bin` directory, for example, `C:\Wrox\bin`. Then, you will write a simple ASP.NET page in Visual Basic .NET:

```
<%@ Import Namespace="Component" %>
<%@ Import Namespace="System.Data" %>
<%@ Import Namespace="System.Data.SqlClient" %>

<Script runat="server">
  Public Sub Page_Load()
    Dim simpleComponent As New Simple()

    Dim dataSet As New DataSet()
    dataSet = simpleComponent.LoadDataSet()

    datagrid1.DataSource = dataSet
    datagrid1.DataBind()
  End Sub
</Script>
<font size=6>
<asp:DataGrid runat="server" id="datagrid1"/>
</font>
```

Let's look at implementing the *Component.Simple* assembly used in the preceding code. This simple page creates a new instance, `simpleComponent,` of an assembly named `Simple`. It then uses the

LoadDataSet method of the simpleComponent to populate a DataSet, which is eventually used to data bind an ASP.NET datagrid server control.

At this point, if you request the page in your browser, you will receive an error message in the detailed compiler output, telling us:

error BC30466: Namespace or type 'Component' for the Imports 'Component' cannot be found.

This is because you have identified a namespace called Component that doesn't exist yet – you will create it now.

Using either Visual Studio .NET or the command line compiler, you can create and compile a simple Visual Basic .NET component named Component.Simple, which will be responsible for implementing the LoadDataSet method – here, we are going to build it using Visual Studio .NET.

Open Visual Studio .NET, and select File | New | Project. Select the Visual Basic Projects type and Class Library for the template. Name the project Component, and implement the following code in the Class1.vb file created as part of the project:

```vb
Imports System.Data
Imports System.Data.SqlClient

Public Class Simple
  Public Function LoadDataSet() As DataSet
    Dim myConnection As SqlConnection
    Dim myCommand As SqlDataAdapter
    Dim products As New DataSet()
    Dim sql As String
    Dim dsn As String

    sql = "SELECT address, city, state FROM Authors"
    dsn = "server=localhost;uid=sa;pwd=;database=pubs"
    myConnection = New SqlConnection(dsn)
    myCommand = New SqlDataAdapter(sql, myConnection)
    myCommand.Fill(products, "myAuthors")

    Return products
  End Function
End Class
```

This Visual Basic .NET class named Simple implements the LoadDataSet method required by this ASP.NET page. Compile the Visual Basic .NET project by selecting Build | Build Component. Now open Windows Explorer and navigate to the location where the project was created. Within this location is a bin directory, where you should find a .dll named Component.dll.

Simply copy the Component.dll file from this location to C:\Wrox\bin. That's all there is to it! The act of copying the file into an application's bin directory registers the component. Yes, it's that easy!

If you now request your simple ASP.NET page again, rather than throwing an error, it finds and uses the component, and returns an HTML table showing the address, city, and state (the columns selected in your Simple component).

So what if you now want to change the component? Perhaps you only want to return the address and state? Well, first you need to change the component's SQL text (as shown in the following snippet), and then you must re-compile it with Visual Studio .NET.

```
sql = "SELECT address, state FROM Authors"
```

Once again, copy the newly compiled component to the `C:\Wrox\bin` directory, and immediately request the ASP.NET page again. The response you see is an HTML table that only shows address and state. Behind the scenes, ASP.NET noticed that the old component was replaced, and restarted the application using the new one.

The `bin` directory dramatically changes the way ASP.NET web applications are built. You no longer require local server access to register components, and ASP.NET never locks those components. You can carry out updates and changes, and ASP.NET will simply restart the application using the new version without requiring you to do anything.

Now that you are somewhat familiar with the `bin` directory, let's move on to another part of the ASP.NET web application, `global.asax`.

Application Code – global.asax

Like ASP, ASP.NET supports a *global file* for each web application. This file is used as an implementation point for global events, objects, and variables. If you are familiar with classic ASP, you will recognize this file as `global.asa`. ASP.NET supports a similar file, called `global.asax`.

> The code contained in `global.asax` constitutes part of our application. It does not contain application configuration information – the `web.config` file deals with this, and is covered in the next chapter.

Running ASP.NET and ASP Together

ASP.NET's `global.asax` file uses a separate extension, distinct from ASP's `global.asa` file. The extension `.asax` is used so as not to interfere with ASP's `global.asa`. This means that both `global.asa` and `global.asax` can reside in the same web application root.

Microsoft worked very hard to ensure that installing ASP.NET does not break any existing ASP applications. However, a caveat of this is that they cannot share any resources. This applies to *all* ASP.NET and ASP resources, not just the `global.asax`/`global.asa` files. ASP.NET maintains its `Application`, `Session`, global events, and so on, in complete isolation from ASP. Additionally, in a manner similar to ASP, there can only be one `global.asax` file per web application, and it *must* be called `global.asax`.

Let's take a look at the `global.asax` file format.

File Format of global.asax

The `global.asax` file follows a similar format to ASP.NET pages. The following snippet is a simple template of what a `global.asax` file looks like:

```
<%@ [Directive] [attribute]=[value] %>

<Script runat="server">
  [Application Event Prototypes]
</Script>
```

A `global.asax` file typically includes directives, events, and user code.

Directives

Similar to ASP.NET pages and web services, `global.asax` supports directives that provide ASP.NET with special instructions used in compilation of the `global.asax` file. The following code snippet is the prototype for directives – note that multiple attribute/value pairs are supported:

```
<%@ [directive name] [attribute]=[value] [attribute]=[value] %>
```

`global.asax` supports three directives, each with its own settings:

❑ `Application`: This allows us to define the base class `global.asax` will use. In addition to this, it supports a simple documentation option. These features are implemented through two attributes, `Inherits` and `Description`:

  ❑ The `Inherits` attribute allows us to name a .NET class that `global.asax` will use as the base class for all compiled instances of `global.asax`. This is useful if we want to add our own methods or properties to `global.asax`. This is quite a powerful feature and one that we will discuss in more detail in the *Advanced Topics* section later in this chapter.

  ❑ The `Description` attribute of the `Application` directive provides a simple way to add some descriptive text about our `global.asax`:

  ```
  <%@ Application Description="A sample global.asax description" %>
  ```

  The value of `Description` is discarded when `global.asax` is compiled.

❑ `Import`: This directive allows us to import .NET namespaces for use in `global.asax`, and makes all interfaces and classes of the imported namespace available to global.asax, without needing to fully qualify their names This directive is similar in function to the `Imports` keyword in Visual Basic .NET or `using` in C#. It simply provides a reference to a namespace that contains classes we wish to make use of.

❑ To use the `Import` directive, we must guarantee that the assembly in which the namespace exists is also available. If it is not, an ASP.NET exception will occur when we run the application. Support for adding the assembly is done either through the `Assembly` directive or the `<compilers>` section of our configuration file (configuration is covered in the next chapter). To reference assemblies that are not available, we can use the `Assembly` directive, outlined next.

The `Import` directive requires a single attribute:

❑ The `Namespace` attribute of `Import` is used to identify an assembly namespace for use in `global.asax`. For example, we could use the `Import` directive, specifying the namespace attribute for the `System.Data` namespace:

```
<%@ Import namespace="System.Data" %>
```

If we include this directive in the `global.asax` file for our web application, we can use classes in `System.Data` without fully qualifying the class name.

For example, to use the `DataSet` class, we can refer to it as `System.Data.DataSet` (fully qualified class name), or use the `Import` directive naming the `System.Data` namespace and refer to the class simply as `DataSet`.

Using the `Import` directive and its `Namespace` attribute saves us from having to fully qualify the name of the class. However, in the event that two namespaces share a common class name (such as `Math`) we can't use the `Import` directive. Instead, we have to fully qualify the names when we use them, for example, `Simple.Math` and `Complex.Math`.

❑ `Assembly`: This directive is used to name assemblies that contain classes we wish to use within our ASP.NET application. An assembly is a compiled unit of code in .NET with the extension `.dll` and exists either in the global assembly cache (covered in Chapter 23) or the `bin` directory of the ASP.NET application.

The `Import` and `Assembly` directives are very different. `Import` assumes that the assembly (for example, `System.Data.dll`) is already available to our application, and allows us to use abbreviated class names for classes within that namespace. `Assembly`, on the other hand, is used to tell ASP.NET that there is an assembly that needs to be loaded.

Assemblies located in the `bin` directory are automatically loaded.

Using the `Assembly` directive is simple. It has one attribute, `Name`, which identifies the assembly we wish to reference as part of our application.

As mentioned previously, some assemblies are available by default:

❑ `mscorlib.dll`: Base classes, such as the definition of `Object`, `String`, and so on.

❑ `System.dll`: Additional base classes, such as the network class libraries

❑ `System.Web.dll`: Classes for ASP.NET

❑ `System.Data.dll`: Classes for ADO.NET

❑ `System.Web.Services.dll`: Classes for ASP.NET Web services

❑ `System.Xml.dll`: Classes for XML

❑ `System.Drawing.dll`: Classes for graphics and drawing

❑ All assemblies within an application's `bin` directory

Included in this list are several `System` assemblies (for example, the assemblies provided as part of the .NET Framework) and those found in application `bin` directories. You would use the `Assembly` directive when an assembly is registered in the global assembly cache, or when you need `System` assemblies not already loaded.

For example, the assembly `System.DirectoryServices.dll` contains classes for working with directory services, such as Microsoft's *Active Directory*. This assembly is not one of the default assemblies loaded. To use the classes provided within it in `global.asax`, you need to use the Assembly directive:

```
<%@ Assembly Name="System.DirectoryServices" %>
```

> **The extension of the assembly (`.dll`) is not included.**

You can now write code in your `global.asax` file that uses classes (such as `DirectorySearcher`) found within this assembly,

The directives for `global.asax` are straightforward to use. Later, in the Advanced Topics section, you will take a closer look at one of these directives. For now, turn your focus to the code you can write within `global.asax`.

Code Declaration

Code is declared in `global.asax` using `<Script runat="server"/>` blocks. These are identical to the script blocks defined in ASP.NET pages, so we won't explain their syntax in detail again.

Later in the chapter, when we discuss global events, we will implant the created events within these script blocks.

There are two additional ways of declaring code in `global.asax`:

❑ **Server-side includes**: `global.asax` supports the use of server-side #include statements using both `File` and `Virtual` as the path type to the filename. Server-side includes are declared using the following syntax:

```
<!--#Include [File | Virtual]="Path to file" -->
```

`File` identifies the path as being on the file system, while `Virtual` identifies a virtual directory provided through the web server. The contents of the file included will be added to the `global.asax` file before it is compiled. Include files, especially those created using the `Virtual` option, can be quite useful as they allow us to define a common directory that can be shared among many applications, which may make our application more portable.

> **If an include file is used within a `global.asax`, the application will automatically be restarted whenever the include file changes.**

While it is possible to use server side includes in your `global.asax` file, it is not recommended. It is supported only for the purpose of backwards compatibility with classic ASP.

❑ **Declarative object tags:** `<Object>` tags enable us to declare and instantiate `Application` and `Session` objects in `global.asax`, using a declarative tag-based syntax. These tags can be used to create .NET assemblies, or COM objects specified by either `ProgID` or `CLSID`.

The type of object to create is identified using one of three different tag attributes:

  ❑ `class`

  ❑ `progid`

  ❑ `classid`

Only one of these tag attributes can be used per `<Object>` tag declaration.

Using Object Tag Declarations

Here is a sample of how object tag declarations are used:

```
<object id="appData" runat="server"
        class="System.Data.DataSet" scope="Application"/>
```

We have declared an `Application` scoped variable named `appData` that is of class type `System.Data.DataSet`. However, the object is not actually created until it is first used. The object then exists for the lifetime of the context in which it is created. In the preceding example, this is the lifetime of the application. Likewise, if the scope were set to `Session`, the object would be valid for the life of the current user session, and once that session terminated, the object would be destroyed.

> **Object tags should be placed outside of script blocks.**

The attributes used in this declaration are:

Attributes	Description
`id`	Unique name to use when referring to the object within the application.
`runat`	Must be set to `server` for the object to execute within ASP.NET.
`scope`	Determines where the object lives. The choices are `Application` for application state, `Session` for session state, or `Appinstance`, allowing each application to receive its own object instance.
`[class, progid, classid]`	Identifies either the assembly, or the COM `ProgID` or `ClassID` of which an instance is to be created.

You have three options for adding code to a `global.asax` file. The first and most common option will be to use the `<script runat="server">` blocks to define application code. You can also define code from an include file and use the `<object/>` tag syntax to declaratively create an object. Now that you are familiar with how to code your `global.asax` file, let's take a quick diversion and discuss application state management before moving on to the supported application events.

Application State Management

State management is the persistence of objects or values throughout the lifetime of a web application or for the duration of a user's interaction with the application. ASP.NET provides four ways to manage state for your application (we will cover each in more detail later in the chapter):

❑ **User state (session)**: User state is controlled through the `Session` object. `Session` allows us to maintain data for a limited duration of time (the configurable default is 20 minutes), for a particular user and isolate that data from other users. For example, we could use `Session` state to track the ad banners we have shown a particular user. If the user doesn't interact with the site within the configurable `Session` time limit, their data expires and is deleted.

❑ **Application state**: Application state is controlled through the `Application` object. `Application` allows us to maintain data for a given ASP.NET application. Settings made in `Application` are accessible to all resources (ASP.NET page, web services, and so on) within our web application. For example, if we wanted to retrieve some expensive records out of a database and share it throughout our application, storing the data using `Application` state would be very useful.

❑ **Transient application state (cache)**: Transient Application state is controlled through the `Cache` object. `Cache` is similar in functionality to `Application`, in that it is accessible (shared memory) for the entire web application. However, it adds some functionality not available to `Application`, in the form of dependencies, callbacks, and expiration. For example, when our ASP.NET application started we might populate an object used by all ASP.NET pages from an XML file. We could store this object in the `Cache` and also create a dependency for that item on the XML file the data originated from. If the XML file changed, ASP.NET will detect the file change and notify the `Cache` to invalidate the entry. Caching is a very powerful feature of ASP.NET. The differences between `Application` and `Cache` are summarized later in the chapter.

❑ **Static variables**: In addition to using the `Application` or `Cache` sytate, we can also use one of the object-oriented facilities of ASP.NET – *static variables*. When we can declare a static variable, only one copy of the variable is created no matter how many instances of the class are created. The static variable is accessible throughout our application and in some cases is more efficient than `Application`. This is an advanced option and is discussed at the end of the chapter.

The use of `Application` and `Session` (and now `Cache`) in ASP.NET is identical to the use of `Application` and `Session` in ASP. You can simply use a string key and set a value:

```
' Set an Application value
Application("SomeValue") = "my value"
' Read an Application value
Dim someString As String
someString = Application("SomeValue")
```

These familiar semantics are carried forward and used for the `Cache`, too:

```
' Set a Cache value
Cache("SomeValue") = "my value"

' Read a Cache value
Dim someString As String
someString = Cache("SomeValue")
```

Let's take a closer look at `Session`, `Application`, and `Cache` and how they relate to building web applications.

Session – Managing User State

Classic ASP's familiar `Session` object is new and improved for ASP.NET. The major caveats for `Session` use in classic ASP are:

❑ **Web farm challenges**: `Session` data is stored in memory on the server it is created on. In a web farm scenario, where there are multiple web servers, a problem could arise if a user was redirected to a server other than the server upon which they stored their `Session` state. Normally, this can be handled by an IP routing solution where the IP address of the client is used to route that client to a particular server. However, some ISPs use farms of reverse proxies, where the client request may come through a different IP on each request. When a user is redirected to a server other than the server that contains their `Session` data, poorly designed applications can break.

❑ **Supporting clients that don't accept HTTP cookies**: Since the Web is inherently a stateless environment, to use `Session` state the client and web server need to share a key that the client can present to identify its `Session` data on subsequent requests. Classic ASP shared this key with the client through an HTTP cookie. While this scenario worked well for clients that accept HTTP cookies, it broke for the one percent of users that rejected HTTP cookies.

Both of these issues have been addressed in ASP.NET's `Session` state, which supports several new features:

❑ **Web farm support**: ASP.NET `Session` now supports storing the `Session` data in-process (in the same memory that ASP.NET uses), out-of-process using Windows NT Service (in separate memory from ASP.NET), and in SQL Server (persistent storage). Both the Windows Service and SQL Server solutions support a web farm scenario where all the web servers can be configured to share a common `Session` store. So, as users get routed to different servers, each server is able to access that user's `Session` data. To the developer using `Session`, this is completely transparent and does not require any changes in the application code. Rather, we must configure ASP.NET to support one of these out-of-process options. We will discuss configuring `Session` state in the next chapter.

❑ **Cookieless mode**: Although somewhat supported in ASP through the use of an ISAPI filter (available as part of the IIS 4.0 SDK), ASP.NET makes cookieless support for `Session` a first class feature. However, by default, `Session` still uses HTTP cookies. When cookieless mode is enabled (details in the next chapter), ASP.NET will munge the URL that it sends back to the client with a `Session` ID, rather than storing the `Session` ID in an HTTP cookie. When the client makes a request using the munged URL containing the `Session` ID, ASP.NET is able to extract it and map the request to the appropriate `Session` data.

We will cover how to configure both of these options in the next chapter, when we discuss ASP.NET configuration. From our perspective as developers coding and using `Session`, these features are completely transparent.

`Session` is dedicated data storage for each user within an ASP.NET application. It is implemented as a `Hashtable` and stores data based on key/value pair combinations.

Setting Session Value

In ASP.NET, the use of `Session` follows the same pattern as in classic ASP. To set a `Session` value in Visual Basic .NET, simply state:

```
Session("[String key]") = Object
```

The C# equivalent is:

```
Session["[String key]"] = Object;
```

You can provide `Session` with a key that identifies the item we are storing. This `Session` stores items of type `Object`. Since all types in .NET inherit from `Object`, this allows you to store anything in `Session`. However, objects that contain live references, such as a `DataReader` containing an open connection to a database, should not be stored in `Session`.

For example, to store the string `Hello World` using a key of `SimpleSession`, write the following code in Visual Basic .NET:

```
Session("SimpleSession") = "Hello World"
```

And in C#:

```
Session["SimpleSession"] = "Hello World";
```

Underneath the covers, the CLR knows that the type `String` originated from the type `Object`, and is able to store that value correctly in memory.

Retrieving Session Value

Since `Session` is available throughout your web application, you can set values in `global.asax` code and access a `Session` value from ASP.NET pages.

For example, to retrieve your `Hello World` value from `Session`, you only need to provide `Session` with your key for it to return the value. This is the Visual Basic .NET code:

```
Dim sessionValue As String
sessionValue = Session("SimpleSession")
```

And in C#:

```
string sessionValue;
sessionValue = Session["SimpleSession"];
```

For types other than `String`, the semantics of accessing the value stored in `Session` are a bit more explicit. Because `Session` stores its data as an `Object` type, giving it the flexibility to store any .NET item, when you wish to retrieve data (other than type `String`) you have to cast the return value to the correct type.

For example, if you stored a custom class you defined called `PurchaseOrder` in `Session`, here is how you would need to retrieve it in Visual Basic .NET:

> **For a class instance to be stored in out-of-process `Session` state, the class must be marked with the `[Serializable]` attribute.**

```
Dim po As PurchaseOrder
po = CType(Session("po"), PurchaseOrder)
```

And in C#:

```
PurchaseOrder po;
po = (PurchaseOrder) Session["po"];
```

In both examples, the `Object` returned is cast by the key `po` to type `PurchaseOrder`.

The `Session` API provides additional properties that you can use in code to determine what mode `Session` is in:

❑ `IsCookieless`: Returns `True` or `False` indicating whether or not `Session` is using cookieless mode to maintain the `Session` ID. By default, this is `False`, meaning that `Session` is using cookies.

❑ `IsReadOnly`: Returns `True` or `False` indicating whether or not `Session` is in read-only mode. Read-only mode is an optimization that does not allow ASP.NET to update `Session` data. This can be particularly useful for out of process modes on pages that only read `Session` state and don't need write access. When a `Session` is read-only, a lock does not have to be maintained and the round-trip back to an out-of-process `Session` store for an update can be skipped. By default, this value is `False`, and `Session` is read/write. We will discuss how to enable `ReadOnly` for `Session` in the next chapter.

❑ `Mode`: Returns the value of an enumeration, `SessionStateMode`, (found in `System.Web.SessionState`) that indicates the storage mode that `Session` is configured for. Values include `InProc`, `Off`, `SQLServer`, and `StateServer`.

ASP.NET session state is quite different from ASP session state. The new capability of session state that is not bound to the ASP.NET process means that developers can begin to use session state in server farm environments without worrying about whether the client is coming through a proxy server. With the cookieless state functionality, it is even easier to use session state and guarantee that all clients can take advantage of the session state feature. In the next chapter, you will learn how to configure Session to support a read-only mode as well the other 'mode' options (in-process, Windows Service, and SQL Server).

Configuring and using Session State is covered in more depth in Chapter 13.

Application – Managing Application State

Unlike Session, which is basically dedicated storage for each user, Application is shared application storage. This shared storage is quite useful, especially if there are resources that all users share, such as an XML representation of a site's shopping catalog. Similar to Session, Application state is simply a Hashtable that stores key/value pair combinations.

Unlike Session, however, Application does not support the concept of storing data separate from the ASP.NET process. Instead, Application stores its data in process with ASP.NET. If the ASP.NET process is recycled (covered in the next chapter) Application data is lost. The trade-off is that storing the data in-process is faster than going to another process, or possibly across the network, to retrieve data.

The syntax used for setting and accessing values with Application is identical to that of Session, with one exception.

Since Application is accessible in a multi-user environment, updates to Application values should be *synchronized*. This simply means that whenever Application data is being updated, you should prevent other users or applications from updating the data simultaneously. Luckily, Application provides you with this capability through a simple set of locking methods. Note these are the same locking methods Lock and UnLock supported in ASP.

Reading and Writing Application Data

We read and write data in Application in a similar manner to Session using key/value pairs, such as the following in Visual Basic .NET:

```
Application("HitCounter") = 10
```

Or in C#:

```
Application["HitCounter"] = 10;
```

Similarly, if you wish to read the value back simply use your key, like this in Visual Basic .NET:

```
Dim HitCount As Integer
HitCount = Application("HitCounter")
```

Or in C#:

```
int HitCount = Application["HitCounter"];
```

However, to update HitCounter you must synchronize access using the Lock and UnLock methods of Application. Otherwise, the potential exists for two requests to attempt to update HitCounter simultaneously, causing a potential deadlock or update failure.

Although this is an illustrative example, when you Lock, you are effectively blocking other applications that may be attempting to update the HitCounter value, causing them to serialize – that is, perform operations one after another. We definitely don't want to Lock/UnLock on each request, as this would negatively affect performance. If the data stored in Application must be updated frequently, it is probably not a good candidate for Application state, unless recreating the data is more costly than the time spent serializing the updates.

Let's look at an illustrative example using `Application.Lock` and `Application.UnLock`, first in Visual Basic .NET:

```
Public Sub Application_OnStart()
  Application("HitCount") = 0
End Sub

Public Sub Application_OnBeginRequest()
  Application.Lock()
  Application("HitCounter") = Application("HitCounter") + 1
  Application.UnLock()
End Sub
```

And now in C#:

```
public void Application_OnStart() {
  Application["HitCounter"] = 0;
}

public void Application_OnBeginRequest(){
  Application.Lock();
  int tmpInt = (int)Application["HitCounter"];
  Application["HitCounter"] = tmpInt + 1;
  Application.UnLock();
}
```

In the preceding code, we call `Application.Lock` to ensure that while we update HitCounter, some other thread cannot update the value simultaneously.

> *When the ASP.NET process is stopped or recycled, `Application` state is lost. However, when the process is recycled, the `Application_OnEnd` event (discussed later) is raised and values can be persisted to a database or file.*

Since ASP.NET is a multi-threaded system, `Application` memory can be accessed by multiple processes simultaneously. To use `Application` and set values, you must either:

❑　Know that the object stored in `Application` is doing its own thread management (not shown).

　　Or

❑　Perform our own synchronization using `Application.Lock` and `Application.UnLock`.

Calling `Lock` instructs ASP.NET to block any other threads from modifying this resource until `UnLock` is called, giving your code exclusive access. However, if you don't explicitly call `UnLock`, ASP.NET will call it when the application completes the request, the request times out, or an unhandled error occurs. Although this is done for us, you should always aim to write code that explicitly calls `UnLock`.

Storing Objects in Application

Classic ASP VB objects could not be hosted in `Application` state due to the default threading model these components supported (*Apartment Model threading*). In effect, accessing an instance of a VB component stored in `Application` would cause ASP to serialize (execute one request after another) access to that component. .NET components are free threaded by default and don't have this thread affinity problem. Therefore, there are no performance penalties for storing a Visual Basic .NET object in `Application` and accessing it across multiple requests.

Next, let's look at a new object, `Cache`, used to store transient application data.

Cache – Managing Transient State

Many developers use `Application` as a cache for frequently used resources, for example, reading an XML file that represents a product catalog and storing the object representing that XML file in `Application` memory.

However, what happens when this XML file representing the product catalog changes? In most cases, developers who use `Application` to manage this data simply force the web application to restart, thus forcing `Application` to get refreshed.

The design goal of the `Cache` was to give developers the benefits of `Application`, but with additional features that went above and beyond those provided by `Application`, such as the ability to evict an item from the `Cache` when a file changes, it is then your responsibility through code to add the item back to the `Cache` if you desire.

Cache Overview

`Cache` is an instance of the `Cache` class found in the namespace `System.Web.Caching`. In addition to being a simple key/value pair `Hashtable` like `Application`, the `Cache` also supports:

- ❑ **Dependency-based expiration**: Dependencies can be other `Cache` keys, files, or a timestamp. When one of the dependencies changes or expires (timestamp), the `Cache` item is invalidated and removed from the `Cache`.

- ❑ **Lock management**: Unlike `Application`, the `Cache` class does its own internal lock management. Therefore, while `Application` required us to explicitly `Lock` and `UnLock` when updating `Application`, `Cache` doesn't require this. Keep in mind that we do still need to manage concurrency for objects stored in the `Cache` just as we do with objects stored in `Application`.

- ❑ **Resource management**: When the `Cache` detects memory pressure, a least recently used algorithm walks the `Cache` and automatically evicts items used less frequently. Therefore, before we request an item, we always need to check if the item exists.

- ❑ **Callbacks**: The `Cache` supports allows us to run code when items are removed from the `Cache`.

The Cache supports two methods of inserting items:

❑ **Implicit**: We are familiar with this syntax from working with Session or Application using the key/value pairs:

In Visual Basic .NET:

```
Dim productDataSet As New DataSet()
' Populate DataSet
Cache("products") = productDataSet
```

And in C#:

```
DataSet productDataSet = new DataSet();
// Populate DataSet
Cache["products"] = productDataSet;
```

❑ **Explicit**: Using the Insert method, it allows us to set up special relationships such as dependencies. In VB.NET, the code to do this is:

```
Dim productDataSet As New DataSet()
' Populate DataSet
Cache.Insert("products", productDataSet, Nothing)
```

In C#:

```
DataSet productDataSet = new DataSet();
// Populate DataSet
Cache.Insert("products", productDataSet, null)
```

The Cache also supports an Add method. The Add method behaves similar to Insert, with the exception that it will only add them item to the Cache if it does not already exist – whereas the Insert method will always add the item into the Cache, even if it already exists.

When using the Cache, you will mostly use the explicit Insert. Let's look at some examples.

Dependency-Based Expiration

Dependency-based expiration is very powerful. It allows you to create a relationship between an item in the Cache and either a file, another Cache key, or a defined point in time. For example, if your site used XML and XSL transforms to control aspects of content, you could load the XML into an XmlDocument class and store the value within the Cache. You could also establish a relationship between the cached XmlDocument and the file that it is reading, using the file-based dependency feature of the Cache. Let's build this sample.

This is the XML file:

```
<?xml version="1.0"?>
<books>
  <book>
    <name>Professional ASP.NET 2nd Edition</name>
    <isbn>1861007035</isbn>
    <publisher>Wrox Press</publisher>
```

```
        <authors>
          <author name="David Sussman"/>
          <author name="Brian Francis"/>
          <author name="Alex Homer"/>
          <author name="Karli Watson"/>
          <author name="Rich Anderson"/>
          <author name="Rob Howard"/>
        </authors>
        <description>
        ASP.NET is a unified web development
        platform that provides the services necessary
        for developers to build enterprise-class web
        applications.
        </description>
      </book>
  </books>
```

The file is saved as `1861007035.xml`, which is the ISBN for the book Professional ASP.NET 1.0 Special Edition. You also have an XSL transform for this file, called `book.xsl`:

```
<xsl:stylesheet
      version="1.0"
      xmlns:xsl="http://www.w3.org/1999/XSL/Transform">
<xsl:output method="html"/>
  <xsl:template match="/">
    <html>
    <head>
      <title><xsl:value-of select="books/book/name"/></title>
    </head>
    <style>
        body { font-family: Arial; font-size: 18; color:white; }
        li { list-style: square outside; }
    </style>
    <body bgcolor="black">
        <xsl:apply-templates/>
    </body>
    </html>
  </xsl:template>
  <xsl:template match="name">
    <h1><font color="red"><xsl:value-of select="."/></font></h1>
  </xsl:template>
  <xsl:template match="description">
    <h6><xsl:value-of select="."/></h6>
  </xsl:template>
  <xsl:template match="isbn">
    <font size="1">ISBN: <xsl:value-of select="."/></font><br/>
  </xsl:template>
  <xsl:template match="publisher">
    <font size="1">Publisher: <xsl:value-of select="."/></font><br/>
  </xsl:template>
</xsl:stylesheet>
```

The following code snippet is the ASP.NET page (`SingleFilevb.aspx`) that uses the `Cache` and creates a file dependency on the XML file only – in this particular example we are not caching the XSL file:

```
<%@ Import Namespace="System.Xml" %>
<%@ Import Namespace="System.Xml.Xsl" %>

<Script runat="server">
Public Sub Page_Load(sender As Object, e As EventArgs)
  Dim dom As XmlDocument
  Dim xsl As New XslTransform()

  ' Do we have the Wrox Pro ASP.NET 2nd Ed book in the Cache?
  If (IsNothing(Cache("1861007035.xml"))) Then
    CacheStatus.Text = "Item not present, updating the Cache..."
    UpdateCache("1861007035.xml")
  Else
    CacheStatus.Text = "Retrieving from Cache"
  End If

  ' Load the transform
  xsl.Load(Server.MapPath("book.xsl"))

  dom = CType(Cache("1861007035.xml"), XmlDocument)

  BookDisplay.Document = dom
  BookDisplay.Transform = xsl

End Sub

Public Sub UpdateCache(strItem As String)

    Dim strPath As String
    Dim dom As New XmlDocument()

    ' Determine the file path of the file to monitor
    strPath = Server.MapPath(strItem)

    ' Load the file into an Xml Dom
    dom.Load(strPath)

    ' Create a CacheDependency on the file
    Dim dependency as New CacheDependency(strPath)

    ' Cache the XML document
    Cache.Insert(strItem, dom, dependency)
End Sub
</Script>
Status: <asp:label id="CacheStatus" runat=server/>
<br>
<asp:xml id="BookDisplay" runat=server/>
```

The interesting code appears in the UpdateCache subroutine, which is called if the Cache key 1861007035.xml is not present. We first map the path to the XML file, which is in the same directory, and load that XML file into an XmlDocument class. Then, we create a new CacheDependency class passing in the path to the XML file. Finally, we use the Cache's Insert method and create a new Cache entry using the name of the file (1861007035.xml), the XmlDocument instance, dom, and the CacheDependency class instance, dependency.

On requesting this page for the first time, you would see the screen shown in Figure 12-9:

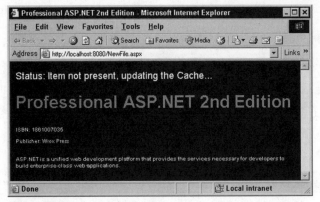

Figure 12-9

On subsequent requests you would see the Status: Retrieving from Cache message.

If you open the 1861007035.xml file and modify the name from Professional ASP.NET 1.0 Special Edition to Pro ASP.NET 1.0, the file change notification would be enforced and the XmlDocument storing the XML from the file would be removed from the Cache. Requesting the ASP.NET page would bring up the screen shown in Figure 12-10:

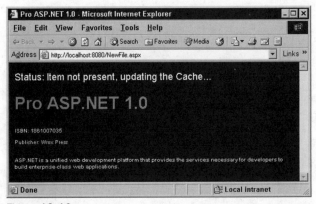

Figure 12-10

What if instead of monitoring a file, you wanted to remove an entry (or series of entries) from the Cache when another item in the Cache changed? This option is supported through a key-based dependency.

The syntax for supporting key-based dependencies is very similar to that used in file-based dependencies. For example, you can easily change the preceding code to support a key-based dependency by modifying only a couple of lines.

If you cached multiple XML documents for each Wrox book on .NET, you could set up a dependency relationship where the Cache entries for the books could be invalidated (and reloaded) whenever a master key, for example booksDependencyKey, changed.

The following code example, called `KeyBasedvb.aspx`, creates such a relationship:

```
<%@ Import Namespace="System.Xml" %>

<Script runat="server">

  Public Sub Create(sender As Object, e As EventArgs)
    ' Create the Cache entry for the dependency relationship
    ' the value of the key doesn't matter
    Cache("booksDependencyKey") = "Book Dependency"

    ' Create a string array with the key names for the
    ' dependencies to be created upon
    Dim dependencyKey(0) As String

    dependencyKey(0) = "booksDependencyKey"

    ' Create a CacheDependency on this key
    Dim dependency as New CacheDependency(nothing, dependencyKey)

    ' Cache the XML document
    Cache.Insert("1861007035.xml", Load("1861007035.xml"), dependency)

    Status()
  End Sub

  Private Function Load(xmlFile As String) As XmlDocument
    Dim dom As New XmlDocument()
    dom.Load(Server.MapPath(xmlFile))
    Return dom
  End Function

  Public Sub Invalidate(sender As Object, e As EventArgs)
    Cache.Remove("booksDependencyKey")
    Status()
  End Sub

  Public Sub Status()
    If (IsNothing(Cache("1861007035.xml"))) Then
      lblStatus1.Text = "No value..."
    Else
      lblStatus1.Text = "Cache entry exists..."
    End If
  End Sub

</Script>
<form runat=server>
  <input type="submit" OnServerClick="Create"
         value="Create Cache Entries" runat="server" />
  <input type="submit" OnServerClick="Invalidate"
         value="Invalidate Key" runat="server" />
</form>
Status for cache key: 1861007035.xml: <b><asp:label id="lblStatus1"
runat=server/></b>
```

When you run this code, you need to press the **Create Cache Entries** button to create the `Cache` entry for the XML file, as well as the dependency relationship. You can then press **Invalidate Key**, which raises the `Invalidate` event. Within this event, we explicitly remove the cache key `booksDependencyKey`. This enforces the dependency and also removes the `Cache` entry for your XML document.

Finally, in addition to file and key-based dependencies, you can also create dependencies on time values. Consider an example where Wrox were to store all of its book titles in a single table in the database, and you knew that this data was only updated once a week. You could cache a `DataSet` that represents this data with an explicit expiration of 60 minutes. This will save you going to the database for every request, but in case an update occurs, you can still guarantee that the data will be fresh within the following hour.

Here's the code from `TimeBasedvb.aspx` that does this:

```
<%@ Import Namespace="System.Data" %>
<%@ Import Namespace="System.Data.SqlClient" %>

<script runat=server>
  Private DSN As String

  Public Sub Page_Load(sender As Object, e As EventArgs)
    Dim strCacheKey As String
    Dim titlesDataSet As DataSet

    strCacheKey = "Titles"

    If (IsNothing(Cache(strCacheKey))) Then
      lblStatus.Text = "Getting data from database..."
      LoadTitles(strCacheKey)
    Else
      lblStatus.Text = "Getting data from Cache..."
    End If

    titlesDataSet = CType(Cache(strCacheKey), DataSet)
    TitleList.DataSource = titlesDataSet
    TitleList.DataBind()

  End Sub

  Public Sub LoadTitles(strCacheKey As String)
    Dim connection As SqlConnection
    Dim command As SqlDataAdapter
    Dim sqlSelect As String
    Dim strDsn As String
    Dim dataset As New DataSet()

    sqlSelect = "SELECT title, pub_id, price, notes, pubdate FROM titles"
    strDsn = "server=localhost;uid=sa;pwd=;database=pubs"

    connection = New SqlConnection(strDsn)
    command = New SqlDataAdapter(sqlSelect, connection)

    command.Fill(dataset, "Author-Titles")
```

```
          Cache.Insert(strCacheKey, dataset, nothing, _
                     DateTime.Now.AddMinutes(60), TimeSpan.Zero)
    End Sub
  </script>
  <font size=6>
  <asp:label id="lblStatus" runat="server"/>
  </font>
  <P>
  <ASP:DataGrid id="TitleList" HeaderStyle-BackColor="#aaaadd"
  BackColor="#ccccff"
                   runat="server" />
```

In this example, we have some logic at the beginning that checks for an entry in the Cache named Titles. If the Cache entry doesn't exist, we then call the subroutine LoadTitles, which connects to a database, performs a select on the titles table, fills a DataSet, and finally inserts the DataSet into the Cache. We are using the explicit Insert method of the Cache:

```
          Cache.Insert(strCacheKey, dataset, nothing, _
                     DateTime.Now.AddMinutes(60), TimeSpan.Zero)
```

This adds a Cache entry with the key titles, the populated dataset, and also instructs the cache to expire the item after 60 minutes.

Cache additionally supports a very useful callback capability. The callback allows you to run your code when an item is removed from the cache, giving you the opportunity to add it back.

We could make the following modification to the preceding code (highlighted), which would guarantee that our item is always served from the cache:

```
      ...
    If (loadedFromCallback) Then
       lblStatus.Text = lblStatus.Text + "loaded from callback"
       loadedFromCallback = false
    End If
    sqlSelect = "SELECT title, pub_id, price, notes, pubdate FROM titles"
    connection = New
  SqlConnection("server=localhost;uid=sa;pwd=00password;database=pubs")
    command = New SqlDataAdapter(sqlSelect, connection)
    command.Fill(dataset, "Author-Titles")
    ' Create the a CacheItemRemovedCallback
    Dim onRemove As New CacheItemRemovedCallback(AddressOf _
                                         Me.RemovedCallback)
    Cache.Insert(strCacheKey, dataset, nothing,
               DateTime.Now.AddMinutes(60), TimeSpan.Zero, _
               CacheItemPriority.High, onRemove)
    End Sub
  ' This method represents the callback
  Public Sub RemovedCallback(key As String, value As Object,
                         reason As CacheItemRemovedReason)
    ' Let's always re-add the item if removed
    LoadTitles(key)
  End Sub
  </script>
```

```
<font size=6>
<asp:label id="lblStatus" runat="server"/>
</font>
<P>
<ASP:DataGrid id="TitleList" HeaderStyle-BackColor="#aaaadd" BackColor="#ccccff"
              runat="server" />
```

Caching adds a lot of powerful new features to manage data that you ordinarily would have stored in `Application` state. Dependencies allow you to set up relationships with items that can invalidate the cache, and callbacks allow you to execute your own code whenever an item is removed from the `Cache`.

State management in ASP.NET should be very familiar to developers who have worked with ASP. Both `Session` and `Application` state remain identical in use and you now have the `Cache` option. It is very important to understand state management and when to use the options provided by it. Here are some basic guidelines:

❑   `Session`: Used to store data that should be available to the user on each request. Be efficient about what you store in `Session`, since each `Session` will get its own individual copy of the data. Remember that class instances stored in out-of-process session state must be attributed with the `[Serializable]` attribute at the class level.

❑   `Application`: Used to store data that needs to be available to the entire application. A good candidate for `Application` is data that remains fairly static and must be available on each request. Remember to use the `Lock` and `Unlock` methods to control access to `Application` when updating the data.

❑   `Cache`: Used to store data that may be used on each request, or data where a dependency relationship needs to be established. In many cases, `Cache` can be used in place of `Application`.

Application Events

Although we don't have to use events in ASP.NET, they do make our lives easier. Events provide great ways to organize and control execution of code. Examples of this include creating instances of objects that you assign to `Application`, `Cache`, or `Session` when your application starts, validating custom user credentials before you allow the user to access the requested resource, or perhaps, implementing a billing feature that will charge the user for each access to a page. The options are endless. The point is that application events allow you to execute your own code while ASP.NET processes the request. We can use application events in one of two ways:

❑   **Implement event prototypes in global.asax**: We will simply add the event prototypes file. This is similar to events we captured in ASP's `global.asa` file such as `Application_OnStart` or `Session_OnEnd`. We will use `global.asax` to demonstrate application events in this chapter.

❑   **Author custom HTTP modules**: An HTTP module is an advanced feature of ASP.NET. It is the equivalent of IIS's ISAPI filter concept. An HTTP module gives us an opportunity to work with the request before it is serviced by an ASP.NET page or web service (or custom HTTP Handler), and again, before the response is sent to the client. For example, we can use HTTP modules to author custom solutions for our ASP.NET applications, such as an authentication system that authenticates users against a Netscape LDAP.

> **ASP.NET application events are multi-cast events. This means that we can have both an HTTP module and `global.asax` respond to the same event.**

ASP.NET supports 18 application events, and also allows you to add your own custom events. ASP.NET also introduces support for asynchronous events. We will discuss these at the end of the chapter in the Advanced Topics section.

Event Syntax and Prototypes

When implementing the event code in `global.asax`, it is a good practice to use `sender` as the `Object` parameter, and `e` as the `EventArgs` parameter. The syntax for Visual Basic .NET:

```
Public Sub Application_OnStart(sender As Object, e As EventArgs)
End Sub
```

And in C#:

```
public void Application_OnStart(Object sender, EventArgs e) {
}
```

The argument provided to your event prototype tells you who raised the event (`sender`). It also provides a mechanism for the `sender` to provide additional event details through an `EventArgs` parameter (`e`).

In addition to using this prototype, you can also use a shorthand event prototype (shorthand since you're not naming the event parameters). The code in VB.NET is:

```
Public Sub Application_OnStart()
End Sub
```

And in C#:

```
public void Application_OnStart() {
}
```

In the preceding event prototypes, you do not have access to the `EventArgs` or the `sender`. Including the parameters is considered best practice. However, remember that the shorthand syntax is supported.

Supported Events

The 18 supported events can be divided into two categories:

- Events that are raised on each request
- Conditional events, such as when an error occurs

The next section lists the two categories of events and provides a brief description of each event. We have also provided a figure that shows the ordering of the events for the per-request events. We will soon implement examples using several events.

Per-Request Application Events

Per-request application events are those raised during each and every request made to an ASP.NET application, such as the events that indicate the beginning or end of the request. Some of these include:

❑ `Application_OnBeginRequest`: This event is raised on *each* request that ASP.NET handles, for example, a page or web service. This is unlike the familiar ASP `Application_OnStart` event, which is only raised *once* when the application is started. We can use the `Application_OnBeginRequest` event to execute code before a page, web service, or any other HTTP Handler gets the opportunity to process the request.

❑ `Application_OnAuthenticateRequest`: This event is raised when ASP.NET is ready to perform authentication on the request (see Chapter 14 for more detail on authentication). Events such as these allow us to easily build custom authentication systems in ASP.NET. Within this event, we can examine the request and execute our own code to determine whether or not the request is authenticated. When enabled, ASP.NET authentication modes such as Windows Forms or Passport use this event.

❑ `Application_OnAuthorizeRequest`: Similar to `OnAuthenticateRequest`, this event is raised when ASP.NET is ready to authorize a request for a resource. We can use this event to examine the request and execute our own code that determines what privileges we grant or deny the request. Similar to the previous event, when enabled, the ASP.NET authorization system relies on this event for its authorization support.

❑ `Application_OnResolveRequestCache`: Although not yet discussed, ASP.NET has a rich page and web service output caching feature that utilizes the `Cache` covered earlier in this chapter. For example, rather than executing a page on each request, the page can be executed once and served statically for future requests. This event is raised when ASP.NET is ready to determine if the request should be served from the cache. Internally, ASP.NET's output cache relies upon this event. We can use it to run application code independently of whether or not the actual response is served from the output cache.

❑ `Application_OnAcquireRequestState`: This event is raised when ASP.NET is ready to acquire `Session` state data from in-process, out-of-process Windows Service, or SQL Server. If we want to provide our own 'custom' `Session`, such as an `XmlSession` object, we could populate the values of that object using this event. Then, when the request is handed to the page or web service, the `XmlSession` would already have its values populated.

❑ `Application_OnPreRequestHandlerExecute`: This event is raised just before the handler servicing the request is called. In most cases, the handler will be the `Page` handler.

After the `Application_OnPreRequestHandlerExecute` event is raised, the HTTP Handler receives the request. The next application event is raised when the handler is finished with the request.

❑ `Application_OnPostRequestHandlerExecute`: This is the first event raised after the handler has completed servicing the request. The `Response` object now has data to be sent back to the client.

❑ `Application_OnReleaseRequestState`: This releases the `Session` data and updates storage if necessary. After this event is raised, we can no longer update `Session` data. In the corresponding `Application_OnRequestState` event, we mentioned populating an `XmlSession` object. In this corresponding `ReleaseState` event, we could write the value of `XmlSession` back to the XML file that represented the session data for a particular user.

❑ Application_OnUpdateRequestCache: This event is raised when ASP.NET updates the output cache with the current request (if it is to be output cached).

❑ Application_OnEndRequest: Once the request is complete, this is the last event raised that allows us to affect the application response before we send the HTTP headers and body.

Figure 12-11 shows the processing of a request by ASP.NET using the ten events just detailed:

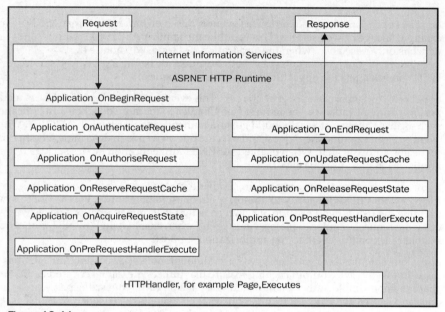

Figure 12-11

As shown, IIS first receives the request and then hands it to ASP.NET. The ASP.NET Application Events are then raised, starting with Application_OnBeginRequest. Immediately before an HTTP Handler (such as default.aspx) is called, the Application_OnPreRequestHandlerExecute event is raised. Immediately after the HTTP Handler has executed the Application_OnPostRequestHandlerExecute is raised. Finally, the Application_OnEndRequest event is raised before the response is handed back to IIS to be sent back to the requestor,.

These ten per-request events are raised in a known order. However, there are two other per-request events that are raised during the processing of the request.

Per-Request Indeterminate Order

Unlike the other per-request events, the following two events are raised as soon as data is ready to be sent back to the client. By default, ASP.NET enables response buffering – this simply means the server will not begin sending data to the requestor until all the data is ready. When buffering is enabled, the following two events are raised after Application_OnEndRequest. However, if buffering is disabled, the response can be sent as data becomes available. In that case, the following two events will be raised when the data is sent to the client.

❑ `Application_OnPreSendRequestHeaders`: This event is raised before the HTTP headers are sent to the client making the request. Once the headers are sent, we cannot modify the content of the response – we have already sent the content size of the response to the client.

❑ `Application_OnPreSendRequestContent`: This event is raised before the HTTP body is sent to the client making the request.

Conditional Application Events

Conditional application events are events that may or may not be raised during the processing of a request. For example, when the application starts, we raise the `Application_OnStart` event, or when an error occurs within our application, we raise the `Application_Error` event. These events are just as useful as our per-request events, sometimes even more so:

❑ `Application_OnStart`: This event is raised when an ASP.NET application first starts unlike `Application_OnBeginRequest` that is raised on each request. We can use this event to carry out tasks that prepare our application to service requests. Examples include opening a connection to the database and retrieving some shared data, adding items to the cache, or simply setting application or static variables to default values. If this event has not yet been raised when a request comes in, it will be raised before the per-request `Application_OnBeginRequest` event.

❑ `Application_OnEnd`: This event is another single occurrence event. It is the reciprocal event to `Application_OnStart` as it is raised when the ASP.NET web application is shutting down. We can use this event for cleaning up code. For example, closing connections to the database, evicting items from the cache, or resetting Application and static variables.

❑ Most of these tasks won't be necessary, however, since once the application ends, the CLR will eventually release the application's memory. However, it is still good practice to do the cleanup ourselves.

❑ `Session_OnStart`: This event is raised when a user's session begins within an ASP.NET application. We can use this event to execute code that is user specific, such as assigning values to `Session`.

❑ `Session_OnEnd`: This is the reciprocal event to `Session_OnStart`, being raised when a user's `Session` ends. If we wish to save the `Session` data, we can use this to walk the object and save interesting information to a SQL database, or other permanent storage medium.

❑ `Application_Error`: This event is raised whenever an unhandled application error occurs. This is a very powerful event, and we will call it in an example later in the chapter. Just as an ASP.NET page supports a `Page_Error` for unhandled page exceptions, the `Application_Error` allows us to catch all unhandled exceptions for the entire application, such as logging an exception to the Windows event log, or sending the administrator an e-mail containing details of the error.

❑ `Application_OnDisposed`: This event is raised when the ASP.NET application is eventually shut down and the CLR removes the application from memory. This event gives us the opportunity to clean up or close any outstanding connections or write any last data back to a database or file system. In most scenarios, this event will not be used.

Although ASP.NET supports 18 events, you don't necessarily have to use all of them. Next, you will look at some examples of the common events that you will want to use most often in ASP.NET applications.

Event Examples

The following code samples demonstrate Application events.

Adding a Footer to All Pages

The `Application_OnEndRequest` event is raised at the end of the request immediately before the response is sent to the requestor. Since this event is the last called, you can use it to run some code before the response is sent, or to modify the response. For example, an ISP running ASP.NET could use the `Application_OnEndRequest` event to add a footer to the bottom of all pages served by ASP.NET.

Here is the `global.asax` code in Visual Basic .NET:

```
<Script runat="server">

  Public Sub Application_OnEndRequest(sender As Object, e As EventArgs)
    Response.Write("<hr size=1>")
    Response.Write("<font face=arial size=2>This page was " _
                                       & "served by ASP.NET</font>")
  End Sub

</Script>
```

In the preceding `global.asax` code, we implemented the `Application_OnEndRequest` event and within the event used `Response.Write` to output a simple statement that says This page was served by ASP.NET.

We can then author an ASP.NET page in Visual Basic .NET:

```
<%@ Import Namespace="System.Data" %>
<%@ Import Namespace="System.Data.SqlClient" %>

<Script runat="server">

  Public Sub Page_Load(sender As Object, e As EventArgs)
    Dim connection As SqlConnection
    Dim command As SqlCommand
    Dim reader As SqlDataReader
    Dim sqlSelect As String
    Dim dsn As String

    ' Name dsn and sql select
    dsn="server=localhost;uid=sa;pwd=;database=pubs"
    sqlSelect="Select * From stores"

    ' Connect to the database
    connection = New SqlConnection(dsn)
    command = New SqlCommand(sqlSelect, connection)

    ' Open the connection
    connection.Open()
    ' Create the reader
    reader = command.ExecuteReader()
```

```
    ' Populate the datagrid
    datagrid1.DataSource = reader
    datagrid1.DataBind()

    ' Close the connection
    connection.Close()
  End Sub

</Script>
<asp:datagrid id="datagrid1" runat="server" />
```

The preceding code connects to a database and populates an ASP.NET `datagrid` with the results. If you save these two files into a web application, the code executed in `Application_OnEndRequest` will be added to the bottom of the requested page, as shown in Figure 12-12:

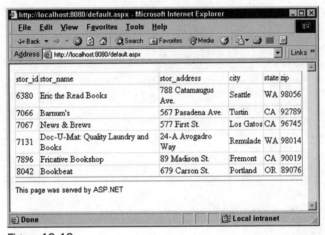

Figure 12-12

When you enable *page tracing* (which we'll learn more about in the following chapter), you output trace details at the end of the request. Internally, tracing is using the `Application_OnEndRequest` to ensure that the output details are the final addition to the request.

In this example, we are using an event to output code, to better illustrate how the event is executed. This works well for ASP.NET pages because the `Response.Write` statements are appended to the end of the page results and simply add additional HTML. However, remember that ASP.NET is no longer simply about displaying HTML pages. Good examples here include the rich set of server controls that can output WML, or ASP.NET Web services that return XML to the caller. The `global.asax` file is global for the ASP.NET application, and if you want to add logic into your `global.asax` file that outputs HTML, you should probably not serve ASP.NET Web services out of that same application, unless you add additional code that checks the request type to see if HTML content can be returned.

Loading Custom User Data

ASP.NET provides some great facilities for storing per-request user state, `Session`, and per-application state – `Application` and `Cache`. However, what if you wanted to also support a scenario that fell somewhere in-between these, such as per-request group data?

Many sites personalize themselves based on the identity of the requestor. What if you didn't want to personalize for an individual user, but instead wanted to group a common set of users together and personalize your site based on group settings? For example, what if you divided your users into groups such as Gold, Silver, and Bronze. You want Gold customers to have access to the common state, but not so for Silver and Bronze customers. Similarly, you would want your Silver customers to only see their data.

We can easily build our own 'state manager' using ASP.NET and use the Application_OnAcquireRequestState event to determine who the request is for and then to fetch the appropriate data. Let's look at a simple example that identifies the customer category from the URL: default.aspx?customerType=Gold, default.aspx?customerType=Silver, and so on.

First, let's code the Visual Basic .NET global.asax file:

```
<%@ Import Namespace="System.Xml" %>
<Script runat="server">

  Public Sub Application_OnAcquireRequestState( _
      sender As Object, e As EventArgs)
    Dim dom As New XmlDocument()
    Dim customerType As String
    ' Grab the customerType from the QueryString
    customerType = Request.QueryString("customerType")

    ' Check for values
    If (IsNothing(customerType)) Then
      customerType = "Bronze"
    End If

    ' Load the appropriate XML file
    Select Case customerType
      Case "Gold"
        dom.Load(Server.MapPath("Gold.xml"))
      Case "Silver"
        dom.Load(Server.MapPath("Silver.xml"))
      Case Else
        dom.Load(Server.MapPath("Bronze.xml"))
    End Select

    Session("WelcomeMsg") = _
      dom.SelectSingleNode("/customer/welcome").InnerText
  End Sub

</Script>
```

The file's Application_OnAcquireRequestState event begins by executing some logic to determine where the current request fits in – we are simply passing a customerType value on the QueryString – and if no customerType is provided, we default to Bronze.

Then the code loads an XML file for the appropriate customer type, for example, Gold.xml, and loads the welcome message from that file. Here are the Gold.xml, Silver.xml, and Bronze.xml files:

```xml
<?xml version="1.0"?>

<customer>
 <welcome>
  You're a Gold customer -- you get a free product sample!
 </welcome>
</customer>


<?xml version="1.0"?>

<customer>
 <welcome>
  You're a Silver customer -- thanks for your business!
 </welcome>
</customer>


<?xml version="1.0"?>

<customer>
 <welcome>
  You're a Bronze customer -- can we interest you in 30 days no interest?
 </welcome>
</customer>
```

Finally, a session value is set for the current request, `Session("WelcomeMsg")`, with the appropriate welcome message for the customer type.

We can then write an ASP.NET page that extracts this session value and displays the welcome message for the correct group:

```
<Script runat="server">
   Public Sub Page_Load(sender As Object, e As EventArgs)
      WelcomeMsg.Text = Session("WelcomeMsg")
   End Sub
</Script>
<asp:label id="WelcomeMsg" runat="server" />
```

Although this is a simple example (we could have written all of this code into our ASP.NET page), it shows how nicely you can encapsulate this inside `global.asax` and not repeat it on each and every application file that wants to use the associated XML file for the customer type. Additionally, when users access the ASP.NET page, the values are already populated.

Finally, let's look at the `Application_Error` event that you can use to catch unhandled exceptions from your ASP.NET application.

Handling Application Errors

Since ASP.NET uses the CLR, you can use any CLR language to build your web application. One of the CLR's features is structured `try`/`catch` exception handling (no more of VB6's `On Error Resume Next`!). As great as this new structured error handling model is, it doesn't prevent you from writing buggy code. For example, you might write some code in your ASP.NET application that connects to and reads from a database. You can also wrap that code in a `try`/ `catch` block so that if you can't connect to the database, you can handle the error appropriately.

However, what happens if an exception occurs outside of a `try`/ `catch` block? If it is not handled, ASP.NET will throw a run-time error (providing you with a detailed overview of where the error occurred and what the application was doing). For ASP.NET pages, you can optionally implement a `Page_Error` event to catch all unhandled page errors. However, if you decide you would rather catch all unhandled ASP.NET errors at the application level, you have that option too, using the `Application_Error` event.

We can use this event as a catch-all whenever an unhandled exception occurs, and log the exception to the Windows event log:

```vb
<%@ Import Namespace="System.Diagnostics" %>

<script language="VB" runat=server>
  Public Sub Application_Error(Sender as Object, E as EventArgs)

    Dim LogName As String = "Web_Errors"
    Dim Message As String
    Message = "Url: " & Request.Path
    Message = Message & " Error: " & Server.GetLastError.ToString

    ' Create event log if it doesn't exist
    If (Not EventLog.SourceExists(LogName)) Then
      EventLog.CreateEventSource(LogName, LogName)
    End if

    ' Fire off to event log
    Dim Log as New EventLog

    Log.Source = LogName
    Log.WriteEntry(Message, EventLogEntryType.Error)

  End Sub
</script>
```

In this example, we first import the namespace `System.Diagnostics` as we will be using some of the classes found in this namespace to write to the event log. We then implement our `Application_Error` event handler and create some local variables. This is done before using the `EventLog` class's static method `SourceExists` to determine if the event log you're going to write to already exists – if it doesn't we create it. Finally, we create a new `EventLog` instance named `Log` and use the `WriteEntry` method to enter our `Message` into the Windows Event Log.

Whenever an error occurs within our application, that error is now logged into a custom event log named `Web_Errors`. Note that we wrote approximately 10 lines of code to accomplish a task that could potentially be 50 to 60 lines in VB/ASP!

Now that we have covered each of the application events, let's look at some advanced topics. These are areas that are left to the more advanced ASP.NET developer and the understanding of these topics is not required to build great ASP.NET applications, but they do help!

Advanced Topics

This section covers four advanced topics related to building superior ASP.NET applications:

❑ **Using static variables**: It is not always necessary to use `Application` to store persistent values in memory. Since ASP.NET is compiled and the application is represented in an object-oriented manner, we can use global static variables in addition to `Application`.

❑ **Using our own base class for `global.asax`**: The earlier discussion of the `Application` directive for `global.asax` mentioned the `Inherits` attribute. We will examine how we can use this to create our own class for `global.asax` to instantiate.

❑ **Mapping file extensions**: If we want ASP.NET to support file extensions other than the defaults, such as the file extension `.wrox`, we must map the extension in IIS first. This is because IIS gets the first look at the request and acts as the router determining where to send requests.

❑ **Asynchronous application events**: Earlier in the chapter, we discussed the application events that ASP.NET supports. What we didn't discuss in detail is the fact that ASP.NET also supports some asynchronous representations of these events.

Static Variables

Another supported attribute of the `Application` directive is `Classname`. This attribute allows you to control the name of the class generated for your `global.asax` code when it is compiled. If you provide a `Classname` value, you can access the instance of `global.asax`.

Since you now have access to the `global.asax` instance, this also means that public methods, properties, or variables declared within it are accessible anywhere in your application. An advanced design choice you can elect to make is to take advantage of one of the object-oriented features of ASP.NET – *static members*.

When a class is created, such as an instance of `global.asax`, each instance of the class also uses its own methods, properties, and variables to perform tasks. You can declare a method, property, or variable *static* and all instances of the class will share the one instance of that method, property, or variable. These static members can be used to store commonly accessed data, for instance, a string array containing the 50 states of the USA.

Using static members is sometimes faster than accessing `Application` state. `Application` is an object, and loading `Application` requires memory allocations, and so on. A simple example that demonstrates this is the discount rate applied to all products for a one-time sale. The following snippet is a sample `global.asax` file in C#:

```
<%@ Application Classname="CommerceApplication" %>

<Script Language="C#" runat="server">
// Set discount to 10%
public static float discountRate = .1F;
</Script>
```

And in Visual Basic .NET:

```
<%@ Application Classname="CommerceApplication" %>

<Script runat="server">
' Set discount to 10%
Public Shared discountRate As Single = .1F
</Script>
```

We first identify the name of the `global.asax`'s class using the `Classname` attribute of the `Application` directive. Then we declare a static member variable, `discountRate`.

We can now write code that accesses this class and its static member, `discountRate`. The following code snippet in VB.NET is a sample ASP.NET page, `default.aspx`:

```
<Script runat="server" >
  Public Sub Page_Load(sender As Object, e As EventArgs)
    ' Calculate the discount rate
    Dim discountRate As Single
    Dim productCost As Single

    ' Determine productCost value
    productCost = 19.99F
    ' Calculate discount rate and apply to product cost
    discountRate = CommerceApplication.discountRate
    productCost = productCost - (productCost * discountRate)

    ' Display calculation
    lblCost.Text = productCost.ToString()

  End Sub
</Script>

The cost of the product is: $<asp:label id="lblCost" runat="server" />
```

Here we have a simple Visual Basic ASP.NET page that calculates a product's cost with the applied discount rate. The value for `discountRate` is obtained from the static member defined in our `global.asax` file `CommerceApplication.discountRate`.

Using Your Own Base Class for global.asax

The `Inherits` attribute of the `global.asax` application directive allows you to name a .NET class that `global.asax` will use as the base class for all compiled instances of `global.asax`. This is useful if you want to add your own methods or properties as part of `global.asax`. It allows you create a `global.asax` file that is customized to a particular application.

For example, a commerce solution may provide a commerce-oriented `global.asax` that exposes properties or methods that are specific to its application, for example, a `global.asax` property such as `AdTargetingEnabled`. Developers who use this commerce framework don't see the implementation of this property. Instead, it's encapsulated within `global.asax` and they just need to know what happens when they set `AdTargetingEnabled = true`.

Inherits

To use `Inherits`, you first need to create your own custom class that inherits from the `HttpApplication` class. `HttpApplication` is the default base class used by `global.asax`, and it is what exposes the application and session events as well as any default properties.

After creating a new class that inherits from `HttpApplication`, and adding the new functionality you desire, you can then use the `global.asax` `Inherits` directive to instruct ASP.NET to use your base class instead of `HttpApplication`. Let's illustrate this with an example.

The following code snippet is a simple class, `MyApplication`, that inherits from `HttpApplication`. The `MyApplication` class implements a `CurrentTime` method that simply returns the current date/time. Using the `Inherits` keyword, you have told the compiler that the `MyApplication` class inherits all the methods, properties, events, and so on, that `HttpApplication` implements. Essentially, all this class does is add one more method:

```
Imports System
Imports System.Web

' To compile: vbc /t:library /r:system.web.dll /r:system.dll Inherits.vb

Public Class MyApplication
  Inherits HttpApplication

  Public Function CurrentTime() As String
    ' Use ToString("r") to show seconds in Now output
    Return DateTime.Now.ToString("r")
  End Function

End Class
```

Next, you need to compile and deploy the generated assembly to your web application's `bin` directory. To compile, you can either create a new Visual Basic .NET Class project in Visual Studio .NET, or you can use the command line compilers. Either will work equally well. Here is the command line compiler command to compile this in case you don't have Visual Studio .NET:

```
> vbc /t:library /r:system.web.dll /r:system.dll Inherits.vb
```

Next, you need to copy the resulting `.dll` to your web application's `bin` directory. Remember, deploying it to the `bin` directory makes it available to your application.

You can then write a `global.asax` file that uses the `Application` directive's `Inherits` attribute to inherit from your custom base class. Then, within your `global.asax` code, you have access to your new method:

```
<%@ Application Inherits="MyApplication" %>

<Script runat="server">
  Public Sub Application_OnBeginRequest()

    Dim TimeStamp As String
    TimeStamp = CurrentTime()
```

```
        Response.Write("Request Beginning TimeStamp: " & TimeStamp)
        Response.Write("<HR size=1>")

    End Sub
</Script>
```

Since we inherited from the `MyApplication` base class (which itself inherits from `HttpApplication`), we have all of the standard behaviors of `global.asax` provided with the addition of a new `CurrentTime` method. In this code example, we created a simple local variable of type `String` named `TimeStamp`, then set `TimeStamp` using the inherited `CurrentTime` method, before returning the result with `Response.Write`.

Mapping File Extensions to ASP. NET

A more advanced (but no more difficult) option that ASP.NET supports is mapping custom file extensions to ASP.NET resources. If for example, instead of using the extension `.aspx` for ASP.NET pages we decided to use the extension `.wrox`, you would need to make two changes to enable ASP.NET to serve `default.wrox`:

❑　First, we must create the following new entry in the `<httpHandlers>` section of either our `web.config` or `machine.config` files – more about these two files and the `<httpHandlers>` settings in the next chapter:

```
<configuration>

  <system.web>
    <httpHandlers>
      <add verb="*" path="*.wrox"
           type="System.Web.UI.PageHandlerFactory.System.Web" />
    </httpHandlers>
  </system.web>

</configuration>
```

❑　Second, we must configure IIS to send requests with the extension `.wrox` to ASP.NET. This is accomplished through the IIS Microsoft Management Console.

Open the IIS MMC, and right-click on a web root or a web application folder (if you want to limit the mapping to a single application) and select the Properties option. Once the dialog is open, press the Configuration button, and select the App Mappings tab, as shown in Figure 12-13:

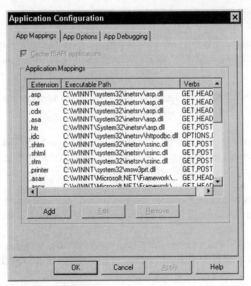

Figure 12-13

This tab lists all the extensions that IIS maps to ISAPI extensions. ISAPI is a low-level API that lets custom applications plug in to IIS. ASP used an ISAPI named `asp.dll`, and ASP.NET uses an ISAPI named `aspnet_isapi.dll`. The ASP.NET ISAPI simply takes the entire request from IIS and hands it to ASP.NET. If you want ASP.NET to handle the `.wrox` extension, you need to map it onto the `aspnet_isapi.dll` so that IIS sends the request to ASP.NET.

To add this application mapping, press the Add button. This brings up the Add/Edit Application Extension Mapping dialog box. You can then name the ASP.NET ISAPI (`aspnet_isapi.dll`), found in the directory `C:\[WINNT]\Microsoft.NET\Framework\[version]\`. You can now name your extension `.wrox`. Your completed entry should look similar to Figure 12-14:

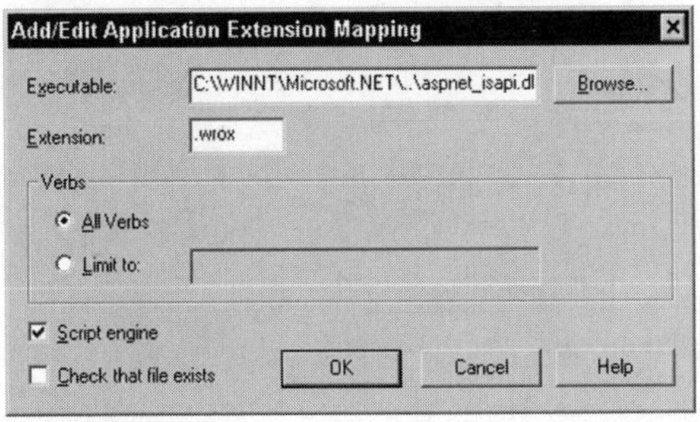

Figure 12-14

In the next chapter, you will look at how to map the `.wrox` extension to ASP.NET resources through the ASP.NET configuration system.

Asynchronous Application Events

This is a more advanced discussion than the previous topics. Understanding asynchronous application events is not necessary to build good ASP.NET applications. It is, however, an advanced feature that can prove very useful in some cases.

As mentioned earlier, ASP.NET code is executed in an ASP.NET worker process, not in the IIS process. Within this worker process, threads are used to execute code.

A thread is a resource, and there are a finite number of threads that ASP.NET will be able to use, otherwise the processor would spend all its time context-switching (that is, switching threads of execution in the processor) rather than executing user code.

ASP.NET creates and manages a *threadpool*, increasing and decreasing the number of threads as required throughout the life of the application. This is in contrast to ASP, which used a fixed number of threads.

In some cases, application code such as network I/O can potentially stall threads in the ASP.NET process. This is because the ASP.NET thread has to wait (it is blocked) until this slow operation is completed.

When a thread is blocked, it can't be used to service requests, resulting in queuing of requests and degraded application performance. The ASP.NET team took this into consideration and added support for asynchronous events in addition to the existing synchronous ones discussed earlier.

The only reason for using these asynchronous events in `global.asax` is in application code (within an event) that performs operations over the network where the network class supports I/O completion ports, such as a web service proxy.

Supported Events

There are ten supported asynchronous events, raised in the following order:

- ❑ `AddOnBeginRequestAsync`
- ❑ `AddOnAuthenticateRequestAsync`
- ❑ `AddOnAuthorizeRequestAsync`
- ❑ `AddOnResolveRequestCacheAsync`
- ❑ `AddOnAcquireRequestStateAsync`
- ❑ `AddOnPreRequestHandlerExecuteAsync`
- ❑ `AddOnPostRequestHandlerExecuteAsync`
- ❑ `AddOnReleaseRequestStateAsync`
- ❑ `AddOnUpdateRequestCacheAsync`
- ❑ `AddOnEndRequestAsync`

No descriptions are given, as these events are synonymous with their synchronous counterparts described earlier.

When to Use Asynchronous Events

In Chapter 19, you will start looking at ASP.NET Web services. In a nutshell, ASP.NET allows you to easily build XML interfaces for application code. All you need to do is write the application logic and mark the methods with the WebMethod attribute.

Web services are very powerful and easy to use. However, since they make calls over the network, and are subject to all the limitations of that network, we don't want to make a lot of web service calls within a web application (this is applicable to any web application, not just ASP.NET) because those network calls can potentially stall the threads used to process ASP.NET requests. For example, if our application gets twenty simultaneous requests and the application code that services each request makes a call to a web service, we will potentially stall and queue subsequent requests as we wait for the threads to return.

However, by using asynchronous events, you could at least free up the threads that ASP.NET isn't using for the web service calls. Let's look at a sample of this.

Sample Web Service

First, you need a sample web service. The following snippet creates a simple StockQuote Web service, in a file named StockQuote.asmx:

```
<%@ WebService Class="QuoteService" %>
Imports System.Web.Services
Public Class QuoteService
  <WebMethod()> Public Function GetQuotes() As QuoteDetails()
    ' Create an array of 3 Quote objects for our return
    Dim quotes(3) As QuoteDetails

    quotes(0) = New QuoteDetails()
    quotes(0).Symbol = "MSFT"
    quotes(0).Price = 89.34F

    quotes(1) = New QuoteDetails()
    quotes(1).Symbol = "SUNW"
    quotes(1).Price = 11.13F

    quotes(2) = New QuoteDetails()
    quotes(2).Symbol = "ORCL"
    quotes(2).Price = 22.93F

    Return quotes
  End Function
End Class

Public Class QuoteDetails
  Public Symbol As String
  Public Price As Single
End Class
```

This particular web service, written in Visual Basic .NET, simply returns an array of QuoteDetails with some pre-populated values. You can then write an ASP.NET application that uses this web service, and calls it asynchronously. When you build the proxy, ASP.NET automatically creates asynchronous implementations of your web service's methods.

Asynchronous Event Prototypes

Implementing asynchronous events is not trivial. Not only do you need to know whether or not the application code you're writing can benefit from asynchronous events, you also need to understand the asynchronous programming model supported by .NET.

To use these events within `global.asax`, you need to wire up the provided event prototype ourselves. This is done by overriding the `Init` method, which is marked as virtual in `HttpApplication`, and replacing it with your wire-up code. Unlike synchronous events, asynchronous event wire-up is not done automatically for us.

The following code, written in Visual Basic .NET, calls the `QuoteService` Web service asynchronously:

```
<%@ Import namespace="System.Threading" %>
<%@ Import namespace="System.Text" %>

<Script runat="server">
  Dim asyncResult As MyAsyncResult
  Public Overrides Sub Init()
    Dim beginEvent As New BeginEventHandler(AddressOf _Begin)
    Dim endEvent As New EndEventHandler(AddressOf _End)
    AddOnBeginRequestAsync(beginEvent, endEvent)
  End Sub
```

First, we override the `Init` method of `HttpApplication` so we can execute our code when `global.asax` is initialized. The code executed is an implementation of `AddOnBeginRequestAsync`. We provide this event with both a `Begin` and an `End` event handler. It is a code path within the begin event where we execute our code. The following code is an implementation for both the `BeginEventHandler` and the `EndEventHandler`:

```
' Begin Event Handler
Public Function _Begin(source As Object, e As EventArgs, _
                     callback As AsyncCallBack, _
                     extraData As Object) As IAsyncResult
  asyncResult = New MyAsyncResult(Context, callback, extraData)
  Return asyncResult
End Function

' End Event Handler
Public Sub _End(ar As IAsyncResult)
End Sub
```

The Begin Event Handler, `_Begin`, is raised when `OnBeginRequest` is called. Within this event handler, we create a new instance of a class called `MyAsyncResult`. It is within this class (defined further in the code) that we implement our code to call the web service.

The `EndEventHandler`, which can be used to clean up resources when the `BeginEventHandler` completes, is not used in this example.

Next, we find the implementation of `MyAsyncResult`. This class is an implementation of the `IAsyncResult` interface. The `IAsyncResult` interface is part of the asynchronous programming pattern defined by the CLR. We provide an implementation (see the product documentation for a description of the implemented properties) that contains the code we want executed:

```vb
' Async implementation class
Private Class MyAsyncResult
  Implements IAsyncResult

  Dim _asyncState As Object
  Dim _callback As AsyncCallback
  Dim _thread As Thread
  Dim _context As HttpContext
  Dim _isCompleted As Boolean = False

  Public Sub New(context As HttpContext, _
                 callback As AsyncCallback, asyncState As Object)
    _callback = callback
    _asyncState = asyncState
    _context = context
    _thread = New Thread(New ThreadStart( _
                          AddressOf CallStockQuoteWebService))
    _thread.Start()
  End Sub

  Public ReadOnly Property AsyncState As Object _
                                   Implements IAsyncResult.AsyncState
    Get
      Return _asyncState
    End Get
  End Property

  Public ReadOnly Property AsyncWaitHandle As WaitHandle _
                            Implements IAsyncResult.AsyncWaitHandle
    Get
      Return Nothing
    End Get
  End Property

  Public ReadOnly Property CompletedSynchronously As Boolean _
                       Implements IAsyncResult.CompletedSynchronously
    Get
      Return False
    End Get
  End Property

  Public ReadOnly Property IsCompleted As Boolean _
                                   Implements IAsyncResult.IsCompleted
    Get
      Return _isCompleted
    End Get
  End Property
```

The constructor for MyAsyncResult creates a new thread and calls the CallStockQuoteWebService on that thread. This subroutine (in the following code snippet) creates a new instance of the proxy to our QuoteService ASP.NET Web service, and uses the asynchronous implementation of the GetQuotes method. It identifies a callback, `QuoteCallBack`, which is called when the I/O completion port is reactivated. Within this callback we again create a new instance of the proxy class and then call its `EndGetQuotes` method. Finally, we save the proxy's `QuoteDetails` return to `Application` state memory so we can access it from anywhere within ASP.NET:

```
Public Sub CallStockQuoteWebService()
  Dim quote As New QuoteService()

  quote.BeginGetQuotes(New AsyncCallback( _
                              AddressOf QuoteCallBack), Nothing)
End Sub

Public Sub QuoteCallBack(ar As IAsyncResult)
  Dim quote As New QuoteService()
  Dim d() As QuoteDetails

  d = quote.EndGetQuotes(ar)
  _context.Application("QuoteDetails") = d
  _isCompleted = true
  _callback(Me)
End Sub

End Class

</Script>
```

We can now write a simple ASP.NET page that retrieves the values from `Application("QuoteDetails")`:

```
<Script runat="server">
  Dim quotes() As QuoteDetails

  Public Sub Page_Load(Sender As Object, e As EventArgs)
    quotes = CType(Application("QuoteDetails"), QuoteDetails())
  End Sub
</Script>

<%
Dim item As QuoteDetails

For Each item in quotes
  Response.Write("Symbol: " + item.Symbol + "<br>")
  Response.Write("Price: " + item.Price.ToString() + "<br>")
  Response.Write("<hr size=1>")
Next
%>
```

Executing this code brings up the screen shown in Figure 12-15:

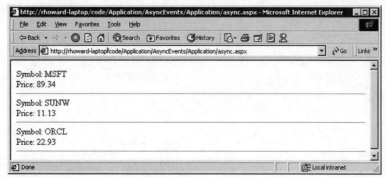

Figure 12-15

Since ASP.NET supports both synchronous and asynchronous application events, you can have more options when building your application. Coding the event to be asynchronous will free the ASP.NET worker thread to service other requests until the code executed on the asynchronous thread completes. The result is better scalability, since you're not blocking the threads ASP.NET uses to service requests.

Summary

We have covered a lot of material in this chapter. We started with a discussion of what a web application is, and how we create a new web application using Internet Information Services (IIS). We moved on to the important topic of developing an understanding of web applications, before we looked at the `bin` directory and the `global.asax` file. We learned that the `bin` directory is where we deploy compiled code in ASP.NET and that `global.asax` allows you to run application-level code. We additionally looked at the file format of `global.asax`.

Next, we discussed application state management and looked at three areas in detail: `Application`, `Session`, and `Cache`. We compared and contrasted `Application` versus `Cache` and gave some code examples showing the implicit and explicit methods used to add items to the Cache. We then looked at a `Cache` file dependency example.

`Application` events were covered next and in this section, we looked at the eighteen events supported by ASP.NET. We gave brief overviews of each, covering their naming and syntax, before looking at specific examples of some of the more important events. One of the examples showed how to use the `Application_Error` event to write to the Windows Event Log.

Finally, we wrapped up the chapter with an Advanced Topics section covering some of the more advanced areas of ASP.NET including asynchronous events, and mapping custom file extensions.

In the next chapter we are going to learn more about how to configure ASP.NET. We will explore topics such as configuring `Session` to support the various modes discussed in this chapter.

Configuration

Whenever you build an application, the storage of details describing the behaviors and settings for the application, also known as configuration information, are required. As it relates to web applications, configuration information includes details such as database connection strings, timeout values, and various other *behaviors* such as how errors should be logged, or how state is to be maintained.

Those of you with a background in developing pages using ASP will no doubt recall that all application configuration information is stored in a binary repository called the *Internet Information Services (IIS) metabase*. To configure an ASP application such as changing the `Session` timeout – an example we'll use throughout the chapter – the metabase needs to be modified, either through script or more commonly through the IIS Microsoft Management Console snap-in.

ASP.NET, unlike ASP, does not require extensive use of the IIS metabase. Instead, ASP.NET uses an XML-based configuration system. As you will see in this chapter, ASP.NET's configuration system is much more flexible, accessible, and easier to use.

The following is a breakdown of what this chapter will cover:

❑ **Configuration overview**: We will start with a high-level overview of configuration, discuss what's new in ASP.NET and how configuration has changed from ASP. We will look at a common example, configuring `Session` state, to better frame the discussion. We will also discuss the new configuration file format in detail.

❑ **Common configuration settings**: Here we will look at several of the most common configuration settings that will be used when working with ASP.NET. These settings include options for `Session` state, security, and management of the ASP.NET worker process. The bulk of this chapter will be spent in this section.

❑ **Advanced topics**: In this section we will discuss some more advanced topics such as the creation of configuration section handler and settings.

Let's get started with an overview of configuration.

Configuration Overview

ASP.NET configuration can be summarized as: *a simple but powerful XML-based configuration system*. Rather than relying upon the IIS metabase as with the ASP applications, ASP.NET uses an XML-based configuration system. XML is used to describe the properties and behaviors for various aspects of ASP.NET applications.

The ASP.NET configuration system supports two types of configuration file:

❑ **Server configuration**: Server configuration information is stored in a `machine.config` file. This file represents the default settings used by all ASP.NET web applications. ASP.NET installs a single `machine.config` file on the server. You can find `machine.config` in `[WinNT\Windows]\Microsoft.NET\Framework\[version]\CONFIG\`.

A single `machine.config` file is installed for each version of ASP.NET installed. For example, if you have both ASP.NET 1.0 and ASP.NET 1.1 installed, you will have two separate version directories, `v1.0.3705` and `v1.1.4322` for version 1.0 and 1.1 respectively, of the .NET Framework. The CLR, and thus ASP.NET, supports the concept of side-by-side execution.

❑ **Application configuration**: Application configuration information is stored in a `web.config` file. This file represents the settings for an individual ASP.NET application. A server can have multiple `web.config` files, each existing in application roots or directories within the application. Settings in a `web.config` file either override or add new settings to the default configuration information provided by `machine.config`. Later in the chapter, you will learn how the administrator can control the settings that a `web.config` file is allowed to override.

We will come back to these configuration files soon and talk more about how to use them. Let's take a quick look at ASP configuration (for those who used ASP).

ASP Configuration

Prior to ASP.NET, ASP web application configuration was either accomplished by a script that modified the IIS metabase or through the IIS Manager.

The metabase is a binary data store that IIS uses for configuration settings.

Let's use a common task (of setting session state timeout from 20 minutes to 10 minutes) to illustrate ASP configuration.

Session State Example

To configure session timeout in ASP, we go through the following steps (note these steps need to repeat for each server in your server farm):

1. Open the Internet Services Manager.

2. Right-click on a web application and select Properties.

3. Select the Home Directory tab.

4. Select Configuration.

5. Select the App Options tab.

Finally, you are presented with a dialog box in which you can configure session settings, as shown in Figure 13-1:

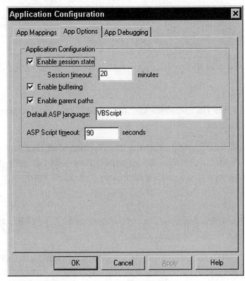

Figure 13-1

You can change the session timeout value from 20 minutes to 10 minutes, press OK, and back out of all the menus. These settings are applied to the metabase, but they don't apply to your application just yet.

To apply these changes to the web application, you need to stop and start the web server by either using the IIS Manager (Stop and Start buttons), or opening a command prompt and running iisreset.

Once these changes have been applied and IIS is restarted, the application has the desired behavior of 10-minute session timeout. If you maintain a web server farm, you need to manually perform these steps for each server.

Ideally, you could replicate the IIS metabase to all the servers in our farm, but due to security reasons, the metabase uses a unique *machine key* to encrypt some of the stored values. Even if you managed to copy the updated metabase to another server, that server would most likely *not* be able to use it. This method is not ideal, especially when running a web server farm!

Application Center can replicate IIS settings to other IIS servers in your farm. Additionally, it includes other web farm manageability tools.

ASP.NET Configuration

For completeness, we need to show the same configuration example of setting session timeout from 20 minutes to 10 minutes for an ASP.NET application.

Session State Example

Fire up your favorite text editor and type the following XML into a file:

```
<configuration>
  <system.web>
    <sessionState timeout="10" />
  </system.web>
</configuration>
```

Save this file as web.config in a web application root (see Chapter 12 for details on creating a web application).

While ASP.NET does not use the IIS metabase for application settings, the administrator is still required to mark folders as web applications.

That's all there is to it – the ASP.NET application will now timeout the Session after 10 minutes of inactivity. Similar to ASP, ASP.NET default session timeout is set to 20 minutes. Although not shown, this default value is set in the server's machine.config file. However, our web.config has overridden that setting to 10 minutes.

Settings such as session timeout made in the IIS metabase via the IIS MMC, as done for the ASP example, do not effect your ASP.NET applications.

To update servers in the farm with these new settings, simply copy this web.config file to the appropriate application directory. ASP.NET takes care of the rest – no server restarts and no local server access is required – and your application continues to function normally, except now with the new settings. As you can clearly see, this new configuration system is very simple and straightforward to use. You simply write a configuration file and save it to a web application, and ASP.NET will automatically apply the changes. More on how all this works later.

Benefits of ASP.NET Configuration

As demonstrated in the preceding section, instead of relying on the metabase for application configuration information, ASP.NET uses XML configuration files. The benefits of this include:

❑ **Human-readable configuration settings**: It is very easy to open an XML file and read (or change) the settings. Tools that work with XML, such as Visual Studio .NET can be used to open the file and settings can easily be identified and updated.

❑ **Updates are immediate**: Unlike ASP, application configuration changes are immediate and do not require the web server to be stopped and restarted for the settings to take effect. Instead, the settings immediately affect a running system and are completely transparent to the end user.

❑ **Local server access is not required**: ASP.NET automatically detects when updates are made to the configuration system, and then creates a new instance of the application. End users are then redirected to the new application and the configuration changes are applied without the need for the administrator to stop and start the web server. Note that this is completely transparent to the end user. Although not covered in great detail, this is done through a CLR feature called *application domains*, mentioned in the previous chapter.

❑ **Easy replication**: Unlike the metabase, which could not easily be replicated since the instance of the metabase is bound to the server it resides upon, ASP.NET configuration files can simply be copied to the appropriate location – they are simply XML files.

The ASP.NET configuration system eliminates 99 percent of the work to be done by the metabase. However, there are two exceptions:

❑ **Creating web applications**: As discussed in the previous chapter, marking a folder, either virtual or physical, through the Internet Service Management Console as an application allows ASP.NET to treat components, files, and configuration information as a web application. This process must still be accomplished either by using script that modifies the IIS metabase, through the IIS Manager snap-in, or automatically when you create a new ASP.NET project with Visual Studio .NET. The task of marking a web application forces the administrator to decide what is or is not an ASP.NET application.

❑ **Custom file extension mappings**: Again, as discussed in the previous chapter, if you wish to use file extensions other than those already supported by ASP.NET, you need to add an entry in the application settings for IIS. For example, to write applications that use the .wrox extension, you have to tell IIS that requests for resources ending with the .wrox extension should be handled by ASP.NET.

Both these exceptions are configuration decisions made when building the server. For all other application and server configuration options, such as configuring Session timeout, the execution timeout (how long an ASP.NET application executes before being timed out), or new settings such as timing out the worker process, we will use the ASP.NET configuration exclusively.

How Configuration Is Applied

When ASP.NET applies configuration settings for a given request, a union of the machine.config *and* any web.config files is applied for a given application. Configuration settings are inherited from parent web applications; machine.config being the root parent. This is depicted in Figure 13-2:

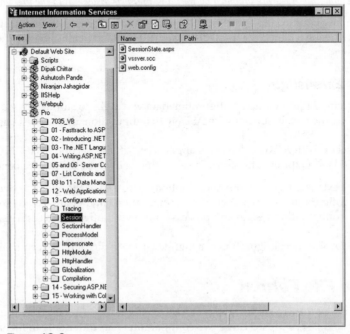

Figure 13-2

The preceding screenshot is of the IIS MMC. The `machine.config` is applied to all web applications on the server. We then see callouts labeled `web.config` that identify locations where a `web.config` file might exist within this server. The three configuration files apply to:

❑ The root of the web – for example, http://localhost/

❑ A sub-application – for example, http://localhost/7035/

❑ A folder within the Wrox application – for example, http://localhost/7035/configuration/Session/

The configuration for each of these applications is unique, but settings are inherited. For example, if the `web.config` file in the root of the web site defines session timeout as 10 minutes (overriding the server's default settings inherited from `machine.config`) and the `web.config` files in `/7035/` and `/7035/configuration/Session/` directories do not override these settings, both these directories will inherit the settings of 10 minute session timeout, in addition to applying their own settings for their respective application.

Detecting Configuration File Changes

ASP.NET detects when files (such as `machine.config` or `web.config`) are changed, by listening for file change notification events provided by the operating system. Behind the scenes, when an ASP.NET application is started, the configuration settings are read and stored in the ASP.NET `Cache`. A file dependency is then placed upon the entry within the `Cache` upon the `machine.config` and/or `web.config` configuration files. When a change is detected, such as an update to `machine.config`, ASP.NET creates a new application domain to service new requests. When the old application domain has completed servicing its outstanding requests, it is destroyed.

An application domain is a feature provided by the CLR, and was discussed in the previous chapter.

There is no longer any need to stop and start IIS to apply configuration settings as with ASP. Instead, changes to ASP.NET configuration are immediate, and are handled behind the scenes through the use of application domains.

Configuration Is Extensible

What happens if your application has configuration data you'd like to store? This wasn't a feasible option in ASP (using the metabase), but with ASP.NET configuration, there are a couple of choices:

❑ **High-level extension**: You can use the application settings section of ASP.NET configuration (discussed later in the chapter) to store key/value pairs representing the configuration settings.

❑ **Low-level extension**: A more advanced option, discussed at the end of the chapter, is to create a custom configuration handler. A custom configuration handler allows you to extend the ASP.NET configuration system and process your own configuration settings.

We have discussed ASP.NET configuration at a high-level – let's dig into the technical details.

Configuration File Format

As previously mentioned, there are two types of XML configuration files used by ASP.NET: `machine.config` and `web.config`. These two configuration files differ only in filename, where they live on the file system, and support of some settings. Both use the same XML format (pseudoschema shown):

Items in brackets [ ] have unique values within the real configuration file.

```xml
<?xml version="1.0" encoding="UTF-8"?>
<configuration>
  <configSections>
    <section name="[sectionSettings]" type="[Class]"/>

    <sectionGroup name="[sectionGroup]">
      <section name="[sectionSettings]" type="[Class]"/>
    </sectionGroup>
  </configSections>

  <[sectionSettings] attribute="[value]"/>

  <[sectionSettings] attribute="[value]">
    <element attribute="[value]"/>
  </[sectionSettings]>

  <[sectionGroup]>
    <[sectionSettings] attribute="[value]"/>

    <[sectionSettings] attribute="[value]">
      <element attribute="[value]"/>
    </[sectionSettings]>
  </[sectionGroup]>
</configuration>
```

Note the camel-casing. The first letter of the first word is always lowercase and the first letter of subsequent words is uppercase – for example, thisIsAnExample. Understanding the casing is very important, since the ASP.NET configuration system is case-sensitive.

The root element of the configuration file is always <configuration>. Within <configuration> there are two important sections:

❑   <section name="[sectionSettings]">: Referred to as a configuration section handler, this defines a class used to interpret the meaning of configuration data. It is important to note that configuration section handlers only need to be declared once for all applications if declared in machine.config (this is because applications inherit the settings in machine.config). Web applications that wish to change the settings for a particular configuration option, such as the Session example shown earlier, do not need to re-declare the configuration section handler.

❑   <[sectionSettings]>: Referred to as configuration section settings, this defines the actual settings for a particular option. The sample web.config file shown earlier defines a configuration section setting for sessionState overriding the default of 20 minutes inherited from machine.config.

These two sections are intimately related. Whereas section settings, such as configuring the timeout value for Session state, define options for a particular feature, section handlers define the code that implements the desired behaviors. We will look at some examples that clarify this.

Each of the section handlers and settings are optionally wrapped in a `<sectionGroup>`. A `<sectionGroup>` provides an organizational function within the configuration file. It allows you to organize configuration into unique groups – for instance, the `<system.web>` section group is used to identify areas within the configuration file specific to ASP.NET.

Configuration Handlers

Section handlers identify .NET classes, which are loaded when the configuration system is loaded. These classes are responsible for reading the settings for their respective features from the configuration section settings.

The `name` attribute of the `<section name="[sectionSettings]">` tag defines the tag name (here, `sessionState`) of the configuration section settings element, (`<sessionState>`). Let's use the `Session` state example to better illustrate how this works.

Session State Example

Within the `machine.config` file, you can find the base definition for the `sessionState` section handler. Remember, since this section handler is defined in `machine.config`, you don't need to re-declare it on each use in `web.config` files.

Here is the XML that defines the `sessionState` section handler (highlighted):

```xml
<?xml version="1.0" encoding="UTF-8" ?>
<configuration>
  <configSections>
    <sectionGroup name="system.web">
      <section name="sessionState"
        type="System.Web.SessionState.SessionStateSectionHandler, System.Web,
        Version=1.0.3300.0, Culture=neutral, PublicKeyToken=b03f5f7f11d50a3a"
        allowDefinition="MachineToApplication"
      />
    </sectionGroup>
  </configSections>
</configuration>
...
```

The `type="System.WebSessionState.SessionStateSectionHandler"` identifies the class responsible for the configuration settings of ASP.NET session state. The `name="sessionState"` value defines the name of configuration section settings `<sessionState>` here, an element found later in the configuration document and `System.Web` identifies the assembly the class resides within.

Once a configuration section handler is declared, it does not need to be redeclared in configuration files that inherit from it. Since all `web.config` application configuration files inherit from `machine.config`, any configuration section handlers declared in `machine.config` are automatically available within `web.config`. In other words, `<sessionState>` settings may be declared in any application's `web.config` file and will be processed using the handler defined in `machine.config`.

You can enforce settings found in the `machine.config` so that `web.config` files can't override settings. For example, if you are running ASP.NET in a hosted environment, the administrator can restrict the `sessionState` settings so they can't be changed in `web.config` files – we'll explore this option later in the chapter in the advanced topics section.

Let's take a look at the section settings that actually define our desired behaviors. We will use the same `sessionState` example.

Configuration Settings

The second section of the configuration file is the configuration session settings. Whereas the handler (described in the preceding section) names a class, the configuration session settings identify properties that affect the behavior of the application. In most cases, you only need to understand the settings for the configuration option you wish to modify, such as the settings for `sessionState`.

Again, this is best explained through revisiting the earlier session state example.

Session State Example

Here, we have the `machine.config` section handler and settings for ASP.NET `sessionState` – the settings are highlighted. We will come back to the values for `<sessionState>` later:

```
<?xml version="1.0" encoding="UTF-8" ?>
<configuration>
  <configSections>
    <sectionGroup name="system.web">
      <section name="sessionState"
        type="System.Web.SessionState.SessionStateSectionHandler, System.Web,
        Version=1.0.3300.0, Culture=neutral, PublicKeyToken=b03f5f7f11d50a3a"
        allowDefinition="MachineToApplication"
      />
    </sectionGroup>
    ...
  </configSections>
  ...
  <system.web>
    <sessionState
      mode="InProc"
      stateConnectionString="tcpip=127.0.0.1:42424"
      stateNetworkTimeout="10"
      sqlConnectionString="data source=127.0.0.1; user id=sa;password="
      cookieless="false"
      timeout="20"
    />
  </system.web>
</configuration>
```

In the session settings, `sessionState` properties are set – for example, `mode`, `cookieless`, `timeout`, and so on. ASP.NET `Session` uses these settings, and when a request is made, ASP.NET knows where to find the necessary resources, as well as how to use those resources. For example, if you were to set `cookieless` to `"true"`, this would instruct ASP.NET to *not* use HTTP cookies to manage the `Session` ID and instead pass a key in the URL.

The preceding example showed both section handlers and session settings. As mentioned earlier, we will use the settings most often as `web.config` files that we build for our applications, to inherit the handlers and settings found in `machine.config`. The following code is a valid `web.config` file that enables cookieless session ID management – note that the handler isn't being redeclared:

```
<configuration>
  <system.web>
    <sessionState
        mode="InProc"
        stateConnectionString="tcpip=127.0.0.1:42424"
        stateNetworkTimeout="10"
        sqlConnectionString="data source=127.0.0.1; user id=sa;password="
        cookieless="true"
        timeout="20"
    />
  </system.web>
</configuration>
```

It is good, but not absolutely necessary, to understand section handlers – we will build our own at the end of the chapter. However, it is very important that you understand the settings. When we build and deploy applications, we will usually create our own web.config files and override the machine.config settings without seeing machine.config. It is recommended to modify web.config files rather than the machine.config, since changing machine.config affects all applications on the server. Let's discuss the most common configuration settings used for our applications.

Common Configuration Settings

If you have examined machine.config, which I would suggest you do, you will find around 30 configuration settings. Here are the most commonly used configuration entries:

- **General configuration settings**: How long a given ASP.NET resource, such as a page, is allowed to execute before being considered timed-out.

- **Page configuration**: ASP.NET pages have configuration options such as whether buffering or viewstate is enabled.

- **Application settings**: A key/value combination that allows you to store data within the configuration system and access it within your application.

- **Session state**: Options for Session state, such as where data is stored, timeout, and support for cookieless state management.

- **Tracing**: Provides a trace of what the application is doing. This is configurable both at the page-level and application-level.

- **Custom errors**: ASP.NET has several options for handling application errors, as well as common HTTP errors (404 file not found, and so on).

- **Security**: Although we will cover security in Chapter 14, we will discuss some of the basic security configuration options.

- **Web services**: The web services section allows you to configure some the options for ASP.NET web services such as the name and location of the DefaultWSDLHelpGenerator.aspx template used to generate an HTML view of the web service.

- **Globalization**: Application-level options for the request/response character encoding for ASP.NET to use.

❑ **Compilation**: The compilation options allow you to control some of the compilation behaviors of ASP.NET, such as changing the default language from Visual Basic .NET to C#.

❑ **Identity**: ASP.NET allows you to impersonate the user that ASP.NET acts on the behalf of.

❑ **HTTP handlers**: HTTP handlers are responsible for servicing requests for a particular extension in ASP.NET such as `.aspx` or `.asmx`. Custom handlers can be added or existing handlers removed within this section.

❑ **HTTP modules**: HTTP modules are responsible for filtering each request/response in an ASP.NET application, such as determining whether a particular request should be served from the cache or directed to an HTTP handler.

❑ **Process model**: By default, ASP.NET runs out-of-process from IIS, and has the capability to recycle by itself. The settings found in this section allow granular control over the behavior of the worker process. We will also discuss the *ASP.NET Worker process* in this section.

❑ **Machine key**: A key used for encryption or hashing of some values such as the data in the cookie used for forms authentication. In a server farm environment, all the servers must share a common machine key.

General Configuration Settings

We use the `<httpRuntime>` configuration settings for general application configuration settings such as how long a request is processed before being considered timed-out, the maximum size of a request, or whether to use fully qualified URLs in redirects (a requirement for some mobile applications):

```
<configuration>
  <system.web>
    <httpRuntime
      executionTimeout="90"
      maxRequestLength="4096"
      useFullyQualifiedRedirectUrl="false"
      minFreeThreads="8"
      minLocalRequestFreeThreads="4"
      appRequestQueueLimit="100"
      enableVersionHeader="true"
    />
  </system.web>
</configuration>
```

There are seven configurable options:

❑ `executionTimeout`

❑ `maxRequestLength`

❑ `useFullyQualifiedRedirectUrl`

❑ `minFreeThreads`

❑ `minLocalRequestFreeThreads`

❑ `appRequestQueueLimit`

❑ `enableVersionHeader` (ASP.NET 1.1 only)

Application Timeout

The `executionTimeout` setting is similar to the timeout option for ASP. The value of this attribute is the amount of time in seconds for which a resource can execute before ASP.NET times the request out. The default setting is 90 seconds.

If a particular ASP.NET page or web service takes longer than 90 seconds to execute, you can extend the time limit in the configuration. A good example here is an application that makes a particularly long database request, such as generating a sales report for an application in a company's intranet. If we know the report takes 120 seconds (on average) to execute, we could set the `timeout="300"` and ASP.NET would not timeout the request prematurely. Similarly, you can set the value to less than 90 seconds, and this will decrease the time ASP.NET is allowed to process the request before timing out.

Controlling the Maximum Request Length

The maximum request length attribute, `maxRequestLength`, identifies the maximum size in KB of the request. By default, the maximum request length is 4 MB.

For example, if your site allows customers to upload files and you expect that content to be larger than 4 MB, you can increase this setting. Good examples here include MP3s, unusually large images such as an X-ray stored as a large uncompressed TIFF for a medical site, and so on.

Controlling the maximum request length is important, since common denial of service attacks involve spamming a web site with unusually large requests.

Fully Qualified URLs for Redirects

Some devices, such as mobile phones, that may use ASP.NET applications require that a redirect URL be fully qualified. The default behavior is for ASP.NET to send an unqualified URL for client redirects, (`/Wrox/Logon.aspx`, for example). Setting `useFullyQualifiedRedirectUrl` to "true" will cause the server to send a redirect as `http://[server name]/Wrox/Logon.aspx`.

Thread Management

Two of the more advanced attributes, `minFreeThreads` and `minLocalRequestFreeThreads`, allow you to control how ASP.NET manages threads.

The `minFreeThreads` attribute indicates the number of threads that ASP.NET guarantees is available within the thread pool, the default value for which is 8. For complex applications that require additional threads to complete processing, this simply ensures that the threads are available and that the application does not need to be blocked waiting for a free thread to schedule more work.

The `minLocalRequestFreeThreads` controls the number of free threads dedicated for local request processing, the default of which is 4.

Managing the Request Queue Limit

The final attribute, `appRequestQueueLimit`, controls the number of client requests that may be queued, or in other words, waiting to be processed. Queuing occurs when the server is receiving requests faster than they can be processed. When the number of requests in the queue reaches this threshold, the server will begin sending a HTTP status code 503 indicating that the server is too busy to handle any more requests. If this occurs, you should consider adding another server to handle the load, or isolate and improve the performance of poorly performing ASP.NET pages or web services. A good way to do this is to take advantage of the caching features.

The 'Powered by ASP.NET' Header

New to ASP.NET 1.1 is the `<httpRuntime>` `enableVersionHeader` flag. This attribute controls whether the ASP.NET reports the version number used on the server. By default, this value is set to true, and when requests are made to a web server using ASP.NET, the server will return several headers:

HTTP/1.1 302 Found

Content-Length: 40959

Date: Thu, 02 Oct 2003 14:45:49 GMT

Location: http://www.asp.net/default.aspx?tabindex=0&tabid=1

Content-Type: text/html; charset=utf-8

Server: Microsoft-IIS/6.0

X-Powered-By: ASP.NET

X-AspNet-Version: 1.1.4322

Cache-Control: private

As you can see, two headers X-Powered-By and X-AspNet-Version, are specific to ASP.NET. If `enableVersionHeader` is set to `false`, the X-AspNet-Version header is simply not returned.

In addition to configuring the application, there are also settings particular to ASP.NET pages.

Page Configuration

The page configuration settings allow you to control some of the default behaviors for all ASP.NET pages. These behaviors include options such as whether the output should be buffered before sending, and whether `Session` state is enabled for pages within the application.

The following `web.config` file mirrors the default settings from `machine.config`:

```
<configuration>
  <system.web>
    <pages buffer="true"
           enableSessionState="true"
           enableViewState="true"
           enableViewStateMac="false"
           autoEventWireup="true"
           smartNavigation="false"
           pageBaseType="System.Web.UI.Page"
```

```
            userControlBaseType="System.Web.UI.UserControl"
            validateRequest="true"
    />
  </system.web>
</configuration>
```

Here is what these settings allow you to control:

❏   buffer: Whether the response to a request is buffered on the server before being sent. If buffer="false", the response to a request is sent as the response is available. In some cases, buffering can be disabled and the end-user will perceive that the application is responding faster. In general, however, buffering should not be disabled and the default setting of true need not be changed.

❏   enableSessionState: By default, Session state is enabled for ASP.NET pages. However, if Session is not going to be used for the application, you should disable Session state. Disabling Session state will conserve resources used by the application.

In addition to true and false settings for this attribute, you can also set enableSessionState to readonly. We will cover the readonly option later in the chapter when we discuss the <sessionState> settings.

❏   enableViewState: By default, viewstate, a means of storing server control data on the client, is round-tripped within a hidden form element (__VIEWSTATE) in ASP.NET pages. If the application will not use viewstate, you can set the value to false in the application's web.config file.

❏   autoEventWireup: ASP.NET can automatically wire up common page events such as Load or Error, allowing you to simply author an event prototype such as Page_Load. Setting autoEventWireup to "false", the default behavior of Visual Studio .NET, forces us (done automatically with Visual Studio .NET) to override the appropriate Page events.

❏   smartNavigation: Smart navigation is a feature that takes advantage of a client's browser (Internet Explorer only) to prevent the flickering/redrawing seen when a page is posted back to itself. Instead, using smart navigation, the request is sent through an IFRAME on the client and IE only redraws the sections of the page that have changed. By default, this is set to false, and when enabled, is only available to Internet Explorer browsers – all other browsers will get the standard behavior.

❏   pageBaseType: An advanced option, this attribute controls the base class that all ASP.NET Pages inherit from. By default, it is set to System.Web.UI.Page. However, if you wish all of your pages to inherit from some other base class – for example ACME.Web.Page – you could configure this option here.

❏   userControlBaseType: An advanced option similar to pageBaseType, this attribute allows you to control the base class that all user controls inherit from. The default is System.Web.UI.UserControl.

❏   validateRequest (ASP.NET 1.1): When validateRequest is set to true, content that is posted back to the server is checks for unencoded HTML. If unencoded HTML is found, an exception is thrown that prevents that data from being posted to the application. This is designed to prevent sites from allowing cross-site scripting attacks by posting content into the application. For more on this feature visit http://www.asp.net/faq/RequestValidation.aspx.

Note that all of the preceding settings can be overridden within a given ASP.NET page. For example, you can disable view state at the control-level on individual pages. See Chapter 5 for more details.

Application Settings

The application settings section, `<appSettings/>`, allows you to store application configuration details within the configuration file without needing to write your own configuration section handler. The use of these key/value pair settings simply populates a hashtable that you can access within your application. The following simple example stores the DSN for a connection to a database and a SQL statement:

```
<configuration>
  <appSettings>
    <add key="DSN"
         value="server=sql1;uid=cust;pwd=8d$net;database=pubs" />
    <add key="SQL_PRODUCTS"
         value="SELECT Name, Price FROM Products" />
  </appSettings>
</configuration>
```

You can then retrieve these settings within your ASP.NET application:

```
<%@ Import Namespace="System.Data" %>
<%@ Import Namespace="System.Data.SqlClient" %>
<script runat="server">
  Private dsn As String
  Private sql As String
  Public Sub Page_Load()
    dsn = ConfigurationSettings.AppSettings("DSN")
    sql = ConfigurationSettings.AppSettings("SQL_PRODUCTS")
    Dim myConnection As New SqlConnection(dsn)
    Dim myCommand As New SqlCommand(sql, myConnection)
    Dim reader As DataReader
    myConnection.Open()

    If (reader.Read) Then
      datagrid1.DataSource = reader
      datagrid1.DataBind()
    End If

    myConnection.Close()
  End Sub
</script>
<asp:DataGrid id=datagrid1 runat="server" />
```

Storing this type of commonly used information within the configuration system allows you to manage common application details in a single location, and if the configuration data changes – such as changing the password value of the DSN or the columns in the `select` statement – the application is automatically restarted and the new values used.

Session State

Session state is dedicated data storage for each user within an ASP.NET application. It is implemented as a Hashtable and stores data, based on key/value pair combinations (for details on how to use the Session programmatically, see the previous chapter).

Classic ASP Session state has two main shortcomings:

❑ **Web farm challenges**: Session data is stored in memory on the server it is created upon. In a web farm scenario, where there are multiple web servers, a problem could arise if a user was redirected to a server other than the server upon which they stored their Session state. Normally this can be managed by an IP routing solution where the IP address of the client is used to route that client to a particular server – in other words 'sticky sessions'. However, some ISPs use farms of reverse proxies, and so the client request may come through a different IP on each request. When a user is redirected to a server other than the server that contains their Session data, poorly designed applications can break.

❑ **Supporting clients that do not accept HTTP cookies**: The Web is inherently a stateless environment. To use Session state, the client and web server need to share a key that the client can present to identify its Session data on subsequent requests. Classic ASP shared this key with the client through the use of an HTTP cookie. While this scenario worked well for clients that accept HTTP cookies, it broke the small minority of users that rejected HTTP cookies.

Both of these issues are addressed in ASP.NET Session, which supports new features to remedy these problems:

❑ **Web farm support**: ASP.NET Session supports storing the Session data either in-process (in the same memory that ASP.NET uses), out-of-process using Windows NT Service (in separate memory from ASP.NET), or in SQL Server (persistent storage). Both the Windows Service and SQL Server solutions support a web farm scenario where all the web servers can be configured to share a common Session store. Thus, as users get routed to different servers, each server is able to access that user's Session data. To the developer programming with Session, this is completely transparent and does not require any changes in the application code. Rather, we simply configure ASP.NET to support one of these out-of-process options.

❑ **Cookieless mode**: Although supported to an extent in ASP through the use of an ISAPI filter (available as part of the IIS 4.0 SDK), ASP.NET makes cookieless support for Session a first class feature. However, by default Session still uses HTTP cookies. When cookieless mode is enabled, ASP.NET will embed the session ID (normally stored in the cookie), into the URL that is sent back to the client. When the client makes a request using the URL containing the Session ID, ASP.NET is able to extract the Session ID and map the request to the appropriate Session data.

Let's take a look at the configuration settings used to enable these options.

Configuration Settings

The sessionState configuration settings within web.config or machine.config allow you to configure how you take advantage of the Session features previously described. The following sample web.config file mirrors the defaults found in machine.config:

```
<configuration>
  <system.web>
    <sessionState
      mode="InProc"
      stateConnectionString="tcpip=127.0.0.1:42424"
      stateNetworkTimeout="10"
      sqlConnectionString="data source=127.0.0.1; user id=sa;password="
      cookieless="false"
      timeout="20"
      lockAttributes="sqlConnectionString, stateConnectionString"
    />
  </system.web>
</configuration>
```

The `<sessionState>` configuration setting supports the following attributes (we will show their use shortly):

❑   mode: The mode setting supports four options: Off, InProc, SQLServer, and StateServer. The InProc option, the default, enables in-process state management. In-process state management is identical to the behavior of ASP Session. There are also two options for out-of-process state management: a Windows NT Service (StateServer) and SQL Server (SQLServer).

❑   stateConnectionString: Identifies the TCP/IP address and port used to communicate with the Windows NT Service providing state management facilities. You must configure the stateConnectionString when mode is set to StateServer.

❑   stateNetworkTimeout: Controls the timeout, in seconds, allowed when attempting to store state in an out-of-process session store.

❑   sqlConnectionString: Identifies the database connection string that names the database used for mode="SQLServer". This includes both the TCP/IP address identified by data source as well as a username and password to connect to the SQL Server database.

❑   cookieless: Enables support for Session key management without requiring HTTP cookies.

❑   timeout: This option controls the life of a user's Session. timeout is a sliding value, and on each request the timeout period is reset to the current time plus the timeout value.

❑   lockAttributes (**ASP.NET 1.1**): This option allows the server owner the lock the attribute values an not allow these values to be overridden in child applications. For example, locking the out-of-process SQL Server connection string would force all users to use the same SQL Server database as opposed to allowing them to specify their own. This is not enabled by default.

Next, let's implement some of the common scenarios encountered when building applications using Session state.

Supporting Web Farms

By default, ASP.NET ships with Session state configured to store Session data in the same process as ASP.NET. This is identical to how ASP Session data is stored. The session web farm feature allows several front-end web servers to share a common storage point for Session data, rather than each web server maintaining its own copy. This creates a scenario in which the client making the request can be serviced from any server within the server farm. Additionally this allows an individual server's process to recycle and access to `Session` data to be maintained.

There are two options for out-of-process `Session` state: a Windows NT Service that stores the data (in memory) in a separate process from ASP.NET (either on the same server or on a different server), and a SQL Server option that stores the data in SQL Server. Let's look at how to configure both of these options.

Out-Of-Process – Windows NT Service

To support the out-of-process Windows Service option (`mode="StateServer"`), you first need to decide which server is going to run the Windows Service used for `Session` state storage. ASP.NET ships with a Windows Service named `aspnet_state` that needs to be running so that `Session` functions in `mode="StateServer"`.

The service can be started by opening a command prompt and entering the following:

```
> net start aspnet_state
The ASP.NET State Service service is starting.
The ASP.NET State Service service was started successfully.
```

Alternatively, you can configure the service using the Services and Applications Microsoft Management Console MMC snap-in (available from Start | Settings | Control Panel | Administrative Tools | Computer Management). If you view the Services item in this tool, you are presented with a list of the available services on the server as shown in Figure 13-3:

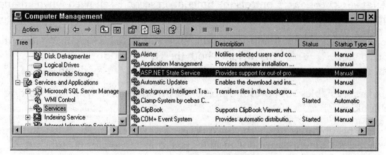

Figure 13-3

Right-clicking on the ASP.NET State Service item opens up a menu that allows you to configure how this service is to be run. You can select the start-up options (whether Windows should automatically start this service for you) as well as use the toolbar Start and Stop buttons to enable or disable this service.

Once the service has been started, ASP.NET must be configured to use this particular service. This is done through your configuration file. You need to tell ASP.NET which server and port to use for communication with the ASP.NET State service, as well as the fact that the Windows Service state option is to be used.

Here is the `web.config`, with the necessary settings highlighted:

```
<configuration>
  <system.web>
    <sessionState
      mode="StateServer"
      stateConnectionString="tcpip=127.0.0.1:42424"
      stateNetworkTimeout="10"
      sqlConnectionString="data source=127.0.0.1; user id=sa;password="
      cookieless="false"
      timeout="20"
    />
  </system.web>
</configuration>
```

In this example, ASP.NET Session is directed to use the Windows Service for state management on the local server (the address 127.0.0.1 is the TCP/IP loop-back address).

The default port that aspnet_state uses to communicate is 42424; you can configure this to any other port you wish, but this configuration must be done through the system registry. To configure the port to 100, run RegEdit.exe and expand HKEY_LOCAL_MACHINE | SYSTEM | CurrentControlSet | Services | aspnet_state | Parameters. Within Parameters, you will find a Port setting, which allows you to configure the TCP/IP port which the aspnet_state service uses to communicate as shown in Figure 13-4:

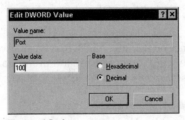

Figure 13-4

In ASP.NET version 1.1, due to security reasons, only local machines can connect to the state server. To allow only non-local host requests in ASP.NET 1.1, open the same registry entry for the port setting HKLM\SYSTEM\CurrentControlSet\Services\aspnet_state\Parameters\. Change AllowRemoteConnection to 1.

To enable state for all of the servers in a server farm to point back to a single state server, you need to change the IP address to reflect the IP address of the server running the Windows NT Service, and each of the server's machine keys must be identical. This last point is very important. Each server, by default, is set to auto-generate its own machine key. This machine key is used to encrypt data or to create unique serverspecific values for data (known as hashing).

The ID used for Session state is created using the machine key. Thus, for the key to be understood by all the servers in the farm, the servers need the same machine key. The machine key has other applications besides sessionState and we will cover it in more detail later in the chapter.

Out-Of-Process – SQL Server

Configuring ASP.NET to support SQL Server for Session state is just as simple as configuring the Windows Service. The only difference is that we will use SQL Server. To configure SQL Server, you need to run a T-SQL script that ships with ASP.NET – InstallSqlState.sql. A T-SQL script (called UninstallSqlState.sql), to uninstall ASP.NET SQL Server support, is also included.

ASP.NET ships with a lightweight version of SQL Server 2000 that has several limitations (such as limited connections, throttled transactions) but is a normal working version of SQL Server 2000 for all practical purposes. You can use this developer version of SQL Server 2000 for development purposes, but to deploy and use SQL Server for state management in a production server farm, use SQL Server 2000 Standard or Enterprise versions for optimal performance.

To run the InstallSqlState.sql script, we will use a tool that ships with SQL Server (and MSDE); OSQL.exe. OSQL allows us to apply a T-SQL script to a SQL Server. The InstallSqlState.sql T-SQL script creates several stored procedures and creates several temporary databases for ASP.NET Session to use.

Version 1.1 of ASP.NET ships with another set of SQL Scripts for storing the session data in permanent SQL table (as opposed to using SQL Server temporary tables). These scripts are named InstallPersistSqlState.sql and UninstallPersistSqlState.sql. Use these scripts to setup replication or failover for Session data – SQL replication/failover support does not exist for data stored in SQL Server temporary tables.

The script only needs to be run once on any given SQL Server, and we will need sa-level (administrator) access to run the script. To run the script, open a command prompt and navigate to the \WINNT\Microsoft.NET\Framework\[version]\ directory and type:

```
> OSQL -S localhost -U sa -P <InstallSqlState.sql
1> 2> 3> 1> 2> 3> 4> 5> 6> 1> 2> 3> 4> 5> 6> 1> 2> 3> 4> 5> 6> 7>
8> 1> 2> 3> 4> 5> 6> 7> 8> 1> 2> 3> 4> 5> 6> 7> 8> 1> 2> 3> 4> 5> 6> 7> 8> 9> 10>
11> 12> 13> 14> 15> 16> 17> 18> 19> 20> 21> 22> 23> 1> 2> 3> 4> The CREATE
DATABASE process is allocating 0.63 MB on disk 'ASPState'.
The CREATE DATABASE process is allocating 0.49 MB on disk 'ASPState_log'.
1> 2> 3> 1> 2> 3> 1> 2> 1> 2> 3> 4> 5> 6> 7> 8> 9> 10> 11> 12> 13> 1> 2> 3> 4> 5>
6> 7> 8> 9> 10> 11> 12> 13> 14> 15> 16> 17> 18> 19> 20> 21> 22> 23> 24> 25> 26>
27> 28> 29> 30> 31> 1> 2> 3> 4> 5> 6> 7> 1> 2> 3> (1 row affected)
Type added.
1> 2> 3> (1 row affected)
Type added.
1> 2> 3> (1 row affected)
Type added.
1> 2> 3> (1 row affected)
Type added.
1> 2> 3> (1 row affected)
Type added.
1> 2> 3> 4> 5> 6> 7> 8> 9> 10> 11> 12> 13> 14> 15> 16> 17> 18> 19> 20> 21> 22> 1>
2> 3> 4> 5> 6> 7> 8> 9> 10> 11> 12> 13> 14> 15> 16> 17> 18> 19> 20> 21> 22> 23>
24> 25> 26> 27> 28> 29> 30> 31> 32> 33> 34> 35> 36> 37> 1> 2> 3> 4> 5> 6> 7> 8> 9>
10> 11> 12> 13> 14> 15> 16> 17> 18> 19> 20> 21> 22> 23> 24> 25> 26> 27> 28> 29>
30> 31> 32> 33> 34> 35> 36> 37> 38> 39> 40> 41> 42>
```

Next, you need to change the configuration settings to use SQL Server (highlighted). First, you set mode to "SQLServer" and then configure the sqlConnectionString to point to the server that has the T-SQL script installed:

```
<configuration>
  <system.web>
    <sessionState
      mode="SQLServer"
      stateConnectionString="tcpip=127.0.0.1:42424"
      stateNetworkTimeout="10"
      sqlConnectionString="data source=127.0.0.1;
                           user id=session;password=&363test"
      cookieless="false"
      timeout="20"
    />
  </system.web>
</configuration>
```

Session data stored in SQL is inaccessible to other applications. It is serialized as a protected type and should not be read or modified by applications other than ASP.NET.

> **ASP.NET accesses the data stored in SQL via stored procedures. By default, session data is stored in the TempDB database. The stored procedures may be modified, for example, if we wished to store to tables other than TempDB. However, this is an option best saved for DBAs.**

From the developer's point of view, writing code that uses Session in any of the preceding modes is completely transparent. However, we should briefly discuss choosing a mode, as the mode selection can impact on the performance of the application.

Choosing a Mode

There are three modes from which you can choose when building an application:

❑ **In-process (default)**: In-process will perform best because the Session data is kept within the ASP.NET process, and local memory access will always be faster than having to go out-of-process. Additional reasons include web applications hosted on a single server, applications in which the user is guaranteed to be redirected to the correct server, or when Session data is not critical (in the sense that it can be easily re-created).

❑ **Windows Service**: This mode is best used when performance is important and there are multiple web servers servicing requests. With this out-of-process mode, you get the performance of reading from memory and the reliability of a separate process that manages the state for all servers.

❑ **SQL Server**: This mode is best used when the reliability of the data is fundamental to the stability of the application, as the data is stored in SQL Server. The performance isn't as fast as the Windows Service, but the tradeoff is the higher level of reliability.

Now that we have examined the supported options for web farms, let's turn to another one of the great new features of ASP.NET `Session`: support for clients that don't accept HTTP cookies.

Cookieless Session

Since HTTP is a stateless environment, both the client and the server need to maintain a key in order to maintain state across requests through `Session`. This key is used to identify the client's `Session` across requests. The server can then use the key to access the data stored for that user. By default, the server gives the client a key using an HTTP cookie. On subsequent requests to that server, the client will present the HTTP cookie and the server then has access to the session key.

However, some clients choose not to accept HTTP cookies for a variety of reasons, a common one being the perceived privacy issue. When this happens, the site has to either *adapt* and not support cookies (and `Session`), or build the application to not require the use of `Session`. A third option, first provided with IIS 4, is an ISAPI filter that can extract the session ID out of the cookie and pass it as part of the URL. This concept is supported by ASP.NET as a first class feature. This feature is known as cookieless `Session` state, and it works with any of the supported `mode` options.

Individual applications can be configured to support either cookie or cookieless states, but not both.

You can enable cookieless `Session` support by simply setting a flag in the configuration system (highlighted):

```
<configuration>
  <system.web>
    <sessionState
      mode="InProc"
      stateConnectionString="tcpip=127.0.0.1:42424"
      stateNetworkTimeout="10"
      sqlConnectionString="data source=127.0.0.1; user id=sa;password="
      cookieless="true"
      timeout="20"
    />
  </system.web>
</configuration>
```

As with all configuration changes in ASP.NET, these settings are applied immediately. After changing cookieless from `false` (the default) to `true`, the session ID is embedded in the URL of the page, as shown in Figure 13-5. As you can see, the session ID `reqe3wvsxfoabvilmkmvq2p` is embedded within the URL:

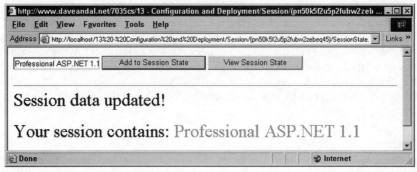

Figure 13-5

The following source in Visual Basic .NET shows this. You will notice that no special changes have been made to the sourcecode to support embedding the Session ID in the URL:

```
<Script runat=server>
  Public Sub Session_Add(sender As Object, e As EventArgs)
    Session("cart") = text1.Value
    span1.InnerHtml = "Session data updated! <P>" + _
                      "Your session contains: <font color=red>" + _
                      Session("cart") + "</font>"
  End Sub

  Public Sub CheckSession(sender As Object, e As EventArgs)
    If (Session("cart") Is Nothing) Then
      span1.InnerHtml = "NOTHING, SESSION DATA LOST!"
    Else
      span1.InnerHtml = "Your session contains:" + _
                        "<font color=red>" + Session("cart") + "</font>"
    End If
  End Sub
</Script>
<form runat=server>
  <input id=text1 type=text runat=server>
  <input type=submit runat=server OnServerClick="Session_Add"
         Value="Add to Session State">
  <input type=submit runat=server OnServerClick="CheckSession"
         Value="View Session State">
</form>
<a href="SessionState_cs.aspx">C# Example</A>
<hr size=1>
<font size=6><span id=span1 runat=server/></font>
```

Additionally, for relative URLs (as viewed by the browser) within the page, such as:

```
<a href="SessionState_cs.aspx">C# Example</a>
```

ASP.NET will automatically add the session ID into the URL. The client receives the following link:

```
<a href="/(yxxn2w555rn13henl2sxd055)/SessionState_cs.aspx">C# Example</a>
```

Note that the ID is added directly after the name of the application root. In this example, you can see that /Session is marked as an application. The new features for Session state in ASP.NET are very powerful. You can configure Session to be stored in a separate process from the ASP.NET worker process, which allows the Session data to be available if a server farm and in the rare case that the web server crashes. In addition to the great support for out-of-process Sessions state, support for cookieless Sessions has also been added. Cookieless session allows you to use Session for clients that don't accept HTTP cookies. Next, let's look at a feature of ASP.NET that replaces Response.Write debugging for ASP pages.

Tracing

Tracing is a new feature introduced with ASP.NET, previously absent in ASP. This feature allows you to trace the execution of an application and later view the trace results. Let's see an example in VB:

```
<Script
runat="server">
  Public Function Add(a As Integer, b As Integer) As Integer
    Return a + b
  End Function
</Script>
Call the Add routine: 4 + 5 = <%=Add(4,5)%>
```

The output of this is:

Call the Add routine: 4 + 5 = 9

Classic ASP Tracing

Although a simple example, what if within the Add function you wished to know the parameters of a and b as the code was executing? ASP developers usually add Response.Write statements in their code to trace the actions of their code as it's executed:

```
<Script runat="server">
Public Function Add(a As Integer, b As Integer) As Integer
  Response.Write("Inside Add() a: " + a.ToString() + "<BR>")
  Response.Write("Inside Add() b: " + b.ToString() + "<BR>")
  Return a + b
End Function
</Script>
Call the Add routine: 4 + 5 = <BR><%=Add(4,5)%>
```

The output of which is:

Call the Add routine: 4 + 5 =

Inside Add() a: 4

Inside Add() b: 5

9

Although this works well, it does introduce unnecessary code into the application. This usually results in bugs that break deployed applications. Examples of this include SQL statements, configuration flags, or output status details, which are all items that were never intended to be shown. You also cannot trace a deployed application, since the users would see the `Response.Write` trace results!

ASP.NET Tracing

Using ASP.NET's new tracing functionality, the `Response.Write` statements are replaced with `Trace.Write` statements:

```
<Script runat="server">
  Public Function Add(a As Integer, b As Integer) As Integer
    Trace.Write("Inside Add() a: ", a.ToString())
    Trace.Write("Inside Add() b: ", b.ToString())
    Return a + b
  End Function
</Script>
Call the Add routine: 4 + 5 = <%=Add(4,5)%>
```

If you request this page, using the default settings of ASP.NET (by default, trace output is not enabled), you would see the following result in the browser:

Call the Add routine: 4 + 5 = 9

Think of tracing as 'debug mode' for ASP.NET applications, since tracing code can be left in your scripts and when tracing is disabled, the trace statements are simply ignored.

Viewing Trace Output

To view the results of the `Trace.Write` statements, you have two options:

❑   Enable page tracing

❑   Enable application tracing

Once tracing is enabled, by default the results are only presented to local clients – this is configurable, as you will see in a moment.

Enable Page Tracing

You can enable page tracing by adding a directive to the top of the ASP.NET Page:

```
<%@ Page Trace="true" %>
  <Script runat="server">
    Public Function Add(a As Integer, b As Integer) As Integer
      Trace.Write("Inside Add() a: ", a.ToString())
      Trace.Write("Inside Add() b: ", b.ToString())
      Return a + b
    End Function
  </Script>
Call the Add routine: 4 + 5 = <%=Add(4,5)%>
```

639

This will add a trace output to the bottom of the requested page. Included with this output, as shown in Figure 13-6, are our `Trace.Write` outputs:

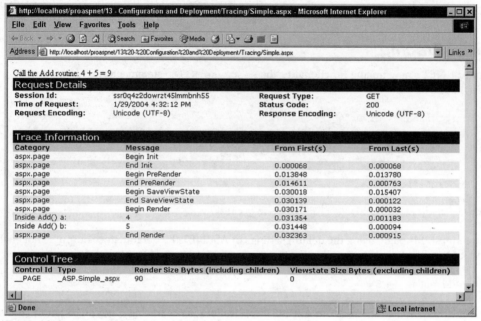

Figure 13-6

Enable Application Tracing

Adding `Trace="true"` statements to the top of ASP.NET pages isn't difficult, but what if you had a larger application consisting of several ASP.NET pages? Or, what if you wanted to trace the output of your application and view the results, but at the same time not output the trace section at the end of each page? Application tracing allows you to accomplish all of this.

You can enable application tracing by creating a `web.config` file with trace settings in it for your web application:

```
<configuration>
  <system.web>
    <trace
        enabled="true"
        requestLimit="10"
        pageOutput="false"
        traceMode="SortByTime"
        localOnly="true"
    />
  </system.web>
</configuration>
```

You can set the enabled flag to true (the inherited machine.config default is false), request the page, and then use a special tool to view the application traces; Trace.axd as shown in Figure 13-7:

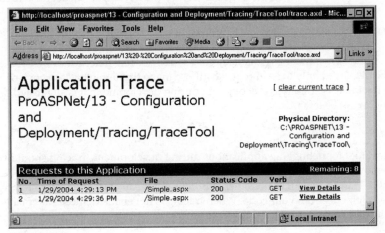

Figure 13-7

Trace.axd is a special HTTP Handler used to view trace output for an application. We will discuss this tool, tracing, and the Trace object in more detail in Chapter 22. Let's turn our attention to the configuration settings found in the web.config file we created.

Trace Configuration Settings

The <trace> section within the configuration file provides us with some additional options not available when enabling tracing on a page. These options include:

❑ enabled: This option can be set to true or false. Tracing is enabled or disabled at an application-level. If you set enabled to "false", page tracing is still supported using the Trace directive discussed earlier. This value is set to false by default.

```
enabled="[true | false]"
```

❑ requestLimit: The total number of trace requests to keep cached in memory on a per application basis. Tracing exposes a special resource, trace.axd, used to view trace output when pageOutput is set to false. By default, the value of requestLimit is 10.

```
requestLimit = "[int]"
```

❑ pageOutput: When tracing is enabled through the configuration file, the administrator is given the option to either enable or disable tracing on each page. pageOutput tracing enables details to be traced for every page within an application. However, pageOutput tracing may be turned off while application level tracing is still enabled (enabled = "true"). This keeps trace requests in memory such that they are available via trace.axd but not within the output of a page. By default, pageOutput is set to false.

```
pageOutput = "[true | false]"
```

❑ traceMode: The tracemode setting gives control over how trace detail information is output. Data may be sorted by time or category, where category is either the settings made by the system or the Trace.Write settings enabled by the developer. By default, traceMode is set to SortByTime.

```
traceMode = "[SortByTime | SortByCategory]"
```

❑ localOnly: When tracing is enabled, the localOnly flag determines whether the trace output is to be displayed only to local requests (those made through http://localhost) or for any request. Since tracing is best used as a debug tool during development, it is suggested that the default setting (true) be left as is.

```
localOnly = "[true | false]"
```

Tracing is a great tool for debugging applications during development. Tracing should not, however, be enabled for deployed applications. When tracing is enabled, it consumes resources, whereas applications should be kept as lean and mean as possible. This does not mean that you need to remove the Trace.Write statements from your code. When tracing is not enabled, these statements are ignored and do not affect the performance of the application.

For deployed applications, the recommendation is to use the Windows Event Log for application logging/tracing. A sample use of the Windows Event Log is shown for the Application_OnError event discussed in the previous chapter.

If you did any amount of coding in ASP, you will no doubt remember those helpful error codes, such as 0x800A01A8. ASP.NET makes some dramatic improvements on the level of detail available when errors occur, however, we don't always want that type of rich data displayed to end users. With ASP.NET's *custom errors* configuration option, we can control how ASP.NET displays application error messages.

Custom Errors

When a runtime or design-time error occurs within the application, ASP.NET will display a very helpful error page. For example, a compilation error (such as forgetting to declare that C# is used) generates an error page that describes the error, highlights the line of code, provides detailed compiler output, and the complete source for the page as shown in Figure 13-8.

While this is useful for aiding in debugging the application, you obviously wouldn't want to display this type of error detail to end-users. By default, this type of error detail is only available to requests to http://localhost:

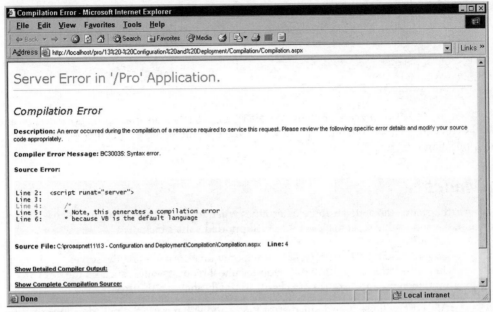

Figure 13-8

Requests from other domains will display a helpful error page, without the details, that describes how to enable the ASP.NET application to show richer error messages to remote clients as shown in Figure 13-9:

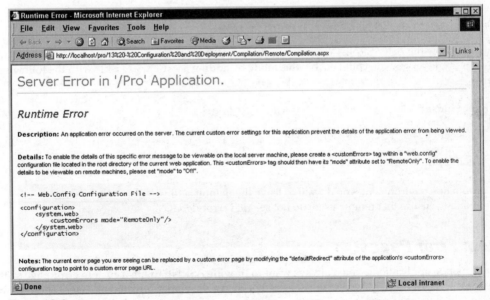

Figure 13-9

This error page describes the `<customErrors>` section of configuration:

```
<configuration>
  <system.web>
    <customErrors mode="Off" />
  </system.web>
</configuration>
```

The `<customErrors>` section defines how ASP.NET behaves when an application error occurs, and provides you with a variety of options for how you want to handle these and other types of errors for your application.

Error Modes

When an error occurs, the `mode` attribute determines whether an ASP.NET error message is displayed. By default, the `mode` value is set to `RemoteOnly`. Supported values include:

❑ `RemoteOnly`: ASP.NET error page is shown only to users accessing the server on the same machine (the localhost or 127.0.0.1). Non-localhost requests will first check the `<error>` settings, then use the `defaultRedirect`, or finally show an IIS error.

❑ `On`: ASP.NET will use user-defined error pages and will not use the rich, developer oriented ASP.NET error page. If a custom error page is not provided, ASP.NET will show the error page describing how to enable remote viewing of errors.

❑ `Off`: ASP.NET will always use ASP.NET's rich error page, with stack traces and compilation issues, when an error occurs.

Always Showing ASP.NET Error Pages

To always show the rich ASP.NET error page, such as cases when a team of developers are working against a single server, you could enable this mode by adding a `web.config` file with the following setting:

```
<configuration>
  <system.web>
    <customErrors mode="Off" />
  </system.web>
</configuration>
```

In a production environment, you'd want to leave the default setting, `mode="RemoteOnly"`, or `mode="On"` to ensure that remote users do not see rich error detail.

Custom Error Pages

For production applications, you'd always want to provide ASP.NET with a custom error page so that the end-user sees a friendly, helpful message rather than a developer-oriented message. There are two ways in which you can support custom error pages:

❑ **Default redirects**: A defined error page that the client is redirected to whenever an error occurs on the system

❑ **Custom redirects**: A defined error page that the client is redirected to whenever a specific HTTP error occurs – for example, the 404 Not Found error

Let's look at both of these starting with default redirects.

Default Redirects

The `defaultRedirect` attribute of `<customErrors>` names the page to be redirected to when an error occurs:

```
<configuration>
  <system.web>
    <customErrors defaultRedirect="/defaultError.aspx"/>
  </system.web>
</configuration>
```

In this example, clients are redirected to the `defaultError.aspx` page whenever an error occurs. This only applies to ASP.NET-specific requests, so if you requested `SomeRandomFile.aspx` – an ASP.NET file that doesn't exist on the *server* – you would be redirected to `defaultError.aspx`. However, if you requested `SomeRandomFile.asp` – an ASP file that doesn't exist *at all* – you'd be redirected to the IIS-defined error page.

What if there is an error in the page we direct to (`defaultError.aspx`) when an error occurs? This could possibly lead to a circular reference; the page we are directed to causes an error and we are sent back to the same page again. ASP.NET detects this and will *not* cause the browser to continuously request the error page.

Custom Redirects

You can also send users to a custom error page depending upon the type of error that occurred. For instance, in case of a 404 Not Found error or an Access Denied error, the client can be routed to a specific error page tailored with an appropriate response – for example 'Sorry, but you must be a valid user to access our site.'

You can create that page, and then instruct ASP.NET to redirect HTTP requests that generate the matching `statusCode` value for the HTTP status code. This is done through an `<error>` sub-element of `<customErrors>`. `<error>` supports two attributes:

❑ `statusCode`: The HTTP status code to match. If a match is found, the request is redirected to the value defined in `redirect`.

❑ `redirect`: The page that clients are redirected to.

Let's look at a compound example that sets a `defaultRedirect` page, leaves `mode` to the default setting of `RemoteOnly`, and defines a `<error>` element for 404 Page Not Found errors.

The `<error>` settings only apply to ASP.NET requests, so the earlier `SomeRandomFile.aspx` example will now be redirected to `FileNotFound.htm`.

```
<configuration>
  <system.web>
    <customErrors defaultRedirect="/defaultError.aspx" mode="RemoteOnly">
      <error statusCode="404" redirect="/FileNotFound.htm"/>
    </customErrors>
  </system.web>
</configuration>
```

Configuring IIS and ASP.NET to Support Same Error Pages

It is possible to configure ASP.NET and IIS to support the same set of error pages. For example, IIS uses the same error page for 404 errors, located at \WINNT\Help\iisHelp\common\404b.htm.

You could create a virtual folder called Errors in the web site, and set the physical path of this virtual folder to \WINNT\Help\iisHelp\common\. You could then modify your ASP.NET <error> as follows:

```
<configuration>
  <system.web>
    <customErrors defaultRedirect="/defaultError.aspx" mode="RemoteOnly">
      <error statusCode="404" redirect="/Errors/404b.htm "/>
    </customErrors>
  </system.web>
</configuration>
```

You could also do the reverse and set up IIS to support an ASP.NET error page, 404.aspx for example. Please see the IIS documentation for how to configure IIS custom errors to specific URLs.

ASP.NET's error handling system is very rich. You can provide a default custom error page to direct all errors to, or can customize the error page depending upon the error case (404 File Not Found, for example). Additionally, you have control over the type of error page shown to a type of request. The default mode, RemoteOnly, shows custom (user-friendly) errors to remote users, but shows rich ASP.NET errors to local clients.

As you can see, ASP.NET is attempting to address many of the shortcomings of ASP. Another of the shortcomings it addresses is authentication and authorization. That is, how to control access to resources served by the web server. Unless we used a custom solution, such as Site Server 3.0 or Commerce Server 2000 (and sometimes with these too), we had to have a good fundamental understanding of Windows security.

ASP.NET still has great support for Windows security, but it extends the options to include Microsoft Passport and HTML Forms-based authentication, as well as providing all the hooks. This allows us to build custom authentication and authorization solutions such as the Application_OnAuthenticate event discussed in the previous chapter.

Application authentication and authorization is, of course, also configured through the ASP.NET configuration system.

Authentication and Authorization

In ASP.NET, authentication is the process of establishing identity between the server and a request, to clearly establish that all the server really has is the data sent to it over HTTP. In other words, the server knows nothing about the client other than what the client sends the server. This is important since the application making a request is not always a browser. In fact, it would be wise to get out of the mentality that only web browsers will be making requests against your server.

To establish the identity of a request, the request must follow a protocol that enables a predefined set of rules to be adhered to. For example, almost all HTTP servers support clear text/basic authentication, the pop-up dialog box that asks for a username and password. Clear text/basic authentication follows a protocol such that the browser can properly formulate and encode the request in the format that the server expects.

ASP.NET provides four distinct options for assigning identity to a request:

- ❑ **Forms authentication**: Allows you to authenticate requests using HTTP cookies and HTML forms. You can validate identity against any resource.

- ❑ **Passport authentication**: Uses Microsoft's single sign-on Passport identity system.

- ❑ **Windows authentication**: Allows you to authenticate requests using Windows Challenge/Response semantics. This consists of the server initially denying access to a request (a challenge) and the requestor responding with a hashed value of their Windows username/password, which the server can then choose to authenticate and/or authorize.

- ❑ **Custom authentication**: Allows you to roll your own authentication system.

Authentication

ASP.NET's authentication system is very flexible. It supports four modes and various settings for each of these modes. The default mode is `Windows`, but you can configure support for the other modes using the `mode` attribute of the `<authentication>` element:

This attribute has four acceptable settings; `Windows`, `Forms`, `Passport`, and `None`. This value determines the authentication mode that ASP.NET will enforce. The default is `Windows`. If the `mode` is set to `Forms`, a child element of `<authentication>` (called `<forms>`) allows you to define behaviors for forms authentication.

Custom HTML Forms Login

Forms authentication allows you to use HTML forms to request credentials, and then issue an HTTP cookie that the requestor may use for identity on subsequent requests. ASP.NET provides the infrastructure to support this, but also gives the flexibility to choose how you wish to validate credentials.

For example, once you obtain the username and password that has been sent to the ASP.NET application via HTTP `POST` (rather than HTTP `GET` as it passes the data on the query string), you can validate the credentials against an XML file, a database, an in memory structure, an LDAP directory, or even through a web service!

The validation of credentials is completely up to you. Once the credentials are validated, you can call some of the APIs provided by forms authentication to issue an HTTP cookie to the requestor. On subsequent requests, the cookie is provided along with the request body, and ASP.NET can use the information in the cookie to recreate a valid identity.

The <forms> element has the following attributes:

❑ name: Forms authentication uses a cookie that contains an ID of the authenticated user. The name of that cookie is defined by the name value of <forms>. The default setting is .ASPXAUTH.

❑ loginUrl: When a request comes into ASP.NET with forms authentication enabled, and the request doesn't present a cookie (new user) or has an invalid value within the cookie, ASP.NET will redirect the request to an ASP.NET page capable of logging in the user and issuing the cookie. loginUrl allows you to configure this value. By default, it is set to login.aspx and you must provide *your* implementation of this file.

❑ protection: The value within the cookie can optionally be encrypted or sent in plain text. For sites that simply use forms authentication as a means of identifying the user, you might choose to use no cookie encryption. Valid settings for protection are All, None, Encryption, and Validation.

❑ timeout: Specifies the time in minutes that the cookie is valid for. The timeout of the cookie is reset on each request to the current time plus the timeout value. The default value is 30 minutes.

❑ path: Specifies the path value of the cookie. By default this is set to /, the root of the server. Cookies are only visible to the path and server that sets the cookie. ASP.NET forms authentication chooses to use the root of the server as the path, since the path value in a cookie is case-sensitive.

❑ requireSSL (**ASP.NET 1.1**): Defaults to false, but when set to true requires that the Forms Authentication cookie is sent using SSL. Using SSL for sending the cookie provides a better measure of security.

Within <forms> there is also a <credentials> sub-element, which can *optionally* be used to define users.

> As you will learn in Chapter 14, when we use forms authentication, you can validate users from any data store.

Defining Users for HTML Forms Authentication

Nested within the <forms> element is a <credentials> element. <credentials> allows you to define users (identities) and passwords directly within your configuration file, although this is completely optional. You can choose to take advantage of this section, or can choose to define identities in another location.

> **Use of the <credentials> section is not required. Instead, the validation of the username and password can be custom-coded, such as validation of username/password pairs stored in a database.**

The <credentials> section allows you to define <user> entries. This section is used to optionally store your usernames and passwords in the configuration file. <credentials> supports a single attribute, passwordFormat. This attribute tells ASP.NET the password format used by the password value of <user>. Supported values include SHA1, MD5, and Clear. However, simply setting this value does not automatically encrypt the value of password. It is the developer/administrator's responsibility to add the value of the SHA1 or MD5 hashed password into the configuration file.

Nested within <credentials> are <user> entries. The <user> entries are used to define valid usernames and passwords against which to authenticate. A <user> entry contains two attributes – name and password – that together are compared against when we attempt to authenticate requests.

If you choose to store your usernames and passwords in the configuration file, you are provided with several options for password hiding. The <credentials> tag supports a single passwordFormat attribute. This attribute can be set to one of three values:

❑ Clear: Value of the password for <user> entries is stored in clear text. For example, password="password".

❑ SHA1: Value of the password for <user> entries is stored as a SHA1 hash. For example, password="5B9FEBC2D7429C8F2002721484A71A84C12730C7" (value is password). Hashing will be discussed in the next chapter.

❑ MD5: Value of the password for <user> entries is stored as an MD5 hash. For example, password="2BF3023F1259B0C2F607E4302556BD72" (value is password).

Rather than storing clear text values within the <credentials> section for <user> entries, you can store hashes of the password. If your configuration file is compromised, the users' passwords are safer than if they were stored as clear text.

An example of storing the username and password in the credentials section is shown next. The passwordFormat is set to SHA1 and the value for password represents a SHA1 hash of the user's password:

```
<configuration>
  <system.web>
    <authentication mode="Forms">
      <forms name=".ASPXAUTH" loginUrl="login.aspx"
             protection="all"  timeout="30" path="/" >
        <credentials passwordFormat="SHA1">
          <user name="SomeUser" password="83jksjfi3983ksl23dscdf"/>
        </credentials>
      </forms>
    </authentication>
  </system.web>
</configuration>
```

Passport Authentication

When Passport is installed on the server, ASP.NET's Passport integration can be utilized to authenticate users, based on whether they present a valid Passport with their request. The Passport is a token granted to a given request that enables the request to be authenticated by applications that trust Passport IDs.

The token is stored in a site-specific cookie after authenticating with `login.passport.com`. You can use the `redirectUrl` attribute of the `<passport>` authentication option to control where non-authenticated Passport users are directed. For example:

```
<passport redirectUrl="/Passport/SignIn.aspx">
```

Depending upon how you configure your site's authorization (discussed next), this may be the only page that Passport users are allowed to access.

We will explore authentication in more detail in Chapter 14.

Authorization

The `<authorization>` configuration settings allow you to set access control permissions, defined as `<allow>` and `<deny>` settings, used to control access to resources. Both follow the same format for entries:

```
<[allow | deny] users="users | * | ?" roles="roles"/>
```

For example:

```
<configuration>
  <system.web>
    <authentication mode="Forms">
      <forms name=".ASPXAUTH" loginUrl="login.aspx"
             protection="all" timeout="30" path="/" >
      </forms>
    </authentication>
    <authorization>
      <allow users="Stephen, Brian, Rob" roles="Administrator, Customer" />
      <deny users="?" roles="BlackList" />
    </authorization>
  </system.web>
</configuration>
```

Note the ordering of the `<allow>` and `<deny>`. This controls how the authorization is enforced, `<deny>` should follow the `<allow>`.

In the configuration settings, we define authorization settings that allow the users `Stephen`, `Brian`, and `Rob` as well as the `Administrator` and `Customer` roles. However, anonymous users (identified by `?`) and users that belong to the `BlackList` role/group will be denied access. Any users or roles that are denied access will be redirected to the `loginUrl` specified in the authentication settings, since the server will attempt to re-authenticate the user.

Web Services

ASP.NET web services allow you to easily expose programmable application logic over the Web using *Simple Object Access Protocol* (*SOAP*). Developers who want to use a web service do not need to know a thing about the implementation of our service. Rather, they simply need to know how to call our service using SOAP and that they will get a SOAP reply in return, if the application is configured to send SOAP replies.

ASP.NET provides a flexible framework for building web services. As part of that framework, you have the ability to configure aspects of ASP.NET web services. Although there are other configuration options for web services, the only one we will address is changing the ASP.NET page used to create the web service Help page:

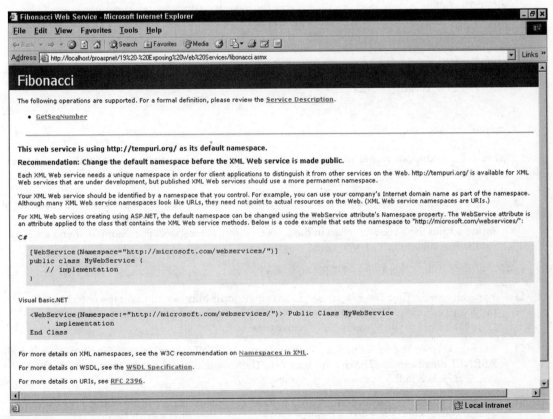

Figure 13-10

The ASP.NET page used to create this view of our web service can be found at `WINNT\Microsoft.NET\Framework\[version]\CONFIG\DefaultWSDLHelpGenerator.aspx`. To customize `DefaultWSDLHelpGenerator.aspx`, you can instruct ASP.NET to use the custom file:

```
<configuration>
  <system.web>
    <webServices>
      <wsdlHelpGenerator href="MyWsdlHelpGenerator.aspx" />
    </webServices>
  </system.web>
</configuration>
```

You could use this `web.config` file in your application and instruct ASP.NET to use a custom template page used to describe an ASP.NET web service.

Internationalization and Encoding

The settings defined within `<globalization>` allow us to configure the culture and encoding options, in other words, the code page used by a request and the code page used by a response for the application. The following `web.config` file mirrors the default settings found in `machine.config`:

```
<configuration>
  <system.web>
    <globalization
      requestEncoding="utf-8"
      responseEncoding="utf-8"
    />
  </system.web>
</configuration>
```

`<globalization>` supports five attributes that allow you to configure various globalization properties for your application:

❑ `requestEncoding`: The `requestEncoding` attribute allows you to set the assumed encoding of each incoming request; the default is `utf-8`. The values allowed for `requestEncoding` can be found within the `Encoding` class in the `System.Text` namespace. For example, if you wish to set the encoding to `utf-7`, you could simply set:

```
<globalization requestEncoding="utf-7"/>
```

❑ `responseEncoding`: The `responseEncoding` attribute allows you to set the encoding of outgoing responses. The default is `utf-8`. The values allowed can be found within the `Encoding` class in the `System.Text` namespace.

❑ `fileEncoding`: The `fileEncoding` attribute lets ASP.NET know the encoding type used for all ASP.NET file resources. The default is `utf-8`. The values allowed can be found within the `Encoding` class in the `System.Text` namespace.

❑ `culture`: The `culture` attribute is used to localize content using culture strings. For example, `en-US` represents United States English, while `en-GB` represents British English. This setting allows for strings to be formatted in both the appropriate language as well as using the appropriate format for dates, and so on.

❑ `uiCulture`: The `uiCulture` attribute is used to define the culture string, used to look up resources.

If, for example, you were building a web application that was used in France, you could configure the following globalization and culture settings:

```
<configuration>
  <system.web>
    <globalization
      requestEncoding="utf-8"
```

```
        responseEncoding="utf-8"
        culture="fr-FR"
        uiCulture="fr-FR"
    />
  </system.web>
</configuration>
```

You could then write a simple ASP.NET page using Visual Basic .NET to test your culture settings, such as ensuring that the current date value is formatted correctly:

```
<Script runat="server">
  Public Sub Page_Load(sender As Object, e As EventArgs)
    ' Use ToString("D") to format display: Week Day, Month Day, Year
    lblDateTime.Text = DateTime.Now.ToString("D")
  End Sub
</Script>
Server Date/Time: <b><asp:label id="lblDateTime" runat="server" /></b>
```

The default settings of culture, en-US, would display:

Server Date/Time: **Tuesday, January 08, 2002**

While the localized setting, using fr-FR, would display:

Server Date/Time: **mardi 8 janvier 2002**

Compilation Options

The settings defined in the <compilation> section of machine.config allow you to control some of the settings that ASP.NET uses to compile ASP.NET resources, such as ASP.NET pages. A common setting that you can change if you don't want Visual Basic .NET to be the default language, is the defaultLanguage option. This is where you can also add additional CLR compilers, such as COBOL or Perl. Within the <compilation> settings, you can also name the assemblies (compiled reusable code libraries) that ASP.NET will link to when compiling ASP.NET application files.

The following code is the default configuration from machine.config:

```
<configuration>
  <system.web>
    <compilation debug="false" explicit="true" defaultLanguage="vb">
      <compilers>
        <compiler language="c#;cs;csharp" extension=".cs"
                  type="Microsoft.CSharp.CSharpCodeProvider,System" />
        <compiler language="vb;visualbasic;vbscript" extension=".vb"
                  type="Microsoft.VisualBasic.VBCodeProvider,System" />
        <compiler language="js;jscript;javascript" extension=".js"
            type="Microsoft.JScript.JScriptCodeProvider,Microsoft.JScript" />
      </compilers>
      <assemblies>
        <add assembly="mscorlib"/>
        <add assembly="System"/>
```

```
            <add assembly="System.Web"/>
            <add assembly="System.Data"/>
            <add assembly="System.Web.Services"/>
            <add assembly="System.Xml"/>
            <add assembly="System.Drawing"/>
            <add assembly="*"/>
        </assemblies>
      </compilation>
    </system.web>
  </configuration>
```

The `<compilation>` tag supports the following attributes:

- ❑   debug
- ❑   defaultLanguage
- ❑   tempDirectory
- ❑   strict
- ❑   explicit
- ❑   batch
- ❑   batchTimeout
- ❑   maxBatchSize
- ❑   maxBatchGeneratedFileSize
- ❑   numRecompilesBeforeAppRestart

The debug attribute enables you to debug ASP.NET application files with the command line debugger or Visual Studio .NET. When you build a project with Visual Studio .NET, it creates its own web.config file and sets the debug to true or false depending on whether the project is in debug mode (a compile option). The default setting is false.

One of the side benefits of setting debug="true" is that ASP.NET will save the source file it generates, which you can then view! Let's look at an example of how this is done. ASP.NET takes a source file, such as the ASP.NET page in the following code snippet, compiles it, and saves the resulting .NET .dll file to disk in a directory under \WINNT\Microsoft.NET\Framework\[version]\Temporary ASP.NET Files\. Directories found within this directory are unique entities that ASP.NET creates automatically.

Let's look at what happens when we set debug="true". First, set debug to "true" in machine.config. Next, you need a simple ASP.NET page. This one is written in VB.NET:

```
<Script runat="server">
  Public Sub Page_Load(sender As Object, e As EventArgs)
    lblHello.Text = "Hello!"
  End Sub
</Script>
<b><asp:label id="lblHello" runat="server" /></b>
```

You then need to request this page through a browser. The URL that I'm using to make the request is http://localhost/Configuration/Compilation/Hello.aspx.

You can then navigate to the ...\Temporary ASP.NET Files\ directory. ASP.NET will create the directory based on the name of the web application. In this case, the Configuration folder is marked as a web application. If you do a file search in the Configuration folder for *.vb, you will find a single Visual Basic file. Mine is named ohgemg-9.0.vb – the name of the file is hashed to create a unique value. If you open this file in Visual Studio .NET, you'll see the screen depicted in Figure 13-11:

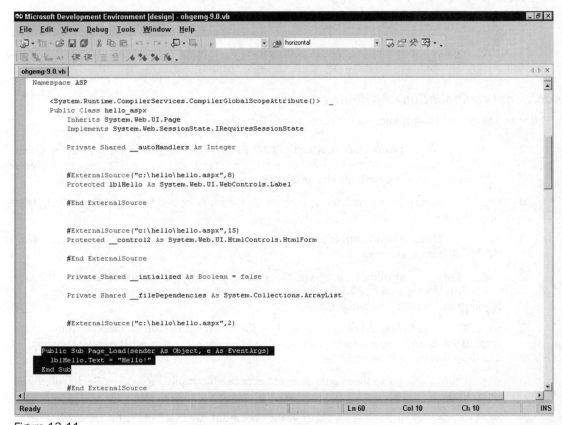

Figure 13-11

Here, you can see your code, lblHello.Text = "Hello!" along with the rest of the code that ASP.NET automatically generated to build the ASP.NET page. If you ever want to know what an ASP.NET page is doing behind the scenes, this is a great resource.

Changing the Default Language

The defaultLanguage attribute of <compilation> allows you to configure the default language that ASP.NET resources use. In code samples within this book, we have been using both page directives and script blocks. When we have shown code examples in C#, or other languages, we have used one of three options to override the default language of Visual Basic .NET.

655

The options are shown here:

```
<%@ Page Language="C#" %>
<%@ WebService Language="C#" %>
<Script Language="C#" runat=server>
  ...
</Script>
```

If you code your application in C#, set the `defaultLanguage` attribute in the `<compilation>` tag:

```
<compilation debug="false" explicit="true" defaultLanguage="C#">
```

The language value specified for `defaultLanguage` must be one of the supported languages named in a `<compiler>` sub-element of `<compilers>`.

Additional `<compilation>` Attributes

Here are the additional attributes for the `<compilation>` element:

❑ `tempDirectory`: The directory in which ASP.NET stores compiled assemblies. By default, this is `\WINNT\Microsoft.NET\Framework\[version]\Temporary ASP.NET Files\`. However, the temporary directory may be changed using this option.

❑ `strict`: This attribute controls the `Option Strict` compile option for Visual Basic .NET. By default it is set to `false`.

❑ `explicit`: This attribute controls the `Option Explicit` compile option for Visual Basic .NET. By default it is set to `true`.

❑ `batch`: The `batch` attribute controls whether batch compilation is supported. By default it is set to `true`, indicating that ASP.NET will attempt to compile all resources found in a given application upon the first request.

❑ `batchTimeout`: The period of time, in seconds, for batch compilation to complete. If the compilation cannot complete within the specified time, only the requested resource is compiled. The default value is 15 seconds.

❑ `maxBatchSize`: Controls the maximum number of batch compiled resources. By default this is set to 1000.

❑ `maxBatchGeneratedFileSize`: Controls the maximum size in KB of the file generated during batch compilation. By default this is set to 3000 KB.

❑ `numRecompilesBeforeAppRestart`: Controls the number of compilations allowed before the application is automatically recycled. The default is 15.

The `<compilation>` setting defines two sub-elements:

❑ `<compilers>`: Section pertaining to the supported .NET language compilers for ASP.NET

❑ `<assemblies>`: Section that allows you to define .NET assemblies that are added to the compilation of ASP.NET application files

<compilers>

The `<compilers>` element is the parent element for `<compiler>` entries. The `<compiler>` element, which is a sub-element of the `<compilers>` tag, allows you to name and configure the languages supported by ASP.NET. By default, ASP.NET supports the three languages that .NET ships with (Visual Basic .NET, C#, JScript .Net).

The `<compiler>` element has four attributes:

- ❏ `language`: The value used when you name the language from `Language = [setting]` within your code files

- ❏ `extension`: Names the extension for the code files when using a codebehind model

- ❏ `type`: Both the `language` and `extension` settings are used so that ASP.NET knows the class named in the type attribute to use to compile the resource

- ❏ `warningLevel`: Controls the compiler warning level setting

For example, to include support for Perl, you'd need to make the following entry:

```
<configuration>
  <system.web>
    <compilation>
      <compilers>
        <compiler language="Perl" extension=".pl"
                   type="[Perl CodeDOM Class]"/>
      </compilers>
    </compilation>
  </system.web>
</configuration>
```

<assemblies>

The `<assemblies>` element is used to add, remove, or clear assemblies that should be used in the compile path of the ASP.NET applications. Assemblies are units of compiled application logic, and contain classes and other information necessary for .NET applications to load and use the compiled application logic.

We need some assemblies to be available intrinsically for ASP.NET, since we rely upon classes found in these assemblies in the ASP.NET applications. The following assemblies are referenced in `machine.config` (and are therefore available in all ASP.NET applications):

- ❏ `mscorlib.dll`: Contains the base classes such as `String`, `Object`, `int`, and so on, and the `Root` namespace of `System`. Additionally, defines other namespaces such as `System.IO`, and so on.

- ❏ `System.dll`: Contains the code generators for C#, Visual Basic .NET, and JavaScript. Extends definition of the `System` namespace, and includes additional namespaces such as `Net` (the namespace for the network class libraries).

- ❏ `System.Web.dll`: The classes and namespaces used and required by ASP.NET, such as `HttpRequest`, `Page`, and namespaces such as `System.Web.UI` for ASP.NET server controls.

- ❑ System.Data.dll: Contains the classes and namespaces belonging to ADO.NET.

- ❑ System.Web.Services.dll: Contains the classes and namespaces such as System.Web.Services used for building ASP.NET web services.

- ❑ System.Xml.dll: Contains the XML classes and namespaces such as XmlDocument or XmlNode, and namespaces, such as the System.Xml.XPath.

- ❑ System.Drawing.dll: Contains classes and namespaces for working with images such as Bitmap.

- ❑ System.EnterpriseServices.dll: Contains classes and namespaces for COM+ integration and transactions.

- ❑ *: The special * entry tells ASP.NET also to include all assemblies found within ASP.NET application bin\ directories. bin\ directories, discussed in the previous chapter, are used to register assemblies that are specific to a web application.

These assemblies are added using an <add> tag within <assemblies> and the .dll extension of the assembly is not included in the reference.

<add>

The <add> tag is used to name .NET assemblies you wish to have available to your ASP.NET applications. For example, to use the classes found in System.DirectoryServices.dll in your web application, you need to add a reference for it in the web.config file (alternatively, you could add it to machine.config, and make it available to all applications):

```
<configuration>
  <system.web>
    <compilation>
      <assemblies>
        ...
          <add assembly="System.DirectoryServices" />
        ...
      </assemblies>
    </compilation>
  </system.web>
</configuration>
```

<remove>

The <remove> tag is used to remove assemblies. This is very useful if machine.config names assemblies using the <add> tag, but you wish to restrict the use of assemblies within the ASP.NET application. For example, machine.config lists System.Drawing as one of the assemblies to include in the compilation of ASP.NET application files. If you didn't need the classes found in System.Drawing.dll, you could ensure that ASP.NET didn't compile the assembly as part of the application. You could add an entry to a web.config file that used the <remove> tag to remove the System.Drawing assembly for only that application:

```
<configuration>
  <system.web>
    <compilation>
      <assemblies>
```

```
        <remove assembly="System.Drawing" />
      </assemblies>
    </compilation>
  </system.web>
</configuration>
```

<clear>

The `<clear>` entry goes one step further than the `<remove>` tag. Whereas the `<remove>` tag removes individual assemblies, `<clear>` removes any and all assembly references. When `<clear>` is used, no inherited assemblies are loaded.

The compilation settings in `machine.config` give a granular control over many settings that apply to ASP.NET application files, such as the default language, support for other compilers, and the assemblies (libraries of code) you want available by default within your application.

Although the compilation settings allow you to control how the application is compiled, they do not allow you to control how the application is run. To control the identity of the process that ASP.NET uses for compiling, processing, and servicing requests of your ASP.NET application, you have the identity settings.

Controlling the Identity of Execution

You can use the `<identity>` setting of `machine.config` (note that `identity` can be set in `web.config` files as well) to define which Windows user to impersonate when making requests from the operating system.

> *This is separate from the trust level assigned to a particular application. The trust level, set in the configuration system for an application, determines what a particular application may or may not do. Trust levels are used to sandbox applications.*

Three attributes are used with `<identity>`:

❏ `impersonate`: The `impersonate` attribute of `<identity>` is a Boolean value that determines the Windows NT user the ASP.NET worker process runs under. If `impersonate="true"`, ASP.NET will run under the identity provided by IIS. If set to `true`, this would be `IUSR[server name]`, or whatever identity that IIS is configured to impersonate. However, if Windows NT authentication is enabled on the web server, ASP.NET will impersonate the authenticated user. Alternatively, you can name a Windows NT user and password for the ASP.NET process to run as. The default setting of `impersonate` is `False`.

❏ `userName`: Available when `impersonate="true"`, the `name` value names a valid Windows NT account to impersonate.

❏ `password`: Complementary to `name`, the password of the user to `impersonate`.

As mentioned, the default setting is `impersonate="false"`. Let's look at some examples where ASP.NET runs with `impersonate="true"` allowing the impersonation to flow from IIS, as well as configuring the user/password for ASP.NET to run as.

Impersonating the IIS User

To impersonate the user that IIS uses, you first need to set `impersonate` to `"true"`:

```
<configuration>
  <system.web>
    <identity impersonate="true" />
  </system.web>
</configuration>
```

To test impersonation, you can use the following ASP.NET page, written in Visual Basic .NET:

```
<%@ Import Namespace="System.Security.Principal" %>

<Script runat="server">
  Public Sub Page_Load(sender As Object, e As EventArgs)
    lblIdentity.Text = WindowsIdentity.GetCurrent().Name
  End Sub
</Script>
Current identity is: <asp:label id="lblIdentity" runat="server" />
```

This code simply uses the `WindowsIdentity` class's `GetCurrent` method to return the name of the Windows user the request is processed as.

On my server, when `impersonate="false"`, the result of a request to this page is:

Current identity is: NT AUTHORITY\SYSTEM

When `impersonate="true"`, the result is:

Current identity is: RHOWARD-LAPTOP\IUSR_RHOWARD-LAPTOP

ASP.NET is impersonating the Windows user that IIS is using to process the request. Here, this is the `IUSR_[machine name]` Windows account that IIS uses for anonymous requests. If you configured IIS to use a different anonymous account, or enabled IIS security to support NTLM authentication, you would see a different result. For example, if we enable NTLM authentication for the server (see Chapter 14 for details on NTLM authentication), when I run the code I see:

Current identity is: REDMOND\RHOWARD

Since NTLM authentication is enabled, as is impersonation with ASP.NET, ASP.NET impersonates the Windows users that IIS NTLM authenticates – in this case, the user RHOWARD in the domain REDMOND.

The last option you can configure with identity is to explicitly name a username and password. Note that the username and password values are stored in clear text in the configuration system:

```
<configuration>
  <system.web>
    <identity impersonate="true"
              username="ASPNET_Anonymous"
```

```
                    password="93%dk12"
      />
   </system.web>
</configuration>
```

In this example, we've identified a user ASPNET_Anonymous as the user for ASP.NET to impersonate.

Keep in mind that the user impersonated needs to have the necessary file access permissions –
ASPNET_Anonymous needs to have access to the necessary ASP.NET files and common directory paths.
Please see the next chapter for more details on ASP.NET security.

Controlling the identity of the impersonation account used by ASP.NET allows you to have granular
system-level control over what a particular user may or may not do. However, you also have to provide
the impersonation account with the appropriate levels of access to be able to accomplish meaningful
work in your system.

Extending ASP.NET with HTTP Handlers

ASP.NET builds upon an extensible architecture known simply as the *HTTP runtime*. The runtime is
responsible for handling requests and sending responses. It is up to individual handlers, such as an
ASP.NET page or web service, to implement the work to be done on a request.

Similar to the way IIS supports a low-level API known as ISAPI, for letting developers implement
custom solutions (such as building a JSP implementation that runs on IIS), ASP.NET implements a
similar concept with HTTP Handlers. A request is assigned to ASP.NET from IIS. ASP.NET then
examines entries in the <httpHandlers> section, based on the extension (.aspx for example) of the
request to determine which handler the request should be routed to.

The most common entry used is the .aspx extension. The following entry in machine.config is for the
HTTP Handler used for the .aspx extension (as well as several other familiar extensions):

```
<configuration>
  <system.web>
    <httpHandlers>
      <add verb="*" path="*.aspx"
           type="System.Web.UI.PageHandlerFactory,System.Web" />
      <add verb="*" path="*.asmx"
           type="System.Web.Services.Protocols.WebServiceHandlerFactory,
                 System.Web.Services" validate="false"/>
      <add verb="*" path="*.ascx"
           type="System.Web.HttpForbiddenHandler,System.Web" />
      <add verb="*" path="*.config"
           type="System.Web.HttpForbiddenHandler,System.Web" />
    </httpHandlers>
  </system.web>
</configuration>
```

In this configuration code, four common handlers are identified (the actual machine.config file
identifies about 18 entries). We have the HTTP handlers for pages (.aspx), web services (.asmx), user
controls (.ascx), and configuration (.config).

Both page and web services map to actual classes, while user controls and configuration map to a special handler called `HttpForbiddenHandler`. This handler explicitly denies access to these extensions when requested directly, so a request for `Address.ascx` or `web.config` will send back an access denied reply.

As mentioned, HTTP Handlers are the ASP.NET equivalent of IIS ISAPI extensions. However, unlike ISAPI, which was only accessible to developers who could code C++, HTTP Handlers can be coded in any .NET language – Visual Basic .NET developers can now author the equivalent of an ISAPI extension.

Let's look at a simple HTTP Handler written in Visual Basic .NET:

```vbnet
Imports System
Imports System.Web

Public Class HelloWorldHandler
  Implements IHttpHandler

  Sub ProcessRequest(ByVal context As HttpContext) _
                     Implements IHttpHandler.ProcessRequest
    Dim Request As HttpRequest = context.Request
    Dim Response As HttpResponse = context.Response

    Response.Write("<html>")
    Response.Write("<body>")
    Response.Write("<h1> Hello " + _
                      Request.QueryString("Name") + "</h1>")
    Response.Write("</body>")
    Response.Write("</html>")
  End Sub

  Public ReadOnly Property IsReusable As Boolean _
                           Implements IHttpHandler.IsReusable
    Get
      Return True
    End Get
  End Property
End Class
```

Here, we have written a Visual Basic .NET `HelloWorldHandler` class, which implements the `IHttpHandler` interface. This interface requires that we implement a single method, `ProcessRequest`, as well as a single property, `IsReusable`. Within the `ProcessRequest` method, which is responsible for processing the request, we `Response.Write` some simple HTML. Within the body of the HTML, we use the `Request` to access the `Name` parameter passed on the query string.

To register this handler, you first must build it using either the command line compilers or Visual Studio .NET. You can then deploy the compiled `.dll` file to an ASP.NET `bin` directory and add the entry into your configuration file (in this particular case, a `web.config` file). The `<add>` tag of `<httpHandlers>` is used.

Adding Handlers

The `<add>` tag is used to name a class that implements either the `IHttpHandler` or the `IHttpHandlerFactory` interface. All HTTP Handlers must implement one of these interfaces so that the HTTP runtime knows how to call them.

The following code snippet shows the format used for this tag:

```
<configuration>
  <system.web>
    <httpHandlers>
      <add verb="[HTTP Verb]" path="[Request Path]" type="[.NET Class]"/>
    </httpHandlers>
  </system.web>
</configuration>
```

There are three attributes within the `<add>` tag that tell ASP.NET how the HTTP Handler is to be interpreted:

❑ verb: This attribute instructs the HTTP runtime about the HTTP verb type that the handler services request. Values for the verb attribute include asterisks (*), which instructs the HTTP runtime to match on all HTTP verbs, or a string value that names an HTTP verb (for example, the HTTP GET verb, `verb="Get"`), or a string value of semi-colon-separated HTTP verbs (for example, `verb="Get; Post; Head"`).

❑ path: This attribute instructs the HTTP runtime as to the request path, for example `/MyApp/test.aspx`, that this HTTP Handler is executed for. Valid values for `path` include asterisks (*) with an extension (`*.aspx`), which instruct the HTTP runtime to match only resources that match the extension, or a string value with an extension. You can name one resource that maps to an HTTP Handler. A good example here is the `Trace.axd` HTTP Handler, which uses the `path="trace.axd"` value.

❑ type: This attribute names the .NET class that implements the HTTP Handler code. The value for type follows the format `[Namespace].[Class], [Assembly name]`.

If you compile the preceding sample, `HelloWorldHandler.vb`, to an assembly named `Simple.dll`, you could make the following entry in a configuration file:

```
<configuration>
  <system.web>
    <httpHandlers>
      <add verb="*" path="HelloWorld.aspx"
           type="Simple.HelloWorldHandler, Simple"/>
    </httpHandlers>
  </system.web>
</configuration>
```

This configuration entry names an assembly, `Simple`, that contains a `HelloWorldHandler` class. ASP.NET will assume that `HelloWorldHandler` implements the `IHttpHandler` interface. We then identify the path and verb that the ASP.NET HTTP runtime uses to route to this handler. In this case, the HTTP runtime has been told that we wish to route on all verbs (via the *) and that we will service requests for `HelloWorld.aspx`.

You could use a custom extension, such as `*.wrox`, *but this would further require you to map this* `.wrox` *extension to ASP.NET in ISS Manager (as discussed in the previous chapter).*

We are now ready to service requests for this handler. If you open a web browser and point it to the web application that contains `bin\Simple.dll` as well as the `web.config` file that we defined, you can make a request for `.../HelloWorld.aspx?Name=Rob` as shown in Figure 13-12:

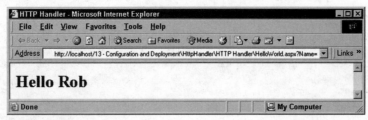

Figure 13-12

ASP.NET maps the request `HelloWorld.aspx` to the HTTP Handler we built called `Simple.dll`. The result is that the HTTP Handler is executed and the request is served. This is a somewhat simple example, but it let's you envision the types of applications that could be created. What if this HTTP Handler was declared in `machine.config` and you didn't want a given application to have access to it? In that case, you can use the `<remove>` tag of the `<httpHandlers>` section.

Removing Handlers

The `<remove>` tag can be used to override `<add>` entries that are either inherited or declared within the same configuration file. This is useful for removing HTTP Handlers from some web applications or commenting out HTTP Handlers so that the functionality is unavailable to end users:

```
<remove verb="[http verb | *]" path="[path]"/>
```

A good example is the `trace.axd` HTTP Handler used for tracing, which you may decide not to support in all of your web applications. `machine.config` defines the following entry for the `trace.axd`:

```
<configuration>
  <system.web>
    <httpHandlers>
      <add verb="*"
        path="trace.axd"
        type="System.Web.Handlers.TraceHandler,System.Web"
      />
    </httpHandlers>
  </system.web>
</configuration>
```

You could remove support of this handler in web applications by creating a `web.config` file and making the following entry using the `<remove>` tag. The web application using this `web.config` file will generate a file not found error when a request is made for `trace.axd`:

```
<configuration>
  <system.web>
    <httpHandlers>
      <remove verb="*" path="trace.axd"/>
    </httpHandlers>
  </system.web>
</configuration>
```

HTTP Handlers allow you, at a low-level, to handle the application request. You can build a simple example, such as the `HelloWorld` example, or could write more complex examples that take over well-known extensions such as `.jpg` to add additional functionality (for example, a request for `chart.jpg?x=10&y=13` could draw a graph). The opportunities are endless! However, what if you simply want to look at the request? Rather than replace the functionality that ASP.NET pages provide you with, you may simply want to examine the request before or after the HTTP Handler processes it. For this, you have HTTP Modules.

Extending ASP.NET with HTTP Modules

Whereas HTTP Handlers allow you to map a request to a specific class to handle the request, HTTP Modules act as filters (note that HTTP Modules are similar in function to ISAPI filters) that you can apply before the handler sees the request or after the handler is done with the request.

ASP.NET makes use of modules for cookieless session state, output caching, and several security-related features. In the advanced topics discussion in Chapter 20, we will look at an HTTP Module that authenticates web service requests. Before the request is 'handled' by the appropriate `.asmx` file, the HTTP Module looks at the request, and determines if it is a SOAP message. If it is a SOAP message, it extracts the username and password values from the SOAP header.

As it relates to configuration, there are the same three settings as for HTTP Handlers: `<add>`, `<remove>`, and `<clear>`. `<add>` is the only tag that differs from HTTP Handlers.

Adding Modules

The `<add>` entry for `<httpModules>` simply names the module and references the class that implements the `IHttpModule` interface and the assembly the class exists within. Just as HTTP Handlers implement a common interface, `IHttpHandler`, we have an interface that modules implement. The following code snippet is an `<httpModules>` entry for the `OutputCache` module from `machine.config`:

```
<configuration>
  <system.web>
    <httpModules>
      <add name="OutputCache"
           type="System.Web.Caching.OutputCacheModule,System.Web" />
    </httpModules>
  </system.web>
</configuration>
```

Similar to HTTP Handlers, HTTP Modules require that you implement an interface. In this case, that interface is `IHttpModule`. If you implement this interface, you can build a simple HTTP Module. Handlers and modules are definitely an advanced feature of ASP.NET. They give complete control over the request and allow you to look at the request as it comes in, execute the request, and then look at the request again as it goes out.

The `machine.config` file gives you access to a number of advanced configuration features such as the two we just examined. Another configuration option found in `machine.config` is the process model setting. The process model settings allow you to configure the ASP.NET Worker Process.

Configuring the ASP.NET Worker Process

Unlike ASP, ASP.NET runs in a separate process from IIS. When code misbehaved in ASP – say we forgot to free memory in a COM object – the leak could degrade the server performance and possibly crash the process ASP ran in. In some cases, this could crash the IIS process, which would result in the application not servicing requests!

ASP.NET, on the other hand, was designed to take into account the errors that can and will occur within the system. Rather than running in process with IIS, ASP.NET runs in a separate worker process, `aspnet_wp.exe`. ASP.NET uses IIS only to receive requests and to send responses (as a request/response broker). IIS is not involved in executing any ASP.NET code. The ASP.NET process can come and go, and it doesn't affect the stability of IIS in any way.

> *When using ASP.NET 1.1 on IIS 6.0, the new IIS worker process settings are used, and the settings in the `<processMode />` section of `machine.config` are ignored.*

You can view the ASP.NET process (`aspnet_wp.exe`) through the Windows Task Manager after a request for an ASP.NET resource has been made, as the process starts when ASP.NET applications are being used. To view the process, first request an ASP.NET resource and then open up the Windows Task Manager (press Control+Shift+Escape). Once the Task Manager is open, switch to the **Processes** tab and look for aspnet_wp.exe in the Image Name column as shown in Figure 13-13:

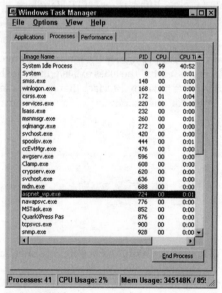

Figure 13-13

Figure 13-13 shows the `aspnet_wp.exe` process, the process ID (PID) of 1744, the CPU usage as 0%, CPU time, and memory usage in KB.

The `<processModel>` section of `machine.config` is used to configure ASP.NET process management. These settings can only be made in `machine.config` as they apply to all ASP.NET applications on that machine. Within the `<processModel>` settings, you can configure options such as which processor each ASP.NET worker process should affinitize with, and can additionally configure settings such as automatically recycling the process after n requests or n amount of time.

*An important but subtle change in the final released version of ASP.NET is the Windows identity that the ASP.NET worker process runs as. In previous beta versions it was the **System** account. The final version uses a special Windows account created when the .NET Framework is installed: **aspnet**. For more details on the implications of these changes, please see the chapter on security. This, of course, is still configurable using the username/password attributes of the `<processModel ...>` settings.*

The following code shows the default `machine.config` settings:

```
<configuration>
  <system.web>
      <processModel
          enable="true"
          timeout="Infinite"
          idleTimeout="Infinite"
          shutdownTimeout="0:00:05"
          requestLimit="Infinite"
          requestQueueLimit="5000"
          restartQueueLimit="10"
          memoryLimit="60"
          webGarden="false"
          cpuMask="0xffffffff"
          userName="machine"
          password="AutoGenerate"
          logLevel="Errors"
          clientConnectedCheck="0:00:05"
          comAuthenticationLevel="Connect"
          comImpersonationLevel="Impersonate"
          responseRestartDeadlockInterval="00:09:00"
          responseDeadlockInterval="00:03:00"
          maxWorkerThreads="25"
          maxIoThreads="25"
          serverErrorMessageFile="[Not Configured]"
      />
  </system.web>
</configuration>
```

As you can see, there are 21 options that you can configure. Let's examine all of these, starting with the `enable` option.

Enabling the ASP.NET Worker Process

The `enable` attribute is a Boolean setting used to determine if ASP.NET should run in a separate worker process, be the default, or in-process with IIS. If you set it to `false`, the `<processModel>` settings are ignored:

```
enable="[true | false]"
```

If you do set `enable` to `"false"`, you won't see the `aspnet_wp.exe` show up in the task manager; it's now loaded in-process with IIS.

> *IIS has to be stopped and restarted if the `enable` option is changed.*

It is recommended that this setting be left as `true` so that applications can reap the benefits that the ASP.NET worker process provides.

Timing Out the Process

The `timeout` attribute determines how long the worker process will live before a new worker process is created to take its place. The default value is `Infinite`. However, you can also set this value to a time using an `HH:MM:SS` format:

```
timeout = "[Infinite | HH:MM:SS]"
```

This value can be extremely useful if a scenario exists where the application's performance starts to degrade slightly after running for several weeks, such as in the case of a memory leak. Rather than having to manually start and stop the process, ASP.NET can restart automatically:

```
<configuration>
  <system.web>
      <processModel
          enable="true"
          timeout="336:00:00"
          idleTimeout="Infinite"
          ...
          serverErrorMessageFile="[Not Configured]"
      />
  </system.web>
</configuration>
```

In this setting, the ASP.NET worker process will recycle itself automatically after approximately 336 hours (two weeks). The clock starts ticking on the life of the process when the process is started (on the first request after the changes have been made).

Shutting Down the Process Automatically

You can shut down the ASP.NET worker process automatically using the `idleTimeout` option. `idleTimeout` is used to shut down the worker process when it has not served any requests within a given period of time. By default, it is set to `Infinite` and once started, will not shut down. You can also set this value to a time using the `HH:MM:SS` format:

```
idleTimeout = "[Infinite | HH:MM:SS]"
```

Starting a process for the first request can make a performance hit on the server. Two scenarios for use of `idleTimout` include:

❑ To release resources that ASP.NET is using when not actively servicing requests.

❑ To recycle processes during down time. You could configure `idleTimout` to shutdown after 20 minutes of no requests. For example, if you don't receive requests between the hours of midnight to 3 a.m., ASP.NET can quietly exit the process. When a new request comes in, a new process is started.

Graceful Shutdown

The `shutDownTimeout` attribute is used to specify how long the worker process is given to shut itself down gracefully before ASP.NET calls the kill command on the process – kill is a low-level command that forcefully removes the process. By default, `shutDownTimeout` is set to five seconds, but this is configurable:

```
shutDownTimeout = "[HH:MM:SS]"
```

This is a very useful configuration setting for processes that have crossed some threshold and appear to have crashed. ASP.NET can kill the process after it is given the opportunity to shutdown gracefully.

Recycling the Process after n Requests

`requestLimit` allows you to configure ASP.NET to recycle after a certain number of requests are served. The default value is `Infinite`, no request limit, but you can also set it to a number:

```
requestLimit = "[Infinite | int]"
```

If the performance of the application degrades after a certain number of requests, for example 5000, you can configure the `requestLimit` property to a threshold of 5000. ASP.NET will then recycle the process after 5000 requests.

You can take this example a step further and see the `requestLimit` being enforced by ASP.NET, if you:

❑ Set the `requestLimit` to 5

❑ Save your `machine.config` file

❑ Open the Windows Task Manager, view the `aspnet_wp.exe` process, and take note of the process ID

Next, if you make more than five requests for an ASP.NET application file, ASP.NET will recycle the process. To see this, go back and check the process ID of `aspnet_wp.exe`; after five requests, you will have a new process ID.

Recycling the Process If Requests Are Queued

The `requestQueueLimit` option instructs ASP.NET to recycle the worker process if the number of queued requests limit is exceeded. ASP.NET uses threads within a process to service user requests. If a thread is blocked or is unable to service requests, requests can be queued. The `requestQueueLimit` option gives you the opportunity to detect if requests are queued and recycle the process if the queued requests exceed the allowed limit. The default setting is 5000:

```
requestQueueLimit = "[int]"
```

Recycling the Process If Too Much Memory is Consumed

The `memoryLimit` option determines how much physical memory the worker process is allowed to consume before it is considered to be misbehaving. The default value is 60 (representing 60 percent):

```
memoryLimit = "[int]"
```

You should never 'leak' memory in a .NET application since the CLR is performing garbage collection (memory management) for you. However, since .NET also supports the use of native code, and is able to interoperate with COM, it is possible to leak memory if either the native code or the COM object is mismanaging memory.

The simplest way to demonstrate the use of `memoryLimit` is with a simple ASP.NET page that fills application state memory with useless information – this simulates a memory leak. The following page is written in Visual Basic .NET:

```
<%@ Import Namespace="System.Diagnostics" %>
<%@ Import Namespace="System.Text" %>
<script runat=server>
  Sub Page_Load(Sender as Object, E as EventArgs)
    Dim i As Integer
    Dim garbage As New StringBuilder
    If Application("garbage") Is Nothing Then
      Dim c As Integer
      For c=1 to 1000
        garbage = garbage.Append("xxxxxxxxxx")
      Next c
      Application("garbage") = garbage
    Else
      garbage = Application("garbage")
    End If

    For i=1 to 500
      ' Make sure we create a unique entry
      Application(i.ToString + DateTime.Now.ToString("r")) = _
                  (garbage.ToString() + DateTime.Now.ToString("r"))
    Next i

    Dim p as ProcessInfo
    p = ProcessModelInfo.GetCurrentProcessInfo()
    ProcessID.Text = p.ProcessID.ToString()
  End Sub
</script>
<html>
  <body>
      <h2>The Process ID serving this request is:
          <asp:label id="ProcessID" forecolor=red runat=server/>
      </h2>
```

```
        <h2>There are <%=Application.Count.ToString()%>
          items in Application state memory.
        </h2>
      </body>
    </html>
```

We can then set `memoryLimit` to a very low threshold, such as 5 percent:

```
<configuration>
  <system.web>
      <processModel
          ...
          restartQueueLimit="10"
          memoryLimit="5"
          webGarden="false"
          ...
      />
  </system.web>
</configuration>
```

Next, we make requests for the ASP.NET page that simulates a leak. Again, watch the `aspnet_wp.exe` worker process in the Task Manager. As the resource is requested, you will see memory increase for the process. Finally, when 5 percent of memory has been utilized, you will see a new process appear next to the old process, which disappears. From the end user's perspective, the application just keeps running. Figure 13-14 shows the process (PID 1572) that has exceeded the memory threshold, and the new process (PID 1972) that has just started:

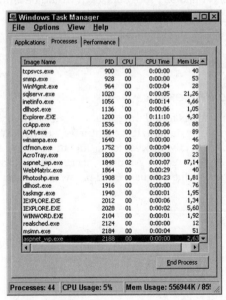

Figure 13-14

This is also evident in the sample ASP.NET page since we display the process ID.

Supporting Multiple Worker Processes

There are usually two ways to scale an application; write tighter and better code, or simply add more hardware. The term *web farm* is used to describe a collection of nearly identical web servers that can be used to service requests. As the user-base grows, we simply add more servers into the server farm and are able to increase the scalability of our application. This is very cost effective since adding a server is, in most cases, less expensive than rewriting the entire application.

When you build a server farm, you essentially put all the required hardware in place to host another process that can service requests. A new option that ASP.NET now supports is a *web garden* – multiple processes on the *same* server.

A web garden lets you host multiple ASP.NET worker processes on a single server, thus providing the application with better hardware scalability.

> *Web garden mode is only supported on multi-processor servers. To support a web garden with ASP.NET, we use two inter-related* `<processModel>` *configuration settings:*

❑   `webGarden`: The `webGarden` attribute determines whether web garden mode is enabled. The default setting is `false`.

```
webGarden = "[true | false]"
```

❑   `cpuMask`: The `cpuMask` (a hexadecimal value) is used to determine which processors should be affinitized to ASP.NET worker processes when `webGarden` is set to `"true"`. The default value is all processors, as `0xFFFFFFFF` is a bit mask of `11111111111111111111111111111111`. In other words, if the server had 32 processors, each would be affinitized to its own ASP.NET worker process.

```
cpuMask="0xffffffff""
```

The settings of `cpuMask` do nothing if `webGarden="false"`.

Setting the Identity of the Process

The `username` and `password` settings found in `<processModel>` are used to control the user that the ASP.NET Worker process runs as. By default, it is a restricted **ASPNET** Windows account. However, by using these settings, you can instruct the process to execute under another Windows identity or the **System** account. For example, if you create a Windows user `ASPNET_WP` with a password of `&dotnet$12`, you could set these as the username and password values:

```
<configuration>
  <system.web>
      <processModel
          ...
          cpuMask="0xffffffff"
          userName="ASPNET_WP"
          password="&dotnet$12"
          logLevel="Errors"
          ...
      />
  </system.web>
</configuration>
```

When you view the process information in the Windows Task Manager, you'll see that the process is executing as user `ASPNET_WP` rather than `ASPNET`. To run as the system account, as previous Beta versions of ASP.NET did, simply change the username/password to the following values:

```
userName="System"
password="AutoGenerate"
```

Logging Process Events

The `logLevel` attribute allows you to configure how the ASP.NET worker process logs events. The default setting is to log only errors:

```
logLevel="[All | None | Errors]"
```

In addition to logging errors that occur, you can also configure to log all events or log none of the events. The events are written to the Windows Application Event Log.

Checking If the Client Is Connected

When an application is slow to respond, some users will simply issue a new request from the browser by hitting page refresh several times. This will force the web server to do unnecessary work, since the client may make 15 requests but only the last request completes – the web server will still do the associated work for the other 14 requests.

The `clientConnectedCheck` setting allows you to check if the client is still connected at timed intervals before performing work. Thus, rather than processing all the requests, ASP.NET will only process requests where the client is expecting a response. The other requests that sit in the queue waiting for work can then be discarded.

The default setting for this attribute is 5 seconds, which means that for requests that are queued, ASP.NET will check if the client is connected every 5 seconds. If not, the request can be discarded from the queue.

The following settings are supported:

```
clientConnectedCheck="[HH:MM:SS | Infinite]"
```

The process model settings of ASP.NET introduce a new level of flexibility and stability for our applications. All of the options for controlling the processing, including the identity that the process runs as, as well as which CPU the process should affinitize to, are provided.

COM Impersonation and Authentication

For COM integration, there are two `<processModel>` attributes that control both authentication level and impersonation level:

- ❑ `comAuthenticationLevel`: Controls the level of authentication for DCOM security. The default is set to `Connect`.

- ❑ `comImpersonationLevel`: Controls the authentication level for COM security. The default is set to `Impersonate`.

Process Restarts due to Deadlock

In some rare scenarios, the ASP.NET worker process may get into a deadlocked state. The process has work to complete (queued requests), but due to some unknown reason, the process is no longer responding to responses. There are two `<processModel>` attributes that control the behavior of the ASP.NET worker process during a deadlock:

❑ `responseDeadlockInterval`: A deadlock is considered to exist when there are requests queued and no responses have been sent during this interval, after which the process is restarted. By default, this is set to 3 minutes. The format is `00:03:00`.

❑ `responseRestartDeadlockInterval`: This interval exists to prevent thrashing, for example, continuous stopping and restarting of processes due to deadlock. By default, this is set to 9 minutes, with the format `00:09:00`. If a process has been restarted due to a deadlock issue, this specifies the amount of time that must elapse before another deadlock process restart is initiated.

Controlling Worker Process Threads

There are two attributes within `<processModel>` that control the maximum number of worker threads and I/O threads used by the ASP.NET worker process:

❑ `maxWorkerThreads`: The maximum number of threads that exist within the thread pool of an ASP.NET worker process. The default is 25. Note that this does not mean that 25 threads exist at all times. Rather, the thread pool dynamically manages the size of the threads available.

❑ `maxIoThreads`: The maximum number of I/O threads that exist within the ASP.NET worker process. The default is 25.

It is recommended that neither of the options be changed unless you understand exactly what the implications are.

Server Unavailable Error Message

When the ASP.NET worker process is recycling, it is possible to encounter a Server Unavailable error message. The process model's `serverErrorMessageFile` attribute allows you to control the contents of the error message. The location of the file is relative to `machine.config`, the contents of which will be returned if a server unavailable error message is required.

Machine Key

ASP.NET uses a key to encrypt or hash some data so that the data is only accessible from the server that created the data. In a single server environment, we will never touch this setting. However, in a multi-server environment in which a request can be directed to a farm of web servers, each server in the farm needs to share the same machine key. This way, server A and server B can both encrypt, decrypt, or hash the same values, so that data created on A can be understood and used on B and vice-versa. The default setting of `<machineKey>`, from `machine.config`, is:

```
<machineKey validationKey="AutoGenerate"
            decryptionKey="AutoGenerate"
            validation="SHA1"
/>
```

There are three settings for <machineKey>:

❑   validationKey

❑   decryptionKey

❑   validation

Let's look at each of these in more detail.

validationKey

The validationKey is used for the validation of data, such as the hash that is done for forms-based authentication cookies. The validationKey is used as part of the hash so that the hash can only be recomputed by ASP.NET applications that have the appropriate validationKey. The default setting is AutoGenerate (ASP.NET automatically creates a value for you), but in a server farm environment, you would need to configure the value and ensure that each server, or application, has the same value. Here are the acceptable settings:

```
validationKey="[AutoGenerate | 40-128 hex Chars]"
```

If a user-defined validationKey is to be used, the recommendation is to use the full 128 chars. This is a valid entry:

```
validationKey="0123456789abcdef0123456789abcdef0123456789abcdef
               0123456789abcdef0123456789abcdef0123456789abcdef
               0123456789abcdef0123456789abcdef"
```

Key lengths shorter than 40 or longer than 128 hex chars will generate an error.

decryptionKey

The decryptionKey is used to encrypt data stored in the Forms Authentication cookie. The default is AutoGenerate (ASP.NET automatically generates the value). In a web farm environment, just as with the validationKey, each server needs to use an identical value for this key. The value of the string should be 16 to 48 hex characters. The validationKey ensures that the information is valid; decryptionKey protects the information from prying eyes.

validation

The validation attribute of <machineKey> is used to determine what type of hash is to be computed. Valid values include MD5, SHA1, and 3DES.

The hash can be sent to the client along with, for example, the Forms Authentication cookie. The data in the cookie can be validated by the server by re-hashing the values with the validationKey, and the appropriate algorithm determined by validation. If the values match, the data is considered valid. If not, the data represented by the hash is considered invalid (it may have been tampered with). The validationKey guarantees the data is valid. Another setting decryptionKey, guarantees that the plain text of the message cannot be read by nontrusted parties.

Advanced Topics

Here, we will cover three advanced topics related to ASP.NET configuration:

❑   Specifying location

❑   Locking down configuration settings

❑   Building a custom configuration handler

Specifying the Location

In all the examples discussed in this chapter, we have either used the `machine.config` file to configure settings for the entire server or the `web.config` file to configure settings for an individual application.

Another option not discussed previously, is to use a `<location>` element within a configuration file. Using the `<location>` element, you can specify application-specific settings in `machine.config` for different applications on our server, rather than creating a web.config file.

For example, if you have a virtual directory named `Wrox` accessible as `http://localhost/Wrox/`, and that virtual directory is marked as an application, you could make the following entry in `machine.config` to configure `Session` settings for all applications as well as `Session` settings specific to the `Wrox` application:

```
<configuration>
  <system.web>
    <sessionState
      mode="InProc"
      stateConnectionString="tcpip=127.0.0.1:42424"
      sqlConnectionString="data source=127.0.0.1; user id=sa;password="
      cookieless="false"
      timeout="20"
    />
  </system.web>
  <location path="Default Web Site/Wrox">
    <system.web>
      <sessionState
        mode="StateServer"
        stateConnectionString="tcpip=127.0.0.1:42424"
        sqlConnectionString="data source=127.0.0.1; user id=sa;password="
        cookieless="true"
        timeout="10"
      />
    </system.web>
  </location>
</configuration>
```

In this snippet from `machine.config`, we have specified a default setting for all applications, and have also provided the settings specific to the `Wrox` application using the `<location>` element.

Setting the Path

The `<location>` element requires that you define a path. If a path is not provided, or the path value is set to an empty string, the settings are applied as normal. In the preceding example, it would be an error to define `<location path="">`. This would cause `machine.config` to have two conflicting settings for `<sessionState>`.

> *The value of path requires that you provide* `[site name]/[application path]`. *The value for* `[site name]` *is the description value of the web site. The description value can be obtained by opening the IIS MMC, right-clicking on a web site, selecting **Properties**, and selecting the **Web Sites** tab. The description value is then visible in the **Description** textbox.*

In addition to using `<location>` to define settings for your application, you can also lock down application configuration settings through the use of `<location>`.

Locking Down Configuration Settings

ASP.NET's configuration system is very flexible. For your applications, you can simply create a `web.config` file specifying the desired configuration options, and the application will behave appropriately.

However, in some cases, as in a hosted environment, you may want to limit the configuration options a particular application is allowed to control. For example, you may decide that some applications cannot change the settings for `Session` state. There are two options for locking down configuration settings:

❑   Use the `<location>` `allowOverride` attribute.

❑   Use the `allowDefinition` attribute on the configuration section handler.

Let's look at both of these.

Locking Down via <location>

In addition to supporting a `path` attribute, you can additionally specify an `allowOverride` attribute in the `<location>` tag. The usage of `allowOverride` is:

```
<location path="[site description]/[application path]"
          allowOverride="[true|false]">
```

Let's look at an example to clarify the use. You could define the following in the `machine.config` file:

```
<configuration>
   ...
   <location path="Default Web Site/Wrox" allowOverride="true">
     <system.web>
       <sessionState
         mode="StateServer"
         stateConnectionString="tcpip=127.0.0.1:42424"
         sqlConnectionString="data source=127.0.0.1; user id=sa;password="
         cookieless="true"
         timeout="10"
```

```
      />
    </system.web>
  </location>
</configuration>
```

Within the `Wrox` application, you could then define a `web.config` file that provides session state settings, overriding the settings inherited from `machine.config`'s `<location>` settings:

```
<configuration>
  <system.web>
    <sessionState
      mode="InProc"
      stateConnectionString="tcpip=127.0.0.1:42424"
      sqlConnectionString="data source=127.0.0.1; user id=sa;password="
      cookieless="false"
      timeout="20"
    />
  </system.web>
</configuration>
```

However, if in `machine.config` you set `allowOverride="false"` in the `<location>` settings for `Wrox`, a `web.config` file for the `Wrox` application that attempted to set `<sessionState>` settings would result in an exception. The application is effectively prevented from 'redefining' the settings for `<sessionState>` configured by the administrator in `machine.config`.

Using the `allowOverride` attribute of `<location>` allows the administrator to control the default settings of a given application, as well as whether that application can change those settings in a `web.config` file. If the default inherited settings from `machine.config` are acceptable, you can also lock down using the attributes on the configuration section handler.

Locking Down via Configuration Section Handler

If the settings specified in `machine.config` are acceptable defaults, and you don't want those settings changed by applications that inherit those settings, you can use the optional `allowDefinition` attribute on the configuration section handler.

Let's look at an example. The following values are taken from `machine.config` for the `sessionState` section handler as well as the `<sessionState>` settings. The section handler is highlighted:

```
<?xml version="1.0" encoding="UTF-8" ?>
<configuration>
  <configSections>
    <sectionGroup name="system.web">
      <section name="sessionState"
               type="System.Web.SessionState.SessionStateSectionHandler",
                     System.Web
      />
    </sectionGroup>
    ...
  </configSections>
  ...
  <system.web>
```

```
        <sessionState
            mode="InProc"
            stateConnectionString="tcpip=127.0.0.1:42424"
            sqlConnectionString="data source=127.0.0.1;
                                 user id=sa;password="
            cookieless="false"
            timeout="20"
        />
      </system.web>
    </configuration>
```

In this configuration, applications can use a web.config file to redefine the configuration settings for <sessionState>. To restrict this, you could use the allowDefinition attribute on the section handler:

```
    <section name="sessionState"
             type="System.Web.SessionState.SessionStateSectionHandler,
                   System.Web"
             allowDefinition="MachineOnly"
    />
```

Applications that use a web.config file attempting to change <sessionState> settings will now receive an error message, and will be prevented from defining <sessionState> settings, just as was done with <location>.

The allowDefinition attribute has three acceptable settings:

❑ Everywhere: Settings for the section handler can be declared in machine.config or within a web.config file. The web.config file may or may not reside within a directory marked as an application.

❑ MachineOnly: Settings for the section handler can be declared only by the machine.config file and cannot be overridden in a web.config file.

❑ MachineToApplication: Settings for the section handler can be declared in either machine.config or a web.config file residing within a directory marked as an application.

If allowDefinition is absent, the default setting is allowDefinition="Everywhere".

Custom Configuration Handler

Earlier in the chapter, we discussed the use of <appSettings> for storing our own configuration data. This allowed us to store simple key/value data in the configuration file and later access it through configuration APIs.

While <appSettings> is definitely useful, in some cases you might want to add more complex configuration data. For this, you can create your own configuration section handler that can read configuration settings. A custom configuration section handler is simply a class that implements the IConfigurationSectionHandler interface.

The IConfigurationSectionHandler interface has one method that we are required to implement:

```
object Create(object parent, object configContext, XmlNode section)
```

Let's write a simple example of a configuration section handler.

Simple Configuration Handler

Let's say you want to provide all pages with a default background color. You also want to store the default value in the configuration system. Instead of using <appSettings> to accomplish this (you could easily use it for this example), you decide to write your own configuration handler.

The following code snippet shows the C# code for the configuration section handler:

```csharp
using System;
using System.Collections;
using System.Xml;
using System.Configuration;
using System.Web.Configuration;

namespace Wrox {
  internal class PagePropertiesHandler : IConfigurationSectionHandler {
    public virtual object Create(Object parent,
                                Object context,
                                XmlNode node) {
      PagePropertiesConfig config;
      config = new PagePropertiesConfig((PagePropertiesConfig)parent);
      config.LoadValuesFromConfigurationXml(node);
      return config;
    }
  }

  public class PagePropertiesConfig {
    string _backColor;
    internal PagePropertiesConfig(PagePropertiesConfig parent) {
      if (parent != null)
        _backColor = parent._backColor;
    }
    internal void LoadValuesFromConfigurationXml(XmlNode node) {
      Exception error = null;
      XmlAttributeCollection attributeCollection = node.Attributes;
      _backColor = attributeCollection["backColor"].Value;
    }

    public string BackColor{
      get {return _backColor;}
    }
  }
}
```

In this code, we have implemented a PagePropertiesHandler class that implements IConfigurationSectionHandler's Create method. We use a public class called PagePropertiesConfig to retrieve and store the values from the configuration settings.

When this handler is created, it will pass in the XmlNode node value, and call LoadValuesFromConfigurationXml to load the backColor setting.

After compiling the source file and deploying it to the application's bin directory, the following web.config file can be written to use this configuration section handler:

```
<configuration>
  <configSections>
    <sectionGroup name="system.web">
      <section name="pageProperties"
               type="Wrox.PagePropertiesHandler, PageProperties" />
    </sectionGroup>
  </configSections>

  <system.web>
    <pageProperties backColor="blue" />
  </system.web>
</configuration>
```

Next, we can write the following ASP.NET page:

```
<%@ Import Namespace="Wrox" %>

<Script runat="server">
  Public backColor As String

  Public Sub Page_Load(sender As Object, e As EventArgs)
    Dim _config As PagePropertiesConfig

    _config = CType(Context.GetConfig("system.web/pageProperties"), _
                  PagePropertiesConfig)

    backColor = _config.BackColor
  End Sub
</Script>

<Body bgcolor="<%=backColor%>">
<Font face="arial" color="white" size=4>
This page has its backcolor set from the ASP.NET configuration system!
</Font>
```

Within the ASP.NET page, we first import the Wrox namespace, as this includes the PagePropertiesConfig. Next, we use the Context object's GetConfig method and request the configuration information for system.web/pageProperties. The return type is cast to PagePropertiesConfig. Finally, we are able to access the BackColor property on the PagePropertiesConfig class, which returns the value set in the web.config file, blue.

As you can clearly see, this is a simple example. However, it does show just how easy plugging into the ASP.NET configuration system is. You could easily write more complex configuration section handlers for personalization features or other extensions that you may want to add to ASP.NET.

Summary

As you learned in this chapter, the ASP.NET configuration system does not rely upon the IIS metabase as ASP did. Instead, ASP.NET uses an XML configuration system. An XML configuration system is human-readable/writable, replicates easily, and does not require local server access, since you can simply FTP the configuration files to your web servers.

ASP.NET's XML configuration system is divided into two distinct files:

- ❑ `machine.config`
- ❑ `web.config`

A server *always* has `machine.config` file to represent the default settings for all web applications on that server. However, that same server may have multiple `web.config` files used to configure applications on an applicationbyapplication basis.

You also learned that configuration files are inherited. The default settings in `machine.config` are inherited in `web.config` files unless overridden, as you saw in the `<sessionState>` examples within this chapter.

After introducing configuration, we then spent the bulk of the chapter discussing various configuration settings used in ASP.NET. We covered topics from internationalization, to HTTP Handlers, to process model settings. The settings covered in this chapter cover 90 percent of all the configuration settings you will want to use for applications.

Finally, we discussed how you could author your own configuration section handler by implementing a class that inherited from the `IConfigurationSectionHandler` interface.

Securing ASP.NET Applications

Most of the pages that you create for a public web site are designed to be accessible to any visitor, so the default settings for ASP.NET pages are ideal – anyone can access the pages from anywhere on the network or the Internet. However, there will always be some pages that you don't want to be publicly available. For example, you might want to limit access to a complete site to users who have paid a subscription, or to limit access to administration pages to specific users only.

In previous versions of ASP, securing your pages was generally done in one of two ways. You could create a custom security system that allowed users to login to your site or application (or a specific part of it). Alternatively, you could rely on the security features of IIS and Windows itself to control which users could access specific pages, folders, or resources.

In ASP.NET, pages run under the .NET Framework, and this introduces new concepts in managing security, while still retaining existing security features. In this chapter, we'll overview all the features that control user access and then concentrate on the specific techniques designed for use with ASP.NET. The main topics in this chapter are:

- ❑ An overview of the security model within Windows and IIS
- ❑ An overview of the new security features in ASP.NET
- ❑ The different types of access control that you can implement with ASP.NET
- ❑ A detailed look at how to apply the ASP.NET security and access control features

Windows 2000 and IIS Security Overview

As this book is about ASP.NET, we'll only be providing an overview of the features in the Windows operating system and IIS for securing your web pages and web applications. Though we will be concentrating on Windows 2000, Windows XP, and Windows 2003 Server here, the concepts, configuration, and usage of these features is virtually unchanged from previous versions of ASP. However, they do provide the basis on which .NET security techniques are founded. If you are not familiar with the material in this section, you may wish to consult other documentation or books to gain a broader understanding.

> **Securing your applications or web sites is one of the most important factors when connecting your server to the Internet. While the basics described here and the techniques you use to control access will provide a secure environment, you must still implement all the other measures that are required for protecting your servers and applications against intruders. This includes physical security (for example, locked doors and windows), internal user security (such as keeping passwords secret and monitoring usage), virus protection, prompt installation of operating system updates and patches, and so on.**

The Need for Security

When you secure your applications, you must first think about what it is you are actually trying to achieve. For example, does your application contain highly sensitive information, or allow users to perform tasks that you absolutely must protect against misuse – such as a bank providing online account access to clients. Or, is the information less sensitive but still valuable, such as content you want visitors to pay a subscription to access.

In the end, it all comes down to quantifying the risks involved and the effect of a security breach. Securing applications is more difficult than allowing everyone access, and can involve using extra hardware to build complex multi-layer systems with firewalls, demilitarized zones, and all kinds of other high security features. However this type of approach is normally used only when the highest levels of security are required, such as when you are protecting whole networks from access by external intruders.

Security, as it concerns the ASP.NET applications, will normally be limited to the configuration of the machine(s) on which they run, and the connected resources such as database servers, etc. This generally involves limiting access to specific folders, files, components, and other resources, to only the appropriate users. These topics are the real focus of this chapter.

If you are building an application that requires the utmost protection from intruders, you must base the ASP.NET servers in a secure environment, as well as configure them correctly. This involves the kinds of extra equipment mentioned earlier, and a thorough understanding of the risks involved. Books such as *Designing Secure Web-based Applications for Windows 2000 (ISBN 0-7356-0995-0)* from *MS Press* are useful. If in doubt, however, employ an experienced professional to design and secure your network and servers as well.

Security Concepts

The basic concepts for securing your applications consist of four main topic areas:

❑ **Authentication**: The process of discovering the individual identity of users, and making them prove that they are who they say they are.

❑ **Authorization**: The process of determining if a particular user is entitled to access the resource they've requested.

❑ **Impersonation**: The process whereby the resource can be accessed under a different identity, usually the context of a remote user.

❑ **Data or functional security**: The process of securing the system through physical means, operating system updates, and use of robust software (this topic is not covered in this chapter).

Many elements of the operating system, IIS, and the .NET Framework combine to provide the features required to implement the first three topics in the preceding list. For example, Windows uses its own list of user accounts to help identify and authenticate users. IIS also identifies users based on the information provided by Windows as they access a web site, and it passes this information on to ASP.NET where it can be used as part of the overall authorization process.

Let's look at these three topics in detail. Just remember that they are all part of the same chain of events involved in allowing or denying users access to resources.

Authentication

To be able to limit access to specific users, you have to be able to identify them. This doesn't mean you need to know everything about them – as in some big-brother scenario – but you do need to be able to tell each user apart, and identify those that should have access and those that should not.

Authentication involves challenging a user to prove that they are who they say they are – usually by means of a username and password, a digital certificate, or perhaps even a *smart card* or a fingerprint reader. In theory, if they can provide a valid username and password combination or some other user-specific *property* that can be identified, then they must be who they say they are. You depend on only one person having access to that particular property.

In the most common case, a user provides their username and matching password when prompted, either when they log onto a machine or when they access the resource. If these details are valid, the user has been identified – they are *authenticated*.

Authorization

Once you know who the user is, you can find out whether they have permission to access the resource they requested. This is done in a range of ways, depending on the resource. In Windows-based systems most resources have an *Access Control List* (*ACL*) that lists the users allowed to access a resource. The list will usually also specify what kind of access each user has (for example, whether they can read it, write to it, modify it, delete it, and so on).

For example, if they request an ASP page, the operating system will check to see if they have read access to the page. If so, it will allow IIS to fetch the page. However, IIS also has authorization settings that control what a user can do with a resource. If it's an ASP page, they will only be able to execute the script in that page if IIS has script execute permission set for the web site, folder or page.

So, in traditional ASP environments, several *layers* can be involved in the authorization process. If the identified user has permission to access the resource in the way they've requested, the process succeeds – they have been *authorized*. If not, they receive an error message of some type, generated by the layer that refused them access to the resource.

Impersonation

There are times when a user will access a resource as though they were someone (or something) else. Microsoft defines this process in the .NET SDK as, "ASP.NET applications can optionally execute with the identity of the client on whose behalf they are operating." When impersonation is enabled for a site, ASP.NET accesses the resources requested by the client using the client's credentials rather than its own.

To understand this, think about when there is no access control in place for a web page – in other words it allows any users to access it. In fact, this is an over-simplification, because Windows never allows anonymous access. All users must be authenticated and authorized using an existing account.

For HTML pages, ASP pages and components in ASP version 3.0 and earlier, this is achieved through the two accounts named *IUSR_machinename* and *IWAM_machinename*. These accounts are set up when IIS is installed, and are automatically added to all the folders in every web site on the server. These accounts still exist in Windows 2003 Server, though (as you'll see later) the accounts that are used for anonymous access are different – depending on the configuration of IIS. In this general discussion of the way that security works in Windows, we'll refer to these accounts as the *anonymous accounts*.

If you allow anonymous access to a resource in IIS, every user will look the same – you won't be able to tell who is who. When IIS receives a request for a web page or other resource for which anonymous access is permitted, it uses its anonymous accounts to access the resources on the user's behalf.

In contrast, ASP.NET – when impersonation is turned off – makes all access to resources under the context of a special ASP.NET process account. When you turn impersonation on, ASP.NET executes every resource under the account of a specified user that is authenticated by IIS when the request is made.

As in a COM+ application running under Windows 2000 or in MTS under Windows NT4, you can specify the account that will be used. If you specify one of the anonymous accounts, ASP.NET will behave like previous versions of ASP, as far as the permissions for accessing resources is concerned.

> **One vital point to bear in mind is that the authentication process used by ASP.NET only applies to resources that are associated with ASP.NET. In other words, access control is only applied to files that are defined as 'application' files in the IIS Application Mappings dialog. By default this includes `.aspx` and `.asax` pages, `.ascx` components, `.vb` and `.cs` code files, web service files, and other resources that are mapped to `aspnet_isapi.dll`. It does not apply to resources such as images, Word documents, zip files, PDF files, and other types of files. These types of files must be protected using standard Windows techniques such as ACLs. You'll see all these topics discussed later in this chapter.**

Security within ASP.NET

From the preceding chapters, you saw how many of the configuration settings (that you used to make within IIS under previous versions of ASP) are now made through one or more instances of the new configuration file named web.config. This applies to most of the settings in the Internet Services Manager interface (within the MMC), because web.config replaces the metabase contents that this interface is used to manipulate.

However, security settings made in IIS are still effective in many areas. This is because, unlike the configuration of application settings, custom errors, etc., IIS is still actively managing the request and performing the base security process in conjunction with the operating system itself. In effect, a request for an ASP.NET page is received by IIS, which in turn uses the *application mappings* defined for the site containing that page to direct the request to ASP.NET.

You can see the application mappings if you open the Application Configuration dialog from the Home Directory page of the Properties dialog for a site or directory in Internet Services Manager, as shown in Figure 14-1. The application mappings for all the ASP.NET resource types point to a file named aspnet_isapi.dll stored in the .NET Frameworks folder:

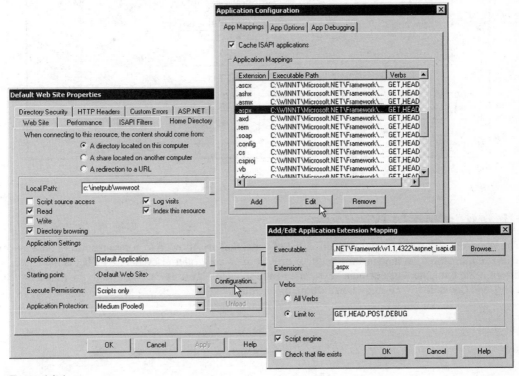

Figure 14-1

As you can see from Figure 14-1, the application mappings rely on file extensions. This is why you can still run existing ASP 3.0 pages on the same server as ASP.NET (they have a different file extension), and (of course) publish other resources such as HTML pages, zip files, documents, and so on that aren't processed by ASP.NET.

IIS first authenticates a user, and then passes the request on to ASP.NET where it can perform its own security processes. The schematic in Figure 14-2 shows the overall flow of the request, and we'll briefly see how each part of the process is carried out in the following sections of this chapter:

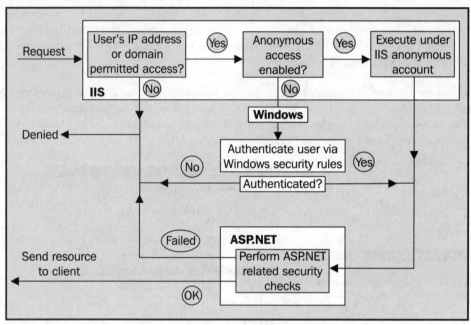

Figure 14-2

Authentication in Windows

The Windows security system maintains a list of users that are allowed to access resources on a machine. This is either stored on the machine itself, or on a domain controller elsewhere. The list is managed through the Computer Management MMC snap-in tool (as in Figure 14-3), or through the Active Directory Users and Computers snap-in tool on a domain controller.

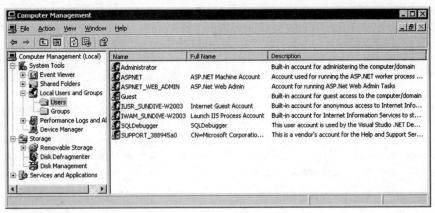

Figure 14-3

You can see the IUSR and IWAM accounts that are used by IIS when anonymous access is enabled in Figure 14-3 (the machine name is SUNDIVE-W2003). Depending on the operating system version and other software you have installed, you'll probably see several other accounts listed as well.

User Groups

The Computer Management and Active Directory Users and Computers snap-in tools also provide a list of account groups on the local machine. You can see this list in Figure 14-4, together with the Properties dialog for the group named IIS_WPG. This dialog displays a list of the members of the selected group:

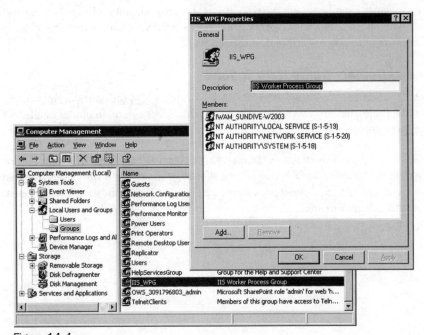

Figure 14-4

The screenshot in Figure 14-4 is taken from a Windows Server 2003 machine, and the special account group IIS_WPG is created automatically on installation. You can see that it contains the IWAM account (as used for anonymous access to COM and COM+ components under ASP 3.0), plus the LOCAL SERVICE and SYSTEM accounts. There is another account in the list, which is created by default only in Windows Server 2003, named NETWORK SERVICE. You'll see how this is used by ASP.NET later in this chapter.

You can create your own account groups, and add new and existing users to them. All accounts are automatically added to the default users group as well. Allocating users to groups provides a way of minimizing the amount of work required to change permissions. For example, if you have 500 users who can access a particular set of resources, you can allocate them all to one group and then give that group permission to access those resources.

The alternative would be to add all 500 users to each resource individually. And any changes to the permissions afterwards would mean changing them for all 500 users, rather than just once for the group as a whole.

Groups are also useful when you use programmatic security. You can detect whether a user is a member of a specific group, and make decisions based on the result. This means that you don't have to hardcode all of the usernames into your application (just the group name), and you don't have to change the code to add or remove individual users. Just configure the group in the ACL for the resource to add users to, or remove them from the group.

Authentication in IIS

When a user requests a resource over the web, IIS receives the request and performs the initial authentication of the user. IIS also performs other checks before deciding whether the user will be allowed access to the resource. We'll look at these next.

IP Address and Domain Name Restrictions

In Windows 2000 Server, Windows Server 2003, and Windows NT4 (but not Windows 2000 Professional or Windows XP Professional), you can specify the IP addresses or domain names of clients that will be allowed access or denied access.

This is achieved using the IP Address and Domain Name Restrictions dialog, shown in Figure 14-5, which is available from the Directory Security page of the Properties dialog for a site or directory. This is useful if you always access the restricted site from a single machine, or if all your users come from a specific set of IP addresses or set of domains.

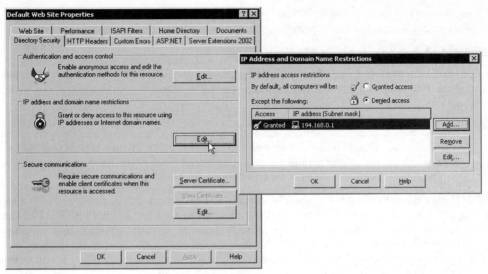

Figure 14-5

Using Certificates to Authenticate Users

You can also use the Properties dialog to set up server certificates that are to be used for a site or directory. As well as enabling secure communication through SSL, these certificates can be used in conjunction with client certificates to identify the machine that is accessing your server. For example, Figure 14-6 shows a configuration where clients can provide a certificate to access the site. We've created a rule so that, if the organization that issued the certificate to the client is our own certificate server, the user will automatically be authenticated using an account named TestUser from a domain named DANDARE:

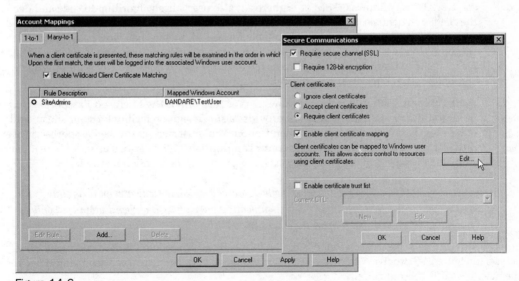

Figure 14-6

You can also access the content of a client certificate using code in an ASP.NET page, through the `Request.ClientCertificate` *collection.*

Specifying the Authentication Method

The third option in the Directory Security page of the Properties dialog for a site or directory enables you to specify the authentication method that should be used. The Authentication Methods dialog provides several options:

❑ **Anonymous Access**: Any user can access the WWW service provided that the settings for their IP address and domain name restrictions don't prevent them. IIS then accesses resources on their behalf using the appropriate anonymous account (such as the IUSR account), and so they will be able to access all resources for which these accounts are valid.

❑ **Basic Authentication**: If anonymous access is disabled, users will be presented with a logon dialog generated by their browser or their client-side user agent application. The username and password they provide are Base64-encoded and passed to IIS. It then looks up this account in Windows (on the server), and will only allow the user to access the resource if the account is valid and has the appropriate permission for that resource. Base64 encoding is not very secure, and so this option is not suitable for high-security applications.

❑ **Digest Authentication**: If anonymous access is disabled, users will be prompted for their credentials (their logon information). The browser combines this with other information stored on the client, and sends an encoded hash (or digest) of it to the server. The server already has a copy of this information, and so can recreate the original details from its own hash and authenticate the user. This method only works with Internet Explorer and .NET web services, but will pass through firewalls, proxy servers, and over the Internet. It is also very secure. The user will be able to access the resource they requested only if the specified account exists in Windows, is valid, and has appropriate permission for that resource.

❑ **Integrated Windows Authentication**: This is the same method as when you log onto your local network. Sometimes called "NTLM" authentication or "Challenge Response" authentication, it can work with Windows NTLM or Kerberos. It also uses a hash algorithm to code and decode the client's credentials. It will *not* work through most proxy servers and firewalls, or through some routers, and so is not generally suitable for use on the Internet. However, it usually works fine on an Intranet or a corporate network. Like digest authentication, this is also a very secure technique. The user will be able to access the resource they requested only if the specified account exists in Windows, is valid, and has appropriate permission for that resource.

❑ **.NET Passport Authentication** (Windows Server 2003 only): The Microsoft Passport service is used to authenticate users, and hence provides a single-sign-on facility for your site and all other sites that support Passport authentication. You must sign up for the Passport service as a provider, and then implement access control appropriate to the various users who visit your site using the same system of permissions as for any other authentication method.

If anonymous access is disabled and the other methods are all enabled, IIS will attempt to use Integrated Windows authentication first, followed by digest authentication, with basic authentication used only as a last resort if the client does not support the other two methods.

You can also use the Authentication Methods dialog to specify which account is used for anonymous access. In Figure 14-7, from a Windows 2000 machine named DANDARE, you can see that the default is the machine's IUSR account:

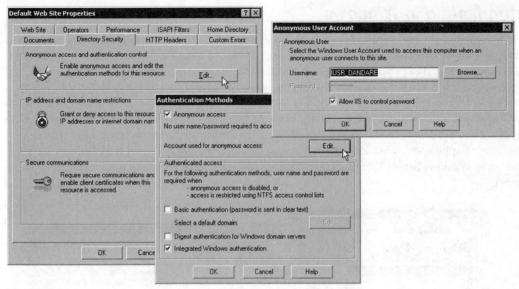

Figure 14-7

When set, the checkbox marked Allow IIS to control password in Figure 14-7 specifies that IIS will automatically extract the correct password for the IUSR account from Windows and use it when requesting resources on behalf of the user. It is checked by default, which means that you won't break the WWW service if you change the password for this account in the Computer Management tool at some point in the future.

Figure 14-8 shows the Authentication Methods dialog in Windows Sever 2003, on a machine named SUNDIVE-W2003. You can see that the .NET Passport authentication option is available in this dialog:

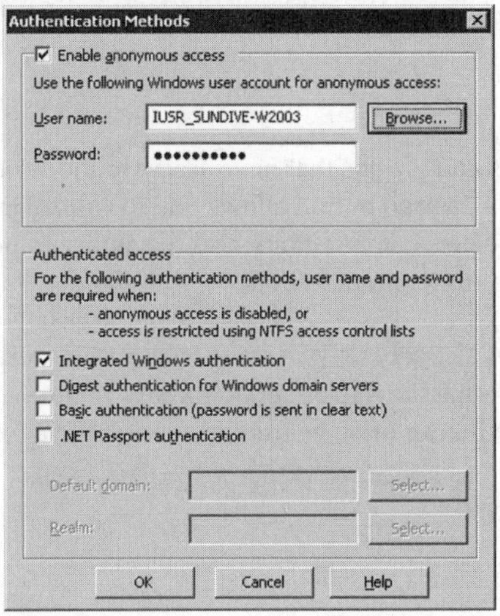

Figure 14-8

Authorization in Windows

So, assuming that your user has been successfully authenticated, what happens next? We mentioned in the previous section that a user will only be able to access the resource they requested if the account they were authenticated with has appropriate permission for that resource. These permissions are held in Access Control Lists (ACLs) that are allocated to every resource.

ACLs are managed in a range of ways – for example, Windows Explorer is used to manage the ACLs for files and folders on local and network drives. Open the Properties dialog for any file or folder in Windows Explorer and select the Security page, as shown in Figure 14-9 (this is a Windows 2000 machine, Windows Server 2003 is slightly different in appearance but works fundamentally the same way).

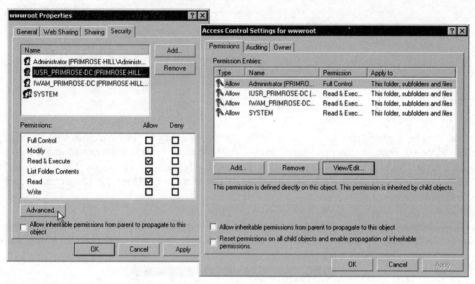

Figure 14-9

This dialog shows the accounts and groups that have access to the selected file or folder, and the permissions for each one. The Advanced button allows you to control the options in more detail, giving up to 13 different read/write/delete combinations, and the ability to propagate the permissions to child objects and inherit permissions from parent folders.

Other applications and services also rely on Windows accounts. For example, as shown in Figure 14-10, Microsoft SQL Server allows permissions to be set up for any Windows account. This means the account that the user is authenticated with can often be used to access all the resources they need:

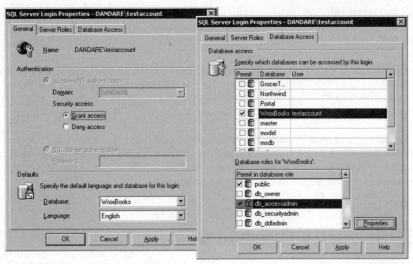

Figure 14-10

Authorization in IIS

There is one other area where security is applied to a web application or web site. IIS accesses resources on behalf of the user with either its own anonymous access account, or with the account credentials that the user provides when anonymous access is disabled. However, on a different level, it also specifies what they can do with the resource they have accessed.

The central section of the Home Directory page of the Properties dialog for a web site or directory specifies the type of operation that the user can perform within this site or directory. As shown in Figure 14-11, you can specify Script source access, Read, and/or Write permissions. The default is just Read:

Figure 14-11

Remember, however, that this is separate from the ACLs that Windows applies to that resource. Also, this setting is applied on a web site or directory basis, and not on a per-user basis. The settings here affect all users.

These settings offer an added layer of protection. For example, by default, users are prevented from writing to a web site directory through IIS, and they are also prevented from downloading any script files. These can only be executed, so that the source code is not visible. Of course, you can change these settings (and the others shown in this dialog) to suit your own application requirements.

However, if you decide to offer Write access for example, you must also set the appropriate permissions on the Windows ACL for the disk folders. As in all security scenarios, when settings for a resource conflict like this, the most restrictive ones will be applied. In other words, if the ACL says you can't write to the folder, allowing write access in IIS will have no effect.

ASP.NET Security Overview

Having briefly overviewed the security features provided by the operating system and IIS, the next step is to understand how these relate to the security features available within ASP.NET. As mentioned earlier, the process of authenticating users and authorizing their requests for resources is like a chain. The operating system and IIS have their own unique parts to play initially, as the request arrives at the server. Afterwards, providing that access is not denied by IIS, the request is passed to ASP.NET for processing and fulfillment.

The ASP.NET Security Process

The schematic in Figure 14-12 shows the process for an ASP.NET request in more detail.

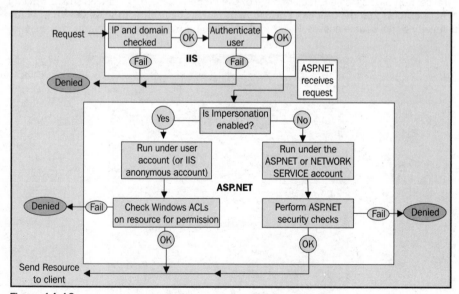

Figure 14-12

After IIS has checked the user's IP address and domain to ensure that they are allowed access, it authenticates the user. Remember that the user may be the IUSR account (the IIS anonymous account) if anonymous access is enabled. At this point IIS spawns an instance of the ASP application that holds the resource the user requested, or passes the request into an already executing instance of the application.

ASP.NET Impersonation

The first step in ASP.NET is to see if the application is configured to use *impersonation*. This is a similar concept to the way that IIS impersonates users with its anonymous account. However, in this case, impersonation is used to decide whether the user's request should be executed under the context of their account, or that of the special account that ASP.NET uses for anonymous requests.

This is confusing at first. The added complexity comes from the fact that ASP.NET uses the dynamic compilation features of the .NET Framework. It needs to write to the drive in various places to create temporary files and compiled assemblies. The IUSR account has only limited permissions on the local machine, and so is not suitable without some reconfiguration. This is intentional because it is also the account used by IIS to access resources like HTML pages, documents, and zip files that are not executed as part of the .NET Framework.

> *The account that is actually used for executing ASP.NET resources when impersonation is not enabled is controlled by the* `<processModel>` *element in the* `machine.config` *configuration file. The* `username` *and* `password` *attributes specify which account is used. The defaults for normal use are* `userName="machine"` *and* `password="AutoGenerate"`. *We'll look at this topic in more detail at the end of the chapter.*

If impersonation *is* enabled in an ASP.NET application:

❏ If anonymous access is enabled in IIS (the default) the request is made under the context of the IIS anonymous access account (`IUSR_machinename` by default).

❏ If anonymous access is not enabled in IIS, the request is made under the context of the authenticated user (their own Windows account).

❏ In either case, permissions for the account are checked in the Windows ACL for the resource(s) the user requested, and the resource is only available if the account is valid for that resource.

If impersonation is *not* enabled in an ASP.NET application (the default), then the request is made under the context of the ASP.NET process account, irrespective of whether anonymous access is enabled or not in IIS. This may be the ASPNET or the NETWORK SERVICE account, depending on the operating system version.

Other security checks are also possible within ASP.NET. The availability of these checks depends on the type of security specified. We'll overview the various options next, and look at these in more detail as we go through the chapter.

Windows Server 2003 and IIS 6.0

With the release of Windows Server 2003, Microsoft has made fundamental changes to the way that IIS works. The new version, IIS 6.0, uses application pools to provide a more scalable and robust architecture compared to previous versions of IIS. The accounts that are used to process requests are also changed in IIS 6.0 compared to earlier versions.

In versions of IIS up to 5.0, ASP.NET resources are accessed under an account named ASPNET. This account is created automatically on the machine when ASP.NET is installed, and given permission to access the services, files, and folders it requires in order to execute ASP.NET pages. When ASP.NET spawns a worker process, this process runs under the LOCAL SYSTEM account.

In IIS 6.0, by default, ASP.NET applications run within one or more application pools (unless you specify otherwise, they run within the default pool for the wwwroot folder and the Default Web Site). Worker processes for the application pools run under a new account called NETWORK SERVICE, which has reduced permissions compared to the LOCAL SYSTEM account. However, as you saw earlier in this chapter (in the section *User Groups*), there is an account group created named IIS_WPG, of which all the accounts required by ASP.NET are members.

This means that you have to configure access to resources based on which operating system you are using. In Windows 2000, Windows XP and Windows NT4 you configure permissions for the ASPNET account. In Windows Server 2003, in the default configuration for IIS 6.0, you configure permissions on resources either directly for the NETWORK SERVICE account, or for the IIS_WPG group so that it applies to all accounts that ASP.NET uses. The latter is the recommendation in the documentation for IIS 6.0.

Application Pools in IIS 6.0

It's clear from the earlier discussions of IIS 6.0 that application pools change the way that IIS behaves. In the IIS Manager snap-in tool for IIS 6.0, you will see a new entry Application Pools in the left-hand tree view. The DefaultAppPool entry denotes the default application pool that is created by IIS, and depending on what other software you have installed you may see others as well (such as MSSharePointAppPool if you have Microsoft SharePoint installed).

All the applications in the same application pool run within the same process space. However you can create more application pools, as required, and allocate your applications to them so that they run in separate process spaces. Just bear in mind that each one uses a separate block of resources, so it's likely that you'll want to run several applications within each pool, and hence divide the pools in such a way that you achieve the best combination of performance and protection.

However, application pools do attempt to minimize resource usage by recycling applications that are not in use. The Properties dialog for each application pool offers a range of configuration options under the Recycling and Performance tabs. You can also specify which process account the applications within each pool will run under.

As shown in Figure 14-13, the Identity page of the Properties dialog allows you to choose a pre-defined service account (the default is Network Service), or specify any other account. The IWAM_machinename account is pre-filled as an option if you wish to use this.

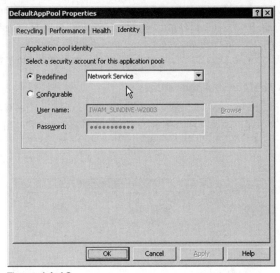

Figure 14-13

Creating a New Application Pool

Creating new application pools is simply a matter of selecting the appropriate menu option, as shown in Figure 14-14, and specifying a name. You can also save an application pool as a template on which to base new application pools (not shown here), or back up and restore the configuration of the application pools and then use the backups to create new application pools (the from file option shown in Figure 14-14).

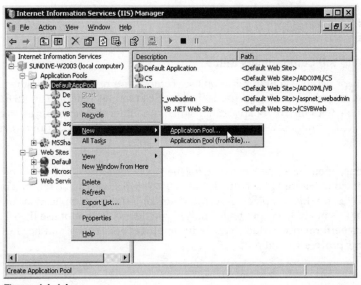

Figure 14-14

If you want to run multiple versions of ASP.NET on the same machine, you must create separate application pools for them. If you try and run two applications that execute under different versions of ASP.NET in the same application pool, you'll get a Server Unavailable error message in the resulting web page, and a message in Windows Event Log indicating the problem in more detail.

Selecting the Application Pool for an Application

You can select which application pool an application will run under in IIS 6.0 using the Application pool drop-down list in the Directory or Home Directory page of the Properties dialog for the application as shown in Figure 14-15. This list contains all the application pools that are currently configured in IIS 6.0 on the server.

Figure 14-15

Running IIS 6.0 in IIS 5.0 Compatibility Mode

If you wish, perhaps because your application uses components or resources that require complete ASP.NET version 1.0 compatibility as regards the process accounts, you can run IIS 6.0 in a mode that makes it compatible with IIS 5.0. All applications then run under the same processes as they would in IIS 5.0, and the ASPNET account is used instead of the NETWORK SERVICE account for access to resources by ASP.NET.

To select this mode, open the Properties dialog for the Web Sites entry in the left-hand tree, and go to the Service tab as shown in Figure 14-16. Note that IIS 5.0 isolation mode can be selected only for the complete WWW Service (the complete server), and not for individual applications or web sites. Also bear in mind that this mode is recommended only if you definitely cannot use IIS 6.0 default mode. It is not as robust, hits performance, reduces scalability, impinges on security, and negates the many advantages of true process separation.

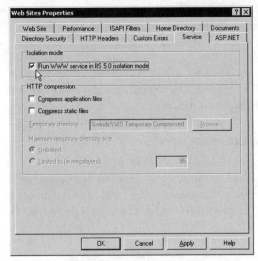

Figure 14-16

Web Service Extensions in IIS 6.0

Another area where configuration of ASP.NET differs between IIS 6.0 and previous versions is in a new feature called Web service extensions. IIS 6.0 controls access to resources for all requests based on the file type (defined by the file extension). IIS Manager contains a section that allows you to configure Web service extensions, allowing or prohibiting files of each specific type (see Figure 14-17).

If the extension is prohibited, the client receives a 404 Not Found message when they try and access a resource with that extension. This security measure protects the server, as it simply appears to the user that the specific file they requested does not exist. There is no external indication that it is in fact blocked by the web service extension.

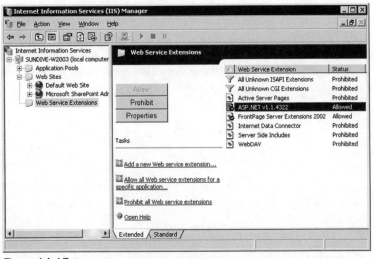

Figure 14-17

701

When you install ASP.NET on Windows Server 2003, it creates a web service extension for that particular version. However, you will usually have to go to the IIS Manager and enable it using the **Allow** button shown in Figure 14-17.

If you are unable to access any ASP.NET files, this is the first place to check. And if you have multiple versions of ASP.NET installed, there will be a separate web service extension for each one, so you can **Allow** or **Prohibit** individual versions if required.

Creating a New Web Service Extension

If the required web service extension does not exist, you can create one using the **Add a new Web service extension** link in the page shown in Figure 14-17. This link opens another dialog, as shown in Figure 14-18, to which you add a reference to the resource that will handle requests for files with this extension or of this type. With ASP.NET, as mentioned before, you can set up web service extensions for different versions.

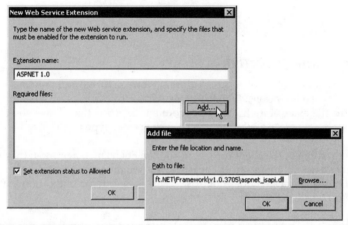

Figure 14-18

Afterwards the new extension appears in IIS Manager, as shown in Figure 14-19. Because the checkbox marked **Set extension to Allowed** is set in the dialog shown in Figure 14-18, the new web service extension is set to **Allowed** automatically:

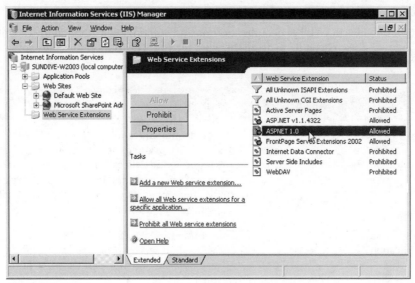

Figure 14-19

The ASP.NET Security Options

ASP.NET provides a range of different options for implementing security and restricting user access in a web application. All these options are configured within the `web.config` file located in the root folder of the application. The main features of `web.config` and its usage were discussed in Chapter 13. In this chapter, we'll focus on just the authentication and authorization sections.

Important Points When Using Security in ASP.NET

Before you get too engrossed in the following ASP.NET security examples, there are a couple of things to keep in mind:

❑ You don't *have* to change any of the default settings in Internet Services Manager, or change the permissions assigned to files or resources when using the security features that are configured for ASP.NET in the `web.config` file. The examples in this chapter work fine with the default settings. However, you can tighten security by editing these settings *as well*, as we describe in the following chapters when looking at the various configuration options.

❑ Many of the options you configure within `web.config` are applied automatically to any directory in which you place the `web.config` file. This applies to the authorization settings you make in the `<authorization>` section. However, *this is not the case* with the authentication security configuration settings in the `<authentication>` section. To use the authentication techniques described here, you *must* place the `web.config` file in the root folder of a web site (the Home Directory) *or* configure the directory that contains the `web.config` file as a virtual root or virtual application in Internet Services Manager. Afterwards, remember to access the application through this alias.

The Types of Authentication and Authorization

ASP.NET itself provides three types of authentication and authorization , though the first of these options (Windows) does rely on IIS to do all the work for you. The four options are shown in the following table:

Type	Name	Description
Windows built-in authentication	Windows	The initial authentication is performed by IIS through Basic, Digest, or Integrated Windows authentication. The requested resources are then accessed under the context of this account. The web.config file can specify the accounts that are valid for the whole or parts of the application.
Passport-based authentication	Passport	This option uses a centralized Web-based authentication service provided by Microsoft, which offers single-sign-on (SSN) and core profile services for member sites.
Forms-based authentication	Forms	Unauthenticated requests are automatically redirected to an HTML form page using HTTP client-side redirection. This is similar to custom authentication methods used in previous versions of ASP, but it provides much of the functionality as part of the framework of ASP.NET. The user provides their login credentials and submits the form. If the application authenticates the request, the system issues a cookie that contains their credentials (in fact, a key for re-acquiring the identity). The client browser then sends the cookie with all subsequent requests, and the user can access the application while they retain this cookie.
Default (IIS) authentication	None	The default. Impersonation can still be used, but access control is limited to that specified within IIS. Resources are accessed under the context of the ASP.NET process account, or the IUSR account if impersonation is enabled.

To specify the type of authentication you want to use in an ASP.NET virtual application or virtual directory, provide the Name shown in the <authentication> section of the web.config file for that site of directory, as shown in the following code:

```
<configuration>
...
<system.web>
  <authentication mode="Windows|Passport|Forms|None">
    authentication options used for the application
```

```
    </authentication>
    <authorization>
      users and roles that have access to the application
    </authorization>
    <identity>
      if application should run under a different account
    </identity>
  </system.web>
  ...
  </configuration>
```

The other two elements within the `<system.web>` section of `web.config` that we're interested in are used to specify the details of how authentication should be carried out. The `<authorization>` section is used to specify which users or groups can and cannot access the application. The `<identity>` section is used to specify if impersonation is enabled – in other words, whether to run under the user (or IUSR) account, the ASP.NET process account, or a different account that you specify. You'll see how to use these sections of the file when you look at each type of authentication in more detail next.

Using Windows Authentication in ASP.NET

Windows authentication is best suited to situations like a corporate Intranet web site or web application where you know in advance which users will be accessing your site. This is because you have to set up an account within Windows for each user, and provide them with the username password (the login credentials) they'll need to access the site. Of course, in an Intranet scenario, or an application where you can classify users into groups, you can set up an account for each group and allow all users who know the relevant username and password to access the application under this single account.

> *Note that we aren't referring to Windows account groups here – we're using the term 'group' simply to signify several users who will have the same access rights as each other.*

An example would be to set up a Windows account named *siteadmins*, and allow all administrators to log into the application using this account. Just bear in mind that this will not allow you to audit the actions of each individual user, as they will all be accessing resources under the same account credentials. However, this can be a suitable solution in many scenarios.

Setting Up Windows Authentication

To set up an application or a section of an application to use Windows authentication, simply specify this authentication mode and then turn on impersonation within the `<identity>` element. Now each user will access resources under the context of the account that they logged into IIS with. The `<identity>` element is only used with Windows authentication, and not with the other types of authentication that we'll meet later.

```
<configuration>
...
<system.web>
  <authentication mode="Windows" />
  <identity impersonate="true" />
</system.web>
...
</configuration>
```

Specifying Users and Groups

As well as simply specifying Windows authentication, you can also provide a list of users and groups that will be able to access the application. This is done within the `<authorization>` section of the `web.config` file, with a series of `<allow>` and `<deny>` elements. The general form of each of these elements is shown in the following code:

```
<allow roles="comma-separated list of Windows account group names"
       users="comma-separated list of Windows user account names"
       verb="GET|POST|HEAD"
/>

<deny roles="comma-separated list of Windows account group names"
      users="comma-separated list of Windows user account names"
      verb="GET|POST|HEAD"
/>
```

The `<allow>` and `<deny>` elements must contain either a `roles` or a `users` attribute. They do not have to contain both, and the `verb` attribute is always optional. To specify a domain user account, include the domain name followed by a backslash and the username, for example `MyDomainName\MyUserName`. There are also special values that refer to built-in account groups, such as `Everyone`, `BUILTIN\Administrators`, etc.

To specify a local (machine) account you can just use the machine name in place of the domain name. There is no way to specify a domain account without the actual domain (there is no short-cut that means 'use the local domain'), so you have to edit the list if you change the domain name or move the application to another domain.

There are also two special symbols that you can use:

❑ An asterisk (*) means all `users`, `roles`, or `verbs`, depending on the attribute it is used in.

❑ A question mark (?) means 'anonymous access'. In the case of Windows authentication, this is the account set up in IIS for anonymous access. This character can only be used within the `users` attribute.

The default configuration for a server is in the file `machine.config`, stored in the directory `C:\WINNT\Microsoft.NET\Framework\[version]\CONFIG\`. It contains a single `<allow>` element that permits all users to access ASP.NET resources:

```
<authorization>
  <allow users="*" />
</authorization>
```

The `<allow>` and `<deny>` elements are merged for all configuration files in the application path, starting with the root (default) configuration file `machine.config`, and including all `web.config` files in folders below this application directory. Rules that are higher up in the hierarchy (that is, nearer the application directory) take precedence over those in `web.config` files below them (nearer the root).

Once the merged list of `<allow>` and `<deny>` elements is created, they are processed from top to bottom and the best match for a user or role is selected. Processing doesn't just stop when the first match is found, but continues throughout all the entries fine-tuning the selection. This means that a specific reference to a user will take precedence over a role, and over a wildcard rule that uses the asterisk character. The merge process also gives `<deny>` elements precedence over `<allow>` elements, so that you can allow a Windows account group using `<allow roles="xxxx" />`, but deny specific users that are within that account group using `<deny users="yyyy" />`.

So, to control access to a specific application or a directory within an application, add a `web.config` file to that directory. For example, the `<authorization>` element shown in the following code permits access to the application for the domain-level account named billjones from the domain named **MyDomainName** and the local (machine) account named marthasmith, plus all members of the domain-level account group named **SalesDept**. All other users will be denied access.

```
<configuration>
...
<system.web>
  <authorization>
    <allow roles="MyDomainName\SalesDept"
           users="MyDomainName\billjones,MyMachineName\marthasmith" />
    <deny users="*" />
  </authorization>
</system.web>
...
</configuration>
```

> The `<allow>` element should always be located before the `<deny>` element.

Specifying HTTP Access Types

You can also use the `<allow>` and `<deny>` elements to control the type of HTTP action that a user can take when accessing an application or directory by using the verb attribute. The example shown in the following code allows the domain-level account named marthasmith to send POST requests to the application (submit an HTML form), but all other users will only be able to send GET requests. And, of course, you can combine this access control setting with the list of groups and users, by adding the verb attribute to the previous example that used the roles and users attributes.

```
<configuration>
<system.web>
  <authorization>
    <allow verb="GET" users="*" />
    <allow verb="POST" users="MyDomainName\marthasmith" />
    <deny verb="POST" users="*" />
  </authorization>
</system.web>
</configuration>
```

You can also use the `<location>` element to specify more than one `<system.web>` section, applying each of these sections to a specific path or file. This is useful for setting different permissions for subfolders or files using a single `web.config` file. For example, the following code shows how you can specify that a file named mypage.aspx will have different authorization settings from the rest of the files in the same folder:

```
<configuration>
...
<system.web>  <!-- default for this application -->
  <authorization>
    <allow verb="GET" users="*" />
    <allow verb="POST" users="MyDomainName\marthasmith" />
    <deny verb="POST" users="*" />
  </authorization>
</system.web>
<location path="mypage.aspx">  <!-- only applies to this file -->
  <system.web>
    <authorization>
      <allow verb="GET" users="*" />
      <allow verb="POST" users="MyDomainName\billjones" />
      <deny verb="POST" users="*" />
    </authorization>
  </system.web>
</location>
...
</configuration>
```

Running Under Another Specific Account

Finally, you can instruct ASP.NET to access resources under a specific account, rather than the user account that was authenticated by IIS or the special ASP.NET process account (which is normally used when impersonation is not enabled).

Here you're specifying that impersonation is enabled but, instead of using the ASP.NET process account, ASP.NET should access all resources under the context of the domain-level account named `MyUserName` from the domain named `MyDomainName`. You also have to provide the password for the account so that ASP.NET can present it to the operating system and other applications and services when it requires access to them.

```
<configuration>
...
<system.web>
  <identity impersonate="true"
            userName="MyDomainName\MyUserName"
            password="MyPassword" />
</system.web>
...
</configuration>
```

> **Remember that the password will be visible in the file, and this could introduce a security risk.**

IIS and Windows Security Settings for Windows Authentication

Remember that access control using the `Windows` authentication method depends on a Windows account being available for ASP.NET to use to access the requested resources. You can tighten security by using the ACLs on resources to allocate permission to just specific users, or to the accounts that the user will be running under. This isn't required, but does provide a second level of protection.

To be able to do this, you must be aware of which account is actually being used to access the resource, and give that account the appropriate permissions while removing any permissions that are not required. The schematic in Figure 14-20 shows which accounts you must set permissions for, depending on the configuration in your `machine.config` and `web.config` files:

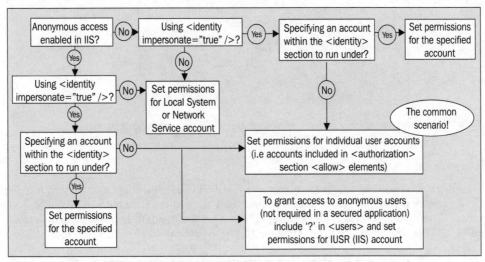

Figure 14-20

The Logon Process in Windows Authentication

When you access a resource in a secured application or virtual directory that does not allow anonymous access, you are always required to log on. However, if you are accessing the application or directory from the local machine or a machine on the same domain, you may not actually see the logon dialog. This is because – providing Integrated Windows authentication is enabled in Internet Services Manager (the default) – your browser will send your current Windows logon details in response to the logon challenge from the web server.

So, it's a good plan if you are building applications for the web (rather than for a corporate Intranet) to access the site from a machine that is not logged into the domain, as well as experimenting with one that is. On a machine that is not on the same domain (and not on a trusted domain), you will see the standard logon dialog, as shown in Figure 14-21:

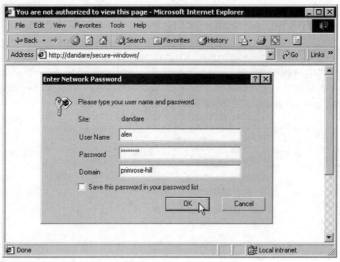

Figure 14-21

One useful way that you can tell what's going on as far as IIS authentication is concerned is to look at the page you get back if you make three attempts to access a secured resource with an invalid username or password. If anonymous access is *not enabled* in IIS, you get the standard IIS error page, as shown in Figure 14-22. This is because you have failed the IIS logon process.

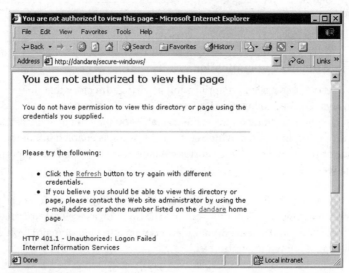

Figure 14-22

However, if anonymous access *is* enabled within Internet Services Manager (the default), you are granted access and the request is passed to ASP.NET. It then detects that you don't have permission to access the resource (because your Windows account username and/or password are invalid) and it sends back its own error page, as shown in Figure 14-23. Later on in this chapter, we'll see an example of Windows authentication that you can use to help configure your applications and virtual directories.

Figure 14-23

Using Passport Authentication in ASP.NET

Windows authentication provides the most secure way of controlling access and securing your ASP.NET applications. However, it falls down if you want to establish a single-sign-on policy for several applications that are distributed across different servers and sites – especially if these are geographically separated. The only solution is to set up the same accounts on all the servers, perhaps by establishing a Windows 2000 *forest* using Active Directory so that all the servers are part of the same enterprise – even if they are on different domains.

But even this fails if you want to enable a system where users can be authenticated using the same credentials across multiple sites that you don't provide yourself. For example, you might want to build a solution where a user can log onto one of the well-known sites like hotmail.com and then come to your site and be automatically authenticated based on the logon credentials they provided when they logged onto Hotmail.

This is possible using *Passport authentication*. Microsoft provides a *Passport Service* that can be used to authenticate users on any passport-enabled site, anywhere on the Internet. When they log onto a participating site, their browser or user agent sends their credentials to the passport service, which authenticates them and places a secure cookie on their machine. Then, when they access another participating site, the browser presents this cookie to the passport service to prove that the user has already been authenticated. The passport service then indicates who that user is to the new site so they can be properly authorized – that is, the new site can check if this user has permission to access the resource they've requested.

So, the power of the passport service is that a user can present the same credentials to any participating site, while only having to log in once during a session. When they close their browser, or indicate that they wish to log off, the cookie is destroyed. They must then log on again to re-access resources on any of the participating sites.

Setting Up Passport Authentication

Unfortunately, passport authentication doesn't come free – someone has to pay the running costs of the service. To set up passport authentication you must subscribe to the service, and install special software on your Web server to allow the process to work. Full details are available from http://www.microsoft.com/net/services/passport/business.asp.

Once you've installed the software and subscribed to the service, you configure passport authentication in the `web.config` file, as shown in the following code. The `<passport>` section supports a single attribute named `redirectUrl`. The default value (before you install and configure passport authentication) is `internal`, which means that unauthenticated requests will receive a generic error message created by your server. Any other string is assumed to be the URL of the passport service that unauthenticated requests will be redirected to for authentication.

```
<configuration>
...
<system.web>
  <authentication mode="Passport">
    <passport redirectUrl="internal|url" />
  </authentication>
</system.web>
...
</configuration>
```

Once passport authentication is enabled, the login process to your server goes something like this:

❑ The user requests a protected resource from your server. If they have already logged into the passport service, there will be an encrypted ticket in a cookie or the query string, and your server will access the passport service to get the user's identity.

❑ If there is no ticket, or if it has expired or is invalid, they are redirected to the passport service's login page on the main passport service servers. They present their credentials, are authenticated, and are redirected back to your server with an appropriate ticket.

❑ Your server can now check the user's authorization and provide the protected resource if they have the relevant permission.

Using Forms-based Authentication in ASP.NET

The third type of authentication available in ASP.NET is an excellent solution for applications where the highest levels of security are not required. *Forms-based authentication* (sometimes referred to as cookie-based authentication) automates many of the tasks that you would normally perform in earlier versions of ASP to build custom authentication solutions. Forms-based authentication also removes the unintuitive Windows Logon dialog, allowing you to replace it with an attractive custom form, or integrate the login controls (basically two text boxes and a button) into existing pages.

The schematic in Figure 14-24 describes the process. As usual, the request is received by IIS, which checks that the IP address and domain of the user are permitted. IIS also authenticates the user if anonymous access is disabled, although in this scenario you will almost always allow anonymous access because the access control is being performed by ASP.NET. Once IIS is happy with the user's request, it passes it to ASP.NET, where the first step is to see if there is an authentication cookie within the request headers.

The forms authentication process generates this cookie when the user logs into the application. If it's present, you know that they have already been authenticated and the cookie contains their identity. ASP.NET then checks whether this user is authorized to access the resource they requested, and if so sends it to them. If not, the user is denied access.

If the cookie is not present in the request headers, the user is automatically redirected to a custom login page that you create yourselves. The user enters their credentials into this login page and submits it to your application where these credentials are automatically checked to authenticate the user. If they are recognized, an authentication cookie is added to the headers and the request is sent to the next stage of the process. ASP.NET checks to see if this user is authorized to access the resource they requested, and if so sends it to them. If not, they are denied access.

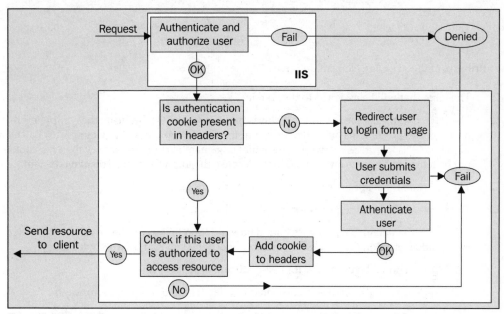

Figure 14-24

Setting Up Forms-Based Authentication

Like all other ASP.NET security settings, forms-based authentication is configured within the web.config file for an application or a virtual directory. As shown in the following code, the <authentication> section carries the value "Forms" for the mode attribute, and within the element itself you can add more elements to specify how the authentication of users will behave:

```
<configuration>
...
<system.web>
  <authentication mode="Forms">
    <forms name="cookie-name"
           path="cookie-path"
           loginurl="url"
           protection="All|None|Encryption|Validation"
```

713

```
                timeout="number-of-minutes"
                requireSSL="true|false"
                slidingExpiration="true|false" >
          <credentials passwordFormat="Clear|SHA1|MD5">
            <user name="user-name" password="user-password" />
            <user name="user-name" password="user-password" />
            ... more users listed here ...
          </credentials>
        </forms>
      </authentication>
      <machineKey validationKey="AutoGenerate[,IsolateApps]|key"
                  decryptionKey="AutoGenerate[,IsolateApps]|key"
                  validation="SHA1|MD5"/>
    </system.web>
    ...
  </configuration>
```

The attributes of the `<forms>` element define:

❑ The `name` that will be assigned to the cookie.

❑ The `path` that the cookie is valid for. This is usually set to "/" to indicate the complete site. If not, and the site contains links that are not in the correct letter case (for example an `<a>` element with `href="mypage.aspx"` where the actual page name is `MyPage.aspx`), then the cookie will not be returned by some browsers. This will cause the login form to be displayed again.

❑ The `loginurl` that specifies the virtual path to the login form page.

❑ The `protection` level required for the cookie. The settings are:

    ❑ `All` (the default), which uses both data validation (based on the `<machineKey>` element) and encryption (Triple DES if available and if the key is at least 48 bytes long)

    ❑ `None` (should be used only for personalization purposes)

    ❑ `Encryption` (the cookie is encrypted but data validation is not performed)

    ❑ `Validation` (validation is performed but the cookie is not encrypted)

❑ The `timeout` in minutes before the cookie expires on the user's machine and the server.

❑ The `requiresSSL` value can be set to `true` to force the use of SSL for any pages that pass the authentication cookie across the wire. The default is `false`. This feature was added in version 1.1.

❑ The `slidingExpiration` value determines if sliding expiration is used. When `true` (the default), each access to a secured page resets the timeout. When `false`, the timeout is enforced from initial login. This feature was added in version 1.1.

Within the `<forms>` element is an optional `<credentials>` element that specifies the encryption algorithm used to encrypt the user's password in the `web.config` file. Within this element there can be a series of optional `<user>` elements, which between them specify the users who will be able to access the protected resources.

Specifying Encryption and Validation Key Generation Methods

You can also specify an optional `<machineKey>` element within the `<system.web>` section, which specifies the keys and method to be used to encrypt the cookie contents. In general you will omit this element and allow a key to be created automatically. However, it can be useful in a situation like a web farm, where you want all machines to use the same key. The key length must match the number of characters required for the encryption level and method that is used. The entry in the default `machine.config` file (in the following code) specifies that the keys are auto-generated:

```
<machineKey validationKey="AutoGenerate,IsolateApps"
            decryptionKey="AutoGenerate,IsolateApps"
            validation="SHA1" />
```

Notice the `IsolateApps` modifier (suffix) on the `validationKey` and `decryptionKey` attribute values. These are new in version 1.1 of ASP.NET, and cause the auto-generated keys to include details of the ASP.NET application that is using Forms authentication (and which is creating the cookie) within the key that is generated. This improves security and application isolation, especially where a server is hosting multiple sites or applications that are not supposed to be able to share authentication cookies.

In reality, it means that different applications using Forms authentication, running on the same machine, will generate different keys for securing their cookies, rather than all using the same key (as was the case in version 1.0). However, the only times that this new behavior is likely to affect your applications are:

❑ Where you rely on shared authentication cookies, perhaps where you have nested applications (an application within a subfolder of another application, with the `Path` of the cookie set to `"/"` in the local `web.config` file).

❑ Where you are passing the viewstate in a page to a different application through some kind of customized form-post. This is because the values in the `<machineKey>` element are used to validate and encrypt the viewstate string that is inserted into a hidden control when an ASP.NET server-side `<form>` is used.

To retain the version 1.0 behavior when running under version 1.1 of the .NET Framework, you can:

❑ Remove the `IsolateApps` modifiers from `machine.config`, or (better) use a local `web.config` file that does not contain the `IsolateApps` modifiers. This gives behavior that is identical to version 1.0.

❑ Change the `validationKey` and `decryptionKey` attribute values to specify an explicit key, rather than auto-generating it. If you are using a web farm or other shared server setup to drive the site, you will be using a specific key that is the same on all the servers anyway, and so the behavior will be identical to version 1.0.

An Example: Forms-Based Authentication Configuration

So, an example `web.config` file might look like that shown in the following code. Remember that the `<credentials>` and `<machineKey>` sections are optional. The example shown also lists some users, and you can see that the passwords are encrypted in this case. You'll see where you get these values from later in the chapter.

```
<configuration>
...
<system.web>
  <authentication mode="Forms">
    <forms name="MyNewApp" path="/" loginUrl="/main/login.aspx"
           protection="All" timeout="30" >
      <credentials passwordFormat="SHA1">
        <user name="billjones"
              password="87F8ED9157125FFC4DA9E06A7B8011AD80A53FE1" />
        <user name="marthasmith"
              password="93FB8A49CC350BAEB2661FA5C5C97959BD328C50" />
        <user name="joesoap"
              password="5469541CA9236F939D889B2B465F9B15A09149E4" />
      </credentials>
    </forms>
  </authentication>
  <!-- keys usually only specified for a Web farm -->
  <machineKey validationKey="3875f9...645a78ff"
              decryptionKey="3875f9...645a78ff"
              validation="SHA1" />
</system.web>
...
</configuration>
```

The `<identity>` *element is not used in forms-based authentication.*

Creating a Login Form

After you've completed the configuration tasks with `web.config`, what about the things you have to do as developers to complete the setup of forms-based authentication? You need a form that will be used to collect the user's credentials, and code to process these credentials. The following code shows a simple example of the HTML section of the page:

```
<%@Page Language="VB" %>
<html>
<body>

<form runat="server">
  UserName: <input id="txtUsr" type="text" runat="server" /><p />
  Password: <input id="txtPwd" type="password" runat="server" /><p />
  <ASP:CheckBox id="chkPersist" runat="server" />
  Remember my credentials<p />
  <input type="submit" value="Login" runat="server"
                       onserverclick="DoLogin" />
  <div id="outMessage" runat="server" />
</form>

</body>
</html>
... script section goes here ...
```

This creates a login form page containing textboxes for the username and password, and a checkbox where the user can specify whether their credentials are to be *remembered* so that they won't have to login again next time they visit the site. Next there is a Login button that fires an event handler named `DoLogin` on the server, followed by a `<div>` element where you display a message if the user's credentials are incorrect. The visual appearance of the page can be seen in Figure 14-25:

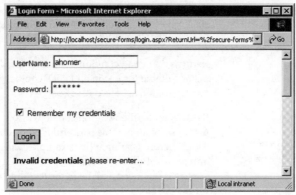

Figure 14-25

> To prevent the user's credentials being passed over the network in clear text, you should consider storing this form in a directory that has SSL (HTTPS) enabled. Once they are validated, the encrypted cookie can be used in the application over HTTP as usual. The content of the authentication cookie is just the encrypted session ticket – it does not contain the username or password.

Writing the Login Code

While forms-based authentication is a clever technology, it can't do everything automatically. You have to write code that authenticates the user and performs the other operations required, such as creating the cookie and redirecting the user to the page they originally requested. However, this is very simple.

All the classes used in ASP.NET security are in the `System.Web.Security` namespace of the class library. The class that handles forms-based authentication is called `FormsAuthentication`, and it exposes a range of `Static` methods and properties that you can use in your code. The most common methods are shown in the following table:

Method	Description
Authenticate (*userid, password*)	Checks to see if a username and password combination is valid by comparing it to the set of users specified within web.config. Returns True or False.
Decrypt (*string*)	Returns an instance of a FormsAuthenticationTicket class, given a valid encrypted authentication ticket obtained from an HTTP cookie as a String.
Encrypt (*ticket*)	Returns a String containing an encrypted authentication ticket suitable for use in an HTTP cookie, given a FormsAuthenticationTicket.
GetAuthCookie (*userid, persistent*) GetAuthCookie (*userid, persistent, path*)	Returns the authentication cookie without adding it to the response headers. This is useful if when customizing the cookie before issuing it (for example changing the path it applies to). Takes the user ID or name, a Boolean value to specify if the logon will be persistent, and optionally a path for the cookie.
GetRedirectUrl (*userid, persistent*)	Returns the URL of the original page that the user requested before being redirected to the login page. Can be used in conjunction with SetAuthCookie to provide custom authentication when the RedirectFromLoginPage method is not being used. Accepts the user ID or name and a Boolean value to specify if the logon will be persistent.
HashPasswordFor Storing InConfigFile (*password, hash-type*)	Creates and returns a String that is the encrypted values of a password, using the specified hash type ("SHA" or "MD5").
RedirectFromLoginPage (*userid, persistent*) RedirectFromLoginPage (*userid, persistent, path*)	Performs all the actions required once a user has been authenticated, including: creating the encrypted cookie, adding it to the request headers, and redirecting the user to the page they originally requested. Takes the user ID or name, a Boolean value to specify if the logon will be persistent, and optionally a path for the cookie.
RenewTicketIfOld (*ticket*)	Takes a FormsAuthenticationTicket and returns it with the sliding expiration conditionally updated.
SetAuthCookie (*userid, persistent*) SetAuthCookie (*userid, persistent, path*)	Creates the encrypted cookie, and adds it to the headers, but doesn't redirect the user. Allows the tasks normally accomplished by the RedirectFromLoginPage method to be performed individually, and tailored to a particular situation. Takes the user ID or name, a Boolean value to specify if the logon will be persistent, and optionally a path for the cookie.
SignOut	Destroys the current encrypted cookie, effectively logging the user out of the application.

The following table lists the read-only static properties of the `FormsAuthentication` class:

Property	Description
FormsCookieName	Returns the name for the cookie as configured for the current application as a `String`.
FormsCookiePath	Returns the path of the cookie as configured for the current application as a `String`.
RequireSSL	Returns a `Boolean` value indicating whether a cookie must be transmitted only over a secure connection. Added in version 1.1.
SlidingExpiration	Returns a `Boolean` value indicating whether sliding expiration is enabled for the cookie as configured for the current application. See the section *How Long Is a Login Valid For?* later in this chapter for more details. Added in version 1.1.

So, to authenticate your user and return them to the page they originally requested, you just need to create an event handler that is executed when the **Login** button is clicked. In your login form, you specified the subroutine `DoLogin` as the value of the `onserverclick` attribute of the login button. Let's start by checking to see if the username and password that were provided are valid within the list of users in `web.config`. If they are, the `Authenticate` method returns `True` and you can call the `RedirectFromLoginPage` method to create the cookie, add it to the request headers, and redirect the user to the page they originally requested. It's as simple as that.

```
Sub DoLogin(objSender As Object, objArgs As EventArgs)
   If FormsAuthentication.Authenticate(txtUsr.Value, txtPwd.Value) Then
      FormsAuthentication.RedirectFromLoginPage(txtUsr.Value, _
                                        chkPersist.Checked)
   Else
      outMessage.InnerHtml = "<b>Invalid credentials</b> please re-enter."
   End If
End Sub
```

How Long Is a Login Valid?

One interesting point is how long the authentication cookie will be valid for. If you don't specify a value for the `timeout` attribute in the `<forms>` element in `web.config`, the cookie will only remain on the user's machine for 30 minutes (the default setting in `machine.config`), or until they close their browser. However, you can set the `timeout` attribute in the `<forms>` element to over ride this setting.

This means that they will be able to leave the site and come back to it again within 30 minutes providing that they haven't closed their browser (or deleted the cookie). Of course, as the user accesses pages within the site, the cookie will be updated with each response from the server, and so the timeout only comes into force the specified number of minutes after the last time they accessed a page. This is called *sliding expiration*. But, even if they leave their browser running, they will be effectively logged out after the timeout period. This provides a better level of security. You also have the option to persist the cookie between sessions. When you call the `RedirectFromLoginPage` method, you need to specify a `Boolean` value for the second parameter. In the example code, this is the value of the `Checked` property of the checkbox control on the login page:

```
FormsAuthentication.RedirectFromLoginPage(username, persist-cookie)
```

Passing the value `True` to the method causes it to create a cookie with a long expiry date and time (50 years from now!) so that the user will not have to log back into the site when they return again. Although most modern browsers store cookies on a per-user basis (providing that the client machine is set up to force users to log in), this can present a security risk. It's not difficult to hijack a cookie, and by doing so the hijacker will automatically be granted access to the site during the lifespan of that cookie. Nevertheless, it is a useful feature for low-security or personalization-only scenarios.

Finally, you can expire a cookie immediately on demand by calling the `SignOut` method. You can place a **Log Off** button or link on a page, and create an event handler that destroys the cookie and prevents the user accessing any other resources until they log in again. In the event handler all that's needed is:

```
FormsAuthentication.SignOut()
```

However, if a user has *stolen* a persistent cookie, this will not detect and remove it. Hence, persistent cookies should never be used for applications other than those performing basic personalization and requiring the minimum level of security.

Authorizing Users with Forms-Based Security

So far, you've only actually *authenticated* (or identified) the user – you haven't specified what resources they will be allowed to access. Unless you are happy for any authenticated user to access any of the resources within the site or directory (an unlikely scenario in a secured application), you must include an `<authorization>` section in `web.config` as well. If not, the default authorization level specified in the `machine.config` file (shown in the following code) will be used:

```
<authorization>
  <allow users="*" />
</authorization>
```

To allow only specified users to access the application, add an appropriate `<authorization>` element to the `web.config` file for this site or directory. The format and content are the same as we described earlier when looking at Windows authentication and authorization – and the same rules apply.

Note that you're using the anonymous access wildcard (?) in the `<deny>` element. In forms-based authentication, this indicates that only users you specifically authenticate will be allowed access. Irrespective of which Windows account the user is running under (generally it will be the ASP.NET process account in this case), they will only be permitted access if they are in the list of users in the `<allow>` element.

```
<configuration>
...
<system.web>
  <authorization>
```

```
        <allow users="billjones,marthasmith,joesoap" verb="GET" />
        <allow users="marthasmith" verb="POST" />
        <deny users="?" />
    </authorization>
</system.web>
...
</configuration>
```

You can also get away with using just the single `<deny>` element that prevents unauthenticated access if you don't want to set any specific access permissions for the users you authenticate. In other words, providing that you are happy for all users that are listed in the `<authentication>` section to have access to all resources in the application using any type of HTTP method (`POST`, `GET`, `HEAD`), you can use the simple configuration setting shown in the following code:

```
<authorization>
    <deny users="?" />
</authorization>
```

> Don't be tempted to try and set Windows ACL permissions on resources for the users you specify when using forms-based authentication. Even if Windows accounts do exist for these users, they are not used when the user logs in via forms-based authentication. All access will be performed under the context of the ASP.NET process account (which must have access to the resource).

Custom Lists of User Credentials

All your forms-based authentication configuration examples so far have used the `<credentials>` section of `web.config` to store the list of users that you authenticate requests against. In many cases this is not practical. Rather than manually editing a text file to add and remove users, you will often want to store user details elsewhere – maybe in a database table, an XML document, or even Active Directory. However, it's still useful to be able to take advantage of the other features that forms-based authentication provides, such as automatic redirection to a login page, encryption and validation of the authentication cookie, and integration with the environment (which allows you to retrieve the user's details elsewhere in your code; more details of this coming up later).

It's easy to accomplish lookups of user credentials in other data stores, as the examples at the end of the chapter demonstrate. For example, you can use the relational data access capabilities of .NET to retrieve values from a relational database using SQL statements or stored procedures, or you can use classes from the `System.Xml` namespace to access XML documents.

Programmatic Security and Personalization

The techniques described so far can be used to control access to resources based on the principle of uniquely identifying a user through *authentication*, and then checking that user's access permission for a resource through *authorization*. This is sufficient to implement the common types of access control requirement for most applications.

However, there are times when you want to be able to control access on a more granular level, or just be able to tell who the current user is within your code. These two techniques are often referred to under the generic terms *programmatic security* and *personalization*. Let's look at them to see how to get information about the currently logged-on user.

Roles and Identity Overview

Once a user has been authenticated, the system knows at least something about that user. At minimum, it knows the username (the *identity*) and the *type of authentication* that was carried out. In the case of `Windows` authentication, it also knows which *roles* (that is, which Windows account groups) the user is a member of.

You can access this information in code, and use it to tailor the way that your applications behave. For example, you can display different pages or change the content of pages depending on the specific user, or on the groups that they are members of. This is a very useful feature, as the only alternative would be to create multiple copies of the page and set up permission to access each page for the appropriate users. And even then, the only way that the user would know which page they could access would be to try them all. Not exactly a user-friendly approach!

There is also the situation where you allow each user to personalize their pages within an application – perhaps to show different content, or just to change the font size, background color, etc. Again, you need to know who the user is so that you can build the appropriate pages. Maybe one user wants to see the current news headlines on their home page in your application, while another just wants the daily Dilbert cartoon.

Getting the User Identity and Role

The technique you use to get the user's identity depends on the type of authentication you used originally. ASP.NET exposes the `IPrincipal` object as the `User` property of the current `HttpContext` object (the context within which the page is executing). Through the `Identity` property, the `User` object exposes a reference to the `IIdentity` object that describes the current user. This object provides properties that you can use to identify the current user, as shown in the following table:

Property	Description
Name	Returns the username or the name of the account that the user logged on with, including the domain name if it was a Windows domain account
IsAuthenticated	Returns True if the current user has been authenticated
AuthenticationType	Returns a string indicating the authentication method used – for example, Forms, NTLM, Basic, Passport

Depending on the type of authentication used, the `Identity` property will actually be an instance of one of three different objects. For Windows authentication, the property returns a `WindowsIdentity` object, for Passport authentication it returns a `PassportIdentity` object, and for Forms-based authentication it returns a `FormsIdentity` object. The three properties listed in the preceding table are common to all these objects:

```
strUserName = User.Identity.Name
blnAuthenticated = User.Identity.IsAuthenticated
strAuthType = User.Identity.AuthenticationType
```

However, the different `Identity` objects also expose properties that are specific to the type of authentication used. For example, the `WindowsIdentity` object exposes properties for the Windows security token and `Boolean` values indicating if the account is a guest account, an anonymous account, or a system account. The `FormsIdentity` object exposes the current user's cookie *ticket* value, and the `PassportIdentity` object exposes a host of properties and methods that are specific to this type of authentication.

The namespace containing the class that implements the `Identity` object (`System.Web.Security`) is imported into ASP.NET pages by default, but to create a specific reference to a `WindowsIdentity` object you also need to import the `System.Security.Principal` namespace:

```
<%@Import Namespace="System.Security.Principal" %>
```

This allows you to cast the `User.Identity` to a `WindowsIdentity` object, and use the extra properties and methods it provides. A full list of all the properties and methods for each object is included in the .NET Framework SDK in the section **Reference | Class Library | System.Security.Principal**.

Checking the User's Role

If Windows authentication was used, it's possible to tell which Windows account group the current user is a member of. Or rather, to be more exact, it's possible to tell if the user is a member of a group that you specify. For security reasons, you can't enumerate the list of groups – instead you specify the group name in a call to the `IsInRole` method. This is a method of the `User` object for the current context:

```
blnResult = User.IsInRole("MyDomainName\SalesDept")
```

This method is useful if you want to change the behavior of a page or application based on the Windows account group that the user is a member of. For example, you can display different menus or links pages for members of the *Administrators* group, or change the appearance of pages for members of a group named *SalesDept* compared to the appearance when a member of the *AccountingDept* group accesses them. To test for a local (machine-level) account group include the machine name instead of the domain name:

```
blnResult = User.IsInRole("MyMachineName\SalesDept")
```

Using Built-in Account Groups

Windows 2000 includes several built-in groups, and it adds users to these groups automatically. For example, all user accounts are automatically members of the built-in Users group, and the administrator account is a member of the built-in Administrators group. To specify one of these built-in groups, you must include the word `BUILTIN` as though it is the domain name, for example:

```
blnResult = User.IsInRole("BUILTIN\Users")
blnResult = User.IsInRole("BUILTIN\Administrators")
```

However, instead of using the name of the group directly, you can substitute values from the enumeration named `WindowsBuiltInRole` to specify the groups that are built into Windows. This is useful because it will detect the groups or individual accounts if they have been renamed, and will also work on platforms other than Windows 2000 and in other localized operating system languages.

For example, using `WindowsBuiltInRole.Administrator` will include the built-in **Administrator** account, even if you have renamed it. The full list of members of this enumeration is shown in the following code:

```
WindowsBuiltInRole.AccountOperator
WindowsBuiltInRole.Administrator
WindowsBuiltInRole.BackupOperator
WindowsBuiltInRole.Guest
WindowsBuiltInRole.PowerUser
WindowsBuiltInRole.PrintOperator
WindowsBuiltInRole.Replicator
WindowsBuiltInRole.SystemOperator
WindowsBuiltInRole.User
```

ASP.NET Security Examples

So far in this chapter we've discussed the theory of authentication and access control in ASP.NET applications. This section looks at some examples that use the different aspects of security we've been exploring. The samples cover:

- ❏ Configuring a web application using Windows authentication
- ❏ Accessing the user's identity within this application
- ❏ Accessing the user's role within this application
- ❏ Configuring a web application using forms-based authentication
- ❏ Using different types of user credentials lists
- ❏ Accessing the user's identity within this application
- ❏ A simple personalization example

Obtaining the Example Files

The example files for this chapter can be downloaded from http://www.daveandal.net/books/8900/. You can also run many of them online at the same URL. The `default.htm` menu page shown in Figure 14-26 provides links to the example pages.

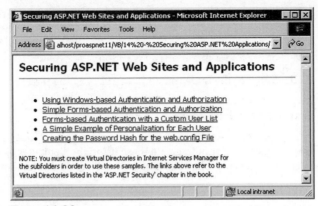

Figure 14-26

Setting Up the Examples on Your Server

Before you can use the examples we provide, there are a couple of things you need to do. First, you must create a virtual root to each of the subfolders containing the example pages within Internet Services Manager. In the Default Web Site entry for your server, create new virtual roots by right clicking and selecting New | Virtual Directory, as shown in Figure 14-27:

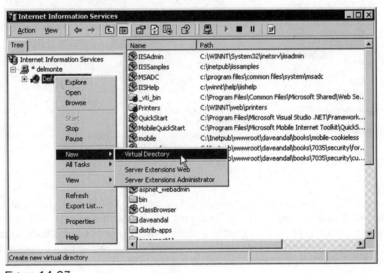

Figure 14-27

In the Wizard that appears, enter the appropriate alias from the following list, select the corresponding directory where you installed the example files, and then ensure that you leave the Read and Run Scripts permissions selected. The four aliases used (and which are included in the links on the `default.htm` menu page) are:

❑   **Secure-forms**: Pointing to the folder in the examples named `security\forms-based`

❑   **Secure-custom-forms**: For the folder named `security\custom-forms-based`

❑   **Secure-windows**: For the folder in `security\windows`

❑   **Secure-personalization**: For the folder named `security\personalization`

Creating the Windows Test Account and Groups

Our Windows authentication example uses a local user account named TestUser, and two local groups named TestGroup and NoMembers. You should create these using the Computer Management utility on your server – avoid using a domain controller machine as it will create domain-level accounts rather than local accounts.

As shown in Figure 14-28, right-click the Users entry in Local Users and Groups, and select New User. Enter the account name TestUser, a simple password that you can remember, uncheck User must change password at next logon, and check User cannot change password:

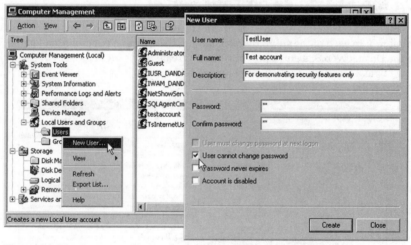

Figure 14-28

Then click Create followed by Close. Now select the Groups entry, right-click, and select New Group, as shown in Figure 14-29. Name the new group TestGroup, click Add, and select the TestUser account and then your own domain or local user account as members of the group. Click Create to create this group, and then enter the name NoMembers for another group and click Create again followed by Close. As the name suggests, you shouldn't add any members to the NoMembers group.

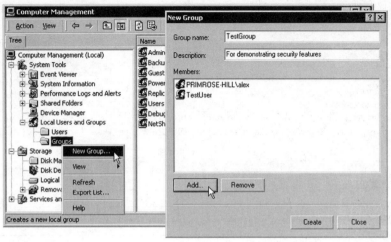

Figure 14-29

Creating the UserList Database

The only other task is to create the database of users for the custom-forms-based and personalization examples. We've provided a SQL script file named `make-security-db.sql` in the `security` folder of the samples that will do this for you. Full instructions on creating the database are included in the file `database-readme.txt` in the same folder as the SQL script. You may need to edit the `web.config` files that are located in the two folders `security\custom-forms-based` and `security\personalization` to specify the name of your database server (if it is not the default on your machine) in the connection string for the `UserList` database:

```
<appSettings>
  <add key="DsnUserList"
       value="Provider=SQLOLEDB; server=.; database=UserList; uid=sa; pw=" />
</appSettings>
```

Finally, you will have to recreate the password hash values and update the database for the final example, as the hash is machine-dependent (it depends on the value of the `machineKey` element in `web.config`, for which the default value is `AutoGenerate, IsolateApps` – as you saw earlier). You can use the sample page described later in this section to create the new hashes for your machine.

Windows Authentication Example

The first example, Using Windows-based Authentication and Authorization, demonstrates how to use Windows authentication and authorization with a web site or web application directory. It uses the `web.config` file.

This instructs the server to authenticate the user through IIS and Windows so they must login using a valid Windows account. It is also specified that you want to use impersonation, so the application will run under the context of this account. Then, in the `<authorization>` section, specify that only members of the built-in Administrators group, the local Administrator account on the machine named

DANDARE, and the local test user account named TestUser (on the same machine) can access the folder and its contents.

```
<configuration>
<system.web>
  <authentication mode="Windows" />
  <identity impersonate="true" />
  <authorization>
    <allow roles="BUILTIN\Administrators"
           users="DANDARE\Administrator,DANDARE\TestUser" />
    <deny users="*" />
  </authorization>
</system.web>
</configuration>
```

Remember to edit the machine name when you run the example on your own server.

If you try and open the page under the context of a different account, access is denied. In Figure 14-30, the page is accessed from a machine that is not on the domain and a username and password combination is specified for an account that does exist on the target server, but which is not included in the list of users specified within the web.config file:

Figure 14-30

If you now log in using a suitable account that is included in the list in the web.config file, you'll see a page that shows your account login name (your username), and a selection of other information about your account.

In Figure 14-31, we've logged in using the TestUser account created earlier, and our own domain account that has the username alex. You can see the account name, complete with the machine or domain name, the authentication method used, the type of account, and the groups that the account is a member of.

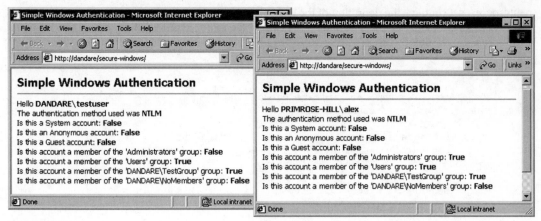

Figure 14-31

To experiment, you can edit the web.config file to specify different accounts and account groups that are to be permitted access to the folder, and see the effects. Remember to close and reopen your browser each time you edit web.config so that you are not trying to access the pages using the previous logon credentials.

How This Example Works

Simply placing the web.config file into the virtual directory containing your restricted pages is enough to look after authentication and authorization. The page you see when you do successfully log into the application (default.aspx) is just responsible for displaying the details of the account you used.

The page includes the Import directives required to use the Windows-based security features. This is needed because you want to be able to access the account information using a WindowsIdentity object:

```
<%@Import Namespace="System.Security.Principal" %>
```

The HTML part of the page contains a single <div> element that is used to display the account details:

```
<div id="msgHello" runat="server" />
```

Checking for Authentication and Accessing the User's Identity

The code that gets information about the current user is in the Page_Load event, so it runs as the page is being created. The first thing to do is check that the user has in fact been authenticated. This will always be the case with the web.config file you're using, but it's a good idea to include this check.

Access the User object via the current context of the page (it is a property of the integral HttpContext object), and get a reference to the user's Identity object from it. The IsAuthenticated property returns True if the user has been authenticated:

Now you can get a reference to the actual WindowsIdentity object for this user. The Identity property returns an Identity object, and you cast this to a WindowsIdentity object (in VB this is done with the CType method). This is why you need to import the System.Security.Principal namespace, as it contains the definition of the `WindowsIdentity` class. From this `WindowsIdentity` object you can get more detailed information by calling the `GetCurrent` method, which also returns a `WindowsIdentity` object.

```
Sub Page_Load()

    'see if the user has been authenticated
    If User.Identity.IsAuthenticated Then

        'create a reference to a WindowsIdentity object that
        'represents this user's Indentity object
        Dim objIdentity = CType(User.Identity, WindowsIdentity)

        'get the current WindowsIdentity object for this user
        'this contains more specific information
        Dim objWinIdentity = objIdentity.GetCurrent()
        ...
```

You can use the original `WindowsIdentity` object returned by the `Users` property instead of creating the second one using the `GetCurrent` method. However, the `GetCurrent` method builds the identity using the operating system-level process token rather than just using the current `HTTPContext` object, and so contains information about the logon account that is not available when impersonation is turned off and you are running under the IIS anonymous account.

Displaying the Account Details

You can now access your `WindowsIdentity` object to display information about this user's account. As shown in the following code, display the username and authentication type from the appropriate properties, and you can tell if the account is a `System`, `Anonymous`, or `Guest` account using three more of the properties of the `WindowsIdentity` object:

```
    ...
    'display the properties
    msgHello.InnerHtml = "Hello " & objWinIdentity.Name & "<br />" _
        & "The authentication method used was " _
        & objWinIdentity.AuthenticationType & "<br />" _
        & "Is this a System account: " _
        & objWinIdentity.IsSystem & "<br />" _
        & "Is this an Anonymous account: " _
        & objWinIdentity.IsAnonymous & "<br />" _
        & "Is this a Guest account: " _
        & objWinIdentity.IsGuest & "<br />" _
    ...
```

Accessing the User's Role

Now you can investigate which roles (that is, which Windows account groups) this user account belongs to. For this, you can use the `IsInRole` method of the `User` object, and specify the account group you're checking against.

Of course, you'll have to edit the code here to specify your own machine name – and you can add checks to see if the account is in other groups that exist on your own server and domain. However, it's easy to see from this how you can use programmatic security techniques to modify the behavior of an application based on the details of the user that are exposed by the `WindowsIdentity` object. We demonstrate a few of these techniques in conjunction with forms-based authentication in the final example of this chapter.

The final few lines in the page complete the `If..Then` construct, and (just for completeness) display a message if the user accessed this page without being authenticated.

```
      ...
      & "Is this account a member of 'Administrators' group: " _
      & User.IsInRole("BUILTIN\Administrators") & "<br />" _
      & "Is this account a member of the 'Users' group: " _
      & User.IsInRole("BUILTIN\Users") & "<br />"
      & "Is this account a member of 'DANDARE\TestGroup' group: " _
      & User.IsInRole("DANDARE\TestGroup") & "<br />" _
      & "Is this account a member of 'DANDARE\NoMembers' group: " _
      & User.IsInRole("DANDARE\NoMembers")
  Else

    msgHello.InnerHtml = "Hello, you were not authenticated"

  End If

End Sub
```

Forms-Based Authentication Examples

The next two examples in this chapter demonstrate forms-based authentication. The first one, Simple Forms-Based Authentication and Authorization, uses the `web.config` file. You can see that we've specified the page named `login.aspx` as the `loginUrl`, so this is the page that will be loaded when a user attempts to access the application when they have not been authenticated.

We also include a `<credentials>` section that specifies the username and passwords for three users that will be permitted access to the application. The `<authorization>` section that follows this specifies that these three users are the only ones that will be permitted access. Include a `<deny users="?">` element to prevent any anonymous access to the application.

```
<configuration>
<system.web>
  <authentication mode="Forms">
    <forms name="MyApp02" path="/" loginUrl="login.aspx"
           protection="All" timeout="30">
      <credentials passwordFormat="Clear">
        <user name="billjones" password="test" />
        <user name="marthasmith" password="test" />
        <user name="joesoap" password="test" />
      </credentials>
    </forms>
  </authentication>
  <authorization>
    <allow users="billjones,marthasmith,joesoap" />
    <deny users="?" />
```

```
    </authorization>
  </system.web>
  </configuration>
```

When you first access the `default.aspx` page in the protected folder, you are redirected to the login page, as shown in Figure 14-32. You must enter the credentials of one of the users specified in the `web.config` file, such as marthasmith and test:

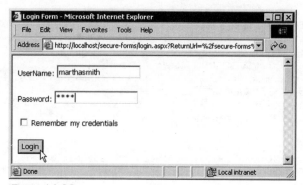

Figure 14-32

For the time being, leave the Remember my credentials checkbox unchecked, and click Login. If you got the username and password right, you'll be redirected to the `default.aspx` page. It displays the username that you entered and the type of authentication used, as shown in Figure 14-33.

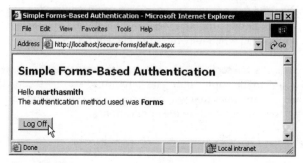

Figure 14-33

If you didn't get them right, you'll see a message appear below the Login button indicating that your credentials were invalid, as shown in Figure 14-34:

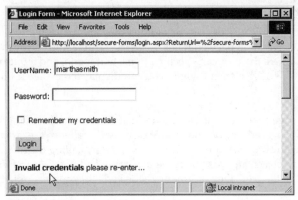

Figure 14-34

Using a Persistent Logon

Now close and reopen you browser and reload the `default.aspx` page. You will be redirected to the login page again. This time, check the **Remember my credentials** checkbox before you click **Login** to store a persistent cookie on your machine. Then close and reopen you browser (do not click the **Log Off** button), and reload the `default.aspx` page again. This time you are not redirected to the login page, and the server can extract and display your username and authentication method as before.

This is because you have the authentication cookie stored on your machine. To see the cookie that is used, open the `Temporary Internet Files` folder. The easiest way is to select **Internet Options** from the **Tools** menu in Internet Explorer, click **Settings** and **View Files**. Find the file named `Cookie:[Windows-user-name]@[your-machine-name]` and double-click to open it and view the contents. You'll see something like Figure 14-35, showing the encrypted ticket that allows you access to the page without requiring an explicit login:

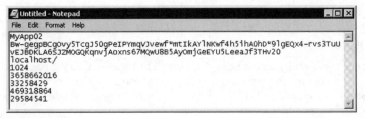

Figure 14-35

Logging Off

Now go back to the page that displays your name and authentication type (the `default.aspx` page), and click the **Log Off** button. You are immediately redirected back to the logon page. The cookie holding your authentication details has been destroyed (not sent back to the browser), and so you must log in again to recreate it before you can access any restricted pages. You can also check your browser's `Temporary Internet Files` folder to confirm that the cookie is no longer there (press F5 to refresh the list).

How This Example Works

When users first access an ASP.NET page in this folder, they are redirected to the page `login.aspx`. The HTML section of the `login.aspx` page contains a `<form>` with textboxes for the username and password, a checkbox where the user can specify a persistent logon, and a button to submit the form to the server. There is also a `<div>` element where you can display a message if the user cannot be authenticated.

The remainder of this page contains a single subroutine that is executed on the server when the user clicks the Login button. This is the same code as we discussed earlier in the chapter. First it checks the credentials provided against the list of users in `web.config` by calling the `Authenticate` method of the `FormsAuthentication` object, and passing it the username and password. If this returns `True`, it redirects the user back to the page they originally requested – in your example this is `default.aspx`.

If the user cannot be authenticated, the `Else` section of the `If..Then` construct displays a message to this effect in the `<div>` element at the bottom of the page.

```
<form runat="server">
  UserName: <input id="txtUsr" type="text" runat="server" /><p />
  Password: <input id="txtPwd" type="password" runat="server" /><p />
  <ASP:CheckBox id="chkPersist" runat="server" />
  Remember my credentials<p />
  <input type="submit" Value="Login" runat="server"
        onserverclick="DoLogin" /><p />
  <div id="outMessage" runat="server" />
</form>
Sub DoLogin(objSender As Object, objArgs As EventArgs)
  If FormsAuthentication.Authenticate(txtUsr.Value, txtPwd.Value) Then
     FormsAuthentication.RedirectFromLoginPage(txtUsr.Value, _
                                          chkPersist.Checked)
  Else
     outMessage.InnerHtml = "<b>Invalid credentials</b> please re-enter."
  End If
End Sub
```

The default.aspx Page

If the user has been successfully authenticated, they will be redirected to the page that they attempted to load originally (`default.apx` in your example). The page contains a `<div>` element where we'll display some details about the user, and an HTML `<form>` on which there is a single submit button labeled `Log Off`:

```
<div id="msgHello" runat="server" /><p />
<form runat="server">
  <input type="submit" Value="Log Off" runat="server"
        onserverclick="DoSignOut" />
</form>
```

Accessing the User's Identity

Getting the user's name and authentication method is easy when using forms-based authentication. First check that they were authenticated (as in the previous Windows authentication example) and if so, you can access the properties of the `User.Identity` object. And again, as before, you can display a message if the user was not authenticated.

```
Sub Page_Load()
    'see if the user has been authenticated
    If User.Identity.IsAuthenticated Then
        'display the properties
        msgHello.InnerHtml = "Hello " & User.Identity.Name & "<br />" _
                           & "The authentication method used was " _
                           & User.Identity.AuthenticationType
    Else
        msgHello.InnerHtml = "Hello, you were not authenticated"
    End If
End Sub
```

Logging a User Out of an Application

The log off button on this page has its `onserverclick` event set to `DoSignOut`. This is the name of the event handler that is executed when the user clicks this button. The code itself is trivial, as you can see from the following code:

```
Sub DoSignOut(objSender As Object, objArgs As EventArgs)
    'destroy the users authentication cookie
    FormsAuthentication.SignOut()
    'and redirect them to the login page
    Response.Clear()
    Response.Redirect(Request.UrlReferrer.ToString())
End Sub
```

And once you've executed the `SignOut` method, you can redirect the browser back to the referring page (in this case the login page). They can then experiment and log on using a different account.

Encrypting the Passwords in web.config

One thing you may have noticed in the `web.config` file used in this example is that the user's passwords are stored in plain text. The following code was used:

```
<credentials passwordFormat="Clear">
    <user name="billjones" password="test" />
    <user name="marthasmith" password="test" />
    <user name="joesoap" password="test" />
</credentials>
```

This would be a security risk if anyone could get to see the `web.config` file. They cannot download the file from the site, as all requests for this file are blocked automatically by ASP.NET. However, local users might access it, and could then see the complete list of username/password combinations that are valid for the site. To prevent this, you can encrypt the passwords within the `web.config` file.

The delightfully named `HashPasswordForStoringInConfigFile` method (exposed by the `FormsAuthentication` object used earlier) provides an easy way to do this. We've included an example page that takes a password and encrypts it using either the SHA1 or MD5 algorithm. These are the two encryption methods supported by ASP.NET.

Password Hashing Example

The page is named `hash-password.aspx` and is in the `security` folder of the samples we provide for this chapter. You can open it from the main menu page (`default.htm`) in the same folder. Simply select the encryption type as shown in Figure 14-36, enter the password, and click the **Create Hash** button.

Figure 14-36

Now you can copy the password hash into the appropriate user's entry in `web.config`, and change the setting for the `passwordFormat` in the `<credentials>` element to suit the encryption method used, as shown in the following code:

```
<credentials passwordFormat="SHA1">
  <user name="billjones"
        password="87F8ED9157125FFC4DA9E06A7B8011AD80A53FE1" />
  <user name="marthasmith"
        password="2E1FA0D4D3B6CA2623EA6AF07624C3CD29D47344" />
  <user name="joesoap"
        password="36854FAFECB73E79DC3DFF61E76CF24CF8B490CC" />
</credentials>
```

How the Password Hashing Example Works

The HTML section of this example page is just a simple `<form>` containing the two radio buttons, the textbox for the password, and a **Create Hash** button. There is also a `<div>` element that is used to display the result.

Next is the code to create the hash, which runs when the **Create Hash** button is clicked. It gets the encryption type from the selected radio button (using the `Request.Form` collection), and passes it and the password to the `HashPasswordForStoringInConfigFile` method. The result is then displayed in the `<div>` element.

```
<form runat="server">
  Password Format:
  <input type="radio" value="SHA1" name="chkFormat"
         checked="true" runat="server" /> SHA1  
  <input type="radio" value="MD5" name="chkFormat" runat="server" /> MD5<p />
```

```
   Password: <input id="txtPwd" type="text" runat="server" /><p />
   <input type="submit" value="Create Hash" runat="server"
           onserverclick="DoHashPassword" /><p />
   <div id="outMessage" runat="server" />
</form>

Sub DoHashPassword(objSender As Object, objArgs As EventArgs)
  Dim strHash, strFormat As String

  'get the format name as a string from the radio button value
  strFormat = Request.Form("chkFormat")

  'create the hash using the password value provided
  strHash = FormsAuthentication.HashPasswordForStoringInConfigFile _
                                         (txtPwd.Value, strFormat)
  'and display the result
  outMessage.InnerHtml = strFormat & " Password Hash is: " & strHash

End Sub
```

Using Different Credential Lists

When looking at how forms-based authentication works, we mentioned that you can substitute your own custom list of logon details for the list held in the web.config file. This is often a more robust solution – for example it allows you to store the list of users in a relational database or an XML document.

In particular, if you allow users to register before being allowed access to resources, or if you're only using authentication to personalize the web site or application, a relational database is an obvious choice for the user list. You can update it with SQL statements or stored procedures on demand.

The example page, Forms-Based Authentication with a Custom User List, demonstrates custom authentication against both an XML file and a relational database. It uses the web.config file shown in the following code:

```
<configuration>
<system.web>

  <authentication mode="Forms">
    <forms name="MyApp01" path="/" loginUrl="login.aspx"
           protection="All" timeout="30">
    </forms>
  </authentication>

  <authorization>
    <deny users="?" />
  </authorization>
</system.web>
</configuration>
```

In this case, you have no list of users (there is no <credentials> section). In the <authorization> section you have omitted the user list as well, simply leaving the <deny users="?" /> element there.

This means that anyone who has been authenticated can access the pages. Remember that the default `machine.config` file allows all users to access all resources unless you override this in an application.

An XML User List Document

A simple format is chosen for the XML user list document to minimize the code required to access it. As shown in the following code, there is a root element `<userlist>`, within which is a list of elements that are the usernames. The value of each element is that user's password.

```xml
<?xml version="1.0" ?>

<userlist>
   <billjones>test</billjones>
   <marthasmith>test</marthasmith>
   <joesoap>test</joesoap>
</userlist>
```

This file, named `userlist.xml`, is placed in the same folder as the login page. You'll see how to use it when you look at the code in that page shortly.

A User List in a Relational Database

We've also set up a simple table named Users in a relational database named `UserList`, as shown in Figure 14-37. It contains the same users, with `varchar`-type columns named UserName and Password. This table is used in the next example as well, so it contains an extra column named `BGColor`.

There are also three more users, and you can see that the Password column values are encrypted for these users. Just ignore all this for the time being.

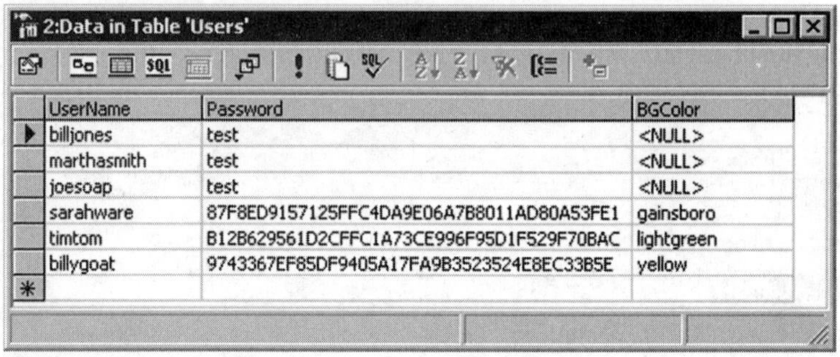

UserName	Password	BGColor
billjones	test	\<NULL\>
marthasmith	test	\<NULL\>
joesoap	test	\<NULL\>
sarahware	87F8ED9157125FFC4DA9E06A7B8011AD80A53FE1	gainsboro
timtom	B12B629561D2CFFC1A73CE996F95D1F529F70BAC	lightgreen
billygoat	9743367EF85DF9405A17FA9B3523524E8EC33B5E	yellow

Figure 14-37

Running the Example

When you first access the example folder to load `default.aspx`, the forms-based security system detects that you haven't been authenticated and redirects you to the login page as shown in Figure 14-38. This is similar to the previous example, but now it contains a pair of radio buttons where you can select the *user store* you want to be authenticated against.

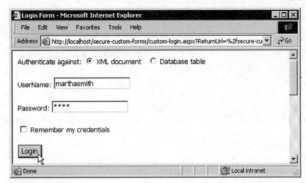

Figure 14-38

*You will have to install the database as described in the section 'Creating the UserList Database' earlier in this chapter to be able to use the **Database table** option.*

Enter the credentials of a suitable account (one with a plain-text password from the database table shown earlier – **marthasmith** with the password **test** will do). If you get it wrong, a message is displayed as in the previous example. If you get it right, as shown in Figure 14-39, you can then access the `default.aspx` page. Again, as in the previous example, this page displays your username and the type of authentication used. It also contains the same **Log Off** button as the previous example:

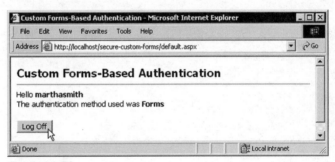

Figure 14-39

How This Example Works

In the `login.aspx` page (where you are redirected if you haven't already been authenticated) first import the namespaces you'll need. As code in this page contains references to classes for accessing relational data and XML documents, you need to add these namespaces to the page.

The HTML section of the page contains a `<form>` within which the same controls are placed as the previous example – textboxes for the username, password, persistent cookie checkbox, and **Login** button. However, at the top of the form also add the two radio buttons that allow you to choose the user list against which you want to be authenticated.

```
<%@Import Namespace="System.Data" %>
<%@Import Namespace="System.Data.OleDb" %>
```

```
<%@Import Namespace="System.Xml" %>
<form runat="server">
  Authenticate against:
  <input type="radio" id="chkXML" name="chkReadFrom" checked="true"
         runat="server" /> XML document  
  <input type="radio" id="chkSQL" name="chkReadFrom"
         runat="server" /> Database table<p />
  UserName: <input id="txtUsr" type="text" runat="server" /><p />
  Password: <input id="txtPwd" type="password" runat="server" /><p />
  <ASP:CheckBox id="chkPersist" runat="server" />
  Remember my credentials<p />
  <input type="submit" Value="Login" runat="server"
         onserverclick="DoLogin" /><p />
  <div id="outMessage" runat="server" />
</form>
```

The Login Code

When the Login button is clicked, the event handler named `DoLogin` is executed. In this first create a suitable connection string to access the database you're using. This value is extracted from the `web.config` file in the root folder of the samples, and you may have to edit this to suit your own setup.

After that, collect the values for the username and password from the form controls, and declare a flag variable to indicate if validation of the user's credentials was successful. Set the default value of this variable to `False`.

```
Sub DoLogin(objSender As Object, objArgs As EventArgs)

  'get the connection string from web.config file
  Dim strConnect As String
  strConnect = ConfigurationSettings.AppSettings("DsnUserList")

  'get username and password from form
  Dim strUsr As String = txtUsr.Value
  Dim strPwd As String = txtPwd.Value

  'set a flag to indicate successful authentication
  Dim blnIsAuthenticated As Boolean = False    'default value
  ...
```

Validating the Credentials against the User List XML Document

Now you can check to see which list of users was selected in the form by checking value of the radio button with the ID of `chkXML`. If this is `Checked`, you are authenticating against an XML document, so you can create the physical path to the document and load it into a new instance of an `XmlDocument` object.

Providing that the file is loaded without an error, you can use the `GetElementsByTagname` method to return an `XmlNodeList` containing the node for this username. From that, you can access the value of the `#text` child node of the element to get the password. If this matches the value entered by the user, you know that they are a valid user so set the `blnIsAuthenticated` flag variable to `True`.

```
...
'see which method we're using to authenticate the user
If chkXML.Checked Then

  'load the XML document containing the user credentials
  Dim strCurrentPath As String = Request.PhysicalPath
  Dim strXMLPath As String = Left(strCurrentPath, _
              InStrRev(strCurrentPath, "\")) & "userlist.xml"

  'create a new XmlDocument object
  Dim objXMLDoc As New XmlDocument()
  Try

    'load the XML file into the XmlDocument object
    objXMLDoc.Load(strXMLPath)

  Catch objError As Exception

    'display error details
    outMessage.innerHTML = "Error accessing XML document.<br />" _
       & objError.Message & "<br />" & objError.Source
    Exit Sub  ' and stop execution

  End Try

  'create a NodeList collection of all matching child nodes
  'there should be only one for this user
  Dim colUser As XmlNodeList
  colUser = objXMLDoc.GetElementsByTagname(strUsr)

  'see if we found an element with this username
  If colUser.Count > 0 Then

    'check if the value of the element (the child #text node)
    'is equal to the password that the user entered
    If strPwd = colUser(0).FirstChild().Value Then
      blnIsAuthenticated = True
    End If

  End If
...
```

Validating the Credentials against the Users' Database Table

If authentication against your database table is selected, the section of code in the `Else` part of the `If..Then` construct will be executed instead of the code that checks against the XML file. However, like that code, checking against a database is quite simple. It follows the techniques we demonstrated in the data access chapters earlier in this book.

So, you can create a suitable SQL statement that will extract the users' password from the row that contains their username and password (you'll see why we chose to return the password shortly). Then create and open a connection to the database and execute the SQL statement returning a `DataReader` object that contains the password if a matching row was found in the database.

Most relational databases are set up to do case-insensitive text matching in a WHERE clause unless you use a specific function or set options before executing the query. It's easier to return the password from the database and do a case-sensitive comparison in the event handler code (unless you aren't bothered about matching case). If the match succeeds, you can set your flag to indicate that this username and password combination is valid, then close the DataReader object and the database connection.

```
...
Else

    'create a suitable SQL statement to retrieve the values
    Dim strSQL As String
    strSQL = "SELECT Password FROM UserTable WHERE UserName='" _
            & strUsr & "' AND Password='" & strPwd & "'"
    Try

        'create a new Connection object and open it
        Dim objConnect As New OleDbConnection(strConnect)
        objConnect.Open()

        'create a new Command using connection object and SQL statement
        Dim objCommand As New OleDbCommand(strSQL, objConnect)

        'declare a variable to hold a DataReader object
        Dim objDataReader As OleDbDataReader

        'execute SQL statement against Command to fill the DataReader
        objDataReader = objCommand.ExecuteReader()

        'if we get a row back, check password for same letter case
        '(usually a SQL SELECT WHERE clause is not case sensitive)
        If objDataReader.Read() Then
            If objDataReader("Password") = strPwd Then
              blnIsAuthenticated = True
            End If
        End If

        'close the DataReader and Connection
        objDataReader.Close()
        objConnect.Close()

    Catch objError As Exception

        'display error details
        outMessage.InnerHtml = "Error accessing database.<br />" _
            & objError.Message & "<br />" & objError.Source
        Exit Sub   ' and stop execution

    End Try

End If
...
```

Authenticating the User

Now you can actually tell ASP.NET that you have validated the user's credentials and that they should be authenticated and receive the appropriate cookie so that they can access your application. If your flag variable is `True`, simply call the `RedirectFromLoginPage` method, and specify the username and whether to persist the authentication cookie on their machine:

```
...
If blnIsAuthenticated Then
    FormsAuthentication.RedirectFromLoginPage(txtUsr.Value, _
                                        chkPersist.Checked)
Else
    outMessage.InnerHtml = Invalid credentials, please re-enter."
End If
End Sub
```

Encrypting the Passwords

Like your first example, you've used un-encrypted passwords in both the database table and the XML document. If there is a risk of these being viewed by unauthorized personnel, you may prefer to encrypt the passwords.

You'll have a problem with this approach if you need to provide passwords for users who forget them, as hashing can't be reversed to get the original value. Of course, if this feature isn't a requirement (or if you'll just issue a new password), the problem goes away.

With encrypted password hashes, the authentication process changes. The steps you would take are:

❑   Encrypt all the user passwords and replace the plain text ones in the database table and/or XML document with the encrypted version.

❑   In your login pages, get the password that the user provides from the login form controls and encrypt this using the same encryption algorithm.

❑   Compare the resulting hash with the encrypted password hash in your database or XML file.

We'll use this technique in the next example.

Simple Personalization Example

The Simple Personalization Example demonstrates how you can implement personalization features much more easily in ASP.NET than in previous versions of ASP. At the same time, it demonstrates more uses for programmatic security.

When you open the example page, as shown in Figure 14-40, it immediately redirects you to the login page, as in the previous examples. You should login using the username timtom and password letmein:

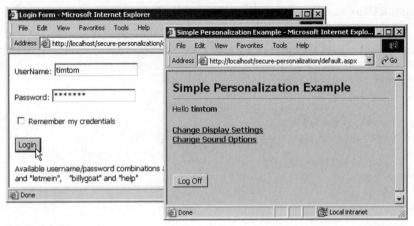

Figure 14-40

After being authenticated, you'll see a simple `default.aspx` page that contains a couple of (dummy) hyperlinks and the customary **Log Off** button. Now log off and login again using the username **sarahware** and password **test**. This time, as shown in Figure 14-41, you get a different colored background and more (dummy) hyperlinks:

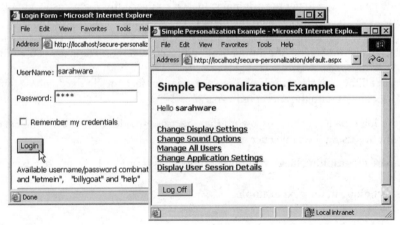

Figure 14-41

The login and `default.aspx` pages used here are basically the same as those used in the previous example, but with a few new twists. A relational database is still used to hold the user's credentials, but now (as you've seen) you can also personalize the pages for each user. Try the username **billygoat** with the password **help** to see another example.

We also use encrypted passwords in the database in this example, as you can see in Figure 14-42 which repeats the screenshot of the database table contents. We include a column that contains the page background color for this user. Remember that you must recreate the password hash values for the final three users (see the section on encrypting the passwords in `web.config` earlier in this chapter), and update the database with the values specific to your machine.

Figure 14-42

How This Example Works

The HTML section of the login page is identical to the earlier forms-based examples, but it contains slightly different code in the `DoLogin` event handler. This time, after you create the connection string and collect the values entered by the user from the form controls, create an SHA1 hash of the password:

```
Sub DoLogin(objSender As Object, objArgs As EventArgs)

    'get connection string from web.config file
    Dim strConnect As String
    strConnect = ConfigurationSettings.AppSettings("DsnUserList")

    'get username and password from form
    Dim strUsr As String = txtUsr.Value
    Dim strPwd As String = txtPwd.Value

    'create the SHA1 hash of the password provided by the user
    Dim strHash As String
    strHash = FormsAuthentication.HashPasswordForStoringInConfigFile( _
                                                  strPwd, "SHA1")

    'set a flag to indicate successful authentication
    Dim blnIsAuthenticated As Boolean = False    'default value
```

Next, declare a variable to hold the value for the page background that you'll be extracting from the database table. Obviously, in your own applications, you'll add code here and in the following SQL statement to extract other values that you store in the table – and use to personalize the application in other ways:

```
    Dim strBGColor As String    'user's saved background color
```

Authenticating the User

To see if the username/password that the user entered is valid, you only have to look up the appropriate row in the database table. If it exists, you know that they can be authenticated. If not, deny them access. In this case, because you've created an SHA1 hash for the password, so you don't have to worry about matching letter case. The actual hash that the algorithm creates takes into account the case of the letters, and a different case for one or more characters will create a different password hash. So, there's no need to extract the password from the database table – your SQL statement just needs to retrieve the personalization value (or values if you've added more personalization settings). If you get a row back, you know that the username/password combination is valid:

```
'create a SQL statement to retrieve personalization values
Dim strSQL As String
strSQL = "SELECT BGColor FROM Users WHERE UserName='" _
       & strUsr & "' AND Password='" & strHash & "'"
```

One point to watch out for here is that users can spoof your page by entering values into the **UserName** *and* **Password** *textboxes that will always evaluate to* True *when the SQL statement is executed. For example, if they enter the text b'or'1'='1 for the user name and password, the result could produce matching rows. To protect from this, you should either parse the strings they enter and remove all single quotes, or use the technique of retrieving the password from the database and comparing it with the value that the user entered.*

Now execute the SQL statement and get the results back in a DataReader. Providing that there is a row returned, you can set your authentication flag and collect the personalization value(s) into the string variable(s) you created earlier:

```
Try
   ...
   'code as used in previous examples to create and open
   'the connection and execute the SQL statement here
   ...
   'if we get a row back we know that the user is authenticated
   If objDataReader.Read() Then
        blnIsAuthenticated = True
        'get user's preferred background color
        strBGColor = objDataReader("BGColor")
        'get other preference values as required
        '... etc ...
   End If
   ...
End Try
```

You can now save the personalization value(s) in the user's Session object so you can access them within the application pages without having to keep going back to the database. Also tell ASP.NET to create the authentication cookie and redirect the user back to the page they originally requested.

```
If blnIsAuthenticated Then
    'save background color in Session object
    Session("BGColor") = strBGColor
    '... save other personalization settings here
    'redirect user to original page
    FormsAuthentication.RedirectFromLoginPage(strUsr, chkPersist.Checked)
Else
    outMessage.InnerHtml = "<b>Invalid credentials</b> please re-enter..."
End If
End Sub
```

The Personalized default.aspx Page

Following a successful login, the user is redirected to the page default.aspx. In it, you can display their user name. Also include the same Log Off button – we won't be describing those features again here.

What is different is the way that you apply any personalization features appropriate to this user. In the example, you set the background color of the page and display an appropriate set of hyperlinks depending on the current username.

The opening <body> tag in the page includes a bgcolor attribute, with the value set to a variable named strColor. This variable is declared in the <script> section of the page, and so is globally available throughout the page. Five ASP.NET Hyperlink controls were also placed within the body of the page to create the HTML hyperlinks you saw in Figure 14-41. The last three of these have their Visible property set to False so they won't normally be visible in the final page.

```
<script language="VB" runat="server">
Dim strColor As String
... rest of script code goes here ...
</script>
<body bgcolor="<% = strColor %>">
...
<ASP:Hyperlink id="lnkUser1" Text="Change Display Settings"
       NavigateUrl="http://dummy" runat="server" /><br />
<ASP:Hyperlink id="lnkUser2" Text="Change Sound Options"
       NavigateUrl="http://dummy" runat="server" /><br />
<ASP:Hyperlink id="lnkAdmin1" Text="Manage All Users"
       Visible="False" NavigateUrl="http://dummy" runat="server" /><br />
<ASP:Hyperlink id="lnkAdmin2" Text="Change Application Settings"
       Visible="False" NavigateUrl="http://dummy" runat="server" /><br />
<ASP:Hyperlink id="lnkAdmin3" Text="Display User Session Details"
       Visible="False" NavigateUrl="http://dummy" runat="server" /><br />
```

The <script> section of the page also contains an event handler that executes as the page is being created in response to the Page-Load event. This first checks that the user has been authenticated, and if so displays the authenticated user name.

Next, it extracts the BGColor value from the user's Session (stored there when they submitted their login details) and sets the strColor variable so that the background color of the page is set to the appropriate color for this user. Finally, you can use the current login username to see if you should display the *administration* hyperlinks. In this example, only display them if the user is sarahware.

```
Sub Page_Load()

   If User.Identity.IsAuthenticated Then

      'display welcome message
      msgHello.InnerHtml = "Hello <b>" & User.Identity.Name & "</b>"

      'set preferred background color to the value that was
      'saved in this user's Session object by the "login" page
      strColor = Session("BGColor")
```

```
      'if user is "sarahware" display admin hyperlinks in page
     If User.Identity.Name = "sarahware" Then
       lnkAdmin1.Visible = True
       lnkAdmin2.Visible = True
       lnkAdmin3.Visible = True
     End If

   End Sub
```

Other Personalization and Programmatic Security Options

This is a very simple example of personalization and programmatic security, but you can see how it can easily be extended. For example you could:

❑ Include more personalization options, such as the text color, font size and style, page layout, page content, and so on.

❑ Include a page containing form controls where the user can select the personalization options and values, and then use a SQL statement or stored procedure to update these in the database.

❑ Store a custom *role* name for each user in the database table, giving you the ability to allocate users to separate roles (rather like Windows account groups). You could then extract the role name for each user as they log in and perform programmatic security checks using this role name rather than the username.

ASP.NET Process Account and Trust Levels

There are several different ways that you can configure reduced permissions in ASP.NET. They all revolve around the ultimate decision that you have to make – which account should you run the pages under? Once you know which account is being used, or specify the one that you want to use, you can use the Windows ACLs on all the resources on your machine to limit and control access.

Specifying the Process Account

The `<processModel>` element in `machine.config` (or in a `web.config` file placed in the application directory) specifies which account is used when impersonation is not enabled:

```
<processModel
  enable="[true | false]"
  userName="[user]"
  password="[AutoGenerate | password]"
/>
```

The default settings in `machine.config` are:

```
<processModel
  enable="true"
  userName="machine"
  password="AutoGenerate"
/>
```

So, by default, all your ASP.NET pages and resources will be executed under the special process account – the account with the *moniker* of ASPNET in Windows 2000, Windows XP, and Windows NT4, or *NETWORK SERVICE* in Windows Server 2003. However, there is another moniker value you can use here instead, namely system, and with the password also set to AutoGenerate. This causes ASP.NET to run under a local SYSTEM account:

```
<processModel
   enable="true"
   userName="system"
   password="AutoGenerate"
/>
```

An alternative is to specify that ASP.NET pages and resources should be processed under the context of some other Windows account by changing the userName and password values in the <processModel> element – either for the entire machine (in machine.config), or for a specific application directory. As a trivial example, you can run your ASP.NET pages and resources under an account (that you create) named "MyProcess" with the password "secret" by specifying this account:

```
<processModel
   enable="true"
   userName="MyProcess"
   password="secret"
/>
```

This approach is useful in a hosting scenario. It allows you to lock down individual applications to the specific accounts of the administrators for each application or site, and prevent them from being able to access other applications or sites. Note that the settings specified in the <processModel> element are only applicable to ASP.NET, and do not affect other types of application or service running under the .NET Framework.

The Identity Element and Impersonation

The <processModel> element provides account details that are used only when impersonation is *not* enabled. Recall from our discussions near the start of this chapter that turning on impersonation means that ASP.NET will run under the context of the account that is authenticated by IIS when a request is received. If IIS is configured to allow anonymous access (the default for a web site), then the context is that of the IUSR account (or the account you specified that IIS use for anonymous access if you changed this).

Simply adding the <identity impersonate="true"> element within the <system.web> section of the machine.config or web.config files means that anonymous access will take place under the IIS anonymous account (IUSR_machinename):

```
<system.web>
   ...
   <identity impersonate="true" />
   ...
</system.web>
```

Another possibility is to use the `userName` and `password` attributes of the `<identity>` element to specify the account that you want ASP.NET resources to be executed under. In this case you also set the `impersonate` attribute to `true`:

```
<system.web>
    ...
    <identity impersonate="true"
              userName="account-name"
              password="account-password"
    />
    ...
</system.web>
```

Note that the settings specified in the `<identity>` element are applicable only to ASP.NET, and *not* to the rest of the .NET Framework. You also might like to consider the wisdom of using this last option where the password must be stored in the file as plain text.

> *In fact there is a little more to it than this. The `<processModel>` element specifies the account under which the worker process is run when it's enabled (it's not in IIS6 in native mode, for example). All threads start as the specified account. When impersonation is enabled, they temporarily take on the impersonated context. Calling the `RevertToSelf` method will always get back to the process account. There are a couple of events that fire without a Request context being available, such as `Application_OnEnd`, and these always run under the context of the process account.*

ASP.NET Process Account Permissions

We've mentioned several times in this chapter how ASP.NET pages and associated resources such as web services, user controls, components, etc., run under the special process accounts ASPNET or NETWORK SERVICE (depending on the operating system version) by default. These accounts have broadly the same privileges as the IUSR_machinename account that is created when IIS is installed (and as used with ASP 3.0). However they require extra privileges beyond that of the IUSR account, due to the fact that ASP.NET takes advantage of dynamic compilation and disk caching features.

If you configure an application to use impersonation (i.e. run under a different account), or change the process account within the `<processModel>` section of `web.config`, the account you use must have the following permissions:

❑ **The ASP.NET installation folder hierarchy** (`%installroot%`): This is where the .NET Framework assemblies and machine configuration files reside. The process account you use must have read access to these folders.

❑ **The folder used for dynamic compilation of ASP.NET pages and resources**: The root folder for this is `%installroot%\ASP.NET Temporary Files`. Application code generation occurs in a discrete directory beneath this folder for each application (the location of this root folder can be configured using the `tempDir` attribute of the `<compilation>` section of `web.config`). The process account you use must have read/write access to these folders.

❑ **The Global Assembly Cache (GAC) folder**: This is where shared assemblies are located (usually `%windir%\assembly`). The process account you use must have read access to this folder.

❑ **The folder used by web services to generate serialization proxies**: By default this is
`%windir%\temp`. The process account you use must have read/write access to this folder.

❑ **The Default web site root folder** (usually `%systemdrive%\inetpub\wwwroot`): The process
account you use must have READ access to the root folder *and* its subfolders. If you want to
write to the disk from an ASP.NET page or other resource, you must enable WRITE permission
for the target folder as well (in the same way as was required under ASP 3.0).

❑ **Your own application directories**: where the application content resides. The process account
you use must have READ access to these folders. If you want to write to the disk from an
ASP.NET page or other resource, you must enable WRITE permission for the target folder as
well (in the same way as was required under ASP 3.0).

Specifying the Trust Level

By default, ASP.NET runs in a mode called *Full Trust* level, which applies few security limits on the code
that can be executed. This is fine for an Intranet scenario or a development machine, but once you place
the server on the Internet you should consider reducing the permissions available to the process that the
ASP.NET pages are running under.

There is another option for controlling the permissions for ASP.NET to process resources. This takes
advantage of the `<trust>` element in `machine.config`, and it can be used to set a more stringent *trust
level*. The default setting is `Full`, specified by this line from the default `machine.config` file:

```
<trust level="Full" originUrl="" />
```

The other options are `High`, `Low`, and `None`, and these apply progressively more stringent limitations on
the permissions that code running under the .NET Framework will have. The `<securityPolicy>`
element specifies which security configuration file applies to each of the trust levels:

```
<securityPolicy>
  <trustLevel name="Full" policyFile="internal" />
  <trustLevel name="High" policyFile="web_hightrust.config" />
  <trustLevel name="Low"  policyFile="web_lowtrust.config" />
  <trustLevel name="None" policyFile="web_notrust.config" />
</securityPolicy>
```

Each of these files has sections that describe the permissions that are available to .NET Framework
applications and code. Some examples of the permissions that can be set are:

❑ Which environment variables the code can query

❑ Which directories the code can write to through the file I/O classes

❑ Whether DNS enquiries are allowed

❑ Whether blank passwords can be used with the ADO.NET data providers

❑ Whether messages can be sent to, and received from, the Message Queue Service

❑ Whether access to a printer is permitted

❑ Which performance counters can be accessed

You can change the trust level and edit the *trust* configuration files to finely control the permissions available to your code and resources. Remember that the settings specified in the `<trust>` element are applicable to the whole of the .NET Framework, not just ASP.NET.

A simple configuration Wizard is provided with the Frameworks that can be used to change the trust level. Select Programs | Administrative Tools | Microsoft .NET Framework 1.1 Wizards, and select the Adjust .NET Security icon, as shown in Figure 14-43:

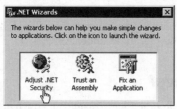

Figure 14-43

The Adjust .NET Security Wizard allows you to specify which trust level each zone should run under. The defaults are shown in Figure 14-44:

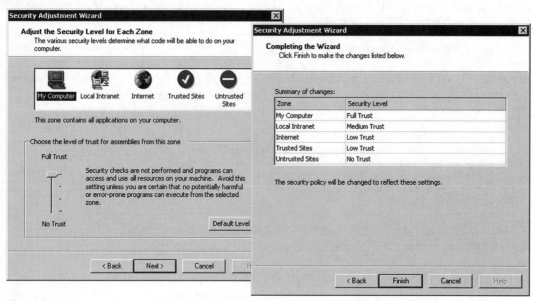

Figure 14-44

For a detailed explanation of the trust model, code-access security, and other related topics check out the SDK that is provided with the .NET Framework. The section *Programming with the .NET Framework* includes a whole subsection *Securing Applications* that is devoted to all the topics we've mentioned in this chapter.

Summary

In this chapter, we've tackled a topic that is often considered to be the most difficult part of building ASP applications, and often doesn't get the attention it deserves (and, from a security point of view, *requires*). As you've hopefully gathered from the theory, explanations, and examples, ASP.NET makes it much easier to set up a secure web site or application to suit every kind of common scenario. But remember that security as a whole involves a lot more than just the topics we've covered here – you also need to consider physical network and server security implications, as well as application security settings and configuration. If in doubt, get an expert in!

Web application security is based around the three fundamental concepts of *authentication* (forcing a user to prove that they are who they say they are), *authorization* (checking if the user has permission to access the resource they requested), and *impersonation* (allowing applications to be executed under the context of a different user).

You looked at each topic in turn, and saw how they are implemented and configured in IIS, in Windows 2000, Windows Server 2003, and in ASP.NET. You also saw the whole chain of events that occur as part of the overall process, and the various access control options that they provide.

We then concentrated on ASP.NET security configuration, and saw how the three fundamental concepts are implemented through the `web.config` files you place in your application folders. We completed this chapter with some examples of creating and configuring secured applications using the various techniques:

❑ Configuring a web application using Windows authentication

❑ Accessing the user's identity within this application

❑ Accessing the user's role within this application

❑ Configuring a web application using forms-based authentication

❑ Using different types of user credentials lists

❑ Accessing the user's identity within this application

❑ A simple personalization example

In the next chapter, we start an in-depth look at some of the base classes that are provided by the framework. In particular, we'll investigate data structures such as collections and lists.

15

Working with Collections and Lists

Over the years Microsoft Windows has grown into an enterprise-caliber operating system that millions of companies and users worldwide depend on daily. Windows NT and Windows 2000 have proved themselves as solid and stable operating systems, providing scalability, reliability, and *return on investment* (*ROI*).

The one area where Windows suffers today compared with its main rivals is the complexity of its developer platform. Yes, Windows has fantastic tools available for development (like Visual Studio), but Windows supports ever-growing numbers of APIs and object models that are increasingly inconsistent, fragmented, and difficult to learn.

The complexity of developing on the Windows platform is a problem that Microsoft has understood for some time. A major objective for .NET was to bring simplicity and consistency to the Windows development platform, making it more competitive with Java in that respect, without sand-boxing developers or sacrificing performance. From a consistency and accessibility viewpoint, the *Common Language Runtime* (*CLR*) provides the foundations that enable this. The .NET Framework uses the CLR to provide a clean object-oriented approach to development by grouping classes within hierarchical namespaces, as well as making the functionality of the platform simple and consistent.

A key part of an object-oriented development platform like .NET is its *Base Class Library*. The classes in this library provide core functionality, with which developers can build applications and class libraries. If you have ever programmed with the C/C++ *Standard Template Library* (*STL*), used the VB.NET scripting runtime objects or the Java SDK, you'll have a good idea of the type of functionality that the .NET Framework base classes provide.

This chapter and the next one will examine some of the commonly used classes in the .NET *Framework Base Class Library* that have been designed to allow applications to be built quickly and elegantly. As such, there are far too many classes in the .NET Framework to cover in just one book.

This chapter focuses on collections, and the next covers files and regular expressions.

Computers have been designed essentially to store and manipulate data, and ever since I started programming (which feels like a very long time ago now) I've spent a sizable chunk of my time writing code to manage sets of data held in different types of data structures, such as queues, dictionaries, and stacks. I doubt that I'm the only developer who's spent time doing this and because working with different data structures is such a universal and common requirement, the .NET Framework provides an impressive class library for dealing with common data structures.

By the end of this chapter, you will:

❑   Understand the support provided by the .NET Framework for working with common data structures such as lists, queues, stacks, and dictionaries

❑   Have a working knowledge of the most important collection interfaces and classes in the `System.Collections` and `System.Collection.Specialized` namespaces

❑   Know how to build strongly typed collection classes

Working with Collections and Lists

The .NET Framework contains thousands of types, a large proportion of which are data structures that are *enumerable* – they support the ability for a contained or associated collection of items to be accessed in a sequential or key-based (random access) way.

To assist in working with enumerable types, the `System.Collections` namespace provides:

❑   Collection interfaces that define standard methods and properties implemented by different types of data structures. These interfaces allow enumerable types to provide consistent functionality, and aid interoperability.

❑   Functionality-rich implementations of many common collection classes such as lists and dictionaries. All these implement one or more of the common collection interfaces.

Collection Interfaces

Dealing with enumerable classes is a common task for developers, so the .NET Framework class library includes a set of interfaces in the `System.Collections` namespace that define contracts (of functionality) that enumerable classes implement. These interfaces provide consistency throughout the framework classes, making the life of a developer easier. Once you know how to work with one enumerable class that supports one or more common interfaces, you should, in theory, be able to work with any other enumerable class that supports the same interface in a uniform way, including the custom types that other developers create.

As developers, it's in your best interest to understand the collection interfaces in the `System.Collections` namespace. There aren't too many, and once you understand how they are organized, you can examine the interfaces that any enumerable type implements or returns from properties or methods, and determine what enumerable support a given type has. For example, any type that implements the `IEnumerable` interface supports forward-only iteration through its contained items. If a collection implements this interface, it also means that you can use the Visual Basic.NET and C# `for each` declaration with it.

> During compilation, compilers convert `for...each` declarations into calls to `IEnumerable` and its associated interface `IEnumerator`.

It's worth mentioning early on that most of the collection classes have many members (methods, properties, and so on) that are *not* defined in standard collection interfaces. The collection interfaces exist to define a common usage pattern across many different collection classes. The implementation of a given data structure, such as a queue, has many unique characteristics that are not defined in a standard interface – they are just members of a particular type.

We'll focus mainly on the members defined by common interfaces in this chapter; however, there are many more methods available on most of the types covered, all of which are documented in the .NET SDK. Let's start by examining the core collection interfaces and some of the classes that implement them.

The System.Collections Core Interfaces

The core collection interfaces defined in the `System.Collections` are:

- ❑ `IEnumerable`
- ❑ `IEnumerator` and `IDictionaryEnumerator`
- ❑ `ICollection`
- ❑ `IList`
- ❑ `IDictionary`

An interface is a specification that defines the members that a type must implement but does not define how the actual functionality of these members will be implemented. Chapter 3 contains more information on interfaces.

The IEnumerable and IEnumerator Interfaces

A type that implements the `IEnumerable` interface indicates to consumers that this type supports the notion of forward-only access to its items, using an *enumerator* object. An enumerator object provides a forward-only read-only cursor for a set of items.

The `IEnumerable` interface has one method, `GetEnumerator`:

```
public interface IEnumerable
{
   IEnumerator GetEnumerator();
}
```

This method returns a new instance of an enumerator object each time it is called. The returned object implements the `IEnumerator` interface, which has methods that can be used to sequentially access the set of `System.Object` types exposed by an enumerable type. The enumerator object supports retrieving the item at the current cursor position, or resetting the cursor back to the beginning of the item set.

The built-in `Array` type supports the `IEnumerable` interface. The following code shows how to declare a simple string array (although any type of array could be used), call the `GetEnumerator` method to create an enumerator object, and use the methods of returned `IEnumerator` interface to sequentially access each item in the array.

Using VB.NET, you would write:

```
Dim authors As String()
authors = New String() {"Richard","Alex","Dave","Rob","Brian","Karli"}
Dim e As IEnumerator
e = authors.GetEnumerator()
Do While e.MoveNext() = True
   Response.Write("<p />" & e.Current)
Loop
```

Using C#, you would write:

```
string[] authors = new string[6]
                {"Richard","Alex","Dave","Rob","Brian","Karli"};
IEnumerator e;
e = authors.GetEnumerator();
while( e.MoveNext() == true )
{
   Response.Write("<p />" + e.Current);
}
```

An example page named `simple-authorlist.aspx` *is provided in the samples that are available for download from* *http://www.daveandal.net/books/8900/* *in both VB.NET and C#. It demonstrates the code shown here.*

In this code, a string array called `authors` was declared that contains the names of six authors. To get an enumerator object for the array, the `authors.GetEnumerator` method is called. All arrays implement the `IEnumerable` interface, so calling `GetEnumerator` *is* possible. Once the enumerator object is created, the `MoveNext` method is called in a `while` loop. This method moves the cursor forward by one logical record. The cursor is always positioned before the first record (think of this as position -1) when an enumerator object is created. This means you must always call `MoveNext` before retrieving the first item using the `Current` property. When the enumerator object is positioned past the last record in a collection, it returns `false`. You can therefore safely loop through all items in the collection by calling `MoveNext` while it returns `true`, exiting when it returns `false`.

The .NET Framework guidelines state that once an enumerator object is created, it takes a snapshot of the items contained within an enumerable object at that point in time. If the original object is changed, the enumerator becomes invalid, and the enumerator object should throw an `InvalidOperationException` the next time one of its methods is called. All .NET Framework classes follow these guidelines, as should the enumerable types that you write. For reasons of performance, the enumerators implemented in the .NET Framework class library don't actually copy all the items when an enumerable object is created. Instead, they just maintain a reference to the enumerable object, and provide a *logical* snapshot. It's much cheaper to maintain a reference and an index to the original enumerable object – copying each and every item would be an expensive process for a large collection.

A simple versioning scheme is used to implement the actual semantics of a logical snapshot. Each time an enumerable object is changed (for example, an author is added or removed from the array), it increments a version number (think of this as a change counter). When an enumerator object is created, it copies the current version number of the enumerable object. Then, each time an enumerator object method is called, the enumerator compares its stored version number to the enumerable object's current version number. If these version numbers are different, the enumerator throws an InvalidOperationException.

The Current property of the IEnumerator interface is defined as the System.Object type. In the earlier code, you didn't have to cast the returned object from Current before using it, since Response.Write will call the ToString method for you. However, to store the underlying string type in the example, you would typically cast it.

For example, using VB.NET, you would write:

```
Dim author As String
author = CType(e.Current, string)
```

Using C#, you would write:

```
string author
author = (string) e.Current;
```

All of the collection interfaces in the System.Collections namespace use the System.Object type, which gives them great flexibility because they can be used with any type. However, this generic approach does mean that the CLR must perform type-conversion checking for most calls, which imposes a small performance overhead.

The for...each Statement

VB.NET and C# both have a statement that calls the enumerator directly. C# has the foreach statement and VB.NET has the For Each..Next statement (we'll refer to these as for..each statements). Both these languages implement their for..each functionality using the IEnumerable and IEnumerator interfaces. This means that you could change the earlier author example to use a for..each rather than a while statement. Using VB.NET, you would write:

```
Dim author As string
For Each author In authors
   Response.Write("<p />" & author)
Next
```

Using C#, you would write:

```
foreach( string author in authors )
{
   Response.Write("<p />" + author );
}
```

Using the `for..each` statement requires less code than using the `IEnumerable` and `IEnumerator` interfaces directly, but there will be times when it is not advisable (or even possible) to use the `for..each` statement.

To create some generic functionality that doesn't deal with concrete types, it would be better to not use the `for..each` statement, and if you had a loop that must be performed across several method invocations, it would not even be possible to use the `for..each` statement.

Provided that a type has a `GetEnumerator` method that returns a type derived from `IEnumerable`, it does not have to implement the `IEnumerable` interface for the `for..each` statement to work with it in C# or VB.NET. However, unless you have a very good reason for not doing so, your enumerable types *should* implement `IEnumerable` – that way they will be in accordance with the guidelines that the rest of the framework follows.

All other enumerable types in the .NET Framework class library derive from the `IEnumerable` interface. This means that although other enumerable types provide additional members for accessing the items they contain, all of them also support the forward-only cursor approach using enumerator objects. The same is true for the `IEnumerator` interface. Thus, all other enumerator interfaces derive from `IEnumerator`. Figure 15-1 shows the interface inheritance for the core interfaces:

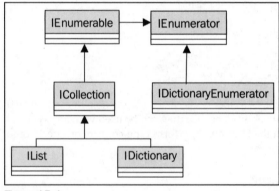

Figure 15-1

This UML class diagram can be read as follows:

❑ The `IList` and `IDictionary` interfaces derive from the `ICollection` interface, which in turn derives from `IEnumerable`.

❑ The `IEnumerable` interface is associated with `IEnumerator`.

❑ The `IDictionaryEnumerator` interface derives from `IEnumerator`.

Types that implement the IEnumerable interface can be enumerated in VB 6 and other COM-aware languages using COM interop, since the `GetEnumerator` method will be exposed with a `DISPID` of −4. Refer to MSDN for more information.

The ICollection and IList Interfaces

Enumerating through a collection sequentially is a common task, and it's also useful to be able to directly access items using a key or an index. For example, to check if a specific author exists in your array of authors from earlier, you could use the static `Array.IndexOf` method.

Using VB.NET, you would write:

```
Dim index As Integer
index = Array.IndexOf(authors, "Richard")
If index <> -1  Then
  Response.Write("<p />" & authors(index) & " is in the author list")
End If
```

Using C# you would write:

```
int index;
index = Array.IndexOf(authors, "Richard");
if (index != -1)
{
  Response.Write("<p />" + authors[index] + " is in the author list");
}
```

The `check-authorlist.aspx` *example page demonstrates the code shown here.*

Here the `Array.IndexOf` method is used to retrieve and store the index of a specific author in `index`. If the value of `index` is not -1 (which would mean that the author was not found), use the index to display the value held at that offset within the array. Under the hood, this method searches the array item by item, performing a comparison against each one. When a match is found, the index is returned.

The `IList` interface defines methods and properties that allow you to work with arrays of `System.Object` items, such as the string array of authors. The `IList` interface defines methods and properties that allow you to:

- ❑ Add an item to the end of the list (using the `Add` method)
- ❑ Insert an item at a specified offset in the list (using the `Insert` method)
- ❑ Determine if an item is contained within a list (using the `Contains` methods)
- ❑ Determine the index of an item within a list (using the `IndexOf` method)
- ❑ Retrieve or add an item by index (using the `Item` property, although in C# you have to use an indexer)
- ❑ Remove an item by reference, or by its index (using the `Remove` or `RemoveAt` methods)
- ❑ Remove all items (using the `Clear` method)
- ❑ Determine if a list is read-only (using the `IsReadOnly` property)
- ❑ Determine if a list is of a fixed size (using the `IsFixedSize` property)

The `IList` interface inherits the members of both `ICollection` and `IEnumerable`, as `IList` derives from `ICollection`, which in turn derives from `IEnumerable`.

The Array and the IList Interface

The built-in `Array` type implements the `IList` interface, but it only implements the `IndexOf`, `Clear`, and `Contains` methods and the `Item` property of the interface. If you try to call any of the other `IList` members, a `NotSupportedException` will be thrown. The other `IList` members are defined as explicit interface member implementations, and you have to access these using an `IList` interface reference.

As you saw in Chapter 3, the author of a type that implements an interface can control whether the members of an interface can be used implicitly (as if they were just part of the type), or if an interface reference has to be used to access them. Typically, the first approach is used, but for types in which specific members of the interface will not be commonly used (or are only required for internal use) the second approach is appropriate, as it keeps the publicly seen members fewer in number and more intuitive to use.

To see `IList` in action rewrite the last example (in which you determined if a specific author existed in an array) to use the `IList.Contains` method to determine if the item is present in the array, the `IList.IndexOf` method to determine the index of the item, and the `IList.Item` property to retrieve the value.

Using VB.NET, you would write:

```
Dim list As IList
list = CType(authors, IList)
If list.Contains("Richard") Then
   index = list.IndexOf("Richard")
   Response.Write("<p />" & list(index) & " is in the author list")
End If
```

Using C#, you would write:

```
IList list = (IList) authors;
if (list.Contains("Richard") == true)
{
   index = list.IndexOf("Richard");
   Response.Write("<p />" + list[index] + " is in the author list");
}
```

The `check-authorlist.aspx` example page demonstrates the code shown here.

As the `Item` property is actually an indexer, in C# you can just use the array-style notation to access items in the list. Using the `IList` interface is pretty simple and the code is certainly no more complex than before. Take a look at the `System.Collections.ArrayList` type to see more of the `IList` methods in use.

The ArrayList Class

An `ArrayList` is capable of holding zero to *n* `System.Object` objects in a dynamically sized array. The total number of objects that can be held in the array is available from the `Capacity` property. The used space (the number of items in the array) is available via the `Count` property. As you add or remove items from the list, the `ArrayList` is automatically resized as required. The key difference between the built-in `Array` type and `ArrayList` is this automatic size management. Internally, the `ArrayList` still uses the `Array` type to implement most of its functionality.

The following code shows how to create an `ArrayList` and populate it with a few items using the `Add` method. This time movie names are used, rather than authors. Using C#, you would write:

```
ArrayList movieList;
movieList = new ArrayList();
movieList.Add("Pulp Fiction");
movieList.Add("Aliens");
movieList.Add("The Good, the Bad and the Ugly");
```

Since `ArrayList` supports any type derived from `System.Object`, you could actually add many different item types to it. For example, using VB.NET, you would write:

```
Dim movieList As ArrayList = New ArrayList()
variedItems.Add("Pulp Fiction")      ' add a string
variedItems.Add(1234)                ' add an integer
variedItems.Add(new ArrayList())     ' add another array list
```

The `ArrayList` class implements the `IList` interface, so all the other `IList` members covered so far are implemented and available to use. The `IList` interface members are implemented *implicitly* as public members by the `ArrayList` type, so there is no need to use an `IList` reference to call them. Most of the types in the .NET Framework do this to make using them simpler. Of course, there's nothing stopping you from using an interface if you want to. Doing so could have advantages if, for example, you are trying to write generic code that works with any implementation of `IList`.

In the following VB.NET code, the `IList` interface of the `ArrayList` is used:

```
Dim movieList As IList
movieList = New ArrayList()
movieList.Add("Pulp Fiction")
movieList.Add("Aliens")
movieList.Add("The Good, the Bad and the Ugly")
```

Using C#, you would write:

```
IList movieList;
movieList = new ArrayList();
movieList.Add("Pulp Fiction");
movieList.Add("Aliens");
movieList.Add("The Good, the Bad and the Ugly");
```

Here a `movieList` variable of type `IList` is declared, and then assigned a newly created `ArrayList` object. You will only be able to use the members defined in the `IList` interface. To use the other `ArrayList` members, you must cast `movieList` to an `ArrayList` (or to some other supported interface).

When you assign a newly instantiated type to a variable in this way, you don't need to specify any casting as the compiler will interrogate the meta data of the type at compile time, and ensure that the interface is supported. If the interface isn't supported, a compile error will occur. However, if you do specify an explicit cast on an assignment such as `new`, this will override the checks performed by the compiler. If the cast then turns out to be invalid at runtime, the CLR will throw an `InvalidCastException`.

Let's write a simple web page that allows a user to enter a list of their favorite movies to demonstrate how to use the various members of `ArrayList`. The page will have options to add and delete movies to a list, as well as to sort the list. Only the important elements of the code for this application are reviewed here. The result is shown in Figure 15-2 – it automatically adds three movies. Notice that there is a [view source] link at the bottom of the page you can use to see the complete source code.

Figure 15-2

The code responsible for creating the visible output in the page (excluding the server-side code for events) is shown next in VB.NET. It is a separate routine named `ShowList`, which can be called when required from anywhere in the page code. The HTML section of the page contains a `<div runat="server">` element with the `outList` ID, into which the list of movies is inserted:

```
Sub ShowList()
  If movieList.Count > 0 Then
    For Each Movie As String In movieList
      outList.InnerHtml &= Movie & "<br />"
    Next
  Else
    outList.InnerHtml = "There are no movies in the list."
  End If
End Sub
```

If there are no movies in the list, the code displays the message There are no movies in the list. If there are movies in the list (the `Count` property of `movieList` is greater than zero), the code renders a list of the titles of the movies. The `For Each` statement is used to enumerate the `ArrayList` that contains the movies. You can do this as `ArrayList` implements `IEnumerable`.

The `movieList` variable is created in the `Page_Load` event handler. You'll see two ways of creating and maintaining state during postbacks, as well as the advantages and disadvantages of each. The first approach creates the list the first time the page is rendered, and places the instantiated object into the

ViewState of the page using a movies key. On subsequent postbacks, the list is retrieved using this key from the ViewState.

Whether a page is being rendered for the first time or not, the instantiated ArrayList is held in a page-level member variable called movieList. We've used a variable in this way to make the subsequent page code more readable, since no casting is needed after it has been retrieved. Using VB.NET, you would write:

```
Dim movieList As ArrayList

Sub Page_Load(Sender As Object, Args As EventArgs)
  If Page.IsPostBack Then
    movieList = CType(ViewState("movies"), ArrayList)
  Else
    movieList = New ArrayList()
    movieList.Add("Pulp Fiction")
    movieList.Add("Aliens")
    movieList.Add("The Good, the Bad and the Ugly")
    ViewState("movies") = movieList
    ShowList()
  End If
End Sub
```

> Collection classes are reference types, not value types. Therefore, when a reference to a collection type is assigned to multiple variables, all those variables will reference the same object on the managed heap.

There are no COM-type threading issues associated with storing objects in the ASP intrinsic objects such as ViewState or Session. It's perfectly safe, and in general you don't have to worry about threading models at all. However, storing an ArrayList in the Session object like this means that, by default, the ArrayList objects reside in memory on a *specific* web server. This means you cannot load-balance requests to such a page across multiple web servers. There are two solutions to this problem. You could tell ASP.NET to use an external state store (this was discussed in Chapter 13) or you can store the list in the ViewState as in this example, instead of the intrinsic Session object.

The following C# code shows how you can implement the Page_Load event handler using the Session object:

```
protected void Page_Load (object sender, EventArgs e)
{
  if (IsPostBack == true)
  {
    movieList = (ArrayList) Session["movies"];
  }
  else
  {
    movieList = new ArrayList();
    Session["movies"] = movieList;
  }
}
```

Now, the ASP.NET page framework will persist the state held in the `ArrayList` in the user's `Session`, rather that as part of the HTML page returned to the client. When the next postback occurs, ASP.NET will automatically recreate the `ArrayList`, restore its state, and make it available to your page.

The `ViewState` approach allows you to load-balance your application, but it does mean that pages sent back to the client will be slightly larger, and that the web server will have to perform a few more CPU cycles in order to create and destroy the objects held in `ViewState`.

> *When you store types in `ViewState`, you should enable tracing to keep an eye on the total `ViewState` size. You can find more details on this in Chapter 4.*

The choice of whether to use `Session` or `ViewState` to hold state should be made on a per-application basis as both have advantages:

❑ The problems associated with `Session` state in ASP 3 are gone, thanks to new external state stores such as SQL Server. A key benefit of using the `Session` object to hold the state is that the contents can survive across multiple pages; they are destroyed only when an ASP.NET session ends or the `Session` variable is deleted. For applications that require features like shopping carts, `Session` state combined with an external state store provides a fine solution.

❑ Unlike `Session` state, `ViewState` cannot be used beyond the scope of a single page. This means that it can't be used to pass data between pages, so any important data must be persisted elsewhere before the user navigates away from a page. However, the advantage of using `ViewState` is that fewer server resources – such as memory – are consumed, which increases the scalability of an application.

You've seen how the page is rendered, and how you can store the list of movies in either `Session` or `ViewState`. Next, let's look at the event handlers that manipulate the list in response to the user's actions.

The MovieList Event Handlers

Users can input a movie name and then select an action to perform using the following HTML form:

```
<form runat=server>

<h3>Movies in List</h3>
<div id="outList" runat="server" EnableViewState="False" /><p />
<b>Movie Name:</b> <asp:TextBox id="MovieName" runat="server" /><p />
<asp:Button OnClick="OnAddMovie" Text="Add Movie" runat="server" />
<asp:Button OnClick="OnDeleteMovie" Text="Delete Movie" runat="server" />
<asp:Button OnClick="OnSortList" Text="Sort List" runat="server" />
<asp:Button OnClick="OnCustomSortList"
            Text="Sort List (custom)" runat="server"/>
</form>
```

Six server controls are used in this form, one for the `<div>` into which the list of movies is inserted, one for the movie name textbox, (`id="MovieName"`), and one for each of the four buttons. Each button is associated with a server-side event handler via the `OnClick` attribute.

When the user hits the Add button, the following event handler is invoked (shown here in VB.NET). This event handler retrieves the value of the `Text` property of the `MovieName` server control and adds it to `movieList` (our `ArrayList`). Then it displays the list with the new movie added by calling the `ShowList` routine you saw earlier:

```
Sub OnAddMovie(Sender As Object, Args As EventArgs)
    movieList.Add(MovieName.Text)
    ShowList()
End Sub
```

When the user hits the Delete button, the following event handler is invoked (shown here in VB.NET). This event handler checks if the movie exists in the list by using the `IndexOf` method. If the movie is found in the list, the `Remove` method of the `ArrayList` is called to delete the movie:

```
Sub OnDeleteMovie(Sender As Object, Args As EventArgs)
    If movieList.IndexOf(MovieName.Text) = -1 Then
        status.InnerHtml = "Movie not found in list"
    Else
        movieList.Remove(MovieName.Text)
    End If
    ShowList()
End Sub
```

If the movie is not found, an error message is displayed by setting the `InnerHtml` property of a `<div>` element with the ID of `status`. This element is represented by a `HtmlGenericControl` control underneath the main form:

```
<div style="color:red" id="status" EnableViewState="False" runat="server" />
```

The `Remove` method doesn't throw any exception if it's called with an argument that's not in the list, and so you wouldn't have to validate the arguments (as done here), unless you wanted to give some type of feedback to the user. The `Remove` method of `ArrayList` actually calls the `IndexOf` method to determine the index of the passed item, and then calls the `RemoveAt` method, which actually removes the item at a specific position from the array. This means that this event handler could be more efficiently written as:

```
Sub OnDeleteMovie(Sender As Object, Args As EventArgs)
    Dim index As Integer = movieList.IndexOf(MovieName.Text)
    If index = -1 Then
        status.InnerHtml = "Movie not found in list"
    Else
        movieList.RemoveAt(index)
    End If
    ShowList()
End Sub
```

Now check for an item's index, store it in the `index` variable, and then use it to delete the item. Small optimizations like this may seem minor, but are well worth doing as the `ArrayList` type isn't particularly efficient. It will sequentially search an array, item by item, until a match is found, which means that for a list with a several hundred items, the scan time can be significant.

When the user hits the Sort List button the following event handler is invoked (shown here in VB.NET):

```
Sub OnSortList(Sender As Object, Args As EventArgs)
   movieList.Sort()
   ShowList()
End Sub
```

This event handler calls the `Sort` method of the `ArrayList`. This method sorts the items in the list by using a QuickSort algorithm (this cannot be changed), which results in the list being efficiently sorted alphabetically – the default for string types. Figure 15-3 shows the result:

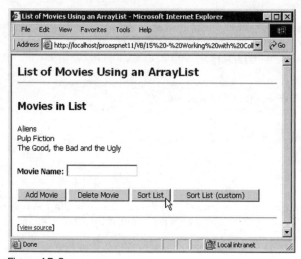

Figure 15-3

The QuickSort algorithm works by dividing a list of items into two partitions based upon a pivot item. Items less than the pivot item end up in the left partition, items greater than the pivot item end up in the right partition, and the pivot item ends up in the middle. By recursively applying this algorithm to each of the left and right partitions that are created until each partition only contains a single item, a list can be sorted with a minimum number of comparisons and exchanges.

Performance and Memory Optimizations

When items are added to an `ArrayList`, the size of its internal array is automatically increased as required. The default *capacity* of an `ArrayList` is sixteen. If a seventeenth item is added to the list, a new internal array is created which is twice the size of the current one, and the original items are copied to the array. It's worth optimizing the initial capacity of a list if you know how many items will be in it, as otherwise the repeated memory allocation and copying of items as the list grows in size could prove expensive.

Most of the framework collection classes can have their initial capacity and size set, and `ArrayList` is no exception. The capacity for an `ArrayList` can be set using the `Capacity` property, which accepts an integer value. For example (in C#):

```
ArrayList list = new ArrayList();
list.Capacity = 128;
```

Alternatively, you can set the capacity when the `ArrayList` is created by using one of the overloaded constructors. For example (in C#):

```
ArrayList list = new ArrayList(128);
```

Once a list is populated with items, you can release any unused slots by calling the `TrimToSize` method. However, calling this method will require a new array to be allocated, and all of the existing items will be copied from the old array to the new one. Accordingly, this method should only be called if a list is likely to remain static in size for a reasonable length of time, or if there are a large number of unused slots that should be freed.

Sorting the List – IComparer and IComparable

Collection classes such as `ArrayList` and `Array` use the `System.Collections.IComparer` interface to determine equality when they are sorting collections. This interface is used to establish if a type instance is less than, equal to, or greater than another type instance and has a single method called `Compare`:

```
public int Compare(object x, object y)
```

Classes that implement this interface should check for equality between the objects passed in, and return one of the following:

- ❑ A negative value if object x is less than object y
- ❑ A positive value is object x is greater than object y
- ❑ Zero if the objects are equal

The default implementation of `IComparer`, which is used by the `ArrayList` and other types, is the `System.Collections.Comparer` class. This class implements its comparison of two objects by using the `System.IComparable` interface of the first object (x) passed in to the `IComparer.Compare` method.

The `IComparable` interface has a single method called `CompareTo`, which has the same return values as the `IComparer.Compare` method:

```
public int CompareTo(object x);
```

Most value types such as string and integer implement the `IComparable` interface, which means that you can compare most types as follows (using VB.NET):

```
Dim s1 As String = "This One"
Dim s2 As String  = "That One"
Dim c1 As IComparable
c1 = CType(s1, IComparable)
If c1.CompareTo(s2) <> 0 Then
  outResult.InnerHtml = "'" & s1 & "' is different to '" & s2 & "'"
End If
If c1.CompareTo(s2) < 0 Then
  outResult.InnerHtml = "'" & s1 & "' is less than '" & s2 & "'"
End If
If c1.CompareTo(s2) > 0 Then
```

```
    outResult.InnerHtml = "'" & s1 & "' is greater than '" & s2 & "'"
End If
```

The `simple-compare.aspx` example page demonstrates the code shown here.

Unless there's a good reason, custom types should implement the `IComparable` interface, so that the type can be sorted easily. However, there is a limitation as to what can be sorted. The `ArrayList` class uses the `System.Collections.Comparer` implementation of `IComparer` to sort its list, which in turn uses the `IComparable` interface of the types within the list. This means that you can only sort an array that contains items that can do equality checks on each other. Most types can only do equality checks against their own type, so by default you can't sort an `ArrayList` that contains different types. For example, the following VB.NET code that tries to compare a string and integer will throw an `ArgumentException`:

```
Dim s1 As String = "richard"
Dim i1 As Integer = 1234
Dim c1 As IComparable
c1 = CType(s1, IComparable)
If c1.CompareTo(i1) <> 0
   outResult.InnerHtml = "You'll never see this line because of the exception."
End If
```

The `error-compare.aspx` example page demonstrates the code shown here.

When the `CompareTo` method is called, the string type checks the type of the argument passed. If the argument is not a string type, it throws an exception. This exception must be caught at runtime. The code will compile without error, as type checking is not possible at design time. While this restriction will not be a problem in most applications, it is possible to sort arrays that contain different types. You can gain complete control over how an array is sorted by using an overload of the `Sort` method that accepts an `IComparer` interface that will be used when equality checks are performed.

This technique is used in the movie list application. Clicking the **Sort List (custom)** button results in the list of movies being displayed in reverse alphabetical order, as shown in Figure 15-4:

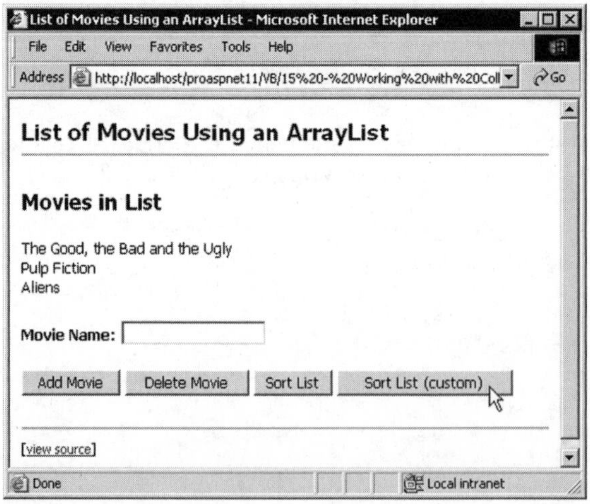

Figure 15-4

The event handler for the Sort List (custom) button invokes the custom sort:

```
Sub OnCustomSortList(Sender As Object, Args As EventArgs)
   Dim custom As IComparer = New MyComparer()
   movieList.Sort(custom)
   ShowList()
End Sub
```

The MyComparer comparer class follows. This class uses the IComparable interface of object x to compare it with object y. The result from the call to CompareTo is then checked, and the sign of the number is inverted if the objects are not equal. By making negative values positive and positive values negative, the list is effectively reverse-sorted. An implementation of IComparer should always treat non-null values as being greater than a null value:

```
Class MyComparer Implements IComparer
   Overridable Function Compare(x As Object, y As Object) As Integer _
             Implements IComparer.Compare
      Dim ic As IComparable
      Dim compareResult As Integer
      ic = CType(x, IComparable)
      compareResult = ic.CompareTo(y)
      If compareResult <> 0
        compareResult = compareResult * -1
      End If
      Return compareResult
   End Function
End Class
```

The ArrayList type actually has a Reverse method, which would normally be used to reverse-sort a list.

Efficient Searching – Using Binary Searching

Searching an ArrayList using methods like IndexOf means that every item in the list is compared with the value being searched for, until a match is found. This 'brute force' approach to searching means that as the number of items in a list increases, so does the number of comparisons that have to be performed to locate an item, particularly when the item being searched for is located towards the end of the list. The result is (pretty much) a linear increase in search times as a list grows. This isn't a problem for small lists, but large lists need a more efficient solution.

You can use a binary search to efficiently search lists. If a list is sorted (which is a prerequisite of performing a binary search), a binary search can locate an item using significantly fewer comparisons, which results in search times that are significantly less than for a regular linear search. The following code shows how you can perform a binary search on an ArrayList:

```
ArrayList someList;
int ItemIndex;
someList = new ArrayList();
// code here to add lots of items to the list...
someList.Sort();
ItemIndex = someList.BinarySearch("Some item");
```

Binary searches do not work on an unsorted list. You won't receive an error if you call the BinarySearch method on an unsorted list, but you *will* get unpredictable results – for example, items that are in the list may not be found. There are two main reasons why the BinarySearch method doesn't just sort the list anyway:

❑ **Performance**: The list may already be sorted, and re-sorting would thus be wasteful.

❑ **Custom sorts**: Sorting the list might require a custom IComparer implementation, which means that the BinarySearch method cannot make any assumptions on how to sort the list.

If you do sort a list using a custom IComparer interface, use the overloaded version of the BinarySearch method that accepts the comparer interface. If you don't use this overload, the search results will be unpredictable.

Indexers and Bounds Checking

When working with an ArrayList, you can treat it just like an array by using an integer index to retrieve a specific item. For example, using VB.NET, you would write:

```
BestMovieOfAllTime = CType(movieList[2], string)
```

Using C#, you would write:

```
BestMovieOfAllTime = (string) movieList[2];
```

You can treat the ArrayList like an array because it implements an *indexer*. Indexers allow a type to be programmatically treated like an array, but under the hood methods are called to set or retrieve values. Indexers can be declared to accept different types, which means that an indexer value could be an integer, a string, or another supported type. For example, the ASP.NET Session object supports both integer and string indexers. Using VB.NET, you would write:

```
Dim SomeValue As String
SomeValue = CType(Session(0), String)
SomeValue = CType(Session("NamedValue"), String)
```

Using C#, you would write:

```
string SomeValue;
SomeValue = (string) Session[0];
SomeValue = (string) Session["NamedValue"];
```

This code shows how you can retrieve the first session variable using either an integer index value (in this case zero), or a named session variable.

Types that support indexers typically throw exceptions when confronted with invalid index values. If you don't know in advance whether an index is valid, always write code that deals with exceptions. For example, using C#, you would write:

```
try
{
    BestMovieOfAllTime = (string) movieList[6];
```

```
    }
    catch( ArgumentOutOfRangeException rangeException )
    {
       BestMovieOfAllTime = "index too big";
    }
```

Since types such as the `ArrayList` will throw an `ArgumentOutOfRangeException` if an index is invalid, you should declare an exception handler to catch an error and give the user some basic feedback. You should also handle the general exception case, since types could throw other unexpected exceptions:

```
    try
    {
       BestMovieOfAllTime = (string) movieList[6];
    }
    catch( ArgumentOutOfRangeException rangeException )
    {
       BestMovieOfAllTime = "index too big";
    }
    catch( Exception e )
    {
       // do something useful here
    }
```

The ICollection Interface

The `ArrayList` class supports three collection interfaces: `IList`, `IEnumerable`, and `ICollection`. We've covered the first two. Turn your attention to `ICollection`. The `ICollection` interface defines methods and properties that allow you to:

❑   Determine how many items are in a collection (using the `Count` property).

❑   Copy the contents of a collection into a specified array at a given offset (using the `CopyTo` method).

❑   Determine if the collection is synchronized and therefore thread-safe.

❑   Determine the synchronization root object for the collection (using the `SyncRoot` property). The synchronization root object is the object that is locked and unlocked as collection operations are performed on a synchronized collection.

The `ICollection` interface derives from the `IEnumerable` interface so it inherits the `GetEnumerator` method.

The ICollection.Count Property

The following code shows how to use the `ICollection.Count` property to display the number of items in the `movieList ArrayList`:

```
    <p>There are <%=movieList.Count%> in the list.</p>
```

For those types in the class library, the implementation of the Count property returns a cached field. It doesn't cause the size of a collection to be recalculated, so it isn't expensive to call, which means that you don't need to worry about caching the Count property in an effort to get efficiency.

The ICollection.CopyTo Method

The ICollection.CopyTo method allows the contents of a collection to be inserted into an array at a specified offset. If the array to which the contents are copied does not have sufficient capacity for the insertion, an ArgumentException will be thrown. The following VB.NET code shows how to copy the contents of the ArrayList into a string array (at the beginning) using the CopyTo method:

```
Dim Animals As ArrayList = New ArrayList()
Dim ArrayOfAnimals() As String
Animals.Add("Cat")
Animals.Add("Dog")
Dim a As Array
ArrayOfAnimals = Array.CreateInstance(GetType(String), 2)
Animals.CopyTo(ArrayOfAnimals, 0)
Dim Animal As String
For Each Animal In ArrayOfAnimals
    Response.Write("<p />" & Animal)
Next
```

Using C#, you would write:

```
ArrayList Animals = new ArrayList();
string[] ArrayOfAnimals;
Animals.Add("Cat");
Animals.Add("Dog");
ArrayOfAnimals = (string[]) Array.CreateInstance(typeof(string), 2);
Animals.CopyTo(ArrayOfAnimals, 0);
foreach( string Animal in ArrayOfAnimals )
{
    Response.Write("<p />" + Animal);
}
```

The array-copyto.aspx example page demonstrates the code shown here.

Here, you create an ArrayList that contains a couple of animals, dynamically create a string array, and then use the CopyTo method of the ArrayList to populate the created array with the contents of the ArrayList.

The ArrayList supports two additional overloads of CopyTo. The first overload doesn't require an index to be specified when the contents of the ArrayList are copied and inserted at the start of an array. The second overload allows a specified number of items, starting from a specified position, to be copied from the ArrayList to a given index within another array.

As the ArrayList class does not expose its internal array, you have to use either its AddRange or InsertRange method when copying data from an array into an ArrayList. The AddRange method accepts an ICollection interface and adds all items within the collection to the end of the array. In the following example, the contents of two arrays are copied into an ArrayList. The code would result in the names being listed in this order: Tom, Mark, Paul, Jon. Using C#, you would write:

```
string[] Friends = {"Tom","Mark"};
string[] CoWorkers = {"Paul","Jon"};
ArrayList MergedList = new ArrayList();
MergedList.AddRange(Friends);
MergedList.AddRange(CoWorkers);
foreach (string Name in MergedList)
{
   Response.Write("<p />" + Name );
}
```

The `InsertRange` method accepts an `ICollection` interface as its second parameter, but expects the first parameter to be the index to which the new items will be copied. To make the names `Paul` and `Jon` appear at the front of the list, you could insert the second array using `InsertRange` with an index value of zero. This code would result in the names being listed in this order: `Paul`, `Jon`, `Tom`, `Mark`:

```
string[] Friends = {"Tom","Mark"};
string[] CoWorkers = {"Paul","Jon"};
ArrayList MergedList = new ArrayList();
MergedList.AddRange(Friends);
MergedList.InsertRange(0, CoWorkers);
foreach( string Name in MergedList )
{
   Response.Write("<p />" + Name);
}
```

The `merging-lists.aspx` example page demonstrates the code shown here.

The ICollection.IsSynchronized Property

ASP.NET enables Web applications to share objects by using the `Application` and `Cache` intrinsic objects. If an object reference is shared this way, it's possible for multiple pages to work simultaneously with the *same* object instance. If this happens, any changes to the object must be synchronized. If two pages try to modify an object at the same time without synchronization, there is a high probability that the object's state will become corrupted. Objects that can safely be manipulated simultaneously are thread-safe. A thread-safe object takes on the responsibility of guarding itself from concurrent access, providing the necessary synchronization.

The `ICollection.IsSynchronized` property can be used to determine if an object is thread-safe. For performance reasons, most objects (including `ArrayList`) are not thread-safe by default. Thus, you should not share types like `ArrayList` in a Web application without performing some form of synchronization. In classic ASP, you could use the `Application.Lock` and `Application.Unlock` methods for synchronization and while they are available in ASP.NET, they're not suitable for this particular task. They provide a coarse-grained lock (which is application-wide) that simply isn't suitable for scalable applications.

To safely share a collection object such as an `ArrayList` between multiple Web pages, you need to use a synchronization helper object. Such a helper object provides the same public interface as a non-thread-safe type, but adds a synchronization wrapper around the methods and properties that would otherwise *not* be thread-safe. Since this is such a common requirement, the collection types (and many other framework classes) follow a common pattern.

Types that need to work in a thread-safe way provide a public, static, method called `Synchronized` that takes a non-thread-safe object reference and creates and returns a thread-safe wrapper that can be used to synchronize calls. Both objects manipulate the same underlying state, so changes made by either the thread-safe or non-thread-safe object will be seen by any other code that holds a reference to either object.

The following VB.NET code shows how a non-thread-safe `ArrayList` adds an item before creating a thread-safe wrapper:

```
Dim NotThreadSafeArrayList As ArrayList
NotThreadSafeArrayList = New ArrayList()
NotThreadSafeArrayList.Add("Hello")
Dim ThreadSafeArrayList As ArrayList
ThreadSafeArrayList = ArrayList.Synchronized(NotThreadSafeArrayList)
If ThreadSafeArrayList.IsSynchronized = True Then
  Response.Write("<p />It's synchronized")
End If
```

Figure 15-5 illustrates how this `ThreadSafeArrayList` works by protecting calls, and then delegating the calls to the non-thread-safe object:

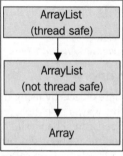

Figure 15-5

The ICollection.SyncRoot Property

When writing thread-safe code, it's common to have a handle or object that's used by all the possible code paths in different threads (web pages) in order to synchronize access to the shared state. The CLR automatically allows any .NET type instance to be a synchronization root (SyncRoot) that can be locked and unlocked to ensure that one or more code statements are only ever executed by a single thread at a time.

In VB.NET, you can use an object reference in conjunction with the `SyncLock` statement to make code thread-safe:

```
Sub DoSomethingWithAList( list as ArrayList )
  SyncLock list
    list.Add("abc")
  End SyncLock
End Sub
```

In C#, you can achieve the same result using the `lock` statement:

```
void DoSomethingWithAList( ArrayList list )
{
  lock(list)
  {
    list.Add("abc");
  }
}
```

Under the hood, both C# and VB.NET use the `System.Threading.Monitor` object to perform their synchronization. Both the C# and VB.NET compilers add exception handling around the statements being executed, to ensure that any exceptions that are not handled in the code do not result in synchronization locks not being released.

Using `SyncLock` (or `lock`) you can achieve a fine-grained level of locking inside ASP.NET pages. Rather than having one global lock, which is effectively what `Application.Lock` and `Application.Unlock` provide, you can have many smaller locks, which reduces lock contention.

The disadvantage to this approach is that it requires that page developers really understand multi-threading. Since the writing of multi-threaded applications is not simple (and something ASP.NET does its best to protect you from), using the `Synchronized` method to automatically make a type thread-safe is often the preferred approach to take.

When acquiring or releasing a `SyncLock`, you need to know what `SyncRoot` object to use. This is the function of the `ICollection.SyncRoot` property. As you cannot assume any implementation knowledge about the type providing an interface, you cannot make any assumptions about which `SyncRoot` object to use either.

Consider this VB.NET code:

```
Dim NotThreadSafeArrayList As ArrayList
NotThreadSafeArrayList = New ArrayList()
NotThreadSafeArrayList.Add("Hello")
Dim ThreadSafeArrayList1 As ArrayList
Dim ThreadSafeArrayList2 As ArrayList
Dim ThreadSafeArrayList3 As ArrayList
ThreadSafeArrayList1 = ArrayList.Synchronized(NotThreadSafeArrayList)
ThreadSafeArrayList2 = ArrayList.Synchronized(NotThreadSafeArrayList)
ThreadSafeArrayList3 = ArrayList.Synchronized(NotThreadSafeArrayList)
```

Here you create an `ArrayList` and then create three synchronization wrapper objects, each of which exposes the `ICollection` interface. Since each of the wrapper objects actually manipulates the same underlying array, the `SyncRoot` object used by each of the wrappers is the non-thread-safe `ArrayList`, as depicted in Figure 15-6:

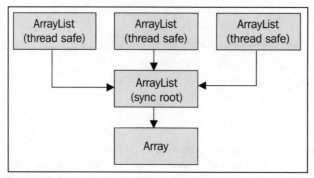

Figure 15-6

To synchronize access to the array in a Web page so that you could perform an atomic operation like adding the contents of the array to a database and clearing it, you'd need to lock out all other threads from using the `ArrayList`. If you only had a reference to an `ArrayList` object or an `ICollection` interface, and didn't know whether or not that type was thread-safe, how could you achieve this?

If you had a thread-safe wrapper, and wrote your code as follows, it would fail miserably:

```
SyncLock ThreadSafeArrayList1
    ' copy list to db and clear list (as an example)
End SyncLock
```

All this code does is acquire a lock on the thread-safe wrapper, not on the underlying list. Anybody using one of the other thread-safe wrappers would still be able to modify the list. The `ICollection.SyncRoot` property solves this problem. The implementation of this property should always return the appropriate `SyncRoot` object. You should therefore rewrite the code as follows:

```
SyncLock ThreadSafeArrayList1.SyncRoot
    ' copy list to db and clear list (as an example)
End SyncLock
```

Working with Dictionary Objects

In ASP.NET, state is managed by the `Session` or `Application` intrinsic objects. The value type stored is of type `System.Object` (rather than `Variant`, as was the case in ASP 3.0). Since all types in .NET derive from `System.Object`, any built-in or custom type can be held in session or application state.

The following code shows a simple example of storing and retrieving state using the `Session` intrinsic object. Using VB.NET, you would write:

```
Session("value1") = "Wrox"
Session("value2") = "Wiley"
Dim value As String
value = CType(Session("value1"), string)
value = CType(Session("value2"), string)
```

Using C#, you would write:

```
Session["value1"] = "Wrox";
Session["value2"] = "Wiley";
string value;
value = (string) Session["value1"];
value = (string) Session["value2"];
```

Here two values are being set using the keys `value1` and `value2`. The values associated with these keys are then retrieved.

The Hashtable Class

The `Hashtable` class represents a dictionary of associated keys and values, implemented as a *hash table*. A hash table is a proven way of efficiently storing and retrieving values using the *hash* of a key value.

Internally, the ASP intrinsic objects such as `Session` use the `System.Collections.Hashtable` class to implement key-based lookup functionality. This class is very similar to the scripting runtime `Dictionary` object used in classic ASP pages, and provides all those methods expected from a dictionary type object.

Using the `Hashtable` class is straightforward. You can create an instance of the `Hashtable` class and use a text indexer to set and retrieve associated keys and values. For example, using C#, you would write:

```
Hashtable ourSession;
ourSession = new Hashtable();
ourSession["value1"] = "Wrox";
ourSession["value2"] = "Wiley";
string value;
value = (string) ourSession["value1"];
value = (string) ourSession["value2"];
```

You can determine if a key is contained within the hash table using the `ContainsKey` method. Using VB.NET, you would write:

```
If ourSession.ContainsKey("value1") = True Then
   Response.Write("The key value1 is in the Hashtable")
End If
```

You could of course use the `Contains` method to determine if a key is present, but since all that does is call the `ContainsKey` method, there is no point. You can determine if a specified value is held within the `Hashtable` using the `ContainsValue` method. Using VB.NET, you would write:

```
If ourSession.ContainsValue("Wrox") = True Then
   Response.Write("The value Wrox is in the Hashtable")
End If
```

Figure 15-7 demonstrates the creation of a `Hashtable`, and the use of the `ContainsKey` and `ContainsValue` methods:

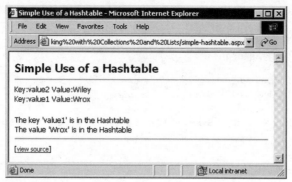

Figure 15-7

Although the `Hashtable` allows any object type to be used as a key, only those types that override `System.Object.GetHashCode` and `System.Object.Equals` should actually be used. All of the primitive types in .NET, such as integer and string, override these methods and are safe to use as keys.

A hash table depends on *hash codes* to uniquely identify keys. Hash codes are numbers that, where possible, uniquely identify a single object instance of a specific type. A perfect hash code algorithm will always return a hash code that is unique to a single instance of a specific type. A good candidate for a hash code is something along the lines of the identity field for a row within a database. The `Hashtable` class uses hash codes to provide efficient and fast lookups. When creating custom types, you also have to implement a good hash code algorithm.

As any type can be used with most of the collections in the .NET Framework class library, the `System.Object` class has a method called `GetHashCode` that returns a hash code for any object instance. The system-provided implementation of this method returns a hash code that uniquely identifies an object instance, but the hash code is not specific to a given type. The returned value is simply an index held internally by the CLR to identify an object. Thus, if the system-provided implementation of `GetHashCode` is not overridden by a type, then by default, two equal hash code values will imply that it's the same object instance, as demonstrated in this C# code:

```
class SomeType {};
SomeType variable1 = new SomeType();
SomeType variable2;
variable2 = variable1;
if ( variable1.GetHashCode() == variable2.GetHashCode() )
{
   Response.Write("The two variables reference the same object");
}
```

Hash codes enable classes like `Hashtable` to efficiently store and retrieve values. When an item is added to a `Hashtable`, the hash code of its associated key is used to determine a slot in which an item can be held. If a key with the same hash code doesn't already exist at the slot located using the hash code, the value can be saved. If the slot is already full, `System.Object.Equals` is called to determine if the key already in the slot is in fact equal to the one used to locate the slot. If both keys are equal, an exception is thrown. If the keys are different, a new key and value is added to the hash table in a different slot.

For these reasons, any type used as a key within a hash table must:

❑ Implement an efficient hash code algorithm that (where possible) uniquely identifies an object of a specific type. This means that you must override `System.Object.GetHashCode`.

❑ Override the `System.Object.Equals` method and provide an efficient comparison of two object instances. Typically, you would implement this by comparing the hash codes (if you can be sure that the hash code is always unique), or key fields that are held within a type as fields.

You can enumerate all of the keys and values in a hash table using the `Keys` or `Values` properties. Both these properties are defined as the `ICollection` type, and so they can be accessed in numerous ways. The following code uses the C# `foreach` statement to enumerate the keys. This code will actually result in a call to `table.Keys.GetEnumerator` (recall that `ICollection` inherits this from `IEnumerable`). This method will return an enumerator object that implements `IEnumerator`, which can then be used to walk through each key value:

```
Hashtable table = new Hashtable();
table["name"] = "Richard";
table["age"] = "Old enough";
foreach (string key in table.Keys)
{
   Response.Write("<br />" + key );
}
```

In VB.NET, you can do the same thing using the `For Each..Next` statement:

```
Dim table As Hashtable = New Hashtable()
Dim value As String
table("name") = "Richard"
table("age") = "Old enough"
For Each value As String In table.Values
   Response.Write("<br />" & value)
Next
```

The `Hashtable` class implements the interface `IEnumerable`, so you can enumerate all its contained keys and items. The enumerator object returned by the `Hashtable`'s implementation of `IEnumerable.GetEnumerator` exposes contained items using the value type `System.Collections.DictionaryEntry`. This value type has properties that allow you to access the associated `Key` and `Value` properties. To list all of the keys and current values held in a `Hashtable`, you could write the following C# code:

```
foreach (DictionaryEntry entry in table)
{
   Response.Write("<br />Key: " + entry.Key + " Value: " + entry.Value);
}
```

The public `GetEnumerator` method of the `Hashtable` object returns the `IDictionaryEnumerator` interface. This enumerator interface has all the methods and properties of `IEnumerator`, in addition to three properties that expose the `Key`, `Value`, and `DictionaryEntry` of the current item. Returning a custom enumerator with these additional properties reduces casting when the `foreach` statement cannot be used. This in turn improves performance of an application, as the CLR must check that a cast is type-safe.

The following C# code shows how you could use the `IDictionaryEnumerator` interface:

```
IDictionaryEnumerator e;
e = table.GetEnumerator();
while (e.MoveNext())
{
  Response.Write("<br />Key: " + e.Key + " Value: " + e.Value );
}
```

When the type implements the `IEnumerable` interface, it still has to implement a version of the `GetEnumerator` method, which returns an `IEnumerator` interface. The following C# code shows how to implement an enumerable type that supports both the standard `IEnumerable.GetEnumerator` method using an explicit interface method definition, and a public `GetEnumerator` method that reduces the need for casting:

```
public class MyCollection : IEnumerable
{
  public MyCustomEnumerator GetEnumerator()
  {
    return new MyCustomEnumerator();
  }
  IEnumerator IEnumerable.GetEnumerator()
  {
    return new MyCustomEnumerator();
  }
}
```

Comparing Hashtable with the Intrinsic ASP.NET Objects

There are a number of differences between using the `Hashtable` class and the ASP.NET intrinsic objects:

❑ The key values for a `Hashtable` are not restricted to strings. Any type can be used, so long as the type used as a key overrides the `System.Object.Equals` and `System.Object.GetHashCode` methods.

❑ String keys are case-sensitive whereas those of the ASP.NET intrinsic objects are not.

❑ When enumerating over an ASP.NET intrinsic object, you enumerate over the keys associated with each contained item value. The `Hashtable` returns both the key and value using the `DictionaryEntry` class.

❑ When enumerating over an ASP.NET intrinsic object, the `Current` property returns a `System.String` object (the key value) and not a `System.Collections.DictionaryEntry` entry.

The IDictionary Interface

The `IDictionary` interface defines methods and properties that allow you to work with an unordered collection of keys and their associated values. Keys and values are both defined in this interface as type

`System.Object`, which means any type can be used as a key, and any type can be used as a value. The `IDictionary` interface defines methods and properties that allow you to:

- Add items to the collection (by passing in the key and value to the `Add` method)

- Delete items from the collection (by passing the key of the value to delete to the `Remove` method)

- Determine if a specified key exists and is associated with an item (using the `Contains` method)

- Empty the collection (by calling the `Clear` method)

- Enumerate all of the keys in the collection (using the `Keys` property, which is defined as an `ICollection`)

- Enumerate all of the values in the collection (using the `Values` property, which is defined as an `ICollection`)

- Enumerate key-value pairs (by using the `GetEnumerator` method, which returns an `IDictionaryEnumerator` interface that is discussed shortly)

- Determine if the collection is read-only (using the `IsReadOnly` property)

- Determine if the collection is of a fixed size (using the `IsFixedSize` property)

The `IDictionary` interface derives from the `ICollection` interface so it inherits all of its methods and properties, as well as those of the basic interface `IEnumerable`.

Case Sensitivity of Keys

With the ASP.NET intrinsic objects, key values are case-insensitive. This means that the following C# code, which uses the intrinsic `Session` object, will happily set and retrieve the value correctly, even though the case in the key is different:

```
Session["key"] = "value";
Response.Write("<p />value is " + Session["KEY"]);
```

The following VB.NET code shows the hash codes for two objects that contain the same string value, but with differing case:

```
Dim name1, name2 As String
name1 = "Richard"
name2 = "RICHARD"
outResult1.InnerHtml &= "Hash code for '" & name1 & "' is " & _
                                        name1.GetHashCode()
outResult1.InnerHtml &= "Hash code for '" & name2 & "' is " & _
                                        name2.GetHashCode()
...
```

Since the .NET Framework is case-sensitive by default, the hash codes for these strings are unique. If you want two strings that differ only by case to be considered the same, you have to implement a hash code provider class that determines hash codes for other types, and can therefore use a different algorithm to create a hash code, one which is not based on case-sensitive letters. Since it's common to have case-insensitive keys, the .NET Framework has a built-in hash code provider that is case-insensitive:

```
...
Dim hcp As IHashCodeProvider
hcp = CaseInsensitiveHashCodeProvider.Default
Response.Write("Hash code for '" & name1 & "' is " & hcp.GetHashCode(name1))
Response.Write("<br />");
Response.Write("Hash code for '" & name2 & "' is " & hcp.GetHashCode(name2))
```

Figure 15-8 demonstrates case-sensitive and case-insensitive hash code generation, using the example code you've just seen, in the display-hashcodes.aspx page:

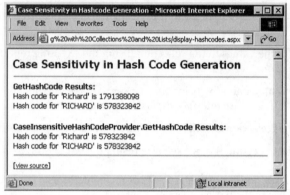

Figure 15-8

Classes such as Hashtable can use hash code providers to override their behavior. The following C# code shows how you can create a hash table that is not case-sensitive (when string keys are used) by using the standard framework classes System.Collections.CaseInsensitiveHashCodeProvider and System.Collections.CaseInsensitiveComparer:

```
Hashtable ourSession;
ourSession = new Hashtable(CaseInsensitiveHashCodeProvider.Default,
                           CaseInsensitiveComparer.Default);
Session["key"] = "value";
Response.Write("value is " + Session["KEY"]);
```

With this code, the value will be correctly displayed in the browser – the value will be found, even though the casing of the key is different.

The CaseInsensitiveHashCodeProvider class provides an implementation of the IHashCodeProvider interface that creates a case-insensitive hash code of string types. For non-string types, the objects default hash code is returned, which means that such types may still be case-sensitive (this depends on the algorithm used to create the hash).

The CaseInsensitiveComparer class provides an implementation of the IComparer interface that will perform a case-insensitive comparison for two string values. If either of the objects being compared is not a string, it uses the default Comparer.Default comparer object, encountered earlier.

Both `CaseInsensitiveHashCodeProvider` and `CaseInsensitiveComparer` have a static property called `Default`, which returns an instance of the class that is shared and always available.

Creating a case-insensitive hash table is a common requirement, and so a helper class, `System.Collections.Specialized.CollectionsUtil`, is provided to assist. For example:

```
Hashtable names;
names = CollectionsUtil.CreateCaseInsensitiveHashtable();
```

> The `System.Collections.Specialized` namespace is imported by default into a ASP.NET page so you do not need to use fully qualified names or an import directive.

The Stack Class

The `Stack` class provides a *Last-In First-Out (LIFO)* collection of `System.Object` types. The last item pushed onto the stack is always the first item retrieved from the stack. The `Stack` class can be extremely useful when you need to perform recursive operations, where you often need to save and restore values in order (such as the context within an XSLT processor) but in which the number of values saved and restored is not necessarily known in advance.

A `Stack` class can also be useful if you simply need to save the values of some variables while performing a temporary calculation, after which you need to recall their original values.

The `Stack` class implements the `ICollection` and `IEnumerable` collection interfaces, and so can be enumerated using the `For Each` and `foreach` statements of VB.NET and C#, have its size determined, have specific items accessed using an indexer, and so on.

The following VB.NET code shows how you can *push* several items on to a stack and then *pop* (retrieve) them:

```
Dim s As Stack = New Stack()

s.Push("Alex")
s.Push("Dave")
s.Push("Rich")
s.Push("Brian")
s.Push("Karli")

While s.Count > 0
   Response.Write(s.Pop() & "<br />")
End While
```

Here, you keep retrieving and displaying items from the stack until the `Count` property tells you that there are no more items. As shown in Figure 15-9, the items are listed in reverse order in the browser, since the last item ("Karli") is retrieved first:

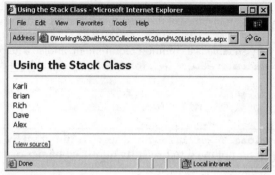

Figure 15-9

If you want to look at an item on the stack without actually removing it, use the `Peek` method:

```
Response.Write(s.Peek())
```

The `Stack` class has a static `Synchronized` method that returns a thread-safe wrapper for a stack, which allows it to be called concurrently from different threads:

```
Dim s As Stack = New Stack()
Dim s2 As Stack
s2 = Stack.Synchronized(s)
```

> **Unless you provide your own synchronization, you should always use a thread-safe wrapper if multiple ASP.NET pages are going to access a shared object using application state.**

The Queue Class

The `Queue` class provides a *First-In First-Out (FIFO)* collection. This is useful when you need to process items in order, such as a list of in-memory work to do. The following VB.NET code shows how to add items to a `Queue` before retrieving and displaying them, checking the `Count` property to ensure there are still items to be processed:

```
Dim q As Queue = New Queue()
q.Enqueue("Wake up")
q.Enqueue("Have a shower")
q.Enqueue("Get dressed")
q.Enqueue("Go to work")
q.Enqueue("Do a great job")
q.Enqueue("Come home and relax")
While q.Count > 0
  Response.Write(q.Dequeue() & "<br />")
End While
```

The output from this example, shown in Figure 15-10, demonstrates that the items are always retrieved in the order they are added:

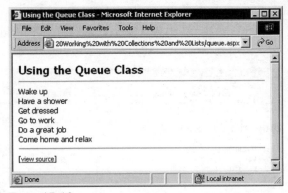

Figure 15-10

Like the `Stack` class the `Queue` class implements the `ICollection` and `IEnumerable` collection interfaces, and so can be enumerated using the `foreach` statements of VB.NET and C#, have its size determined, have specific items accessed using an indexer, and so on.

The `Queue` class has a `Synchronized` method that can return a thread-safe wrapper for a queue, which enables it to be called concurrently from different threads:

```
Dim q As Queue = New Queue()
Dim q2 As Queue
q2 = Queue.Synchronized(q)
```

Again, a thread-safe wrapper should always be used if multiple ASP.NET pages are going to access a shared object using application state.

The SortedList Class

The `SortedList` class is an interesting collection class, as it's a cross between a `Hashtable` and an `ArrayList`. It implements the `IDictionary` interface and maintains key-value pairs like the `Hashtable`, but internally holds items in two sorted arrays. The following VB.NET code shows how to create and use a `SortedList`:

```
Dim alphabet As New SortedList()

alphabet = CollectionsUtil.CreateCaseInsensitiveSortedList()

alphabet.Add("Z", "The Letter Z")
alphabet.Add("A", "The Letter A")
alphabet.Add("S", "The Letter S")

For Each letter As DictionaryEntry In alphabet
  outResult.InnerHtml &= "Key:" & letter.Key & " - Value:" _
                    & letter.Value & "<br />"
Next
```

This code creates an instance of the SortedList class, adds three items that represent some letters of the alphabet, and then uses the For Each statement to display the items. The result can be seen in Figure 15-11:

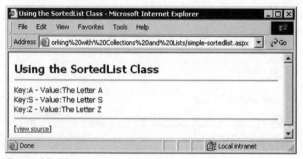

Figure 15-11

A SortedList always maintains a sorted collection of items. When an item is inserted, a binary search is performed to see if the specified key already exists. If the key is already in use, an ArgumentException is thrown since keys must be unique. If the key is not in use, the return code from the binary search (from the Array.BinarySearch method) is used to determine the insert point of the new item.

The sort order for a SortedList is determined by the implementation of IComparer that is used. The default comparer is System.Collections.Comparer. As discussed earlier, this implementation uses the IComparable interface of the left object passed into the IComparer.Compare method. In this example, the key is a string type, so the result is that the list is sorted alphabetically in ascending order (it will also be case-sensitive), as that's how the string type implementation of IComparable works.

An overloaded constructor of SortedList allows you to specify a custom IComparer interface if you need to override the sort order for a list of items. For example:

```
IComparer ic = new SomeCustomTypeThatImplementsIComparer();
SortedList alphabet = new SortedList(ic);
```

If you need to create a case-insensitive sorted list, you could use the System.Collections.Comparer with this overload, or you could use the CreateCaseInsensitiveSortedList static method of the CollectionsUtil class (which basically just saves some typing):

```
SortedList alphabet;
alphabet = CollectionsUtil.CreateCaseInsensitiveSortedList();
```

The SortedList class implements the IDictionary and IEnumerable interfaces. The IEnumerable.GetEnumerator method returns an IDictionaryEnumerator type.

Accessing items using an indexer or searching for an item is performed very quickly but adding items to a sorted list can be slower than adding them to unsorted lists, since the SortedList class holds keys and values in two different arrays. Arrays are held contiguously in memory, so when an item is inserted between two existing items, the items to the right of the insertion point have to be moved to make room.

This copying can be relatively slow for large lists, so it might be necessary to consider an alternative approach.

Creating an Indexed or Sorted View of an Existing Collection

The `SortedList` class has a constructor that accepts an `IDictionary` parameter. This constructor will copy the contents of the specified collection. This provides a great way of indexing and sorting existing collections of items, without having to change the source collection. The following C# code creates an unordered list of names using a `Hashtable`, and then creates a sorted list using the `SortedList` class:

```
Dim names As New Hashtable()
names.Add("RA", "Richard Anderson")
names.Add("DS", "David Sussman")
names.Add("RH", "Rob Howard")
names.Add("AH", "Alex Homer")
names.Add("KW", "Karli Watson")
names.Add("BF", "Brian Francis")

For Each name As DictionaryEntry In names
  outResult1.InnerHtml &= "Key:" & name.Key & " - Value:" _
                      & name.Value & "<br />"
Next

Dim sortedNameList As New SortedList(names)
For Each name As DictionaryEntry In sortedNameList
  outResult2.InnerHtml &= "Key:" & name.Key & " - Value:" _
                      & name.Value & "<br />"
Next
```

The output of this code is shown in Figure 15-12:

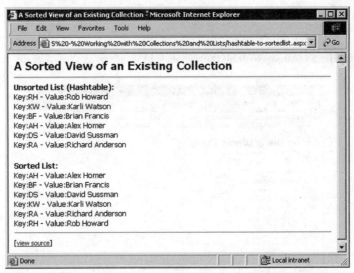

Figure 15-12

When a `SortedList` copies the contents of a source collection using the `IDictionary` interface, the list capacity is automatically resized to match the source. Once copied, no link between the collections is maintained. Changes made to one of the collections do not affect the other. Like the `Stack` and `Queue` classes, the `SortedList` class has a `Synchronized` method that can return a thread-safe wrapper for a given `SortedList`.

The BitArray Class

The `BitArray` class provides an efficient way of creating and manipulating a compact array of bit values. The bit array can be any size, and individual bits are represented as `Boolean` values, where `True` equals bit set (1), and `False` equals bit not set (0). The following C# code shows how you can create a bit array that contains eight bits:

```
BitArray b = new BitArray(8);
```

By default all bits are set to `False`. However, you *can* use an overloaded constructor to set the default value to `True`:

```
BitArray b = new BitArray(8, true);
```

The `BitArray` class implements the `IEnumerable` and `ICollection` interfaces, so by using the `IEnumerable` interface, you can display the values of the bit array. This VB.NET code creates a new `BitArray` with all the values set to `False`:

```
Dim b As BitArray = new BitArray(8, False)
Dim index As Integer
outResult.InnerHtml = "Count property is " & b.Count & "<br />"
index = 0
For Each value As Boolean in b
   index += 1
   outResult.InnerHtml &= "Bit " & index & " - value is " & value & "<br />"
Next
```

Figure 15-13 shows the `BitArray` with all the values set to `False`, as shown in the preceding code:

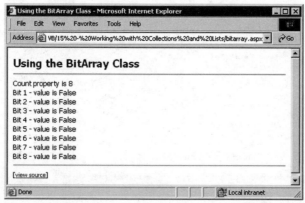

Figure 15-13

To set a bit, you can use an indexer or the `Set` method. Following VB.NET code sets bit 2 and bit 7 using both approaches:

```
Dim b As BitArray = new BitArray(8, False)
Dim index As Integer
outResult.InnerHtml = "Count property is " & b.Count & "<br />"
index = 0
b(2) = True
b.Set(7,True)
For Each value As Boolean in b
    index += 1
    outResult.InnerHtml &= "Bit " & index & " - value is " & value & "<br />"
Next
```

Figure 15-14 shows the `BitArray` after this code runs, with bits 2 and 7 set as expected:

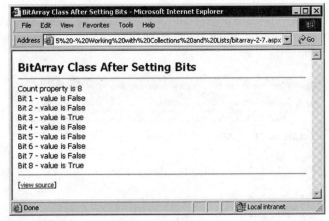

Figure 15-14

Note that the code displays the `Bit` numbers starting from 1, whereas (like all .NET collections) the values are actually indexed starting from zero.

The `BitArray` class provides several methods that allow logical bit operations to be performed against a `BitArray`. These include:

❑ `And`: Performs a bitwise `AND` operation on the elements in the current `BitArray` against the corresponding elements in another `BitArray`

❑ `Not`: Inverts all bits in the array such that any 1's (`True`) become 0 (`False`) and vice versa

❑ `Or`: Performs a bitwise `OR` operation on the elements in the current `BitArray` against the corresponding elements in another `BitArray`

❑ `Xor`: Performs a bitwise `Exclusive OR` (`XOR`) operation on the elements in the current `BitArray` against the corresponding elements in another `BitArray`

All of these logical operations work in the same way. The following C# code extends the previous example by creating a second bit array, setting bits 0, 1, and 6, and then performing an `Xor` operation:

```
Dim b As BitArray = new BitArray(8, False)
Dim b2 As BitArray = new BitArray(8, False)
Dim index As Integer
outResult.InnerHtml = "Count property is " & b.Count & "<br />"
index = 0
b(2) = True
b.Set(7,True)
b2(0) = True
b2(1) = True
b2(6) = True
b.Xor(b2)

For Each value As Boolean in b
  index += 1
  outResult.InnerHtml &= "Bit " & index & " - value is " & value & "<br />"
Next
```

The expected result of an Xor is that a given bit is set to 1 if only one of the input bits is 1. If both bits are 0 or 1, the value should be zero. Figure 15-15 shows the BitArray from the previous example after the Xor operation has taken place:

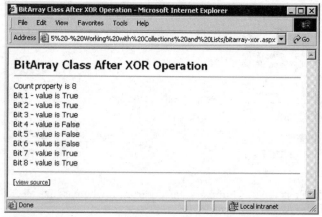

Figure 15-15

System.Collections.Specialized Namespace

The System.Collections.Specialized namespace contains collection classes that are suited to specialized tasks, as well as collection classes that are strongly typed, which, although it limits the types that can be contained, reduces the amount of casting needed.

The StringCollection Class

The System.Collections.Specialized.StringCollection class provides an implementation of an ArrayList that can only contain string values. This class implements all of the functionality of

`ArrayList`, but does all of the casting behind the scenes. Like `ArrayList`, `StringCollection` implements the `IList` interface.

Here is a simple example of using the `StringCollection` class in C#:

```
StringCollection names = new StringCollection();
names.Add("Richard");
names.Add("Sam");
names.Add("Richard");
names.Add("Sam");
foreach (String name in names)
{
    Response.Write("<br />" + name);
}
```

The StringDictionary Class

The `System.Collections.Specialized.StringDictionary` class provides an implementation of a hash table, in which the key and value are always of type `System.String`. The key is also case-insensitive. Internally, this class uses the `Hashtable` class for its implementation. If you're interested only in dealing with string values, you should use this class.

The following C# code shows how to use `StringDictionary` to locate the surname of a given person:

```
StringDictionary names;
string surname;
names = new StringDictionary();
names["Richard"] = "Anderson";
names["Alex"] = "Homer";
surname = names["Alex"];
Response.Write("The surname for alex is " + surname);
```

Strongly Typed Collections

The fact that most of the collections classes in the .NET Framework class library are designed to work with the `System.Object` type makes them very versatile. However, this flexibility can also be viewed as a minor problem, since it means you have to do a lot of casting (assuming you know the type in the first place). For example, assuming a `Hashtable` contains a number of items of the type `Product`, you have to cast each item you retrieve. Using C#, you would write:

```
Hashtable products;
Product p;
p = (Product) product["ProductCode"];
```

Using VB.NET, you would write:

```
Dim products As Hashtable
Dim p As Product
p = CType(products("ProductCode"), Product)
```

Casting types like this isn't difficult, but it can make code less readable, and often leads to silly compiler errors when you forget to cast. Strongly typed collections can resolve these problems. Rather than directly using the collection classes such as `Hashtable` in your class, you should instead provide a custom type that encapsulates the collection type being used, and also removes the need for casting.

For example, using C# you would write:

```
ProductCollection products;
Product p;
p = products["ProductCode"];
```

Using VB.NET, you would write:

```
Dim products As ProductCollection
Dim p As Product
p = products("ProductCode")
```

Implementing a strongly typed collection like this is relatively simple, and it allows you to build in additional rules and error handling, saving you from duplicating them throughout the code.

To a strongly typed collection, you have to:

❑   Define the custom type of the item held in the collection

❑   Create the collection class, and implement the `Add`, `Remove`, and `GetEnumerator` methods, as well as the `Item` property

Let's look at each of these in turn.

Defining the Custom Type

In the strongly typed example, a `Product` type was used. When implementing a collection, you should always have a custom type, and a collection for that custom type in which the collection name is simply the custom type name appended with `Collection`; for example, `Product` and `ProductCollection`, or `Address` and `AddressCollection`.

Here is a class definition for a `Product` type, written using VB.NET:

```
Public Class Product

    ' private fields
    Private _code As string
    Private _description As string
    Private _price As Double

    ' constructor
    Public Sub New(initialCode As String, _
                   initialDescription As String, _
                   initialPrice As Double)
        Code = initialCode
        Description = initialDescription
```

```
      Price = initialPrice
   End Sub

   Public Property Description As String
     Get
        Description = _description
     End Get
     Set
        _description = Value
     End Set
   End Property

   Public Property Code As String
     Get
        Code = _code
     End Get
     Set
        _code = Value
     End Set
   End Property

   Public Property Price As Double
     Get
        Price = _price
     End Get
     Set
        _price = Value
     End Set
   End Property

End Class
```

The `Product` type has three public properties:

- ❑   `Code`: A unique code assigned to the product
- ❑   `Description`: A description of the product
- ❑   `Price`: The cost of the product

All of the properties have a get and set accessor, and their implementation simply stores or retrieves the property value in a private field. The field name is the same as the property name, but prefixed with an underscore. The `Product` type has a constructor that accepts three parameters, allowing quick initialization. For example:

```
Dim p As Product
p = New Product("PROASP3", "Professional ASP 3.0", 39.99)
```

For the purposes of this example, let's define the classes within the ASP.NET page. Typically, you would define these in a separate compiled assembly. That topic was introduced in Chapters 3 and 4, and is covered in more detail in Chapter 17.

Creating the Collection Class

The `ProductCollection` class will support two key features:

❑   Unordered enumeration of all the contained products

❑   Direct access of a product using a product code

Since the `Hashtable` class provides the collection functionality necessary for implementing these features, you can use a `Hashtable` internally within your collection class for holding items. Then, you can aggregate the functionality of `Hashtable` and expose it, to provide access to your items in a type safe way that doesn't require casting.

Since an internal `Hashtable` is being used to hold the `Product` items, define a private field called `_products` of type `Hashtable` within the collection class. A new object instance is assigned to this field in the constructor:

```
Dim _products as Hashtable
Public Sub New()
  _products = New Hashtable()
End Sub
```

Implementing the Add Method

The `Add` method allows a new `Product` to be added to the collection:

```
Public Sub Add( Item as Product )
  If Item Is Nothing Then
    Throw New ArgumentException("Product cannot be null")
  End If
  _products.Add(Item.Code, Item)
End Sub
```

This method throws an `ArgumentException` if a `null` item parameter is passed. If the parameter is not `null`, the `Code` property of the passed `Product` is used as the key for the `Product` in the contained `Hashtable`. Depending on your requirements, you could perform additional business logic validation here and throw additional exceptions.

Implementing the Remove Method

The `Remove` method removes a `Product` from the collection. The implementation of the method simply calls the `Remove` method of the `Hashtable`:

```
Public Sub Remove(Item as Product)
  _products.Remove(Item.Code)
End Sub
```

Implementing the Item Property

The `Item` property allows a `Product` to be retrieved from, or added to the collection by specifying the product code:

```
Public Default Property Item(Code as String) as Product
   Get
      Item = CType(_products(Code), Product)
   End Get
   Set
      Add(Value)
   End Set
End Property
```

The implementation of the Set accessor calls the Add method in order to add the new product to the internal Hashtable. The process is implemented in a way so that any business logic in the Add method (such as the Null check) is neither duplicated nor missed.

Implementing the GetEnumerator Method

To use your collection class with the for..each statements in VB.NET and C#, your collection class must have a method called GetEnumerator. Although not strictly necessary, the IEnumerable interface is also implemented using the VB.NET Implements keyword. This is good practice and requires very little work:

```
Public Class ProductCollection
      Implements IEnumerable
   ' ...
   ' implement an enumerator for the products
   Public Function GetEnumerator() As IEnumerator
         Implements IEnumerable.GetEnumerator
      GetEnumerator = _products.Values.GetEnumerator()
   End Function
   ' ...
End Class
```

The GetEnumerator method has to return an enumerator object that implements the IEnumerator interface. You could implement this interface by creating another class, but since your collection class is using a Hashtable internally, it makes much more sense to reuse the enumerator object provided by that class when its values are enumerated. The Hashtable.Values property returns an ICollection interface and since the ICollection interface derives from IEnumerable, you can call GetEnumerator to create an enumerator object for the collection of values.

Using the Collection Class

With the Product and ProductCollection classes created, you can use them just like the other collections in this chapter, but this time with no casting. For example:

```
' Page-level variable
Dim _products as ProductCollection = New ProductCollection

Sub Page_Load(sender as Object, events As EventArgs)
   ' Runs when page is loaded

   Dim products As New ProductCollection()
   Dim p As product
```

```
p = New Product("CAR", "A New Car", 19999.99)
products.Add(p)

p = New Product("HOUSE", "A New House", 299999.99)
products.Add(p)

p = New Product("BOOK", "A New Book", 49.99)
products(p.Code) = p

For Each p In products
  outResult1.InnerHtml &= p.Code & " - " & p.Description _
                        & " - $" & p.Price & "<br />"
Next

products.Remove( products("HOUSE") )

For Each p In products
  outResult2.InnerHtml &= p.Code & " - " & p.Description _
                        & " - $" & p.Price & "<br />"
Next


outResult3.InnerHtml = "Description for code CAR is: " _
                    & products("CAR").Description

End Sub
```

The complete code for this example is contained in the samples available for download, in both VB.NET and C#. The result of running this page is shown in Figure 15-16:

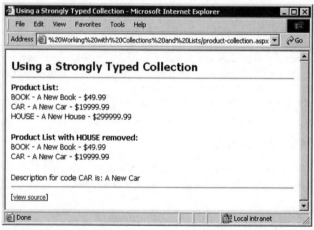

Figure 15-16

The DictionaryBase and CollectionBase Classes

The `DictionaryBase` and `CollectionBase` classes allow you to create a `Hashtable` or `ArrayList` collection that can validate, and therefore restrict, the types it contains. It's a simple process to create your own collection class by deriving from these classes.

This simple ASP.NET page defines a `MyStringCollection` collection class, adds three strings and one integer, and then displays the contents:

```
'our custom collection
Class MyStringCollection
  Inherits CollectionBase
  ... implementation goes here...
End Class

  Dim names As IList

  names = New MyStringCollection

  names.Add("Richard")
  names.Add("Alex")
  names.Add("Dave")

  Try
    names.Add(2002)
  Catch e As Exception
    outResult1.InnerHtml = "Error: " & e.Message
  End Try

  For Each name As String in names
    outResult2.InnerHtml &= name & "<br />"
  Next
```

The `Collection` base class implements the `IList` and `ICollection` interfaces. All the members of these interfaces are defined explicitly, which is why in the sample code the `names` variables have been defined as type `IList`.

Each of the collection base classes provides a number of virtual functions that are called when the collection is modified. For example, `OnClear` is called when a collection is cleared; `OnInsert` is called when an item is added; `OnRemove` when an item is deleted, and so on. By overriding one of these methods, you can perform additional checks and throw an exception if an undesired condition arises. For example, in the collection class, you could implement an `OnInsert` method that throws an `ArgumentException` if anything other than a string is added:

```
Class MyStringCollection
    Inherits CollectionBase
  Overrides Protected Sub OnInsert(index as Integer, item as Object)
    If Not(TypeOf item Is String) Then
      Throw New ArgumentException("My collection only supports strings")
    End If
  End Sub
End Class
```

Figure 15-17 shows the results of running this code:

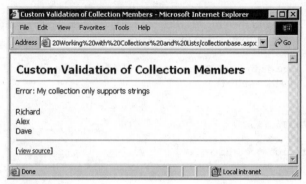

Figure 15-17

The `DictionaryBase` class is used in the same way as the `CollectionBase` class and implements the `IDictionary` and `ICollection` interfaces.

The ReadOnlyCollectionBase Class

The `ReadOnlyCollectionBase` class provides functionality for exposing a read-only collection. The class implements the `ICollection` and `IEnumerable` interface. The items exposed are internally held in a protected `ArrayList` variable called `InnerList`. To use this class, you have to derive your own class from it, and populate the contents of the `InnerList` array.

Disposable Enumerators

When you enumerate a collection, the enumerator objects that implement the `IEnumerator` interface may require expensive resources. For example, depending on how underlying items are stored, a custom enumerator could be using a database connection, or be holding temporary files on disk. In these scenarios, it is important that the enumerable object releases resources it holds as soon as possible.

Due to the non-deterministic way the CLR releases object references, any code you write that directly uses an `IEnumerator` interface must always check if the enumerator objects that provided the interface support the `IDisposable` interface. You must then call the `Dispose` method when you've finished with the enumerator. If you do not do this, the resources held by the enumerator may not be released for some time. When you use the `for..each` language statement in C# and VB.NET, this is done automatically .

When you use the `IEnumerator` interface directly (or any other enumerable type), if you do not know whether an enumerator object supports the `IDisposable` interface, always check once you have finished with it. For example, in C#, you might write:

```
IEnumerator e = c.GetEnumerator();
try
{
  while (e.MoveNext())
  {
```

```
        Foo x = e.Current;
          // ...
        }
    }
finally
{
    IDisposable d = e as IDisposable;
    if (d != null) d.Dispose();
}
```

If you know that an enumerator object supports `IDisposable`, you can call it directly:

```
IEnumerator e = c.GetEnumerator();
try
{
  while (e.MoveNext())
    {
     Foo x = e.Current;
     // ...
    }
}
finally
{
    ((IDisposable)e).Dispose();
}
```

Summary

This chapter covered most of the interfaces and classes that comprise the `System.Collections` and `System.Collection.Specialized` namespaces. We examined the standard interfaces such as `IEnumerable`, `IEnumerator`, and `ICollection`, and have discussed how these interfaces work together to provide a consistent way of creating and using collections. We've not covered every single collection class or method in this chapter, but hopefully have given you a pretty good feel for the type of functionality available.

This chapter looked at:

❑   How to use the standard collection classes such as `ArrayList`, `Hashtable`, `Queue`, and `Stack`.

❑   How to derive from collection base classes to quickly implement your own collection classes that restrict contained types.

❑   How to create strongly typed collections that make using collections more intuitive for specific applications, which leads to more readable code thanks to fewer casts.

The next chapter looks at the classes provided by the .NET Framework class library for working with text files, sockets, and regular expressions.

Working with Other Base Classes

16

The last chapter introduced the .NET Framework class library and spent a fair amount of time looking at the collection classes it provides for dealing with common data structures such as lists, queues, and stacks. In this chapter, we'll continue our examination of the class library, this time looking at the classes it provides for working with directories, files, regular expressions, and web requests.

This chapter will cover:

- ❑ The contents of the file system, working with directories and files
- ❑ Reading and writing data from backing stores such as the file system or memory
- ❑ Retrieving data in a generic way using stream objects
- ❑ Using regular expressions to parse text and extract values using captures

Let's look at the classes used for working with the file system.

Working with Directories and Files

The .NET Framework class library makes working with directories and files an easy and painless experience. It provides an easy-to-understand set of classes located in the `System.IO` namespace. These classes can be used to:

- ❑ Retrieve and change information about directories and files
- ❑ Manipulate paths, including combining them and extracting individual elements
- ❑ Read and write bytes of data from generic streams such as files and memory buffers

It's important to understand early on that the classes in System.IO are not designed for working just with the file system. They work with any number of backing stores that are accessed using *stream* objects. A backing store is the .NET Framework term used to define a source which data can be read from or written to using a stream object. Each backing store provides a Stream object that is used to communicate with it. For example, the FileStream class (the Stream object) can be used to read and write data to the file system (the backing store), and the MemoryStream class can be used to read and write data to memory.

All stream classes derive from a common Stream base class, and (just like the collection interfaces described in the previous chapter) once you know what the common System.IO classes are and how they're organized, you'll find working with new data sources a breeze.

Class Overview

The following classes are commonly used when working with directories, files, and streams:

Class	Description
Directory	Provides static (shared) methods for enumerating directories and logical drives
DirectoryInfo	Used to work with a specific directory and its subdirectories
File	Provides static methods for working with files
FileInfo	Used to work with a specific file
Stream	Base class used to read from and write to a backing store, such as the file system or network
StreamReader	Used in conjunction with a stream to read characters from backing store
StreamWriter	Used in conjunction with a stream to write characters to a backing store
TextReader	Abstract class used to define methods for reading characters from any source (backing store, string, and so on)
TextWriter	Abstract class used to define methods to write characters to any source
BinaryReader	Used to read primitive types such as strings, integers, and Booleans from a stream
BinaryWriter	Used to write primitive types such as strings, integers, and Booleans to a stream
FileStream	Used to read and write data in the file system
MemoryStream	Used to read and write data in a memory buffer

DirectoryInfo and Directory

The base class library provides two classes for working with directories: `Directory` and `DirectoryInfo`. The `Directory` class contains a number of static methods (in VB.NET. these are known as shared methods) that can be used to manipulate and query information about any directory. The `DirectoryInfo` class contains a series of instance methods (also known as non-static or non-shared methods) and properties that can be used to manipulate and work with a single named directory.

For the most part, these classes have equivalent functionality and can be used to:

- ❑ Create and delete directories

- ❑ Determine if a directory exists

- ❑ Get a list of subdirectories and files for a given directory

- ❑ Get information about directories, such as creation times and attributes, and modify it

- ❑ Get and set the current working directory (`Directory` class only)

- ❑ Get a list of available drives (`Directory` class only)

- ❑ Move directories

Having two classes, although confusing at first, actually simplifies and increases the performance of your applications. For example, to determine whether a given directory existed, you could use the static `Exists` method of the `Directory` class as follows (written here in VB.NET):

```
<%@ Page Language="VB" %>
<%@ Import Namespace="System.IO" %>
<%
If Directory.Exists("C:\Wrox") Then
  Response.Write("C:\Wrox directory exists")
Else
  Response.Write("C:\Wrox directory does not exist")
End If
%>
```

The `Exists` method is static, so declaring a variable and instantiating an instance of the `Directory` class is not necessary. This makes the code more readable, and also saves a few CPU cycles.

The constructor of the `Directory` class is declared as private, so it is not possible to instantiate an instance of the class.

To check if a directory exists using the `DirectoryInfo` class, you have to instantiate an instance of the `DirectoryInfo` class, passing the directory name you want into the constructor. Then call the `Exists` property. Using VB.NET, you would write:

```
<%@ Page Language="VB" %>
<%@ Import Namespace="System.IO" %>
<%
Dim dir As DirectoryInfo
dir = New DirectoryInfo("C:\Wrox")
```

```
    If dir.Exists = True Then
       Response.Write("C:\Wrox directory exists")
    Else
       Response.Write("C:\Wrox directory does not exist")
    End If
    %>
```

As the `DirectoryInfo` class has instance members (that is, they are not static) you have to use an object reference to access them. If all you want to do is check for the existence of a directory, using `DirectoryInfo` is overkill – you'd be better off using the `Directory` class. However, if you want to perform several operations against a single directory, then using the `DirectoryInfo` class is the correct approach. Use of this class means that the readability and general style of the code is improved, as demonstrated by this additional line of code that displays the creation time of a directory (if it exists):

```
<%@ Page Language="VB" %>
<%@ Import Namespace="System.IO" %>
<%
Dim dir As DirectoryInfo
dir = New DirectoryInfo("C:\Wrox")
If dir.Exists = True Then
   Response.Write("C:\Wrox directory exists")
   Response.Write("<br />Created: " & dir.CreationTime )
Else
   Response.Write("<br />C:\Wrox directory does not exist")
End If
%>
```

Instantiating an object in this way and then using its members, or passing it as a parameter to method calls is a fundamental concept in object-oriented programming. This is something familiar from classic ASP, where objects like ADO `Connection` or `Recordset` were used. To write a method to display the contents of a directory in ASP.NET, I'd probably design the method to accept a `DirectoryInfo` object rather than a string that represented the directory name. It looks neater, feels right, and can have performance benefits if the method was going to use the `DirectoryInfo` class to do a lot of work. Also, why create a new instance of the `DirectoryInfo` class when the caller might already have one?

Another subtler benefit of using the `DirectoryInfo` class is that it will typically execute multiple operations against a single directory in an efficient manner. Once instantiated, it can maintain state such as the creation time and last modification date of a directory. Then, when members such as the `CreationTime` property are used, this state can be used to provide the results. The `Directory` class cannot do this. It must go out and retrieve information about a directory each time a method is called.

Although traditionally this wasn't a terribly expensive operation, with the advent of the CLR this type of operation requires code access permissions to be granted by the runtime, which means that the runtime has to ensure that the code calling the method is allowed to know about the directory. These checks can be relatively expensive to perform and their use should be minimized. Accordingly, using the `DirectoryInfo` class wherever possible makes good coding sense. The `DirectoryInfo` class performs different code access permission checks depending on the methods called. While some methods will not cause permission checks, others, such as `Delete`, always will.

File and FileInfo

You can use the `File` and `FileInfo` classes to discover information about files, as well as to get access to a stream object that allows you to read from and write to the contents of a file.

The `File` and `FileInfo` classes provide equivalent functionality and can be used to:

❑ Create, delete, open, copy, and move files (these classes are not used to read, write, append to, or close files)

❑ Retrieve information – such as creation times and attributes – about files, and modify it

Like the `Directory` class, the `File` class has a series of static methods to manipulate or query information about a file. The `FileInfo` class has a series of instance methods and properties that can be used to manipulate and work with a single named file.

Here is a simple (VB.NET) code example that shows how to use the `File` class to determine if a file exists:

```
<%@ Page Language="VB" %>
<%@ Import Namespace="System.IO" %>
<%
If File.Exists("C:\Wrox\Hello.txt") = True Then
   Response.Write("C:\Wrox\Hello.Txt file exists")
Else
   Response.Write("C:\Wrox\Hello.Txt file does not exist")
End If
%>
```

The `Exists` method returns `true` if the file exists, and `false` if it does not. Here is the equivalent VB.NET code using `FileInfo`, although this time the file's creation time is also shown (as in the earlier `DirectoryInfo` sample):

```
<%@ Page Language="VB" %>
<%@ Import Namespace="System.IO" %>
<%
Dim myfile As FileInfo
myfile = New FileInfo("C:\Wrox\Hello.Txt")
If myfile.Exists = True Then
   Response.Write("C:\Wrox\Hello.Txt file exists")
   Response.Write("<br />Created: " & myfile.CreationTime)
Else
   Response.Write("<br />C:\Wrox\Hello.Txt file does not exist")
End If
%>
```

As with the `DirectoryInfo` class, `FileInfo` is the preferred class to use when you need to perform multiple operations as it results in greater readability, style, and performance.

Common Directory and File Tasks

Having introduced the various directory and file classes, let's look at some examples of how they can be used to perform common tasks, as well as some of the common exceptions that can be thrown.

Setting and Getting the Current Directory

When an ASP.NET page is executed, the thread used to execute the code that generates the page will, by default, have a current working directory of `%windir%\system32`. If you pass a relative filename into any class in the `System.IO` namespace, the file is assumed to be located within the current working directory.

Retrieving and changing the current working directory is a function of the `Directory` class. The following example shows how the working directory can be changed using `SetCurrentDirectory` and retrieved again using `GetCurrentDirectory`:

```
<%@ Page Language="VB" %>
<%@ Import Namespace="System.IO" %>
<%
  Directory.SetCurrentDirectory("C:\Wrox")
  Response.Write("The current directory is " & _
                 Directory.GetCurrentDirectory() )
%>
```

When writing an ASP.NET page, make no assumptions about the current working directory. Typically, you should never need to change it, since you should not use relative filenames within ASP.NET pages. Rather, you should use the `Server.MapPath` method to create a fully qualified filename from a relative filename.

Common Exceptions

In most of the code samples for this chapter, exception handling is not included. This is done to keep the examination of the methods as clear as possible. However, like most other classes in .NET, the `System.IO` classes throw exceptions when an error condition occurs. The most common exceptions include:

❑   `IOException`: Indicates that a general problem has occurred during the method

❑   `ArgumentException`: Indicates that one or more of the method input parameters are invalid

❑   `UnauthorizedAccessException`: Indicates that a specified directory, file, or other resource is read-only and cannot be accessed or modified

❑   `SecurityException`: Indicates that the code calling the method doesn't have enough runtime privileges to perform the operation

When writing production code, always use exception handling, as discussed in Chapter 22.

Listing Available Logical Drives

The `GetLogicalDrives` method of the `Directory` class returns a string array that contains a list of the available drives. Using VB.NET, you could write:

```
<%@ Page Language="VB" %>
<%@ Import Namespace="System.IO" %>
<%
Dim Drives() As string
Dim Drive As string
Drives = Directory.GetLogicalDrives()
For Each Drive in Drives
  Response.Write(drive)
  Response.Write("<br />")
Next
%>
```

This code displays the server-side logical drives returned by the method call, as seen in Figure 16-1 (your system will probably display drives different from these):

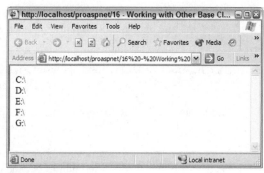

Figure 16-1

Creating a Directory

The following VB.NET code shows how to create a hierarchy of directories in a single method call by using `Directory.CreateDirectory`:

```
<%@ Page Language="VB" %>
<%@ Import Namespace="System.IO" %>
<%
  Directory.CreateDirectory("C:\Create\Several\Directories")
%>
```

When the `CreateDirectory` method is called, it first checks if the `C:\Create` directory exists; it will be created if it doesn't exist. Next, the method will check if the `Several` directory exists within the `Create` directory. Again, it will be created if it doesn't exist. Finally, the method will check if the `Directories` directory exists within the `Several` directory, again creating it if it doesn't exist. The `DirectoryInfo` class also has a `Create` method that provides the same functionality.

If you try to create a directory that already exists, an exception will *not* be thrown. An `ArgumentException` will be thrown only if part of the directory path is invalid. Use the `Directory.Exists` method to determine if a directory exists.

Listing the Contents of a Directory

The `Directory` class has the following methods that can be used to retrieve a list of a directory's contents:

Method Name	Parameters	Description
GetDirectories	Pathname	Returns a string array filled with the fully qualified names of each contained directory
GetDirectories	Pathname, Search path	Returns a string array filled with the fully qualified names of each contained directory that matches the search pattern
GetFiles	Pathname	Returns a string array filled with the fully qualified names of each contained file
GetFiles	Pathname, Search path	Returns a string array filled with the fully qualified names of each contained file that matches the search pattern
GetFile SystemEntries	Pathname	Returns a string array filled with fully qualified names of each contained directory and file
GetFile SystemEntries	Pathname, Search path	Returns a string array filled with the fully qualified names of each contained directory and file that matches the search pattern

The following VB.NET code demonstrates how to use the `GetDirectories` method:

```
<%@ Page Language="VB" %>
<%@ Import Namespace="System.IO" %>
<%
  Dim dir As string
  Dim subdirs() As string

  ' Get all child directories of C:\ and enumerate each one
  subdirs = Directory.GetDirectories("c:\")
  For Each dir In subdirs
    Response.Write(dir & "<br />")
  Next

  ' Get all child directories that start with a 't' and enumerate each one
  subdirs = Directory.GetDirectories("c:\","t*")
  For Each dir In subdirs
    Response.Write(dir & "<br />")
  Next
%>
```

The following code demonstrates how to use the `GetFiles` method:

```
<%@ Page Language="VB" %>
<%@ Import Namespace="System.IO" %>
<%
  Dim f As string
  Dim files() As string
  files = Directory.GetFiles("C:\Wrox\")
  For Each f In files
    Response.Write(f & "<br />")
  Next
  files = Directory.GetFiles("C:\Wrox\","h*")
  For Each f in files
    Response.Write(f & "<br />")
  Next
%>
```

The following code demonstrates how to use the `GetFileSystemEntries` method:

```
<%@ Page Language="VB" %>
<%@ Import Namespace="System.IO" %>
<%
  Dim item As string
  Dim items() As string
  ' Get all files & directories in C:\Wrox and enumerate them
  items = Directory.GetFileSystemEntries("C:\Wrox\")
  For Each item In items
    Response.Write(item & "<br />")
  Next
  ' Get all files & directories in C:\Wrox starting with 'h' and enum them
  items = Directory.GetFileSystemEntries("C:\Wrox\","h*")
  For Each item in items
    Response.Write(item & "<br />")
  Next
%>
```

The `DirectoryInfo` class also has `GetDirectories`, `GetFiles`, and `GetFileSystemEntries` methods. These provide equivalent functionality, but with two important differences:

❑ No pathname is passed as an argument to these methods, as the class already knows the path (it was passed in as a parameter to the constructor).

❑ These methods do not return string arrays. The `GetDirectories` method returns an array of `DirectoryInfo`. The `GetFiles` method returns an array of `FileInfo`. The `GetFileSystemEntries` method returns an array of `FileSystemInfo` (which will be discussed shortly).

Deleting a Directory

A directory can be deleted using the `Directory.Delete` or `DirectoryInfo.Delete` methods. For example, you could write the following VB.NET code:

```
<%@ Page Language="VB" %>
<%@ Import Namespace="System.IO" %>
```

```
<%
   Directory.Delete("C:\Create")
   Dim dir As DirectoryInfo
   dir = New DirectoryInfo("C:\Create")
   dir.Delete()
%>
```

If you attempt to delete a non-existent directory, a `DirectoryNotFound` exception will be thrown. If you attempt to delete a directory that contains other files or directories, an `IOException` will be thrown, unless you use an overloaded version of the `Delete` method that allows you to specify whether any contained files or directories should also be deleted. For example:

```
<%@ Page Language="VB" %>
<%@ Import Namespace="System.IO" %>
<%
   Directory.Delete("C:\Create",True)
   Dim dir As DirectoryInfo
   dir = New DirectoryInfo("C:\Create")
   dir.Delete(True)
%>
```

Deleting a File

You can delete a file using the `File.Delete` or `FileInfo.Delete` methods. For example:

```
<%@ Page Language="VB" %>
<%@ Import Namespace="System.IO" %>
<%
   File.Delete("C:\myfile.txt")
   Dim f As FileInfo
   f = New FileInfo("myfile.txt")
   f.Delete()
%>
```

If you attempt to delete a file that does not exist, no exceptions are thrown unless part of the path does not exist (in which case, a `DirectoryNotFoundException` is thrown).

Properties and Attributes of Files and Directories

Directories and files share common operations (such as deleting them) that can be performed on them. They also share common properties, such as their creation time, fully qualified name, and attributes.

The `FileSystemInfo` class defines members that are common to both files and directories. Both the `DirectoryInfo` and `FileInfo` classes are derived from this class. The `FileSystemInfo` class has the following properties:

Name	Type	Read/ Write	Description
Attributes	FileAttributes	Read/ Write	The attributes such as hidden, archive, and read-only that are set for this file.
CreationTime	System.DateTime	Read/ Write	The time that the file or directory was created.
LastAccessTime	System.DateTime	Read/ Write	The time that the file or directory was last accessed.
LastWriteTime	System.DateTime	Read/ Write	The time that the file or directory was last updated.
Exists	Boolean	Read	Indicates if the file or directory exists.
Extension	String	Read	Returns the file or directory extension, including the period. For a directory, the extension is the text located after last period in the name.
Name	String	Read	Returns the name of the file/directory relative to its containing directory. This includes the extension.
FullName	String	Read	Returns the fully qualified name for the file or directory.

The FileSystemInfo class has the following methods:

Name	Description
Delete	Deletes the file or directory
Refresh	Updates any cached state such as creation time and attributes with those present on disk
Exists	Determines whether the file or directory exists

To know how to use attributes, and some interesting methods and properties of the `DirectoryInfo` and `FileInfo` classes, let's take a look at the code required to write a simple Web-based file browser. Here the file browser is being used to display information about the `C:\program files\internet explorer` directory, as shown in Figure 16-2:

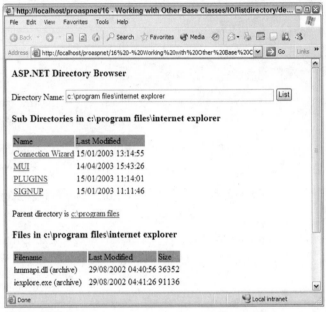

Figure 16-2

This application takes a path and then lists any directories and files it contains. It also displays the last time that each directory and file was modified, and their various attributes (such as whether they have been archived). The application uses an HTML form to capture the path to be examined. This has an input control (marked as a server control using the `runat="server"` attribute) with an `id` of `DirName`:

```
<form runat="server">
   Directory Name: <input type="text" id="DirName" size="60"
                          value="c:\program files\internet explorer"
                          runat="server">
   <input type="submit" value="List">
</form>
```

When the page is rendered, it uses the `DirName.Value` server control property to initialize an instance of the `DirectoryInfo` class:

```
Dim dir As DirectoryInfo
Dim anchor As String
dir = New DirectoryInfo(DirName.Value)
```

The `DirectoryInfo` class is used rather than the `Directory` class, since you want to display details about the contained directories and files, such as their last modification date. The `GetDirectories` method of `Directory` does not give this information–it only provides the name.

The first block of rendering logic for the application outputs a table that lists the name of the directory being listed and its subdirectories. The subdirectories are retrieved using the GetDirectories method of the dir object:

```
Response.Write("<h3>Sub Directories in " & DirName.Value & "</h3>")
Response.Write("<table>")
Response.Write("<tr bgcolor=cornflowerblue>")
Response.Write("<td>Name</td>")
Response.Write("<td>Last Modified</td>")
Response.Write("</tr>")
Dim SubDir as DirectoryInfo
For Each SubDir In dir.GetDirectories()
  anchor = "<a href='" & "default.aspx?dir=" & _
  SubDir.FullName & "'>" & SubDir.Name & "</a>"
  Response.Write("<tr>")
  Response.Write("<td>" & anchor & "</td>" )
  Response.Write("<td>" & SubDir.LastWriteTime & "</td>" )
  Response.Write("</tr>")
Next
Response.Write("</table>")
```

As you list each contained directory, output an anchor tag that points back to your page with a URL containing a dir parameter that holds the fully qualified name of the subdirectory. This fully qualified name is returned by the FullName property. The actual text of the anchor is just the directory's relative name within its parent, which is accessed using the Name property:

```
For Each SubDir In dir.GetDirectories()
  anchor = "<a href='" & "default.aspx?dir=" & _
           SubDir.FullName & "'>" + SubDir.Name & "</a>"
Next
```

If the dir parameter is present in the query string when a postback occurs, the Page_Load event handler sets the value of the DirName.Text property to the value of dir. This allows the application to navigate down to subdirectories and to list their contents:

```
<script runat="server">
  Sub Page_Load(sender As Object, e As EventArgs)
    If Not Request.Form("dir") Is Nothing Then
      DirName.Value = Request("dir")
    End If
  End Sub
</script>
```

The next section of the page has an anchor tag that displays the parent directory of that being listed. This is determined using the Parent property. This value will be null if there isn't a parent directory, so the following code checks for this:

```
If (Not dir.Parent Is Nothing) Then
  anchor = "<a href='" & "default.aspx?dir=" & dir.Parent.FullName & _
           "'>" & dir.Parent.FullName & "</a>"
  Response.Write("<p>Parent directory is " + anchor)
End If
```

The parent directory is displayed using an anchor tag, which also uses the `dir` parameter, this time to allow the user to navigate up from the current directory to the parent directory.

The final section of the page uses the `GetFiles` method (see the sourcecode for details) to list the files within the directory. Apart from displaying the name and last modified date of the file, this code also shows what attributes are set on the file (such as if it's a system file or is hidden). These attributes are available from the `Attributes` property of the `FileInfo` class (which returns a `FileAttributes` enumeration). The code uses the bit-wise `and` operator to determine if these attributes are set for a given file. If they are, some simple custom formatting is done to shows its presence:

```
Dim f as FileInfo
For Each f in dir.GetFiles()
  Response.Write("<tr>")
  Response.Write("<td>" & f.Name )

  If ((f.Attributes And FileAttributes.ReadOnly) <> 0) Then
    Response.Write(" (read only)")
  End If
  If ((f.Attributes And FileAttributes.Hidden) <> 0) Then
    Response.Write(" (hidden)")
  End If
  If ((f.Attributes And FileAttributes.System) <> 0) Then
    Response.Write(" (system)")
  End If
  If ((f.Attributes And FileAttributes.Archive) <> 0) Then
    Response.Write(" (archive)")
  End If
  Response.Write("<td>" & f.LastWriteTime & "</td>")
  Response.Write("<td>" & f.Length.ToString() & "</td>")
  Response.Write("</tr>")
Next
```

All enumeration types support the ability to convert a numeric enumeration value into a text value. This is a very useful technique for use in debugging. If you don't want any custom formatting in your application, replace your explicit checks for given attributes with a call to the `ToString` method. Then the enumeration type will do the conversion for you. For example, this would list out each of the attributes specified separated by a comma:

```
Response.Write( f.Attributes.ToString() )
```

Working with Paths

When working with files and directories, you often need to manipulate paths. The `Path` class allows you to:

❑ Extract the elements of a path, such as the root path, directory, filename, and extension

❑ Change the extension of a file or directory

❑ Combine paths

❑ Determine special characters, such as the path and volume separator characters

❑ Determine if a path is rooted or has an extension

The `Path` class has the following methods:

Method	Parameters	Description
ChangeExtension	Path, Extension	Takes a path (with or without an extension) and a new extension (with or without the period) as input and returns a new path with the new extension.
Combine	Path1, Path2	Concatenates two paths. The second path should not be rooted. For example, `Path.Combine("c:\rich", "anderson")` returns `c:\rich\anderson`.
GetDirectoryName	Path	Returns the directory or directories within the path.
GetExtension	Path	Returns the extension of the path (if present).
GetFileName	Path	Returns the filename if present.
GetFileNameWithoutExtension	Path	Returns the filename without its extension.
GetFullPath	Path	Given a non-rooted path, returns a rooted path name based on the current working directory. For example, if the path was `test` and the working directory was `c:\wrox`, the return path would be `c:\wrox\test`.
GetPathRoot	Path	Returns the root path (excludes any filename).
GetTempFileName	None	Returns a temporary filename, located in the temporary directory returned by `GetTempPath`.
GetTempPath	None	Returns the temporary directory name.
HasExtension	Path	Returns a Boolean value that indicates whether a path has an extension or not.
IsPathRooted	Path	Returns a Boolean value that indicates if a path is rooted or not.

The `Path` class uses a number of static constants to define the special characters that are used with paths (the values shown in the table are for the Windows platform):

Constant	Type	Description
DirectorySeparatorChar	Char	The default character used to separate directories within a path. Returns the backslash character \.
AltDirectorySeparatorChar	Char	Alternative character that can be used to separate directories within a path. Returns forward slash character /.
PathSeparator	Char	The character used when a string contains multiple paths. This returns the semicolon character ;.
VolumeSeparatorChar	Char	The character used to separate the volume name from the directory and/or filename. This returns the colon character :.
InvalidPathChars	Char array	Returns all of the characters that cannot be used in a path because they have special significance.

The application shown in Figure 16-3 accepts a path, and displays the component parts of that path:

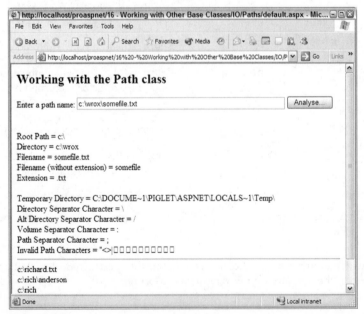

Figure 16-3

Note the entire path including the root path (logical drive), the directory, filename, and extension.

The code for this page shows how to use the various methods and constant properties of the `Path` class:

```
If (Page.IsPostBack) Then
  Response.Write("<br />Root Path = ")
  Response.Write(Path.GetPathRoot(PathName.Text))
  Response.Write("<br />Directory = ")
  Response.Write(Path.GetDirectoryName(PathName.Text))
  Response.Write("<br />Filename = ")
  Response.Write(Path.GetFileName(PathName.Text))
  Response.Write("<br />Filename (without extension) = ")
  Response.Write(Path.GetFileNameWithoutExtension(PathName.Text) )
  If (Path.HasExtension(PathName.Text)) Then
    Response.Write("<br />Extension = ")
    Response.Write(Path.GetExtension(PathName.Text))
  End If

  Response.Write("<br />Temporary Directory = ")
  Response.Write(Path.GetTempPath())
  Response.Write("<br />Directory Separator Character = ")
  Response.Write( Path.DirectorySeparatorChar)
  Response.Write("<br />Alt Directory Separator Character = ")
  Response.Write(Path.AltDirectorySeparatorChar)
  Response.Write("<br />Volume Separator Character = ")
  Response.Write(Path.VolumeSeparatorChar)
  Response.Write("<br />Path Separator Character = ")
  Response.Write(Path.PathSeparator)
  Response.Write("<br />Invalid Path Characters = ")
  Response.Write(HttpUtility.HtmlEncode(new String(Path.InvalidPathChars)))
End If
```

Here the `HttpUtility.HtmlEncode` method is used to encode the `Path.InvalidPathChars` character array so that the characters it contains are suitable for display within HTML. This is done because the characters returned would otherwise be interpreted as HTML elements (the returned character array contains the greater than > and less than < characters).

Reading and Writing Files

The `File` and `FileInfo` classes provide a number of helper methods that can open and create files. These methods don't actually perform the reading and writing of files, rather they instantiate and return other classes such as:

❑　`FileStream`: For reading and writing bytes of data to and from a file

❑　`StreamReader`: For reading characters from a stream

❑　`StreamWriter`: For writing characters to a stream

The following code example shows how to open a text file using the static `OpenText` method of the `File` class and then read several lines of text from it:

```
<%@ Import Namespace="System.IO" %>
<html>
```

```
<body>
<%
  Dim myfile As StreamReader
  Dim name As String
  myfile = File.OpenText(Server.MapPath("names.txt"))
  name = myfile.ReadLine()
  Do While Not name Is Nothing
    Response.Write(name & "<br />")
    name = myfile.ReadLine()
  Loop

  myfile.Close()
%>
</body>
</html>
```

Here the `File.OpenText` method is used to open the `names.txt` file. If successful, this method returns a `StreamReader` object that can be used to read characters (not bytes) from the file. The code uses the `ReadLine` method, which reads all characters up to the next carriage return line feed. Although this method reads the carriage return line feeds from the stream, they are not returned as part of the return string. When the end of the file is reached, a null string (`Nothing` in VB.NET) is returned. This is checked and used to terminate the `While` loop. Calling the `Close` method closes the file.

To ensure that the code remains scalable, you should always close files as soon as possible.

The following code shows how to create a new text file and write a few lines to it:

```
<%@ Page Language="VB" %>
<%@ Import Namespace="System.IO" %>
<%
  Dim books As StreamWriter
  books = File.CreateText(Server.MapPath("books.txt"))
  books.WriteLine("Professional ASP.NET")
  books.WriteLine("Professional C#")
  books.Close()
%>
```

Here, the `File.CreateText` method is used to create a new file. This method returns a `StreamWriter` object that you can use to write data to the file. You then call the `WriteLine` method of the object (which is inherited from the base class, `TextWriter`) and output the names of the two books. Finally, the `Close` method is called to close the connection to the file.

Once you've written code to read or write data from a backing store (such as the file system) using the `StreamReader` or `StreamWriter` classes, you can easily read and write character data from other backing stores (such as memory buffers or network connections) using the *same* classes. This consistency makes working with streams of data easy.

The main role of the `StreamReader` and `StreamWriter` classes is essentially to convert bytes of data into characters. Different character encoding types, such as Unicode, ASCII, or UTF-8, use different byte sequences to represent their characters, but no matter where bytes are read from, or written to, the same translations are performed, so it makes sense to always use the same classes for this purpose. To support this, the classes read and write bytes of data using a `Stream` class, as shown in the Figure 16-4:

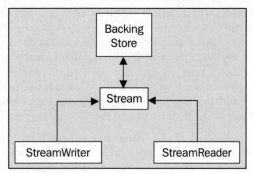

Figure 16-4

This generic model is very powerful. To support reading character data from different backing stores, all you require is a stream object for each backing store. Each of these stream objects inherits from the `Stream` class and overrides several abstract methods that can be used to read and write bytes of data, provide the current position in the stream as well as change it, determine the length of the stream, and expose the capabilities of the backing store (for example, whether it is read-only, or write-only). Figure 16-5 shows how reading and writing from the file system, network sockets, and memory buffers is supported by this model:

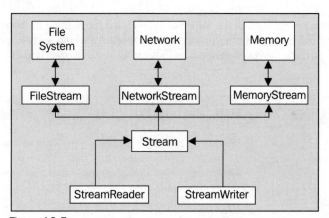

Figure 16-5

The `FileStream`, `NetworkStream`, and `MemoryStream` classes all derive from the `Stream` class. The `StreamReader` and `StreamWriter` classes contain a reference to the stream object they use to access the associated backing store. This reference is held in the `BaseStream` property (defined as type `Stream`). If you had a reference to a `StreamReader` and knew the backing store was actually a `FileStream`, you could use this property to get a reference to the original `FileStream` object:

```
Dim myfile As StreamReader
Dim backingStore As FileStream
' assuming backingStore and myfile are already initialized...
backingStore = CType(myfile.BaseStream, FileStream)
backingStore.Seek(0, SeekOrigin.Begin)
```

The capabilities of a stream object will depend on the backing data store. For example, if you're using a `StreamReader` to read data from a socket (for example, a web page over HTTP), you cannot change the position of the stream since you cannot push data back into a socket once it has been read. To determine the capability of a backing store, the `Stream` class has a number of read-only properties:

❑ `CanRead`: Determines if data can be read from a stream. If this property returns `true`, the `Read` method can be used to read a specified number of bytes from the `Stream` into a byte array at a given offset, or the `ReadByte` method can be used to read a single byte.

❑ `CanWrite`: Determines if data can be written to a stream. If this property returns `true`, the `Write` method can be used to write a specified number of bytes from a byte array to the `Stream`, or the `WriteByte` method can be used to write a single byte.

❑ `CanSeek`: Indicates if a stream supports random access. If it does, the `Position` property of the stream class can be used to set the stream position. Alternatively, the `Seek` method can be used to set a relative position from the start of the stream, the end of the stream, or the current position of the stream. The `SetLength` method can also be called to change the size of the underlying backing data store object.

Consider `Stream` *in .NET to be the replacement of the* `IStream` *interface in COM. In future versions of .NET, the* `Stream` *object will automatically expose the* `IStream` *interface through COM interop.*

FileStream

The `FileStream` class provides all of the functionality needed for reading and writing data to files. It derives from the `Stream` class, so it inherits all of the properties and methods just discussed. The `FileStream` class has the following constructors that can be used to open and create files in various modes:

Parameters	Description
path as string, mode as FileMode	Specifies a path/file and how you want to work with it. `FileMode` is an enumeration that defines how you want to work with a file, and what actions you want to take if it already exists. The values of `FileMode` will be covered after this table, when we look at an example of creating a `FileStream`.
path as string, mode as FileMode, access as FileAccess	As for the previous constructor, but also allows you to specify permissions to read, write, or read *and* write from the stream. Values for `FileAccess` are `Read`, `ReadWrite`, and `Write`. The default is `ReadWrite`.
path as string, mode as FileMode, access as FileAccess, share as FileShare	As with the previous constructor, but also allows you to specify what access other people will have to the file while you're working with it. Values for `FileShare` are `None`, `Read`, `ReadWrite`, `Write`, and `Inheritable`. The default is `None` (nobody else can access the file).

Parameters	Description
path as string, mode as FileMode, access as FileAccess, share as FileShare, bufferSize as Integer	As with the previous constructor, but also allows you to specify the size of the internal buffer used to reduce the number of calls to the underlying operation system. The default value is 4KB. You should not change the size of this buffer unless you have good reasons to do so.
path as string, mode as FileMode, access as FileAccess, share as FileShare, bufferSize as Integer, useAsync as Boolean	As with the previous constructor, but also tells the class the application calling it is using asynchronous IO. This can result in better performance for large reads and writes. The default value of this parameter is False.

The following code shows how to create a new text file using the `FileStream` class:

```
<%@ Page Language="VB" %>
<%@ Import Namespace="System.IO" %>
<%
  Dim fs As FileStream
  fs = New FileStream("MyFile.Txt", FileMode.Create)
  fs.Close()
%>
```

Since the `FileMode.Create` parameter is specified, any existing file called `MyFile.Txt` will be truncated (that is, all existing content will be overwritten) when the file is opened. The values of `FileMode` include:

- ❑ `Append:` Opens the specified file and seeks to the end of the stream. If a file does not exist, it is created.
- ❑ `CreateNew:` Creates the specified file. If the file already exists, an `IOException` is thrown.
- ❑ `Create:` Creates the specified file, truncating the file content if it already exists.
- ❑ `Open:` Opens the specified file. If the file doesn't exist, a `FileNotFound` exception is thrown.
- ❑ `OpenToCreate:` Opens the specified file, and creates it if it doesn't already exist.
- ❑ `Truncate:` Opens the specified file and clears the existing contents. If the file doesn't exist, a `FileNotFound` exception is thrown.

Once a file is opened and you have a `FileStream` object, you can create a reader or writer object to work with the file's contents. The following code shows how to write a few lines of text to a file using the `StreamWriter` class:

```
<%@ Page Language="VB" %>
<%@ Import Namespace="System.IO" %>
```

```
<%
  Dim fs As FileStream
  Dim sw As StreamWriter
  fs = New FileStream("MyFile.Txt", FileMode.Create)
  sw = New StreamWriter(fs)
  sw.WriteLine("Professional ASP.NET")
  sw.WriteLine("Professional C#")
  sw.Close()
%>
```

To use a writer object to write data to a stream, use only one writer. You should never have multiple writers per stream. Writer objects buffer data in an internal cache to reduce the number of calls to the underlying backing store, and having multiple writers active on one stream will result in unpredictable results.

The lifetime of the writer is tied to that of the stream. When the writer is closed, the stream is also closed by the writer, which is why you call sw.Close rather than fs.Close in this code.

When a stream is closed (assuming the writer didn't close it), the writer can no longer write to the stream. The same is true for reader objects. Any attempt to perform an operation on a closed stream will result in an exception.

The following code shows how to open an existing file using the FileStream class and read lines of text from it using the StreamReader class:

```
<%@ Page Language="VB" %>
<%@ Import Namespace="System.IO" %>
<%
  Dim fs As FileStream
  Dim sr As StreamReader
  Dim line As String
  fs = New FileStream("MyFile.Txt", FileMode.Open)
  sr = New StreamReader(fs)
  line = sr.ReadLine()
  Response.Write(line & "<br />")
  line = sr.ReadLine()
  Response.Write(line & "<br />")
  sr.Close()
%>
```

In this code the FileMode.Open parameter is being used to tell the FileStream that you're opening an existing file. Use the ReadLine method to read two lines from the file and write them to your ASP.NET page using Response.Write.

MemoryStream

A memory stream allows you to read and write bytes of data from memory. It has several constructors that allow you to initialize the buffer to a given size (default is 256 bytes) that indicate whether the buffer is read-only (and can therefore not be written to), and copy specified data from an existing array.

The following code demonstrates how you can use the MemoryStream class to create a byte array containing the text "Professional ASP.NET". Although something of an esoteric example, it demonstrates how to use a stream writer to fill the memory stream with some text, and then create a byte array containing that text:

```
<%@ Page Language="VB" %>
<%@ Import Namespace="System.IO" %>
<%
   Dim memstream As MemoryStream
   Dim writer As StreamWriter
   Dim array() As Byte
   memstream = New MemoryStream()
   writer = New StreamWriter(memstream)
   writer.Write("Professional ASP.NET")
   writer.Flush()
   array = memstream.ToArray()
   writer.Close()
%>
```

The `StreamWriter` class uses an internal 1KB buffer to write blocks of data to the underlying stream (and its associated backing store) more efficiently. Calling its `Flush` method causes any buffered data to be written to the underlying stream (before the 1KB limit is reached), and resets the buffer to an empty state. The `Flush` method is automatically called by the `Close` method of the `StreamWriter`.

In your code use the `ToArray` method of `MemoryStream` to convert the memory buffer into a byte array. You have to explicitly call the `Flush` method before calling this method, since the amount of data written to the stream using the `Write` method is less than 1KB. If you didn't call `Flush` first, you'd simply end up with an empty array, as no data would have actually been written to the memory stream. In this case, you have to call `Flush`, since calling the `ToArray` method *after* the `Close` method would also result in an empty array, as the memory stream releases its resources (memory) when the `Close` method is called.

The `Capacity` property can be used to determine the amount of data a memory stream can hold before it will need to reallocate its buffer. This property can be set to increase or shrink the size of the memory buffer. However, you cannot set the capacity of the memory stream to be less than the current length of the memory stream, as the length reflects how much data has already been written to the memory stream. To determine how much data is currently in a memory stream, use the read-only `Length` property.

The `MemoryStream` class automatically manages its own capacity expansion. A memory stream is full it doubles in size, allocating a new buffer and copying the old data across.

> When using classes such as `StreamWriter` to populate a memory stream, the memory stream's `Length` property will not be accurate until the stream writer's `Flush` method is called (because of the buffering it performs).

TextReader and TextWriter

The `StreamReader` class derives from the *abstract* `TextReader` class. This class defines the base methods that are useful to applications that need to read character data. It does not define any methods for opening or connecting to an underlying data source (backing store), those are provided by derived classes such as `StringReader` and `StreamReader`.

The `TextReader` class has the methods shown in the following table:

Method Name	Parameters	Description
`Close`	None	Closes the underlying backing store connection and dispose of any held resources.
`Read`	None	Reads the next character from the input stream.
`Read`	`Char array, index, count`	Reads a specified number of characters from the input stream into an array at the specified offset. The number of characters read is returned.
`ReadBlock`	`Char array, index, count`	Reads a specified number of characters from the input stream into an array at the specified offset. The number of characters read is returned. This method will block (that is, the method will not return) until data is available.
`ReadLine`	None	Returns a string containing the next line of characters.
`ReadToEnd`	None	Reads all of the remaining content from the input stream into a string. You should not use this method for large streams, as it can consume a lot of memory.
`Synchronized`	`TextReader`	Accepts a `TextReader` object as input and returns a thread-safe wrapper. This is a static method.

One of the reasons the `TextReader` class exists is so that non-stream-oriented backing stores such as a `string` can have an interface consistent with streams. It provides a mechanism by which classes can expose or consume a text stream without having to be aware of where the underlying data stream is. The following C# code shows how a function can output the data read from a text-oriented input stream using an ASP.NET page :

```
<script runat="server">
  protected void WriteContentsToResponse(TextReader r)
  {
    string line;
    line = r.ReadLine();
    while (line != null)
    {
      Response.Write(line);
      Response.Write("<br />");
      line = r.ReadLine();
    }
  }
</script>
```

This function is passed a `TextReader` and reads lines of text using the `ReadLine` method. It then writes that back to the client browser using the `Response.Write` method. As the HTML standard defines line breaks using the `<br />` element, it is written after each line.

The `StringReader` class derives from `TextReader` in order to provide a way of accessing the contents of a string in a text-stream-oriented way. The `StreamReader` class extends `TextReader` to provide an implementation that makes it easy to read text data from a file. You can derive your own classes from `TextReader` to provide an implementation that makes it easy to read from your internal data source. This same model is used for the `TextWriter` class. The `StreamWriter` class derives from the abstract `TextWriter` class. `StreamWriter` defines methods for writing character data. It also provides many overloaded methods for converting primitive types like `bool` and `integer` into character data:

Method Name	Parameters	Description
Close	None	Closes the underlying backing store connection and disposes of any resources that are held.
Flush	None	Flushes any buffered data to the underlying backing store.
Synchronized	TextWriter	Accepts a TextWriter object as input and returns a thread safe wrapper. This is a static method.
Write	Numerous overloads	Writes the passed parameter to the underlying data stream. The primitive types string, char, char array, bool, integer, unsigned integer, long, unsigned long, float, and decimal are valid parameter types. If a string and an object parameter are passed, the string is assumed to contain formatting specifications, so the String.Format method is called. There are method overloads for formatting that take either between one and three object parameters, or an array of objects as input.
WriteLine	Numerous overloads	Implemented as per the Write method, but also outputs the carriage return line feed characters.

Following VB.NET code shows how to use the `Write` method to write formatted strings using the various available overloads:

```
<%@ Page Language="VB" %>
<%@ Import Namespace="System.IO" %>
<%
  Dim myfile As TextWriter
  myfile = File.CreateText("c:\authors.txt")
  myfile.WriteLine("My name is {0}", "Richard")
  myfile.WriteLine("My name is {0} {1}", "Richard", "James")
```

```
myfile.WriteLine("My name is {0} {1} {2}", "Richard", "James", "Anderson")
Dim authors(5) as Object
authors(0) = "Alex"
authors(1) = "Dave"
authors(2) = "Rich"
authors(3) = "Brian"
authors(4) = "Karli"
authors(5) = "Rob"
myfile.WriteLine( "Authors:{0},{1},{2},{3},{4},{5}", authors)
myfile.Close()
%>
```

The contents of the `authors.txt` file created by this code are:

```
My name is Richard
My name is Richard James
My name is Richard James Anderson
Authors:Alex,Dave,Rich,Brian,Karli,Rob
```

StringReader and StringWriter

The `StringReader` derives from the `TextReader` class and uses a string as the underlying input stream. The string to read from is passed in as a parameter to the constructor.

The `StringWriter` class derives from the `TextWriter` class and uses a string as the underlying output stream. For reasons of efficiency, this underlying string is actually built using a string builder. Optionally, you can pass in your `StringBuilder` object as a constructor parameter if you want to add data to existing strings.

The following code shows how to build a multi-line string using the `StringWriter` class:

```
<%@ Page Language="VB" %>
<%@ Import Namespace="System.IO" %>
<html>
<body>
<%
   Dim sw As StringWriter = New StringWriter()
   sw.WriteLine("The Cow")
   sw.WriteLine("Jumped Over")
   sw.WriteLine("The Moon")
   Response.Write("<pre>")
   Response.Write(sw.ToString())
   Response.Write("</pre>")

   sw.Close()
%>
</body>
</html>
```

Here, you allocate a `StringWriter` and use the `WriteLine` method to build up the contents of the string. Retrieve the string using the `ToString` method, and render it within an HTML <pre> element to ensure that the carriage return line feeds within the string are not ignored by the browser, as shown in Figure 16-6:

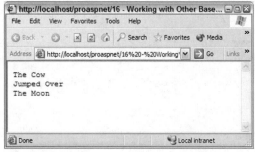

Figure 16-6

Reading and Writing Binary Data

When working with streams of binary data, you often need to read and write primitive types. For this, you can use the `BinaryReader` and `BinaryWriter` classes respectively. The following C# code demonstrates how to use a `BinaryWriter` with a `FileStream` to write a few primitive types to a file:

```
<%@ Page Language="C#" %>
<%@ Import Namespace="System.IO" %>
<%
  BinaryWriter bw;
  FileStream fs;
  string filename;

  filename = Server.MapPath("myfile.bin");
  fs = new FileStream(filename, FileMode.Create);
  bw = new BinaryWriter(fs);

  string s = "a string";
  long l = 0x123456789abcdef;
  int i = 0x12345678;
  char c = 'c';
  float f = 1.5f;
  Decimal d = 100.2m;

  bw.Write(s);
  bw.Write(l);
  bw.Write(i);
  bw.Write(c);
  bw.Write(f);
  bw.Write(d);

  fs.Close();
%>
```

The following C# code shows how to re-read the created binary file using the `BinaryReader` class:

```
<%@ Page Language="C#" %>
<%@ Import Namespace="System.IO" %>
<%
  BinaryReader br;
  FileStream fs;
  string filename;
  filename = Server.MapPath("myfile.bin");
  fs = new FileStream( filename, FileMode.Open );
  br = new BinaryReader( fs );

  string s = br.ReadString();
  long l = br.ReadInt64();
  int i = br.ReadInt32();
  char c = br.ReadChar();
  float f = br.ReadSingle();
  Decimal d = br.ReadDecimal();
  fs.Close();
%>
```

Methods of Encoding

The `StreamReader` class will, by default, attempt to determine the encoding format of a file. If one of the supported methods of encoding (such as UTF-8 or Unicode) is detected, it will be used. If the encoding is not recognized, the default encoding of UTF-8 will be used. Depending on the constructor you call, you can change the default encoding used, and even turn off encoding detection.

The following VB.NET code shows how you can specify a default encoding of `Unicode` to use to read from a file:

```
Dim Reader As StreamReader
Reader = new StreamReader("somefile.txt", System.Encoding.Text.Unicode);
```

The default encoding for `StreamWriter` is also UTF-8, and you can override it in the same manner as the `StreamReader` class. For example, the following C# code creates a file using each supported encoding:

```
<%@Page Language="C#"%>
<%@Import Namespace="System.IO" %>
<%@Import Namespace="System.Text" %>
<%
  StreamWriter stream;
  char HiChar;
  HiChar = (char) 0xaaaa;
  stream = new StreamWriter(Server.MapPath("myfile.utf8"), false,
                            System.Text.Encoding.UTF8);
  stream.Write("Hello World");
  stream.Write(HiChar);
  stream.Close();

  stream = new StreamWriter(Server.MapPath("myfile.utf7"), false,
                            System.Text.Encoding.UTF7);
  stream.Write("Hello World");
  stream.Write(HiChar);
```

```
    stream.Close();

    stream = new StreamWriter(Server.MapPath("myfile.ascii"), false,
                            System.Text.Encoding.ASCII);
    stream.Write("Hello World");
    stream.Write(HiChar);
    stream.Close();
    stream = new StreamWriter(Server.MapPath("myfile.unicode"), false,
                            System.Text.Encoding.Unicode);
    stream.Write("Hello World");
    stream.Write(HiChar);
    stream.Close();
%>
```

The size of each created file varies due to the way the different methods of encoding work. The largest is the Unicode-encoded file at 26 bytes. The smallest file is the ASCII file at 12 bytes. However, since ASCII encoding can only encode 8-bit characters, and you've got a 16-bit character (0xaaaa) you're actually losing data. Avoid ASCII encoding whenever possible and stick with the default UTF-8 encoding, or use Unicode. UTF-8 encoding is preferred since it typically requires less space than Unicode (17 bytes compared to 26 bytes in this example) and is the standard encoding for Web technologies such as XML and HTML.

BufferedStream

The BufferedStream class reads and writes data to another stream through an internal buffer, the size of which can be specified in the constructor. This class is designed to be composed with other stream classes that do not have internal buffers, enabling you to reduce potentially expensive calls by reading data in large chunks and buffering it. The BufferedStream class should not be used with the FileStream or MemoryStream classes because they already buffer their own data.

Copying between Streams

One of the functions of the stream object *not* included in version 1.0 of .NET is the ability to write the content of one stream into another. Here is some C# code that shows how it can be implemented:

```
public static long Pump(Stream input, Stream output)
{
  if (input == null)
  {
    throw new ArgumentNullException("input");
  }
  if (output == null)
  {
    throw new ArgumentNullException("output");
  }

  const int count = 4096;
  byte[] bytes = new byte[count];
  int numBytes;
  long totalBytes = 0;

  while((numBytes = input.Read(bytes, 0, count)) > 0)
```

```
  {
    output.Write(bytes, 0, numBytes);
    totalBytes += numBytes;
  }

  return totalBytes;
}
```

This code uses a 4KB buffer to read data from the input stream and write it to the output stream. If the copy is successful, the total number of bytes copied is returned. The method throws an `ArgumentNullException` if the input parameters are invalid.

Always Call Close, and Watch for Exceptions

In the non-deterministic world of .NET, *always* make sure that you call the `Close` method on your streams. If you don't call `Close`, the time at which the buffered contents of a stream will be written to the underlying backing store is not predictable (due to the way the CLR garbage collector works). Furthermore, since garbage collection does not guarantee the order in which objects are finalized, you may also find that your data is not written correctly and is corrupted. For example, it is possible for a stream to be closed before a writer object has flushed its data.

Because of this non-deterministic behavior, always add exception handling to your code when using streams. There is no performance overhead at runtime for doing this in cases when exceptions are not thrown, and by putting your stream cleanup code in the `finally` section of the exception handler, you can ensure resources aren't held for an unpredictable amount of time (in the unlikely case that error conditions *do* arise).

For C# code, it's worth considering the `using` statement, which can be used to automatically close a stream when it goes out of scope, even if an exception is thrown. The following code shows the `using` statement in action:

```
<%@ Page Language="C#" %>
<%@ Import Namespace="System.IO" %>
<%
  FileStream fs = new FileStream("MyFile.Txt", FileMode.Create );
  using(fs)
  {
    //...
  }
%>
```

In this code you create a file stream, and then begin a new scope by using the `using` statement. When this `using` statement is exited (either normally or if an exception occurs), the resources held by the stream are released. Under the hood, the `using` statement causes code to be generated that calls the `IDiposable.Dispose` method implemented by the `FileStream`.

ASP.NET and Streams

The ASP.NET page framework allows you to read and write content to a page using a stream:

❑   `Page.Response.Output` property: Returns a `TextWriter` that can be used to write text content into the output stream of a page

❑   `Page.Response.OutputStream` property: Returns a `Stream` object that can be used to write bytes to the output stream of a page

❑   The `Page.Request.InputStream` property: Returns a `Stream` object that can be used to read bytes of data from a posted request

Suppose content, such as an XML file, was posted to an ASP.NET page. The following VB.NET shows how you could read and display the data using the `Page.Request.InputStream` property:

```
<%@ Page Language="VB" %>
<%@ Import Namespace="System.IO" %>
<%
  Dim reader As StreamReader
  Dim line As String
  reader = New StreamReader(Page.Request.InputStream)
  line = reader.ReadLine()
  Do While Not line Is Nothing
    Response.Write(line & "<br />")
    line = reader.ReadLine()
  Loop
%>
```

Writing Custom Streams

Depending on the type of applications or components that you write, you may want to create your own stream class. Custom streams are fairly easy to write, and can be used just like the other stream classes (such as `FileStream`) as well as in conjunction with classes like `StreamReader` and `StreamWriter`.

There are essentially two types of streams you are likely to write:

❑   Streams that provide access to a custom backing store

❑   Streams that are composed of other streams in order to provide services such as filtering, compression, or encryption

To implement either of these, you need to create a new class that derives from the `Stream` class and overrides the following properties:

Name	Get/Set	Type
CanRead	Get	Bool
CanWrite	Get	Bool
CanSeek	Get	Bool
Length	Get	Long
Position	Get/Set	Long

It also needs to override the `Close`, `Flush`, `Seek`, `SetLength`, `Read`, and `Write` methods. The other methods of the `Stream` object such as `ReadByte` and `WriteByte` use these overridden members. You can override these methods to provide custom implementation (which could have performance benefits).

Here is a simple custom stream implementation (written in C#) that you can compose from other stream objects. It accepts a `Stream` object as a constructor parameter, and implements all of the stream members (except the `Read` and `Write` methods) by directly delegating to that object:

```csharp
using System;
using System.IO;
namespace CustomStreams
{
  public class UpperCaseStream : Stream
  {
    Stream _stream;
    public UpperCaseStream(Stream stream)
    {
      _stream = stream;
    }

    public override bool CanRead
    {
      get { return _stream.CanRead; }
    }

    public override bool CanSeek
    {
      get { return _stream.CanSeek; }
    }

    public override bool CanWrite
    {
      get { return _stream.CanWrite; }
    }

    public override long Length
    {
      get { return _stream.Length; }
    }

    public override long Position
    {
      get { return _stream.Position; }
      set { _stream.Position = value; }
    }

    public override void Close()
    {
      _stream.Close();
    }

    public override void Flush()
    {
      _stream.Flush();
    }
```

```
public override long Seek(long offset, System.IO.SeekOrigin origin)
{
  return _stream.Seek(offset, origin);
}

public override void SetLength(long length)
{
  _stream.SetLength(length);
}
```

The Read and Write methods scan the data passed in to them and convert any lowercase characters to uppercase. In the case of the Read method, this is done *after* the Read method of the contained stream class is called. For the Write method, it is done *before* the Write method of the contained stream is called:

```
public override int Read(byte[] buffer, int offset, int count)
{
  int bytesRead;
  int index;
  // let base class do the read
  bytesRead = _stream.Read(buffer, offset, count);
  // if something was read
  if ( bytesRead > 0)
  {
    for(index = offset; index < (offset+bytesRead); index++)
    {
      if (buffer[index] >= 'a' && buffer[index] <= 'z')
      {
        buffer[index] = (byte) (buffer[index] - 32 );
      }
    }
  }
  return bytesRead;
}

public override void Write(byte[] buffer, int offset, int count)
{
  int index;
  // if something was to be written
  if ( count > 0)
  {
    for(index = offset; index < (offset+count); index++)
    {
      if ( buffer[index] >= 'a' && buffer[index] <= 'z')
      {
        buffer[index] = (byte) (buffer[index] - 32);
      }
    }
  }
  // write the content
  _stream.Write( buffer, offset, count );
}
}
}
```

The following code shows how you could create this custom stream and then use it to interact with a `FileStream` in order to automatically read and convert the characters contained within a file to uppercase:

```
public static void Main()
{
    UpperCaseStream customStream;

    // Create our custom stream, passing it a file stream
    customStream = new UpperCaseStream(new FileStream("file.txt",
                                                   FileMode.Open));
    StreamReader sr = new StreamReader(customStream);
    Console.WriteLine("{0}",sr.ReadToEnd());
    customStream.Close();
}
```

The following code shows how to use this custom stream, in conjunction with a `FileStream`, to automatically convert written data to uppercase:

```
public static void Main()
{
    UpperCaseStream customStream;
    customStream = new UpperCaseStream(new FileStream("fileout.txt",
                                                   FileMode.Create));
    StreamWriter sw = new StreamWriter( customStream,
    System.Text.Encoding.ASCII );
    sw.WriteLine("Hello World!");
    sw.Close();
}
```

The `fileout.txt` file will now contain the text HELLO WORLD!

This is a fairly simple custom stream implementation, but you could use the same technique to write a more sophisticated class, perhaps to dynamically compress, or secure data. Although not covered in this book, the `System.Security` namespace contains a `CryptoStream` class to encrypt data, and third-party vendors are already working on compression streams.

Web Request Classes and Streams

Once it's understood that streams provide a generic mechanism by which data can be read and written to a backing store, and that reader and writer objects provide higher-level functions to a stream such as the ability to read and write text, it's easy to work with the numerous backing stores in .NET.

To demonstrate how classes in other namespaces in the .NET Framework build upon this stream paradigm, let's take a brief look at the `HttpWebRequest` and `HttpWebResponse` classes in the `System.Net` namespace. These classes make it easy to download a file over HTTP. However, we're not going to examine the `System.Net` namespace in depth, since it's outside the scope of this book.

To make an HTTP request, you need to create an instance of the `HttpWebRequest` class using the static `WebRequest.Create` method. This is a factory method that accepts the URI of an Internet resource and then, based upon that protocol, creates an instance of a protocol-specific request object. All protocol-specific request objects derive from the abstract `WebRequest` class.

If a URI uses HTTP, the actual concrete class created by the `WebRequest.CreateRequest` method will be of type `HttpWebRequest`. So, when you write code to create a URI starting with `http://`, you can safely cast the object returned from `WebRequest.CreateRequest` back to `HttpWebRequest`.

Once you have a request object, use the `GetResponse` method to retrieve the resource. As with request objects, each protocol has its own response object that derives from a common abstract class, `WebResponse`. This is the type returned by the `GetResponse` method of the request object. For the HTTP protocol, the response object can be cast back to the concrete `HttpWebResponse` class.

The `HttpWebResponse` class has a `GetResponseStream` method, which returns a `Stream` object. This `Stream` object can be used to read the response data in exactly the same way that you would read data from a file, or any other stream. The following VB.NET code shows how to download the Amazon.com home page using the `System.Net` classes:

```
<%@ Import Namespace="System.IO" %>
<%@ Import Namespace="System.Net" %>
<h3>HTML for http://www.amazon.com</h3>
<%
  Dim myRequest As HttpWebRequest
  Dim myResponse As HttpWebResponse
  Dim sr As StreamReader
  Dim line As String
  myRequest = CType(WebRequest.Create("http://www.amazon.com"), _
                    HttpWebRequest)

  myResponse = CType(myRequest.GetResponse(), HttpWebResponse)

  sr = New StreamReader(myResponse.GetResponseStream())
  line = sr.ReadLine()
  Do While Not line Is Nothing
    line = HttpUtility.HtmlEncode(line)
    If line.Length <> 0 Then
        Response.Write(line & "<br />")
    End If
    line = sr.ReadLine()
  Loop
  sr.Close
%>
```

Figure 16-7 shows the output generated by this page:

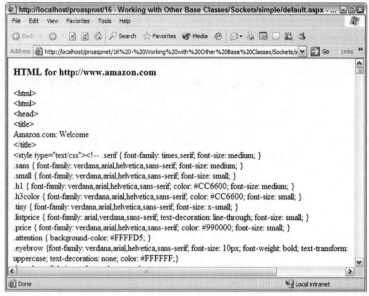

Figure 16-7

Let's take a look a closer look at what this code does. It initially constructs a web request using `WebRequest.Create`, and casts the returned object back to an `HttpWebRequest`:

```
myRequest = CType(WebRequest.Create("http://www.amazon.com"),HttpWebRequest)
```

Next, the request is executed and the response object is retrieved. Once again, the `Response` object is safely cast back to `HttpWebResponse` since you know the protocol being used:

```
myResponse = CType(myRequest.GetResponse(), HttpWebResponse)
```

Once you have the web response object, the `GetResponseStream` method is called to get a `Stream` object that can be used to read the contents of the web page:

```
sr = new StreamReader(myResponse.GetResponseStream())
```

To output the underlying HTML in a useful form, create a `StreamReader` object that can be used to read the web page line-by-line. `HttpUtility.HtmlEncode` method is used for escaping characters that would otherwise be interpreted by the browser (if you want the user to see the underlying HTML):

```
line = sr.ReadLine()
Do While Not line Is Nothing
  line = HttpUtility.HtmlEncode(line)
  If line.Length <> 0 Then
    Response.Write(line & "<br />")
  End If
  line = sr.ReadLine()
Loop
```

Finally, the stream is closed using the `Close` method of the `StreamReader`.

The `HttpWebRequest` and `HttpWebResponse` classes make it really simple to work with resources located anywhere over the Internet or a local network. They don't use the `WinInet` APIs under the hood, so they can be safely used in ASP.NET without any worries about affecting the scalability of applications.

To round off our coverage of the `HttpWebRequest` and `HttpWebResponse` classes, and to introduce our next topic, *regular expressions*, let's create a simple application that can determine the ranking of a book on Amazon.com. The technique shown is often called screen scraping and should give an idea of how you can apply these classes in real-world applications.

Our application accepts the URL of a book on Amazon.com and displays the book rank along with details about the response such as the content length, encoding, and HTTP response code (see Figure 16-8):

Figure 16-8

The application works by downloading the specified page and placing the retrieved HTML into a string. To get the page content into a string we create a `StreamReader` object and call its `ReadToEnd` method, which returns a string that contains the complete content of the stream:

```
HttpWebRequest myRequest;
HttpWebResponse myResponse;
Stream s;
myRequest = (HttpWebRequest) WebRequest.Create(URLToRead.Value);
myResponse = (HttpWebResponse) myRequest.GetResponse();
s = myResponse.GetResponseStream();
_HtmlContent = new StreamReader(s).ReadToEnd();
s.Close();
```

Once the page content is retrieved, the string that contains the HTML is processed and regular expressions are used to extract the ranking:

```
void RenderStreamIntoPage()
{
  Regex re;
  Match m;

  re =
    new Regex("(?<x>Amazon.com Sales Rank: </b> )(?<rank>.*)</font><br>");
  m = re.Match(_HtmlContent);
  // Check for multiple matches
  while(m.Success == true)
  {
    foreach(Capture c in m.Captures)
    {
      Response.Write("<br />Ranking : " + m.Result("${rank}" ));
    }
    m = m.NextMatch();
  }
}
```

Regular Expressions

Regular expressions often generate a lot of confusion, but are extremely useful if you have to deal with any form of text input or need to process some text. Chapter 5 discussed validation controls, including the regular expression validator that uses a regular expression to check the value of an email entry field. This works very well to validate entry fields, but there are times when you need to process text outside of the validators, probably when writing custom text or screen scraping applications.

For example, without regular expressions, how easy would it be to extract all the links from the HTML of a web page? You could search for the "href" string, but then you would have to be flexible about the contents of the attribute string. Regular expressions allow this flexibility, by way of *pattern matching*.

Pattern Matching

Regular expressions allow you to search, extract, or replace substrings based on an expression, or a pattern. These expressions are where the power of regular expressions lies. The patterns available in regular expressions use special characters and sequences to identify what is being searched for. The following table lists some of the main pattern elements:

Element	Description
*	A quantifier construct, when used it indicates that zero or more matches for a specific expression
+	A quantifier construct, when used it indicates that one or more matches for a specific expression
( )	Captures the matched substring into the next available capture group (a capture group is zero, one, or more strings)
(?<name>)	Captures matched substring into capture group identified by name
\n	Return the nth captured group
|	Either of the expressions separated by the | character
.	Any character (except newline)
[]	Any single character within the brackets
[^]	Any single character not within the brackets
\s	Any whitespace character
\S	Any non-whitespace character
\d	Any digit character
\D	Any non-digit character

The following table shows some examples of regular expressions, and content those expressions match:

Example	Matches
abc*	abc followed by none or more 'c' characters
abc+	abc followed by one or more 'c' characters
abc(def)ghi	abcdefghi, and places def in the first capture group
Ab(cd)ef(gh)i	abcdefghi, places cd into capture group 1, and gh into capture group 2
hello|goodbye	Either hello or goodbye
[abcdef]	Any of the characters abcdef
[a-f]	Any of the characters abcdef
[^a-f]	Any character other than abcdef

Pattern Ordering and Length

There are two important points to note about searching for patterns. The searched pattern will be the largest available, which may not be what is expected. For example, consider the following string:

```
Alex Homer is an author. Despite his years, he's not the Homer that wrote
Greek epics.
```

Let's say we use the following expression:

```
Homer(.*)
```

This expression looks for the word `Homer`, and places any characters found after it in a capture group. The thing to watch for is that the first expression found in the search string is used. So, what's captured is the following:

```
 is an author. Despite his years, he's not the Homer that wrote Greek epics.
```

There are two instances of `Homer`, and it's the first one that is matched. This rule changes when the search expression is widened to include any characters at the start of the search string. If you use the following expression:

```
.*Homer(.*)
```

This looks for any characters, followed by `Homer`, and places any characters found after it in a capture group. However, since the entire expression is widened, it now matches a larger number of characters. The largest match is returned, but the group now contains less characters. In this case, the following is captured:

```
 that wrote the Greek epics.
```

The rules for these matches are entirely consistent, and they mean that you have to be careful in selecting match strings.

Text Replacement

If you are using patterns to search and replace within a string, remember that the replacement text may invalidate the expression that was used to perform the search. You should therefore be careful of search patterns that pick the widest match. It's nearly always best to be as explicit as possible, by using narrow patterns.

Pattern Example

You've seen how to use the network classes to retrieve a web page from Amazon.com and extract the sales ranking for a book. Let's take a look at part of the HTML that the Amazon.com web page uses:

```
<b>Amazon.com Sales Rank: </b> 52,504 </font><br>
```

Notice that this is all on one line, so you need to extract the rank from the middle of text, rather than from a line on its own. Here's the search expression, this time only using one group, since you really only require the sales rank:

```
<b>Amazon.com Sales Rank: </b>(?<rank>.*)</font></b>
```

There are several parts to this, some of which aren't directly relevant to the ranking. However, let's take the whole expression so you can see exactly what it's built from. Firstly you'll notice that you have two groups (these are the parts contained within parentheses), each of which is given a name. The name is defined by use of the ? character followed by a name contained within angle brackets. So you have x and rank. The groupings don't affect how the expression is parsed – they are just used to allow easy access to parts of the expression once parsing has taken place.

It's clear which characters you need to match–those after : </b> and before the closing font tag. These are extracted by the group labeled rank.

The Regular Expression Classes

The System.Text.RegularExpressions namespace contains eight classes for the manipulation of regular expressions. These are:

Class	Represents
Regex	A regular expression
Match	The results from a single expression match
MatchCollection	A collection of results from iteratively applied matches
Group	The results from a single captured group
GroupCollection	A collection of captured groups
Capture	The results from a single sub-expression capture
CaptureCollection	A collection of captured sub-expressions
RegexCompilationInfo	Information about the compilation of expressions

Like the pattern matching, we're not going to cover an exhaustive list of all the classes, properties, and methods. Instead we'll concentrate on the most useful scenarios.

The Regex Class

Regex is the root class for regular expressions, and represents an individual regular expression. It contains a number of methods to allow the creation and matching of expressions. For example:

```
Dim expr As String = "hello"
Dim re As New Regex(expr)
re.Match("Hello everyone, hello one and all.")
```

This creates an expression and then uses the `Match` method to match the expression with the supplied string. In this case, there would only be one match – the second `hello` – since the matching is, by default, case-sensitive.

The `Regex` class constructor can be overloaded, to allow options to be specified. For example:

```
Dim expr As String = "hello"
Dim re   As New Regex(expr, RegexOptions.IgnoreCase)
re.Match("Hello everyone, hello one and all.")
```

Now there are two matches, since case is being ignored!

The options to specify can be from the `RegexOptions` shown in the following table (or set the `Options` property of the class):

RegexOption	Description
Compiled	Specifies that the expression should be compiled to MSIL
ECMAScript	Enables `ECMAScript`-compliant behavior for the expression
ExplicitCapture	Only captures explicitly named or numbered groups, allowing parentheses to be matched without escaping
IgnoreCase	Case-insensitive match
IgnorePattern Whitespace	Ignores un-escaped whitespace in the pattern
Multiline	Make ^ and $ match the beginning and end of any line, rather than the entire string
None	No options are set
RightToLeft	Searches from right to left. This sets the `RightToLeft` property of the class
SingleLine	Treat the search string as a single line (where all characters are matched, including new line)

The Match Class

The `Match` class contains the details of a single expression match, as returned by the `Match` method of the `Regex` class. For example:

```
Dim mt As Match
Dim expr As String = "hello"
Dim re As New Regex(expr, RegexOptions.IgnoreCase)
mt = re.Match("Hello everyone, hello one and all.")
```

You can then use the `Success` property to determine if any matches were made, and examine the `Groups` and `Captures` collections to identify what were matched.

The Group Class

The `Group` class identifies a single captured group. Since an expression can contain multiple groups, the `Match` class has a `Groups` collection that contains a `Group` object for each group matched. For example, consider the match expression:

```
(he(ll)o)
```

This contains two explicit groups. One is for the entire word `hello`, and the other for the two `l` characters. There is also a third group, which is the entire expression. So, as far as matching is concerned, this expression is equivalent to:

```
he(ll)o
```

The only difference is the number of groups created.

Unlike the sales-ranking examples, these groups aren't explicitly named, so they are given names equivalent to their position in the collection (1, 2, and so on). You can access the groups directly, or through an enumeration. For simple expressions, it's marginally quicker to allow the class name the groups, but for more complex expressions, explicit names make it clear exactly which groups correspond to which match expression.

For example, consider the following expression:

```
(l)+
```

This expression matches one or more occurrences of the `l` character.

The following example demonstrates simple grouping in use:

```
<%@ Page Language="VB" %>
<%
  Dim mt As Match
  Dim gp As Group
  Dim expr As String = "h(e(ll)o) "
  Dim re As New Regex(expr, RegexOptions.IgnoreCase)
  mt = re.Match("Hello everyone, hello one and all.")
  For Each gp In mt.Groups
    Response.Write("<br />")
    Response.Write(gp.Value)
  Next
%>
```

This returns the following:

```
hello
ello
ll
```

There are three matches. The first is the entire match expression, the second corresponds to the group within the first set of parentheses, and the third is the group within the second set of parentheses.

The `Group` class also includes `Index` and `Length` properties, which indicate the position of the match within the search string, and the length of string that is matched.

The Capture Class

The `Capture` class represents a single sub-expression capture. Each `Group` can have multiple captures. The `Capture` class really comes into its own when quantifiers are used within expressions. *Quantifiers* add an optional quantity to finding patterns. Examples of quantifiers are * for zero or more occurrences and + for one or more occurrences. For example, consider the following expression, which searches for the first occurrence of one or more 1 characters:

```
(1)+
```

Putting this into a full example, you have:

```
<%@ Page Language="VB" %>
<%
  Dim mt As Match
  Dim gp As Group
  Dim cp As Capture
  Dim expr As String = "(1)+"
  Dim re As New Regex(expr, RegexOptions.IgnoreCase)
  mt = re.Match("Hello everyone, hello one and all.")
  For Each gp In mt.Groups
    Response.Write("Group: " & gp.Value)
    Response.Write("<br />");
    For Each cp In gp.Captures
      Response.Write("  Capture: " & cp.Value)
      Response.Write("<br />");
    Next
  Next
%>
```

This gives the following result:

```
Group: ll
  Capture: ll
Group: l
  Capture: l
  Capture: l
```

Both a single 1 and multiple 1 characters are matched, because the + quantifier specifies one or more. So, the first group matches the 11 in the first `Hello`. For the second group, there are two occurrences of single 1 characters. This becomes clearer with another example. Let's consider the following:

```
(abc)+
```

This matches one or more occurrences of the string abc. When matched against QQQabcabcabcWWWEEEabcab you get the following output:

```
Group: abcabcabc
  Capture: abcabcabc
Group: abc
  Capture: abc
  Capture: abc
  Capture: abc
```

The first group matches the widest expression, and there is only one occurrence of this. The second group matches the explicit group, and there are three occurrences of this.

Substitutions

When using groups in expressions, you can reuse the group without having to retype it. This is known as *substitution*. For example, consider the expression:

```
(abc)def
```

This matches abcdef but places abc into the first group. Then, to match abcdefabc, you'd use:

```
(abc)def\1
```

Summary

We've covered a lot of useful classes and techniques in this chapter. The .NET Framework class library is full of useful feature-rich classes, and over the last two chapters, we've picked out and studied those that you'll use most frequently when creating ASP.NET applications. Specifically, we looked at:

- ❑ The File and Directory classes, which provide static methods for enumerating files and directories.

- ❑ The FileInfo and DirectoryInfo classes, which enable you to work with a single file or directory. For the most part, they provide equivalent functionality to File and Directory classes, but deal with a single object.

- ❑ How backing stores are responsible for the physical storage and management of bytes of data.

- ❑ How the Stream class is the programmatic interface used to communicate to a backing store. Each backing store such as the file system or memory buffer provides its own class derived from Stream. This implements the basic functionality required from a backing store, and can also provide additional methods and properties specific to a given backing store.

- ❑ How the reader and writer classes layer functionality over a stream to abstract you from the underlying byte representation of primitive types, such as characters, strings, and floats.

- ❑ How the reader and writer classes use internal buffers for performance reasons.

- ❑ The System.Net classes, and how they provide a powerful way of writing network applications. The classes are safe to use in an ASP.NET page and are scalable.

- ❑ How to use regular expressions as a means of searching data using simple or very complex patterns.

In the next chapter, we'll look at building business objects.

17

.NET Components

Even with the great changes that Microsoft has cooked into the Common Language Runtime and the .NET Framework, there are still some basics of application design that remain constant. One of those constants is the benefit of *components*. Even with the advent of compiled ASP.NET pages written in multiple languages, good application design still requires the use of components.

While you may no longer gain the absolute benefits of speed seen when moving to COM components from scripted ASP pages, you can still gain the benefits of encapsulation and reusability that components provide. I don't know who came up with the adage that says, 'just because you can doesn't mean that you should', but that definitely holds true with the .NET platform when it comes to application design.

In the past, one of the main reasons for moving script code to components was to gain execution speed. Now, with pages being compiled and executed, that benefit is gone. So, does this mean that you should forego good application design and throw all code into ASP.NET pages? Just because you can doesn't mean that you should!

Components are still critical in the .NET Framework. This chapter won't go into detail about why you *should* use components; it will talk about *how* to use them. It is important to know how to build components, how to use the features of the CLR to extend components, and importantly how to deploy them.

In this chapter, we will look at building and deploying .NET components for use within ASP.NET applications. Specifically, you will look at:

- ❑ Writing *business objects* using the .NET Framework

- ❑ Creating a class in one language, and then inheriting from that class in a different language

- ❑ Using COM+ Services, such as transactions, from within .NET components

- ❑ Deploying components in .NET

Writing Business Objects

First, let's look at creating business objects that can be used by .NET applications. These business objects will perform the same types of functions that business objects in COM or other objects models do, plus they will be able to make use of all of the advantages offered by the .NET architecture and the CLR.

This section looks at how to create an object and then extend that object through inheritance. Then it looks at how to extend the functionality of an existing class and also how to utilize some of the COM+ component services within the .NET object. After creating the object, you compile it and place it in an assembly. Once the assembly is created, you will create an ASP.NET page to test the new object.

There are two concurrent examples through the chapter. They share exactly the same functionality, except that one is written in Visual Basic .NET and the other is written in C#. These objects will be tested from an ASP.NET page, but could just as easily be tested from a Windows Forms application or from a command line application. Use a simple text editor to create the files, and the command line compilers and tools to create the assemblies.

Building the Object

To create the object, you need to look at the:

- ❏   Guidelines for creating a component
- ❏   Attributes that can be set to describe a component

With all of that out of the way, you can move to actually creating the example objects.

Class Design Guidelines

When writing components for .NET, some of the existing component design guidelines can still be used. However, just as the .NET Framework is different from COM and COM+, some of the design guidelines you have used in the past are now implemented in a different way. In the past, there may have even been different guidelines depending on the language used. Now with .NET, those guidelines are unified. One of the other keys to using these design guidelines is that they have been adhered to by Microsoft in the creation of the System Frameworks themselves, along with all of the sample code that comes with the SDK.

Error Handling

Now that robust error handling (including structured exception handling) is part of the CLR, and therefore available to all languages supported by the CLR, you should use it wherever possible. The former practice of using error codes and checking return values or even `On Error Goto` has been replaced with catching exceptions and handling the errors at that point.

This doesn't mean you should use exceptions everywhere – exceptions are designed to handle *errors*, not something you should expect to happen. However, there are instances where error codes can come in handy. For example, if you are trying to open a file and the file doesn't exist, return a null value, since that error could be expected in normal use. But if the file system returns an I/O error, throw an exception, since that condition isn't normally expected.

Properties versus Methods

One of the most difficult choices in designing a component is choosing what type of interface to use. This holds true for all component-based architectures, not just .NET. Knowing when to use a property as opposed to a method and vice versa, is as much a matter of personal taste as are the following of design guidelines. The basic guidelines to follow are:

❑   If there is an internal data member being exposed outside the component, use a property.

❑   If the execution of the code causes some measurable side effect to the component or the environment, use a method.

❑   If the order of code execution is important, use a method. Since the CLR has the ability to short-circuit expression testing, a property may not be accessed when you expect it will. Let's look at an example of a short-circuited expression.

An object X has two properties, A and B. These properties do more than just expose an internal data member–they actually do some work as they return a value. For this example, they each return an integer between 1 and 10. They are being used in code that looks like this:

```
if (X.A > 5) AndAlso (X.B < 7) then
   ... ' do something
end if
```

If the evaluation of X.A returns a 4, then the first part of the Boolean expression is False. In order for an AndAlso statement to be True, both parts have to be True. The CLR knows this too, and seeing that the first part is False, it will skip or short-circuit the evaluation of X.B, since its value doesn't matter. However, because the code violated good design principles and did work during the evaluation of B, that work will not be performed in this case. This is probably not the desired effect.

Memory Management

Memory management is one of the most difficult things that most programmers face. Now that the operating system has gone to a flat memory model, developers don't have the issues from the days of Windows 3.1 about allocating memory. However, they still have had to deal with how and when to discard the memory. With the CLR handling most of the memory management for .NET components, there are only a few things that developers need to do differently when dealing with memory than in the past.

The CLR has the ability to create small, short-lived objects very quickly and cheaply. Thus you shouldn't be worried about creating objects that make the development easier to follow. According to performance testing done by Microsoft, the runtime can allocate nearly 10 million objects per second on a moderately fast machine. Also, objects running in the CLR will be garbage-collected by the runtime after they are no longer being referenced. This happens automatically, and keeps the developer from having to deal with memory leaks from improperly-freed objects. While automatic garbage collection does deal with a lot of headaches, there still have to be processor cycles dedicated to the garbage collector running. When it actually runs is also unpredictable, and could cause a temporary hiccup in performance.

Using Attributes

Attributes in the CLR allow developers to add additional information to the classes they have created. These are then available to the application using the component through the System.Reflection classes. You can use attributes to provide hints or flags to a number of different systems that may be using the component. Attributes can be used as compiler flags to tell the compiler how to handle the compilation of the class. They can be used by tools to provide more information about the usage of the component at design-time. This means developers can get away from having to embed comments in code simply as clues for the tool to know where certain parts of the code are. Attributes can also be used to identify the transaction characteristics of a class when interacting with the *Components Services* feature of the operating system.

The following two tables show the standard attributes for properties and events that are defined in the `System.ComponentModel` namespace in the CLR. As these attributes are already defined, they can be used by the developer without having to create a corresponding class for a custom attribute.

Here are the attributes common to events *and* properties:

Attribute	Description	Usage – default in bold
Browsable	Declares if this property should appear in the property window of a design tool.	`[Browsable (false | `**`true`**`)]`
Category	Used to group properties when being displayed by a design tool.	`[Category (categoryName)]`
Description	Help text displayed by the design tool when this property or event is selected.	`[Description (descriptionString)]`

The attributes for properties are as follows:

Attribute	Description	Usage – default in bold
Bindable	Declares if data should be bound to this property.	`[Bindable (`**`false`**` | true)]`
DefaultProperty	Indicates that this is the default property for the class.	`[DefaultProperty]`
DefaultValue	Sets a default value for the property.	`[DefaultValue (value)]`
Localizable	Indicates that a property can be localized. The compiler will cause all properties with this attribute to store the property in a resource file. The resources file can then be localized without having to modify any code.	`[Localizable (`**`false`**` | true)]`

The attribute for events is:

Attribute	Description	Usage
DefaultEvent	Specifies the default event for the class.	[DefaultEvent]

Sample Object

In this section you will see how to create a sample object,which will be used to encapsulate business and data access functionality – this is the typical usage for objects in the applications that most developers are creating. The business object will encapsulate the interaction with the IBuyAdventure database that is used in the case study discussed in Chapter 24. Since this is an example of how to build components rather than a full case study on a business and data component, the component will have limited functionality.

The component will have one property:

Property	Type	Usage
DatabaseConnection	String	The database connection string

The component will have three methods:

Method	Returns	Parameters	Usage
GetProductTypes	String Collection	*none*	Returns a string collection of all of the product types in the database.
GetProducts	DataSet	productType	Returns a DataSet containing the records for a specific product type.
AveragePrice	Single	productType	Returns a single value that represents the average price of the items of a specific product type.

With the interface defined, it is now time to write the component. As stated earlier, the component will be developed in both Visual Basic .NET and in C#. Let's start with the Visual Basic .NET version.

Visual Basic .NET Class Example

Here is how the final class looks when written in Visual Basic .NET:

```
Option Explicit
Option Strict

Imports System
Imports System.Data
Imports System.Data.SqlClient

Namespace BusObjectVB

  Public Class IBAProducts

    Private m_DSN As String

    Public Sub New ()
      MyBase.New
      m_DSN = ""
    End Sub

    Public Sub New(DSN As string)
      MyBase.New
      m_DSN = DSN
    End Sub

    Public Property DatabaseConnection As string
      Set
        m_DSN = value
      End Set
      Get
        Return m_DSN
      End Get
    End Property

    Public Function GetProductTypes () As DataSet
      If m_DSN = "" Then
        Throw(New ArgumentNullException("DatabaseConnection", _
                        "No value for the database connection string"))
      End If
      Dim myConnection As New SqlConnection(m_DSN)
      Dim sqlAdapter1 As New SqlDataAdapter("SELECT DISTINCT ProductType " _
                                & "FROM Products", myConnection)

      Dim types As New DataSet()
      sqlAdapter1.Fill(types, "ProdTypes")

      Return types
    End Function

    Public Function GetProducts ( productType As String) As DataSet
      If m_DSN = "" Then
        Throw(New ArgumentNullException("DatabaseConnection", _
```

```
                               "No value for the database connection string"))
           End If
           Dim myConnection As New SqlConnection(m_DSN)
           Dim sqlAdapter1 As New SqlDataAdapter("SELECT * FROM Products WHERE " _
                         & "ProductType='" & productType & "'", myConnection)

           Dim products As New DataSet()
           sqlAdapter1.Fill(products, "products")

           Return products
       End Function

       Public Function AveragePrice ( productType As string) As Double
           If m_DSN = "" Then
             Throw(New ArgumentNullException("DatabaseConnection", _
                           "No value for the database connection string"))
           End If
           Dim myConnection As New SqlConnection(m_DSN)

           Dim sqlAdapter1 As New SqlDataAdapter("SELECT AVG(UnitPrice) AS " _
                         & "AveragePrice FROM Products WHERE " _
                         & "ProductType='"+productType+"'", myConnection)

           Dim AvgPrice As New DataSet()
           sqlAdapter1.Fill(AvgPrice, "AveragePrice")

           Dim priceTable As DataTable
           priceTable = AvgPrice.Tables("AveragePrice")
           If (Not priceTable.Rows(0).IsNull("AveragePrice")) Then
             Return CDbl(priceTable.Rows(0)("AveragePrice"))
           Else
             Return 0
           End If
       End Function
     End Class
End Namespace
```

Let's break down each part and describe what it does and how.

Look at the object in detail. The first two statements are unique to Visual Basic. With its roots as a loosely-typed language, Visual Basic .NET has had some directives added to it to tell the compiler that it should do some level of type checking when compiling the application. The `Option Explicit` statement is familiar to Visual Basic programmers. It forces the declaration of all variables before they are used, and will generate a compiler error if a variable is used before it is declared. The `Option Strict` statement is introduced with Visual Basic .NET. It greatly limits the implicit data type conversions that Visual Basic has been able to do in the past. `Option Strict` also disallows any late binding. This will increase the performance in components since types are checked at compile-time, and not at runtime.

```
Option Explicit
Option Strict
```

The next section states which parts of the System Frameworks will be used in this object:

```
Imports System
Imports System.Data
Imports System.Data.SqlClient
```

You can actually use any part of the System Frameworks at any time in the code by simply referencing the full path to it – `System.Data.SqlClient.DataTable` – but that would begin to make the code cumbersome and unnecessarily long. By explicitly stating which parts of the System Frameworks the component will use, you can refer to the particular class without having to state the full path – `DataTable` – as shown in the example.

This object uses the `System` namespace, which contains the necessary base classes to build the object. The `System.Data` namespace contains the classes that make up the ADO.NET data access architecture. Since the component accesses data in a SQL Server 2000 database, the component also includes the `System.Data.SqlClient` namespace. This namespace contains the classes to access the SQL Server-managed provider.

The object will be encapsulated in its own unique namespace, `BusObjectVB`, so first declare all of the classes that make up the object within that namespace. The business component is defined as a class – after creating an instance of it in the program it will then be an object:

```
Namespace BusObjectVB

    Public Class IBAProducts
```

Within the object, there will be one private variable, which will be used to hold the database connection string. The next two methods are the constructors for the class. The constructor is automatically called by the runtime when an object is instantiated. There are actually two constructors. The first one takes no parameters and is therefore called the default constructor:

```
    Private m_DSN As String

    Public Sub New ()
      MyBase.New
      m_DSN = ""
    End Sub
```

The second constructor takes a parameter, `DSN`, and will set the database connection string at the same time as the object is created:

```
    Public Sub New(DSN As string)
      MyBase.New
      m_DSN = DSN
    End Sub
```

Since a constructor cannot return any values, it is declared as a `Sub` rather than a `Function`. In Visual Basic, you must *explicitly* call the constructor for the base class, using the `MyBase.New` statement.

While the second constructor sets the database connection string when the object is created, the object needs to provide a way to set and read it at other times. Since the member variable holding this data is marked as private, there is a property function to set and retrieve the value. The external name of the property is `DatabaseConnection`:

```
Public Property DatabaseConnection As String
  Set
    m_DSN = value
  End Set
  Get
     Return m_DSN
  End Get
End Property
```

Next, look at the methods that work with the information in the database.

The first method, `GetProductTypes`, will retrieve a listing of the product types for the products stored in the database. This will return the listing to the calling program in a `DataSet`. A `DataSet` represents an in-memory cache of data. This means that it is a *copy* of the data in the database, so there is no underlying connection to the stored data. To access the database, you first need to connect to it. The `SqlConnection` object provides this functionality and when the `Open` method is called, it will connect to the database using the connection string that was stored in the private member variable `m_DSN`.

It is therefore important that this value be set properly. If the user of the component does not set the value of the `DatabaseConnection` property, the object won't be able to open the database. The best way to indicate this is to throw an exception. The object uses the `Throw` statement and passes it an instance of the `ArgumentNullException` class. This version of the constructor for this class takes two strings–the parameter that was Null and a text description of the error:

```
Public Function GetProductTypes () As DataSet
  If m_DSN = "" Then
    Throw(New ArgumentNullException("DatabaseConnection", _
                     "No value for the database connection string"))
  End If
  Dim myConnection As New SqlConnection(m_DSN)
```

To retrieve the desired information from the database, use a SQL query. To process the query, use the `SqlDataAdapter`. When you create the object, pass in the text of the SQL query that will be executed by this object. Also, tell the object which database connection object to use to access the data. That is the object that was created in the previous steps. The creation of this object will automatically open the database connection:

```
Dim sqlAdapter1 As New SqlDataAdapter("SELECT DISTINCT ProductType " _
                        & "FROM Products", myConnection)
```

With the mechanism for retrieving the data from the database, you need a place to store it to pass it back to the caller. This will be in a `DataSet` object. Create a new instance of this class and call it `types`. The data will be placed in this object by using the `Fill` method of the `SqlDataAdapter` class. This method takes the destination `DataSet` object as well as a name to represent the data within the data set. To send the data back to the caller, return the `DataSet` object `types`:

```
Dim types As New DataSet()
sqlAdapter1.Fill(types, "ProdTypes")

Return types
End Function
```

The next method, GetProducts, shown in the following code will retrieve the list of products for a specified product type. Specify the product type by passing in the product type string. The list of products will be returned as a DataSet. The main part of the method is the same as the previous method; connect to the database and fill up a DataSet object with the information needed:

```
Public Function GetProducts ( productType As String) As DataSet
    If m_DSN = "" Then
        Throw(New ArgumentNullException("DatabaseConnection", _
                        "No value for the database connection string"))
    End If
    Dim myConnection As New SqlConnection(m_DSN)
    Dim sqlAdapter1 As New SqlDataAdapter("SELECT * FROM Products WHERE " _
                & "ProductType='" & productType & "'", myConnection)

    Dim products As New DataSet()
    sqlAdapter1.Fill(products, "products")

    Return products
End Function
```

The resulting filled DataSet object can then be returned to the calling application.

Next, look at the method to calculate the average selling price of the items of a particular type:

```
Public Function AveragePrice ( productType As string) As Double
    If m_DSN = "" Then
        Throw(New ArgumentNullException("DatabaseConnection", _
                        "No value for the database connection string"))
    End If
    Dim myConnection As New SqlConnection(m_DSN)

    Dim sqlAdapter1 As New SqlDataAdapter("SELECT AVG(UnitPrice) AS " _
                & "AveragePrice FROM Products WHERE " _
                & "ProductType='"+productType+"'", myConnection)
```

The method to calculate the average selling price for a product type will pass that value back as a return value of type double. Just as with the previous method, the one parameter for this method will be the product type of the desired product group. The database access code is again very similar – the primary difference being that the SQL statement calculates an average rather than returning a set of rows from the database:

```
Dim AvgPrice As New DataSet()
sqlAdapter1.Fill(AvgPrice, "AveragePrice")

Dim priceTable As DataTable
priceTable = AvgPrice.Tables("AveragePrice")
```

With the results of the database query in the DataSet object, take a look at the contents of the data to see what the average price was. To examine the data directly, first grab the table that contains the result of the query from the DataSet. In the Fill method, ADO.NET put the results of the query into a table named AveragePrice. Then to get a reference to that specific table from the DataSet, retrieve that table by name from the Tables collection.

If there was no data returned, you will have a table with no rows in it. If this is the case, then return the average price as 0. If there is one row in the table – a SQL statement to calculate an average will return at most one row – then look at the value contained in the field named `AveragePrice` and return that value as the average price for the product type. The field named `AveragePrice` does not exist in the physical database, but is an alias that is created with the SQL `SELECT` statement to hold the results of the `AVG` function:

```
        If (Not priceTable.Rows(0).IsNull("AveragePrice")) Then
          Return CDbl(priceTable.Rows(0)("AveragePrice"))
        Else
          Return 0
        End If
      End Function
    End Class
End Namespace
```

This is the end of the Visual Basic .NET class. Before compiling and testing it, let's look at the same component coded in C#.

C# Class Example

Here is the same class written in C#:

```
using System;
using System.Data;
using System.Data.SqlClient;

namespace BusObjectCS {

public class IBAProducts {

  private string m_DSN;

  public  IBAProducts () {
    m_DSN="";
  }

  public  IBAProducts (string DSN) {
    m_DSN = DSN;
  }

  public string DatabaseConnection {
    set { m_DSN = value; }
    get { return m_DSN; }
  }
  public DataSet GetProducts (string productType) {
    if (m_DSN == "")
    {
        throw new ArgumentNullException("DatabaseConnection",
                      "No value for the database connection string");
    }
    SqlConnection myConnection = new SqlConnection(m_DSN);
    SqlDataAdapter sqlAdapter1 = new SqlDataAdapter(
```

```
            "SELECT * FROM Products WHERE ProductType='"+productType+"'", myConnection);
        DataSet products = new DataSet();
        sqlAdapter1.Fill(products, "products");

        return products;
    }

    public DataSet GetProductTypes () {

        if (m_DSN == "")
        {
            throw new ArgumentNullException("DatabaseConnection",
                            "No value for the database connection string");
        }
        SqlConnection dbConnection = new SqlConnection(m_DSN);
        dbConnection.Open();

        SqlDataAdapter sqlAdapter1 = new SqlDataAdapter(
                "SELECT DISTINCT ProductType FROM Products", dbConnection);

        DataSet types = new DataSet();
        sqlAdapter1.Fill(types, "ProdTypes");

        return types;
    }

    public Double AveragePrice (string productType) {
        if (m_DSN == "")
        {
            throw new ArgumentNullException("DatabaseConnection",
                            "No value for the database connection string");
        }
        SqlConnection dbConnection = new SqlConnection(m_DSN);
        dbConnection.Open();

        SqlDataAdapter sqlAdapter1 = new SqlDataAdapter(
            "SELECT AVG(UnitPrice) AS AveragePrice FROM Products WHERE " +
            "ProductType='" + productType + "'", dbConnection);

        DataSet AvgPrice = new DataSet();
        sqlAdapter1.Fill(AvgPrice, "AveragePrice");

        DataTable priceTable;
        priceTable = AvgPrice.Tables["AveragePrice"];
        if (priceTable.Rows.Count > 0)
        {
            return (Double)priceTable.Rows[0]["AveragePrice"];
        }
        else
            return 0;
    }
}
}
```

Let's look at this object in detail. Focus on the differences between the C# version and the Visual Basic .NET version. The functionality is exactly the same.

The first set of statements is used to specify the System Framework namespaces that will be used by this class. Rather than using the Visual Basic .NET `Imports` keyword, C# uses the `using` keyword. As before, use the same three namespaces as the Visual Basic .NET version. In the Visual Basic .NET version, you had `Option Explicit` and `Option Strict` statements. Since by default C# is a strongly-typed language, these statements (or rather a C# equivalent) are not necessary:

```
using System;
using System.Data;
using System.Data.SqlClient;
```

The next step is to declare the namespace and the class. Note that the name of the class is the same as the Visual Basic .NET version. This is OK, and both can even run at the same time, because of the namespace. Class names only need to be unique *within* a namespace.

```
namespace BusObjectCS {
public class IBAProducts {
```

The next major difference in the two implementations comes with the way that constructors are defined. In C#, a constructor is defined with a method that has the same name as the class. In Visual Basic .NET, the constructor for a class is always named `New`. In C#, the base class constructor is called automatically by the compiler:

```
private string m_DSN;

public  IBAProducts () {
  m_DSN="";
}

public  IBAProducts (string DSN) {
  m_DSN = DSN;
}
```

A property is defined in a similar way to Visual Basic .NET, but uses a different syntax to declare the accessor methods. Where C# uses a `set` (or `get`) statement followed by a block delimited by braces, Visual Basic .NET uses a specific `Set...End Set` (or `Get...End Get`) block to denote the accessor methods:

```
public string DatabaseConnection {
  set { m_DSN = value; }
  get { return m_DSN; }
}
```

The remainder of the component is identical to the C# version, except for the syntax differences. With both of the components created, let's move on to the next step: compilation.

Compiling the Classes

As seen earlier in the book, the .NET architecture executes code stored in the MSIL format. This intermediate language is created from the sourcecode of the various languages supported by the CLR. You have already created the sourcecode for your components. The next step is to compile this sourcecode into the MSIL version. This is done by executing the appropriate compiler with the proper arguments, based on the language and the destination.

Compiling the VB.NET Class

To compile the Visual Basic .NET component, use a batch file that should be run from the command line. This file is named `makevb.bat` and is as follows:

```
vbc /out:bin\BusObjectvb.dll /t:library sampleObject.vb /r:System.Data.dll
/r:System.dll /r:System.XML.dll
```

Take a look at the parameters that are passed to the compiler. The first parameter, `/out`, defines the output file that the MSIL code will be placed in. In this example, the compiled output is placed in the file named `BusObjectvb.dll`, and stored in the `bin` subdirectory below the directory where the source file resides. If the command did not include an `/out` parameter, the compiler would have automatically created the filename based on the name of the source file and the target type and placed it in the current directory.

The next parameter, `/t`, is used to specify the type of output file format the compiler should create. This is a shortened version of the `/target` parameter; either version can be legally used. There are four possible values for this parameter:

- ❑ `/target:exe`: This tells the compiler to create a command line executable program. This is the default value, so if the `/target` parameter is not included, an `.exe` file will be created.

- ❑ `/target:library`: This tells the compiler to create a DLL file that will contain an assembly that consists of all the source files passed to the compiler. The compiler will also automatically create the manifest for this assembly.

- ❑ `/target:module`: This tells the compiler to create a DLL, but not to create a manifest for it. In order for the module to be used by the .NET Framework, it will need to be manually added to an assembly using the Assembly Generation tool (`AL.EXE`). This tool allows you to create the assembly manifest information manually, and then add modules to it.

- ❑ `/target:winexe`: This tells the compiler to create a Windows Forms application.

The next parameter is the name of the file to be compiled. In your example, the source file is named `sampleObject.vb`. The file extension is not critical, but it does make it easier to recognize the type of source file without having to open it up. If there are multiple source files, specify multiple source files on the same command line. They will be combined into the file type specified by the `/target` parameter. The final set of parameters indicates the other assemblies that are referenced from within the component.

Compiling the C# Class

To make it easier to run the compiler during development, create a batch file that will execute the C# compiler with all of the proper parameters. This file is called `makecs.bat` and looks like this:

```
csc /out:bin\BusObjectcs.dll /t:library sampleObject.cs /r:System.Data.dll
/r:System.dll /r:System.XML.dll
```

As you can see, it is identical to the `makevb.bat` file except for three small changes. First, since the batch file calls the C# compiler rather than the Visual Basic .NET compiler, the file to execute is `csc` instead of vbc. The next difference is the name of the output file; since the C# component is in a separate assembly, it gets a different name of `BusObjectcs.dll`. Finally, the source file that contains the C# sourcecode is called `sampleObject.cs`.

Testing the Class

Now that you have created the two identical objects, the next step is to test them. For this test, access these components from within an ASP.NET page.

The first page, `ProductTypes.aspx`, will test the `GetProductTypes` method. This page will simply be used to display the results of a call to this method. The sourcecode for the page looks like this:

```
<%@ Page Language="C#" Description="Component Test Program" %>
<%@ Import Namespace="System.Data" %>
<%@ Import Namespace="BusObjectCS" %>
<%@ Import Namespace="BusObjectVB" %>
<html>
<script language="C#" runat="server">

void Page_Load(Object sender, EventArgs evArgs){
//  BusObjectCS.IBAProducts objProducts = new BusObjectCS.IBAProducts();
   BusObjectVB.IBAProducts objProducts = new BusObjectVB.IBAProducts();

   String dsn = "server=localhost;uid=sa;pwd=;database=IBuyAdventure";

   objProducts.DatabaseConnection = dsn;

   DataSet prodTypes = objProducts.GetProductTypes();

   productList.DataSource = prodTypes;
   productList.DataBind();

}

</script>

<body>
   <h3><font face="Verdana">List of Product Types</font></h3>
   <asp:DataList id="productList" runat="server">
     <HeaderTemplate>
       <table border="1">
         <tr><th>Click to Display list of products</th></tr>
     </HeaderTemplate>

     <ItemTemplate>
       <tr>
         <td align="center">
         <%# DataBinder.Eval(Container.DataItem, "ProductType",
           "<a href=\"displayProducts.aspx?PID={0}\">{0}</a>") %>
         </td>
       </tr>
     </ItemTemplate>

     <FooterTemplate>
       </table>
     </FooterTemplate>
```

```
        </asp:DataList>
    </body>
</html>
```

The first part of the page sets up the language to use, as well as the namespaces of the assemblies that will be used on the page:

```
<%@ Page Language="C#" Description="Component Test Program" %>
<%@ Import Namespace="System.Data" %>
<%@ Import Namespace="BusObjectCS" %>
<%@ Import Namespace="BusObjectVB" %>
```

The code in this page is written using C#. The language used in the ASP.NET page does not have to correlate to the language that was used in the business components. Since both the page and the components will be compiled down to MSIL before they are executed, the language they are written in does not need to correspond.

Also include the namespaces of the assemblies being used. Even though the component is not calling any of the methods from the `System.Data` namespace, it is using one of the classes (`DataSet`) as a return value from the method in the component. In order for the page to understand how to deal with this class, add the namespace that contains it as an `@Import` to the page. Since this page will be used to test both the C# and Visual Basic .NET versions of the component, import the namespaces for both. There are no drawbacks in doing this, as the different namespaces guarantee that there will be no name conflicts, and the compiler is smart enough not to load a namespace if there is nothing in the code that references it.

The `Page_Load` method will be working with the data provided by the business component. This test page will be used to test both components. Since each component has *exactly* the same interface (properties and methods), you can use the same local variable to represent the object to test. You can simply have two lines (of which one is commented out) in the page that create the object in the language you are testing with. In the test page, the first line creates the C# version of the component, and the second the Visual Basic .NET version:

```
void Page_Load(Object sender, EventArgs evArgs){
//  BusObjectCS.IBAProducts objProducts = new BusObjectCS.IBAProducts();
    BusObjectVB.IBAProducts objProducts = new BusObjectVB.IBAProducts();
```

The component needs to know from where to retrieve its data. Pass in a database connection string as the `DatabaseConnection` property of the object. This value is simply stored in the page as a string. In a production environment, values like database connection strings are usually stored in the `web.config` file for the ASP.NET application:

```
String dsn = "server=localhost;uid=sa;pwd=;database=IBuyAdventure";

objProducts.DatabaseConnection = dsn;
```

This example uses the database from the IBuyAdventure case study in Chapter 24. Follow the instructions in the `readme.txt` file in the database folder to set up the database in SQL Server 2000.

Once the instance of the class has been created and initialized with the proper database connection string, call the `GetProductTypes` method to return the list of product types. This data will be passed back as a `DataSet`, which in turn will serve as the data source for the `asp:DataList` element named `productList` that will actually display the data. By calling the `DataBind` method, the values in the `DataSet` will be rendered out into the `DataList` element:

```
DataSet prodTypes = objProducts.GetProductTypes();
productList.DataSthece = prodTypes;
productList.DataBind();
```

The `asp:DataList` will use a template to add some formatting to the data. The header and footer will simply begin and end the `TABLE` element being used to display the data. The `ItemTemplate` template sets up the format for each row in the table. In each row, there will be one column. This will be the product type string as a hyperlink to the page named `displayProducts.aspx`. The value of the product type will be passed to this page as part of the query string:

```
<ItemTemplate>
  <tr>
    <td align="center">
    <%# DataBinder.Eval(Container.DataItem, "ProductType",
      "<a href=\"displayProducts.aspx?PID={0}\">{0}</a>") %>
    </td>
  </tr>
</ ItemTemplate>

<FooterTemplate>
  </table>
</ FooterTemplate>
```

When this page is displayed in the browser, it shows Figure 17-1:

Figure 17-1

When the user clicks on any of the hyperlinks, they will be taken to the detail test page called `displayProducts.aspx`. The page's sourcecode looks like this:

```
<%@ Page Language="VB" Description="Component Test Program" Debug="true" %>
<%@ Import Namespace="BusObjectCS" %>
<%@ Import Namespace="BusObjectVB" %>
<%@ Import Namespace="System.Data" %>

<html>
<script runat="server">
Sub Page_Load(sender As Object, evtArgs As EventArgs)
   Dim dsn As String = "server=localhost;uid=sa;pwd=;database=IBuyAdventure"

'  Dim objProducts = New BusObjectCS.IBAProducts()
   Dim objProducts = New BusObjectVB.IBAProducts()

   objProducts.DatabaseConnection = dsn

   Dim products As DataSet = objProducts.GetProducts(Request.Params("PID"))

   prodGrid.DataSthece = products
   prodGrid.DataBind()

   avgPrice.Text = objProducts.AveragePrice(Request.Params("PID")).ToString()
End sub

</script>

<body>

<h2>Average price for products in this category =
   <asp:Label runat="server" id="avgPrice" /></h2>

   <h3>List of Products</h3>

<asp:DataGrid id="prodGrid" runat="server" ShowHeader="False">
</asp:DataGrid>

</body>
</html>
```

In this page, we use the final two methods of the business component. The first thing to do in the page, however, is to make sure that the proper namespaces are included with it:

```
<%@ Page Language="VB" Description="Component Test Program" Debug="true" %>
<%@ Import Namespace="BusObjectCS" %>
<%@ Import Namespace="BusObjectVB" %>
<%@ Import Namespace="System.Data" %>
```

The methods in this page will be returning a double value from one and a `DataSet` object from the other. In order for the code on this page to understand how to work with the `DataSet` class, import the `System.Data` namespace into the page. As in the previous page, import both the C# and Visual Basic .NET versions of the components.

The first part of the `Page_Load` method is the same as the previous page. There are statements to create the object in both Visual Basic .NET and in C#, but only one of these will be active when the page is run, the other will be commented out. In fact, if for some reason both lines were left in the page when it was executed, the C# object will be created first. Then the VB object will be created and assigned to the same variable name. When that happens, the C# object will be marked for disposal, and will be destroyed the next time the CLR garbage collector is run. So the page ends up with a Visual Basic .NET component:

```
Sub Page_Load(sender As Object, evtArgs As EventArgs)
   Dim dsn As String = "server=localhost;uid=sa;pwd=;database=IBuyAdventure"

'  Dim objProducts = New BusObjectCS.IBAProducts()
   Dim objProducts = New BusObjectVB.IBAProducts()

   objProducts.DatabaseConnection = dsn
```

Retrieve the list of products for the requested product type by using the `GetProducts` method. The product type has been passed in on the URL, and can be retrieved from the `Request.Params` collection. The information is returned as a `DataSet` object. Use the values in this collection as the source to populate the `DataGrid`:

```
Dim products As DataSet = objProducts.GetProducts(Request.Params("PID"))

prodGrid.DataSthece = products
prodGrid.DataBind()
```

The other piece of information to display on the page is the average price for all of the products of this product type. This is retrieved by calling the `AveragePrice` function of the business component. This method will return a double value. Since the `Text` property of the `Label` control requires a string, convert the double value to a string using the `ToString` function:

```
avgPrice.Text = objProducts.AveragePrice(Request.Params("PID")).ToString()
End sub
```

All of the difficult work in the page is done in the `Page_Load` method. All that needs to be done in the display portion is provide the proper server-side controls to display the information. The `asp:Label` element is a server-side control that is used to display the average selling price for the product type. The `asp:DataGrid` element will display a simple table that contains the list of products for that product type:

```
<h2>Average price for products in this category =
   <asp:Label runat="server" id="avgPrice" /></h2>

   <h3>List of Products</h3>

<asp:DataGrid id="prodGrid" runat="server" ShowHeader="False">
</asp:DataGrid>
```

On selecting a hyperlink from the previous page, the browser will show something like Figure 17-2:

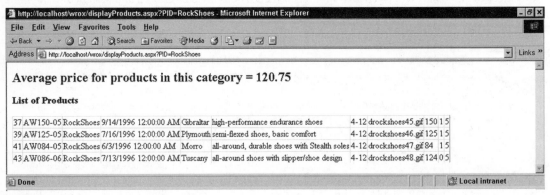

Figure 17-2

Cross-Language Inheritance

In the past, it has been quite difficult (nearly impossible, actually) to have components written in one language subclass and extend a component written in another. You couldn't take a class written in C++ and inherit from it in Visual Basic to create a new object – things like that just weren't possible. You also had no way of taking a compiled binary component – even one written in the same language – and deriving a new object from it, without having the sourcecode for the parent object, or at least a header file. It came down to the fact that there just wasn't enough information about the compiled components embedded in them to allow you to derive a new object.

Now with the CLR however, you have the ability to do just that. The metadata that is associated with a .NET class provides enough information, even in compiled form, to allow you to derive a new class from an existing class. The other cool thing that the CLR allows is for you to derive a new class in a different language. In the past, you actually had to have the sourcecode for the base class in order to derive a new class–and that new class had to be written in the same language as the base class. But since all CLR languages compile down to an intermediate language – MSIL – the new class can be in whatever CLR-compliant language you choose.

Cross-language inheritance, as this is known, also makes debugging much easier. It doesn't matter what language the code was written in when debugging. Simply run the debugger on the code, and then the CLR will trace from one language to the next *automatically*, *transparent* to the developer. It can even handle exceptions across languages and not worry about translating or modifying the information as it switches languages – the CLR makes that all transparent.

The other key advantage of cross-language inheritance is that it makes a great way to create class libraries. If you cast your memory back a few years to the *Microsoft Foundation Classes* (MFC) introduced by Microsoft to build Windows applications, you have an example of a class library. MFC was written in C++, so it could be used to create C++ Windows applications or components. Since MFC is innately tied to C++, a Visual Basic developer could not directly use any of the capabilities of MFC, though. With the .NET Framework, Microsoft has written those in C#, but the cross-language inheritance capabilities of the CLR allow any supported language to both use the framework as well as create new classes that inherit from classes within the framework.

Cross-Language Inheritance Example

To show how cross-language inheritance works, let's look at a quick example component. In this example, take the C# class that was created earlier in the chapter and derive another class from it. This class will be written in Visual Basic .NET and will override the function that calculates the average selling price. The first step is to modify the C# class so that the function can be overridden.

To do this, add the `virtual` modifier to the function declaration for the `AveragePrice` function in the C# class. In C#, properties and methods are non-virtual by default, which means that they can't be overridden in any derived classes. Without the `virtual` keyword, you would get an error message when compiling the derived class that was trying to override this method:

```
public virtual Double AveragePrice (string productType) {
```

This points out an interesting design dilemma when creating the classes. If there are methods that you think might be overridden in a derived class, it probably makes sense to mark these as `virtual` when you first create the class. In the previous example, this wasn't done, so now you have to go back and re-deploy the original component. Likewise, if there is a function that you don't want overridden in a derived class, make sure that it is not defined as `virtual`, and anyone that derives from the class will not be able to override it.

Next, let's look at the new class, written in Visual Basic .NET, derived from this C# class:

```vb
Option Explicit
Option Strict

Imports BusObjectCS
Imports System.Data

Namespace SubBusinessClass
   Public Class SubIBAProducts
   Inherits IBAProducts
   Public Overrides Function AveragePrice ( productType As String) As Double

      Dim iAverage As Double

      iAverage = MyBase.AveragePrice(productType)

      Return CDbl(iAverage * 0.65)
   End Function

   Public Function GetNewestProduct (productType As String) As String

      Dim myProducts As DataSet
      myProducts = GetProducts(productType)

      Dim myDataView As DataView = New DataView(myProducts.Tables("products"))
      myDataView.Sort = "ProductIntroductionDate DESC"
```

```
        Return myDataView(0)("ProductCode").ToString()

    End Function

    End Class
End Namespace
```

As with all Visual Basic .NET components, set both `Option Explicit` and `Option Strict` so that the compiler takes care of a lot of the error checking and code validation. These will greatly help to reduce any runtime errors that may occur.

Since this class will be derived from the C# version of the business component, import the namespace for that class so that the compiler will understand the references to that class that are made in the new component:

```
Imports BusObjectCS
Imports System.Data
```

There will also be a `DataSet` object in the derived class, so import the namespace containing that class as well. This is an important concept. Even though the base class imported this namespace, you still need to import it here. This is because the namespaces are not inherited by the derived class – they are internally used by the base class, but not available externally.

The next two lines in the code are nearly identical to the VB.NET component created earlier. Define a `SubBusinessClass` namespace, and within that namespace create a public class called `SubIBAProducts`. Remember that class names only need to have unique names within the same namespace.

This means that you could have named the class `IBAProducts`, as in both original classes, and still no naming conflicts will occur. The key line in this class is the next line. The `Inherits` statement defines the class that the class being defined is inheriting from. It must be the *first* line in the class definition after the class declaration:

```
Namespace SubBusinessClass
    Public Class SubIBAProducts
    Inherits IBAProducts
```

The first method in the derived class will be the one to override. When defining a derived class, any public properties and methods from the parent class automatically become public properties or methods of the derived class. This automatically produces the two constructors of the parent class, along with the one property and three methods:

```
Public Overrides Function AveragePrice ( productType As String) As Double

    Dim iAverage As Double

    iAverage = MyBase.AveragePrice(productType)

    Return CDbl(iAverage * 0.65)
End Function
```

However, this derived class changes the implementation of the third method. This is why in the base class the virtual keyword was added to the method declaration – to allow for changing its implementation. The new implementation will not have the virtual keyword (unless you want to further derive from this class and override the method again) but rather an Overrides keyword. This keyword means that the function declared here will replace the base class version of this function. In order to override a function in a base class, the overriding function must have the same declaration – function name, parameter list, and return type.

In the body of the function, utilize some of the functionality of the base class implementation. To do this, call the base class version of the function directly. Use the MyBase keyword as a preface to the function call so that the compiler knows which version to call. The value that is returned from the function is then modified and returned as the new return value for this function. There is no requirement to use any of the base class implementation; sometimes it is better to leverage the code that is in there rather than having to rewrite it.

The other method in the derived class (shown in the following snippet) is not found in the base class. This new method will only be accessible to instances of the derived class. In this method, calculate the newest product in a specific product category. There are two ways to do this. First, write a whole new method from scratch that had all of the database code necessary to execute the proper SQL query to obtain this information. This would in essence duplicate a great deal of code from the base class – not normally the most efficient way to write code.

```
Public Function GetNewestProduct (productType As String) As String

    Dim myProducts As DataSet
    myProducts = GetProducts(productType)

    Dim myDataView As DataView = New DataView(myProducts.Tables("products"))
    myDataView.Sort = "ProductIntroductionDate DESC"

    Return myDataView(0)("ProductCode").ToString()

End Function
```

The other way to do this is to leverage a method from the base class – GetProducts – and perform some other work to determine the newest product. Notice that the call to GetProducts does not have to be prefaced with MyBase. This is because there isn't a function declared in the class that overrides the function in the base class. The compiler automatically figures out that it needs to call the implementation of this method from the base class.

With the DataSet that contains all of the products for a particular product type, next obtain a DataView that represents the table containing the information. Sorting the DataView in reverse order by ProductIntroductionDate ensures that the first product in the table is the newest. You can then just grab that row's ProductCode and return it from the new function.

To test this component, first compile it and then modify the test ASP.NET page so that this component is used instead of the original component. When executing displayProducts_ovr.aspx (the modified page), see that the new value for average price is now displayed.

Then, add some code to display the newest product as shown in Figure 17-3:

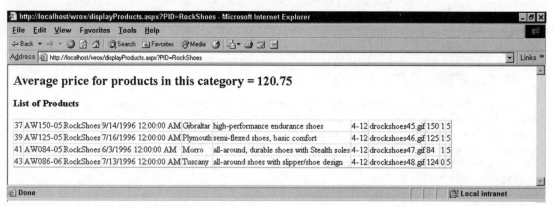

Figure 17-3

Transactions in .NET

To provide integration with COM+, the CLR provides the same declarative transaction model. This allows managed objects to participate in existing transactions. Use these transactions from within ASP.NET pages, and also from within .NET components.

At the ASP.NET page level, you can add a page-level directive for this:

```
<%@ Page Transaction="Required" %>
```

The allowable values are:

Value	Description
Disabled	Transactional context will be ignored. This is the default.
NotSupported	The page does not run within a transaction. The object context is created without a transaction.
Supported	The page runs within the scope of an existing transaction, if one is active. If no transaction scope is active, the page runs without a transaction.
Required	The page runs within the scope of a transaction, either an existing one, or creating one if no existing transaction exists.
RequiresNew	The page requires a new transaction, and one will be created for each page request.

To participate in the transaction success or failure, you can either rely on transaction `AutoComplete` or explicitly commit or abort the transaction. With `AutoComplete` enabled, the page will vote to commit the transaction if the page runs without throwing an exception. `AutoComplete` is enabled by default on a page, so if the page completes successfully, then the page will vote to commit.

Explicitly control the transaction result by calling the methods of the `ContextUtil` class. To vote to abort a transaction, call:

```
ContextUtil.SetAbort()
```

And, to vote to commit a transaction, call:

```
ContextUtil.SetComplete()
```

For transacted components, create a serviced component.

Serviced Components

A *serviced component* is one that is automatically serviced by the Windows Component Services, allowing managed classes to live within the existing `ObjectContext`. The key thing here is that the code is still managed, so you get all of the managed benefits, with the addition of transactional integration. A serviced component is a .NET component, but it is hosted inside of a COM+ application, and therefore can access the services offered by COM+.

A serviced component has its configuration information held by the COM+ catalog. When using a serviced component within an application, COM+ will create a context service layer based on the attributes you have assigned to the serviced component. Basically, the context service layer runs within COM+ Services, and communicates with the serviced components, which are still running within .NET.

There are several steps to go through to create serviced components:

1. Derive the class from the `System.EnterpriseServices.ServicedComponent` class.

2. Add the `TransactionAttribute` to the class.

3. Create a *strong name* for the assembly.

4. Add assembly attributes to identify the strong name, and the COM+ application name.

5. Register the assembly with the COM+ catalog. This can be manually done, or under certain circumstances, done automatically (this is called *lazy registration*).

Creating a Serviced Component Class

Creating the class and adding the attributes is simple. Here is an example written in Visual Basic .NET:

```
Option Explicit
Option Strict

Imports System.EnterpriseServices
Imports System.Reflection

<assembly:AssemblyKeyFile("BankVB.snk")>
```

```
<assembly:ApplicationName("DotNetBank")>

Namespace Wrox

<Transaction(TransactionOption.RequiresNew)> Public Class BankVB
  Inherits ServicedComponent

    Public Sub Transfer(FromAC As String, ToAC As String, Amt As Decimal)
      Dim f As String = "Transferring " & Amt.ToString() & " from " _
                        & FromAC & " to " & ToAC
      ContextUtil.SetComplete()
    End Sub

  End Class

End Namespace
```

Look at the attributes that have been added to this class. The first two are:

```
<assembly:AssemblyKeyFile("BankVB.snk")>
<assembly:ApplicationName("DotNetBank")>
```

The `AssemblyKeyFile` attribute is used to indicate the file that contains the public and private keys for the strong name for this assembly. Later in this chapter, you will look at strong-named assemblies. These types of assemblies are required to have multiple versions of an assembly executable at the same time on the same system. The `ApplicationName` attribute defines the COM+ application that this .NET component will execute within. If the application is not found, then COM+ will create an application with the name supplied – in this case `DotNetBank`.

The other attribute that has been included with this component is the `Transaction` attribute. This attribute specifies the transaction parameter for this component. In this case, make sure that the component executes inside a new transaction. The parameter passed is an enum defined as `TransactionOption.RequiresNew`:

```
<Transaction(TransactionOption.RequiresNew)>
```

The C# version of the serviced component is nearly identical to the Visual Basic .NET version. The only difference is the syntax that is used to denote the attributes within the code. Whereas the Visual Basic .NET version uses `<...>` to delineate the attributes, the C# version uses `[...]` to indicate the attributes:

```
using System.EnterpriseServices;
using System.Reflection;

[assembly:AssemblyKeyFile("BankCS.snk")]
[assembly:ApplicationName("DotNetBank")]

namespace Wrox

  [Transaction(TransactionOption.Required)]
  public class BankVB : ServicedComponent
  {
    public void Transfer(string FromAC, string ToAC, decimal Amt)
    {
      string f = "Transferring " + Amt.ToString() + " from " +
```

```
                                        FromAC + " to " + ToAC;

            ContextUtil.SetComplete();
        }
    }
}
```

Additional Assembly Attributes

As well as the `ApplicationName` attribute, you can also add COM+ component details such as:

- ❏   `ApplicationActivation`, to determine how the assembly is activated (`Library` or `Server`)
- ❏   `ApplicationID`, to specify a GUID
- ❏   `Description`, to give the assembly a description

For example, in Visual Basic .NET these would be:

```
<assembly:ApplicationActivation(ActivationOption.Library)>
<assembly:ApplicationID("guid")>
<assembly:Description(".NET bank assembly")>
```

Accessing COM+ Context

Use the `System.EnterpriseServices.ContextUtil` class to access the COM+ context from the .NET-serviced component. There are no major performance penalties since the cost to transition into COM+ context is very small. The context (including transactions) flows with the call, so transactions automatically flow.

Registering the Serviced Component

Classes using COM+ services must be registered, which can be done using the Register Services tool. The syntax is:

```
regsvcs [Options] AssemblyName
```

Where `Options` can be one of the following:

Option	Description
/fc	Find or create a target application. This is a default.
/c	Create the target application, generating an error if it already exists.
/exapp	Expect an existing application.
/tlb:tlbfile	Filename for the exported type library.
/appname:name	Use the specified name for the application.

Table continued on following page

Option	Description
/parname:*name*	Use the specified name or ID for the target partition.
/extlb	Use an existing type library.
/reconfig	Reconfigure the existing target application. This is a default.
/noreconfig	Do not reconfigure the existing target application.
/u	Uninstall the target application.
/componly	Configure only the components, not methods or interfaces.
/nologo	Suppress logo output.
/quiet	Suppress logo and success output.

Using this utility performs the following actions:

❏ Loads the assembly

❏ Registers the assembly

❏ Generates a type library

❏ Registers the type library

❏ Installs the type library into the COM+ application

❏ Configures the COM+ application

For example, to register the bank assemblies, you will use the regsvcs command line tool, as seen in Figure 17-4:

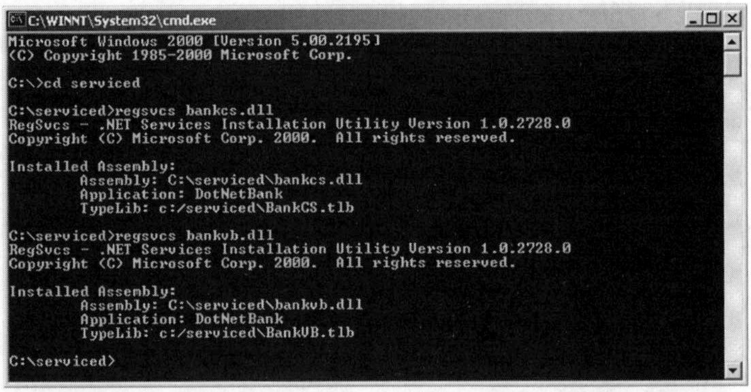

Figure 17-4

In examining the COM+ Component Services, you'll see the .NET components as in Figure 17-5:

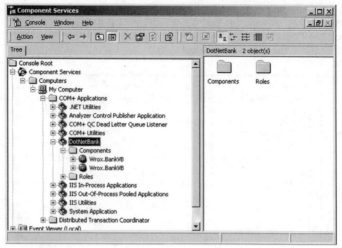

Figure 17-5

These can be treated like any other transactional COM+ component.

Lazy Registration

If a serviced component is used from managed code and it is not already registered as part of a COM+ application, then the registration and configuration is performed automatically. This may seem like an ideal solution, but it does require administrative privileges, so is not suitable for all scenarios. By and large, it is best to manually register components, perhaps as part of the installation.

Serviced Component Security

Integration with COM+ security is also provided as part of serviced components, allowing access to the SecurityContext object of the COM+ application. For this to succeed, the managed code needs to obtain an NT security token and perform impersonation before calling the .NET object.

Component Deployment

An assembly is used by the .NET architecture to support the sharing and reuse of code. All classes must exist within an assembly in order to be creatable by the CLR. The assembly contains the metadata that the CLR uses to allow the object to function. Without an assembly, the component cannot function. In the past, you could store code in a DLL and use DLLs as loadable modules within an application. The difference is in the metadata. A DLL was just a block of code – there was no knowledge of what it did outside of the developer that was familiar with it. The metadata associated with an assembly provides that kind of information.

What Are Assemblies?

There is no concept of an assembly as a file – there is no such thing as a .assembly file to worry about now. The assembly is a collection of files that together make up the assembly. The only requirement is that these files need to all reside in the same directory on the disk. When they are placed into an assembly, the CLR treats all these as a single unit.

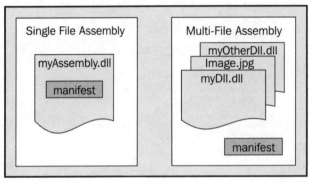

Figure 17-6

As shown in Figure 17-6, the manifest is what is used to describe the contents of the application. The manifest can either be embedded within a single DLL, as seen in the single file assembly, or can be in a separate file, as is the case with the multi-file assembly. When looking at DLLs in .NET, they are just a bit different from what they were in COM or Win32. While the extension is the same, they are executed by the CLR, instead of being executed as native code.

The assembly can be thought of as a logical DLL. In the past, the developer could distribute components or resources through the deployment of a DLL. Now, the developer can distribute the pieces of an assembly in the same way. The main difference is that the DLL needed some other information somewhere – usually in the registry – to tell the system that it was there ready to run. With an assembly, it carries that information along with it, in its metadata.

An assembly is *not* an application. An application is built from one or more assemblies. The assemblies that make up an application can be deployed in a number of different ways. Since an assembly contains its own metadata, it is capable of telling the operating system all about itself. It does not rely on entries into the registry to describe itself.

This association of metadata with executable code simplifies the distribution of an application. All the developer needs to do to deploy an application is simply to copy all of the assemblies that make up the application to a directory on the disk. This is known as *XCOPY deployment*, since the only tool required to deploy the files to disk is the XCOPY console command. When the application is first executed, the metadata within the assemblies tells the system all that it needs to know in order to execute the application. As seen earlier, this may not always be the case. If the application uses serviced components, these need to be registered with COM+.

.NET applications can also use more traditional installation mechanisms to distribute applications built out of assemblies. This includes building an .msi file and using the Windows Installer to deploy the files into the correct location. Likewise, you can build a .CAB file and have a browser download the file to the system and execute the application. In either case, all that the installation mechanism is responsible for is getting the proper files into the proper location on the destination system – no information about the assemblies needs to be added to the registry of the target system.

Assemblies and Versioning

There are currently two problems with the Win32 architecture that have combined to create what is known as *DLL Hell*. In DLL Hell, there is no control entity that is responsible for all of the DLL files installed onto a system. Information about a COM DLL is held in the registry. It can be easily overwritten by another application. For DLLs that aren't COM DLLs, there is no entry whatsoever in the registry. An application install program can also overwrite an existing DLL. This can play havoc with any existing application that was relying on that particular DLL performing a specific function when a method is called.

One of the specific problems with Win32 is that there is no system-level enforcement of versioning rules between components. It is left up to 'best practices' coding, which says that once an interface is published it can never be changed, but there is nothing in the operating system that explicitly prevents this from happening.

The other problem is that there is no common way for an application to say that it needs version 1.2.1.1234 of a particular component. It is left up to the developer to check the version of a DLL before calling into it. If that check is not done, and the application finds a different version, the code that it is relying on may no longer be there, or it may not perform the function that it expects, even if the interface is still intact. To combat this, Windows 2000 added System File Protection. This is an OS feature that can stop any installation program from overwriting any system DLLs.

The CLR extends this support by allowing developers to specify the specific version of a component for their application to use. It provides all of the support to make sure that the proper version is located and used for the requesting application. In doing this, it also allows for the execution of code from two similar components, only differing in version. This is known as side-by-side execution and is discussed a bit later in the chapter.

Assembly Manifest

In order for an assembly to describe itself to the CLR, it must contain a set of metadata. This metadata is contained in the assembly's manifest. The manifest contains the metadata required to specify:

- ❑ The assembly version
- ❑ The security information for the assembly
- ❑ The scope of the assembly
- ❑ Information to resolve references to the resources and classes of the assembly

The manifest for an assembly can either be stored in an EXE or DLL file, or in a standalone file. Remember that the assembly can be made up of one or more files – in which case there isn't a specific file that contains the entire assembly. In a single file assembly, the manifest is part of the DLL or EXE file that is the assembly.

The manifest of an assembly lists all of the files and resources that make up the assembly. It also lists all the classes and types defined in the assembly, and specifies which resources or files within the assembly map to which classes or types. The manifest also identifies any other assemblies on which it is dependent.

In creating a multi-file assembly, the Assembly Generation tool (AL.EXE) is used to create the manifest for the assembly. To create a multi-file assembly, compile the individual source files without an assembly. Then the AL tool is used to read through the compiled modules and create an assembly for the full set of modules.

Metadata

The manifest will specifically contain these pieces of metadata:

- ❑   Assembly name
- ❑   Version information
- ❑   Assembly file list
- ❑   Type reference information
- ❑   Referenced assemblies

Let's look at each of them in detail.

Assembly Name

This is a textual string name that identifies the assembly. When an assembly is used by one application, the developer can generally enforce a unique name for each assembly, thus preventing name collisions. However, when an assembly is designed to be shared, a more unique naming method must be used. This is called a *strong name*, and creating one allows the assembly to be stored in the *global assembly cache*. The global assembly cache is used to store assemblies that can be used by several applications on a machine.

To store an assembly into the global assembly cache, there are three steps to be followed:

1.   Create a strong name for the assembly using the SN.EXE tool. This tool will generate a file that contains the necessary public and private keys to define a strong name.

2.   Pass the contents of that file to the Assembly Generation Tool (AL.EXE) to create an assembly with a strong name associated with it.

3.   Use the Global Assembly Cache Tool (GACUTIL.EXE) to install the assembly into the global assembly cache. This is a tool that is used to manipulate the contents of the global assembly cache, including adding components to the GAC.

Version Information

The components of the version number are the major and minor version numbers, a build number, and a revision number. This is represented as a set of four numbers with the format:

```
<major version>.<minor version>.<build number>.<revision>
```

When the CLR is checking to see if an assembly is the proper version, it first checks the major and minor version numbers. These *must* match in order for the assembly to be compatible. If these two numbers match but the build number is different, then as long as the build number of the assembly is greater than the build required by the application, it can be assumed to be backwards-compatible with the version expected by the application.

Assembly File List

This lists each file contained in the assembly, along with the relative path to the file. For version 1 of the .NET Framework, all files in an assembly must be in the same directory as the manifest file. This only holds true for a multi-file assembly.

Type Reference Information

Maps all of the types included in the assembly to the specific file in the assembly that contains the type. This is necessary so that any types referenced within the classes contained in the assembly can be resolved by the runtime.

Referenced Assemblies

This lists all of the other assemblies that are statically referenced within the types contained in this assembly. Each entry contains the name of the assembly along with the required version information.

Custom Metadata

There is also custom metadata that can be included by the developer. Only the developer can use this information–the CLR does not use this information in any way. There are two sets of custom assembly metadata. The first set is made up of nine classes from the `System.Reflection` namespace. Use this namespace to query the values for this metadata at runtime. `System.Reflection` metadata includes:

- ❑ Company information
- ❑ Build information, such as 'Retail' or 'Debug'
- ❑ Copyright information
- ❑ Additional naming and version information
- ❑ Assembly title and description
- ❑ Product and Trademark information

The second set is made up of classes from the `System.Runtime.CompilerServices` namespace. This metadata includes:

- ❑ Cultures or spoken languages supported by the assembly, but not programming languages.
- ❑ Operating systems and processors the assembly has been built to support. Version 1 of the CLR does not use this information.

Self-Describing Components

With other application architectures, the only way for components to communicate is through a binary interface. If these components were written in different languages, there is a good chance that the way the data was stored is different as well. This leads to problems in the communication between these two components. In the .NET architecture, the metadata that is presented by each assembly helps to alleviate this confusion. The confusion is further alleviated through the common types of the CLR.

Since the components within an assembly are so thoroughly defined by the metadata, the developer can even define a new class that inherits from an existing class directly from the compiled code–you don't need to access the sourcecode to do this. In fact, the components do not even need to be in the same language, as long as both are managed components. This was seen in an example earlier in the chapter.

The assemblies and the components within them are said to be *self-describing*. This means that they carry all the information that other components need to know in order to interact with them. This information is all carried within the metadata of the assembly. There are no more IDL files in the .NET Architecture or public header files that get out of sync with the executables, and you can always be sure that the metadata information being used by the runtime is the proper metadata for the code being executed, since they are held together in the assembly.

Side-by-Side Execution

The ability to run multiple versions of the same component at the same time is a very valuable feature of the CLR. It can even execute two versions of the same component within the same process. The ability to do this is called *side-by-side execution*. By allowing this, the .NET architecture offers the developer an advantage over architectures such as COM. While there have been ways in the past to do side-by-side execution, its implementation in .NET frees the developer from most of the worries associated with doing it. By handling it in the plumbing of the CLR, the developer only has to worry about the business-specific code in their application.

When creating new versions of a component, a developer doesn't have to worry as much about maintaining compatibility with previous versions. Since the older component can run right alongside the new component, and the application using the component knows which version of the component to use, both can co-exist peacefully on the same machine. There are some precautions that the developer must take into account when having components that will run side-by-side with previous versions.

For example, if the component is relying on a physical file as a data cache, two components executing side-by-side will try to access the same file. The components would need to be written such that they keep the file in a location that is dependent on the version of the component being executed.

Summary

The flexibility and power of the .NET architecture extends beyond just creating applications, web services, and ASP.NET pages. Developers can create powerful business components using the .NET Framework and the CLR that have just as much power and flexibility as COM objects. In some cases, the capabilities offered by the CLR provide distinct advantages over COM. Now developers can actually derive new objects from classes written in different languages. And this can be done even if all that is available is the compiled version of the base class. However, that doesn't mean that COM and .NET can't work together in the same application.

This chapter specifically looked at:

❑   How to write a business object in two different languages, and then use the same test program to work with both objects

❑   How to take a class written in one language and extend its functionality by deriving a new class in a totally different language

❑   How to make use of transactions in ASP.NET pages and within .NET components

❑   How assemblies and metadata provide a way to package the executable code along with detailed descriptions of the code being packaged

In the next chapter, we will look at building ASP.NET Server controls, and how they mark a considerable improvement of previous methods of reusing code in your ASP.NET applications.

Building ASP.NET Server Controls

Since the early days, COM developers around the world have been building reusable visual controls. In the early 90's, building such controls required significant time and investment in understanding the myriad of COM interfaces that a control had to implement and use.

Later in the decade, C/C++ Frameworks like the *Microsoft Foundation Classes* (*MFC*) and the *Active Template Library* (*ATL*) made control development a little easier. They provided reusable classes and templates that implemented a lot of plumbing code required for controls. But the true breakthrough in popular control development didn't really happen until 1996, when the release of the Visual Basic Control Creation edition made control creation far simpler, and consequently very popular globally.

The upside of control development, and the reason why people still write so many controls today, is reusability. Once you have conquered visual control development, the reward of being able to write a control once (the grid control being the canonical example) and then reuse it in numerous *control containers* (such as Word and Excel) makes it worth all the pain. You can, of course, reuse the control in your own suite of products, not to mention that you could make a good living selling them to other developers. These same advantages apply in the world of ASP.NET controls, but there is one big difference: *ASP.NET controls are easy to get started with.*

ASP.NET allows you to build reusable visual controls that can render themselves as HTML or any other markup language such as WML. Many high-level similarities can be drawn between COM controls and ASP.NET controls, as they both enable reuse within UIs. But in reality, they are very different in the way they are implemented. ASP.NET provides a clean and easy-to-use class hierarchy for implementing controls, and there are no esoteric interfaces or threading models that are difficult to understand. ASP.NET still uses interfaces, but there really aren't more than a couple you'll use on a regular basis.

In this chapter, we'll look at ASP.NET control development covering:

❑ When, why, and how to build ASP.NET controls in both Visual Basic .NET and C#

❑ How controls form the basis of *all* page-rendering in ASP.NET

❑ How controls persist state across page invocation

❑ How controls interact with postback and can raise events.\

❑ Building controls that themselves use other controls to render their UI

Writing a Simple Control

To demonstrate the basic principles of control development and to show how easy ASP.NET control development is, we'll kick off this chapter by writing a simple Label control, which can render a text message. We'll initially develop the control in C#, review the code, and then rewrite it using VB.NET. This example will hopefully prove to you that control development really isn't that difficult, and it is, at the very least, worth understanding how controls are written so you can better understand how ASP.NET renders pages.

Creating a C# Control

Fire up your text editor or IDE of choice and enter the following C# code:

```csharp
using System;
using System.Web;
using System.Web.UI;
namespace WroxControls
{
    public class MyFirstControl : Control
    {
        protected override void Render(HtmlTextWriter writer)
        {
            writer.Write("<h1>ASP.NET Control Development in C#</h1>");
        }
    }
}
```

Save the file as `MyFirstControl.cs`. Let's briefly examine the code. The first few lines import three *namespaces* that controls typically use:

❑ `System`: Contains core system classes like `String`. The code will compile without this, but as most controls make use of the core classes, it is always good practice to include it.

❑ `System.Web`: The parent namespace for all ASP.NET classes. It contains classes such as `HttpRequest` (the ASP.NET `Request` object) and `HttpResponse` (the ASP.NET `Response` object). Again, the code will compile without this, but as with the `System` namespace, most control classes will use the ASP.NET intrinsic objects, and so it is good practice to include it.

❑ `System.Web.UI`: Contains the ASP.NET control classes, many of which are divided up into namespaces based upon their family (`System.Web.UI.WebControls`, `System.Web.UI.HtmlControls`, and so on). This reference is needed as you are using the
• `Control` and `HtmlTextWriter` classes.

The next line of the code marks the beginning scope of a new namespace called `WroxControls` chosen for the control:

```
namespace WroxControls
{
```

Anything declared within the next section of the code until the end of the namespace seven lines later is a member of the `WroxControls` namespace. This means that the full namespace-qualified reference to the control is `WroxControls.MyFirstControl`. Any code using our class must use this complete name unless the `Using` directive is included to import all definitions within the namespace into its default scope.

The next few lines of code declare the class for the server control:

```
public class MyFirstControl : Control
{
    protected override void Render(HtmlTextWriter writer)
    {
        writer.Write("<h1>ASP.NET Control Development in C#</h1>");
    }
}
```

The class is called `MyFirstControl`. It's derived from the `Control` class (which is part of the `System.Web.UI` namespace) declared as `public`, and has one protected method called `Render`. The `Control` class implements the basic plumbing code required by a server control to be used within an ASP.NET page.

The name of the class is arbitrary, and you can call your controls whatever you like, as they are defined in *your* namespace. Avoid using names that are already used by ASP.NET (or any other part of the runtime), as name conflicts will occur if two namespaces are imported using the `@Import` directive by a page, or the `using` directive inside of a source file. If you decided to create *your* label control, do not call it `Label`; call it `MyLabel` or some other meaningful name such as `WroxLabel`.

> *By marking your class public, you state that anybody can create an instance of the class and use it. If you specify that it is private (by omitting the public attribute), the class will only be usable by other classes within the same namespace. If an ASP.NET page attempts to access a private class, the runtime will raise an error saying the class/type is not defined. This is somewhat confusing when trying to track down an error, so it is always worth checking the access control of a class as it is easy to forget to add the public keyword when developing.*

The `Render` method is declared using the `override` keyword. This keyword tells the compiler that the `Control` base class implements the `Render` member, but our class wants to override the method so that it can control the output created at runtime itself. The implementation of this method calls the `Write` method of the `HtmlTextWriter` object, which results in the HTML "`<h1>ASP.NET Control Development in C#</h1>`" being written to the page output stream.

Once you have created a server control and compiled it (as we'll demonstrate shortly), you can use it in an ASP.NET page. To do this, use the `@Register` page directive to associate a tag prefix with a namespace containing a server control, and then use the tag prefix plus the class name of a server control, as shown here:

```
<%@ Register TagPrefix="Wrox" Namespace="WroxControls"
              Assembly="MyFirstControl" %>
<html>
<body>
<Wrox:MyFirstControl runat="server" />
</body>
</html>
```

This page tells the ASP.NET page compiler that when it sees any element starting with `Wrox:`, it should search the `WroxControls` namespace for a class whose name matches the element name (`MyFirstControl`). Furthermore, the assembly attribute defines the physical assembly in which the class is contained. At runtime, assuming ASP.NET located the class, it creates an instance of it, and calls its `Render` method to allow it to write data to the output stream being created (for example, the page).

The position of the HTML that a control creates in the final page depends upon where that control is declared inside the ASP.NET page code. In this page we'd expect the server controls output to be rendered after the body tag.

In this example, once the control has inserted its HTML into the output stream, the final page sent down to the client browser will look as follows:

```
<html>
<body>
<h1>ASP.NET Control Development in C#</h1>
</body>
</html>
```

The actual rendering is shown in Figure 18-1:

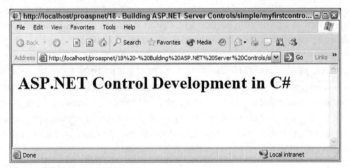

Figure 18-1

To test the ASP.NET page yourself and view the output, you need to compile the C# sourcecode to create an assembly. This is placed in the `bin` directory of the application on the web server, causing the ASP.NET runtime to scan the assembly and make an internal note of the namespaces and classes/controls within it.

Compiling the C# Control and Creating an Assembly

To compile the server control class, bring up your text editor, enter the following batch commands, and save the file as make.bat:

```
set outdir=..\bin\MyFirstControl.dll
set assemblies=System.dll,System.Web.dll
csc /t:library /out:%outdir% /r:%assemblies% MyFirstControl.cs
```

For the class to compile correctly, you'll need to change the outdir *parameter in line one, to match a directory configured as a virtual directory on your machine.*

The first two lines of the make.bat file declare a couple of variables. These make the line that actually does the compilation more readable. The compiler options are discussed in Chapter 3. The important points to note about this file are:

❑ A reference to the System.dll and System.Web.dll assemblies is added using the /r parameter. This is done so that the compiler knows where to search for the namespaces or classes being imported into the control with the using directive. If you do not add a reference to the assembly containing referenced classes, you'll get a compile error.

❑ The compiler's output (MyFirstControl.dll) is placed directly into the Web application's bin directory. When ASP.NET has to create a class at runtime, this directory is searched. Using the meta data contained in your assembly, ASP.NET will know where to locate the WroxControls namespace specified in the page's @Register directive. By compiling the control directory to the bin directory, you are less likely to forget to copy the assembly.

Run the make.bat file, and you'll see some output, as in Figure 18-2:

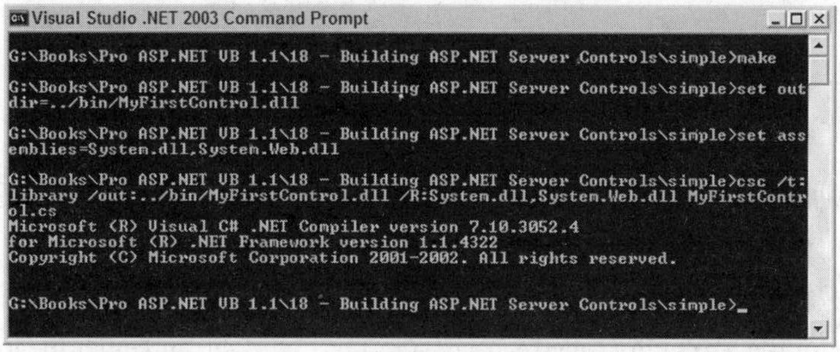

Figure 18-2

If all goes well, the bin directory should contain the compiled assembly, and you should be able to open the ASP.NET page created earlier and see the output of the control.

Although the C# control we've just developed is about as simple as it gets, and doesn't really have any practical use as yet, you've just seen the full development cycle required for a simple ASP.NET control. Hopefully, you now realize that control development is nothing like it was in the COM days, and that control development seems worth checking out in more detail. Things will get more advanced from here on in, but all of the code is clean and fairly easy to understand once you've grasped the basic concepts.

To show that control development in Visual Basic is just as painless, we'll create an almost identical control called `MyFirstControlInVB`.

Control Development in Visual Basic

One of the great things about Visual Basic.NET is that the language has arrived in the 21st Century with a bang. It now has all the *object-oriented* (*OO*) features that make it a first-class programming language. However, as expected, the VB team and C# teams at Microsoft are competing with each other for adopters, and as a result have used different names for certain attributes and directives within their respective languages that they feel to be more suitable for their audience of programmers. This is fair enough, but it does mean that switching between the languages can be initially a little confusing.

Here are a few language differences that should help you convert any of the samples in this chapter between C# and VB:

C# Example	VB Example
`using System;`	`Imports System`

`namespace WroxControls {`
`...`
`};`
	`Namespace WroxControls`
	`...`
	`End Namespace`

`public class A : B {`
`...`
`}`
	`Public Class A`
	`  Inherits B`
	`...`
	`End Class`

`public class A : B {`
`...`
`}`
	`Public Class A`
	`  Implements B`
	`...`
	`End Class`

This chapter will mainly discuss samples in C#, but whenever a new technique is introduced, the equivalent VB.NET code will also be shown.

Creating an ASP.NET Server Control in VB.NET

Create a new file for the VB control called `MyFirstControlInVB.vb` and enter the following code:

```
Imports System
Imports System.Web
Imports System.Web.UI
Namespace WroxControls
  Public Class MyFirstControlInVB
  Inherits Control
    Overrides Protected Sub Render(writer as HtmlTextWriter)
      writer.Write("<h1>ASP.NET Control Development in VB</h1>")
    End Sub
  End Class
End Namespace
```

Using the comparison table, you should be able to see how the code has been translated from C#. The main changes are:

❑ All references to `using` have been replaced with `Imports`.

❑ All the trailing C-style syntax semicolons have been removed.

❑ All opening curly brackets have been removed, and the closing curly brackets replaced with the more verbose VB syntax of `End Class`, `End Namespace`, and so on.

❑ The `Class` declaration has had the trailing `: Control` text removed, and a separate line, `Inherits Control`, has replaced it.

❑ The method declaration order has been switched around, as VB declares the name of a variable before the type, unlike C#.

The other change to note is that the HTML output says **VB** rather than **C#**, so the browser output is now rendered as in Figure 18-3:

Figure 18-3

To build the assembly containing this new class, create a `makevb.bat` file and enter the following commands:

```
set outdir=..\..\bin\MyFirstControlInVB.dll
set assemblies=System.dll,System.Web.dll
vbc /t:library /out:%outdir% /r:%assemblies% MyFirstControlInVB.vb
```

Again, substitute the '..' in the first line to point to your virtual directory.

This is similar to the C# `make` file except that the compiler name is now `vbc` rather than `csc`, and the output file is `MyFirstControlInVB.dll`. Run the `make` file to compile the control, and then bring up your text editor and enter the following ASP.NET page code, and save it, replacing the original:

```
<%@ Register TagPrefix="Wrox" Namespace="WroxControls"
             Assembly="MyFirstControlInVB" %>
<html>
<body>
<Wrox:MyFirstControlInVB runat="server" />
</body>
</html>
```

The page is pretty much identical to the ASP.NET page that used the C# version of the control, but the assembly directive and line in the `<body>` element is changed to specify the class `MyFirstControlInVB` instead of `MyFirstControl`.

Two Controls on One Page

After you have viewed the page to and confirmed your VB control is working, update the page with the additional lines shown here:

```
<%@ Register TagPrefix="Wrox" Namespace="WroxControls"
            Assembly="MyFirstControlInVB" %>
<%@ Register TagPrefix="WroxCSharp" Namespace="WroxControls"
            Assembly="MyFirstControl" %>
<html>
<body>
<Wrox:MyFirstControlInVB runat="server" />
<WroxCSharp:MyFirstControl runat="server" />
</body>
</html>
```

The additional `register` directive associates the assembly containing the C# control with the `WroxCSharp` tag prefix. This needs to be done since the controls used on this page are in different assemblies. If two controls were in the same assembly, you'd only need one directive.

View this updated page in the browser, and you should see the output from the two controls as shown in Figure 18-4:

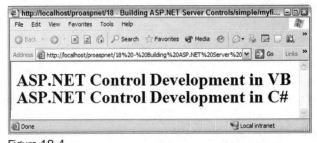

Figure 18-4

As expected, both controls have rendered themselves in the output stream depending upon their location in the ASP.NET page. The ASP.NET page framework doesn't care what language the controls are written in, as long as they are directly or indirectly derived from the `Control` class.

Multi-Step Page Rendering

The rendering of a control is just one of many events that occur during its lifetime. As we progress, we'll discuss the other events that occur, and how these events are fired during the lifetime of an ASP.NET page. Unlike ASP, where a page essentially had one execution step, *render*, an ASP.NET page has many executions steps or phases. As such, control events are fired during different execution stages within a page.

Control Properties

For a server control to be useful, it needs to allow a page developer to influence how the control renders its UI. In ASP.NET pages, the basic way of achieving this is using attributes. For example, assuming you had a server control called `MyLabel`, which had a `Text` attribute specifying a label to be printed, you could declare the control a couple of times and make different labels appear:

```
<%@ Register TagPrefix="Wrox" Namespace="WroxControls"
             Assembly="MyLabel" %>
<html>
<body>
<Wrox:MyLabel runat="server" Text="Hello" />
<Wrox:MyLabel runat="server" Text="World" />
</body>
</html>
```

When the ASP.NET page framework processes attributes of an HTML element that are part of a server control declaration, it maps them to the *public properties* of the associated class. These values of the properties are set in the *initialization stage* of a page. During this stage, for each control, the OnInit method is called once all properties for a control have been set. In this method a control can perform validation of the properties and other operations such as default values.

During the initialization stage, a control should not try to access other server controls declared on a page, except child controls. Until the initialization stage is reached, other controls on the page will be in an inconsistent state.

The following code implements the MyLabel control discussed:

```
using System;
using System.Web;
using System.Web.UI;
namespace WroxControls
{
    public class MyLabel : Control
    {
        string _text;
        public string Text
        {
            get{ return _text; }
            set{ _text = value; }
        }
        protected override void OnInit(EventArgs e)
        {
            base.OnInit(e);
            if ( _text == null )
                _text = "Here is some default text";
        }
        protected override void Render(HtmlTextWriter writer)
        {
            writer.Write("<h1>" + _text + "</h1>" );
        }
    }
}
```

The main areas of interest in this code are:

❑ The Text property allows the value of the label to be set and retrieved.

❑ The OnInit method sets the Text property to a default value if it's not specified. For our example, this shows that properties of the class are set just before OnInit is called.

❑ The `Render` method has been updated to write the control's `Text` property out between the `<h1>` elements.

With these code changes in place, we can create a new ASP.NET page that has three `MyLabel` controls:

```
<%@ Register TagPrefix="Wrox" Namespace="WroxControls"
              Assembly="MyLabel" %>
<html>
<body>
<Wrox:MyLabel runat="server" Text="Hello" />
<Wrox:MyLabel runat="server" Text="World" />
<Wrox:MyLabel runat="server"/>
</body>
</html>
```

This page should render two `<h1>` elements with the text Hello and World, and one `<h1>` element with the text Here is some default text, since not specifying the `Text` attribute should result in the default text appearing.

Figure 18-5 shows the output from this page:

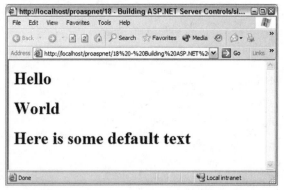

Figure 18-5

Attribute Value Conversion

When ASP.NET matches an attribute to a property, it will perform intelligent conversion of the attribute value. If a class property is a `string`, ASP.NET will just do a simple mapping and initialize the attribute. If the property is an `integer` or `long`, the attribute value will be converted to a number, and then set. If a value is an enumeration, ASP.NET will match the `string` value against an *enumeration name*, and then set the correct enumeration value. The same type of logical conversion occurs for other types, such as `Boolean`. If a value cannot be converted–for example, if you try and use a `string` value for a numeric property–ASP.NET will generate a parse error.

To see some of these conversions, add a `RepeatCount` property to the control, which is defined as an `integer`, and a `ForeColor` property defined as `System.Drawing.Color`. These new properties will enable page developers to specify how many times a label should appear, and the color used for the text.

In this updated page, use the `RepeatCount` attribute to tell the first label to draw itself three times. Set the second label to `Green` and the third label to `Orange`, using the `ForeColor` attribute. Since no `ForeColor` attribute is specified for the first label, it will appear as the default color selected (`Blue`):

```
<%@ Register TagPrefix="Wrox" Namespace="WroxControls"
            Assembly="MyLabel" %>
<html>
<body>
<Wrox:MyLabel runat="server" RepeatCount="3" Text="Hello" />
<Wrox:MyLabel runat="server" Text="World" ForeColor="Green" />
<Wrox:MyLabel runat="server" ForeColor="Orange" />
</body>
</html>
```

The output for this new page is shown in Figure 18-6, where Hello now appears three times, and the text is in different colors:

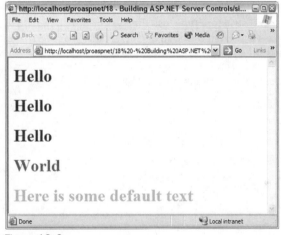

Figure 18-6

Implementing these new properties in the server control is straightforward because ASP.NET provides all of the conversion processing, keeping the code clean and simple. There is nothing specific to ASP.NET in the code:

```
public class MyLabel : Control
{
    int _repeatCount = 1;
    public int RepeatCount
    {
        get { return _repeatCount; }
        set { _repeatCount = value; }
    }

    Color _foreColor = Color.Blue;
    public Color ForeColor
```

```
        {
            get { return _foreColor; }
            set { _foreColor = value; }
        }
    }
```

The Color *enumeration is defined in the* System.Drawing *namespace. So, you have to add a using statement for this to the code.*

In this code, the default RepeatCount is made equal to 1, and the default color Blue. Both these defaults are set using member initializers rather than by adding code to the OnInit method. Typically, this is the best way to specify default values for a variable. You only really need to add initialization code in OnInit for more complex initialization. For example, in OnInit you could ensure the RepeatCount is within a valid range, throwing an ArgumentException if the count exceeds a reasonable number.

With these new properties in place, the Render method is updated to output the <h1> element and its associated text RepeatCount times. The color of the text will be set using a style attribute and a color selector. To convert the Color structure type, use the System.Drawing.ColorTranslator class. The ToHtml method of this class is used in the code to convert the _foreColor enumeration value into the HTML color value. Here is the updated Render method:

```
protected override void Render(HtmlTextWriter writer)
{
    int loop;

    for( loop=0; loop < _repeatCount; loop++ )
    {
        writer.Write("<h1 style='color:" +
                ColorTranslator.ToHtml(_foreColor) +
                "'>" + _text + "</h1>" );
    }
}
```

Using HtmlTextWriter Rendering Services

The label server control has started becoming more useful now as we've enabled basic customizations such as the repeat count and foreground color. The only problem with these customizations is that they have increased the complexity of the created HTML. As the number of attributes a control supports increases, so does the complexity of the HTML it has to emit, and the code that needs to be created. To keep the code readable and to reduce the likelihood of HTML formatting errors, use the rendering services of the HtmlTextWriter class to manage HTML tag and attribute creation.

The HtmlTextWriter class provides services for:

❑ Writing HTML or other markup languages to the output stream

❑ Managing the creation of well formed elements

❑ Creating attributes

❑ Creating a style attribute

Using the services of the `HtmlTextWriter`, you can rewrite the `Render` method as follows:

```
protected override void Render(HtmlTextWriter writer)
{
    int loop;
    for( loop=0; loop < _repeatCount; loop++ )
    {
        writer.AddStyleAttribute( "color",
            ColorTranslator.ToHtml(_foreColor) );
        writer.RenderBeginTag("h1");
        writer.Write( _text );
        writer.RenderEndTag();
    }
}
```

This code is much more readable, maintainable, and less error prone, since the `HtmlTextWriter` class takes on the responsibility of formatting the HTML. The call to `AddStyleAttribute` tells the `HtmlTextWriter` that the next element it starts should have a `color` style element with a specified value. You can call this multiple times, and the `HtmlTextWriter` will automatically emit a matching style element.

The call to `RenderBeginTag` tells the `HtmlTextWriter` to output a start tag for the `<h1>` element, outputting any attributes that have previously been added using `AddStyleAttribute`, or `AddAttribute`. `AddAttribute` can be used to output a normal HTML attribute.

The call to `Write` tells the `HtmlTextWriter` to output the specified content to the HTML stream. Various overloads for `Write` allow you to pass in any type. All types will be converted to a `string` and written to the output stream. If there is not a specific overload for a type, the `Object.ToString` method will be used. The `RenderEndTag` call tells the `HtmlTextWriter` to output the close tag for the last tag opened using `RenderBeginTag`. These two methods automatically stack and recursively manage element tags, and can be used to emit complex nested HTML elements.

The HTML output from our page using the rendering services of `HtmlTextWriter` looks like this:

```
<html>
<body>
<h1 style="color:Blue;">
  Hello
</h1><h1 style="color:Blue;">
  Hello
</h1><h1 style="color:Blue;">
  Hello
</h1>
<h1 style="color:Green;">
  World
</h1>
<h1 style="color:Orange;">
  Here is some default text
</h1>
</body>
</html>
```

As you can see, the `HtmlTextWriter` also performs automatic indentation of the markup it creates.

Object Properties

Server controls can expose other objects *and* primitive types, as properties. A server control declaration within an ASP.NET page can directly set the properties of an object in two ways. The first method of setting object properties is using the *object walker syntax* for attribute names, when a hyphen (-) character is used instead of a period (.) to specify an object's property:

```
<Wrox:MyFirstControl MyObject-A="hello" MyObject-B="World"
                    runat="server" />
```

The object walker syntax can walk any number of sub-objects of an object property too:

```
<Wrox:MyFirstControl MyObject-AnotherObject-A="hello"
                    runat="server" />
```

Supporting an object property is straightforward. For example, this simple class definition allows two string values to be set using the properties `A` and `B`:

```
public class SampleClassProperty {
    string _valueA;
    string _valueB;
     public string A {
        get {
            return _valueA;
        }
        set {
            _valueA = value;
        }
    }

    public string B {
        get {
            return _valueB;
        }
        set {
            _valueB = value;
        }
    }
}
```

A server control could use it for one of its object properties, `MyObject`, as follows:

```
SampleClassProperty _exampleObjectProperty
    = new SampleClassProperty();
public SampleClassProperty MyObject
{
    get { return _exampleObjectProperty; }
}
```

By enabling object properties to be initialized, server controls can group together logically related attributes and can easily expose them on one or more controls, with very little code. The `style` object, used by most ASP.NET controls, is a good example of this.

Another way of initializing object properties within a server control is by using nested elements:

```
<Wrox:MyFirstControl runat="server">
    <MyObject A="Hello" B="Hello" />
</Wrox:MyFirstControl>
```

Most ASP.NET Web controls support this. However, you need to annotate your server control class definition with the `ParseChildren` attribute, specifying a value of `true`:

```
namespace WroxControls
{
    [
        ParseChildren(true)
    ]
    public class MyLabel : Control
    ...
```

When the ASP.NET page compiler sees this attribute, the *default control builder* that ASP.NET uses to parse sub-content for a server control declaration knows that each element is an object property. If you do not specify this attribute, or specify `false`, ASP.NET assumes that nested elements should be added as child controls (covered later in this chapter).

> *A control builder is the parser used by ASP.NET to process the inner content of a server control declaration. Control builders are an advanced topic covered at the end of this chapter.*

If sub-elements of control declarations also contain elements, such elements are assumed to be object properties of the outer object property. For example, assuming the mythical `MyObject` element mapped to an object called `MyObject`, which had two object properties called `SomeObjectPropertyA` and `SomeObjectPropertyB`, you could declare and initialize the control as follows:

```
<Wrox:MyFirstControl runat="server">
    <MyObject A="Hello" B="Hello">
    <SomeObjectPropertyA  SomeAttribute="Another value" />
    <SomeObjectPropertyB  SomeAttribute="Another value" />
    </MyObject>
</Wrox:MyFirstControl>
```

You could also use the object walker syntax, although that is less readable for complex server control declarations:

```
<Wrox:MyFirstControl MyObject-A="hello" MyObject-B="World"
        MyObject-SomeObjectPropertyA-SomeAttribute="Another value"
        MyObject-SomeObjectPropertyB-SomeAttribute="Another value"
        runat="server" />
```

To demonstrate using object properties in a server control let's take a look at the `Style` object.

Using the System.Web.UI.WebControls.Style Object

The `Style` class has methods and properties that make working with style attributes more intuitive, and very consistent through all server controls. This class handles style attributes such as those for colors, borders, and fonts. If your server control is to expose style elements, it should use the `Style` class.

To use the style object, you can add a new member variable called `_style` to the control, along with a read-only property accessor to enable the ASP.NET pages to access it:

```
Style _style = new Style();
public Style LabelStyle
{
    get { return _style; }
}
```

As you'd be using the `Style` object for building the `style` attribute eventually rendered down to the browser, it's necessary to change the `ForeColor` property accessor to use the `Style` object to set and retrieve the `ForeColor` value. This removes the need for the `_foreColor` member variable, and so it can be deleted. The updated `ForeColor` property accessor code looks like this:

```
public Color ForeColor
{
    get { return _style.ForeColor; }
    set { _style.ForeColor = value; }
}
```

Finally, update the `Render` method to use the `AddAttributesToRender` method of the `Style` class. This takes an `HtmlTextWriter` object as an input parameter, and calls `AddStyleAttribute` depending on the various style attributes that have been set using the `Style` object:

```
protected override void Render(HtmlTextWriter writer)
{
    int loop;
    for( loop=0; loop < _repeatCount; loop++ )
    {
        _style.AddAttributesToRender( writer );
        writer.RenderBeginTag("h1");
        writer.Write( _text );
        writer.RenderEndTag();
    }
}
```

With these changes in place, you can create a label with the text **Server Controls Are Cool**, displayed in a yellow font, on a black background, using a 36-point font size as follows:

```
<%@ Register TagPrefix="Wrox" Namespace="WroxControls"
            Assembly="MyLabel" %>
<html>
<body>
<Wrox:MyLabel runat="server"
            ForeColor="Yellow"
            LabelStyle-BackColor="Black"
```

```
                          LabelStyle-Font-Size="36"
                          Text="Server Controls Are Cool" />
    </body>
    </html>
```

The rendered output is shown in Figure 18-7:

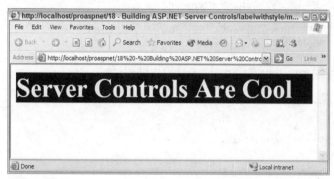

Figure 18-7

Using the WebControl Class for Server Controls That Use Style

For controls, such as the label, that need style management, derive from the WebControl class in the System.Web.UI.WebControls namespace. This class adds the following functionality to a server control:

- ❑ Exposes properties that allow style colors to be set using properties like ForeColor, BackColor, and Font.

- ❑ Allows expando attributes (attributes that are not pre-defined properties of the control) to be specified in a server-control declaration. Expando attributes are not interpreted and are written directly to the output HTML stream. By default, the Control class throws an exception if an attribute is not a property of the server control.

- ❑ Provides consistency with the standard ASP.NET Web controls since they derive from the WebControl class.

- ❑ Persists the style object and any settings or state during postbacks, using view state. In the control example earlier, when the style object was used, any style changes made in event handlers or in other code would not have been remembered after a postback, since the state of the style object was not being round tripped using viewstate. For the control to remember any style changes (because it is derived from Control), you'd need to implement custom statement management, by overriding the LoadViewState and SaveViewState methods. Viewstate is discussed later in the chapter.

The WebControl class is designed to either assist with the rendering of a control, or take complete control of the rendering. For a simple control such as the label, the WebControl class can replace most of the code written.

To use the WebControl class, make the following changes to the code:

❑ Derive from the `WebControl` class rather than `Control` class.

❑ Declare a public constructor that calls the base constructor, specifying which HTML element to render.

❑ Override the `RenderContents` method to emit the content you want within your `<h1>` element. The `WebControl` class takes responsibility for rendering the attributes as well as the begin and end-tags, so the `Render` method is removed.

❑ Remove all of the style properties implemented earlier, since the `WebControl` will automatically have implemented them.

After making these changes, the C# control code looks like this:

```csharp
using System;
using System.Web;
using System.Web.UI;
using System.Web.UI.WebControls;
namespace WroxControls
{
    public class MyLabel : WebControl
    {
        string _text;
        public MyLabel() : base ("H1")
        {
        }
        public string Text
        {
            get{ return _text; }
            set{ _text = value; }
        }
        protected override void OnInit(EventArgs e)
        {
            base.OnInit(e);
            if ( _text == null)
                _text = "Here is some default text";
        }
        protected override void RenderContents(HtmlTextWriter writer)
        {
            writer.Write( _text);
        }
    }
}
```

The same control in VB.NET:

```vbnet
Imports System
Imports System.Web
Imports System.Web.UI
Imports System.Web.UI.WebControls
Namespace WroxControls
    Public Class MyLabel
        Inherits WebControl
        Private _text As String
```

```
        Public Sub New()
            MyBase.New("H1")
        End Sub 'New

        Public Property Text As String
            Get
                Return _text
            End Get
            Set
                _text = value
            End Set
        End Property

        Protected Overrides Sub OnInit(e As EventArgs)
            MyBase.OnInit(e)
            If _text Is Nothing Then
                _text = "Here is some default text"
            End If
        End Sub

        Protected Overrides Sub RenderContents(writer As HtmlTextWriter)
            writer.Write(_text)
        End Sub
    End Class
End Namespace
```

With these changes, you need to change the ASP.NET page, since the available properties names for the control have changed. Use the `WebControl` class documentation to get a list of all the available properties.

Here is the updated page, which now uses properties consistent with all the server controls provided as part of ASP.NET, which were discussed in Chapter 5:

```
<%@ Register TagPrefix="Wrox" Namespace="WroxControls"
             Assembly="MyLabel" %>
<html>
<body>
<Wrox:MyLabel runat="server"
             ForeColor="Yellow"
             BackColor="Black"
             Font-Size="36"
             Text="Web Controls" />
</body>
</html>
```

For controls that require only one HTML root element to be rendered, the updated control code provides a good model to follow when building server controls. Your server controls should always derive from the `WebControl` class unless they do not render any UI, in which case the services provided by `WebControl` do not provide any benefit.

You can use all the other techniques to render HTML so far with server controls derived from `WebControl`, the only difference is that your code is moved to the `RenderContents` method.

In this revised code demonstrating the use of `WebControl`, I have removed support for the `RepeatCount` property, since that would require one or more HTML elements to be rendered at the root level (you can have any number of controls within the root element). This is something a basic Web control can do. To do this, you have to override the `Render` method.

To implement the `RepeatCount` property in the implementation, the overridden `Render` method calls the base implementation of `Render` a number of times. Let's see the necessary calling code in C# and VB.NET.

The following C# code just calls the base `Render` method thrice to demonstrate the technique:

```csharp
protected override void Render(HtmlTextWriter writer)
{
    for(int i=0; i < 3; i++ )
    {
        base.Render( writer );
    }
}
```

In VB.NET:

```vbnet
Protected Overrides Sub Render(writer As HtmlTextWriter)
    Dim i As Integer
    For i = 0 To 2
        MyBase.Render(writer)
    Next i
End Sub 'Render
```

As expected, the control renders the label three times, as shown in Figure 18-8:

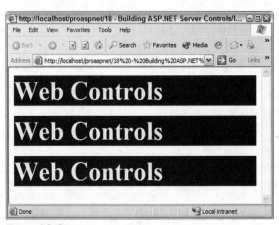

Figure 18-8

The server control can also be programmatically manipulated, just like any other ASP.NET server control provided out of the box. The following ASP.NET page sets all the properties of the server-control properties within the `Page_Init` event:

```
<%@ Register TagPrefix="Wrox" Namespace="WroxControls"
               Assembly="MyLabel" %>
<%@ Import Namespace="System.Drawing" %>
<script runat="server" language="C#">
  void Page_Init( object sender, EventArgs e )
    {
      ourLabel.Text = "Web Controls";
      ourLabel.ForeColor = Color.Yellow;
      ourLabel.BackColor = Color.Black;
      ourLabel.Font.Size = 36;
    }
</script>
<html>
<body>
    <Wrox:MyLabel runat="server" id="ourLabel" />
</body>
</html>
```

Now that we've created a couple of server controls that generate their UI by emitting HTML, let's take a look at composite controls. These controls render their UI by reusing other server controls. An ASP.NET page is a good example of a composite control. So let's take a look at how they work in detail.

Composite Controls

All ASP.NET dynamic pages are created by the ASP.NET runtime using ASP.NET controls. You may not have realized it, but we have already built several ASP.NET controls in the earlier chapters just by creating ASP.NET pages and user controls. The ASP.NET page framework automatically converts and compiles pages into server controls contained within a dynamically created assembly the first time a page is requested, as shown in Figure 18-9:

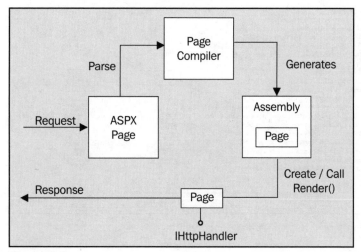

Figure 18-9

This server control is then used to render the page. Subsequently, when a page is requested, the precompiled server control can be instantiated and called, resulting in great performance, as Figure 18-10 suggests:

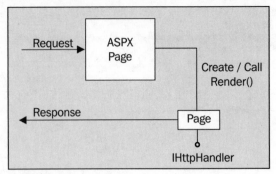

Figure 18-10

The assemblies created for ASP.NET pages are automatically managed for you. If you search around your Windows system directory, you'll find a `Temporary ASP.NET Files` directory. Within this you'll find subdirectories for the various web sites on your machine, which in turn contain the assemblies for ASP.NET pages.

Open up one of these generated assemblies using the ILDASM tool (Figure 18-11). You'll see that they typically contain a single class with the same name as the ASP.NET page. This class extends (derives from) the `System.Web.UI.Page` class (see the sixth item from the root in the tree control):

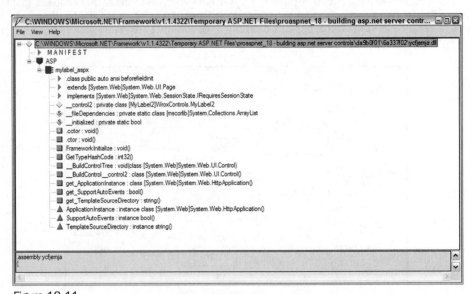

Figure 18-11

The `Page` object (located in the `System.Web.dll` assembly) derives from the `TemplateControl` class, which in turn derives from the `Control` class. Figure 18-12 shows the main ASP.NET control classes and their inheritance hierarchy:

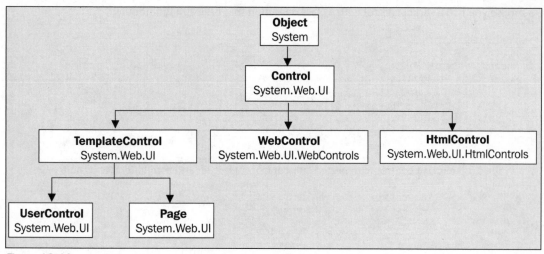

Figure 18-12

Here is a brief description of each of these classes:

- ❑   `Control`: Provides a common base class for all other control types.

- ❑   `WebControl`: Provides methods and properties for dealing with the style. This class is the base class for all ASP web controls. These are always declared in an ASP.NET page using an `ASP:` prefix.

- ❑   `HtmlControl`: The base class for standard HTML elements, such as `input`. Typically, you will never derive from this control.

- ❑   `TemplateControl`: Contains functionality that is shared between user controls and pages, such as support for loading user controls (`.ascx`) or templates.

- ❑   `UserControl`: The base class from which all user controls derive.

- ❑   `Page`: The base class from which all dynamically compiled ASP.NET pages derive.

The actual code generated by ASP.NET for these dynamically generated classes is not that different from the code we have just written for the label control. One key difference is that it uses *control composition* to actually generate the page. This means that a page is a server control that uses other server controls to render its UI.

Building a Composite Control

A server control can be a *container* for other controls. The `Control` class has a `Controls` property of the `ControlsCollection` type. This collection class can hold zero or more child controls. When a control is rendered, each of its child controls is called upon to render itself. If these child controls contain child controls, this process repeats until all controls have been rendered.

By default, if you derive a server control from the `Control` class, nested elements declared within an ASP.NET page will be added to the `Controls` collection, assuming you haven't used the `ParseChildren` attribute discussed earlier to change the default behavior.

Suppose you had a server control with a class definition that basically did nothing:

```
using System;
using System.Web;
using System.Web.UI;
namespace WroxControls
{
    public class CompositeControl : Control
    {
    }
}
```

And then declared that control with nested sub-controls (a button and some literal text) on a page:

```
<%@ Register TagPrefix="Wrox" Namespace="WroxControls"
             Assembly="MyFirstControl" %>
<html>
<body>
<form runat="server">
  <Wrox:CompositeControl runat="server">
    <asp:button Text="A Button" runat="server" />
    Some Text
  </Wrox:CompositeControl>
</form>
</body>
</html>
```

The ASP.NET page parser automatically creates a `LiteralControl` for each block of text or significant whitespace.

The control would actually render the button and the literal text, since the default `Render` implementation invokes the `Render` method of each control in the `Controls` collection, as shown in Figure 18-13:

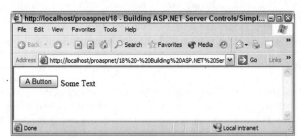

Figure 18-13

When writing a composite control, the control itself typically decides on what child controls to create, rather than the user. If the user is going to create all the UI, you should use a `User` control rather than a custom server control.

Server controls override the `CreateChildControls` method and populate the `Controls` collection. The ASP.NET Framework calls this method to signal to a control that it should create its child controls. Which controls you populate the control's collection with will depend on the UI your control renders. Any class can be used as long as it derives from the `Control` class.

The code required to implement our first server control using control composition is shown here:

```
using System;
using System.Web;
using System.Web.UI;
namespace WroxControls
{
    public class CompositeControl : Control, INamingContainer
    {
        protected override void CreateChildControls()
        {
          LiteralControl text;
          text = new LiteralControl(
                    "<h1>ASP.NET Control Development in C#</h1>" );
          Controls.Add(text);
        }
    }
}
```

In this code, we have removed the Render method and replaced it with the CreateChildControls method. When called, this code creates a single LiteralControl and adds it to the child control collection. The class has also been modified to derive from the INamingContainer interface to indicate that it is a *naming container*. We'll discuss naming containers in more detail later in this chapter, but as a general rule, all composite controls should implement this.

By removing the Render method from the class, the default implementation of the Render method defined in the Control class is called during the render phase of a page. The default Render method enumerates the Controls collection and invokes the RenderControl method of each child control in turn. This effectively causes a control's UI to be drawn, by allowing each child control to output their own HTML, by either using the HtmlTextWriter object, or by using child controls.

When deriving from the WebControl class and overriding the RenderContents methods, always call the base implementation of RenderContents if your WebControl uses control composition, as this method calls its base classes' (the Control class) Render method. The same is true if you derive from Control and override Control.Render (assuming you want child controls declared in a page to be rendered).

CreateChildControls

The CreateChildControls method can be called at different stages in the life cycle of a composite control, but it will only be called once per instantiation of the control, unless you explicitly reset the state of a control using the ChildControlsCreated property. In this respect, it is a non-deterministic event that occurs during the lifetime of a control, unlike the Init and Render events already discussed, which occur at fixed times in the life cycle of a page, and thus are deterministic.

If not called before, the CreateChildControls method will always be called in the pre-render stage of a page. The method will be called prior to this if either the public FindControl method of the control is called, or if the Control itself calls the protected EnsureChildControls method. The FindControl method is used when pushing postback data into a control, so CreateChildControls will also be called during the postback stage of a page, if there is postback data associated with a given control.

As a control author, always use the EnsureChildControls method if you need to populate your controls collection prematurely. This method calls CreateChildControls only if the ChildControlsCreated public property is false. If the property is false, it is set to true once CreateChildControls is called. This method ensures child controls are only created once.

If the ChildControlsCreated property is set to false, all child controls are released automatically. Subsequently, CreateChildControls may be called again.

ASP.NET Pages and Composite Controls

An ASP.NET page is essentially compiled into a composite control. Consider this simple page:

```
<html>
  <body>
    <form method="post" runat="server">
        Name: <asp:textbox runat="server"/>
    </form>
  </body>
</html>
```

When compiled, the page is rendered using the server controls (shown in Figure 18-14), which effectively form a hierarchical tree of server controls:

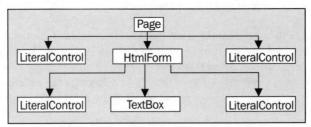

Figure 18-14

The Page object's Controls collection contains the LiteralControl, HtmlForm, and LiteralControl child controls. The HtmlForm control contains the LiteralControl, TextBox, and LiteralControl child controls. When the page is rendered, each of these controls is rendered in turn, starting at the top, recursively rendering each child control before moving on to the next sibling. So, for this page the rendering sequence would be Page, LiteralControl, HtmlForm, LiteralControl, TextBox, LiteralControl, LiteralControl.

Control Tree Navigation

A server control tree can be navigated using different methods of the Control class. To navigate down one level, you use the Control.Controls collection. To navigate up the tree one level, from a control to its parent, you use the Parent property. To navigate from a Control to the container Page, you use the Control object's Page property. To recursively search down the tree for a control, you use the Control object's FindControl method.

The Advantages of Control Composition

Using control composition for simple controls really doesn't have much advantage over rendering the HTML directly using `HtmlTextWriter`. To see when there is a much greater benefit, let's create a more complex control. This control will create an HTML table below an `<h1>` element. The table will contain ten rows, each with five cells. You can render this using the `HtmlTextWriter` or by creating lots of `LiteralContent` objects, but it makes a lot more sense to use the high-level ASP.NET web controls seen in earlier chapters. Although we have typically only made references to these controls in ASP.NET pages before, creating these controls dynamically within a control is straightforward:

```
using System;
using System.Web;
using System.Web.UI;
using System.Web.UI.WebControls;
namespace WroxControls
{
    public class CompositeTableControl : Control, INamingContainer
    {
      Table _table;  // Make table a member so we can access it at any point

      protected override void CreateChildControls()
      {
          LiteralControl text;
          text = new LiteralControl(
                    "<h1>ASP.NET Control Development in C#</h1>");
          Controls.Add(text);
          TableRow row;
          TableCell cell;

          // Create a table and set a 2-pixel border
          _table = new Table();
          _table.BorderWidth = 2;
          Controls.Add(_table);

          // Add 10 rows each with 5 cells
          for(int x = 0; x < 10; x++) {

              // Create a row and add it to the table
              row = new TableRow();
              _table.Rows.Add(row);

              // Create a cell that contains the text
              for(int y = 0; y < 5; y++) {
                  text = new LiteralControl("Row: " + x + " Cell: " + y);
                  cell = new TableCell();
                  cell.Controls.Add(text);
                  row.Cells.Add(cell);
                  }
              }
          }
    }
}
```

This code may look at bit complex a first, but what it's doing is very simple. Firstly, it adds the `LiteralControl` containing the `<h1>` element as a child control. Next, it creates a `Table` object (`System.Web.UI.WebControls.Table`), sets the border width to two pixels, and adds that as a child control:

```
_table = new Table();
_table.BorderWidth = 2;
 Controls.Add(_table);
```

The table is then populated with rows by running a `for` loop for ten iterations, creating, and adding a `TableRow` object using the `Rows` collection property:

```
row = new TableRow();
_table.Rows.Add(row);
```

Finally, for each row added, an inner loop is executed for five iterations adding a `TableCell` object that has a `LiteralControl` as its child. The `Text` of the `LiteralControl` is set to indicate the current row and cell. Compiling and executing this code produces the results shown in Figure 18-15:

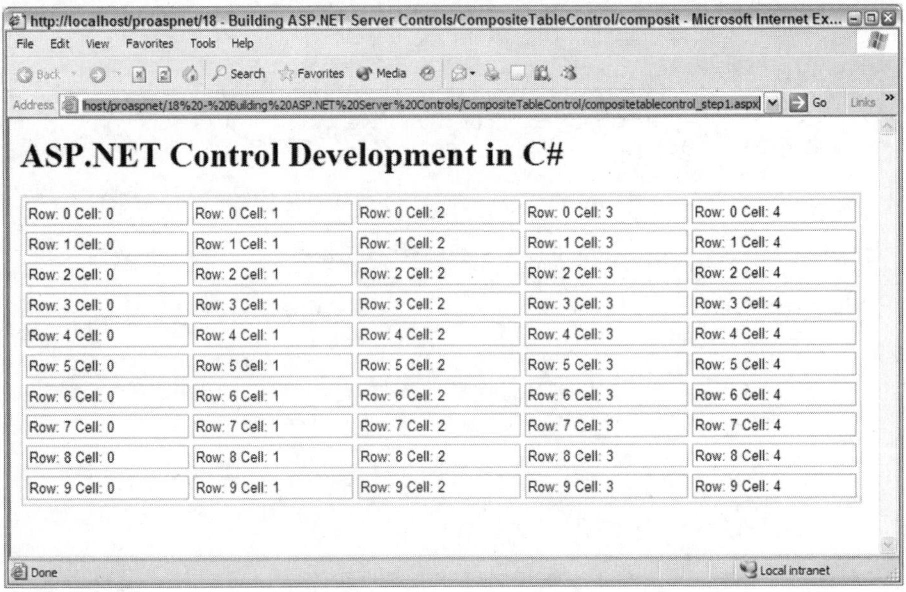

Figure 18-15

All of the controls used (such as `Table`, `TableRow`, and `TableCell`,) derive from the `Control` class somewhere in their inheritance hierarchy. Each of these controls also uses control composition to render its UI. The control tree for the page actually looks like Figure 18-16:

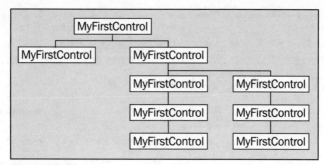

Figure 18-16

If you view the source for this generated page, you'll see around 130 lines of HTML, none of which have been manually created. There are a number of key advantages of using control composition over direct rendering:

❑ You save yourselves a great deal of error-prone HTML creation via code, and therefore save time and increase productivity.

❑ You programmatically create objects, call methods, and set properties. The code written is therefore simple to read and easily extendable at a later date.

❑ You have not been exposed to the underlying HTML generated by the various controls used.

❑ The fact that they actually render table, tr, and td HTML elements to the page is an implementation detail that you don't have to worry about. In theory, the output can just as easily be WML or any other markup language–the control will still work fine.

The argument for using composite controls becomes more apparent as the child controls you use–such as the Table control–provide more and more functionality and hence save more time and effort. As an example, let's modify the table so the user can edit each cell within it, by using a TextBox control (rather than a LiteralControl) within the TableCell control:

```
for( int y=0; y < 5; y++ ) {
    TextBox textbox;
    textbox = new TextBox();
    textbox.Text = "Row: " + x + " Cell: " + y;

    cell = new TableCell();
    cell.Controls.Add(textbox);
...
```

By changing four lines of code, we now have an editable table as shown in Figure 18-17:

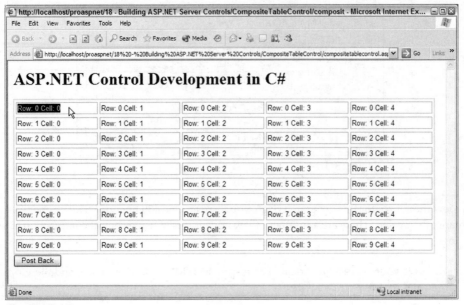

Figure 18-17

The underlying HTML generated by our control is now even more complex, with the child controls creating all the input elements needed within the td elements:

```html
<html>
<body>
<form name="ctrl0" method="post" action="compositetablecontrol.aspx"
id="ctrl0">
<input type="hidden" name="__VIEWSTATE" value="dDwtNTMxODUzMzMxOzs+" />
  <h1>ASP.NET Control Development in C#</h1>

  <table border="0" style="border-width:2px;border-style:solid;">
    <tr>
      <td>
        <input name="grid:ctrl2" type="text" value="Row: 0 Cell: 0" />
      </td><td>
        <input name="grid:ctrl3" type="text" value="Row: 0 Cell: 1" />
      </td><td>
        <input name="grid:ctrl4" type="text" value="Row: 0 Cell: 2" />
      </td><td>
        <input name="grid:ctrl5" type="text" value="Row: 0 Cell: 3" />
      </td><td>
        <input name="grid:ctrl6" type="text" value="Row: 0 Cell: 4" />
      </td>
    </tr><tr>...
```

You'll notice within this HTML that each of the input elements has a name attribute. By default, these ids are assigned sequentially by ASP.NET as the child controls are created and added to the control.

When a postback occurs, ASP.NET uses these `ids` to automatically push *postback* data into server controls that are created with the same `id`. This automatic management of postback data is part of the magic that gives the impression to page developers that controls are intelligent–developers don't have to write lots of code to manually make controls (like a textbox) remember their state. Of course, under the hood, a control author has to implement some code that maps the postback data to properties, but once that is done, page developers and custom control writers can simply reuse an intelligent self-maintaining control.

Writing a TextBox Control

To understand some of the more advanced development aspects of server control, it is useful to actually write a simple control like a textbox. Although this isn't the most exciting control to write, especially since it already exists, it clearly demonstrates some important aspects that control authors need to understand including:

❑   Interacting with postback

❑   Using viewstate

❑   Raising events from a control

To render a textbox, the server control needs to output an HTML `input` element with a `type` attribute containing the value `"text"`. Using the `WebControl` as our control's base class makes this first task simple. We have to perform several main tasks:

❑   Create a new class that derives from the `WebControl` class.

❑   Implement a public constructor that calls the base class constructor specifying that our server control should output an `input` element.

❑   Override the `AddAttributesToRender` method. This is called to allow derived classes to add attributes to the root element (`input`).

❑   Add the `type` attribute with a value of `text`.

❑   Add a `name` attribute whose value is derived from the `UniqueID` property. This property is used by ASP.NET to hold the unique `id` of each control. We have to output the name property containing this value since an HTML form will not postback the value entered into an input field without a name.

Here is the sourcecode that implements these steps:

```
using System;
using System.Web;
using System.Web.UI;
using System.Web.UI.WebControls;
namespace WroxControls
{
    public class MyTextBox : WebControl
    {
        public MyTextBox() : base("input")
```

```
        {
        }
        protected override void AddAttributesToRender(HtmlTextWriter writer)
        {
            base.AddAttributesToRender(writer);
            writer.AddAttribute(HtmlTextWriterAttribute.Name, UniqueID);
            writer.AddAttribute(HtmlTextWriterAttribute.Type, "input" );
        }
    }
}
```

The implementation of the `AddAttributesToRender` method calls the base-class implementation. This is called since the base-class implementation will add various other attributes, such as style attributes, to your element depending on other properties that have been set in the base class.

Once compiled, you can use the following ASP.NET page to reference your control (assuming the control is called `MyTextBox` and is compiled to the `MyTextBox.dll` assembly):

```
<%@ Register TagPrefix="Wrox" Namespace="WroxControls"
              Assembly="MyTextBox" %>
<html>
<body>
<form runat="server">
  <H3>TextBox Control</H3>
  <P>Enter a value: <Wrox:MyTextBox runat="server" />
  <BR>
  <ASP:Button Text="Postback" runat="server" />
</form>
</body>
</html>
```

In this ASP.NET page we've declared an instance of the `MyTextBox` control, and a button within a form element so that we can cause a postback to occur. When viewed in the browser, this page initially renders as shown in Figure 18-18:

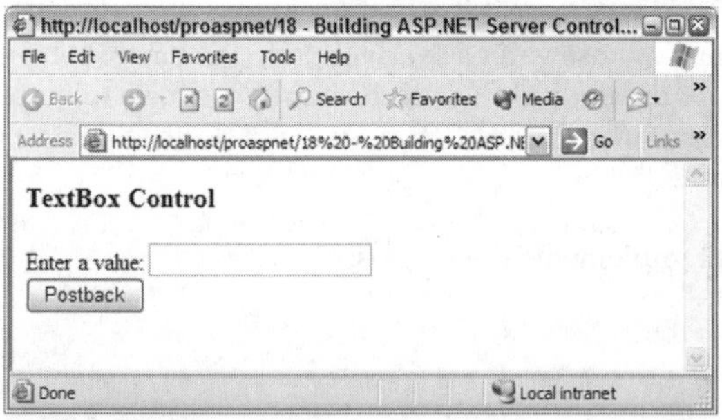

Figure 18-18

Enter some text into the textbox and click the Postback button. You will find that after the postback occurs, the textbox is blank again. This demonstrates that as a control developer, you have to do some work for a control to become intelligent.

For an intelligent textbox, you need to access the postback data submitted as part of a form. If data is present for the control, add a `value` attribute to the `input` element. Assuming you can populate a member variable `_text` with the postback for the textbox, you could add the following code to output a `value` attribute:

```
public MyTextBox() : base ("input")
{
}
string _value;
protected override void AddAttributesToRender(HtmlTextWriter writer)
{
    base.AddAttributesToRender(writer);
    writer.AddAttribute(HtmlTextWriterAttribute.Name, UniqueID);
    writer.AddAttribute(HtmlTextWriterAttribute.Type, "input" );
    if ( _value != null )
        writer.AddAttribute( "value", _value );
}
```

To access postback data, a server control has to implement the `IPostBackDataHandler` interface.

The IPostBackDataHandler Interface

The `IPostBackDataHandler` interface has two methods:

```
bool IPostBackDataHandler.LoadPostData(string postDataKey,
                                        NameValueCollection postCollection);
void IPostBackDataHandler.RaisePostDataChangedEvent()
```

The `LoadPostData` method is called when postback occurs and a control has postback data. The method is called in sequence for all controls on a page that need to access postback data. If a control does not have any postback data (for example, if the control was disabled), the method is not called. A control can explicitly ask for this method to be called even if does not have postback, by calling the `RegisterRequiresPostBack` method of the `Page` class.

The `LoadPostData` call passes all of the postback data submitted in a form using a `NameValueCollection`. A control can access any of the data in this collection. To access the specific postback data item associated with a control, the `postDataKey` variable is used as the key into the collection. The value of this key field is the *unique name* assigned to the control either automatically by ASP.NET, or the value assigned by a user if an `id` attribute was specified in the control declaration.

The `LoadPostData` method returns a `Boolean` value. If `true` is returned, the `RaisePostDataChangedEvent` method will be called after the `LoadPostData` method has been called for all other server controls on a page with postback data. If a `false` value is returned, the `RaisePostDataChangedMethod` will not be called.

A control should return `true` in the `LoadPostData` method to raise an event as the result of certain data being present, or changes to data caused as a result of postback data. Events must be raised in the `RaisePostDataChangedEvent` method since raising events in `LoadPostData` will cause unpredictable results. Any event handler that caught and processed an event raised in `LoadPostData` would not be able to depend on consistent state being present in other controls, since such controls may not have initialized or updated their state based upon postback.

To make your textbox control intelligent, implement the `IPostBackDataHandler` **interface as follows:**

```
bool IPostBackDataHandler.LoadPostData(string postDataKey,
                                        NameValueCollection postCollection)
{
    _value = postCollection[postDataKey];
    return false;
}

void IPostBackDataHandler.RaisePostDataChangedEvent()
{
}
```

The `NameValueCollection` class is defined in the `System.Collections.Specialized` namespace, and so it has to be imported into any class files before this code will compile.

The `LoadPostData` method uses the `postDataKey` variable to copy the postback data for the control into the `_value` variable. Since this variable is already being used to render a value, if present, the textbox should now appear intelligent. We return `false` from `LoadPostData` since we're not yet interested in raising any events. For the same reason, the implementation of the `RaisePostDataChangedEvent` is also empty.

With these changes in place, enter a value into the textbox, and hit the **Postback** button to cause a roundtrip to the server. Any value entered will be remembered, since the value attribute will be emitted by our control, as seen in Figure 18-19:

Figure 18-19

If you look at the HTML output for this page, you'll see the value attribute, which is why the value redisplays correctly:

```
<html>
<body>

<form name="_ctl0" method="post" action="mytextbox.aspx" id="_ctl0">
<input type="hidden" name="__VIEWSTATE"
value="dDwtMzM4NzUxNTczOzs+YFp06wUt7ZoMN2kDeJMiO1YBg9U=" />

  <H3>TextBox Control (VB)</H3>
```

```
    <P>Enter a value: <input id="name" name="name" type="input" />
    <BR>

    <input type="submit" name="_ctl1" value="Postback" />

    <P>
    <span id="status"></span>

</form>

</body>
</html>
```

If you declared a couple more of `MyTextBox` controls in the ASP.NET page, entered values, and used the button to cause postback, you would see that they all remember their state, just as with other standard server controls in earlier chapters. Each declared server control has a unique name assigned to it, so each manages its own postback and renders itself correctly, without interfering with other controls. All control behavior added to the textbox is encapsulated and reusable. This makes server controls very powerful, and makes complex page development much simpler. Once individual controls are written, they take care of all the plumbing code to remember their state.

Raising Events from Controls

ASP.NET provides a powerful server-side event model. As a page is being created, server controls can fire events that are caused either by aspects of a client-side postback, or by controls responding to page code that is calling their methods or changing properties. These events can be captured in an ASP.NET page, or can be caught by other server controls.

ASP.NET server controls support events using delegates, just like any other .NET class does. With ASP.NET, the `EventHandler` delegate is used when defining most events. The standard definition for this delegate defines a method signature with two parameters–the first parameter of type `object`, and the second of type `EventArgs`–that you will have seen many times in event handlers like `Page_Load`. When a server control raises an event, the first parameter of the event method will contain a reference to the server control. Supplying a reference to the control that raised the event allows event methods to handle events from multiple controls.Depending on the parameters you need your controls to raise, you can replace the `EventHandler` delegate with a custom delegate.

To demonstrate events, we'll add an event to our textbox control that is raised when its value changes.

Events in Action

To support an event in the textbox control, first define a public `event` of the type `EventHandler` called `TextChanged`. The code in C# will look as follows:

```
public event EventHandler TextChanged;
```

In VB:

```
Event TextChanged As EventHandler
```

919

Next, change the `LoadPostData` implementation to always return `true`:

```
bool IPostBackDataHandler.LoadPostData(string postDataKey,
                                       NameValueCollection postCollection)
{
    _value = postCollection[postDataKey];
    return true;
}
```

This will cause the `RaisePostDataChangedEvent` to be called, from which it is safe to raise events caused by postback.

In this method, we use the delegate to raise a `TextChanged` event, assuming there are listeners (for example, the delegate is not `null`):

```
void IPostBackDataHandler.RaisePostDataChangedEvent()
{
    if ( TextChanged != null )
        TextChanged( this, EventArgs.Empty );
}
```

You're probably wondering if these changes will always raise a `TextChanged` event when postback occurs, even if the text has not changed. As it stands, this is precisely what will happen. We'll shortly refine the event handler to only call the event when the value actually changes. But for now, let's just see how events are raised.

To use the new event, declare an event handler called `OnNamedChanged` in the ASP.NET page:

```
<script runat="server" language="C#">
    private void OnNameChanged( object sender, EventArgs e )
    {
        status.Text = "Value changed to " + name.Text;
    }
</script>
```

To wire the event handler up to the text changed event, add an `OnTextChanged` attribute and specify the name of the method to be called when the event is fired (in this case, `OnNameChanged`):

```
<P>Enter a value: <Wrox:MyTextBox id="name" runat="server"
                                  OnTextChanged="OnNameChanged" />
```

Prefix an event name with `'On'` to associate event handlers with server-control events in server control declarations. If your control had an additional event called `TextInvalid`, the event name would be `OnTextInvalid`.

The `OnNameChanged` event handler displays the value of text in a label field when the event is fired:

```
<asp:Label runat="server" id="status" />
```

For your event handler code to work, you have to declare a `Text` property on your server control that exposes the held value so it can be displayed:

```
      public string Text
      {
         get { return _value; }
      }
```

With all these changes in place, entering a value of Events in ASP.NET in the textbox and calling the Postback button will cause a message to appear below the Postback button, as shown in Figure 18-20:

Figure 18-20

The following code shows how to implement a server-side control that supports events in VB:

```
Imports System
Imports System.Web
Imports System.Web.UI
Imports System.Web.UI.WebControls
Imports System.Collections.Specialized

Namespace WroxControls
  Public Class MyTextBoxVB
    Inherits WebControl
    Implements IPostBackDataHandler

    Public Sub New()
       MyBase.New("input")
    End Sub 'New

    Public Event TextChanged As EventHandler
    Private _value As String
    Public ReadOnly Property Text As String
      Get
         Return _value
      End Get
    End Property

    Protected Overrides Sub AddAttributesToRender(writer As HtmlTextWriter)
      MyBase.AddAttributesToRender(writer)
      writer.AddAttribute(HtmlTextWriterAttribute.Name, UniqueID)
      writer.AddAttribute(HtmlTextWriterAttribute.Type, "input")
      If Not (_value Is Nothing) Then
```

```
                   writer.AddAttribute("value", _value)
            End If
        End Sub

        Function LoadPostData(postDataKey As String, _
                        postCollection As NameValueCollection) As Boolean
            Implements IPostBackDataHandler.LoadPostData
            _value = postCollection(postDataKey)
            Return True
        End Function

        Sub RaisePostDataChangedEvent()
            Implements IPostBackDataHandler.RaisePostDataChangedEvent
            RaiseEvent TextChanged(Me, EventArgs.Empty)
        End Sub
    End Class
End Namespace
```

The Framework Event Pattern

When supporting events, classes in the .NET Framework define a protected method called OnEventName, which actually raises the event. The reason for this is that it enables derived classes to perform event handling by overriding a method instead of attaching a delegate. This is simpler and more efficient. To follow this pattern for the TextChange event, you could implement the IPostBackDataHandler.RaisePostDataChangedEvent method as follows:

```
void IPostBackDataHandler.RaisePostDataChangedEvent()
{
    OnTextChanged(EventArgs.Empty );
}
protected void OnTextChanged (EventArgs e)
{
    if ( TextChanged != null )
        TextChanged ( this, e);
}
```

In this code, the RaisePostDataChangedEvent method calls the OnTextChanged method to raise the event. Derived classes that want to raise events can simply override the OnTextChanged method to catch the event, and optionally call the base-class implementation if they want other listeners to receive the event.

Causing Postback from Any Element–IPostBackEventHandler

In HTML, only the button and imagebutton elements can actually cause a postback to occur. When designing controls, you may want other elements of a control's user interface such as an anchor element to cause postback. You may also want a control's user interface to be able to raise different types of postback events, which the control can process to manipulate its user interface. For example, a calendar control may want to have previous-month and next-month events.

To show how to support postback events, we'll write a simple counter control. The control's user interface displays a counter (starting at 50) and provides two hyperlinks that enable you to increase or decrease the value (see Figure 18-21):

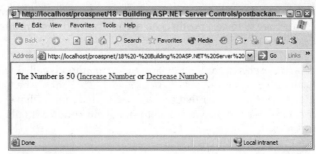

Figure 18-21

If you click **Increase Number** twice, the count would increase to 52, as shown in Figure 18-22:

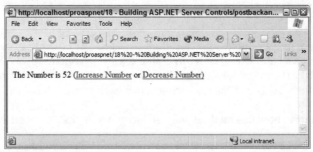

Figure 18-22

If you click **Decrease Number** four times, the number goes down to 48 (see Figure 18-23):

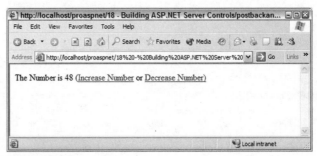

Figure 18-23

This control is raising postback events to itself. To achieve this, a control must do two things:

❑   Derive from the `IPostBackEventHandler` interface and implement the `RaisePostBackEvent` method.

❑ Call the `Page` class' `GetPostBackEventReference` method to create some script code that can be rendered into a page to force a postback to occur. This of course means the browser must support JavaScript for this feature.

The `IPostBackEventHandler` class's `RaisePostBackEvent` method is called when a postback is caused by script code calling `Page` class's `GetPostBackEventReference`. The `RaisePostBackEvent` method accepts a single `string` parameter that can be used to determine what event has been raised. In the case of the counter control, we use the value `inc` to signal our counter should be increased, and `dec` to signal it should be decreased:

```
public void RaisePostBackEvent(string eventArgument)
{
    if ( eventArgument == "inc" )
        Number = Number + 1;
    if ( eventArgument == "dec" )
        Number = Number - 1;
}
```

When a control renders its user interface, it calls the `Page` class's `GetPostBackEventReference` method passing itself as a parameter. The return value is a string containing JavaScript code that will cause a postback event to be raised when it is called. In our control, this JavaScript is placed into an anchor element, so when the user clicks the anchor, a postback occurs.

The following code shows how this method was used to generate the `inc` postback event:

```
writer.Write("<a href=\"javascript:" +
    Page.GetPostBackEventReference(this,"inc") +
    "\"'>Increase Number</a>");
```

Here is the complete sourcecode for the counter control:

```
using System;
using System.Web;
using System.Web.UI;
namespace WroxControls
{
  public class MyFirstControl : Control,
      IPostBackEventHandler
  {
    public int Number
    {
      get
      {
        if ( ViewState["Number"] != null )
          return (int) ViewState["Number"];
        return 50;
      }
      set
      {
        ViewState["Number"] = value;
      }
    }
```

```
    public void RaisePostBackEvent(string eventArgument)
    {
      if ( eventArgument == "inc" )
        Number = Number + 1;
      if ( eventArgument == "dec" )
        Number = Number - 1;
    }

    protected override void Render(HtmlTextWriter writer)
    {
      writer.Write("The Number is " + Number.ToString() + " (" );
      writer.Write("<a href=\"javascript:" +
                   Page.GetPostBackEventReference(this,"inc") +
                   "\"'>Increase Number</a>");
      writer.Write(" or " );
      writer.Write("<a href=\"javascript:" +
                   Page.GetPostBackEventReference(this,"dec") +
                   "\">Decrease Number)</a>");
    }
  }
}
```

This control demonstrates how to:

❑   Derive and implement the `IPostBackEventHandler`

❑   Use the `Page.GetPostBackEventReference` to raise two events

The next section in the chapter covers viewstate, so for now ignore the implementation of the `Number` property.

The control renders the following HTML:

```
<html>
<body>

<form name="_ctl0" method="post" action="myfirstcontrol.aspx" id="_ctl0">
<input type="hidden" name="__VIEWSTATE"
value="dDwxMjc4NDMyNjExO3Q8O2w8aTwxPjs+O2w8dDw7bDxpPDE+Oz47bDx0PHA8bDxiZXI
7PjtsPGk8NDg+Ozs+Oz4+Ozs+Oz4+Oz6XT9F3HCi1voCIwAsaNszynaGM2w==" />

The Number is 48 (<a href="javascript:__doPostBack('_ctl1','inc')">Increase
Number</a> or <a href="javascript:__doPostBack('_ctl1','dec')">Decrease
Number)</a>

<input type="hidden" name="__EVENTTARGET" value="" />
<input type="hidden" name="__EVENTARGUMENT" value="" />
<script language="javascript">
<!--
  function __doPostBack(eventTarget, eventArgument) {
    var theform;
    if (window.navigator.appName.toLowerCase().indexOf("netscape") > -1) {
```

```
      theform = document.forms["_ctl0"];
    }
    else {
      theform = document._ctl0;
    }
    theform.__EVENTTARGET.value = eventTarget.split("$").join(":");
    theform.__EVENTARGUMENT.value = eventArgument;
    theform.submit();
  }
// -->
</script>
</form>

</body>
</html>
```

Notice how the following script block containing the `__doPostBack` function is automatically rendered into the output stream when an ASP.NET server control calls the `Page.GetPostBackEventReference` reference:

```
<script language="javascript">
<!--
  function __doPostBack(eventTarget, eventArgument) {
    var theform;
    if (window.navigator.appName.toLowerCase().indexOf("netscape") > -1) {
      theform = document.forms["_ctl0"];
    }
    else {
      theform = document._ctl0;
    }
    theform.__EVENTTARGET.value = eventTarget.split("$").join(":");
    theform.__EVENTARGUMENT.value = eventArgument;
    theform.submit();
  }
// -->
</script>
```

This function is called by the script code returned from `Page.GetPostBackEventReference`:

```
<a href="javascript:__doPostBack('_ctl1','inc')">
```

Now that we have covered handling postback and events, let's look at how a control can persist state during postback using viewstate.

Using ViewState

After an ASP.NET page is rendered, the page object, which created the page and all of its server controls, is destroyed. When a postback occurs, a new page and server-control objects are created.

When writing a server control you often need to store and manage state. Since a control is created and destroyed with each page request, any state held in object member variables will be lost. If a control needs to maintain state, it has to do so using another technique. As you have seen with the textbox control, one way of managing state is to use postback. When a postback occurs, any postback data associated with a control is made available to it via the `IPostBackData` interface. A control can therefore repopulate its class variables, making the control appear to be stateful.

Using postback data to manage the state of a control is a good technique when it can be used, but there are some drawbacks. The most obvious one is that only certain HTML elements, such as `input`, can use postback. If you had a label control that needed to remember its value, you couldn't use postback.

Also, postback is only really designed to contain a single item of data. For example, our textbox control needs to remember its last value so it can raise a `TextChanged` event when the value changes. To maintain this additional state, one option would be to use hidden fields. When a control renders its output, it could also output hidden fields with other values that need to be remembered. When a postback occurs, these values would be retrieved into the `LoadPostData` method. This approach would work for a single control, but could be problematic in cases where many instances of the same control were on a page (for example, what would you call the hidden fields? How could you ensure the names do not clash with names a page developer may have used?)

To resolve the problems of managing state ASP.NET has a feature called viewstate. In a nutshell, viewstate is a hidden input field that can contain state for any number of server controls. This hidden field is automatically managed for you, and as a control author you never need to access it directly.

Introducing the StateBag

All server controls have a `ViewState` property. This is defined in the `Control` class as the `StateBag` type, and allows server controls to store and retrieve values that are automatically round-tripped and recreated during a postback.

During the *save state stage* of a page, the ASP.NET Framework enumerates all server controls within a page and persists their *combined state* into a hidden field called __VIEWSTATE. If you view any rendered ASP.NET containing a form element, you will see this field:

```
<input type="hidden" name="__VIEWSTATE" value="dDwtMTcxOTc0MTI5NDs7Pg==" />
```

When a postback occurs, ASP.NET decodes the __VIEWSTATE hidden field and automatically repopulates the viewstate for each server control as they are created. This reloading of state occurs during the *load state stage* of a page for controls that are declared on an ASP.NET page.

If a control is dynamically created, either on a page or within another composite control, the state will be loaded at the point of creation. ASP.NET keeps track of what viewstate hasn't been processed, and when a new control is added to the `Controls` property of a `Control` (remember a page is a control), it checks to see if it has any viewstate for the control. If it has, it is loaded into the control at that point.

To see viewstate in action, change your textbox control to store its current value in viewstate, rather than the _value field. By doing this, when `LoadPostData` is called to enable the textbox control to retrieve its new value, you can compare it with the old value held in viewstate. Return `true` if the values are different. This will cause a `TextChanged` event to be raised in `RaisePostDataChangedEvent`. If the values are the same, return `false`, so that `RaisePostDataChangedEvent` is not called, and no event is raised.

The StateBag class implements the IDictionary interface, and for the most part is used just like the Hashtable class with a string key. All items stored are of the System.Object type, and thus, *any* type can be held in the viewstate, and casting is required for retrieving an item.

In the earlier textbox control, we used a _value string member variable to hold the current value of the textbox. Delete that variable and rewrite the property to use viewstate:

```
public string Text
{
  get
  {
    if ( ViewState["value"] == null )
      return String.Empty;
    return (string) ViewState["value"];
  }
  set
  {
    ViewState["value"] = value;
  }
}
```

Since you've deleted the _value member variable and replaced it with this property, you need to change all references to it, with the Text property. You could directly reference the ViewState where you previously used _value, but it's good practice to use properties to encapsulate your usage of viewstate, making the code cleaner and more maintainable (for example, if you changed the viewstate key name used for the text value, you'd only have to do it in one place).

With this new property in place, you can revise the LoadPostData to perform the check against the existing value as discussed:

```
bool IPostBackDataHandler.LoadPostData(string postDataKey,
                                       NameValueCollection postCollection)
{
  bool raiseEvent = false;
  if ( Text != postCollection[postDataKey] )
    raiseEvent = true;
  Text = postCollection[postDataKey];
  return raiseEvent;
}
```

Before testing this code to prove that the TextChanged event is now only raised when the text changes, you need to make a small change to the ASP.NET page. As you'll recall from earlier, we have an event handler that sets the contents of a label to reflect our textbox value when TextChanged is raised:

```
<script runat="server" language="C#">
private void OnNameChanged( object sender, EventArgs e )
{
  status.Text = "Value changed to " + name.Text;
}
</script>
```

The label control uses viewstate to remember its value. When a postback occurs, even if this event is not raised, the label will still display the text from the previous postback, making it look like an event was raised. So, to know if an event really was raised, reset the value of the label during each postback. You could do this within the page `init` or `load` events, but since the label uses viewstate to retain its value, you can simply disable viewstate for the control using the `EnableViewState` attribute as follows:

```
<ASP:Label runat="server" EnableViewState="false" id="status" />
```

During the save state stage of a page, the ASP.NET page framework will not persist viewstate for the controls with an `EnableViewState` property of `false`. This change to the page will therefore make the label forget its value during each postback.

> Setting `EnableViewState` to `false` does not prevent a control from remembering state using postback, as the state is rendered to the browser as the `Text` property of the control, and resubmitted during postback As such, should you need to reset the value of a textbox, you'd have to clear the `Text` property in a page's `init` or `load` event.

With all these changes made, if you enter a value of **Wrox Press** and press the **Postback** button, you will see that during the first postback our event is fired, and our label control displays the value (see Figure 18-24):

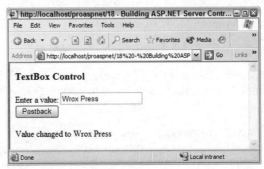

Figure 18-24

If you click the postback button again, the textbox control will use its viewstate to determine that the postback value has not changed, and it will not fire its `TextChanged` event. Since the label control does not remember its state, as viewstate was disabled for it, the value-changed message will not appear during the second postback since the label will default back to its original blank value (see Figure 18-25):

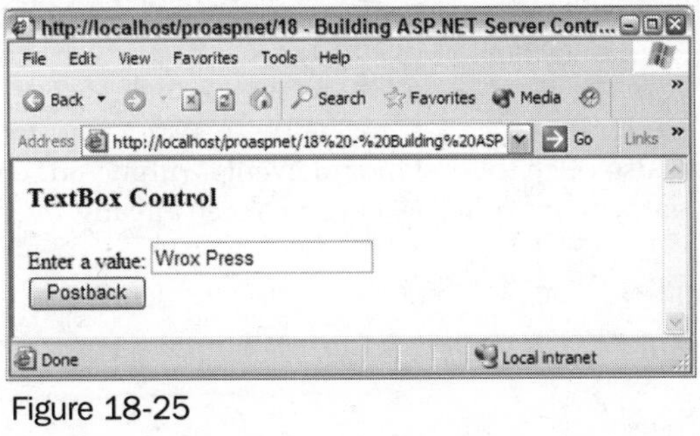

Figure 18-25

Our textbox control is now pretty functional for a simple control–it can remember its value during postback, can raise events when its text changes, and can have style properties applied in the same way as other Web controls using the various style attributes:

```
<Wrox:MyTextBox id="name" runat="server"
                BackColor="Green"
                ForeColor="Yellow"
                BorderColor="Red"
                OnTextChanged="OnNameChanged" />
```

More on Events

Any server control that derives from the `Control` base classes automatically inherits several built-in events that page developers can also handle:

- ❑ `Init`: Called when a control has to be constructed and its properties have been set

- ❑ `Load`:Called when a control's viewstate is available

- ❑ `DataBinding`:Called when a control bound to a data source should enumerate its data source and build its control tree

- ❑ `PreRender`:Called just before the UI of a control is rendered

- ❑ `Unload`: Called when a control has been rendered

- ❑ `Disposed`:Called when a control is destroyed by its container

These events behave just like any other event. For example, you could catch the `PreRender` event of the `TextBox` and restrict its length to seven characters, by adding an `OnPreRender` attribute to the control declaration:

```
<P>Enter a value: <Wrox:MyTextBox id="name" runat="server"
                            BackColor="Green"
                            ForeColor="Yellow"
                            BorderColor="Red"
                            OnTextChanged="OnNameChanged"
                            OnPreRender="OnPreRender" />
```

And an event handler that restricts the size of the `TextBox` value if it exceeds seven characters:

```
private void OnPreRender( object sender, EventArgs e )
{
  if ( name.Text.Length > 7 )
    name.Text = name.Text.Substring(0,7);
}
```

As a control author, you can also catch these standard events within your controls. Do this by either wiring up the necessary event wire-up code, or, as you've seen already, overriding one of these methods:

- ❑ `OnInit(EventArgs e)`

- ❑ `OnLoad(EventArgs e)`

- ❏ OnDataBinding(EventArgs e)
- ❏ OnPreRender(EventArgs e)
- ❏ OnUnload(EventArgs e)
- ❏ Disposed()

The default implementation of each of these methods raises the associated events listed earlier. For example, OnInit fires the Init event, and OnPreRender fires the PreRender event. When overriding one of these methods, you should call the base-class implementation of the method so that events are still raised, assuming that is the behavior you want:

```
protected override void OnInit(EventArgs e)
{
    base.OnInit(e);
    if ( _text == null )
        _text = "Here is some default text";
}
```

Event Optimization in C# Using the EventHandlerList

When an event is declared within a class definition, additional memory must be allocated for an object instance at runtime for the field containing the event. As the number of events a class supports increases, the memory consumed by each and every object instance increases. Assuming that a control supports ten events (six built-in and four custom events), and assuming an event declaration requires roughly 16 bytes of memory, each object instance will require 160 bytes of memory. If nobody is interested in any of these events, this is a lot of overhead for a single control.

To only consume memory for events that are in use, ASP.NET controls can use the EventHandlerList class. The EventHandlerList is an optimized list class designed to hold delegates. The list can hold any number of delegates, and each delegate is associated with a key. The Control class has an Events property that returns a reference to an instance of the EventHandlerList. This instantiates the class on demand, so if no event handlers are in use, there is almost no overhead:

```
protected EventHandlerList Events
{
    get
    {
        if (_events == null)
            _events = new EventHandlerList();

        return _events;
    }
}
```

The EventHandlerList class has two main methods:

```
void AddHandler( object key, Delegate handler );
```

And:

```
void RemoveHandler( object key, Delegate handler );
```

AddHandler is used to associate a delegate (event handler) with a given key. If the method is called with a key for which a delegate already exists, the two delegates will be combined and both will be called when an event is raised. RemoveHandler simply performs the reverse of AddHandler.

Using the Events property, a server control should implement support for an event using a property declared as the type event:

```
private static readonly object _textChanged = new object();
public event EventHandler TextChanged
{
    add { Events.AddHandler(EventPreRender, value); }
    remove { Events.RemoveHandler(EventPreRender, value); }
}
```

Since this property is declared as an event, you have to use the add and remove property accessor declarations, rather than get and set. When add or remove are called, the value is equal to the delegate being added or removed, so we use this value when calling AddHandler or RemoveHandler.

> As Visual Basic .NET does not support the add/remove accessor, you can't use optimized event handlers in Visual Basic .NET.

To create a unique key for your events, which will not clash with any events defined in your base classes, define a static, read-only member variable called _textChanged, and instantiate it with an object reference. You could use other techniques for creating the key, but this approach adds no overhead for each instance of the server control, and is also the technique used by the built-in ASP.NET server controls. By making the key value static, there is no per-object overhead.

Checking and raising an event using the Events property is done by determining if a delegate exists for the key associated with an event. If it does, you can raise it to notify one or more subscribed listeners:

```
void IPostBackDataHandler.RaisePostDataChangedEvent()
{
    EventHandler handler = (EventHandler) Events[_textChanged];
    if (handler != null)
        handler(this, EventArgs.Empty);
}
```

Using the EventHandler technique, a control can implement many events without causing excessive overhead for controls that do not have any event listeners associated with them. Since the Control class already implements most of the work for you, it makes sense to always implement your events in this way.

Tracking ViewState

When adding and removing items from viewstate, they are only persisted by a control if its viewstate is being tracked. This tracking only occurs after the initialization phase of a page is completed. This means if a server control makes any changes to itself or to another control *before* this phase, and the OnInit event has been raised, the changes will not be saved.

Types and ViewState

We mentioned earlier that the `StateBag` method used for implementing viewstate allows any type to be saved and retrieved from it. While this is true, this does *not* mean that you can use *any* type with it. Only types that can be safely persisted can be used. As such, types that maintain resources such as database connections or file handles should not be used.

`ViewState` is optimized and designed to work with the following types:

❑   `Int32`, `Boolean`, `String`, and other primitive types

❑   Arrays of `Int32`, `Boolean`, `String`, and other primitive types

❑   `ArrayList`, `Hashtable`.

❑   Types that have a *type converter*. A type converter is a class derived from `System.ComponentModel.TypeConverter` that can convert one type into another. For example, the type converter for the `Color` class can convert the string `red` into the enumeration value for red. ASP.NET requires a type converter that can convert a type to and from a string.

❑   Types that are *serializable* (marked with the serializable attribute, or support the serialization interfaces).

❑   `Pair`, `Triplet` (defined in `System.Web.UI`, and respectively hold two or three of the other types listed).

`ViewState` is converted from these types into a string by the *Limited Object Serialization* (*LOS*) formatter class (`System.Web.UI.LosFormatter`).

The LOS formatter used by ASP.NET encodes a hash code into viewstate when a page is generated. This hash code is used during postback to determine if the static control declarations in an ASP.NET page have changed (for example, the number and ordering of server controls declared within an ASP.NET page). If a change is detected, all viewstate is discarded, since viewstate cannot be reliably processed if the structure of a page has changed. This limitation stems from the fact that ASP.NET automatically assigns unique identifiers to controls, and uses these identifiers to associate viewstate with individual given controls. If a page structure changes, so do the unique identifiers assigned to controls, and therefore the viewstate-control relationship is meaningless. In case you're wondering, yes, this is one technical reason why ASP.NET only allows a page to postback to itself.

More on Object Properties and Template UI

Earlier, we discussed how the default control builder of a server control would automatically map sub-elements defined within a server-control declaration to public properties of that control. For example, consider the following server-control declaration:

```
<Wrox:ICollectionLister id="SessionList" runat="server">
   <HeadingStyle ForeColor="Blue">
      <Font Size="18"/>
   </HeadingStyle>
   <ItemStyle ForeColor="Green" Font-Size="12"/>
</Wrox:ICollectionLister>
```

The control builder of the ICollectionLister control shown here would try to initialize the HeadingStyle and ItemStyle object properties, determining the type of the object properties by examining the meta data of the ICollectionLister class using reflection. As the HeadingStyle element in this example has a Font sub-element, the control builder would determine that the HeadingStyle object property has an object property of Font.

Using the ICollectionLister Server Control

The ICollectionLister server control is a simple composite control that can enumerate the contents of any collection class implementing the ICollection. For each item in the collection, it creates a Label control, and sets the text of the label using the ToString method of the current item in the collection. This causes a linebreak because for each item in the collection, the label starts with <BR>. The control also has a fixed heading of ICollection Lister Control which is also created using a label control.

The ICollectionLister control has three properties:

❑ DataSource: A public property of the ICollection type. When CreateChildControls is called, this property is enumerated to generate the main output of the control.

❑ HeadingStyle: A public property of the Style type. This allows users of the control to specify the style attributes used for the hard-coded heading text. The Style.ApplyStyle method is used to copy this style object into the Label control created for the header.

❑ ItemStyle: A public property of the Style type. This allows users of the control to specify the style attributes used for each of the collections that is rendered. The Style.ApplyStyle method is used to copy this style object into the Label control created for each item.

The code for this server control is shown here:

```
using System;
using System.Web;
using System.Web.UI;
using System.Collections;
using System.Web.UI.WebControls;
namespace WroxControls
{
    public class ICollectionLister : WebControl, INamingContainer
    {
        ICollection _datasource;
        public ICollection DataSource
        {
            get { return _datasource; }
            set { _datasource = value; }
        }

        Style _headingStyle = new Style();
        public Style HeadingStyle
        {
            get{ return _headingStyle; }
        }

        Style _itemStyle = new Style();
        public Style ItemStyle
```

```
      {
        get{ return _itemStyle; }
      }

      protected override void CreateChildControls()
      {
        IEnumerator e;
        Label l;

        // Create the heading, using the specified user style
        l = new Label();
        l.ApplyStyle( _headingStyle );
        l.Text = "ICollection Lister Control";
        Controls.Add( l );

        // Create a label for each key/value pair in the collection
        if ( _datasource == null )
          throw new Exception("Control requires a datasource");

        e = _datasource.GetEnumerator();
        while( e.MoveNext() )
        {
          l = new Label();
          l.ApplyStyle( _itemStyle );
          l.Text = "<BR>" + e.Current.ToString();
          Controls.Add( l );
        }
      }
    }
  }
}
```

There is nothing new in this code that hasn't already been discussed. Refer to Chapter 15 for an explanation of using IEnumerator and ICollection.

The following ASP.NET page uses the ICollectionLister control to list the contents of a string array. This array is created in the Page_Load event and associated with a server control which has been given a name/Id of SessionList in this page:

```
<%@ Register TagPrefix="Wrox" Namespace="WroxControls"
        Assembly="DictionaryLister" %>
<script runat="server" language="C#">
  void Page_Load( object sender, EventArgs e )
  {

    string[] names = new string[3];
    names[0] = "Richard";
    names[1] = "Alex";
    names[2] = "Rob";
    SessionList.DataSource = names;
  }
</script>

<Wrox:ICollectionLister id="SessionList" runat="server">
```

```
    <HeadingStyle ForeColor="Blue">
      <Font Size="18"/>
    </HeadingStyle>

    <ItemStyle ForeColor="Green" Font-Size="12"/>
  </Wrox:ICollectionLister>
```

The output from this page (if viewed in color) is a blue header with green text for each item in the collection:

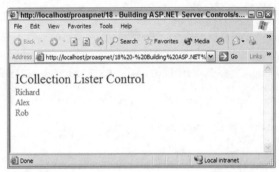

Figure 18-26

For controls that have fixed style and layout requirements, initializing them using object properties as we have in the ICollectionLister control is a good approach. You will have seen the same approach used throughout the standard ASP.NET server controls, such as the data grid and data list. However, for a control to provide ultimate flexibility, it's better to enable the user of the control to define what the UI of a control looks like by using templates. You've seen this in earlier chapters, with controls such as the data grid.

Using Templates

As you saw in Chapter 7, templates allow the users of a control to define how chunks of its UI–such as the header or footer–should be rendered.

Templates are classes that implement the ITemplate interface. As a control developer, you declare public properties of the ITemplate type to support one or more templates. When the default control builder sees a property of this type, it knows to dynamically build a class that supports the ITemplate interface, which can be used to render the section of UI the template defines.

Supporting template properties in a server control is relatively straightforward, although when using them within a data-bound control, things can initially seem a little complex, since the creation of child controls has to be handled slightly differently.

Let's introduce templates by rewriting the ICollectionLister control to support a heading and item template. Make the following changes to your code:

❑ Change the HeadingStyle and ItemStyle properties to the ITemplate type.

❑ Make the `HeadingStyle` and `ItemStyle` properties writeable. This has to be done since the objects implementing the `ITemplate` interface are dynamically created by the ASP.NET page and then associated with the server control.

❑ Use the `TemplateContainer` attribute to give the control builder a hint about the type of object within which your templates will be instantiated. This reduces the need for casting in databinding syntax.

The changed code is shown here:

```
ITemplate _headingStyle;
[TemplateContainer(typeof(ICollectionLister))]
public ITemplate HeadingStyle
{
  get{ return _headingStyle; }
  set{ _headingStyle = value; }
}
ITemplate _itemStyle;
[TemplateContainer(typeof(ICollectionLister))]
public ITemplate ItemStyle
{
  get{ return _itemStyle; }
  set{ _itemStyle = value; }
}
```

At runtime, if a user specifies a template, the properties will contain a non-null value. Null means no template has been specified.

The `ITemplate` interface has one method called `InstantiateIn`. This method accepts one parameter of the type `Control`. When called, this method populates the `Controls` collections of the control passed in with one or more server controls that represent the UI defined within a template by a user. Any existing controls in the collection are not removed, so you can instantiate a template against another server control one or more times.

A server control could use the `Page` class' `LoadTemplate` method (string filename) to dynamically load templates, but this is not recommended. It is very slow and is known to be unreliable. If you need dynamic templates, you should write your own class that implements the `ITemplate` interface.

Using the `InstantiateIn` method, you can change the `CreateChildControls` to use your new template properties to build the server controls for the header and each item. Since we're not supporting the data-binding syntax yet, the UI created for each item in the collection will not contain any useful values.

In the following code, the `InstantiateIn` method is called only if a template is not null. If a template is null, we throw an exception to let the user know the control needs a data source:

```
protected override void CreateChildControls()
{
    IEnumerator e;
    if ( _headingStyle != null )
       _headingStyle.InstantiateIn( this );
    if ( _datasource == null )
```

```
      throw new Exception("Control requires a data source");
  e = _datasource.GetEnumerator();
  while( e.MoveNext() )
  {
    if( _itemStyle != null)
      _itemStyle.InstantiateIn( this);
  }
}
```

With the new template properties and revised `CreateChildControls`, you can now declare a page that uses templates to style your controls UI. Here is a basic example that uses a `<H3>` element for the heading, and some bold text for each item (remember we're not showing the item value yet):

```
<Wrox:ICollectionLister id="SessionList" runat="server">
  <HeadingStyle>
    <h3>ICollection Lister</H3>
  </HeadingStyle>

  <ItemStyle>
    <BR><Strong>An item in the collection</Strong></BR>
  </ItemStyle>
</Wrox:ICollectionLister>
```

With these changes, the UI will now render as shown in Figure 18-27:

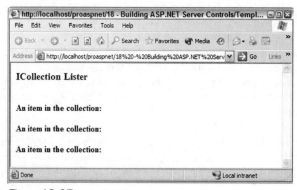

Figure 18-27

Although not visually stunning, these changes allow the UI of our control to be completely controlled and changed by the user in their declaration of our server control. As you've seen in previous chapters, this is a very powerful technique.

Your controls template support can use data-binding syntax without any additional changes. However, it is limited to the data it can access. You can access public properties or methods on the page within which the control is declared, or any public property or method of any other server control you have access to. For example, if you had a `Name` public property declared in your ASP.NET page, you could bind your item template to this using the databinding syntax introduced in Chapter 7:

```
<ItemStyle>
  <BR><Strong>An item in the collection: <%#Name%></Strong></BR>
</ItemStyle>
```

When this expression is evaluated, ASP.NET will try and locate the Name property on the naming container first (the control in which the template was instantiated in this case); if it's not found there, it will check the ASP page. Assuming you defined this property to return a Templates Rock string, you'd see Figure 18-28 as the output from the control:

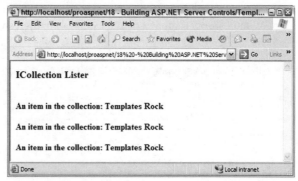

Figure 18-28

To bind to a text field called mylabel declared within the same page, use the following syntax:

```
<ItemStyle>
  <BR><Strong>An item in the collection: <%#mylabel.Text%></Strong></BR>
</ItemStyle>
```

To bind to the naming container in which the template is instantiated, use the Container. syntax:

```
<ItemStyle>
  <BR><Strong>An item in the collection: <%#Container.DataItem%></Strong></BR>
</ItemStyle>
```

Using the last syntax, you could be forgiven for thinking you could enable the item template to access the current collection item being enumerated. To achieve this, it looks as if you'd simply add a public object property to your DataItem server control:

```
object _dataitem;
public object DataItem
{
    get{   return _dataitem; }
}
```

After this, set that property to the current item being enumerated in the loop that instantiates the item template, as follows:

```
...
e = _datasource.GetEnumerator();
while( e.MoveNext() )
```

```
{
  if ( _itemStyle != null )
  {
    // Set the current item
    _dataitem = e.Current;
    _itemStyle.InstantiateIn( this );
  }
}
...
```

But if you made these changes and compiled them, you'd encounter an interesting problem, as seen in Figure 18-29:

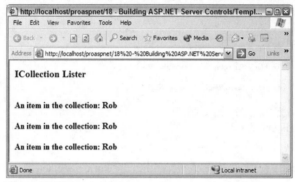

Figure 18-29

Each template item instantiated has the same value! This occurs because the data binding for controls instantiated using a template, or just added using `Controls.Add` by hand, are not data bound *unless* the parent control is data-bound. This means your collection has already been enumerated, and the `DataItem` will always point to the last item in the collection, as the controls instantiated by the item templates are data-bound. To resolve this problem, instantiate your template on a control that has a `DataItem` property that holds the correct value. This control will not render any UI, and will do very little except expose the `DataItem` property:

```
public class CollectionItem : WebControl, INamingContainer
{
  object _dataitem;
  public object DataItem
  {
    get{ return _value; }
  }
  public CollectionItem(object value)
  {
    _dataitem = value;
  }
}
```

The class derives from the `WebControl` since it will be the container for the controls instantiated by the item template. It also implements the `INamingContainer` interface to signal that it is a naming container for any child controls. This is important. Without this, the data-binding syntax would still refer to the parent control.

Using this new class, you can change your enumeration code to create an instance of the class for each item enumerated in the collection, passing in the current item being enumerated as a parameter to the constructor. The item template is then instantiated against the `CollectionItem` object created, before being added as a child control of the `ICollectionLister`.

Here is the revised section of the enumeration code:

```
...
e = _datasource.GetEnumerator();
CollectionItem item;
while( e.MoveNext() )
{
  if ( _itemStyle != null )
  {
    item = new CollectionItem( e.Current );
    _itemStyle.InstantiateIn( item );
    Controls.Add( item );
  }
}
...
```

The end result of these changes is that the server control hierarchy shown in Figure 18-30 will be created:

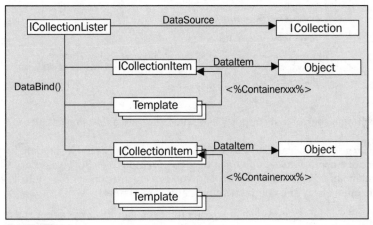

Figure 18-30

At the top of this diagram is the instance of the `ICollectionLister` control declared on the page. Assuming the `DataSource` associated with the control only contained two items, the `CollectionItem` object would have two `CollectionItem` child server controls. Each of these child server controls has a `DataItem` property that exposes the associated collection item, passed in via the constructor. The item template is instantiated within each of the `CollectionItem` objects, so its child controls vary depending on the "what's defined in the item" template. However, any data-binding using the `Container` syntax will always refer back to its parent `CollectionItem`, and therefore the correct `DataItem`.

Your *item template* is now being instantiated within the `CollectionItem` class. Thus, you have to update the `TemplateContainer` attribute declared on the `ItemTemplate` property to reflect this. Without this, ASP.NET would throw a cast exception when evaluating a data-binding expression:

```
ITemplate _itemStyle;
[TemplateContainer(typeof(CollectionItem))]
public ITemplate ItemStyle
{
  get{ return _itemStyle; }
  set{ _itemStyle = value; }
}
```

With these changes in place, your UI renders each item in the collection and displays its value, as shown in Figure 18-31:

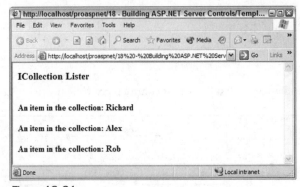

Figure 18-31

When implementing a control that supports templates, here are a few simple rules you should follow:

❑ If you are going to instantiate a template more than once, *do not* instantiate it against the same instance of a control unless you have very good reason to do so. For example, if a template does not contain any data-binding syntax and you can ensure none of the controls will be assigned an `id` (ids must always be unique within a naming container).

❑ If a control will be supporting a header template, it should *always* support a footer template. This is important for scenarios where a user may want to create an HTML table (or any other item that has a start element, several items, and then an end item).

❑ Be consistent with the intrinsic controls, and follow the same naming conventions that they use.

DataBind and OnDataBinding

When a server control can be data-bound, it should support a couple of additional features:

❑ The ability for the page developer to determine when (and *if*) a control should data-bind itself. This high degree of control over when a control accesses its data source, allows a page developer to optimize data source usage keeping it to a minimum.

❑ The ability to recreate itself and all child controls during postback, without being connected to its data source. The goal here is to reduce load on the data source provider.

To signal a control to connect to its data source and create its child controls, a page developer calls the `Control.DataBind` method. This call results in the `Control.OnDataBinding` method being called and the `DataBinding` event being raised. This behavior is in line with all other stages of pages.

When a server control's `OnDataBinding` method is called, it should create its child control tree as we did previously in the `CreateChildControls` method, but with a few changes:

❑ The number of controls instantiated (the numbers of items in the collection) is remembered using `ViewState`. You have to do this, as you need to recreate the same number of controls when a postback occurs. All other state will automatically be remembered by the other server controls instantiated as part of the template.

❑ Because `OnDataBinding` may be called one or more times, the `ClearChildViewState` and `Controls.Clear` methods are called to clear any existing viewstate for the control, and delete all child controls.

❑ The `ChildControlsCreated` property is set to `true`. Setting this flag ensures that `CreateChildControls` is not subsequently called.

The following code implements these changes:

```
protected override void OnDataBinding( EventArgs args )
{
  base.OnDataBinding(args);
  if ( _datasource == null )
    throw new Exception("Control requires a data source");

  // Clear all controls and state
  ClearChildViewState();
  Controls.Clear();
  IEnumerator e;
  int iCount;

  if ( _headingStyle != null )
    _headingStyle.InstantiateIn( this );

  e = _datasource.GetEnumerator();
  CollectionItem item;
  while( e.MoveNext() )
  {
    if ( _itemStyle != null )
    {
      item = new CollectionItem( e.Current );
      _itemStyle.InstantiateIn( item );
      Controls.Add( item );
      iCount++;
    }
  }

  // Remember the number of controls, so we can recreate the
```

```
// same controls, without the data source.
ViewState["count"] = iCount;

// stop CreateChildControls() being called again

ChildControlsCreated = true;

// Ensure viewstate is being tracked
TrackViewState();
}
```

When a postback occurs, a server control's `CreateChildControls` method will typically be called, unless a page developer explicitly calls `DataBind`. This method should recreate the control tree, using only information stored in viewstate.

Here is the implementation of `CreateChildControls`. The basic creation logic is similar to `OnDataBinding`, except that the data source is not at all used:

```
protected override void CreateChildControls()
{
    int iCount;
    int i;
    CollectionItem item;

    if ( _headingStyle != null )
      _headingStyle.InstantiateIn( this );

    iCount = (int) ViewState["count"];
    for( i=0; i< iCount; i++ )
    {
      if ( _itemStyle != null )
      {
        item = new CollectionItem( null );
        _itemStyle.InstantiateIn( item );
        Controls.Add( item );
      }
    }
}
```

The changes in this code are:

❑ The data source hasn't been used.

❑ The number of controls to create was determined by the `count` property held in viewstate.

❑ A null value was passed to the constructor of `CollectionItem`, since the `DataItem` will not be used.

With these changes in place, you have a data-bound templated control. The control should behave just like any of the built-in controls you have used.

Miscellaneous Topics

In this section, you'll see some useful techniques, depending on the types of server controls you write.

Accessing the ASP.NET Intrinsics

The `Control` class has a `Context` property that enables a server control to access ASP.NET intrinsic objects such as `Application`, `Session`, `Request`, `Response`, `Error`, and `Cache`. The `Context` property is defined as the `System.Web.HttpContext` type, which is the same type as the `Page.Context` property, which means it is used in the same way (such as for tracing).

The following code shows a simple server control that will output HTML to display the keys and values held in the application and session intrinsics:

```
using System;
using System.Web;
using System.Web.UI;
using System.Web.UI.WebControls;
namespace WroxControls
{
  public class IntrinsicDisplay : WebControl
  {
    protected override void Render(HtmlTextWriter writer)
    {
      writer.Write("<H3>Application Variables</H3>");
      foreach( string key in Context.Application )
      {
        writer.Write( "<BR>Key = '" + key +
               "' , Value = '" +
                 Context.Application[key] + "'" );
      }

      writer.Write("<H3>Session Variables</H3>");
      foreach( string key in Context.Session )
      {
        writer.Write( "<BR>Key = '" + key +
            "' , Value = '" +
            Context.Session[key] + "'" );
      }
    }
  }
}
```

For example, the following ASP.NET page sets some application and session variables in the `Page_Load` event and declares an instance of the `IntrinsicDisplay` control:

```
<%@ Register TagPrefix="Wrox" Namespace="WroxControls"
        Assembly="Intrinsic" %>
<script runat="server" language="VB">
  Sub Page_Load( sender as object, args as EventArgs )
    Application("Name") = "Richard"
    Application("Age") = "27"
    Session("Year") = "1972"
    Session("Car") = "Audi"
  End Sub
</script>
```

```
<html>
<body>
<Wrox:IntrinsicDisplay runat="server" />
</body>
</html>
```

Our control would render the output shown in Figure 18-32:

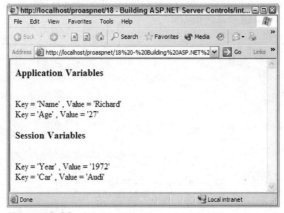

Figure 18-32

Writing Adaptive Controls

When writing a server control, the HTML (or other markup) that a control generates can be varied depending on the capabilities of the client browser. Using the Browser property of the Page object property, a control can determine the capabilities of the browser that is requesting the page. Most of the built-in ASP.NET server controls use this capability to reduce postback when a browser supports client-side JavaScript.

Here is a simple server control that determines the capabilities of a browser and reports some of them back to the client browser:

```
using System;
using System.Web;
using System.Web.UI;
using System.Web.UI.WebControls;
using System.ComponentModel;
namespace WroxControls
{
  public class AdaptiveControl: WebControl
  {
    override protected void Render( HtmlTextWriter objWriter )
    {
      objWriter.Write("<BR>");
      objWriter.Write("Browser is: ");
      objWriter.Write(Page.Request.Browser.Browser );
```

```
        objWriter.Write("<BR>");
        objWriter.Write("Browser version is: ");
        objWriter.Write(Page.Request.Browser.Version );
        objWriter.Write("<BR>");
        if  ( Page.Request.Browser.JavaScript == true )
        {
          objWriter.Write("Browser supports JavaScript");
        }

        if  ( Page.Request.Browser.VBScript == true )
        {
          objWriter.Write("Browser supports VBScript");
        }

        if  ( Page.Request.Browser.Browser == "IE" )
        {
          objWriter.Write("<BR>IE rocks!");
        }

        if  ( Page.Request.Browser.Browser == "Netscape" )
        {
          objWriter.Write("<BR>Netscape rolls!");
        }
      }
   }
}
```

The output from this server control, when viewed in IE is shown in Figure 18-33:

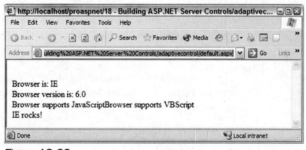

Figure 18-33

The output from the same server control when viewed in a Mozilla browser is shown in Figure 18-34:

Figure 18-34

947

Using the `HttpBrowserCapabilities` class exposed through the `Page.Browser` property allows a server control to become adaptive. For example, if the `Page.Request.Browser.JavaScript` property returns `true`, a textbox control could generate some client-side JavaScript to perform an advanced client-side behavior–such as limiting the number or type of characters that can be entered.

Control Attributes

When developing server controls, you can annotate your classes with attributes that instruct the ASP.NET page compiler on how the control should be compiled and used. Attributes can also influence the way your control is displayed by a visual designer such as Visual Studio.NET.

The following table lists a few of the common attributes used by ASP.NET server controls:

Attributes	Description
Bindable	Determines whether a property should be displayed in the DataBindings dialog in VS.NET. The default value is `false`.
Category	If the property grid is sorted by category, this determines which category the property should appear in. The default value is `Default`.
DefaultValue	The default value of the property. The default value is the name of the control.
Description	The text describing the property. This appears at the bottom of the property grid in the Description box. The default value is `String.Empty`.
PersistenceMode	How (or whether) changes made to the value of the property should be persisted. The default value is `EncodedDefaultInnerProperty`.
Browsable	Determines whether a property is displayed in the designer. The default value is `Yes`.
TypeConverter, Editor	Hooks up extended UI for setting the property.

The following example shows the use of the `Browsable` property for hiding the `SomeProperty` from the properties window:

```
[
Browsable(false),
]
protected virtual string SomeProperty
{
```

```
    get { ... }
  }
```

Custom Control Builders

A custom control builder is a class that derives from the class `ControlBuilder`, and overrides one or more methods that influence how a server deals with declaration within an ASP.NET page.

The following control builder class overrides the `AllowWhitespaceLiterals` method and returns `false` to indicate that spaces are not significant. If this method returned `true`, a `LiteralControl` containing spaces would be created and added to the `Controls` collection:

```
public class NoWhiteSpaceBuilder: ControlBuilder
{
  public override bool AllowWhitespaceLiterals()
  {
    return false;
  }
}
```

A control builder is associated with a given server control by making use of the `ControlBuilder` attribute:

```
[
ControlBuilderAttribute(typeof(NoWhiteSpaceBuilder)),
Designer("System.Web.UI.Design.WebControls.XmlDesigner, " +
AssemblyRef.SystemDesign)
]
public class SomeControl : Control {…}
```

User Controls

Although we have not explicitly discussed creating user controls in this chapter (see Chapter 4 for more on user controls), all of the features shown can be pretty much applied to them.

A key benefit of user controls is that complex sections of the UI can be declared using only control declarations. In a server control, you'd have to write code to achieve this. Although not difficult, this can be time consuming–changing or maintaining it can take longer–and also is more error-prone.

Why Create Your Own Server Controls?

"Why create your own controls?" isn't really the right question to ask. Instead, the decision you have to make as an ASP.NET developer is whether you let ASP.NET build server controls automatically for you (by just building your sites using ASP.NET pages and/or user controls), or whether you take over some of the control creation yourself. In the latter case, you can build your site using a mixture of ASP.NET pages, user controls, and custom server controls.

Thus, there's no *right* answer to the original question. However, a few pointers should help you decide for yourself:

❑ ASP.NET controls enable a fine-grained level of black-box reuse. ASP.NET user controls and pages can also provide this reuse, but since they are far more coarse-grained and typically have fixed UI traits (pages don't support templates, although user controls can), they are likely to provide far less reuse.

❑ ASP.NET controls ultimately provide the most flexibility, but take longer to write and require more coding skill.

❑ If you want a custom control, but are not 100% sure, start with a user control; you can always change it to become a custom control later. All the code you write will work as a control, but you will need to convert any HTML sections of your user control into code using control composition.

❑ Only custom controls and user controls can be *lookless*, and therefore support templates. If you want people to be able to extend and manage your control's UI, use these control types.

❑ User controls and custom controls can be written in different languages, and then used within the same hosting page. At present, only one language can be used directly within any single ASP.NET page.

❑ Only custom controls are compiled. You may therefore want to use them if you need to protect your sourcecode.

Summary

In this chapter, we've examined how to develop ASP.NET server controls using C# and VB. There are many topics, such as advanced state management, that we've not covered in this chapter but we've hopefully given you enough information to start developing server controls.

We started the chapter by looking at how to develop a really elementary server control with a hardcoded user interface. We then evolved this into a more useful label control supporting attributes to allow the text content of a label to be specified, along with server style attributes to define font size and text control.

Then you saw how the WebControl class is designed for server controls that require styles and also want to provide an object model consistent with the built-in ASP.NET server controls. Next you saw how server controls can interact with postback and use viewstate to become intelligent–automatically round-tripping their values in the browser, and raising events to allow server-side event handlers to react to changes in state.

You also saw several miscellaneous topics, including how to use attributes to influence the design-time experience of a server control, and how to determine the capabilities of a browser to enable a control's user interface to be adaptive. Finally, we looked at some of the reasons why you might want to write server controls in preference to user controls or plain ASP.NET pages.

The next chapter deals with exposing web services, allowing you to share information across networks and the Internet.

Exposing Web Services

Web services aren't a new concept. They allow distributed applications to share business logic over a network. A classic web service example scenario is a stock quote service: one company provides a service that can accept requests for stock symbols and responds with stock quote details. A company building an investment site can then use the application logic provided by the stock quote company to retrieve stock quote details.

This problem sounds relatively simple, but has proven quite difficult to solve in the past. That's largely due to proprietary protocol formats, such as RMI, and the lock-down of open ports to only port 80 (for HTTP) and port 443 (for HTTPS).

What is new is the use of XML and HTTP, which are open standards, rather than proprietary serialization formats such as DCOM, RMI, or CORBA (although CORBA isn't proprietary, each vendor's CORBA implementation is unique to the vendor).

By using standard Web protocols such as HTTP, and data description languages such as XML, to exchange data over common ports, web services can utilize the ubiquitous HTTP infrastructure support that is already in place.

The technical definition of a web service is programmable application logic accessible via standard Web protocols. Behind this definition are two important points:

- **Programmable application logic**: Web service is non-specific to implementation. The application logic can be implemented by components, by Perl scripts, or by any other mechanism that supports XML.

- **Standard web protocols**: Web services use Internet transport protocols such as HTTP or SMTP. The union of XML and HTTP forms *Simple Object Access Protocol* (*SOAP*). SOAP is a W3C submitted note (as of May 2000) that uses HTTP and XML to encode and transmit application data.

Consumers of a web service don't need to know anything about the platform, object model, or programming language used to implement the service; they only need to understand how to send and receive SOAP messages.

ASP.NET makes building web services easy, and since it uses the standard ASP development model, ASP developers already have the skills required to build web services with ASP.NET. Although a web service makes use of XML and HTTP as part of the plumbing, ASP.NET abstracts this and makes building SOAP-based end-points as simple as coding application logic. The plumbing is still accessible if you need to work with the transport or serialization mechanisms for some reason.

Here's what we'll cover in this chapter:

- ❑ We'll start with an overview of what a web service is, look at some of the common problems associated with building distributed applications, and briefly discuss the public specifications used for building web services.

- ❑ We'll look at how we build web services with ASP.NET, starting with enabling some simple application logic, and going on to look at the additional attributes and classes you can use when creating ASP.NET web services.

- ❑ ASP.NET web services support three protocols for exchanging data through a web service: HTTP GET and POST, and SOAP. We'll look at these protocols and the supported data types.

- ❑ We'll look at some strategies for building web services and tracing web service requests, as well as how to build services that operate asynchronously on the server. We'll also look at some of the general ASP.NET features that we can leverage.

> **In this chapter, any discussion of web services implies the use of SOAP unless otherwise stated.**

Let's get started with an overview of web services.

Web Services Overview

Today the most common way to access information on the Internet is via a browser that sends and receives messages via HTTP. The browser receives HTML that is then parsed and used to render the user interface.

The web browser only begins to scratch the surface of what can be done with the Internet when it comes to building applications. You can already see a migration to other Internet applications that use a similar set of underlying protocols but don't always rely on HTML to control the user interface or exchange data. Examples include PDAs, cellular phones, blackberry devices, and rich-client peer-to-peer applications.

Web services are designed to facilitate the move to this next generation of the Internet. Using web services it's simple to enable peer-to-peer and distributed application development, as you can use a common protocol for all these applications. It's easy to envision applications that use a broad set of web services for authentication, email, buddy lists, and so on.

As the protocol format is standardized, any application that understands SOAP can take advantage of web services. For example, if eBay built an auction web service, or Hotmail built an email web service, SOAP-aware applications would be able to utilize these services. However, various implementations can *interpret* the meaning of the SOAP specification differently. Microsoft has worked to ensure that ASP.NET web services are compatible with other common SOAP implementations. As great as all this sounds, there are some common issues and questions that surround web services.

Common Issues

Solving the problem of exposing application logic and details of services through XML and HTTP isn't difficult. You could use classic ASP, Java, and Perl (to name a few) to write a simple application that exposed data via XML. For example, you could use ASP to write a simple application that accepted values passed on the query string, and generated an XML return document that represented a specific database table. Other applications could then make calls against an end-point (say a URL exposing your database tables) to fetch, parse, and derive values from the document.

However, designs like this are tightly coupled. The client expects a highly structured XML document, and if the application providing this document is changed, the client implementations may be broken. In most cases, this can be addressed by using public XML schemas, but maintaining a set of schemas for each application would be cumbersome. Also, the XML document will be dependent upon the server implementation.

Typically, even minor changes to the application logic can require large changes in the code used to expose that application logic as an XML document. The classic example of this problem is encountered with screen-scraping, in which the HTML of a site is parsed for specific values. As long as the HTML remains static, the known values can easily be extracted, but if the HTML changes, it usually breaks the application that consumes the HTML. Other common issues include:

- ❑ **Publishing the service**: Once the service is available, how do clients find or *discover* the web service? Just as web sites such as MSN and Yahoo, which publish the location of web sites, shouldn't there be something similar for web services?

- ❑ **Describing the service**: How do consumers of the service *call* the service? For example, what protocol does the service support? How does the protocol serialize data? What data types does the service support? Does the web service require a schema?

- ❑ **The network**: One of the problems with other protocols such as DCOM, RMI, or CORBA is that they use TCP/IP ports that are closed or restricted, or in some cases require additional software or a specific operating system. Administrators use firewalls to lock down their Internet exposure, usually leaving only ports 80 and 443 open for HTTP and HTTPS traffic, respectively. If the required ports are not accessible or are blocked, building successful distributed applications becomes difficult. Additionally, most web applications are an amalgamation of technologies and operating systems.

- ❑ **The development framework and tools**: Given some application logic, is there a common development framework – as opposed to a choice of language, or even platform – that can be used to easily create web services?

These challenges are not particularly difficult to overcome. In fact, Microsoft, IBM, Intel, and HP (to name just a few) have worked to address many of these issues through development frameworks (such as Microsoft .NET) or through specifications that have been submitted to standards organizations. The specifications form part of the solution to the problems we listed. Rather than each company driving its own view of the world, they can agree on a single specification and provide an implementation of it. Standards-based specifications work especially well at the network level since each application can then leverage all the features provided by its native platform.

Specifications

To solve these types of integration, protocol, discovery, and description problems, Microsoft is working with companies that believe that web services are the key to building the next generation of web applications. The specifications they are creating fall into three categories:

❑ **Discovery**: There are two specifications that address the discovery of web services. *Universal Description, Discovery and Integration (UDDI)* – see http://www.UDDI.org for more details – is a directory that you can use to publish and discover public web services. Another specification, *DISCO* (abbreviated from *Discovery*) can also be used to group common services together on a server and provide links to the schema documents that may be required by the services it describes. We'll discuss both of these in the next chapter.

❑ **Description**: *Web Service Description Language (WSDL)*, another Microsoft co-submitted W3C specification, defines an XML grammar for describing web services. This description includes details such as where to find the web service (its URI), what methods and properties that service supports, the data types, and the protocols used to communicate with the service. Tools can consume this WSDL and build proxy objects that clients use to communicate with the web services. We'll talk more about what proxies are and how to build them in the next chapter. The WSDL specification is available at http://www.w3.org/TR/wsdl.

❑ **Protocol**: As already mentioned, SOAP describes an extensible XML serialization format that uses HTTP to transport data. We will discuss SOAP in this chapter, but not in any great detail. The specification is available at http://www.w3.org/TR/SOAP.

Using Discovery, Description, and Protocols

Figure 19-1 shows a scenario for using a Credit Card Validation Web service:

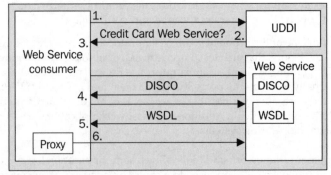

Figure 19-1

When building a web service, UDDI, DISCO, and WSDL are for the most part the technologies to be used at design time. The steps here are as follows:

1. A consumer's interest in a Credit Card Web service is communicated to a UDDI node (nodes maintain the available services), either through UDDI's public web services, or through the browser.

2. UDDI responds with a listing of credit card services (if they're available – let's assume they are).

3. The list of services returned by UDDI provides URIs that map to either DISCO or WSDL documents. We'll use the DISCO documents. In addition to the programmatic details provided by UDDI, you can also discover documentation for the web service at one of the UDDI.org nodes. Hopefully the provider of the service would provide additional details about what the service offered.

4. Follow the URI for the DISCO document. A listing of the location of WSDL documents is given within the DISCO document.

5. After parsing the DISCO document, follow the URI for the WSDL document related to the Credit Card Validation Web service.

6. Parse the WSDL document, and build a proxy object based on the details provided within the WSDL.

Although the DISCO and the WSDL documents can reside on the same server as the web service, it is not a requirement. The DISCO document can be stored anywhere since it is only responsible for linking to WSDL documents. Similarly, the WSDL document can exist anywhere as long as it accurately describes the web service (the description includes the end-point of the web service).

You now have a proxy object that can be used locally within the code, which looks and feels like the application logic it represents – it exposes the same methods and properties, but rather than the application logic executing locally, the proxy *encapsulates* the calls to the web service. You're now ready to use the web wervice at runtime.

You can build an application that uses the proxy (let's call it the CreditCardWebService proxy). The proxy encapsulates all the details of how to use the remote web service. From our perspective, we're working with a local object. If the company providing the Credit Card Web service decides to add some more functionality to the web service, it can simply update the WSDL. If it only adds new members, and doesn't change the signatures of existing members, our proxy will continue to work fine.

A lot of companies, including Microsoft and IBM, believe strongly that web services will be the next great enabler of the Internet. Support for web services is one of the most important features in ASP.NET. In the next chapter, you'll look at how to use the services you build. First though, we need to discuss *how* to use ASP.NET to build web services.

Building ASP.NET Web Services

Like ASP.NET Pages, ASP.NET Web services are compiled on their first request, and support a code-behind model, in which the code for the web service can reside in a pre-compiled .NET Assembly.

In this section, we'll discuss the programming model. Our emphasis will be on how to expose application logic as a web service, rather than upon the application logic itself.

> **ASP.NET Web service files are simply source files (that are part of an ASP.NET application) with a `.asmx` file extension.**

A Simple Web Service

Consider a simple class that calculates the value of an index in a Fibonacci series. A Fibonacci series is a series of numbers beginning with 0 and 1, in which the next number in the sequence is calculated by adding the previous two numbers. So, the third number in the sequence is 0 + 1 = 1, the fourth number is 1 + 1 = 2, and so on. The first seven numbers of the Fibonacci series are 0, 1, 1, 2, 3, 5, and 8. Let's implement this in code.

Fibonacci Application Logic

The following logic allows you to interact with a Fibonacci series. Using VB.NET, you could write:

```
Public Class Fibonacci

  Public Function GetSeqNumber (fibIndex As Integer) As Integer

    If (fibIndex < 2) Then
      Return fibIndex
    End If

    Dim FibArray(2) As Integer
    Dim i As Integer

    FibArray(0) = 0
    FibArray(1) = 1

    For i = 2 To fibIndex
      FibArray(1) = FibArray(1) + FibArray(0)
      FibArray(0) = FibArray(1) - FibArray(0)
    Next

    Return FibArray(1)
  End Function
End Class
```

Using C#, you could write:

```
public class Fibonacci {

  public int GetSeqNumber(int fibIndex){

    if (fibIndex < 2)
      return fibIndex;
```

```
      int[] FibArray = {0,1};

      for (int i = 1; i< fibIndex; i++){
        FibArray[1] = FibArray[0] + FibArray[1];
        FibArray[0] = FibArray[1] - FibArray[0];
      }

      return FibArray[1];
    }
  }
```

Both these sections of code create a `Fibonacci` class with a single method, `GetSeqNumber`, that accepts a single parameter, `fibIndex`, of type `Integer`(or `int` in C#), and returns the value of the index in the Fibonacci series. The index into the series begins with 0. So, for example, `GetSeqNumber(6)` returns 8.

A two-element array is created and initialized with the first series values of 0 and 1. For these numbers in the series, the value is the same as the index number, and so we can just use that as a return value. If the `fibIndex` parameter is greater than 1, we iterate in a `For Next` (VB) or `for` loop (C#), performing the necessary math to calculate the current values. Finally, we return the requested element (the last value calculated in the loop) in the array.

This is simply application logic, and is no different from the type of application logic authored when building ASP.NET pages or components. However, there are some special considerations that you need to be aware of when designing application logic to be a web service, such as supported data types and behaviors specific to web services. We'll cover those later in the chapter.

Next, let's see what needs to be done to enable this simple application logic as a web service, using ASP.NET. You'd want another application to be able to easily call and use *your* `Fibonacci` class. The difference is that this `Fibonacci` class needs to be able to communicate using SOAP. Fortunately, ASP.NET helps to do that very easily.

Fibonacci ASP.NET Web Service

You can use ASP.NET to expose your application logic as a web service by simply adding attributes to your code. An attribute is *declarative* code that adds additional behavior (such as the ability to support SOAP) to the code without having to add new *programmatic* code that changes the behavior of the application logic. It sounds complicated, but it's really not.

There are several attributes that a web service makes use of. The most notable of them is the `WebMethod` attribute. The methods or properties that have this attribute are treated as web services. They can receive, process, and respond with XML messages. All of the internal serialization and deserialization (that is, how the data being sent back and forth as XML is represented) is handled internally.

Let's look at the Fibonacci code, reworked as an ASP.NET Web service: Using VB.NET, you would write:

```
<%@ WebService class="Fibonacci"%>
Imports System.Web.Services
Public Class Fibonacci
  <WebMethod> Public Function GetSeqNumber (fibIndex as Integer) as Integer
    If (fibIndex < 2) Then
      Return fibIndex
    End If
```

```
      Dim FibArray(2) as Integer
      Dim i as Integer

      FibArray(0) = 0
      FibArray(1) = 1

      For i = 2 To fibIndex
        FibArray(1) = FibArray(1) + FibArray(0)
        FibArray(0) = FibArray(1) - FibArray(0)
      Next

      Return FibArray(1)
   End Function
End Class
```

Using C# you would write:

```
<%@ WebService Language="C#" class="Fibonacci" %>
using System.Web.Services;
public class Fibonacci : WebService{
   [WebMethod]
   public int GetSeqNumber(int fibIndex){

      if (fibIndex < 2)
        return fibIndex;

      int[] FibArray = {0,1};

      for (int i = 1; i< fibIndex; i++){
        FibArray[1] = FibArray[0] + FibArray[1];
        FibArray[0] = FibArray[1] - FibArray[0];
      }

      return FibArray[1];
   }
}
```

The application logic for both files remains identical. The difference is that the code now exists within an ASP.NET Web service source file (`Fibonacci_vb.asmx` or `Fibonacci_cs.asmx`, depending on the language used and has some additional declarative code, such as the use of the `WebMethod` attribute. The details of these changes will be discussed in a moment, but first let's test the web service.

Testing the Web Service

The Fibonacci ASP.NET Web service code is now a functional web service. To test its functionality, you can use a browser and request the URL that is represented by the ASP.NET Web service file.

A web service is not intended to service requests for web browsers. The web browser functionality shown is only for testing purposes, or design-time information. In the next chapter, we'll look at an IE 5.5 behavior that allows you to consume web services for rich browser clients.

To run the `fibonacci_vb.asmx` or `fibonacci_cs.asmx` (*the filename_cs and filename_vb naming convention has been eliminated in this chapter hence*), you must make it accessible through a web server, just as you would do for an ASP.NET page.

Once you've saved the code to a file on your web server, you can navigate to it with your browser. You should see the screen shown in Figure 19-2:

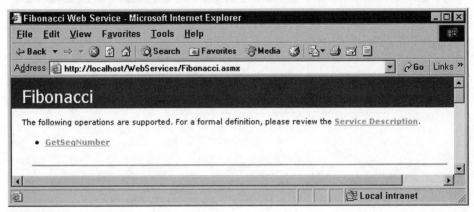

Figure 19-2

ASP.NET provides an ASP.NET Web service Help file template. On receiving an HTTP GET request, the web service Help file template programmatically examines the code in the .asmx file (using reflection), and generates the UI. This includes details such as the class and method name. Later, you'll see how to get even more information out of this file. The UI also provides some handy ways of testing the functionality of the web service.

The template page that does this is called `DefaultWsdlHelpGenerator.aspx`, and can be found in the `\WinNt\Microsoft.NET\Framework\[version]` directory. As it's just an ASP.NET page, it can easily be customized for the application. You can, in fact, have custom Help file templates files for different ASP.NET applications.

The Service Description link in Figure 19-2 provides the WSDL (the XML contract for this web service). The WSDL for any ASP.NET Web service is available as `[webservice name].asmx?WSDL`: so in this case, you can access it as `fibonacci.asmx?WSDL`.

> *We'll return to WSDL in the next chapter, where we discuss how to use the WSDL to build a proxy to use a web service.*

The other link on the page names the `GetSeqNumber` method. This represents the method that marked as a `WebMethod` in the `Fibonacci` class. If you select this link, you will be presented with information about the `GetSeqNumber` method exposed as a web service, as shown in Figure 19-3:

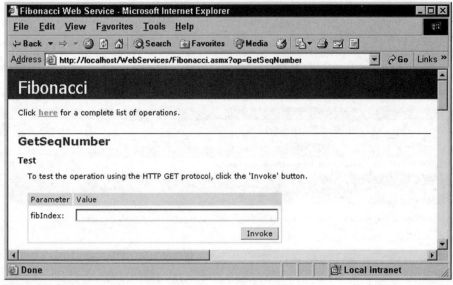

Figure 19-3

You can use the HTML form provided to pass values to the GetSeqNumber method. Enter a value for the parameter textbox and press the Invoke button to view the results.

The .NET Framework 1.1 changed the behavior of how web services can be accessed through the browser. In .NET Framework 1.0, the default behavior was to allow any browser to perform an HTTP-POST or HTTP-GET for testing purposes. In .NET Framework 1.1, this behavior was changed to only allow for localhost. *This new 1.1 behavior can be changed by modifying the configuration settings for web services.*

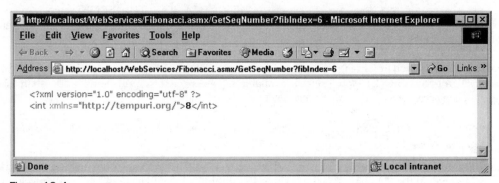

Figure 19-4

Figure 19-4 shows the XML returned from the GetSeqNumber method call. The element is named `<int/>`, and the return value is 8. Note that the value of fibIndex=6 is passed as an argument in the query string. You could change this argument's value directly, and the web service would return the appropriate result.

This isn't a SOAP return; it's another protocol type that ASP.NET Web services support: HTTP-GET. The web service help page generates a simple HTML form that makes a `GET` request to the `Fibonacci.asmx` file. When you build proxies to use the web service, the default protocol will be SOAP.

Let's take a closer look at the changes just made to the code in order to implement it as a web service.

Coding ASP.NET Web Services

The `.asmx` file format is very straightforward. You have two options for exposing application logic as an ASP.NET Web service. Both options involve creating a file with a `.asmx` extension:

❑   **Inline**: The application logic exists within the `.asmx` file.

❑   **Code-behind**: The application logic exists outside the `.asmx` file.

Using Inline Code

The first option (and the one used for our examples) is to code the application logic within the `.asmx` file. This is similar to inline ASP.NET pages – we take the Fibonacci VB.NET or C# code, and create the corresponding `Fibonacci_vb.asmx` and `Fibonacci_cs.asmx`.

Using Code-Behind

We have a code-behind option for ASP.NET Web services just as that for ASP.NET pages. Code-behind is the default behavior for ASP.NET Web services created with Visual Studio.NET. Rather than the application logic existing within the `.asmx` file, the application logic is stored in an external assembly.

To be able to reference an external assembly, the assembly must reside in the ASP.NET application's `bin` directory. The `bin` directory is a special directory used by the ASP.NET application, to which assemblies can be deployed and *automatically* registered.

To use the code-behind option, simply create a small ASP.NET Web service `.asmx` file (which we'll call `Fibonacci_Codebehind.asmx`) that contains a single line:

```
<%@ WebService Codebehind="Fibonacci.vb" Class="Fibonacci" %>
```

You need an implementation of the `Fibonacci` class in a separate assembly, either compiled and deployed in the ASP.NET application's `bin` directory, or as part of an assembly named directly in the configuration file. Here's what the source would look like for the VB.NET version of the Fibonacci example (`Fibonacci.vb`):

```
Imports System
Imports System.Web
Imports System.Web.Services


Public Class Fibonacci
  <WebMethod()> Public Function GetSeqNumber(fibIndex As Integer) As Integer
```

```
      If (fibIndex < 2) Then
         Return fibIndex
      End If

      Dim FibArray(2) As Integer
      Dim i As Integer

      FibArray(0) = 0
      FibArray(1) = 1

      For i = 2 To fibIndex
         FibArray(1) = FibArray(1) + FibArray(0)
         FibArray(0) = FibArray(1) - FibArray(0)
      Next

      Return FibArray(1)
   End Function
End Class
```

You can simply use the following command line to compile the source into a .NET assembly:

```
vbc /t:library /r:System.Web.dll /r:System.Web.Services.dll Fibonacci.vb
```

The result of this is a single file, `Fibonacci.dll`, which you need to place in a `bin` directory that is located below the root directory of the application. You can easily deploy the assembly (`Fibonacci.dll`) so that both ASP.NET pages and web services may use it – it's simply a component with a `WebMethod` attribute.

For example, if you decide that the functionality encapsulated within a class would make a great web service, you can simply make some minor changes to the assembly's application logic and create a one-line ASP.NET Web service `.asmx` file (as shown), to enable the application logic as a SOAP-based end-point.

As code-behind is the default behavior, the use of the `Codebehind` statement in `Fibonacci.asmx` is optional. Visual Studio .NET will use the `Codebehind` attribute, but you can just as easily remove it and still achieve the same functionality, so long as the assembly contains the class the ASP.NET Web service references. Also, there is no difference in performance between using inline code or code-behind.

Further discussion of web services will use the inline style, unless otherwise noted. The only tangible benefits of using code-behind over the inline style are:

❑   Code is compiled, and the source cannot be viewed once deployed.

❑   Since the code-behind option is an assembly, the assembly can also be used in ASP.NET pages.

Both the inline and code-behind options share a common set of directives that are used to give ASP.NET special instructions when handling ASP.NET Web service requests.

The WebService Directive

Like ASP.NET pages, ASP.NET Web services support directives that instruct ASP.NET how to process the request. For example, when the Fibonacci examples were converted to ASP.NET Web services, we first added a directive at the top of the `.asmx` file.

Using VB.NET, we wrote:

```
<%@ WebService Class="Fibonacci" %>
```

And using C#:

```
<%@ WebService Language="C#" Class="Fibonacci" %>
```

The `WebService` directive is a required addition for all ASP.NET Web services. We'll look at the directive syntax, and then at the attributes we'll use most often.

Syntax

The directive syntax is identical to that of ASP.NET pages. The declaration is contained within `<%@` and `%>` tags, contains a single directive, and may contain multiple attributes that apply to that directive:

```
<%@ DirectiveName Attribute="Value" %>
```

Or:

```
<%@ WebService Attribute="Value" Attribute="Value"%>
```

An ASP.NET Web service may contain multiple classes. However, only one of the classes can contain methods marked with `WebMethod` attributes. This relationship is enforced with a `WebService` directive attribute named `Class`.

The Class Attribute

The `Class` attribute is special, since it is required and forces us to always declare the `WebService` directive within a `.asmx` file. Fortunately, it's not complicated. The `Class` attribute simply names the .NET class, whether inline or code-behind, that contains exposed methods or properties:

```
<%@ WebService Class="[Namespace.Class | Class]" %>
```

Using the Class Attribute

The `Fibonacci` class must be named in the `Class` attribute as the class contains the logic to be exposed:

```
<%@ WebService Class="Fibonacci" %>
```

If the `Fibonacci` class existed within a namespace, you'd need to further qualify it:

```
<%@ WebService Language="C#" Class="MyMath.Fibonacci" %>
namespace MyMath{
  public class Fibonacci{
    // implementation
  }
}
```

In addition to the class attribute, you need to use the language attribute if you use a language other than the ASP.NET default language, VB.NET. To use C# as the language for the Fibonacci implementation, add a `Language` directive:

```
<%@ WebService Language="C#" Class="Fibonacci"%>
```

That's all you need for coding simple ASP.NET Web services. Next, we'll look at the changes to be made to the application logic.

Application Code

Whether the application code for an ASP.NET Web service exists inline or in an assembly named through the code-behind support, the requirements for both resources remain the same. You must:

❑ Include a reference to the `System.Web.Services` namespace

❑ Use attributes found within the `System.Web.Services` namespace to identify those methods and properties that should be Web-callable

❑ Optionally inherit from the `WebService` base class

The System.Web.Services Namespace

The `System.Web.Services` namespace contains classes that ASP.NET relies upon to enable ASP.NET Web services. Declare the use of this namespace in your ASP.NET Web service file differently depending upon the language you code the logic with. Using VB.NET, you would write:

```
Imports System.Web.Services
```

Using C#, you would write:

```
using System.Web.Services;
```

Importing the `System.Web.Services` namespace is required, as this namespace contains the `WebMethod` attribute.

The WebMethod Attribute

The `WebMethod` attribute is the declarative code used to enable the application logic to be Web-callable. Thus, you'd be able to support serialization and deserialization of XML, mapping of XML values to correct types, and transporting of requests and responses – the 'infrastructure' that enables web services.

Again, the syntax of the attribute declaration varies from language to language. For VB.NET, declare the attribute inline with the function or property declaration:

```
<WebMethod> Public Function GetSeqNumber (fibIndex as Integer) as Integer
```

For C#, declare the attribute on the line preceding the method or property declaration:

```
[WebMethod]
public int GetSeqNumber(int fibIndex)
```

Using the WebMethod Attribute

The following is an example of using `WebMethod` in VB.NET (`WebMethod1.asmx`) that returns the sum of two integers provided by the user:

```
<%@ WebService class="WebMethod1" %>

Imports System.Web.Services

Public Class WebMethod1
  <WebMethod> Public Function Add(a As Integer, b As Integer) As Integer
    Return a + b
  End Function
End Class
```

Once the `WebMethod` attribute is added, the `Add` method is Web-callable, and when the `.asmx` is requested through a browser, the method is available to select as shown in Figure 19-5:

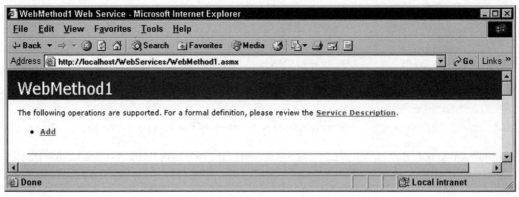

Figure 19-5

The last change you might need to make to the application code is to inherit from the `WebService` base class (also contained in the `System.Web.Services` namespace). You only need to do this if the web service requires the properties that the base class make available, as discussed next.

WebService Base Class

An ASP.NET Web service is part of the ASP.NET application it resides in. Just as we have application-specific configuration, session, and data for ASP.NET pages, we have the same capabilities for ASP.NET Web services.

You have a couple of choices for how you gain access to the ASP.NET-intrinsic objects, such as `Application` or `Session`. The easiest way to enable access to ASP.NET intrinsic objects within a web service is to inherit from the `WebService` base class.

Using the WebService Base Class

In the following VB.NET code, we use the `Inherits` keyword to inherit from the `WebService` base class. This base class for example, gives access to an `Application` property, just as we would expect to find when coding an ASP.NET page:

```
<%@ Webservice class="WebServiceBaseClass" %>

Imports System.Web.Services

Public class WebServiceBaseClass
  Inherits WebService

  <WebMethod> Public Sub SetApplicationState(state As String)
    Application("state") = state
  End Sub

  <WebMethod> Public Function GetApplicationState() As String
    Return Application("state").ToString()
  End Function
End Class
```

This code (`WebServiceBaseClass1.asmx`) exposes two Web-callable methods:

❑   `SetApplicationState`: Accepts a string value and sets an application key/value pair to the value passed in

❑   `GetApplicationState`: Simply retrieves the value of the data set in `SetApplicationState`

It's important to note that an ASP.NET page has access to the same application state memory that ASP.NET Web services do (the same is also true with `Cache` and `Session`). Therefore, items added to application state memory, or to the cache, can be shared between the page and web services. This allows for powerful reuse. For example, an e-commerce site can load the store catalog into `Application` state memory from the database a single time, and then both the ASP.NET pages and web services can share that data.

The `WebService` base class adds five public (not Web-callable) properties that you are already familiar with from ASP.NET pages:

❑   `Application`: Application state memory

❑   `Context`: Instance class passed throughout the life of the request

❑   `Server`: Server-intrinsic, provides us with access to methods such as `CreateObject`

❑   `Session`: Session state memory

❑   `User`: Identity of the user making the request (security feature)

Classes *do not need to* inherit from the `WebService` base class in order to be a functional web service – it is only for convenience. In fact, since an ASP.NET Web service is simply another ASP.NET resource, the `HttpContext`, which contains the raw information for the request and response, is already available by default. So, classes that do not inherit from the `WebService` base class can still implement similar functionality – for example, accessing the `Application` intrinsic object.

Accessing Application State without Inheriting from the WebService Base Class

Let's take, for example, the same code as before, but without inheriting from `WebService`:

```
<%@ Webservice class="WebServiceBaseClass" %>
Imports System.Web
Imports System.Web.Services
Public class WebServiceBaseClass

    <WebMethod()> Public Sub SetApplicationState(state As String)
        Dim Application As HttpApplicationState
        Application = HttpContext.Current.Application
        Application("state") = state
    End Sub

    <WebMethod()> Public Function GetApplicationState() As String
        Dim Application As HttpApplicationState
        Application = HttpContext.Current.Application
        Return Application("state").ToString()
    End Function

End Class
```

In this example (`WebServiceBaseClass2.asmx`), we're using the web service's instance of the `HttpContext` to retrieve the intrinsic `Application` object. This means we have to import the `System.Web` namespace in the code, since `HttpContext` is defined in the `System.Web` namespace.

The `HttpContext` instance can then be used to access the intrinsic `Application` object, which is set to a local variable of type `HttpApplicationState` named `Application`. The code then uses the intrinsic `Application` object in an identical manner to the code that inherited from the `WebService` base class.

Since a class can only inherit from a single base class, the advantage of not using the `WebService` base class can be seen when inheriting from a different class.

You now have all the basic knowledge necessary for building ASP.NET Web services. You could now skip directly to consuming ASP.NET Web services. However, there are more options available in building ASP.NET Web services. For example, the `WebMethod` attribute has configurable properties, and it's not the only attribute you can use.

Before looking at these options, we need to talk a little about the protocols and data types supported by web services.

Protocols

Protocols define how communication between systems takes place. ASP.NET supports three default protocols – HTTP-GET, HTTP-POST, and SOAP – but can be extended to support others.

The first two protocols, HTTP-GET and HTTP-POST, are implemented primarily as helper protocols, and for backward-compatibility, accepting parameters through GET or POST mechanisms, and returning an XML document. We will use these protocols to test web services and to provide a mechanism for existing ASP applications to build and immediately use ASP.NET technologies.

ASP.NET supports this exact same behavior, but in a more robust manner. If you're used to authoring ASP applications that emit XML, this should be a simple transition. However, for communication between applications, SOAP is the default protocol, and thus is the protocol that you need to be most familiar with. SOAP combines XML and HTTP to provide a simple but powerful mechanism, which allows developers to build applications that can communicate using strongly typed XML documents.

HTTP-GET

The implementation of the HTTP-GET protocol is the one that you see most often when building an ASP.NET Web service. That's because HTTP-GET is the protocol used in the page generated by DefaultWsdlHelpGenerator.aspx.

For example, when we built the Fibonacci Web service, viewed it through the browser, and called the method, the result received was a simple XML document as shown in Figure 19-6:

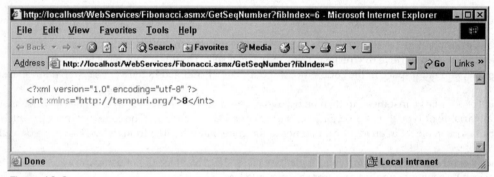

Figure 19-6

However, this document has nothing to do with SOAP. Instead, parameters are passed on the query string in the form GetSeqNumber?fibIndex=6. You can also modify the query string directly, and get different results.

Our web service help page only supports HTTP-GET (the default) and HTTP-POST. The reason for this is that a simple HTML form POST/GET mechanism cannot support the POST format used by SOAP. SOAP requires the body of the POST to be an XML SOAP document. However, an HTML form POST will attempt to send a name/value pair, which cannot be used to generate a valid XML document in the POST body.

HTTP-POST

The output from HTTP-POST is similar to HTTP-GET. The only difference is how HTTP-POST is input – that is, how the data is sent to the endpoint. Rather than passing data in the query string, the data is posted as name/value pairs within the body of the HTTP request. You'd expect the result to be an XML document identical to the one we got through the HTTP-GET request earlier.

To use HTTP-POST in your web service description Help page, and have it provide an HTML form similar to that created for HTTP-GET, you can modify `DefaultWsdlHelpPage.aspx` by setting the `showPost` flag to `true`.

SOAP

We won't cover SOAP in great detail. Firstly because there are other great resources (such as the specification at http://www w3 org/TR/soap12-part1/) for learning about SOAP, and secondly because it's a protocol and this chapter is about building solutions. To learn more about SOAP, you'll find some useful resources listed at the end of the chapter.

The W3C has officially created the XML Protocol Activity using SOAP 1.1, and updated it to SOAP 1.2. The XML Protocol Group has four deliverables:

- ❑ Protocol envelope
- ❑ Mechanism for serializing abstract data models
- ❑ Convention for use with RPC
- ❑ Binding to HTTP

Several companies have developed solutions using the SOAP 1.1 and 1.2 specifications, including Microsoft .NET, Microsoft Soap Toolkit Version 2, and the Apache Soap Toolkit (from IBM). The Microsoft Soap Toolkit v1 was intended to be an SDK. Version 2 is a supported solution, but with the availability of .NET you would be wise to use ASP.NET.

Implementation Details

A SOAP protocol message contains four parts:

- ❑ An envelope
- ❑ Encoding rules
- ❑ RPC representation
- ❑ Protocol bindings

The implementation of SOAP in ASP.NET uses HTTP as a transport, and thus is two-way – you send a message and receive a response. This is a design feature of HTTP and not of SOAP.

The SOAP envelope is the basic unit of exchange between the listener and sender of the SOAP message. Envelopes can be nested, in which case the outer envelope is considered to be active to the receiving SOAP end-point.

Headers are one of the extensibility mechanisms of SOAP, and are used to pass additional information about the envelope, or data that pertains to the particular protocol exchange. A good example of using SOAP headers is for authentication. For example, rather than passing an identification token as part of the envelope, which would assume the token was part of a method in ASP.NET, the token can be passed as part of the header. You'll learn more about SOAP later in this chapter, and in Chapter 20 you'll see how you can use the header to pass authentication information, which can then be used to verify credentials and authorize actions. You've seen the supported protocols for web services, now let's look at the supported data types.

Data Types

ASP.NET Web services support all the primitive types supported in the CLR. In addition to the simple primitive types, arrays of primitives are also supported. More interesting, however, is the support for user-defined classes and structs. Essentially, anything that can be represented by an XSD schema can be a parameter or return type of an ASP.NET Web service.

Custom Types

Suppose you want to build an ASP.NET Web service that returns a user-defined class named `CustomerRecord`. This returns some string and integer values, as well as an array of another, user-defined, class named `Order`:

```
Public Class CustomerRecord
   Public Customer As String
   Public Address1 As String
   Public Address2 As String
   Public Phone As String
   Public Email As String
   Public CustomerOrder(2) As Order
End Class

Public Class Order
   Public OrderNumber As Integer
   Public Name As String
   Public Cost As String
   Public ShipDate As String
End Class
```

You could write the following `WebMethod` that returned an instance of `CustomerRecord`:

```
Public Class OrderDetails
   <WebMethod()> Public Function RequestOrderDetails() As CustomerRecord
     Dim customerRecord As New CustomerRecord
     ' Set data...
     customerRecord.Customer = "JohnDoe"
     customerRecord.Address1 = "22913 Crestpark Dr"
     customerRecord.Address2 = "Houston, Tx 79043"
     customerRecord.Phone = "281-475-0938"
     customerRecord.Email = "john@customer.com"
     customerRecord.CustomerOrder(0) = New Order()
     customerRecord.CustomerOrder(0).OrderNumber = 12
     customerRecord.CustomerOrder(0).Name = "Product A"
     customerRecord.CustomerOrder(0).Cost = "$23.45"
     customerRecord.CustomerOrder(0).ShipDate = "8/6/01"

     customerRecord.CustomerOrder(1) = New Order()
```

```
        customerRecord.CustomerOrder(1).OrderNumber = 15
        customerRecord.CustomerOrder(1).Name = "Product C"
        customerRecord.CustomerOrder(1).Cost = "$13.41"
        customerRecord.CustomerOrder(1).ShipDate = "7/1/01"

        Return customerRecord
    End Function
End Class
```

As long as the user-defined class represents its data using primitive types, and those types are public, the data will be sent correctly to the caller. If, however, the class used `Get/Set` properties and modified private variables within the class, the data would not be sent correctly – XML is not used to describe the binary representation of the object in memory. Now that you're more familiar with the data types and the general ASP.NET Web service `.asmx` file, let's take a deeper look at two of the attributes used most often when building ASP.NET Web services.

WebMethod and WebService Attributes

Although the `WebMethod` attribute will be used most often when authoring ASP.NET Web services, there are other attributes at your disposal that provide additional functionality. Apart from marking a method or property with an attribute, you can set some attribute properties that influence the behavior of attributes, and which in turn affect the target of the attribute. We'll use the following syntax to set attribute properties. Using VB.NET, you would write:

```
... <AttributeName(PropertyName:="Value")> ...
```

Note the colon after `PropertyName:="Value"`. This syntax is only required for VB.NET. Using C#, you would write:

```
[AttributeName(PropertyName="Value")]
```

We won't discuss all the available attributes here – we'll concentrate on the `WebMethod` and `WebService` attributes. Let's take a detailed look at the `WebMethod` attribute.

The WebMethod Attribute

The `WebMethod` attribute is used to mark a method or property as Web-callable, and is represented by the `WebMethodAttribute` class. There are six properties on the `WebMethod` attribute that you can manipulate:

- ❑   `Description`
- ❑   `EnableSession`
- ❑   `MessageName`
- ❑   `TransactionOption`
- ❑   `CacheDuration`
- ❑   `BufferResponse`

Let's examine each of these in turn.

Commenting the WebMethod

The Description property is used to provide a brief description of the functionality of the Web-callable method or property. Using VB.NET, you could write:

```
...<WebMethod(Description:="[string]")>...
```

Using C#, you could write:

```
[WebMethod(Description="[string]")]
```

The value of the Description property is added to the WSDL and to the web service Help page.

Using the Description Property

If you add a Description property to the Fibonacci example and then request this through the browser, the description shows up under the link for the Web-callable method:

```
<%@ WebService Language="C#" class="Fibonacci" %>
using System.Web.Services;

public class Fibonacci : WebService{
  [WebMethod(Description="Returns value of index into Fibonacci series")]
    public int GetSeqNumber(int fibIndex){

    if (fibIndex < 2)
      return fibIndex;

    int[] FibArray = {0,1};

    for (int i = 1; i< fibIndex; i++){
      FibArray[1] = FibArray[0] + FibArray[1];
      FibArray[0] = FibArray[1] - FibArray[0];
    }

    return FibArray[1];
  }
}
```

When the .asmx file is requested by a browser, the screen shown in Figure 19-7 appears:

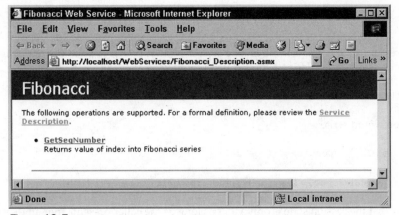

Figure 19-7

If you view the Service Description (WSDL), you can also see the description as shown in Figure 19-8:

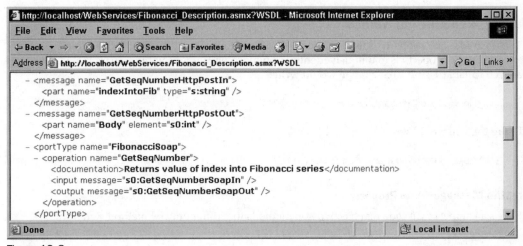

Figure 19-8

The entries in the `Description` property may contain HTML formatting. This formatting is then used to display a description in the Help page. However, keep in mind that the description text is entered into the WSDL. Other applications may consume the WSDL, and they might not understand the HTML tags found in the description.

Enabling Session State

Classes that inherit from the `WebService` base class or use the `HttpContext` can take advantage of session state to maintain state between calls. Session state, however, involves additional overhead, and is bound to the HTTP protocol since it uses HTTP cookies. Although SOAP is theoretically transport-independent, it relies on the transport protocol for application functionality when HTTP cookies are used. If you moved the SOAP message to SMTP, you wouldn't have the HTTP cookies functionality available.

By default, session state is disabled. To enable session state support, you can use one of the `WebMethod` properties, `EnableSession`. Using VB.NET, you would write:

```
...<WebMethod(EnableSession:="[true/false]")>...
```

Using C#, you would write:

```
[WebMethod(EnableSession="[true/false]")]
```

To enable session state, `EnableSession` is set to `true` (it is `false` by default).

One caveat is that the session state is only valid as long as the caller presents the same session ID. In the next chapter, when we build proxies to use against our web services, session state is available only for the duration of the existence of the proxy instance. The HTTP cookie is never stored on disk, and a new session is created for each new proxy instance, since the proxy, by default, doesn't persist the session cookie containing the ID. We'll also look at an example of how to persist and reuse the session cookie.

Aliasing Web Method Names

The `MessageName` property is used to alias method or property names. The most common use of the `MessageName` property is to uniquely identify polymorphic methods within a class that is to be marked as web-callable. Using VB.NET, you would write:

```
...<WebMethod(MessageName:="[string]")>...
```

Using C#, you would write:

```
[WebMethod(MessageName="[string]")]
```

Using the MessageName Property

Here's a snippet of C# code that has two `Add` methods that differ only by method signature:

```
...
[WebMethod]
public int Add(int a, int b){
  return a+b;
}
[WebMethod]
public int Add(int a, int b, int c){
  return a+b+c;
}
...
```

This generates an exception when requested through the browser. Both `Int32 Add(Int32, Int32, Int32)` and `Int32 Add(Int32, Int32)` use the message name Add. You can use the `MessageName` property of the custom `WebMethod` attribute to specify unique message names for the methods. The problem is that ASP.NET cannot differentiate between the two methods, and requires the use of the `MessageName` property to differentiate between the method names:

```
...
[WebMethod]
public int Add(int a, int b){
  return a+b;
}
[WebMethod(MessageName="Add2")]
public int Add(int a, int b, int c){
  return a+b+c;
}
...
```

Additionally, the WSDL that is generated must also be able to uniquely identify the element name when it is used to construct a message. When you use the `MessageName` property, this is reflected in your WSDL, as shown in Figure 19-9:

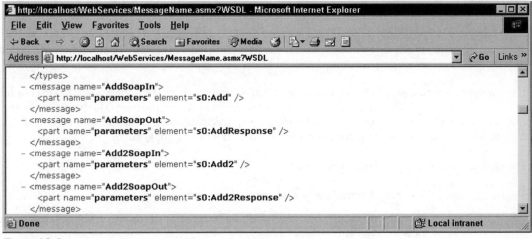

Figure 19-9

The `MessageName` property simply aliases our method name.

Building Transacted Web Services

ASP.NET Web services support transactions, but only ones that the web service originates. A transaction cannot be started by another application and then flow into a web service.

Using VB.NET, you would write:

```
...<WebMethod(TransactionOption:="[TransactionOption]")>...
```

Using C#, you would write:

```
[WebMethod(TransactionOption="[TransactionOption]")]
```

975

Using the TransactionOption Property

Suppose you had a banking transaction, in which the client makes a web service remote call to a method named `DebitAccount`, the transaction started by the client cannot be stretched through the web service remote call. The schematic diagram is shown in Figure 19-10:

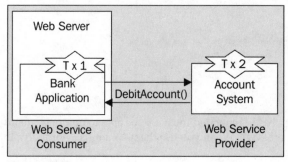

Figure 19-10

In this diagram, a **Bank Application** begins a transaction (**Tx1**). It then calls a web service, which begins another transaction (**Tx2**). The transaction (**Tx1**) started by the **Bank Application** does not flow through the web service.

If the web service transaction (**Tx2**) succeeds, it will allow the application's transaction (**Tx1**) to continue. However, failure of the `DebitAccount` call will fail the application's transaction. The `DebitAccount` call, which provides the web service, can also choose to participate in a transaction, but it is a new transaction context, not the transaction context started by the calling application.

The options for using transacted web methods are:

- ❑ `Disabled`: We cannot control automatic transactions on the object.
- ❑ `NotSupported`: The object does not run within the scope of a transaction, irrespective of whether a transaction already exists or not.
- ❑ `Supported`: If a transaction exists, the object runs in the context of that transaction. If there is no existing transaction, the object runs without one.
- ❑ `Required`: The object requires a transaction in order to execute. It will either use an existing transaction, or create a new one if none exists. `Required` is the default.
- ❑ `RequiresNew`: The object requires a new transaction, so a new transaction is created for each request.

Calling `SetComplete` or `SetAbort` in code is no longer necessary. Simply raising an exception is considered as a `SetAbort`, and successful completion of the call is considered a `SetComplete`.

The `SetAbort` and `SetComplete` methods are used to indicate to MTS or COM+ whether a transaction completed or failed.

Caching Web Services

Like ASP.NET pages, ASP.NET Web services support output caching. Output caching allows for the result of a particular resource to be saved to a cache rather than executed on each request. High traffic resources whose data changes infrequently can take advantage of caching for better scalability and performance.

The use of caching for web services is configured on a method-by-method basis through the use of the WebMethod attribute's CacheDuration property. Using VB.NET, you would write:

```
...<WebMethod(CacheDuration:=[int])>...
```

Using C#, you would write:

```
[WebMethod(CacheDuration=[int])]
```

Using the CacheDuration Property

The following is a VB.NET example use of CacheDuration (WebMethodCacheDuration.asmx):

```
<%@ WebService class="CacheDurationExample" %>

Imports System
Imports System.Web.Services

Public Class CacheDurationExample
  <WebMethod(CacheDuration:=30)> Public Function TimeLastCached As String
    Return DateTime.Now.ToString("r")
  End Function
End Class
```

This simple sample returns the value of the current time on its first execution. This result is then cached for 30 seconds, and the same result is returned until the cached entry has expired (30 seconds after the initial call), at which time the code will execute again.

Although this simple example highlights that caching is working, what would happen in a more complex example in which the WebMethod had parameters? You obviously wouldn't want to serve the same response for all requests; you'd rather vary the response on the basis of the request.

For example, if the result that the web service returned from a SQL Server database was dependent on one of the parameters of the WebMethod, you might not only want to cache the result (for the performance gain), but would also want different variations of that cached result based on the supplied parameters. This is supported by default.

Let's take a look at a VB.NET code sample to illustrate this better (WebMethodCacheData.asmx):

```
<%@ WebService class="DataExample" %>

Imports System.Web.Services
Imports System.Data
Imports System.Data.SqlClient
```

```
Public Class DataExample : Inherits WebService
  <WebMethod(CacheDuration:=30)> Public Function _
                  GetDataSet(City As String) As DataSet
    If (Application("ProductData" + City) Is Nothing) Then
      Application("ProductData" + City) = LoadDataSet(City)
    End If

    Return CType(Application("ProductData" + City), DataSet)
  End Function

  Private Function LoadDataSet(City As String) As DataSet
    Dim dsn As String
    Dim sql As String

    dsn = "server=localhost;uid=sa;pwd=;database=pubs"
    sql = "SELECT * FROM Authors WHERE City = '" + City + "'"
    Dim myConnection As New SqlConnection(dsn)
    Dim myCommand As New SqlDataAdapter(sql, myConnection)

    Dim products As New DataSet

    myCommand.Fill(products, "products")

    Return products
  End Function
End Class
```

You might have to alter the server name in the preceding code to reflect your own database.

Here, a `GetDataSet` WebMethod accepts a single parameter: `City`. The result from the request will be output cached. The ASP.NET Web service is executed once and served statically on subsequent requests for 30 seconds, and the cache will vary based on the different value for `City`. If you have a request where the value of `City` is `Dallas`, the web service will execute once and the result will be cached. If there is another request for `Dallas` within the allotted time period of 30 seconds, it will be served from the cache – the ASP.NET Web service does not need to execute and query the database.

This can be a serious performance enhancement, but should be used wisely – only items that vary by a few parameters are good candidates for web services output caching.

Buffering the Server Response

Buffering allows the server to buffer the output from the response, and transmit it only once the response is completely buffered. This might not be optimal for long running methods – you'd rather want to send the response as you receive it rather than wait for the complete response.

By default, ASP.NET Web services buffer the response before sending it, as this is usually most optimal for the server. However, the `BufferResponse` property allows you to configure ASP.NET Web services to not buffer the response. By default, this property is set to `true`.

Using VB.NET, you would write:

```
...<WebMethod(BufferResponse:="[true|false]")>...
```

Using C#, you would write:

```
[WebMethod(BufferResponse="[true|false]")]
```

The other attribute we'll look at, the `WebService` attribute, gives additional control over the *class* that contains the Web-callable methods rather than the *individual methods*.

The WebService Attribute

The `WebService` attribute is used to configure properties for the class – rather than the method or property – named in the `WebService` directive. These properties apply to the web service Help page as well as the WSDL. It *does not*, however, mark the methods within the class as Web-callable.

There are three properties of the `WebService` attribute that you can manipulate:

- ❑   `Description`
- ❑   `Namespace`
- ❑   `Name`

Commenting the Web Service

The `Description` property is used to provide a brief description of the functionality of the class that contains Web-callable methods and properties. It's similar to the `Description` property of the `WebMethod` attribute, but it's a description for the entire class, not individual methods and properties. Using VB.NET it would be written as:

```
<WebService (Description:="[string]")> Public Class [Class Name]
```

Using C# it would be written as:

```
[WebService(Description="[string]")]
public class [Class Name]
```

Using the Description Property of the WebService Attribute

The value from the `Description` property is added to the WSDL, and is also added to the output generated when the ASP.NET Web service is requested by the browser. For example, you can add a `Description` property to the `Fibonacci` example (`WebServiceDescription.asmx`):

```
<%@ WebService Language="C#" class="Fibonacci" %>
using System.Web.Services;
[WebService(Description=
            "This class contains methods for working with Fib series")]
public class Fibonacci : WebService{
  [WebMethod]
  public int GetSeqNumber(int fibIndex){

    if (fibIndex < 2)
      return fibIndex;
```

```
    int[] FibArray = {0,1};
    for (int i = 1; i< fibIndex; i++){
      FibArray[1] = FibArray[0] + FibArray[1];
      FibArray[0] = FibArray[1] - FibArray[0];
    }
    return FibArray[1];
  }
}
```

The output would be as shown in Figure 19-11:

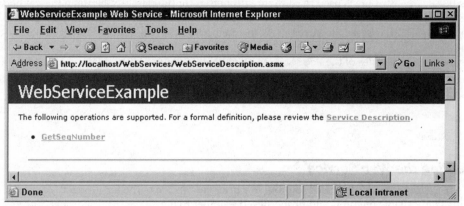

Figure 19-11

In the WSDL, it would appear as shown in Figure 19-12:

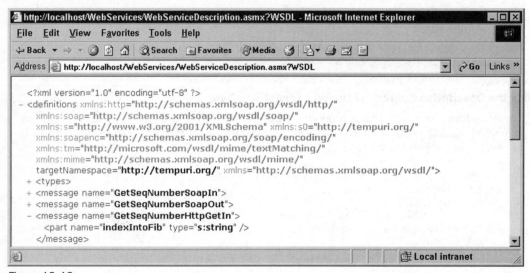

Figure 19-12

Controlling the Namespace

XML uses namespaces to uniquely identify sections of an XML document. Multiple documents can share markup vocabularies to describe particular regions of information. For example, in the case of two XML documents that both contain an `<Add>` element, how can software differentiate between the two elements in the composite document?

Organizations may qualify their markup vocabulary with a universal name that is unique to their markup vocabulary through the use of XML namespaces.

The default namespace that ASP.NET assigns to ASP.NET Web services is http://tempuri.org. tempuri.org will be discussed in the WSDL section of the next chapter. For now, the `Namespace` property of the `WebService` attribute can be used to change the namespace value to a value of your choosing.

Using VB.NET, it would be written as:

```
<WebService(Namespace:="[string]")> Public Class [Class Name]
```

Using C#, it would be written as:

```
[WebServiceNamespace="[string]")]
public class [Class Name]
```

Using the Namespace Property

If you viewed the WSDL from either the VB or C# Fibonacci Web service, you would see http://tempuri.org/ used for the value of the namespace. To change the namespace to http://rhoward/Fibonacci/, you could make the following change to the code (`WebServiceNamespace.asmx`):

```
<%@ WebService Language="C#" class="Fibonacci" %>
using System.Web.Services;
[WebService(Namespace="http://rhoward/Fibonacci/")]
public class Fibonacci : WebService{

  [WebMethod]
  public int GetSeqNumber(int fibIndex){

    if (fibIndex < 2)
      return fibIndex;
    int[] FibArray = {0,1};

    for (int i = 1; i< fibIndex; i++){
      FibArray[1] = FibArray[0] + FibArray[1];
      FibArray[0] = FibArray[1] - FibArray[0];
    }

    return FibArray[1];
  }
}
```

Now the WSDL appears as shown in Figure 19-13:

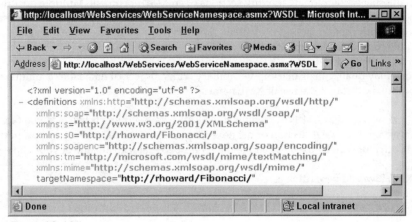

Figure 19-13

This affects what our SOAP message looks like, as shown in Figure 19-14:

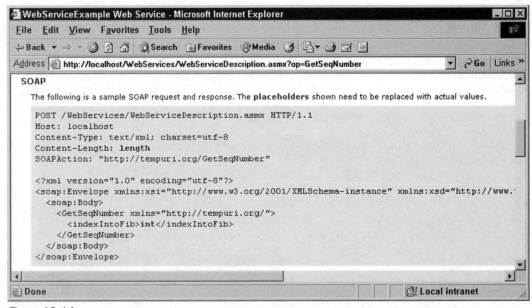

Figure 19-14

Changing the Name of the Web Service

When the WSDL is generated for an ASP.NET Web service, the name of the class is used for the `service name` value within the WSDL. When a proxy uses the WSDL and builds a proxy class, the name of the class generated corresponds to the `name` value of `service`. The `Name` property of the `WebService` attribute allows you to override the default value.

Using VB.NET, you would write:

```
<WebService(Name:="[string]")> Public Class [Class Name]
```

Using C#, you would write:

```
[WebService(Name="[string]")]
```

Using the Name Property

If you viewed the WSDL of the `Fibonacci` class, you would see the output as shown in Figure 19-15:

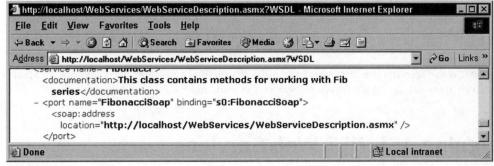

Figure 19-15

If you set the `Name` value to `WebServiceExample` in the `WebService` attribute (as in `WebServiceName.asmx`):

```
[WebService(Name="WebServiceExample")]
```

You would see the change in the WSDL as shown in Figure 19-16. All instances of `Fibonacci` in the WSDL have been replaced with `WebServiceExample`.

This property is useful if you want to control the name of the class that proxies generate, as tools that consume the WSDL to build the proxy will now build a `WebServiceExample` class as the proxy instead of building a class with the name `Fibonacci`.

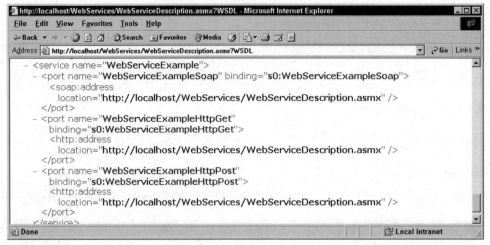

Figure 19-16

Now that we've seen the two attributes used most often to build ASP.NET Web services, let's discuss how to go about designing web services, and look at some more advanced issues involved.

Designing ASP.NET Web Services

Web services provide access to application logic, and application logic can take many forms – from stored procedures to components. Although ASP.NET Web services take the form of classes with implementations, this should not imply that normalized object-oriented design principles must be adhered to. A web service should never be considered as a class, method, or property. Rather, a web service is an end-point that data is sent to and received from.

While designing ASP.NET Web services, you need to compare many aspects (we've presented a few here). Let's start the discussion of building ASP.NET Web services by discussing API design, namely *chunky versus chatty* patterns.

Chunky versus Chatty

Web services rely on XML and HTTP to encode and transmit serialized application data. The combination of these two technologies provides a powerful means to create cross-platform distributed applications, as well as the ability to push application requests through proxies.

However, there are some downsides to this technology as well. It's an extremely verbose way of describing what should be a simple exchange of data between two applications, and it's stateless. Thus, the design recommendation is that you should try to reduce the number of network calls to the web service wherever possible.

Stateless versus Stateful

HTTP is a stateless protocol, and this doesn't change for ASP.NET Web services that use HTTP to transport SOAP messages. ASP.NET provides workarounds for this stateless barrier, but the workarounds rely on the use of a session token which can either be stored in an HTTP cookie, or embedded within the URL.

The stateless nature of HTTP should definitely be taken into account when building web applications. If that stateless problem needs to be solved with a solution such as `Session` state, it's worth considering the implications to the web service – using HTTP cookies builds reliance on the protocol rather than the SOAP message.

The discussion of stateless versus stateful applies most to discussions of design – how will your application logic be exposed (for example, will you use *methods* or *properties*) and how would end-users interact with that logic?

Using Methods or Properties

ASP.NET Web services use a class with methods marked with the `WebMethod` attribute to enable us to send and receive SOAP messages. Not only can the `WebMethod` attribute be applied to methods within the class, but it can also be applied to properties:

```
<%@ WebService Class="MethodsAndProperties" %>

Imports System.Web.Services

Public Class MethodsAndProperties
  Private Dim _name As String
  Public Property YourName() As String
    <WebMethod()> Get
      Return _name
    End Get

    <WebMethod()> Set
      _name = value
    End Set
  End Property
End Class
```

In this VB.NET code (`StatelessMethodsAndProperties.asmx`), the `WebMethod` attribute has been applied to `Get` and `Set` of the `YourName` property.

It's best not to mark properties with the `WebMethod` attribute. Although functionally the behavior can be made to work, it requires that the class instance hold state. For example, running the last code example, (using the handy web service description Help page) you can call `set_YourName` and pass it `Rob`. If you then call `get_YourName`, you get no result. Since ASP.NET Web services are stateless, the instance of our `MethodsAndProperties` class is created and destroyed for each request.

This can be fixed by enabling session state (`StatefulMethodsAndProperties.asmx`):

```
<%@ WebService Class="MethodsAndProperties" %>
Imports System.Web.Services
```

```
Public Class MethodsAndProperties
   Private Dim _name As String
   Public Property YourName() As String
      <WebMethod(EnableSession:=true)> Get
         Return _name
      End Get

      <WebMethod(EnableSession:=true)> Set
         _name = value
      End Set
   End Property
End Class
```

However, this solution will only work when you use a proxy to access this web service (which you *will* in the next chapter). Even with these changes, you still won't get the desired behavior when you test this code in your web service help page. The recommendation is that web services should be designed to be stateless, and that consequently using properties in web services is usually bad design.

Caching versus Static

Caching is another feature that can really help build great ASP.NET Web services. It's ideal for data that is requested often and doesn't change frequently. As you've already seen, caching can be controlled using the `CacheDuration` property of the `WebMethod` attribute.

Response Caching

The `CacheDuration` property allows you to specify a time duration within which the response to the request should be served from the ASP.NET cache. Serving requests from the cache can dramatically improve the performance of your application, since you no longer need to execute code on each request. Requests to a Web-callable method using the `CacheDuration` property will vary the entries for the response in the cache based upon the request. So, for a SOAP request, the contents of the cache will depend on the POST data.

Data Caching

In some cases, caching the entire response simply doesn't make sense. In such cases, you can use the cache API to cache interesting data within your web service. Consider the following VB.NET code (`DataCaching.asmx`):

```
<%@ WebService class="DataCachingExample" %>
Imports System.Web.Services
Imports System.Data
Imports System.Data.SqlClient
Imports System.Web.Caching
Imports System.Web

Public Class DataCachingExample
   <WebMethod()> Public Function GetDataSet(column As String) As DataSet
      Dim AppCache As Cache
      AppCache = HttpContext.Current.Cache
      If (AppCache(column) Is Nothing) Then
```

```
         AppCache(column) = LoadDataSet(column)
      End If

      Return CType(AppCache(column), DataSet)
   End Function

   Private Function LoadDataSet(column As String) As DataSet
      Dim myConnection As SqlConnection
      Dim myCommand As SqlDataAdapter
      Dim products As DataSet

      myConnection = _
         New SqlConnection("server=localhost;uid=sa;pwd=;database=pubs")
      myCommand = _
         New SqlDataAdapter("select " + column + " from Authors", myConnection)
      products = New DataSet()

      myCommand.Fill(products, "products")

      Return products
   End Function
End Class
```

Although this code would work equally well with the `WebMethod` attribute's `CacheDuration` property set, it does illustrate how you can use the lower-level cache API to save work. In this example, we accept a single parameter: the name of a column in a database. This parameter is then used to create a `DataSet`, which is then added to the cache. On subsequent requests, they can be serviced dynamically, but it results in a serious performance benefit since the data does not need to be fetched from the database.

Although caching is recommended when (and where) possible for performance enhancements, you need to understand how the resources within the web service are being cached. For example, in the previous database example, we had a fairly simple matrix of items to be served from the cache (limited by the number of columns in a particular database table). However, caching is useless for application logic that might have an unlimited amount of variations – for example, `Add(a As Integer, b As Integer)`.

Asynchronous versus Synchronous

Web services can be designed to be synchronous or asynchronous:

- ❑ A synchronous design allows the ASP.NET thread of execution to run until it's complete. If an action within the code has the potential to block, such as network I/O or an extensive database lookup, this can stall the ASP.NET worker thread. Since a thread is a resource, and there are only a limited number of resources available on the system, this can force other requests to be queued. This all translates to an impact on the performance and scalability of the system.

- ❑ An asynchronous design, on the other hand, allows the ASP.NET thread of execution to start up another thread, which can call back onto an ASP.NET thread when the work is complete. Thus, the ASP.NET application is not stalled because of resource constraints on available threads.

Advanced ASP.NET Web Services

This section will focus on some of the esoteric areas of web services. We'll cover topics such as integrating with Windows DNA, and shaping the SOAP/XML document exposed by our web services.

Controlling and Shaping the XML

ASP.NET provides several additional attributes (not discussed earlier) that allow you to shape the XML generated by the XML serializer used by ASP.NET. There are two separate types of attributes: those that apply to the XML documents generated by the HTTP-GET and HTTP-POST protocols, and those that apply to SOAP. It is *not* an error to use the attributes together. The following table lists these attributes, along with a brief description of their purpose:

Attribute	Description
XML Documents: `XmlAttribute` SOAP Documents: `SoapAttribute`	Allows you to control the XML attribute representation, or convert an XML element into an attribute
XML Documents: `XmlElement` SOAP Documents: `SoapElement`	Allows you to control the XML element representation, or convert an XML attribute into an element
XML Documents: `XmlArray` SOAP Documents: `SoapArray`	Allows you to treat elements as an XML array

These attributes allow us to have fine granular control over the shape of the XML document used as part of the HTTP-GET, HTTP-POST, or SOAP responses. These attributes are very straightforward, and are most often used when you return an instance of a class. Returning classes have not been discussed yet, so a brief example is necessary. Consider a simple ASP.NET Web service (`Books.asmx`) that returns a `Books` class:

```
<%@ WebService Class="ReturnBooks" %>
Imports System.Web.Services
Public Class ReturnBooks
  <WebMethod()> Public Function GetBooks() As Books
    Dim b As New Books
    b.Title = "Professional ASP.NET"
    b.Price = 59.99
    b.Description = "This book covers Microsoft's ASP.NET technology " & _
                    "for building Web Applications"
    ReDim b.Authors(5)
    b.Authors(0) = "Alex Homer"
    b.Authors(1) = "David Sussman"
    b.Authors(2) = "Rob Howard"
    b.Authors(3) = "Brian Francis"
    b.Authors(4) = "Rich Anderson"
    b.Authors(5) = "Karli Watson"
```

```
      Return b
   End Function
End Class

Public Class Books
   Public Title As String
   Public Description As String
   Public Price As Double
   Public Authors() As String
End Class
```

Calls made to the `GetBooks` WebMethod will return an XML document with a root node of `<Book>`, and elements within `<Book>`, such as `<Authors>`, `<Title>`, `<Price>`, and so on, for each of our classes members. Figure 19-17 shows an XML document returned from an HTTP-GET request:

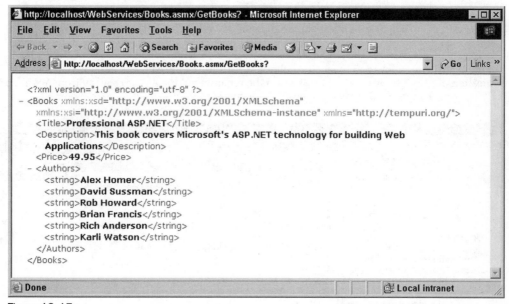

Figure 19-17

To change the shape of the XML document – say by returning the title as an attribute of Books, and renaming the <Price> element to <DiscountPrice> – use the XmlAttribute and XmlElement attributes. To influence the SOAP message, you need to add the SOAP equivalent attributes. Two changes have to be made to the `Books` class. First, add the `System.Xml.Serialization` namespace, as it contains both the `XmlAttribute` and `XmlElement` attributes. Second, add the attributes to the `Books` class member variables you want them applied to (`Books2.asmx`):

```
<%@ WebService Class="ReturnBooks" %>
Imports System.Web.Services
Imports System.Xml.Serialization
Public Class ReturnBooks
   <WebMethod()> Public Function GetBooks() As Books
      Dim b As New Books
```

```
        b.Title = "Professional ASP.NET"
        b.Price = 59.99
        b.Description = "This book covers Microsoft's ASP.NET technology " & _
                        "for building Web Applications"
        ReDim b.Authors(5)
        b.Authors(0) = "Alex Homer"
        b.Authors(1) = "David Sussman"
        b.Authors(2) = "Rob Howard"
        b.Authors(3) = "Brian Francis"
        b.Authors(4) = "Rich Anderson"
        b.Authors(5) = "Karli Watson"
        Return b
    End Function
End Class
Public Class Books
    <XmlAttribute> Public Title As String
    Public Description As String
    <XmlElement("DiscountedPrice")> Public Price As Double
    <XmlArray("Contributors")> Public Authors() As String
End Class
```

All of these attributes allow you to rename either the attribute or the element, as shown in the
modification of Price to DiscountedPrice and the renaming of the Authors array from Authors to
Contributors. Figure 19-18 shows the new XML document:

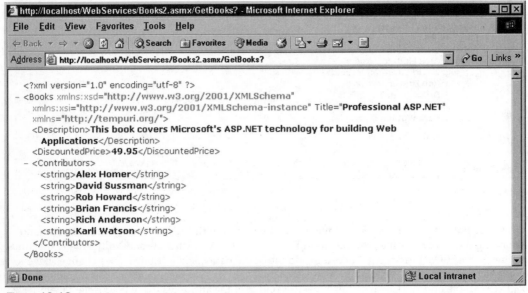

Figure 19-18

Modifying the Web Service Help Page

The default web service Help page is the template used for all ASP.NET Web services when a request is
made through the browser to a particular web service. Chapter 16 (ASP.NET Configuration) discussed

how each application could support its own web service – it's simply a configuration option to tell the application which ASP.NET page to use. Since the web service Help page is implemented as an ASP.NET page, it can be modified. For example, the page can be customized with graphics specific to the application, or provide additional details about the web services that the server provides.

Remember that any changes to the server's `DefaultWsdlHelpGenerator.aspx` will apply to all ASP.NET Web services on that server, unless you alter the ASP.NET configuration. However, there are some changes that can be made to this file, which will be useful in debugging the ASP.NET Web service.

HTML Form (Post Support)

If an ASP.NET Web service is capable of supporting the HTTP-POST protocol, and that functionality needs to be tested, `DefaultWsdlHelpGenerator.aspx` can be opened and modifications be made to the `showPost` flag:

```
// set this to true if you want to see a
// POST test form instead of a GET test form
bool showPost = false;
```

By default, this flag is set to `false`, but when set to `true` it will generate another HTML form available on the detail page for a particular `WebMethod` supporting HTTP-POST.

Protocol Request/Response Sample

When you drill into a particular `WebMethod` detail page, you are provided with a view of what the protocol request and response messages should look like. Within `DefaultWsdlHelpGenerator.aspx`, there are three flags that can be altered to change how these protocol messages are displayed:

Flag	Default Value	Description
dontFilterXml	false	By default, the XML shown in protocol messages is not URL-encoded. If the flag is set to `true`, you can view the URL encoded XML in the message.
maxObjectGraphDepth	4	This setting allows you to control the depth objects to show. This would be applicable for the `Books` class if it contained a public member `Authors` that was another class, and `Authors` contained a public member which was another class, and so on.
maxArraySize	2	This option allows you to control the maximum number of array element examples shown within the protocols. For example, the `Books` class contained an array of six authors. The array representing these items in the protocol samples would, by default, only show two items.

Next, let's look at one of the features of SOAP headers, which can be used to send out-of-band information.

SOAP Headers

The use of headers is supported only within the SOAP protocol, and not HTTP-GET or HTTP-POST. ASP.NET Web services that are created using SOAP as the default protocol for application-to-application communication. For example, consider the SOAP response to a call to the Fibonacci Web service:

```xml
<?xml version="1.0"?>
<soap:Envelope xmlns:xsi="http://www.w3.org/2000/10/XMLSchema-instance"
               xmlns:xsd="http://www.w3.org/2000/10/XMLSchema"
               xmlns:soap="http://schemas.xmlsoap.org/soap/envelope">
  <soap:Body>
    <GetSeqNumber xmlns="http://tempuri.org/">
      <FibIndex>6</FibIndex>
    </GetSeqNumber>
  </soap:Body>
</soap:Envelope>
```

The HTTP headers have been stripped out, and what remains is the body of an HTTP request containing the SOAP message. The SOAP message contains an envelope (<soap:Envelope ...>) that encapsulates a body (<soap:Body>) and optional headers (<soap:Headers>). To use SOAP headers, you need to specify a SoapHeader attribute on the Web-callable method or property.

The SoapHeader attribute allows you to optionally set a SOAP header, on the consumer *or* provider of the service. SOAP does not define headers for you: they are simply an extensibility mechanism that can be used in your ASP.NET Web services.

For example, consider the following SOAP message for the Fibonacci example along with a simple header:

```xml
<?xml version="1.0"?>
<soap:Envelope xmlns:xsi="http://www.w3.org/2000/10/XMLSchema-instance"
               xmlns:xsd="http://www.w3.org/2000/10/XMLSchema"
               xmlns:soap="http://schemas.xmlsoap.org/soap/envelope">
  <soap:Header>
    <SimpleSoapHeader xmlns="http://tempuri.org/">
      <value>string</value>
    </SimpleSoapHeader>
  </soap:Header>
  <soap:Body>
    <GetSeqNumber xmlns="http://tempuri.org/">
      <FibIndex>int</FibIndex>
    </GetSeqNumber>
  </soap:Body>
</soap:Envelope>
```

To use SOAP headers, it is necessary to create a class that inherits from the SoapHeader base class. In the following code, both a SoapHeader attribute and the SoapHeader class will be used. They are two separate classes – it's just that with attributes it's not necessary to explicitly add Attribute onto the end of the attribute on declaration (as SoapHeaderAttribute).

The SoapHeader Class

To make use of a SOAP header, you need to create a class that derives from SoapHeader, which can be found in the System.Web.Services.Protocols namespace:

```
public abstract class SoapHeader{
   public bool MustUnderstand{get; set;}
   public string Actor{get; set;}
   public bool DidUnderstand{get; set;}
}
```

Here's a simple example of a class that inherits from SoapHeader (written in VB.NET):

```
Imports System.Web.Services.Protocols

Public Class SimpleSoapHeader
  Inherits SoapHeader
  Public value As string
End Class
```

Within this class is defined a single public member, value. Applications that wish to use this SOAP header can pass data within value.

Let's add this class to the Fibonacci example (FibonnaciSOAP.asmx):

```
<%@ WebService class="Fibonacci"%>

Imports System.Web.Services
Imports System.Web.Services.Protocols

Public Class SimpleSoapHeader
  Inherits SoapHeader

  Public value As string
End Class
Public Class Fibonacci
  Public simpleHeader As SimpleSoapHeader

  <WebMethod, SoapHeader("simpleHeader")> Public Function _
                      GetSeqNumber (fibIndex as Integer) as Integer
    If (fibIndex < 2) Then
      Return fibIndex
    End If

    Dim FibArray(2) As Integer
    Dim i As Integer

    FibArray(0) = 0
    FibArray(1) = 1
```

```
      For i = 2 To fibIndex
         FibArray(1) = FibArray(1) + FibArray(0)
         FibArray(0) = FibArray(1) - FibArray(0)
      Next

      Return FibArray(1)
   End Function
End Class
```

This cannot be tested in the same way as the earlier examples – you'll see why.later.

In this modified `Fibonacci` class, we declared a local member variable `simpleHeader`, of type `SimpleSoapHeader`:

```
   Public simpleHeader As SimpleSoapHeader
```

This represents an instance of the custom SOAP header that a client will set. Next, we used the `SoapHeader` attribute, which has been added to `GetSeqNumber`, and passed in the name of the member variable, `simpleHeader`:

```
   <WebMethod, SoapHeader("simpleHeader")> Public Function _
                           GetSeqNumber (fibIndex as Integer) as Integer
```

Setting the `SoapHeader` attribute to `simpleHeader` creates a SOAP header containing a single item (named `value`) that you can set, as defined in the `SimpleSoapHeader` class. When we created the `SimpleSoapHeader` class, the class inherited from the `SoapHeader` class. Let's take a look at the inherited properties the class receives.

Properties Inherited from SoapHeader

The `SoapHeader` class provides three additional properties. We won't discuss them in detail, but you can review the SOAP 1.2 specification (http://www.w3.org/TR/soap12-part1/) to learn more about why they exist. The properties are:

❑   `Actor`: Section 5.2.2 of the SOAP 1.2 specification states that a `role` header message may be used by a SOAP document to name the intended recipient, as a SOAP message can pass through many applications capable of routing the message. The `Actor` property allows you to set the URI value – the endpoint that the SOAP message is ultimately going to be routed to. Alternatively, you can set a special URI – http://www.w3.org/2003/05/soap-envelope/role/next as defined by the SOAP 1.2 specification – that indicates that the next recipient of the SOAP message should process the message.

Note that the SOAP 1.1 defines the SOAP header attribute as `Actor`, but this has been renamed to `Role`. The `SoapHeader` property will remain as `Actor` for backward-compatibility.

❑   `mustUnderstand`: Section 5.2.3 of the SOAP 1.2 specification states that a SOAP header can use an attribute, `mustUnderstand`, to indicate whether it is mandatory or optional for a recipient to process the header entry. This value is set to `false` by default.

❑   `DidUnderstand`: A Boolean flag that the receiver of the SOAP message may set if the SOAP header was understood.

When we applied the `SoapHeader` attribute, we set a value that represents a property of a `SoapHeader` attribute called `MemberName`. Let's take a look at `MemberName` *and* the other properties supported by the `SoapHeader` attribute.

The SoapHeader Attribute

The `SoapHeader` attribute is the attribute added to Web-callable methods or properties to instruct those methods and properties to support SOAP headers. You've already seen that to use a SOAP header, you need to create a class that inherits from the `SoapHeader` base class. After this, you expose a member variable whose type is that of your class (which inherits from `SoapHeader`).

Consumers of your web service use the member variable to create an instance of your class and to set values. The `SoapHeader` attribute is provided with the name of this class – for example, `<SoapHeader("simpleHeader")>` – and is thus able to access the class instance. This constructor sets the `MemberName` property of the `SoapHeader` attribute.

The `SoapHeader` attribute supports three properties:

❑   `MemberName`

❑   `Direction`

❑   `Required`

The MemberName Property

The `MemberName` property identifies the name of the member (within the class) for which the header is to be created. This is best demonstrated by revisiting the example code:

```
public simpleHeader As SimpleSoapHeader

<WebMethod, SoapHeader("simpleHeader")> public Function
                        GetSeqNumber (FibIndex as Integer) as Integer
```

`simpleHeader` is a variable of type `SimpleSoapHeader` (which is the class that inherits from the `SoapHeader` base class).

Next, you see the `SoapHeader` attribute and the value passed in its constructor – the name of the `SimpleSoapHeader` variable, `simpleHeader`. `simpleHeader` is the name of the member that represents the `SimpleSoapHeader` class. When we discuss consuming web services in the next chapter, you'll see how the consumer can create an instance of `SimpleSoapHeader`, set its `value` property, and assign that instance to `simpleHeader`.

In a nutshell, the `MemberName` property allows the `SoapHeader` attribute to name the class variable that it will be a type of.

The Direction Property

SOAP headers are, by default, inbound only; the server servicing SOAP requests expects to receive SOAP headers, but not to set or send SOAP headers. This becomes apparent if you try to test the example (the Fibonacci Web service with a simple SOAP header, shown in Figure 19-19) using the web service's Help page. The HTML form for testing the results is no longer available:

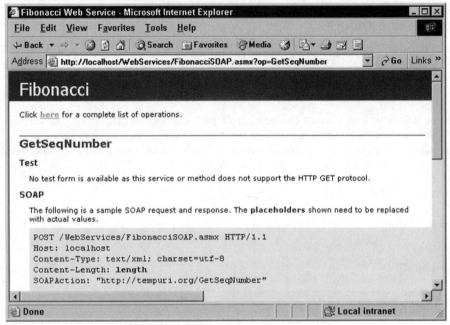

Figure 19-19

The `Direction` property allows this to be configured. This property uses the `SoapHeaderDirection` enumeration to determine the direction of the header. Using VB.NET, you could write:

```
<SoapHeader("simpleHeader", Direction:=SoapHeaderDirection.InOut)>
```

Using C#, you could write:

```
[SoapHeader("simpleHeader", Direction=SoapHeaderDirection.InOut)]
```

The `SoapHeaderDirection` enumeration supports three values. Their names describe their use:

- ❑ `SoapHeaderDirection.In`
- ❑ `SoapHeaderDirection.Out`
- ❑ `SoapHeaderDirection.InOut`

The Required Property

Headers defined by a method are required by default, which means that if they are not present in the request, an exception will be generated. Setting the `Required` property to `false` allows headers to be optional. Using VB.NET, you would write:

```
<SoapHeader("simpleHeader", Required:="false")>
```

Using C#, you would write:

```
[SoapHeader("simpleHeader", Required="false")]
```

Summary

In this chapter you've learned that ASP.NET's support for XML includes technologies such as SOAP, which Microsoft has identified as important for the future evolution of Internet services. In the very near future, we can expect to see a plethora of third-party web services such as credit card validation *and* verification, address verification, billing services, and so on.

We illustrated how you can build web services easily with ASP.NET. Specifically, we discussed:

❑ Some of the common issues associated with building applications that can share data, and how web services address these by using a common protocol, SOAP, that all parties can adhere to.

❑ Some of the public specifications in addition to SOAP, namely WSDL and UDDI, and how all these pieces should fit together in an application.

❑ How to build a simple ASP.NET Web service using some straightforward application logic. We walked through examples both in VB and C#, and showed how (with just a few small modifications) your application logic can be web service enabled. We tested the logic by calling it through a browser, and examined the description of the service that ASP.NET was able to generate for us.

❑ The details of the ASP.NET .asmx file, which is the file format used to expose our application logic. We discussed the directives, the System.Web.Services namespace, and the WebMethod and WebService attributes, including the properties that each supports.

❑ Design suggestions, and some of the more advanced aspects of ASP.NET Web services – specifically how to shape the XML document and create SOAP Headers.

In the next chapter we'll look at how you can consume the web services built in this chapter, as well as the security issues associated with ASP.NET Web services.

20

Using Web Services

In the previous chapter, we discussed how to create web services with ASP.NET. You learned that you could simply author application logic and use the `WebMethod` attribute to enable methods as SOAP end points.

This chapter will look at how to put web services to use in your applications. Web services are independent of platform and technology. This means that solutions built with ASP.NET, or with other technologies such as IBM's Apache SOAP module must all adhere to the SOAP specification. That way, they will be able to interoperate.

In addition to examining how to use the web services created in the previous chapter, we will also discuss some concepts related to ASP.NET Web services, specifically HTML screen-scraping and security.

You'll be looking at:

❑ **Finding and describing web services**: When building a web service, developers face the problem of describing what the capabilities of the service are, and where the server that hosts the service can be found. We'll discuss how UDDI and WSDL address these problems.

❑ **Building web service proxies**: You don't have to serialize and deserialize SOAP messages, or understand the various transport protocols for SOAP messages. Rather, you'll build proxy (or stub) objects that applications can use. You'll look at how to build proxies with both Visual Studio .NET and the `WSDL.exe` command line tool.

❑ **Using the .NET proxy class**: The proxy class generated for you by either Visual Studio .NET or `WSDL.exe` has properties and methods to control aspects of how the proxy calls the web service, including the length of the request, timeout, and access to the HTTP cookies collections.

❑ **HTML screen-scraping**: Using regular expression pattern-matching, you can extract information from a web page. You'll look at how to create a custom WSDL document, and then use that document with either of your .NET proxy generation tools to create a proxy that is capable of extracting information from any web page, effectively turning any web page into a web service that can be programmed.

❑ **Design decisions**: We'll discuss some common design decisions that are encountered when building applications that use web services.

❑ **Web services security**: We'll look at how you can use the security options provided by .NET to secure your web services.

❑ **Advanced topics**: We'll discuss custom authentication and authorization strategies for web services, as well as *Soap Extensions*–a feature of ASP.NET that allows you to interact with .NET Web services at a low level.

Let's get started by discussing how you can find and describe web services.

Finding and Describing Web Services

If you're building an application and decide that you'd like to use a web service to provide certain functionality, how do you find a web service that meets your needs? Just as you would use a tool such as Google to find web pages, use a similar directory-oriented tool to find web services: it's called *Universal Description, Discovery, and Integration (UDDI)*. UDDI is a well-known location to find and register web services.

Universal Description, Discovery, and Integration

Microsoft, IBM, and Ariba jointly announced UDDI in September 2000. UDDI is a project that strives to define how businesses describe and publish web services and consists of two main elements:

❑ **UDDI XML schema for business description**: This schema is used to define XML documents that describe various elements of a business; for example, contact information, business categorization, and web services offered. When you search UDDI for a service, you are searching against XML documents that conform to *this* schema.

❑ **Web-based registry**: The business description data is available either through a standard browser interface, or through published, SOAP-based Web services. You can use the web services to interact programmatically with the UDDI schema repository.

Further details about UDDI can be found at http://www.uddi.org, along with the public specifications.

In a manner similar to a phone book, you can use the UDDI web services directory as the yellow, white, and green pages to find web services offered by organizations. For example, a company that provides a credit card web service can register the service at http://UDDI.org. Then, customers who need a credit card web service can visit http://UDDI.org and query the registry for the existence of suitable credit card services through UDDI's public SOAP-based Web services or through their browser. If services matching the criteria of the request are found, the company will have the necessary information (the location and description of the web service) to access them.

UDDI Implementations

UDDI allows organizations to register and discover web services that other organizations have registered. The specification at the time of writing is implemented by Microsoft at http://uddi.microsoft.com/ and by IBM at http://www-3.ibm.com/services/uddi/.

UDDI nodes mirror each other. If one node is unavailable, another node can be used, thus eliminating single points of failure. In the future, additional UDDI nodes should become available. It's also possible that private UDDI servers will be made available. This would allow organizations to host their own intranet UDDI nodes for intra-organizational web service registration and discovery.

We won't look at how to use UDDI programmatically, but will discuss the steps involved in finding web services using a browser at one of the existing UDDI nodes. We'll look at Microsoft's UDDI node, available at http://uddi.microsoft.com.

Microsoft UDDI Node

When you navigate to http://uddi.microsoft.com, you're served a simple HTML page that contains news and information about the UDDI project. You can search this node for services, after logging in through Passport.

Searching the Microsoft UDDI Node

The Search link brings up another web page that details how you can search for services. An HTML form is provided for entering the search parameters. Since we're looking for web services offered by Microsoft, we can search for the value Microsoft from the Providers tab. Other search options include:

Option	Searches by	Example
Business location	Location of the business.	Redmond
tModel name	Services that support a certain type of service.	SOAP
Business identifier	A D-U-N-S reference number for business lookup.	08-146-6849 for Microsoft
Discovery URL	The location of the service. You can check if a known service is registered with UDDI.	A URL for a service that we already know exists: reverse lookup
GeoWeb Taxonomy	By geographic classification.	North America
NAICS Codes	North American Industry Classification.	Software Publisher
SIC Codes	Standard Industrial Classification.	Classification code used to classify business types
UNSPSC Codes	Universal Standard Products and Services Codes.	Software

After querying UDDI, you are presented with the results. In our case, the Results present a link to a page that describes the registered services for Microsoft. Follow this link.

Details Tab

The Details tab lists details entered by the web service owner, such as a unique provider key as well as a name and description of the service.

Bindings Tab

The Binding tab lists any web service end-points. Using the information provided in the bindings, you can use the technologies found in .NET to easily build proxy classes that can use these SOAP-based web services.

> UDDI allows you to search a common repository for published web services. If you find a web service that meets your needs, you can then access that web service using the binding details provided by UDDI.

UDDI solves the problem of web service discovery. However, even after you've found the web service, some issues need to be addressed:

❑ How to describe what the web service can, and can't, do

❑ What does the SOAP request look like

❑ What does the SOAP response look like

❑ What data types does the web service support

❑ Does the web service require an XML schema

While UDDI makes finding web services easy, *Web Service Description Language* (WSDL) is used to describe the capabilities of a web service and it is WSDL that answers these questions.

Web Service Description Language

WSDL is a W3C submitted specification (at the time of writing it is not yet a W3C standard) supported by a number of industry leaders, including Microsoft and IBM.

> The public specification, available at *http://msdn.microsoft.com/xml/general/wsdl.asp*, states, "Web Service Description Language is an XML format for describing network services as a set of end-points operating on messages containing either document-oriented or procedure-oriented information."

WSDL is an XML document that describes:

❑ **How a web service is used**: For example, how both the client and the server send and receive messages

❑ **The location of a web service**: For example, the URI to which messages are sent, in order to interact with the web service

❑ **The nature of the message exchange**: SOAP allows for either an XML document or XML RPC view of messages.

If you come from an object development background and have used Interface Definition Language (IDL) to describe an object, its methods, and the interfaces it supports, you'll find that WSDL is similar in concept but uses XML and describes a web service rather than a component.

Interoperability between Web Services

Web services are interoperable at network level. The implementation of a web service is completely independent of the operating system or the technology used to implement the service, and the description of the web service is encapsulated in an XML document (WSDL).

For example, if JSP developers wanted to use ASP.NET Web services in their application, they would simply need to examine the WSDL for the web service and format the correct message to a named end-point. The return message could then also be interpreted (again using WSDL) and the appropriate value extracted. However, it doesn't need to be this complicated. With .NET, using web services requires a trivial amount of work.

WSDL is an incredibly important technology for enabling web service interoperability because it fully describes the capabilities and use of the service. In fact, the description is so complete that tools can use WSDL to automate the creation of code. Let's look at a sample WSDL document that describes the Fibonacci Web service implemented in the previous chapter.

Using WSDL with the Fibonacci Web Service

Recall from the previous chapter that an ASP.NET Web service provides a Web Service Description help page that allows you to interact and test the web service through a browser.

The help page provides a link called Service Description. This requests the current document, and appends ?WSDL to the request URL. Selecting the Service Description link provides us with WSDL. The WSDL document that describes the Fibonacci ASP.NET Web service follows. We implemented the web service in both C# and VB.NET, but this is completely abstracted by the WSDL.

Sections of the WSDL that describe the use of the HTTP-GET and HTTP-POST protocols have been removed in this example (to decrease the size). This WSDL document only describes web services using SOAP:

```
<?xml version="1.0" encoding="utf-8"?>
<definitions xmlns:s="http://www.w3.org/2001/XMLSchema"
             xmlns:http="http://schemas.xmlsoap.org/wsdl/http/"
             xmlns:mime="http://schemas.xmlsoap.org/wsdl/mime/"
             xmlns:urt="http://microsoft.com/urt/wsdl/text/"
             xmlns:soap="http://schemas.xmlsoap.org/wsdl/soap/"
             xmlns:soapenc="http://schemas.xmlsoap.org/soap/encoding/"
             xmlns:s0="http://tempuri.org/"
             targetNamespace="http://tempuri.org/"
             xmlns="http://schemas.xmlsoap.org/wsdl/">
  <types>
    <s:schema attributeFormDefault="qualified"
              elementFormDefault="qualified"
              targetNamespace="http://tempuri.org/">
      <s:element name="GetSeqNumber">
        <s:complexType>
          <s:sequence>
```

```
            <s:element minOccurs="1"
                       maxOccurs="1"
                       name="fibIndex"
                       type="s:int" />
          </s:sequence>
        </s:complexType>
      </s:element>
      <s:element name="GetSeqNumberResponse">
        <s:complexType>
          <s:sequence>
            <s:element minOccurs="1"
                       maxOccurs="1"
                       name="GetSeqNumberResult"
                       type="s:int" />
          </s:sequence>
        </s:complexType>
      </s:element>
      <s:element name="int" type="s:int" />
    </s:schema>
  </types>
  <message name="GetSeqNumberSoapIn">
    <part name="parameters" element="s0:GetSeqNumber" />
  </message>
  <message name="GetSeqNumberSoapOut">
    <part name="parameters" element="s0:GetSeqNumberResponse" />
  </message>
  <portType name="FibonacciSoap">
    <operation name="GetSeqNumber">
      <input message="s0:GetSeqNumberSoapIn" />
      <output message="s0:GetSeqNumberSoapOut" />
    </operation>
  </portType>
  <binding name="FibonacciSoap" type="s0:FibonacciSoap">
    <soap:binding
        transport="http://schemas.xmlsoap.org/soap/http" style="document" />
    <operation name="GetSeqNumber">
      <soap:operation
            soapAction="http://tempuri.org/GetSeqNumber" style="document" />
      <input>
        <soap:body use="literal" />
      </input>
      <output>
        <soap:body use="literal" />
      </output>
    </operation>
  </binding>
  <service name="Fibonacci">
    <port name="FibonacciSoap" binding="s0:FibonacciSoap">
      <soap:address location="http:// ... /Fibonacci_cs.asmx" />
    </port>
  </service>
</definitions>
```

This WSDL document is divided into five major sections:

❑ `<types>`: This section of the WSDL is simply an XML schema used by the web service to define the schema for the message sections. The XML schema defines a set of rules for how XML data should be formatted. The resulting XML can be validated against the schema.

❑ `<message>`: For each web service described in the WSDL, there will be at least one `<message>` element. There may be only one as a web service can be one-way (read-only) as well as two-way (request/response). In our example, the `GetSeqNumber` Web service is two-way, and so we have both a request message (`GetSeqNumberSoapIn`) and a response message (`GetSeqNumberSoapOut`).

The `<message>` element describes the format that the web service expects to receive the request in, as well as the format the web service will use when it responds. Both the examples in this WSDL support parameters and use an XSD (XML Schema) to describe the message format defined in the `<types>` element.

❑ `<portType>`: The WSDL may describe multiple web services. The `<portType>` element is used to describe the request and response messages (defined by `<message>` elements) that these web services support. In this example, the only web service described is `GetSeqNumber`. This is the value of the `name` attribute of the `<operation>` element in the `<portType>` element. If we exposed additional web methods, we would expect to find a definition for them as well. Within the `<operation>` tag, we then find the `<input>` and `<output>` elements, which reference `<message>` elements within the WSDL.

❑ `<binding>`: This element describes the message format, as either SOAP section 5 RPC-style encoding, or XML document-style encoding. Each method supported by the web service can vary in its support of message encoding and thus each web service described by the WSDL receives its own section within `<binding>`. The only web service described in this WSDL is `GetSeqNumber`.

❑ `<service>`: The name of the web service is defined in the `<service>` element's `name` attribute. Also defined in the `<service>` element is the `<port>` element, which identifies the location of the web service (that is, the end-point that the service calls) as well as any bindings that the web service uses. The values in the `<port>` element are further described by the `<binding>` and `<portType>` elements. By default, the service name corresponds to the classname of the ASP.NET Web service we authored but is configurable using the `WebService` attribute on the web service.

XML namespaces are used extensively in WSDL and we'll discuss them next.

Applying Namespaces to WSDL

XML uses namespaces to uniquely identify sections of an XML document. Namespaces are *Universal Resource Indicators (URIs)* such as http://microsoft.com and allow the markup language used to be unique within a given namespace.

> *Even though a URI might take the shape of an http:// address, this does not imply that some value or meaning exists at this end-point, it is simply a unique string.*

Software can use namespaces to differentiate between a `<GetSeqNumber>` element from Microsoft and a `<GetSeqNumber>` element from a third party. The default namespace ASP.NET assigns to web services is http://tempuri.org, as is evident in the previous WSDL (you saw in the previous chapter how to use the `Namespace` property of the `WebService` attribute to change the default namespace).

The WSDL generated by ASP.NET describes three protocols: SOAP, HTTP-POST, and HTTP-GET (all described in the previous chapter). You don't actually need a thorough understanding of WSDL to build web services. With ASP.NET the WSDL is created automatically.

We've had a foundation in UDDI and WSDL; let's shift our discussion towards using WSDL to build a proxy class capable of calling a web service.

Building Web Service Proxies

A *proxy* works on behalf of others. A good example is proxy web server software. Users configure their web browser to use a proxy server and make requests for Internet resources (such as http://msdn.microsoft.com/) to the proxy. The proxy then makes a request on the behalf of the browser to the requested URL.

> *You can use proxy classes to represent the web service you want to call.*

In the previous chapter, we created a `Fibonacci` class that supports a single method called `GetSeqNumber`. The class was compiled into a .NET assembly and deployed to an ASP.NET application's `\bin` directory (on the server).

This assembly can be used as both a web service and a local class inside an ASP.NET page. For example, you could write the following ASP.NET page (using VB.NET):

```
<script runat="server">

  Public Sub Page_Load(sender As Object, e As EventArgs)
    Dim fibonacci As New Fibonacci()
    result.Text = Fibonacci.GetSeqNumber(5)
  End Sub

</script>

Index of 5 in the Fibonacci Series is:
<asp:literal id="result" runat="server"/>
```

However, this class was implemented as a web service as well, which means that you also have the ability to call the `GetSeqNumber` method via SOAP over a network.

The question is can we expect applications that wish to use *our* Fibonacci Web service to work with the raw SOAP messages (the HTTP and XML) directly? Probably not! Consumers of our web service should *not* have to formulate their own XML messages, and then encapsulate those messages in HTTP in order to send them to the appropriate destination. The same is true for receiving messages. Consumers should use a proxy representation of the web service.

Fibonacci Proxy

The WSDL describes the web service and you can create a .NET class using tools that are capable of reading and parsing the WSDL. For example, you can build a proxy class for the Fibonacci Web service that will have a class named `Fibonacci` and a `GetSeqNumber` method.

The proxy class does not contain the actual implementation (the code that calculates the sequence number), since this is not described in the WSDL. The implementation still resides within the called web service. However, programmatically the proxy has the same public methods. Its classname, method names, and parameters are the same as those for a local `Fibonacci` class, but the methods wrap calls to the remote `Fibonacci` Web service. As an example, consider the VB.NET pseudocode for a proxy implementation of `Fibonacci`:

```
Public Class Fibonacci
   Inherits SoapHttpClientProtocol

   Public Sub New()
     MyBase.New
     Me.Url = "http://[Server]/Fibonacci_cs.asmx"
   End Sub

   Public Function GetSeqNumber(ByVal fibIndex As Integer) As Integer
     Dim results() As Object = Me.Invoke("GetSeqNumber", _
                                         New Object() {fibIndex})
     Return CType(results(0),Integer)
   End Function

End Class
```

This pseudocode contains a class named `Fibonacci` and a single `GetSeqNumber` function.

The proxy function name and parameters look identical to the web service implementation, but the actual implementation (highlighted) is obviously different. Here we have two lines of code. The first line uses the `Invoke` function to call the web service and return a result. The second line uses the VB.NET `CType` function to cast the return data, `results(0)`, to an `Integer` type:

```
Public Function GetSeqNumber(ByVal fibIndex As Integer) As Integer
   Dim results() As Object = Me.Invoke("GetSeqNumber", _
                                       New Object() {fibIndex})
   Return CType(results(0),Integer)
End Function
```

Let's expand this a little further. Imagine if the Fibonacci Web service was implemented on a server residing in New York, while the application that wished to call it was in Seattle. The Seattle application could examine the WSDL of the New York Fibonacci Web service and construct a proxy class similar to the preceding example. The application could then write an ASP.NET page that, when requested, would use the local proxy to call the Fibonacci Web service in New York. The New York Web service would then perform the work and return the result to the application in Seattle that called it:

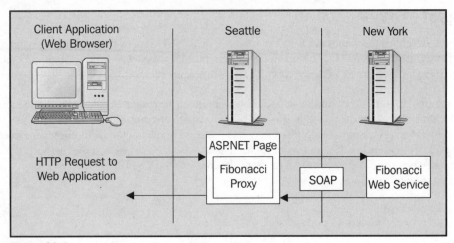

Figure 20-1

The ASP.NET page that uses the Fibonacci proxy might look as follows (written using VB.NET):

```
' Seattle ASP.NET application
<script runat="server">
  Public Sub Page_Load(sender As Object, e As EventArgs)
    Dim fibonacci As New Fibonacci()
    lblResult = Fibonacci.GetSeqNumber(5)
  End Sub
</script>
Index of 5 in the Fibonacci Series is:
<asp:label id="lblResult" runat="server"/>
```

To the Seattle developer who is coding the application, it appears as if Fibonacci is a local class, when in fact the class is a proxy of the New York Web service.

Now that we know what a proxy is used for, let's discuss how to automate its creation.

Creating Proxy Classes

There are four ways to create proxies for web services:

❑   Use Visual Studio .NET and add a **Web Reference** to a new project.

❑   Use the wsdl.exe command-line utility available with the .NET Framework SDK.

❑   Use the Microsoft SOAP toolkit.

❑   As long as the platform is capable of sending and receiving HTTP and is capable of parsing strings (or supports XML), you've got everything necessary for communicating with a web service, so you could roll your own using the technology of your choice.

Although all the examples in this chapter use ASP.NET Web services, the .NET technology used for creating the proxies could be applied to any web service so long as it uses SOAP.

Because this book is about .NET, we'll focus only on the first two options for building proxies: Visual Stuido.NET and the `wsdl.exe` command-line tool. However, using Visual Studio .NET is by far the easiest method available.

Let's start by looking at how we build a proxy using Visual Studio .NET. After we use Visual Studio .NET and the command-line tool to build and use a proxy, we'll come back and examine the auto-generated proxy class in more detail. For both examples we'll use the Fibonacci Web service created in the previous chapter.

Using Visual Studio .NET

If you've built an application using Visual Basic 6, you're probably familiar with the Add Reference option, available from any VB project under Project | Add Reference, which allowed for referencing a component you wanted to include in your project.

Including a reference allows you to early-bind to the object, instead of late-binding. Early binding simply allows you to know the data types at both runtime and compile-time, while late binding would force the code to determine the data types at runtime. For example, late-bound code would be as follows (this code is written in Visual Basic 6 and so makes use of the `Object` data type):

```
Dim objAdo As Object
Set objAdo = CreateObject("ADODB.Connection")
```

With late-bound code, an instance of `ADODB.Connection` would be treated as an `Object` type, and VB would be responsible for calling the appropriate methods at runtime. Late-binding is expensive, and we want to avoid it where possible.

Instead of writing late-bound code, you could use the Add Reference option in VB to add a reference at design-time. The code would then become:

```
Dim objAdo As New ADODB.Connection
```

VB would treat `objAdo` as an instance of type `ADODB.Connection` at runtime.

Visual Studio .NET continues to support the concepts of early and late binding, as well as the Project | Add Reference option. However, there's a new option specifically designed for web services: Project | Add Web Reference.

Add Web Reference

Visual Studio .NET supports the capability to early-bind to web services.

When you add a Web Reference to a Visual Studio .NET project (the Add Web Reference option is available to all Visual Studio .NET projects and languages), Visual Studio .NET will do all the work required to connect to the web service, parse the WSDL, and will generate a proxy class that you can use.

Using the Fibonacci Web Service

Let's look at an example using our Fibonacci Web service. Before you can create the Web Reference, you need to know the location of the WSDL for referencing the web service. For example, the address of the

WSDL for the VB.NET Fibonacci implementation of the ASP.NET Web service on my server is http://localhost/WebServices/Fibonacci_vb.asmx?WSDL.

Next, let's create a new Visual Studio .NET project. Since this book is about ASP.NET, we'll create a new ASP.NET Web application using Visual Basic .NET as the language. Once Visual Studio .NET creates the new application, you're presented with a design page. You can drag-and-drop elements onto this page. For this example, you'll need a textbox, a label, and a button, as shown in Figure 20-2:

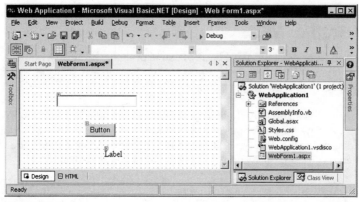

Figure 20-2

Leave the names of each of these items the same, that is, TextBox1, Button1, and Label1. Now you're ready to add the Web Reference.

You have two options: you can either select Project | Add Web Reference or you can right-click on the References in the Solution Explorer and select Add Web Reference. Both open the Add Web Reference dialog box shown in Figure 20-3:

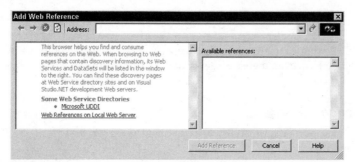

Figure 20-3

Within this dialog box, you can browse services provided by UDDI (the link to Microsoft UDDI takes you to the Microsoft UDDI implementation), browse Web References on the Local Web Server (for web services created with Visual Studio .NET), or enter the address.

Enter the address of the Fibonacci Web service, as shown in Figure 20-4:

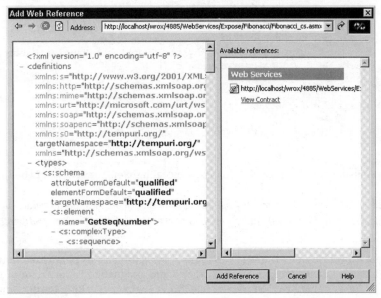

Figure 20-4

On the left-hand side of the **Add Web Reference** dialog, you can view the WSDL. Essentially Visual Studio .NET has fetched the WSDL from the specified location, and has validated it. The **Add Reference** button is now enabled and we are able to add a reference to the web service described by this WSDL to the current project (at which point Visual Studio .NET will create a proxy).

Click on **Add Reference**. Visual Studio .NET will create a new section in the **Solution Explorer** entitled **Web References**. Behind the scenes, Visual Studio .NET has parsed the WSDL, created a proxy object that represents the web service (the namespace of the proxy is the name of the server the WSDL was served from, which is localhost in this case), and cached a local copy of the WSDL. This is all visible if you expand the **Web References** section with the **Solution Explorer** shown in Figure 20-5:

Figure 20-5

You can now write code in the web application to use the Fibonacci Web service. Double-click on **Button1** and write some code for the `Button1_Click` event handler. Once the code view is open, write the following to call the `GetSeqNumber` of the `Fibonacci` Web service:

```
Private Sub Button1_Click(ByVal sender As System.Object,
                          ByVal e As System.EventArgs) Handles Button1.Click
    Dim fibonacci As New localhost.Fibonacci()
    Dim indexIntoSeries As Integer

    indexIntoSeries = TextBox1.Text

    Label1.Text = fibonacci.GetSeqNumber(indexIntoSeries)
End Sub
```

We first create an instance of the proxy, `fibonacci`, by calling `New localhost.Fibonacci`.

> *Changing the namespace in this example from* localhost *to some more meaningful value, such as* MathServices, *is as simple as right-clicking on* localhost *in the* Solution Explorer *and selecting* rename.

Next, we declare a local variable, `indexIntoSeries`. This is used as the parameter value for the call to `GetSeqNumber`. The value from `TextBox1` is extracted and assigned to `indexIntoSeries`–so the user must enter an `Integer` value. We then use our instance, `fibonacci`, calling the `GetSeqNumber` method and passing in the value of `indexIntoSeries`. When the call completes, an `Integer` is returned, the value of which is assigned to `Label1.Text`.

Here's a high-level rundown of what occurs when you run this application and click on `Button1`:

1. ASP.NET creates an instance of the proxy and calls it, passing in the value of `TextBox1`.
2. The proxy calls the Fibonacci Web service via SOAP, which computes the result and sends it back to the proxy via SOAP.
3. The proxy then deserializes the SOAP message (converts the values within the SOAP message to .NET types) and returns an `Integer` value, which is displayed to the end user.

Let's take a look at the sourcecode that Visual Studio .NET created.

Viewing the Source for the Proxy

Visual Studio .NET has obviously done a lot of work for us–it's created the proxy that can send and receive the SOAP requests and responses.

You can access and modify the sourcecode that Visual Studio .NET creates and compiles for the proxy. It's not available by default, but if you right-click on the project in Solution Explorer and select Add Existing Item, a file selection dialog box is opened. The file dialog box is currently accessing the root directory of the project. You should see a folder named `localhost` (or another name if you renamed the Web Reference). If you open this folder, you'll find the source to your proxy. On my server, the source file is `Fibonacci_cs.vb` (Figure 20-6):

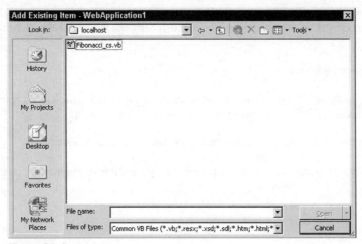

Figure 20-6

The proxy is created in the language the project is using. For this particular example, the proxy source is in VB.NET, as we'd created a VB.NET ASP.NET Web application.

If you open this source file, it'll be added to your current project and you can view or modify its source.

Creating a proxy using Visual Studio .NET is simple. As long as you have the URL to the WSDL, Visual Studio .NET can take care of the rest. You can write code and call methods just as you would expect to with a local class, when in fact the proxy is exchanging SOAP messages with a web service.

While Visual Studio .NET definitely makes using web services easy, it isn't required for creating proxy classes. If you're using .NET, but don't have a copy of Visual Studio .NET, you can still automate the process of building proxies to web services using the wsdl.exe command-line tool.

Using wsdl.exe

The wsdl.exe command-line tool is installed by the .NET Framework and used to generate proxy classes from WSDL contracts. Using wsdl.exe to generate a proxy for a .NET application isn't as easy as it is with Visual Studio .NET. For example, the output of wsdl.exe is always a source file, which then has to be compiled. However, the command-line tool gives you more options, such as the language (which can be any .NET language) that should be used for the proxy source file.

Creating the Source File

Let's start by using wsdl.exe to generate a proxy for a WSDL document available at http://localhost/wrox/4885/WebServices/Expose/Fibonacci/Fibonacci_cs.asmx?WSDL. At the command prompt, run the following command:

```
wsdl http://localhost/.../Fibonacci_cs.asmx?WSDL
```

The result is a source file (by default written in C#) named Fibonacci.cs.

By default, if you name an HTTP-based WSDL location, `wsdl.exe` will use the proxy settings configured for Internet Explorer. Alternatively, you can copy the WSDL locally and then run it through `wsdl.exe`:

wsdl Fibonacci_vb.wsdl

The result is the same – a C# source file that represents the proxy. The language is configurable, and to generate the proxy in VB.NET, you simply need to set the `language` flag:

wsdl /language:VB http://localhost/.../Fibonacci_cs.asmx?WSDL

When you open up the source files, you are presented with similar implementations that differ in language. The VB.NET file contains:

```
Option Strict Off
Option Explicit On

Imports System
Imports System.ComponentModel
Imports System.Diagnostics
Imports System.Web.Services
Imports System.Web.Services.Protocols
Imports System.Xml.Serialization

<System.Diagnostics.DebuggerStepThroughAttribute(), _
 System.ComponentModel.DesignerCategoryAttribute("code"), _
 System.Web.Services.WebServiceBindingAttribute(Name:="FibonacciSoap",
[Namespace]:="http://tempuri.org/")>  _
Public Class Fibonacci
    Inherits System.Web.Services.Protocols.SoapHttpClientProtocol

    Public Sub New()
        MyBase.New
        Me.Url = "http://localhost/WebServices/Fibonacci_vb.asmx"
    End Sub

<System.Web.Services.Protocols.SoapDocumentMethodAttribute("http://tempuri.org/Get
SeqNumber", RequestNamespace:="http://tempuri.org/",
ResponseNamespace:="http://tempuri.org/",
Use:=System.Web.Services.Description.SoapBindingUse.Literal,
ParameterStyle:=System.Web.Services.Protocols.SoapParameterStyle.Wrapped)>
    Public Function GetSeqNumber(ByVal fibIndex As Integer) As Integer
        Dim results() As Object = Me.Invoke("GetSeqNumber", New Object()
                        {fibIndex})
        Return CType(results(0),Integer)
    End Function

    Public Function BeginGetSeqNumber(ByVal fibIndex As Integer, ByVal callback As
System.AsyncCallback, ByVal asyncState As Object) As System.IAsyncResult
        Return Me.BeginInvoke("GetSeqNumber", New Object() {fibIndex}, callback,
                        asyncState)
    End Function
```

```
        Public Function EndGetSeqNumber(ByVal asyncResult As System.IAsyncResult) As
            Integer
            Dim results() As Object = Me.EndInvoke(asyncResult)
            Return CType(results(0),Integer)
        End Function
    End Class
```

The C# file contains:

```
using System.Diagnostics;
using System.Xml.Serialization;
using System;
using System.Web.Services.Protocols;
using System.ComponentModel;
using System.Web.Services;

[System.Diagnostics.DebuggerStepThroughAttribute()]
[System.ComponentModel.DesignerCategoryAttribute("code")]
[System.Web.Services.WebServiceBindingAttribute(Name="FibonacciSoap",
Namespace="http://tempuri.org/")]
public class Fibonacci : System.Web.Services.Protocols.SoapHttpClientProtocol {

    public Fibonacci() {
        this.Url = "http://localhost/WebServices/Fibonacci_vb.asmx";
    }

[System.Web.Services.Protocols.SoapDocumentMethodAttribute("http://tempuri.org/Get
SeqNumber", RequestNamespace="http://tempuri.org/",
ResponseNamespace="http://tempuri.org/",
Use=System.Web.Services.Description.SoapBindingUse.Literal,
ParameterStyle=System.Web.Services.Protocols.SoapParameterStyle.Wrapped)]
    public int GetSeqNumber(int fibIndex) {
        object[] results = this.Invoke("GetSeqNumber", new object[] {
                fibIndex});
        return ((int)(results[0]));
    }

    public System.IAsyncResult BeginGetSeqNumber(int fibIndex,
                                        System.AsyncCallback callback,
                                        object asyncState) {
        return this.BeginInvoke("GetSeqNumber", new object[] {
                fibIndex}, callback, asyncState);
    }

    public int EndGetSeqNumber(System.IAsyncResult asyncResult) {
        object[] results = this.EndInvoke(asyncResult);
        return ((int)(results[0]));
    }
}
```

Compiling the Source File

Now that you have the proxy source files, you need to compile them. Included with .NET are comm
and-line compilers for C# (csc.exe) and VB.NET (vbc.exe). We'll use these to build the proxy classes
into assemblies.

Compiling the VB.NET Source

To compile the VB.NET source file, execute the following statement at a command prompt (note that this command is all *one* line):

```
vbc /t:library /out:Fibonacci_vb.dll
/reference:System.Web.Services.dll,System.Xml.dll,System.dll Fibonacci.vb
```

This instructs the VB.NET compiler to create a library (.dll), rather than an executable, and to create a file named `Fibonacci_vb.dll`. Finally the VB.NET compiler is instructed to use `Fibonacci.vb` as the input source file. The result is a `Fibonacci_vb.dll` file.

Compiling the C# Source

To compile the C# source file, execute the following command (note that this command is all *one* line):

```
csc /t:library /out:Fibonacci_cs.dll Fibonacci.cs
```

The syntax for the VB.NET and C# compilers is identical, and after executing this statement the result is a .dll file named `fibonacci_cs.dll`.

You can copy either of these .dll files (you need only *one* of them) to an ASP.NET application's \bin directory. You can then build an ASP.NET application that uses this proxy, just as with Visual Studio .NET. For example:

```
<Script runat="server">
Private Sub Page_Load(sender As Object, e As EventArgs)
  Dim fibonacci As New Fibonacci ()

  lblResult.Text = fibonacci.GetSeqNumber(6)
End Sub
The value of the 6th element in the Fibonacci series is:
<asp:label id="lblResult" runat="server"/>
```

In the Visual Studio .NET version of this example, we used a Fibonacci proxy that was part of the `localhost` namespace. Our example of the proxy using the command-line tool didn't use a namespace. This is a choice we made. You could make the previous class part of a namespace with another simple command-line switch: `namespace`. For example:

```
wsdl /namespace:localhost http://localhost/../Fibonacci_cs.asmx?WSDL
```

The `namespace` and `language` parameters are just two of the parameters that `wsdl.exe` supports. Let's look at the others.

Using wsdl.exe

There are several parameters that can be used to configure the behavior of the `wsdl.exe` tool. A description of these parameters can be found by typing the following at a command prompt:

```
wsdl.exe /?
```

This returns a full listing of the switches the tool supports:

Parameters	Description
`<url or path>`	The URL or file path to one of these supported document types that `WSDL.exe` recognizes (WSDL Contract, XSD Schema, or DISCO Document).
`/nologo`	Hides the banner output when the tool is run.
`/language:<language>`	The `language` option (short form `/l:`) allows you to create the proxy in any .NET language. Three languages are available as part of the SDK that the tool supports: C# (`/language:CS`), VB.NET (`language:VB`), and JScript.NET (`/language:JS`). The default language is C#. To use a language other than these three, you must name the class implementing the `ICodeGenerator` interface. For example, to use Perl, you would use a `CodeDOM` class provided by the .NET Perl compiler.
`/server`	By default, `wsdl.exe` will create client proxies for a given WSDL document. However, if you use the `/server` option, `wsdl.exe` will generate a source file with abstract members that represents the server implementation of the web service. This option is useful if several organizations agree upon the structure of the web service (as defined by the WSDL), but would like to provide their own implementations.
`/namespace:<namespace>`	The `/namespace` (short form `/n:`) option allows you to set the namespace that the proxy class is generated within. By default, no namespace is used. For example, you can generate a proxy class within a namespace of `MathSamples` by simply setting `/n:MathSamples`.
`/out:<filename>`	The `/out` parameter allows you to name the source file created by `wsdl.exe`. By default, the name of this source file is `[service name].[language extension]`.
`/protocol:<protocol>`	ASP.NET Web services support three protocols: `HTTPGet`, `HTTPPost`, and `SOAP`. By default, SOAP is used for client proxies and is what WSDL will instruct the proxy class to use (through attributes in the source). You can override this setting by specifying one of these protocols: `HttpGet`, `HttpPost`, or `SOAP`.

Table continued on following page

Parameters	Description
/username:<username>	The /username parameter (short form /u:) is set when you use a URL to access the WSDL, DISCO, or XSD Schema, and the server requires authentication.
/password:<password>	The /password parameter (short form /p:) is set when you use a URL to access the WSDL, DISCO, or XSD Schema and the server requires authentication for a user.
/domain:<domain>	The /domain parameter (short form /d:) is set when you use a URL to access the WSDL, DISCO, or XSD Schema, and the server requires authentication.
/proxy:<url>	The proxy server used for HTTP requests. By default the proxy settings defined for Internet Explorer are used.
/proxyusername:<username>	The name of the user to authenticate to the proxy server with.
/proxypassword:<password>	The value of the proxy user's password to authenticate to the proxy server with.
/proxydomain:<domain>	The name of the proxy user's domain to authenticate to the proxy server with.
/appsettingsurlkey:<key>	Rather than hardcoding the URL specified in the WSDL document, a URL can be stored in ASP.NET configuration system's <appSettings> section. You can use the appsettingsurlkey parameter with wsdl.exe to name the key that corresponds to the value stored in the configuration file.
/appsettingsbaseurl:<baseurl>	When used in conjunction with the appsettingsurlkey, this parameter allows you to name the base URL for the web service.

Now that you know how to use both Visual Studio .NET and wsdl.exe to create a proxy class, we can discuss the proxy that's generated. It inherits some properties and methods from a base class, and as you'll see, these properties and methods give even more control over how we interact with the web service that the proxy represents.

Using the Proxy Class

If you build and use the proxy class in Visual Studio .NET, you can see (through statement completion) that the class contains additional methods and properties beyond the methods used in the web service. For example, the `Fibonacci` class supported a `GetSeqNumber` method. However, if you examine the proxy for `Fibonacci` in Visual Studio .NET, you'll see several other methods and properties that `Fibonacci` supports. This is because the `Fibonacci` proxy class inherits these methods and properties from a base class.

> *A proxy inherits from* `SoapHttpClientProtocol`, *which inherits from* `HttpWebClientProtocol`, *which in turn inherits from* `WebClientProtocol`.

Let's examine some of the common methods and properties we might use.

Controlling Timeout

We still need to write applications so that they behave correctly when the web service is not performing correctly. For example, the network connection between the provider and the consumer of the service could become saturated so that responses start to take too long. Requests are issued, and the consumer of the service simply waits until the request times out. The default timeout for a request from our proxy is ninety seconds.

The following VB.NET code illustrates a simple `Add` Web service that performs slowly due to a call to `Thread.Sleep(20000)` that forces the thread to wait 20 seconds before continuing:

```
<%@ WebService Class="Timeout" %>

Imports System.Threading
Imports System.Web.Services

Public Class Timeout
  <WebMethod()> Public Function Add(a As Integer, b As Integer) As Integer
    Thread.Sleep(20000)

    Return a + b
  End Function
End Class
```

This code introduces false latency into the application. However, if this latency were real, the client using the web service would probably not want to wait 20 seconds for a response.

One of the inherited properties in the proxy class is `Timeout`. If you use a proxy named `Timeout` for the `Add` Web service, you could write the following VB.NET code to time the request out if the web service did not respond within five seconds:

```
<Script runat="server">
Public Sub Page_Load(sender As Object, e As EventArgs)
  Dim example As New Timeout()
  example.Timeout = 5000

  Try
```

```
        lblResult.Text = example.Add(4,5)
    Catch err As Exception
        lblResult.Text = err.Message
    End Try
End Sub
</Script>
The result of 4 + 5 is: <asp:label id="lblResult" runat="server" />
```

This code demonstrates the use of a `Try...Catch` block surrounding a web service call. We'll talk more about handling web service exceptions later in the chapter. A timeout is an exception, and if it's not handled, an error will be generated.

Using the `Timeout` property of the proxy ensures that the application won't wait for a slow web service. Another inherited property of the proxy, `Url`, allows you to set the end-point URL that the proxy sends requests to.

Setting the URL

When you build a proxy from a WSDL document generated by ASP.NET, the default end-point of the service is already provided. Here's a snippet of the WSDL for the Fibonacci Web service:

```
<service name="Fibonacci">
  <port name="FibonacciSoap" binding="s0:FibonacciSoap">
    <soap:address location="http:// ... /Fibonacci_cs.asmx" />
  </port>
</service>
```

The `location` attribute defined in `<soap:address/>` names the end-point to which SOAP calls are sent. The proxy that is generated uses this setting. As an example, consider the constructor of the VB.NET code:

```
Public Sub New()
  MyBase.New
  Me.Url = "http://localhost/WebServices/Fibonacci_cs.asmx"
End Sub
```

The equivalent C# code:

```
public Fibonacci() {
    this.Url = "http://localhost/WebServices/Fibonacci_cs.asmx";
}
```

Both constructors set the `Url` property to the value of `location` in the WSDL. Although the value is 'pre-configured' for you in the proxy, you can either remove this setting or reset the value of the property at runtime using the `Url` property of the proxy.

As you can reset the `Url` that the proxy uses, you can dynamically choose the web service you want to use, or use a common proxy for multiple web services. For example, if you built an e-commerce site and wanted to use web services for credit card validation, you could use the `Timeout` and the `Url` properties together. If a given call to a service timed out (for example, a call to a Credit Card Web service), you could write code that changes the `Url` to a web service provided by another vendor and call that backup service. Of course, this assumes that either the proxy supports all these services, or all the services implement a common web service API.

Proxy Web Server Access

By default the web service proxy will use the settings configured for Internet Explorer to access the Internet. However, you can set your own proxy using the `Proxy` property.

To use the `Proxy` property, you need to set its value to a class that implements `IWebProxy`, such as the `WebProxy` class found in the `System.Net` namespace. For example, if the local network requires you to use a proxy server named `AcmeCoProxy` through port 80, you could write the following VB.NET code:

```
<%@ Import Namespace="System.Net" %>
<Script runat="server">
Private Sub Page_Load(sender As Object, e As EventArgs)
   Dim fibonacci As New Fibonacci()
   Dim webProxy As New WebProxy("AcmeCoProxy", 80)

   Fibonacci.Proxy = webProxy
   lblResult.Text = fibonacci.GetSeqNumber(6)
End Sub
The value of the 6th element in the Fibonacci series is: <asp:label id="lblResult"
runat="server"/>
```

Calls made through the `Fibonacci` proxy object are now routed to the `AcmeCoProxy` server on port 80. The Web proxy server then issues the request and returns the result to the caller. If the Web proxy server requires credentials, these can be set as part of the `System.Net.WebProxy` class.

Maintaining State

ASP.NET Web services use HTTP as the transport protocol for messages. Additional transport protocols can be used to route SOAP, including SMTP and UDP, but HTTP will be the most commonly used protocol. Accordingly, the proxy provides with access to common HTTP protocol features, such as cookies.

Just as you would with a browser-based application, you can use HTTP cookies to pass *additional* data along with SOAP messages. The most common use of cookies in an ASP.NET Web service would be to maintain a `Session` on the server that is providing the web service. For example, the following web service (written using VB.NET) uses `Session` state to retain values on the server:

```
<%@ WebService Class="SessionStateExample" %>

Imports System.Web.Services

Public Class SessionStateExample
   Inherits WebService

   <WebMethod(EnableSession:=true)> _
   Public Function SetSession(key As String, item As String)
```

```
      Session(key) = item
   End Function

   <WebMethod(EnableSession:=true)> _
   Public Function GetSession(key As String) As String
     Return Session(key)
   End Function
End Class
```

This ASP.NET Web service has two functions defined as web services:

❑   SetSession: Allows you to pass a key and item (both strings) and uses the key value to create an entry in Session for the value

❑   GetSession: Allows you to pass the key and retrieve the result of the item stored for that key

The WebMethod attribute explicitly enables Session (which is *not enabled*, by default) by setting EnableSession:="true" for each of the methods. The server will issue a Session cookie to the caller that contains a unique Session ID. On each subsequent request, the caller (in this case the web service proxy) presents the cookie, and the server is able to load the appropriate Session data.

There are two caveats for using HTTP cookies with the proxy:

❑   If you create a proxy for a web service, and the web service requires the use of HTTP cookies, you need to explicitly support HTTP cookies within our proxy. This is done by creating an instance of a CookieContainer class and assigning that instance to the proxy's CookieContainer property.

❑   If you intend to maintain state through the use of ASP.NET session state within the web service, you need to re-present the HTTP cookie on each subsequent use of the proxy by your application. The Cookie that the proxy receives is only valid for the life of the proxy. When the proxy instance goes out of scope or is destroyed, the cookie is lost and on subsequent requests you no longer have access to the Session (since you no longer have the Session cookie to send to the server).

The following VB.NET code illustrates both these caveats:

```
<Script runat="Server">
Public Sub Page_Load(sender As Object, e As EventArgs)
   Dim sessionExample As New SessionStateExample()

   sessionExample.SetSession("name", "rob")
   lblSession1.Text = sessionExample.GetSession("name")
End Sub
</Script>
<Font face="arial">
Value: <asp:label id="lblSession1" runat="server"/>
</Font>
```

In the Page_Load event handler, we create an instance of SessionStateExample and create a new Session on the web service by calling SetSession. We then retrieve the value by calling GetSession("name"). In this case, no value is returned, because the proxy is not using HTTP cookies and so lblSession1 would not contain a value.

Supporting Cookies within a Web Service Proxy

To enable cookie support within the web service proxy, you need to create a `CookieContainer`. Here is the fixed VB.NET code:

```
<%@ Import Namespace="System.Net" %>
<Script runat="Server">
Public Sub Page_Load(sender As Object, e As EventArgs)
   Dim sessionExample As New SessionStateExample()
   Dim cookieContainer As New CookieContainer()
   sessionExample.CookieContainer = cookieContainer
   sessionExample.SetSession("name", "rob")
   lblSession1.Text = sessionExample.GetSession("name")
End Sub

</Script>
<Font face="arial">
   Value: <asp:label id="lblSession1" runat="server"/>
</Font>
```

Here, we first import the `System.Net` namespace, which contains the necessary `CookieContainer` class. Then, within the `Page_Load` event handler we add two lines of code to create an instance of the `CookieContainer` class and set that instance to the `CookieContainer` property of the web service proxy. When this code is executed, we get the desired result. The `GetSession` call returns the value set by `SetSession`.

Although this is a simple example, it effectively illustrates how to maintain state through the use of an HTTP cookie using a web service proxy. Let's go one step further.

Persisting the Web Service Cookie for Multiple Requests

Since the proxy does not persist the Session cookie, to use Session state in your web service across multiple requests, you'd need to do your own cookie persistence. Take the following VB.NET example:

```
<%@ Import Namespace="System.Net" %>
<script runat="server">

Public Sub Page_Load(sender As Object, e As EventArgs)
   Dim sessionExample As New SessionStateExample()
   Dim cookieContainer As New CookieContainer()
   Dim sessionCookie As Cookie
   Dim cookieCollection As New CookieCollection()
   sessionExample.CookieContainer = cookieContainer
   sessionCookie = CType(session("sessionCookie"), Cookie)

   If (IsNothing(sessionCookie)) Then
     sessionExample.SetSession("name", "rob")
     cookieCollection = sessionExample.CookieContainer.GetCookies( _
          New Uri("http://localhost"))
     Session("sessionCookie") = cookieCollection("ASP.NET_SessionId")
   Else
     sessionExample.CookieContainer.Add(sessionCookie)
   End If
```

```
      lblSession1.Text = sessionExample.GetSession("name")
End Sub

</script>
<Font face="arial">
  Value: <asp:label id="lblSession1" runat="server"/>
</Font>
```

This is a more advanced example that demonstrates how you can store the web service's Session cookie in Session state with the web application that is using the web service. The code uses two new local variables, `sessionCookie` and `cookieCollection`, to store the web service's Session cookie.

The code tries to retrieve a value for `sessionCookie` by attempting to access a local Session variable. The code then determines if `sessionCookie` references an instance of a `Cookie`. If it does not, it walks through the procedure of calling the proxy's `SetSession` method and then stores the web service's Session cookie. Alternatively, you could simply add the `sessionCookie` to the existing proxy's `CookieContainer` and call the `GetSession` method. We've encapsulated all of this work in one ASP.NET page, but it could just as easily be applied to an entire web application, which would allow us to use ASP.NET Session state for web services across an application.

Let's look at another feature that ASP.NET Web services make easy – converting any web site into a web service.

From Web Site to Web Service

HTML screen-scraping is the practice of connecting to a web site, retrieving a result, (usually HTML), and then sifting through the unstructured data to extract a useful value. For example, to find the current sales rank for this book, you could look it up by ISBN (0-7645-5890-0) using http://shop.barnesandnoble.com/booksearch/isbnInquiry.asp?isbn=0764558900 on Barnes and Noble.

You could then view the HTML source and search for 'sales rank'. You would find something like:

```
<font size="-1">sales rank: 1,823</font>
```

In the past, to automate this through code, we would write a small application that would connect to BarnesAndNoble.com through `WinInet`, or the `XMLHttp` component, and request the document. Then we'd write some code to search the HTML for a string that matched `<font size="-1">sales rank:` and also search for a string immediately following the previous string of `</font>`. Anything found between these two strings would be the result.

This isn't efficient, and the code to perform this match would be very fragile. If the HTML changed, your code would no longer function correctly.

.NET makes a lot of this much easier. For example, there is support for regular expression pattern-matching. Finding the sales rank value in the preceding string is now simply a matter of creating the appropriate regular expression syntax, and then searching the document:

```
"size=.-1.>sales rank:.(.*?)</"
```

This regular expression search string returns the sales rank.

You can find more information on regular expressions and pattern-matching in Chapter 16.

While regular expressions simplify searching for strings, you still need to write all the other code to access the site and return the HTML, as well as wrapping all of this in a friendly API.

ASP.NET Web services automates much of this by allowing you to build custom WSDL documents that specify the location, parameters, regular expression to match, and return types. You can then use one of your proxy generation tools, such as Visual Studio .NET or wsdl.exe, to generate a proxy object to encapsulate this.

Authoring the WSDL

Let's write an example that returns the sales rank for any book, for a provided ISBN. First, the WSDL:

```xml
<?xml version="1.0"?>
<definitions xmlns:s="http://www.w3.org/2000/10/XMLSchema"
             xmlns:http="http://schemas.xmlsoap.org/wsdl/http/"
             xmlns:mime="http://schemas.xmlsoap.org/wsdl/mime/"
             xmlns:soapenc="http://schemas.xmlsoap.org/soap/encoding/"
             xmlns:soap="http://schemas.xmlsoap.org/wsdl/soap/"
             xmlns:s0="http://tempuri.org/"
             targetNamespace="http://tempuri.org/"
             xmlns="http://schemas.xmlsoap.org/wsdl/"
             xmlns:msType="http://microsoft.com/wsdl/mime/textMatching/">
  <types/>
  <message name="GetBookDetailsHttpGetIn">
    <part name="isbn" type="s:string"/>
  </message>
  <message name="GetBookDetailsHttpGetOut"/>
  <portType name="BarnesAndNobleHttpGet">
    <operation name="GetBookDetails">
      <input message="s0:GetBookDetailsHttpGetIn"/>
      <output message="s0:GetBookDetailsHttpGetOut"/>
    </operation>
  </portType>
  <binding name="BarnesAndNobleHttpGet" type="s0:BarnesAndNobleHttpGet">
    <http:binding verb="GET"/>
    <operation name="GetBookDetails">
      <http:operation location="/booksearch/isbnInquiry.asp"/>
      <input>
        <http:urlEncoded/>
      </input>
      <output>
        <msType:text>
          <msType:match name="Rank"
                        pattern="size=.-1.&gt;sales rank:.(.*?)&lt;/"
                        ignoreCase="true"/>
        </msType:text>
      </output>
    </operation>
  </binding>
```

```
    <service name="BarnesAndNoble">
      <port name="BarnesAndNobleHttpGet" binding="s0:BarnesAndNobleHttpGet">
        <http:address location="http://shop.barnesandnoble.com"/>
      </port>
    </service>
</definitions>
```

This WSDL defines a `<service>` named `BarnesAndNoble`, which also names the end-point, http://shop.barnesandnoble.com that we'll make queries against. This service does not use SOAP, but instead uses HTTP GET to make requests. There are two other areas of interest in the WSDL elements you just saw: `<binding>` and `<message name="GetBookDetailsHttpGetIn">`.

The `<binding>` element defines an operation, `GetBookDetails`, that further qualifies the end-point to which the HTTP-GET request is sent (`/booksearch/isbnInquiry.asp`). It also defines, in the `<output>` section, a `<msType:match ...>` element. Within a `<match>` element, we declare the regular expression syntax used for our string match. The value of the `name` attribute allows you to control the name of the property the proxy will create, which will be used to access the 'sales rank' of a given ISBN. The `pattern` value is the regular expression pattern used for searching the document and returning results with.

The other section of interest is the `<message name="GetBookDetailsHttpGetIn">` element, which is used to define parameters that we want to send as part of the HTTP GET request. The defined value, `isbn` (which is of type `string`) will be used to formulate a request, such as, http://shop.barnesandnoble.com/booksearch/isbnInquiry.asp?isbn=1861004753, or http://shop.barnesandnoble.com/booksearch/isbnInquiry.asp?isbn=1861004885.

We're now ready to build a proxy for this WSDL.

Building the Proxy

Open a command prompt and move to the directory where the WSDL was created. Then issue the following command:

wsdl.exe /language:VB bn.wsdl

If there were no errors in the WSDL, you should have a VB.NET source file named `BarnesAndNoble.vb`. Let's look at the source of this file (some elements not relevant to this discussion, namely comments and the asynchronous methods, have been removed):

```
Option Strict Off
Option Explicit On

Imports System
Imports System.ComponentModel
Imports System.Diagnostics
Imports System.Web.Services
Imports System.Web.Services.Protocols
Imports System.Xml.Serialization

<System.Diagnostics.DebuggerStepThroughAttribute(),  _
```

```
    System.ComponentModel.DesignerCategoryAttribute("code")> _
Public Class BarnesAndNoble
    Inherits System.Web.Services.Protocols.HttpGetClientProtocol

    Public Sub New()
        MyBase.New
        Me.Url = "http://shop.barnesandnoble.com"
    End Sub

<System.Web.Services.Protocols.HttpMethodAttribute(GetType(System.Web.Services._
                                    Protocols.TextReturnReader),
GetType(System.Web.Services.Protocols.UrlParameterWriter))> _
    Public Function GetBookDetails(ByVal isbn As String) As GetBookDetailsMatches
        Return CType(Me.Invoke("GetBookDetails", (Me.Url +
                    "/booksearch/isbnInquiry.asp"),
                    New Object() {isbn}),GetBookDetailsMatches)
    End Function

    Public Function BeginGetBookDetails(ByVal isbn As String, ByVal callback As
        System.AsyncCallback, ByVal asyncState As Object) As System.IAsyncResult
        Return Me.BeginInvoke("GetBookDetails", (Me.Url +
        "/booksearch/isbnInquiry.asp"), New Object() {isbn}, callback, asyncState)
    End Function

    Public Function EndGetBookDetails(ByVal asyncResult As System.IAsyncResult) As
        GetBookDetailsMatches
        Return CType(Me.EndInvoke(asyncResult),GetBookDetailsMatches)
    End Function
End Class

Public Class GetBookDetailsMatches
    <System.Web.Services.Protocols.MatchAttribute("size=.-1.>sales rank:.(.*?)</",
        IgnoreCase:=true)> _
    Public Rank As String
End Class
```

This auto-generated source file contains two classes. The first class, BarnesAndNoble, has a single function called GetBookDetails that accepts an ISBN as a parameter and returns an instance of GetBookDetailsMatches. The returned type, GetBookDetailsMatches, is the second class defined in the source file. It contains a single member variable Rank. The Rank member variable has an attribute applied to it that represents the regular expression syntax declared in the WSDL.

Compile this source file by executing the following command (note that this command should be typed all on one line):

```
vbc.exe /t:library /r:System.dll /r:System.Web.dll /r:System.Web.Services.dll
                                    /r:System.Xml.dll BarnesAndNoble.vb
```

This will generate an assembly named BarnesAndNoble.dll.

Using the Screen Scrape Proxy

Now that an assembly is built, you can deploy it to the \bin directory of a web application. You can then write the following ASP.NET page (using VB.NET here) that loads and uses the BarnesAndNoble proxy:

```
<%@ Import Namespace="System.Net" %>

<Script runat=server>
Public Sub GetSalesRank(sender As Object, e As EventArgs)
  Dim bn As New BarnesAndNoble()
  Dim match As GetBookDetailsMatches
  match = bn.GetBookDetails(isbn.Value)

  rank.Text = match.Rank
End Sub
</Script>
<font face=arial>
  <form runat=server>
    ISBN number: <input type=text id="isbn" runat=server/>
    <input type=submit id=submit onserverclick="GetSalesRank" runat=server/>
  </form>
  Sales Rank: <font color=red><b><asp:label id=rank runat=server/></b></font>
</font>
```

Using C#, you would write:

```
<%@ Page Language="C#" %>
<%@ Import Namespace="System.Net" %>

<Script runat="server">
public void GetSalesRank(Object sender, EventArgs e) {
  BarnesAndNoble bn = new BarnesAndNoble();
  GetBookDetailsMatches match;
  match = bn.GetBookDetails(isbn.Value);
  rank.Text = match.Rank;
}
</Script>

<font face=arial>
  <form runat=server ID="Form1">
    ISBN number: <input type=text id="isbn" runat=server NAME="isbn"/>
    <input type=submit id=submit onserverclick="GetSalesRank" runat=server
                          NAME="submit"/>
  </form>
  Sales Rank: <font color=red><b><asp:label id=rank runat=server/></b></font>
</font>
```

This ASP.NET page creates a new instance of the BarnesAndNoble proxy object in the GetSalesRank event handler for when the input button is clicked. The BarnesAndNoble instance, bn, is used to call the GetBookDetails method (passing in the ISBN number):

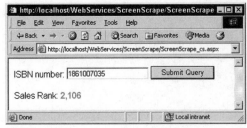

Figure 20-7

In the screenshot shown in Figure 20-7 you can see that the ASP.NET page has successfully queried BarnesAndNoble.com for the sales rank of this book.

This screen-scraping feature of ASP.NET Web services allows you to turn any web site into a web service. You can simply author the WSDL, and VS.NET or `wsdl.exe` *takes care of the rest.*

Design Decisions

Just as there are design decisions to be made when you build a web service, there are design decisions related to how to use a web service. One of the most obvious is handling exceptions.

SOAP Exceptions

In an ideal scenario, whenever you call a web service, some type of application logic is executed performing the desired task according to the request. However, code often has bugs. SOAP takes this fact into account and defines the response that a web service should use when an error occurs. This error takes the form of a SOAP message, and it is known as a *SOAP Exception*.

Requests to ASP.NET Web services that generate an exception will return a SOAP exception. Within the `System.Web.Services.Protocols` namespace is a class named `SoapException`. Clients using .NET can wrap `try...catch` blocks around calls to web services and catch SOAP Exceptions as instances of a `SoapException` class. Let's look at an example. The following is a simple web service (written using VB.NET) that can generate a runtime 'divide by zero' error:

```
<%@ WebService Class="ExceptionExample" %>

Imports System.Web.Services

Public Class ExceptionExample
  <WebMethod()> Public Function Divide(a As Integer, b As Integer) As Integer
    Return a / b
  End Function
End Class
```

Using Visual Studio .NET or `wsdl.exe`, you can build a proxy class. Let's name it `ExceptionExample`, deploy it to a web application's `bin` directory, and call the `ExceptionExample` Web service. Using VB.NET, you could write:

```
<Script runat="server">
Public Sub Page_Load(sender As Object, e As EventArgs)
  Dim example As New ExceptionExample()

  lblDiv1.Text = example.Divide(6,2)
  lblDiv2.Text = example.Divide(5,0)
End Sub
</Script>
The result of 6 divided by 2 is: <asp:label id="lblDiv1" runat="server" />
<br>
The result of 5 divided by 0 is: <asp:label id="lblDiv2" runat="server" />
```

If you execute this code, the statement `example.Divide(6,2)` is valid, and should execute. However, the statement `example.Divide(5,0)` results in a divide-by-zero error. Figure 20-8 the result:

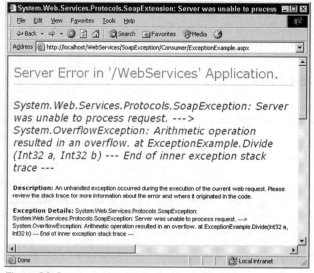

Figure 20-8

The code raises an unhandled exception on line 6 in our call to `Divide(5,0)`. The exception that is bubbled up and displayed in the ASP.NET error page is of type `SoapException`. Let's make a few modifications to the code to handle this exception:

```
<%@ Import Namespace="System.Web.Services.Protocols" %>

<Script runat="server">
Public Sub Page_Load(sender As Object, e As EventArgs)
  Dim example As New ExceptionExample()

  Try
    lblDiv1.Text = example.Divide(6,2)
  Catch err As SoapException
    lblDiv1.Text = "Unable to compute..."
  End Try
```

```
    Try
       lblDiv2.Text = example.Divide(5,0)
    Catch err As SoapException
       lblDiv2.Text = "Unable to compute..."
    End Try

  End Sub
  </Script>
  The result of 6 divided by 2 is: <asp:label id="lblDiv1" runat="server" />
  <br>
  The result of 5 divided by 0 is: <asp:label id="lblDiv2" runat="server" />
```

Unlike an ASP/VBScript combination, ASP.NET supports structured error-handling (so no more On Error Resume Next) thanks to the CLR. In our code we've made a few modifications to catch exceptions: we've added a namespace, System.Web.Services.Protocols, which contains the SoapException class and have added try...catch blocks around the code. Now, if an exception of type SoapException occurs, we can catch the exception and display a meaningful result.

When you run the modified code, you get the following result, as shown in Figure 20-9:

Figure 20-9

Another design decision is whether to use SOAP headers to send additional data with the web service. In the previous chapter, we examined how to support SOAP headers on the server. Now, let's look at how to use SOAP headers with the proxy.

Using SOAP Headers

The following is a simple ASP.NET Web service (written in VB.NET) that implements a SOAP header:

```
<%@ WebService Class="UsingSoapHeaders" %>

Imports System.Web.Services
Imports System.Web.Services.Protocols

Public Class MySoapHeader : Inherits SoapHeader
  Public Value As String
End Class

Public Class UsingSoapHeaders
  Public sHeader As MySoapHeader
```

```
    <WebMethod(), SoapHeader("sHeader")> _
    Public Function GetValueOfSoapHeader() As String
        Return sHeader.Value
    End Function
End Class
```

Here, `GetValueOfSoapHeader` returns the value of the SOAP header that the caller presents.

Described in WSDL

The information for `SimpleSoapHeader` is described in the WSDL for the service, as the application using the web service will require knowledge of the `SoapHeader`, in order to call the service:

```
<s:element name="MySoapHeader" nillable="true" type="s0:MySoapHeader" />
<s:complexType name="MySoapHeader">
  <s:sequence>
    <s:element minOccurs="1"
               maxOccurs="1"
               name="Value"
               nillable="true"
               type="s:string" />
  </s:sequence>
</s:complexType>
```

This WSDL uses an XML Schema to define a SOAP header, `MySoapHeader`. The proxy generator (Visual Studio .NET or `wsdl.exe`) will then create a class `MySoapHeader` with a single member variable `Value`.

SOAP Header Proxy

The following is the VB.NET code generated by Visual Studio .NET for the WSDL preceding the web service:

```
Namespace Simple

  <WebServiceBindingAttribute(Name:="UsingSoapHeadersSoap")
                             [Namespace]:="http://tempuri.org/")>
  Public Class UsingSoapHeaders
    Inherits SoapHttpClientProtocol
    Public MySoapHeaderValue As MySoapHeader
    Public Sub New()
      MyBase.New
      Me.Url = "http://localhost/.../SoapHeaders_vb.asmx"
    End Sub

    <SoapHeaderAttribute("MySoapHeaderValue")> _
    <SoapDocumentMethodAttribute("http://tempuri.org/GetValueOfSoapHeader",
                               Use:=SoapBindingUse.Literal,
                               ParameterStyle:= SoapParameterStyle.Wrapped)>
    Public Function GetValueOfSoapHeader() As String
      Dim results() As Object = Me.Invoke("GetValueOfSoapHeader", _
                                           New Object(0) {})
      Return CType(results(0),String)
    End Function
```

```
    End Class

    <XmlRootAttribute([Namespace]:="http://tempuri.org/", IsNullable:=true)>
    Public Class MySoapHeader
      Inherits SoapHeader

      Public Value As String
    End Class
  End Namespace
```

The proxy class contains a `MySoapHeader` subclass, which has a member variable, `Value`. The proxy class also contains a member variable, `MySoapHeaderValue`, which is used to set the SOAP header.

Using the SOAP Header

Let's look at how to use this proxy, along with its SOAP header to send additional data with the web service request. The following is a simple ASP.NET page (written in VB.NET) that uses the proxy:

```
<%@ Import Namespace="Simple" %>

<script runat="server">
Public Sub Page_Load(sender As Object, e As EventArgs)
  ' Create a new instance of the UsingSoapHeaders
  ' proxy class used to call the remote .asmx file
  Dim soapHeaderExample As New UsingSoapHeaders()

  ' Create a new instance of the mySoapHeader class
  Dim myHeader As New MySoapHeader()

  ' Set the value of myHeader
  myHeader.Value = "Sample Header Text"

  ' Set the MySoapHeader public member of the
  ' UsingSoapHeaders class to myHeader
  soapHeaderExample.MySoapHeaderValue = myHeader

  ' Get the result of the call
  Dim result As String
  result = soapHeaderExample.GetValueOfSoapHeader()
  span1.InnerHtml = result
End Sub
</script>
<font size=6>The value of the SOAP header is: <font color="red">
<span id="span1" runat="server"/></font></font>
```

In the `Page_Load` event handler, we create a new instance of the web service proxy, `soapHeaderExample`. We also create an instance of `MySoapHeader` that represents the SOAP header (`myHeader`). The `Value` field of `myHeader` is set to `Sample Header Text`.

Next, we set `myHeader` to the `soapHeaderExample` member variable `MySoapHeaderValue`. Finally, we call the `GetValueOfSoapHeader` Web service. The `MySoapHeader` class instance `myHeader` is serialized as a SOAP header for the message and is sent along with the request. When the call completes, the value that was sent as a SOAP header is displayed.

Using SOAP headers is easy. The WSDL of the service describes what the SOAP header is, and the proxy generation tool turns the XML description found in the WSDL into a .NET class that you can program with. SOAP headers are very powerful since they allow you to pass out-of-band data (data that is part of the request, but doesn't belong as part of the method marked as a web service). For example, to send a user ID with each request, you obviously wouldn't want to design each of the methods in the web service to accept that user ID as a parameter. It would be much easier to simply make use of a SOAP header.

This example is relatively simple, but it's enough to allow us to demonstrate how we could build some meaningful applications that use SOAP headers. Later, you'll see a real-world example of how to use SOAP headers. Specifically, you'll see how you can use SOAP headers to send authentication details with each request. Using SOAP headers for authentication is obviously a custom implementation of authentication and authorization, and so you should start by reviewing the security features that are already available.

Web Services Security

Security, as it relates to web services, almost seems to be a taboo topic. Individuals and companies are still trying to understand exactly what they can build with web services, but still aren't quite sure how they should protect those investments.

Fortunately, because ASP.NET Web services are simply part of an ASP.NET application, we can take advantage of all the security features provided by ASP.NET including solutions for granting or denying access to resources based on the identity of the user (username, password, and the groups/roles that the user may belong to) as well as protecting the data through the use of encryption, such as using *Secure Sockets Layer (SSL)* with HTTP (HTTPS). We can also step outside the bounds of what ASP.NET provides and implement some custom solutions, which will be discussed at the end of the chapter.

Let's start with the authentication and authorization security features provided by ASP.NET

ASP.NET Authentication and Authorization

As shown in Chapter 14, ASP.NET has several offerings for authenticating and authorizing access to ASP.NET resources:

- ❑ **Windows authentication**: Uses existing Windows users, groups and security concepts, such as an *Access Control List (ACL)*, to protect resources. To enable Windows authentication or authorization, IIS must also enforce Windows authentication, either through NTLM or Clear-Text/Basic authentication.

- ❑ **Forms authentication**: Uses user-defined users and roles and ASP.NET's URL authorization features. Using the ASP.NET configuration system, the developer defines what a given user or role is allowed to access. ASP.NET then enforces these permissions and redirects the user to a login page if they do not present a valid forms authentication cookie.

❑ **Passport authentication**: Uses a distributed authentication store to validate usernames and passwords.

Windows Authentication

To enable Windows authentication for our web service, we need to instruct IIS to use Windows authentication. This is done through the IIS Administration tool (Start | Programs | Administrative Tools | Internet Services Manager). You then find the resource that you want to enforce Windows security upon, such as `/WebServices/BasicAuthentication/Server`. Right-click on the resource, select Properties from the menus, and then select the Directory Security tab shown in Figure 20-10:

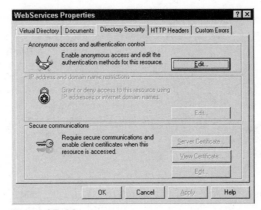

Figure 20-10

From here we'll select the Edit button for Anonymous access and authentication control. This brings up the Authentication Methods dialog depicted in Figure 20-11:

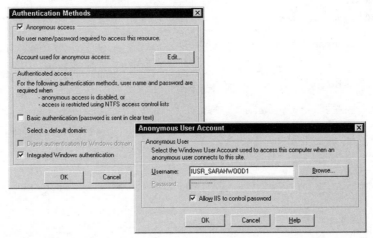

Figure 20-11

You can see the default settings. **Anonymous access** is checked and **Authenticated Access** is set to use **Integrated Windows** authentication. With Anonymous access checked, IIS will not, by default, require the client to present identity to the server. Instead the server will treat all requests, including web services, as anonymous – unless the requested resource, such as a file, does not allow anonymous access, in which case the client will be challenged for credentials.

Uncheck **Anonymous access**, and leave **Integrated Windows** authentication checked. This will instruct IIS to enforce NTLM authentication challenges for resources requested in the `/Wrox/WebServices/BasicAuthentication/Server` directory. You can then write a simple ASP.NET Web service (shown here in VB.NET) to validate the credentials used:

```
<%@ WebService Class="SecureSample" %>

Imports System.Web.Services

Public Class SecureSample
  Inherits WebService

  <WebMethod> _
  Public Function WhoAreYou() As String
    Return User.Identity.Name
  End Function
End Class
```

This web service simply uses the ASP.NET `User` object's `Identity.Name` property to return the name of the authenticated user back to the caller. You can now build a proxy for this web service and test to see if the credentials are enforced. The following is a simple ASP.NET page (written in VB.NET) that uses the proxy to call the `SecureSample` Web service:

```
<%@ Import Namespace="System.Net" %>

<Script runat="server">
Public Sub Page_Load(sender As Object, e As EventArgs)
  ' Create an instance of the SecureSample proxy
  Dim secureSample As New SecureSample()

  ' Create a new NetworkCredential class
  Dim credentials As New NetworkCredential()

  ' Set username and password values
  credentials.UserName = "demo"
  credentials.Password = "00password"
  credentials.Domain = "rhoward"

  ' Set the credentials
  secureSample.Credentials = credentials

  ' Call its WhoAreYou() function
  lblSecureSample.Text = secureSample.WhoAreYou()
End Sub

</Script>
<asp:label id="lblSecureSample" runat="server"/>
```

This code creates an instance of the `SecureSample` proxy and then creates an instance of `NetworkCredentials`. The `NetworkCredentials` class is used to specify a `UserName`, `Password`, and `Domain`. These credentials are then used along with the network request. For the proxy class, we assign the `NetworkCredentials` instance to an inherited property of the proxy, `Credentials`. Then we can make our request to the Windows authenticated web service. If the credentials are valid, the users are authenticated; otherwise, they are denied access.

This example uses NTLM authentication. When you make a request to the web server, the web server determines that Windows authentication is required and issues a challenge response back to the caller. The caller then has the opportunity to send a hashed value of the username, password, and domain to the server. The server will then attempt to create the same hash. If the values match, the user is considered authenticated. Sometimes, however, NTLM authentication can't be used. For example, your client could be a non-Windows application, in which case you might decide to use Clear-Text/Basic authentication.

Clear-Text/Basic Authentication

Whereas Windows NTLM authentication sends a hash of the credentials, this hash can only be computed by an application that is able to create the hash. Some web service clients may not wish to use NTLM authentication, but are likely still to be able to use Clear-Text/Basic authentication.

Clear-Text/Basic authentication works in a manner similar to NTLM in that the server issues a challenge, but rather than sending a hashed value of the credentials, the client Base64-encodes the values. The format is `BASIC: Domain\Username:Password`. Basic authentication hides the data, but the credentials can be easily extracted. The value is sent using the `AUTHORIZATION` HTTP header and the value of this header is the Base64-encoded value. Clear-Text/Basic authentication, by itself, is not considered a secure form of authentication. However, when used with HTTPS, which encrypts all communication between the client and server, it is quite useful.

You can enable this authentication option in IIS, by revisiting the Authentication methods dialog and selecting only Basic authentication, shown in Figure 20-12:

Figure 20-12

When you enable Basic authentication, IIS will display a warning that this authentication method will pass credentials in clear text. You can use the proxy class to make calls to the web service. However, instead of using a secure authentication mechanism, your credentials are passed in Base64-encoded clear text.

Another option is to use ASP.NET Forms authentication to validate the user. However, you have to make some special arrangements to use this type of authentication with web services. This is because Forms authentication uses cookies, and you have already seen how a cookie is kept in memory and is lost when the proxy is destroyed. Additionally, Forms authentication makes use of HTTP redirects to an HTML form for unauthenticated users.

Forms Authentication

ASP.NET Forms authentication allows you to use an HTML form to request the credentials for a user. The submitted credentials can then be validated against any data store, and if the credentials are considered valid, an HTTP cookie is sent to the client. This cookie is used on subsequent requests to authenticate the user.

While Forms authentication is a very flexible system, it is somewhat cumbersome to use with web services. The main issue is that when configured for Forms authentication, ASP.NET will redirect requests to an HTML forms login page. This will cause problems for a web service proxy that is expecting a SOAP response. To use Forms authentication with ASP.NET Web services, you have to bend the rules a little. To look at how this is done, let's use the same SecureSample Web service we used earlier with *one* minor modification:

```
<%@ WebService Class="SecureSample" %>
Imports System.Web.Services
Imports System.Web.Security

Public Class SecureSample
  Inherits WebService
  <WebMethod> _
  Public Function WhoAreYou() As String
    Return User.Identity.Name
  End Function

  <WebMethod> _
  Public Function Authenticate(username As String, password As String)
    If (username = "John") AND (password = "password") Then
      FormsAuthentication.SetAuthCookie(username, true)

      Return true
    End If

    Return false
  End Function
End Class
```

We've added a new function, Authenticate, which accepts both a username and a password. We then have to write code to determine the validity of the username and password values, and have used the FormsAuthentication SetAuthCookie static method to write the Forms authentication cookie to the client. We also need a web.config file that configures this web service to use Forms authentication:

```
<configuration>
  <system.web>
```

```
      <authentication mode="Forms">
        <forms name=".ASPXAUTH" loginUrl="login.aspx"
               protection="All"  timeout="30" path="/" />
      </authentication>
    </system.web>
</configuration>
```

We don't specify an `<authorization>` section. This allows us to get around the problem of redirecting the user to `login.aspx`, but still allows us to use the Forms authentication cookie for validation purposes.

After you authenticate by calling the web service `Authenticate` method, you can call the `WhoAreYou` method and see that the ASP.NET `User` object recognizes you as a valid user. You can then authorize actions for this user in the code. For example, for users in the 'customer' role, you could allow access to direct database requests, but for users in the 'anonymous' role, you could send them cached data.

Yet another solution to the authentication problem is to use *client certificates*. Client certificates usually go hand-in-hand with SSL, so we'll discuss them together.

HTTPS Encryption and Client Certificates

The recommended strategy for hiding data in transmission is to use the HTTPS protocol. HTTPS uses public/private asymmetric cryptography to provide a secure communication between the caller and the server.

> *Refer to the IIS documentation for directions on how to install and use a server certificate for secure communication.*

Once a server certificate is installed, you can enforce the use of the certificate on your web application by simply opening the properties dialog for the web application, selecting the Directory Security tab, clicking the Edit button under Secure Communications, and then checking the Require secure channel (SSL) checkbox, as Figure 20-13 depicts:

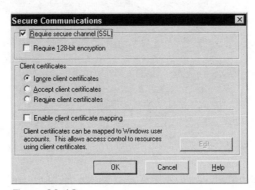

Figure 20-13

Requests to this web application will now require HTTPS to request data from the server, thus encrypting content. You can simply add an ASP.NET Web service to this application and the use of HTTPS will be transparent.

An ASP.NET Web service served from a web application with HTTPS enabled will generate WSDL that correctly identifies the web service as using HTTPS (described via the `location` attribute of the port setting in the WSDL). When you build a proxy using the WSDL, the proxy will automatically be configured to use HTTPS for secure communication with the server.

Another option, which is only available when the server has an installed certificate, is to enable the server to recognize client certificates.

Client Certificates

Server certificates are issued by a third party to ensure that the identity of the server is valid and can be trusted. A client certificate is also issued by a trusted third party, but is used to ensure that the identity of the client is valid and can be trusted. A client can send a request to the server along with the client certificate. The server can then determine if the certificate is trusted, and can use the certificate to authenticate and authorize the client.

The most common use of client certificates is a certificate installed with the browser. For example, if you obtain a client certificate, you can view the certificate in Internet Explorer. For Internet Explorer 6, this is done by selecting Tools | Internet Options. This opens the Internet Options dialog. Next, select the Content tab shown in Figure 20-14:

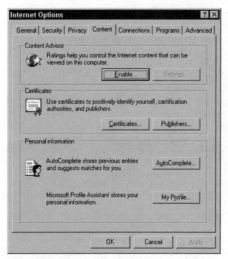

Figure 20-14

If you press the Certificates button, you'll be provided with a list of the installed client certificates.

You can require the use of client certificates on the server by configuring your web application through the same Secure Communication dialog box used for enabling HTTPS (note that this requires that you have a server certificate as well). To enable support for client certificates, simply check the **Require** or **Accept client certificates** option.

Clients that make requests to this web application are then required to present a client certificate. If the client does not present a certificate, access is denied. If certificates are accepted, the onus is on us to determine whether or not to authenticate the request. We validate the certificate through code, as you'll see in a moment.

Before using the certificate from our proxy, we'll test the certificate using a browser that has a client certificate installed, and access an ASP.NET Web service on a server that requires the use of client certificates–this all happens transparently within our code.

If client certificates are installed, we can also write some code on the server that examines the certificate and extracts meaningful information from it. The following is a simple ASP.NET Web service (written in VB.NET) that accesses certificates presented by the client and extracts meaningful details:

```
<%@ WebService Class="CertExample" %>

Imports System.Security.Principal
Imports System.Web.Services
Imports System.Web
Imports System

Public Class CertExample
  <WebMethod> _
  Public Function GetCertDetails() As CertDetails
    Dim request As HttpRequest = HttpContext.Current.Request
    Dim cert As New CertDetails()

    cert.Issuer = Request.ClientCertificate.Issuer
    cert.Subject = Request.ClientCertificate.Subject
    cert.Valid = Request.ClientCertificate.IsValid
    cert.KeySize = Request.ClientCertificate.KeySize
    cert.PublicKey = Convert.ToBase64String(Request.ClientCertificate.PublicKey)
    cert.Cookie = Request.ClientCertificate.Cookie

    Return cert
  End Function
End Class

Public Class CertDetails
  Public Issuer As String
  Public Subject As String
  Public Valid As Boolean
  Public KeySize As Integer
  Public PublicKey As String
  Public Cookie As String
End Class
```

If you test this web service through a browser and the client presents a certificate, you should see a result similar to that shown in Figure 20-15:

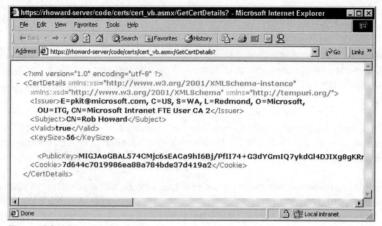

Figure 20-15

This example demonstrates how a certificate sent by the client is used on the server to recognize the client's identity. Let's now look at the same example, but instead of using a browser to present the certificate, we'll use the ASP.NET proxy to present it along with the request.

Using Client Certificates with Web Services

To use client certificates with the proxy, you need to export the client certificate. If you select Tools | Internet Options from Internet Explorer, select the Content tab, and view the installed certificates (as you did earlier), you can select a certificate and export it.

If you select the certificate and press the Export button, the Certificate Export Wizard will open. You can simply press the Next button, accepting the defaults, until you arrive at the File to Export dialog. Here, you need to provide a filename for the exported certificate as well as a location, for example C:\cert.cer. Click the Finish button, and your certificate is exported.

You now need to modify the application that's using the web service proxy to supply the certificate with the call:

```
<%@ Import Namespace="System.Security.Cryptography.X509Certificates" %>

<script runat="server">
  Public Sub Page_Load(sender As Object, e As EventArgs)
    Dim cert As new CertExample()
    Dim details As CertDetails
    Dim x509 As X509Certificate.CreateFromCertFile("c:\\cert.cer")

    cert.ClientCertificates.Add(x509)

    details = cert.GetCertDetails()

    lblIssuer.Text = details.Issuer
    lblSubject.Text = details.Subject
    lblValid.Text = details.Valid
```

```
      lblKeySize.Text = details.KeySize
      lblPublicKey.Text = details.PublicKey
      lblCookie.Text = details.Cookie
    End Sub
</script>
Issuer: <asp:label id="lblIssuer" runat="server"/>
<br>
Subject: <asp:label id="lblSubject" runat="server"/>
<br>
Valid: <asp:label id="lblValid" runat="server"/>
<br>
KeySize: <asp:label id="lblKeySize" runat="server"/>
<br>
PublicKey: <asp:label id="lblPublicKey" runat="server"/>
<br>
Cookie: <asp:label id="lblCookie" runat="server"/>
```

In this code, the `X509Certificate` class is used to load the client certificate from the `C:\cert.cer` file. Then the certificate is added to the proxy, and the request is issued.

In the next section, we'll delve a bit deeper into web service security issues.

Advanced Topics

All of the security options we've discussed so far rely upon the HTTP transport protocol for the security details: Windows NTLM, Basic, and Forms authentications, all rely on either an HTTP header or an HTTP cookie.

Now, we'll look at an advanced example that demonstrates a custom authentication and authorization example using SOAP headers.

Custom Authentication and Authorization

SOAP headers provide a great way to send out-of-band data. We use HTTP headers to send details that aren't directly part of the body with the HTTP message, and can do the same thing with SOAP headers. This allows us to decouple application details, such as session cookies and authentication, from the transport protocol and instead pass them as part of the SOAP message. This way, no matter what transport the SOAP message is sent over, these details remain with the message instead of being lost when transport protocols change.

We'll look at an example that uses SOAP headers (rather than relying upon a cookie or an HTTP header) to send an 'authentication' header. This example shows several great features of ASP.NET:

- ❑ **Custom authentication**: Bypass the authentication features that ASP.NET offers, such as Forms or Windows, and plug our own authentication system into ASP.NET.

- ❑ **SOAP headers**: Use SOAP headers to transmit credentials and decouple the information from the HTTP headers, making the message transport-independent.

❑ **HTTP module**: Use of an HTTP module that looks at each request and determines if it is a SOAP message.

❑ **Custom application events**: The HTTP module raises a custom `global.asax` event, within which we implement our application logic to verify credentials.

Let's start by examining the web service.

ASP.NET Web Service

The following is the code for a web service (written in VB.NET) that implements an authentication SOAP header:

```
<%@ WebService Class="SecureWebService" %>

Imports System
Imports System.Web.Services
Imports System.Web.Services.Protocols

Public Class Authentication : Inherits SoapHeader
  Public User As String
  Public Password As String
End Class

Public Class SecureWebService : Inherits WebService
  Public authentication As Authentication

  <WebMethod> _
  <SoapHeader("authentication")> _
  Public Function ValidUser() As String
    If User.IsInRole("Customer") Then
      Return "User is in the Customer role..."
    Else If User.Identity.IsAuthenticated Then
      Return "User is valid..."
    Else
      Return "Not authenticated"
    End If
  End Function

End Class
```

This code implements a single `WebMethod`, `ValidUser`, which simply uses the ASP.NET `User` intrinsic object to determine if the request is from a validated user:

❑ If the user is in the `Customer` role, the function returns `User is in the Customer role....`

❑ If the user is simply authenticated but is *not* in the `Customer` role, the function returns `User is valid....`

❑ If the user is not authenticated, the function returns `Not authenticated`.

The code is quite simple. The web service uses the ASP.NET `User` intrinsic object to validate the authentication of a request.

The web service also defines a SOAP header, `Authentication`. Applications using the web service will set this header with appropriate values, and our application will validate the credentials and create a valid `User` object. Let's see how that's done.

Sample Application

The following VB.NET code is for a simple ASP.NET page that makes use of a proxy, `SecureWebService`. The proxy is used to make calls to the ASP.NET Web service we just created:

```
<%@ Import Namespace="Security"%>
<%@ Import Namespace="System.Web.Services.Protocols" %>
<script runat="server">
  Public Sub Page_Load(sender As Object, e As EventArgs)
    span1.InnerHtml = ""
    span2.InnerHtml = ""
  End Sub
  Public Sub Authenticate_Click(sender As Object, e As EventArgs)
    Dim secureWebService As New SecureWebService()

    ' Create the Authentication header and set values
    Dim authenticationHeader As New Authentication()
    authenticationHeader.User = user.Value
    authenticationHeader.Password = password.Value

    ' Assign the Header
    secureWebService.AuthenticationValue = authenticationHeader
    ' Call method
    Try
      span1.InnerHtml = s.ValidUser()
    Catch soap As SoapException
      span2.InnerHtml = soap.Message
    End Try
  End Sub
</script>
```

This ASP.NET page simply renders an HTML form that allows the user to enter credentials. These credentials are then made part of the request sent to the server. Here is the SOAP message that a caller makes to the server (minus the HTTP headers):

```
<?xml version="1.0" encoding="utf-8"?>
<soap:Envelope xmlns:soap="http://schemas.xmlsoap.org/soap/envelope/"
               xmlns:xsi="http://www.w3.org/2001/XMLSchema-instance"
               xmlns:xsd="http://www.w3.org/2001/XMLSchema">
  <soap:Header>
    <Authentication xmlns="http://tempuri.org/">
      <User>John</User>
      <Password>password</Password>
    </Authentication>
  </soap:Header>
  <soap:Body>
    <ValidUser xmlns="http://tempuri.org/" />
  </soap:Body>
</soap:Envelope>
```

And here is the response (again, minus HTTP headers):

```
<?xml version="1.0" encoding="utf-8"?>

<soap:Envelope xmlns:soap="http://schemas.xmlsoap.org/soap/envelope/"
               xmlns:xsi="http://www.w3.org/2001/XMLSchema-instance"
               xmlns:xsd="http://www.w3.org/2001/XMLSchema">
  <soap:Body>
    <ValidUserResponse xmlns="http://tempuri.org/">
      <ValidUserResult>Not authenticated</ValidUserResult>
    </ValidUserResponse>
  </soap:Body>

</soap:Envelope>
```

The SOAP header is passed in clear-text – we'll address encryption shortly.

Calls to the web service are obviously getting processed. However, we've left a few details out, including how the credentials are authenticated. Let's look at that now.

Validating SOAP Header Credentials

The ASP.NET Web service requires a `global.asax` file in its application root. Here's what the `global.asax` file contains:

```
<%@ Import Namespace="Microsoft.WebServices.Security" %>
<%@ Import Namespace="System.Security.Principal" %>

<script runat=server>
  Public Sub WebServiceAuthentication_OnAuthenticate(sender As Object, _
                                      e As WebServiceAuthenticationEvent)
    If (e.User = "bwhite@bar.com") And (e.Password = "password") Then
        e.Authenticate()
    Else If (e.User = "sswienton@foo.com") _
        And (e.Password = "password") Then
      Dim s(1) As String
      s(0) = "Customer"
      e.Authenticate(s)
    End If
  End Sub
</script>
```

Our `global.asax` file implements a `WebServiceAuthentication_OnAuthenticate` event handler that is raised whenever a request is made to a web service within the current application. Inside the event, application logic is used to determine the validity of a given set of credentials. In this case, we have two hardcoded cases. One simply authenticates the user and the other authenticates the user and also adds the user to the `Customer` role. Although the usernames and passwords are hardcoded into the logic, it is easy to envision replacing this with calls to a database, an XML file, or another resource that you want to verify credentials against.

The actual event is raised by a custom HTTP module. The HTTP module looks at each request, and for requests that are web services, the HTTP module opens the message, parses the SOAP value for an authentication header (and values), raises a custom event, and finally implements the necessary calls to authenticate a user *and* add a given user to the role. By the time the request actually reaches the web service, all of this has already taken place.

WebServiceAuthentication HTTP Module

The HTTP module encapsulates all the work of authenticating the request. Although all of the work done by the module could be achieved using `global.asax`, this method provides a clean level of abstraction and allows the developer to focus on authenticating the request.

The HTTP module listens for an ASP.NET authenticate event (discussed in Chapter 12). When this ASP.NET application event is raised, the HTTP module has the opportunity to execute code. In this case, the module raises its own `OnEnter` event.

The `OnEnter` event handler starts by examining the request for the `HTTP_SOAPACTION` header. The existence of this header is required by the SOAP 1.1 specification, but the value it contains is optional. If the header exists, we know the HTTP request contains a SOAP message. The code is shown here in C#:

```
void OnEnter(Object source, EventArgs eventArgs) {
    HttpApplication app = (HttpApplication)source;
    HttpContext context = app.Context;
    Stream HttpStream = context.Request.InputStream;

    // Current position of stream
    long posStream = HttpStream.Position;

    // If the request contains an HTTP_SOAPACTION
    // header we'll look at this message
    if (context.Request.ServerVariables["HTTP_SOAPACTION"] == null)
      return;

    // Load the body of the HTTP message
    // into an XML document
    XmlDocument dom = new XmlDocument();
    string soapUser;
    string soapPassword;
    try {
      dom.Load(HttpStream);
```

If the request is a valid SOAP message, we will attempt to load the SOAP message into an XML document. If this succeeds, we'll reset the location in the stream (so that the ASP.NET Web service still has the chance to read the request). Then we'll attempt to read the `User` and `Password` values of the `Authentication` header. As these operations are wrapped in a `try...catch` block, if it fails, an exception is thrown.

```
    // Reset the stream position
    HttpStream.Position = posStream;

    // Bind to the Authentication header
    soapUser = dom.GetElementsByTagName("User").Item(0).InnerText;
```

```
        soapPassword = dom.GetElementsByTagName("Password").Item(0).InnerText;
} catch (Exception e) {
    // Reset Position of stream
    HttpStream.Position = posStream;

    // Throw exception
    throw soapException
}
```

If no exceptions are raised, we'll call the code to raise the event that we can listen for in `global.asax`:

```
    // Raise the custom global.asax event
    OnAuthenticate(new WebServiceAuthenticationEvent(context,
                                                      soapUser,
                                                      soapPassword));

    return;
}
```

Finally, the function returns, and the processing of the request is handed to the ASP.NET `.asmx` handler.

This example demonstrates how to use SOAP headers to pass additional information, such as authentication details, as part of the SOAP message–decoupling those details from the transport. In this particular example, we passed the data in clear text, obviously a less than ideal solution. However, this example is only meant to be a conceptual sample that you can extend, not a solution in itself.

Next, we'll look at another advanced feature of ASP.NET Web services: SOAP extensions.

SOAP Extensions

ASP.NET provides a great programming model for working with and building web services, and in some ways it has trivialized the work required to build SOAP-based applications. We simply author the application logic, sprinkle some `WebMethod` attributes on the functions, and it's done.

However, life isn't always so easy. The use of the `WebMethod` is simple, but it also abstracts a lot of what is happening behind the scenes. A special base class, `SoapExtension`, allows for implementing our own custom extensions that are able to manipulate ASP.NET Web services at a very low level.

The `SoapExtension` base class, which our class *must* inherit from, requires that we implement some virtual functions. The most important function that we must implement is `ProcessMessage`.

The `ProcessMessage` method allows you to look at the raw message before and after it is serialized from a .NET class into SOAP or deserialized from SOAP back into a .NET class. This functionality is available for the web service *and* the proxy.

Let's look at a simple SOAP extension that enables us to trace the SOAP request/response data to disk. This is a very helpful attribute written by some of the developers on the ASP.NET Web services team.

Tracing

One of the most frustrating aspects of developing web services is the lack of tools available to view the SOAP message exchange. The trace extension (the source of which follows) outputs the incoming and outgoing SOAP message to a file.

The trace extension can be used as follows:

```
<WebMethod()> _
<TraceExtension(Filename:="c:\\trace.log")> _
Public Function Add(a As Integer, b As Integer) As Integer
  Return a + b
End Function
```

We simply compile the trace extension attribute and deploy it to our application's \bin directory. We then use the attribute, as shown, providing it with the name of a file to log results to. The result of this is:

```
================================= Request at 6/6/2001 2:10:20 AM
<?xml version="1.0" encoding="utf-8"?>
<soap:Envelope xmlns:soap="http://schemas.xmlsoap.org/soap/envelope/"
               xmlns:xsi="http://www.w3.org/2001/XMLSchema-instance"
               xmlns:xsd="http://www.w3.org/2001/XMLSchema">
  <soap:Body>
    <Add xmlns="http://tempuri.org/">
      <a>10</a>
      <b>5</b>
    </Add>
  </soap:Body>
</soap:Envelope>

--------------------------------- Response at 6/6/2001 2:10:20 AM
<?xml version="1.0" encoding="utf-8"?>
<soap:Envelope xmlns:soap="http://schemas.xmlsoap.org/soap/envelope/"
               xmlns:xsi="http://www.w3.org/2001/XMLSchema-instance"
               xmlns:xsd="http://www.w3.org/2001/XMLSchema">
  <soap:Body>
    <AddResponse xmlns="http://tempuri.org/">
      <AddResult>15</AddResult>
    </AddResponse>
  </soap:Body>
</soap:Envelope>
```

You can see the trace results of a request to the Add Web service and the response. Here's the C# source to the trace extension attribute:

```
using System;
using System.IO;
using System.Web.Services.Protocols;

[AttributeUsage(AttributeTargets.Method)]
public class TraceExtensionAttribute : SoapExtensionAttribute {
  private string filename = "c:\\log.txt";
  private int priority;
```

```
    public override Type ExtensionType {
      get { return typeof(TraceExtension); }
    }
    public override int Priority {
      get { return priority; }
      set { priority = value; }
    }

    public string Filename {
        get {
        return filename;
      }
      set {
        filename = value;
      }
    }
  }
}
```

In the `TraceExtensionAttribute` class, we inherit from `SoapExtensionAttribute`, implementing both our public property for configuring the filename used for logging (`Filename`), and the `Extension` type attribute, which returns a class of type `TraceExtension`:

```
public class TraceExtension : SoapExtension {

  Stream oldStream;
  Stream newStream;
  string filename;

  public override object GetInitializer(LogicalMethodInfo methodInfo,
                                        SoapExtensionAttribute attribute) {
    return ((TraceExtensionAttribute) attribute).Filename;
  }

  public override object GetInitializer(Type serviceType){
    return typeof(TraceExtension);
  }

  public override void Initialize(object initializer) {
    filename = (string) initializer;
  }
```

In the `TraceExtension` class, we override some methods that are marked as `virtual` in `SoapExtension`. The most important of these is `ProcessMessage`, which allows you to interact with the message at four different stages of processing:

❑   `BeforeSerialize`: Allows you to interact with the message before you serialize the data as a SOAP message.

❑   `AfterSerialize`: Allows you to interact with the message after you serialize the data as a SOAP message. In our case, we call the `WriteOutput` function to write the current SOAP message to our log during this stage.

❑ `BeforeDeserialize`: Allows you to interact with the message before you deserialize the SOAP message back into .NET data types. Here, we call `WriteInput` to write the current SOAP message to the log.

❑ `AfterDeserialize`: Allows you to interact with the message after you deserialize the SOAP message back into .NET data types.

The code for these methods follows:

```
public override void ProcessMessage(SoapMessage message) {
  switch (message.Stage) {

  case SoapMessageStage.BeforeSerialize:
    break;

  case SoapMessageStage.AfterSerialize:
    WriteOutput( message );
    break;

  case SoapMessageStage.BeforeDeserialize:
    WriteInput( message );
    break;

  case SoapMessageStage.AfterDeserialize:
    break;

  default:
    throw new Exception("invalid stage");
  }
}

public override Stream ChainStream( Stream stream ){
  oldStream = stream;
  newStream = new MemoryStream();
  return newStream;
}

public void WriteOutput( SoapMessage message ){
  newStream.Position = 0;
  FileStream fs = new FileStream(filename, FileMode.Append, FileAccess.Write);
  StreamWriter w = new StreamWriter(fs);
  w.WriteLine("--------------------------- Response at " + DateTime.Now);
  w.Flush();
  Copy(newStream, fs);
  fs.Close();
  newStream.Position = 0;
  Copy(newStream, oldStream);
}

public void WriteInput( SoapMessage message ){
  Copy(oldStream, newStream);
  FileStream fs = new FileStream(filename, FileMode.Append, FileAccess.Write);
  StreamWriter w = new StreamWriter(fs);
  w.WriteLine("============================= Request at " + DateTime.Now);
```

```
        w.Flush();
        newStream.Position = 0;
        Copy(newStream, fs);
        fs.Close();
        newStream.Position = 0;
    }
    void Copy(Stream from, Stream to) {
        TextReader reader = new StreamReader(from);
        TextWriter writer = new StreamWriter(to);
        writer.WriteLine(reader.ReadToEnd());
        writer.Flush();
    }
}
```

It should be clear how powerful SOAP extensions are. You could, for example, have written the custom authentication example demonstrated earlier using SOAP extensions. Another possibility would have been to use SOAP extensions to perform custom encryption of data.

Custom Encryption

This example was originally written to demonstrate an alternative to using HTTP/SSL to send data. Consider this: as long as the SOAP message is sent via HTTP, you can use a complementary protocol such as HTTPS to encrypt the data. However, if the SOAP message is routed between various servers, each of those servers must have a trust relationship with the others as each will have to establish a new SSL connection to transmit the data to the next server.

We want to route over *public* networks, but exchange *private* data. The custom encryption attribute discussed next allows a valid SOAP message to be routed over the public network, but the contents of that SOAP message can be encrypted. For example, you could write the following web service and use the tracing extensions to see exactly what is exchanged via SOAP on the wire:

```
...
<WebMethod()>
<TraceExtension(Filename:="c:\\trace.log")>
Public Function SayHello() As String
    Return "Secret message"
End Function
...
```

The log result of the exchange follows:

```
--------------------------------- Response at 6/7/2001 3:11:47 AM
<?xml version="1.0" encoding="utf-8"?>
<soap:Envelope xmlns:soap="http://schemas.xmlsoap.org/soap/envelope/"
               xmlns:xsi="http://www.w3.org/2001/XMLSchema-instance"
               xmlns:xsd="http://www.w3.org/2001/XMLSchema">
  <soap:Body>
    <SayHello xmlns="http://tempuri.org/" />
  </soap:Body>
</soap:Envelope>
================================= Request at 6/7/2001 3:11:49 AM
<?xml version="1.0" encoding="utf-8"?>
```

```
<soap:Envelope xmlns:soap="http://schemas.xmlsoap.org/soap/envelope/"
               xmlns:xsi="http://www.w3.org/2001/XMLSchema-instance"
               xmlns:xsd="http://www.w3.org/2001/XMLSchema">
  <soap:Body>
    <SayHelloResponse xmlns="http://tempuri.org/">
      <SayHelloResult>Secret message</SayHelloResult>
    </SayHelloResponse>
  </soap:Body>
</soap:Envelope>
```

To prevent prying eyes from examining the details of your message exchange, you could:

❑   Use HTTPS and encrypt the entire data exchange

❑   Use a custom SOAP extension and encrypt only part of the data

Let's look at a custom SOAP extension that is capable of encrypting only part of the data:

```
...
<WebMethod()>
<EncryptionExtension(Encrypt=EncryptMode.Response)>
<TraceExtension(Filename:="c:\\trace.log")>
Public Function SayHello() As String
  Return "Secret message"
End Function
...
```

We've now added an `EncryptionExtension` attribute to the `SayHello` function, and also set a property (in this new attribute) that sets `EncryptMode.Response`. Now, when we make a SOAP request to this service and trace the result, our data is encrypted:

```
--------------------------------- Response at 6/7/2001 3:18:25 AM
<?xml version="1.0" encoding="utf-8"?>
<soap:Envelope xmlns:soap="http://schemas.xmlsoap.org/soap/envelope/"
               xmlns:xsi="http://www.w3.org/2001/XMLSchema-instance"
               xmlns:xsd="http://www.w3.org/2001/XMLSchema">
  <soap:Body>
    <SayHello xmlns="http://tempuri.org/" />
  </soap:Body>
</soap:Envelope>
================================== Request at 6/7/2001 3:18:27 AM
<?xml version="1.0" encoding="utf-8"?>
<soap:Envelope xmlns:soap="http://schemas.xmlsoap.org/soap/envelope/"
               xmlns:xsi="http://www.w3.org/2001/XMLSchema-instance"
               xmlns:xsd="http://www.w3.org/2001/XMLSchema">
  <soap:Body>
    <SayHelloResponse xmlns="http://tempuri.org/">
      <SayHelloResult>
        158 68 233 236 56 189 240 27 73 27 17 214 65 142 207 77
      </SayHelloResult>
    </SayHelloResponse>
  </soap:Body>
</soap:Envelope>
```

The value of the `<SayHelloResult>` element is now an array of bytes. These bytes are a single-pass, symmetric encryption using *Data Encryption Standard* (*DES*) of the string `"Secret Message"`.

The `EncryptionExtension` attribute that is added to the function encrypts the value after the message is serialized into SOAP. This allows us to send a valid SOAP message that can be routed between various intermediaries *and* sent over alternative protocols. Our data remains secure, as it is sent over the network.

To decrypt the message, we use the same attribute, but add it to the proxy used by the application using our service:

```
<EncryptionExtension(Decrypt=DecryptMode.Request)> _
<SoapDocumentMethodAttribute("http://tempuri.org/SayHello",
                    Use:=SoapBindingUse.Literal,
                    ParameterStyle:= SoapParameterStyle.Wrapped)> _
Public Function SayHello() As String
  Dim results() As Object = Me.Invoke("SayHello", New Object(0) {})
  Return CType(results(0),String)
End Function
```

Instead of setting an `Encrypt` property in the `EncryptionExtension` attribute, we now set a `Decrypt` property. This instructs the `EncryptionExtension` to decrypt any incoming messages. The result is that data is encrypted on the wire as it's exchanged, and decrypted again by the intended recipient.

The `ProcessMessage` function of `EncryptionExtension` follows:

```
public override void ProcessMessage(SoapMessage message) {
  switch (message.Stage) {

    case SoapMessageStage.BeforeSerialize:
      break;

    case SoapMessageStage.AfterSerialize:
      Encrypt();
      break;

    case SoapMessageStage.BeforeDeserialize:
      Decrypt();
      break;

    case SoapMessageStage.AfterDeserialize:
      break;

    default:
      throw new Exception("invalid stage");
  }
}
```

It's very similar to the tracing extension we saw earlier. However, instead of writing the SOAP message to a file, this extension is capable of using DES encryption to both encrypt and decrypt the SOAP message. Here's the `Encrypt` routine that is called:

```
private void Encrypt() {
  newStream.Position = 0;

  if (encryptMode == EncryptMode.Response)
    newStream = EncryptSoap(newStream);
    Copy(newStream, oldStream);
  }
```

If the `Encrypt` property of the attribute is set to `EncryptMode.Response`, the `Encrypt` function will call another routine, `EncryptSoap`:

```
public MemoryStream EncryptSoap(Stream streamToEncrypt) {
  streamToEncrypt.Position = 0;
  XmlTextReader reader = new XmlTextReader(streamToEncrypt);
  XmlDocument dom = new XmlDocument();
  dom.Load(reader);

  XmlNamespaceManager nsmgr = new XmlNamespaceManager(dom.NameTable);
  nsmgr.AddNamespace("soap", "http://schemas.xmlsoap.org/soap/envelope/");
  XmlNode node = dom.SelectSingleNode("//soap:Body", nsmgr);
  node = node.FirstChild.FirstChild;

  byte[] outData = Encrypt(node.InnerText);

  StringBuilder s = new StringBuilder();

  for(int i=0; i<outData.Length; i++) {
    if(i==(outData.Length-1))
      s.Append(outData[i]);
    else
      s.Append(outData[i] + " ");
  }

  node.InnerText = s.ToString();

  MemoryStream ms = new MemoryStream();
  dom.Save(ms);
  ms.Position = 0;

  return ms;
}
```

`EncryptSoap` reads in the memory stream that represents the SOAP message and navigates down to the appropriate node. Once this is found, the `Encrypt` method that accepts a string and returns the DES encrypted byte array is called. Afterwards, `EncryptSoap` simply converts the encrypted byte array to a string and adds that string back into the SOAP message stream, which is then returned.

Although this is quite a complex sample, it should provide you with an excellent starting point with which to build more secure web services. Here are some recommendations:

❑ Ideally, this encryption extension should be using asymmetric encryption, rather than having both the web service and the proxy sharing the same key.

❑ A SOAP header should be used to send additional details about the message relating to the encryption; for example, details of the public key (if you were to re-implement this to support asymmetric encoding), as well as an encrypted timestamp to prevent replay attacks.

❑ Currently, the message exchange only supports clear-text requests (from the proxy) and encrypted results. Ideally, the extension should support encrypted requests.

These suggestions are beyond the scope of what can be covered in this chapter. However, hopefully they will be implemented in the near future and released into the public domain.

Summary

We started this chapter by discussing the general problem of finding web services that we might want to use. To address the problem, we looked at UDDI, and how organizations can use it to find and register web services. We then stepped through the use of UDDI, using Microsoft's UDDI node, to demonstrate its typical use in discovering SOAP Web services.

After discussing the uses of UDDI, we mentioned that there still needs to be a way of describing the capabilities of web services, such as the protocols they support as well as the data types and XML schemas that may be used. To address this problem, we introduced WSDL.

Thanks to WSDL, we can build software based on the XML blueprint of a web service. We discussed the use of both Visual Studio .NET, and the wsdl.exe command-line tool to create this proxy software. After creating proxies with both of these tools, we demonstrated how to use them and stepped through some common scenarios, including setting the timeout value and using HTTP cookies.

Following our discussion of building .NET proxies for web services, we went on to HTML screen-scraping and how we could use a simple WSDL document and the support for regular expressions in .NET to easily turn any web site into a web service.

Next, we saw several design decisions for web services. We looked at handling exceptions and how to use SOAP headers to send out-of-band data (that is, data that doesn't belong as part of the body of the SOAP message).

Finally, we discussed security–both the options provided by ASP.NET, such as Forms or Windows authentication, and some custom security and encryption options that can be implemented.

That completes our coverage of web services. In the next chapter we'll turn our attention to Mobile Controls.

21

Mobile Controls

ASP.NET Mobile Controls are an extension to the controls available in the .NET framework that add support for mobile devices. They are a collection of controls that vary their output depending on the browsing device, and allow for content types other that HTML, such as WML (Wireless Markup Language) and cHTML (Compact HTML).

> *Prior to version 1.1 of the .NET Framework, these controls were available as a separate download known as the Mobile Internet Toolkit. Version 1.1 of the framework includes these controls as part of the standard installation.*

This chapter details these controls and gives examples of their use. We'll start with a tour of the wireless Web, with a look at what is available and a discussion of WAP. Next you'll look at the mobile controls, including a reference section on the controls available. Moving on, we'll see some of the more advanced techniques you can use to streamline mobile Web applications, before finishing off with a few guesses as to what the future holds for mobile controls, and wireless Internet access.

A Summary of the Wireless Web

Recently, there has been a huge surge of interest in wireless Internet access, and indeed in mobile computing in general. As everyone has become increasingly dependent on the World Wide Web, there is a desire to access it from anywhere. The technology now exists to enable you to do this, although the exact nature of this access is quite different from 'traditional' Internet access.

This difference has caused many problems, both for device manufacturers and consumers, as it has frequently been overlooked. Often, consumers have expected to get an all-singing, all-dancing, Web-surfing gadget, and have been disappointed with what they ended up with. However, the underlying potential of such devices is unquestionable. In order to make sense of this you need to look at features inherent in the devices that can be used for mobile Internet access. The most obvious of these features is that the device will be small. It follows on from this that:

❑ Display area is limited, being far smaller than a PC monitor. Color capability is becoming standard (due to improved display technologies, power consumption, and battery life), but display legibility is still partly reliant on viewing angle and lighting conditions.

❑ Processing power and memory is unlikely to compete with PCs.

❑ Multimedia capabilities will be severely challenged.

Already it's obvious that you cannot expect the sort of Web experience you are accustomed to using Web browsers on your PC. To further illustrate this, consider Figure 21-1, which shows the Wrox web site displayed on the screen of an Internet capable mobile phone:

Figure 21-1

You'd have a hard time navigating through this site – if you could even read it!

Of course, larger screened devices are available, such as the (significantly more expensive) Personal Digital Assistant (PDA) type devices out there. Some of the cutting edge ones support resolutions up to 640x480 pixels, so perhaps there is hope for viewing complex HTML pages. Most standard PDAs with smaller screens are also capable of viewing HTML, although the experience can be quite different from using a traditional Web browser.

There are also concerns when you consider the 'wireless' aspect of mobile Internet access. Put plainly, you can never expect the sort of bandwidth that is possible in hardwired systems. Not only that, but the signal quality is likely to be variable – you might temporarily lose communications; while driving through a tunnel, for example.

Most current (second generation, or 2G) systems allow a data transfer rate of around 9.6Kbps (9600 bits per second), which is comparable to the modems of yesteryear, and about six times slower than you might expect on a standard modem line (and orders of magnitude slower than more professional systems). Although many mobile networks are now implementing systems allowing for faster access in the future, speeds are for the most part slower than you can achieve on a PC. GPRS (a so-called 2.5G technology), for example, is capable of speeds up to 115Kbps by using several channels simultaneously, although in practice you are more likely to achieve data transfer rates of 14.4-56Kbps, comparable to modem speeds. Third generation (3G) services are starting to become available, which while expensive, boast bandwidths of up to 2Mbps (2000Kbps), but at the time of writing are not universally available, and are having commercial teething troubles. When this is taken into account you can hardly expect streaming multimedia Web sites on mobile devices just yet, unless there is some interesting paint drying nearby that you can watch while things download.

These were the bad points. After reading them you may well be asking yourself how mobile Internet access will ever got off the ground. However, there are many things that are possible with mobile devices that aren't with PCs. It is only when you consider these possibilities that the true power becomes clear. The key point to remember is that mobile Internet access is *mobile*. It is available anywhere and anytime, without having to lug much hardware around with you. In addition, the fact that you carry it with you means that you are likely to be interested in information that pertains to your current situation and position (such as "Where's the closest Indian restaurant?"). In theory this kind of 'location-dependent' information should be accessible without actually entering information about where you are. After all, the network operator knows more or less where you are from the network cell you are in. Unfortunately, this kind of application has been slow to get going. It seems that network operators aren't too keen on handing out this information, although developments are occurring regularly, and I wouldn't be surprised if this capability was far more prevalent by the time you read this.

Even though mobile Internet access is a good idea, in the face of all the problems mentioned earlier, how do you make it work? Luckily, this isn't something you have to work out for yourselves. A lot of serious thought has been expended to come up with standards to get things moving. One solution that has taken off in Japan and is starting to spread into the rest of the world is i-Mode. This technology uses a cut-down version of HTML known as i-Mode cHTML (similar but not identical to the W3C cHTML standard). The standard that has the greatest prominence in Europe and the United States is the Wireless Application Protocol (WAP).

WAP

If you've had any experience using mobile devices to connect to Internet services, you've more than likely used a WAP-enabled device. Not only that, but I'd say it was very likely that you've heard the term 'WAP' on TV, seen it in magazines, and heard how much people seem to hate it. However, if you analyze the problems that people have with WAP, such as "It's too slow", "There's no color", "All the WAP sites look rubbish", and so on, you may notice that these can in all cases be explained by the limitations looked at in the last section – and we weren't even considering WAP there.

Even so, it seems perfectly reasonable to wonder why you should bother with WAP at all.

In actual fact, WAP does quite a good job of dealing with these limitations, but the end result is still not enough to satisfy the e-generation. However, WAP is ready for the next generation of mobile communication networks – without major changes – and is likely to start to become more accepted as bandwidth increases. Of course, many people ask whether WAP will be here at all, or whether it will be replaced with something else. In order to address this point you need to take a step back and look at exactly what WAP is, and how it works.

The objective of WAP is, logically enough, to get information from the Internet to a mobile client. This isn't exactly simple, not least due to the fact that there is no physical connection between the Internet and the wireless network. In addition, building up any communication protocol is a lengthy process (I, for one, wouldn't fancy sitting down and reading through the specifications drawn up for Internet communications, even if I did have a spare month or two). Deciding what form data should take, what security measures should be taken, how data should be compressed and transmitted, etc. is by no means simple.

This is one thing that you can relax about though; the architects of WAP (the WAP forum) have analyzed the issues involved, and the results work fine. To summarize, the gap between the Internet and the wireless network is filled by what is known as a WAP gateway, which acts primarily as a protocol converter. Resources on the Internet are accessed by this gateway in much the same way as Internet clients do – using HTTP. The gateway does this when it receives a request from a WAP enabled device, which is transmitted using WAP protocols. Once it has fetched the resource required, the gateway may perform additional processing (such as compressing files to optimize transmission) if necessary, and then will transmit the result back to the mobile client, again using WAP protocols. This is illustrated in Figure 21-2:

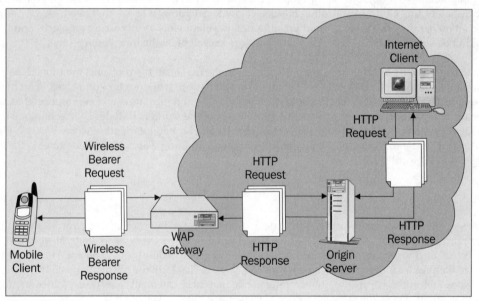

Figure 21-2

This leads to a few questions, such as "What form do WAP resources take on the Internet?" and "How is security propagated between the mobile client and the origin server?" Again, these questions have been thought of already, which is part of the reason why the WAP specification (freely available from www.wapforum.org) is so large and consists of so many sections. The latest version of this specification released (in July 2001) was WAP 2.0, but for now most browsers use the older version, 1.1, with a few using version 1.2, last updated June 2000. Version 1.1 is the version we'll concentrate on here. Instead of listing all the documents, I'll just point out the categories to which they belong:

- ❑ **General WAP technologies**: A selection of documents setting out the objectives of the WAP specification, and the various enabling technologies.

- ❑ **The WAP protocol stack and WAP gateways**: The means by which information is exchanged with the Internet, optimized to be as efficient as possible in a low bandwidth environment.

- ❑ **WAP language specifications**: Specifics on the way in which applications may be created for WAP-enabled devices.

The WAP push specification – information on server-initiated WAP exchanges (that is, how information may be transmitted to WAP enabled devices without a direct request for it).

Much of this specification is advanced, certainly more advanced than we want to get into here, but it's reassuring to know that it is there.

Consider the WAP language specification section. This is the part of the specification that details how resources should be formatted on servers (as well as how they may be compressed for wireless transmission). From the discussion in the last section, it shouldn't be too much of a surprise that HTML isn't the language used by WAP devices. HTML is a relatively heavyweight language, containing much functionality that just doesn't fit in with the idea of quick mobile Internet access. It makes far more sense to create something new for the bulk of cheap mobile devices, something relatively simple, optimized for the considerations you looked at earlier, and lightweight. Something, in fact, like WML – the Wireless Markup Language. We'll take a look at this in the next section.

Note that more complex devices, such as PDAs, don't suffer from quite such strict limitations when it comes to Internet content. Since they typically have larger screens than WAP enabled mobile phones they are more suited to HTML – or at least very simple HTML to avoid the low bandwidth problem. Other options include cHTML, a variant of which is used in i-Mode as noted earlier, and the XHTML standard used in WAP version 2.0.

In case you are worried that omitting a full discussion of the new XHTML dialect is not 'future proofing' you, rest assured that enough of the key concepts and structure of WML survives. Learning WML will stand you in good stead for later XHTML devices. Also, as explained, using the mobile controls is to some extent language independent, so there's even less to worry about.

After looking at all this, I hope I can convince you that WAP is here to stay. So many technical challenges have been overcome and so much groundwork is in place, that launching a new and completely different means of wireless Internet access would be like reinventing the wheel. Of course, there are places where improvements may be made, but WAP is much more likely to evolve than to die.

WML

The *Wireless Markup Language (WML)* is the WAP forum's solution to the problem of formatting content for display on WAP browsers. It is an XML application and shares some features with HTML, although comparisons between these languages aren't that simple to draw. As mentioned earlier, a Web 'page' (taken here as the atomic unit of a Web site) isn't an obvious choice for a fragment of a WAP site. For a start, many Web pages contain far more information than would be usable on a mobile device, and the concept of separate frames containing extra information is also not easily translatable.

A single WML file is often called a deck, and contains one or more cards. Each card can be thought of as a screen-full of information, complete with text, graphics, hyperlinks, and so on. Depending on the characteristics of the browser, and the device used to display a given card, this 'screen' may fit completely into the device display area, be accessible via scrolling keys, or require other modes of user intervention to navigate through. Navigation between cards may be within a single deck, or between decks, as shown in Figure 21-3:

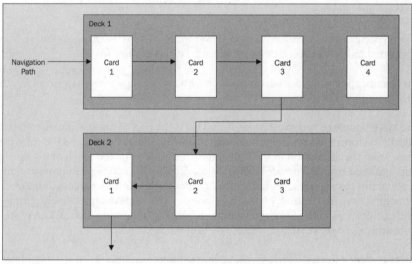

Figure 21-3

Owing to the limitations detailed earlier, a size restriction has been placed on WML decks. A compiled WML deck may be no larger than 1,440 bytes. This is quite a small limit, and means that complete WML applications will rarely fit into a single deck, unless they are very simple. Also, as is apparent from the diagram in the last section, WML files may be stored on any existing Web server, such as IIS, PWS, Apache, etc. All that is required in order to do this is to configure the MIME types for WML and compiled WML files. When doing this it is worth adding the other MIME types that are used by WAP, as shown in the following table:

Description	MIME Type	Associated Extension
Plain WML file	`text/vnd.wap.wml`	`.wml`
Compiled WML file	`application/vnd.wap.wmlc`	`.wmlc`
WMLScript file	`text/vnd.wap.wmlscript`	`.wmls`
Compiled WMLScript file	`application/vnd.wap.wmlscriptc`	`.wmlsc`
Wireless Bitmap Image	`image/vnd.wap.wbmp`	`.wbmp`

WAP browsers may then access WML files using standard URL format.

Here is an example of a WML deck. This file can be found in the downloadable code for this chapter with the filename `example1.wml`:

```
<?xml version="1.0"?>
<!DOCTYPE wml PUBLIC "-//WAPFORUM//DTD WML 1.1//EN"
                     "http://www.wapforum.org/DTD/wml_1.1.xml">

<wml>
    <card id="first" title="First Card">
        <p>
            Welcome!<br/>
            <a href="#second">Continue</a>
        </p>
        <do type="accept" label="Next">
            <go href="#second"/>
        </do>
    </card>
    <card id="second" title="Second Card">
        <p>
            Now into content...
        </p>
        <do type="prev">
            <prev/>
        </do>
    </card>
</wml>
```

Before analyzing this code let's have a quick look at the results on a WAP device simulator. For this example we'll use the Nokia WAP toolkit version 3.0 (the most recent version at the time of writing) simulating a Nokia 5100 phone. This toolkit is freely available at http://forum.nokia.com/ if you register for it, and comes with all the documentation necessary to set up and use the device simulators included (for brevity I won't cover this aspect here). Upon loading the example deck into the simulator, you see the content of the first card, shown in Figure 21-4:

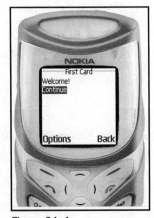

Figure 21-4

Here you have two choices – you can follow the highlighted Continue link by pressing the default selection button on the device (on the simulator this involves clicking the mouse on it) or select Options by pressing the button beneath this text. A labeled button such as Options is called a softkey. If you follow the Continue link you'll reach the next card in the deck, as shown in Figure 21-5:

Figure 21-5

This card has no hyperlink but contains text content and an additional softkey – Back. This softkey will take you one place back in the history stack and return you to the first card. The code starts with the standard XML declaration necessary for any XML file:

```
<?xml version="1.0"?>
```

Next you have the DOCTYPE for the XML file. This resource specifies the WML 1.1 syntax and enables validation:

```
<!DOCTYPE wml PUBLIC "-//WAPFORUM//DTD WML 1.1//EN"
                     "http://www.wapforum.org/DTD/wml_1.1.xml">
```

Note that WML 1.2 is not used here. This is because most current devices (and emulators) don't support it. Using this version isn't a problem, as the code in this chapter is not WML 1.2 specific.

Next you have the root element, <wml>, which contains the WML deck:

```
<wml>
   ...
</wml>
```

The two cards that make up the deck are within this root element:

```
<card id="first" title="First Card">
   ...
</card>
<card id="second" title="Second Card">
   ...
</card>
```

Each of these `card` elements has two attributes (there are many more possible, but these two are fine for a simple example):

❑   `id`: This identifies each card within the deck, and is essential for navigation between cards.

❑   `title`: This provides a string for the browser to use in the presentation of the card. The Nokia 5100 places this text at the top of its display area as shown in the earlier screenshots, but this is not always the case – some browsers will display this in alternative ways; some will ignore it completely.

This kind of behavior is discussed in more detail in the section on device interoperability.

Next, look at each card in turn, starting with the one with the `id` attribute of `first`. This card contains two elements: `<p>`, a paragraph element that contains (among other things) text to display, and `<do>`, which defines a softkey:

```
<p>
    Welcome!<br/>
    <a href="#second">Continue</a>
</p>
<do type="accept" label="Next">
    <go href="#second"/>
</do>
```

The paragraph element contains the simple text `Welcome!`, a line break using the `<br/>` empty element (note that the trailing slash here is used to signify that the element is empty, unlike the similar `<br>` tag in HTML), and a hyperlink. WML hyperlinks use either the `<anchor>` element or the slightly less versatile `<a>` element. Here the `<a>` element is used, as this is enough for simple navigation. Enclosed in the element is the text that we want to display for the link, `Continue`, and the navigation itself is detailed by the element attributes.

The only attribute used here, `href`, contains the destination for the link. This link is meant to provide navigation to the other card in the deck, which has an `id` of `second`, so this is used for the attribute value. Note the use of a # symbol here, which is essentially XML fragment syntax, and points the browser at a specified card within a deck.

You could use a fully qualified URL here, such as http://www.somewhere.com/somedeck.wml#card1. If you point at a separate deck in this way, the card specifying section (#card1) is optional. If omitted, the first card contained in the target deck will be navigated to.

The `<do>` element is a versatile one, and allows several different types of softkey to be created, the type being chosen by the type attribute. Here the type `accept` is used, which means this is a simple *press to activate* type key.

The `label` attribute is used when displaying the softkey. The Nokia 5100 browser requires the user to access the **Options** menu to activate `accept` type softkeys, where they are placed along with built in device options; see Figure 21-6:

Figure 21-6

The Next softkey is shown highlighted in the preceding list.

The functionality of this softkey is determined by the content of the <do> element. In this case the element contains a <go> element that specifies navigation. This code uses the same destination for the softkey as for the #second hyperlink and so there are two ways of navigating to the other card in the deck. If there is more text contained in the <p> element, so that the Continue hyperlink doesn't appear without scrolling down, this softkey provides an alternative and possibly quicker method of getting to the second card.

The second card contains another <p> element, this time containing just some simple text, and another <do> element:

```
<p>
    Now into content...
</p>
<do type="prev">
    <prev/>
</do>
```

This time the <do> element is of type prev and contains a simple empty element, <prev/>. This is a quick way of adding a Back link to a card, and is really worth using! The Nokia 5100 simulator shown here adds Back links by default, but this isn't always the case.

That completes the brief WML example, which although only scratches the surface of what is possible does show you the basics, and gives a general idea of the structures used.

For completeness, just remember that WML is a language similar to JavaScript (it is in fact a subset of ECMAScript) and enables simple client-side calculations. This can save round trips to the server (important in the low-bandwidth WAP world), and is useful for simple user input validation, for example.

However, this knowledge isn't essential to use the techniques found in the rest of this chapter, although it may be useful to get a wider understanding of wireless Internet access.

Device Interoperability

Before moving on to look at the ASP.NET mobile controls, it is worth considering what is probably the main problem with WML. WML was designed to specify content, not layout, meaning that different devices will often display the same WML in different ways. In itself this isn't a real problem, as in most cases the information contained in a file will be preserved. However, in certain situations usability may be severely hampered. In some cases, WML code that works fine on one device may be difficult or even impossible to make sense of when rendered on others.

In addition, many devices have certain quirks that may be exploited to enhance usability, but the syntax for these varies greatly. In particular, devices equipped with the Openwave (the new name for Phone.com) browser may use a proprietary set of WML extensions, requiring a different DTD file (DOCTYPE). If files using these are loaded into other browsers they will likely fail to work at all.

As a simple demonstration, look at an example from the last section on the Openwave Simulator (also available free of charge, from http://developer.phone.com/download/index.html, and comes with full instructions for use). The most recent version at the time of writing is version 6.2.2, and that is the version used for screenshots in this chapter. The first card looks like Figure 21-7:

Figure 21-7

Figure courtesy Openwave Systems Inc.

Here there is a *tick* softkey, which appears because the Continue link is selected, and enables you to follow this link. Note that the softkey defined by the <do> element is not displayed. Figure 21-8 shows how the screen looks when the hyperlink isn't selected:

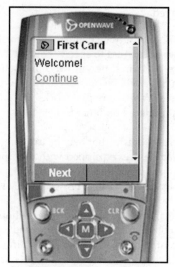

Figure 21-8
Figure courtesy Openwave Systems Inc.

A **Next** softkey appears – which is the one specified by the `<do>` element. `accept` type `<do>` elements on this browser are overridden by, among other things, softkeys created to follow hyperlinks.

The other card in the deck is shown in Figure 21-9:

Figure 21-9
Figure courtesy Openwave Systems Inc.

Note that no **Back** softkey is displayed. Devices equipped with this browser are expected to have a button for going back (an example of which can be seen in the first screenshot in this section, labeled **Bck**), meaning that this functionality is always available.

Before moving on, look at Figure 21-10, which shows the `example1.wml` file displayed on a Pocket PC 2003 device (this simulator is available as a download from MSDN):

Figure 21-10

The first thing to realize here is that the title attribute for the `<card>` element isn't displayed. In fact, the WAP specification says that this attribute is optional and only intended as a suggestion to the browser to be used for display purposes if it chooses. This can cause problems, however, if you've only tested a WAP application on a browser that displays these titles, and are using them as an important source of information for the user. This is an example of a common pitfall to avoid when developing in WML – you must test code on multiple browsers!

Another point to note here is that the **Next** softkey is successfully rendered as a clickable field at the bottom of the display.

> *These browser comparisons are very basic, but they do illustrate some of the differences that often occur between browsers (although not fatal ones in this case). There are many more of these, but an in-depth discussion of the situation is beyond the scope of this chapter.*

There are several solutions to this problem. The simplest, but also the hardest to maintain, is to provide different WML files for different devices. It is possible to detect the browser type by examining the `HTTP_USER_AGENT` header and then redirect the browser accordingly.

Slightly more advanced is the technique of generating WML dynamically, using ASP.NET or any other code generation technology. However, this can be tricky to implement, as many minor things need changing, which can make the code very confusing. This may also result in you creating more work for yourself as different decks may end up with quite different processing.

Another strategy is to make use of the fact that WML is an XML application and transform raw data with XSLT, using different stylesheets for different browsers. This can be used to good effect, although it is tricky to get started and requires a great deal of foresight to structure your stylesheets in an appropriate fashion.

Finally, you can use ASP.NET mobile controls. These may not allow as much versatility as other methods, but certainly seem to work OK and require much less effort on your part. As well as being able to generate WML they also cater for HTML and i-Mode browsers, making them suitable for sites that should work on WAP enabled devices, HTML browsers on PDAs, and i-Mode handsets. In theory this means that knowledge of WML is unnecessary, although I feel that a basic knowledge of the structure of WML pages can help you to design mobile Web forms in a better way. The rest of this chapter is dedicated to examining these controls.

Introduction to Mobile Controls

Mobile controls are the ASP.NET solution to creating Web applications that are usable by multiple platforms. The current release supports HTML 3.2, WML 1.1, and cHTML browsers, and allows third party customization for other types of output (such that the controls could be extended to cover whatever odd Internet access technologies might appear in the future). The motivation behind this is to create a set of controls that will perform equally well on multiple devices and yet be programmable using device independent syntax.

The techniques for using mobile controls are similar to those required for other ASP.NET controls, so much of the code may look familiar to you, particularly that required for event handling etc. However, there are differences in the way pages are structured to contain mobile Web controls, many of which are due to the limitations of mobile devices as discussed earlier. In particular, multiple forms can be contained within a single mobile control Web page, necessary to create a system analogous to multiple WML cards in a single deck.

As is often the case when trying to explain a new programming paradigm, it is easiest to start with an example to show the basic operation of mobile controls in action.

Simple Example

For this example we'll create a mobile controls page similar to the simple example discussed earlier in the chapter. The code, `example1.aspx`, is as follows:

```
<%@ Page Inherits="System.Web.UI.MobileControls.MobilePage" Language="VB" %>
<%@ Register TagPrefix="mobile" Namespace="System.Web.UI.MobileControls"
    Assembly="System.Web.Mobile" %>

<mobile:Form Runat="server" id="first" Title="First Page">
    Welcome!<br/>
    <mobile:Link Runat="server" NavigateURL="#second">
        Continue
    </mobile:Link>
    <mobile:Link Runat="server" NavigateURL="http://www.somewhere.com/">
        Home
    </mobile:Link>
</mobile:Form>

<mobile:Form runat="server" id="second" Title="Second Page">
    Now into content...
</mobile:Form>
```

The first two lines of code are required for any mobile Web form application, setting up the base class for the page:

```
<%@ Page Inherits="System.Web.UI.MobileControls.MobilePage" Language="VB" %>
```

And the mobile controls namespace:

```
<%@ Register TagPrefix="mobile" Namespace="System.Web.UI.MobileControls"
    Assembly="System.Web.Mobile" %>
```

These two lines of code are often called the *prolog* of a mobile Web form.

Note that the `TagPrefix` attribute here specifies mobile as the prefix for mobile controls. Although you can use a different prefix, this is not advised as this may cause compatibility problems with pages made using Visual Studio .NET.

The body of the page consists of two `<mobile:Form>` controls. Each of these can be thought of as a card for display on a WAP device, or a page for display in an HTML browser. The first of these forms contains some plain text and two `<mobile:Link>` controls, to display hyperlinks – complete with `NavigateURL` attributes pointing to the second form and an external link. The second form just contains some text.

Don't worry too much about the exact functionality of these controls for now; all of this will be covered later in the chapter.

Again, take a brief look at the results, first on the Nokia 5100 simulator shown in Figure 21-11:

Figure 21-11

Points to notice for this device (in comparison with the earlier example and in a general sense):

❑   A back link is placed in both cards. The mobile controls automatically place these in every card generated.

❑   Both links are generated as hyperlinks.

❑   Links appear in the same line of text if there is enough space.

Next look at the Openwave Simulator in Figure 21-12:

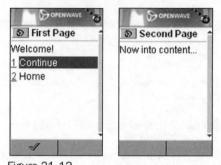

Figure 21-12
Figure courtesy Openwave Systems Inc.

Although it looks slightly different, the functionality is the same. However, the code produced by the controls is quite different, as you will see in the next section. Figure 21-13 shows this page on the Sony Ericsson T610 Simulator (available from http://www.ericsson.com/mobilityworld/):

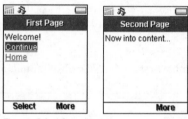

Figure 21-13

Finally, as mobile control pages can also generate HTML, you can look at the results in an HTML browser on a PDA. One way of doing this, and the method I'll use, is to use the Pocket PC 2003 Emulator described earlier. You could also use Microsoft Explorer and simply reduce the window size, but this way is more accurate (Figure 21-14):

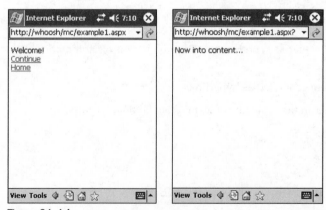

Figure 21-14

The first page shows the specified text along with a hyperlink to the second page, while the second simply produces the expected string.

The HTML results here do look quite bare, but it is possible to customize HTML output such that it could be considered for a professional Web site – using templates and style properties.

Viewing Generated Code

In each browser used in the last section, different code was generated. Most browsers enable you to view the sourcecode for the page being displayed (that is, the code generated by the ASP.NET processor, not the ASP.NET code itself). However, this is not always the case.

It can be useful to see the code generated by an ASP.NET page containing mobile controls, to see exactly what is happening and enabling you to further customize your code as required. The easiest way to do this is to impersonate the device from a separate ASP.NET page, which will call pages containing mobile controls sending the required headers (HTTP_USER_AGENT, HTTP_ACCEPT, and a few others related to device capabilities) to get the tailored response.

Well, to save you the trouble I've created just such a page: impersonate.aspx, which is available in the code download for this chapter. The interface is shown in Figure 21-15:

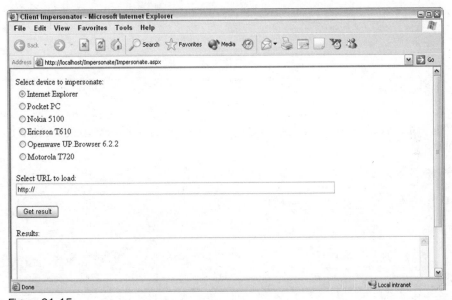

Figure 21-15

If you select a device (I've included a few more browsers here – it's simple enough to add more to the code if you know the HTTP headers for a device), enter a URL (try the example from the last section) and press Get Result you will see the resultant code in the text box as shown in Figure 21-16:

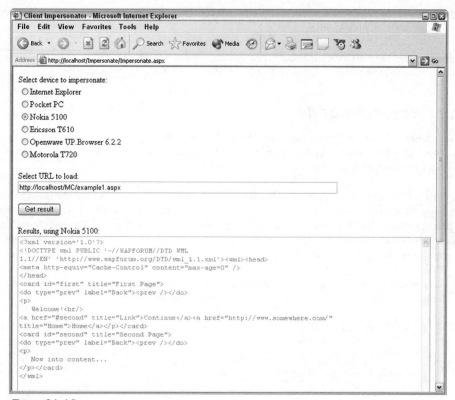

Figure 21-16

Using this tool you can see the code generated for the two devices in the last section. This is the result for the Nokia 5100:

```
<?xml version='1.0'?>
<!DOCTYPE wml PUBLIC '-//WAPFORUM//DTD WML 1.1//EN'
'http://www.wapforum.org/DTD/wml_1.1.xml'>

<wml>
   <head>
      <meta http-equiv="Cache-Control" content="max-age=0" />
   </head>

   <card id="first" title="First Page">
      <do type="prev" label="Back">
         <prev />
      </do>
      <p>
         Welcome!
         <br/>
         <a href="#second" title="Link">Continue</a>
         <a href="http://www.somewhere.com/" title="Home">Home</a>
      </p>
```

```
      </card>

      <card id="second" title="Second Page">
        <do type="prev" label="Back">
          <prev />
        </do>
        <p>
          Now into content...
        </p>
      </card>
    </wml>
```

This is the result for the Openwave Simulator:

```
<?xml version='1.0'?>
<!DOCTYPE wml PUBLIC '-//WAPFORUM//DTD WML 1.1//EN'
'http://www.wapforum.org/DTD/wml_1.1.xml'>

<wml>
  <head>
    <meta http-equiv="Cache-Control" content="max-age=0" />
  </head>

  <card id="first" title="First Page">
    <p>
      Welcome!
      <do type="accept" label="Go">
        <go href="/MC/example1.aspx" method="post">
          <postfield name="__EVENTTARGET" value="first" />
          <postfield name="__EVENTARGUMENT" value="$(first)" />
        </go>
      </do>
      <select name="first">
        <option onpick="#second">Continue</option>
        <option onpick="http://www.somewhere.com/">Home</option>
      </select>
    </p>
  </card>

  <card id="second" title="Second Page">
    <do type="accept">
      <noop />
    </do>
    <p>
      Now into content...
    </p>
  </card>
</wml>
```

As you can see, the two versions are quite different. Don't worry about any WML elements you don't recognize – in most cases you don't need to know exactly what they mean. However, it is worth looking at those that make up the main differences between these pieces of code.

The `<select>` and `<option>` elements are used by WML to build list selection fields. On the Openwave Simulator these are rendered as numbered lists, allowing selection either by hitting a softkey or by pressing the appropriately numbered button on the device – a quick and intuitive solution to lists of up to 10 choices. Unfortunately, list selection fields aren't rendered like this on other devices. It can be tricky to select an item from these on, for example, the Nokia 5100, and no numeric keypad shortcuts are available. This is why hyperlinks are used instead on the Nokia simulator, and the `<a>` element is used as shown in the preceding code.

Also the code for the Openwave Simulator contains code that is common to ASP.NET pages – the postback information. This isn't required for simple links such as the one used for the Nokia 7110 simulator. But, when you use many controls to generate more complex pages it is worth keeping an eye on this added info. Remember that there is quite a small size limit for WML pages – if the compiled version is larger than around one and a half KB you'll start to run into problems. As a final note on this link rendering, be aware that the code generated can vary in certain circumstances – see the notes on the `<mobile:Link>` control in the control reference section of this chapter.

This is the first example we've seen of different WML being generated for different devices – without any intervention on our part. This is good – you can relax in the knowledge that (assuming the mobile controls development team do their job properly and keep up with current devices) the code you write will be effectively tailored for multiple client devices.

Wherever WML code is detailed in this chapter, it has been extracted using this simple tool, which will save you the effort of downloading and installing multiple WAP browsers. Note, however, that some devices are not supported by the version of the mobile controls available at the time of writing. If you generate code using these, you will see the HTML code as generated for IE. It is possible to extend the configuration of the mobile controls yourself to cater for such devices, but this is an advanced topic that I don't want to get into here.

Mobile Control Forms

All mobile controls in ASP.NET pages are held in `<mobile:Form>` forms. As you saw in the last example, each of these corresponds to a single display. The form currently being displayed is held in the `ActiveForm` property of the page, which you can set programmatically to change the display – something you will often do in event handlers for controls.

You can see a quick example of this by making use of one of the events that `<mobile:Form>` forms generate. They create two events, which (unsurprisingly) occur when a given form is activated or deactivated, and are called `OnActivate` and `OnDeactivate` accordingly. You can assign event handlers for these controls using identically named attributes on any given form, and create event handlers in the standard way. So, to view the id for the currently active form you could use the following (not particularly useful, but illustrative) code:

```
<%@ Page Inherits="System.Web.UI.MobileControls.MobilePage" Language="VB" %>
<%@ Register TagPrefix="mobile" Namespace="System.Web.UI.MobileControls"
    Assembly="System.Web.Mobile" %>

<mobile:Form runat="server" id="first" OnActivate="first_OnActivate">
    Now in form:
    <mobile:Label runat="server" id="content"/>
</mobile:Form>
```

```
<script runat="server" language="VB">
    Sub first_OnActivate(sender As Object, e As System.EventArgs)
        content.Text = ActiveForm.ID
    End Sub
</script>
```

Here the Text property for the <mobile:Label> control with the ID attribute of content to the ID property of the currently active form – in this case first. The result for this is shown in Figure 21-17:

Figure 21-17

As this is simple text there is no need to show the result in other browsers (throughout this chapter I'll only show multiple browsers where the results are pertinent).

In addition to the runat, id, title, OnActivate, and OnDeactivate attributes for forms there are a few more you should take a brief look at. Several of these enable you to set styles for form content. These are common to all mobile controls, and any that are set for a form will propagate down into contained controls. You can also set up common style references elsewhere using simple stylesheets, and use the StyleReference attribute of a form or contained control to set up multiple style properties simultaneously, using reusable styles. This is covered in the Styling section later in this chapter.

For now, here is a list of the common style attributes, shared by all the mobile controls:

- ❑   StyleReference
- ❑   Font (broken down into sub-properties as per standard server controls)
- ❑   ForeColor
- ❑   BackColor
- ❑   Alignment
- ❑   Wrapping

As well as sharing the preceding attributes, all mobile controls also share the following three:

- ❑   BreakAfter
- ❑   EnableViewState
- ❑   Visible

`BreakAfter` determines whether a control should have a line break after its own rendering, `EnableViewState` whether the control should store its own state between postbacks, and `Visible` whether it should be rendered at all. All of these attributes may be `True` or `False`, where the default is `True`.

`Form` controls also have some properties concerning pagination. As you can't fit huge amounts of text on a mobile screen, it is often useful to split text over several cards, and perhaps even decks. The pagination properties are as follows:

❑   `Paginate`

❑   `OnPaginate`

We'll look at the use of these later in the chapter, in the section on pagination. However, other pagination-related attributes appearing on other controls will be noted in the following section for later reference.

Finally, there are two properties controlling the postback operation of the form:

❑   `Action`

❑   `Method`

`Action` is used to specify an alternative URL to use for posting information if required, and `Method` selects the HTTP method (`Get` or `Post`) used for postback information.

Control Reference

In this section you will look at each of the controls available in the mobile controls collection (with the exception of `<mobile:StyleSheet>`, which is examined in the Styling section) along with examples of their usage and details of their properties and available events. We'll start with the simpler visual controls and finish up with the validation controls, which are similar to their standard ASP.NET control counterparts.

Note that all controls contain the standard `id` and `runat` attributes (where `runat` must be `server` for all controls) as well as the styling attributes listed in the last section, so these won't be listed with the attributes for each control. Also, attributes pertaining to events will be listed in a separate Events section where appropriate.

<mobile:Label>

This is a simple control, allowing you to output simple text to a browser. You can do this using plain text as we've already seen, but this control lets you make programmatic changes to its text via the `Text` property, in the same way as the `<asp:Label>` control does for non-mobile ASP.NET pages.

On WAP devices this control will result in text being placed inside a `<p>` element in the card created by the `<mobile:Form>` form that contains the `<mobile:Label>` control. For HTML, output text is inserted as a simple literal.

Attributes

Attribute	Description
Text	The text to output to the browser.

Code Generated

On the WAP simulators this generates the following code in a card:

```
<p>
    Text<br/>
</p>
```

For HTML browsers the following code is generated:

```
Text
```

This is contained inside the `<form>` for the page.

Example Usage

As you saw in the earlier example:

```
<mobile:Form runat="server" id="frmFirst">
    <mobile:Label runat="server">Welcome!</mobile:Label>
</mobile:Form>
```

The label text may be set either by the `Text` attribute or by enclosing text inside the element (although the attribute value always takes precedence). The preceding code could be rewritten, with no change to the results, as:

```
<mobile:Form runat="server" id="frmFirst">
    <mobile:Label runat="server" Text="Welcome!"/>
</mobile:Form>
```

As this example generates simple text, the likes of which you have already seen, we won't show screenshots of the resultant displays here.

<mobile:Link>

This control is another one that you have already seen in action, and generates the UI code required to create a simple hyperlink.

Attributes

Attribute	Description
NavigateUrl	The destination URL for the link. If preceded with a # character this refers to the id of a mobile form within the current page.
SoftkeyLabel	The label to display on a softkey when the link is selected, if supported on the target browser.
Text	The text to output to the browser.

Code Generated

This control can generate three types of code, depending on whether the target of the link is another form in the same page, whether further processing is required for a second page, and whether several links are placed next to each other in a single form. In simple cases, the WML generated for a single link control will be as follows:

```
<a href="NavigateURL" title="SoftKeyLabel">Text</a>
```

On some WAP devices, a softkey alternative will also be generated, meaning the link can be followed even if it isn't visible on screen owing to scrolling. In this case the code generated will be:

```
<do type="accept" label="SoftKeyLabel">
   <go href="NavigateURL" />
</do>
```

The HTML generated is generally along the lines of:

```
<a href="NavigateURL">Text</a>
```

OR:

```
<a href="javascript:__doPostBack('ctrl5','frmSecond')">Text</a>
```

depending on the task required and the various forms that postback operations can take (simply adding a SoftkeyLabel attribute will result in the latter code). There will also be a __doPostBack() function defined on the page, together with the usual hidden data for the viewstate, etc.

As demonstrated in the earlier example, the WML created for multiple links can vary a great deal depending on the device, and may be rendered as several <a> elements or a <select> / <option> list.

Example Usage

The following code generates simple, postback, and <select> / <option> links depending on the browser:

```
<mobile:Form runat="server" id="first" Title="First">
   <mobile:Link runat="server"
             NavigateUrl="http://www.somewhere.com/somefile.aspx">
```

```
        External Link
    </mobile:Link>
    <mobile:Link runat="server"
                NavigateUrl="http://www.somewhere.com/somefile.aspx"
                SoftkeyLabel="Ext">
      External Link with label
    </mobile:Link>
    <mobile:Link runat="server" NavigateUrl="#second">
      Internal Link
    </mobile:Link>
    <mobile:Link runat="server" NavigateUrl="#second" SoftkeyLabel="Int">
      Internal Link with label
    </mobile:Link>
</mobile:Form>

<mobile:Form runat="server" id="second" Title="Second">
    2nd Card
</mobile:Form>
```

Try using this along with additional forms, etc. to see the various code generated, using `Impersonate.aspx`.

<mobile:Image>

This control enables you to embed images in your forms. WAP supports a single image format, known as Wireless Bitmap Images, or WBMPs. This format is (once again) optimized for low bandwidth systems, as it can display only two color (one bit) images. Various editors are available on the Web for creating such images, and various plugins are available for existing image editors.

This control requires you to make a choice of image based on the browser being used. Later in the chapter this is covered more detail, but for now look at the simple case of distinguishing between HTML and WML browsers.

The mobile controls require you to add filters to the `web.config` file for your application in order to check against device capabilities stored in `machine.config`. A simple filter for WML1.1 and HTML3.2 devices requires the following code to be added to `web.config`:

```
<?xml version="1.0" encoding="utf-8" ?>
<configuration>
    <system.web>

        ...
```

```
        <deviceFilters>
            <filter name="isHTML32" compare="preferredRenderingType"
                    argument="html32" />
            <filter name="isWML11" compare="preferredRenderingType"
                    argument="wml11" />
        </deviceFilters>
    </system.web>
</configuration>
```

Note that creating mobile Web forms in Visual Studio .NET will result in several device filters being added to your initial `web.config` file by default, including the preceding code.

You can then refer to these filters by placing a `<DeviceSpecific>` element inside the `<mobile:Image>` element, which in turn contains one or more `<Choice>` elements. These `<Choice>` elements allow you to make modifications to the `<mobile:Image>` control, based on specified filters. These modifications take the form of overriding properties of the `<mobile:Image>` control. The following usage selects one of two images depending on whether the browser is WML 1.1:

```
<mobile:Image runat="server" ImageUrl="NonWML1.1URL">
   <DeviceSpecific>
      <Choice ImageUrl="WML1.1URL" Filter="isWML11"/>
   </DeviceSpecific>
</mobile:Image>
```

Attributes

Attribute	Description
AlternateText	Text to display if no image can be displayed in the browser being used (rendered as a label control).
ImageUrl	URL of image to display for the command. The default is `null`.
NavigateUrl	A URL to navigate to if the image is interacted with, if desired (and supported).
SoftkeyLabel	The label to display on a softkey when the image is selected, if supported on the target browser.

Code Generated

The code generated is identical for all browsers, as the WML syntax is identical to the HTML syntax:

```
<img src="Filename" alt="AlternateText"/>
```

The only difference in the generated code will be the filename specified.

Example Usage

The following code displays a picture I took of a friend's lizard, in one of two formats, depending on the browser used:

```
<mobile:Form runat="server" id="first">
   <mobile:Image runat="server" AlternateText="Lizard" ImageUrl="lizard.bmp">
      <DeviceSpecific>
         <Choice ImageUrl="lizard.wbmp" Filter="isWML11"/>
      </DeviceSpecific>
   </mobile:Image>
</mobile:Form>
```

The results are shown in Figure 21-18:

Pocket PC

Nokia 5100

Openwave SDK

Figure courtesy Openwave Systems Inc.

Figure 21-18

<mobile:Command>

This control enables you to place a UI element that the user can interact with in some way, resulting in a call to an event handler (either a simple click event or a custom item event, which will be bubbled up to parent controls). For HTML output this control results in a button; the WML result varies.

Attributes

Attribute	Description
CausesValidation	Whether the control is authenticated; True (the default) or False.
CommandArgument	The argument associated with the command in OnItemCommand.
CommandName	The name that identifies the command in OnItemCommand.
Format	Can be Button or Link. Sets the rendering style for the control.
ImageUrl	URL of image to display for the command. The default is null.
SoftkeyLabel	The label to display on a softkey when the link is selected, if supported on the target browser.
Text	The text to output to the browser.

1083

Events

Event	Description
OnItemCommand	Occurs when the user interacts with the UI element generated and bubbled up to parent controls, if any.
OnClick	Occurs when the user interacts with the UI element generated.

Code Generated

For HTML pages this results in an `<input>` element if format is set to Button, for example:

```
<input name="id" type="submit" value="Text"/>
```

or a simple `<a>` element if format is set to Link.

The WML varies. A softkey may be generated:

```
<do type="accept" label="Text">
   <go href="command.aspx?631151558034057424" method="post">
      <postfield name="__VIEWSTATE"
    value="YjU2NTJiNTktODVlNS00YTVhLThjZWMtYWJjYmRkZmIzOTQ3LDA=f0da65f6" />
      <postfield name="__EVENTTARGET" value="id" />
      <postfield name="id" value="$(id)" />
   </go>
</do>
```

Alternatively, and particularly on the Openwave Simulator, a `<select>` list may be generated with an `<option>` element allowing the command to be called, in much the same way as for `<mobile:Link>`.

Note that the `ImageUrl` property, which determines an image to display on a device if that device supports graphics, works in the same way as the equivalent property of the `<mobile:Image>` control, with device-specific rendering supported in the same way.

Example Usage

The following code contains some text that changes when the **Press** button is pressed:

```
<mobile:Form runat="server" id="first" Title="First">
   <mobile:Label runat="server" id="result">
      Button not pressed.
   </mobile:Label>
   <mobile:Command runat="server" id="button1" Text="Press"
                   SoftkeyLabel="Press" OnClick="button1_OnClick"/>
</mobile:Form>
<script runat="server" Language="VB">
Sub button1_OnClick(sender As Object, e As System.EventArgs)
   result.Text = "Button pressed!"
End Sub
</script>
```

Figure 21-19 shows how the button appears on various devices:

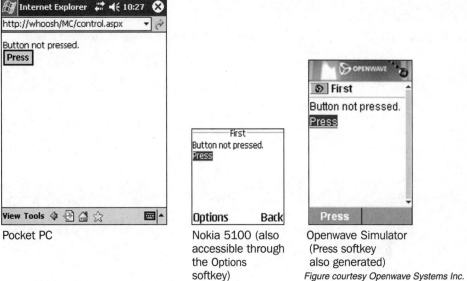

Pocket PC

Nokia 5100 (also accessible through the Options softkey)

Openwave Simulator (Press softkey also generated)

Figure courtesy Openwave Systems Inc.

Figure 21-19

<mobile:TextBox>

This control enables user input. The output in all cases will be a text box, although the functionality of the WML rendition of this varies significantly between browsers.

It is possible to change the type of textbox displayed using the Numeric and Password attributes. If both of these are false you get a plain text box, setting Numeric to true gives a number only textbox, and setting Password to True renders a password mode text box, where asterisks are written to the screen to prevent unwanted reading of passwords.

However, I personally think that the Password type only causes confusion on mobile devices, as it makes the already awkward text input even harder (it's easy to lose your place) and – to be honest – who's likely to read your password over your shoulder on a tiny LCD screen?

Attributes

Attribute	Description
MaxLength	The maximum number of characters allowed in the text box.
Numeric	`True` or `False`. Indicates whether the text box is numeric.
Password	`True` or `False`. Indicates whether the text box acts in password mode.
Size	The size of the control in characters.
Text	The text to output to the browser.

Events

Event	Description
OnTextChanged	Occurs when the user modifies the text in the text box (and a post back is triggered)

Code Generated

For HTML and WML browsers (again, the syntax is identical):

```
<input name="id" [type="password"]/>
```

Example Usage

The following code uses text input for a simple login page:

```
<mobile:Form runat="server" id="first">
   Enter name:
   <mobile:TextBox runat="server" id="name"/>
   Enter password:
   <mobile:TextBox runat="server" id="password" Password="true"/>
   <mobile:Link runat="server" NavigateUrl="#second" Text="Login"
               SoftkeyLabel="Login"/>
</mobile:Form>
<mobile:Form runat="server" id="second" OnActivate="second_OnActivate">
   <mobile:Label runat="server" id="result"/>
</mobile:Form>
<script runat="server" Language="VB">
Sub second_OnActivate(sender As Object, e As System.EventArgs)
   if ((name.Text = "Karli") AND (password.Text = "Cheese")) then
      result.Text = "Welcome Karli!"
   Else
      result.Text = "Sorry, " & name.Text & ", your password is not " _
                  & "recognized."
   End If
End Sub
</script>
```

The first form takes a name and password; the second displays the login result. This result is calculated by `frmSecond_OnActivate()`, which is called when the name and password are submitted (or, more accurately, when `frmSecond` is activated). The simple algorithm used simply checks if the name is `Karli` and the password is `Cheese`, else it displays a failure message.

It is worth noting another fairly major difference between browsers here. Although the code generated for different WAP devices is very similar, the user experience can vary a great deal. Most browsers display the input boxes in a form-like interface, for example the Nokia 5100 shown in Figure 21-20:

Figure 21-20

Here, selecting a field in the Nokia simulator takes you to a separate data entry screen, and when you return the fields are updated.

However, the Openwave Simulator interface allows direct input to the fields displayed. Once the *pencil* softkey is selected, you can use the rest of the keys on the phone to type text directly on screen, much like in a Pocket PC form (Figure 21-21):

Figure 21-21
Figure courtesy Openwave Systems Inc.

When text is entered and the ➡ softkey is selected, the display moves on to the password entry field, and finally to the Login link. The end effect is the same, but the routes there can vary.

<mobile:List>

This control allows for simple non-interactive lists of items in plain text, a list of commands, or a list of links. Whatever you want to do with this control you can specify the items it contains using `<Item>` elements within the control, or programmatically (using the exposed `Items` collection). A very simple list, used for display only, might therefore look like this:

```
<mobile:List runat="server">
   <Item Text="Richard Anderson"/>
   <Item Text="Brian Francis"/>
   <Item Text="Alex Homer"/>
   <Item Text="Dave Sussman"/>
   <Item Text="Karli Watson"/>
</mobile:List>
```

Each of the `<Item>` elements may also have a `Value` property, which specifies a destination when link lists are used. To obtain a link list, simply set the `ItemsAsLinks` property to `true`:

```
<mobile:List runat="server" ItemsAsLinks="true">
   <Item Text="Richard Anderson" Value="http://www.richardanderson.com/"/>
   <Item Text="Brian Francis" Value="http://www.brianfrancis.com/"/>
   <Item Text="Alex Homer" Value="http://www.alexhomer.com/"/>
   <Item Text="Dave Sussman" Value="http://www.davesussman.com/"/>
   <Item Text="Karli Watson" Value="http://www.karliwatson.com/"/>
</mobile:List>
```

Alternatively, you can specify an event handler to execute when an item is selected using `OnItemCommand`, although this won't work properly if `ItemsAsLinks` is `true`. The control also supports standard ASP.NET data binding.

Attributes

Attribute	Description
DataMember	When databinding, this attribute specifies the table of a `DataSet` to use.
DataSource	When databinding, this attribute specifies the data source to use.
DataTextField	When databinding, this attribute specifies the field to use for item text values.
DataValueField	When databinding, this attribute specifies the field to use for item-value values.
Decoration	`None`, `Bulleted`, or `Numbered` – allows for extra formatting of item text by adding bullet marks or numbering items.
ItemCount	The amount of items to display when using pagination, where a value of 0 means to choose this value automatically.
ItemsAsLinks	`True` or `False`. Whether to render items as links.
ItemsPerPage	The number of items to display per page when using pagination, where a value of 0 means to use the default value.

Events

Event	Description
OnItemCommand	Occurs when an individual list item generates a command event. Note that this won't work if ItemsAsLinks is true.
OnItemDataBind	Occurs when an item is databound.
OnLoadItems	Occurs when pagination is being used and the items to display are requested.

Code Generated

Obviously, this control can generate varied code. For simple lists the output will be plain text, with appropriate line breaks, or formatted as a table. Link lists will generate code appropriate to the device, such as `<select>` fields or anchors. For example, the preceding code generates the following HTML on a Pocket PC:

```
<table>
   <tr>
      <td>
         <a href="http://www.richardanderson.com/">Richard Anderson</a>
      </td>
   </tr>
   <tr>
      <td>
         <a href="http://www.brianfrancis.com/">Brian Francis</a>
      </td>
   </tr>
   <tr>
      <td>
         <a href="http://www.alexhomer.com/">Alex Homer</a>
      </td>
   </tr>
   <tr>
      <td>
         <a href="http://www.davesussman.com/">Dave Sussman</a>
      </td>
   </tr>
   <tr>
      <td>
         <a href="http://www.karliwatson.com/">Karli Watson</a>
      </td>
   </tr>
</table>
```

The WML generated on a Nokia 5100 is as follows:

```
<a href="http://www.richardanderson.com/">Richard Anderson</a>
<a href="http://www.brianfrancis.com/">Brian Francis</a>
<a href="http://www.alexhomer.com/">Alex Homer</a>
<a href="http://www.davesussman.com/">Dave Sussman</a>
```

```
<a href="http://www.karliwatson.com/">Karli Watson</a>
```

And the WML generated on Openwave browsers is along the lines of:

```
<do type="accept" label="Go">
   <go href="example.aspx?__ufps=631274647595414160" method="post">
      <postfield name="__VIEWSTATE"
                  value="aDxfX1A7QDw7MmI1YjhiMTgtYWROGExOTg1LDA7Pjs+" />
      <postfield name="__EVENTTARGET" value="ctrl0" />
      <postfield name="__EVENTARGUMENT" value="$(ctrl0)" />
   </go>
</do>
<select name="ctrl0">
  <option onpick="http://www.richardanderson.com/">Richard Anderson</option>
  <option onpick="http://www.brianfrancis.com/">Brian Francis</option>
  <option onpick="http://www.alexhomer.com/">Alex Homer</option>
  <option onpick="http://www.davesussman.com/">Dave Sussman</option>
  <option onpick="http://www.karliwatson.com/">Karli Watson</option>
</select>
```

Each of these pieces of code is entirely appropriate for the target device. If you are generating a list of commands then appropriate post back code will also be generated.

Example Usage

As a quick example of a command list, consider the following modified code:

```
<mobile:Form runat="server" id="first">
   <mobile:List runat="server" id="List1"
            OnItemCommand="List1_OnItemCommand">
      <Item Text="Richard Anderson"
            Value="http://www.richardanderson.com/"/>
      <Item Text="Brian Francis"
            Value="http://www.brianfrancis.com/"/>
      <Item Text="Alex Homer"
            Value="http://www.alexhomer.com/"/>
      <Item Text="Dave Sussman"
            Value="http://www.davesussman.com/"/>
      <Item Text="Karli Watson"
            Value="http://www.karliwatson.com/"/>
   </mobile:List>
</mobile:Form>

<mobile:Form runat="server" id="second">
   Follow this link for <mobile:Label runat="server" id="name"/> homepage:
   <mobile:Link runat="server" id="homepage" Text="Link"
            SoftkeyLabel="Link"/>
</mobile:Form>

<script runat="server" Language="VB">

Sub List1_OnItemCommand(sender As Object, _
                 e As System.Web.UI.MobileControls.ListCommandEventArgs)
```

```
        name.Text = e.ListItem.Text & "'s"
        homepage.NavigateURL = e.ListItem.Value
        ActiveForm = second
    End Sub

    </script>
```

When the user selects an item from the list they are redirected to the second card by the command event handler, which also provides a link to the homepage specified in the item value attributes.

Note that the `ActiveForm` property is set to the `id` of the target form without enclosing the `id` in double quotes.

<mobile:SelectionList>

This control is similar to `<mobile:List>`, but has a few important differences. First, it doesn't support pagination. Second, multiple item selection is permitted, aided by the fact that selecting individual items doesn't necessarily trigger a postback. Third, it maintains a list of what items are selected. Finally, the UI is different.

There are two methods of accessing selected items. For single selection lists you can look at the `Selection` and `SelectedIndex` properties of the control. However, for multiple selection lists you must examine the `Selected` property of each item in the `Items` collection of the control.

Attributes

Attribute	Description
DataMember	When databinding, this attribute specifies the table of a `DataSet` to use.
DataSource	When databinding, this attribute specifies the data source to use.
DataTextField	When databinding, this attribute specifies the field to use for item text values.
DataValueField	When databinding, this attribute specifies the field to use for item value values.
Rows	For HTML and cHTML devices, this attribute gets or sets the number of rows displayed in the selection list.
SelectType	`DropDown` (the default), `ListBox`, `Radio`, `MultiSelectListBox`, or `CheckBox`. Determines the rendering style.
Title	Text used for selection list title in some WML devices.

Events

Event	Description
OnItemDataBind	Occurs when an item is data bound.
OnSelectedIndexChanged	Occurs when a post back is performed and the selected items have changed.

Code Generated

The code generated for this control varies a great deal from HTML output, to cater for the various input methods, although for WML it is always a `<select>` / `<option>` list. As a postback isn't generated by default you also need to add a method of doing this manually, such as a button or link.

Example Usage

The following code generates a multiple selection check box list and displays the items selected when a `<mobile:Command>` control is manipulated:

```
<mobile:Form runat="server" id="first">
   <mobile:SelectionList runat="Server" id="List1" runat="server"
                         SelectType="CheckBox" Title="Authors">
     <Item Text="Richard Anderson" />
     <Item Text="Brian Francis" />
     <Item Text="Alex Homer" />
     <Item Text="Dave Sussman" />
     <Item Text="Karli Watson" />
   </mobile:SelectionList>
   <mobile:Command id="nextForm" runat="server" SoftkeyLabel="Next"
                   Text="Next" onClick="nextForm_click"/>
</mobile:Form>

<mobile:Form runat="server" id="second">
   Selected:
   <mobile:Label id="names" runat="server"/>
</mobile:Form>

<script runat="server" Language="VB">

Sub nextForm_click(sender As Object, e As System.EventArgs)
   Dim selectionCount As New Integer()
   Dim item As MobileListItem
   selectionCount = 0
   names.Text = ""
   For Each item In List1.Items
      If item.Selected Then
         If selectionCount <> 0 Then
            names.Text += ", "
         End If
         names.Text += item.Text
         selectionCount += 1
      End If
```

```
        Next
        If selectionCount = 0 Then
            names.Text = "None"
        End If
        ActiveForm = second
    End Sub

</script>
```

Remember that you can only use the `Selection` and `SelectedIndex` properties of `List1` to get information on single selection lists, hence the `For...Each` loop is used in the previous code to interrogate all items in the list.

On the Pocket PC this is rendered as shown in Figure 21-22:

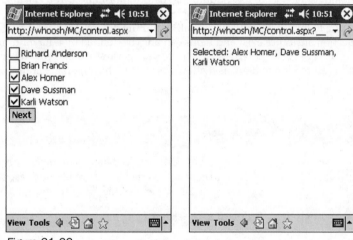

Figure 21-22

The rendering on the Sony Ericsson T610 Simulator is shown in Figure 21-23:

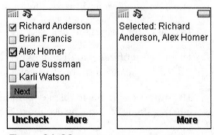

Figure 21-23

The Nokia 5100 interface is slightly trickier to use and involves more steps, but it still works. One advantage, though, is that the `Title` attribute (`Author`) is recognized and displayed, as shown in Figure 21-24:

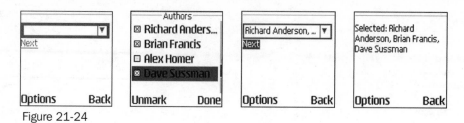

Figure 21-24

<mobile:ObjectList>

This control enables more complex lists to be defined, where each item is the visual representation (this may vary significantly between browsers)of an object.. This object enables a lot more flexibility – even in its default usage it allows the user to view additional object information. You can also define multiple fields to view and commands to execute for items, leading to interesting possibilities, as you will see in the next example. Due to this additional functionality, and the difference in rendering when compared to simple lists, no selection attributes exist and items can only be defined by data binding. However, you still have access to the `Selection` and `SelectedIndex` properties of a list, which becomes important once a command is executed for an item, as it allows us to tell which item generated the command.

Attributes

Attribute	Description
AutoGenerateFields	`True` or `False` – If `True` (the default value), then object properties are automatically converted into extra fields for each `ObjectListItem` object that the list contains.
BackCommandText	Text used for **Back** link.
DataMember	When data binding to a `DataSet`, this attribute specifies the table to use.
DataSource	This attribute specifies the data source to use.
DefaultCommand	The default command to execute for an item.
DetailsCommandText	Text used for **Details** link.
ItemCount	The amount of items to display when using pagination, where a value of 0 means to choose this value automatically.
ItemsPerPage	The number of items to display per page when using pagination, where a value of 0 means use the default value.
LabelField	The field to use for primary display purposes.
MoreText	Text used for **More** link.
TableFields	The fields to display in table view, as a series of identifiers separated by semicolons.

Events

Event	Description
OnItemCommand	Occurs when an individual list item generates a command event.
OnItemDataBind	Occurs when an item is databound.
OnItemSelect	Occurs when an item is selected.
OnLoadItems	Occurs when pagination is being used and user requests more data.
OnShowItemCommands	Occurs when the defined commands for an item are rendered.

Example Usage

To illustrate this object, let's expand the author list from the last section such that information about each author is stored in an object. First of all, you need to define an author class:

```vb
<script runat="server" Language="VB">

Public Class author
    Private authorName, authorInitials, authorFavoritefood As String

    Public Sub New(ByVal name As String, ByVal initials As String, _
                ByVal favoritefood As String)
        authorName = name
        authorInitials = initials
        authorFavoritefood = favoritefood
    End Sub

    Public ReadOnly Property name() As String
        Get
            Return authorName
        End Get
    End Property

    Public ReadOnly Property initials() As String
        Get
            Return authorInitials
        End Get
    End Property

    Public ReadOnly Property favoritefood() As String
        Get
            Return authorFavoritefood
        End Get
    End Property
End Class
```

You can then populate the list control, itemList, with an array of author objects. The easiest place to do this is in the Page_Load() event handler (although you only need to do this once, so you can check to see if there is a postback going on):

```
Public Sub Page_Load(o As Object, e As EventArgs)
   If (IsPostBack = False) Then
      Dim authors As New ArrayList
      authors.Add(new author("Richard Anderson", "RJA", "Pizza"))
      authors.Add(new author("Brian Francis", "BF", "Pasta"))
      authors.Add(new author("Alex Homer", "AH", "Steak "))
      authors.Add(new author("Dave Sussman", "DS", "Whisky"))
      authors.Add(new author("Karli Watson", "KCW", "Fondue"))
      lstItems.DataSource = authors
      lstItems.DataBind()
   End If
End Sub

</script>
```

The code for the form itself is very simple. The only thing you need to add is a LabelField attribute, which specifies which field to use for the primary list display:

```
<mobile:Form runat="server" id="frmFirst">
   <mobile:ObjectList runat="server" id="lstItems" LabelField="name"/>
</mobile:Form>
```

The result of all this is more complex than you might expect. Figure 21-25 shows the output on the Pocket PC:

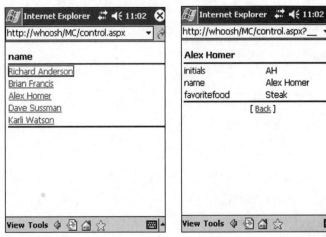

Figure 21-25

Clicking on an author name now has the default effect for this control (we haven't implemented our own handler), which is to show additional information on the author using automatically created fields. Notice that the field names are exactly the same as the class property names. This is because

`AutoGenerateFields` is set to `True` – the default. If you change this to `False`, you can specify how fields are rendered or even if they are rendered at all. This is done by adding `<Field>` elements inside the control. Each of these elements specifies a field to add to the `ObjectListItems` in the control. You specify these by what property they should represent (using the `DataField` attribute), the display name for the field (using the `Title` attribute), and an `id` for accessing the field. You can also use the `Visible` attribute to control whether a given field appears when you follow the automatically generated author name links:

```
<mobile:Form runat="server" id="first">
    <mobile:ObjectList runat="server" id="lstItems"
                     AutoGenerateFields="False" LabelField="fName">
      <Field Name="fName" Title="Author Name"
            DataField="name" Visible="True"/>
      <Field Name="fInitials" Title="Author Initials"
            DataField="initials" Visible="True"/>
      <Field Name="fFood" Title="Author's Favorite Food"
            DataField="favoritefood" Visible="False"/>
    </mobile:ObjectList>
</mobile:Form>
```

These changes result in the output shown in Figure 21-26:

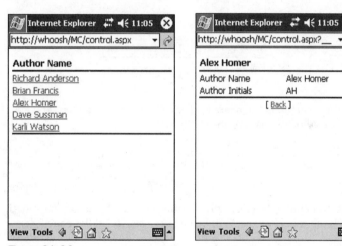

Figure 21-26

As well as adding fields you can also define commands for the items, using `<Command>` elements. Let's add two commands, to query for a biography or a favorite food:

```
<mobile:Form runat="server" id="frmFirst">
    <mobile:ObjectList runat="server" id="lstItems"
                     AutoGenerateFields="False" LabelField="name">
      <Field id="fName" Title="Author Name" DataField="name"
            Visible="True"/>
      <Field id="fInitials" Title="Author Initials" DataField="initials"
            Visible="True"/>
```

```
            <Field id="fFood" Title="Author's Favorite Food"
                DataField="favoritefood" Visible="False"/>
        <Command Name="Bio" Text="Author biography"/>
        <Command Name="Food" Text="Find out the author's favorite food!"/>
    </mobile:ObjectList>
</mobile:Form>
```

These commands appear as shown in Figure 21-27:

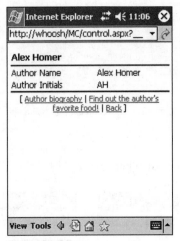

Figure 21-27

In order to hook up the commands (there are two now) use the `OnItemCommand` event. First specify a handler by modifying the opening tag for the control:

```
<mobile:ObjectList runat="server" id="lstItems"
                AutoGenerateFields="False" LabelField="fName"
                OnItemCommand="lstItems_itemCommand">
```

Next you implement the handler. Here, simply use the item data to specify information for two new forms, shown beneath the code that goes in the `<script>` section of the page:

```
Public Sub lstItems_itemCommand(sender As Object, _
                            e As ObjectListCommandEventArgs)
    Dim currentAuthor As author
    If (e.CommandName = "Food") Then
        foodLabel.Text = lstItems.Selection.Item("fName") & _
                    "'s favorite food is " & _
                    lstItems.Selection.Item("fFood") & "!"
        ActiveForm = second
    Else
        bioLabel.Text = lstItems.Selection.Item("fName") & " biography..."
        ActiveForm = third
    End If
End Sub
```

```
<mobile:Form runat="server" id="second">
   <mobile:Label runat="server" id="foodLabel"/>
</mobile:Form>

<mobile:Form runat="server" id="third">
   <mobile:Label runat="server" id="bioLabel"/>
</mobile:Form>
```

Clicking on an author name then yields the first screenshot in Figure 21-28, and on a 'favorite food' link the second:

Figure 21-28

This is all very well, but how does it appear on a WAP device? Well, on the Nokia 5100 Simulator you see the following card first (Figure 21-29):

Figure 21-29

When you select an author you get to see the available commands (Figure 21-30):

Figure 21-30

and these links take you to the relevant command generated forms as shown in Figure 21-31:

Figure 21-31

This is a very powerful control, as you can do far more with the commands than just display information. You could trigger whole chains of business logic in this manner. Again, I'll leave it to you to play with that!

<mobile:PhoneCall>

This control allows the user to call a phone number. Obviously, this isn't appropriate for all devices, so provision is made for those without this capability.

Attributes

Attribute	Description
AlternateFormat	Text to output to devices incapable of making a phone call. This text should include the two placeholders {0} and {1}, which will be replaced with Text and PhoneNumber respectively. The default is "{0} {1}".
AlternateUrl	Target URL for non-calling devices. If specified, the text in AlternateFormat will be rendered as a hyperlink pointing at this URL.
PhoneNumber	Phone number to dial.
Text	Descriptive text to output to the browser.

Code Generated

If the device cannot dial a number then the AlternateFormat text will be output. If the AlternateURL attribute is specified, then the text will be rendered as a hyperlink pointing at the specified URL.

Devices that can dial numbers fall into two categories: some devices, including those using the Openwave Browser, such as the Openwave Simulator, make use of Wireless Telephony Application Interface (WTAI) type commands, in which case the following WML code will do the job:

```
<a href="wtai://wp/mc;PhoneNumber" title="Text">Text</a>
```

Other devices enable the user to use a number that appears in text, in which case the number will simply be rendered to the screen:

```
<p>Text PhoneNumber</p>
```

Example Usage

You could use this control in code such as:

```
<mobile:Form runat="server" id="first">
    <mobile:PhoneCall runat="server" Text="Call Karli's mum"
                   PhoneNumber="555-1234" AlternateFormat="{0} on: {1}"/>
</mobile:Form>
```

The Pocket PC simply renders text as shown in Figure 21-32, as it cannot dial phone numbers (it renders links if you specify `AlternateURL`):

Figure 21-32

The Openwave Simulator renders a link that will dial the number, as shown in Figure 21-33:

Figure 21-33

Image courtesy Openwave Systems Inc.

And the Nokia 5100 renders the phone number such that it can be selected with the **Use Number** menu option shown in Figure 21-34:

Figure 21-34

<mobile:Calendar>

This control is basically the same as the web control with the same name, but is capable of enabling date selection from WAP devices. The UI required to do this is quite different from the HTML version, due to the impossibility of fitting a similar calendar onto a WAP device screen and keeping functionality intact.

The WML version of this control allows you to select dates in two different ways. You can either type one in manually, following the suggested format of MM/DD/YYYY, or choose one by selecting a month, a week, and a day (although not a year for some reason.)

All of the attributes associated with the standard ASP.NET `Calendar` control are also available, although not declaratively. You can gain access to these using the `WebCalendar` property of this control, which returns a Web forms calendar control that you can manipulate.

Attributes

Attribute	Description
CalendarEntryText	Text for link into date selection where multiple steps are required (such as in WML browsers).
FirstDayOfWeek	The first day of the week (such as `Sunday`). The default value (default) uses the locale settings to determine this attribute.
SelectedDate	The currently selected date, which defaults to `TodaysDate`.
SelectionMode	`day`, `dayweek`, `dayweekmonth`, `none` – what selections are possible from the calendar. The default is `day`.
ShowDayHeader	`true` or `false`. Whether to show day names or just date numbers.
VisibleDate	The month to display – set by choosing any date in a given month.

Events

Event	Description
OnSelectionChanged	Occurs when a selection is made.

Code Generated

Once again, the code generated by this control is complex, and voluminous. Knowing exactly what this code is doesn't really tell you anything useful, and it would waste a lot of space!

Example Usage

As an example, let's create a page that asks the user what their birthday is. To start off with, I'll initialize the calendar to my birthday (once you know what it is you can all send me presents), and then prompt for a selection. When the OnSelectionChanged event is raised the user will be asked to confirm the date, which will either complete the procedure or take the user back to the calendar selection. The code is as follows:

```
<script runat="server">

Public Sub Page_Load(o As Object, e As EventArgs)
   If (IsPostBack = False) Then
      birthdayCal.SelectedDate = New DateTime(2004, 9, 17)
      birthdayCal.VisibleDate = birthdayCal.SelectedDate
   End If
End Sub

Public Sub birthdayCal_selectionChanged(sender As Object, _
                                    e As System.EventArgs)
   confirmLabel.Text = "Your birthday is " & _
                   birthdayCal.SelectedDate.Month.ToString() & "/" & _
                   birthdayCal.SelectedDate.Day.ToString() & "?"
   ActiveForm = confirm
End Sub

</script>

<mobile:Form runat="server" id="calendar">
   When is your birthday?
   <mobile:Calendar runat="server" id="birthdayCal"
                   OnSelectionChanged="birthdayCal_selectionChanged"/>
</mobile:Form>

<mobile:Form runat="server" id="confirm">
   <mobile:Label runat="server" id="confirmLabel"/>
   <mobile:Link runat="server" NavigateURL="#done" Text="Yes"/>
   <mobile:Link runat="server" NavigateURL="#calendar" Text="No"/>
</mobile:Form>

<mobile:Form runat="server" id="done">
   Done.
</mobile:Form>
```

Using the Pocket PC you see the calendar display shown in Figure 21-35:

Figure 21-35

From here you can select a date easily by following any of the day links.

The starting screen in the Nokia 5100 Simulator is shown in Figure 21-36:

Figure 21-36

When you follow this link you get three more options as shown in Figure 21-37:

Figure 21-37

The first link, which shows the currently selected date, allows you to confirm a date choice. The other two allow the user to enter a date, either by manually typing it in as shown in Figure 21-38 (with an error message appearing if you enter an invalid date):

Figure 21-38

or via a series of selection screens as shown in Figure 21-39:

Figure 21-39

Whichever method is used, the same confirmation message appears, where you can choose to keep or discard the selected date.

This control also supports advanced styling using style objects if you extract the Web form control from `WebCalendar`.

<mobile:TextView>

This control is designed for displaying large volumes of text set at runtime. The only time this control is useful is when you have text containing formatting elements such as <i> and <b>, which aren't allowed in `Label` controls.

<mobile:AdRotator>

This control is practically identical to the ASP control of the same name, including the way it gets data from an XML file. The only difference is that it can render WML – it just outputs the `AlternateText` text for the advert chosen. Since this is the case I will not reiterate its functionality here.

<mobile:Panel>

This control can be used as a container for other controls, including other panels. The main reason for using panels is that they can be useful for grouping controls together. When you do this and use pagination then panel contents will be displayed on single pages if at all possible.

Validation Controls

The Mobile Web SDK contains the following validation controls:

- ❏ `<mobile:RequiredFieldValidator>`

- ❏ `<mobile:RangeValidator>`

- ❏ `<mobile:CompareValidator>`

- ❏ `<mobile:RegularExpressionValidator>`

- ❏ `<mobile:CustomValidator>`

- ❏ `<mobile:ValidationSummary>`

If these look familiar, it's probably because they are once again very similar to their non-mobile counterparts. As such, we're not going to go into a huge amount of detail about these controls, save providing an example of their use and the results they provide.

Example Usage

Let's use a couple of controls in a login form:

```
<mobile:Form runat="server" id="first">
   Enter name:
   <mobile:TextBox runat="server" id="name"/>
   Enter password:
   <mobile:TextBox runat="server" id="password" Password="true"/>
   Confirm password:
   <mobile:TextBox runat="server" id="confirm" Password="true"/>
   <mobile:Command runat="server" id="enter" Onclick="enter_click"
                 Text="Enter"/>
   <mobile:RequiredFieldValidator runat="server" ControlToValidate="name"
                                ErrorMessage="Please enter a name" />
   <mobile:RequiredFieldValidator runat="server"
                                ControlToValidate="password"
                                ErrorMessage="Please enter a password" />
   <mobile:RequiredFieldValidator runat="server" ControlToValidate="confirm"
                              ErrorMessage="Please confirm your password" />
   <mobile:CompareValidator runat="server" ControlToValidate="confirm"
                          ControlToCompare="password"
                          ErrorMessage="Confirmation must match password" />
</mobile:Form>

<mobile:Form runat="server" id="second">
   <mobile:ValidationSummary runat="server" formToValidate="first"
                           HeaderText="Invalid input"/>
</mobile:Form>
<mobile:Form runat="server" id="third">
   <mobile:Label runat="server">Input accepted.</mobile:Label>
</mobile:Form>

<script runat="server">

Public Sub enter_click(sender As Object, e As System.EventArgs)
   If (Page.IsValid) Then
```

```
        ActiveForm = third
    Else
        ActiveForm = second
    End If
End Sub

</script>
```

We prompt for a name, a password, and a password confirmation, then check to see if the input is valid. If it is, then a confirmation message is displayed, otherwise the `<mobile:ValidationSummary>` control is used to output the reasons why the input is invalid. This code also uses the `Page.IsValid` property to see whether a validation summary is required.

Advanced Mobile Control Topics

We've now covered all of the controls and their basic usage. However, there will often be times when you want to display them in better ways, particularly in HTML pages to avoid them looking too bland, or change their default behavior in some way. There are four ways you can achieve this:

❑ **Styling**: All the controls give us a degree of influence over the way they look, from basic color schemes to more involved styling.

❑ **Using device capabilities**: The controls give us access to many of the capabilities specific to a device, so you can tailor content accordingly.

❑ **Templating**: Adding templates to controls allows you to add extra code to output, both HTML and WML.

❑ **Pagination**: Splitting lengthy text over several pages

Styling

As mentioned earlier, all the mobile controls have a set of styling attributes you can use. The basic ones are:

Attribute	Description
Alignment	NotSet, Center, Left, or Right – for text alignment.
BackColor	The background color for the control.

Attribute	Description
ForeColor	The foreground color for the control.
Font	The font to use for text display. This is split into Font-Name, Font-Size (Normal, Small, or Large), Font-Bold (true or false), and Font-Italic (true or false).
Wrapping	Wrap, or NoWrap. Whether to 'wrap' text, where wrapping text means to place it on multiple lines if possible.

Most of these are self explanatory, but bear in mind that WAP browsers will ignore many of these attributes. As an example, let's look at a very simple <mobile:Label> control with added formatting:

```
<mobile:Form runat="server" BackColor="Azure">
    <mobile:Label runat="server" ForeColor="BlueViolet" Alignment="Center"
            Font-Bold="true" Font-Size="large"
            Font-Name="Arial">This is some formatted text.</mobile:Label>
</mobile:Form>
```

Figures 21-40 shows the results on various browsers:

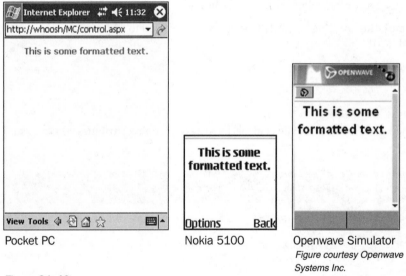

Pocket PC   Nokia 5100   Openwave Simulator
Figure courtesy Openwave Systems Inc.

Figure 21-40

The BackColor attribute from the form propagates through to the label. Notice, also, that neither the Nokia 5100 nor the Openwave simulator apply color formatting. This is because they are using the WML version of the output, not the HTML version. Even though the devices support color, it isn't used by the mobile controls in this case.

In addition to the attributes shown in the preceding code, there is one more: `StyleReference`. This attribute enables you to refer to a separate style, defined in a `<mobile:StyleSheet>` control by a `<Style>` element. `<mobile:StyleSheet>` controls result in no rendering at all, and are not contained in `<mobile:Form>` controls, but they allow you to specify named collections of style attributes that you can apply to multiple controls in your page. For example, you could rewrite the preceding code as:

```
<mobile:StyleSheet runat="server">
    <Style Name="textStyle" ForeColor="BlueViolet" Alignment="Center"
            Font-Bold="true" Font-Size="large" Font-Name="Arial"
            BackColor="Azure"/>
</mobile:StyleSheet>

<mobile:Form runat="server" StyleReference="textStyle">
    This is some formatted text.
</mobile:Form>
```

You can define as many styles as you want in this way and use them in as many controls as you like.

Using Device Capabilities

In the earlier discussion of `<mobile:Image>`, we capitalized on the fact that a filter can detect whether a browser supports HTML or WML. The use of `<DeviceSpecific>` and `<Choice>` elements along with information added to `web.config` allowed us to customize the output of mobile controls. In actual fact we've only scratched the surface of what is possible here so far.

If you look in your `machine.config` you'll see that a large volume of text there applies to mobile controls. Much of this is concerned with determining the capabilities of connecting devices by interrogating the HTTP headers received.

There is no worldwide standard implemented for this. Some browsers such as the Openwave send additional device capability headers to servers. Others, like the Motorola T720, don't. Because of this, many capabilities have been found out manually, and are hard coded in `machine.config`. The reasoning goes that if you have enough information to identify a device then you can specify its capabilities.

> *One emerging standard (not yet supported by ASP.NET mobile controls) is to pass a `HTTP_X_WAP_PROFILE` header specifying a remote XML document specifying device capabilities. The Ericsson T610, for example, directs browsers to http://wap.sonyericsson.com/UAProf/T610R101.xml. This document is a Composite Capabilities/Preferences Profile (CC/PP), which is in turn an application of the Resource Description Framework (RDF). This approach shows a lot of promise, and if you would like to learn more about it see http://www.ccpp.info.*

The list of capabilities that is set in `machine.config` is quite a long one, and I won't reproduce it here. It includes entries as simple as whether a device has a color screen (`isColor`), entries on specific WML rendering characteristics (such as `rendersBreaksAfterWmlAnchor`), screen dimensions (including `defaultScreenPixelsWidth`), and so on. There are sections for many current devices, for example Nokia, which starts by assigning some general Nokia browser characteristics:

```
<!-- Nokia -->
<case match="Nokia.*">
    browser = "Nokia"
```

```
mobileDeviceManufacturer = "Nokia"
preferredRenderingType = "wml11"
preferredRenderingMime = "text/vnd.wap.wml"
preferredImageMime = "image/vnd.wap.wbmp"
defaultScreenCharactersWidth = "20"
defaultScreenCharactersHeight = "4"
defaultScreenPixelsWidth="90"
defaultScreenPixelsHeight="40"
screenBitDepth = "1"
isColor = "false"
inputType = "telephoneKeypad"
numberOfSoftkeys = "2"
hasBackButton = "false"
rendersWmlDoAcceptsInline = "false"
rendersBreaksAfterWmlInput = "true"
requiresUniqueFilePathSuffix = "true"
maximumRenderedPageSize = "1397"
canInitiateVoiceCall = "true"
requiresPhoneNumbersAsPlainText = "true"
rendersBreaksAfterWmlAnchor = "true"
canRenderOneventAndPrevElementsTogether = "false"
canRenderPostBackCards = "false"
canSendMail = "false"
isMobileDevice="true"
```

and has additional sections for individual devices, such as the 7110:

```
<case
      match="Nokia7110/1.0 \((?'versionString'.*)\)">
      type = "Nokia 7110"
      version = ${versionString}
      <filter
            with="${versionString}"
   match="(?'browserMajorVersion'\w*)(?'browserMinorVersion'\.\w*).*">
            majorVersion = ${browserMajorVersion}
            minorVersion = ${browserMinorVersion}
      </filter>
      mobileDeviceModel = "7110"
      optimumPageWeight = "800"
      screenCharactersWidth="22"
      screenCharactersHeight="4"
      screenPixelsWidth="96"
      screenPixelsHeight="44"
</case>
```

Here the match attributes are compared with the HTTP_USER_AGENT header to identify the device, and set the capabilities accordingly.

The important thing to realize here, is that this is an extensible system. There are plenty of devices already in this file, but you can add your own, perhaps including the capabilities of the browser built into your fridge or whatever. You could even add devices that support some odd proprietary format should you wish to.

The ASP.NET mobile controls team at Microsoft also release periodical updates to these device definitions via http://msdn.microsoft.com/vstudio/device/mobilecontrols/aspmobiledrivers.aspx. However, even the latest of these at the time of writing (Device Update 3.0) doesn't include most of the browsers examined in this chapter. This explains one or two of the quirks you have seen, such as the lack of support for color displays. XHTML rendering is one of the features added by this update, shown in Figure 21-41:

Figure 21-41
Figure courtesy Openwave Systems Inc.

Once device capabilities have been set, you have access to them from your code in two ways. The simplest is through the `System.Mobile.MobileCapabilities` class.

This class has a number of properties that relate to device characteristics, such as the number of characters that can fit in a screen row, whether color is supported, and what markup language is preferred. `<Choice>` elements can access these properties via their `capability` attribute, which is how the preferred markup type was chosen earlier. We were actually testing for the value of the `preferredRenderingType` property of the `MobileCapabilities` object containing information about the current browser.

You can also access these capabilities programmatically. The following code outputs the value of `preferredRenderingType` to the screen:

```
<mobile:Form runat="server" id="first" OnActivate="first_activate">
   <mobile:Label runat="server" id="devCaps"/>
</mobile:Form>

<script runat="server">

Public Sub first_activate(o As Object, e As EventArgs)
   devCaps.Text = "preferredRenderingType = " & _
                Device.PreferredRenderingType
End Sub

</script>
```

This results in the output shown in Figure 21-42:

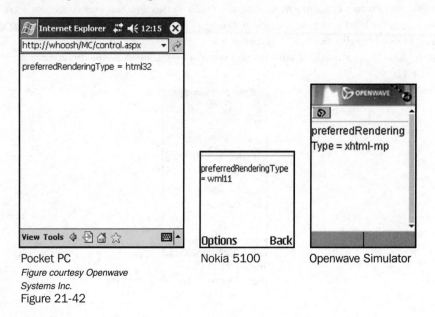

Pocket PC   Nokia 5100   Openwave Simulator

Figure courtesy Openwave
Systems Inc.
Figure 21-42

Using this method you can make dynamic choices in your code based on device capabilities.

The other method is the one you briefly saw earlier, involving setting up filters and using them declaratively in your code. Setting filters involves adding `<filter>` elements to the `<deviceFilters>` section, of the `<system.web>` section, of the `web.config` file for your application.

The format of these `<filter>` elements is simple:

```
<filter name="filterName" compare="devCap" argument="compareString" />
```

Specify a name for the `filter` with `filterName`, a device capability (as specified in `machine.config`) with `devCap`, and a string to compare with the string content of the capability. The filters set up earlier are now pretty self-explanatory:

```
<deviceFilters>
    <filter name="isHTML32" compare="preferredRenderingType"
            argument="html32" />
    <filter name="isWML11" compare="preferredRenderingType"
            argument="wml11" />
</deviceFilters>
```

Once you have configured your filters you can use them in any mobile control with `<DeviceSpecific>` and `<Choice>` elements. The simplest use of these is to override or provide extra attributes, as with the earlier example:

```
<mobile:Image runat="server" AlternateText="Lizard" ImageURL="lizard.bmp">
   <DeviceSpecific>
      <Choice ImageURL="lizard.wbmp" Filter="isWML11"/>
   </DeviceSpecific>
</mobile:Image>
```

Here, the only attribute of `<Choice>` that is specific to the `<Choice>` element is `Filter`, all others are applied to the parent control. This means that the `ImageUrl` attribute is overridden here.

`<Choice>` elements can also be used to contain templates, which are the subject of the next section.

Templates

Much like the standard ASP.NET controls, it is possible to extend the way mobile controls are displayed using templates. Unlike ASP.NET controls, you can do this on a device-by-device basis using the `<DeviceSpecific>` and `<Choice>` elements discussed in the last section.

A given template will specify markup to use for display purposes, which, for example, might be as simple as specifying a section of HTML that is always output prior to the standard HTML output of a mobile control in a Web browser, or might be more complex.

There are five mobile controls that allow templating: `<mobile:Form>`, `<mobile:Panel>`, `<mobile:Image>`, `<mobile:List>`, and `<mobile:ObjectList>`. There are eight available templates:

- ❑ `ContentTemplate`: Markup for replacing entire control output

- ❑ `HeaderTemplate`: Markup to place before the control

- ❑ `FooterTemplate`: Markup to place after the control

- ❑ `LabelTemplate`: Markup to use for rendering the label of an item in an `ObjectList`

- ❑ `ItemTemplate`: Markup to use for each item contained in the control

- ❑ `AlternatingItemTemplate`: Markup to use for every other item contained in the control

- ❑ `ItemDetailsTemplate`: Markup to use for rendering the details for an item in an `ObjectList`

- ❑ `SeparatorTemplate`: Markup to place between each item contained in the control

These apply to the templatable controls as shown in the following table.

	Template							
Control	ContentTemplate	HeaderTemplate	FooterTemplate	LabelTemplate	ItemTemplate	AlternatingItemTemplate	ItemDetailsTemplate	SeparatorTemplate
`<mobile:Form>`	Y	Y	Y	N	N	N	N	N
`<mobile:Panel>`	Y	N	N	N	N	N	N	N
`<mobile:Image>`	Y	N	N	N	N	N	N	N
`<mobile:List>`	N	Y	Y	N	Y	Y	N	Y
`<mobile:ObjectList>`	N	Y	Y	Y	Y	Y	Y	Y

Templates are specified within elements having the same name as the template in question, and contain markup to use.

The clever part here is that these elements are contained within `<Choice>` elements, allowing you to provide different templates for different devices (in much the same way as different images were used in the `<mobile:Image>` control), for example:

```
<mobile:Form runat="server" id="first" title="Back to Front">

    <DeviceSpecific>
        <Choice Filter="isHTML32">
            <HeaderTemplate>
                <table width="100%" cellpadding="4" cellspacing="2"
                        bgcolor="black">

                    <tr>
                        <td align="center" colspan="2" bgcolor="blanchedalmond">
                            <font face="Arial Black" size="5" color="black">
                        Back to Front
```

```
                    </font>
                </td>
            <tr>
                <td width="25%" bgcolor="Gold" valign="top">
                    <font face="Verdana, sans-serif" size="2"><b>
                        <a href="/index.aspx">Home</a><br>
                        <a href="/links.aspx">Links</a><br>
                        <a href="/about.aspx">About</a><br>
                        <a href="/discuss.aspx">Discuss</a><br>
                        <a href="/contact.aspx">Contact</a>
                    </b></font>
                </td>
                <td bgcolor="coral" valign="top">
        </HeaderTemplate>
        <FooterTemplate>
                </td>
            <tr>

            </table>
        </FooterTemplate>
    </Choice>
  </DeviceSpecific>

  The site that talks about what you don't want to hear about in a way that
  makes it too confusing to follow anyway!

</mobile:Form>
```

This code uses the header and footer templates to customize form layout. It requires the following filter in `web.config`:

```
<filter name="isHTML32" compare="preferredRenderingType"
        argument="html32" />
```

On a WML browser the HTML template is ignored as shown in Figure 21-43:

Figure 21-43

However, on an HTML browser such as the Pocket PC you can make better use of the available capabilities, as shown in Figure 21-44:

Figure 21-44

The other templates when used with lists, can also be used to create excellent results, but an example of this isn't given here as their use is identical to formatting lists using the standard ASP.NET controls (although using a structure like the previous example's).

Templates can also be placed in stylesheets such that they can be reused in multiple forms. The template used in the last example is a good candidate for this, as it provides a structure for containing body text that might apply well to several forms.

Pagination

Pagination is specified and controlled from `<mobile:Form>` controls. In most cases the pagination functionality supplied by default is enough for us, so `Paginate` is set to off'. It can be turned on as follows:

```
<mobile:Form runat="server" id="first" Paginate="True">
   ...
</mobile:Form>
```

Any text you specify in the form will then be split across screens where appropriate. For example:

```
<mobile:Form runat="server" id="first" Paginate="true">
Tyger! Tyger! burning bright<br/>
In the forest of the night<br/>
What immortal hand or eye<br/>
Could frame thy fearful symmetry?<br/>
<br/>
In what distant deeps or skies<br/>
Burnt the fire of thine eyes?<br/>
On what wings dare he aspire?<br/>
What the hand dare seize the fire?<br/>
<br/>
And what shoulder, and what art,<br/>
Could twist the sinews of thy heart?<br/>
And when thy heart began to beat,<br/>
What dread hand? and what dread feet?<br/>
<br/>
```

```
What the hammer? what the chain?<br/>
In what furnace was thy brain?<br/>
What the anvil? what dread grasp<br/>
Dare its deadly terrors clasp?<br/>
<br/>
When the stars threw down their spears,<br/>
And watered heaven with their tears,<br/>
Did he smile his work to see?<br/>
Did he who made the lamb make thee?<br/>
<br/>
Tyger! Tyger! burning bright<br/>
In the forests of the night,<br/>
What immortal hand or eye<br/>
Dare frame thy fearful symmetry?<br/>
</mobile:Form>
```

This text is rendered over several pages on the Openwave, Nokia, and Ericsson browsers, with Next and Previous links added automatically., as shown in Figure 21-45:

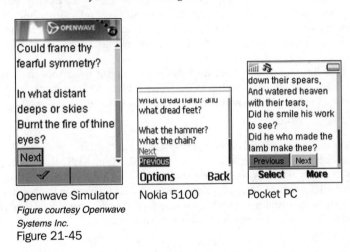

Openwave Simulator
Figure courtesy Openwave Systems Inc.
Figure 21-45

Nokia 5100

Pocket PC

The Pocket PC fits all this on one page as shown in Figure 21-46:

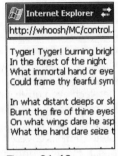

Figure 21-46

This device does support pagination, but can fit more text in one page. In fact, it will fit another two paragraphs on the end of the Blake poem I've used here.

Summary and Future Possibilities

To conclude this chapter I'd like to take a quick peek into the future and attempt to predict the fortunes of the mobile Web and mobile controls.

The Future of the Mobile Internet

One thing is certain – the mobile Web is here to stay. In fact, it may become so pervasive that the future may be entirely wireless. However, this situation is a long way off, so let's just consider the next few years for now.

For a start, more and more people will gain mobile Internet access. More devices will be available at a lower cost and will be more useful. You can expect the available bandwidth to increase rapidly, and enhanced usability will come with this speed and with packet networks. It will soon become essential for most organizations with a Web presence to develop for mobile devices.

However, many of the limitations of mobile devices are impossible to surmount. There will always be a tiny display area when compared to desktop PCs – at least until you can display information directly onto the human retina I suppose! You will also be hampered when it comes to other capabilities important for multimedia applications.

The upshot of this is that you will still need to design classic and mobile Web applications in different ways – even if you don't end up using WML. In fact, WAP 2.0 uses XHTML (although the dialect used looks very similar to and works in a similar way as WML). This may mean that it will be easier for Web designers to make the leap to mobile applications, but still doesn't change the fact that a single Web application is unlikely to be suitable for all browsers unless specific customizations are made; and, of course, one candidate for this could rely on mobile controls.

The Future of the Mobile Controls

The mobile controls provide a viable alternative to low-level mobile application design. Although traditional Web designers may find them tricky to use, their power is obvious. However, there are problems.

For a start, there are currently many devices with many browsers and subtle differences. The best developer team in the world would surely have a tough time keeping up with developments. This means that interoperability issues will continue to abound, particularly so when proprietary device enhancements are taken into account. To maximize usability it is often desirable to make use of these, resulting in significant code differences between even quite similar devices. Can mobile controls account for this? In theory, they can. However, this may mean a fair bit of effort is required on the part of developers to write device specific code. Mind you, the extensibility framework is in place, so all is not lost! Perhaps, in a few years time, the mobile controls covered here will form the basis of a significant amount of multi-browser Web applications. If the development team at Microsoft continues to develop them, then I for one will be very interested in the results.

22

Tracing, Error Handling, Debugging, and Performance

I often wonder whether the panacea of error-free software will ever happen. Humans aren't error free, so while we are writing software, it is likely we will make at least one mistake. Software companies have teams of people testing their products because developers are fallible. Not only do mistakes happen, but also compatibility between components can cause other errors. One of the error handling specifications for ASP.NET says, 'Errors happen. Deal with it', and one developer I know says, 'Errors suck.' Both are true – however bad errors are, they do happen, and you have to find ways to track them down and prevent further errors.

This chapter looks at the features ASP.NET provides as help during the development cycle. In particular you will look at:

❑ **Tracing**: How to track progress through ASP.NET pages and components

❑ **Debugging**: How to find errors, and use the debugger

❑ **Error handling**: How to handle errors gracefully, and prevent further ones

❑ **Profiling**: How to identify areas of slow performance

These topics were all available in ASP, but they were always hampered by the environment or language. The .NET platform has freed developers from some of the constraints and restrictions that ASP imposed, and the languages have improved other areas. Overall, .NET not only presents a far better way of developing applications but also better facilities for making those applications as robust and error free as possible.

Tracing

Tracing is the art of tracking the progress of an application – finding out what's happening and when. It is a safe bet to use tracing – scattering `Response.Write` statements through your code. It may not be elegant, but it works. There are, however, problems with this approach:

❑ **Where to output the tracing information?**
Putting it inline just makes the output hard to read and the trace statements hard to interpret. Ways of getting around this are to build a string of tracing information, and then output that as the last thing on the page, or write the tracing information externally (such as to a text file, database or event log).

❑ **How to enable or disable tracing?**
There are two ways to achieve this in ASP. The first is the laborious method of just commenting out the tracing information. This is time consuming, not very flexible, and error-prone (ever commented out too many lines?). The second approach is to encapsulate the tracing within a procedure in an include file. You can then just comment out the code in one place, or replace the procedure with one that does nothing, but this is also inefficient. Alternatively, you can use a switch (perhaps a registry setting or configuration file) to identify whether tracing is enabled, but, again, this can lead to performance problems.

❑ **How to have tracing, but not have it visible to users?**
When testing applications, you often want to trace the path of execution without your users being aware of the information. Writing output to a text file or database would probably be the best solution here.

You can actually create some quite elegant solutions for tracing, but with ASP.NET, everything is neatly encapsulated for you. What's particularly cool is that you can decide if you want tracing managed on a page-by-page basis, or for the entire application.

Page-Level Tracing

Page-level tracing is achieved by adding a page-level directive. For example, consider the following page (called `SimpleTrace.aspx`):

```
<html>
  <body>
    This is a simple page showing tracing in action.
    <br/>
    At the moment the page does nothing.
    <br/>
  </body>
</html>
```

It doesn't do anything, and you can see there are just a couple of lines of text. To enable tracing for this page, set the `Trace` attribute of the `Page` directive to `True`:

```
<%@ Page Trace="True" %>
```

Adding this to the top of your ASP.NET page will give you the output shown in Figure 22-1:

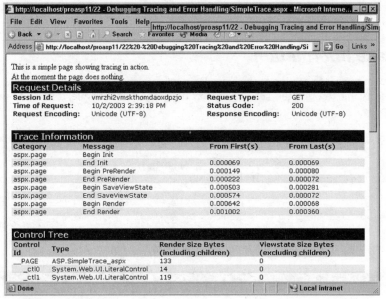

Figure 22-1

This information is all automatically generated and added to the bottom of the page, and consists of the following sections (not all of which are shown in Figure 22-1, purely due to the screen size):

Section	Contains
Request Details	Information about the request, such as the type, HTTP code.
Trace Information	Details of execution order, showing the time taken to execute for each section. When adding your own custom message (you will see how to do that in a short while), they will appear in this section.
Control Tree	Hierarchical list of all controls on the page, including their size.
Session State	Details of each item (if any) held in Session state.
Application State	Details of each item (if any) held in Application state.
Cookies Collection	Details of each cookie.
Headers Collection	The HTTP headers.
Forms Collection	Name and value of each Form variable.
QueryString Collection	Name and value (if applicable) of each QueryString variable.
Server Variables	A complete list of all server variables and their contents.

Not all sections appear for all pages. For example, if your page doesn't contain Form or QueryString information, these sections are not rendered.

Writing Trace Information

To add your own trace information to the Trace Information section you can use the `TraceContext` object, made available through the `Trace` property of a page. For example, if you add the following to your simple page:

```
<script language="VB" runat="server">

Sub Page_Load(Sender As Object, E As EventArgs)
  Trace.Write("Page_Load", "Here we are")
End Sub

</script>
```

Upon refreshing the page, the trace information now looks like Figure 22-2:

Trace Information			
Category	**Message**	**From First(s)**	**From Last(s)**
aspx.page	Begin Init		
aspx.page	End Init	0.000073	0.000073
Page_Load	Here we are	0.001264	0.001191
aspx.page	Begin PreRender	0.001385	0.000121
aspx.page	End PreRender	0.001459	0.000073
aspx.page	Begin SaveViewState	0.001762	0.000303
aspx.page	End SaveViewState	0.001834	0.000072
aspx.page	Begin Render	0.001902	0.000068
aspx.page	End Render	0.002279	0.000377

Figure 22-2

You can see that your line of text has been added. If you now add a button to the page, such as:

```
<form runat="server">

  <asp:Button id="btn" Text="Click Me!" OnCLick="btn_Click" runat="server"/>
  <br/>
  <asp:Label id="foo" runat="server"/>

</form>
```

And have the following as the event:

```
Sub btn_Click(Sender As Object, E As EventArgs)

  Trace.Warn("btn_Click", "Button was pressed")

End Sub
```

Upon postback you will see Figure 22-3:

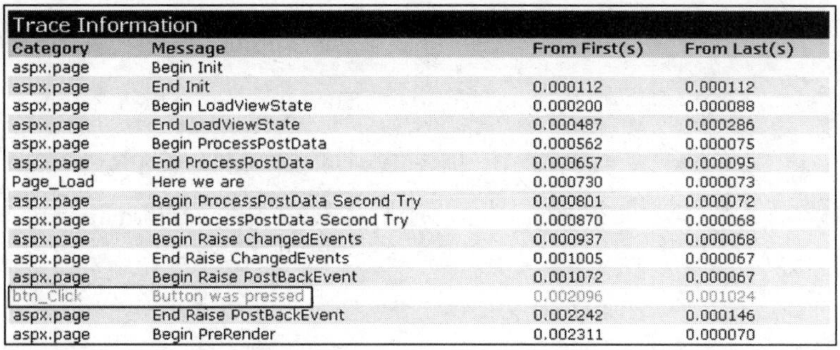

Figure 22-3

The new line has been added in red because you used the `Warn` method (trust me – it really is red!), and you can see the extra events that are called as part of the postback. Using `Warn` method allows you to easily spot lines in the trace information.

The TraceContext Object

Tracing is actually handled by the `TraceContext` object, which has two properties and two methods:

Property/Method	Description
IsEnabled	Indicates whether or not tracing is enabled, and equates to the page-level directive. This is a read/write property, so it can be used to enable or disable tracing from within code.
TraceMode	Indicates the sort order of messages in the Trace Information section, and can be either `SortByCategory` or `SortByTime`. Like `IsEnabled`, this is also available through a page-level directive.
Write	Writes information to the Trace Information section.
Warn	The same as `Write`, except that the text is shown in red.

Both methods for writing to the log can be overloaded:

```
Trace.Write (message)
Trace.Write (category, message)
Trace.Write (category, message, exceptionInfo)
Trace.Warn (message)
Trace.Warn (category, message)
Trace.Warn (category, message, exceptionInfo)
```

The three parameters are as follows:

Parameter	Type	Description
category	String	The category for the message
message	String	The message to display
exceptionInfo	System.Exception	Any exception information, to be displayed after the message

The following code example shows all three parameters in action. The first two with the `Write` method and the third with the `Warn` method:

```
Trace.Write("A simple message")
Trace.Write("Button", "Message here")
Try
   ' some code goes here
Catch E As Exception
   Trace.Warn("Error", "Message here", E)
End Try
```

Turning Off Tracing

One of the problems with the old ASP method of tracing was that you had to remove the trace statements when you were done. With ASP.NET, all you do is turn off tracing either by setting the page directive or using the `IsEnabled` property. You don't have to remove the `Trace` statements themselves, or comment them out, because if tracing isn't enabled, the compiler automatically removes them. So, this is where the great improvement comes – you are free to put as many trace statements into your code as you feel is warranted, without the worry of having to clean them up after testing, and without worrying about performance.

You can even make the tracing *dynamic*, perhaps by use of the query string. For example, consider the following code:

```
Sub Page_Load(Sender As Object, E As EventArgs)
   If Request.QueryString("Trace") = "True" Then
      Trace.IsEnabled = True
   End If
End Sub
```

You could then call a page with http://localhost/TestPage.aspx?Trace=True, which would turn on tracing, but if called normally, no tracing would appear. Alternative solutions such as using the registry or a configuration file to identify whether tracing is enabled are also possible.

Tracing from Components

The same method of tracing is available to components called from an ASP.NET page, allowing them to integrate seamlessly with your pages. To access the `Trace` functionality, you have to import the `System.Web` namespace, reference the current `HttpContext` object, and get its `Trace` property. For example:

```
Imports System
Imports System.Web
Namespace People
  Public Class PersonTrace
    Private ctx As HttpContext
    Public Sub New()
      ctx = HttpContext.Current
      ctx.Trace.Write("PersonTrace", "New")
    End Sub
```

These messages just become part of the existing trace messages, appearing in the order in which they are called. See Figure 22-4:

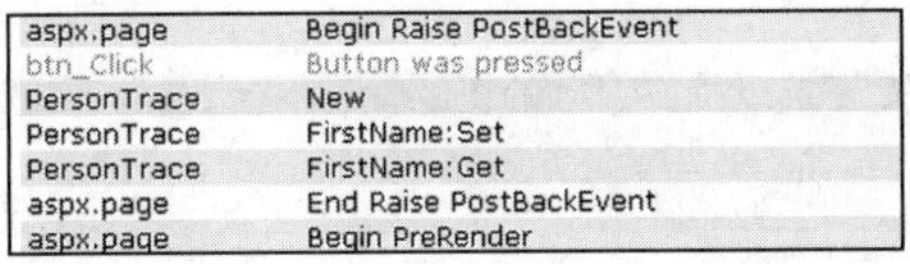

aspx.page	Begin Raise PostBackEvent
btn_Click	Button was pressed
PersonTrace	New
PersonTrace	FirstName:Set
PersonTrace	FirstName:Get
aspx.page	End Raise PostBackEvent
aspx.page	Begin PreRender

Figure 22-4

Tracing output is only displayed if tracing is turned on for the page in which the component is called.

Application-Level Tracing

Application-level tracing expands on the page idea, but allows tracing to be controlled for an entire application. To configure this option, you need to create, or edit, the `web.config` file in the root directory of your application. Application-level tracing works by collecting the trace information for each request, which can be optionally displayed in each page, or just collected for later examination. You can add a `Trace` element as part of the `<system.web>` section. It takes the following attributes:

Attribute	Default	Description
enabled	False	Indicates whether or not application-level tracing is enabled.
requestLimit	10	The number of HTTP requests for which to store tracing information in the trace log. This works on a rolling system, where the last requests are kept.
pageOutput	False	Indicates whether or not the tracing information is displayed at the end of each page. The information is still collected whether or not it is displayed.
traceMode	SortByTime	Indicates the sort order of messages in the Trace Information section, and can be either `SortByCategory` or `SortByTime`.
localOnly	True	Indicates whether the trace information is only shown to local clients, or is available to remote clients as well.

The interesting thing about application-level tracing is that the trace details are collected for each request (up to the number set in the `requestLimit` attribute), irrespective of whether they are shown on the page. This means that tracing can be enabled for a live application without the users seeing anything.

> **Page-level tracing overrides application-level tracing. Therefore, if your page has a `Trace` attribute, application tracing will not work for that page.**

To view the trace information, navigate to `trace.axd` held in the root directory of the application. This file doesn't actually exist, but is instead a special URL that is intercepted by ASP.NET. It will give you a list of requests as seen in Figure 22-5:

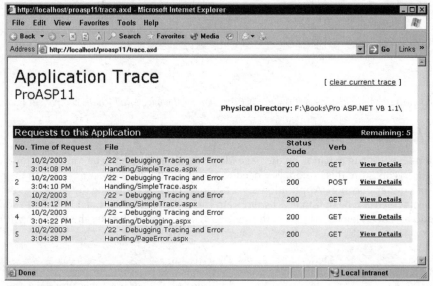

Figure 22-5

Clicking on the View Details link for a request will show the same trace details that would normally be shown at the end of each page.

Error Handling

Error handling has always been a bit of a juggling act – that fine line between what you need to protect your code against and what you don't. While it would be nice to assume that all data handled by your code is correct (it *was* validated wasn't it?) and that all resources will be available, that's not something you can take for granted. As applications become more complex, they rely on other programs, components, external resources, and so on, and you have to assume that at some point something might go wrong. Taking this defensive attitude will lead to more robust applications, as well as making development easier in the future.

In previous versions of ASP you probably relied upon the VBScript `On Error` statement (or `Try...Catch` if you are one of the few who used JScript server-side). While acceptable, it was never a good solution, as it was difficult to build centralized error routines and provide a neat way to manage the errors. The CLR has solved this by providing support for *structured exception handling*.

Structured Exception Handling

Structured exception handling is a fundamental part of the CLR, and provides .NET programmers with a great way of managing errors, and has a good set of features:

❑   It is cross-language; therefore exceptions can be raised in one language and caught in another.

❑   It is cross-process and cross-machine, so even when remote .NET components raise exceptions, they can be caught locally.

❑   It is a hierarchical system, allowing exceptions to be layered, with each exception able to encompass another. This means that components can trap exceptions from underlying objects (such as data access layers), and raise their own exception, including the original as part of it. This allows programs to trap exceptions at a high-level, but drill-down through the exception list to find more fine-grained exception information.

❑   It obviates the need to check for return values from every function or method call – errors that are raised as exceptions will never be missed.

❑   There is no performance downside unless an exception is raised.

All exceptions in the CLR are derived from a single base class, and many of the classes in the framework extend from this to provide finer-grained errors.

The Exception Class

The `Exception` class provides the following properties to detail the problem:

Property	Description
HelpLink	A URN or URL indicating the help file associated with this error.
HResult	For COM interoperability, the Windows 32-bit HRESULT.
InnerException	For nested exceptions, an exception object representing the inner exception.
Message	The textual error message.
Source	The name of the application, or object, that raised the error. This will be the assembly name if left blank by the application throwing the exception.
StackTrace	A string containing the stack trace.
TargetSite	A MethodBase object detailing the method that raised the exception.

There is also one method, GetBaseException (for use with nested exceptions), that returns the original exception that was raised.

Try...Catch

You can manage exceptions by use of the Try...Catch statement. In Visual Basic .NET, the general syntax is:

```
Try
   ' code block to run
[Catch [exception [As type]] [When expression]
   ' code to run if the exception generated matches
   ' the exception and expression defined above
   [Exit Try]
]
Catch [exception [As type]] [When expression]
   ' code to run if the exception generated matches
   ' the exception and expression defined above
   [Exit Try]
[Finally
   ' code that always runs, whether or not an exception
   ' was caught, unless Exit Try is called
]
End Try
```

There can be multiple Catch blocks to allow for fine-grained control over exceptions. For example, imagine a function that returns the contents of a file:

```
Public Function GetFileContents(fileName As String) As String
   Dim fileContents As String = ""
   Try
     Dim sr As New StreamReader(fileName)
     fileContents = sr.ReadToEnd()
     sr.Close()
   Catch exArg As ArgumentException
     ' argument not supplied
   Catch exFNF As FileNotFoundException
     ' file wasn't found - handle error
   Finally
     Return fileContents
   End Try
End Function
```

When using multiple Catch blocks, you should put the finest-grain exception first, and the widest (the base class Exception, for example) last. This is because these blocks are tried in the order of declaration. So, putting the widest exception first could hide a narrower one.

The Finally block will always be run, except when you use Exit Try to exit from the block, whether or not an exception is thrown. Even if used within a procedure, and the procedure is exited from within a Catch block, the Finally block still runs.

Raising Exceptions

To raise exceptions use the `Throw` statement. For example, if you forget the file name to the constructor of the `StreamReader` you normally get the message shown in Figure 22-6:

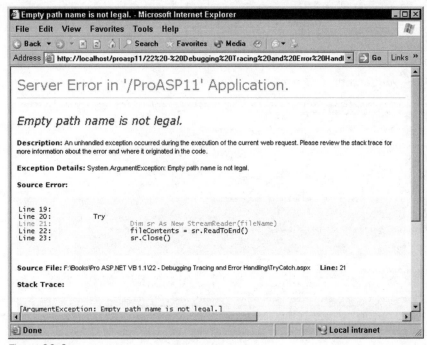

Figure 22-6

In this example, the error is being thrown again – back to the calling procedure. This is why the `Try...Catch` block is visible in the code.

If you wanted to provide your own error message, you could throw a new error containing the new details:

```
Public Function GetFileContents(fileName As String) As String
  Dim fileContents As String = ""
  Try
    Dim sr As New StreamReader(fileName)
    fileContents = sr.ReadToEnd()
    sr.Close()
  Catch exArg As ArgumentException
    Throw New ArgumentException("Doh - you forgot the filename!")
  Finally
    Return fileContents
  End Try
End Function
```

This gives you the results shown in Figure 22-7:

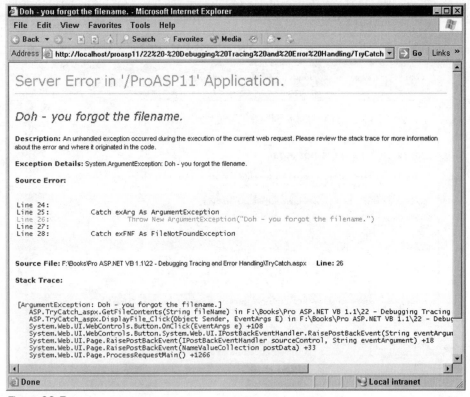

Figure 22-7

This gives you the new error message, but the source error is shown on the line where you raised the error, rather than where the error was actually generated. If this isn't acceptable, you can pass in the original exception as an argument when you throw the new exception. For example:

```
Catch exArg As ArgumentException
    Throw New ArgumentException("Doh - you forgot the filename.", exArg)
```

The result is shown in Figure 22-8:

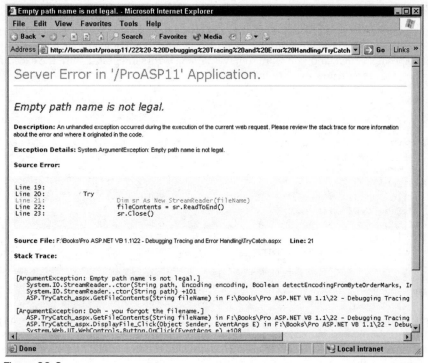

Figure 22-8

Hmm, but wait a minute – where has the new error message gone? You have re-thrown the error using the original exception details, which is why you are now on the correct line, but your error message isn't shown. Well, if you look at the stack trace you will see it as in Figure 22-9:

```
Stack Trace:

[ArgumentException: Empty path name is not legal.]
   System.IO.StreamReader..ctor(String path, Encoding encoding, Boolean detectEncodingFromByteOrderMarks,
   System.IO.StreamReader..ctor(String path) +101
   ASP.TryCatch_aspx.GetFileContents(String fileName) in F:\Books\Pro ASP.NET VB 1.1\22 - Debugging Tracir

[ArgumentException: Doh - you forgot the filename.]
   ASP.TryCatch_aspx.GetFileContents(String fileName) in F:\Books\Pro ASP.NET VB 1.1\22 - Debugging Tracir
   ASP.TryCatch_aspx.DisplayFile_Click(Object Sender, EventArgs E) in F:\Books\Pro ASP.NET VB 1.1\22 - Del
   System.Web.UI.WebControls.Button.OnClick(EventArgs e) +108
   System.Web.UI.WebControls.Button.System.Web.UI.IPostBackEventHandler.RaisePostBackEvent(String eventArg
   System.Web.UI.Page.RaisePostBackEvent(IPostBackEventHandler sourceControl, String eventArgument) +18
   System.Web.UI.Page.RaisePostBackEvent(NameValueCollection postData) +33
   System.Web.UI.Page.ProcessRequestMain() +1266
```

Figure 22-9

The original exception is shown first, and your error is shown next. It is probably not a scenario you would use that often, but the reason for generating exceptions is so that you can catch them and take some appropriate action, such as displaying a message to the user (who doesn't need to see the stack trace or the errors).

Custom Exceptions

Taking the custom error message one step further allows you to create your own exception class, derived not from the `Exception` class, but from `ApplicationException`. For example, consider a parser for a text file of a specific format, and you want to have parsing errors integrated with the exception handling system. You could create a new exception like this:

```
Imports System
Namespace Wrox
   Public Class InvalidContentException
      Inherits ApplicationException
      Public Sub New()
         MyBase.New()
      End Sub
      Public Sub New(message As String)
        MyBase.New(message)
      End Sub
      Public Sub New(message As String, inner As Exception)
        MyBase.New(message, inner)
      End Sub
   End Class
End Namespace
```

This simply defines a new class derived from `ApplicationException`. The class can be any name, but by convention it should end in `Exception`. Within this class the three standard constructors are implemented to call the base class constructors. Now, when you throw this exception you get the results shown in Figure 22-10:

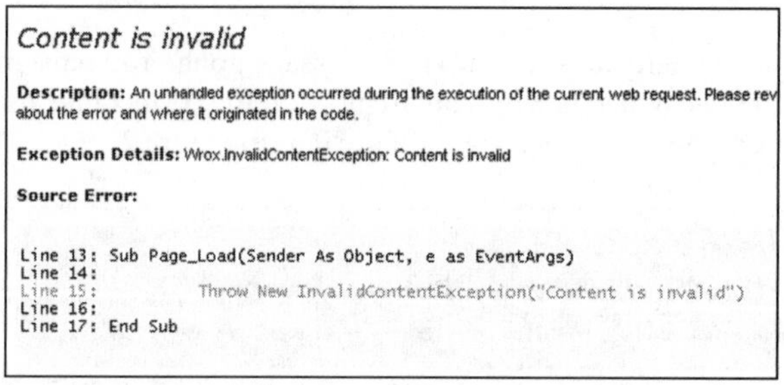

Content is invalid

Description: An unhandled exception occurred during the execution of the current web request. Please rev about the error and where it originated in the code.

Exception Details: Wrox.InvalidContentException: Content is invalid

Source Error:

```
Line 13: Sub Page_Load(Sender As Object, e as EventArgs)
Line 14:
Line 15:         Throw New InvalidContentException("Content is invalid")
Line 16:
Line 17: End Sub
```

Figure 22-10

Notice this is the same layout as standard exceptions – the only difference is that your exception name is used. The advantage of this system is that you can just trap your custom exception. For example:

```
Try
   ' run custom parser
Catch ex As InvalidContentException
   ' notify user of error
End Try
```

Within the new exception class you can do more than just call the base class methods. For example, you could add extra tracing information, or even overload the properties to provide further information.

Exception Types

Many of the internal classes define their own exceptions that you can catch. For example, when connecting to SQL Server, a data access problem might raise a SQLException. Although the documentation details what exceptions will be raised, the simplest way to find a list of the exceptions available is to use a tool like WinCV, and search for exception. This gives you a list as shown in Figure 22-11:

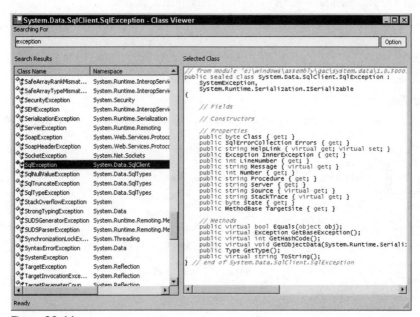

Figure 22-11

Here you can see exactly what exceptions are available, and to which namespace they belong. WinCV is in the bin directory of the SDK install.

Exceptions and COM

The exception handling system in .NET integrates well with the error handling of COM components, whatever type of interoperability you are performing. If you are using .NET components from COM, then exceptions raised in the .NET component will lead to a Windows HRESULT being passed to the COM component. If you are using COM components from .NET, and the COM component returns an HRESULT, this will be mapped to a .NET exception. The type of exception depends on the HRESULT – for example, the HRESULT E_ACCESSDENIED error will be mapped to UnauthorizedAccessException, while unknown instances of HRESULTs will be mapped to COMException. Additionally, COM components that support IErrorInfo will have these details mapped to the properties of the exception.

This topic is covered in more detail in Chapter 23 where you look at migration and interoperability.

ASP.NET Error Handling

In addition to the CLR exception system, ASP.NET also provides ways of handling errors. There are three ways in which this can be done:

❑ At the **page-level error event** for errors on an individual page

❑ At the **application-level error event** for errors in an application

❑ In the **application configuration** file to perform declarative error handling for an application

Which method you use depends on what you want to do when handling errors and what sort of structure you wish your application to have.

Page_Error Event

At the page level you can use the `Page_Error` event to trap errors on a page. For example:

```
<%@ Import Namespace="System.Data.SqlClient" %>
<script runat="server">
  Sub Page_Load(Sender As Object, E As EventArgs)
    Dim conn As SqlConnection
    Response.Write(conn.ToString())
  End Sub
  Sub Page_Error(Sender As Object, E As EventArgs)
    Dim err As String = "Error in: " & Request.Url.ToString() & "<p/>" & _
                        "Stack Trace Below:<br/>" & _
                          Server.GetLastError().ToString()
    Response.Write(err)
    Server.ClearError()
  End Sub
</script>
```

This uses the `Page_Load` event to generate a runtime error (by trying to display the connection string details when the connection hasn't been opened), which can be caught by the `Page_Error` event. The error details are available by calling the `GetLastError` method to return the exception object generated by the error. In this case, just output the details, but you could log the error or notify the web site administrator (see the Notifying Administrators of Errors section a little later in this chapter for details).

Application_Error Event

Like the `Page_Error` event, there is also an `Application_Error` event, which is declared in the `global.asax` file. For example, the following block uses similar code as seen in the previous section:

```
Sub Application_Error(Sender As Object, E As EventArgs)

  Dim err As String = "<h1>Application Error</h1>" & _
                      "Error in: " & Request.Url.ToString() & "<p/>" & _
                      "Stack Trace Below:<br/>" & _
                      Server.GetLastError().ToString()
  Response.Write(err)
  Server.ClearError()
End Sub
```

This event will be run if no `Page_Error` event traps the error. This event is one place where you could put application-wide error logging information.

Application Error Configuration

As well as programmatic handling of errors, there is also the declarative method utilizing the `web.config` file. This method is for handling HTTP errors or errors not handled elsewhere in the application, and providing a simple way to return custom error pages. It is configured with the `customErrors` element of the `system.web` section in the configuration file:

```
<system.web>
  <customErrors defaultRedirect="url" mode="On|Off|RemoteOnly">
    <error statusCode="code" redirect="url"/>
  </customErrors>
</system.web>
```

The `defaultRedirect` attribute indicates the page that should be shown if no other errors are trapped. It should be the last resort page for completely unexpected errors. The mode can be:

- ❑ `On`: To specify that custom errors be enabled
- ❑ `Off`: To specify that custom errors be disabled
- ❑ `RemoteOnly`: To specify that custom errors are only enabled for remote clients

The `RemoteOnly` option allows you to define custom errors for all users, except those accessing the page locally. This allows users to see a nice error page while you can log onto the server and see the exception details and stack trace.

The `error` sub-element allows individual pages to be shown for individual errors. For example:

```
<system.web>
  <customErrors defaultRedirect="DefaultErrorPage.aspx" mode="RemoteOnly">
    <error statusCode="404" redirect="FileNotFound.aspx"/>
  </customErrors>
</system.web>
```

Here, the 404 (not found) error will redirect to `FileNotFound.aspx`, while all other unhandled errors will go to `DefaultErrorPage.aspx`. You can have multiple `error` elements to cater to multiple HTTP errors.

Notifying Administrators of Errors

The rich set of error handling that ASP.NET provides is a great way to trap errors, but the users aren't the only people who need to know that something has gone wrong. A user will see the error page, but administrators and developers also need to know when things go wrong. There are many ways in which you can do this, but by far the simplest is to automatically write an event to the *event log* or to mail the administrator. Both of these are techniques you could add to the error pages so that whenever an error occurs, the details are logged somehow.

One important point to note about the event log is that you require special permissions to create new logs. In Chapter 14, we discussed the ASPNET account that, by default, all ASP.NET pages run under, and this account doesn't have permissions to create new event logs. This is because creation of new logs requires write permission in the registry, and by default, the ASPNET account doesn't require this. By and large you shouldn't need to create new logs within your ASP.NET pages, since this should really be an installation task. Once the log is created, then you don't need any special permission to write to the log.

If you do need to create a new log from within ASP.NET then you have two options, both of which involve the account under which ASP.NET runs. This first option is to modify the configuration file so that ASP.NET runs under a different account – perhaps the system account. This account allows the creation of event logs, but means that your entire application is now running in a less secure environment, which isn't recommended. Alternatively, you can move just the event log pages to a new directory and create a `web.config` file to allow impersonation for just this task, adding the following lines:

```
<configuration>
  <system.web>
    <identity impersonate="true" userName="RegWriter" password="iRule" />
  </system.web>
<configuration>
```

The user name should be an account with permissions to write to the registry.

Writing to the Event Log

Writing to the event log is extremely simple, as there is an `EventLog` class in the `System.Diagnostics` namespace. Consider the following function:

```
<%@ Import Namespace="System.Diagnostics" %>
    ... ' rest of page here
    Sub WriteToEventLog(LogName As String, Message As String)
      ' Create event log if it doesn't exist
      If (Not EventLog.SourceExists(LogName)) Then
        EventLog.CreateEventSource(LogName, LogName)
      End if
      ' Fire off to event log
      Dim Log as New EventLog(LogName)
      Log.Source = LogName
      Log.WriteEntry(Message, EventLogEntryType.Error)
    End Sub
```

This first creates a custom event log if it doesn't already exist, and then writes a new entry into the log. You could call this function like this:

```
Try
   ' do something here
Catch ex As Exception
   WriteToEventLog("Wrox", ex.ToString())
End Try
```

The result appears in the event log like any other event (Figure 22-12). Notice that this is in a custom log.

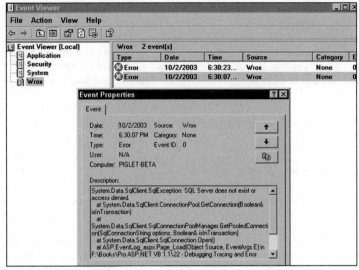

Figure 22-12

Sending Email Error Notifications

An alternative approach would be to send an automatic mail message, using the `MailMessage` class of the `System.Web.Mail` namespace. For example:

```
<%@ Import Namespace="System.Web.Mail" %>
  ... ' rest of page here
  Public Sub SendMail(message As String)
    Dim MyMessage as New MailMessage
    MyMessage.To = "webmaster@yourcompany.com"
    MyMessage.From = "ASPApplication@yourcompany.com"
    MyMessage.Subject = "Unhandled ASP.NET Error"
    MyMessage.BodyFormat = MailFormat.Text
    MyMessage.Body = message
    SmtpMail.SmtpServer = "YourSMTPServer"
    SmtpMail.Send(MyMessage)
  End Sub
```

Notice that the `Send` method is a static method, and therefore you don't need to create an instance of the `SmtpMail` component.

You could call this like so:

```
Try
  ' do something here
Catch ex As Exception
  SendMail(ex.ToString())
End Try
```

Debugging

With previous versions of ASP, debugging has always been a bit of a chore. `Response.Write` was the primary method of finding out what's going on in a program, and even the **Script Debugger** was weak in comparison to the debuggers that Windows developers had for Visual Basic and C++ code. All that has now changed with .NET, as the CLR provides integrated debugging for all applications. The primary goals of this were:

❑ Both in-process and out-of-process debugging

❑ Remote process debugging

❑ Managed and unmanaged code debugging

❑ Mixed language support

❑ Edit-and-Continue

Some of these aren't actually implemented as part of the CLR, but the rest of the framework provides the required support. There are two ways to perform debugging in the .NET Framework. The first is to use the SDK debugger, and the second is to use Visual Studio .NET. This section isn't going to give a comprehensive list of all debugger features, as most are fairly obvious. What we will concentrate on are the most used features.

The SDK Debugger

The SDK debugger (`DbgCLR.exe`) ships with the .NET SDK, and can be found in the `GuiDebug` directory. It provides the same features as the Visual Studio .NET debugger, except that it doesn't support remote debugging or Edit-and-Continue. Despite the lack of these two features, it is far better than anything you have been used to in the ASP world.

Enabling Debugging

Earlier in this chapter, we showed that to allow tracing you added a `Page` directive to your web pages. The same is true for debugging, where the `Debug` attribute is set to `True`:

```
<%@ Page Debug="True" %>
```

This tells the compiler to emit debugging symbols into the compiled page, and allows the debugger to attach to the running program.

The debug symbols are also required for components, and to enable them use the `/debug` flag on the compiler (the flag is the same whichever language compiler you are using). When you compile with this an extra file is created, ending in `.pdb` – this contains the debugging symbols. You don't have to do anything with this file, as it is only used by the debugger.

Before using the debugger, you will also need to view the web page in the browser so that the debugging symbols are loaded for the page. You can still start the debugger and load the page, but you won't be able to do any debugging until the page has been compiled once with the debugging enabled.

Remember to disable debugging and compile components without the debug symbols when you deploy applications to reduce any overhead.

Starting Debugging

To start debugging your ASP.NET applications, launch the debugger, and from the Tools menu select Debug Process..., to show the dialog in Figure 22-13:

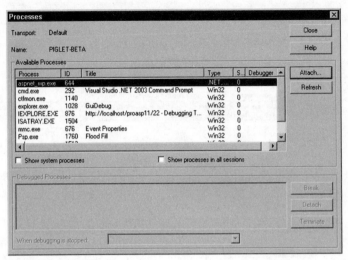

Figure 22-13

This shows the processes you can pick to debug. Make sure you have the Show system processes checkbox box selected, and pick the aspnet_wp.exe process – this is the ASP.NET worker process. Click the Attach... button to attach the debugger to the process, and then close the dialog. You can now load a page into the debugger (by using File | Open) and set breakpoints by clicking in the gray margin as shown in Figure 22-14:

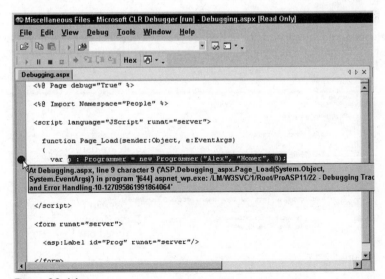

Figure 22-14

This shows a breakpoint in a simple ASP.NET page coded using JScript (unlikely for most people, but there's a point to it – bear with me). This page simply instantiates a class called `Programmer`. If you now hit the page, you are flipped into the debugger at the set line as shown in Figure 22-15:

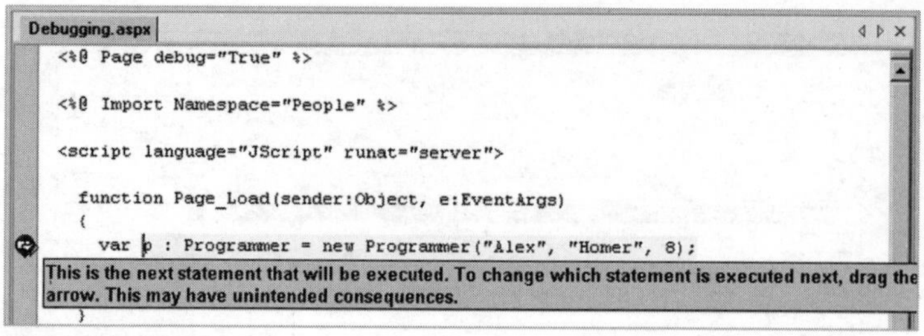

```
Debugging.aspx                                                    ◁ ▷ ✕

   <%@ Page debug="True" %>

   <%@ Import Namespace="People" %>

   <script language="JScript" runat="server">

   function Page_Load(sender:Object, e:EventArgs)
   {
      var p : Programmer = new Programmer("Alex", "Homer", 8);
      This is the next statement that will be executed. To change which statement is executed next, drag the
      arrow. This may have unintended consequences.
   }
```

Figure 22-15

You can now step into the code for the component (assuming it was compiled with the `/debug` option), as shown in Figure 22-16:

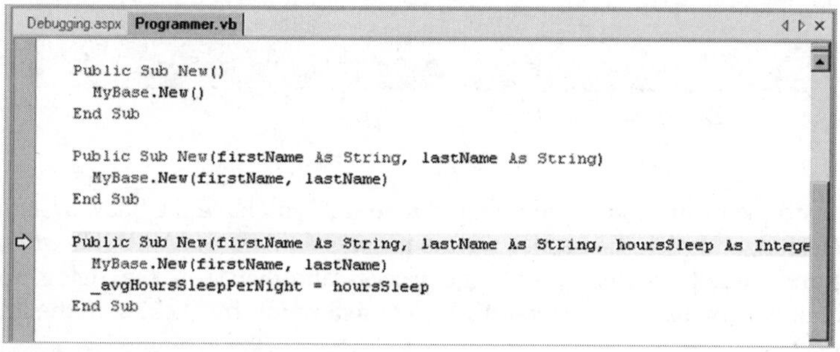

```
Debugging.aspx  Programmer.vb                                     ◁ ▷ ✕

      Public Sub New()
         MyBase.New()
      End Sub

      Public Sub New(firstName As String, lastName As String)
         MyBase.New(firstName, lastName)
      End Sub

 ⇨    Public Sub New(firstName As String, lastName As String, hoursSleep As Intege
         MyBase.New(firstName, lastName)
         _avgHoursSleepPerNight = hoursSleep
      End Sub
```

Figure 22-16

Now you've stepped into the constructor of the `Programmer` class. Notice that it is a Visual Basic class. You are almost at that point I was trying to make – let's go one step further and step into the base class. See Figure 22-17:

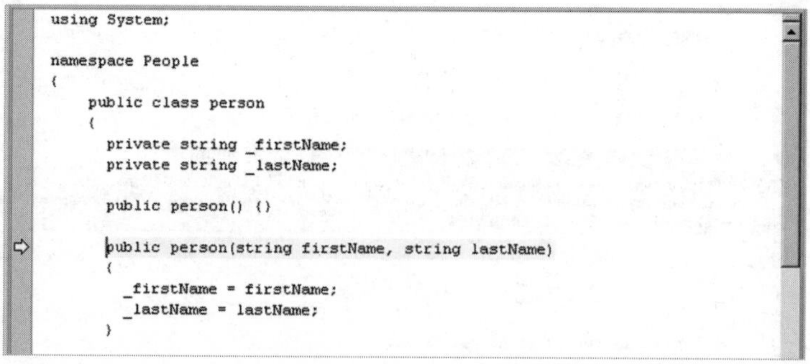

```
   using System;

   namespace People
   {
      public class person
      {
        private string _firstName;
        private string _lastName;

        public person() {}

 ⇨      public person(string firstName, string lastName)
        {
           _firstName = firstName;
           _lastName = lastName;
        }
```

Figure 22-17

Now the point is made. You have a base class written in C#, which is sub-classed by a Visual Basic class, and used in a JScript ASP page. This becomes obvious when examining the call stack as shown in Figure 22-18:

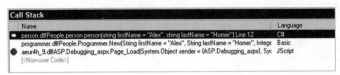

Figure 22-18

This really reinforces the concept of language equality in the runtime, since you can debug through components written in different languages. Even if it were restricted to a single language, the fact that you have such a good debugger would be a great benefit in itself.

SDK Debugger Features

The SDK debugger has all of the great features that you'd expect from a high-end development environment, including:

- ❑ Stepping into, out of, and over code

- ❑ Setting breakpoints on specific lines

- ❑ Setting breakpoints on specific exceptions

- ❑ Setting breakpoints on expressions

- ❑ Viewing contents of variables

- ❑ Viewing the call stack, threads, and modules

The two major features that aren't supported are debugging remote processes and Edit-and-Continue. No support for Edit-and-Continue means that the SDK debugger is a read-only debugger, so you can't edit code inline and continue the debugging process. You can only edit code externally, and the debugger recognizes that the file has changed (and will reload it if you desire), but the new changes will not take effect until the request is rerun. For these features you need the Visual Studio .NET debugger.

Debugging in Visual Studio .NET

In Visual Studio .NET debugging is just a part of working with an integrated development tool. When building an application, all you have to do is set a breakpoint from within the code editor window and run your application. You'll see a view that looks similar to the SDK debugger, and supports the same set of features such as stepping and viewing of code and variables.

Edit-and-Continue

Edit-and-Continue gives you the ability to alter code while programs are running. This is due to the ability of the runtime to inject code into a running process. There are, however, some limitations:

❑ For running functions (anywhere in the call stack) you are limited to 64 bytes of additional variables. Outside of the call stack there is no limit.

❑ You cannot change resource files.

❑ You cannot change exception-handling blocks.

❑ You cannot change data types.

❑ You cannot remove functions.

In most cases you couldn't really call these *limitations*, as they are the sorts of alterations that would require more than a simple change.

There's nothing special you have to do to enable this functionality. There are options to disable Edit-and-Continue, and to specify its various functions, but the defaults are all acceptable. All you have to do is retype code in the debugger when in break mode and the new code takes effect.

Remote Debugging

Remote debugging works in the same way as local debugging, except you have the option to debug a remote process. This is useful in situations where you have a separate server hosting the application. A full description of remote debugging is beyond the scope of this book, but consult the .NET documentation, under the section titled *Remote Debugging Setup*.

Profiling and Performance

Profiling is often one of those areas that never seem to have great value in some people's minds, but in certain respects it is the most important area of development. A slow web site is a great way to put off users and lose customers, and remains the bane of many administrators' lives. The simple fact is that performance testing often gets cut due to time constraints as, when deadlines get tight, people cut things that don't have an immediate impact. The attitude is often to get the product shipped, and then release a performance-enhanced version at a later date. The reality is, of course, that users expect great things from a first release, and there should be no excuses for not delivering the best-performing application.

So, if you want the best possible performance from an application, how do you go about it? How do you find the areas of an application that need improvement, and go about testing those areas? Profiling is the act of gathering that data about an application, allowing you to see which areas take longest to execute.

Performance testing isn't only about seeing how well an application performs in its current incarnation, but also includes:

❑ **Baselining**: This is the act of collecting performance data to be used as a comparison for future tests. Collecting metrics is important as applications and loads change – you need to have some base figures against which you can compare future analysis.

❑ **Loading**: Application performance decreases as the load increases, so you need to see how your application will perform under increasing load. That's the thing about web sites – the load is never guaranteed to stay the same – it can increase and decrease sharply as usage trends change.

❑ **Stability**: Web sites need to have constant availability as they have global reach. It is not possible to assume that no one will use your site at night, because your night may be your user's day. Therefore, you have to ensure your application stays stable, especially under load.

As applications become more complex, so does testing. This is especially true now, where ASP.NET applications may be written with interoperability in mind to provide integration with, or reuse of existing technology. An example of this is the reuse of an existing COM data layer. This layer may be performing optimally in a current application, but when used from a .NET application does it become a bottleneck? At this stage, you have to ask if performance could be improved by rewriting the layer. This sort of question is discussed further in Chapter 23, where we look at migration and interoperability issues.

There are three steps in the process of profiling:

❑ **Instrumentation**: Where you add profiling to your code. This could be adding Windows performance counters, or custom profiling statements to identify the execution of the code, as well as logging and tracing information.

❑ **Sampling**: Where you run your application to collect the profiling data.

❑ **Analysis**: Where you examine the collected data, and validate it against your baseline data.

We will be concentrating on the first of these, although we will discuss the latter two options to show how the instrumentation process is used.

Instrumentation

Instrumentation is a bit like Schrödinger's Cat, where the act of viewing changes the outcome. In performance testing, you are examining how your application performs under certain conditions, and you add profiling to detect this. However, the profiling you add affects those very things you are testing – the performance metrics. The more profiling code you add to applications, the more you affect performance. So, the act of instrumentation is one that should be carefully handled. There is no harm in adding large amounts of profiling code as long as you understand the implications.

The `Trace` class shown earlier provides some performance data for events, but this has to be manually viewed, and is not really designed for profiling. To profile, you want a simple way of adding profiling code as well as collecting information. This is provided by *Performance Monitor Counters*. Both the .NET Framework and ASP.NET have counters (which you'll look at under the *Analysis* section), but to provide custom profiling you will need to create custom counters.

Security

The ASPNET account does not have sufficient privileges to read performance counter data, although it does have privilege to write performance counter data. To read performance counter data, the process requires *Administrator* or *Power User* permissions. To enable reading of data from counters, your ASP.NET pages will need to run under impersonation. Placing these pages in a separate directory and modifying the configuration file will allow this.

When to Create and Remove Counters

The creation and removal of counters is something you should think carefully about, as they are really installer and uninstaller features. If your application requires custom counters, then the counters should be created when the application is installed, and removed when the application is uninstalled. One problem with this approach is fitting it into ASP.NET applications where the xcopy deployment method is used. The ways to solve this could be to:

❑ Create an application installer so that the counters are created and removed in the correct place.

❑ Create a separate script or page to create and remove the counters.

❑ Check for the existence of counters in your application (perhaps the Application_OnStart event), and if missing create them. This leaves the problem of removing counters if the application is uninstalled, as well as a performance problem since you are checking for them every time the application starts.

Of these solutions, the first option is certainly the best.

Along with the question of when to create counters, there is the question of why? The answer is simple – create custom counters when you need to profile areas within your application. The supplied counters are perfect for looking at the application or ASP.NET as a whole, but isn't fine-grained enough to show you how the individual parts of your application are performing. So, it is only if you need this amount of information that you need to create custom counters. For example, imagine you have an e-commerce site, and you need to know how well the order processing section is performing. You will probably be storing the orders in a database, so you can see how many orders you have, but unless you also keep time information you can't see any performance metrics. Adding instrumentation to the order processing allows fine grained monitoring of this information.

Custom Performance Counters

The base class library supplies a set of classes for interacting with the Windows performance monitor, allowing both read-and-write access, as well as the creation of custom objects and counters. These objects are as follows:

Object	Description
PerformanceCounterCategory	A counter category to contain individual counters.
PerformanceCounter	The details of an individual performance counter.
CounterCreationData	The details required for the creation of a counter.
CounterCreationDataCollection	A collection of performance counter creation details, for creating multiple counters in a category.
CounterSample	A sample of data from a counter.

The first two of these objects are easy to relate to, by looking at the Add Counters screen of the Windows Performance Monitor. See Figure 22-19:

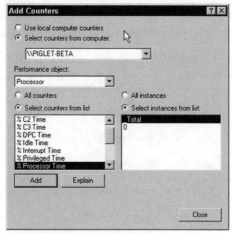

Figure 22-19

The performance object drop-down list on the dialog corresponds to the PerformanceCounterCategory, and the counters list corresponds to the PerformanceCounter. Just like the dialog in Figure 22-19, the use of the counter objects isn't limited to the local machine – many of the methods allow the addition of a machine name, allowing manipulation of counters on remote machines (assuming the correct permissions).

The PerformanceCounterCategory Object

Let's first look at the category object, as this contains details for the category itself, allowing creation of new categories and counters as well as the retrieval of category and counter information. It has three properties as follows:

Property	Description
CategoryName	The name of the category
CategoryHelp	Text describing the category
MachineName	The machine upon which the category is installed

The methods are more extensive:

Method	Description
CounterExists	Indicates whether or not the selected counter exists
Create	Creates a category and a counter or counters
Delete	Deletes a category and counters
Exists	Indicates whether or not the category exists
GetCategories	Returns an array of categories
GetCounters	Returns an array of counters for the category
GetInstanceNames	Returns an array of names of counter instances
InstanceExists	Indicates whether or not the counter instance exists
ReadCategory	Returns a collection of all category and instance data

Many of these methods are overloaded, allowing several forms of use. For example, the `CounterExists` method has three forms:

```
CounterExists(CounterName)
CounterExists(CounterName, CategoryName)
CounterExists(CounterName, CategoryName, MachineName)
```

The first case of these requires the `PerformanceCounterCategory` object to have been initialized to an existing category. For example:

```
Dim PC As New PerformanceCounterCategory("Wrox")
If PC.CounterExists("MyCounter") Then ...
    ...
End If
```

The latter two cases are static methods, and don't require an object instance. For example:

```
If PerformanceCounterCategory.CounterExists("MyCounter", "Wrox") Then ...
    ...
End If
```

Or:

```
If PerformanceCounterCategory.CounterExists("MyCounter", "Wrox", "Eeyore") Then
    ...
End If
```

Creating Custom Performance Counters

The first point to note about creating counters is that they can only be created in new categories. This means that you cannot modify any of the existing categories, and that if you want to add counters to a custom category, you need to remove the category first. To create counters, use the `Create` method of the `PerformanceCounterCategory` object, which has several forms:

```
Create(CategoryName, CategoryHelp, CounterName, CounterHelp)
Create(CategoryName, CategoryHelp, CounterName, CounterHelp, MachineName)
Create(CategoryName, CategoryHelp, CounterCreationDataCollection)
Create(CategoryName, CategoryHelp, CounterCreationDataCollection, MachineName)
```

The first two of these allow a category and a single counter to be created. For example:

```
PerformanceCounterCategory.Create("Wrox", "Wrox Press Counters", _
                               "Counter1", "This counter is counter 1")
```

The second two methods use a collection of `CounterCreationData` objects, allowing the creation of multiple counters, as well as being able to specify the type of counter (which defaults to `RateOfCountsPerSecond32` – more on types later). This object can be constructed like so:

```
Dim CCD As CounterCreationData
CCD = New CounterCreationData("Counter1", "This counter is counter 1", _
                               PerformanceCounterType.NumberOfItems32)
```

or, alternatively using the properties:

```
Dim CCD As New CounterCreationData()
CCD.CounterName = "Counter1"
CCD.CounterHelp = "This counter is counter 1"
CCD.CounterType = PerformanceCounterType.NumberOfItems32
```

Once created, the object can be added to the collection:

```
Dim CCDC As New CounterCreationDataCollection()
CCDC.Add(CCD)
PerformanceCounterCategory.Create("Wrox", "Wrox Press Counters", CCDC)
```

This process can be abbreviated by combining creation and addition into one line, making adding multiple counters easier to read:

```
Dim CCDC As New CounterCreationDataCollection()
CCDC.Add(New CounterCreationData("Counter1", "This counter is counter 1", _
                               PerformanceCounterType.NumberOfItems32)
CCDC.Add(New CounterCreationData("Counter2", "This counter is counter 2", _
                               PerformanceCounterType.NumberOfItems32)
CCDC.Add(New CounterCreationData("Counters/sec", _
                               "Counters per second", _
                          PerformanceCounterType.RateOfCountersPerSecond32)
PerformanceCounterCategory.Create("Wrox", "Wrox Press Counters", CCDC)
```

The allowable values for `PerformanceCounterType` are as follows:

Type	Description
AverageBase	Used as the base data in the computation of time or count averages (AverageCounter64 and AverageTimer32).
AverageCount64	A count that usually gives the bytes per operation when divided by the number of operations.
AverageTimer32	A timer that usually gives time per operation when divided by the number of operations.
CountPerTimeInterval32	Count per time interval. Typically used to track number of items queued or waiting.
CountPerTimeInterval64	Large count per time interval. Typically used to track number of items queued or waiting.
CounterDelta32	Difference between two counters.
CounterDelta64	Large difference between two counters.
CounterMultiBase	Used as the base data for the Multi counters. It defines the number of similar items sampled.
CounterMultiTimer	Timer sampling of multiple but similar items. Result is an average sampling among the items.
CounterMultiTimer100Ns	Timer sampling of multiple , but similar items, every 100 nanoseconds. Result is an average sampling among the items.
CounterMultiTimer 100NsInverse	The inverse of CounterMultiTimer100Ns. Used when the object is not in use.
CounterMultiTimer Inverse	The inverse of CounterMultiTimer. Used when the object is not in use.
CounterTimer	A common timer for percentage values.
CounterTimerInverse	The inverse of CounterTimer. Used when the object is not in use.
ElapsedTime	The data is the start time of the item being measured.
NumberOfItems32	A raw counter value.
NumberOfItems64	A large raw counter value.
NumberOfItemsHEX32	A raw counter value for display in hexadecimal.
NumberOfItemsHEX64	A large raw counter value for display in hexadecimal.

Type	Description
RateOfCounts PerSecond32	Rate of counter per second.
RateOfCounts PerSecond64	Large rate of counts per second.
RawBase	Used as the base data for `RawFraction`. The counter value holds the denominator of the fraction value.
RawFraction	Instantaneous value, to be divided by the base data (`RawBase`).
SampleBase	Used as the base data for `SampleCounter` and `SampleFraction`.
SampleCounter	A count that is either 1 or 0 on each sampling. The counter value is the counter of 1s sampled.
SampleFraction	A count that is either 1 or 0 on each sampling. The counter value is the counter of 1s sampled. For display in terms of a percentage.
Timer100ns	Timer sampling every 100 nanoseconds.
Timer100nsInverse	The inverse of `Timer100ns`. Used when the object is not in use.

The type of counter you create depends upon what you are trying to measure. For simple count values (for example, the total number of orders in an e-commerce system) you can use `NumberOfItems32` or `NumberOfItems64` (the difference being the magnitude of number allowed). For a performance metric (such as the number of orders per second) you can use `RateOfCountsPerSecond32` or `RateOfCountsPerSecond64`. The difference between the large and normal counters (those ending in `32` and `64`) is the size of data they can hold. Those ending in `32` are 32 bits wide (holding 4 bytes) and those ending in `64` are 64 bits wide (holding 8 bytes).

The counter type also comes into effect when you look at sampling, as explained later in the chapter.

Creating Counter Instances

The term *instance* can be confusing when dealing with performance counters, as it is easy to think in terms of class instantiation giving you an instance of a class. This is, in fact, the right way to think of it – the difference is that an instance of a performance counter is reflected as part of the instrumentation. For example, consider the Performance Monitor application, where you have the choice to add counters (Figure 22-19). At the bottom right of this dialog you see instances of a counter dealing with the `Process` object. The instances here reflect the number of processors in the monitored machine (sadly I only have 1 CPU). There is also a `_Total` instance, which aggregates the values for other instances. Some counters, such as `Memory`, don't have specific instances, as they are concerned with a single object. What's especially noteworthy about this is the instances apply to a `Performance` object (or category), and not to individual counters. You cannot have two counters in the same category with different instances.

Creating instances is different from creating the counters themselves, because instances are created for existing custom counters. Use the `PerformanceCounter` object for this:

```
Dim pc As New PerformanceCounter("Wrox", "Counter1")
Dim pc As New PerformanceCounter("Wrox", "Counter1", "Instance1")
Dim pc As New PerformanceCounter("Wrox", "Counter1", "Instance2")
Dim pc As New PerformanceCounter("Wrox", "Counter1", "_Total")
```

The first line creates a counter with the default instance. The latter three lines show the creation of explicit instances. These examples create read-only counters – the constructor is overloaded to allow a Boolean flag to indicate a read/write counter:

```
Dim pc As New PerformanceCounter("Wrox", "Counter1", "Instance2", True)
```

There is also another form allowing the addition of a machine name:

```
Dim pc As New PerformanceCounter("Wrox", "Counter1", "Instance2", _
                                 "EEYORE", True)
```

You will look at the use of counters in more detail a little later when we discuss updating counter values and sampling.

Counter Lifetime

It is important to understand that performance counter values are *values* rather than *entries* – when you write a value to a performance counter, you are not making a permanent entry in the counter, as you do when you write an entry to an event log. Rather, performance counter values are transitory, and reflect a point in time. When the last `PerformanceCounter` component to reference a particular system counter is disposed of, the counter resets itself to zero.

There are several ways you can manage the lifetime of a performance counter if you want to retain values for a longer period of time than the default counter behavior allows:

❑ You can run the Performance Monitor application on the server where the counter lives. As long as the Performance Monitor is open, the reference to the counters is maintained and counter values continue to accumulate.

❑ You can make sure that there is always an instance of the `PerformanceCounter` component connected to the particular counter for which you want to maintain values.

❑ You can write a Windows service that keeps a reference to the counter.

While these solutions are perfectly acceptable, you should realize that performance counters aren't meant to hold stateful data. Their very nature is for measuring metrics at a particular point in time. So, if no one is running your application, it makes sense for the counter values to be 0, or even to not exist at all.

Removing Counters

Custom counters can be removed by use of the `Delete` method of the `PerformanceCounterCategory` object, which removes the category and all counters associated with it. For example:

```
PerformanceCounterCategory.Delete("Wrox")
```

What's important to remember is the lifetime of counters, because the counter will not be removed if another application is using the same. The counters use shared memory underneath, so this memory won't be released until all monitoring and instrumentation applications have been closed. This means that you could remove counters, and then recreate them immediately, and the old values would be retained. To guarantee their instant removal you can use the `CloseSharedResources` method of the performance counter object. For example:

```
Dim cat As New PerformanceCounterCategory("Wrox")
Dim pc As New PerformanceCounter
For Each pc In cat.GetCounters()
  pc.CloseSharedResources()
Next
PerformanceCounterCategory.Delete("Wrox")
```

The trouble with this code is that you would need to add more to check for instances. As a general rule it is best to just use the `Delete` method to delete the category and counters – the counter values will be reset once all references are removed.

Updating Performance Counter Values

Once your counters have been created, there are several ways to update counter values. The first is to simply set the `RawValue` property:

```
Dim pc As New PerformanceCounter("Wrox", "Counter1", True)
pc.RawValue = 10
```

The other ways all rely on a similar set of methods:

```
pc.Increment()
pc.IncrementBy(5)
pc.Decrement()
pc.DecrementBy(5)
```

These just increment or decrement the counter, either by 1 or by a supplied value.

Sampling

The .NET Framework doesn't provide any new tools for performance testing, but instead, integrates with the Windows Performance Log, so you can use existing tools to track how your application performs. If you don't have an existing performance-testing tool, then the *Web Application Stress Tool (WAST)* is freely available from Microsoft at http://www.microsoft.com/downloads/ – search for *webtool*. This allows you to run automated tests against a web site, simulating large numbers of users. A description of WAST is outside the scope of this book. If you have the Enterprise Version of Visual Studio .NET you will have Application Center Test, which is the new version of WAST.

Monitoring custom counters with the Performance Monitor is just the same as for Windows counters – you just pick your custom category and counters as shown in Figure 22-20:

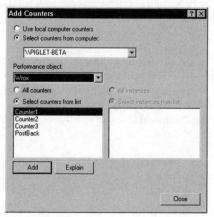

Figure 22-20

This in itself is an acceptable form of monitoring, but if you want to build some form of custom graphs, you will need to take sample data and perform calculations on it.

Custom Sampling

There are several ways in which you can extract the values from performance counters. The simplest, and quickest, is to examine the value of the RawValue property, which gives the uncalculated value of the counter. When using this value, you should remember that it represents the counter value at its last sampling, and may only represent a transient state. For example, a counter measuring CPU utilization may have high fluctuations, and the RawValue property will only reflect this if you happen to sample at the same point as the fluctuation. You can also use the NextSample method to fetch the next raw value for the counter. For example:

```
Dim pc As New PerformanceCounter("Wrox", "Counter1", True)
Dim ValueNow As Integer
Dim ValueNew As Integer
ValueNow = pc.RawValue
ValueNew = pc.NextSample().RawValue
```

This example introduces the concept of the CounterSample object, which contains the following properties:

Property	Description
BaseValue	Returns the base value. Only for samples that are based upon multiple counters.
CounterFrequency	Returns the frequency at which the counter is read. This is the number of milliseconds between samples.
CounterTimeStamp	The time at which the sample was taken.
CounterType	The type of counter. This will be one of the PerformanceCounterType constants.
RawValue	Returns the raw value of the counter.
SystemFrequency	The frequency at which the system reads from the counter.
TimeStamp	The system timestamp.
TimeStamp100nsec	The system timestamp, to within 0.1 milliseconds.

There is also a single method, Calculate, to calculate sample values:

```
Dim pc      As New PerformanceCounter("Wrox", "Counter1", True)
Dim samp1   As CounterSample
Dim result  As Single
samp1 = pc.NextSample()
result = CounterSample.Calculate(samp1)
```

You can also use this method to calculate between two samples:

```
Dim pc      As New PerformanceCounter("Wrox", "Counter1", True)
Dim samp1   As CounterSample
Dim samp2   As CounterSample
Dim result  As Single
samp1 = pc.NextSample()
samp2 = pc.NextSample()
result = CounterSample.Calculate(samp1, samp2)
```

This takes two samples, and then uses the Calculate method to perform the calculation between them. When dealing with counters that could have fluctuations sampling gives a more accurate picture of the trends within your application.

The calculation performed depends upon the type of counter from the PerformanceCounterType enumeration, and the details are shown next:

AverageCount64 is a standard average counter, giving the result of the average count per operation:

```
(NewSample-OldSample)/(NewCount-OldCount)
```

`AverageTimer32` is the average of a time value, giving the result of the average time per operation:

```
((NewSample-OldSample)/SampleFrequency)/(NewTime-OldTime)
```

`CountPerTimeInterval32` and `CountPerTimeInterval64` represent the number of counts per time interval:

```
(NewSample-OldSample)/(NewTime-OldTime)
```

`CounterDelta32` and `CounterDelta64` represent the difference between two counter values:

```
NewSample-OldSample
```

`CounterMultiTimer` gives the result of an average sampling among multiple items:

```
100.((NewSample-OldSample)/((NewTime-OldSample)/SampleFrequency))
```

`CounterMultiTimerInverse` is simply the inverse of `CounterMultiTimer`:

```
100.NumberOfItemsSampled-CounterMultiTimer
```

`CounterMultiTimer100ns` is an average sample among multiple items per 100 nanoseconds:

```
100.((NewSample-OldSample)/((NewTime-OldTime)/100ns))/NumberOfItemsSampled
```

`CounterMultiTimer100nsInverse` is the inverse of `CounterMultiTimer100ns`:

```
100.NumberOfItemsSampled-CounterMultiTimer100ns
```

`CounterTimer` is the percentage of items over the sample period:

```
100.((NewSample-OldSample)/(NewTime-OldTime))
```

`CounterTimerInverse` is the inverse of `CounterTimer`:

```
100-CounterTimer
```

`ElapsedTime` is the elapsed time for the measurement:

```
(SampleTime-SampleStartTime)/SampleFrequency
```

The `NumberOfItems32`, `NumberOfItems64`, `NumberOfItemsHEX32`, `NumberOfItemsHEX64` counters have no calculation since they indicate fixed values.

`RateOfCountsPerSecond32` and `RateOfCountsPerSecond64` are the number of counts per time base:

```
((NewSample-OldSample)/(NewTime-OldTime))/SampleFrequency
```

The `RawFraction` counter returns the raw fraction between two values:

```
100.(Sample/BaseValue)
```

`SampleCounter` is the difference between samples:

```
(NewSample-OldSample)/(NewBaseValue-OldBaseValue)
```

`SampleFraction` returns the fractional difference between samples:

```
100.((NewSample-OldSample)/(NewBaseValue-OldBaseValue))
```

`Timer100ns` gives the percentage of time (in 100ns units) for the counter:

```
100.((NewSample-OldSample)/(NewTime100ns-OldTime100ns))
```

`Timer100nsInverse` is the inverse of `Timer100ns`:

```
100-Timer100ns
```

Analysis

There are two sets of information you can use to evaluate the performance of your web applications – the .NET performance counters, and custom counters. ASP.NET has an extensive list of counters, which are well documented in the framework SDK.

Analysis of custom counters is application-specific, and there are no hard rules as to what you should analyze. It really depends upon what counters you have created and when you update them. Remember that custom counters can easily be tracked in the Performance Monitor.

Using tools such as WAST, you can test your application and collect performance counters for analysis, perhaps in a spreadsheet. You can also use the `PerformanceCounter` object to query counters, although this is a task best left to applications other than ASP.NET. This is because accurate monitoring depends on regular sampling of data, and this isn't a task that ASP.NET is suited to. In this case you'd be better off building a Windows Forms application that could sample the data at regular intervals.

Summary

In this chapter you have examined the less exciting parts of development – those things that many programmers find a drudge, but in some respects are the most important. Maybe these topics have always been shied away from because you just haven't had the facilities to make their implementation and use easy. After all, that was pretty much the case with ASP. It's a great product, but the surrounding toolset wasn't industrial strength. With ASP.NET you have that strength – great support for error handling and tracing, and a fully featured debugger.

In particular we have see:

- ❑ **Tracing**: And how you can trace the flow of your applications.
- ❑ **Error handling**: To show how robust applications can be created.

❑ **Debugging**: With the rich debuggers allowing cross-language and cross-machine application debugging.

❑ **Profiling**: Seeing how to add performance counters so performance and scalability can be assessed.

Together these features provide a great environment for developing applications. Now it's time to turn our attention to migrating from existing ASP and COM applications.

23

Migration and Interoperability

Wouldn't it be great if, when a new version of a development product was released, you could forget about all your existing projects using old versions of the software? Unfortunately, for the majority of people, existing applications take up a good deal of their time and rightly so. If you restarted development with every new version of a product, then you'd never get anything finished. Organizations have a duty to their staff and shareholders, so throwing away existing investment (in both products and expertise) is not something that can be done lightly. Therefore new developments may have to work alongside and in cooperation with existing products.

This chapter is about how to manage getting .NET to work with the pre -.NET world. In particular you will look at:

❑   Migrating ASP applications to ASP.NET

❑   Changing from VBScript to their Visual Basic .NET

❑   Using existing COM components from .NET

❑   Using .NET components from COM

Despite the fact that ASP.NET is such a radical change from ASP, there's an excellent migration path, as well as great support for working alongside existing applications.

Migration from ASP.NET 1.0 to 1.1 is covered in Appendix C.

Migrate, Integrate, or Rewrite?

The first question that needs to be asked is, should you migrate at all? Is the effort going to be worth it? No one can deny that ASP.NET is better than ASP in many (if not all) areas for developers. The whole environment promotes cleaner code, better reuse, and faster applications –

many developers would love to work in this better world. However as you move forward with your development, there will be costs involved, and you must weigh up those costs carefully to decide which option you should choose.

For example, ask yourself the following questions:

❑ Is the application purely ASP pages?

❑ Does it use COM components?

❑ Do you have a data tier in MTS or COM+ Services?

❑ Which browsers is it targeted at?

❑ Does it use client-side script?

❑ Do you need to migrate at all?

The answers to these questions will help you decide the action you need to take. Unfortunately, there's no simple answer – almost every application is unique, and must be considered independently. The one thing that's critical about the process of migration is to set your expectations at the right level. Don't think you can just rename your pages to `.aspx` and expect miracles to happen.

Migrate

Migration can be described as the movement of all parts of an application to a new environment, with the minimal amount of code change. This is often the goal many people aim for, but it can have hidden costs.

For example, will the new application be easily maintainable? Will you add code to bring the application into line with ASP.NET, but in doing so leave code that is even more confusing than it was before? The short-term cost of performing the least work might actually turn out to be more expensive, if, further down the line, more work is required. You should analyze the cost of this approach, comparing it to the cost of rewriting, and see which has the greatest long-term benefit.

Integrate

Integration gives you the ability to add new ASP.NET features to existing ASP applications, or perhaps to migrate only selected parts of an application. In many ways this is a good approach, but it also comes with pitfalls, the two most obvious of which are:

❑ **Built-in session and application state cannot be shared** between ASP and ASP.NET applications.

❑ **Sluggish performance**, as crossing the managed/un-managed code boundary incurs a minor performance cost.

Usually you'll find that the latter is acceptable for your particular application – after all, the application will still work, and the new ASP.NET code will run faster, so the benefit of using new code might equal out any performance drop. Also, when all things are considered, the boundary crossing is light compared to some other actions (such as database access). The first bullet point, though, is a big problem

– you can easily integrate ASP.NET pages into an ASP application, but there's no way of sharing built-in state. So, unless your application uses its own form of session storage (such as a database), or doesn't use the in-built state handling, your options are limited.

Integrating ASP.NET applications with existing COM components only suffers from the minor performance hit of the unmanaged/managed code boundary, unless they use the ASP context. In this case you may need to alter your ASP.NET pages. We'll look at this topic later, when we look at the `ObjectContext` object in the Intrinsic Objects section.

Rewrite

Rewriting is the option many of you would like. Starting again from scratch is not only a great opportunity to get the best from the new platform, but it's also a chance to cure some of those things about the original application that you never liked. This option will, of course, get the best from .NET, and in the long run may be the cheapest solution. One of the reasons why the ASP.NET team decided to break compatibility with ASP was because you have more Internet time ahead of you than behind you; the future of the Internet is more important that its past. Microsoft wants a platform that will last for a long time. Of course, one of the big problems with the rewrite method isn't with the code itself, it's with education. With a new technology such as .NET, it's often the training and experience that prove too much of a hindrance to this option.

Do Nothing

No matter how much you might want to take one of the preceding methods doing nothing might actually be the best bet for your applications. After all, do you really need to move to .NET? What sort of business case can you put forward to justify it? How much will it cost? Conversion (whatever form it takes) means time (and therefore money) for developers, testers, bug fixing, and so on. The whole development cycle has to be gone through again. Remember the old adage – "if it ain't broke, don't fix it". It's nice to play with new toys, but sometimes a good old-fashioned wooden train set works fine.

ASP.NET

There are many changes to take into account when looking purely at ASP pages. The most obvious are the server controls and the postback architecture. These have been covered extensively in earlier chapters of the book, so now we'll move on to other features that still exist in ASP.NET, but are different from ASP. We'll also abbreviate explanations of changes that are explained in detail elsewhere in this book, and instead provide a summary and reference to them. Since ASP.NET is fully class-based, we'll also provide references to the underlying classes, so you can easily find full information in the documentation, or look up the classes in tools such as WinCV and ILDasm.

Preparing the Way

Before we delve into the changes in detail, here's a quick list of things you can do now, in your current ASP pages, to pave the way for migrating to ASP.NET:

- ❏ Use only a single language within each ASP page

- ❏ Use `Option Explicit` to enforce declaration of variables

- ❏ Use `<script>` blocks for function declaration instead of `<% %>` blocks

- ❏ Avoid render functions

- ❏ Use the `Call` keyword for calling functions, to force the use of parentheses around arguments

- ❏ Avoid default properties, such as `Recordset("column")` instead of `Recordset.Fields("column").Value`

- ❏ Explicitly close open resources (such as the file system or recordsets)

These are only relevant to server-side code – client-side code is still browser related.

Many of these are best practices anyway, but we all tend to take shortcuts. Adhering to this list will ease your migration path. You'll be looking at these in detail as you go through the chapter.

Intrinsic Objects

Most ASP intrinsic objects remain available and unchanged, providing excellent support for existing applications. However, there are changes to some properties and methods, as well as the addition of new ones. One significant change is the removal of the `ASPError` object, as error handling is now managed by exceptions.

The Application Object

ASP.NET application state handling is implemented by the `HttpApplicationState` class in the `System.Web` namespace. Although ASP.NET supports ASP functionality by way of the `Contents` and `StaticObjects` collections, there are some minor differences that may confuse you if you check the documentation. The reason is `HttpApplicationState` is a first class object that implements a collection (used to hold the items in application state). Therefore methods such as `Remove` and `RemoveAll` are members of the `HttpApplicationState` object itself. However, to preserve compatibility, there is also a `Contents` property, which simply points back to the parent object. Thus, the following lines of code are equivalent.

In VB.NET, the code is:

```
Application.Remove("Item1")
Application.Contents.Remove("Item1")
```

The code in C# is:

```
Application.Remove("Item1");
Application.Contents.Remove("Item1");
```

The first line in these code examples is what you'd see in .NET code samples, whereas the second line is how you'd do it in ASP. However, because compatibility has been preserved, they both work.

New features of the application object are shown in the following table. Note that although there are explicit `Add` and `Get` methods, the existing way of accessing the collection still works fine:

Property/Method	Description
AllKeys	Returns an array of strings containing the names of stored application state members.
Count	Returns a count of items in application state.
Add	Adds a new item to the state.
Clear	Removes all items from the state. This is equivalent to RemoveAll, and is provided as part of the standard collection handling features.
Get	Returns an individual item (either by name or by ordinal).
GetKey	Returns the key for the supplied ordinal.
Set	Updates the value of a stored item.

Objects in Application State

In ASP it was always taboo to store single-threaded objects in application state, which was a real problem for Visual Basic programmers developing components. Given that the .NET languages (including Visual Basic) allow the production of free-threaded components, has this problem now gone away? Well, to a degree yes, as long as you understand the following:

❑ You can store free-threaded components as long as they provide thread synchronization.

❑ You can store single-threaded components if you use Lock and Unlock to protect against thread blocks.

❑ Application state has no guaranteed durability. The application domain can be torn down at any time (synchronized restart for example), so for durability you need an external store.

By and large, the storage of objects in Application state is discouraged because of the resources used, and the potential for scalability and performance problems. However, the storage of scalar type data (such as string) is a great way to get some performance improvement, as long as it is used carefully. You might think that the classic case of wanting to store Recordsets in application state is now easy, since you can store the XML from a DataSet, but remember that memory (although cheap) is finite. Frequent use of a 10Mb set of data stored in application state may give great benefits, but 100Mb may not. This sort of scenario needs full testing before the implications are really known.

The Session Object

Session state is implemented by the HttpSessionState class in the System.Web.SessionState namespace. The Contents and StaticObjects follow the same rules as Application state – the structure of the class is different from ASP, but access works in the same way. Thus, the following examples are equivalent. In VB.NET:

```
Session.Remove("Item1")
Session.Contents.Remove("Item"1)
```

In C#:

```
Session.Remove("Item1");
Session.Contents.Remove("Item1");
```

The *changed* and new features of the session object are shown in the following table:

Property/Method	Description
Count	Returns a count of items in session state.
IsCookieless	Indicates whether or not session state is being handled in a cookieless manner.
IsNewSession	Indicates whether or not the session has been created with the current request.
IsReadOnly	Indicates whether or not the session is read -only.
IsSynchronized	Indicates whether or not access to the session state values is thread safe.
Mode	Indicates how session state is being stored. Will contain one of the SessionStateMode constants: InProc, for in process Off, for no session state StateServer, for the out -of -process state service SQLServer, for SQL Server
SessionID	In ASP.NET the SessionID property returns a String (as opposed to a Long in ASP)
SyncRoot	An object that provides synchronous access to the session contents.
Add	Adds a new item to the session state.
Clear	Removes all items from the session state. This is equivalent to RemoveAll, and is provided as part of the standard collection handling features.
CopyTo	Copies the contents of the session state to an array of strings.
Equals	Compares an object in session state with the supplied one to see if they are the same.
Remove	In ASP, the Remove method could take either the key name of the item or its index. In ASP.NET, you can only supply the name. To remove by index use the RemoveAt method.
RemoveAt	Removes an item at the selected ordinal.

The Request Object

The request is implemented by the `HttpRequest` class in the `System.Web` namespace. All of the existing properties and methods are supported, although there are some notable exceptions regarding the use of collections (see in the following table) where the appropriate ASP 3.0 `ServerVariables` equivalent has been mentioned. New and *changed* properties or methods are detailed in corresponding fonts as follows:

Property	Description
AcceptTypes	Returns a string array of the MIME types supported by the client. For ASP this could be extracted from the comma separated `ServerVariables` `HTTP_ACCEPT` entry.
ApplicationPath	The virtual application path.
Browser	Returns an `HttpBrowserCapabilities` object describing the features of the browser.
ClientCertificate	Returns an `HttpClientCertificate` object (as opposed to an array of values in ASP).
ContentEncoding	The character set of the entity body.
ContentLength	The length (in bytes) of the request. Equivalent to `CONTENT_LENGTH`.
ContentType	The MIME type of the request. Equivalent to `CONTENT_TYPE`.
Cookies	Returns an `HttpCookieCollection` object (as opposed to an array of values in ASP).
FilePath	The virtual path of the request. Equivalent to `SCRIPT_NAME`.
Files	Returns an `HttpFileCollection` of uploaded files (for multi-part form posts).
Filter	Identifies the stream filter to use for the request. All content will be passed through the filter before being accessible by the page.
Form	Returns a collection (`NameValueCollection`) of `Form` contents. Accessing this collection is different from accessing the `Form` collection under ASP (see the *Request Collections* sections).
Headers	A collection (`NameValueCollection`) of HTTP headers. In ASP these values are space -separated *name*: *value* pairs; in .NET they can be accessed via `HTTP_name`.
HttpMethod	The HTTP method used for the request. Equivalent to `REQUEST_METHOD`.
InputStream	A `Stream` containing the input for the request.

Table continued on following page

Property	Description
IsAuthenticated	Indicates whether or not the user has been authenticated.
IsSecureConnection	Indicates whether or not the connection is using HTTPS. Equivalent to HTTPS in ASP.
Params	A combined collection of QueryString, Form, ServerVariables, and Cookies.
Path	The virtual path of the request. Equivalent to PATH_INFO.
PathInfo	Additional path information.
Physical ApplicationPath	The physical path of the application root. Equivalent to APPL_PHYSICAL_PATH.
PhysicalPath	The physical path of the request. Equivalent to PATH_TRANSLATED.
QueryString	Returns a collection (NameValueCollection) of QueryString contents. Accessing this collection is different from accessing the QueryString collection under ASP (see the *Request Collections* section later in the chapter).
RawUrl	The raw URL of the request. Equivalent to RAW_URL.
RequestType	The HTTP method used for the request. Equivalent to REQUEST_METHOD.
TotalBytes	The number of bytes in the input stream.
Url	A Uri object containing details of the request. A Uri object (from the System namespace) encapsulates information about a specific resource, such as port and DNS information.
UrlReferrer	A Uri object detailing referrer information.
UserAgent	The browser user agent string. Equivalent to HTTP_USER_AGENT.
UserHostAddress	The IP address of the user. Equivalent to REMOTE_ADDR.
UserHostName	The DNS name of the user. Equivalent to REMOTE_NAME.
UserLangauges	An array of langauges preferences. Equivalent to HTTP_ACCEPT_LANGUAGE.
BinaryRead	Returns a Byte array containing the binary information sent to the server. In ASP the return type is variant.
MapImage Coordinates	Maps the image -field parameter to *x* and *y* coordinates.

Property	Description
MapPath	Maps the virtual path to a physical path. The method is now overloaded taking two forms. The first is the same as ASP where the parameter is the URL of the virtual path. The second takes three parameters: the virtual path, the virtual base directory for relative resolution, and a `Boolean` indicating whether or not the virtual path may belong to another application.
SaveAs	Saves the HTTP request to disk.

Some of this information is still available through the `ServerVariables` collection, but has now been abstracted out into more accessible properties.

The `Request` object supports collections for accessing the contents of a form or query string, and there are some major implications where those contents contain elements of the same name. This is typically the case where check boxes, radio buttons, or multi-select list boxes are used. For example, consider the following ASP form:

```
<form action="foo.asp" method="post">
  Select your favorite editor:
  <select name="editor" multiple="multiple">
    <option>Notepad
    <option>Textpad
    <option>Visual Studio .NET
  </select>
  <p/>
  <input type="submit" value="Send">
</form>
```

To extract the selected values from the multi-select list you could use:

```
For item = 1 To Request.Form("editor").Count
  Response.Write Request.Form("editor")(item) & "<br/>"
Next
```

However, this code will not work in ASP.NET, as a `NameValueCollection` represents the form contents. There are two points about this:

❑ The collection is zero based

❑ You have to explicitly get the values

For example:

```
Dim item As Integer
For item = 0 To Request.Form.GetValues("editor").Length - 1
  Response.Write (Request.Form.GetValues("editor")(item) & "<br/>")
Next
```

Here you have to use the GetValues() method of the collection, and index into that (using a base of 0) to get the required value.

The Response Object

The response to a request is implemented by the HttpResponse class. Like the request, all existing functionality is kept, with the following *changes* or additions:

Property/Method	Description
BufferOutput	Indicates whether or not to buffer output. This is the same as the Buffer property, and is the preferred method of changing buffering in ASP.NET.
Cache	Returns an HttpCachePolicy object, containing details about the caching policy of the current response.
CacheControl	Although still supported, this property is deprecated in favor of the HttpCachePolicy methods.
ContentEncoding	Identifies the character set of the output. The value can be one of those listed in the Encoding enumeration (ASCIIEncoding, UnicodeEncoding, UTF7Encoding, UTF8Encoding).
Cookies	Returns a collection (HttpCookieCollection) of HttpCookie objects (as opposed to an array of attributed values in ASP). The ASP cookie attributes appear as properties of the HttpCookie object.
Expires	Although still supported, this property is deprecated in favor of the HttpCachePolicy methods.
ExpiresAbsolute	Although still supported, this property is deprecated in favor of the HttpCachePolicy methods.
Filter	The Stream object that acts as the output filter. All output will go through this filter before being returned to the client.
Output	Returns a TextWriter object through which custom output can be returned to the client.
OutputStream	Returns a Stream object representing the raw data of the content body.
Status	Sets the HTTP status code to return to the client. This property has been deprecated in favor of the StatusDescription property.
StatusCode	The HTTP status code of the response.

Property/Method	Description
SuppressContent	Indicates whether or not content is to be returned to the client.
AddFileDependencies	Adds a group of file names to the dependency list upon which the response is based. Changes to these files will invalidate the output cache.
AddFileDependency	Adds a single file name to the dependency list upon which the response is based. Changes to this file will invalidate the output cache.
AddHeader	This method has been deprecated in favor of the AppendHeader method.
AppendHeader	Appends an HTTP header to the content stream. This method is preferred over AddHeader.
ApplyAppPathModifier	Applies the Cookieless Session ID to a given relative or virtual path. This allows HREFS with fully qualified names to be modified to include the current Session ID.
BinaryWrite	Writes binary data (a Byte array) to the output stream. In ASP this is a variant array.
ClearContent	Clears the content from the buffer stream.
ClearHeaders	Clears the headers from the buffer stream.
Close	Closes the socket connection to the client.
Redirect	This method is now overloaded. The first form is the same as ASP, taking a URL, and the second form takes a URL and a Boolean indicating whether or not Response.End is called after the redirection.
Write	This method is overloaded, and can take one of four sets of parameters: A Char An Object A String A Char array, along with the start index and number of characters to write
WriteFile	Writes the specified file directly to the output stream.

The Server Object

The `Server` object is implemented by the `HttpServerUtility` class in the `System.Web` namespace. The additions and *changes* are detailed as follows:

Property/Method	Description
MachineName	Returns the name of the server.
ClearError	Clears the previous exception.
CreateObject	This method is now overloaded. The original form taking a string of the `ProgID` is still allowed, as well as the new form taking a `Type` object.
CreateObjectFromClsid	Creates an instance of a COM object from the Class identifier (`CLSID`).
Execute	This method is now overloaded. The original form taking a string of the path of the new request is still allowed, as well as the new form taking the path and a `TextWriter` used to capture the output. This allows requests to be executed and then manipulated.
GetLastError	This now returns an `Exception` object (as opposed to an `ASPError` object in ASP).
HtmlDecode	Decodes an HTML encoded string.
HtmlEncode	This method is now overloaded, with an additional form taking a `string` to encode and a `TextWriter` into which the encoded text should be placed.
Transfer	This method is now overloaded, with an additional form taking a `string` for the path, and a `Boolean` to indicate whether or not the `Form` and `QueryString` collections should be preserved across the transfer.
UrlDecode	Decodes an HTML encoded URL.
UrlPathEncode	Encodes only the URL portion of a string (as opposed to `UrlEncode` which encode the URL and any `QueryString`).
UrlEncode	This method is now overloaded, with an additional form taking a `string` of the URL to encode, and a `TextWriter` into which the encoded URL is placed.

The ASPError Object

The `ASPError` object has been removed, as errors are now represented by exceptions. For example, the following code extracts the last error:

```
Dim lastError As Exception
lastError = Server.GetLastError()
Response.Write("Error was: " & lastError.Message)
```

The ObjectContext Object

The `ObjectContext` object in ASP is designed for the integration of ASP pages with external transacted components, such as those in *Microsoft Transaction Server (MTS)* or COM+ Services. Within ASP.NET you have the ability to run pages with *ASP Page Compatibility*, by setting a page directive:

```
<%@ Page AspCompat="true" %>
```

This allows the page to be run on a single threaded apartment (STA) thread, allowing it to call STA components, such as those written in VB6. This is particularly useful for those components that reference the ASP intrinsic objects and generate HTML.

The Page Object

The `Page` object (in the `System.Web.UI` namespace) was not a part of ASP, but plays an important role in ASP.NET. The `Page` is the parent object for the objects mentioned above, apart from the `ObjectContext`. Many of the features of the page you'll already have seen (such as the `IsPostBack` and `IsValid` properties), and the rest are extensively documented in the help files. We mention this object here in case you see code such as `Page.Session`, `Page.Response`, or `Page.Request`, and wonder how the objects relate.

Page Changes

Along with changes to the common objects, the structure and usage of ASP pages have changed. You've already seen how the event model and postback architecture changes the layout of pages, so what you'll concentrate on here are the things that need changing from existing ASP pages.

Single Language Per Page

I've never actually seen any code that used more than one server-side language, but with ASP.NET you must use a single language per page. If you need to use multiple languages you'll have to use User Controls or custom controls, which can be in any language.

The single language per page rule only affects individual pages – multiple pages in an application can be in different languages.

Script Blocks

Procedures in ASP.NET pages have to reside within proper script tags. So, the following is no longer allowed:

```
<%
  Sub Foo()
    ...
  End Sub
%>
```

Instead you must use:

```
<script language="VB" runat="server">
  Sub Foo()
    ...
  End Sub
</script>
```

You can still use the `<% %>` tags for inline placement of variables or function results.

Code Render Functions

The changes to script block usage mean that render functions are no longer allowed. Render functions are where the body of a function actually contains HTML. For example:

```
<% Sub ShowSeparator() %>
  <img src="sep.gif" width="100%"></img>
<% End Sub %>
```

This now has to be:

```
<script language="VB" runat="server">
  Sub ShowSeparator()
    Response.Write("<img src='sep.gif' width='100%'></img>")
  End Sub
</script>
```

Language Changes

One of the major changes in .NET has been in the use of languages. You looked at the specifics of these in Chapter 2, but let's reiterate some of them here.

Visual Basic probably has the changes that affect people most, purely because most ASP pages are written in VBScript. Microsoft made a brave (but correct) move in updating the language – breaking functionality in certain areas and adding functionality in others. The main reasons for this are to bring Visual Basic into the fold of the .NET CLR, and to take the opportunity to update the language with some much-needed features.

The details listed in Chapter 2 regarding Visual Basic related to the language as a whole. This section looks at the differences between VBScript and Visual Basic .NET and the sort of things you'll need to change when migrating applications.

Variables and Strong Typing

The first point is that VBScript is no longer used as it is replaced by Visual Basic .NET. This means you now have the ability to have data types. For example:

```
Dim Name As String
Dim Age  As Integer
```

The second point about variables is that by default they have to be declared, as the `explicit` option is set to `true`. You can set this option on a page-by-page basis by:

```
<%@ Page Explicit="False" %>
```

Alternatively it can be set in the `web.config` file:

```
<compilation explicit="false"/>
```

As a general rule, explicit variable declaration is better, as it reduces the potential for errors.

Variant and Data Type Conversion

The `Variant` data type has been removed, and replaced by a generic `Object`. For example, in VBScript you could do this:

```
Dim o
o = 1
Response.Write "o=" & o & "<br/>"
o = "hello"
Response.Write "o=" & o & "<br/>"
```

And the output would be:

o=1
o=hello

In Visual Basic .NET, you can declare a variable as type `Object`, although the effect this has depends on whether you have strict typing enabled or not. This can be set either at the page level with:

```
<%@ Page Strict="True" %>
```

or in the `web.config` file:

```
<compilation strict="true"/>
```

Without strict typing the following code works fine:

```
Dim o As Object
o = 1
Response.Write("o=" & o & "<br/>")
o = "hello"
Response.Write("o=" & o & "<br/>")
```

That's because the object type automatically converts its value to a `string`. With strict typing, however, the code needs to be changed to:

```
Dim o As Object
o = 1
Response.Write("o=" & o.ToString() & "<br/>")
o = "hello"
Response.Write("o=" & o.ToString() & "<br/>")
```

Automatic conversion cannot be done on the `Object` type with strict conversion, so you have to convert explicitly. Implicit conversion is limited to widening, for example from an `Integer` to a `Long`.

Explicit Type Conversion

To perform data type conversion use the `CType` function or the `cast` keywords:

```
CType (expression, DataType)
```

The *expression* is the variable to be converted, and *DataType* is the new type. For example:

```
Dim d As Double = 123.456
Dim i As Integer = CType(d, Integer)
```

The alternative method of conversion is to use the cast types:

```
Dim i As Integer = CInt(d)
```

Since every primitive data type ultimately inherits from `Object`, you can also utilize the `ToString()` method provided by `Object`. For example:

```
Dim d As Double = 123.456
Response.Write(d.ToString())
```

There is also a `Convert` class (in the `System` namespace), which provides methods for data type conversions.

Methods

The main change to methods has been the way in which they are called. In Visual Basic .NET all methods must be surrounded by parentheses, as opposed to VBScript, where parentheses were only required for functions. For example, the following is no longer allowed:

```
Response.Write "Hello there"
```

And has to be replaced by:

```
Response.Write("Hello there")
```

This has its biggest impact when switching between the ASP and ASP.NET environments.

Method Arguments

By default, arguments to methods in Visual Basic .NET are now passed by value, rather than by reference. Thus the following code will not work as expected:

```
Sub Foo(X As Integer)
   X = X + 1
End Sub
Dim Y As Integer = 3
Foo(Y)
Response.Write("Y=" & Y.ToString())
```

The output here will be 3, rather than 4. To correct this you need to change the procedure declaration to:

```
Sub Foo(ByRef X As Integer)
```

Default Properties

The use of default properties is not allowed in Visual Basic .NET. This doesn't affect .NET components, since there's no way to define a default property, but it has an impact when accessing COM objects. For example, the following would not be allowed:

```
Dim rs   As New ADODB.Recordset
Dim Name As String
rs.Open("...", "...")
Name = rs("Name")
```

The last line in .NET would be:

```
Name = rs("Name").Value
```

This means more typing, but makes the code much more explicit, and therefore less prone to errors.

Set and Let

The Set and Let keywords are no longer required for object references. For example, the following is now the accepted syntax:

```
Dim conn As SQLConnection
conn = SQLConnection
```

Single and Multiple Lines

In Visual Basic .NET, all If statements must be constructed across multiple lines. For example, in VBScript you could do this:

```
If x > y Then foo()
```

In Visual Basic .NET this becomes:

```
If x > y Then
   foo()
End If
```

Interoperability

No matter how much you'd like to do all your coding in .NET, you have to face reality. There is an enormous amount of traditional ASP and COM code being used, and businesses cannot afford to just throw that away. The success of MTS/COM+ Services as a middle-tier business object layer has led to a large number of COM objects being used as data layers, abstracting the data management code from the ASP code. With .NET, Microsoft has provided good interoperability for several reasons:

❑ **To preserve existing investment**: Compatibility with existing applications means you can continue to use existing code, as well as preserve your existing investment.

❑ **Incremental migration**: There is no need to migrate everything at once if your new code can exist alongside other applications.

❑ **Some code will never change**: There is probably plenty of code where the investment, time, or skill to migrate is not available.

Although .NET is independent from COM, Microsoft realized the need for interoperability, and provided ways to use COM objects from within .NET, and also .NET components from within COM. They've realized that there had to be a way to call down to the Windows API, for those that need to.

This chapter gives an introduction into the interoperability issues. For a detailed look consult the book *Professional Visual Basic Interoperability - COM and VB6 to .NET, ISBN 1 -861005 -65 -2, by Apress.*

This chapter uses the term COM as a generic term for COM and COM+ purely to improve legibility.

Crossing the Boundary

You know that .NET code is managed by the CLR, and that COM code is not, so there has to be some way to cross the managed/unmanaged code boundary. This is one of the major problems is the conversion of data types, but the CLR handles this for us, as shown in Figure 23 -1:

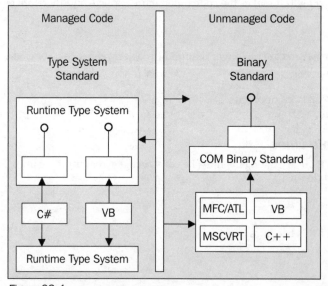

Figure 23-1

When crossing this boundary you have to think about the differences between the two systems. Architecturally, these are:

Unmanaged Code has ...	Managed Code has ...
Binary standard	Type standard
Type libraries	Meta data
Immutable types	Version binding
DLL hell	Versioned assemblies
Interface based	Object based
HResults	Exceptions
GUIDS	String names

Additionally, the programming differences are as follows:

Unmanaged Code has ...	Managed Code has ...
CoCreateInstance	new operator
QueryInterface	Cast operator
Reference counting	Memory management and garbage collection
GetProcAddress	Static methods

The unmanaged way of doing things doesn't affect ASP or ASP.NET, but does affect those of you who also write COM and use components.

Data Type Marshalling

When you cross the managed/unmanaged boundary, the wrappers automatically perform data type mapping for you. So, although you don't need to know how this works, it's useful to see what language types map to in .NET. There are two kinds of data types as far as marshalling goes:

❑ **Blittable types**: These are the same on both sides of the boundary, and therefore don't need any conversion.

❑ **Non-Blittable types**: These are different on either side of the boundary, and therefore require conversion.

The following table details the pre-.NET data types, and what they map into in .NET:

C++	Visual Basic 6	.NET	Blittable
signed char	Not supported	SByte	Yes
unsigned char	Byte	Byte	Yes
short	Integer	Short	Yes
unsigned short	Not supported	UInt16	Yes
int	Long	Integer	Yes
unsigned int	Not supported	UInt32	Yes
__int64	Not supported	Long	Yes
unsigned __int64	Not supported	UInt64	Yes
float	Single	Single	Yes
double	Double	Double	Yes
BSTR	String	String	No
BOOL	Boolean	Boolean	No
VARIANT	Variant	Object	No
IUnknown	object	UnmanagedType.IUknown	No
DATE	Date	Date	No
CURRENCY	Currency	Decimal	No
__wchar_t	Char	Char	Yes
void	Not supported	Void	Yes
HANDLE	Long	IntPtr	Yes

Simple arrays (single dimensional arrays of blittable types) are themselves defined as blittable types.

Custom Type Marshalling

For blittable types, the marshaller always knows both the managed and unmanaged type, but this isn't so for non-blittable types (such as strings or multi-dimensional arrays). By default the following conversion takes place:

Managed Type	Unmanaged Type
Boolean	A 2 or 4 byte value (VARIANT_BOOL or Win32 BOOL); True being 1 or –1.
Char	A Unicode or ANSI char (Win32 CHAR or CHAR).
String	A Unicode or ANSI char array (Win32 LPWSTR/LPSTR), or a BSTR.
Object	A Variant or an interface.
Class	A class interface.
Value Type	Structure with fixed memory layout.
Array	Interface or a SafeArray.

For non-blittable types, you can specify how they are marshalled across the boundary. This is really beyond the scope of this book, but is well detailed in the .NET SDK help file, under Programming with the .NET Framework, Interoperating with Unmanaged Code, and Data Marshalling.

HRESULTS

In Windows, the standard method of handling errors is via the use of HRESULTS. When crossing the boundary to .NET these are automatically converted to exceptions, with the HRESULT details being stored as part of the exception object. This means you can use COM objects without sacrificing the structured exception handling in .NET. For this to work the COM object must support the ISupportErrorInfo and IErrorInfo interfaces.

Using COM Objects from .NET

Using COM components from .NET is extremely simple, as there is a tool that takes a COM component or type library and creates a managed assembly (a callable wrapper) to manage the boundary transition for you. Figure 23-2 shows how this wrapper is used:

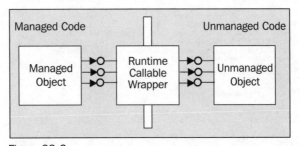

Figure 23-2

From the programming perspective all you have to do is call methods and access properties as you would with the COM component. The difference is that you'll be calling the wrapper class, which will take the .NET types, convert them to COM types, and call the COM interface methods. The CLR maintains the reference to the COM object, so COM reference counting works as expected, while also providing the simplicity of garbage collected references for the .NET usage of the object.

There are several ways in which you can generate the wrapper class:

❑   Adding a reference in Visual Studio .NET

❑   Using the type library import tool

❑   Using the type library convert class

❑   Creating a custom wrapper

Of these, the first two are by far the easiest.

Using Visual Studio .NET

In Visual Studio .NET all you have to do is create a reference to the COM object, and the wrapper class is created for you. First, select References from the Solution Explorer, and then pick Add Reference..., as shown in Figure 23-3:

Figure 23-3

Then, from the dialog that appears, select the COM tab, and pick your COM object, as shown in Figure 23-4:

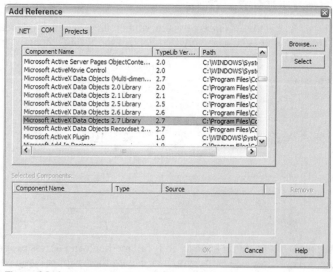

Figure 23-4

Once you've clicked **Select** and then **OK**, the reference is added. The wrapper class (in this case it would be `ADODB.dll`) is placed in the `bin` directory of the application.

The Type Library Import Tool

If you don't have Visual Studio .NET (or are a die-hard Notepad user) then you can use the type library import tool to create the wrapper class for you. The syntax is:

```
tlbimp TypeLibrary [Options]
```

where *Options* can be:

Option	Description
/out:FileName	The filename of the wrapper assembly to create.
/namespace:Namespace	Namespace of the assembly to be produced.
/asmversion:version	Version number of the assembly to be produced.
/reference:FileName	Assembly filename used to resolve references. This can be specified multiple times for multiple references.
/publickey:FileName	Filename containing the strong name public key.
/keyfile:FileName	Filename containing the strong name key pair.
/keycontainer:FileName	Key container holding the strong name key pair.
/delaysign	Force strong name delay signing.
/unsafe	Produce an interface without runtime security checks.
/nologo	Don't display the logo.
/silent	Don't display output, except for errors.
/sysarray	Map COM `SafeArray` to the .NET `System.Array` class.
/verbose	Display full information.
/primary	Produce a primary interop assembly.
/strictref	Only use assemblies specified with `/reference`.

By default the output name will be the same as the COM type library, not the filename. For example:

```
tlbimp msado15.dll
```

will produce a wrapper assembly called `ADODB.dll`, *not* `msado15.dll`. The resulting assembly can then be copied into the application `bin` directory (or installed in the Global Assembly Cache), and referenced as with other .NET assemblies:

```
<%@ Import Namespace="ADODB" %>
```

The Type Library Convert Class

The `System.Runtime.InteropServices` namespace contains a class called `TypeLibConverter`, which provides methods to convert COM classes and interfaces into assembly meta data. This is really only useful if you are building tools that examine COM type libraries at runtime, and is outside the scope of this book.

Custom Wrappers

If your COM component doesn't have a type library then it's possible to create a custom wrapper that directly calls the COM component. This is outside the scope of the book, but for more information, see the topics "Programming with the .NET Framework", "Interoperating with Unmanaged Code", and "Customizing Standard Wrappers" in the SDK help file.

Using the Wrapper Assembly

Using the wrapper assembly is simply a case of treating it like any other managed assembly. For example, if you import the ADO namespace, you can use it in your ASP.NET pages like so:

```
<%@ Import Namespace="ADODB" %>
<html>
<script language="VB" runat="server">
  Sub Page_Load(Sender As Object, e as EventArgs)
    Dim rs As New ADODB.Recordset
    rs.Open("publishers", "Provider=SQLOLEDB; Data Source=.; " & _
                          "Initial Catalog=pubs; User Id=sa")
    While Not rs.EOF
      Response.Write(rs.Fields("pub_name").Value & "<br/>")
      rs.MoveNext()
    End While
    rs.Close
  End Sub

</script>
</html>
```

Deploying Applications That Use COM

However great the COM interoperability story is, it doesn't get around the fact that COM components need to be registered. This is not a fault of .NET, more an issue of the way COM works, and you don't need to do anything other than the standard COM registration. However, the big problem this causes is with the xcopy deployment model, for which it isn't suitable. You can still xcopy the deployment, but you'd need to provide some form of script to register the COM components before the application is activated.

Using .NET Components from COM

The interoperability story doesn't end with using COM code in .NET, as the reverse is also possible. This allows the new language and class features to be used, but without getting rid of old applications. The workings of the wrapper class are shown in Figure 23-5 – it marshals the COM calls through to the managed object:

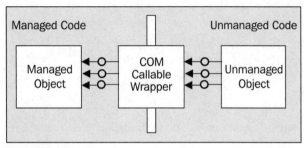

Figure 23-5

The story is very similar to its opposite that was just examined, as COM type libraries are created for the .NET assemblies. The difference is that there's slightly more work, as you have to explicitly decide which interfaces and methods you want exposed to COM. This is a crucial point, because for .NET components to be available in COM they have to have an *Interface* (see Chapter 3 for more details on Interfaces), and there are two ways to have this exposed – manually or automatically. Manually Created Interfaces

Manually creating interfaces means you use the language features to explicitly declare the interface. For example, consider a `Person` class with two properties (`FirstName` and `LastName`) and one method (`FullName`). The interface and class in Visual Basic .NET could be defined as follows:

```vb
Public Interface IPersonVB
   Property FirstName() As String
   Property LastName()  As String
   Function FullName()  As String
End Interface

Public Class PersonVB
   Implements IPersonVB
   Private _firstName As String
   Private _lastName  As String

   Public Sub New()
      ' default constructor - required for interop
   End Sub

   Public Property FirstName() As String Implements IPersonVB.FirstName
      Get
         FirstName = _firstName
      End Get
      Set
         _firstName = value
      End Set
```

```
      End Property

   Public Property LastName() As String Implements IPersonVB.LastName
      Get
         LastName = _lastName
      End Get
      Set
         _lastName = value
      End Set
   End Property

   Public Function FullName() As String Implements IPersonVB.FullName
      Return _firstName & " " & _lastName
   End Function
End Class
```

One thing to notice is that the class must have a public default constructor. In C#, the interface and class could be defined as follows:

```csharp
public interface IPersonCS
{
   string FirstName{get; set;}
   string LastName{get; set;}
   string FullName();
}

public class PersonCS : IPersonCS
{
   private string _firstName;
   private string _lastName;

   // default constructor - required for interop
   public PersonCS() {}

   public string FirstName
   {
      get { return _firstName; }
      set { _firstName = value; }
   }

   public string LastName
   {
      get { return _lastName; }
      set { _lastName = value; }
   }

   public string FullName()
   {
      return _firstName + " " + _lastName;
   }
}
```

Automatic Interfaces

The alternative approach is to use the *Interop Services* attributes to have an interface automatically created from the class. To do this you must use the `InteropServices` namespace, and then add an attribute in front of the class. This attribute will be one of the `ClassInterfaceType` attributes, which can be one of:

Attribute	Description
None	No class interface is generated for the class. Using COM `QueryInterface` for `IDispatch` will fail. An interface needs to be manually created.
AutoDispatch	An interface that supports `IDispatch` is created for the class. However, no type information is produced, so `DispIds` cannot be cached.
AutoDual	A dual interface is created for the class. `Typeinfo` is produced and made available in the type library.

The use of this attribute form in Visual Basic .NET is as follows:

```
Imports System.Runtime.InteropServices
<ClassInterfaceAttribute(ClassInterfaceType.AutoDual)> _
Public Class PersonVB
```

And in C#, it is:

```
using System.Runtime.InteropServices;
[ClassInterfaceAttribute(ClassInterfaceType.AutoDual)]
public class PersonCS
```

The attribute can also be applied to the assembly, whereby it affects all classes within it.

In addition to the `ClassInterfaceAttribute`, there are others that control how various parts of the assembly are exposed to COM. For example, the attribute `GuidAttribute` allows you to specify the GUID of the exposed item (class, interface, or assembly), and `ComVisibleAttribute` can be used to hide .NET types from COM.

Attributes that relate to the marshalling of data are covered in the API Calls section, a little later in the chapter, while the others are fully covered in the SDK help, under "Programming with the .NET Framework", "Interoperating with Unmanaged Code", "Exposing .NET Framework Components to COM", and "Applying Interop Attributes".

Which Interface Method to Use

You've seen that there are three forms of interface creation, and each has its own advantages and disadvantages. The real problem that arises is that of versioning – as COM interfaces are immutable, and .NET has the ability to bind to version interfaces. So, the type of interface you expose to COM depends on how your .NET components are going to change over time. For example, consider the following code blocks.

In Visual Basic .NET:

```
Public Class A
   Public Sub Foo()
   End Sub
End Class
Public Class B
     Inherits A
   Public Sub Foo()
   End Sub
End Class
```

In C#:

```
public class A
{
   public void Foo(){}
}
public class B : A
{
   public void Foo(){}
}
```

Since class interfaces do not support versioning, consider what happens if class A is updated to version 2 by adding a new method. Managed users of the class are unaffected, but for unmanaged users of either class A or class B the code will break. This affects both early-bound clients (who rely on the layout of the class interface being immutable) as well as late-bound clients (who use `DispIds`, which change between versions). So, there are great dangers in exposing class interfaces.

By and large the safest option is for the manual creation of interfaces – although it involves more work, you get complete control over the interface. The pros and cons of each method are explained in the following sections.

ClassInterfaceType.None and Manual Interface

Its advantages are as follows:

❑ There are no versioning problems because users can only call through explicitly created interfaces.

❑ The class author has full control over versioning of the class.

Its disadvantages are as follows:

❑ More work, as the interface has to be created manually for each class.

❑ No scripting support.

❑ Less design time support from some RAD tools.

ClassInterfaceType.AutoDispatch

Its advantages are as follows:

❑ No versioning problems because classes only support late binding, but without caching `DispIds`.

❑ Does not require user to create separate interface for each class.

❑ Supports scripting.

Its disadvantages are as follows:

❑ More work for class user.

❑ Less support in Visual Basic, as everything must be of type `Object`.

❑ Slower.

ClassInterfaceType.AutoDual

Advantages:

❑ No extra work for class author or user.

❑ Easy to use from all COM clients.

Disadvantage:

❑ Does not support versioning at all. Any class changes will break COM clients.

Exporting the Type Library

Once the .NET assembly has been created, you need to create a COM type library so that COM clients can set references to the classes. This is done using the Type Library Export tool, the syntax of which is:

```
tlbexp AssemblyName [Options]
```

where *Options* can be:

Option	Description
/out:*FileName*	The filename of the type library to create.
/names:*FileName*	Use the specified file to specify capitalization of names in the type library.
/nologo	Don't display the logo.
/silent	Don't display output, except for errors.
/verbose	Display full information.

For example, if the `Person` class were compiled into a `Person.dll` assembly, you would use:

```
tlbexp Person.dll
```

By default this creates `Person.tlb`.

Registering the DLL for Local Use

Once the type library is created, the class needs to be registered in the Registry. Even though it's a .NET class, which ordinarily doesn't require registration, its use with COM means the wrapper must be registered. The registration is done using the `regasm` tool:

```
regasm AssemblyName [Options]
```

where *Options* can be:

Option	Description
`/unregister`	Unregister the type.
`/tlb[:FileName]`	Export the assembly to the specified type library, and then register it.
`/regfile[:FileName]`	Generate a registry merge file with which the type library can be registered.
`/codebase`	Set the code base in the registry.
`/registered`	Only refer to type libraries that are already registered.
`/nologo`	Don't display the logo.
`/silent`	Don't display output, except for errors.
`/verbose`	Display full information.

For example, the `Person` class could be registered with:

```
ragasm Person.dll
```

You could also save on the explicit `tlbexp` step by doing:

```
regasm /tlb:Person.tlb Person.dll
```

This creates the type library and then registers it.

Once registered, the classes can be used as if they were COM-created classes. The DLL created must be in the same directory as the application executable.

Registering the DLL for Global Use

If you wish the .NET assembly to be used in multiple applications, then it must be registered in the Global Assembly Cache (GAC). This applies not only to .NET components used from .NET, but also to .NET components used from COM.

Generating a Strong Name

Before adding assemblies to the GAC they need to be strongly named. A *Strong Name* consists of the assembly identity (name, version, and culture), plus a public key and digital signature. A strong name is useful for several reasons:

- ❑ **Guarantees uniqueness**: Key pairs are globally unique, and no two will ever be the same.

- ❑ **Guarantees version protection**: Because the key pairs include a digital signature, they ensure protection against spoofed versions of code.

- ❑ **Guarantees code integrity**: The digital signature is part of the procedure that ensures code hasn't been changed since it was built.

You can create strong names with the sn utility, which has the following syntax:

```
sn [ -q(quiet)] Options [parameters]
```

There are plenty of options (detailed in the help), but the one we are interested in is the generation of key pairs:

```
sn -k Person.snk
```

This generates a key pair and stores it in the file named Person.snk. The suffix can be anything, although by convention it is .snk.

At this stage the assembly doesn't know anything about the strong name. To guarantee the link between the assembly and the strong name file you need to add an attribute to the assembly. In Visual Basic .NET:

```
<assembly:AssemblyKeyFile("Person.snk")> _
Namespace People
```

And in C#:

```
[assembly:AssemblyKeyFile("PersonCS.snk")]
namespace People
```

Installing in the Global Assembly Cache

Once the key pair has been constructed the assembly can be installed into the GACeither by using the:

- ❑ Windows Installer or

- ❑ Global Assembly Cache tool (gacutil).

Use the latter of these, with either the /i switch to install the assembly, or /u to uninstall the assembly. For example:

```
gacutil /i Person.dll
```

or:

```
gacutil /u Person
```

You can also use the /l option to list all assemblies in the cache. Alternatively, you can use the Assembly Cache Viewer (search the SDK for more information on this).

Using the .NET Component from COM

Once the .NET component is created and made available to COM (either in the application directory or the GAC), it's available for use. All you have to do is reference it in the usual way from the Project References dialog in Visual Studio. The component can then be used like so:

```
Dim p As New PersonVB.PersonVB
p.FirstName = "Dave"
p.LastName = "Sussman"
MsgBox p.FullName
```

API Calls

The compatibility story doesn't stop with COM, as .NET provides a way to access DLLs that aren't COM based, using the *Platform Invoke Services (P/Invoke)*. This gives you the ability to call APIs in a manner similar to the way Visual Basic 6 does it – by specifying the DLL and API call before it's used.

The Visual Basic .NET syntax is the same as Visual Basic 6:

```
Declare StringConversionType (Function | Sub) _
    MethodName Lib "DllName" ([Args]) As Type
```

Where:

❑ *StringConversionType* identifies the type of conversion that takes place for strings. This can be Ansi (the default) to convert all strings to ANSI values, Unicode to convert all strings to Unicode values, or Auto to convert strings according to the .NET runtime rules.

❑ *MethodName* is the name of the API to call.

❑ *DllName* is the name of the DLL.

❑ *Args* are any arguments to the API call.

❑ *Type* is the return type of the API call.

For example:

```
Declare Auto Function GetSystemMetrics _
            Lib "User32.dll" (nIndex As Integer) As Integer
```

You can place this within a class if you wish to encapsulate several API calls:

```
Namespace Wrox
  Public Class Metrics
    Declare Auto Function GetSystemMetrics _
               Lib "User32.dll" (nIndex As Integer) As Integer
  End Class
End Namespace
```

You can then call this API like so:

```
Dim mt  As New Metrics
Dim val As Integer
val = mt.GetSystemMetrics(SM_CXSCREEN)
```

Alternatively, you can wrap the API call in a class method, giving you the option of pre- or post-processing the data:

```
Namespace Wrox
  Public Class Metrics
    Declare Auto Function GetSystemMetrics _
               Lib "User32.dll" (nIndex As Integer) As Integer
    Public Function GetMetrics(Index As Integer) As Integer
      Return GetSystemMetrics(Index)
    End Function
  End Class
End Namespace
```

This approach allows you to wrap many API calls into a single class.

For C# use the DllImport attribute, using the following syntax:

```
[DllImport("LibraryName", CallingConvention := "CallingConvention", _
                         CharSet := "CharSet", _
                         EntryPoint := "EntryPoint", _
                         ExactSpelling := "ExactSpelling", _
                         PreserveSig := "PreserveSig", _
                         SetLastError := "SetLastError")> _
       static extern FunctionName(Arguments)
```

The fields of DllImport are detailed in the following table:

Field	Description
CallingConvention	Indicates the value to use when passing method arguments. This can be one of the CallingConvention enumerations: Cdecl, to use the __cdecl format, allowing the calling of functions with varargs.
	FastCall, to use the __fastcall format. This format is not supported by the initial release of the .NET Framework, but is included here for completeness.
	StdCall, to use the __stdcall format. This is the default for calling functions in unmanaged code.
	ThisCall, to use the this call format, for the calling of methods on classes exported from unmanaged code.
	Winapi, to use the default platform calling convention (StdCall on Windows or Cdecl on Windows CE).
	For Win32 API calls you should use StdCall, which is the default.
CharSet	Indicates the character set to use for names and string passing. This can be one of the CharSet enumerations:
	Ansi, to marshal strings as ANSI 1-byte characters.
	Auto, to automatically marshal strings appropriate to the target system.
	None, to indicate no specific marshalling.
	Unicode, to marshal string as Unicode 2-byte characters. This also appends the letter 'A' to the EntryPoint, in convention with many Windows API calls.
	The default is Ansi.
EntryPoint	The name, or ordinal, of the entry point in the DLL to be called.
ExactSpelling	Indicates whether or not the name of the EntryPoint should be modified to correspond with the CharSet. The default value is False.
PreserveSig	Indicates whether or not the HRESULT from the API call should be converted to a managed failure. The default is True.
SetLastError	Indicates whether or not the GetLastError API call can be called to determine if an error occurred. The default is False.

For many Win32 API calls you can accept the default values, for example:

```
[DllImport("User32.dll")]
static extern int GetSystemMetrics(int nIndex);
```

This can be wrapped in a class to allow external use:

```
namespace Wrox
{
  public class Metrics
  {
    [DllImport("User32.dll")]
    static extern int GetSystemMetrics(int nIndex);
  }
}
```

Alternatively you can wrap the API call in a class method, giving you the option of pre- or post-processing the data:

```
namespace Wrox
{
  public class Metrics
  {
    [DllImport("User32.dll")]
    static extern int GetSystemMetrics(int nIndex);
    public int GetMetrics(int Index)
    {
      return GetSystemMetrics(Index);
    }
  }
}
```

Using the API Class

Using this API class wrapper is just like using any other class. For example, consider the following ASP.NET page:

```
<%@ Import Namespace="Wrox" %>
<html>
<script Language="VB" runat="server">
  Sub Page_Load(Sender As Object, E As EventArgs)
    Dim mt     As New Metrics()
    Dim Width  As Integer = mt.GetMetrics(MetricsValues.SM_CXSCREEN)
    Dim Height As Integer = mt.GetMetrics(MetricsValues.SM_CYSCREEN)

    VBScreen.Text = "VB Screen = " & Width.ToString() & " * " & _
                                     Height.ToString()
  End Sub
</script>
<asp:Label id="Screen" runat="server"/>
</html>
```

This displays the current screen resolution of the server. The values passed into the `GetMetrics()` method are defined in the class as an `enum` (see the Platform SDK under **GetSystemMetrics** for more details on these).

Type Marshalling

When dealing with API calls you often have to pass structures into the call, and the structure gets filled with the appropriate information. When doing this you need to tell the CLR how the structure is going to be arranged in memory, so that it matches the equivalent Win32 structure. Use the StructLayout attribute to do this.

For example, consider the `GetSystemTime` API call in Visual Basic .NET:

```
<StructLayout(LayoutKind.Sequential)> Public Structure SystemTime
  Public wYear         As Short
  Public wMonth        As Short
  Public wDayOfWeek    As Short
  Public wDay          As Short
  Public wHour         As Short
  Public wMinute       As Short
  Public wSecond       As Short
  Public wMilliseconds As Short
End Structure
Public Class API
  Declare Auto Sub GetSystemTime _
               Lib "Kernel32.dll" (ByRef sysTime As SystemTime)
End Class
```

The API call could then be used like this:

```
Dim st As New SystemTime()
Dim t  As New API()
t.GetSystemTime(st)
Response.Write("Month = " & st.Month)
```

In C#, you also specify attributes on the API arguments:

```
[StructLayout(LayoutKind.Sequential)]
public class SystemTime
{
  public short wYear;
  public short wMonth;
  public short wDayOfWeek;
  public short wDay;
  public short wHour;
  public short wMinute;
  public short wSecond;
  public short wMilliseconds;
}
public class API
{
  [DllImport("Kernel32.dll")]
  public static extern void GetSystemTime(
```

```
                    [Out, MarshalAs(UnmanagedType.LPStruct)]SystemTime sysTime)
    }
```

The API call could then be used like this:

```
SystemTime st = new SystemTime();
API.GetSystemTime(st);
Response.Write("Month = " + st.Month);
```

Marshalling Attributes

The `StructLayout` attribute determines how the CLR aligns the members of a class, allowing them to line up with their unmanaged equivalent. The possible values are:

Type	Description
Automatic	Allows the runtime to choose the most appropriate layout.
Explicit	Used in conjunction with the `FieldOffsetAttribute` to allow exact positioning of each member.
Sequential	To layout members sequentially, in the order they are declared.

The `MarshalAs` attribute gives the CLR explicit instructions on how the type is to be marshalled. The possible values for the `UnmanagedType` enum are:

Type	Description
AnsiBStr	Length prefixed ANSI (single byte) character string.
AsAny	The type is determined at runtime.
Bool	4-byte Boolean, where `False` is 0, and `True` is not 0.
BStr	Length prefixed Unicode (double byte) character string.
ByValArray	An array of items whose type (an `UnmanagedType` value) is defined by the `ArraySubType` field.
ByValTStr	Fixed length character array within a structure.
Currency	Used to marshal a `System.Decimal` type to an unmanaged Currency type.
CustomMarshaller	A custom marshaller type.
Error	A signed or unsigned integer, equivalent to an `HRESULT`.
FunctionPtr	A function pointer.

Table continued on following page

Type	Description
I1	A 1 -byte signed integer.
I2	A 2 -byte signed integer.
I4	A 4 -byte signed integer.
I8	An 8 -byte signed integer.
IDispatch	A COM IDispatch pointer.
Interface	A COM interface pointer.
IUnknown	A COM IUnknown pointer.
LPArray	An array whose size is determined at runtime.
LPStr	An ANSI (single byte) character string.
LPStruct	A pointer to a C -style structure.
LPTStr	A platform -dependent character string (ANSI on Win9x, Unicode on NT/Windows 2000/XP).
LPWStr	A Unicode (double byte) character string.
R4	A 4 -byte floating point number.
R8	An 8 -byte floating point number.
RPrecise	Size agnostic floating point number.
SafeArray	A self -describing array.
Struct	A C -style structure.
SysInt	Platform -dependent signed integer (4 -bytes on 32 -bit Windows, 8 -bytes on 64 -bit Windows).
SysUInt	Hardware natural sized unsigned integer.
TBStr	Length prefixed platform -dependent character string (ANSI on Windows 9x, Unicode on Windows NT/2000/XP).
U1	A 1 -byte unsigned integer.
U2	A 2 -byte unsigned integer.
U4	A 4 -byte unsigned integer.
U8	An 8 -byte unsigned integer.
VariantBool	An 8 -byte unsigned integer.
VBByRefStr	Visual Basic specific array passed by reference.

Dangers of P/Invoke

When calling DLLs through the P/Invoke method, you should be aware that the CLR cannot apply any security checks to unmanaged code. With managed code you have great security control (safe types, no unmanaged memory, code security, versioning, and so on), but none of these are available in unmanaged code.

This issue shouldn't be confused with the integration of Windows Component Services security, which is covered in the *Serviced Components* section in Chapter 17.

Summary

There's no denying that .NET is an exceptional platform for application development. Throughout this book you've seen the great features ASP.NET provides for writing first-class applications, and how those applications will have less code, be more reusable, and provide easier maintenance. It would have been easy for Microsoft to leave it there, and just provide a great new platform, but the reality of life means that this platform has to interoperate with existing applications. There's a huge investment, not only in ASP, but also in Visual Basic and COM, and this cannot be thrown away.

So, Microsoft has provided a way to integrate that existing investment with new development on the .NET platform. In this chapter we've examined the differences between ASP and ASP.NET, and how moving from VBScript to Visual Basic .NET can be achieved with the least pain. We've also examined how to allow .NET to leverage existing COM infrastructures, as well as showing how COM can use .NET. So, if the features of .NET weren't enough to persuade you that this is a great platform, maybe the ability to run alongside existing applications will tip the balance.

Case Study
IBuyAdventure.NET

The previous chapters of this book have looked at the individual features of ASP.NET, such as web controls, data binding, configuration, and security. Powerful though they are, these features are like pieces of a jigsaw puzzle; the final objective is to figure out how to put them together to create the big picture.

This chapter will explain how to use ASP.NET to create a simple n-tier e-commerce application that is scalable, yet still relatively simple to code and understand. Along the way, the chapter will discuss and review:

- ❏ How to design and write an n-tier e-commerce application on the .NET platform

- ❏ Using HTML form-based authentication to secure an e-commerce application

- ❏ Scalability considerations when creating an e-commerce site that must scale in a web farm

- ❏ Using business objects to encapsulate business logic and data access

- ❏ Using 'code behind' to share common page logic

Overview of the Application

For those who can remember back to ASP 2.0, you may recall that it shipped with a sample application called *AdventureWorks*. This application allowed you to shop for climbing equipment suitable for extreme conditions. AdventureWorks featured all the basic features of a typical e-commerce application, including product viewing and selection, user registration, and a shopping basket. This chapter will use ASP.NET to extend the AdventureWorks application into a new one called *IBuyAdventure.NET*, or *IBA* for short. The rest of this chapter will review the code and the functionality of this application, and discuss some of the design decisions made while creating it.

All the files for the IBuyAdventure.NET application are available for download from the Wrox website, http://www.wrox.com/, and include set up and installation instructions.

IBuyAdventure.NET (IBA.NET)

If you haven't seen or used the old ASP AdventureWorks application before, don't worry. This chapter will be covering the IBA.NET application from the ground up, and you will only be porting a small subset of features from the original application. This approach will demonstrate how to use ASP.NET to create real world e-commerce applications, without getting distracted by too many application specific features that would simply dilute the goals of the chapter.

If you do have access to the original AdventureWorks application, spend some time comparing the original ASP code and ASP.NET code in this chapter. Sections such as the shopping basket and page layout code really show the power and simplicity of ASP.NET.

The Target Audience

The IBA.NET application is aimed at allowing climbing enthusiasts to check out and buy the latest climbing equipment over the Internet from the comfort of their home, or tent! The application will let customers view different products grouped by category (boots, pants, tents, and so on), and enable them to add items to their shopping cart at any time. The application uses just-in-time registration, so customers can fill their shopping carts with products and not have to register or login until they actually proceed to the checkout. This approach is pretty common on most major sites like Amazon.com, and is a must-have feature in any e-commerce application today.

Scalability – Web Solution Platform

The IBA.NET application needs to be *scalable* and capable of supporting hundreds, if not thousands, of concurrent users. To achieve this goal, the application has been designed according to the guidelines set by the *Microsoft Web Solution Platform* (http://microsoft.com/business/products/webplatform). The application therefore adopts an n-tier architecture as described by Windows DNA, where the application is split into a number of tiers for presentation, business logic, and data:

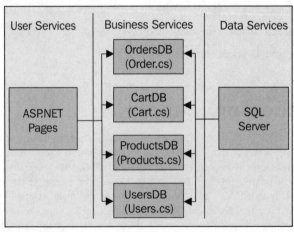

Figure 24-1

By adopting an n-tier approach, as shown in Figure 24-1, the IBuyAdventure.NET application can easily be deployed on a single machine or multiple machines (one or more physical tiers). Using this architecture it should be possible to deploy ASP.NET pages, .NET components, and SQL Server on their own dedicated servers. All the ASP.NET pages in IBuyAdventure.NET access the back end database using a set of .NET components that enforce business logic and encapsulate the underlying database. These components are fairly thin, and for the most part, simply wrap a series of ADO.NET routines, similar to those that were covered in Chapter 8, returning a `DataSet` from the methods that are called to retrieve data.

Designing for Enterprise Scalability

To cater for enterprise-level scalability (the use of web farms), the application uses *no* ASP.NET session level state. All state is either stored client side within hidden fields, or in the back end SQL Server database. When a user first visits the site, the ASP.NET session ID is used to track users and any shopping items they add to their shopping cart. This information is stored in the database, and the session ID is used as the primary key to identify the user.

While this is not normally recommended, the transient nature of the shopping cart data makes it pretty safe. Alternatively, the application could generate a GUID and use that to track the anonymous users. After registering or logging in, any references to the ASP.NET session ID stored in the database are updated with the customer name.

By taking this approach, the application can easily be deployed in a web farm without the need to use session state that is specific to an individual server. Each web server receiving a request can simply use the session ID or user name (provided by the forms based authentication) to look up user details and cart items from a central database.

> 'Sticky sessions' is a term used to describe ASP/ASP.NET user sessions that must always be redirected to the same front-end web server in a web farm. Generally, sticky sessions are required in applications that depend upon state stored in the `Session` object. This is typically a bad design decision because if the machine hosting the sticky session crashes or has to be restarted, all session state is lost and the user effectively has to start again.

Using a database to store session state (such as the shopping cart) does add a degree of overhead to the application, but makes it more resilient in the case of failures. If a web server, or two, fails during a user's request, another server can handle it and no information will be lost. If the application had used a session-based shopping cart, the customers would lose everything created during their session if the machine hosting that session failed.

> ASP.NET was designed around the principle that servers do fail and applications/components do leak memory and crash from time to time. By designing the IBuyAdventure application to use no session state, the application works well with the ASP.NET philosophy.

The Business Objects and Assemblies

Four business objects written in C# provide the various ASP.NET pages with all the business logic and data access code they require. As all of the .NET classes are fairly similar in terms of structure and the ADO.NET code they use to access the SQL server database, we won't review every single method of every single object. Instead you will look at one of the components in detail (ProductsDB) to see the basic structure of the components, and then use the ILDASM utility to show the methods and properties of each of the remaining business objects for reference purposes. As you encounter pages that use these functions, we will expand on their purposes.

ProductsDB Business Object

The ProductsDB class provides functions for retrieving product information. The complete C# code for the class is shown here:

```csharp
using System;
using System.Data;
using System.Data.SqlClient;

namespace IBuyAdventure
{
    public class ProductsDB
    {
        string m_ConnectionString;
        public ProductsDB( string dsn ) {
            m_ConnectionString = dsn;
        }

        public DataSet GetProduct(string productCode) {

            SqlConnection myConnection = new SqlConnection(m_ConnectionString);
            SqlDataAdapter sqlAdapter1 = new SqlDataAdapter("SELECT * FROM "
                + "Products WHERE ProductCode='"+productCode+"'", myConnection);

            DataSet products = new DataSet();
            sqlAdapter1.Fill(products, "products");

            return products;
        }

        public DataSet GetProducts(string category) {

            SqlConnection myConnection = new SqlConnection(m_ConnectionString);
            SqlDataAdapter sqlAdapter1 = new SqlDataAdapter("SELECT * FROM "
                + "Products WHERE ProductType='"+category+"'", myConnection);

            DataSet products = new DataSet();
            sqlAdapter1.Fill(products, "products");

            return products;
        }
        public DataSet GetProductCategories() {
```

```
        SqlConnection myConnection = new SqlConnection(m_ConnectionString);
        SqlDataAdapter sqlAdapter1 = new SqlDataAdapter("SELECT DISTINCT "
            + "ProductType FROM Products", myConnection);
        DataSet products = new DataSet();
        sqlAdapter1.Fill(products, "products");
        return products;
    }
  }
}
```

This class has four methods, including the constructor:

❑   `ProductsDB`: Initializes the class with a data source string

❑   `GetProduct`: Returns a dataset containing details for a single product

❑   `GetProducts`: Returns a dataset containing the details for all products in a specified category

❑   `GetProductCategories`: Returns a dataset containing the list of product categories

The first three lines of the component declare the namespaces used:

```
using System;
using System.Data;
using System.Data.SqlClient;
```

All of the class files have these lines and they indicate that the application is using the standard system namespace, the namespaces for ADO.NET, and the SQL Server specific parts of ADO.NET (`System.Data.SqlClient`). The application uses the SQL Server specific elements of ADO.NET because they provide high performance SQL Server access using TDS (Tabular Data Stream) via the classes `SqlConnection` and `SqlDataAdapter`. If the application needed to support a different back-end database, the developer could recode the classes to use the `OleDbConnection` and `OleDbDataAdapter` classes, which perform database access through OLEDB. These classes were discussed in Chapter 8.

One important point to note about all of the ADO.NET code in the business object is that it does not contain any exception handlers. It is therefore up to the code that uses these classes to catch exceptions like `SqlException`, which can be thrown if any error occurs when performing the data access (such as the existence of duplicate rows, and so on). No exception handling is included in these ASP.NET pages (to keep them terse), but the basic format is shown here:

```
try
{
    someObject.SomeMethodUsingAdoDotNet()
}
catch (SqlException e)
{
    if (e.Number == 2627)
        Message.InnerHtml = "Record exists with the same primary key";
    else
        Message.InnerHtml = e.Message;
}
```

This code checks for a known SQL Server error code using the `SqlException Number` property. If the error code the app is checking for is matched, it displays a custom error message. If the known error code is not encountered, it displays the exception's `Message` property. The `Message` property of an exception object typically contains very descriptive and helpful text that can help resolve a problem quickly. In your applications, you are unlikely to check for specific error codes, unless you want to perform some type of action. For example, you may check for the preceding error code if you want to delete a row that may already exist.

> You should always proactively add exception handling code to your production applications. The ADO.NET classes (including `SqlException`) are located in the assembly `System.Data.dll`. Use the IL Disassembler (`ildasm.exe`) tool, the WinCV class viewer, or the class browser example from the Quick Start to explore the classes in more detail.

The Connection String Constructor

The `ProductsDB` class has a constructor that accepts the connection string used to establish a connection to the back-end database. By passing the string in like this, the app prevents people from forgetting to specify it, and hopefully prevents the business objects from containing hard coded strings, which is always bad practice.

The string passed in is stored in the member `m_ConnectionString` in the constructor code:

```
...
string m_ConnectionString;

public ProductsDB( string dsn ) {
    m_ConnectionString = dsn;
}
...
```

The `m_ConnectionString` member is then used when constructing the `SqlConnection` object:

```
        public DataSet GetProduct(string productCode) {

            SqlConnection myConnection = new SqlConnection(m_ConnectionString);
            SqlDataAdapter sqlAdapter1 = new SqlDataAdapter("SELECT * FROM "
               + "Products WHERE ProductCode='"+productCode+"'", myConnection);

            DataSet products = new DataSet();
            sqlAdapter1.Fill(products, "products");

            return products;
        }
```

Anybody using the `ProductsDB` business object (and any of the other business objects) must therefore pass the connection string when creating an instance of the class:

```
    IBuyAdventure.ProductsDB inventory =new IBuyAdventure.ProductsDB(getConnStr());
```

The `getConnStr` function in this example retrieves the connection string from the `web.config` file:

```
<configuration>

  <appSettings>
    <add key="connectionString"
         value="server=localhost;uid=sa;pwd=;database=IBuyAdventure" />
    <add key="specialOffer" value="AW048-01" />
  </appSettings>
...
```

By using the `web.config` file to store the connection string for the components (and, in the previous example, another application-level value) the application does not have connection strings duplicated throughout business objects and ASP.NET pages, making it much easier to manage the connection string should you decide to rename the database or change any of the connection string properties.

> The `getConnStr` function is implemented using a 'code behind' class that will be reviewed when creating the `Page` class. You could, alternatively, use an include file to define such functions in your application, but the 'code behind' approach is my preferred option.

After reviewing the `ProductsDB` class, let's take a brief look at a couple of ILDASM screenshots showing the methods for the other business objects.

Figure 24-2 shows the ILDASM output for the `IBuyAdventure.dll` assembly:

Figure 24-2

The ILDASM Output for IBuyAdventureCart.dll

Figure 24-3 shows the ILDASM output for the IBuyAdventureCart.dll assembly:

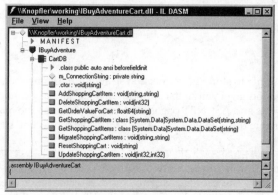

Figure 24-3

Assemblies

As discussed in Chapter 17, *assemblies* are the key deployment mechanism in ASP.NET applications. As shown in Figure 24-4 the business objects for IBuyAdventure.NET are divided into two assemblies that are both dependent upon the System.Data.dll assembly, because they use ADO.NET.

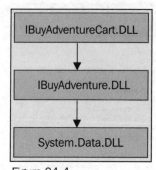

Figure 24-4

The IBuyAdventureCart.DLL contains the CartDB business object, which is used for manipulating the shopping cart. This is dependent upon the ProductsDB class contained within the IBuyAdventure.DLL assembly.

> Although assemblies have a .dll extension, they are, for the most part, not DLLs! The extension was kept only to aid interoperability between COM+ managed code and classic COM unmanaged code.

The IBuyAdventureCart.dll assembly isn't strictly necessary, but it does show that partitioning classes into different assemblies in an ASP.NET application isn't a difficult task. The decision as to when to create assemblies will typically be influenced by a number of real life factors:

❑ **The functionality of the classes within the assembly**: Assemblies should ideally contain functionally related classes.

❑ **The number of developers working on an application**: Assemblies are key units of deployment in ASP.NET applications, so it makes sense for different development teams to create their own assemblies to ease co-development.

Compiling the Assemblies

All of the business object sourcecode for the IBuyAdventure application is located in the components directory. This directory contains the file make.bat that uses the C# command line compiler (csc.exe) to create the two assemblies:

```
csc /out:..\bin\IBuyAdventure.dll /t:library productsdb.cs ordersdb.cs
usersdb.cs /r:System.Data.dll,System.dll,System.Xml.dll

csc /out:..\bin\IBuyAdventureCart.dll /t:library cartdb.cs
/r:System.Data.dll,System.dll,System.Xml.dll /r:..\bin\IBuyAdventure.dll
```

The first statement compiles the business objects ProductsDB, OrdersDB, and UsersDB, which are located within the files productdb.cs, ordersdb.cs, and usersdb.cs respectively. The output from this statement is the IBuyAdventure.dll assembly. The second statement compiles the business CartDB, which is located in the file cartdb.cs. The output from this is the IBuyAdventureCart.dll assembly. Both assemblies are compiled into the ASP.NET application bin directory so that they are available to the ASP.NET pages.

Naming Conventions

The IBuyAdventure business objects ProductsDB, OrdersDB, and UsersDB are declared within the namespace IBuyAdventure. This reflects the name of the assembly they are contained in, making it easy to locate and determine what files to ship when it comes to deploying an application that contains pages that are dependent upon those classes. The same naming convention applies to the CartDB business object, which is declared within the namespace IBuyAdventureCart, and contained in the assembly IBuyAdventureCart.dll. Microsoft also uses this naming convention for most of its assemblies. The exceptions to the rule are core classes, such as strings, which tend to live in assemblies called mscor[*].dll.

The IBuyAdventure .NET Database

IBuyAdventure is driven by a SQL Server 7 or 2000 database, with four tables (Accounts, Products, ShoppingCarts, and Orders) as shown in the Figure 24-5:

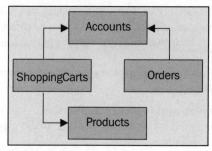

Figure 24-5

The business objects encapsulate each of these tables, so the ASP.NET pages never perform direct database access.

The Accounts Table

The Accounts table is used to store the login information for registered customers and has the following structure:

Column Name	Type	Length	Description
CustomerName	nvarchar	50	The name or email address of the registered user. This field is used as the key against all of the tables, and should therefore be unique.
Password	nvarchar	30	The password specified by the user during registration.

The Orders Table

The Orders table stores a summary of all the orders made by customers and has the following structure:

Column Name	Type	Length	Description
CustomerName	nvarchar	50	The name or email address of the registered user. This field is used as the key against all of the tables, and should therefore be unique.
Ordered	datetime	8	The date the order was placed.
TotalValue	float	8	The total value of the order.

When a user hits the **Confirm Order** button, and moves to the checkout page to confirm an order, an entry is added to this table. The individual items within the shopping cart are not saved to the database when an order is confirmed, although this would be a requirement for a commercial application.

The Products Table

The `Products` table contains a list of all products that a customer can purchase from IBuyAdventure. The table has the following structure:

Column Name	Type	Length	Description
ProductID	int	4	A unique ID for the product.
ProductCode	nvarchar	10	The unique code for the product.
ProductType	nvarchar	20	The category for the product.
Product Introduction Date	small datetime	4	The date when the product was first added to the catalog.
ProductName	nvarchar	50	The name of the product shown in the catalog.
Product Description	nvarchar	255	A description of the product.
ProductSize	nvarchar	5	The size of the product.
ProductImageURL	varchar	255	The URL of the image to display for the product.
UnitPrice	float	8	The price for this product.
OnSale	int	4	A flag to indicate whether or not the unit price is a sale price: 1 = on sale, 0 = not on sale.
Rating	float	8	A rating out of five for this product in terms of overall quality.

IBuyAdventure has slightly less than 50 products, grouped in 12 categories.

The ShoppingCarts Table

The `ShoppingCarts` table holds all of the current product details for each user's shopping cart. The table has the following structure:

Column Name	Type	Length	Description
ShoppingCartID	int	4	Auto-generated ID field.
ProductCode	nvarchar	10	The unique code for the product.
ProductName	char	50	The name of the product.
Description	nvarchar	255	A description of the product.
UnitPrice	money	8	The price for this product.
Quantity	int	4	The number of units wanted.
CustomerName	nvarchar	50	The name or email address of the registered user who currently has the specified product in their basket. If the user is not currently registered or logged in, this is a GUID to represent the anonymous user.

Every time an item is added to a user's shopping cart, an entry is added to this table.

> The IBuyAdventure sample application does not clean up the database, or remove rows that are associated with sessions that have expired. This would need to be done in a production application. You could handle the `Session_OnEnd` event and do your database cleanup there.

The Application User Interface

When a user first visits the IBuyAdventure site they are presented with an ASP.NET page that gives them a brief introduction to the site contents, and provides all the standard promotion material, special offers, and navigation buttons you'd expect from an e-commerce application:

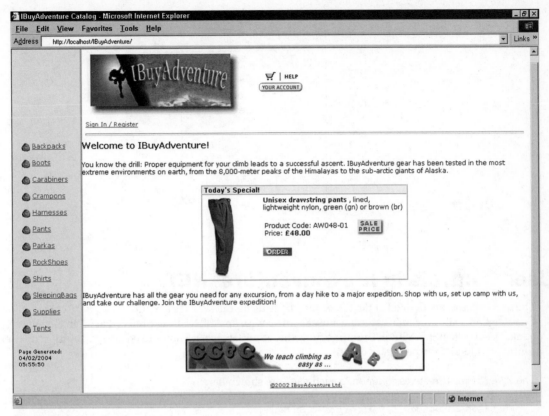

Figure 24-6

The welcome page shown in Figure 24-6 provides a fairly intuitive user interface that should enable customers to browse, register, and buy goods. The top of the page contains the IBuyAdventure logo and navigation buttons that let the user register, log in, and view their current/previous orders.

The left-hand side of the screen details all of the product categories that are defined in the IBuyAdventure database. The bottom of the screen contains the product advertising banner and the rest of the screen's middle section contains the special offers.

All pages on the site have the same basic structure as the front page, so each page uses at least three user controls as shown in Figure 24-7:

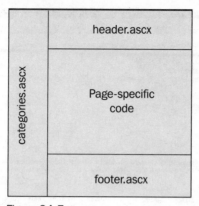

Figure 24-7

User Controls in IBuyAdventure .NET

The user controls are defined at the top of each page using the @ Register directive. As discussed in Chapter 4, this allows you to associate a user control with an ASP.NET tag prefix (that is, an element namespace). When the ASP.NET runtime finds these special tags, it knows to create the appropriate user control and render the necessary output.

The @ Register directives common to each page are shown here:

```
<%@ Page Language="C#" Inherits="IBuyAdventure.PageBase"
         src="components/stdpage.cs" %>
<%@ Register TagPrefix="IBA" TagName="Header" Src="UserControl\Header.ascx" %>
<%@ Register TagPrefix="IBA" TagName="Categories"
             src="UserControl\Categories.ascx" %>
<%@ Register TagPrefix="IBA" TagName="Special" src="UserControl\Special.ascx"
%>
<%@ Register TagPrefix="IBA" TagName="Footer" src="UserControl\Footer.ascx" %>
```

The user controls that you have registered are then inserted into a page in the same way as seen in previous chapters:

```
<IBA:Header id="Header" runat="server" />
```

Most of the pages in the IBuyAdventure application have the same basic format, containing an HTML table. Therefore let's review the complete page code for default.aspx that shows all of the user controls being declared, the language, 'code behind' page directive, the default output cache directive, and the basic HTML page structure:

```
<%@ Page Language="C#" Inherits="IBuyAdventure.PageBase"
src="components/stdpage.cs" %>
<%@ Register TagPrefix="IBA" TagName="Header" src="UserControl\Header.ascx" %>
<%@ Register TagPrefix="IBA" TagName="Categories"
             src="UserControl\Categories.ascx" %>
```

```
<%@ Register TagPrefix="IBA" TagName="Special" src="UserControl\Special.ascx" %>
<%@ Register TagPrefix="IBA" TagName="Footer" src="UserControl\Footer.ascx" %>
<%@ OutputCache Duration="60" VaryByParam="*" %>

<script language="C#" runat="server" >

    private String GetCustomerID() {
        if (Context.User.Identity.Name != "")
            return Context.User.Identity.Name;
        else {
            if (Session["AnonUID"] == null)
                Session["AnonUID"] = Guid.NewGuid();
            return Session["AnonUID"].ToString();
        }
    }

    void Page_Load(Object sender, EventArgs e) {
        if (Request.Params["Abandon"] == "1")
        {
            IBuyAdventure.CartDB cart = new IBuyAdventure.CartDB(
                ConfigurationSettings.AppSettings["connectionString"]);
            cart.ResetShoppingCart(GetCustomerID());
            Session.Abandon();
            FormsAuthentication.SignOut();
        }
    }
</script>

<html>
  <head>
    <title>IBuyAdventure Catalog</title>
  </head>

  <body background="images/back_sub.gif">
    <form runat="server">
    <font face="Verdana, Arial, Helvetica" size="2">

      <table border="0" cellpadding="0" cellspacing="0">
        <tr>
          <td colspan="5">
            <IBA:Header id="Header" runat="server"/>
          </td>
        </tr>
        <tr>
          <td colspan="3" align="left" valign="top">
            <IBA:Categories id="Categories" runat="server"/>
          </td>
          <td>
              
          </td>
          <td align="left" valign="top">
            <h3>Welcome to IBuyAdventure!</h3>
            <p>
            <font face="Verdana, Arial, Helvetica" size="2">
```

```
                    You know the drill: Proper equipment for your climb leads to
                    a successful ascent. IBuyAdventure gear has been tested in
                    the most extreme environments on earth, from the 8,000-meter
                    peaks of the Himalayas to the sub-arctic giants of Alaska.
                <p>
                <IBA:Special runat="server"/>
                <p>
                    IBuyAdventure has all the gear you need for any excursion,
                    from a day hike to a major expedition. Shop with us, set up
                    camp with us, and take our challenge. Join the IBuyAdventure
                    expedition!
                <br>
                <br>
                <br>
                <IBA:footer runat="server"/>
                </font>
            </td>
        </tr>
        </table>
    </font>
</form>
</body>
</html>
```

Although the appearance of the front page is fairly rich, the amount of code within the page is actually quite small because much of the HTML and code is encapsulated within the three user controls. `default.aspx`, like most pages, uses the `@ OutputCache` directive to specify that pages be cached for 60 seconds. This reduces database overhead, but you should consider the following issues:

❑ Cached information is stored in memory so the amount of memory used by your application will be larger.

❑ The same page will be cached multiple times if it has different query parameters, so you will have to allow for that increase in the working set.

❑ If a page is cached, then all the output for that page is also cached. This might seem obvious, but it does mean that, for example, the `AdRotator` control for the Adventure Work application doesn't rotate as often as a normal site (the advert changes once every 60 seconds on the pages that use caching). If you wanted portions of the page to be cached, while the rest is rendered afresh every time, use *fragment caching*. Fragment caching works by caching the information in a user control. The `.aspx` page is rendered each time, but when the time comes to add the contents of the user control to a page, those contents are drawn from the cache.

Single Server-Side <form> Element

One important point to note about the `default.aspx` page is that it contains a single `<form>` element with the `runat="server"` attribute. This form contains the majority of the page's HTML. None of the user controls have a server side `<form>` element. This is important because `<form>` elements *cannot* be nested, so the single form must include *all* user control code. If you attempt to define a `<form>` element with the `runat="server"` attribute anywhere within the outer `<form>` element, this will generate an error.

Using C# for the User Controls and Code

The first line of all your pages in IBuyAdventure contains the @Page directive:

```
<%@ Page Language="C#" Inherits="IBuyAdventure.PageBase"
        src="components/stdpage.cs" %>
```

This kind of directive was first seen in Chapter 4. The one used here informs the ASP.NET compiler of two key points about the pages:

❑ All of the page code is written using C# (although you could just as easily have used other languages).

❑ Each page uses 'code behind', and derives from the .NET class PageBase that provides common functionality.

The main motivation for using C# to write the IBuyAdventure application was to show that it really isn't so different from JScript and Visual Basic, and it is easy to read and understand. ASP.NET itself is written in C#, which indicates that it has a solid future ahead of it. Since all .NET languages compile down to MSIL before they are executed. It really doesn't matter which language the code is written in –use the one that you're most comfortable with.

The 'code behind' class specified using the Inherits and src attributes, causes the ASP.NET compiler to create a page that derives from the class PageBase rather than Page. The implementation of PageBase is very simple:

```csharp
using System;
using System.Collections;
using System.Web.UI;
using System.Web.Security;
using System.Configuration;

namespace IBuyAdventure
{
    public class PageBase : Page
    {
        public string getConnStr() {
        string dsn;
        dsn = ConfigurationSettings.AppSettings["connectionString"];
        return dsn;
        }
    }
}
```

By deriving each page from this class the getConnStr function is made available within each of the ASP.NET pages. This function retrieves the database connection string from the web.config file, and is called in pages when constructing business objects that connect to the back-end data source. The web.config file is cached, so accessing it frequently in the pages should not have any detrimental effect on performance. Should you want to cache just the connection string you could use the data cache to hold it, only accessing the web.config file initially to retrieve the value when creating the cache entry:

```
public String getConnStrCached() {
    string connectionString;

    // Check the Cache for the ConnectionString
    connectionString = (string) Context.Cache["connectionString"];

    // If the ConnectionString is not in the cache, fetch from Config.web
    if (connectionString == null) {
        connectionString =
            ConfigurationSettings.AppSettings["connectionString"];

        //store to cache
        Cache["connectionString"] = connectionString;
    }
    return connectionString;
}
```

One point to consider when using the data cache is that the values held within it *will* be updated if somebody changes the web.config file. ASP.NET automatically creates a new application domain and essentially restarts the web application to handle all new web requests when the web.config file is changed. As this results in a new data cache being created, the new connection string will be cached after the first call to getConnStrCached.

> As discussed in Chapter 13, applications settings should always be stored in the appsettings section of web.config. Values within that section are cached automatically.

However, should you decide to store application configuration in another location (maybe your own XML file on a central server) you can still invalidate the cache when your files change by creating a file dependency. This allows a cache item to be automatically flushed from the cache when a specific file changes:

```
//store to cache
Cache.Insert("connectionString", connectionString,
    new CacheDependency(Server.MapPath("\\someserver\myconfig.xml")));
```

File dependencies are just one of the cache dependency types ASP.NET supports. The other types supported include:

❑   **Scavenging**: Flushing cache items based upon their usage, memory consumption, and rating

❑   **Expiration**: Flushing cache items at a specific time or after a period of inactivity/access

❑   **File and key dependencies**: Flushing cache items when either a file changes or another cache entry changes

For more details about caching see Chapter 12.

The Specials User Control – special.ascx

As you might have noticed, the `default.aspx` page seen earlier that implements the welcome page, actually uses an additional user control (`UserControl\Special.ascx`) to display today's special product, so the page structure is slightly more complex than it would otherwise. See Figure 24-8:

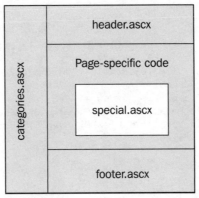

Figure 24-8

The product on offer is stored in the `web.config` file, making it easy for the site administrator to change the product displayed:

```
<configuration>
  <appSettings>
    <add key="connectionString"
         value="server=localhost;uid=sa;pwd=;database=IBuyAdventure" />
    <add key="specialOffer" value="AW048-01" />
  </appSettings>
  ...
</configuration>
```

The `Special` user control reads this value in its `Page_Load` event handler, retrieving the product information using the `ProductDB` component, and then updates the page using server-side controls:

```
...
<%@ Control Inherits="IBuyAdventure.ControlBase"
           src="../components/stdctrl.cs" %>
<%@ Import Namespace="System.Data" %>
<%@ Import Namespace="System.Configuration" %>

<script language="C#" runat="server">

    void Page_Load(Object sender, EventArgs e) {
        // Obtain today's special product.
        IBuyAdventure.ProductsDB inventory =
            new IBuyAdventure.ProductsDB(getConnStr());
        string specialOffer;
        specialOffer = ConfigurationSettings.AppSettings["specialOffer"];
```

```
                DataSet specialDetails = inventory.GetProduct(specialOffer);
                // Update UI with product details
                ProductImageURL.Src = Context.Request.ApplicationPath + "/images/" +
                    (String) specialDetails.Tables[0].Rows[0]["ProductImageURL"];
                ProductName.Text =
                    (String) specialDetails.Tables[0].Rows[0]["ProductName"];
                ProductDescription.Text =
                    (String) specialDetails.Tables[0].Rows[0]["ProductDescription"];
                ProductCode.Text =
                    (String) specialDetails.Tables[0].Rows[0]["ProductCode"];
                UnitPrice.Text = String.Format("{0:C}",
                    specialDetails.Tables[0].Rows[0]["UnitPrice"]);
                OrderAnchor.HRef = Request.ApplicationPath +
                    "/ShoppingCart.aspx?ProductCode=" +
                    (String) specialDetails.Tables[0].Rows[0]["ProductCode"];
                if ( (int) specialDetails.Tables[0].Rows[0]["OnSale"] == 0 )
                    sale.Visible = false;
        }

</script>

<table width="400" align=center border="1" cellpadding="0" cellspacing="0">
  <tr bgcolor="#F7EFDE">
    <td>
      <font face="verdana" size="2" ><b>  Today's Special! </b></font>
    </td>
  </tr>
  <tr>
    <td>
      <table>
        <tr>
          <td align="left" valign="top" width="1"10>
             <img id="ProductImageURL" runat="server">
          </td>
          <td align="left" valign="top">
            <font size="2">
              <b><asp:label id="ProductName" runat="server"/></b>,
              <asp:label id="ProductDescription" runat="server"/><br><br>
              <table>
                <tr>
                  <td>
                  <font size="2">
                    Product Code: <asp:label id="ProductCode" runat="server"/><br>
                    Price: <b><asp:label id="UnitPrice" runat="server"/></b>
                  </font>
                  </td>
                  <td>
                      
                    <img src="../images/saleTag1.gif" id="sale" runat="server" >
                  </td>
                </tr>
              </table>
              <br>
              <a id="OrderAnchor"
```

```
                     href='../ShoppingCart.aspx?ProductCode=AW109-15'
                     runat="server">
                  <img src="images/order.gif" width="55" height="15"
                        alt="Order" border="0">
               </a><br><br>
            </font>
         </td>
      </tr>
   </table>
  </td>
 </tr>
</table>
```

The user control code is very simple and just updates the server controls with values from the `DataSet` returned by the function call to `GetProduct`. The `String.Format` function is called using a format string of `{0:C}` to show the `UnitPrice` as a numerical value that represents a localespecific currency amount.

The Categories User Controls – categories.ascx

The product category list (`categories.ascx`), shown on the left hand side of most of the pages (it is not on the checkout or account pages), is dynamically built using the `asp:DataList` control and the `ProductsDB` business object. The `DataSource` property for the control is set in the `Page_Load` event:

```
<%@ Control Inherits="IBuyAdventure.ControlBase"
src="../components/stdctrl.cs" %>
<%@ OutputCache Duration="60" VaryByParam="none" %>

<script language="C#" runat="server">

   void Page_Load( Object sender, EventArgs e ) {
      String dsn = getConnStr();
      IBuyAdventure.ProductsDB inventory =
         new IBuyAdventure.ProductsDB(getConnStr());
      CategoryList.DataSource = inventory.GetProductCategories();
      CategoryList.DataBind();
   }

</script>
```

The `ItemTemplate` for this data list control is detailed in the user control, and specifies the layout of the data:

```
<asp:datalist id="CategoryList" border="0" runat="server">
  <itemtemplate>
    <tr>
      <td valign="top">
        <asp:image imageurl="/IBuyAdventure/images/bullet.gif"
                   alternatetext="bullet" runat="server" />
      </td>
      <td valign="top">
        <font face="Verdana, Arial, Helvetica" size="2">
```

```
            <asp:hyperlink
            NavigateURL='<%# "/IBuyAdventure/catalogue.aspx?ProductType=" +
            DataBinder.Eval( Container.DataItem, "ProductType" )%>'
            Text='<%# DataBinder.Eval( Container.DataItem, "ProductType" )%>'
            runat="server"/>
        </font>
      </td>
    </tr>
  </itemtemplate>
</asp:datalist>
```

The `asp:DataList` control was first seen in Chapter 7. It is bound to a data source of items in a collection, and renders the `ItemTemplate` for each of them.

The `asp:DataList` control outputs an HTML table; so the `ItemTemplate` outputs a `<tr>` element containing two columns (`<td>` elements), which ensure the table and page are correctly rendered. The first column contains an `asp:image` control that renders the small 'rock' bullet bitmap, the second column contains an `asp:hyperlink` control that has two fields (`NavigateURL` and `Text`). These fields are bound to the current row of the `DataSet` returned by the `ProductDB` business object.

The hyperlink rendered in `ItemTemplate` allows the user to view the product details for a specific category. The `NavigateURL` attribute is a calculated field consisting of a fixed URL (`/IBuyAdventure/catalogue.aspx`) and a dynamic query parameter, `ProductType`, whose value is set to equal the `ProductType` field in the current dataset row. Finally, the `Text` attribute is a simple attribute with its value also assigned to equal the `ProductType` field in the current dataset row.

The `DataBinder` class is used to retrieve the values stored in these properties. In case you are wondering, the `DataBinder` class is just a helper class provided by ASP.NET to keep the code simpler (fewer casts) and more readable, especially if you also need to format a property.

Alternatively, the app could also have directly accessed the current `DataSet` row and retrieved the `ProductType` value using the following code:

```
((DataRowView)Container.DataItem)["ProductType"].ToString()
```

This format is slightly more complex, but may be preferable if you are happy using casts and prefer the style. One advantage of this code is that it is early-bound, so it will execute faster than the late bound `DataBinder` syntax.

When one of the product category hyperlinks is clicked, the ASP.NET page `Catalogue.aspx` is displayed:

Figure 24-9

As you can see in Figure 24-9, this page shows the products for the selected category by using the
`ProductType` query string parameter in the `Page_Load` event to filter the results returned from the
`ProductDB` component:

```
void Page_Load(Object sender, EventArgs e) {
    if (!IsPostBack) {
        // Determine what product category has been specified and update
        // section image
        String productType = Request.Params["ProductType"];
        CatalogueSectionImage.Src = "images/hd_" + productType + ".gif";

        // User business object to fetch category products and databind
        // it to a <asp:datalist> control
        IBuyAdventure.ProductsDB inventory =
            new IBuyAdventure.ProductsDB(getConnStr());
        MyList.DataSource = inventory.GetProducts(productType);
        MyList.DataBind();
    }
}
```

A design issue here is that the application uses a hyperlink, and not a postback, to change the products shown.

Each of the products displayed for the selected category has a number of details:

❑ **Product name**: The name of the product (Everglades, Rockies, and so on).

❑ **Product info**: Facts about the product that will interest customers and help them make purchasing decisions (whether the item is waterproof, its color, and so on).

❑ **Product code**: The unique ID for the product across the site.

❑ **Price**: The price of the product.

❑ **On sale**: If the price is reduced, the SALE PRICE image is displayed.

❑ **Order button**: To add the product to the shopping basket the user clicks the Order image.

The main body of this page is also generated using an `asp:DataList` control, by setting the data source in the `Page_Load` event and using an `ItemTemplate` to control the rendering of each product. Unlike the category's User Control, the `asp:datalist` on this page takes advantage of the `RepeatDirection` and `RepeatColumns` attributes:

```
<asp:datalist id="MyList" BorderWidth="0" RepeatDirection="vertical"
    RepeatColumns="2" runat="server" OnItemDataBound="DataList_ItemBound">
```

These attributes automatically perform the page layout for us, and make the application look professional. Your `ItemTemplate` will define a two-column table that contains the image in the first column, and the details in the second. The `asp:DataList` control then works out how to flow the rows – so changing the page to use horizontal flowing is simply a matter of changing one attribute value:

```
<asp:datalist id="MyList" BorderWidth="0" RepeatDirection="horizontal"
    RepeatColumns="2" runat="server" OnItemDataBound="DataList_ItemBound">
```

Now, the app shows a different layout of the items. See Figure 24-10:

Figure 24-10

Without the `asp:DataList` control providing this functionality, you would have to write considerable amount of code to achieve this.

> *If you review the original ASP Adventure Works application, you will see it required around 100 lines of code in total!*

When an item is on sale, the bitmap shown in Figure 24-11 is displayed:

Figure 24-11

To determine whether or not this image is displayed, you need to handle the `OnItemDataBound` event of the `asp:DataList` object. This event is raised whenever an item in the datalist is created. To do this, set the `Visible` property of the `saleItem` server control (the `img` element) to `false` if the `OnSale` property is equal to zero. In order to get a reference to the `saleItem` control, use the `FindControl` method of the `DataList` item object. This method will search all the child controls of the `DataList` item being added to the page to get a reference to the `saleItem` control of that item:

```
...
void DataList_ItemCreated(Object sender , DataListItemEventArgs e ) {

    DataRowView myRowView;
    DataRow myRow;

    myRowView = (DataRowView) e.Item.DataItem;
    myRow = myRowView.Row;

    if  ( (int) myRow["OnSale"] == 0 )
       e.Item.FindControl("saleItem").Visible = false;
...

<img src="images/saleTag1.gif" id="saleItem" runat="server" />

...
```

By setting the `Visible` *property to* `false`*, the ASP.NET runtime does not render the control or any child controls – as it would if the application used something like a* `<span>` *element to contain the image and text. This is a very powerful approach for preventing partial page generation, and is much cleaner than the inline* `if...then` *statements that classic ASP required you to write.*

An advantage of this approach is that the code is somewhat cleaner and easier to maintain, but more importantly, any changes made by the code to controls that persist their state survive postbacks. As inline code is executed during the render phase of ASP.NET page, viewstate (state saved by the page and/or any child controls) has *already* been saved, so any changes made in inline code will not be round-tripped during a postback. The reason for using inline code in this chapter is to show that while ASP.NET applications can still make use of inline code, better (and sometimes mandatory) alternative approaches exist that allow you to maintain a much stronger separation of code from content.

Product Details

For each product shown in the `catalogue.aspx` page, the product name is rendered as a hyperlink. If a customer finds the product overview interesting, they can click the link to see more details about it (admittedly, there is not a great deal of extra detail in the sample application):

Figure 24-12

The additional information on this screen includes the date when the product was first introduced and a product rating assigned by the reviewer team at IbuyAdventure as you can see in Figure 24-12. The team always tests out the gear it sells first hand and assigns a rating. The `Rating` field in the `Products` table determines the rating bar shown for each product. The bar itself is generated using a custom server control written for IBuyAdventure. The sourcecode for this rating meter control is located in the `controls` directory, and should be easily understood if you have read Chapter 18. Like the `components` directory, the `controls` directory contains a `make.bat` file for building the control.

The control is registered and assigned an element name (tag prefix) at the top of the details page:

```
<%@ Register TagPrefix="Wrox" Namespace="WroxControls" %>
```

Although it only shows a single product, the `details.aspx` page still uses an `asp:DataList` control. The motivation for this was that future versions of IBuyAdventure could potentially allow multiple products to have their details viewed at the same time for product comparison purposes. The rating control is therefore declared within the `ItemTemplate` for the `asp:DataList` control as the `Score` property, using the field named `Rating` in the database table:

```
<Wrox:RatingMeter runat="server"
                  Score=<%#(double)DataBinder.Eval(Container.DataItem, "Rating")%>
Votes="1"
MaxRating="5"
CellWidth="51"
CellHeight="10" />
```

While the properties of the rating control may seem a little confusing at first, you should understand that it is a generic control that is suitable for many tasks. If you have seen the ASPToday.com article rating system it will probably make sense, but if not, consider the case where 200 people have rated a product, so you have 200 votes. For each vote a score between 0 and MaxRating is assigned, and the Score attribute reflects the overall average for all votes.

The rating control actually supports more functionality than is needed by the IBuyAdventure application, so set the Votes property to 1, since only a single staff member rates the products. The idea is that future versions of the application will support customer ratings and reviews.

The functionality of the rating control will not be covered any further in this chapter, but here is a run down of the properties of this control:

Property	Description
CellWidth	The size of each cell within the bar.
MaxRating	The maximum rating that can be assigned by a single vote. This value determines the number of cells that the bar has.
CellHeight	The height of each cell.
Votes	The number of votes that have been cast.
Score	The current score or rating.

The Shopping Cart

When surfing through the site, a customer can add items to their shopping basket at any time by hitting the Order image button shown in Figure 24-13:

Figure 24-13

This image button is inserted into the catalogue.aspx page as it is created, and clicking it results in the browser navigating to the ShoppingCart.aspx page:

```
<asp:ImageButton runat="server" id="OrderButton"
                 ImageUrl="images/order.gif"
                 OnCommand="OrderButton_Command"
                 CommandName="Order"/>
```

Two additional pieces of code need to be added to the page to support this button. First, since this button will appear multiple times on the page, you will need to tie each instance to the specific product. This will allow the app to figure out which product the user selected when the button is clicked.

```
void DataList_ItemBound(Object sender , DataListItemEventArgs e ) {

    DataRowView myRowView;
    DataRow myRow;
    myRowView = (DataRowView) e.Item.DataItem;
    myRow = myRowView.Row;
    if ( (int) myRow["OnSale"] == 0 )
        e.Item.FindControl("saleItem").Visible = false;
    ((ImageButton)e.Item.FindControl("OrderButton")).CommandArgument =
        myRow["ProductCode"].ToString();
    ((ImageButton)e.Item.FindControl("OrderButton")).AlternateText =
        "Click to order " + myRow["ProductName"];

}
```

The `DataList_ItemBound()` method is called every time a product from the database is added to the `DataList` control. Set the `CommandArgument` property for the specific `ImageButton` to be the product code for the specific product. You will see later how this is used to select the proper product. Also, use the `AlternateText` property to set the tooltip that will appear when the user hovers the mouse over the order button.

Next, handle the postback event that occurs when users click an order button for the product they want to purchase. This will trigger a server roundtrip and fire the `OrderButton_Command` event:

```
void OrderButton_Command(object sender, CommandEventArgs e) {

    if (e.CommandName == "Order") {
        String prodCode = e.CommandArgument.ToString();
        Response.Redirect ("ShoppingCart.aspx?ProductCode=" + prodCode);
    }

}
```

When this event is handled, check to see what the `CommandName` of the button firing this event is. If it matches `Order`, then the app knows it was caused by the user pressing the order button for a specific product. The `CommandArgument` property will contain the product code for this product. Then you can redirect the execution to the `ShoppingCart.aspx` page and pass the product code as a parameter.

You can see the `ShoppingCart.aspx` page in Figure 24-14:

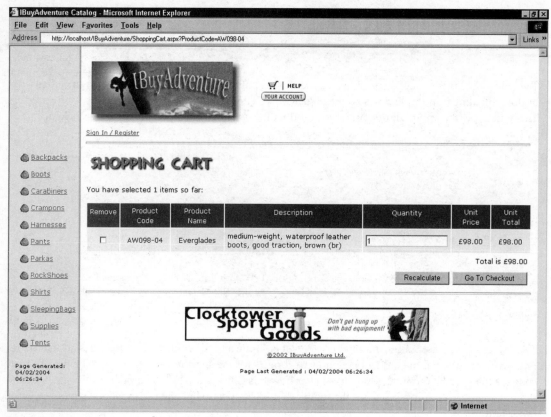

Figure 24-14

When the `ShoppingCart.aspx` page is being generated, the `Page_Load` event checks to see if a new product is being added to the cart, by looking for a `Request` parameter called `ProductCode`. This is added to the URL as a query string by the code in the `Catalogue.aspx` page (as shown earlier). The `AddShoppingCartItem` function of the `CartDB` object is then invoked to add it to the shopping cart for the current user.

The `Page_Load` event handler for the `ShoppingCart.aspx` page is shown here:

```
void Page_Load(Object sender, EventArgs e) {

    IBuyAdventure.CartDB cart = new IBuyAdventure.CartDB(getConnStr());
    // If page is not being loaded in response to postback
    if (Page.IsPostBack == false) {
        // If a new product to add is specified, add it
        // to the shopping cart
        if (Request.Params["ProductCode"] != null) {
            cart.AddShoppingCartItem(
                GetCustomerID(), Request.Params["ProductCode"]);
        }
        PopulateShoppingCartList();
```

```
                  UpdateSelectedItemStatus();
              }
          }
```

The `ProductCode` parameter is optional because the shopping cart can also be displayed by clicking on the shopping cart symbol shown in the navigation bar. If this is the method by which the page is accessed, then don't add any items to the shopping cart. The `CustomerID` function used here returns the unique ID for the current customer, which is then passed as a parameter to the `AddShoppingCartItem` function. If the customer has not registered and logged in, the ID returned by the `CustomerID` function is the current ASP.NET session ID; otherwise it is the current user name:

```
String GetCustomerID() {
    if (User.Identity.Name != "") {
        return Context.User.Identity.Name;
    }
    else {
        if (Session["AnonUID"] == null)
            Session["AnonUID"] = Guid.NewGuid();
        return Session["AnonUID"].ToString();
    }
}
```

The implementation of the `AddShoppingCartItem()` method of the `CartDB` business object is worth reviewing at this point, because it contains two interesting sections of code:

```
public void AddShoppingCartItem(string customerName, string productCode) {

    DataSet previousItem = GetShoppingCartItem(customerName, productCode);

    if (previousItem.Tables[0].Rows.Count > 0) {
        UpdateShoppingCartItem((int)
            previousItem.Tables[0].Rows[0]["ShoppingCartID"],
            ((int)previousItem.Tables[0].Rows[0]["Quantity"]) + 1);
    }
    else {

        IBuyAdventure.ProductsDB products;
        products = new IBuyAdventure.ProductsDB(m_ConnectionString);
        DataSet productDetails = products.GetProduct(productCode);

        String description =
            (String) productDetails.Tables[0].Rows[0]["ProductDescription"];
        String productName =
            (String) productDetails.Tables[0].Rows[0]["ProductName"];
        double unitPrice =
            (double) productDetails.Tables[0].Rows[0]["UnitPrice"];
        String insertStatement = "INSERT INTO ShoppingCarts (ProductCode, "
            + "ProductName, Description, UnitPrice, CustomerName, "
            + "Quantity) values ('" + productCode + "', @productName, "
            + "@description, " + unitPrice + ", '" + customerName + "' , 1)";

        SqlConnection myConnection = new SqlConnection(m_ConnectionString);
        SqlCommand myCommand = new SqlCommand(insertStatement, myConnection);
```

```
          myCommand.Parameters.Add(
             new SqlParameter("@ProductName", SqlDbType.VarChar, 50));
          myCommand.Parameters["@ProductName"].Value = productName ;

          myCommand.Parameters.Add(
             new SqlParameter("@description", SqlDbType.VarChar, 255));
          myCommand.Parameters["@description"].Value = description;
          myCommand.Connection.Open();
          myCommand.ExecuteNonQuery();
          myCommand.Connection.Close();
       }
    }
```

The first interesting point about the code is that it checks whether the item is already in the shopping cart by calling GetShoppingCartItem, and if it does already exist, simply increases the quantity for that item and updates it in the database using the UpdateShoppingCartItem function.

The second interesting point comes about because the ADO.NET code that adds a new cart item uses the SqlCommand class. Since the IBuyAdventure product descriptions can contain single quotes, the app needs to ensure that any quotes within the description do not conflict with the quotes used to delimit the field. To do this the SqlCommand object is used to execute the query, making use of parameters in the SQL, like @description, to avoid any conflict. The values for the parameters are then specified using the Parameters collections of the SqlCommand object:

```
          myCommand.Parameters.Add(
             new SqlParameter("@description", SqlDbType.VarChar, 255));
```

Once the SQL statement is built, the command object can be connected, the statement executed, and then disconnected:

```
          myCommand.Connection.Open();
          myCommand.ExecuteNonQuery();
          myCommand.Connection.Close();
```

Displaying the Shopping Cart and Changing an Order

The shopping cart allows customers to specify a quantity for each product in the cart, and displays the price per item, and total price for the quantity ordered. At any time, a customer can change the order quantity or remove one or more items from the cart by checking the **Remove** box and clicking **Recalculate**. An item will also be removed if the customer enters a quantity of zero.

To implement this functionality, use the asp:Repeater control. Implementing this functionality in straight ASP pages isn't an easy task, and requires significant code. In ASP.NET it is fairly simple.

The asp:Repeater control was used as the base for building the shopping cart as it doesn't need to use any of the built-in selection and editing functionality provided by the other list controls such as the asp:DataList and asp:DataGrid. All of the items are always checked and processed during a postback, and the cart contents (the dataset bound to the asp:Repeater control) is always generated during each postback.

The asp:Repeater control is also 'lookless' (it only generates the HTML element specified using templates), which fits in well with the design of the shopping cart page– a complete table does not need to be generated by the control (the table's start and header rows are part of the static HTML).

The shopping cart data source is provided by the CartDB component, which is bound to the myList asp:repeater control:

```
void PopulateShoppingCartList() {

    IBuyAdventure.CartDB cart = new IBuyAdventure.CartDB(getConnStr());
    DataSet ds = cart.GetShoppingCartItems(GetCustomerID());

    MyList.DataSource = ds;
    MyList.DataBind();
...
```

The HTML used to render the shopping cart, including the ItemTemplate rendered for each item in the MyList.DataSource is shown next, although some parts of the HTML page formatting (for example the font settings) have been removed to keep it short and easily readable:

```
<table colspan="8" cellpadding="5" border="0" valign="top">
<tr valign="top">
  <td align="center" bgcolor="#800000">Remove</td>
  <td align="center" bgcolor="#800000">Product Code</td>
  <td align="center" bgcolor="#800000">Product Name</td>
  <td align="center" bgcolor="#800000" width="250">Description</td>
  <td align="center" bgcolor="#800000">Quantity</td>
  <td align="center" bgcolor="#800000">Unit Price</td>
  <td align="center" bgcolor="#800000">Unit Total</td>
</tr>

<asp:Repeater id="MyList" runat="server">

  <itemtemplate>
    <tr>
    <td align="center" bgcolor="#f7efde">
      <asp:checkbox id="Remove" runat="server" />
    </td>
    <td align="center" bgcolor="#f7efde">
      <input id="ShoppingCartID" type="hidden"
      value='<%#DataBinder.Eval(Container.DataItem,"ShoppingCartID", "{0:g}")%>'
      runat="server" />
      <%#DataBinder.Eval(Container.DataItem, "ProductCode")%>
    </td>
    <td align="center" bgcolor="#f7efde">
      <%#DataBinder.Eval(Container.DataItem, "ProductName")%>
    </td>
    <td align="center" bgcolor="#f7efde">
      <%#DataBinder.Eval(Container.DataItem, "Description")%>
```

```
      </td>
      <td align="center" bgcolor="#f7efde">
        <asp:textbox id="Quantity"
                text='<%#DataBinder.Eval(Container.DataItem, "Quantity","{0:g}")%>'
                width="30"
                runat="server" />
      </td>
      <td align="center" bgcolor="#f7efde">
        <asp:label id="UnitPrice" runat="server">
          <%#DataBinder.Eval(Container.DataItem, "UnitPrice", "{0:C}")%>
        </asp:label>
      </td>
      <td align="center" bgcolor="#f7efde">
        <%# String.Format("{0:C}",
          (((int)DataBinder.Eval(Container.DataItem, "Quantity"))
          * ((double) DataBinder.Eval(Container.DataItem, "UnitPrice")) )) %>
      </td>
    </tr>
  </itemtemplate>

</asp:Repeater>

<tr>
  <td colspan="6"></td>
  <td colspan="2" align="right">
  Total is <%=String.Format(fTotal.ToString(), "{0:C}") %>
  </td>
</tr>

<tr>
  <td colspan="8" align="right">
    <asp:button text="Recalculate" OnClick="Recalculate_Click" runat="server" />
    <asp:button text="Go To Checkout" OnClick="Checkout_Click" runat="server" />
  </td>
</tr>

</table>
```

This code is similar to that seen earlier, so it should be easy to follow. The important point to note is that all the fields that need to be available when a postback occurs are marked with the id and runat="server" attributes.

When the customer causes a postback by pressing the Recalculate button, the ASP.NET page can access the Remove checkbox control, the database cart ID hidden field control, and the Quantity field control for each list item, and update the database accordingly.

For each row in the ShoppingCarts table for this customer, the asp:Repeater control will contain a list item containing these three controls, which can be programmatically accessed. Refer to Figure 24-15 to get a better understanding:

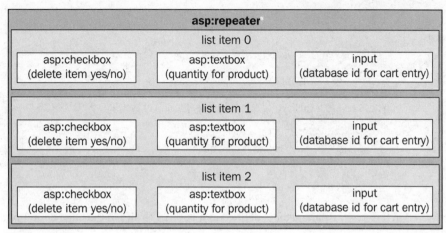

Figure 24-15

To associate each list item within the `asp:Repeater` control with a specific database cart item, a hidden field is used to store the unique ID for the entry:

```
<input id="ShoppingCartID" type="hidden"
       value='<%#DataBinder.Eval(
               Container.DataItem, "ShoppingCartID", " {0:g}") %>'
       runat="server">
```

As discussed earlier, the contents of the shopping cart are always stored in the SQL Server table named `ShoppingCarts`, and manipulated using the business object named `CartDB`. To populate the shopping cart with items, the ASP.NET page invokes the `PopulateShoppingCartList` function. This occurs when the page is loaded for the first time (that is, when `Page.PostBack` is `false`), and after each postback that leads to the database being modified– items added, deleted, or changed. To retrieve the cart items and data bind the `asp:Repeater` control, this function uses the `GetShoppingCartItems` method of the `CartDB` object:

```
void PopulateShoppingCartList() {

    IBuyAdventure.CartDB cart = new IBuyAdventure.CartDB(getConnStr());

    DataSet ds = cart.GetShoppingCartItems(GetCustomerID());

    MyList.DataSource = ds;
    MyList.DataBind();
    ...
```

Once the list is bound, the dataset is then enumerated to calculate the total value of the items within the cart:

```
    DataTable dt;
    dt = ds.Tables[0];

    int lIndex;
```

```
        double UnitPrice;
        int Quantity;

        for ( lIndex =0; lIndex < dt.Rows.Count; lIndex++ ) {

            UnitPrice = (double) dt.Rows[lIndex]["UnitPrice"];

            Quantity = (int) dt.Rows[lIndex]["Quantity"];

            if ( Quantity > 0 ) {
                fTotal += UnitPrice * Quantity;
            }
        }
    }
```

The total stored in the `fTotal` parameter is defined as a `Double` earlier in the page definition:

```
// Total for shopping basket
double fTotal = 0;
```

and then referenced by inline code that executes just after the `asp:Repeater` control:

```
...
</asp:repeater>
<tr>
  <td colspan="6"></td><td colspan="2" align="right">
    Total is <%=String.Format("{0:C}", fTotal ) %>
  </td>
</tr>
...
```

When customers change the order quantity for products in their cart, or mark items to be removed, they click the Recalculate button. This button was created using the `asp:button` control with its `OnClick` event wired up to the `Recalculate_Click` function:

```
<asp:button text="Recalculate" OnClick="Recalculate_Click" runat="server" />
```

The `Recalculate_Click` function updates the database based on the changes users made to the quantities, and the items they have added or deleted. It then retrieves the updated cart items from the database, rebinds the repeater control to the updated data set, and finally creates a status message informing the user how many items (if any) are currently in the cart. These functions are, in turn, delegated within the event handler to three different functions:

```
void Recalculate_Click(Object sender, EventArgs e) {
    // Update Shopping Cart
    UpdateShoppingCartDatabase();
    // Repopulate ShoppingCart List
    PopulateShoppingCartList();
    // Change status message
    UpdateSelectedItemStatus();
    }
```

The `UpdateShoppingCartDatabase` method is called first in the event handler, when the postback data for the `asp:Repeater` control describing the cart, and any changes made, will be available. The function can therefore access this postback data and make any database updates and deletions that may be required. Next, calling `PopulateShoppingCartList` causes the shopping cart to be re-read from the database and bound to the `asp:Repeater` control. This will cause the page to render an updated view of the cart to the user.

To perform the required database updates, the `UpdateShoppingCartDatabase` function iterates through each of the list items (the rows) within the `asp:Repeater` control and checks each item to see if it should be deleted or modified:

```
void UpdateShoppingCartDatabase() {

    IBuyAdventure.ProductsDB inventory =
        new IBuyAdventure.ProductsDB(getConnStr());
    IBuyAdventure.CartDB cart = new IBuyAdventure.CartDB(getConnStr());
    for (int i=0; i<MyList.Items.Count; i++) {
        TextBox quantityTxt =
            (TextBox) MyList.Items[i].FindControl("Quantity");
        CheckBox remove =
            (CheckBox) MyList.Items[i].FindControl("Remove");
        HtmlInputHidden shoppingCartIDTxt =
        (HtmlInputHidden) MyList.Items[i].FindControl("ShoppingCartID");

        int Quantity = Int32.Parse(quantityTxt.Text);

        if (remove.Checked == true || Quantity  == 0)
            cart.DeleteShoppingCartItem(
                Int32.Parse(shoppingCartIDTxt.Value));
        else {
            cart.UpdateShoppingCartItem(
                Int32.Parse(shoppingCartIDTxt.Value), Quantity );
        }
    }
}
```

This code takes a brute-force approach by updating every item in the shopping cart that isn't marked for deletion. In a commercial application, consider having a hidden field that stores the original quantity and only updates items when the two quantity fields differ. This could potentially reduce database I/O considerably if you have users who keep changing their order quantities and deleting items. Another alternative would be to handle the `OnChange` events for the controls in the list, and only update the database when events are invoked.

Checkout Processing and Security

When customers are ready to commit to purchasing the goods that are currently in their shopping cart, they can click the Go to Checkout button in the shopping cart page, or click the shopping basket image located on the navigation bar. The security system used in IBuyAdventure takes advantage of forms based authentication (also called cookie-based security), as introduced in Chapter 14. When a customer hits any of the pages that require authentication, if they haven't already signed in, the page `login.aspx` is displayed. The `login.aspx` page is as shown in Figure 24-16:

Figure 24-16

The ASP.NET runtime knows to display this page if a user is not logged in because all pages that require authentication are located in a directory called SECURE. It contains a web.config file, which specifies that anonymous access is *not* allowed:

```
<configuration>
  <system.web>
    <authorization>
      <deny users="?" />
    </authorization>
  </system.web>
</configuration>
```

Remember that "?" means 'anonymous users'.

Using a specific directory to contain secure items is a simple yet flexible way of implementing security in ASP.NET applications. When the ASP.NET runtime determines that an anonymous user is trying to access a page in a secure directory of the application, it knows which page to display because the web.config file located in the root directory has a cookie element with a loginurl attribute that specifies it:

```
<configuration>
  <system.web>
    <authentication mode="Forms">
      <forms name=".ibuyadventurecookie" loginUrl="login.aspx"
             protection="All" timeout="60">
      </forms>
    </authentication>
```

```
      <authorization>
        <allow users="*" />
      </authorization>
    </system.web>
</configuration>
```

This configuration basically says, if the `.ibuyadventurecookie` cookie is present and it has not been tampered with, the user has been authenticated and so can access secure directions, if authorized; if not present, redirect to the URL specified by `loginurl`.

Forms-Based Authentication in Web Farms

For forms-based authentication to work within a web farm environment, the `decryptionkey` attribute of the `cookie` element must be set, and not left blank or specified as the default value of `autogenerate`. The `decryptionkey` attribute should be set the same on all machines within the farm. The length of the string is 16 characters for DES encryption (56/64 bit), or 48 characters for Triple DES encryption (128 bit). If you do use the default value it will cause a different encryption string to be generated by each machine in the farm, and cause the session authentication to fail between different machines as a user moves between servers. If this happens a `CryptographicException` will be thrown and the user will be presented with a screen saying the data is bad, or could not be decoded.

The Login.aspx Page Event Handlers

The Login button on the login form is created using an `asp:button` control, which has the `OnClick` event wired up to the `LoginBtn_Click` event handler:

```
...
<td colspan="2" align="right">
  <asp:button Text=" Login " OnClick="LoginBtn_Click" runat="server" />
</td>
```

When the button is clicked, the `LoginBtn_Click` event handler is invoked. It validates users, and then redirects them to the original page. The validation and redirection code is shown here:

```
void LoginBtn_Click(Object sender, EventArgs e) {
    IBuyAdventure.UsersDB users = new IBuyAdventure.UsersDB(getConnStr());
    IBuyAdventure.CartDB cart = new IBuyAdventure.CartDB(getConnStr());

    if (users.ValidateLogin(UserName.Text, Password.Text)) {

        cart.MigrateShoppingCartItems(Session.SessionID, UserName.Text);
        FormsAuthentication.RedirectFromLoginPage(
            UserName.Text, Persist.Checked);
    }
    else {
        Message.Text =
            "Login failed, please check your details and try again.";
    }
}
```

The code initially creates the two business objects that are required, using the 'code behind' function `getConnStr` to collect details of the data source to connect to. Once the `UsersDB` object is created, its

`ValidateLogin` method is invoked to determine if the user credentials are OK (the user details are stored in the `Account` table rather than the `web.config` file). If the details are invalid, the `Text` property of the `Message` control is updated to show the error. If the login is successful, the following steps occur:

1. The client is marked as authenticated by calling the `RedirectFromLoginPage` method of the `FormsAuthentication` object, which was discussed in Chapter 14.

2. This causes the cookie named `.ibuyadventurecookie` to be sent back to the client, so from here on it indicates that the client has been authenticated.

3. The user is redirected back to the page that initially caused the login form to be displayed.

If customers have previously registered, they can login via the `Login` page. This will then redirect them back to the original page that caused the `Login` page to be displayed. This redirection code is actually implemented by the `Login` page, and does require some extra code.

Handling Page Return Navigation During Authentication

When the ASP.NET runtime determines that a secure item has been accessed, it will redirect the user to the `Login` page, and include a query string parameter named `ReturnURL`. As the name suggests, this is the page that users will be redirected to once they are allowed access to it. When displaying the page, save this value, as it will be lost during the postbacks where the user is validated. The approach used is to store the value in a hidden field during the `Page_Load` event:

```
void Page_Load(Object sender, EventArgs e)
{
   // Store Return Url in Page State
   if (Request.QueryString["ReturnUrl"] != null)
   {
      ReturnUrl.Value = Request.QueryString["ReturnUrl"];
         ((HyperLink)RegisterUser).NavigateUrl =
            "Register.aspx?ReturnUrl=" + ReturnUrl.Value;
   }
}
```

The hidden field is defined as part of the `Login` form, and includes the `runat="server"` attribute so that the app can programmatically access it in its event handlers:

```
<input type="hidden" value="/advworks/default.aspx"
       id="ReturnUrl" runat="server" />
```

The hidden field is given a default value, as it is possible for the user to go directly to the login page via the navigation bar. Without a default value, the redirection code that is executed after login would not work.

So, when customers click the Login button, you can validate their details and then redirect them to the page whose value is stored in the `ReturnUrl` hidden control.

First Time Customer – Registration

If customers have not registered with the application before, they can click the Registration hyperlink, and will be presented with a user registration form to fill in. See Figure 24-17:

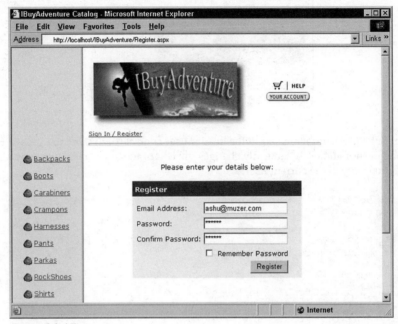

Figure 24-17

The form is kept simple for this case study, and only asks for an e-mail address and password. In a commercial application, this form would probably include additional information such as the name and address of the customer.

As the registration page (`Register.aspx`) is opened from a hyperlink in the login page (`login.aspx`), ensure that the app passes on the `ReturnUrl` parameter, so that the registration page knows where to redirect users once they have completed the form. To do this, dynamically create the hyperlink in the registration form during the `Page_Load` event of the login page:

```
((HyperLink)RegisterUser).NavigateUrl =
    "Register.aspx?ReturnUrl=" + ReturnUrl.Value;
```

Also, make sure that the hyperlink is marked as a server control in the `login.aspx` page:

```
...
<font size="2">
<asp:HyperLink NavigateUrl="Register.aspx" id="RegisterUser" runat="server" />
  Click Here to Register New Account
</asp:hyperlink>
</font>
...
```

Those of you with a keen eye will have spotted that customers can actually log in at any time by clicking the Sign In / Register hyperlink located in the page header. Once a user is successfully authenticated, this hyperlink changes to say Sign Out as shown in Figure 24-18:

Figure 24-18

The sign in or out code is implemented in the header user control (UserControl/header.ascx) where the Page_Load event handler dynamically changes the text of the signInOutMsg control, depending on the authentication state of the current user:

```
<%@ Import Namespace="System.Web.Security" %>
<script language="C#" runat="server">

    private void Page_Load( Object Sender, EventArgs e ) {
        updateSignInOutMessage();
    }

    private void SignInOut( Object Sender, EventArgs e ) {

        if ( Context.User.Identity.Name != "" ) {
            IBuyAdventure.CartDB cart =
                new IBuyAdventure.CartDB(
                    ConfigurationSettings.AppSettings["connectionString"]);
            cart.ResetShoppingCart(GetCustomerID());
            FormsAuthentication.SignOut();
            Response.Redirect("/IBuyAdventure/default.aspx");
        }
        else {
            Response.Redirect("/IBuyAdventure/login.aspx");
        }
    }
private void updateSignInOutMessage() {

    if ( Context.User.Identity.Name != "" ) {
        signInOutMsg.Text = "Sign Out (" + Context.User.Identity.Name+ ")";
    }
    else {
        signInOutMsg.Text = "Sign In / Register";
    }


    }
</script>
...
```

The `updateSignInOutMessage` function actually updates the text, and the `SignInOut` method is called when the user clicks the sign in/out text. If a user is signing out, the `CookieAuthentication.SignOut` function is called to invalidate the authentication cookie. If signing in, the user is redirected to the login page.

The `SignInOut` code is wired up as part of the control declaration:

```
...
<td>
  <asp:linkbutton style="font:8pt verdana" id="signInOutMsg"
                  runat="server" OnClick="SignInOut" />
</td>
...
```

Checkout Processing

Once a customer is authenticated, they are taken to the checkout page (`secure/checkout.aspx`), presented with their shopping list, and asked to confirm that the list is correct. Figure 24-19 illustrates the `Checkout.aspx` page:

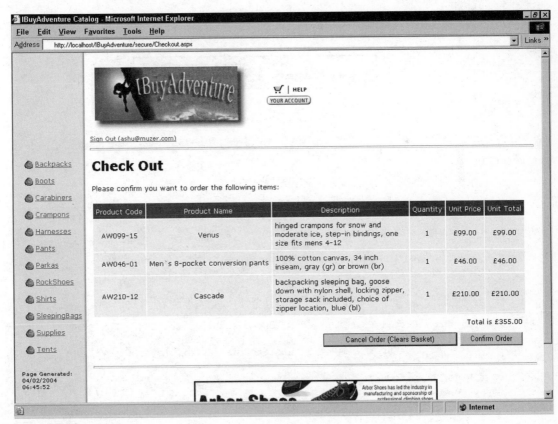

Figure 24-19

The checkout page uses very similar code to the `ShoppingCart.aspx` page, except for the controls that allow the customer to remove items or edit the order quantities. If the customer confirms an order by pressing the Confirm Order button, a new database record is created for the order containing the date, and the total order value. Then the current shopping basket is cleared, and the customer is presented with a confirmation screen as shown in Figure 24-20:

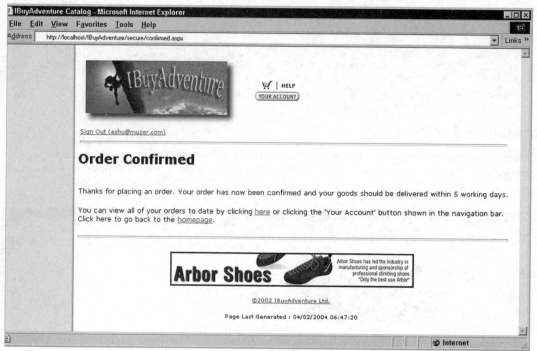

Figure 24-20

The code invoked for confirming an order is as follows:

```
void Confirm_Order(Object sender, EventArgs e) {

    IBuyAdventure.CartDB cart = new IBuyAdventure.CartDB(getConnStr());
    double totalOrderValue;

    totalOrderValue = cart.GetOrderValueForCart(GetCustomerID());

    IBuyAdventure.OrdersDB orders = new IBuyAdventure.OrdersDB(getConnStr());
    orders.AddNewOrder(GetCustomerID(), DateTime.Now.ToString("G",
                    DateTimeFormatInfo.InvariantInfo), totalOrderValue );

    cart.ResetShoppingCart( GetCustomerID() );
    Response.Redirect("confirmed.aspx");
}
```

Case Study – IBuyAdventure.NET

The total value of the order is calculated using the `GetOrderValueForCart` function of the `CartDB` object. The customer name that is passed into this function, as returned by a call to `GetCustomerID`, will always be the name that the user entered when registering, as it is not possible to access this page without being authenticated.

Once the total value of the order has been calculated, the `AddNewOrder` function of the `OrdersDB` object is called to create an entry in the `orders` table. Since the app will be adding the date and time of the order to the database make sure that the date is in a known format–as the standard formatting routines take into account the locale of the server, the app may end up with a date format that SQL Server doesn't recognize.

To get around this, use an overloaded version of the `ToString()` method. Usually, this method takes no parameters, but in this case you will use two. The first specifies the general date and time format. The `DateTimeFormatInfo.InvariantInfo` is a static object that ensures that the date string will be formatted the same regardless of the locale of the server. Finally, the shopping cart contents are cleared from the database and the browser is redirected to the order confirmation screen.

> In a commercial application you would want to keep the contents of the shopping cart so you could actually process the order. As this is only a simple demonstration application, this is not implemented here.

Canceling the Order

If an order is canceled before it is completed, the current shopping cart is cleared and the customer is taken back to the IBuyAdventure home page (`default.aspx`). The code for canceling an order is shown here:

```
void Cancel_Order(Object sender, EventArgs e) {

    IBuyAdventure.ProductsDB inventory =
        new IBuyAdventure.ProductsDB(getConnStr());
    IBuyAdventure.CartDB cart = new IBuyAdventure.CartDB(getConnStr());
    cart.ResetShoppingCart( GetCustomerID() );

    Response.Redirect("/IBuyAdventure/default.aspx");
}
```

Order History and Your Account

Customers can review their order history at any time by clicking the Your Account image located at the top of each page. When clicked, this page displays all the orders they have previously placed to date, showing the date when the order was created and the total value of the order as shown in Figure 24-21:

Figure 24-21

This page is generated using the `asp:Repeater` control, and simply shows the entries in the `Orders` table for the current customer. The `PopulateOrderList` function databinds the controls just as in previous pages:

```
void PopulateOrderList() {

    IBuyAdventure.OrdersDB orders = new IBuyAdventure.OrdersDB(getConnStr());

    DataSet ds = orders.GetOrdersForCustomer(GetCustomerID());

    MyList.DataSource = ds;
    MyList.DataBind();

    if ( MyList.Items.Count == 0 ) {
        ClearButton.Visible = false;
        MyList.Visible = false;
        Status.Text = "No orders have been placed to date.";
    }
}
```

The last few lines of the code hide the **Clear Order History** button if there are no orders for the customer. If there are orders, then clicking this button invokes the `ClearOrderHistory()` function:

```
void ClearOrderHistory(Object sender, EventArgs e) {

    IBuyAdventure.OrdersDB orders = new IBuyAdventure.OrdersDB(getConnStr());
    orders.DeleteOrdersForCustomer( GetCustomerID() );
    PopulateOrderList();
}
```

This code clears all orders for the customer by calling the `DeletesOrdersForCustomer()` function provided by the `OrdersDB` object.

Summary

That's it, your first ASP.NET e-commerce application!

This chapter has shown how clean and easy it is to write an e-commerce application using ASP.NET. The rich server side control and event model makes ASP.NET development much more like traditional Visual Basic event based programming, which dramatically reduces the amount of code you have to write.

The chapter has not had the space to cover every single feature that you could potentially use in an application in this chapter. Hopefully, however, the code presented here covers the most common aspects of an application, and when combined with the information provided in the other chapters, will give you the confidence to build your own applications.

The Common System Namespaces

Due to the huge number of classes that make up the .NET Class Library, we don't have room to list them all, let alone their properties, methods, and events. The SDK provided with the Framework contains a full reference section, which you can access under Reference | Class Library in the .NET SDK documentation. However, to help you find the classes you need, a list of the most commonly used namespaces has been provided, together with a description of the classes they contain.

Fundamental System Namespaces

System	Fundamental classes and base classes that define commonly-used value and reference data types, events and event handlers, interfaces, attributes, and processing exceptions. It also contains services that support data type conversion, method parameter manipulation, mathematics, remote and local program invocation, application environment management, and supervision of managed and unmanaged applications.
System.Collections	Interfaces and classes that define various collections of objects, such as the List, Queue, ArrayList, HashTable, and Dictionary objects.
System. ComponentModel	Classes that are used to implement the runtime and design-time behavior of components and controls. Includes the base classes and interfaces for implementing attributes, type converters, binding to data sources, and licensing components.
System. Configuration	Classes that are used to configure an assembly and allow custom installers to be created.

Table continued on following page

System.Configuration	Classes that are used to configure an assembly and allow custom installers to be created.
System.IO	Classes and types that provide synchronous and asynchronous reading from and writing to data streams and files.
System.Reflection	Classes and interfaces providing a managed view of loaded types, methods, and fields, with the ability to dynamically create and invoke types.
System.Security	Classes that provide the underlying structure for the CLR security system, including base classes for permissions.
System.Text	Classes representing ASCII, Unicode, UTF-7, and UTF-8 character encodings, abstract base classes for converting blocks of characters to and from blocks of bytes, and a helper class that manipulates and formats `String` objects without creating intermediate instances.
System.Text.RegularExpressions	Classes that provide access to the .NET Framework regular expression engine.
System.Threading	Classes and interfaces to enable multi-threaded programming, including the `ThreadPool` class, a delegate timer class and the `Mutex` class. Also contains classes for thread scheduling, wait notification, and deadlock resolution.
System.Timers	Contains the programmable `Timer` component, which allows events to be raised at specified intervals.

.NET Languages Namespaces

Microsoft.CSharp	Classes that support compilation and code generation for the C# language.
Microsoft.JScript	Classes that support compilation and code generation for the JScript language.
Microsoft.VisualBasic	Classes that support compilation and code generation for the Visual Basic language.

Data Management Namespaces

`System.Data`	Classes that constitute the ADO.NET relational data access and management architecture for multiple data sources.
`System.Data.Common`	Classes that form the basis for the provider specific classes such as DataReader, Connection, DataAdapter, etc. within the subsidiary namespaces.
`System.Data.Odbc`	Classes that support the ODBC .NET data provider.
`System.Data.OracleClient`	Classes that support the Oracle .NET data provider.
`System.Data.SqlServerCe`	Classes that support the SQL Server on WIndows Compact Edition.
`System.Data.OleDb`	Classes that support the OLE DB .NET data provider.
`System.Data.SqlClient`	Classes that support the SQL Server .NET data provider.
`System.Data.SqlTypes`	Classes for native data types within MS SQL Server.
`System.Xml`	Classes that provide standards-based support for processing XML.
`System.Xml.Schema`	Classes that provide standards-based support for processing XML schemas.
`System.Xml.Serialization`	Classes that can be used to serialize and deserialize objects as XML.
`System.Xml.XPath`	Contains the `XPath` parser and evaluation engine.
`System.Xml.Xsl`	Classes that provide support for XSL/T transformations.

Debugging and Monitoring Namespaces

`System.Diagnostics`	Classes for debugging applications and for tracing code execution, starting system processes, reading and writing to event logs, and monitoring system performance using performance counters.
`System.Management`	Classes for working with Windows Management Instrumentation (WMI).

Application Services Namespaces

`System. DirectoryServices`	Classes that provide access to the active directory.
`System. EnterpriseServices`	Classes that are used to manage component activation and associated activities in an enterprise scenario.
`System.Messaging`	Classes for working with message queues, sending messages to queues, and receiving or peeking messages from queues. Note that this is not used for SMTP messaging.

Graphics and Printing Namespaces

`System.Drawing`	Provides access to GDI and basic graphics functionality.
`System.Drawing. Design`	Classes that extend design-time user interface logic and drawing.
`System.Drawing. Drawing2D`	Advanced 2-dimensional and vector graphics classes.
`System.Drawing. Imaging`	Advanced GDI and imaging classes.
`System.Drawing. Printing`	Classes that allow customized printing.
`System.Drawing.Text`	Advanced GDI and typography classes for creating and using fonts.

Fundamental Networking Namespaces

`System.Net`	Provides simple programming interfaces to many common network protocols. Includes the `WebRequest` and `WebResponse` classes that enable applications to use Internet resources.
`System.Net.Sockets`	Provides a managed implementation of the Windows Sockets interface in the same way as the Winsock API.

Windows Forms Application Namespaces

`System.Windows. Forms`	Classes for creating Windows-based executable applications to run under the .NET Framework.
`System.Windows. Forms.Design`	Classes for extending design-time support for Windows Forms.

Fundamental Web Application Namespaces

`System.Web`	Classes and interfaces to enable browser-server communication. Includes `HTTPRequest` and `HTTPResponse`, and the `HTTPServerUtility` object that provides access to server-side utilities and processes. Also includes classes for cookie manipulation, file transfer, exception information, and output cache control.
`System.Web.Caching`	Classes for caching frequently used resources on the server.
`System.Web.Configuration`	Classes that are used to configure ASP.NET applications.
`System.Web.Hosting`	Classes for working with application domains, worker requests and interfacing with IIS.
`System.Web.Mail`	Classes for creating and managing SMTP e-mail messages and attachments.
`System.Web.Security`	Classes that implement security in ASP.NET applications.

Web Forms Application Namespaces

`System.Web.UI`	Classes and interfaces for creating user interface pages and controls in web applications. Includes the `Control` base class, the `Page` class and classes to implement data binding, viewstate management, and control parsing.
`System.Web.UI.Design`	Classes for extending design-time support for Web Forms.
`System.Web.UI.Design.WebControls`	Classes for extending design-time support for Web Controls.
`System.Web.UI.HtmlControls`	Classes for creating HTML server controls that map directly to standard HTML elements.
`System.Web.UI.WebControls`	Classes for creating ASP.NET Web Controls, which provide a consistent and abstracted interface.

Web Service Application Namespaces

`System.Web.Services`	Classes for building and using Web Services.
`System.Web.Services.Description`	Classes for publicly describing Web Services via the Web Service Description Language (WSDL).
`System.Web.Services.Discovery`	Classes for implementing Web Service Discovery.
`System.Web.Services.Protocols`	Classes that define the data transmission protocols between ASP.NET Web Services and clients.

Scott Guthrie's Top Performance Tips

With thanks to Scott Guthrie, the inventor of ASP.NET.

Here are Scott's top tips for maximizing performance of your ASP.NET applications, plus a few things to watch out for.

In general, ASP.NET pages take longer to respond on the first 'hit' due to the extra instantiation and compilation sequence. However, after they are first compiled, they are faster for all subsequent accesses. Although pages with very little code may provide around the same performance as ASP 3.0 pages, more complex pages are actually a lot faster due to the compilation of the code they contain.

The best benefit/cost ratio for an ASP.NET server is achievable on a two-processor machine. With ADO.NET data access, a four-processor machine can be beneficial, but is far more costly–two to three thousand dollars will buy a good twin-processor server, whereas a four-processor machine is in the twenty thousand dollar price range.

Manage Your ViewState

Depending on the size of the viewstate, transmitting your viewstate across a network can entail a performance hit. You can check the viewstate for any control on the complete page by enabling tracing using the Page directive:

```
<%@ Page Trace="true" ... %>
```

To disable viewstate maintenance for a page, use the following Page directive:

```
<%@ Page EnableViewState="false" ... %>
```

To disable viewstate maintenance for a single control, use the `EnableViewState` property:

```
<ASP:Datagrid EnableViewState="false" ... runat="server"/>
```

To disable viewstate maintenance for an entire application, change the setting in `web.config`:

```
<pages enableViewState="false" ... />
```

Manage Your Session State

Use sessions where they are actually required for the application. Turn them off in pages that don't require access to them. Alternatively, use read-only session state where you don't need to update the values.

To disable session state maintenance for a page, use the following `Page` directive:

```
<%@ Page EnableSessionState="false" %>
```

To disable session state maintenance for an entire application, change the setting in `web.config`:

```
<sessionState mode="off" />
<pages enableSessionState="false" ... />
```

To specify read-only session state maintenance for a page, use the following `Page` directive:

```
<%@ Page EnableSessionState="ReadOnly" %>
```

To specify read-only session state maintenance for an entire application, change the setting in `web.config`:

```
<pages enableSessionState="ReadOnly" ... />
```

Wherever possible, use the default in-process session management. The out-of-process state service can produce a performance hit of 20 percent over the in-process session manager, and the remote SQL Server state management session adds around another 50 percent performance hit over out-of-process session state management – use it only for a web farm.

Use Output Caching

The judicious use of output caching can provide a ten-fold performance increase, depending on whether or how much of a page can be cached and how many variations there are for different users. To enable output caching for a page, use the `OutputCache` directive:

```
<%@ OutputCache Duration="#ofseconds"
    Location="Any | Client | Downstream | Server | None"
    VaryByControl="control-name" VaryByCustom="browser | custom-string"
    VaryByHeader="headers" VaryByParam="parameter-name" %>
```

Use Server Controls Only When Appropriate

If you need to access an HTML element's properties, methods, or events in server-side code, you have to declare it as a server control. It is always worth considering *which* elements actually need to be server controls when you build a page. For example, the following situations *do not* require a server-side control:

❏   When the element is only used to run some client-side script–for example, a button that opens a new browser window, or interacts with a client-side ActiveX control or Java applet, or calculates some value for display in the page using DHTML, or in an `alert` dialog.

❏   When the element is a hyperlink that opens a different page or URL and there is no need to process the values for the hyperlink on the server.

❏   When access to the element's properties, methods, or events in server-side code is not required.

A page containing server controls will take a performance hit compared to one that does not use server controls, perhaps as much as 30 percent. However, using code to set or access the element content directly will also cause a performance hit, so if you do need to access the element programmatically (even just to set the text or value), use a server control for that element.

Use a DataReader Instead of a DataSet

In general, the only times that a `DataSet` must be used in preference to a `DataReader` are:

❏   When the data will be remoted (that is, sent as a disconnected package) to the client or a remote instance of the application or a component–for example, when using a web service that returns a `DataSet`.

❏   When you need to retrieve and store more than one set of rows, and, optionally, the relationships between them.

A `DataReader` can be used as the source for data binding controls if required.

Use the SQL TDS Classes for Data Access

There are several sets of objects for accessing a data source:

❏   Objects prefixed `OleDb` (from the `System.Data.OleDb` namespace) use an OLEDB provider to access that data store.

❏   Objects prefixed `Odbc` (from the `System.Data.Odbc` namespace) use an ODBC driver to access that data store.

❏   Objects prefixed `Oracle` (from the `System.Data.OracleClient` namespace) use an Oracle-specific provider to access that data store.

❏   Objects prefixed `Sql` (from the `System.Data.SqlClient` namespace) use the Microsoft SQL Server *Tabular Data Stream* (*TDS*) interface to access that data store.

In general, the `Sql`-prefixed objects are much faster and more efficient, and should always be used where you know that the data store will be Microsoft SQL Server. All the data access classes automatically provide connection pooling.

Use Data Binding Where Possible

Traditionally, ASP has been used to iterate through a rowset, extracting values and placing them in the page. In ASP.NET, the list controls can do this automatically through data binding, and provide a huge performance increase.

Compared to using ASP 3.0 with ADO to create an HTML table explicitly from a `Recordset`, ASP.NET with a data-bound `DataList` control fed by a `DataReader` object using the `OleDb` data provider can be three times quicker. Switch to the `Sql` TDS data provider and it can be up to five times faster than the ASP 3.0 approach.

If you do need to bind to a `DataSet`, use the `DataMember` property of the control to specify the table rather than creating a `DataView` object first.

Use Option Explicit or Strict in Visual Basic

Early binding provides much better performance than late binding. To ensure that only early binding is used, always include the `Option Explicit` statement in code to force variables to be pre-declared. By default, ASP.NET pages are automatically compiled with the equivalent to `Option Explicit` set.

Also, always specify a data type for variables when they are declared. This provides strong typing of variables for best performance. For example, use:

```
Dim intThis As Integer
```

Rather than:

```
Dim intThis
```

As a comparison, failing to declare variable types and therefore forcing late binding can lead to performance that is about the same as using VBScript in ASP 3.0.

It's also worth using `Option Strict` where possible to enforce strict variable typing. This means that variables must be explicitly cast to the correct data type for each operation that requires a type conversion. Again, it can provide better performance, though it does involve more code and so may not always be appropriate. In ASP.NET, `Strict` compilation is enabled using:

```
<%@ Page Language="VB" Strict="true" %>
```

Use Early Binding to Components

Early binding provides a noticeable performance increase for components that are used in ASP.NET pages. The actual performance hit from late-bound components depends on the amount of transferred data. However, for a component that has to marshal strings, an approximate measure of performance can be gauged from the following comparisons:

❑ COM or COM+ components using late binding provide around the same level of performance as in ASP 3.0 with VBScript.

❑ COM or COM+ components using early binding (for example, components wrapped with the `tlbimp` utility) provide around 50 percent better performance than in ASP 3.0 with VBScript.

❑ Early-bound .NET components provide around three times better performance than the equivalent COM or COM+ components using late binding in ASP 3.0 with VBScript.

All the .NET objects provided by the framework, including all ASP.NET server controls, are automatically early-bound. The *instantiate/destroy cycle* is also very efficient under the .NET framework, and *stateful* components (components that cannot be pooled in Component Services or MTS) are acceptable.

Avoid ASP Compatibility

To use an apartment-threaded component in an ASP.NET page, you must set the compatibility mode to `ASP` using the `AspCompat="true"` page directive. This allows the page to be executed on a *single-threaded apartment (STA)* thread, so that it can call into STA components (for example a component developed with VB6.0). However, in this mode, performance of the ASP.NET page can be quite severely degraded.

Remember the New Request and Response Objects

In ASP.NET, the `Request` and `Response` objects have been extended to provide many new features that can improve performance. For example, to write the contents of a disk file into a page, use the new `Response.WriteFile` method rather than opening the file, reading it from disk and writing it to the `Response`.

Finally, avoid the `ServerVariables` collection where possible by using the new `Request` properties like `Request.Url`, `Request.Referrer`, `Request.PhysicalPath`, `Request.UserAgent`, and so on.

Summary of Changes to ASP.NET in Version 1.1

This appendix summarizes the major changes to the .NET Framework between versions 1.0 and 1.1 that affect developers of ASP.NET Web sites and Web applications. It does not include the multitude of changes that affect compiled executable application development, or tools such as Visual Studio.

New Namespaces

Three new namespaces containing data access classes and managed providers have been added to the Framework. `System.Data.Odbc` implements the ODBC Data Provider, replacing the previous Beta version available as `Microsoft.Data.Odbc`. `System.Data.OracleClient` implements the .NET Data Provider for Oracle. `System.Data.SqlServerCe` implements access to SQL Server CE for the .NET Compact Framework.

The ASP.NET Mobile Controls from the Microsoft Mobile Internet Toolkit are now integrated into the class library, without requiring a separate installation. `System.Web.Mobile` contains the core classes, authentication and error-handling features. `System.Web.UI.MobileControls` contains the controls themselves. `System.Web.UI.MobileControls.Adapters` contains the core control adapter classes you can use to build you own mobile controls.

Changes in the System Namespace

The `System.Array` class now supports array dimensions up to 64-bits (`Long` index values).

The `System.DateTime` class now supports date/times for file timestamps as Universal Time Coordinate (UTC) values.

The `System.Uri` class now correctly parses complex URLs that contain a hash (#) character.

Changes in the System.Data Namespaces

The `DataReader` classes expose a new property named `HasRows` that returns a `Boolean` value indicating if the result set contains any rows.

The `Connection` class exposes a new method named `EnlistDistributedTransaction`. If a component is pooled with an open connection, it will not automatically enlist in any new transactions that are started while the component is active. The `EnlistDistributedTransaction` method can be used to enlist it into a transaction.

Changes in the System.IO Namespace

The `System.IO.File` and `System.IO.Directory` classes gain six new methods for handling file timestamps in UTC format: `GetCreationTimeUtc`, `GetLastAccessTimeUtc`, `GetLastWriteTimeUtc`, `SetCreationTimeUtc`, `SetLastAccessTimeUtc` and `SetLastWriteTimeUtc`.

The `System.IO.FileInfo`, `System.IO.FileSystemInfo` and `System.IO.DirectoryInfo` classes gain three new read/write properties: `CreationTimeUtc`, `LastAccessTimeUtc` and `LastWriteTimeUtc`.

The `System.IO.Path.GetDirectoryName` method now correctly returns the current folder for a path that ends with "`\.`" (a backslash and a single period), instead of returning the parent folder as it did In version 1.0.

Changes in the System.Net Namespace

The `System.Net.HttpWebRequest` class gains two new properties that set the value for the size of the HTTP headers that the `HttpWebRequest` class will read. The `MaximumResponseHeadersLength` property sets the value for specific instances of the class, and the `DefaultMaximumResponseHeadersLength` sets the defaul value. In both cases, the value is an `Integer` representing the number of KB (multiples of 1,024 bytes). To allow any length of header, set the value to`-1`. Setting it to zero will cause all requests to fail. The values can also be set in `machine.config` and `web.config`:

```
<httpRequest maximumResponseHeadersLength="integer" />
```

The `System.Net.HttpWebRequest` class gains a new property `UnsafeAuthenticatedConnectionSharing` that can be set to `True` to allow an authenticated connection to be shared between requests.

The `System.Net.WebExceptionStatus` enumeration gains two new values. `MessageLengthLimitExceeded` indicates that the headers of the request exceed the currently enforced limits. `UnknownError` indicates that the Framework cannot determine the actual reason for the error.

Changes in the System.Web Namespaces

ASP.NET pages now automatically validate all input sent with the request (including any `Form`, `QueryString` and `Cookies` collection contents) against a hard-coded list of undocumented but potentially dangerous string values, and raise an exception if any potentially dangerous content is detected. Input validation can be disabled using a `Page` directive:

```
<%@Page Language="VB" ValidateRequest="false" %>
```

or in `machine.config` / `web.config`:

```
<pages validateRequest="false" ... />
```

The `System.Web.HttpRequest` class gains a new method named `ValidateInput` that checks if the values submitted to the page are potentially dangerous. Used when automatic input validation is disabled for a page, and raises an exception if any potentially dangerous content is detected.

The `System.Web.UI.Page` class gains a new property named `ViewStateUserKey` to which a value that is unique to the current user can be assigned. It is encoded into the viewstate of the page, and when the page is submitted, the viewstate will only be valid if this value is present.

The `ListControl`, `DropDownList`, `CheckBoxList`, `RadioButtonList` and `ListBox` classes from the `System.Web.UI.WebControls` namespace gain a new property named `SelectedValue` that returns the `Value` property for the first selected `ListItem` object in the list. It can also be used to select an item in these controls by assigning the required `String` value to the property.

The `System.Web.HttpContext.RewritePath` method gains a new overload that accepts three `String` parameters: the new path, any extra path information, and the query string to be passed to the requested resource.

The `System.Web.HttpBrowserCapabilities` class gains a new method named `GetClrVersions` that returns an array of `Version` instances indicating the .NET Framework versions installed on the client.

The `System.Web.HttpResponse` class gains a new property named `RedirectLocation` that sets or returns the location that the client will be redirected to (the value of the `Location` HTTP header).

The `System.Web.HttpRuntime` class gains a new method named `UnloadAppDomain` that forces the current ASP.NET application to be unloaded and restarted when the next request is received.

The `System.Web.HttpUtility` class gains a new method named `UrlPathEncode` that encodes only the path section of a URL string, producing a URL in a format that is suitable for use within hyperlinks and other HTML elements within the page.

The System.Web.Mail.MailMessage class gains a new property named Fields that is a reference to a Dictionary object that containing additional information on the contents of the message that is not available from the existing properties.

The System.Web.Caching.HttpCachePolicy class gains a new method named SetAllowInBrowserHistory which, when set to True, instructs the client to cache the response in their History folder or document cache. This means that the Back and Forward commands in the browser will not request a new version of the page each time.

The System.Web.Caching.HttpCacheability enumeration gains two now values. ServerAndNoCache specifies that the content is cached at the origin server, but all other caching systems are explicitly denied the ability to cache the response. ServerAndPrivate indicates that the response is cached at the server and at the client, but nowhere else (proxy servers and other shared caching systems are not allowed to cache the response).

The System.Web.Security.FormsAuthentication class gains two new read-only properties that return information about the configuration of Forms authentication. The RequireSSL property returns a Boolean value indicating if the cookie must only be sent over a secure SSL-encrypted channel. The SlidingExpiration property returns a Boolean value indicating if the timeout is reset with each page request (True), or is treated as a fixed value from the initial login (False). Two new attributes are added to the <forms> element in machine.config and web.config that specify if SSL is required and if sliding expiration is enabled:

```
<authentication mode="Forms">
  <forms requireSSL="true|false" slidingExpiration="true|false" ... />
</authentication>
```

The default <machineKey> element within the <system.web> section of the machine.config and web.config files now applies a modifier named IsolateApps to the validation and decryption keys:

```
<machineKey validationKey="AutoGenerate,IsolateApps"
            decryptionKey="AutoGenerate,IsolateApps"
            validation="SHA1"/>
```

The IsolateApps modifier causes these keys to include details of the ASP.NET application that is using Forms authentication and creating the cookie, so different applications that use Forms authentication will each generate different keys for securing their cookies and encoding viewstate in the pages.

Changes to the Web Services Classes

The System.Web.Services.Discovery.DiscoveryClientProtocol class gains a new property named UnsafeAuthenticatedConnectionSharing that can be set to True to allow an authenticated connection to be shared between requests.

The System.Web.Services.Protocols.HttpGetClientProtocol class gains a new property named UnsafeAuthenticatedConnectionSharing that can be set to True to allow an authenticated connection to be shared between requests.

The `System.Web.Services.Protocols.HttpPostClientProtocol` class gains a new property named `UnsafeAuthenticatedConnectionSharing` that can be set to `True` to allow an authenticated connection to be shared between requests.

The `System.Web.Services.Protocols.HttpSimpleClientProtocol` class gains a new property named `UnsafeAuthenticatedConnectionSharing` that can be set to `True` to allow an authenticated connection to be shared between requests.

The `System.Web.Services.Protocols.HttpWebClientProtocol` class gains a new property named `UnsafeAuthenticatedConnectionSharing` that can be set to `True` to allow an authenticated connection to be shared between requests.

The `System.Web.Services.Protocols.SoapHttpClientProtocol` class gains a new property named `UnsafeAuthenticatedConnectionSharing` that can be set to `True` to allow an authenticated connection to be shared between requests.

The `System.Web.Services.Protocols.SoapMessage` class gains a new property named `ContentEncoding` that can be used to provide supplementary details about the content without having to set the Content-Type HTTP header for the complete response.

The `System.Web.Services.Protocols.SoapClientMessage` class gains a new property named `ContentEncoding` that can be used to provide supplementary details about the content without having to set the Content-Type HTTP header for the complete response.

The `System.Web.Services.Protocols.SoapServerMessage` class gains a new property named `ContentEncoding` that can be used to provide supplementary details about the content without having to set the Content-Type HTTP header for the complete response.

Changes in the System.Xml Namespaces

The `ReadInnerXML` and `ReadOuterXml` methods of the `System.Xml.XmlReader` class now validate the content they return against a schema or DTD if present.

Several overloads of the the `Load` and `Transform` methods of the `System.Xml.Xsl.XslTransform` class are now obsolete. Stylesheets should be loaded through an instance of the existing `XmlUrlResolver` class or the new `XmlSecureResolver` class unless they are from a fully trusted source.

New overloads are available for the `System.Xml.Schema.XmlSchema.Compile` method and the `System.Xml.Schema.XmlSchemaCollection.Add` method that accept an `XmlUrlResolver` or `XmlSecureResolver` instance.

References and Further Information

Although .NET is a new product, there are already many Web sites that provide discussion groups, reference information, community support, components, and other useful resources. Some of those that were available when this book went to press are listed below.

ASP.NET Web Sites and Discussion Lists

MSDN .Net Start Page	**http://msdn.microsoft.com/net/**
Visual Studio	**http://msdn.microsoft.com/vstudio/**
ASP.NET	**http://msdn.microsoft.com/asp.net/**
Wrox Press ASP discussion list	**http://p2p.wrox.com/**
Microsoft Framework team web site	**http://www.asp.net/**
ASPNG ASP.NET community site	**http://www.aspng.com/**
A Tale of Two Authors	**http://daveandal.com/**
.NET Advocacy Discussion Lists	**http://discuss.develop.com/dotnet-advocacy.html**
.NET101	**http://www.dotnet101.com/**
.NETWire	**http://www.dotnetwire.com/**
123aspx.com	**http://www.123aspx.com/**

Table continued on following page

411 ASP.NET Directory	**http://www.411asp.net/**
4GuysFromRolla.com	**http://www.4guysfromrolla.com/**
ActiveZ.com (in Turkish)	**http://activez.cu.edu.tr/**
Angry Coder	**http://www.angrycoder.com/**
ASP Index	**http://www.aspin.com/**
ASP Wire	**http://www.aspwire.com/**
ASP101.com	**http://www.asp101.com/**
aspalliance	**http://www.aspalliance.com/**
ASPFree.com	**http://www.aspfree.com/aspnet/Default.aspx**
ASPNextGen.com	**http://www.aspnextgen.com/**
ASPToday.com	**http://www.asptoday.com/**
BipinJoshi.com	**http://www.bipinjoshi.com/**
C# Corner	**http://www.c-sharpcorner.com/**
Coalesys Inc.	**http://www.coalesys.com/**
Code Guru	**http://www.codeguru.com/**
DevX.com	**http://www.devx.com/dotnet/**
DotNET French .NET news portal	**http://www.dotnet-fr.org/**
Learn C# The Easy Way	**http://learncsharp.cjb.net/**
Mailing list DOTNET (in French)	**http://www.neoxia.com/fr/mailing-lists.php3**
St. Louis .NET User Group	**http://www.stlnet.org/**
TopXML.com	**http://www.vbxml.com/**
Visual.NET Advisor	**http://www.advisor.com/www/VisualNetAdvisor/**
VSJ	**http://www.net.vsj.co.uk/**

Third-Party ASP.NET Component Vendors

Software Artisans	http://softwareartisans.com/
Combit	http://www.combit.net/us/default.asp?content=/us/support/msdotnet.asp
Component Source	http://www.componentsource.com/
Dart Communications	http://www.dart.com/dotnet.asp
Dataphor	http://www.dataphor.com/
Desaware Inc.	http://www.desaware.com/
Developer Express	http://devexpress.com/index.shtm
DevPower Components	http://www.devpower.com/net/
FarPoint Technologies	http://www.fpoint.com/
Infragistics	http://www.infragistics.com/
LEADTOOLS Imaging Development	http://www.leadtools.com/
Mabry Software	http://www.mabry.com/dotnet.htm
Sax Software Corporation	http://www.saxsoft.net/
Software FX - Chart FX	http://www.softwarefx.com/
VisualSoft Technologies	http://www.visualmart.com/dotnetreq.asp
WebGecko Software	http://www.webgecko.com/products/dotnet.asp
Xceed Software Inc.	http://www.xceedsoft.com/dotnet/

ASP.NET Hosting

2COOLWEB	http://www.2coolweb.com/
Brinkster.com	http://www.brinkster.com/aspxinfo.asp
Eraserver.net	http://www.eraserver.net/
Extreme Web Works	http://extremewebworks.com/
Franklins.net	http://www.franklins.net/
IIS Host List	http://www.actionjackson.com/hosts/
MaximumASP.com	http://www.maximumasp.com/
ORCSWEB.com	http://www.orcsweb.com/
SecureWebs.com	http://shop.securewebs.com/

Index

A Guide to the Index

The index is arranged hierarchically, in alphabetical order, with symbols preceding the letter A. Most second-level entries and many third-level entries also occur as first-level entries. This is to ensure that users find the information they require however they choose to search for it.